Essentials of Management Information Systems, second edition, illustrates how the Internet is transforming business and redefining the role of information systems. The Internet is integrated throughout the text and the entire learning package.

The new Chapter 9, "Enterprise Networking and the Internet," describes the underlying technology, capabilities, and benefits of the Internet with numerous illustrations from real-world companies.

Internet Coverage in Every Chapter. The Internet is introduced in Chapter 1. Every chapter contains a "Window On" box, case study, or in-text discussion of how the Internet is changing a particular aspect of information systems.

The Internet Connection with Interactive Projects. The Internet Connection in each chapter links organizations and topics discussed in each chapter to sites on the World Wide Web. Students can use many of these sites for managerial problem-solving projects.

Here are some organizations featured in the Internet Connections and how they make use of the Internet.

- Onsale and Lombard Institutional Brokerage uses the Internet for electronic commerce
- Cygnus Support uses its intranet for organizational communication and coordination
- Trane Co. used the Internet to re-engineer its production process
- Sun Microsystemsi Java and the Internet are revolutionizing software development and delivery
- Federal Express uses the World Wide Web to reduce operating expenses
- Hyatt Hotels uses the World Wide Web for market research
- United Parcel Service links its World Wide Web site to internal databases

Other Web sites provide additional case studies, demonstrations of important MIS concepts, or new information resources.

- Citicorp
- Federal Express
- Ernst & Young
- Electronic Privacy Information Center
- Sun Microsystems
- Microsoft Corporation
- GeoSystems Global Corp.
- Oracle Corporation
- Goodyear Tire & Rubber Company
- Hyatt Hotels
- Andersen Consulting
- SAP A.G.
- National Aeronautic and Space Administration (NASA)
- Neural Applications Corporation
- Fidelity Investments
- McAfee Associates
- Digicash
- EUROPAGES Business Directory
- UK Business Directory

Please visit the book's Web site at http://www.prenhall.com/~laudon

Essentials of
Management
Information
Systems

Second Edition

Essentials of Management Information Systems

Organization and Technology

Kenneth C. Laudon
New York University

Jane Price Laudon
Azimuth Corporation

PRENTICE HALL International, Inc.

Senior Acquisitions Editor: Jo-Ann DeLuca
Assistant Editor: Audrey Regan
Editorial Assistant: Marc Oliver
Editor-in-Chief: Richard Wohl
Executive Marketing Manager: Nancy Evans
Sales Specialist: Audra Silverie
Editorial/Production Supervision: Kelli Rahlf/Carlisle Publishers Services
Production Coordinator: David Cotugno
Managing Editor: Katherine Evancie
Senior Manufacturing Supervisor: Paul Smolenski
Manufacturing Manager: Vincent Scelta
Senior Designer: Suzanne Behnke
Design Director: Patricia Wosczyk
Interior Design: Suzanne Behnke
Cover Design: Maureen Eide
Composition: Carlisle Communications, Ltd.
Cover Art: Valerie Sinclair

 Copyright © 1997, 1995 by Prentice-Hall, Inc.
A Simon & Schuster Company
Upper Saddle River, New Jersey 07458

All rights reserved. No part of this book may be reproduced, in any form or by any means, without written permission from the Publisher.

Photo credits for this book are listed on page 563.

This edition may be sold only in those countries to which it is consigned by Prentice Hall-International. It is not to be re-exported and it is not for sale in the U.S.A., Mexico, or Canada.

ISBN 0-13719493-5

Prentice-Hall International (UK) Limited, *London*
Prentice-Hall of Australia Pty. Limited, *Sydney*
Prentice-Hall Canada, Inc., *Toronto*
Prentice-Hall Hispanoamericana, S.A., *Mexico*
Prentice-Hall of India Private Limited, *New Delhi*
Prentice-Hall of Japan, Inc., *Tokyo*
Simon & Schuster Asia Pte. Ltd., *Singapore*
Editora Prentice-Hall do Brasil, Ltda., *Rio de Janeiro*
Prentice-Hall, *Upper Saddle River, NJ*

Printed in the United States of America

10 9 8 7 6 5 4

for
Erica
and
Elisabeth

Brief Table of Contents

Part One   **Organizational Foundations of Information Systems**

Chapter 1   Information Systems: Challenges and Opportunities   *1*
Chapter 2   The Strategic Role of Information Systems   *29*
Chapter 3   Information Systems, Organizations, and Management   *61*
Chapter 4   Ethical and Social Impact of Information Systems   *93*

Part Two   **Technical Foundations of Information Systems**

Chapter 5   Computers and Information Processing   *124*
Chapter 6   Information Systems Software   *162*
Chapter 7   Managing Data Resources   *195*

Part Three   **Communications and Networks**

Chapter 8   Telecommunications   *228*
Chapter 9   Enterprise Networking and the Internet   *266*

Part Four   **Building Information Systems: Contemporary Approaches**

Chapter 10   Redesigning the Organization with Information Systems   *298*
Chapter 11   Approaches to Systems-Building   *336*

Part Five   **Management and Organizational Support Systems**

Chapter 12   Managing Knowledge   *368*
Chapter 13   Enhancing Management Decision Making   *403*

Part Six   **Managing Information Systems**

Chapter 14   Controlling Information Systems   *430*
Chapter 15   Managing International Information Systems   *458*

International Case Studies   *486*

Appendix A: Functional Information Systems   *519*

Glossary   *525*

Name Index   *539*

Organizations Index   *541*

International Organizations Index   *543*

Subject Index   *544*

Contents

Part One   **Organizational Foundations of Information Systems**

Chapter 1   **Information Systems: Challenges and Opportunities**   *1*
The Internet Levels the Playing Field   *1*

1.1 Why Information Systems?   *3*
The Competitive Business Environment, 3 • *What Is an Information System?,* 6 • *A Business Perspective on Information Systems,* 7 • **Window on Technology:** *UPS Competes Globally with Information Technology,* 8

1.2 Contemporary Approaches to Information Systems   *11*
Technical Approach, 11 • *Behavioral Approach,* 12 • *Approach of This Text: Sociotechnical Systems,* 12

1.3 The New Role of Information Systems in Organizations   *13*
The Widening Scope of Information Systems, 13 • *The Soaring Power of Information Technology,* 14 • *New Options for Organizational Design,* 16 • **Window on Management:** *Custom Manufacturing: The New Automation,* 20 • **Window on Organizations:** *The Internet: The New Electronic Marketplace,* 21 • *The Changing Management Process,* 21

1.4 The Challenge of Information Systems: Key Management Issues   *22*

Summary   25, *Key Terms*   25, *Review Questions*   25, *Discussion Questions*   26, *Group Project*   26, *Case Study: David Battles Goliath for the Power of Information on the Internet*   26, *References*   27.

Chapter 2   **The Strategic Role of Information Systems**   *29*
Information Systems Keep Gillette on the Cutting Edge   *29*

2.1 Key System Applications in the Organization   *31*
Different Kinds of Systems, 31 • *Six Major Types of Systems,* 33 • **Window on Technology:** *Odense Shipyards Speeds Up Product Design,* 37 • *Relationship of Systems to One Another: Integration,* 42

2.2 The Strategic Role of Information Systems   *43*
What Is a Strategic Information System?, 43 • *Countering Competitive Forces,* 43 • **Window on Organizations:** *Mining Data for Profits,* 45 • *Leveraging Technology in the Value Chain,* 47 • *Implications for Managers and Organizations,* 49

2.3 How Information Systems Promote Quality   *50*
What Is Quality?, 50 • *How Information Systems Contribute to Total Quality Management,* 50 • **Window on Management:** *Building an Organization to Sell Flowers,* 52

Management Challenges   53, *Summary*   53, *Key Terms*   54, *Review Questions*   54, *Discussion Questions*   55, *Group Project*   55, *Case Study: Greyhound Seeks Salvation in a Strategic Reservation System*   56, *References*   58

Chapter 3 **Information Systems, Organizations, and Management** *61*
PanCanadian Awakens with Information Systems *61*

3.1 Organizations and Information Systems *63*
What Is an Organization?, 64 • Why Organizations Are So Much Alike: Common Features, 65 • Why Organizations Are So Different: Unique Features, 67

3.2 The Changing Role of Information Systems *70*
The Evolution of Information Systems, 70 • Why Organizations Build Information Systems, 72 • How Information Systems Affect Organizations, 72 • **Window on Organizations:** *Schneider Responds to the New Rules of the Trucking Game, 73 •* **Window on Management:** *Managing the Virtual Office, 76 • Implications for the Design and Understanding of Information Systems, 77*

3.3 The Role of Managers in the Organization *78*
Classical Descriptions of Management, 78 • Behavioral Models, 78 • **Window on Technology:** *Managers Turn to the Internet, 80 • Implications for System Design, 80*

3.4 Managers and Decision Making *81*
The Process of Decision Making, 82 • Individual Models of Decision Making, 84 • Organizational Models of Decision Making, 84 • Implications for System Design, 85

***Management Challenges** 86, **Summary** 86, **Key Terms** 87, **Review Questions** 88, **Discussion Questions** 88, **Group Project** 88, **Case Study: Can Sears Reinvent Itself?** 88, **References** 90*

Chapter 4 **Ethical and Social Impact of Information Systems** *93*
What Price Should Workers Have to Pay for Technology? *93*

4.1 Understanding Ethical and Social Issues Related to Systems *95*
A Model for Thinking About Ethical, Social, and Political Issues, 95 • Five Moral Dimensions of the Information Age, 96 • Key Technology Trends That Raise Ethical Issues, 97

4.2 Ethics in an Information Society *98*
Basic Concepts: Responsibility, Accountability, and Liability, 98 • Ethical Analysis, 99 • Candidate Ethical Principles, 99 • Professional Codes of Conduct, 100 • Some Real-World Ethical Dilemmas, 100

4.3 The Moral Dimensions of Information Systems *102*
Information Rights: Privacy and Freedom in an Information Society, 102 • Property Rights: Intellectual Property, 104 • **Window on Organizations:** *A Corporate Software Code of Ethics, 106 • Accountability, Liability, and Control, 106 •* **Window on Organizations:** *Liability on the Internet, 108 • System Quality: Data Quality and System Errors, 109 • Quality of Life: Equity, Access, Boundaries, 110 •* **Window on Management:** *Whither the Downsized Society?, 114 •* **Window on Management:** *Managing RSI, 116 • Management Actions: A Corporate Code of Ethics, 117 •* **Window on Technology:** *The Coming of a National Digital Superhighway Raises Many Ethical and Social Issues, 118*

***Management Challenges** 118, **Summary** 119, **Key Terms** 119, **Review Questions** 119, **Discussion Questions** 120, **Group Projects** 120, **Case Study: Who Is Responsible?** 120, **References** 122*

Part Two   **Technical Foundations of Information Systems**

Chapter 5   **Computers and Information Processing**   *124*
EMI Tunes Its Information Technology   *124*

     5.1   **What Is a Computer System?**   *126*
System Configuration, 126 • Bits and Bytes: How Computers Represent Data, 126 • Time and Size in the Computer World, 128

     5.2   **The CPU and Primary Storage**   *131*
Primary Storage, 131 • Types of Semiconductor Memory, 132 • Arithmetic-Logic Unit, 133 • Control Unit, 133

     5.3   **The Evolution of Computer Hardware**   *134*
Generations of Computer Hardware, 134 • What Is a Microprocessor? What Is a Chip?, 135

     5.4   **Mainframes, Minicomputers, Microcomputers, Workstations, and Supercomputers**   *137*
Mainframes, Minis, and Micros, 137 • Downsizing and Cooperative Processing, 138 • **Window on Management:** *Deutsche Bank Decides to Stay with Mainframes, 140 • Microcomputers and Workstations, 141 • Supercomputers and Parallel Processing, 141 •* **Window on Technology:** *Parallel Processing Goes Commercial, 142*

     5.5   **Secondary Storage**   *143*
Magnetic Tape, 143 • Magnetic Disk, 144 • Optical Disks, 146

     5.6   **Input and Output Devices**   *148*
Input Devices, 148 • Batch and On-Line Input and Processing, 150 • Output Devices, 150

     5.7   **Information Technology Trends**   *152*
Multimedia, 152 • Superchips, 154 • **Window on Organizations:** *Multimedia Kiosks Educate the Public, 155 • Fifth-Generation Computers, 155*

Management Challenges   *157, Summary*   *157, Key Terms*   *158, Review Questions*   *158, Discussion Questions*   *159, Group Project*   *159, Case Study: Bar Codes Become a Strategic Business Weapon*   *159, References*   *161*

Chapter 6   **Information Systems Software**   *162*
Sand Dollar Saves Many Dollars Through Mailing Software   *162*

     6.1   **What Is Software?**   *164*
Software Programs, 164 • Major Types of Software, 164

     6.2   **System Software**   *165*
Functions of the Operating System, 165 • Multiprogramming, Virtual Storage, Time Sharing, and Multiprocessing, 166 • Language Translation and Utility Software, 168 • Graphical User Interfaces, 169 • Microcomputer Operating Systems, 170 • Selecting a Microcomputer Operating System, 172 • **Window on Management:** *NASA Selects Operating Systems, 174*

     6.3   **Application Software**   *173*
Generations of Programming Languages, 173 • Popular Programming Languages, 175 • Fourth-Generation Languages, 178 • **Window on Organizations:** *Bell Quebec Repairs Its Pay Phones by Magic, 180*

     6.4   **New Software Tools and Approaches**   *184*
Object-Oriented Programming, 184 • **Window on Technology:** *Power Short-Circuits in Object-Oriented Development, 186 • Java and the Software Revolution, 187*

Management Challenges   190, Summary   190, Key Terms   191, Review Questions   191, Discussion Questions   192, Group Project   192, Case Study: A Geographic Information System Adds Zest to Sonny's Bar-B-Q   192, References   194

Chapter 7   Managing Data Resources   195
A Land Title System That Makes a Difference   195

7.1   Organizing Data in a Traditional File Environment   197
File Organization Terms and Concepts, 197 • Accessing Records from Computer Files, 199 • Problems with the Traditional File Environment, 200

7.2   A Modern Database Environment   203
Database Management Systems (DBMS), 203 • Logical and Physical Views of Data, 206 • Advantages of Database Management Systems, 207

7.3   Designing Databases   207
Hierarchical Data Model, 208 • Network Data Model, 208 • Relational Data Model, 209 • Advantages and Disadvantages of the Three Database Models, 210 • **Window on Organizations:** *Denmark Runs on DB2, 211 • Creating a Database, 212*

7.4   Database Trends   213
Distributed Processing and Distributed Databases, 213 • Object-Oriented and Hypermedia Databases, 215 • **Window on Technology:** *Volkswagen Opts for an Object-Oriented Database, 217 • Multidimensional Databases, 217 • Data Warehousing, 218 •* **Window on Management:** *Linking Databases to the Internet, 221*

7.5   Management Requirements for Database Systems   220
Data Administration, 222 • Data Planning and Modeling Methodology, 222 • Database Technology and Management, 222 • Users, 222

Management Challenges   223, Summary   223, Key Terms   224, Review Questions   224, Discussion Questions   224, Group Project   225, Case Study: Can Migration to a Relational Database Management System Help a German Home Loan Lender?   225, References   226

Part Three   Communications and Networks

Chapter 8   Telecommunications   228
Networks Promote Global Trade   228

8.1   The Telecommunications Revolution   230
The Marriage of Computers and Communications, 230 • The Information Superhighway, 231 • **Window on Organizations:** *Telephone Companies Face an Expansive Future, 232*

8.2   Components and Functions of a Telecommunications System   233
Telecommunications System Components, 233 • Types of Signals: Analog and Digital, 234 • Types of Communications Channels, 235 • Characteristics of Communications Channels, 240 • Communications Processors, 242 • Telecommunications Software, 243

8.3   Types of Telecommunications Networks   243
Network Topologies, 243 • Private Branch Exchanges and Local-Area Networks (LANs), 245 • Wide-Area Networks (WANs), 248 • Value-Added Networks (VANs), 249

8.4 How Organizations Use Telecommunications for Competitive Advantage *250*
Facilitating Applications, 251 • **Window on Management:** *Monitoring Employees on Networks: Unethical or Good Business?, 252* • **Window on Technology:** *Intelligent Agents: Network Valets, 254* • *Electronic Data Interchange, 255* • *Groupware, 256*

8.5 Management Issues and Decisions *257*
The Telecommunications Plan, 257 • *Implementing the Plan, 258*

Management Challenges 259, *Summary* 259, *Key Terms* 260, *Review Questions* 260, *Discussion Questions* 261, *Group Project* 261, *Case Study: Goodyear Automates Its Sales Force* 261, *References* 265

Chapter 9 Enterprise Networking and the Internet *266*
Michigan Transportation Department Reinvents Itself with Networked Computers *266*

9.1 Enterprise Networking *268*
The Client/Server Model of Computing, 270 • *Business Drivers of Enterprise Networking, 271* • *Electronic Commerce, 271*

9.2 The Internet *272*
Internet Capabilities, 273 • *Internet Benefits to Organizations, 278* • **Window on Organizations:** *The Internet Becomes the Middleman, 281* • **Window on Technology:** *The Internet for EDI?, 282* • *Intranets, 282* • *Internet Challenges, 284*

9.3 Connectivity and Standards *285*
Models of Connectivity for Networks, 285 • *Other Networking Standards, 287* • *Operating System Standards: The Open Systems Movement, 288*

9.4 Implementing Enterprise Networking *289*
Problems Posed by Enterprise Networking, 289 • *Some Solutions, 291* • **Window on Management:** *Bass Beer Serves a Client/Server Environment, 292*

Management Challenges 293, *Summary* 293, *Key Terms* 294, *Review Questions* 294, *Discussion Questions* 295, *Group Project* 295, *Case Study: Unilever Tries to Unify World Operations* 295, *References* 297

Part Four Building Information Systems: Contemporary Approaches

Chapter 10 Redesigning the Organization with Information Systems *298*
New Zealand Designs for Paperless Tax Returns *298*

10.1 Systems as Planned Organizational Change *300*
Linking Information Systems to the Business Plan, 300 • *Establishing Organizational Information Requirements, 301* • *Systems Development and Organizational Change, 304* • *Business Reengineering, 306* • **Window on Technology:** *Redesigning with the Internet, 307*

10.2 Overview of Systems Development *310*
Systems Analysis, 311 • *Systems Design, 313* • *Completing the Systems Development Process, 314* • **Window on Organizations:** *Europcar Struggles to Migrate Its Systems, 317*

10.3 System Implementation: Managing Change *318*
Implementation Success and Failure, 318 • *Managing Implementation, 320* • **Window on Management:** *Hoechst Heads Off a Reengineering Disaster, 323* • *Designing for the Organization, 324*

10.4 Understanding the Business Value of Information Systems *326*
Capital Budgeting Models, 326 • *Nonfinancial and Strategic Considerations, 327*

***Management Challenges** 329, **Summary** 329, **Key Terms** 330, **Review Questions** 331, **Discussion Questions** 331, **Group Project** 331, **Case Study: Curing Chaos at Methodist Hospital** 332, **References** 333*

Chapter 11 **Approaches to Systems-Building** *336*
ClubCorp Serves Its Members with a Rapid Method of Developing Applications *336*

11.1 The Traditional Systems Lifecycle *338*
Stages of the Systems Lifecycle, 338 • *Limitations of the Lifecycle Approach, 340*

11.2 Alternative System-Building Approaches *340*
Prototyping, 340 • *Application Software Packages, 342* • **Window on Technology:** *Can Saab Find Happiness with a Manufacturing Package from a Tiny, Unknown Vendor?, 346* • *End-User Development, 347* • *Outsourcing, 349* • **Window on Management:** *Ford Europe Makes Its Outsourcing Contractors Part of Its Team, 351*

11.3 System-Building Methodologies *352*
Structured Methodologies, 352 • *Object-Oriented Software Development, 356* • *Computer Aided Software Engineering (CASE), 358* • **Window on Organizations:** *Air Canada Overhauls Its Web Site, 360* • *Software Reengineering, 360*

***Management Challenges** 362, **Summary** 362, **Key Terms** 363, **Review Questions** 364, **Discussion Questions** 364, **Group Project** 364, **Case Study: Can a German Software Giant Provide Client/Server Solutions?** 364, **References** 366*

Part Five **Management and Organizational Support Systems**

Chapter 12 **Managing Knowledge** *368*
The Electronic Hospital *368*

12.1 Knowledge Management in the Organization *370*
Information Systems and Knowledge Management, 370 • *Knowledge Work and Productivity, 371*

12.2 Information and Knowledge Work Systems *372*
Distributing Knowledge: Office Information Systems, 372 • *Creating Knowledge: Knowledge Work Systems, 374* • **Window on Technology:** *Flying High with CAD, 376* • *Sharing Knowledge: Group Collaboration Systems, 377* • *Group Collaboration Via the Internet, 378*

12.3 Artificial Intelligence *380*
What Is Artificial Intelligence?, 380 • *Why Business Is Interested in Artificial Intelligence, 381* • *Capturing Knowledge: Expert Systems, 381* • *Organizational Intelligence: Case-Based Reasoning, 386* • **Window on Management:** *Enabling Reuse of Designs Through Artificial Intelligence, 388*

12.4 Other Intelligent Techniques *387*
Neural Networks, 387 • **Window on Organizations:** *The Neural Network Approach to Stock Picking, 391* • *Fuzzy Logic, 391* • *Genetic Algorithms, 393*

***Management Challenges** 395, **Summary** 395, **Key Terms** 396, **Review Questions** 396, **Discussion Questions** 397, **Group Project** 397, **Case Study: Designing the Paperless Airplane** 397, **References** 400*

Chapter 13 **Enhancing Management Decision Making** *403*
The Ideal Investment Portfolio: What Does the System Say? *403*

13.1 Decision-Support Systems (DSS) *405*
What Are Decision-Support Systems?, 405 • Examples of DSS Applications, 408 • Components of DSS, 411 • **Window on Management:** *Practicing Decision Making, 411 • Building DSS, 412*

13.2 Group Decision-Support Systems (GDSS) *413*
What Is a GDSS?, 413 • **Window on Organizations:** *The Hohenheim CATeam Room, 414 • Characteristics of GDSS, 415 • GDSS Software Tools, 416 • How GDSS Can Enhance Group Decision Making, 418*

13.3 Executive Support Systems (ESS) *420*
The Role of ESS in the Organization, 420 • Developing ESS, 421 • **Window on Technology:** *Fighting Infoglut, 422 • Benefits of ESS, 423 • Examples of ESS, 423*

Management Challenges 425, Summary 425, Key Terms 426, Review Questions, 426, Discussion Questions 426, Group Project 426, Case Study: Zeneca Searches for Decisions 427, References 428

Part Six **Managing Information Systems**

Chapter 14 **Controlling Information Systems** *430*
Broadcast Storms Bring Swissair Network to a Halt *430*

14.1 System Vulnerability and Abuse *432*
Why Systems Are Vulnerable, 432 • **Window on Organizations:** *Uprooting the Internet Hackers, 434 • Concerns for System Builders and Users, 435 • System Quality Problems: Software and Data, 437 •* **Window on Management:** *Client/Server Disaster Planning, 438*

14.2 Creating a Control Environment *441*
General Controls, 442 • Application Controls, 444 • Developing a Control Structure: Costs and Benefits, 447 • The Role of Auditing in the Control Process, 448

14.3 Ensuring System Quality *449*
Software Quality Assurance, 449 • **Window on Technology:** *British Customs Tests Its GUIs, 451 • Data Quality Audits, 451*

Management Challenges 453, Summary 453, Key Terms 454, Review Questions 454, Discussion Questions 454, Group Project 454, Case Study: Can We Trust Mutual Fund Pricing? 455, References 456

Chapter 15 **Managing International Information Systems** *458*
Molex Goes Global *458*

15.1 The Growth of International Information Systems *460*
Developing the International Information Systems Infrastructure, 460 • The Global Environment: Business Drivers and Challenges, 462 • **Window on Organizations:** *The 800-Pound Gorilla of Transnational Technological Change, 465 • State of the Art, 466*

15.2 Organizing International Information Systems *467*
Global Strategies and Business Organization, 467 • Global Systems to Fit the Strategy, 468 • Reorganizing the Business, 469

15.3 Managing Global Systems *470*
A Typical Scenario: Disorganization on a Global Scale, 470 • Strategy: Divide, Conquer, Appease, 471 • Implementation Tactics: Cooptation, 473 • Wrapping

Up: The Management Solution, 473 • **Window on Management:** *Traveling Down the Road of International Technology Infrastructure Mergers, 476*

15.4 Technology Issues and Opportunities 474
Main Technical Issues, 474 • **Window on Technology:** *Is the Internet a World Tool?, 479* • *New Technical Opportunities, 480*

Management Challenges 481, Summary 481, Key Terms 482, Review Questions 482, Discussion Questions 482, Group Project 482, Case Study: Global Information Systems to Support Nestlé's Global Business Strategy 483, References 484

International Case Studies 426

From Geelong and District Water Board to Barwon Water: An Integrated IT Infrastructure **Joel B. Barolsky and Peter Weill, University of Melbourne (Australia),** 487

Ginormous Life Insurance Company **Len Fertuck, University of Toronto (Canada),** 496

Kone Elevators **Tapio Reponen, Turku School of Economics and Business Administration (Finland),** 499

Festo Pneumatic **Helmut Krcmar and Bettina Schwarzer, University of Hohenheim (Germany),** 504

Corning Telecommunications Division **Andrew Boynton, University of North Carolina at Chapel Hill and the International Institute for Management Development (Switzerland) and Michael E. Shank, Renaissance Vision,** 508

Appendix A: Functional Information Systems, 519

Glossary, 525

Name Index, 539

Organizations Index, 541

International Organizations Index, 543

Subject Index, 544

Windows on MIS

Chapter 1	**Window on Technology** UPS Competes Globally with Information Technology *8*	
	Window on Management Custom Manufacturing: The New Automation *20*	
	Window on Organizations The Internet: The New Electronic Marketplace *21*	
Chapter 2	**Window on Technology** Odense Shipyards Speeds Up Product Design *37*	
	Window on Organizations Mining Data for Profits *45*	
	Window on Management Building an Organization to Sell Flowers *52*	
Chapter 3	**Window on Organizations** Schneider Responds to the New Rules of the Trucking Game *73*	
	Window on Management Managing the Virtual Office *76*	
	Window on Technology Managers Turn to the Internet *80*	
Chapter 4	**Window on Organizations** A Corporate Software Code of Ethics *106*	
	Window on Organizations Liability on the Internet *108*	
	Window on Management Whither the Downsized Society? *114*	
	Window on Management Managing RSI *116*	
	Window on Technology The Coming of a National Digital Superhighway Raises Many Ethical and Social Issues *118*	
Chapter 5	**Window on Management** Deutsche Bank Decides to Stay with Mainframes *140*	

xvii

Window on Technology
Parallel Processing Goes Commercial *142*

Window on Organizations
Multimedia Kiosks Educate the Public *155*

Chapter 6 ### Window on Management
NASA Selects Operating Systems *174*

Window on Organizations
Bell Quebec Repairs Its Pay Phones by Magic *180*

Window on Technology
Power Short-Circuits in Object-Oriented Development *186*

Chapter 7 ### Window on Organizations
Denmark Runs on DB2 *211*

Window on Technology
Volkswagen Opts for an Object-Oriented Database *217*

Window on Management
Linking Databases to the Internet *221*

Chapter 8 ### Window on Organizations
Telephone Companies Face an Expansive Future *232*

Window on Management
Monitoring Employees on Networks: Unethical or Good Business? *252*

Window on Technology
Intelligent Agents: Network Valets *254*

Chapter 9 ### Window on Organizations
The Internet Becomes the Middleman *281*

Window on Technology
The Internet for EDI? *282*

Window on Management
Bass Beer Serves a Client/Server Environment *292*

Chapter 10 ### Window on Technology
Redesigning with the Internet *307*

Window on Organizations
Europcar Struggles to Migrate Its Systems *317*

Window on Management
Hoechst Heads Off a Reengineering Disaster *323*

Chapter 11 ### Window on Technology
Can Saab Find Happiness with a Manufacturing Package from a Tiny, Unknown Vendor? *346*

Window on Management
Ford Europe Makes Its Outsourcing Contractors Part of Its Team *351*

Chapter 12

Window on Organizations
Air Canada Overhauls Its Web Site *360*

Window on Technology
Flying High with CAD *376*

Window on Management
Enabling Reuse of Designs Through Artificial Intelligence *388*

Window on Organizations
The Neural Network Approach to Stock Picking *391*

Chapter 13

Window on Management
Practicing Decision Making *411*

Window on Organizations
The Hohenheim CATeam Room *414*

Window on Technology
Fighting Infoglut *422*

Chapter 14

Window on Organizations
Uprooting the Internet Hackers *434*

Window on Management
Client/Server Disaster Planning *438*

Window on Technology
British Customs Tests Its GUIS *451*

Chapter 15

Window on Organizations
The 800-Pound Gorilla of Transnational Technological Change *465*

Window on Management
Traveling Down the Road of International Technology Infrastructure Mergers *476*

Window on Technology
Is the Internet a World Tool? *479*

Preface

Essentials of Management Information Systems: Organization and Technology (Second Edition) is based on the premise that professional managers in both the private and public sectors cannot afford to ignore information systems. In today's business environment, information systems have become essential for creating competitive firms, managing global corporations, and providing useful products and services to customers. Briefly, it is difficult—if not impossible—to manage a modern organization without at least some grounding in the fundamentals of what information systems are, how they affect the organization and its employees, and how they can make businesses more competitive and efficient.

Accordingly, we have written this book to provide a concise introduction to management information systems that undergraduate and MBA students will find vital to their professional success. *Essentials of Management Information Systems* has many of the same features of our larger text book, *Management Information Systems: Organization and Technology (Fourth Edition)*. However, core MIS concepts are presented in 15 chapters, making the text especially well-suited for introductory MIS courses, courses lasting less than one semester, and courses requiring a smaller MIS text to combine with hands-on software, case studies or other projects.

THE INFORMATION REVOLUTION IN BUSINESS AND MANAGEMENT

This book reflects three powerful trends that have recast the role of information systems in business and management:

- The Internet and other global communications networks link together key participants in the value chain of a business—vendors, manufacturers, distributors, and customers. We can now design global business organizations linking factories, offices, and mobile sales forces around the clock. A few years ago this was a dream.

- Globalization of markets puts new emphasis on organizational design and management control. When parts originate in Korea, assembly occurs in Mexico, and finance, marketing and general counsel are in New York, companies face tough challenges in designing the proper organization and managing the work.

- The transformation of the United States and other advanced industrial countries into full-fledged information economies puts new emphasis on productivity of knowledge workers, short product lifecycles, and knowledge and information as a source of competitive advantage.

In essence, the work of an organization—and its employees—depends on what its information systems are capable of doing. Increasing market share, becoming the high-quality or low-cost producer, developing new products, and increasing employee productivity, depend more and more on the kinds and quality of information systems in the firm. Information systems can lead to more efficient and effective organizations, new styles and procedures of management, new strategies, and new organizational roles.

NEW TO THE SECOND EDITION

This edition maintains the strengths of earlier editions while showing how the Internet and related technologies are transforming information systems and business organizations. The second edition was reworked from start to finish to integrate the issues surrounding the growing use of the Internet more fully into the MIS course. This new direction is reflected in the following changes:

THE INTERNET. An entirely new chapter on the Internet and enterprise networking (Chapter 9) describes the underlying technology, capabilities, and benefits of the Internet with numerous illustrations from real-world companies. The chapter carefully analyzes the benefits and limitations of this world-wide network of networks.

INTERNET INTEGRATED INTO EVERY CHAPTER. Every chapter contains a Window On box, case study, or in-text discussion of how the Internet is changing a particular aspect of information systems. Strategic uses of the Internet, electronic commerce, intranets, Java software, intelligent agents, Internet-based group collaboration, and Internet security are among the topics given detailed coverage.

THE INTERNET CONNECTION AND INTERACTIVE INTERNET PROJECTS. **The Internet Connection** can be found in each chapter. The Internet Connection interactively shows students how to use the Internet for research and management problem-solving and helps professors integrate the Internet into the MIS course.

The Internet Connection icon in the text directs students to various sites on the World Wide Web of the Internet where they can find interactive projects, additional case studies, or resources related to topics and organizations discussed in the chapter. Students might be asked to use an interactive Web site to work on a project such as planning a sales conference, to conduct research, or to see a demonstration of an important MIS concept. The user first links to the Laudon-Laudon Home Page [http://www.prenhall.com/~laudon] via either a university or home Internet service. From the Laudon-Laudon Home Page the user can link directly to the Web resources specified for each Internet Connection session.

NEW LEADING-EDGE TOPICS. Full chapters address the challenges and opportunities created by information systems in today's global networked environment: Enterprise Networking and the Internet (Chapter 9); Managing Knowledge (Chapter 12); and Managing International Information Systems (Chapter 15); address these themes. The text includes up-to-date coverage of topics such as:

The Internet and the information superhighway

Electronic commerce

Intranets

Java and the software revolution

Systems for knowledge management

Virtual organizations

Data warehousing and multidimensional data analysis

Intelligent agents

Genetic algorithms

EXPANDED TREATMENT OF BUSINESS REENGINEERING, ORGANIZATIONAL CHANGE, AND ORGANIZATIONAL DESIGN USING INFORMATION TECHNOLOGY. Chapter 10 contains a detailed discussion of redesigning businesses processes using information technology. Experiences of real-world organizations performing business reengineering are described in this chapter and integrated throughout the text. The entire text reflects a heightened emphasis on the use of information technology in organizational change and organizational design.

ATTENTION TO SMALL BUSINESSES AND ENTREPRENEURS. We have expanded the text to devote more attention to the specific management, organization, and technology issues relevant to small businesses and entrepreneurs using information systems. Specially designated chapter-opening vignettes, Window On boxes, and ending case studies highlight the experiences of small businesses using information systems.

UNIQUE FEATURES OF THIS TEXT

Essentials of Management Information Systems: Organization and Technology (Second Edition) has many unique features designed to create an active, dynamic learning environment.

- **Interactive Multimedia Edition:** The textbook is available in a new multimedia interactive format on CD-ROM. The Multimedia Edition features the full 15 chapters of the printed text plus 10 additional videos explaining key concepts, simulations, interactive exercises, audio previews, line art, and research articles. With specially prepared "BulletText" summaries, hyperlinked graphics, and complete hypertext linking of concepts, definitions, and applications, the multimedia version can be used independently of the hard cover version or in conjunction with the hard cover text as an interactive study guide. All supplements for the printed version may be used with the Multimedia Edition.

- **An integrated framework for describing and analyzing information systems.** An integrated framework portrays information systems as being composed of management, organization and technology elements. This framework is used throughout the text to describe and analyze information systems and information system problems. A special diagram accompanying each chapter-opening vignette graphically illustrates how management, organization, and technology elements work together to create an information system solution to the business challenges discussed in the vignette. The diagram can be used as a starting point to analyze any information system problem.

- **Real-World Examples:** Real-world examples drawn from business and public organizations are used throughout to illustrate text concepts. Each chapter opens with a vignette illustrating the themes of the chapter by showing how a real-world organization meets a business challenge using information systems. More than 100 companies in the United States and over 80 organizations in Canada, Europe, Australia, Asia, and Africa are discussed (see the Organizations and International Organizations indexes).

Each chapter contains three WINDOW ON boxes (WINDOW ON MANAGEMENT, WINDOW ON ORGANIZATIONS, WINDOW ON TECHNOLOGY) that present real-world examples illustrating the management, organization, and technology issues in the chapter. Each WINDOW ON box concludes with a section called *To Think About* containing questions for students to apply chapter concepts to management problem solving. The themes for each box are:

WINDOW ON MANAGEMENT: Management problems raised by systems and their solution; management strategies and plans; careers and experiences of managers using systems.

WINDOW ON TECHNOLOGY: Hardware, software, telecommunications, data storage, standards, and systems-building methodologies.

 **WINDOW ON ORGANIZATIONS:** Activities of private and public organizations using information systems; experiences of people working with systems.

- **A truly international perspective:** In addition to a full chapter on Managing International Information Systems, all chapters of the text are illustrated with real-world examples from over eighty corporations in Canada, Europe, Asia, Latin America, Africa, Australia, and the Middle East. Each chapter contains at least one WINDOW ON box, case study or opening vignette drawn from a non-U.S. firm, and often more. The text concludes with five major international case studies contributed by leading MIS experts in Canada, Europe, and Australia—Andrew Boynton, International Institute for Management Development (Switzerland); Len Fertuck, University of Toronto (Canada), Helmut Krcmar and Bettina Schwarzer, Hohenheim University (Germany); Tapio Reponen, Turku School of Economics and Business Administration (Finland); and Peter Weill and J.B. Barolsky, University of Melbourne, (Australia).
- **Pedagogy to encourage active learning and management problem-solving.**

Essentials of Management Information Systems contains many features that encourage students to actively learn and to engage in management problem-solving.

GROUP PROJECTS: At the end of each chapter is a group project that encourages students to develop teamwork and oral and written presentation skills. The group project exercise asks students to work in groups of three or four to research a specific topic, analyze the pros and cons of an issue, write about it, and orally present the group's findings to the class. For instance, students might be asked to work in small groups to analyze a business and to suggest appropriate strategic information systems for that particular business or to develop a corporate ethics code on privacy that considers E-mail privacy and employers' use of information systems to monitor work sites.

MANAGEMENT CHALLENGES SECTION: Each chapter concludes with several challenges relating to the chapter topic that managers are likely to encounter. These challenges are multifaceted and sometimes pose dilemmas. They make excellent springboards for class discussion. Some of these Management Challenges are the organizational obstacles to building a database environment, agreeing on quality standards for information systems, and major risks and uncertainties in systems development.

TO THINK ABOUT QUESTIONS: Concluding every WINDOW ON box, these questions require students to apply chapter concepts to real-world scenarios. These questions frequently ask students to assume the role of managers, use multiple perspectives, consider different alternatives, and think creatively. The questions can be used for class discussion or for short written projects.

CASE STUDIES: Each chapter concludes with a case study based on a real-world organization. These cases help students synthesize chapter concepts and apply this new knowledge to real-world problems and scenarios. International case studies concluding the text provide additional opportunities for management problem-solving. Additional case studies and projects are provided on-line through the Internet Connection. Professors can assign these case studies for class discussion or for term projects.

INTERACTIVE LEARNING: The CD-ROM version provides an interactive, computer-managed instruction component that lets students learn at their own pace. Students apply text concepts to management problems in interactive exercises. Additional interactive learning projects are provided through the Internet Connection.

BOOK OVERVIEW

The six parts of the book are designed to be relatively independent of each other. Each instructor may choose to emphasize different parts.

Part One is concerned with the organizational foundations of systems and their emerging strategic role. It provides an extensive introduction to real-world systems, focusing on their relationship to organizations, management, and important ethical and social issues.

Parts Two and Three provide the technical foundation for understanding information systems, describing hardware, software, storage, and telecommunications technologies. Part Three concludes by describing how all of the information technologies work together in enterprise networking and internetworking with other organizations through the Internet.

Part Four focuses on the process of redesigning organizations using information systems, including reengineering of critical business processes. We see systems analysis and design as an exercise in organizational design, one that requires great sensitivity to the right tools and techniques, quality assurance and change management.

Part Five describes the role of information systems in capturing and distributing organizational knowledge and in enhancing management decision-making. It shows how knowledge management, work group collaboration, and individual and group decision making can be supported by the use of knowledge work, artificial intelligence, decision support, and executive support systems.

Part Six concludes the text by examining the special management challenges and opportunities created by the pervasiveness and power of contemporary information systems: ensuring security and control and developing global systems. Throughout the text emphasis is placed on using information technology to redesign the organization's products, services, procedures, jobs, and management structures, with numerous examples drawn from multinational systems and global business environments.

CHAPTER OUTLINE

Each chapter contains the following:
- A detailed outline at the beginning to provide an overview.
- An opening vignette describing a real-world organization to establish the theme and importance of the chapter.
- A diagram analyzing the opening vignette in terms of the management, organization, and technology model used throughout the text.
- A list of learning objectives .
- Marginal glosses of key terms in the text.
- Management challenges.
- An Internet Connection icon directing students to related material on the Internet.
- A chapter summary keyed to the learning objectives.
- A list of key terms that the student can use to review concepts.
- Review questions for students to test their comprehension of chapter material.
- A set of discussion questions that can be used for class discussion or for research topics.
- A group project to develop teamwork and presentation skills.
- A chapter-ending case study that illustrates important themes.
- A list of references for further research on topics.

INSTRUCTIONAL SUPPORT MATERIALS:

Software

A series of optional management software cases called *Solve it! Management Problem Solving with PC Software* has been developed to support the text. *Solve it!* consists of 10 spreadsheet and 10 database cases drawn from real-world businesses, a data diskette with the files required by the cases, and several Internet projects. The cases are graduated in difficulty. The case book contains complete tutorial documentation showing how to use spreadsheet and database software to solve the problems. There are separate *Solve it!* case books for Windows and DOS software tools. A new version of *Solve it!* with all new cases is published every year. *Solve it!* must be adopted for an entire class. It can be purchased directly from the supplier, Azimuth Corporation, 124 Penfield Ave., Croton-on-Hudson, New York 10520 (Telephone 914-271-6321).

Instructor's Manual

The Instructor's Manual written by Dr. Glenn Bottoms of Gardner-Webb University, features teaching suggestions, Internet Resources, lecture outlines and answers to key terms, review and discussion questions, case studies and group projects. This supplement is also available on disk.

Test Item File

New to this edition is a separate, expanded Test Item File, written by Dr. Bindiganavale Vijayaraman of the College of Business Administration, University of Akron. This edition includes true/false, multiple choice, fill-ins and essay questions, rated according to level of difficulty.

Computerized Test Bank

Prentice Hall Custom Test allows instructors to create and design tests as well as maintain student records. The Custom Test is comprised of the questions from the Test Item File. It is PC compatible.

Video Cases

Nine video cases based on the real-world corporations and organizations including selections from *computer chronicles* are available to adopters. The video cases illustrate the concepts in the text, and can be used for class discussion or written projects.

Powerpoint Slides

Over 100 electronic color slides created by Dr. Edward Fisher of Central Michigan University are available to adopters. The slides, which illuminate and build upon key concepts in the text, can be customized to suit class needs.

Transparencies

One hundred full-color transparency acetates are also available to adopters. These transparencies, taken from figures in the text, provide additional visual support to class lectures.

The New York Times "Themes of the Times"

To enhance access to important new items, a compilation of relevant Information Systems articles is available through an exclusive arrangement between Prentice Hall and The New York Times. Professors may order class quantities through their Prentice Hall sales representative.

Interactive Multimedia Edition

The Multimedia edition features the full 15 chapters of the printed text plus 10 additional videos explaining key concepts, simulations, interactive exercises, audio previews, line art and research articles.

Web Site

Please visit this book's Web Site for online exercises at http://www.prenhall.com/~laudon.

ACKNOWLEDGMENTS

The production of any book involves many valued contributions from a number of persons. We would like to thank all of our editors for encouragement, insight, and strong support for many years. We are grateful to our editor, Jo-Ann DeLuca for her energy in guiding the development of this edition, to Richard Wohl for supporting the project, and to Nancy Evans for her tireless marketing work. We thank Audrey Regan for directing the preparation of ancillary materials and commend Katherine Evancie of the Prentice Hall Production Department for guiding production of this text.

We are deeply indebted to Marshall R. Kaplan for his invaluable assistance in the preparation of this edition. Special thanks to Professors Glenn Bottoms, Bindiganavale Vijayaraman and Edward Fisher for their work on the supporting materials.

The Stern School of Business at New York University and the Information Systems Department provided a very special learning environment, one in which we and others could rethink the MIS field. Special thanks to Vasant Dhar, Ajit Kambil, Robert Kauffman, and Stephen Slade for providing critical feedback and support where deserved. Professor Norm White was especially helpful in commenting on the technical chapters and we thank him. Professor William H. Starbuck of the Management Department at NYU provided valuable comments and insights.

The late professor James Clifford of Stern's Information Systems Department made valuable recommendations for improving our discussion of files and databases. Jim was a wonderful friend and colleague, and we will miss him deeply.

Professor Al Croker of Baruch College and NYU, Professor Kenneth Marr of Hofstra University, Professor Edward Roche of Seton Hall University, Professor Sassan Rahmatian of California State University, Fresno, Ashok Malhotra and Emilio Collar of IBM, Jiri Rodovsky, and Russell Polo provided additional suggestions for improvement.

We are truly grateful to our colleagues in the MIS field who shared their expertise and comments with us. We want to thank Len Fertuck, Andrew Boynton, Helmut Krcmar, Tapio Reponen, Bettina Schwarzer, Joel Barolsky and Peter Weill for contributing case studies. They deeply enrich the text.

One of our goals for *Essentials of Management Information Systems* was to write a book which was authoritative, synthesized diverse views in the MIS literature, and helped define a common academic field. A large number of leading scholars in the field were contacted and assisted us in this effort. Reviewers and consultants for *Essentials of Management Information Systems* are listed in the back end papers of the book. We thank them for their contributions. Consultants for this new edition are: Jason Chen, Gonzaga University; Werner Schenk, University of Rochester; Doug Brinkley, Naval Postgraduate School; Tung Bui, Naval Postgraduate School; Gerald Kohers, Sam Houston State University; Don Springer, University of Portland; Erma Wood, University of Arkansas-Little Rock; William Harrison, Oregon State University; Barbara Libby, Niagara University; and Susan Kinney, Wake Forest University. It is our hope that this group endeavor contributes to a shared vision and understanding of the MIS field.

About the Authors

Kenneth C. Laudon is a Professor of Information Systems at New York University's Stern School of Business. He holds a B.A. in Economics from Stanford and Ph.D. from Columbia University. He has authored fourteen books dealing with information systems, organizations, and society. Professor Laudon has also written over seventy-five articles concerned with the social, organizational, and management impacts of information systems, privacy, ethics, and multimedia technology.

Professor Laudon's current research focuses on four areas: understanding the value of knowledge work; the social and organizational uses of information technology; privacy of personal information; and the development of multimedia, interactive digital higher education materials. He has received grants from the National Science Foundation to study the evolution of national information systems at the Social Security Administration, the IRS, and the FBI. A part of this research is concerned with computer-related organizational and occupational changes in large organizations, changes in management ideology, changes in public policy, and understanding productivity change in the knowledge sector.

Ken Laudon has testified as an expert before the United States Congress. He has been a researcher and consultant to the Office of Technology Assessment (United States Congress) and to the Office of the President, several executive branch agencies, and Congressional Committees. Professor Laudon also acts as a consultant on systems planning and strategy to several Fortune 500 firms and as an educator for major consulting firms in the U.S..

Ken Laudon's hobby is sailing.

Jane Price Laudon is a management consultant in the information systems area and the author of seven books. Her special interests include systems analysis, data management, MIS auditing, software evaluation, and teaching business professionals how to design and use information systems.

Jane received her Ph.D. from Columbia University, her M.A. from Harvard University, and her B.A. from Barnard College. She has taught at Columbia University and the New York University Graduate School of Business. She maintains a lifelong interest in Oriental languages and civilizations.

The Laudons have two daughters, Erica and Elisabeth.

Essentials of Management Information Systems: Organization and Technology reflects a deep understanding of MIS research and teaching as well as practical experience designing and building real world systems.

Chapter 1

Information Systems: Challenges and Opportunities

The Internet Levels the Playing Field

1.1 Why Information Systems?
The Competitive Business Environment
What Is an Information System?
Window on Technology:
UPS Competes Globally with Information Technology
A Business Perspective on Information Systems

1.2 Contemporary Approaches to Information Systems
Technical Approach
Behavioral Approach
Approach of This Text: Sociotechnical Systems

1.3 The New Role of Information Systems in Organizations
The Widening Scope of Information Systems
The Soaring Power of Information Technology
New Options for Organizational Design
Window on Management:
Custom Manufacturing: The New Automation
Window on Organizations:
The Internet: The New Electronic Marketplace
The Changing Management Process

1.4 The Challenge of Information Systems: Key Management Issues

Summary
Key Terms
Review Questions
Discussion Questions
Group Project
Case Study: David Battles Goliath for the Power of Information on the Internet
References

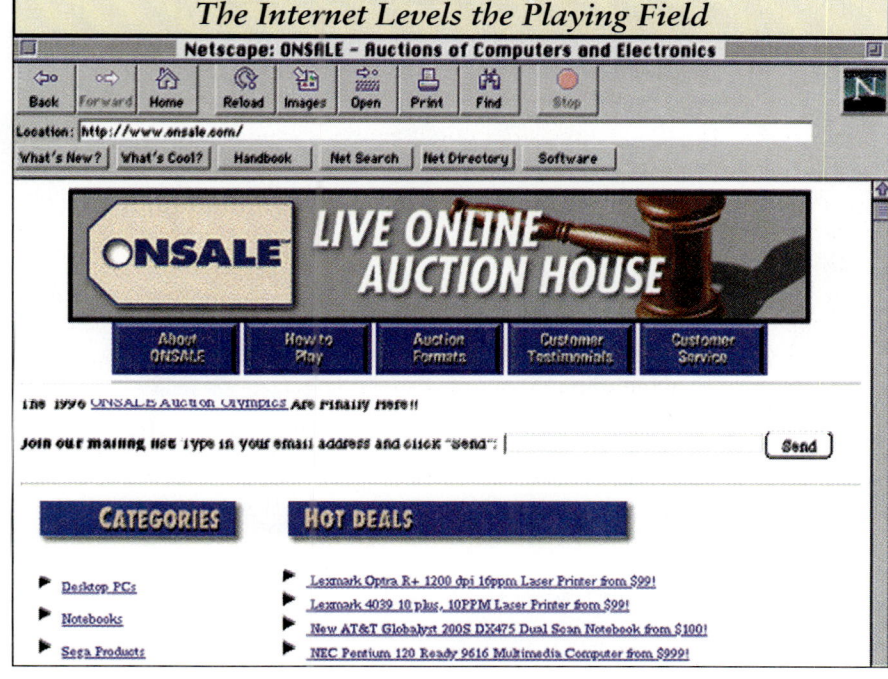

How can tiny computer startup companies compete against giants like Microsoft and Apple? Often they can't. Even with $75 million in financing from IBM and AT&T, Jerry Kaplan's first venture, Go Corporation, never brought its pen-based computing system to market. But from the ashes of failure rose the idea for a new venture, one that had low startup costs and could take advantage of the new business opportunities created by the Internet. Why not a home shopping channel for computer buffs? Kaplan then set about to create an on-line auction forum called Onsale where goods can be bought and sold using the Internet. It looks as if this time Kaplan's idea is working.

Onsale uses some of the interactive features of the Internet so that people can make on-line bids for items such as computer equipment, sports collectibles, wines, rock concert tickets, and electronic items. The mix of merchandise is pitched to young higher-income males between 20 and 45, who are the most typical Internet users. Kaplan runs Onsale so that it has the appeal of a real-life money game where winners walk away with incredible deals. Users are said to get a "voyeuristic thrill" in logging on to check what's on the auction block every day because the winning bidders' initials appear on screen along with their home cities. Onsale's information system accepts bids for items entered on the Internet, evaluates the bids, and identifies the highest bidder. Onsale's e-mail system automatically notifies high bidders when they have been outbidded and warns them about how much time they have left to raise the ante. To pay for the merchandise, successful bidders can submit their credit card numbers over the Internet or telephone them in using a toll-free number.

Even with a limited range of offerings, Onsale's sales are rising 50 percent a month, 20 percent of which comes from international buyers. Some days it moves more than 100 computers. To keep growing at that rate, Kaplan knows he'll have to add more interactivity, animation, and three-dimensional graphics to make Onsale look even more like a video game. He would like to find more cut-rate merchandise to sell and widen his audience. Onsale is ready to sell whatever its customers want to buy. ■

Source: Christopher Koch, "Where the Auction Is," *Webmaster*, January/February 1996.

Onsale's innovative use of the Internet demonstrates how information systems can help both small and large companies compete in today's global business environment. Information systems and global networks help companies such as Onsale extend their reach to faraway locations, offer new products and services, reshape jobs and work flows, and perhaps profoundly change the way they conduct business. An understanding of information systems is essential for today's managers because most organizations need information systems to survive and prosper. This chapter starts our investigation of information systems and organizations by describing information systems from both technical and behavioral perspectives and by surveying the changes they are bringing to organizations and management.

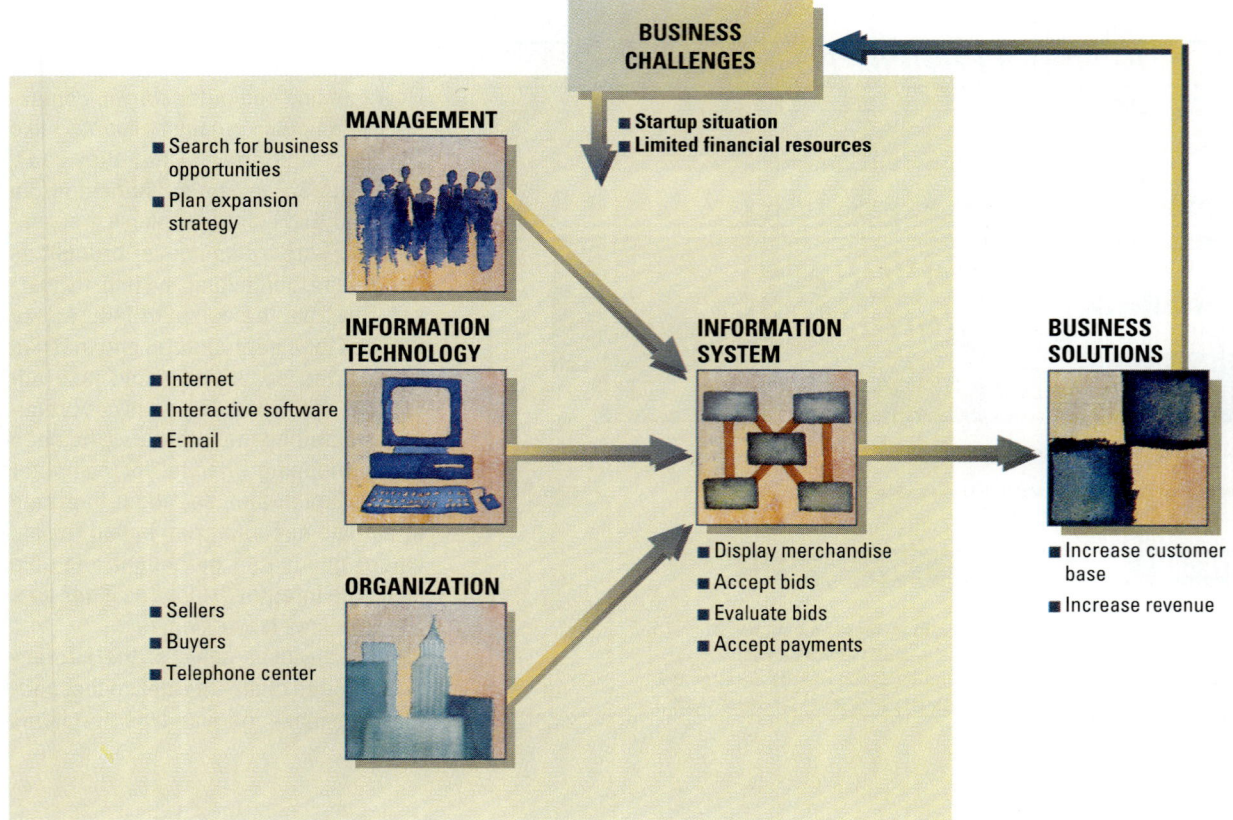

> **Learning Objectives**
>
> *After completing this chapter, you will be able to:*
>
> 1. Define an information system.
> 2. Explain the difference between computer literacy and information systems literacy.
> 3. Explain why information systems are so important today and how they are transforming organizations and management.
> 4. Identify the major management challenges to building and using information systems in organizations.

1.1 WHY INFORMATION SYSTEMS?

Until recently, there was little need for this textbook or course. Information itself was not considered an important asset for the firm. The management process was considered a face-to-face, personal art and not a far-flung, global coordination process. But today few managers can afford to ignore how information is handled by their organization.

THE COMPETITIVE BUSINESS ENVIRONMENT

Three powerful worldwide changes have altered the environment of business. The first change is the emergence and strengthening of the global economy. The second change is the transformation of industrial economies and societies into knowledge- and information-based service economies. The third is the transformation of the business enterprise. These changes in the business environment and climate, summarized in Table 1.1, pose a number of new challenges to business firms and their management.

Emergence of the Global Economy

A growing percentage of the American economy—and other advanced industrial economies in Europe and Asia—depends on imports and exports. Foreign trade, both exports and imports, accounts for a little over 25 percent of the goods and services produced in the United States, and even more in countries like Japan and Germany. This percentage will grow in the future. The success of firms today and in the future depends on their ability to operate globally.

Globalization of the world's industrial economies greatly enhances the value of information to the firm and offers new opportunities to businesses. Today, information systems provide the communication and analytic power that firms need for conducting trade and managing businesses on a global scale. Controlling the far-flung global corporation—communicating with distributors and suppliers, operating 24 hours a day in different national environments, servicing local and international reporting needs—is a major business challenge that requires powerful information system responses.

Globalization and information technology also bring new threats to domestic business firms: Because of global communication and management systems, customers now can shop in a worldwide marketplace, obtaining price and quality information reliably, 24 hours a day. This phenomenon heightens competition and forces firms to play in open, unprotected worldwide markets. To become effective and profitable participants in international markets, firms need powerful information and communication systems.

Transformation of Industrial Economies

The United States, Japan, Germany, and other major industrial powers are experiencing a third economic revolution. In the first revolution, the United States had by 1890

Table 1.1	The Changing Contemporary Business Environment
Globalization	
Management and control in a global marketplace	
Competition in world markets	
Global work groups	
Global delivery systems	
Transformation of Industrial Economies	
Knowledge- and information-based economies	
Productivity	
New products and services	
Knowledge a central productive and strategic asset	
Time-based competition	
Shorter product life	
Turbulent environment	
Limited employee knowledge base	
Transformation of the Enterprise	
Flattening	
Decentralization	
Flexibility	
Location independence	
Low transaction and coordination costs	
Empowerment	
Collaborative work and teamwork	

transformed itself from a colonial backwater to an agrarian powerhouse capable of feeding large segments of the world population. In the second revolution, the United States had by 1920 transformed itself from an agrarian nineteenth-century society to a first-class industrial power. In the third revolution, now in progress, the country is transforming itself into a knowledge- and information-based service economy.

The knowledge and information revolution began at the turn of the twentieth century and has gradually accelerated. By 1976 the number of white-collar workers employed in offices surpassed the number of farm workers, service workers, and blue-collar workers employed in manufacturing (see Figure 1.1). Today, most people no longer work in farms or factories but instead are found in sales, education, health care, banks, insurance firms, and law firms; they also provide business services like copying, computer software development, or deliveries. These jobs primarily involve working with, distributing, or creating new knowledge and information. In fact, knowledge and information work now account for a significant 75 percent of the American gross national product and nearly 70 percent of the labor force.

In a knowledge- and information-based economy, information technology and systems take on great importance. For instance, information technology constitutes more than 70 percent of the invested capital in service industries like finance, insurance, and real estate. Information systems are needed to optimize the flow of information and knowledge within the organization and to help management maximize the firm's knowledge resources.

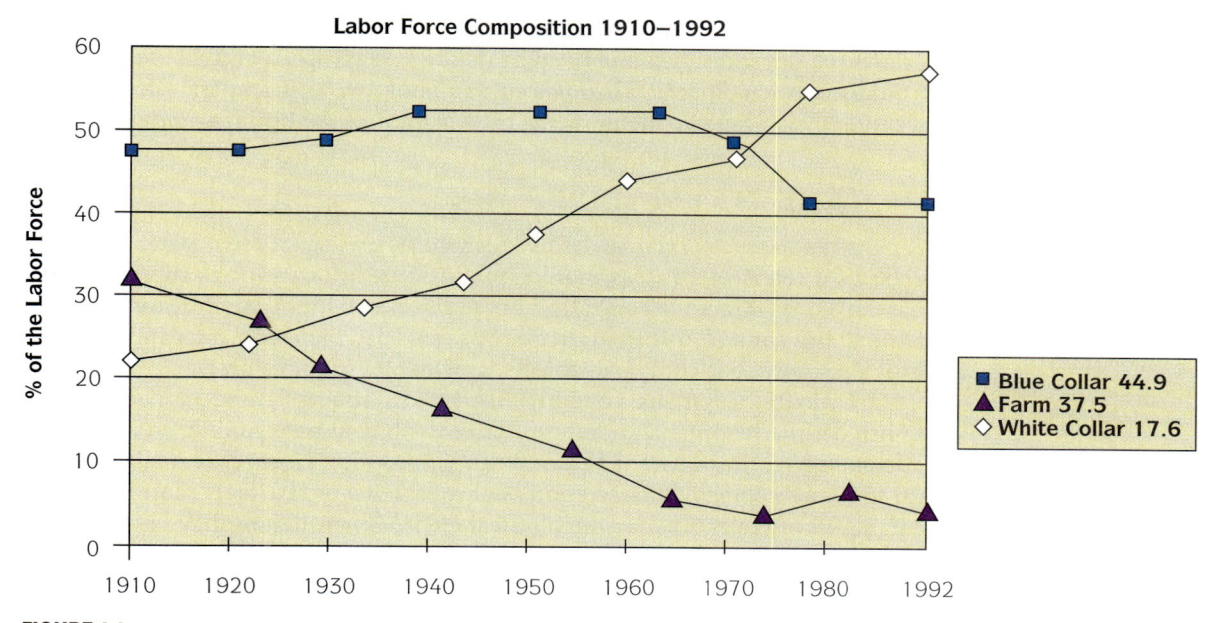

FIGURE 1.1
The growth of the information economy. Since the turn of the century, the United States has experienced a steady decline in the number of farm workers and blue-collar workers who are employed in factories. At the same time, the country is experiencing a rise in the number of white-collar workers who produce economic value using knowledge and information.
Sources: Adapted from U.S. Department of Commerce, Bureau of the Census, Statistical Abstract of the United States, 1994, *Table 644 and* Historical Statistics of the United States, Colonial Times to 1970, *Vol. 1, Series D 182-232.*

Because the productivity of employees will depend on the quality of the systems serving them, management decisions about information technology are critically important to the prosperity and survival of a firm. Consider also that the growing power of information technology makes possible new services of great economic value. Credit card use, overnight package delivery, and worldwide reservation systems are examples of services that are based on new information technologies. Information and the technology that delivers it have become critical, strategic assets for business firms and their managers (Leonard-Barton, 1995).

Transformation of the Business Enterprise

The third major change in the business environment is the very nature of organization and management. There has been a transformation in the possibilities for organizing and managing. Some firms have begun to take advantage of these new possibilities.

The traditional business firm was—and still is—a hierarchical, centralized, structured arrangement of specialists that typically relies on a fixed set of standard operating procedures to deliver a mass-produced product (or service). The new style of business firm is a flattened (less hierarchical), decentralized, flexible arrangement of generalists who rely on nearly instant information to deliver mass-customized products and services uniquely suited to specific markets or customers. This new style of organization is not yet firmly entrenched—it is still evolving. Nevertheless, the direction is clear, and this new direction would be unthinkable without information technology.

The traditional management group relied—and still does—on formal plans, a rigid division of labor, formal rules, and appeals to loyalty to ensure the proper operation of a firm. The new manager relies on informal commitments and networks to establish goals (rather than formal planning), a flexible arrangement of teams and individuals working in task forces, a customer orientation to achieve coordination among employees, and appeals to professionalism and knowledge to ensure proper operation of the firm. Once again, information technology makes this style of management possible.

Information technology is bringing about changes in organization that make the firm even more dependent than in the past on the knowledge, learning, and decision making of individual employees. Throughout this book, we describe the role that information technology is now playing in the transformation of the business enterprise form.

WHAT IS AN INFORMATION SYSTEM?

An **information system** can be defined technically as a set of interrelated components that collect (or retrieve), process, store, and distribute information to support decision making and control in an organization. In addition to supporting decision making, coordination, and control, information systems may also help managers and workers analyze problems, visualize complex subjects, and create new products.

Information systems contain information about significant people, places, and things within the organization or in the environment surrounding it (see Figure 1.2). By **information** we mean data that have been shaped into a form that is meaningful and useful to human beings. **Data,** in contrast, are streams of raw facts representing events occurring in organizations or the physical environment before they have been organized and arranged into a form that people can understand and use.

Three activities in an information system produce the information that organizations need for making decisions, controlling operations, analyzing problems, and creating new products or services. These activities are input, processing, and output. **Input** captures or collects raw data from within the organization or from its external environment. **Processing** converts this raw input into a more meaningful form. **Output** transfers the processed information to the people or activities where it will be used. Information systems also require **feedback,** which is output that is returned to appropriate members of the organization to help them evaluate or correct the input stage. In the information system used by Onsale to evaluate bids, the raw input consists of bid data. The computer processes these data into reports of bids made for an item up for auction that become output. The system thus provides meaningful information such as the highest bid, maximum and minimum bids, number of items sold, and total sales for the day.

Our interest in this book is in formal, organizational **computer-based information systems (CBIS)** like those designed and used by Onsale. **Formal systems** rest on accepted and fixed definitions of data and procedures for collecting, storing, processing, disseminating, and using these data. The formal systems we describe in this text are structured; that is, they operate in conformity with predefined rules that are relatively fixed and not easily changed. For instance, Onsale's auction bidding system requires that all bids be identified with the bidder's address and the amount of the bid.

Informal information systems (such as office gossip networks) rely, by contrast, on implicit agreements and unstated rules of behavior. There is no agreement on what

---

information system Interrelated components working together to collect, process, store, and disseminate information to support decision making, coordination, control, analysis, and visualization in an organization.

information Data that have been shaped into a form that is meaningful and useful to human beings.

data Streams of raw facts representing events occurring in organizations or the physical environment before they have been organized and arranged into a form that people can understand and use.

input The capture or collection of raw data from within the organization or from its external environment for processing in an information system.

processing The conversion, manipulation, and analysis of raw input into a form that is more meaningful to humans.

FIGURE 1.2
Functions of an information system. An information system contains information about an organization and its surrounding environment. Three basic activities—input, processing, and output—produce the information organizations need. Feedback is output returned to appropriate people or activities in the organization to evaluate and refine the input.

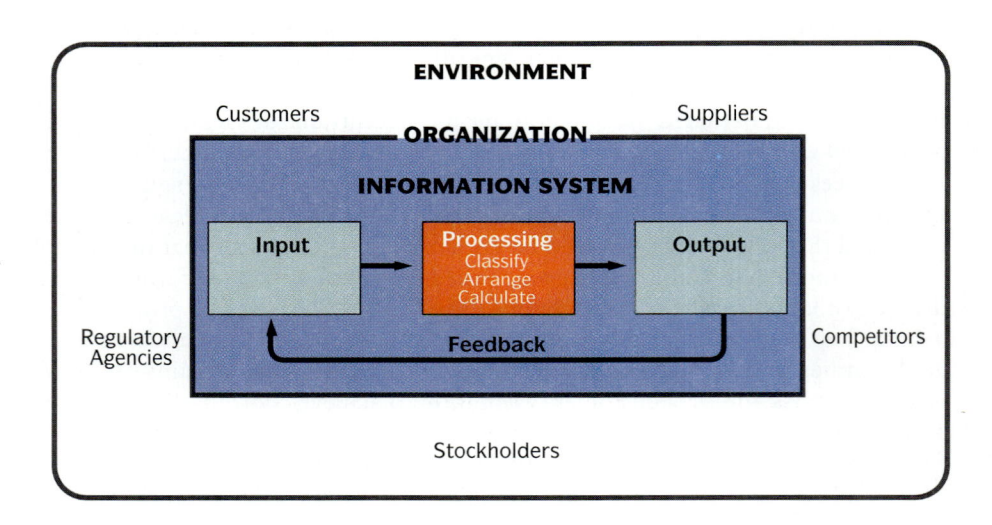

is information, or on how it will be stored and processed. Such systems are essential for the life of an organization, but an analysis of their qualities is beyond the scope of this text.

Formal information systems can be either computer-based or manual. Manual systems use paper and pencil technology. These manual systems serve important needs, but they too are not the subject of this text. Computer-based information systems, in contrast, rely on computer hardware and software technology to process and disseminate information. From this point on, when we use the term *information systems* we will be referring to computer-based information systems—formal organizational systems that rely on computer technology. The Window on Technology describes some of the typical technologies used in computer-based information systems today.

Although computer-based information systems use computer technology to process raw data into meaningful information, there is a sharp distinction between a computer and a computer program on the one hand, and an information system on the other. Electronic computers and related software programs are the technical foundation, the tools and materials, of modern information systems. Computers provide the equipment for storing and processing information. Computer programs, or software, are sets of operating instructions that direct and control computer processing. Knowing how computers and computer programs work is important in designing solutions to organizational problems, but computers are only part of an information system.

Housing provides an appropriate analogy. Houses are built with hammers, nails, and wood, but these do not make a house. The architecture, design, setting, landscaping, and all of the decisions that lead to the creation of these features are part of the house and are crucial for finding a solution to the problem of putting a roof over one's head. Computers and programs are the hammer, nails, and lumber of CBIS, but alone they cannot produce the information a particular organization needs. To understand information systems, one must understand the problems they are designed to solve, their architectural and design elements, and the organizational processes that lead to these solutions. Today's managers must combine computer literacy with information systems literacy.

A BUSINESS PERSPECTIVE ON INFORMATION SYSTEMS

From a business perspective, an information system is an organizational and management solution, based on information technology, to a challenge posed by the environment. Examine this definition closely because it emphasizes the organizational and management nature of information systems: To understand information systems—to be information systems literate as opposed to computer literate—a manager must understand the broader organization, management, and information technology dimensions of systems (see Figure 1.3) and their power to provide solutions to challenges and problems in the business environment.

Review the diagram at the beginning of the chapter, which reflects this expanded definition of an information system. The diagram shows how Onsale's information systems provide a solution to the business challenges posed by the company's limited resources. The diagram also illustrates how management, technology, and organization elements work together to create these systems. We begin each chapter of the text with a diagram like this one to help you analyze the opening case. You can use this diagram as a starting point for analyzing any information system or information system problem you encounter.

Organizations

Information systems are a part of organizations. Indeed, for some companies, such as credit reporting firms, without the system there would be no business. The key elements of an organization are its people, structure and operating procedures, politics, and culture. We introduce these components of organizations here and describe them in greater detail in Chapter 3. Formal organizations are composed of different levels

output The distribution of processed information to the people or activities where it will be used.

feedback Output that is returned to the appropriate members of the organization to help them evaluate or correct input.

computer-based information systems (CBIS) Information systems that rely on computer hardware and software for processing and disseminating information.

formal system System resting on accepted and fixed definitions of data and procedures, operating with predefined rules.

Window on Technology

UPS COMPETES GLOBALLY WITH INFORMATION TECHNOLOGY

United Parcel Service, the world's largest air and ground package distribution company, started out in 1907 in a closet-sized basement office. Jim Casey and Claude Ryan—two teenagers from Seattle with two bicycles and one phone—promised the "best service and lowest rates." UPS has used this formula successfully for nearly 90 years.

UPS still lives up to that promise today, delivering close to 3 billion parcels and documents each year to any address in the United States and to more than 185 countries and territories. Critical to the firm's success has been its investment in advanced information technology. Technology has helped UPS boost customer service while keeping costs low and streamlining its overall operations.

Using a handheld computer called a Delivery Information Acquisition Device (DIAD), UPS drivers automatically capture customers' signatures along with pickup, delivery, and timecard information. The drivers then place the DIAD into their truck's vehicle adapter, an information-transmitting device that is connected to the cellular telephone network. Package tracking information is then transmitted to UPS's computer network for storage and processing in UPS's main computer in Mahwah, New Jersey. From there, the information can be accessed worldwide to provide proof of delivery to the customer. The sys-

> **To Think About:** What are the inputs, processing, and outputs of UPS's package tracking system? What technologies are used? How are these technologies related to UPS's business strategy? What would happen if these technologies were not available?

tem can also generate a printed response to queries by the customer.

Through its automated package tracking system, UPS can monitor packages throughout the delivery process. At various points along the route from sender to receiver, a bar code device scans shipping information on the package label; the information is then fed into the central computer. Customer service representatives can check the status of any package from desktop computers linked to the central computer and are able to respond immediately to inquiries from customers. UPS customers can also access this information directly from their own microcomputers, using either the Internet or special package tracking software supplied by UPS.

UPS's Inventory Express, launched in 1991, warehouses customers' products and ships them overnight to any destination the customer requests. Customers using this service can transmit electronic shipping orders to UPS by 1:00 A.M. and expect delivery by 10:30 that same morning.

UPS is enhancing its information system capabilities so that it can guarantee that a particular package or group of packages will arrive at its destination at a specified time. If requested by the customer, UPS will be able to intercept a package prior to delivery and have it returned or rerouted.

Sources: Jeff Moad, "Can High Performance Be Cloned? Should It Be?" *Datamation*, March 1, 1995; Linda Wilson, "Stand and Deliver," *Information Week*, November 23, 1992; and UPS Public Relations, "High Tech Advances Lead UPS into the Paperless Age," April 1992.

and specialties. Their structures reveal a clear-cut division of labor. Experts are employed and trained for different functions, including sales and marketing, manufacturing, finance, accounting, and human resources. Table 1.2 describes these functions.

An organization coordinates work through a structured hierarchy and formal, standard operating procedures. The hierarchy arranges people in a pyramidal structure of ris-

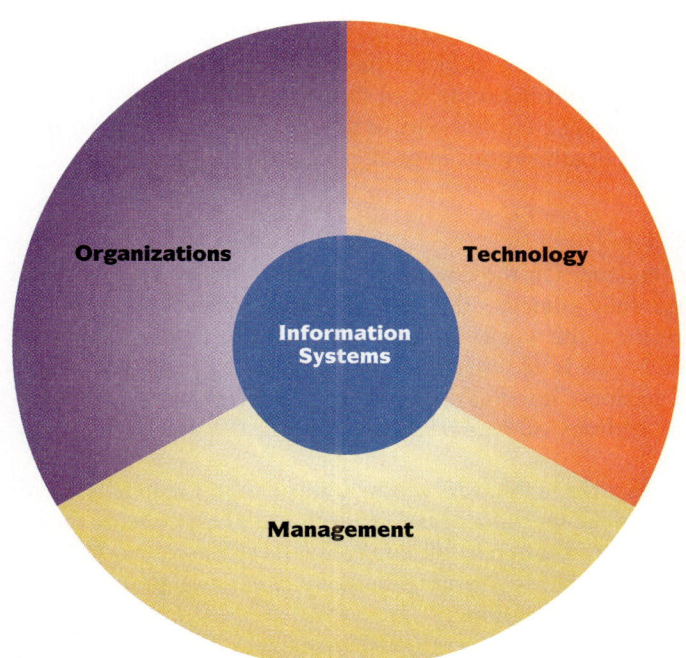

FIGURE 1.3
Information systems are more than computers. Using information systems effectively requires an understanding of the organization, management, and information technology shaping the systems. All information systems can be described as organizational and management solutions to challenges posed by the environment.

ing authority and responsibility. The upper levels of the hierarchy consist of managerial, professional, and technical employees, whereas the lower levels consist of operational personnel.

Standard operating procedures (SOPs) are formal rules for accomplishing tasks that have been developed over a long time; these rules guide employees in a variety of procedures, from writing an invoice to responding to complaining customers. Most procedures are formalized and written down, but many others are informal work practices. Many of a firm's SOPs are incorporated into information systems—such as how to pay a supplier or how to correct an erroneous bill.

Organizations require many different kinds of skills and people. In addition to managers, **knowledge workers** (such as engineers, architects, or scientists) design products or services and create new knowledge, and **data workers** (such as secretaries, bookkeepers, or clerks) process the organization's paperwork. **Production** or **service workers** (such as machinists, assemblers, or packers) actually produce the products or services of the organization.

Each organization has a unique *culture,* or fundamental set of assumptions, values, and ways of doing things, that has been accepted by most of its members. Parts of an organization's culture can always be found embedded in its information systems. For instance, the concern with putting service to the customer first is an aspect of the organizational culture of United Parcel Service that can be found in the company's package tracking systems.

standard operating procedures (SOPs) Formal rules for accomplishing tasks that have been developed to cope with expected situations.

knowledge workers People such as engineers or architects who design products or services and create knowledge for the organization.

data workers People such as secretaries or bookkeepers who process the organization's paperwork.

production or **service workers** People who actually produce the products or services of the organization.

Table 1.2 Major Organizational Functions

Function	Purpose
Sales and marketing	Selling the organization's products and services
Manufacturing	Producing products and services
Finance	Managing the organization's financial assets (cash, stocks, bonds, etc.)
Accounting	Maintaining the organization's financial records (receipts, disbursements, paychecks, etc.); accounting for the flow of funds
Human resources	Attracting, developing, and maintaining the organization's labor force; maintaining employee records

Different levels and specialties in an organization create different interests and points of view. These views often conflict. Conflict is the basis for organizational politics. Information systems come out of this cauldron of differing perspectives, conflicts, compromises, and agreements that are a natural part of all organizations. In Chapter 3 we will examine these features of organizations in greater detail.

Management

Managers perceive business challenges in the environment; they set the organizational strategy for responding, and they allocate the human and financial resources to achieve the strategy and coordinate the work. Throughout, they must exercise responsible leadership. Management's job is to "make sense" out of the many situations faced by organizations. The business information systems described in this book reflect the hopes, dreams, and realities of real-world managers. These are managers' conventional responsibilities.

But less understood is the fact that managers must do more than manage what already exists. They must also create new products and services and even re-create the organization from time to time. A substantial part of management is creative work driven by new knowledge and information. Information technology can play a powerful role in redirecting and redesigning the organization.

Chapter 3 describes the activities of managers and management decision making in detail. It is important to note that managerial roles and decisions vary at different levels of the organization. **Senior managers** make long-range strategic decisions about products and services to produce. **Middle managers** carry out the programs and plans of senior management. **Operational managers** are responsible for monitoring the firm's daily activities. All levels of management are expected to be creative: to develop novel solutions to a broad range of problems. Each level of management has different information needs and information system requirements.

Technology

Information systems technology is one of many tools available to managers for coping with change. CBIS use computer hardware, software, storage, and telecommunications technologies.

Computer hardware is the physical equipment used for input, processing, and output activities in an information system. It consists of the following: the computer processing unit; various input, output, and storage devices; and physical media to link these devices together. Chapter 5 describes computer hardware in greater detail.

Computer software consists of the detailed preprogrammed instructions that control and coordinate the computer hardware components in an information system. Chapter 6 explains the importance of computer software in information systems.

Storage technology includes both the physical media for storing data, such as magnetic or optical disk or tape, and the software governing the organization of data on these physical media. More detail on physical storage media can be found in Chapter 5, whereas Chapter 7 treats data organization and access methods.

Telecommunications technology, consisting of both physical devices and software, links the various pieces of hardware and transfers data from one physical location to another. Computers and communications equipment can be connected in networks for sharing voice, data, images, sound, or even video. A **network** links two or more computers to share data or resources such as a printer. Chapters 8 and 9 provide more details on telecommunications and networking technology and issues.

Let us return to UPS's package tracking system in the Window on Technology and identify the organization, management, and technology elements. The organization element anchors the package tracking system in UPS's sales and production functions (the main product of UPS is a service—package delivery). It identifies the required proce-

---

senior managers People occupying the topmost hierarchy in an organization who are responsible for making long-range decisions.

middle managers People in the middle of the organizational hierarchy who are responsible for carrying out the plans and goals of senior management.

operational managers People who monitor the day-to-day activities of the organization.

computer hardware Physical equipment used for input, processing, and output activities in an information system.

computer software Detailed, preprogrammed instructions that control and coordinate the work of computer hardware components in an information system.

storage technology Physical media and software governing the storage and organization of data for use in an information system.

telecommunications technology Physical devices and software that link various computer hardware components and transfer data from one physical location to another.

network Two or more computers linked to share data or resources such as a printer.

dures for identifying packages with both sender and recipient information, taking inventory, tracking the packages en route, and providing package status reports for UPS customers and customer service representatives. The system must also provide information to satisfy the needs of managers and workers. UPS drivers need to be trained in both package pickup and delivery procedures and in how to use the package tracking system so that they can work more efficiently and effectively. UPS's management is responsible for monitoring service levels and costs and for promoting the company's strategy of combining low cost and superior service. Management decided to use automation to increase the ease of sending a package via UPS and of checking its delivery status, thereby reducing delivery costs and increasing sales revenues. The technology supporting this system consists of handheld computers, bar code scanners, wired and wireless telecommunications networks, desktop computers, UPS's central computer, and storage technology for the package delivery data. The result is an information system solution to a business challenge.

1.2 CONTEMPORARY APPROACHES TO INFORMATION SYSTEMS

Multiple perspectives on information systems show that the study of information systems is a multidisciplinary field; no single theory or perspective dominates. Figure 1.4 illustrates the major disciplines that contribute problems, issues, and solutions in the study of information systems. In general, the field can be divided into technical and behavioral approaches. Information systems are sociotechnical systems. Though they are composed of machines, devices, and "hard" physical technology, they require substantial social, organizational, and intellectual investments to make them work properly.

TECHNICAL APPROACH

The technical approach to information systems emphasizes mathematically based, normative models to study information systems, as well as the physical technology and formal capabilities of these systems. The disciplines that contribute to the technical approach are computer science, management science, and operations research. Computer science is concerned with establishing theories of computability, methods of computation, and methods of efficient data storage and access. Management science emphasizes the development of models for decision-making and management practices. Operations research focuses on mathematical techniques for optimizing selected parameters of organizations such as transportation, inventory control, and transaction costs.

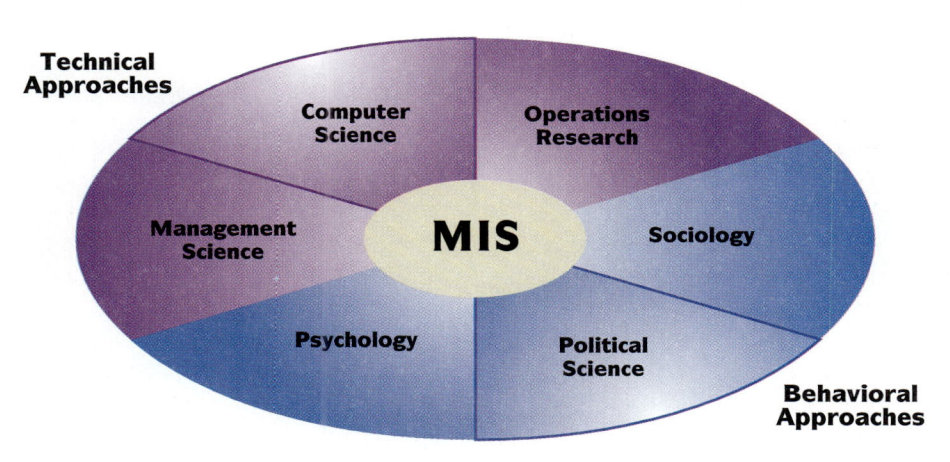

FIGURE 1.4
Contemporary approaches to information systems. The study of information systems deals with issues and insights contributed from technical and behavioral disciplines.

BEHAVIORAL APPROACH

A growing part of the information systems field is concerned with behavioral problems and issues. Many behavioral problems, such as system utilization, implementation, and creative design, cannot be expressed with the normative models used in the technical approach. Other behavioral disciplines also play a role. Sociologists focus on the impact of information systems on groups, organizations, and society. Political science investigates the political impacts and uses of information systems. Psychology is concerned with individual responses to information systems and cognitive models of human reasoning.

The behavioral approach does not ignore technology. Indeed, information systems technology is often the stimulus for a behavioral problem or issue. But the focus of this approach is generally not on technical solutions; it concentrates rather on changes in attitudes, management and organizational policy, and behavior (Kling and Dutton, 1982).

APPROACH OF THIS TEXT: SOCIOTECHNICAL SYSTEMS

The study of management information systems (MIS) arose in the 1970s to focus on computer-based information systems aimed at managers (Davis and Olson, 1985). MIS combines the theoretical work of computer science, management science, and operations research with a practical orientation toward building systems and applications. It also pays attention to behavioral issues raised by sociology, economics, and psychology.

Our experience as academics and practitioners leads us to believe that no single perspective effectively captures the reality of information systems. Problems with systems—and their solutions—are rarely all technical or all behavioral. Our best advice to students is to understand the perspectives of all disciplines. Indeed, the challenge and excitement of the information systems field is that it requires an appreciation and tolerance of many different approaches.

A sociotechnical systems perspective helps to avoid a purely technological approach to information systems. For instance, the fact that information technology is rapidly declining in cost and growing in power does not necessarily or easily translate into productivity enhancement or bottom-line profits.

In this book, we stress the need to optimize the performance of the system as a whole. Both the technical and behavioral components need attention. This means that technology must be changed and designed in such a way as to fit organizational and individual needs. At times, the technology may have to be "de-optimized" to accomplish this fit. Organizations and individuals must also be changed through training, learning, and planned organizational change in order to allow the technology to operate and prosper (see, for example, Liker et al., 1987). People and organizations change to take advantage of new information technology. Figure 1.5 illustrates this process of mutual adjustment in a sociotechnical system.

FIGURE 1.5
A sociotechnical perspective on information systems. In a sociotechnical perspective, the performance of a system is optimized when both the technology and the organization mutually adjust to one another until a satisfactory fit is obtained.
Source: Tornatsky et al., 1983.

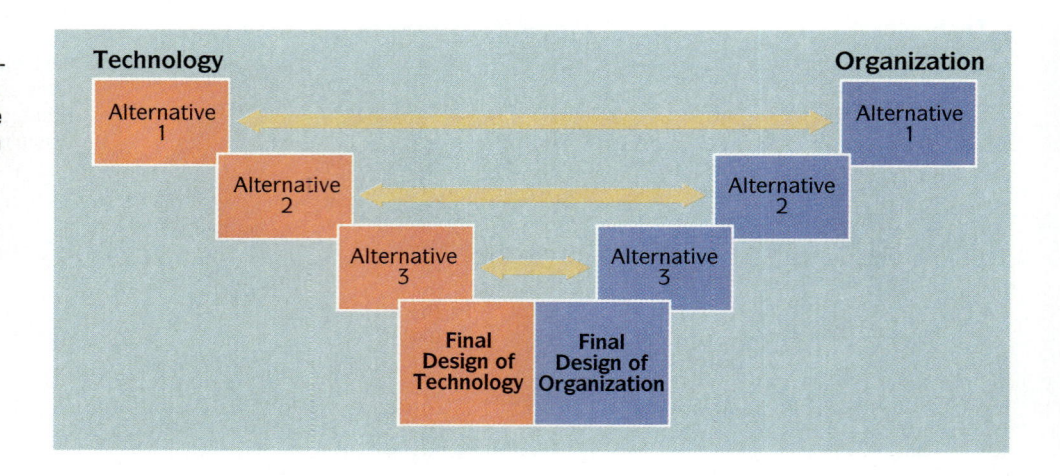

1.3 THE NEW ROLE OF INFORMATION SYSTEMS IN ORGANIZATIONS

Information systems cannot be ignored by managers because they play such a critical role in contemporary organizations. Digital technology is transforming business organizations. The entire cash flow of most Fortune 500 companies is linked to information systems. Today's systems directly affect how managers decide, how senior managers plan, and in many cases what products and services are produced (and how). They play a strategic role in the life of the firm. Responsibility for information systems cannot be delegated to technical decision makers.

THE WIDENING SCOPE OF INFORMATION SYSTEMS

Figure 1.6 illustrates the new relationship between organizations and information systems. There is a growing interdependence between business strategy, rules, and procedures on the one hand, and information systems software, hardware, databases, and telecommunications on the other. A change in any of these components often requires changes in other components. This relationship becomes critical when management plans for the future. What a business would like to do in five years is often dependent on what its systems will be able to do. Increasing market share, becoming the high-quality or low-cost producer, developing new products, and increasing employee productivity depend more and more on the kinds and quality of information systems in the organization.

A second change in the relationship of information systems and organizations results from the growing complexity and scope of system projects and applications. Building systems today involves a much larger part of the organization than it did in the past (see Figure 1.7). Whereas early systems produced largely technical changes that affected few people, contemporary systems bring about managerial changes (who has what information about whom, when, and how often) and institutional "core" changes (what products and services are produced, under what conditions, and by whom).

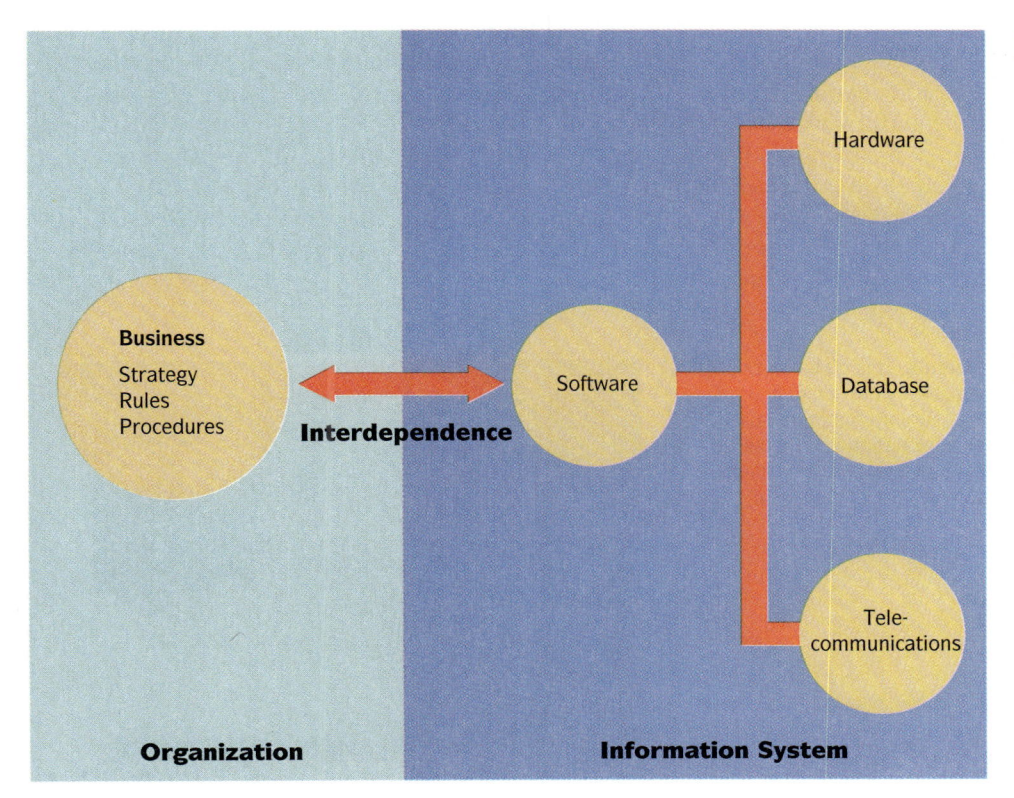

FIGURE 1.6
The interdependence between organizations and information systems. In contemporary systems there is a growing interdependence between organizational business strategy, rules, and procedures and the organization's information systems. Changes in strategy, rules, and procedures increasingly require changes in hardware, software, databases, and telecommunications. Existing systems can act as a constraint on organizations. Often, what the organization would like to do depends on what its systems will permit it to do.

FIGURE 1.7
The widening scope of information systems. Over time, information systems have come to play a larger role in the life of organizations. Early systems brought about largely technical changes that were relatively easy to accomplish. Later systems affected managerial control and behavior; ultimately systems influenced "core" institutional activities concerning products, markets, suppliers, and customers.

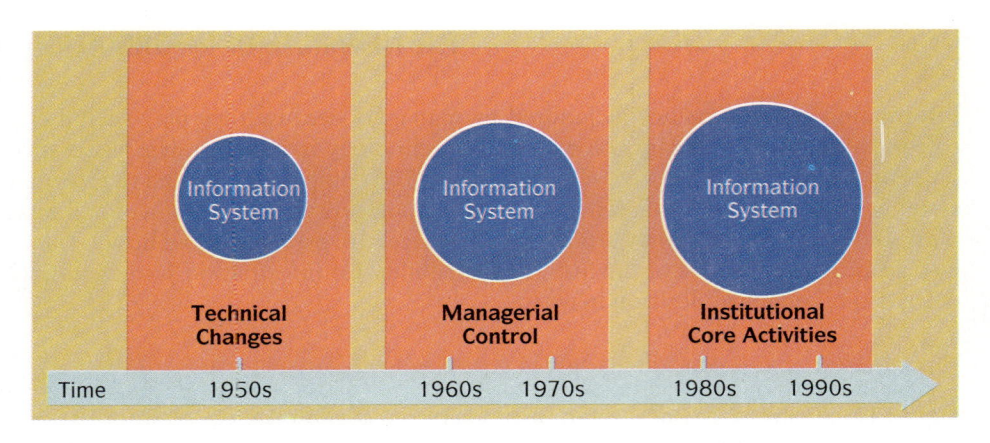

In the 1950s, employees in the treasurer's office, a few part-time programmers, a single program, a single machine, and a few clerks might have used a computerized payroll system. The change from a manual to a computer system was largely technical—the computer system simply automated a clerical procedure such as check processing. In contrast, today's integrated human resources system (which includes payroll processing) may involve all major corporate divisions, the human resources department, dozens of full-time programmers, a flock of external consultants, multiple machines (or remote computers linked by telecommunications networks), and perhaps hundreds of end users in the organization who use payroll data to make calculations about benefits and pensions and to answer a host of other questions. The data, instead of being located in and controlled by the treasurer's office, are now available to hundreds of employees via desktop computers, each of which is as powerful as the large computers of the mid–1980s. This contemporary system embodies both managerial and institutional changes.

THE SOARING POWER OF INFORMATION TECHNOLOGY

One reason why systems play a larger role in organizations, and why they affect more people, is the soaring power and declining cost of the computer technology that is at the core of information systems. Computing power has been doubling every 18 months, so that the performance of microprocessors has improved 25,000 times since their invention 25 years ago. In today's organization, it is now possible to put the power of a large mainframe computer, which at one time took up nearly an entire floor of a company, on every desktop. With powerful, easy-to-use software, the computer can crunch numbers, analyze vast pools of data, or simulate complex physical and logical processes with animated drawings, sounds, and even tactile feedback.

The Internet. This global network of networks provides a highly flexible platform for information-sharing. Digital information can be distributed at almost no cost to millions of people throughout the world.

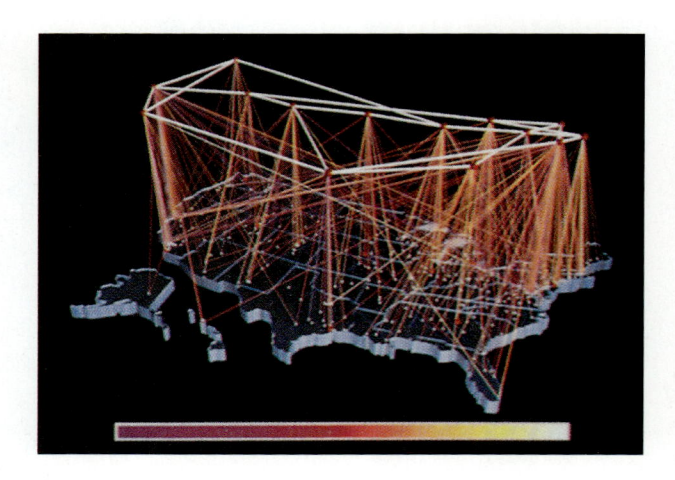

14   CHAPTER 1   Information Systems: Challenges and Opportunities

The revolution in computer technology has spawned powerful communication networks that organizations can use to access vast storehouses of information from around the world and to coordinate activities across space and time. These networks are transforming the shape and form of business enterprises and even our society.

The world's largest and most widely used network is the **Internet.** The Internet is an international network of networks that are both commercial and publicly owned. At last estimate, the Internet connected more than 100,000 different networks from nearly 200 countries around the world. More than 35 million people working in science, education, government, and business organizations use the Internet to exchange information or perform business transactions with other organizations around the globe.

Internet International network that is a collection of more than 31,000 private or public networks.

The Internet is extremely elastic. If networks are added or removed or failures occur in parts of the system, the rest of the Internet continues to operate. Through special communication and technology standards, any computer can communicate with virtually any other computer linked to the Internet using ordinary telephone lines. Companies and private individuals can use the Internet to exchange business transactions, text messages, graphic images, and even video and sound, whether they are located next door or on the other side of the globe. Table 1.3 describes some of the Internet's capabilities.

The Internet is creating a new "universal" technology platform upon which to build all sorts of new products, services, strategies, and organizations. Its potential for reshaping the way information systems are being used in business and daily life is vast and rich, and it is just beginning to be tapped. By eliminating many technical and geographic barriers, the Internet is accelerating the information revolution, inspiring organizations to find new ways to incorporate information systems into their business model.

Table 1.3 What You Can Do on the Internet

	Function	Description
	Communicate and collaborate	Send electronic mail messages; transmit documents and data
	Access information	Search for documents, databases, and library card catalogues; read electronic brochures, manuals, books, and advertisements
	Participate in discussions	Join interactive discussion groups; conduct primitive voice transmission
	Obtain information	Transfer computer files of text, computer programs, graphics, animations, or videos
	Find entertainment	Play interactive video games; view short video clips; read illustrated and even animated magazines and books
	Exchange business transactions	Advertise, sell, and purchase goods and services

In Chapter 9 we discuss Internet capabilities in greater detail. We will also be discussing relevant features of the Internet throughout the text because the Internet affects so many aspects of information systems in organizations.

NEW OPTIONS FOR ORGANIZATIONAL DESIGN

Information systems can become powerful instruments for making organizations more competitive and efficient. Information technology can be used to redesign and reshape organizations, transforming their structure, scope of operations, reporting and control mechanisms, work practices, work flows, products, and services. We now describe some of the major organizational design options that information technology has made available.

Flattening Organizations

Large, bureaucratic organizations developed before the explosive growth of information technology in the 1980s and 1990s. Today, such organizations are often inefficient, slow to change, and uncompetitive. Some of these organizations have downsized, reducing the number of employees and the number of levels in their organizational hierarchies. For example, by 1994 heavy equipment manufacturer Caterpillar, Inc., was producing the same level of output as it did 15 years earlier, but with 40,000 fewer employees.

Flatter organizations have fewer levels of management, with lower-level employees being given greater decision-making authority (see Figure 1.8). Those employees are empowered to make more decisions than in the past, they no longer work standard 9-to-5 hours, and they no longer necessarily work in an office. Moreover, such employees may be scattered geographically, sometimes working half a world away from the manager.

Modern information systems have made such changes possible. They can make more information available to line workers so they can make decisions that previously had been made by managers. Networks of computers have made it possible for em-

FIGURE 1.8
Flattening organizations. Information systems can reduce the number of levels in an organization by providing managers with information to supervise larger numbers of workers and by giving lower-level employees more decision-making authority.

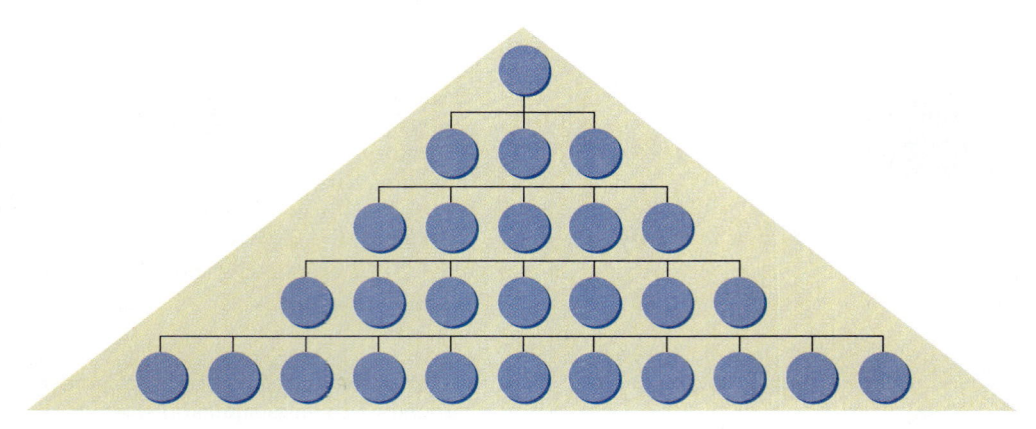

A traditional hierarchical organization with many levels of management

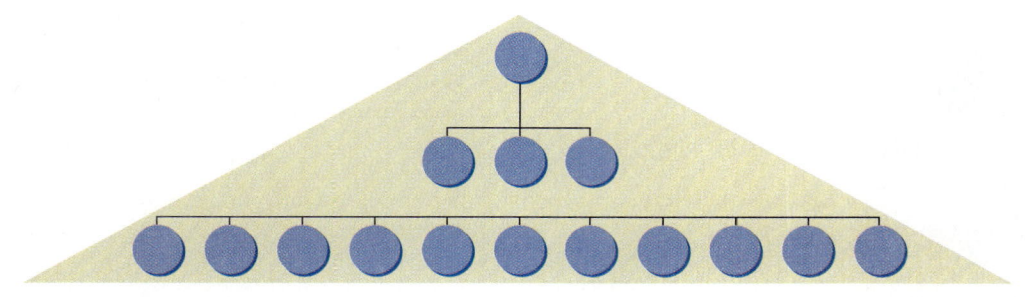

An organization that has been "flattened" by removing layers of management

ployees to work together as a team, another feature of flatter organizations. With the emergence of global networks like the Internet, team members can collaborate closely even from distant locations. These changes mean that the management span of control has also been broadened, allowing high-level managers to manage and control more workers spread over greater distances. Many companies have eliminated thousands of middle managers as a result of these changes. AT&T, IBM, and General Motors are just a few of the organizations that have eliminated more than 30,000 middle managers in one fell swoop.

Separating Work from Location

It is now possible to organize globally while working locally: Information technologies like e-mail, the Internet, and video conferencing to the desktop permit tight coordination of geographically dispersed workers across time zones and cultures. Entire parts of organizations can disappear: Inventory (and the warehouses to store it) can be eliminated as suppliers tie into the firm's computer systems and deliver just what is needed and just in time.

Modern telecommunications technology has eliminated distance as a factor for many types of work in many situations. Salespersons can spend more time in the field—with customers—and yet have more up-to-date information with them and while carrying much less paper. Many employees can work remotely from their homes, or cars, and companies can reserve space at a much smaller central office for meeting clients or other employees.

Collaborative teamwork across thousands of miles has become a reality as designers work on the design of a new product together even if they are located on different continents. Ford Motor adopted a cross-continent collaborative model when it undertook the design of the 1994 Ford Mustang. Supported by high-capacity communications networks and computer-aided design (CAD) software, Ford designers launched the Mustang design in Dunton, England. The design was worked on simultaneously by designers at Dearborn, Michigan, and Dunton, with some input from designers in Japan and Australia. Once the design was completed, Ford engineers in Turin, Italy, used it to produce a full-sized physical model.

Companies are not limited to physical locations for providing products and services. Networked information systems are allowing companies to coordinate their geographically distributed capabilities as virtual corporations (or **virtual organizations**), sometimes called networked organizations. Virtual organizations use networks to link people, assets, and ideas, allying with suppliers and customers (and sometimes even competitors) to create and distribute new products and services without being limited by traditional organizational boundaries or physical location. One company can take advantage of the capabilities of another company without actually physically linking to that company. Each company contributes its core competencies, the capabilities that it does the best. These networked organizations last as long as the opportunity remains profitable. For example, one company might be responsible for product design, another for assembly and manufacturing, and another for administration and sales. Figure 1.9 illustrates the concept of a virtual corporation.

For example, Calyx and Corolla, which has its headquarters in San Francisco, created a networked organization to sell fresh flowers directly to customers, bypassing the traditional flower shop. The company takes orders via a toll-free telephone number and enters them into a central computer, which transmits them directly to grower farms. Farmers pick the flowers and place them in waiting Federal Express refrigerated vans. Calyx and Corolla flowers are delivered within a day or two to their final destination. They are weeks fresher than flowers provided by traditional florists.

virtual organization Organization using networks linking people, assets, and ideas to create and distribute products and services without being limited by traditional organizational boundaries or physical location.

Increasing Flexibility of Organizations

Modern telecommunications technology has enabled many organizations to organize in more flexible ways, increasing the ability of those organizations to respond to changes

FIGURE 1.9
A virtual corporation. Networked information systems enable different companies to join together to provide goods and services.

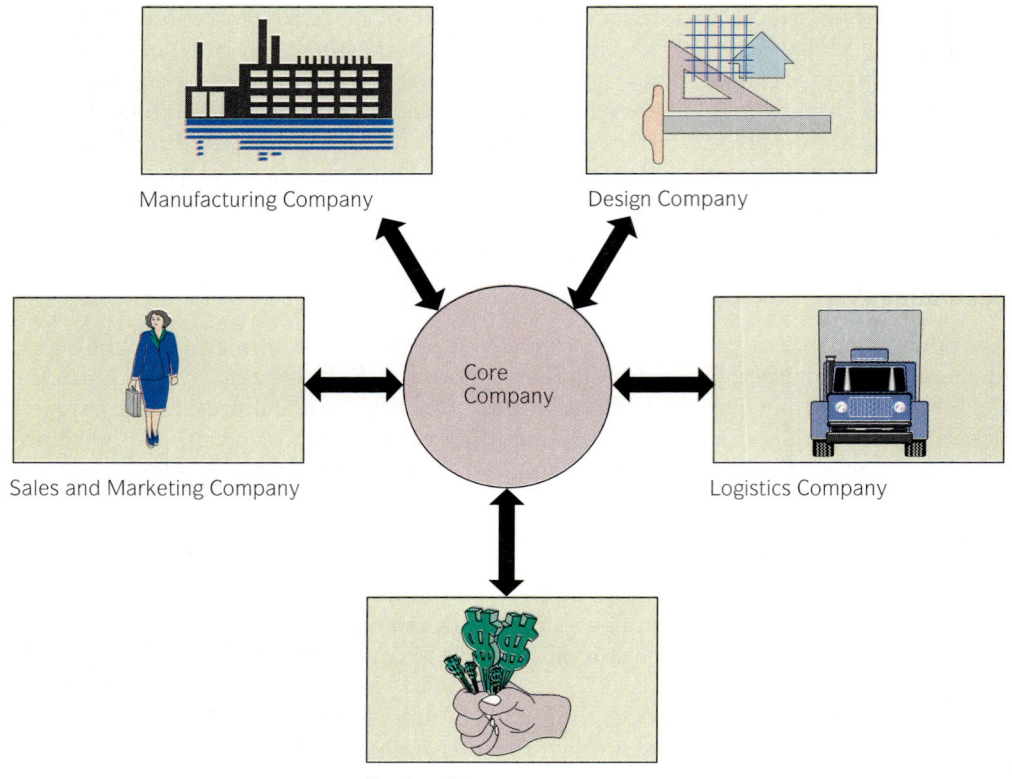

Manufacturing Company   Design Company

Sales and Marketing Company   Core Company   Logistics Company

Finance Company

in the marketplace and to take advantage of new opportunities. Information systems can give both large and small organizations additional flexibility to overcome some of the limitations posed by their size. Table 1.4 describes some of the ways in which information technology can help small companies act big and help big companies act "small." Small organizations such as Onsale (described in the chapter-opening vignette) can use information systems to acquire some of the muscle and reach of larger organizations. They can perform coordinating activities such as processing bids or keeping track of inventory with very few clerks and managers. Large organizations can use information technology to achieve some of the agility and responsiveness of small organizations.

The Window on Management explores one aspect of this phenomenon—custom manufacturing. In **custom manufacturing**, software and computer networks are used to link the plant floor tightly with orders, design, and purchasing and to finely control production machines. The result is a dynamically responsive environment in which products can be turned out in greater variety and easily customized with no added cost for small production runs.

custom manufacturing Use of software and computer networks to finely control production so that products can be easily customized with no added cost for small production runs.

Redefining Organizational Boundaries and Electronic Commerce

Telecommunications-based information systems enable transactions such as payments and purchase orders to be exchanged electronically among different companies. Organizations can also share business data, catalogues, or mail messages through such systems. These networked information systems can create new relationships between an organization, its customers, and suppliers, redefining their organizational boundaries. For example, the Chrysler Corporation is networked to suppliers, such as the Budd Company of Rochester, Michigan. Through this electronic link, the Budd Company monitors Chrysler production and ships sheet metal parts exactly when needed, preceded by an electronic shipping notice. Chrysler and its suppliers have thus become linked business partners with mutually shared responsibilities.

Table 1.4	How Information Technology Increases Organizational Flexibility

Small Companies

Desktop machines, inexpensive computer-aided design (CAD) software, and computer-controlled machine tools provide the precision, speed, and quality of giant manufacturers.

Information immediately accessed by telephone and communications links eliminates the need for research staff and business libraries.

Managers can more easily obtain the information they need to manage larger numbers of employees in widely scattered locations.

Large Companies

Custom manufacturing systems allow large factories to offer customized products in small quantities.

Massive databases of customer purchasing records can be analyzed so that large companies can know their customers' needs and preferences as easily as local merchants.

Information can be easily distributed down the ranks of the organization to empower lower-level employees and work groups to solve problems.

The information system linking Chrysler and its suppliers is called an interorganizational information system. Systems linking a company to its customers, distributors, or suppliers are termed **interorganizational systems** because they automate the flow of information across organizational boundaries (Barrett, 1986–1987; Johnston and Vitale, 1988). Such systems allow information or processing capabilities of one organization to improve the performance of another or to improve relationships among organizations.

Interorganizational systems that provide services to multiple organizations by linking together many buyers and sellers create an **electronic market**. Through computers and telecommunications, these systems function like electronic middlemen, with lowered costs for typical marketplace transactions such as selecting suppliers, establishing prices, ordering goods, and paying bills. (Malone, Yates, and Benjamin, 1987). Buyers and sellers can complete purchase and sale transactions digitally regardless of their location.

The Internet is creating a global electronic marketplace where a vast array of goods and services are being advertised, bought, and exchanged worldwide. Fueling commercial use of the Internet is a capability called the World Wide Web, which allows companies to combine graphics, text, and sound into eye-catching electronic brochures, advertisements, product manuals, and order forms. All kinds of products and services are available on the Web, including fresh flowers, books, real estate, musical recordings, electronics, steaks, and automobiles.

Many retailers operate independently on the Web, such as Absolutely Fresh Flowers (http://www.cts.com/~flowers/). Discovering such independent retailers can be difficult, however, so most prefer to offer their products through one of the electronic shopping malls. One such mall is the Internet Shopping Network (http://www2.internet.net/directories.html), which is owned by the Home Shopping Network. Customers can locate products on this mall either by manufacturer, if they know what they want, or by product type.

Even financial trading has arrived on the Web, offering electronic trading in stocks, bonds, and other financial instruments. The Window on Organizations examines the growing interest in Internet trading.

interorganizational systems Information systems that automate the flow of information across organizational boundaries and link a company to its customers, distributors, or suppliers.

electronic market A marketplace that is created by computer and communication technologies that link many buyers and sellers via interorganizational systems.

Reorganizing Work Flows

Since the first uses of information technology in business in the early 1950s, information systems have been progressively replacing manual work procedures with automated work procedures, work flows, and work processes. Electronic work flows have reduced

Window on Management

CUSTOM MANUFACTURING: THE NEW AUTOMATION

For two decades after World War II, mass production reigned supreme. Mass-production techniques pushed companies into standardized, one-size-fits-all products, long product life cycles, and rigid manufacturing emphasizing efficiency and low cost over flexibility. Special orders and made-to-order products cost more. But today's consumers are very choosy. They want quality, value, and products specially tailored to their needs—at the lowest possible price. Enter custom manufacturing.

Custom manufacturing uses state-of-the-art information technology to produce and deliver products and services designed to fit the specifications of individual customers. Companies can customize products in quantities as small as one with the same speed and low cost as mass-production methods. Custom manufacturing systems use information taken from the customer to control the flow of goods. For example, Motorola manufactures handheld pagers to individual customer specifications. Retailers use Macintosh microcomputers to help customers design the pager features they want. At Motorola's Boynton Beach, Florida, plant, orders stream in over toll-free telephone lines or e-mail for different colors and models. The data are digitized and flow immediately to the assembly line. Within 80 minutes, pick-and-place robots select the proper components for each order, and humans assemble them into the final product. Often the customer can have his or her pager the same day or the day after. Instead of manufacturing, Motorola thinks of this process as rapidly translating data from customers into products.

The John Deere Harvester Works manufacturing plant in Moline, Illinois, produces a wide variety of crop planters, many

> **To Think About:** How does custom manufacturing change the way these companies do business? What are the management benefits of custom manufacturing?

of which sell for more than $100,000. Customers can choose from scores of options, including liquid or dry fertilizer and row count, which amount to thousands of different configurations. Until 1992, the plant was a typical mass-production operation. It kept an inventory of about 300 planters, based on projected demand and production forecasts, because it could not respond quickly to individual orders. Then Deere equipped the factory with new manufacturing scheduling software that would provide shorter lead times and greater flexibility. With this new system, the Deere plant can reschedule production each day in response to customer orders. The plant needs to keep only 20 finished machines in inventory.

Production lines at IBM's Charlotte, North Carolina, plant can turn out up to 27 different products at once—handheld bar code scanners, fiber-optic connectors for mainframes, portable medical computers, and satellite communications devices for truck drivers. Workers are surrounded by "kits" of parts that have been assembled to match production orders. Each worker has a computer screen tied into the factory network that displays an up-to-the-minute checklist of the parts required for the product being worked on at the moment. The worker can ask the computer to display information to guide the assembly steps if he or she needs help. When the task is finished, the worker punches a button, and the information system moves the product on a conveyor to the next bench on the line.

Sources: Jeff Moad, "Let Customers Have It Their Way," *Datamation,* April 1, 1995; and Gene Bylinsky, "The Digital Factory," *Fortune,* November 14, 1994.

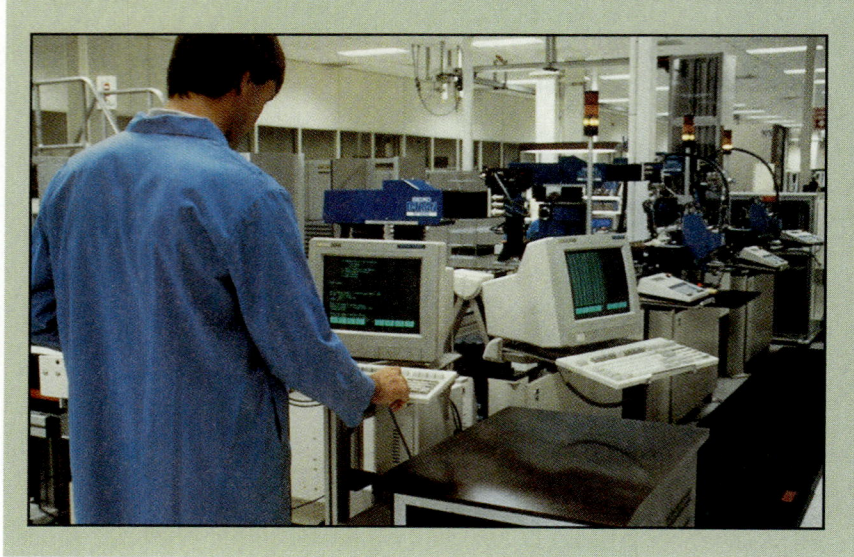

---

the cost of operations in many companies by displacing paper and the manual routines that accompany it. Improved workflow management has enabled many corporations not only to cut costs significantly but also to improve customer service at the same time. For instance, insurance companies can reduce processing of applications for new insurance from weeks to days (see Figure 1.10).

Window on Organizations

THE INTERNET: THE NEW ELECTRONIC MARKETPLACE

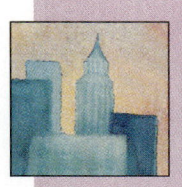

Merrill Lynch and Co.'s worst nightmare could be a small investor like Ed Harrison. He makes several stock trades a week, but he doesn't use a conventional brokerage firm. Instead he buys and sells stocks directly from his desktop computer, using the Internet.

Originally investors could choose among full-service brokers only. That changed in the 1980s when Charles Schwab Inc. began offering brokerage fee discounts of 50% and more to customers who make their own investment decisions. Discount brokers save by eliminating large research departments. People who actively trade stocks have flocked to the discount brokers because they make their own decisions and need a broker only to enter trades. Next, in the mid-1990s, some of the discount firms began offering deeper discounts to traders who enter their trades electronically via networked computers. Electronic trades obviate human contact, further reducing brokerage personnel costs. Now the newest step, use of a World Wide Web brokerage firm, has begun and may be the next revolution.

Internet trading offers further savings because Internet brokerage houses offer a bare-bones service. They maintain no research departments and have few offices, since customers linked to the Internet can access their broker from their desktops. Because these companies link their account data to the Internet, their customers are able to monitor their portfolios via the Net at any time. They see the same up-to-the-minute information that their broker sees. Finally, these brokerage houses never "close." Customers enter their trades any time of the day or night, any day of the year. Internet brokerage sites also offer links to other sites where the investor can obtain stock quotes, charts, investment news, and all kinds of advice on-line. One Internet-accessible firm, Lombard Institutional Brokerage

> **To Think About:** How has the Internet changed the brokerage business? In what ways can using the Internet as an electronic marketplace affect other organizations?

(http://www.lombard.com), offers free 30-minute delayed stock quotes and even stock graphs. Clients can use Lombard's Internet capabilities to make their home computers look like the same flashy terminals used by high-powered Wall Street traders.

Will investor trading via the Internet replace conventional financial trading? Internet security is not yet adequate, so Net brokerage houses bill customers the old-fashioned way, through the mail. Also, government regulations are few, so the industry is unsure if it can accept orders by e-mail. Most of all, however, usage is still tiny—about 800,000 of more than 60 million brokerage accounts in the United States. Most Internet traders are young and computer literate. But over the years, as the population comfortable with computers expands, Internet securities trading will grow, and the traditional brokerage firms will have to adapt.

Source: Leah Nathans Spiro and Linda Himelstein, "With the World Wide Web, Who Needs Wall Street?" *Business Week,* April 29, 1996.

Redesigned work flows can have a profound impact on organizational efficiency and can even lead to new organizational structures, products, and services. We will be discussing the impact of restructured work flows on organizational design in greater detail in Chapters 3 and 10.

THE CHANGING MANAGEMENT PROCESS

Information technology is recasting the process of management, providing powerful new capabilities to help managers strategize and plan, organize, lead, and control. For instance, it is now possible for managers to obtain information on organizational performance down to the level of specific transactions from just about anywhere in the organization at any time. Product managers at Frito-Lay Corporation, the world's largest manufacturer of salty snack foods, can know within hours precisely how many bags of Fritos sold on any street in America at its customers' stores, how much they sold for, and what the competition's sales volumes and prices are. This new intensity of information makes possible far more precise planning, forecasting, and monitoring. Information technology has also opened up new possibilities for leading. By distributing information through electronic networks, the new manager can effectively communicate frequently

Paper system insurance application

11 clerical steps + 6 professional steps = 33 Days

Imaging system insurance application: New streamlined workflow

3 clerical steps + 4 professional steps = 5 Days

FIGURE 1.10
Redesigned workflow for insurance underwriting. An application requiring 33 days in a paper system would only take 5 days using computers, networks and a streamlined workflow.

with thousands of employees and even manage far-flung task forces and teams—tasks which would be impossible in face-to-face traditional organizations.

New People Requirements

Managers must deal with new people issues because the changes brought about by information technology really require a new kind of employee. Employees need to be more highly trained than in the past as work shifts from production of goods to production of services and as more tasks become automated. High on this skill set is the ability to work in an electronic environment; the ability to digest new information and knowledge, and act upon that information; and the ability and willingness to learn new software and business procedures. Most important is the willingness to engage in a lifelong learning process. The new global worker, whether in factories or offices, is a multitalented college graduate who is exceptionally productive because of an ever-changing set of skills and competencies.

1.4 THE CHALLENGE OF INFORMATION SYSTEMS: KEY MANAGEMENT ISSUES

One message of this text is that despite, or perhaps because of, the rapid development of computer technology, there is nothing easy or mechanical about building workable information systems. Building, operating, and maintaining information systems are challenging activities for a number of reasons. We believe that managers should heed five key challenges:

1. **The Strategic Business Challenge: How can businesses use information technology to design organizations that are competitive and effective?** Investment in information technology amounts to more than half of the annual capital expenditures of most large service sector firms. Yet despite investing more in computers than any other country, the United States is grappling with a serious productivity challenge. Until recently, America's productivity growth rate of just under 2% per year has been far below those of other industrial countries. The productivity lag has been especially pronounced in the service sector. During the 1980s, white-collar productivity increased at an annual rate of only .28% (Roach, 1991).

Technical change moves much faster than humans and organizations are changing. The power of computer hardware and software has grown much more rapidly than the ability of organizations to apply and use this technology. To stay competitive, many organizations actually need to be redesigned. They will need to use information technology to simplify communication and coordination, eliminate unnecessary work, and eliminate the inefficiencies of outmoded organizational structures. If organizations merely automate what they are doing today, they are largely missing the potential of information technology. Organizations need to rethink and redesign the way they design, produce, deliver, and maintain goods and services.

2. The Globalization Challenge: How can firms understand the business and system requirements of a global economic environment? The rapid growth in international trade and the emergence of a global economy call for information systems that can support both producing and selling goods in many different countries. In the past, each regional office of a multinational corporation focused on solving its own unique information problems. Given language, cultural, and political differences among countries, this focus frequently resulted in chaos and the failure of central management controls. To develop integrated multinational information systems, businesses must develop global hardware, software, and communications standards and create cross-cultural accounting and reporting structures (Roche, 1992).

3. The Information Architecture Challenge: How can organizations develop an information architecture that supports their business goals? Creating a new system now means much more than installing a new machine in the basement. Today, this process typically places thousands of terminals or microcomputers on the desks of employees who have little experience with them, connecting the devices to powerful communications networks, rearranging social relations in the office and work locations, changing reporting patterns, and redefining business goals. Briefly, new systems today often require redesigning the organization and developing a new information architecture.

Information architecture is the particular form that information technology takes in an organization to achieve selected goals or functions. Information architecture includes the extent to which data and processing power are centralized or distributed. Figure 1.11 illustrates the major elements of information architecture that managers will need to develop. Although the computer systems base is typically operated by technical personnel, general management must decide how to allocate the resources it has assigned to hardware, software, and telecommunications. Resting upon the computer systems base are the major business application systems, or the major islands of applications. Because managers and employees directly interact with these systems, it is critical for the success of the organization that these systems meet business functional requirements now and in the future.

Here are typical questions regarding information architecture facing today's managers: Should the corporate sales data and function be distributed to each corporate remote site, or should they be centralized at headquarters? Should the organization purchase stand-alone microcomputers or build a more powerful centralized mainframe environment within an integrated telecommunications network? Should the organization build its own data communications utility to link remote sites or rely on external providers like the telephone company? There is no one right answer to these questions (see Allen and Boynton, 1991).

Even under the best of circumstances, combining knowledge of systems and the organization is itself a demanding task. For many organizations, the task is even more formidable because they are crippled by fragmented and incompatible computer hardware, software, telecommunications networks, and information systems. Integrating islands of information and technology into a coherent architecture is now a priority.

4. The Information Systems Investment Challenge: How can organizations determine the business value of information systems? A major problem raised by the development of powerful, inexpensive computers involves not technology but rather management and organizations. It's one thing to use information technology to design, produce, deliver, and maintain new products. It's another thing to make money doing it. How can organizations obtain a sizable payoff from their investment in information systems?

Engineering massive organizational and system changes in the hope of positioning a firm strategically is complicated and expensive. Is this an investment that pays off? How can you tell? Senior management can be expected to ask these questions: Are we receiving the kind of return on investment from our systems that we should be? Do our

information architecture The particular form that information technology takes in a specific organization to achieve selected goals or functions.

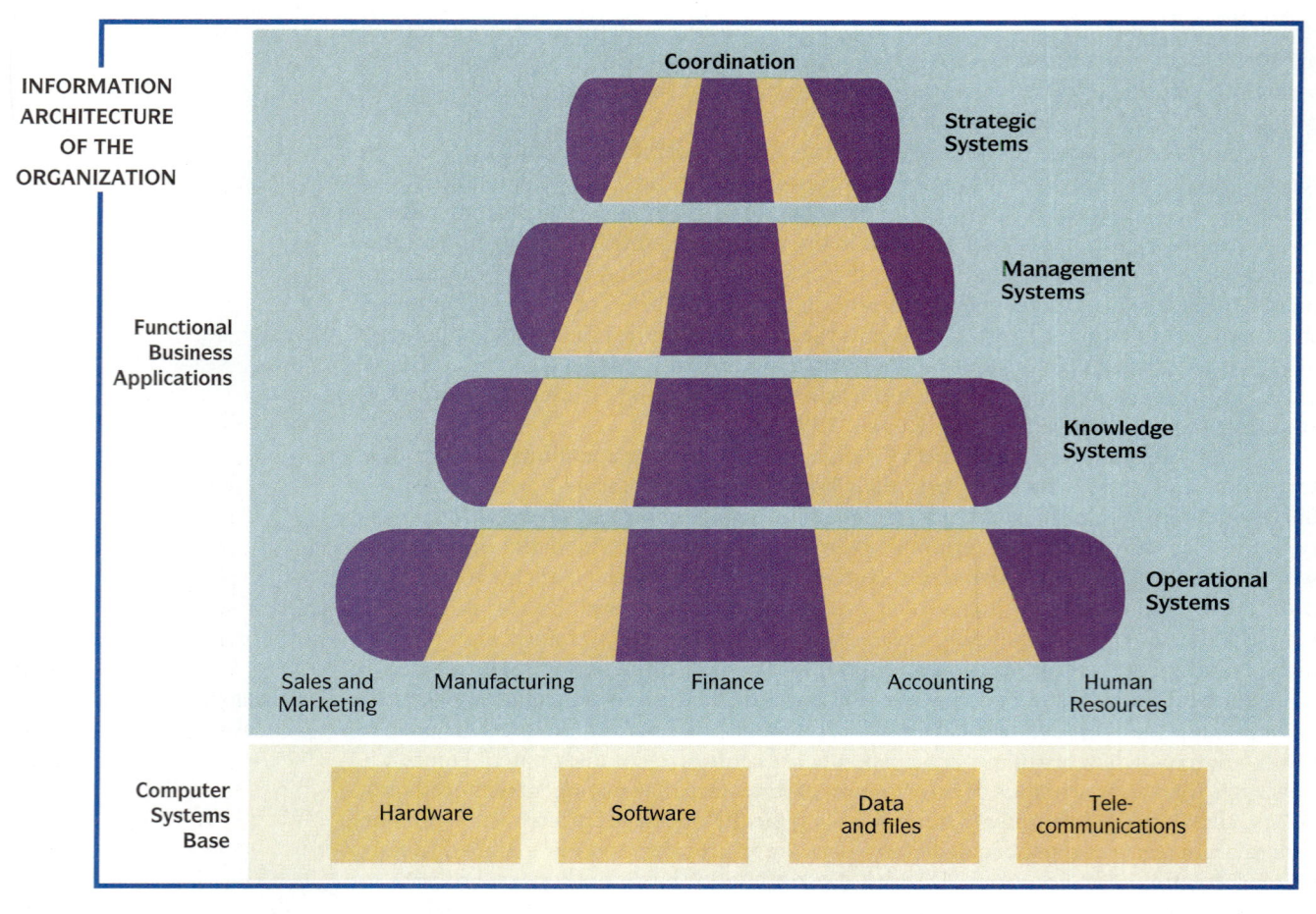

FIGURE 1.11
The information architecture of the firm. Today's managers must know how to arrange and coordinate the various computer technologies and business system applications to meet the information needs of each level of their organization, as well as the needs of the organization as a whole.

competitors get more? While understanding the costs and benefits of building a single system is difficult enough, it is daunting to consider whether the entire systems effort is "worth it." Imagine, then, how a senior executive must think when presented with a major transformation in information architecture—a bold venture in organizational change costing tens of millions of dollars and taking many years.

5. **The Responsibility and Control Challenge: How can organizations design systems that people can control and understand? How can organizations ensure that their information systems are used in an ethically and socially responsible manner?** Information systems are so essential to business, government, and daily life that organizations must take special steps to ensure that they are accurate, reliable, and secure. Automated or semi-automated systems that malfunction or are poorly operated can have extremely harmful consequences. A firm invites disaster if it uses systems that don't work as intended, that don't deliver information in a form that people can interpret correctly and use, or that have control rooms where controls don't work or where instruments give false signals. The potential for massive fraud, error, abuse, and destruction is enormous.

Information systems must be designed so that they function as intended and so that humans can control the process. When building and using information systems, organizations should consider health, safety, job security, and social well-being as carefully as they do their business goals. Managers will need to ask: Can we apply high quality assurance standards to our information systems as well as to our products and services?

Can we build information systems that respect people's rights of privacy while still pursuing our organization's goals? Should information systems monitor employees? What do we do when an information system designed to increase efficiency and productivity eliminates people's jobs?

This text is designed to provide future managers with the knowledge and understanding required to deal with these challenges. To further this objective, each succeeding chapter concludes with a Management Challenges box that outlines the key issues of which managers should be aware.

Summary

1. **Define an information system.** The purpose of a CBIS is to collect, store, and disseminate information from an organization's environment and internal operations for the purpose of supporting organizational functions and decision making, communication, coordination, control, analysis, and visualization. Information systems transform raw data into useful information through three basic activities: input, processing, and output.

2. **Explain the difference between computer literacy and information systems literacy.** Information systems literacy requires an understanding of the organizational and management dimensions of information systems as well as the technical dimensions addressed by computer literacy. Information systems literacy draws on both technical and behavioral approaches to studying information systems. Both perspectives can be combined into a sociotechnical approach to systems.

3. **Explain why information systems are so important today and how they are transforming organizations and management.** The kinds of systems built today are very important for the overall performance of the organization, especially in today's highly globalized and information-based economy. Information systems are driving both daily operations and organizational strategy. Powerful computers, software, and networks have helped organizations become more flexible, eliminate layers of management, separate work from location, and restructure work flows, giving new powers to both line workers and management. The Internet and other networks have redefined organizational boundaries, opening new opportunities for electronic markets and electronic commerce. To maximize the advantages of information technology, there is a much greater need to plan for the overall information architecture of the organization.

4. **Identify the major management challenges to building and using information systems in organizations.** There are five key management challenges in building and using information systems: (1) designing systems that are competitive and efficient; (2) understanding the system requirements of a global business environment; (3) creating an information architecture that supports the organization's goals; (4) determining the business value of information systems; and (5) designing systems that people can control, understand, and use in a socially and ethically responsible manner.

Key Terms

Information system
Information
Data
Input
Processing
Output
Feedback
Computer-based information systems (CBIS)
Formal systems
Standard operating procedures (SOPs)
Knowledge workers
Data workers
Production or service workers
Senior managers
Middle managers
Operational managers
Computer hardware
Computer software
Storage technology
Telecommunications technology
Network
Internet
Virtual organization
Custom manufacturing
Interorganizational systems
Electronic market
Information architecture

Review Questions

1. Distinguish between a computer, a computer program, and an information system. What is the difference between data and information?

2. What activities convert raw data to usable information in information systems? What is their relationship to feedback?

3. What is information systems literacy?
4. What are the organization, management, and technology dimensions of information systems?
5. Distinguish between a behavioral and a technical approach to information systems in terms of the questions asked and the answers provided.
6. What major disciplines contribute to an understanding of information systems?
7. Why should managers study information systems?
8. What is the relationship between an organization and its information systems? How is this relationship changing over time?
9. Why have powerful communications networks, including the Internet, enhanced the role played by information systems in organizations?
10. Describe some of the major changes that information systems are bringing to organizations.
11. How are information systems changing the management process?
12. What do we mean by the information architecture of the organization?
13. What are the key management challenges involved in building, operating, and maintaining information systems today?

Discussion Questions

1. Some people argue that the creation of CBIS is fundamentally a social process. Hence, a person who is an expert in information technology may not be suited to design a CBIS. Discuss and comment.

2. Most of the problems we have with information systems will disappear when computers become faster and cheaper. Discuss and comment.

Group Project

In a group with three or four classmates, find a description in a computer or business magazine of an information system used by an organization. Describe the system in terms of its inputs, processes, and outputs and in terms of its organization, management, and technology features. Present your analysis to the class.

Case Study

DAVID BATTLES GOLIATH FOR THE POWER OF INFORMATION ON THE INTERNET

In an information-based economy, control of information is the key to power. Many believe that is the source of the 1995 conflict between the London Stock Exchange and a tiny startup, Electronic Share Information Ltd. The London Stock Exchange (LSE), the Goliath in the battle, was formally organized 250 years ago to replace a 150-year-old informal system of trading shares in London coffee houses. LSE has undergone some computerization, but some of its activities are still manual and paper-based. Today, although LSE is one of the five premier stock exchanges in the world, it is coming under increasing competitive pressure. The European Association of Securities Dealers plans an automated screen-based trading system soon, while Tradepoint Financial Networks has already established a stock exchange that delivers its services electronically.

Electronic Share Information (ESI), the David in the battle, was established in June 1993 for the purpose of becoming the "world's first cyberspace stock market." Being a British company, it planned to start with British stocks, going head-to-head with the LSE. The new company's leadership was convinced that the Internet would change the way people do business, and it saw an opportunity to develop new tools to support the globalization of the financial markets.

The conflict originated with the plans of ESI to create the first on-line stock exchange. Its founders wanted to phase in the exchange, beginning with a conventional Internet-based information service that provided up-to-the-minute stock prices, company news, and analyst reports. During phase two they would develop an on-line stock exchange for small companies. Their planned service required them to deliver instant real-time market data to the computers of paying customers. The only source for the data was the London Stock Exchange. In the spring of 1995 the LSE signed a contract to supply ESI with market data for a year. Originally ESI planned to develop the whole system itself. However, the World Wide Web of the Internet grew far faster than any of them (or anyone else) expected, and ultimately they decided to base their service on the Web.

Although ESI would not become a stock exchange during its first phase, it did need to offer a brokerage service to transact orders, something that it was not licensed to do. So it turned to David Jones, the founder and chief executive officer of ShareLink Ltd., an established retail brokerage firm that uses modern telecommunications in order to reduce the cost of brokerage services, thus enabling discount prices. Jones agreed to provide ESI with a Web-based full brokerage service, including client portfolio-tracking.

With everything in place the pilot began on May 20, 1995. The ESI pilot site offered free stock market information, including delayed stock prices, price histories, and company data. By the end of August, 3,000 potential clients had registered, a positive enough response for ESI to decide to launch the service. The launch was scheduled for September 8.

On September 4 the LSE backed out, announcing its decision to discontinue the data feed to ESI and to end the contract to supply ESI with real-time market data. Without real-time data, ESI could not continue in business—real-time prices are a linchpin to any market trading service in the electronic information age. The feed was not cut immediately, and ESI decided to go ahead with the launch as planned but to challenge the LSE by publicizing its action to explain its (ESI's) own lack of service. ESI also decided to fight the stock exchange because ESI's contract with it still had eight months to run.

On September 8, Jones gave a public TV interview in which he alleged that the LSE had improperly changed the terms of its contract with ESI. On September 11, the LSE cut its price feed in the middle of the afternoon, and on September 13 it held a press conference at which it rejected allegations that it had cut the feed in order to prevent a new competitor from being established. It announced a defamation suit against Jones, claiming that Jones's remarks on September 8 constituted "conduct detrimental to the interests of the Exchange."

The Office of Fair Trading, a British regulatory body, quickly undertook an investigation into whether the LSE's cancellation of the ESI contract was "intended to distort, restrict or prevent competition." With this great pressure on the LSE, secret negotiations commenced, and on September 27, both sides dropped their legal proceedings and the contract between them was renewed. The details of the settlement remain secret, but on September 28, the data feed to the ESI Web site resumed and soon thereafter Jones publicly apologized.

Jones later indicated his belief that the episode was a battle for control of information. He stated that the Internet undermines control of information, and so power, by giving individuals more direct access to information. The London Stock Exchange continues to claim that the whole affair was merely a contract dispute. Observers point out that the LSE is certainly unable to control the new Internet technology and has reason to be concerned about being undermined.

By early November 1995, ESI had 8,500 users registered for the free service and 250 customers paying for access to the full on-line service, including real-time data and brokerage services. The company indicated that it expected to break even by the end of 1995, and early in 1996, ESI began another round of raising investment capital in order to begin the second phase, the development of a cyberspace stock market for small capitalized companies. By early 1996 the company already had 17 inquiries from groups in various countries interested in franchising its virtual stock exchange model. ∎

Sources: E. E. Baatz, "Hostile Exchanges," *WebMaster*, January/February 1996; Faegre & Benson Limited Liability Partnership, "London Stock Exchange—New Market to be Launched," http://www.faegre.com/areas/area_ib5.html.

Case Study Questions

1. How are the Internet and information technology changing the way stock exchanges are conducting business?
2. How important is the role of information systems in ESI's new venture? Discuss.
3. Describe the management, organization, and technical challenges to building this cyberspace stock exchange.

References

Ackoff, R. L. "Management Misinformation System." *Management Science* 14, no. 4 (December 1967), B140–B116.

Alavi, Maryam, and Patricia Carlson. "A Review of MIS Research and Disciplinary Development." *Journal of Management Information Systems* 8, no. 4 (Spring 1992).

Allen, Brandt R., and Andrew C. Boynton. "Information Architecture: In Search of Efficient Flexibility." *MIS Quarterly* 15, no. 4 (December 1991).

Anthony, R. N. *Planning and Control Systems: A Framework for Analysis*. Cambridge, MA: Harvard University Press (1965).

Armstrong, Arthur, and John Hagel III. "The Real Value of On-line Communities." *Harvard Business Review* (May–June 1996).

Bakos, J. Yannis. "A Strategic Analysis of Electronic Marketplaces." *MIS Quarterly* 15, no. 3 (September 1991).

Barrett, Stephanie S. "Strategic Alternatives and Interorganizational System Implementations: An Overview." *Journal of Management Information Systems* (Winter 1986–1987).

Benjamin, Robert and Rolf Wigand. "Electronic Markets and Virtual Value Chains on the Information Superhighway." *Sloan Management Review* (Winter 1995).

Brown, Carol V. and Sharon L. Magill. "Alignment of the IS Functions with the Enterprise: Toward a Model of Antecedents." *MIS Quarterly* 18, no. 4 (December 1994).

Cash, James I., F. Warren McFarlan, James L. McKenney, and Lynda M. Applegate. *Corporate Information Systems Management*, 3rd ed. Homewood, IL: Irwin (1992).

Clark, Thomas D., Jr.. "Corporate Systems Management: An Overview and Research Perspective." *Communications of the ACM* 35, no. 2 (February 1992).

Davis, Gordon B., and Margrethe H. Olson. *Management Information Systems: Conceptual Foundations, Structure, and Development,* 2nd ed. New York: McGraw-Hill (1985).

Deans, Candace P., and Michael J. Kane. *International Dimensions of Information Systems and Technology*. Boston, MA: PWS-Kent (1992).

Fedorowicz, Jane and Benn Konsynski. "Organization Support Systems: Bridging Business and Decision Processes." *Journal of Management Information Systems* 8, no. 4 (Spring 1992).

Gorry, G. A., and M. S. Scott Morton. "A Framework for Management Information Systems." *Sloan Management Review* 13, no. 1 (1971).

Johnston, Russell and Michael J. Vitale. "Creating Competitive Advantage with Interorganizational Information Systems." *MIS Quarterly* 12, no. 2 (June 1988).

Keen, Peter G. W. *Shaping the Future: Business Design Through Information Technology*. Cambridge, MA: Harvard Business School Press (1991).

King, John. "Centralized vs. Decentralized Computing: Organizational Considerations and Management Options." *Computing Surveys* (October 1984).

Kling, Rob, and William H. Dutton. "The Computer Package: Dynamic Complexity," in *Computers and Politics*, edited by James Danziger, William H. Dutton, Rob Kling, and Kenneth Kraemer. New York: Columbia University Press (1982).

Laudon, Kenneth C. "A General Model for Understanding the Relationship Between Information Technology and Organizations." Working paper, Center for Research on Information Systems, New York University (1989).

Leonard-Barton, Dorothy. *Wellsprings of Knowledge*. Boston, MA: Harvard Business School Press (1995).

Liker, Jeffrey K., David B. Roitman, and Ethel Roskies. "Changing Everything All at Once: Work Life and Technological Change." *Sloan Management Review* (Summer 1987).

Lucas, Henry C., Jr., and Jack Baroudi. "The Role of Information Technology in Organization Design." *Journal of Management Information Systems* 10, no. 4 (Spring 1994).

Malone, Thomas W., JoAnne Yates, and Robert I. Benjamin. "Electronic Markets and Electronic Hierarchies." *Communications of the ACM* (June 1987).

———. "The Logic of Electronic Markets." *Harvard Business Review* (May–June 1989).

McFarlan, F. Warren, James L. McKenney, and Philip Pyburn. "The Information Archipelago—Plotting a Course." *Harvard Business Review* (January–February 1983a).

———. "Governing the New World." *Harvard Business Review* (July–August 1983b).

McKenney, James L., and F. Warren McFarlan. "The Information Archipelago—Maps and Bridges." *Harvard Business Review* (September–October 1982).

Niederman, Fred, James C. Brancheau, and James C. Wetherbe. "Information Systems Management Issues for the 1990s." *MIS Quarterly* 15, no. 4 (December 1991).

Orlikowski, Wanda J., and Jack J. Baroudi. "Studying Information Technology in Organizations: Research Approaches and Assumptions." *Information Systems Research* 2, no. 1 (March 1991).

Rayport, J. F. and J. J. Sviokla. "Managing in the Marketspace." *Harvard Business Review* (November–December 1994).

Roach, Stephen S. "Technology and the Services Sector: The Hidden Competitive Challenge." *Technological Forecasting and Social Change* 34 (1988).

———. "Services Under Siege—The Restructuring Imperative." *Harvard Business Review* (September–October, 1991).

Roche, Edward M. "Planning for Competitive Use of Information Technology in Multinational Corporations." AIB UK Region, Brighton Polytechnic, Brighton, UK, Conference Paper, March 1992. Edward M. Roche, W. Paul Stillman School of Business, Seton Hall University.

Rockart, John F. "The Line Takes the Leadership—IS Management in a Wired Society." *Sloan Management Review* 29, no. 4 (Summer 1988).

Rockart, John F., and James E. Short. "IT in the 1990s: Managing Organizational Interdependence." *Sloan Management Review* 30, no. 2 (Winter 1989).

Scott Morton, Michael, ed. *The Corporation in the 1990s*. New York: Oxford University Press (1991).

Strassman, Paul. *The Information Payoff—The Transformation of Work in the Electronic Age*. New York: Free Press (1985).

Tornatsky, Louis G., J. D. Eveland, Myles G. Boylan, W. A. Hertzner, E. C. Johnson, D. Roitman, and J. Schneider. "The Process of Technological Innovation: Reviewing the Literature." Washington, DC: National Science Foundation (1983).

Chapter 2

The Strategic Role of Information Systems

Information Systems Keep Gillette on the Cutting Edge

2.1 Key System Applications in the Organization
Different Kinds of Systems
Six Major Types of Systems
Window on Technology:
Odense Shipyards Speeds Up Product Design
Relationship of Systems to One Another: Integration

2.2 The Strategic Role of Information Systems
What Is a Strategic Information System?
Countering Competitive Forces

Window on Organizations:
Mining Data for Profits
Leveraging Technology in the Value Chain
Implications for Managers and Organizations

2.3 How Information Systems Promote Quality
What Is Quality?
How Information Systems Contribute to Total Quality Management
Window on Management:
Building an Organization to Sell Flowers

Management Challenges
Summary
Key Terms
Review Questions
Discussion Questions
Group Project
Case Study: Greyhound Seeks Salvation in a Strategic Reservation System
References

Information Systems Keep Gillette on the Cutting Edge

In the early 1900s, when the Gillette Company introduced the first safety razor, it recognized right away that its products were vulnerable to competition. Anyone could obtain a piece of steel at a reasonable price. The way to stay ahead of the pack was to shape that same piece of steel into a sharper, sturdier blade at the lowest possible cost and to be the first to bring a superior product to market. Gillette has pursued this strategy ever since.

Gillette has 64% of the U.S. wet-shaving market and is a market leader in the rest of the world as well. Gillette has 70% of the market share in Europe and 80% in Latin America. This is a cutthroat market where a price difference of a few pennies can spell the difference between success and failure, especially since razors and blades have accounted for nearly 40% of Gillette's sales and 70% of its operating profit.

Information systems have helped Gillette stay ahead as both a low-cost, high-quality producer and as an innovator of new shaving products. With advanced technology, Gillette can cut fractions of a cent off the cost of manufacturing a blade cartridge yet produce a high-quality product. When you're making a billion razor blades a year, shaving a few tenths of a cent off the cost of each blade creates many millions of dollars in savings.

Virtually everything in Gillette's Boston manufacturing plant is automated. The firm's 3,000 workers spend most of their time monitoring equipment, checking report printouts, or searching for bottlenecks in the production process. With computerized process control devices, Gillette can control temperature, pressure, and other machine settings more precisely while optimizing output. The result: Both blade cartridge and razor parts can be fashioned much faster and with higher quality than they could five or ten years ago. A "cycle" in the production process that used to take ten seconds is now down to seven or eight.

Gillette uses information systems to enforce scrupulous quality control standards. For instance, a high-resolution microscopic camera linked to a minicomputer examines every mounted twin blade for Gillette's Sensor razor. The minicomputer compares the images captured by the camera with the image of correctly mounted blades stored in its memory, rejecting blades that are not absolutely parallel. Since an infinitesimal change in angle will give an unsatisfactory shave, the system rejects blades that are off by a couple of microns.

Information systems help detect weak links in the production process as well. Gillette increased output of its Sensor razors by 4% by improving a small clip resembling a staple that anchors the cartridge assembly. Engineers found out that the gap in the clip was too narrow by analyzing computerized data from millions of cartridge assemblies.

Information systems have also helped Gillette capture market share with innovative new razors and speed its product development process. Ten Gillette designers used three-dimensional computer-aided design software running on networked workstations to design the Sensor cartridge, which uses independently suspended twin blades to deliver a closer shave. Sensor became an instant hit and the top seller in the nondisposable razor market, with 43% of market share. Gillette wants to increase this market share even more and rolled out an improved version of the Sensor, called the SensorExcel, that features tiny rubber fins which stretch the skin so that hair jumps out of the follicle. ∎

Sources: Barbara Carton, "Gillette Looks Beyond Whiskers to Big Hair and Stretchy Floss," *The Wall Street Journal*, December 14, 1994; Lawrence Ingrassia, "The Cutting Edge," *The Wall Street Journal*, April 6, 1992; and "Gillette Holds Its Edge by Endlessly Searching for a Better Shave," *The Wall Street Journal*, December 10, 1992.

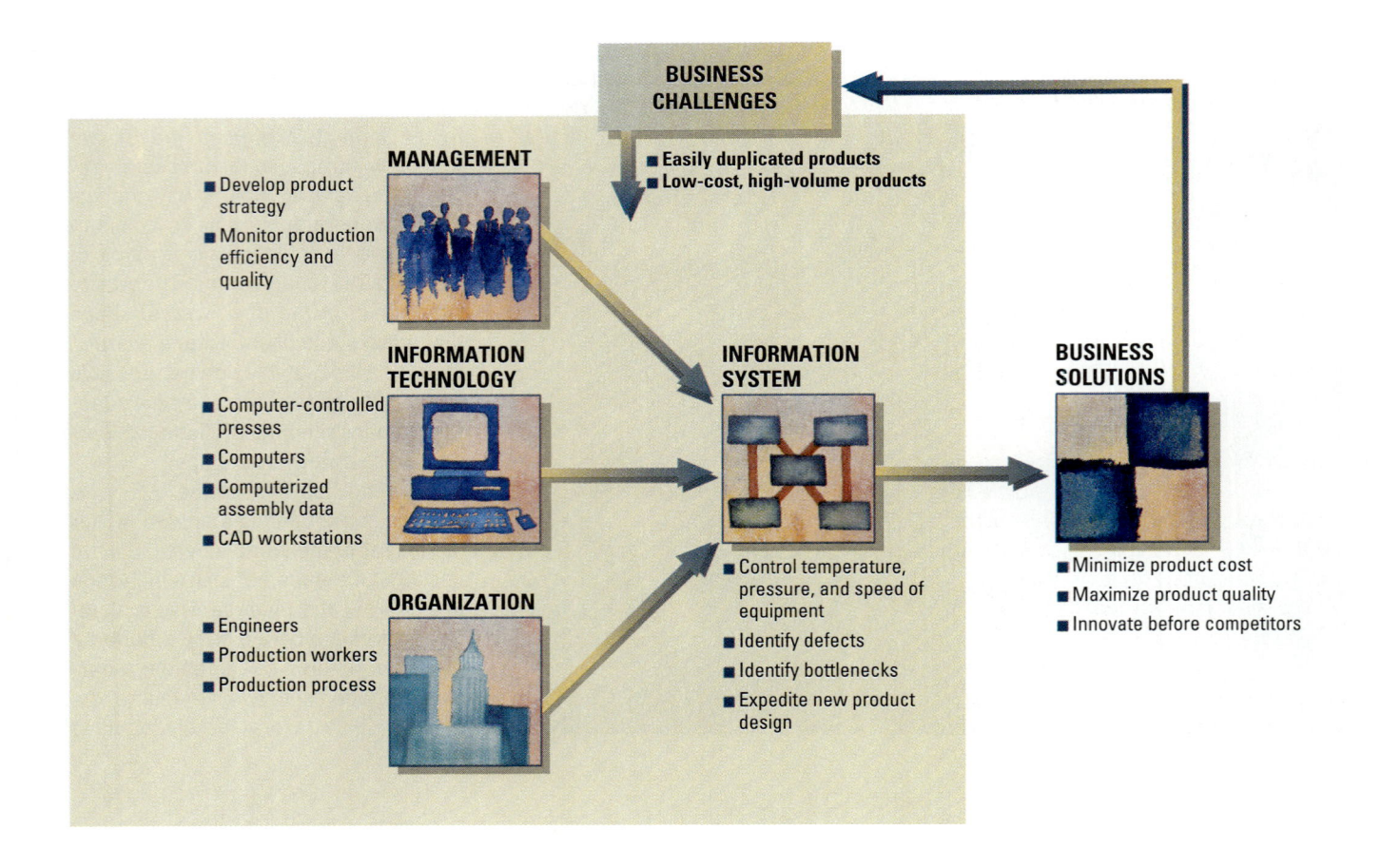

BUSINESS CHALLENGES
- Easily duplicated products
- Low-cost, high-volume products

MANAGEMENT
- Develop product strategy
- Monitor production efficiency and quality

INFORMATION TECHNOLOGY
- Computer-controlled presses
- Computers
- Computerized assembly data
- CAD workstations

ORGANIZATION
- Engineers
- Production workers
- Production process

INFORMATION SYSTEM
- Control temperature, pressure, and speed of equipment
- Identify defects
- Identify bottlenecks
- Expedite new product design

BUSINESS SOLUTIONS
- Minimize product cost
- Maximize product quality
- Innovate before competitors

The Gillette Company's intensive use of information systems illustrates how critical they have become for supporting organizational goals and for enabling firms to stay ahead of the competition. In this chapter we show the role played by the various types of information systems in organizations. We then look at the problems firms face from competition and the ways in which information systems can provide competitive advantage. The Gillette Company used information systems to maximize the quality and originality of its products while minimizing costs. Information systems can be used to pursue other competitive strategies as well. And because quality has become so important in today's competitive environment, we describe the various ways that information systems can contribute to the quality goals of the firm.

> **Learning Objectives**
>
> *After completing this chapter you will be able to:*
>
> 1. Describe the role played by the six major types of information systems in organizations.
> 2. Discuss the relationship between the various types of information systems.
> 3. Describe how the competitive forces and value chain models can be used to identify opportunities for strategic information systems.
> 4. Explain why strategic information systems are difficult to build and to sustain.
> 5. Describe how organizations can use information systems to enhance quality in their operations, products, and services.

2.1 KEY SYSTEM APPLICATIONS IN THE ORGANIZATION

Because there are different interests, specialties, and levels in an organization, there are different kinds of systems. No single system can provide all the information an organization needs. Figure 2.1 illustrates one way to depict the kinds of systems found in an organization. In the illustration, the organization is divided into strategic, management, knowledge, and operational levels and then is further divided into functional areas such as sales and marketing, manufacturing, finance, accounting, and human resources. Systems are built to serve these different organizational interests (Anthony, 1965).

DIFFERENT KINDS OF SYSTEMS

Four main types of information systems serve different organizational levels: operational-level systems, knowledge-level systems, management-level systems, and strategic-level systems. **Operational-level systems** support operational managers by keeping track of the elementary activities and transactions of the organization, such as sales, receipts, cash deposits, payroll, credit decisions, and the flow of materials in a factory. The principal purpose of systems at this level is to answer routine questions and to track the flow of transactions through the organization. How many parts are in inventory? What happened to Mr. Williams's payment? To answer these kinds of questions, information generally must be easily available, current, and accurate. Examples of operational-level systems include a system to record bank deposits from automatic teller machines or one that tracks the number of hours worked each day by employees on a factory floor.

Knowledge-level systems support knowledge and data workers in an organization. The purpose of knowledge-level systems is to help the business firm integrate new knowledge into the business and to help the organization control the flow of paperwork. Knowledge-level systems, especially in the form of workstations and office systems, are the fastest-growing applications in business today.

operational-level systems Information systems that monitor the elementary activities and transactions of the organization.

knowledge-level systems Information systems that support knowledge and data workers in an organization.

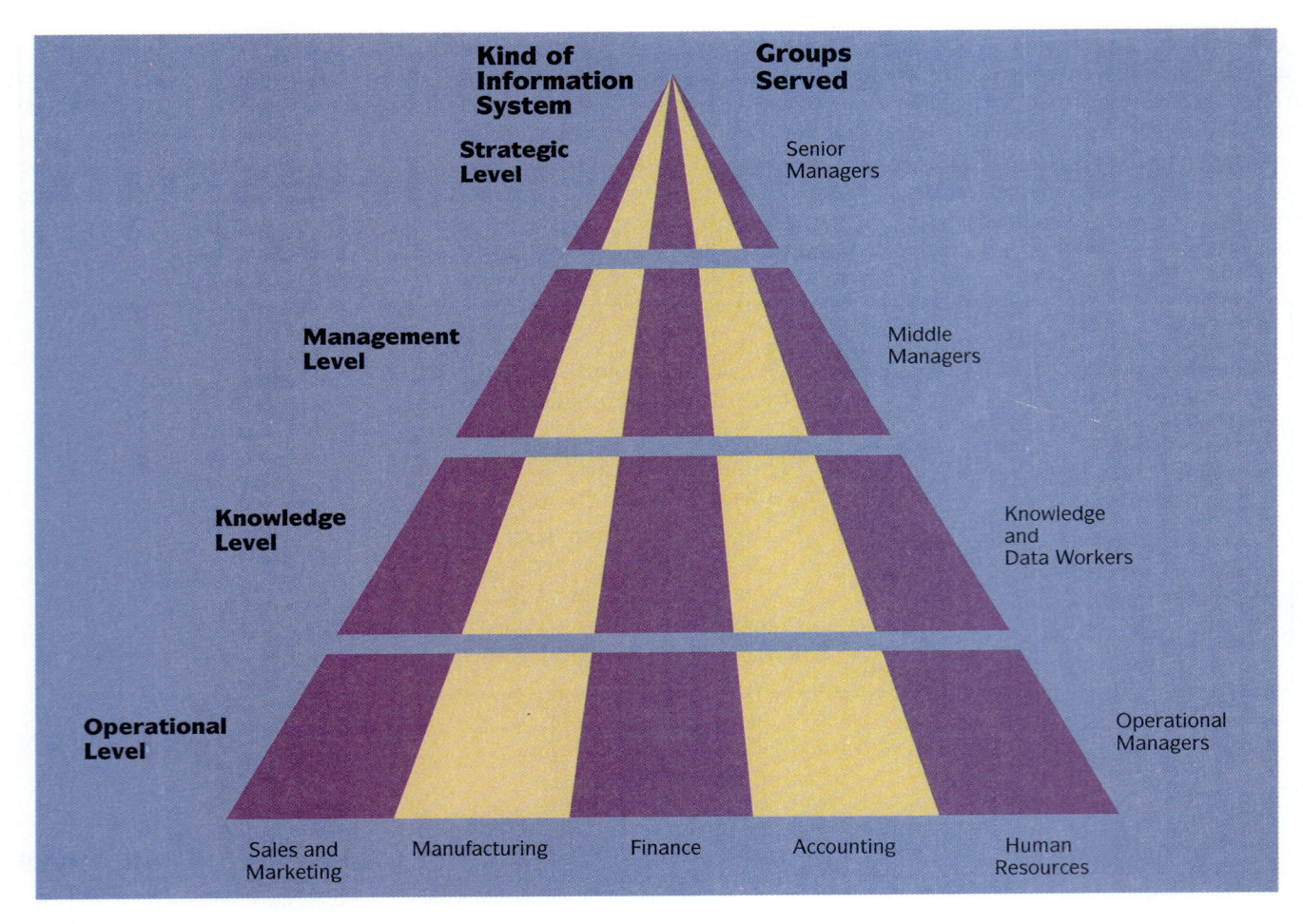

FIGURE 2.1
Types of information systems. Organizations and information systems can be divided into strategic, management, knowledge, and operational levels. They can be divided further into five functional areas: sales and marketing, manufacturing, finance, accounting, and human resources. Information systems serve each of these levels and functions. Strategic-level systems help senior managers with long-term planning. Management-level systems help middle managers monitor and control. Knowledge-level systems help knowledge and data workers design products, distribute information, and cope with paperwork. Operational-level systems help operational managers keep track of the firm's day-to-day activities.

management-level systems Information systems that support the monitoring, controlling, decision-making, and administrative activities of middle managers.

Management-level systems are designed to serve the monitoring, controlling, decision-making, and administrative activities of middle managers. The principal question addressed by such systems is: Are things working well? Management-level systems typically provide periodic reports rather than instant information on operations. An example is a relocation control system that reports on the total moving, house-hunting, and home financing costs for employees in all company divisions, noting wherever actual costs exceed budgets.

Some management-level systems support nonroutine decision making (Keen and Morton, 1978). They tend to focus on less structured decisions for which information requirements are not always clear. These systems often answer "what if" questions: What would be the impact on production schedules if we were to double sales in the month of December? What would happen to our return on investment if a factory schedule were delayed for six months? Answers to these questions frequently require new data from outside the organization, as well as data from inside that cannot be drawn from existing operational-level systems.

strategic-level systems Information systems that support the long-range planning activities of senior management.

Strategic-level systems help senior management tackle and address strategic issues and long-term trends, both in the firm and in the external environment. Their principal concern is matching changes in the external environment with existing organizational

32 CHAPTER 2 The Strategic Role of Information Systems

capability. What will employment levels be in five years? What are the long-term industry cost trends, and where does our firm fit in? What products should we be making in five years?

Information systems may also be differentiated by functional specialty. Major organizational functions, such as sales and marketing, manufacturing, finance, accounting, and human resources, are each served by their own information systems. In large organizations, subfunctions of each of these major functions also have their own information systems. For example, the manufacturing function might have systems for inventory management, process control, plant maintenance, computer-aided engineering, and material requirements planning.

A typical organization has operational-, management-, knowledge-, and strategic-level systems for each functional area. For example, the sales function generally has a sales system on the operational level to record daily sales figures and to process orders. A knowledge-level system designs promotional displays for the firm's products. A management-level system tracks monthly sales figures by sales territory and reports on territories where sales exceed or fall below anticipated levels. A system to forecast sales trends over a five-year period serves the strategic level.

Finally, different organizations have different information systems for the same functional areas. Because no two organizations have exactly the same objectives, structures, or interests, information systems must be custom-made to fit the unique characteristics of each. There is no such thing as a universal information system that can fit all organizations. Every organization does the job somewhat differently.

Information systems can thus be classified by functional specialty or by the organizational level they serve. Throughout this text are examples of systems supporting the various functional areas—sales systems, manufacturing systems, human resources systems, finance and accounting systems. For professors and students requiring deeper analysis of information systems from a functional perspective, we have included additional material in Appendix A. This chapter analyzes the key applications of the organization primarily in terms of the organizational level and types of decisions they support.

SIX MAJOR TYPES OF SYSTEMS

In this section we describe the specific categories of systems serving each organizational level and their value to the organization. Figure 2.2 shows the specific types of information systems that correspond to each organizational level. The organization has executive support systems (ESS) at the strategic level; management information systems (MIS) and decision-support systems (DSS) at the management level; knowledge work systems (KWS) and office automation systems (OAS) at the knowledge level; and transaction processing systems (TPS) at the operational level. Systems at each level in turn are specialized to serve each of the major functional areas. Thus, the typical systems found in organizations are designed to assist workers or managers at each level and in the functions of sales and marketing, manufacturing, finance, accounting, and human resources.

Table 2.1 summarizes the features of the six types of information systems. It should be noted that each of the different kinds of systems may have components that are used by organizational levels and groups other than their main constituencies. A secretary may find information on an MIS, or a middle manager may need to extract data from a TPS.

Transaction processing systems (TPS) are the basic business systems that serve the operational level of the organization. A transaction processing system is a computerized system that performs and records the daily routine transactions necessary to the conduct of the business. Examples are sales order entry, hotel reservation systems, payroll, employee record keeping, and shipping.

At the operational level, tasks, resources, and goals are predefined and highly structured. The decision to grant credit to a customer, for instance, is made by a lower-level supervisor according to predefined criteria. All that must be determined is whether the customer meets the criteria.

transaction processing systems (TPS) Computerized systems that perform and record the daily routine transactions necessary to conduct the business; they serve the operational level of the organization.

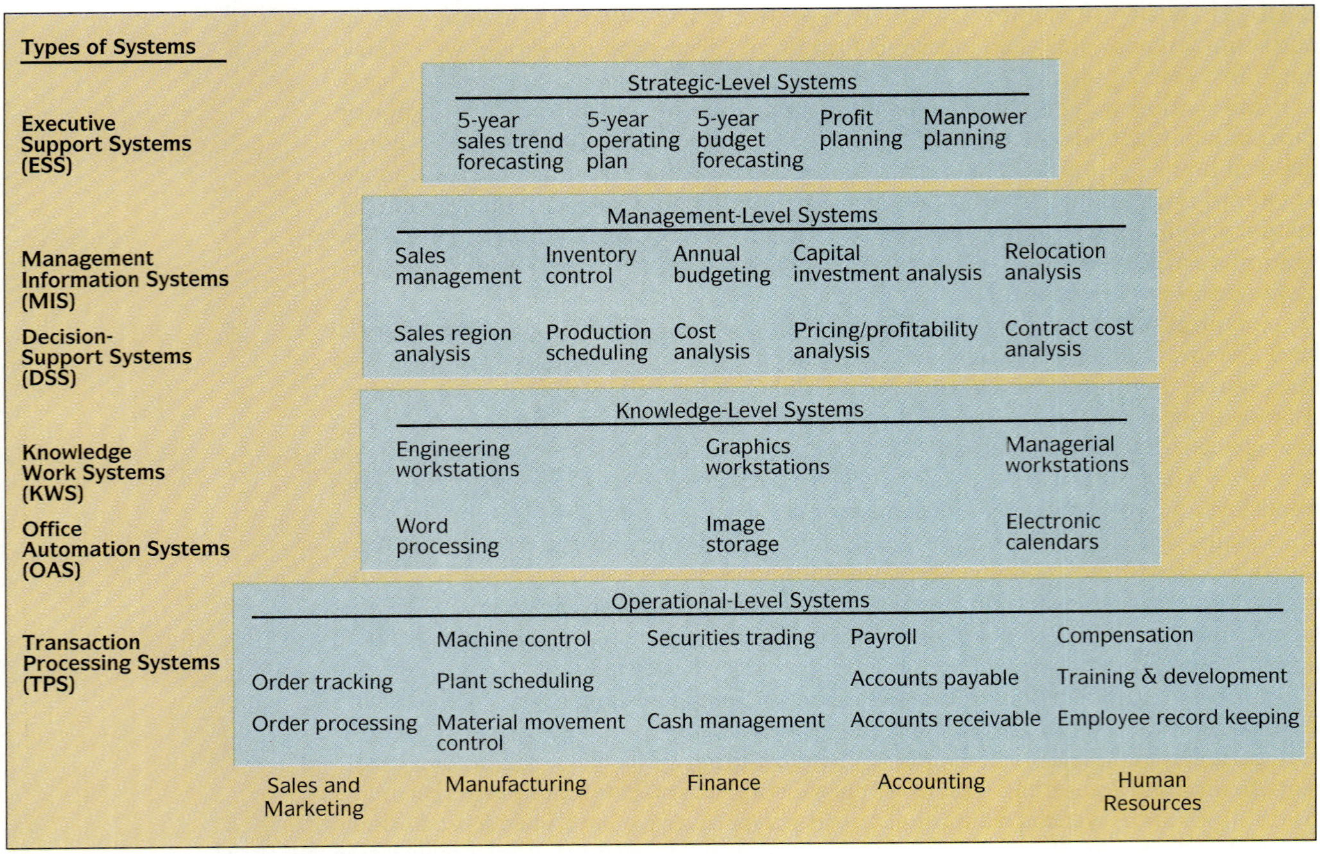

Types of Systems

	Strategic-Level Systems				
Executive Support Systems (ESS)	5-year sales trend forecasting	5-year operating plan	5-year budget forecasting	Profit planning	Manpower planning

	Management-Level Systems				
Management Information Systems (MIS)	Sales management	Inventory control	Annual budgeting	Capital investment analysis	Relocation analysis
Decision-Support Systems (DSS)	Sales region analysis	Production scheduling	Cost analysis	Pricing/profitability analysis	Contract cost analysis

	Knowledge-Level Systems		
Knowledge Work Systems (KWS)	Engineering workstations	Graphics workstations	Managerial workstations
Office Automation Systems (OAS)	Word processing	Image storage	Electronic calendars

	Operational-Level Systems				
Transaction Processing Systems (TPS)		Machine control	Securities trading	Payroll	Compensation
	Order tracking	Plant scheduling		Accounts payable	Training & development
	Order processing	Material movement control	Cash management	Accounts receivable	Employee record keeping
	Sales and Marketing	Manufacturing	Finance	Accounting	Human Resources

FIGURE 2.2
The six major types of information systems needed for the four levels of an organization. Information systems are built to serve each of the four levels of an organization. Transaction processing systems (TPS) serve the operational level of an organization. Knowledge work systems (KWS) and office automation systems (OAS) serve the knowledge level of an organization. Decision-support systems (DSS) and management information systems (MIS) serve the management level of the organization. Executive support systems (ESS) serve the strategic level of an organization.

Table 2.1 Characteristics of Information Processing Systems

Type of System	Information Inputs	Processing	Information Outputs	Users
ESS	Aggregate data; external, internal	Graphics; simulations; interactive	Projections; responses to queries	Senior managers
DSS	Low-volume data; analytic models	Interactive; simulations, analysis	Special reports; decision analyses; responses to queries	Professionals; staff managers
MIS	Summary transaction data; high-volume data; simple models	Routine reports; simple models; low-level analysis	Summary and exception reports	Middle managers
KWS	Design specifications; knowledge base	Modeling; simulations	Models; graphics	Professionals; technical staff
OAS	Documents; schedules	Document management; scheduling; communication	Documents; schedules; mail	Clerical workers
TPS	Transactions; events	Sorting; listing; merging; updating	Detailed reports; lists; summaries	Operations personnel; supervisors

Figure 2.3 depicts a payroll TPS, which is a typical accounting transaction processing system found in most firms. A payroll system keeps track of the money paid to employees. The master file is composed of discrete pieces of information (such as a name, address, or employee number) called data elements. Data are keyed into the system, updating the data elements. The elements on the master file are combined in different ways to make up reports of interest to management and government agencies and paychecks sent to employees. These TPS can generate other report combinations of existing data elements.

Other typical TPS appplications are identified in Figure 2.4. The figure shows that there are five functional categories of TPS: sales/marketing, manufacturing/production, finance/accounting, human resources, and other types of TPS that are unique to a particular industry. The UPS package tracking system described in Chapter 1 is an example of a manufacturing TPS. UPS sells package delivery services; the system keeps track of all of its package shipment transactions.

All organizations have these five kinds of TPS (even if the systems are manual). Transaction processing systems are often so central to a business that TPS failure for a few hours can spell the demise of a firm and perhaps other firms linked to it. Imagine what would happen to UPS if its package tracking system were not working! What would the airlines do without their computerized reservation systems?

Managers need TPS to monitor the status of internal operations and the firm's relations with the external environment. TPS are also major producers of information for the other types of systems. (For example, the payroll system illustrated here along with other accounting TPS supplies data to the company's General Ledger System, which is responsible for maintaining records of the firm's income and expenses and for producing reports such as income statements and balance sheets.)

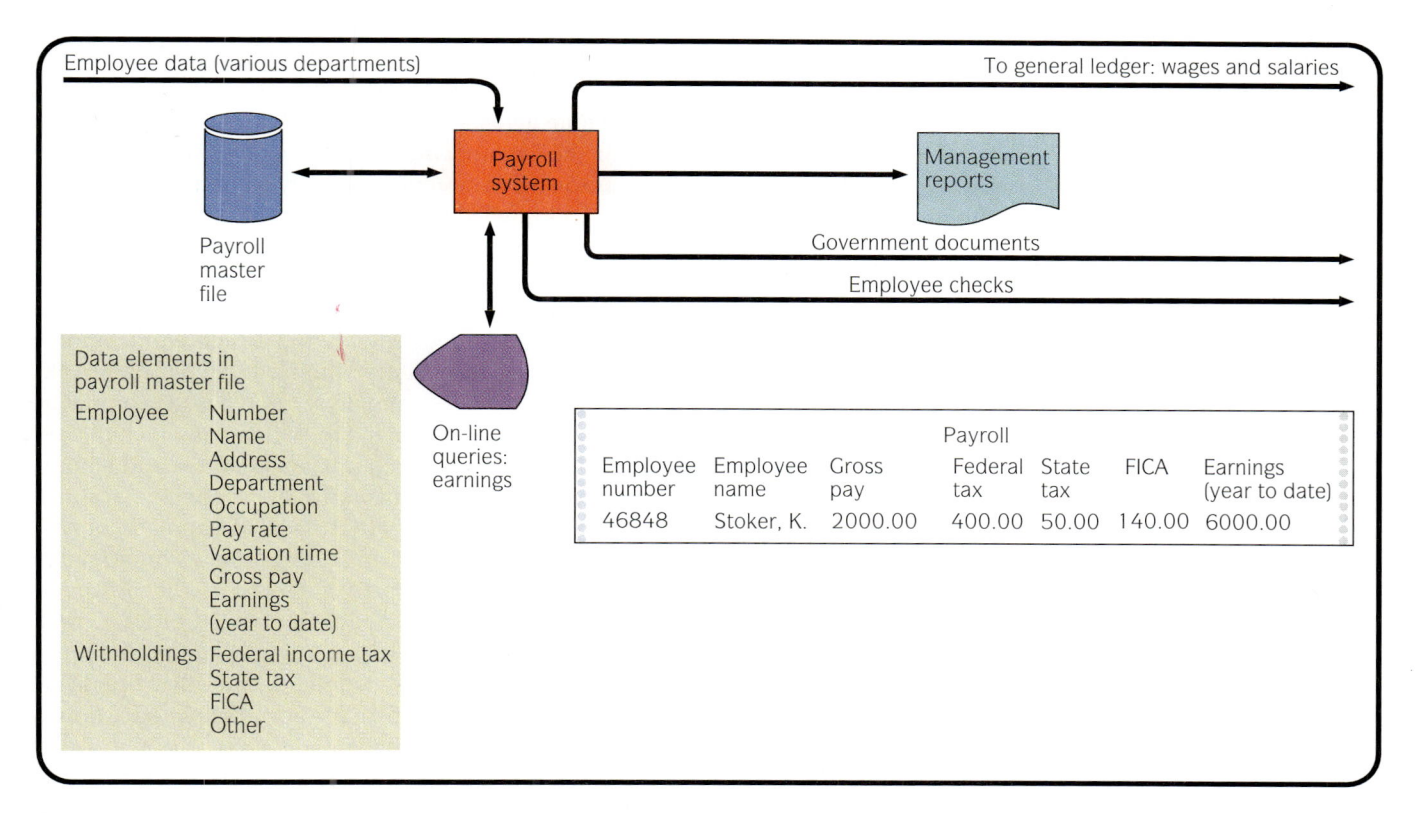

FIGURE 2.3
A symbolic representation for a payroll system TPS.

2.1 Key System Applications in the Organization

	Type of TPS System				
	Sales/ marketing systems	Manufacturing/ production systems	Finance/ accounting systems	Human resources systems	Other types (e.g., university)
Major functions of system	Sales management	Scheduling	Budgeting	Personnel records	Admissions
	Market research	Purchasing	General ledger	Benefits	Grade records
	Promotion	Shipping/receiving	Billing	Compensation	Course records
	Pricing	Engineering	Cost accounting	Labor relations	Alumni
	New products	Operations		Training	
Major application systems	Sales order information system	Materials resource planning systems	General ledger	Payroll	Registration system
	Market research system	Purchase order control systems	Accounts receivable/payable	Employee records	Student transcript system
	Pricing system	Engineering systems	Budgeting	Benefit systems	Curriculum class control systems
		Quality control systems	Funds management systems	Career path systems	Alumni benefactor system
				Personnel planning systems	

FIGURE 2.4
Typical applications of TPS. There are five functional categories of TPS: sales/marketing, manufacturing/production, finance/accounting, human resources, and other types of systems specific to a particular industry. TPS support most business functions in most organizations. Within each of these major functions are subfunctions. For each of these subfunctions (e.g., sales management) there is a major application system.

Knowledge Work and Office Automation Systems

knowledge work systems (KWS) Information systems that aid knowledge workers in the creation and integration of new knowledge in the organization.

office automation systems (OAS) Computer systems, such as word processing, electronic mail systems, and scheduling systems, that are designed to increase the productivity of data workers in the office.

word processing Office automation technology that facilitates the creation of documents through computerized text editing, formatting, storing, and printing.

Knowledge work systems (KWS) and **office automation systems (OAS)** serve the information needs at the knowledge level of the organization. Knowledge work systems aid knowledge workers, whereas office automation systems primarily aid data workers (although they are also used extensively by knowledge workers).

In general, *knowledge workers* are people who hold formal university degrees and who are often members of a recognized profession, like engineers, doctors, lawyers, and scientists. Their jobs consist primarily of creating new information and knowledge. Knowledge work systems (KWS), such as scientific or engineering design workstations, promote the creation of new knowledge and ensure that new knowledge and technical expertise are properly integrated into the business. One example of a KWS is the computer-aided design system used by Odense Shipyards described in the Window on Technology.

Data workers typically have less formal, advanced educational degrees and tend to process rather than create information. They consist primarily of secretaries, accountants, filing clerks, or managers whose jobs are principally to use, manipulate, or disseminate information. Office automation systems (OAS) are information technology applications designed to increase the productivity of data workers in the office by supporting the coordinating and communicating activities of the typical office. Office automation systems coordinate diverse information workers, geographic units, and functional areas: The systems communicate with customers, suppliers, and other organizations outside the firm and serve as a clearinghouse for information and knowledge flows.

Typical office automation systems handle and manage documents (through word processing, desktop publishing, and digital filing), scheduling (through electronic calendars), and communication (through electronic mail, voice mail, or videoconferencing). **Word processing** refers to the software and hardware that creates, edits, formats, stores, and prints documents (see Chapter 6). Word processing systems represent the

Window on Technology

ODENSE SHIPYARDS SPEEDS UP PRODUCT DESIGN

Odense Steel Shipyards in Denmark is not one of the world's larger shipyards, but it specializes in building the world's biggest ships. After the mid-1970s, Odense nearly ran aground. Its labor costs were too high compared with those of competitors from Japan, South Korea, Italy, and East Germany.

By 1979 Odense had laid off all but 800 of its 6,000 workers. It decided to make a comeback by building double-hulled oil tankers that would be more resistant to oil spills in collisions and by building giant ships holding metal cargo containers. To keep costs low and competitive, Odense turned to information systems.

Today, only 15 people run its main steel-construction facility. A less automated facility would require 300 people to do the same job. Most of the work on steel parts is performed by computer-controlled machines. Metal arms slice preprogrammed curves into the steel. Eighty-foot-wide radio-programmed lifters swoop down from ceilings to grab lawn-size plates and position them between machines. Dozens of robots move across the plates, performing some 150 miles of welds for each ship. Workstations throughout the facility display windows showing the progress of jobs.

The data driving all of this automation come from computer-aided design models. Computer-aided design (CAD) eliminates much of the manual drafting and building of physical prototypes that used to slow down the design process by per-

> **To Think About:** How did implementing a computer-aided design system change the way Odense Shipyards conducted its business?

forming much of the design work on the computer. Before CAD, Odense designers used to spend six months building a one-fifteenth scale model of the pumping arrangement in the engine room and surrounding maze of pipes to make sure that everything was connected properly and fit the space. Now, a designer merely needs to indicate two endpoints and the function of the pipe, and the CAD system picks out the appropriate type of pipe and lays a path for it—all on the computer. The process takes one-sixth the time of building a physical model. The prototyped designs can automatically feed the design specifications to Odense's computerized manufacturing systems. Odense can now generate six different designs that meet the speed and size requirements of the customer and select the one that is the most efficient and durable.

When the CAD model for a ship is complete, the system generates a complete list of the 400,000 parts needed, ranging from steel plates to butterfly valves. The system breaks down the list according to supplier and required delivery date and monitors shipment schedules. The system helps Odense schedule parts deliveries for the precise date when they will be used. It also helps Odense schedule its labor force, listing every manual task required by a new ship with an estimate of how much time each task will take. Odense can move several hundred people from one task to another with a precise estimate of costs.

Automobile manufacturers can use software to simulate an assembly line to make sure that welding robots can maneuver. Computer-aided design (CAD) systems eliminate many manual steps in design and production by performing much of the design work on the computer.

Source: David Freedman, "Bits to Ships," *Forbes ASAP*, December 5, 1994.

FIGURE 2.5
United Services Automobile Association's (USAA) imaging network. Scanners enter mail received by USAA's policy department into the imaging system, which stores and distributes the digitally processed image of the document electronically. Service representatives have immediate on-line access to clients' data.

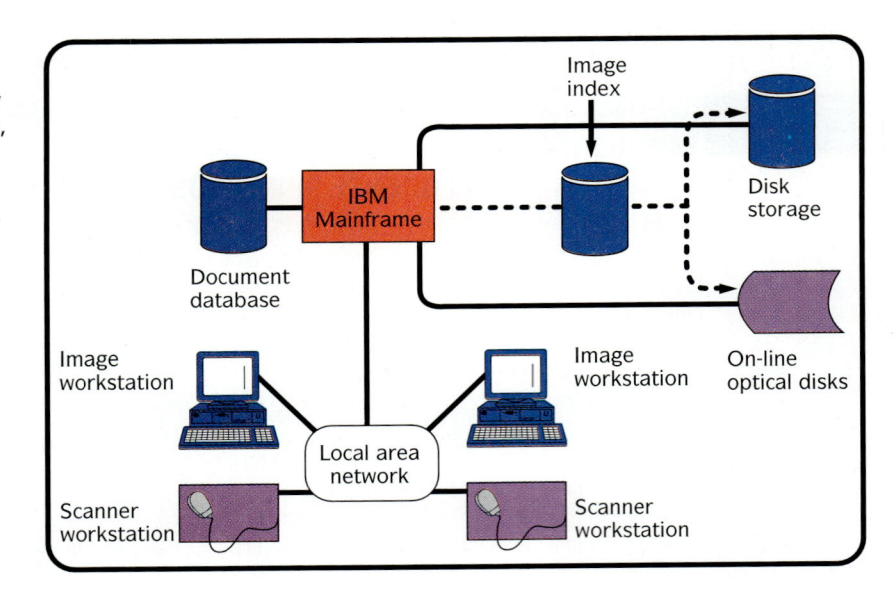

---

desktop publishing Technology that produces professional-quality documents combining output from word processors with design, graphics, and special layout features.

document imaging systems Systems that convert documents and images into digital form so that they can be stored and accessed by the computer.

single most common application of information technology to office work, in part because producing documents is what offices are all about. **Desktop publishing** produces professional publishing–quality documents by combining output from word processing software with design elements, graphics, and special layout features.

Document imaging systems are another widely used knowledge application. **Document imaging systems** convert documents and images into digital form so that they can be stored and accessed by the computer. Figure 2.5 illustrates the imaging system used by the United Services Automobile Association, the largest direct writer of property and casualty insurance in the United States. USAA receives more than 100,000 letters and mails more than 250,000 items daily. USAA has developed the largest imaging system in the world, storing 1.5 billion pages. All incoming mail received each day by the policy department is scanned and stored on optical disk. The original documents are thrown away. Six of USAA's major regional offices across the country are hooked up to its imaging network. The network consists of image scanners, optical storage units, a mainframe computer, and a local area network to link service representatives' workstations and the scanner workstations located in the firm's mailroom. Service representatives can retrieve a client's file on-line and view documents from desktop computers. About 2000 people use the network. Users believe that the imaging system reduces the amount of time their work would take with a paper-based system by one-third, saving paper and storage costs. Customer service has been improved because electronic documents can be accessed more rapidly. (Lasher, Ives, and Jarvenpaa, 1991; "USAA Insuring Progress," 1992).

Management Information Systems

management information systems (MIS) Information systems at the management level of an organization that serve the functions of planning, controlling, and decision making by providing routine summary and exception reports.

Management information systems (MIS) serve the management level of the organization, providing managers with reports and, in some cases, with on-line access to the organization's current performance and historical records. Typically, they are oriented almost exclusively to internal, not environmental or external, events. MIS primarily serve the functions of planning, controlling, and decision making at the management level. Generally, they are dependent on underlying transaction processing systems for their data.

MIS summarize and report on the basic operations of the company. The basic transaction data from TPS are compressed and are usually presented in long reports that are produced on a regular schedule. Figure 2.6 shows how a typical MIS transforms transaction level data from inventory, production, and accounting into MIS files that are used to provide managers with reports. Figure 2.7 shows a sample report from this system.

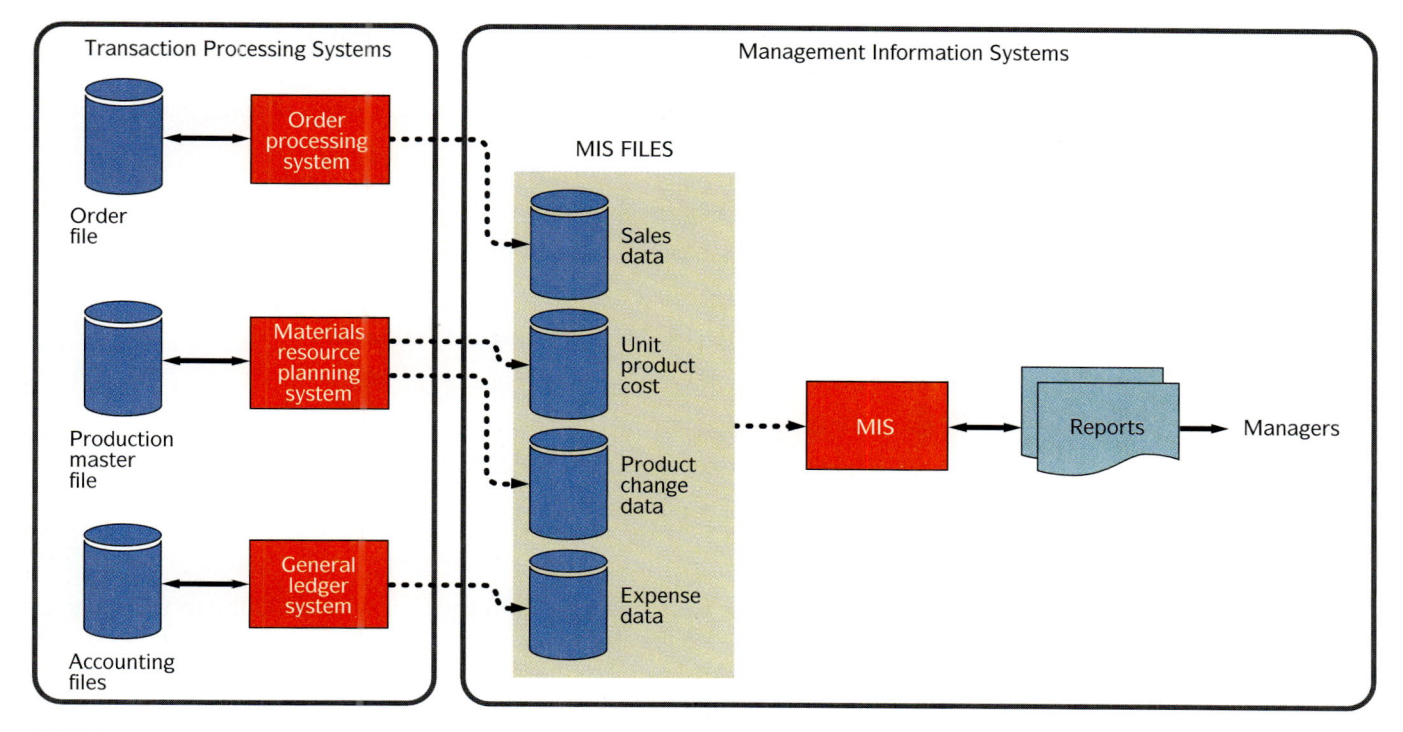

FIGURE 2.6
How management information systems obtain their data from the organization's TPS. In the system illustrated by this diagram, three TPS supply summarized transaction data at the end of the time period to the MIS reporting system. Managers gain access to the organizational data through the MIS, which provides them with the appropriate reports.

MIS usually serve managers interested in weekly, monthly, and yearly results—not day-to-day activities. MIS generally address structured questions that are known well in advance. These systems are generally not flexible and have little analytical capability. Most MIS use simple routines such as summaries and comparisons, as opposed to sophisticated mathematical models or statistical techniques. Table 2.2 describes the characteristics of typical management information systems.

Some researchers use the term MIS to include all of the information systems that support the functional areas of the organization (Davis and Olson, 1985). However, in

Consolidated Consumer Products Corporation
Sales by Product and Sales Region: 1997

PRODUCT CODE	PRODUCT DESCRIPTION	SALES REGION	ACTUAL SALES	PLANNED	ACTUAL VS. PLANNED
4469	Carpet Cleaner	Northeast	4,066,700	4,800,000	0.85
		South	3,778,112	3,750,000	1.01
		Midwest	4,867,001	4,600,000	1.06
		West	4,003,440	4,400,000	0.91
		TOTAL	16,715,253	17,550,000	0.95
5674	Room Freshener	Northeast	3,676,700	3,900,000	0.94
		South	5,608,112	4,700,000	1.19
		Midwest	4,711,001	4,200,000	1.12
		West	4,563,440	4,900,000	0.93
		TOTAL	18,559,253	17,700,000	1.05

FIGURE 2.7
A sample report that might be produced by the MIS system in Figure 2.6

Table 2.2	Characteristics of Management Information Systems

1. MIS support structured and semi-structured decisions at the operational and management control levels. However, they are also useful for planning purposes of senior management staff.
2. MIS are generally reporting and control oriented. They are designed to report on existing operations and therefore to help provide day-to-day control of operations.
3. MIS rely on existing corporate data and data flows.
4. MIS have little analytical capability.
5. MIS generally aid in decision making using past and present data.
6. MIS are relatively inflexible.
7. MIS have an internal rather than an external orientation.
8. Information requirements are known and stable.
9. MIS often require a lengthy analysis and design process.

this book we prefer to use computer-based information systems (CBIS) as the umbrella term for all information systems and to consider management information systems as those that are specifically dedicated to management-level functions.

Decision-Support Systems

decision-support systems (DSS) Information systems at the management level of an organization that combine data and sophisticated analytical models to support semi-structured and unstructured decision making.

Decision-support systems (DSS) also serve the management level of the organization. DSS help managers make decisions that are semi-structured, unique, or rapidly changing, and not easily specified in advance. DSS have to be responsive enough to run several times a day in order to correspond to changing conditions. While DSS use internal information from TPS and MIS, they often bring in information from external sources, such as current stock prices or product prices of competitors. Table 2.3 shows how contemporary DSS differ from MIS and TPS systems.

Clearly, by design, DSS have more analytical power than other systems; they are built explicitly with a variety of models to analyze data. DSS are designed so that users can work with them directly; these systems explicitly include user-friendly software. DSS systems are interactive; the user can change assumptions and include new data.

An interesting, small, but powerful DSS is the voyage-estimating system of a subsidiary of a large American metals company that exists primarily to carry bulk cargoes of coal, oil, ores, and finished products for its parent company. The firm owns some vessels, charters others, and bids for shipping contracts in the open market to carry general cargo. A voyage-estimating system calculates financial and technical voyage details. Financial calculations include ship/time costs (fuel, labor, capital), freight rates for various types of cargo, and port expenses. Technical details include a myriad of factors such as ship cargo capacity, speed, port distances, fuel and water consumption, and loading patterns (location of cargo for different ports). The system can answer questions such as the following: Given a customer delivery schedule and an offered freight rate, which

Table 2.3	Characteristics of Decision-Support Systems

1. DSS offer users flexibility, adaptability, and a quick response.
2. DSS allow users to initiate and control the input and output.
3. DSS operate with little or no assistance from professional programmers.
4. DSS provide support for decisions and problems whose solutions cannot be specified in advance.
5. DSS use sophisticated analysis and modeling tools.

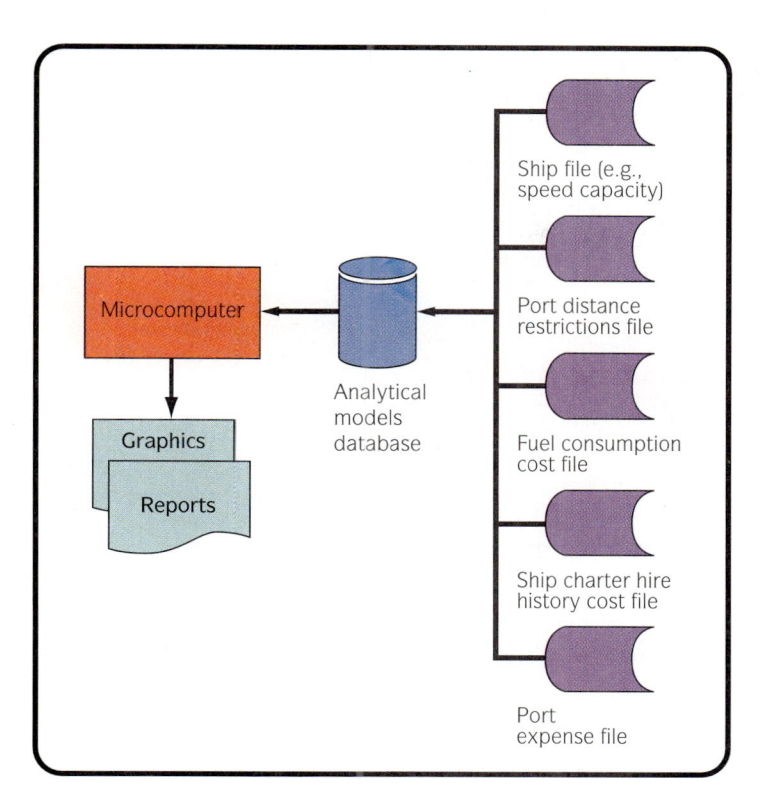

FIGURE 2.8
Voyage estimating decision-support system. This DSS operates on a powerful microcomputer. It is used daily by managers who must develop bids on shipping contracts.

vessel should be assigned at what rate to maximize profits? What is the optimum speed at which a particular vessel can optimize its profit and still meet its delivery schedule? What is the optimal loading pattern for a ship bound for the U.S. west coast from Malaysia? Figure 2.8 illustrates the DSS built for this company. The system operates on a powerful desktop microcomputer, providing a system of menus that makes it easy for users to enter data or obtain information.

Executive Support Systems

Senior managers use a category of information systems called **executive support systems (ESS)** to make decisions. ESS serve the strategic level of the organization. They address unstructured decisions and create a generalized computing and communications environment rather than providing any fixed application or specific capability. ESS are designed to incorporate data about external events such as new tax laws or competitors, but they also draw summarized information from internal MIS and DSS. They filter, compress, and track critical data, emphasizing the reduction of time and effort required to obtain information useful to executives. ESS employ the most advanced graphics software and can deliver graphs and data from many sources immediately to a senior executive's office or to a boardroom.

Unlike the other types of information systems, ESS are not designed primarily to solve specific problems. Instead, ESS provide a generalized computing and telecommunications capacity that can be applied to a changing array of problems. While DSS are designed to be highly analytical, ESS tend to make less use of analytical models.

Questions ESS assist in answering include the following: What business should we be in? What are the competitors doing? What new acquisitions would protect us from cyclical business swings? Which units should we sell to raise cash for acquisitions? (Rockart and Treacy, 1982). Figure 2.9 illustrates a model of an ESS. It consists of workstations with menus, interactive graphics, and communications capabilities that can access historical and competitive data from internal corporate systems and external databases such as Dow Jones News/Retrieval or the Gallup Poll. Because ESS are designed to be used by senior managers who often have little, if any, direct contact or experience

executive support systems (ESS) Information systems at the strategic level of an organization designed to address unstructured decision making through advanced graphics and communications.

FIGURE 2.9
Model of a typical executive support system. This system pools data from diverse internal and external sources and makes them available to executives in an easy-to-use form.

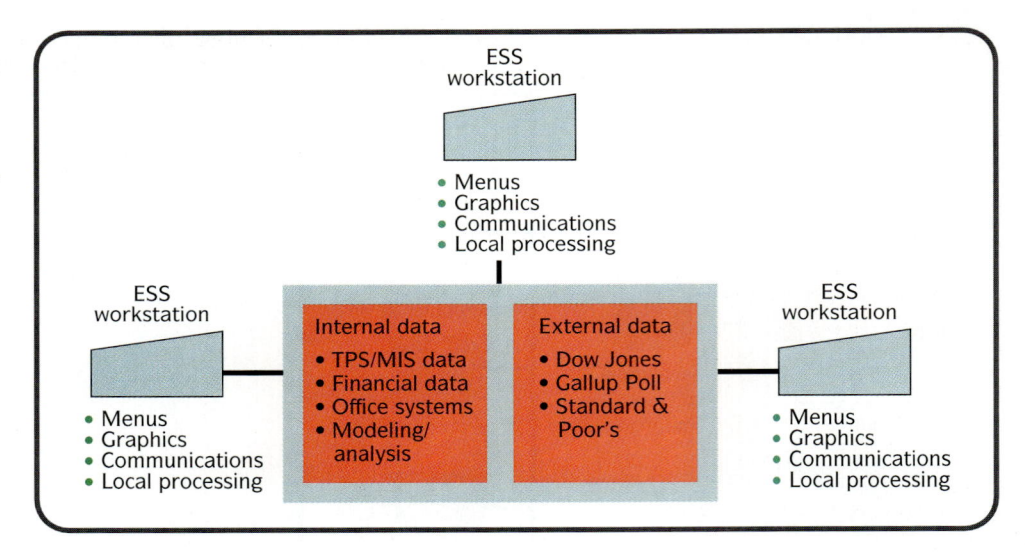

with computer-based information systems, they incorporate easy-to-use graphic interfaces. More details on leading-edge applications of DSS and ESS can be found in Chapter 13.

RELATIONSHIP OF SYSTEMS TO ONE ANOTHER: INTEGRATION

Figure 2.10 illustrates how the various types of systems in the organization are related to one another. TPS are typically a major source of data for other systems, whereas ESS are primarily a recipient of data from lower-level systems. The other types of systems may exchange data among one another as well.

But how much can or should these systems be integrated? This is a very difficult question to answer. It is definitely advantageous to have some measure of integration so that information can flow easily among different parts of the organization. But integration costs money, and integrating many different systems is extremely time-consuming and complex. Each organization must weigh its needs for integrating systems against dif-

FIGURE 2.10
Interrelationships among systems. The various types of systems in the organization do not work independently; rather, there are interdependencies between the systems. TPS are a major producer of information that is required by the other systems which, in turn, produce information for other systems. These different types of systems are only loosely coupled in most organizations.

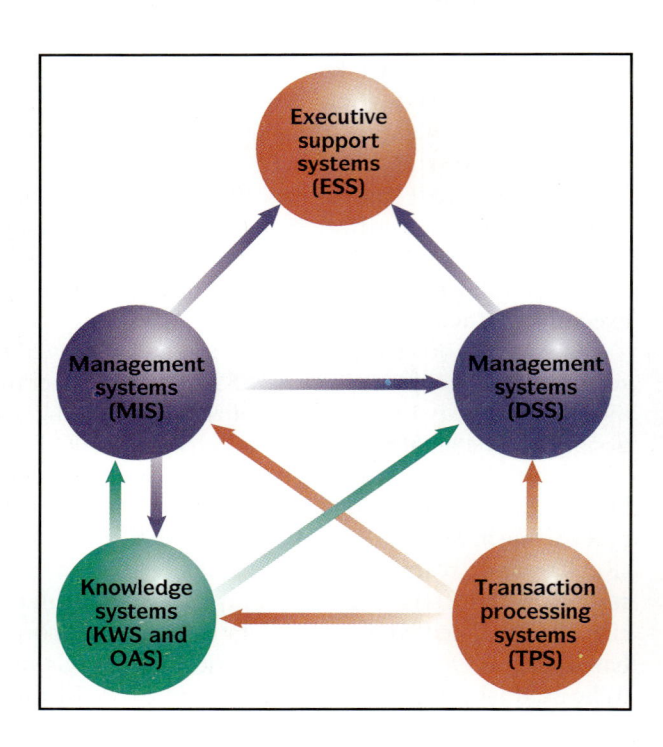

42 CHAPTER 2 The Strategic Role of Information Systems

ficulties of mounting a large-scale systems integration effort. There is no "one right level" of integration or centralization (Allen and Boynton, 1991; King, 1984).

2.2 THE STRATEGIC ROLE OF INFORMATION SYSTEMS

Each of the major types of information systems described previously is valuable for helping organizations solve an important problem. In the past few decades, some of these systems have become especially critical to the firm's long-term prosperity and survival. Such systems, which are powerful tools for staying ahead of the competition, are called strategic information systems.

WHAT IS A STRATEGIC INFORMATION SYSTEM?

Strategic information systems change the goals, operations, products, services, or environmental relationships of organizations to help them gain an edge over competitors. Systems that have these effects may even change the business of organizations. For instance, State Street Bank and Trust Co. of Boston transformed its core business from traditional banking services, such as customer checking and savings accounts and loans, to electronic record keeping, providing data processing services for securities and mutual funds, and services for pension funds to monitor their money managers (Rebello, 1995).

Strategic information systems should be distinguished from strategic-level systems for senior managers that focus on long-term decision-making problems. Strategic information systems can be used at all levels of the organization and are more far-reaching and deep-rooted than the other kinds of systems we have described. Strategic information systems fundamentally change the firm's goals, products, services, or internal and external relationships. Strategic information systems profoundly alter the way a firm conducts its business or the very business of the firm itself.

In order to use information systems as competitive weapons, one must first understand where strategic opportunities for businesses are likely to be found. Two models of the firm and its environment have been used to identify areas of the business where information systems can provide advantages over competitors. These are the competitive forces model and the value chain model.

strategic information systems Computer systems at any level of the organization that change goals, operations, products, services, or environmental relationships to help the organization gain a competitive advantage.

COUNTERING COMPETITIVE FORCES

In the **competitive forces model,** which is illustrated in Figure 2.11 (Porter, 1980), a firm faces a number of external threats and opportunities: the threat of new entrants into its market, the pressure from substitute products or services, the bargaining power of customers, the bargaining power of suppliers, and the positioning of traditional industry competitors.

Competitive advantage can be achieved by enhancing the firm's ability to deal with customers, suppliers, substitute products and services, and new entrants to its market, which in turn may change the balance of power between a firm and other competitors in the industry in the firm's favor. Businesses can use four basic competitive strategies to deal with these competitive forces: product differentiation, focused differentiation, developing tight linkages to customers and suppliers, and becoming the low-cost producer. A firm may achieve competitive advantage by pursuing one of these strategies or by pursuing several strategies simultaneously. For instance, the Gillette Company, described earlier, is competing on quality, innovation, and cost. We now describe how information systems can support these competitive strategies.

competitive forces model Model used to describe the interaction of external influences, specifically threats and opportunities, that affect an organization's strategy and ability to compete.

Product Differentiation

Firms can develop brand loyalty by **product differentiation**—creating unique new products and services that can easily be distinguished from those of competitors, and that existing competitors or potential new competitors can't duplicate.

product differentiation Competitive strategy for creating brand loyalty by developing new and unique products and services that are not easily duplicated by competitors.

FIGURE 2.11
The competitive forces model. There are various forces that affect an organization's ability to compete and therefore greatly influence a firm's business strategy. There are threats from new market entrants and from substitute products and services. Customers and suppliers wield bargaining power. Traditional competitors constantly adapt their strategies to maintain their market positioning.

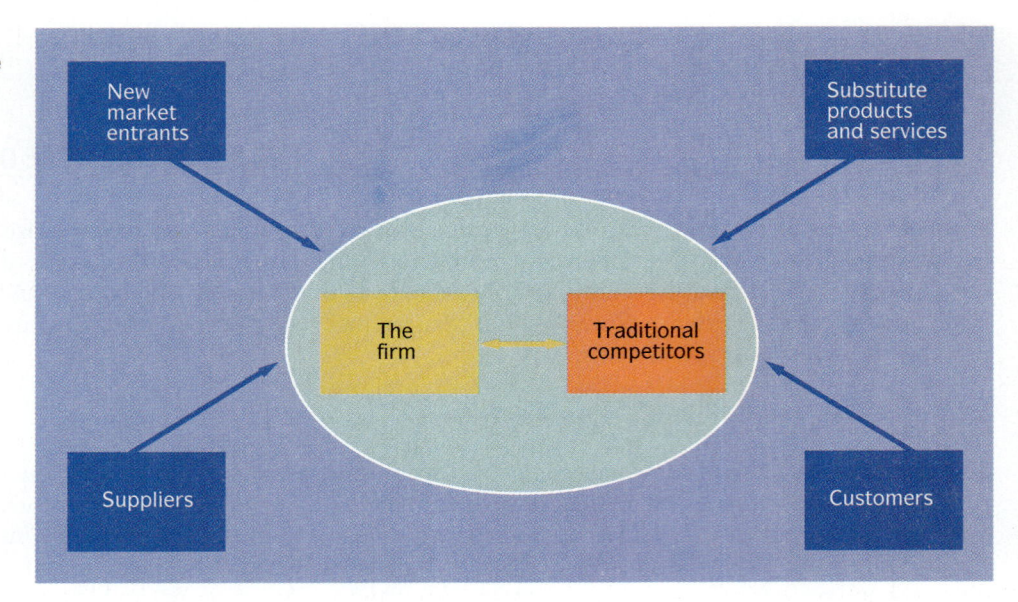

Financial institutions pioneered in using information systems to create new products and services. Citibank developed automatic teller machines (ATMs) and bank debit cards in 1977. As a leader in this area, Citibank became at one time the largest bank in the United States.

Manufacturers are starting to use information systems to create products and services that are custom-tailored to fit the precise specifications of individual customers. Levi Strauss began equipping retail stores with an option called Personal Pair, which allows customers to design jeans to their own specifications, rather than picking them off the rack. Customers enter their measurements into a microcomputer, which then transmits the customer's specification to Levi's plants. Levi Strauss is able to produce the custom jeans on the same lines that manufacture its standard items (Moad, 1995).

Focused Differentiation

focused differentiation
Competitive strategy for developing new market niches for specialized products or services where a business can compete in the target area better than its competitors.

Businesses can create new market niches by **focused differentiation**—identifying a specific target for a product or service that it can serve in a superior manner. The firm can provide a specialized product or service that serves this narrow target market better than existing competitors and that discourages potential new competitors.

An information system can give companies a competitive advantage by producing data to improve their sales and marketing techniques. Such systems treat existing information as a resource that can be "mined" by the organization to increase profitability and market penetration. Classic examples are the sophisticated data mining systems described in the Window on Organizations.

The cost of acquiring a new customer has been estimated to be five times that of retaining an existing customer. By carefully examining transactions of customer purchases and activities, firms can identify profitable customers and win more of their business. Likewise, companies can use these data to identify nonprofitable customers (Clemons and Weber, 1994).

Developing Tight Linkages to Customers and Suppliers

switching costs The expense a customer or company incurs in lost time and expenditure of resources when changing from one supplier or system to a competing supplier or system.

Firms can create ties to customers and suppliers that "lock" customers into the firm's products and that tie suppliers into a delivery timetable and price structure shaped by the purchasing firm. This raises **switching costs** (the cost for customers to switch to competitors' products and services) and reduces customers' bargaining power and the bargaining power of suppliers.

44 CHAPTER 2 The Strategic Role of Information Systems

Window on Organizations

MINING DATA FOR PROFITS

Marketing has come a long way from its early exclusive reliance on mass marketing, where the same message is directed at virtually everyone. The newest approach, commonly known as *data mining*, consists of personal or individualized messages based upon likely individual preferences. Massive quantities of data are gathered on consumers and then analyzed to locate customers with specific interests or to determine the interests of a specific group of customers. The data come from a range of sources.

American Express had a gigantic pool of data culled from $350 billion in credit card purchases in 1991 and continually updated since. One way it uses this data is in *relationship billing*. If, for example, a customer purchases a dress at Saks Fifth Avenue department store, American Express might include in her next billing an offer of a discount on a pair of shoes purchased at the same store and charged on her American Express card. The two goals are to increase the customer use of her American Express card and also to expand the presence of American Express at Saks. A cardholder residing in London, England, who recently took a British Airways flight to Paris might find an offer in a newsletter for a special discounted "getaway" weekend to New York.

Fingerhut Co., a catalogue retailer that has its headquarters in Minnetonka, Minnesota, has a database with 25 million customers. It might search through the data to locate all who bought patio furniture this season to attempt to sell them a gas barbecue grill. Kraft General Foods has built a database of 30 million customers who have responded to coupons and other promotions. It augments the data by surveying customers and learning about their interests and tastes. Then, based upon their profiles, Kraft sends them selected coupons with appropriate tips on nutrition and exercise, as well as recipes that include Kraft brand products.

Holiday Inn Worldwide stores the details of every hotel stay at Holiday Inn and Crown Plaza hotels. It uses the data to examine customer patterns—the length of their stay, how much they paid, whether they used a travel agent. The results of the data analysis are used in promotional programs for Holiday Inn's most frequent customers and to measure customer satisfaction.

To Think About: How could data mining change the way organizations conduct their business? What benefits does data mining provide? What problems might it create?

Sources: Barbara DePompa, "There's Gold in Databases," *Information Week*, January 8, 1996; Jonathan Berry, John Verity, Kathleen Kerwin, and Gail DeGeorge, "Database Marketing," *Business Week* (September 5, 1994); Laurie Hays, "Using Computers to Divine Who Might Buy a Gas Grill," *The Wall Street Journal* (August 16, 1994).

Baxter Healthcare International, Inc. has developed a "stockless inventory" and ordering system to prevent customers from switching to competitors. Participating hospitals become unwilling to switch to another supplier because of the system's convenience and low cost. Baxter supplies nearly two-thirds of all products used by U.S. hospitals. Terminals tied to Baxter's own computers are installed in hospitals. When hospitals want to place an order, they do not need to call a salesperson or send a purchase order—they simply use a Baxter computer terminal on-site to order from the full Baxter supply catalogue. The system generates shipping, billing, invoicing, and inventory information, and the hospital terminals provide customers with an estimated delivery date. With more than 80 distribution centers in the United States, Baxter can make daily deliveries of its products, often within hours of receiving an order.

This system is similar to the just-in-time delivery systems developed in Japan and now being used in the American automobile industry. In these systems, automobile manufacturers such as GM or Chrysler enter the quantity and delivery schedules of specific automobile components into their own information systems. Then these requirements are automatically entered into a supplier's order entry information system. The supplier must respond with an agreement to deliver the materials at the time specified. Thus, automobile companies can reduce the cost of inventory, the space required for warehousing components or raw materials, and construction time.

Baxter has even gone one step further. Delivery personnel no longer drop off their cartons at a loading dock to be placed in a hospital storeroom. Instead, they deliver orders directly to the hospital corridors, dropping them at nursing stations, operating

FIGURE 2.12
A comparison of traditional inventory and delivery practices to the *just-in-time supply method* and the *stockless inventory method*. Strategic systems for linking customers and suppliers have changed the way in which some companies handle the supply and inventory requirements of their businesses. The just-in-time supply method reduces inventory requirements of the customer while stockless inventory allows the customer to eliminate inventories entirely, resulting in a decided competitive advantage.
Adapted from "Removing the Warehouse from Cost-Conscious Hospitals," The New York Times, March 3, 1991. Reprinted by permission of NYT Graphics.

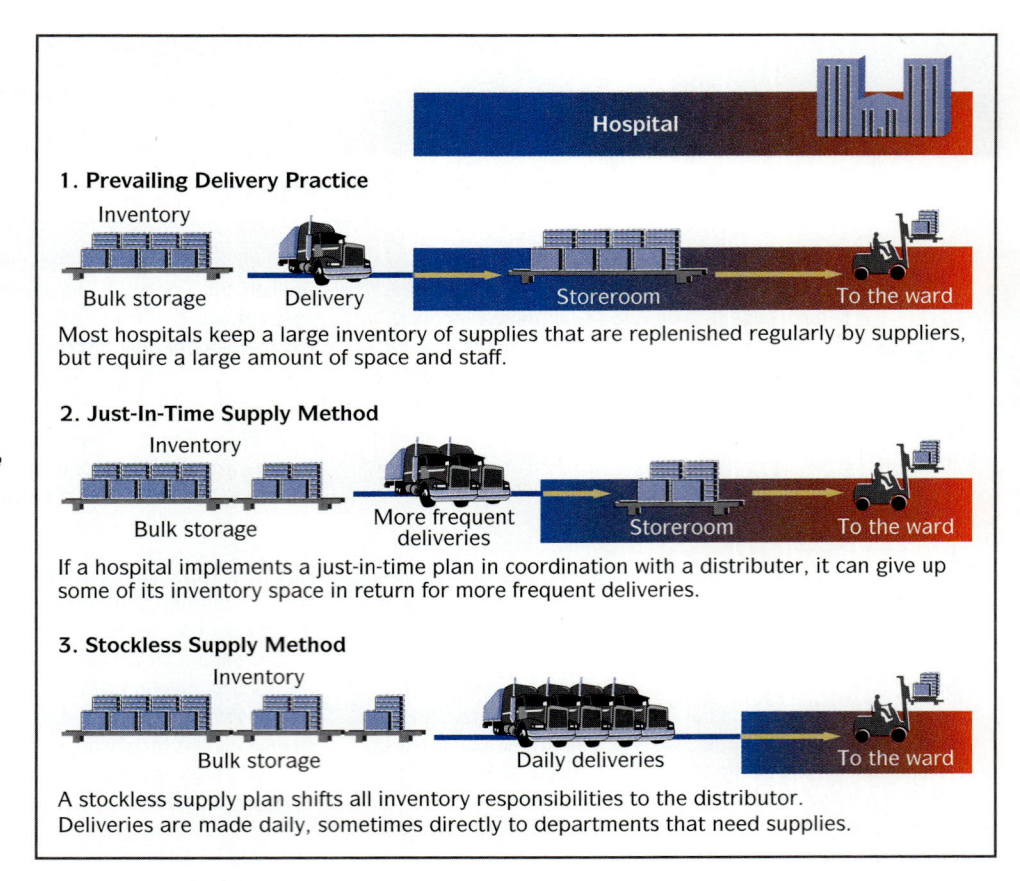

1. Prevailing Delivery Practice

Bulk storage → Delivery → Storeroom → To the ward

Most hospitals keep a large inventory of supplies that are replenished regularly by suppliers, but require a large amount of space and staff.

2. Just-In-Time Supply Method

Bulk storage → More frequent deliveries → Storeroom → To the ward

If a hospital implements a just-in-time plan in coordination with a distributer, it can give up some of its inventory space in return for more frequent deliveries.

3. Stockless Supply Method

Bulk storage → Daily deliveries → To the ward

A stockless supply plan shifts all inventory responsibilities to the distributor. Deliveries are made daily, sometimes directly to departments that need supplies.

rooms, and stock supply closets. This has created in effect a "stockless inventory," with Baxter serving as the hospitals' warehouse (Caldwell, 1991). Figure 2.12 compares stockless inventory with the just-in-time supply method and traditional inventory practices.

While just-in-time inventory allows customers to reduce their inventories, stockless inventory allows them to eliminate their inventories entirely. All inventory responsibilities shift to the distributor, who manages the supply flow. The stockless inventory is a powerful instrument for binding customers, giving the supplier a decided competitive advantage.

Strategic systems aimed at suppliers are designed to maximize the firm's purchasing power (and minimize costs) by having suppliers interact with its information system to satisfy the firm's precise business needs. Suppliers that are unwilling to go along with this system may lose business to other suppliers that can meet these demands.

Becoming the Low-Cost Producer

To prevent new competitors from entering their markets, businesses can produce goods and services at a lower price than competitors. Certain strategically oriented information systems help firms significantly lower their internal costs, allowing them to deliver products and services at a lower price (and sometimes with higher quality) than their competitors can provide.

By keeping prices low and shelves well-stocked, Wal-Mart has become the leading retail business in the United States. Wal-Mart uses a legendary inventory replenishment system triggered by point-of-sale purchases that is considered the best in the industry. The "continuous replenishment system" sends orders for new merchandise directly to suppliers as soon as consumers pay for their purchases at the cash register. Point-of-sale terminals record the bar code of each item passing the checkout counter and send a purchase transaction directly to a central computer at Wal-Mart headquarters. The com-

Wal-Mart's continuous inventory replenishment system uses sales data captured at the checkout counter to transmit orders to restock merchandise directly to its suppliers. The system enables Wal-Mart to keep costs low while fine-tuning its merchandise to meet customer demands.

puter collects the orders from all of the Wal-Mart stores and transmits them to suppliers. Because the system can replenish inventory with lightning speed, Wal-Mart does not need to spend much money on maintaining large inventories of goods in its own warehouses. The system also allows Wal-Mart to adjust purchases of store items to meet customer demands. Competitors such as Sears spend nearly 30% of each dollar in sales to pay for overhead (that is, expenses for salaries, advertising, warehousing, and building upkeep). Kmart spends 21% of sales on overhead. But by using systems to keep operating costs low, Wal-Mart pays only 15% of sales revenue for overhead.

Table 2.4 shows how the Internet can be used to support each of the competitive strategies.

LEVERAGING TECHNOLOGY IN THE VALUE CHAIN

The **value chain model** highlights specific activities in the business where competitive strategies can be best applied (Porter, 1985) and where information systems are most likely to have a strategic impact. The value chain model can supplement the competitive forces model by identifying specific, critical leverage points where a firm can use information technology most effectively to enhance its competitive position. Exactly where can it obtain the greatest benefit from strategic information systems—what

value chain model Model that highlights the primary or support activities that add a margin of value to a firm's products or services where information systems can best be applied to achieve a competitive advantage.

Table 2.4 Strategic Uses of the Internet

Strategy	Internet Application
Product differentiation	Virtual banking: Security First Network Bank allows customers to view account statements, pay bills, check account balances, and obtain 24-hour customer service through the World Wide Web.
Focused differentiation	Hyatt Hotels' TravelWeb provides electronic information on participating hotels in North America. Hyatt can analyze TravelWeb usage patterns to tailor hospitality-related products more closely to customer preferences. (See Chapter 9.)
Links to customers and suppliers	Federal Express maintains a World Wide Web site where customers can track the status of their packages any time of the day, anywhere in the world by entering their package tracking numbers.
Low-cost producer	Avex Electronics, Inc., is reducing costs by exchanging quotes, bills, and design drawings for electronics components and parts with customers and suppliers electronically on the Internet.

specific activities can be used to create new products and services, enhance market penetration, lock in customers and suppliers, and lower operational costs? This model views the firm as a series or "chain" of basic activities that add a margin of value to a firm's products or services. These activities can be categorized as either primary activities or support activities.

Primary activities are most directly related to the production and distribution of the firm's products and services that create value for the customer. Primary activities include inbound logistics, operations, outbound logistics, sales and marketing, and service. Inbound logistics include receiving and storing materials for distribution to production. Operations transforms inputs into finished products. Outbound logistics entail storing and distributing products. Marketing and sales includes promoting and selling the firm's products. The service activity includes maintenance and repair of the firm's goods and services. **Support activities** make the delivery of the primary activities possible and consist of organization infrastructure (administration and management), human resources (employee recruiting, hiring, and training), technology (improving products and the production process), and procurement (purchasing input).

Organizations have a competitive advantage when they provide more value to their customers or when they provide the same value to customers at a lower price. An information system could have strategic impact if it helped the firm provide products or services at a lower cost than competitors or if it provided products and services at the same cost as competitors but with greater value. Gillette's systems, described in the chapter-opening vignette, create value by both lowering production costs and raising the level of quality of Gillette razors and blades. The value activities that add the most value to products and services depend on the features of each particular firm. Businesses should try to develop strategic information systems for the value activities that add the most value to their particular firm. Figure 2.13 illustrates the activities of the value chain, showing examples of strategic information systems that could be developed to make each of the value activities more cost effective.

For instance, a firm such as Wal-Mart could save money in the inbound logistics activity by having suppliers make daily deliveries of goods to its stores, thereby lowering the costs of warehousing and inventory. A computer-aided design system might support the technology activity, helping a firm to reduce costs and perhaps to design more high-quality products than the competition produces. Gillette's computer-controlled machining supports the operations activity, reducing costs and boosting quality.

primary activities Activities most directly related to the production and distribution of a firm's products or services.

support activities Activities that make the delivery of the primary activities of a firm possible. Consist of the organization's infrastructure, human resources, technology, and procurement.

FIGURE 2.13
Activities of the value chain. Various examples of strategic information systems for the primary and support activities of a firm that would add a margin of value to a firm's products or services.

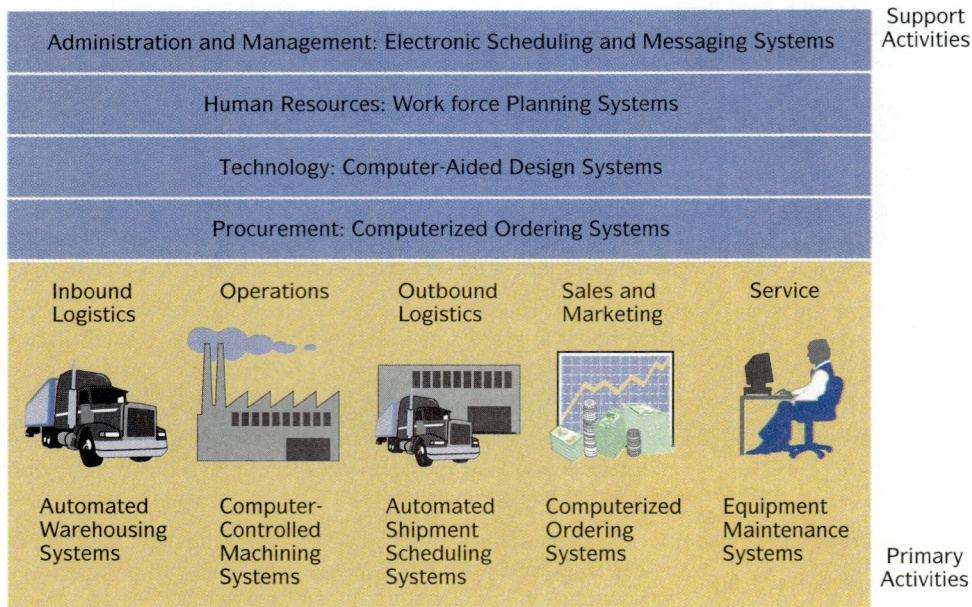

Support Activities:
- Administration and Management: Electronic Scheduling and Messaging Systems
- Human Resources: Work force Planning Systems
- Technology: Computer-Aided Design Systems
- Procurement: Computerized Ordering Systems

Primary Activities:
- Inbound Logistics: Automated Warehousing Systems
- Operations: Computer-Controlled Machining Systems
- Outbound Logistics: Automated Shipment Scheduling Systems
- Sales and Marketing: Computerized Ordering Systems
- Service: Equipment Maintenance Systems

IMPLICATIONS FOR MANAGERS AND ORGANIZATIONS

Strategic information systems often change the organization as well as its products, services, and internal procedures, driving the organization into new behavior patterns. Such changes often require new managers, a new work force, and a much closer relationship with customers and suppliers.

Strategic Alliances and Information Partnerships

Companies are increasingly using information systems for strategic advantage by entering into strategic alliances with other companies in which both firms cooperate by sharing resources or services. Such alliances are often **information partnerships** in which two or more firms share data for mutual advantage (Konsynski and McFarlan, 1990). They can join forces without actually merging. American Airlines has an arrangement with Citibank to award one mile in its frequent flier program for every dollar spent using Citibank credit cards. American benefits from increased customer loyalty, while Citibank gains new credit card subscribers and a highly creditworthy customer base for cross-marketing. Northwest Airlines has a similar arrangement with First Bank of South Dakota. American and Northwest have also allied with MCI, awarding frequent flier miles for each dollar of long-distance billing.

> **information partnership** Cooperative alliance formed between two corporations for the purpose of sharing information to gain strategic advantage.

Managing Strategic Transitions

Adopting the kinds of systems described in this chapter generally requires changes in business goals, relationships with customers and suppliers, internal operations, and information architecture. These sociotechnical changes, affecting both social and technical elements of the organization, can be considered **strategic transitions**—a movement between levels of sociotechnical systems. Managers struggling to boost competitiveness will need to redesign various organizational processes to make effective use of leading-edge information systems technology. They will require new mechanisms for coordinating their firms' activities with those of customers and suppliers (Kambil and Short, 1994). Such changes often entail blurring of organizational boundaries, both external and internal. Suppliers and customers may become intimately linked and may share each other's responsibilities. For instance, in Baxter International's stockless inventory system, Baxter has assumed responsibility for managing its customers' inventories (Johnston and Vitale, 1988). Over time, Baxter has redesigned its work processes numerous times to continually improve its overall service level and business relationship with customers (Short and Venkatraman, 1992).

> **strategic transitions** A movement from one level of sociotechnical system to another. Often required when adopting strategic systems that demand changes in the social and technical elements of an organization.

Other organizational changes may be required as well. Gillette found that its sophisticated new machines that produced its redesigned razors raised the level of technology so much that operators needed more training. The operators didn't understand the reports on quality and production rates produced by these machines and how to make appropriate adjustments to the equipment. Gillette revised its employee development policies to provide education before introducing new equipment. Not all strategic information systems require massive change, but clearly, many do.

What Managers Can Do

Managers must take the initiative to identify the types of systems that would provide a strategic advantage to the firm. Some of the important questions managers should ask are:

- How is the industry currently using information systems? Which organizations are the industry leaders in the application of information systems technology?
- Are significant strategic opportunities to be gained by introducing new information systems technology? Where would new information systems provide the greatest value to the firm?

- What is the current business strategic plan, and how does that plan mesh with the current strategy for information services?
- Does the firm have the technology and capital required to develop a strategic information systems initiative? (Kettinger et al., 1994)

2.3 HOW INFORMATION SYSTEMS PROMOTE QUALITY

Global competition is forcing companies to focus more than ever on using quality in their competitive strategies. There are many ways in which information systems can help organizations achieve higher levels of quality in their products, services, and operations.

WHAT IS QUALITY?

quality Conformance to producer specifications and satisfaction of customer criteria such as quality of physical product, quality of service, and psychological aspects.

Quality can be defined from both a producer and a customer perspective. From the perspective of the producer, **quality** signifies conformance to specifications (or the absence of variation from those specifications). A wristwatch manufacturer, for example, might include a specification for reliability which requires that 99.995 percent of the watches will neither gain nor lose more than one second per month. Simple tests will enable the manufacturer to measure precisely against these specifications.

A customer's definition of quality is much broader. First, customers are concerned with the quality of the physical product—its durability, safety, ease of use, and installation. Second, customers are concerned with the quality of service, by which they mean the accuracy and truthfulness of advertising, responsiveness to warranties, and ongoing product support. Finally, customer concepts of quality include psychological aspects: the company's knowledge of its products, the courtesy and sensitivity of sales and support staff, and the reputation of the product.

total quality management (TQM) A concept that makes quality control a responsibility to be shared by all people in an organization.

Today more and more businesses are turning to an idea known as total quality management. **Total quality management (TQM)** is a concept that makes quality the responsibility of all people within an organization. TQM holds that the achievement of quality control is an end in itself. Everyone is expected to contribute to the overall improvement of quality—the engineer who avoids design errors, the production worker who spots defects, the sales representative who presents the product properly to potential customers, and even the secretary who avoids typing mistakes. Total quality management encompasses all of the functions within an organization.

TQM derives from quality management concepts developed by American quality experts such as W. Edwards Deming and Joseph Juran, but it was popularized by the Japanese. Japanese management adopted the goal of zero defects, focusing on improving their product or service prior to shipment rather than correcting them after they have been delivered. Japanese companies often give the responsibility for quality consistency to the workers who actually make the product or service, as opposed to a quality control department. Studies have repeatedly shown that the earlier in the business cycle a problem is eliminated, the less it costs the company. Thus the Japanese quality approach not only brought a shift in focus to the workers and an increased respect for product and service quality, but it also lowered costs.

HOW INFORMATION SYSTEMS CONTRIBUTE TO TOTAL QUALITY MANAGEMENT

Information systems can help firms achieve their quality goals by helping them simplify products or processes, meet benchmarking standards, make improvements based on customer demands, reduce cycle time, and increase the quality and precision of design and production.

Simplifying the Product, the Production Process, or Both

Quality programs usually have a "fewer is better" philosophy—the fewer steps in a process, the less time and opportunity for an error to occur. A few years ago the Carrier Corporation, the Syracuse, New York, manufacturing giant, was faced with an eroding market share. One reason: a 70% error rate in using its manual order entry system, which was used to match customers and products when ordering Carrier's commercial air conditioning units. The system required so many steps to process an order that mistakes were all but inevitable. Errors sometimes went undetected until the end of the manufacturing line, where workers might discover a wrong coil or some other similar problem. Big mistakes occasionally affected customers. In 1988, the company finally instituted a TQM program in which information technology played a large role. Carrier now coordinates everything from sales to manufacturing by using an artificial intelligence system (LaPlante, 1992). When information systems helped reduce the number of steps, the number of errors dropped dramatically, manufacturing costs dropped, and Carrier found itself with happier customers.

Benchmark

Many companies have been effective in achieving quality by setting strict standards for products, services, and other activities, and then measuring performance against those standards. This procedure is called benchmarking. Companies may use external industry standards, standards set by other companies, internally developed high standards, or some combination of the three. L.L. Bean Inc., the Freeport, Maine, mail order clothing company, uses benchmarking to achieve an order shipping accuracy of 99.9%.

To provide better information for benchmarking, information systems specialists can work with business specialists either to design new systems or to analyze quality-related data in existing systems. For instance, L.L. Bean carefully designed its information systems so it could analyze the data embedded in customer return transactions. Bean's return forms require customers to supply "reason codes" explaining why each item was returned. A report from these systems showing return transaction frequency and dollar value summarized by week or month and broken down by the reason for the returns helps management target areas where mistakes are being made.

Use Customer Demands as a Guide to Improving Products and Services

Improving customer service, making customer service the number one priority, will improve the quality of the product itself, as is clear from the Carrier example described earlier. The Window on Management shows how one small business, 1-800-FLOWERS, addressed the question of customer satisfaction in a quality program. It also shows the contribution of information systems in building a system and making needed information available when required.

Reduce Cycle Time

Experience indicates that the single best way to address quality problems is to reduce the amount of time from the beginning of a process to its end (cycle time). Reducing cycle time usually results in fewer steps. Shorter cycles mean that errors are often caught earlier in production (or logistics or design or whatever the function), often before the process is complete, eliminating many hidden costs. Iomega Corporation in Roy, Utah, a manufacturer of disk drives, was spending $20 million a year to fix defective drives at the end of its 28-day production cycle. Reengineering the production process allowed the firm to reduce cycle time to a day and a half, eliminating this problem and winning the prestigious Shingo Prize for Excellence in American Manufacturing in the process.

Improve the Quality and Precision of the Design

Quality and precision in design will eliminate many production problems. Computer-aided design (CAD) software has made dramatic quality improvements possible in a wide range of businesses from aircraft manufacturing to production of razor blades. Alan R. Burns, a mining engineer from Perth, Australia, was able to use CAD to invent and design a new tire product. His concept was a modular tire made up of a series of replaceable modules or segments so that if one segment were damaged, only that segment, not

Window on Management

BUILDING AN ORGANIZATION TO SELL FLOWERS

Jim McCann bought 1-800-FLOWERS in 1987 because it was the best marketing idea he had seen. But the company was $7 million in debt and spending way too much money attracting new customers. It relied on a large and costly telemarketing center and expensive national advertising. McCann recognized that selling flowers is a "nickel-and-dime business" that cannot afford expensive advertising. To be successful, he would have to rely on repeat customers. The underlying problem was that few customers came back because of poor service and inconsistent quality. So McCann rebuilt his organization to give customers quality service, service that would bring them back repeatedly. 1-800-FLOWERS is now the world's largest florist.

Before McCann pruchased the company, 1-800-FLOWERS had a network of 8,000 florists around the country to design and deliver all orders. McCann decided that he needed fewer florists, but these florists must be held to high standards for design, flower freshness, and delivery. He replaced the existing network with 2,500 florists who agreed to his standards, including a guarantee of same-day delivery for all orders received by 1:00 P.M. McCann then hired a staff of 15 quality-control experts who spot-checked the florists to make certain they sold only fresh flowers. Next, he moved the 1-800-FLOWERS telemarketing center from its 55,000-

> **To Think About:** How did technology promote quality at 1-800-FLOWERS? Could technology alone have solved 1-800-FLOWERS' quality problems? What was the relationship between quality, technology, and 1-800-FLOWERS' business strategy?

square-foot facility in Dallas, Texas, to much smaller facilities in Bayside, New York. He added 30 more telephone representatives to his staff and trained them in customer service, instructing them to personalize each conversation. 1-800-FLOWERS offered customer guarantees that floral arrangements would last a minimum of 7 days; arrangements the customer didn't like could be returned when they arrived.

Making a sale required a number of steps: writing the order, obtaining credit card approval, determining which 1-800-FLOWERS florist is closest to the delivery location, describing and deciding on a floral arrangement, and forwarding the order to the florist. Each step in the manual process increased the chance of human error, and thus the possibility of a wrong delivery. McCann purchased a $4 million NCR midrange computer to centrally process orders more efficiently. The system reduces processing time from ten minutes to less than five. The computer system includes computer images of floral arrangements that the telereps can use to aid them as they talk with customers. The organization of 2,500 florists was brought into the whole process by being connected to the network. A computer, a modem (to connect them to the network), and a printer were installed in each florist shop. McCann found that the data from the computer system had other uses as well. For example, by tracking the orders, he has been able to anticipate the volume on any given day, allowing both 1-800-FLOWERS and the 2,500 florists to have available added staff and product on days of predicted high volume.

Sources: Richard D. Smith, "From One Little Shop, an 1-800-Flowers Garden Grows," *The New York Times*, January 8, 1995; Leah Ingram, "One Blooming Business," *Profit* (May/June 1994).

---

the whole tire, would need replacing. The modules are not pneumatic and so cannot deflate. Moreover, they can be changed quickly and easily by one person. Burns discovered that his new tire would likely find a ready market in the heavy equipment vehicle market (such as the backhoes and earth movers used in construction) and established a company, called Airboss. He first established quality performance measurements for such key tire characteristics as load, temperature, speed, wear life, and traction. He then entered these data into a CAD software package, which he used to design the modules.

Using the software he was able iteratively to design and test until he was satisfied with the results. He did not need to develop an actual working model until the iterative design process was almost complete. Because of the speed and accuracy of the CAD software, the product he produced was of much higher quality than would have been possible through manual design and testing.

Increase the Precision of Production

For many products, one key way to achieve quality is to tighten production tolerances. Computer-aided design (CAD) software often includes a facility to translate design specifications into specifications both for production tooling and for the production process itself. In this way, products with more precise designs can also be produced more efficiently. Once his tire segment design was completed, Burns used the CAD software to design his manufacturing process. In testing by computer he discovered, for example, that the segment would cool unevenly. He was able to correct the problem even before developing the production equipment. He was also able to design a shorter production cycle, improving quality while increasing his ability to meet customer demand more quickly.

Komag of Milpitas, California, the world's largest supplier of 5¼-inch and smaller sputtered thin-film disks for disk drives in all types of computers, must control hundreds of variables in its manufacturing process, which transforms uncoated aluminum disks into highly technical precision products. Komag needed more precision in its production process. It implemented MESA, from Camstar Systems Inc., a Manufacturing Execution System (MES). This system allows Komag to monitor hundreds of process manufacturing execution steps to analyze yield, productivity, and machine utilization. System capabilities include real-time lot movement and inventory tracking, generation of process control charts, lot history, process data, application of process parameters per operation step, and immediate response to out-of-control process variances and yield problems. Managers can obtain data on key production variables by product, process, machine, and shift. Within six months after implementing the new system, Komag doubled output (Komag, 1994).

Management Challenges

1. Integration. On the one hand, it is necessary to design different systems for different levels and functions in the firm—TPS, MIS, DSS, OAS, KWS, and ESS. On the other hand, integrating the systems so that they can freely exchange information can be technologically difficult and costly. Managers need to determine what level of system integration is required and how much it is worth in dollars.

2. Sustainability of competitive advantage. The competitive advantages conferred by strategic systems do not necessarily last long enough to ensure long-term profits. Competitors can retaliate and copy strategic systems. Moreover, these systems are often expensive; costs saved by some systems are expended immediately to maintain the system. Competitive advantage isn't always sustainable. Market conditions change. The business and economic environment changes. Technology and customers' expectations change. The classic strategic information systems—American Airlines' SABRE computerized reservation system, Citibank's ATM system, and Federal Express' package tracking system—benefited by being the first in their respective industries. But then rival systems emerged. NYCE banks blunted Citibank's ATM edge. United Parcel Service, described in Chapter 1, is challenging Federal Express' domination of the overnight package market. Information systems alone cannot provide an enduring business advantage (Kettinger et al., 1994; Mata et al., 1995; Hopper, 1990). Systems originally intended to be strategic frequently become tools for survival, something every firm has in order to stay in business. Rather than conferring long-term competitive advantage, they become critical for a company just to keep abreast of the competition.

Summary

1. Describe the role played by the six major types of information systems in organizations. There are six major types of information systems in contemporary organizations that are designed for different purposes and different audiences. Operational-level systems are transaction processing systems (TPS), such as payroll or order processing, that track the flow of the daily routine transactions that are necessary to conduct business. Knowledge-level systems support clerical, managerial, and professional workers. They consist of office automation systems for increasing the productivity of data workers and knowledge work systems for enhancing the productivity of knowledge workers.

Management-level systems (MIS and DSS) provide the management control level with reports and access to the organization's current performance and historical records. Most MIS reports condense information from TPS and are not highly analytical. Decision-support systems (DSS) support management decisions when these decisions are unique, rapidly changing, and not specified easily in advance. They have more advanced analytical models than MIS and often draw on information from external as well as internal sources.

Executive support systems (ESS) support the strategic level by providing a generalized computing and communications environment to assist senior management's decision making. They have limited analytical capabilities but can draw on sophisticated graphics software and many sources of internal and external information.

2. Discuss the relationship between the various types of information systems. The various types of systems in the organization exchange data with one another. TPS are a major source of data for other systems, especially MIS and DSS. ESS is primarily a recipient of data from lower-level systems. However, the different systems in an organization are only loosely integrated. The information needs of the various functional areas and organizational levels are too specialized to be served by a single system.

3. Describe how the competitive forces and value chain models can be used to identify opportunities for strategic information systems. The competitive forces and value chain models can help identify areas of a business where information systems can supply a strategic advantage. The competitive forces model describes a number of external threats and opportunities faced by firms that they must counter with competitive strategies. Information systems can be developed to cope with the threat of new entrants into the market, the pressure from substitute products, the bargaining power of buyers, the bargaining power of suppliers, and the positioning of traditional industry competitors. The value chain model highlights specific activities in the business where competitive strategies can best be applied and where information systems are most likely to have a strategic impact. This model views the firm as a series or "chain" of basic activities that add a margin of value to a firm's products or services. Information systems can have a strategic impact on the activities that add the most value to the firm.

4. Explain why strategic information systems are difficult to build and to sustain. Not all strategic systems make a profit; they can be expensive and risky to build. Many strategic information systems are easily copied by other firms, so that strategic advantage is not always sustainable. Implementing strategic systems often requires extensive organizational change and a transition from one sociotechnical level to another. Such changes are called strategic transitions and are often difficult and painful to achieve.

5. Describe how organizations can use information systems to enhance quality in their operations, products, and services. Information systems can help organizations simplify their products and the production process, meet benchmarking standards, improve customer service, reduce production cycle time, and improve the quality and precision of design and production.

Key Terms

Operational-level systems	**Word processing**	**Strategic information system**	**Information partnership**
Knowledge-level systems	**Desktop publishing**	**Competitive forces model**	**Strategic transitions**
Management-level systems	**Document imaging systems**	**Product differentiation**	**Quality**
Strategic-level systems	**Management information systems (MIS)**	**Focused differentiation**	**Total quality management**
Transaction processing systems (TPS)	**Decision-support systems (DSS)**	**Switching costs**	
Knowledge work systems (KWS)	**Executive support systems (ESS)**	**Value chain model**	
Office automation systems (OAS)		**Primary activities**	
		Support activities	

Review Questions

1. Identify and describe the four levels of the organizational hierarchy. What types of information systems serve each level?

2. List and briefly describe the major types of systems in organizations. How are they related to one another?

3. What are the five types of TPS in business organizations? What functions do they perform? Give examples of each.
4. Describe the functions performed by knowledge work and office automation systems and some typical applications of each.
5. What are the characteristics of MIS? How does MIS differ from TPS? From DSS?
6. What are the characteristics of DSS? How do they differ from those of ESS?
7. What is a strategic information system? What is the difference between a strategic information system and a strategic-level system?
8. Define and compare the competitive forces and value chain models for identifying opportunities for strategic systems.
9. What are the four basic competitive strategies? How can information systems help firms pursue each of these strategies?
10. Why are strategic information systems difficult to build?
11. Explain the advantages of an information partnership.
12. How can managers find strategic applications in their firm?
13. What is total quality management?
14. How can companies use information systems to promote total quality management?

Discussion Questions

1. In what way is the United Parcel Service package tracking system described in Chapter 1 an example of a TPS? Describe the transactions used in the system. What data do they capture? What do they do with these data? How could these data be used in an MIS?
2. Several information systems experts have claimed, "There is no such thing as a sustainable strategic advantage." Discuss.
3. How do the following kinds of systems give each company a strategic advantage? What competitive strategy does each support?
   a. Mazda Motors of America distributes software to its dealerships; the software compiles customer data on trade-ins and used-car sales.
   b. Citibank has arranged with Federal Express to replace lost credit cards within 24 hours. Federal Express and Citibank computers networked together can track the creation and shipment of new cards to customers through the Federal Express hub in Memphis.
   c. Shell Oil Corporation in Houston introduced ATMs in its gas stations.
   d. The Food Emporium supermarket chain is starting to use video screens attached to shopping carts. As shoppers stroll down the aisles, a sensor activates video commercials and store specials on the video screen using software attached to a computer in the store. In addition to providing information about items for sale, the video screens can give brief weather and news reports.

Group Project

Form a group with two or three classmates. Research a business using annual reports or business publications such as *Fortune, Business Week,* and *The Wall Street Journal.* Analyze the business using the competitive forces and value chain models. Suggest appropriate strategic information systems for that particular business. Present your findings to the class.

Case Study

GREYHOUND SEEKS SALVATION IN A STRATEGIC RESERVATION SYSTEM

Greyhound Lines Inc., headquartered in Dallas, Texas, has long been the leading transcontinental bus company in the United States. However, the company share of interstate travel dropped from 30% in 1960 to 6% in the late 1980s, because of the rise in ownership of automobiles and discount airline service. The following chronology lists events that appear to be relevant to the problems Greyhound underwent.

July 1991

- Frank Schmieder becomes Greyhound chief executive. Schmieder gained a reputation as an intelligent though volatile boss. Union negotiators found him to be affable and were pleased that he occasionally rode the bus.
- J. Michael Doyle, a former financial officer at Phillips Petroleum Co., becomes chief financial officer and works closely with Schmieder to run Greyhound.

August 1991

- Schmieder begins to cut costs, upgrade buses and facilities, and settle labor disputes. Schmieder and Doyle policies include cutting the bus fleet from 3,700 to 2,400 and replacing current regional executives. They also replace most terminal workers with part-time workers who are paid about $6 an hour, whether they sweep floors or serve customers. These part-time workers are offered little opportunity to get a raise. Over the next 3 years, annual staff turnover of 30% becomes common, with some terminals reaching 100% annual turnover.

October 1991

- The Greyhound business plan includes a commitment to a computerized reservation system that financial market analysts focus on as the key to remaining competitive in the national market. The plan includes system support for more efficient use of buses and drivers.

Bus customers traditionally do not reserve seats in advance but rather arrive at the terminal, buy a ticket, and take the next bus. Few buses ever reserve seats. The primary use of bus customer telephone lines has been to disseminate schedule information, not for reserving seats as is the case in the airline industry. Traditionally, clerks plotted journeys manually from thick bus schedule log books (Greyhound buses stop in several thousand towns in the United States). The process was very slow. Computerizing all of the routes and stops would theoretically greatly reduce the time needed to plot journeys and issue tickets. The goals of an automated system were not only to speed the issuing of tickets, thereby reducing company service counter costs, but also simultaneously to improve customer service and customer relations.

The company had to manage several thousand buses and their drivers nationwide, making certain they were in the right locations at the right time. Greyhound assigned buses and bus drivers by hand, using data that were usually months old. The company kept buses and drivers in reserve in order to meet peak period demand, thereby enabling the company to remain the premier continent-wide bus company.

The new system, called Trips, was to handle both reservations and bus and driver allocations together because they were seen as tightly linked. The traditional bus strategy of no reservations, just walk-in riders, meant that many times buses departed nearly empty. Management hoped that adopting a reservation approach would allow them to reduce the number of near-empty buses. They also expected that the reservation portion of the system would provide Greyhound with reliable customer data so schedules could be more efficiently organized and so planners could determine where and when to reduce prices in order to fill seats. The plan for Trips was received very positively in the financial markets, giving Greyhound the ability to borrow funds and to offer new shares to raise capital.

Early Spring 1992

- The Trips project begins with a staff of 40 or so and a $6 million budget; Thomas Thompson, Greyhound senior vice president for network planning and operations, is placed in charge of Trips development.

A bus reservation system, by the nature of the operation of buses, is far more complex than airline reservation systems. A passenger might make one or two stops on an airline flight and cross the United States with none to two stops only, whereas bus passengers may make ten or more stops on a trip, and a cross-country trip might involve scores of stops. Greyhound technicians estimated that a bus management system would need to manage ten times the number of vehicle stops per day of an airline vehicle management system.

The average bus passenger is much less affluent than the average airline passenger. Several Greyhound executives later claimed to have raised the questions of how many bus passengers would have credit cards to enable them to purchase tickets in advance by telephone, and even how many have telephones available. American Airlines' SABRE reservation system had taken three years to develop and had cost several hundred million dollars, and the project had included a staff many times the size of the Trips staff.

November–December 1992

- Greyhound stock price reaches $13.50.
- Greyhound management actively promotes Trips to investors, lenders, and security analysts as a key to the future success of Greyhound. Management publicly promises to launch the system in time for the 1993 summer busy season.

Trips had been developed by a consulting firm. Planned users of the system such as ticket clerks required 40 hours of training to learn to use it. Clerks had to deal with many screens in order to plot a trip between any two points. The system data bank was incomplete, with the result that clerks often had to pull out the log books and revert to plotting a ticket purchaser's planned trip manually. Clerk time to issue tickets doubled when they used the system. The system also crashed repeatedly.

Thompson decided to redesign the system and to introduce it in the Northeast corridor in the spring of 1993. After that initial introduction, no new sites would be added until the autumn of 1993, when the busiest travel season would be behind Greyhound. This approach would also give the team time to work out the bugs before the system was introduced nationally. However, he was overruled by Doyle, who had promised the new system to the financial community.

- Greyhound reports a profit of $11 million, its first profit since 1989.

May 1993

- Rollout of Trips begins, using the failed version because Thompson did not have enough time to develop the new version. When Trips reaches 50 locations, the computer terminals begin to freeze unpredictably.
- Greyhound stock hits a post–Chapter 11 high of $22.75. Securities analysts had been praising Greyhound management for reengineering the company and for cutting costs.

June 1993

- The rollout of Trips continues.
- Doyle exercises an option to purchase 15,000 shares of Greyhound stock at $9.81.
- Greyhound stock holds above $20 as formal introduction of Trips nears.
- Doyle exercises options on 22,642 shares at $9.81 and immediately sells them at a profit of $179,000.

July 1993

- The new toll-free number telephone system begins serving the 220 terminals already hooked up to Trips to be used for making reservations.

The system could not handle all the calls, with many customers receiving busy signals. Customers often had to call as many as a dozen times to get through. The busy signals were caused by the switching mechanism and by the slow response time of Trips. The computer in Dallas sometimes took as long as 45 seconds to respond to just a single keystroke and could take up to five minutes to print a ticket. The system also crashed numerous times, causing many tickets to be written manually.

At some bus terminals, the passengers who arrived with manual tickets were told to wait in line so that they could be reissued a ticket by the computer. Long lines, delays, and confusion resulted. Many passengers missed their connections; others lost their luggage.

- On the same day as the initiation of the telephone system, Greyhound announces an increase in earnings per share and ridership and the introduction of a new discount-fare program; Greyhound stock rises 4.5%.

August 1993

- Doyle sells 15,000 shares of stock at $21.75 on August 4.
- Two other Greyhound vice presidents sell a total of 21,300 shares of stock.

September 1993

- Trips is closed down west of the Mississippi River because of its continuing problems and delays.
- On September 23, Greyhound announces ridership down by 12% in August and earnings also down; the press release does not mention Trips and blames the fall in ridership on the national economic environment.
- Greyhound stock, which was down 12% in August, falls to $11.75, or 24% in one day.

- Thompson is relieved of his duties on Trips; another vice president takes over responsibility.

May 1994

- The company offers a $68 ticket for a trip anywhere in the United States with a three-day advance purchase. The crush of potential customers brings Trips to a halt. Buses and drivers are not available in some cities, resulting in large numbers of frustrated passengers stranded in terminals.

July 1994

- On-time bus performance falls to 59% versus 81% at its peak.
- First half operating revenues fall 12.6%, accompanied by a large dropoff in ridership; the nine largest regional carriers in the United States show an average rise in operating revenue of 2.6%.

August 1994

- Schmieder and Doyle both resign.
- Thomas G. Plaskett, a 50-year-old Greyhound director, is appointed interim CEO; Plaskett was the chairman and CEO of Pan Am Corporation and a former managing director of Fox Run Capital Associates investments.
- The stock price falls to about $6.

November 1994

- Greyhound creditors file suit to attempt to force Greyhound back into protection under Chapter 11 of the Federal Bankruptcy Act.
- Greyhound stock falls to $1.875 per share.
- Greyhound announces its fourth consecutive quarterly loss.
- A financial restructuring agreement is reached that gives creditors 45% ownership of Greyhound. The agreement allows the company to avoid Chapter 11 bankruptcy.
- Craig Lentzcsh is appointed Greyhound's new permanent CEO.

January 1995

Greyhound announces that the Securities and Exchange Commission is investigating the company and former directors, officers, and employees for possible securities law violations. The investigation is examining possible insider trading, the adequacy of the firm's internal accounting procedures, and the adequacy of public disclosures related to the Trips system and the company's disappointing earnings in 1993. Greyhound says that it does not believe it has violated any securities laws and is cooperating fully. In addition to the SEC investigation, Greyhound is facing a raft of investors' lawsuits involving similar allegations and a Justice Department antitrust investigation into its terminal agreements with smaller carriers.

- By January 25, Greyhound stock has dropped to $1.563 per share.

Greyhound continues trying to improve the Trips system. It has started to de-emphasize advance reservations and to use the system for more efficient dispatching. ■

Sources: Robert Tomsho, "Greyhound Says SEC Is Investigating Possible Violations of Securities Law," *The Wall Street Journal*, January 26, 1995; "How Greyhound Lines Re-Engineered Itself Right into a Deep Hole," *The Wall Street Journal*, October 20, 1994; Wendy Zellner, "Greyhound Is Limping Badly," *Business Week*, August 22, 1994.

Case Study Questions

1. Use the competitive forces and value chain models to analyze Greyhound's situation. What competitive forces did Greyhound have to deal with? What was Greyhound's business strategy? What kinds of strategic information systems did Greyhound attempt to use?
2. How much strategic advantage would Trips have provided had it been designed and implemented successfully? Why?
3. What management, organization, and technology factors contributed to Greyhound's problems?
4. If you were a Greyhound manager, what solutions would you recommend? Would you suggest new information systems applications? If so, what would be the functions of those systems?

References

Allen, Brandt R., and Andrew C. Boynton. "Information Architecture: In Search of Efficient Flexibility." *MIS Quarterly* 15, no. 4 (December 1991).

Anthony, R. N. *Planning and Control Systems: A Framework for Analysis.* Cambridge, MA: Harvard University Press (1965).

Bakos, J. Yannis, and Michael E. Treacy. "Information Technology and Corporate Strategy: A Research Perspective." *MIS Quarterly* (June 1986).

Barua, Anitesh, Charles H. Kriebel, and Tridas Mukhopadhyay. "An Economic Analysis of Strategic Information Technology Investments." *MIS Quarterly* 15, no. 5 (September 1991).

Beath, Cynthia Mathis, and Blake Ives. "Competitive Information Systems in Support of Pricing." *MIS Quarterly* (March 1986).

Bower, Joseph L., and Thomas M. Hout. "Fast-Cycle Capability for Competitive Power." *Harvard Business Review* (November–December 1988).

Caldwell, Bruce. "A Cure for Hospital Woes." *Information Week* (September 9, 1991).

Cash, J. I., and Benn R. Konsynski. "IS Redraws Competitive Boundaries." *Harvard Business Review* (March–April 1985).

Cash, J. I., and P. L. McLeod. "Introducing IS Technology in Strategically Dependent Companies." *Journal of Management Information Systems* (Spring 1985).

Clemons, Eric K. "Evaluation of Strategic Investments in Information Technology." *Communications of the ACM* (January 1991).

Clemons, Eric K., and Michael Row. "McKesson Drug Co.: Case Study of a Strategic Information System." *Journal of Management Information Systems* (Summer 1988).

———. "Sustaining IT Advantage: The Role of Structural Differences." *MIS Quarterly* 15, no. 3 (September 1991).

———. "Limits to Interfirm Coordination through IT." *Journal of Management Information Systems* 10, no. 1 (Summer 1993).

Clemons, Eric K., and Bruce W. Weber. "Segmentation, Differentiation, and Flexible Pricing: Experience with Information Technology and Segment-Tailored Strategies." *Journal of Management Information Systems* 11, no. 2 (Fall 1994).

Copeland, Duncan G., and James L. McKenney. "Airline Reservations Systems: Lessons from History." *MIS Quarterly* 12, no. 3 (September 1988).

Culnan, Mary J. "Transaction Processing Applications as Organizational Message Systems: Implications for the Intelligent Organization." Working paper no. 88-10, Twenty-second Hawaii International Conference on Systems Sciences (January 1989).

Davis, Gordon B. and Margrethe H. Olson. *Management Information Systems: Conceptual Foundations, Structure, and Development*, 2nd ed. New York: McGraw-Hill (1985).

Feeny, David F., and Blake Ives. "In Search of Sustainability: Reaping Long-Term Advantage from Investments in Information Technology." *Journal of Management Information Systems* (Summer 1990).

Henderson, John C., and John J. Sifonis. "The Value of Strategic IS Planning: Understanding Consistency, Validity, and IS Markets." *MIS Quarterly* 12, no. 2 (June 1988).

Hopper, Max. "Rattling SABRE—New Ways to Compete on Information." *Harvard Business Review* (May–June 1990).

Houdeshel, George, and Hugh J. Watson. "The Management Information and Decision Support (MIDS) System at Lockheed Georgia." *MIS Quarterly* 11, no. 1 (March 1987).

Huber, George P. "Organizational Information Systems: Determinants of Their Performance and Behavior." *Management Science* 28, no. 2 (1984).

Ives, Blake, and Gerald P. Learmonth. "The Information System as a Competitive Weapon." *Communications of the ACM* (December 1984).

Ives, Blake, and Michael R. Vitale. "After the Sale: Leveraging Maintenance with Information Technology." *MIS Quarterly* (March 1986).

Johnston, H. Russell, and Shelley R. Carrico. "Developing Capabilities to Use Information Strategically." *MIS Quarterly* 12, no. 1 (March 1988).

Johnston, Russell, and Paul R. Lawrence. "Beyond Vertical Integration—The Rise of the Value-Adding Partnership." *Harvard Business Review* (July–August 1988).

Johnston, Russell, and Michael R. Vitale. "Creating Competitive Advantage with Interorganizational Information Systems." *MIS Quarterly* 12, no. 2 (June 1988).

Kambil, Ajit, and James E. Short. "Electronic Integration and Business Network Redesign: A Roles-Linkage Perspective." *Journal of Management Information Systems* 10, no. 4 (Spring 1994).

Keen, Peter G. W. *Competing in Time: Using Telecommunications for Competitive Advantage*. Cambridge, MA: Ballinger Publishing Company (1986).

———. *Shaping the Future: Business Design Through Information Technology*. Cambridge, MA: Harvard Business School Press (1991).

Keen, Peter G. W. and M. S. Morton. *Decision Support Systems: An Organizational Perspective*. Reading, MA: Addison-Wesley (1978).

Kettinger, William J., Varn Grover, Subashish Guhan, and Albert H. Segors. "Strategic Information Systems Revisited: A Study in Sustainability and Performance." *MIS Quarterly* 18, no. 1 (March 1994).

King, John. "Centralized vs. Decentralized Computing: Organizational Considerations and Management Options." *Computing Surveys* (October 1984).

"Komag Chooses MES for Production Control." *Datamation* (September 15, 1994).

Konsynski, Benn R., and F. Warren McFarlan. "Information Partnerships—Shared Data, Shared Scale." *Harvard Business Review* (September–October 1990).

LaPlante, Alice. "For IS, Quality Is 'Job None'." *Computerworld* (January 6, 1992).

Lasher, Donald R., Blake Ives, and Sirkka L. Jarvenpaa. "USAA-IBM Partnerships in Information Technology: Managing the Image Project." *MIS Quarterly* 15, no. 4 (December 1991).

McFarlan, F. Warren. "Information Technology Changes the Way You Compete." *Harvard Business Review* (May–June 1984).

Main, Thomas J., and James E. Short. "Managing the Merger: Building Partnership Through IT Planning at the New Baxter." *MIS Quarterly* 13, no. 4 (December 1989).

Mata, Franciso J., William L. Fuerst, and Jay B. Barney. "Information Technology and Sustained Competitive Advantage: A Resource-Based Analysis." *MIS Quarterly* 19, no. 4 (December 1995).

Millar, Victor E. "Decision-Oriented Information." *Datamation* (January 1984).

Moad, Jeff. "Let Customers Have It Their Way." *Datamation* (April 1, 1995).

Porter, Michael. *Competitive Strategy.* New York: Free Press (1980).

———. *Competitive Advantage.* New York: Free Press (1985).

———. "How Information Can Help You Compete." *Harvard Business Review* (August–September 1985a).

Rackoff, Nick, Charles Wiseman, and Walter A. Ullrich. "Information Systems for Competitive Advantage: Implementation of a Planning Process." *MIS Quarterly* (December 1985).

Rebello, Joseph. "State Street Boston's Allure for Investors Starts to Fade." *The Wall Street Journal* (January 4, 1995).

Rockart, John F., and Michael E. Treacy. "The CEO Goes On-Line." *Harvard Business Review* (January–February 1982).

Short, James E., and N. Venkatraman. "Beyond Business Process Redesign: Redefining Baxter's Business Network." *Sloan Management Review* (Fall 1992).

Sprague, Ralph H., Jr., and Eric D. Carlson. *Building Effective Decision Support Systems.* Englewood Cliffs, NJ: Prentice-Hall (1982).

"USAA Insuring Progress." *Information Week* (May 25, 1992).

Vitale, Michael R. "The Growing Risks of Information System Success." *MIS Quarterly* (December 1986).

Wiseman, Charles. *Strategic Information Systems.* Homewood, IL: Richard D. Irwin (1988).

Chapter 3

Information Systems, Organizations, and Management

PanCanadian Awakens with Information Systems

3.1 Organizations and Information Systems
What Is an Organization?
Why Organizations Are So Much Alike: Common Features
Why Organizations Are So Different: Unique Features

3.2 The Changing Role of Information Systems
The Evolution of Information Systems
Why Organizations Build Information Systems
Window on Organizations:
Schneider Responds to the New Rules of the Trucking Game
How Information Systems Affect Organizations
Window on Management:
Managing the Virtual Office
Implications for the Design and Understanding of Information Systems

3.3 The Role of Managers in the Organization
Classical Descriptions of Management
Behavioral Models
Window on Technology:
Managers Turn to the Internet
Implications for System Design

3.4 Managers and Decision Making
The Process of Decision Making
Individual Models of Decision Making
Organizational Models of Decision Making
Implications for System Design

Management Challenges
Summary
Key Terms
Review Questions
Discussion Questions
Group Project
Case Study: Can Sears Reinvent Itself?
References

PanCanadian Awakens with Information Systems

PanCanadian Petroleum in Calgary, Alberta, used to be known as a "sleeping giant." Although the company owned 25 million acres of potentially oil-bearing land, it drilled fewer wells, produced less oil, and took in less money than its competitors in western Canada. Today, PanCanadian drills more earth than any other Canadian oil company. Its oil production has doubled since 1990. PanCanadian has been able to produce a profit even when the price of crude oil has sunk because it uses information systems to lower the cost of finding, pumping, and distributing oil.

PanCanadian's turnaround began when David O'Brien became its CEO in January 1990. O'Brien trimmed 15% of the company's work force, replaced 8 of the company's 15 officers, and restructured the company geographically instead of along functional lines. O'Brien moved to computerize virtually all aspects of PanCanadian's operations, appointing David Tuer, former assistant deputy minister of energy for the province of Alberta, in charge of the effort.

The oil industry believes that there aren't any large pools of oil in western Canada that haven't already been discovered. The goal of oil exploration thus is to find the small pools or find ways of getting more oil out of large pools that are nearly tapped out. Because the payoff from tapping such sources is modest, oil companies must be selective about the sites in which they invest drilling resources.

One way information systems can help is by providing field geologists and engineers with seismic data that can be translated by a supercomputer into a rough picture of rock layers that includes pockets that might contain trapped oil. PanCanadian had seismic data and state-of-the-art drilling tools, but it still lacked the information that would provide the whole picture of each prospective drilling site. Each type of information was stored in a different source—different computer files as well as paper files. Tuer and his staff consolidated all of this information in a Geological Information System that makes all available information about existing or potential well sites immediately available through the computer. Anyone researching a site merely needs to type in a location and select the kind of data desired. Tuer put microcomputers and workstations on the desks of engineers, geologists, and managers and linked them together in a network.

The system has allowed PanCanadian to push decision making further down the organization. Field geologists and engineers used to have to wait for managers to approve their choices for drilling sites. Now, with instant access to a vast array of data, PanCanadian's exploration professionals have been given the authority to make their own decisions. In 1995, PanCanadian used the World Wide Web of the Internet to create a bulletin board for employees to share information with each other.

PanCanadian now drills three times as many wells as before. Its success rate has risen from 85% to 93%. With the new access to information, management believes that the company will be able to double its rate of drilling in shallow sites and quadruple its rate of drilling in deep sites.

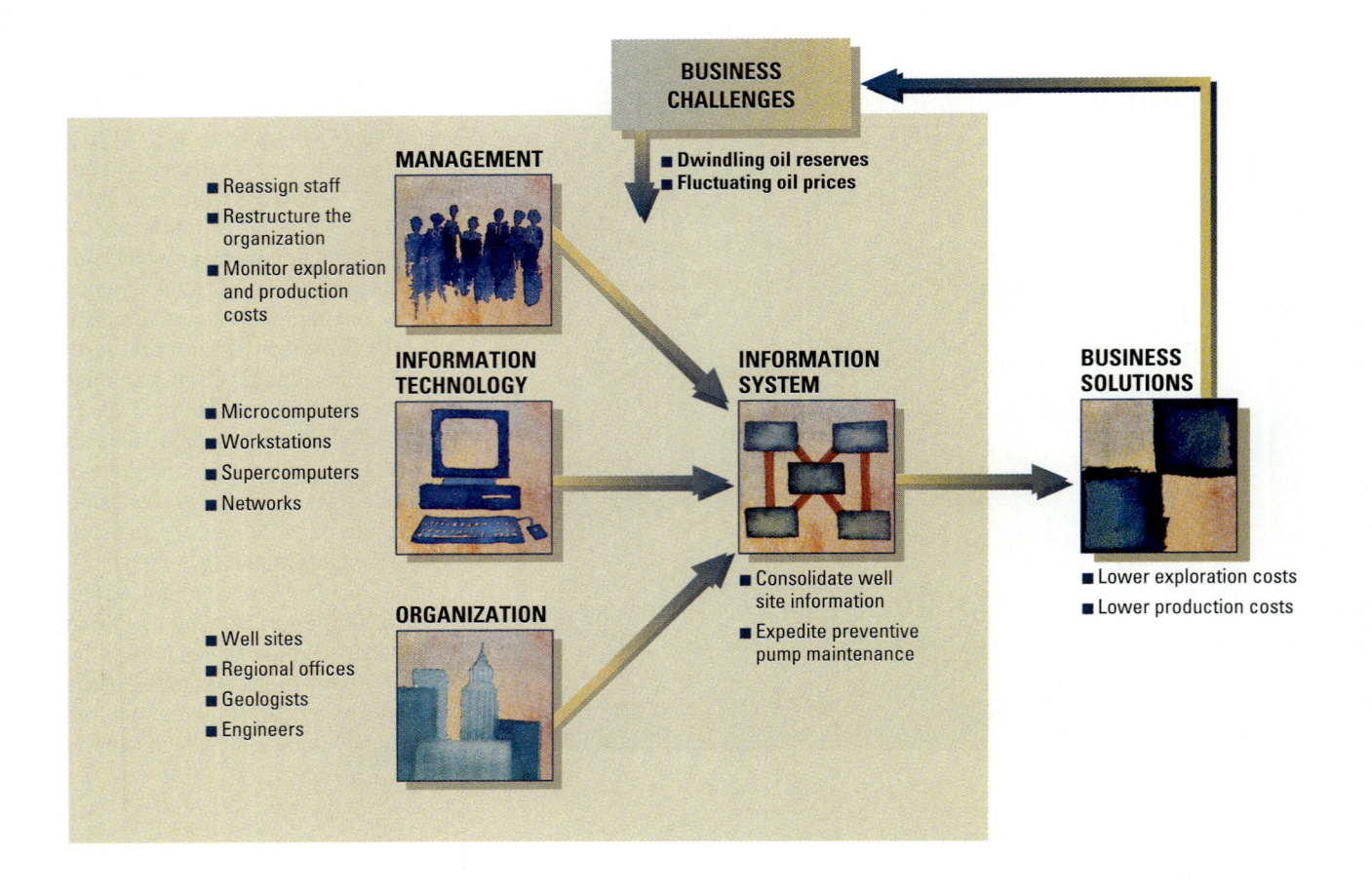

Besides lowering exploration costs, information systems are helping PanCanadian lower its production costs by keeping its oil pumps running at optimum rates. PanCanadian used to assign 400 people throughout western Canada to show up at regional headquarters in the morning, fan out to the wells to read pump-monitoring equipment and look for repairs, and finally return to the office to write up four different kinds of reports. With most of their time spent doing bookkeeping (3 hours daily) or traveling, the well maintenance staff spent only two hours per day working on pumps. PanCanadian addressed this problem by placing microcomputers with special report-writing software at its seven regional offices. When well maintenance staff return from the wells, they type in the new data on the various wells that they gathered. The software produces the four required reports and transmits them via telephone links to headquarters for consolidation and management review. This system has made information accessible and has cut bookkeeping time to one half hour. ∎

Sources: James Enjeneski and Rick Barry, "Internet @ PanCanadian Petroleum Ltd.," *CIP Scene* (November 1995) and David Freedman, "Savvy IT Lets PanCan Dance," *Forbes ASAP*, October 10, 1994.

The experience of PanCanadian Petroleum illustrates the interdependence of business environments, organizational structure, management strategy, and the development of information systems. PanCanadian developed new information systems in response to changes in competitive pressures from its surrounding environment, but it needed to change its organizational structure and management before it could use its new systems successfully. The information systems in turn changed the way PanCanadian ran its business and made management decisions.

In this chapter we explore the complex relationship between organizations, management, and information systems. We introduce you to the features of organizations that you will need to know about as a manager when you envision, design, build, and operate information systems. We also scrutinize the role of a manager and try to identify areas where information systems can contribute to managerial effectiveness. The chapter concludes with an examination of the types of decisions managers make and the process of decision making by individuals and organizations.

Learning Objectives

After completing this chapter you will be able to:

1. Describe the salient characteristics of organizations.
2. Describe the relationship between information systems and organizations.
3. Contrast the classical and contemporary models of managerial activities and roles.
4. Describe how managers make decisions in organizations.
5. Describe the implications of the relationship between information systems, organizations, and management decision making for the design and implementation of information systems.

3.1 ORGANIZATIONS AND INFORMATION SYSTEMS

Let us start with a simple premise based on observation and a great deal of research: Information systems and organizations have a mutual influence on each other. On the one hand, information systems must be aligned with the organization to provide information needed by important groups within the organization. At the same time, the organization must be aware of and open itself to the influences of information systems in order to benefit from new technologies.

The interaction between information technology and organizations is very complex and is influenced by a great many mediating factors, including the organization's structure, standard operating procedures, politics, culture, surrounding environment, and management decisions (see Figure 3.1). Managers must be aware that information systems can markedly alter life in the organization. They cannot successfully design new systems or understand existing systems without understanding organizations. Managers do decide what systems will be built, what they will do, how they will be implemented, and so forth. Sometimes, however, the outcomes are the result of pure chance and of both good and bad luck.

In this chapter our primary focus will be the impact of information systems upon the organization. However, we will see the reverse—the impact of organizations on information systems—throughout this chapter and the rest of the text as we examine the applications and technology that organizations select in order to serve their business needs.

FIGURE 3.1
The two-way relationship between organizations and information technology. This complex two-way relationship is mediated by many factors not the least of which are the decisions made—or not made—by managers. Other factors mediating the relationship are the organizational culture, bureaucracy, politics, business fashion, and pure chance.

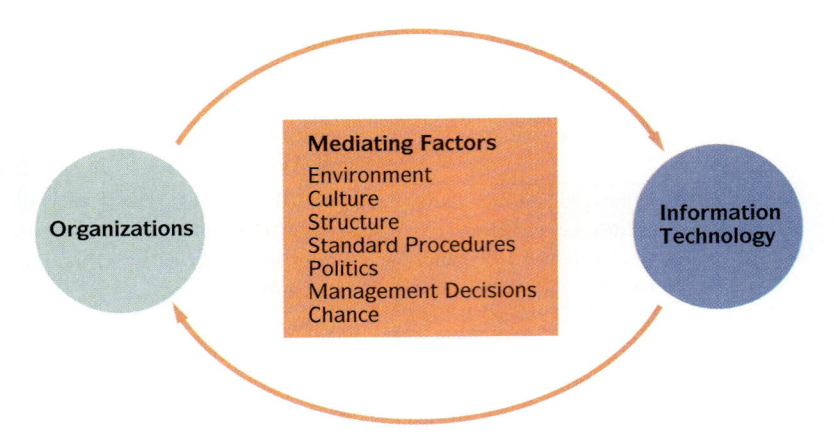

Mediating Factors
Environment
Culture
Structure
Standard Procedures
Politics
Management Decisions
Chance

Organizations ↔ Information Technology

WHAT IS AN ORGANIZATION?

Before describing the impact of information systems upon organizations, we must first review the distinguishing features of organizations. An **organization** is a stable, formal social structure that takes resources from the environment and processes them to produce outputs. This technical definition focuses on three elements of an organization. *Capital* and *labor* are primary production factors provided by the environment. The organization (the firm) transforms these inputs into products and services in a *production function*. The products and services are *consumed by environments* in return for supply inputs (see Figure 3.2). An organization is *more stable* than an informal group in terms of longevity and routineness. Organizations are *formal* legal entities, with internal rules and procedures, that must abide by laws. Organizations are also *social structures* because they are a collection of social elements, much as a machine has a structure—a particular arrangement of valves, cams, shafts, and other parts.

This definition of organizations is powerful and simple, but it is not very descriptive or even predictive of real-world organizations. A more realistic behavioral definition of an organization is that it is a collection of rights, privileges, obligations, and responsibilities that are delicately balanced over a period of time through conflict and conflict resolution (see Figure 3.3). In this behavioral view of the firm, people who work in organizations develop customary ways of working; they gain attachments to existing relationships; and they make arrangements with subordinates and superiors about how work will be done, how much work will be done, and under what conditions. Most of these arrangements and feelings are not discussed in any formal rule book.

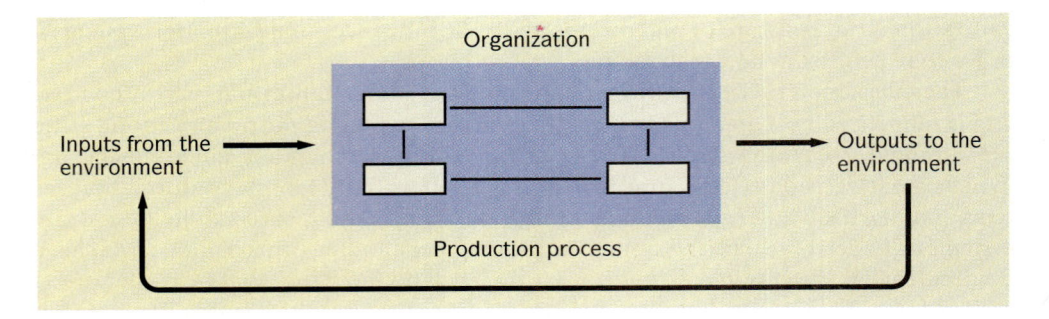

organization (technical definition) A stable, formal social structure that takes resources from the environment and processes them to produce outputs.

organization (behavioral definition) A collection of rights, privileges, obligations, and responsibilities that are delicately balanced over a period of time through conflict and conflict resolution.

FIGURE 3.2
The technical microeconomic definition of the organization. In the microeconomic definition of organizations, capital and labor (the primary production factors provided by the environment) are transformed by the firm through the production process into products and services (outputs to the environment). The products and services are consumed by the environment, which supplies additional capital and labor as inputs in the feedback loop.

CHAPTER 3 Information Systems, Organizations, and Management

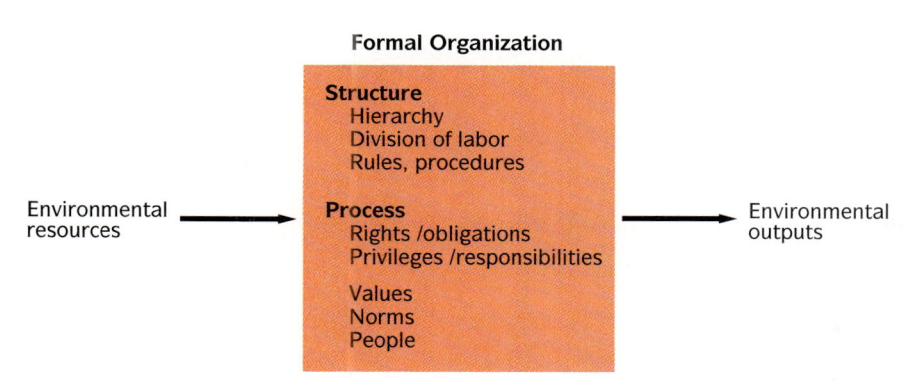

FIGURE 3.3
The behavioral view of organizations. The behavioral view of organizations emphasizes group relationships, values, and structures.

Formal Organization

Structure
Hierarchy
Division of labor
Rules, procedures

Process
Rights /obligations
Privileges /responsibilities

Values
Norms
People

Environmental resources → [box] → Environmental outputs

How do these definitions of organizations relate to information system technology? A technical view of organizations encourages us to focus upon the way inputs are combined into outputs when technology changes are introduced into the company. The firm is seen as infinitely malleable, with capital and labor substituting for each other quite easily. But the more realistic behavioral definition of an organization suggests that building new information systems or rebuilding old ones involves much more than a technical rearrangement of machines or workers—that some information systems change the organizational balance of rights, privileges, obligations, responsibilities, and feelings that has been established over a long period of time.

Technological change requires changes in who owns and controls information, who has the right to access and update that information, and who makes decisions about whom, when, and how. For instance, PanCanadian's new information systems empowered field geologists and engineers to make decisions about drilling sites. This more complex view forces us to look at the way work is designed and the procedures used to achieve outputs.

The technical and behavioral definitions of organizations are not contradictory. Indeed, they complement each other: The technical definition tells us how thousands of firms in competitive markets combine capital, labor, and information technology, whereas the behavioral model takes us inside the individual firm to see how that technology affects the inner workings of the organization. Section 3.2 describes how theories based on each of these definitions of organizations can help explain the relationship between information systems and organizations.

Some features of organizations are common to all organizations; others distinguish one organization from another. Let us look first at the features common to all organizations.

WHY ORGANIZATIONS ARE SO MUCH ALIKE: COMMON FEATURES

You might not think that Apple Computer, United Airlines, and the Aspen, Colorado, Police Department have much in common, but they do. In some respects, all modern organizations are alike because they share the characteristics that are listed in Table 3.1. A German sociologist, Max Weber, was the first to describe these "ideal-typical" characteristics of organizations in 1911. He called organizations **bureaucracies** that have certain "structural" features. According to Weber, all modern bureaucracies:

- have a clear-cut *division of labor and specialization*;
- arrange specialists in a *hierarchy* of authority;
- limit authority and action by abstract *rules or procedures* (standard operating procedures, or SOPs);
- create a system of *impartial and universalistic decision making*;
- hire and promote employees on the basis of *technical qualifications and professionalism* (not personal connections);
- are devoted to the *principle of efficiency*: maximizing output using limited inputs.

bureaucracy Formal organization with a clear-cut division of labor, abstract rules and procedures, and impartial decision making that uses technical qualifications and professionalism as a basis for promoting employees.

Table 3.1 Structural Characteristics of All Organizations

Clear division of labor

Hierarchy

Explicit rules and procedures

Impartial judgments

Technical qualifications for positions

Maximum organizational efficiency

According to Weber, bureaucracies are prevalent because they are the most efficient form of organization. They are much more stable and powerful than mercurial charismatic groups or formal aristocracies held together by the right of birth. Other scholars have supplemented Weber, identifying additional features of organizations. All organizations develop standard operating procedures, politics, and a culture.

Standard Operating Procedures

Organizations that survive over time become very efficient, producing a limited number of products and services by following standard routines. These standard routines become codified into reasonably precise rules, procedures, and practices called **standard operating procedures (SOPs)** that are developed to cope with virtually all expected situations. Some of these rules and procedures are written, formal procedures. Most are "rules of thumb" to be followed in selected situations.

These standard operating procedures have a great deal to do with the efficiency that modern organizations attain. For instance, in the assembly of a car, managers and workers develop complex standard procedures to handle the thousands of motions in a precise fashion, permitting the finished product to roll off the assembly line. Any change in SOPs requires an enormous organizational effort. Indeed, the organization may need to halt the entire production process, or even create a new and expensive parallel system, which must then be tested exhaustively, before the old SOPs can be retired.

For example, difficulty in changing standard operating procedures is one reason Detroit auto makers have been slow to adopt Japanese mass-production methods. Until recently, U.S. auto makers followed Henry Ford's mass-production principles. Ford believed that the cheapest way to build a car was to churn out the largest number of autos by having workers repeatedly perform a simple task. By contrast, Japanese auto makers have emphasized "lean production" methods whereby a smaller number of workers, each performing several tasks, can produce cars with less inventory, less investment, and fewer mistakes. Workers have multiple job responsibilities and are encouraged to stop production in order to correct a problem.

Organizational Politics

People in organizations occupy different positions with different specialties, concerns, and perspectives. As a result, they naturally have divergent viewpoints about how resources, rewards, and punishments should be distributed. These differences matter to members of organizations, both managers and employees, and they result in political struggle, competition, and conflict within every organization. Political resistance is one of the great difficulties of bringing about change in organizations—especially the development of new information systems. Virtually all information systems that bring about significant changes in goals, procedures, productivity, and personnel are politically charged and will elicit serious political opposition.

Organizational Culture

All organizations have bedrock, unassailable, unquestioned (by the members) assumptions that define the goals and products of the organization. **Organizational culture** is this

---

standard operating procedures (SOPs) Precise rules, procedures, and practices developed by organizations to cope with virtually all expected situations.

organizational culture The set of fundamental assumptions about what products the organization should produce, how and where it should produce them, and for whom they should be produced.

set of fundamental assumptions about what products the organization should produce, how it should produce them, where, and for whom. Generally, these cultural assumptions are taken totally for granted and are rarely publicly announced or spoken about. They are simply assumptions that few people, if any, would question (Schein, 1985).

You can see organizational culture at work by looking around your university or college. Some bedrock assumptions of university life are that professors know more than students, the reason students attend college is to learn, and classes follow a regular schedule. Organizational culture is a powerful unifying force that restrains political conflict and promotes common understanding, agreement on procedures, and common practices. If we all share the same basic cultural assumptions, then agreement on other matters is more likely.

At the same time, organizational culture is a powerful restraint on change, especially technological change. Most organizations will do almost anything to avoid making changes in basic assumptions. At first, new technologies are almost always used in ways that support existing cultures, and any technological change that threatens commonly held cultural assumptions usually meets a great deal of resistance. For instance, one key longstanding assumption—that management should be very authoritarian and does not need to listen to the opinions of workers—is another reason U.S. auto makers have been slow to switch to "lean production."

On the other hand, there are times when the only sensible way is to employ a new technology that directly opposes an existing organizational culture. When this occurs, the technology is often stalled while the culture slowly adjusts.

WHY ORGANIZATIONS ARE SO DIFFERENT: UNIQUE FEATURES

Although all organizations do have common characteristics, no two organizations are identical. Organizations have different structures, goals, constituencies, leadership styles, tasks, and surrounding environments.

Different Organizational Types

One important way in which organizations differ is in their structure or shape. The differences among organizational structures are characterized in many ways. Mintzberg's classification, described in Table 3.2, identifies five basic kinds of organizations (Mintzberg, 1979).

Table 3.2 Organizational Structures

Organizational Type	Description	Example
Entrepreneurial structure	Young, small firm in a fast-changing environment. It has a simple structure and is managed by an entrepreneur serving as its single chief executive officer.	Small startup business
Machine bureaucracy	Large bureaucracy existing in a slowly changing environment, producing standard products. It is dominated by a centralized management team and centralized decision making.	Mid-sized manufacturing firm
Divisionalized bureaucracy	Combination of multiple machine bureaucracies, each producing a different product or service, all topped by one central headquarters.	Fortune 500 firms such as General Motors
Professional bureaucracy	Knowledge-based organization where goods and services depend on the expertise and knowledge of professionals. Dominated by department heads with weak centralized authority.	Law firms, school systems, hospitals
Adhocracy	"Task force" organization that must respond to rapidly changing environments. Consists of large groups of specialists organized into short-lived multidisciplinary teams and has weak central management.	Consulting firms such as the Rand Corporation

Environments

Organizations have different environments, each exerting a powerful influence on the organization's structure. Generally, adhocracies and entrepreneurial structures have the flexibility to perform well in fast-changing environments. They are not saddled with large bureaucracies and can delegate considerable authority to subordinates. Machine bureaucracies and divisionalized bureaucracies tend to fare better in stable environments.

Most people do not realize how fragile and short-lived formal organizations really are. The main reasons for organizational failure are an inability to adapt to a rapidly changing environment and the lack of resources—particularly among young firms—to sustain even short periods of troubled times (Freeman et al., 1983). New technologies, new products, and changing public tastes and values put strains on any organization's culture, politics, operating procedures, and people. Fast-changing technologies, like information technology, pose a particular threat to organizations. At times, technological changes occur so radically that they either enhance or destroy the competence of firms in an industry (Tushman and Anderson, 1986). Under such circumstances, most organizations fail to adapt, and many go out of existence, freeing up resources for new, younger organizations. For instance, Wang Laboratories, a leading manufacturer of mid-sized minicomputers and word processors, was a dominant force in the computer industry during the 1970s and early 1980s. But when powerful desktop microcomputers reduced the need for minicomputers, Wang nearly went out of business. It had failed to adapt its products to the new technology.

Other Differences among Organizations

Organizations have different shapes or structures for many other reasons also. They differ in their ultimate goals and the types of power used to achieve them. Some organizations have coercive goals (e.g., prisons); others have utilitarian goals (e.g., businesses). Still others have normative goals (universities, religious groups). Organizations also serve different groups or have different constituencies, some primarily benefiting their members, others benefiting clients, stockholders, or the public. The nature of leadership differs greatly from one organization to another—some organizations may be more democratic or authoritarian than others.

Another way organizations differ is by the tasks they perform and the technology they use. In some cases, organizations use routine tasks that could be programmed—that is, tasks may be reduced to formal rules that require little judgment. (An example would be inventory reordering.) Organizations that primarily perform routine tasks are typically hierarchical and run according to standard procedures. In other cases, organizations work primarily with nonroutine tasks. (An example might be a consulting company that creates strategic plans for other companies.)

Levels of Analysis

As Chapters 1 and 2 make clear, all organizations have different levels, occupations, divisions, and groups, each with different concerns. The impact of information systems will probably be different for different levels and groups within an organization. This can be seen in Figure 3.4, which describes typical organizational levels and the principal concerns at each level, providing examples of information systems that are appropriate for each level.

At the individual and small-group levels of organization, information systems apply to a particular job, task, or project. At the department and division levels, information systems deal with a particular business function, product, or service. At the organization, inter-organization, and organizational network levels, information systems support multiple products, services, and goals and facilitate alliances and coordination between two or more different organizations or groups of organizations.

Perhaps one of the most important and least heralded contributions of information systems is their support of a large variety of work groups that spring up in organizations and that are not even part of the formal organization chart. While organization

Organizational Level		Activity	Example Support System
Individual	•	Job, task	Microcomputer application; personal client database; decision-support systems
Group	◇	Project	Product scheduling; access to mainframe data; access to external data sources; dynamic information requirements; group DSS
Department	⧉	Major function	Accounts payable; warehouse; payroll; human resources; marketing; stable information requirements; MIS; major transaction systems
Division	⧈	Major product or service	Systems to support production, marketing, administration, and human resources; access to organizational financial and planning data; MIS; major transaction systems; on-line interactive systems
Organization	▲	Multiple products, services, and goals	Integrated financial and planning systems; MIS; on-line interactive systems; ESS
Inter-organization	▲▲	Alliance Competition Exchange Contact	Communication systems; intelligence, observation, and monitoring systems
Organizational network	▲▲▲▲	Sector of economy: related products, services; interdependencies	Informal communication systems; industry and sector-level formal reporting systems

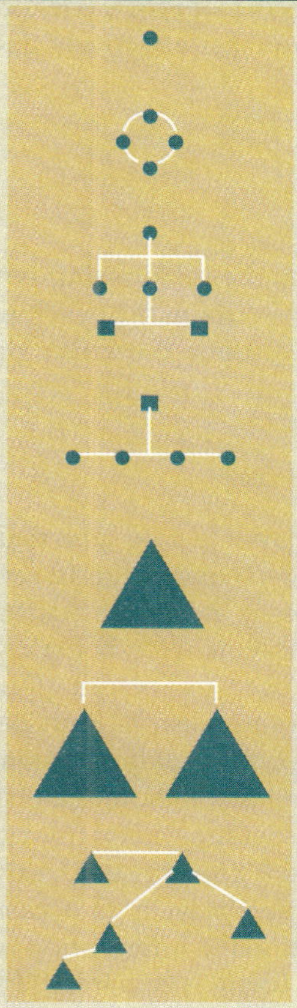

FIGURE 3.4
Organizational levels and support systems. Systems are designed to support various levels of the organization.

charts show the formal reporting relationships in organizations, much of the work of organizations is done by informal work groups such as task forces, interdepartmental committees, project teams, and committees. Recently developed system tools directed at support of work groups are discussed in Chapters 8 and 12.

As you can see in Table 3.3, the list of unique features of organizations is longer than the common features list. It stands to reason that information systems will have a

Table 3.3 A Summary of Salient Features of Organizations

Common Features	Unique Features
Formal structure	Organizational type
Standard operating procedures (SOPs)	Environments
Politics	Goals
Culture	Power
	Constituencies
	Function
	Leadership
	Tasks
	Technology
	Levels

different impact on different types of organizations. Different organizations in different circumstances will experience different effects from the same technology. Only by close analysis of a specific organization can a manager effectively design and manage information systems.

3.2 THE CHANGING ROLE OF INFORMATION SYSTEMS

You are now ready to look more closely at the relationship between information systems and organizations. We will begin by describing the developing role of information systems within organizations before we examine the effect that information system technology has upon organizations.

THE EVOLUTION OF INFORMATION SYSTEMS

In Chapters 1 and 2 we described the expanding role information systems have been playing within organizations. Information systems began in the 1950s as operational-level systems designed to handle elementary but vital transactions such as paying checks. By the late 1960s, management systems were being used for monitoring and controlling; and in the 1970s they were used for planning and simulations. By the 1980s, information systems had expanded into custom-built decision-support systems and early strategic planning systems. Today, information systems are helping to create and disseminate knowledge and information throughout the organization through new knowledge work systems, applications providing companywide access to data, and communications networks linking the entire enterprise. Organizations now are critically dependent upon systems and could not survive even occasional breakdowns.

Changes in the technical and organizational configuration of systems have brought computing power and data much closer to the ultimate end users (see Figure 3.5). Isolated "electronic accounting machines" with limited functions in the 1950s gave way in the 1960s to large, centralized mainframe computers that served corporate headquarters and a few remote sites. In the 1970s, mid-sized minicomputers located in individual departments or divisions of the organization were networked to large centralized computers. Desktop microcomputers first were used independently and then were linked to minicomputers and large computers in the 1980s.

In the 1990s, the architecture for a fully networked organization emerged. In this new architecture, computers coordinate information flowing among desktops, between desktops, among minicomputers and mainframes, and perhaps among hundreds of smaller local networks. In many cases, these networks are linking the firm to other organizations. Information systems have become integral, on-line, interactive tools deeply involved in the minute-to-minute operations and decision making of large organizations. Chapters 5 through 9 provide detailed discussions of technology of information systems and networks.

The position and role of information system specialists have also evolved over time. The formal organizational unit or function that has emerged is called an **information systems department**. In the early years, the information systems group was composed mostly of **programmers**, highly trained technical specialists who wrote the software instructions for the computer. Today a growing proportion of staff members are **systems analysts**, who constitute the principal liaison between the information systems group and the rest of the organization. It is the systems analyst's job to translate business problems and requirements into information requirements and systems. **Information systems managers** are leaders of teams of programmers and analysts, project managers, physical facility managers, telecommunications managers, and heads of office automation groups. They are also managers of computer operations and data entry staff. **End users** are representatives of departments outside of the information systems group for which applications are developed. These users are playing an increasingly large role in the design and development of information systems.

---

information systems department The formal organizational unit that is responsible for the information systems function in the organization.

programmers Highly trained technical specialists who write computer software instructions.

systems analysts Specialists who translate business problems and requirements into information requirements and systems, acting as liaison between the information systems department and the rest of the organization.

information systems managers Leaders of the various specialists in the information systems department.

end users Representatives of departments outside the information systems group for whom applications are developed.

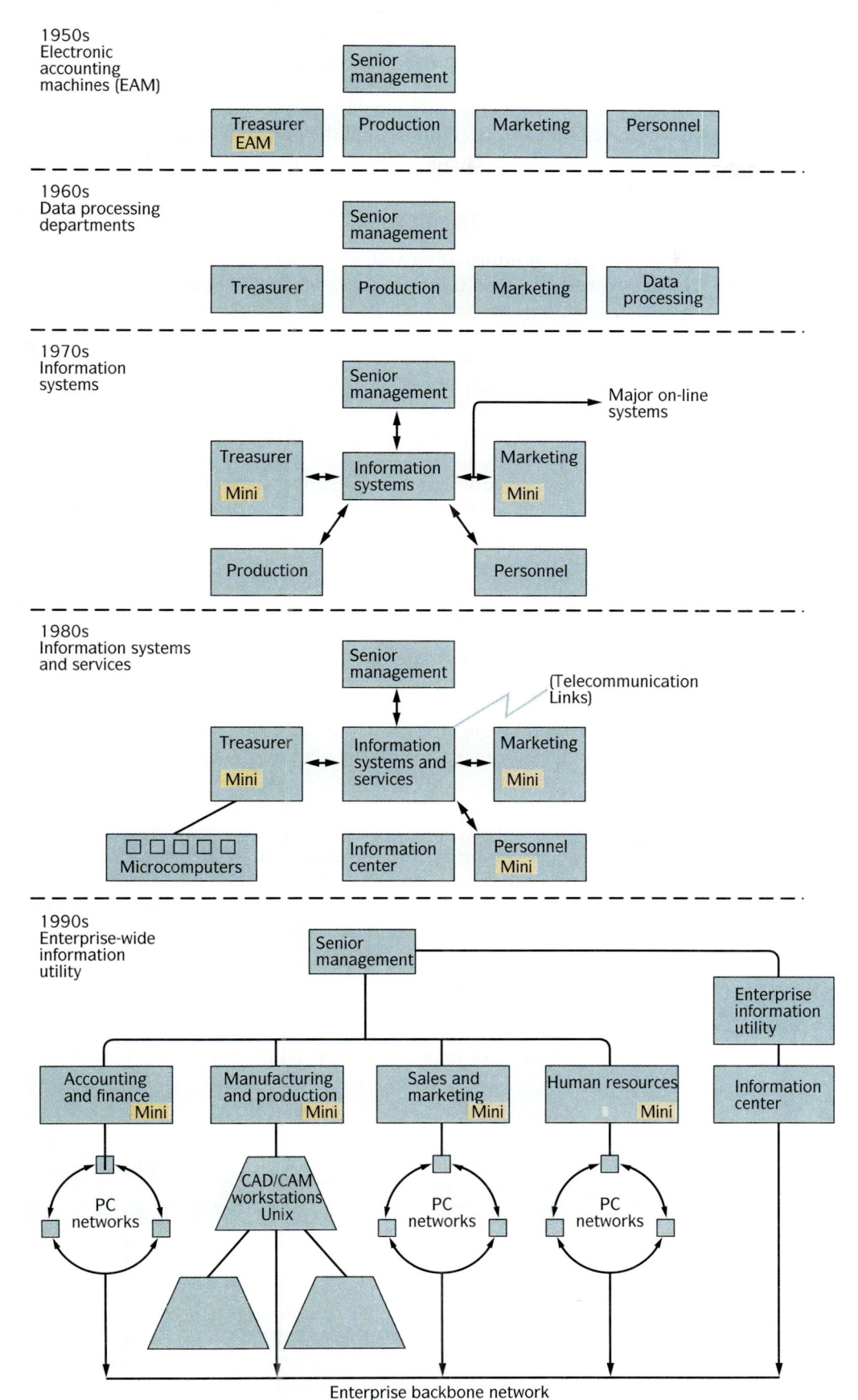

FIGURE 3.5
The development of information architecture of organizations. The last five decades have seen dramatic changes in the technical and organizational configurations of systems. During the 1950s organizations were dependent on computers for a few critical functions. The 1960s witnessed the development of large centralized machines. By the late 1970s and into the 1980s information architecture became complex and information systems included telecommunications links to distribute information. During the 1990s information architecture is an enterprise-wide information utility.

3.2 The Changing Role of Information Systems

The size of the information systems department can vary greatly, depending on the role of information systems in the organization and on the organization's size. Today, information systems groups often act as powerful change agents within the organization, suggesting new business strategies and new information-based products and coordinating both the development of technology and the planned changes in the organization.

WHY ORGANIZATIONS BUILD INFORMATION SYSTEMS

Obviously, organizations adopt information systems to become more efficient, to save money, and to reduce the work force. Information systems have become vitally important simply to stay in business and may even be a source of competitive advantage. However, this may not be the only or even the primary reason for adopting systems.

Some organizations build certain systems simply because they are more innovative than others. They have values that encourage any kind of innovation, regardless of its direct economic benefit to the company. In other cases, information systems are built to satisfy the ambitions of various groups within an organization. And in some cases such as that of PanCanadian Railways, described in the chapter-opening vignette, and Schneider National, described in the Window on Organizations, changes in an organization's environment—including changes in government regulations, competitors' actions, and costs—demand a computer system response.

Figure 3.6 illustrates a model of the systems development process that includes many considerations other than economic. This model divides the explanations for why organizations adopt systems into two groups: *external environmental factors* and *internal institutional factors* (Laudon, 1985; King et al., 1994).

environmental factors Factors external to the organization that influence the adoption and design of information systems.

Environmental factors are factors external to the organization that influence the adoption and design of information systems. Examples of *external constraints* would be the rising costs of labor or other resources, the competitive actions of other organizations, and changes in government regulations. Examples of *external opportunities* include new technologies, new sources of capital, the demise of a competitor, or a new government program.

institutional factors Factors internal to the organization that influence the adoption and design of information systems.

Institutional factors are factors internal to the organization that influence the adoption and design of information systems. They include values, norms, and vital interests that govern matters of strategic importance to the organization. For instance, the top management of a corporation can decide that it needs to exercise much stronger control over the inventory process and therefore decide to develop an inventory information system. (For a similar model, see Kraemer et al., 1989.)

HOW INFORMATION SYSTEMS AFFECT ORGANIZATIONS

Having described the evolution of information systems and the reasons that organizations build them today, we now shall look at another question: How do information

FIGURE 3.6
The systems development process. External environmental factors and internal institutional factors influence the types of information systems that organizations select, develop, and use.

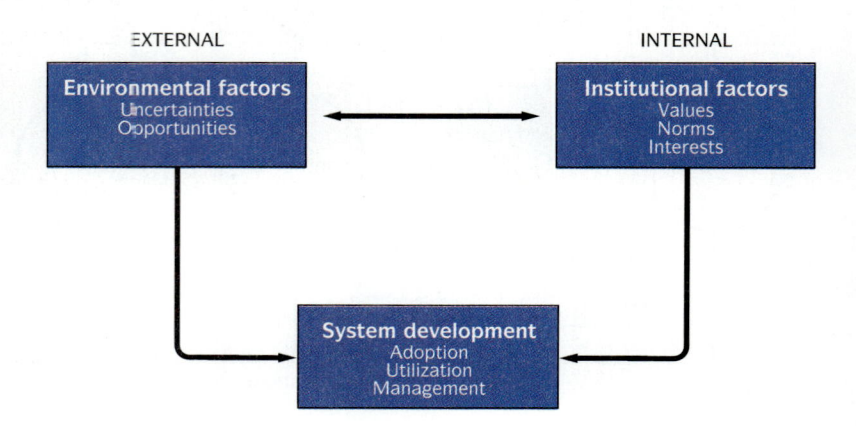

Window on Organizations

SCHNEIDER RESPONDS TO THE NEW RULES OF THE TRUCKING GAME

Deregulation revolutionized the business environment for the trucking industry overnight. Competition for customers heated up. Interstate trucking firms no longer had to follow the rules of a regulatory bureaucracy about what kinds of freight to carry and where to take it. These same rules had also made it difficult for customers to change carriers because only certain trucking firms could meet these regulations. Large retailers and manufacturers were installing just-in-time delivery systems. They wanted to use trucking firms that could transport their shipments right away.

Schneider National, North America's biggest carrier of full-truckload cargoes, responded to these demands with a two-pronged strategy. First, it tried to make sweeping changes in its corporate culture. Schneider sought to replace its regulated-utility mentality with quick reflexes and an urgency to get things done. CEO Don Schneider democratized the organization by calling all employees "associates" and eliminating status symbols like reserved parking places. He encouraged everyone, from drivers on up, to speak out on ways to improve operations. He also instituted an extra bonus paycheck based solely on performance.

Second, Schneider deployed new information systems to support these changes. In 1988, the firm equipped each truck with a computer and a rotating antenna. A satellite tracks every rig, making sure it adheres to schedule. When an order comes

> **To Think About:** How did information systems support Schneider's new business strategy? How did they change the way Schneider ran its business?

into headquarters, dispatchers know exactly which truck to assign to the job. The dispatchers send an order directly by satellite to the driver's on-board terminal, complete with directions to the destination, instructions on what gate to use, and papers to collect with the merchandise. Within 15 to 30 minutes of sending an order to Schneider's computer, customers know which trucks to expect and when.

For example, when Procter & Gamble advises that a trailer of detergent for Omaha will be ready in Cincinnati at 4:00 P.M., the system lists drivers headed for Cincinnati and their arrival times, updating the information every two hours. The system passes driver 11743, who is available, but who has been driving since 4:00 A.M. and needs a break. After selecting an appropriate driver, the system beams the time and place of pickup to the driver's cab, relieving him of the need to phone in. The computer even registers the driver's speed. (Exceeding Schneider's 55-mile-per-hour speed limit can cost drivers their monthly bonuses.)

Information systems now play such a powerful role in Schneider's operations that the firm has been described as "an information system masquerading as a trucking line." Don Schneider himself has observed that "people get the mistaken impression that our business is running trucks." Several other competitors responded to deregulation by merely lowering rates. They went bankrupt.

Sources: Mark Levinson, "Riding the Data Highway," *Newsweek* (March 21, 1994); Stephen Barr, "Delivering the Goods," *CFO* (August 1994); Myron Magnet, "Meet the New Revolutionaries," *Fortune* (February 24, 1992).

systems affect organizations? To answer this question, we need to summarize a large body of research and theory. Some researchers base their work on economics; others take a behavioral approach.

Economic Theories

From an economic standpoint, information system technology can be viewed as a factor of production that can be freely substituted for capital and labor. As the cost of information systems technology falls, it is substituted for labor, which historically has a rising cost. Hence, in microeconomic theory, information technology should result in a decline in the number of middle managers and clerical workers as information technology substitutes for their labor.

Information technology also helps firms contract in size because it can reduce transaction costs— the costs incurred by a firm when it buys on the marketplace what it does not make itself. According to **transaction cost theory**, firms have sought to reduce transaction costs by getting bigger: hiring more employees, vertically integrating (as General Motors did), buying their own suppliers and distributors, and taking over smaller companies. Information technology, especially the use of networks, helps firms lower the cost of market participation (transaction costs) and makes it worthwhile for firms to contract with external suppliers instead of using internal sources of supply. For example, by using computer links to suppliers, the Chrysler Corporation can achieve economies by obtaining more than 70% of its parts from external suppliers. As a result, the size of firms (measured by the number of employees) could stay constant or contract even though they increased their revenues.

Another cost impact of information technology is on internal management costs. According to **agency theory**, organizations incur agency costs, the cost of supervising and managing employees. As firms grow in size, agency costs rise because owners must spend more and more effort monitoring employees. Information technology, by reducing the costs of acquiring and analyzing information, permits organizations to reduce agency costs because it is easier for managers to oversee a greater number of employees.

transaction cost theory Economic theory stating that firms grow larger because they can conduct marketplace transactions internally more cheaply than they can with external firms in the marketplace.

agency theory Economic theory that views the firm as a nexus of contracts among self-interested individuals who must be supervised and managed.

Behavioral Theories

While economic theories try to explain how large numbers of firms act in the marketplace, behavioral theories from sociology, psychology, and political science are more useful for describing the behavior of individual firms. Behavioral research has found little evidence that information systems automatically transform organizations, although the systems may be instrumental in accomplishing this goal once senior management decides to pursue this end. Instead, researchers have observed an intricately choreographed relationship in which organizations and information technology mutually influence each other.

Behavioral researchers have theorized that information technology could change the hierarchy of decision making in organizations by lowering the costs of information acquisition and broadening the distribution of information. Information technology could bring information directly from operating units to senior managers, thereby eliminating middle managers and their clerical support workers. Information technology could permit senior managers to contact lower-level operating units directly through the use of networked telecommunications and computers, eliminating middle management intermediaries. Alternatively, information technology could distribute information directly to lower-level workers, who could then make their own decisions based on their own knowledge and information without any management intervention. Some research even suggests that computerization increases the information given to middle managers, empowering them to make more important decisions than in the past, thus reducing the need for large numbers of lower-level workers (Shore, 1983).

In post-industrial societies, authority increasingly relies on knowledge and competence, and not on mere formal position. Hence, the shape of organizations should "flatten," since professional workers tend to be self-managing; and decision making should become more decentralized as knowledge and information become more widespread throughout (Drucker, 1988). Information technology may encourage "task force" networked organizations in which groups of professionals come together—face-to-face or electronically—for short periods of time to accomplish a specific task (e.g., designing a new automobile); once the task is accomplished, the individuals join other task forces.

Some organizations may also become flatter and more horizontal by reshaping themselves around business processes instead of the traditional, discrete functional departments. Figure 3.7 shows the differences between a traditional vertical organization where groups are arranged by function and the proposed horizontal organization where teams are arranged by cross-functional processes. For instance, instead of focusing independently on the manufacturing function in order to reduce the cost to produce each unit, management might look at the entire logistics process from receipt of raw material to receipt of final product by the customer. Information systems can help organizations achieve great efficiency by automating parts of these processes or by helping organizations rethink and streamline these processes. Chapter 10 will treat this subject in greater detail as it examines the role of new information systems in organizational design.

Who makes sure that self-managed teams do not head off in the wrong direction? Who decides which person works on what team and for how long? How can managers judge the performance of someone who is constantly rotating from team to team? How do people know where their careers are headed? The Window on Management explores some of these questions as it examines the impact of "virtual offices" and anytime, anywhere work environments.

No one knows the answers to these questions, and it is not clear that all modern organizations will undergo this transformation—General Motors, for example, will have many self-managed knowledge workers in certain divisions, but it still will have a manufacturing division structured as a large, traditional bureaucracy. In general, the shape of organizations historically changes with the business cycle and with the latest management fashions. When times are good and profits are high, firms hire large numbers of supervisory personnel; when times are tough, they let go many of these same people (Mintzberg, 1979). It is not known if the shrinkage of some firms' middle management in the early 1990s resulted from hard times or from computerization.

Another behavioral approach views information systems as the outcome of political competition between organizational subgroups for influence over the policies, procedures, and resources of the organization (Laudon, 1974; Keen, 1981; Kling, 1980; Laudon,

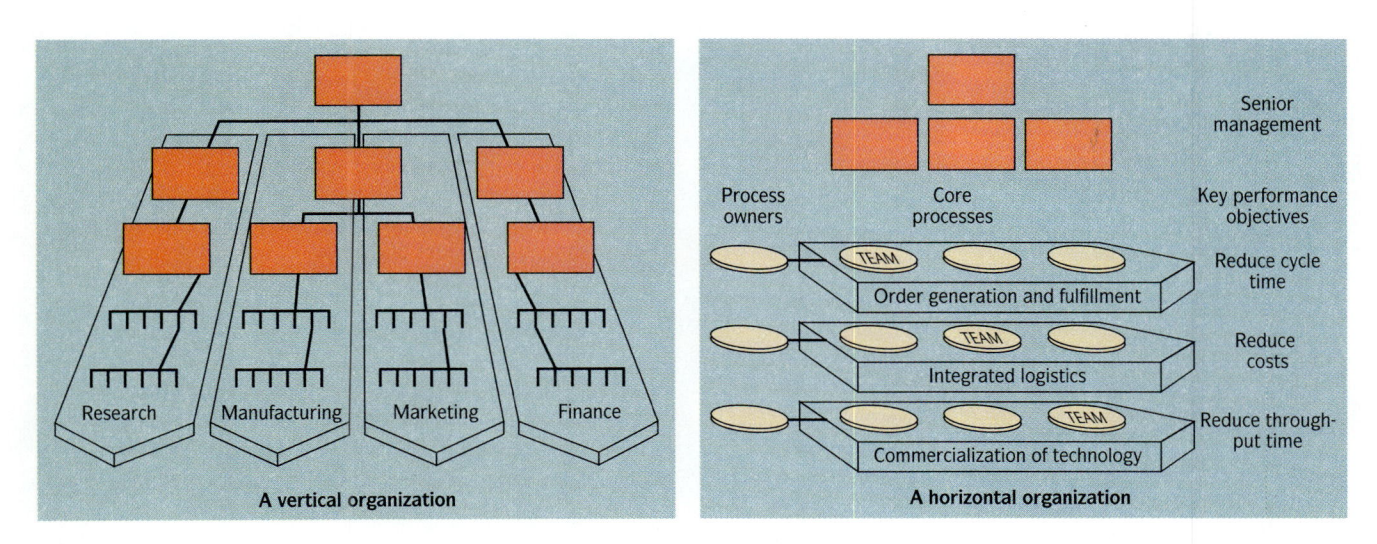

FIGURE 3.7
Some researchers and popular writers argue that information technology allows firms to reorganize themselves from vertical organizations to horizontal organizations where groups of people are arranged by processes. *Source: John Pepper, "Horizontal Organization," InformationWeek, August 17, 1992.*

Window on Management

MANAGING THE VIRTUAL OFFICE

"Work is something you do, not a place to go" at Chiat/Day Inc., an advertising agency based in Los Angeles and New York. Chiat/Day is eliminating its offices and letting its employees work from any location they choose. It is being joined by Ernst & Young, IBM, and other companies. Some of their employees are supposed to work in "virtual offices," any place like a car, plane, train, or home where they can get work done. Virtual offices are possible because of cellular telephones, fax machines, portable computers, and other mobile computing and communications devices.

Chiat/Day armed its employees with laptop computers and cellular car telephones and eliminated private offices and assigned desks. It redesigned its work spaces to create a feeling of creative unrest. There are workrooms dedicated to specific

> **To Think About:** What management, organization, and technology issues must be addressed when converting to a virtual office? Can all companies use virtual offices?

clients; 10 small project workrooms; a library; several large open common areas for meetings, screenings, or socializing; and audio/video and print production centers. Employees keep all of their personal items in assigned lockers. Chiat/Day employees can check in whenever they want or work part of the time at home. Chiat/Day believes that this architecture and structure support the organizational need to be nimble and fast in today's fast-changing business environment.

Ernst & Young, the accounting firm, began moving its Chicago-based accountants and consultants, including senior managers, from offices into a "hoteling" system in June 1992 in an effort to reduce office space and costs. Office spaces must be reserved at least one day in advance to bring in all the equipment and files required to do the work. Ernst & Young hopes to eliminate one million of the seven million square feet of office space it rents nationwide, a savings of $40 million per year.

Eliminating private offices can cut down on real estate costs and increase the amount of time employees spend with customers. It may help firms comply with the U.S. government's Clean Air Act requiring companies with 200 or more employees in major metropolitan areas to reduce commuter automobile mileage by 25%. "Virtual office" employees have more flexibility and control over their own time. But is the virtual office a better way of working? What is its impact on individual identity, worker satisfaction, and the corporate community?

Some employees fear that the virtual office will lead to downsizing, part-time work, and eventually the loss of their jobs. Others respond to the loss of daily social contact. A Bell Telephone study of employees working from home found that productivity and morale plunged precipitously unless they kept in very close personal contact with the office. On the other hand, Ernst & Young reported 99% employee approval of its hoteling arrangement, with increased interaction among employees from different areas and between employees and their bosses.

Sources: Montieth M. Illingworth, "Virtual Managers," *Information Week* (June 13, 1994); Phil Patton, "The Virtual Office Becomes Reality," *The New York Times*, (October 28, 1993).

The giant lips frame an electronic dispensary where employees of Chiat/Day's virtual office sign up for work spaces and pick up their computers.

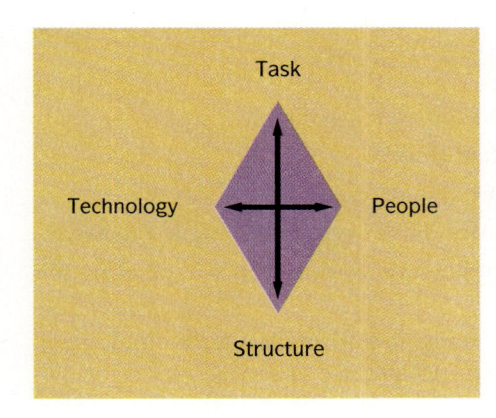

FIGURE 3.8
Organizational resistance and the mutually adjusting relationship between technology and the organization. Implementing information systems has consequences for task arrangements, structures, and people. According to this model, in order to implement change, all four components must be changed simultaneously. *Source:* Leavitt, 1965.

1986). Information systems inevitably become bound up in the politics of organizations because they influence access to a key resource—namely, information. Information systems can affect who does what to whom, when, where, and how in an organization. For instance, a major study of the efforts of the FBI to develop a national computerized criminal history system (a single national listing of the criminal histories, arrests, and convictions of more than 36 million individuals in the United States) found that the state governments strongly resisted the FBI's efforts. This information would give the federal government, and the FBI in particular, the ability to monitor how states use criminal histories. The states resisted the development of this national system quite successfully (Laudon, 1986).

Because information systems potentially change an organization's structure, culture, politics, and work, there is often considerable resistance to them when they are introduced. There are several ways to visualize organizational resistance. Leavitt (1965) used a diamond shape to illustrate the interrelated and mutually adjusting character of technology and organization (see Figure 3.8). Here, changes in technology are absorbed, deflected, and defeated by organizational task arrangements, structures, and people. In this model, the only way to bring about change is to change the technology, tasks, structure, and people simultaneously. Other authors have spoken about the need to "unfreeze" organizations before introducing an innovation, quickly implementing it, and "re-freezing" or institutionalizing the change (Kolb, 1970; Alter and Ginzberg, 1978).

IMPLICATIONS FOR THE DESIGN AND UNDERSTANDING OF INFORMATION SYSTEMS

What is the importance of these theories of organizations? The primary significance of this section is to show that you cannot take a narrow view of organizations and their relationship to information systems. Experienced systems observers and managers approach systems change very cautiously. In order to reap the benefits of technology, organizational innovations—changes in the culture, values, norms, and interest-group alignments—must be managed with as much planning and effort as technology changes.

You should develop a checklist of factors to consider in your systems plans. In our experience, the central organizational factors in rough rank order of importance are these:

The *environment* in which the organization must function.

The *structure* of the organization: hierarchy, specialization, standard operating procedures.

The *culture and politics* of the organization.

The *type* of organization.

The *nature and style* of leadership.

The extent of support and understanding of *top management*.

The *level* of organization at which the system resides.

The principal *interest groups* affected by the system.

The *kinds of tasks and decisions* that the information system is designed to assist.

The *sentiments and attitudes* of workers in the organization who will be using the information system.

The *history of the organization*: past investments in information technology, existing skills, important programs, and human resources.

3.3 THE ROLE OF MANAGERS IN THE ORGANIZATION

Managers play a key role in organizations. Their responsibilities range from making decisions, to writing reports, to attending meetings, to arranging birthday parties. To determine how information systems can benefit managers, we must first examine what managers do and what information they need for decision making and their other functions. We must also understand how decisions are made and what kinds of decisions can be supported by formal information systems.

CLASSICAL DESCRIPTIONS OF MANAGEMENT

classical model of management
Traditional description of management that focused on its formal functions of planning, organizing, coordinating, deciding, and controlling.

The **classical model of management**, which describes what managers do, was largely unquestioned for the more than 70 years since the 1920s. Henri Fayol and other early writers first described the five classical functions of managers as *planning, organizing, coordinating, deciding,* and *controlling*. This description of management activities dominated management thought for a long time, and it is still popular today.

But these terms actually describe managerial functions and are unsatisfactory as a description of what managers actually do. The terms do not address what managers do when they plan, decide things, and control the work of others. We need a more fine-grained understanding of how managers actually behave.

BEHAVIORAL MODELS

Contemporary behavioral scientists have discovered from observation that managers do not behave as the classical model of management led us to believe. Kotter (1982), for example, describes the morning activities of the president of an investment management firm.

7:35 A.M. Richardson arrives at work, unpacks her briefcase, gets some coffee, and begins making a list of activities for the day.

7:45 A.M. Bradshaw (a subordinate) and Richardson converse about a number of topics and exchange pictures recently taken on summer vacations.

8:00 A.M. They talk about a schedule of priorities for the day.

8:20 A.M. Wilson (a subordinate) and Richardson talk about some personnel problems, cracking jokes in the process.

8:45 A.M. Richardson's secretary arrives, and they discuss her new apartment and arrangements for a meeting later in the morning.

8:55 A.M. Richardson goes to a morning meeting run by one of her subordinates. Thirty people are there, and Richardson reads during the meeting.

11:05 A.M. Richardson and her subordinates return to the office and discuss a difficult problem. They try to define the problem and outline possible alternatives. She lets the discussion roam away from and back to the topic again and again. Finally, they agree on a next step.

In this example, it is difficult to determine which activities constitute Richardson's planning, coordinating, and decision making. **Behavioral models** state that the actual behavior of managers appears to be less systematic, more informal, less reflective, more reactive, less well-organized, and much more frivolous than students of information systems and decision making generally expect it to be.

behavioral models Descriptions of management based on behavioral scientists' observations of what managers actually do in their jobs.

Observers find that managerial behavior actually has five attributes that differ greatly from the classical description: First, managers perform a great deal of work at an unrelenting pace—studies have found that managers engage in more than 600 different activities each day, with no break in their pace. Second, managerial activities are fragmented; most activities last for less than 9 minutes; only 10% of the activities exceed one hour in duration. Third, managers prefer speculation, hearsay, gossip—they want current, specific, and ad hoc information (printed information often will be too old). Fourth, they prefer oral forms of communication to written forms because oral media provide greater flexibility, require less effort, and bring a faster response. Fifth, managers give high priority to maintaining a diverse and complex web of contacts that acts as an informal information system.

From his real-world observations, Kotter argues that effective managers are actually involved in only three critical activities:

- First, general managers spend significant time establishing personal agendas and goals, both short- and long-term.
- Second—and perhaps most important—effective managers spend a great deal of time building an interpersonal network composed of people at virtually all levels of the organization, from warehouse staff to clerical support personnel to other managers and senior management.
- Third, Kotter found that managers use their networks to execute personal agendas, to accomplish their own goals.

Analyzing managers' day-to-day behavior, Mintzberg found that it could be classified into ten managerial roles. **Managerial roles** are expectations of the activities that managers should perform in an organization. Mintzberg found that these managerial roles fell into three categories: interpersonal, informational, and decisional.

managerial roles Expectations of the activities that managers should perform in an organization.

INTERPERSONAL ROLES. Managers act as figureheads for the organization when they represent their companies to the outside world and perform symbolic duties such as giving out employee awards. Managers act as leaders, attempting to motivate, counsel, and support subordinates. Managers also act as a liaison between various levels of the organization; within each of these levels, they serve as a liaison among the members of the management team. Managers provide time and favors, which they expect to be returned.

interpersonal roles Mintzberg's classification for managerial roles where managers act as figureheads and leaders for the organization.

INFORMATIONAL ROLES. Managers act as the nerve centers of their organization, receiving the most concrete, up-to-date information and redistributing it to those who need to be aware of it. Managers are therefore information disseminators and spokespersons for their organization.

informational roles Mintzberg's classification for managerial roles where managers act as the nerve centers of their organizations, receiving and disseminating critical information.

DECISIONAL ROLES. Managers make decisions. They act as entrepreneurs by initiating new kinds of activities; they handle disturbances arising in the organization; they allocate resources to staff members who need them; and they negotiate conflicts and mediate between conflicting groups in the organization.

decisional roles Mintzberg's classification for managerial roles where managers initiate activities, handle disturbances, allocate resources, and negotiate conflicts.

The Window on Technology describes some of the ways that the Internet can support these managerial roles.

Window on Technology

MANAGERS TURN TO THE INTERNET

Cushman & Wakefield (C&W), a large New York real estate firm, has 2,000 employees and six major offices around the United States, plus many other smaller offices around the country and the world. The firm manages office buildings, factories, and other commercial properties in addition to being commercial brokers. Its management problem was the logistics nightmare of keeping personnel, benefits and legal policies and procedures up to date at all its sites, particularly given the need to update them many times a year. C&W already had a proprietary network installed, and it also had many employees already using the Internet. The solution was obvious: Why not take advantage of the low cost and interactive features of the Internet to create an internal network for employee communication?

To set up the new network, all C&W needed to do was develop the software. No new hardware or wires were needed; this new network would run over the company's existing network infrastructure. Moreover, the software was easy to develop. The policies and procedures were already being stored electronically as Microsoft Word documents. C&W purchased commercial software to convert the documents directly into documents that could be displayed on the World Wide Web of the Internet. C&W's Employee Resource System (ERS) was completed within three months and cost less than $10,000 to develop. Once the policies were on-line, it became easy to keep every office up to date—just type the new document using Microsoft Word, convert it through the conversion software, and it is done. No complex distribution is required. In addition, many employees found it easy to learn because they were already using the Internet.

The ease of creating, accessing, and updating the ERS made it obvious that the new network could have many other uses. The next system to be added calculates employee commissions. The system had been run on a departmental midframe

To Think About: How can the Internet help managers manage? Suggest management uses for it other than those described here. What managerial roles do Cushman and Wakefield's systems support?

computer, which meant that only a few employees had direct access to its data. Now, however, the system is accessible through the internal Internet-based network. Employee agents, and even contract brokers, can see the commission data they want. C&W plans to provide employees with Internet capabilities for on-line discussions and e-mail as well.

Site Solutions, C&W's property tracking system, will be the biggest system made available through the internal network. This system maintains detailed data on the thousands of commercial properties worldwide that the company manages, including available office space. It also contains data on all their commercial real estate ventures worldwide, whether planned, under construction, or completed. This system will be accessible by brokers throughout the company. Eventually C&W will also make the database available to clients as well as to employees. It will be easy for clients to access because the Internet is so widely used.

Source: Clinton Wilder, "Location, Location, Location," *Information Week* (March 25, 1996).

IMPLICATIONS FOR SYSTEM DESIGN

What are the implications for the organization's use of information systems? While managers do use formal information systems to plan, organize, and coordinate, these systems may be more limited in their impact on managers than was heretofore believed. Managers appreciate verbal, current, flexible sources of information. They will want to use information systems for such vital (to their work) tasks as interpersonal communication, setting and carrying out personal agendas, and establishing a network throughout the organization. Ad hoc (less formal) information systems that can be built quickly, use more current and up-to-date information, and can be adjusted to the unique situations of a specific group of managers will be highly valued by the modern manager.

Table 3.4, based upon Mintzberg's role classifications, is one look at where systems can help managers and where they cannot. The table shows that information systems do not as of yet contribute a great deal to many areas of management life. These areas will undoubtedly provide great opportunities for future systems and system designers.

Corporate chief executives learn how to use laptop computers during a "technology retreat." Many senior managers lack computer knowledge or experience and require systems that are extremely easy to use.

Table 3.4	Managerial Roles and Supporting Information Systems	
Role	Behavior	Support Systems
Interpersonal Roles		
Figurehead		None exist
Leader	Interpersonal	None exist
Liaison		Electronic communication systems
Informational Roles		
Nerve center		Management information systems
Disseminator	Information	Mail, office systems
Spokesman	processing	Office and professional systems Workstations
Decisional Roles		
Entrepreneur		None exist
Disturbance handler	Decision	None exist
Resource allocator	making	DSS systems
Negotiator		None exist

Source: Authors and Henry Mintzberg, "Managerial Work: Analysis from Observation," *Management Science* 18 (October 1971).

3.4 MANAGERS AND DECISION MAKING

Decision making remains one of the more challenging roles of a manager. Information systems have helped managers communicate and distribute information; however, they have provided only limited assistance for management decision making. Because decision making is an area that system designers have sought most of all to affect (with mixed success), we now turn our attention to this issue.

strategic decision making
Determining the long-term objectives, resources, and policies of an organization.

management control Monitoring how efficiently or effectively resources are utilized and how well operational units are performing.

operational control Deciding how to carry out specific tasks specified by upper and middle management and establishing criteria for completion and resource allocation.

knowledge-level decision making Evaluating new ideas for products, services, ways to communicate new knowledge, and ways to distribute information throughout the organization.

THE PROCESS OF DECISION MAKING

Decision making can be classified by organizational level, corresponding to the strategic, management, knowledge, and operational levels of the organization introduced in Chapter 2. **Strategic decision making** determines the objectives, resources, and policies of the organization. Decision making for **management control** is principally concerned with how efficiently and effectively resources are used and how well operational units are performing. **Operational control** decision making determines how to carry out the specific tasks set forth by strategic and middle management decision makers. **Knowledge-level decision making** deals with evaluating new ideas for products and services, ways to communicate new knowledge, and ways to distribute information throughout the organization.

Within each of these levels of decision making, researchers classify decisions as *structured* and *unstructured*, as we do in this book. **Unstructured decisions** are those in which the decision maker must provide judgment, evaluation, and insights into the problem definition. Each of these decisions are novel, important, and nonroutine, and there is no well-understood or agreed-upon procedure for making them (Gorry and Scott-Morton, 1971). **Structured decisions,** by contrast, are repetitive and routine and involve a definite procedure for handling them so that they do not have to be treated each time as if they were new. Some decisions are semi-structured; in such cases, only part of the problem has a clear-cut answer provided by an accepted procedure.

Combining these two views of decision making produces the grid shown in Figure 3.9. In general, operational control personnel face fairly well-structured problems. In contrast, strategic planners tackle highly unstructured problems. Many of the problems en-

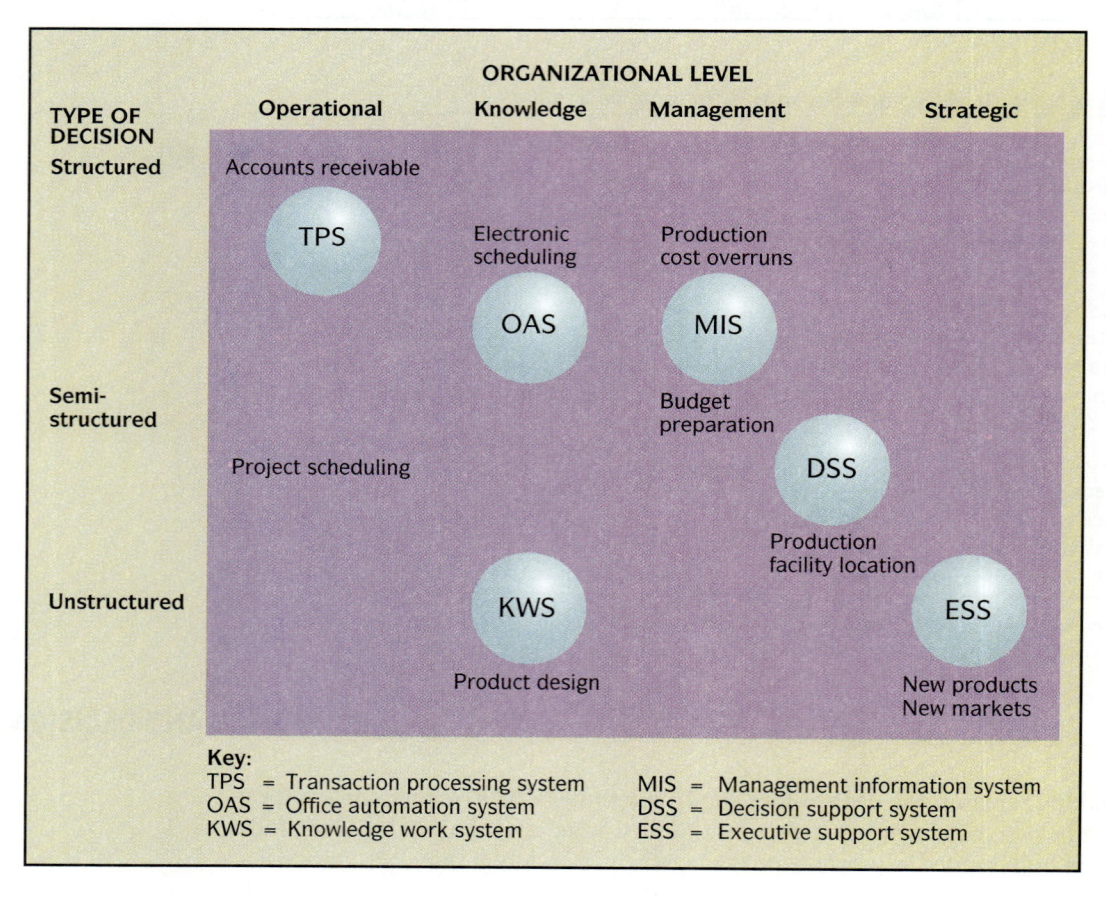

FIGURE 3.9
Different kinds of information systems at the various organization levels support different types of decisions.
Source: Gorry and Scott-Morton (1971).

countered by knowledge workers are fairly unstructured as well. Nevertheless, each level of the organization contains both structured and unstructured problems.

Stages of Decision Making

Making decisions is not a single activity that takes place all at once. The process consists of several different activities that take place at different times. Simon (1960) described four different stages in decision making: intelligence, design, choice, and implementation.

Intelligence consists of *identifying and understanding* the problems occurring in the organization—why the problem, where, and with what effects. Traditional MIS systems that deliver a wide variety of detailed information can help identify problems, especially if the systems report exceptions.

During solution **design,** the individual *designs* possible solutions to the problems. Smaller DSS systems are ideal in this stage of decision making because they operate on simple models, can be developed quickly, and can be operated with limited data.

Choice consists of *choosing* among solution alternatives. Here the decision maker might need a larger DSS system to develop more extensive data on a variety of alternatives and to use complex analytic models needed to account for all of the costs, consequences, and opportunities.

During solution **implementation,** when the decision is put into effect, managers can use a reporting system that delivers routine reports on the progress of a specific solution. Support systems can range from full-blown MIS systems to much smaller systems as well as project-planning software operating on microcomputers.

In general, the stages of decision making do not necessarily follow a linear path. Think again about the decision you made to attend a *specific* college. At any point in the decision-making process, you may have to loop back to a previous stage (see Figure 3.10). For instance, one can often come up with several designs but may not be certain about whether a specific design meets the requirements for the particular problem. This situation requires additional intelligence work. Alternatively, one can be in the process of implementing a decision, only to discover that it is not working. In such a case, one is forced to repeat the design or choice stage.

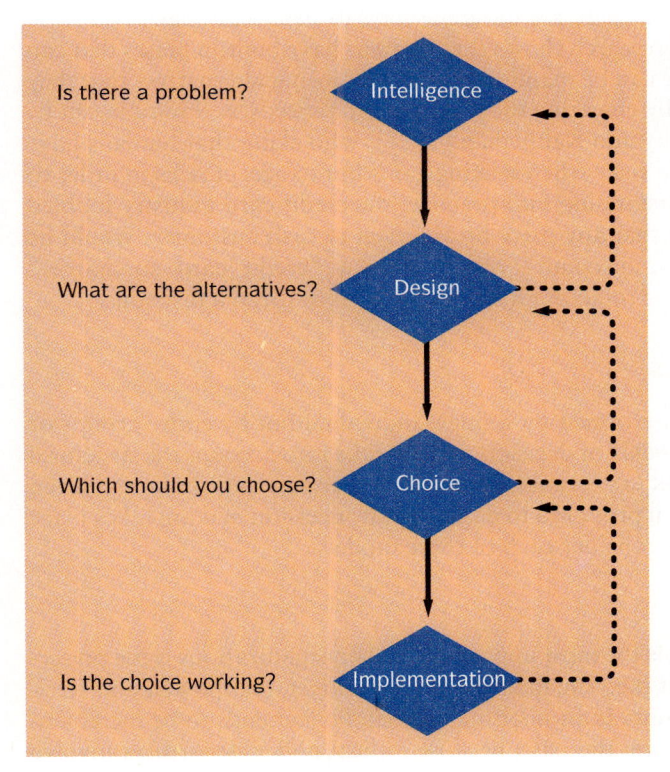

FIGURE 3.10
The decision-making process. Decisions are often arrived at after a series of iterations and evaluations at each stage in the process. The decision maker often must loop back through one or more of the stages before completing the process.

unstructured decisions Non-routine decisions in which the decision maker must provide judgment, evaluation, and insights into the problem definition; there is no agreed-upon procedure for making such decisions.

structured decisions Decisions that are repetitive, routine, and have a definite procedure for handling them.

intelligence The first of Simon's four stages of decision making, when the individual collects information to identify problems occurring in the organization.

design Simon's second stage of decision making, when the individual conceives of possible alternative solutions to a problem.

choice Simon's third stage of decision making, when the individual selects among the various solution alternatives.

implementation Simon's final stage of decision making, when the individual puts the decision into effect and reports on the progress of the solution.

INDIVIDUAL MODELS OF DECISION MAKING

A number of models attempt to describe how people make decisions. Some of these models focus on individual decision making, whereas others focus on decision making in groups.

The basic assumption behind individual models of decision making is that human beings are in some sense rational. The **rational model** of human behavior is built on the idea that people engage in basically consistent, rational, value-maximizing calculations. Under this model, an individual identifies goals, ranks all possible alternative actions by their contribution to those goals, and chooses the alternative that contributes most to those goals.

Criticisms of this model show that in fact people cannot specify all of the alternatives, and that most individuals do not have singular goals and so are unable to rank all alternatives and consequences. Perhaps the most basic criticism is that many decisions are so complex that calculating the choice (even if done by computer) is virtually impossible. One modification to the rational model states that instead of searching through all alternatives, people actually choose the first available alternative that moves them toward their ultimate goal. Another modification alters the rational model by suggesting that in making policy decisions, people choose policies most like the previous policy (Lindblom, 1959). Finally, some scholars point out that people do not make choices, but that decision making is a continuous process in which final decisions are always being modified.

Modern psychology has further qualified the rational model by research which finds that humans differ *in how they maximize their values* and in the *frames of reference* they use to interpret information and make choices. **Cognitive style** describes underlying personality dispositions toward the treatment of information, the selection of alternatives, and the evaluation of consequences. McKenney and Keen (1974) described two decision-making cognitive styles: systematic versus intuitive types. **Systematic decision makers** approach a problem by structuring it in terms of some formal method. They evaluate and gather information in terms of their structured method. **Intuitive decision makers** approach a problem with multiple methods, using trial and error to find a solution. They tend not to structure information gathering or evaluation. Neither style is considered superior to the other. There are different ways of being rational.

More recent psychological research shows that humans have built-in biases that can distort decision making. People can be manipulated into choosing alternatives that they might otherwise reject simply by changing the *frame of reference*. One example can be found in the research of Tversky and Kahneman (1981), who claim that humans have a deep-seated tendency to avoid risks when seeking gains but to accept risks in order to avoid losses. Putting this understanding into practice, the credit card industry lobbied retailers aggressively to ensure that any price break given to cash customers would be presented publicly as a "cash discount" rather than a "credit card surcharge." Consumers would be less willing to accept a surcharge than to forgo a discount.

ORGANIZATIONAL MODELS OF DECISION MAKING

Decision making is often not performed by a single individual but by entire groups or organizations. **Organizational models** of decision making take into account the structural and political characteristics of an organization. Bureaucratic, political, and even "garbage can" models have been proposed to describe how decision making takes place in organizations. We shall now consider each of these models.

Bureaucratic Models

According to **bureaucratic models** the most important goal of organizations is the preservation of the organization itself (i.e., the maintenance of budget, manpower, and territory). The reduction of uncertainty is another major goal. Policy tends to be incremental, only marginally different from the past, because radical policy departures involve

---

rational model Model of human behavior based on the belief that people, organizations, and nations engage in basically consistent, value-maximizing calculations or adaptations within certain constraints.

cognitive style Underlying personality dispositions toward the treatment of information, selection of alternatives, and evaluation of consequences.

systematic decision makers Cognitive style that describes people who approach a problem by structuring it in terms of some formal method.

intuitive decision makers Cognitive style that describes people who approach a problem with multiple methods in an unstructured manner, using trial and error to find a solution.

organizational models of decision making Models of decision making that take into account the structural and political characteristics of an organization.

bureaucratic models of decision making Models of decision making where decisions are shaped by the organization's standard operating procedures (SOPs).

too much uncertainty. These models depict organizations generally as not "choosing" or "deciding" in a rational sense. Rather, according to bureaucratic models, whatever organizations do is the result of standard operating procedures (SOPs) honed over years of active use.

Organizations rarely change these SOPs because they may have to change personnel and incur risks (who knows if the new techniques work better than the old ones?). SOPs thus constitute the range of short-term effective actions that leaders of organizations can take. Although senior management and leaders are hired to coordinate and lead the organization, they are effectively trapped by the organization's standard solutions. As President John F. Kennedy discovered during the Cuban missile crisis, his actions were largely constrained not by his imagination but by what his naval commanders were trained to do (Allison, 1971).

Some organizations do, of course, change; they learn new ways of behaving; and they can be led. But all of these changes require a long time. Look around and you will find many organizations doing pretty much what they did 10, 20, or even 30 years ago.

Political Models of Organizational Choice

Power in organizations is shared; even the lowest-level workers have some power. At the top, power is concentrated in the hands of a few. For many reasons, leaders differ in their opinions about what the organization should do, and, as we made clear earlier in this chapter, these differences do matter.

Each individual in an organization, especially at the top, is a key player in the game of politics. In **political models** of decision making, what an organization does is a result of political bargains struck among key leaders and interest groups. Actions are not necessarily rational, except in a political sense. The outcome is not what any individual necessarily wanted. Instead, policy-organizational action is a compromise, a mixture of conflicting tendencies. Organizations do not come up with "solutions" that are "chosen" to solve some "problem." They come up with compromises that reflect the conflicts, the major stakeholders, the diverse interests, the unequal power, and the confusion that constitute politics.

political models of decision making Models of decision making where decisions result from competition and bargaining among the organization's interest groups and key leaders.

"Garbage Can" Model

A relatively new theory of decision making, called the **"garbage can" model,** states that organizations are not rational. Decision making is largely accidental and is the product of a stream of solutions, problems, and situations that are randomly associated.

If this model is correct, it should not be surprising that the wrong solutions are applied to the wrong problems in an organization or that, over time, a large number of organizations make critical mistakes that lead to their demise. The Exxon Corporation's delayed response to the 1989 Alaska oil spill is an example. Within an hour after the Exxon tanker *Valdez* ran aground in Alaska's Prince William Sound on March 29, 1989, workers were preparing emergency equipment; however, the aid was not dispatched. Instead of sending out emergency crews, the Alyeska Pipeline Service Company (which was responsible for initially responding to oil spill emergencies) sent the crews home. The first full emergency crew did not arrive at the spill site until at least 14 hours after the shipwreck, by which time the oil had spread beyond effective control. Yet enough equipment and personnel had been available to respond effectively. Much of the 10 million gallons of oil fouling the Alaska shoreline in the worst tanker spill in American history could have been confined had Alyeska acted more decisively (Malcolm, 1989).

"garbage can" model Model of decision making that states that organizations are not rational and that decisions are solutions that become attached to problems for accidental reasons.

IMPLICATIONS FOR SYSTEM DESIGN

The research on decision making shows that it is not a simple process even in the rational individual model. Decision situations differ from one another in terms of the clarity of goals, the types of decision makers present, the amount of agreement among them, and the frames of reference brought to a decision-making situation. Information systems do not make the decision for humans but rather support the decision-making process. How this is done will depend on the types of decisions, decision makers, and frames of reference.

Research on organizational decision making should alert students of information systems to the fact that decision making in a business is a group and organizational process. Systems must be built to support group and organizational decision making. Moreover, systems must do more than merely promote decision making. They must also make individual managers better managers of existing routines, better players in the bureaucratic struggle for control of an organization's agenda, and better political players. Finally, for those who resist the "garbage can" tendencies in large organizations, systems should help bring a measure of power to those who can attach the right solution to the right problem.

As a general rule, research on decision making indicates that information systems designers should design systems that have the following characteristics:

- They are flexible and provide many options for handling data and evaluating information.
- They are capable of supporting a variety of styles, skills, and knowledge.
- They are powerful in the sense of having multiple analytical and intuitive models for the evaluation of data and the ability to keep track of many alternatives and consequences.
- They reflect understanding of group and organizational processes of decision making.
- They are sensitive to the bureaucratic and political requirements of systems.
- They reflect an honest and professional awareness of the limits of information systems.

Management Challenges

1. The difficulties of managing change. Bringing about change through the development of information technology and information systems is slowed considerably by the natural inertia of organizations. Of course, organizations do change, and powerful leaders are often required to bring about these changes. Nevertheless, the process, as leaders eventually discover, is more complicated and much slower than is typically anticipated.

2. Fitting technology to the organization (or vice-versa). On the one hand, it is important to align information technology to the business plan, to senior management's strategic business plans, and to standard operating procedures in the business. Information technology is, after all, supposed to be the servant of the organization. On the other hand, these business plans, senior managers, and SOPs may all be very outdated or incompatible with the envisioned technology. In such instances, managers will need to change the organization to fit the technology or to adjust both the organization and the technology to achieve an optimal "fit."

3. Unstructured nature of important decisions. Many important decisions, especially in the areas of strategic planning and knowledge, are not structured and require judgment and examination of many complex factors. Solutions cannot be provided by computerized information systems alone. System builders need to determine exactly what aspects, if any, of a solution can be computerized, and exactly how systems can support the process of arriving at a decision.

Summary

1. Describe the salient characteristics of organizations. All modern organizations are hierarchical, specialized, and impartial. They use explicit standard operating procedures to maximize efficiency. All organizations have their own culture and politics arising from differences in interest groups. Organizations differ in goals, groups served, social roles, leadership styles, incentives, surrounding environments, and types of tasks performed.

These differences create varying types of organizational structures.

2. Describe the relationship between information systems and organizations. The impact of information systems on organizations is not unidirectional. Information systems and the organizations in which they are used interact with and influence each other. The introduction of a new information system will affect the organizational structure, goals, work design, values, competition between interest groups, decision making, and day-to-day behavior. At the same time, information systems must be designed to serve the needs of important organizational groups and will be shaped by the structure, tasks, goals, culture, politics, and management of the organization. The power of information systems to transform organizations radically by flattening organizational hierarchies has not yet been demonstrated for all types of organizations.

3. Contrast the classical and contemporary models of managerial activities and roles. Early classical models of management stressed the functions of planning, organizing, coordinating, deciding, and controlling. Contemporary research has examined the actual behavior of managers to show how managers get things done.

Mintzberg found that managers' real activities are highly fragmented, variegated, and brief in duration, with managers moving rapidly and intensely from one issue to another. Other behavioral research has found that managers spend considerable time pursuing personal agendas and goals and that contemporary managers shy away from making grand, sweeping policy decisions.

4. Describe how managers make decisions in organizations. Decisions can be structured, semi-structured, or unstructured, with structured decisions clustering at the operational level of the organization and unstructured decisions at the strategic planning level. The nature and level of decision making are important factors in building information systems for managers.

Decision making itself is a complex activity at both the individual and the organizational level. Individual models of decision making assume that human beings can accurately choose alternatives and consequences based on the priority of their objectives and goals. The rigorous rational model of individual decision making has been modified by behavioral research which suggests that rationality is limited. People select alternatives biased by their cognitive style and frame of reference. Organizational models of decision making illustrate that real decision making in organizations takes place in arenas where many psychological, political, and bureaucratic forces are at work. Thus, organizational decision making may not necessarily be rational.

5. Describe the implications of the relationship between information systems, organizations, and management decision making for the design and implementation of information systems. Salient features of organizations that must be addressed by information systems include organizational levels, organizational structures, types of tasks and decisions, the nature of management support, and the sentiments and attitudes of workers who will be using the system. The organization's history and external environment must be considered as well.

Implementation of a new information system is often more difficult than anticipated because of organizational change requirements. Because information systems potentially change important organizational dimensions, including the structure, culture, power relationships, and work activities, there is often considerable resistance to new systems.

If information systems are built properly, they can support individual and organizational decision making. Up to now, information systems have been most helpful to managers for performing informational and decisional roles; the same systems have been of very limited value for managers' interpersonal roles. Information systems that are less formal and highly flexible will be more useful than large, formal systems at higher levels of the organization.

Information systems can best support managers and decision making if such systems are flexible, with multiple analytical and intuitive models for evaluating data and the capability of supporting a variety of styles, skills, and knowledge.

Key Terms

Organization	**Environmental factors**	**Management control**	**Systematic decision**
Bureaucracy	**Institutional factors**	**Operational control**	**makers**
Standard operating	**Transaction cost theory**	**Knowledge-level decision**	**Intuitive decision makers**
procedures (SOPs)	**Agency theory**	**making**	**Organizational models of**
Organizational culture	**Classical model of**	**Unstructured decisions**	**decision making**
Information systems	**management**	**Structured decisions**	**Bureaucratic models of**
department	**Behavioral models**	**Intelligence**	**decision making**
Programmers	**Managerial roles**	**Design**	**Political models of**
Systems analysts	**Interpersonal roles**	**Choice**	**decision making**
Information systems	**Informational roles**	**Implementation**	**"Garbage can" model**
managers	**Decisional roles**	**Rational model**	
End users	**Strategic decision making**	**Cognitive style**	

Review Questions

1. What is an organization? How do organizations use information?
2. Compare the technical definition of organizations with the behavioral definition.
3. What features do all organizations have in common?
4. In what ways can organizations differ?
5. How have the roles of information systems and information systems specialists changed in organizations?
6. Describe the two factors that explain why organizations adopt information systems.
7. Describe each of the major theories that help explain how information systems affect organizations.
8. How can information systems change organizational structure?
9. Why is there considerable organizational resistance to the introduction of information systems?
10. What are the five functions of managers described in the classical model?
11. Behavioral research has identified five characteristics of the modern manager. How do these characteristics relate to the classical model?
12. What specific managerial roles can information systems support? Where are information systems particularly strong in supporting managers, and where are they weak?
13. Define structured and unstructured decisions. Give three examples of each.
14. What are the four stages of decision making described by Simon?
15. Describe each of the organizational choice models. How would the design of systems be affected by the choice of model employed?

Discussion Questions

1. You are an information systems designer assigned to build a new accounts receivable system for one of your corporation's divisions. What organizational factors should you consider?
2. It has been said that implementation of a new information system is always more difficult than anticipated. Discuss.
3. At your college or university, identify a major decision made recently by a department, an office, or a bureau. Try to apply each of the organizational models of decision making to the decision. How was information used by the various organizational participants? What are the implications for the design of information systems?

Group Project

With a group of two or three students, examine an organization such as a local drugstore or the bookstore, cafeteria, or registrar's office in your college or university. Describe some of the features of this organization, such as its standard operating procedures, culture, structure, and interest groups. Identify an information system or series of information systems that might improve the performance of this organization, and describe the changes that the organization would have to make in order to use information technology successfully.

Case Study

CAN SEARS REINVENT ITSELF?

On January 25, 1993, Sears Roebuck, the nation's largest retailer, announced that it was dropping its famous "big book" catalogues, closing 113 of its stores, and eliminating 50,000 jobs. Four months earlier Sears had announced plans to dispose of its Dean Witter securities business, Discover credit card, and Coldwell Banker real estate operations and to sell up to 20% of the stock in its Allstate insurance subsidiary. These moves were designed to make Sears a much smaller, leaner concern that could recapture its leadership in retailing.

What is ironic is that Sears' board of directors chose to retain its underperforming operations while it got rid of the profitable parts, and that the underperforming part represents the longtime core of the company. The spotlight now falls on reinvigorating Sears' retail business. Sears has steadily lost ground in retailing, moving from the number one position to number three behind discounters Wal-Mart Stores, Inc., and Kmart Corporation. Sears had been slow to remodel stores, trim costs, and keep pace with current trends in selling and merchandising. Sears could not keep up with the discounters and with specialty retailers such as Toys 'R' Us, Home Depot, Inc., and Circuit City Stores, Inc., which focus on a wide selection of low-price merchandise in a single category. Nor could Sears compete with trend-setting department stores.

Strategies that worked well for competitors fizzled at Sears. J.C. Penney successfully refocused its business to emphasize moderately priced apparel. Everyday low pricing, the pricing strategy used by Wal-Mart and other retailers, bombed at Sears because the firm's cost structure, one of the highest in the industry, did not allow for rock-bottom prices. Everyday low pricing has become "everyday fair pricing" supplemented by frequent sales.

Sears' catalogue sales also stagnated. While the Sears "big book" catalogue, founded in 1887, had the largest revenues of any mail-order business, sales had not been profitable for twenty years. The catalogue had lost ground to specialty catalogues such as those of L. L. Bean and Lands' End.

Yet Sears is heavily computerized—it spends more on information technology and networking than other noncomputer firms in the United States except the Boeing Corporation. Why hasn't this translated into competitive advantage?

One big problem is Sears' high cost of operations. Nearly 30% of each dollar in sales is required to cover overhead (e.g., expenses for salaries, light bills, and advertising), compared with 15% for Wal-Mart and about 21% for Kmart. Sears now hopes to cut costs by streamlining distribution systems and by combining merchandising functions so that there are only two or three general merchandising managers instead of six. Sears also realizes that it can't compete with discounters such as Wal-Mart Corporation on price alone and hopes to build a competitive edge through superior service.

In early 1992, Sears embarked on the Store-Simplification Program, a $60 million automation project intended to make Sears stores more efficient, attractive, and convenient by bringing all transactions closer to the sales floor and centralizing every store's general offices, cashiers, customer services, and credit functions. The program makes many changes in Sears' traditional retail sales efforts:

New point-of-sale (POS) terminals allow sales staff to issue new charge cards, accept charge card payments, issue gift certificates, and report account information to card holders. These innovations will increase savings by reducing the size of Sears' charge card group operations while making shopping more convenient for customers.

Some stores installed automatic teller machines to give customers cash advances against their Sears Discover credit cards. Telephone kiosks have been installed throughout the Sears retail network. Customers can use them to inquire about service, parts, and credit, check the status of their car in the tire and auto center, or call the manager.

Customer service desks are being eliminated. Sales personnel are authorized to handle refunds and returns, eliminating the need for two separate staffs. A customer who forgets his or her charge card can obtain immediate credit by telling the cashier his or her name and address and presenting identification.

Streamlining of patterns of work in back rooms and loading docks will also trim staff and create savings. The entire simplification effort is expected to eliminate $50 million in annual back office costs, 6,900 jobs, and the customer service desks at all stores. Changes will also increase the ratio of selling space to non-selling space at Sears, so that more space can be used to generate revenues.

Sears has also been trying to reduce costs by moving its 6,000 suppliers to an electronic ordering system similar to that described for Baxter Health Care (see Chapter 2). By linking its computerized ordering system directly to that of each supplier, Sears plans to eliminate paper throughout the order process and hopes to expedite the flow of goods into its stores.

To help turn Sears around and refocus on retailing, CEO Edward A. Brennan hired executive Arthur C. Martinez away from Saks Fifth Avenue in September 1992 (and named Martinez his successor as Sears chairman and chief executive officer two years later). Martinez ordered the company to combine its half-dozen disparate customer databases to find out who was really shopping at Sears. It turned out that Sears' biggest shoppers were not men looking for Craftsmen tool belts but women aged 25 to 50 in the market for everything from skirts to appliances.

Under Martinez, Sears stopped trying to sell everything and started focusing on six core types of merchandise—men's, women's, and children's clothing; home furnishings; home improvement; automotive services and supplies; appliances; and consumer electronics. The company is rearranging its merchandise displays to resemble those of more upscale department stores and is focusing on selling women's apparel, which is considered the most profitable segment of Sears' merchandising. Sears is stocking more upscale women's clothing and cosmetics, using advertising campaigns inviting women to see "the softer side of Sears." And it is relieving managers and clerks of some reporting and administrative tasks so that they have more time to actually sell. Beginning in 1996, every employee's compensation includes a measurement for customer service.

Will all these efforts make customers happier with Sears? Will Sears be able to prosper? Since Martinez arrived, earnings have rebounded from their dismally low levels of 1992. The question is whether Sears can sustain this momentum. Its operating expenses are still high compared with those of industry leaders. Market research indicates that Sears continues to be the destination of choice for consumers seeking lawn mowers, wrenches, washing machines, and other "hard" goods—and its tools and appliance businesses are posting large sales gains. But Sears has not yet secured itself as a place for fashionable women's clothing. Can Sears break out of its "retailing no-man's land," caught between fashionable apparel retailers and big-time discounters?

Martinez must also combat Sears' stodgy culture. Sears managers and executives have been indoctrinated in tales of Sears' past glories and entrenched in a massive bureaucracy in which change takes a long time. Some observers believe that Sears' biggest challenge is to transform its culture. ∎

Sources: "Yes, He's Revived Sears. But Can He Reinvent It?" *The New York Times* (January 7, 1996); Susan Chandler, "Sears' Turnaround Is for Real—For Now," *Business Week* (August 15, 1994); Stephanie Strom, "Sears Eliminating Its Catalogues and 50,000 Jobs," *The New York Times* (January 26, 1993), and "For Sears' Stores, Do-or-Die Time," *The New York Times* (September 30, 1992); Barnaby J. Feder, "Sears Will Return to Retailing Focus," *The New York Times* (September 30, 1992); Bruce Caldwell, "Sears Shops for Competitive Edge," *Information Week* (January 13, 1992).

Case Study Questions

1. What management, organization, and technology factors were responsible for Sears' poor performance?
2. Do you believe that the Store-Simplification Program solves these problems? How successful do you think it will be? Why?
3. What management, organization, and technology factors were addressed by the Store-Simplification Program?
4. What theories about the relationship of information systems and organizations are illustrated by this case?
5. Put yourself in the place of a Sears merchandising executive. List five steps you would take in the next year to implement the new Sears strategy.
6. Visit a Sears store and observe sales patterns. What image or market message is being conveyed in the store? How is it implemented? How might it be improved? (You might make a comparison stop at Penney's, Wal-Mart, or Kmart.)

References

Adams, Carl. R., and Jae Hyon Song. "Integrating Decision Technologies: Implications for Management Curriculum." *MIS Quarterly* 13, no. 2 (June 1989).

Allison, Graham T. *Essence of Decision—Explaining the Cuban Missile Crisis.* Boston: Little, Brown, 1971.

Alter, Steven, and Michael Ginzberg. "Managing Uncertainty in MIS Implementation." *Sloan Management Review* 20, no. 1 (Fall 1978).

Anthony, R. N. *Planning and Control Systems: A Framework for Analysis.* Cambridge, MA: Harvard University Press, 1965.

Argyris, Chris. *Interpersonal Competence and Organizational Effectiveness.* Homewood, IL: Dorsey Press, 1962.

Barnard, Chester. *The Functions of the Executive.* Cambridge, MA: Harvard University Press, 1968.

Beer, Michael, Russell A. Eisenstat, and Bert Spector. "Why Change Programs Don't Produce Change." *Harvard Business Review* (November–December 1990).

Bell, Daniel. *The Coming of Post-Industrial Society.* New York: Basic Books, 1973.

Bikson, T. K., and J. D. Eveland. "Integrating New Tools into Information Work." The Rand Corporation, 1992. RAND/RP-106.

Blau, Peter, and W. Richard Scott. *Formal Organizations.* San Francisco: Chandler Press, 1962.

Brzezinski, Z. *The Technetronic Society.* New York: Viking Press, 1970.

Charan, Ram. "How Networks Reshape Organizations—For Results." *Harvard Business Review* (September–October 1991).

Cohen, Michael, James March, and Johan Olsen. "A Garbage Can Model of Organizational Choice." *Administrative Science Quarterly* 17 (1972).

DiMaggio, Paul J., and Walter W. Powell. "The Iron Cage Revisited: Institutional Isomorphism and Collective Rationality in Organizational Fields." *American Sociological Review* 48 (1983).

Drucker, Peter. "The Coming of the New Organization." *Harvard Business Review* (January–February 1988).

El Sawy, Omar A. "Implementation by Cultural Infusion: An Approach for Managing the Introduction of Information Technologies." *MIS Quarterly* (June 1985).

Etzioni, Amitai. *A Comparative Analysis of Complex Organizations.* New York: Free Press, 1975.

Fayol, Henri. *Administration industrielle et generale.* Paris: Dunods, 1950 (first published in 1916).

Freeman, John, Glenn R. Carroll, and Michael T. Hannan. "The Liability of Newness: Age Dependence in Organizational Death Rates." *American Sociological Review* 48 (1983).

George, Joey. "Organizational Decision Support Systems." *Journal of Management Information Systems* 8, no. 3 (Winter 1991–1992).

Gorry, G. Anthony, and Michael S. Scott-Morton. "A Framework for Management Information Systems." *Sloan Management Review* 13, no. 1 (Fall 1971).

Gouldner, Alvin. *Patterns of Industrial Bureaucracy.* New York: Free Press, 1954.

Gurbaxani, V., and S. Whang, "The Impact of Information Systems on Organizations and Markets." *Communications of the ACM* 34, no. 1 (Jan. 1991).

Herzberg, Frederick. *Work and the Nature of Man.* New York: Crowell, 1966.

Huber, George P. "Cognitive Style as a Basis for MIS and DSS Designs: Much Ado About Nothing?" *Management Science* 29 (May 1983).

———. "The Nature and Design of Post-Industrial Organizations." *Management Science* 30, no. 8 (August 1984).

Huff, Sid L., and Malcolm C. Munro. "Information Technology Assessment and Adoption: A Field Study." *Management Information Systems Quarterly* (December 1985).

Isenberg, Daniel J. "How Senior Managers Think." *Harvard Business Review* (November–December 1984).

Ives, Blake, and Margrethe H. Olson. "Manager or Technician? The Nature of the Information Systems Manager's Job." *MIS Quarterly* (December 1981).

Jaques, Elliott. "In Praise of Hierarchy." *Harvard Business Review* (January–February 1990).

Jensen, M., and W. Mekling. "Theory of the Firm: Managerial Behavior, Agency Costs, and Ownership Structure." *Journal of Financial Economics* 3 (1976).

Jessup, Leonard M., Terry Connolly, and Jolene Galegher. "The Effects of Anonymity on GDSS Group Process with an Idea-Generating Task." *MIS Quarterly* 14, no. 3 (September 1990).

Keen, P. G. W. "Information Systems and Organizational Change." *Communications of the ACM* 24, no. 1 (January 1981).

Keen, P. G. W., and M. S. Morton. *Decision Support Systems: An Organizational Perspective*. Reading, MA: Addison-Wesley, 1978.

King, J. L., V. Gurbaxani, K. L. Kraemer, F. W. McFarlan, K. S. Raman, and C. S. Yap. "Institutional Factors in Information Technology Innovation." *Information Systems Research* 5, no. 2 (June 1994).

Kling, Rob. "Social Analyses of Computing: Theoretical Perspectives in Recent Empirical Research." *Computing Survey* 12, no. 1 (March 1980).

Kling, Rob, and William H. Dutton. "The Computer Package: Dynamic Complexity." In *Computers and Politics*, edited by James Danziger, William Dutton, Rob Kling, and Kenneth Kraemer. New York: Columbia University Press, 1982.

Klotz, B. *Industry Productivity Projections: A Methodological Study*. U.S. Department of Labor, Bureau of Labor Statistics, 1966.

Kolb, D. A., and A. L. Frohman. "An Organization Development Approach to Consulting." *Sloan Management Review* 12, no. 1 (Fall 1970).

Kotter, John T. "What Effective General Managers Really Do." *Harvard Business Review* (November–December 1982).

Kraemer, Kenneth, John King, Debora Dunkle, and Joe Lane. *Managing Information Systems*. Los Angeles: Jossey-Bass, 1989.

Laudon, Kenneth C. *Computers and Bureaucratic Reform*. New York: Wiley, 1974.

———. *Dossier Society: Value Choices in the Design of National Information Systems*. New York: Columbia University Press, 1986.

———. "Environmental and Institutional Models of Systems Development." *Communications of the ACM* 28, no. 7, (July 1985).

———. "A General Model of the Relationship Between Information Technology and Organizations." Center for Research on Information Systems, New York University. Working paper, National Science Foundation, 1989.

Lawrence, Paul, and Jay Lorsch. *Organization and Environment*. Cambridge, MA: Harvard University Press, 1969.

Leavitt, Harold J. "Applying Organizational Change in Industry: Structural, Technological and Humanistic Approaches." In *Handbook of Organizations*, edited by James G. March. Chicago: Rand McNally, 1965.

Leavitt, Harold J., and Thomas L. Whisler. "Management in the 1980s." *Harvard Business Review* (November–December 1958).

Leifer, Richard. "Matching Computer-Based Information Systems with Organizational Structures." *MIS Quarterly* 12, no. 1 (March 1988).

Lindblom, C. E., "The Science of Muddling Through." *Public Administration Review* 19 (1959).

Malcolm, Andrew H. "How the Oil Spilled and Spread: Delay and Confusion Off Alaska." *The New York Times*, April 16, 1989.

March, James G., and Herbert A. Simon. *Organizations*. New York: Wiley, 1958.

Markus, M. L. "Power, Politics, and MIS Implementation." *Communications of the ACM* 26, no. 6 (June 1983).

Martin, J. *The Telematic Society*. Englewood Cliffs, NJ: Prentice-Hall, 1981.

Masuda, Y. *The Information Society*. Bethesda, MD: World Future Society, 1980.

Mayo, Elton. *The Social Problems of an Industrial Civilization*. Cambridge, MA: Harvard University Press, 1945.

McKenney, James L., and Peter G. W. Keen. "How Managers' Minds Work." *Harvard Business Review* (May–June 1974).

Michels, Robert. *Political Parties*. New York: Free Press, 1962. Original publication: 1915.

Millman, Zeeva, and Jon Hartwick. "The Impact of Automated Office Systems on Middle Managers and Their Work." *MIS Quarterly* 11, no. 4 (December 1987).

Mintzberg, Henry. "Managerial Work: Analysis from Observation." *Management Science* 18 (October 1971).

———. *The Nature of Managerial Work*. New York: Harper & Row, 1973.

———. *The Structuring of Organizations*. Englewood Cliffs, NJ: Prentice-Hall, 1979.

Olson, Margrethe H. "The IS Manager's Job." *MIS Quarterly* (December 1981).

Parsons, Talcott. *Structure and Process in Modern Societies*. New York: Free Press, 1960.

Perrow, Charles. *Organizational Analysis*. Belmont, CA: Wadsworth, 1970.

Pindyck, Robert S., and Daniel L. Rubinfield. *Microeconomics*. New York: Macmillan, 1992.

Porat, Marc. *The Information Economy: Definition and Measurement*. Washington, DC: U.S. Department of Commerce, Office of Telecommunications (May 1977).

Roethlisberger, F. J., and W. J. Dickson. *Management and the Worker*. Cambridge, MA: Harvard University Press, 1947.

Schein, Edgar H. *Organizational Culture and Leadership*. San Francisco: Jossey-Bass, 1985.

Scott Morton, Michael S. *The Corporation of the 1990s*. New York: Oxford University Press, 1991.

Shore, Edwin B. "Reshaping the IS Organization." *MIS Quarterly* (December 1983).

Simon, H. A. *The New Science of Management Decision*. New York: Harper & Row, 1960.

Simon, Herbert A. "Applying Information Technology to Organization Design." *Public Administration Review* (May/June 1973).

Starbuck, William H. "Organizations as Action Generators." *American Sociological Review* 48 (1983).

Straub, Detmar, and James C. Wetherbe. "Information Technologies for the 1990s: An Organizational Impact Perspective." *Communications of the ACM* 32, no. 11 (November 1989).

Thompson, James. *Organizations in Action*. New York: McGraw-Hill, 1967.

Toffler, Alvin. *Future Shock*. New York: Random House, 1970.

Turner, Jon A. "Computer Mediated Work: The Interplay Between Technology and Structured Jobs." *Communications of the ACM* 27, no. 12 (December 1984).

Turner, Jon A., and Robert A. Karasek, Jr. "Software Ergonomics: Effects of Computer Application Design Parameters on Operator Task Performance and Health." *Ergonomics* 27, no. 6 (1984).

Tushman, Michael L., William H. Newman, and Elaine Romanelli. "Convergence and Upheaval: Managing the Unsteady Pace of Organizational Evolution." *California Management Review* 29, no. 1 (1986).

Tushman, Michael L., and Philip Anderson. "Technological Discontinuities and Organizational Environments." *Administrative Science Quarterly* 31 (September 1986).

Tversky, A., and D. Kahneman. "The Framing of Decisions and the Psychology of Choice." *Science* 211 (January 1981).

Weber, Max. *The Theory of Social and Economic Organization*. Translated by Talcott Parsons. New York: Free Press, 1947.

Williamson, Oliver E. *The Economic Institutions of Capitalism*. New York: Free Press, 1985.

Woodward, Joan. *Industrial Organization: Theory and Practice*. Oxford: Oxford University Press, 1965.

Wrapp, H. Edward. "Good Managers Don't Make Policy Decisions." *Harvard Business Review* (July–August 1984).

Chapter 4

Ethical and Social Impact of Information Systems

What Price Should Workers Have to Pay for Technology?

4.1 Understanding Ethical and Social Issues Related to Systems
A Model for Thinking about Ethical, Social, and Political Issues
Five Moral Dimensions of the Information Age
Key Technology Trends That Raise Ethical Issues

4.2 Ethics in an Information Society
Basic Concepts: Responsibility, Accountability, and Liability
Ethical Analysis
Candidate Ethical Principles
Professional Codes of Conduct
Some Real-World Ethical Dilemmas

4.3 The Moral Dimensions of Information Systems
Information Rights: Privacy and Freedom in an Information Society
Property Rights: Intellectual Property
Window on Organizations:
A Corporate Software Code of Ethics
Accountability, Liability, and Control
Window on Organizations:
Liability on the Internet
System Quality: Data Quality and System Errors
Quality of Life: Equity, Access, Boundaries
Window on Management:
Whither the Downsized Society?

Window on Management:
Managing RSI
Window on Technology:
The Coming of a National Digital Superhighway Raises Many Ethical and Social Issues
Management Actions: A Corporate Code of Ethics

Management Challenges
Summary
Key Terms
Review Questions
Discussion Questions
Group Projects
Case Study: Who Is Responsible?
References

What Price Should Workers Have to Pay for Technology?

In 1992 the order processors employed at Pizza Pizza Ltd. began to notice that their ranks were slowly thinning, that there were fewer and fewer of them as time went by. Canada's Pizza Pizza Ltd. of Toronto, a large fast-food delivery franchising company, had employed a staff of 150 unionized order processors, members of United Food and Commercial Workers' (UFCW) Local 175-633. They worked at a Pizza Pizza office processing phone orders through terminals hooked up to Pizza Pizza's computer. Finally, in August 1992, the company informed the remaining order processors that they would no longer have jobs because Pizza Pizza simply did not have enough work for them. A union investigation quickly uncovered a different reason—that in fact the company had been slowly replacing the unionized order processors with non-union workers who were working out of their homes. The company supplied the new home workers with computer terminals linked by telephone to the corporate computer. These home workers were paid a lower wage than the unionized workers, and in addition the company saved on office expenses. According to the union, the company expects to be saving $4 per hour per worker. UFCW members went out on strike to try to win those jobs back for their members who had been clandestinely replaced. In the end they were only partially successful. About 25 of the fired workers were rehired by Pizza Pizza, but only under the same conditions as the non-union workers—they had to work at home, and at the lower wage.

Once the strike was settled, the former office workers who were now working at home discovered that their work isolated them. They had to use their own telephone lines to connect to the company's computer (the company paid for the cost of the calls), which meant that they were unable to receive outside calls. UFCW wants to know if these isolated workers have a right to use the Pizza Pizza terminals in their home for any purpose other than processing orders. The home workers were unable to use the terminals to contact anyone outside of Pizza Pizza because these terminals were "dumb," able to operate only when connected to the Pizza Pizza computer.

Marc Bélanger, who runs SoliNet, Canada's nationwide labor union computer network, believes that workers should and do have such a right. "If you take people out of a social work setting, then you should have a cyberspace setting so they can interact," he argues. This social interaction aspect of many workers' jobs is sacrificed, he believes, if they are forced to work at home and given no method of interacting with other employees of the company. SoliNet itself provides conputer conferencing capabilities to its members, who belong to the Canadian Union of Public Employees and 20 other unions. But the issue of isolation is one being faced by more and more workers as telecommuting becomes technologically more feasible and is adopted by more companies. ∎

Source: Montieth M. Illingworth, "Workers on the Net, Unite!" *Information Week* (August 22, 1994).

Pizza Pizza has a right to reduce its expenses and to use information systems technology to make that possible. However, the very telecommunications technology that allowed the company to cut expenses also cost a number of workers their jobs. In addition, those who were able to keep their jobs found themselves working at lower pay and in an environment of enforced isolation. Technology can be a double-edged sword. The choice faced by Pizza Pizza management is an example of an ethical dilemma made possible by the use of information systems, one that is shared by many organizations today.

Balancing the need for efficiency with responsibility toward employees is one of many ethical and social issues faced by organizations using information systems. Others include

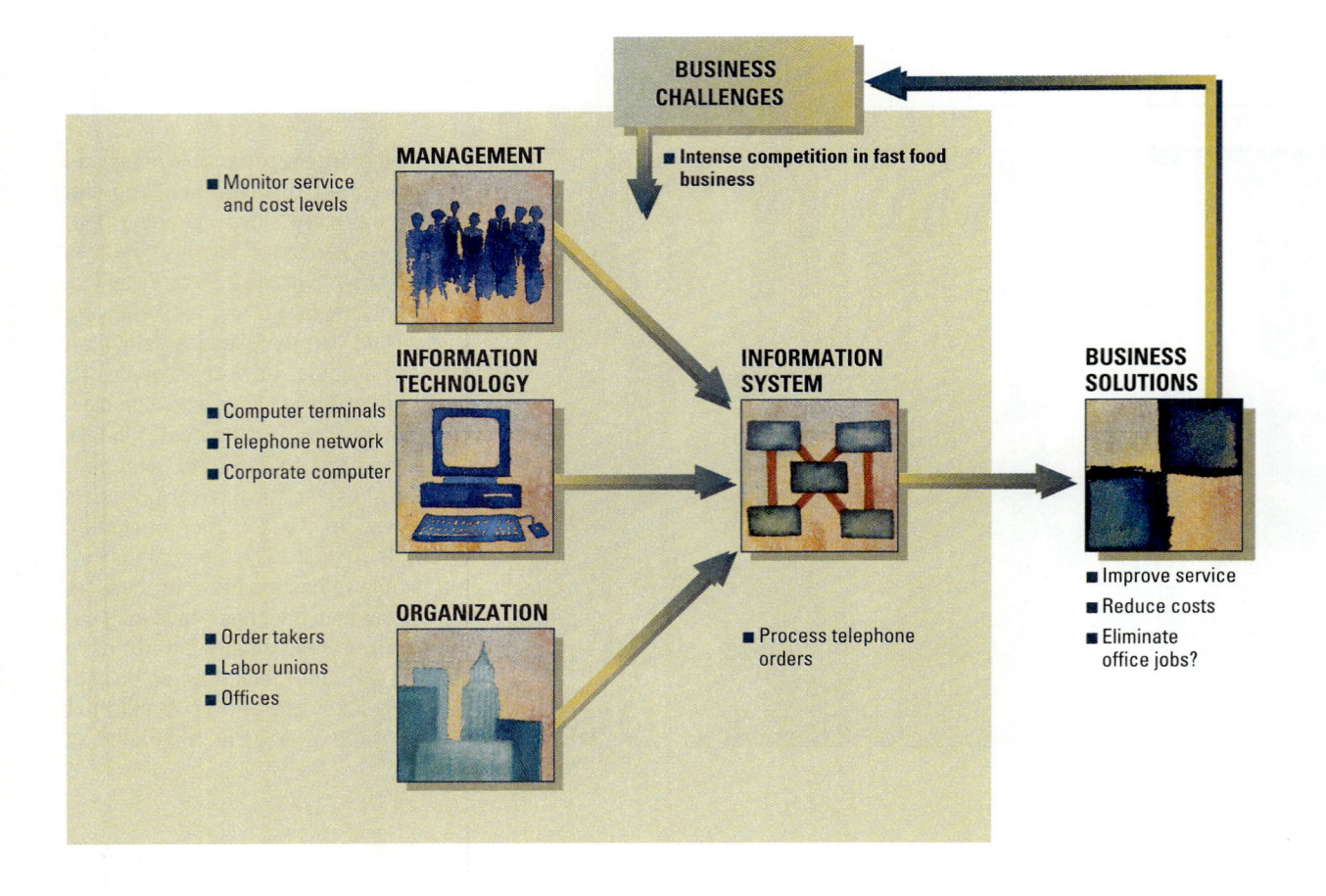

BUSINESS CHALLENGES
- Intense competition in fast food business

MANAGEMENT
- Monitor service and cost levels

INFORMATION TECHNOLOGY
- Computer terminals
- Telephone network
- Corporate computer

ORGANIZATION
- Order takers
- Labor unions
- Offices

INFORMATION SYSTEM
- Process telephone orders

BUSINESS SOLUTIONS
- Improve service
- Reduce costs
- Eliminate office jobs?

establishing information rights, including the right to privacy; protecting intellectual property rights; establishing accountability for the consequences of information systems; setting standards to safeguard system quality that protect the safety of individuals and society; and preserving values and institutions considered essential to the quality of life in an information society. This chapter describes these issues and suggests guidelines for dealing with these questions.

> **Learning Objectives**
>
> *After completing this chapter, you will be able to:*
>
> 1. Understand the relationship among ethical, social, and political issues raised by information systems.
> 2. Identify the main moral dimensions of an information society.
> 3. Employ an ethical analysis to difficult situations.
> 4. Understand specific ethical principles for conduct.
> 5. Develop corporate policies for ethical conduct.

4.1 UNDERSTANDING ETHICAL AND SOCIAL ISSUES RELATED TO SYSTEMS

Ethics refers to the principles of right and wrong that can be used by individuals acting as free moral agents to make choices to guide their behavior. Information technology and information systems raise new ethical questions for both individuals and societies because they create opportunities for intense social change, threatening existing distributions of power, money, rights, and obligations. Like other technologies, such as steam engines, electricity, telephone, and radio, information technology can be used to achieve social progress, but it can also be used to commit crimes and threaten cherished social values. The development of information technology will produce benefits for many, and costs for others. In this situation, what is the ethical and socially responsible course of action?

ethics Principles of right and wrong that can be used by individuals acting as free moral agents to make choices to guide their behavior.

A MODEL FOR THINKING ABOUT ETHICAL, SOCIAL, AND POLITICAL ISSUES

Ethical, social, and political issues are of course tightly coupled together. One way to think about these relationships is given in Figure 4.1. Imagine society as a more or less calm pond on a summer day, a delicate ecosystem in partial equilibrium with individuals and with social and political institutions. Individuals know how to act in this pond because social institutions (family, education, organizations) have developed well-honed rules of behavior, and these are backed up by laws developed in the political sector that prescribe behavior and promise sanctions for violations. Now toss a rock into the center of the pond. But imagine instead of a rock that the disturbing force is a powerful shock of new information technology and systems hitting a society more or less at rest. What happens? Ripples, of course.

Suddenly individual actors are confronted with new situations often not covered by the old rules. Social institutions cannot respond overnight to these ripples—it may take years to develop etiquette, expectations, "socially responsible," "politically correct" attitudes, or approved rules. Political institutions also require time before developing new laws and often require the demonstration of real harm before they act. In the meantime, you may have to act. You may be forced to act in a legal "gray area."

We can use this model as a first approximation to the dynamics that connect ethical, social, and political issues. This model is also useful for identifying the main moral

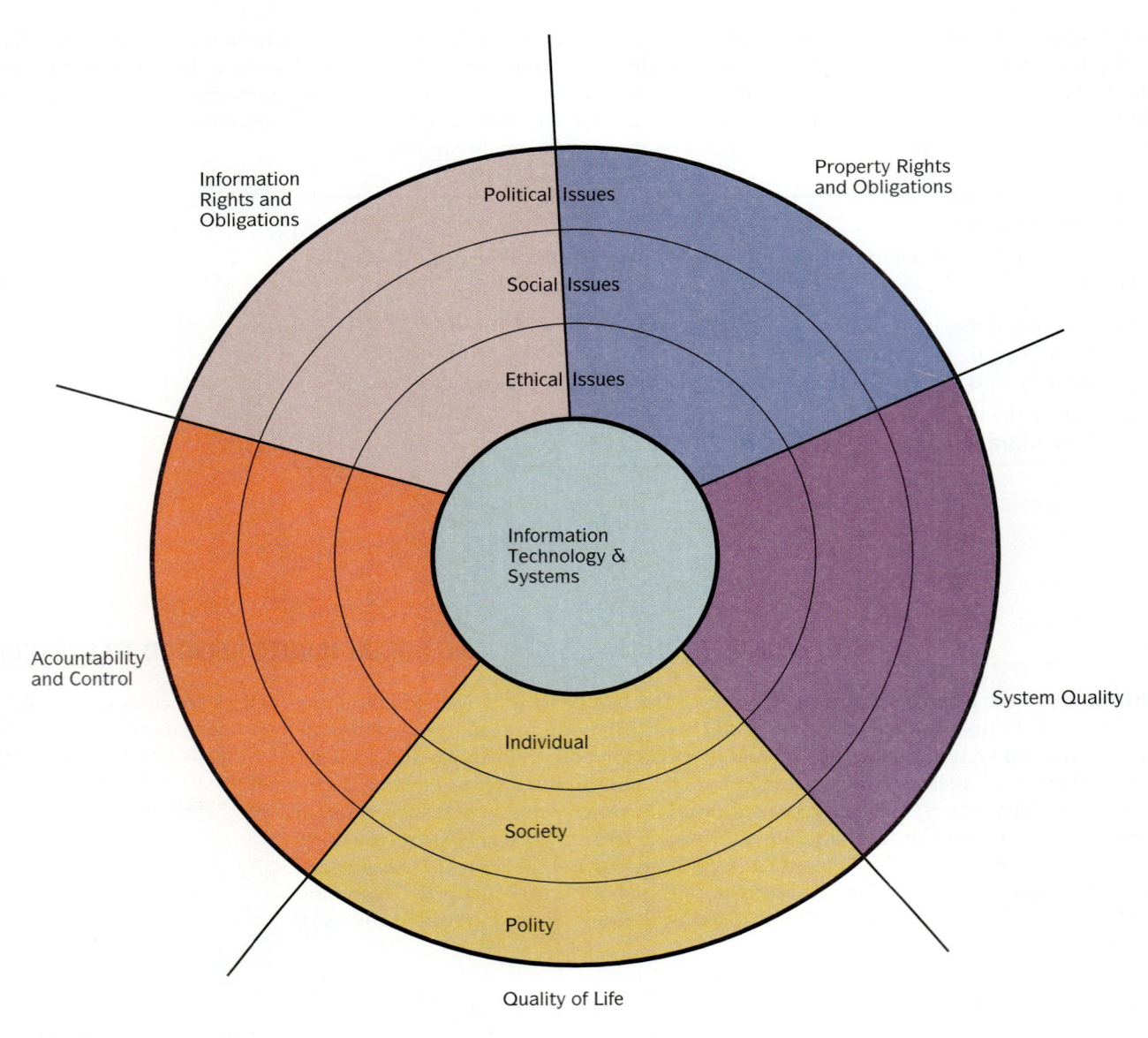

FIGURE 4.1
The relationship between ethical, social, and political issues in an information society. The introduction of new information technology has a ripple effect, raising new ethical, social, and political issues that must be dealt with on the individual, social, and political levels. These issues have five moral dimensions: information rights and obligations, property rights and obligations, system quality, quality of life, and accountability and control.

dimensions of the "information society" that cut across various levels of action—individual, social, and political.

FIVE MORAL DIMENSIONS OF THE INFORMATION AGE

A review of the literature on ethical, social, and political issues surrounding systems identifies five moral dimensions of the information age that we introduce here and explore in greater detail in Section 4.3. The five moral dimensions are as follows:

- *Information rights and obligations*: What **information rights** do individuals and organizations possess with respect to information about themselves? What can they protect? What obligations do individuals and organizations have concerning this information?

information rights The rights that individuals and organizations have with respect to information that pertains to themselves.

96   CHAPTER 4   Ethical and Social Impact of Information Systems

- *Property rights:* How will traditional intellectual property rights be protected in a digital society where tracing and accounting for ownership is difficult, where ignoring such property rights is so easy?
- *Accountability and control:* Who can and will be held accountable and liable for the harm done to individual and collective information and property rights?
- *System quality:* What standards of data and system quality should we demand to protect individual rights and the safety of society?
- *Quality of life:* What values should be preserved in an information- and knowledge-based society? What institutions should we protect from violation? What cultural values and practices are supported by the new information technology?

Before going on to analyze these dimensions, we should briefly review the major technology and system trends that have heightened concern about the foregoing issues.

KEY TECHNOLOGY TRENDS THAT RAISE ETHICAL ISSUES

These ethical issues long preceded information technology—they are the abiding concerns of free societies everywhere. Nevertheless, information technology has heightened ethical concerns, put stress on existing social arrangements, and made existing laws obsolete or severely crippled. There are four key technological trends responsible for these ethical stresses.

The doubling of computing power every 18 months since the early 1980s has made it possible for most organizations to use information systems for their core production processes. As a result, our dependence on systems and our vulnerability to system errors and poor data quality have increased. Occasional system failures heighten public concern over our growing dependence on some critical systems. Social rules and laws have not yet adjusted to this dependence. Standards for ensuring the accuracy and reliability of information systems (see Chapter 14) are not universally accepted or enforced.

Advances in data storage techniques and rapidly declining storage costs have been responsible for the multiplying databases on individuals—employees, customers, and potential customers—maintained by private and public organizations. These advances in data storage have made the routine violation of individual privacy both cheap and effective. For example, EMASS Storage Systems of Dallas produces mass data storage systems capable of holding nearly 500 trillion characters of data in a 54 square foot space, and a record access time of a few seconds (Datamation, 1993 and http://www.emass.com/). Consider that the Social Security Master Beneficiary File with over

Making a purchase with a credit card can make personal information available to market researchers, telephone marketers, and direct mail companies. Advances in information technology facilitate the invasion of privacy.

4.1 Understanding Ethical and Social Issues Related to Systems

50 million names could be put on the EMASS system and take up only a fraction of the space! Already massive data storage systems are cheap enough for regional and even local retailing firms to use in identifying customers.

Advances in data mining techniques for large databases are a third technological trend that heightens ethical concerns. The Window on Technology in Chapter 5 describes how parallel supercomputers are used by Wal-Mart Stores Inc., American Express, and others to rapidly identify buying patterns of customers and suggest appropriate responses. One retailer examined customer "buying trips" as the unit of analysis. They discovered that if someone in the Midwest buys disposable diapers at 5:00 P.M., the most common thing next purchased is a six-pack of beer. The retailer decided, therefore, to put beer and snacks next to the diapers rack (*The Wall Street Journal*, December 23, 1992).

Last, *advances in telecommunications infrastructure* like ISDN (Integrated Services Digital Network—see Chapter 9), the Internet, and proposed national telecommunications networks like the National Research Education Network (NREN) described in the Window on Technology promise to reduce greatly the cost of moving large data sets and open the possibility of mining large data sets remotely using smaller desktop machines.

In a few years it is conceivable that such information technology advances will permit the invasion of privacy on a scale and precision unimaginable to us now. Even the Census Bureau would lose its shelter: With commonly available census data on blocks, along with other data, we could easily pick out information about individuals with great regularity.

The development of global digital superhighway communication networks widely available to individuals and businesses poses many ethical and social concerns. Who will account for the flow of information over these networks? Will you be able to trace information collected about you? What will these networks do to the traditional relationships between family, work, and leisure? How will traditional job designs be altered when millions of "employees" become subcontractors using mobile offices that they themselves must pay for?

In the next section we will consider some ethical principles and analytical techniques for dealing with these kinds of ethical and social concerns.

4.2 ETHICS IN AN INFORMATION SOCIETY

Ethics is a concern of humans who have freedom of choice. Ethics is about individual choice: When faced with alternative courses of action, what is the correct moral choice? What are the main features of "ethical choice"?

BASIC CONCEPTS: RESPONSIBILITY, ACCOUNTABILITY, AND LIABILITY

Ethical choices are decisions made by individuals who are responsible for the consequences of their actions. Responsibility is a feature of individuals and is a key element of ethical action. **Responsibility** means that you accept the potential costs, duties, and obligations for the decisions you make. **Accountability** is a feature of systems and social institutions: It means that mechanisms are in place to determine who took responsible action, who is responsible. Systems and institutions where it is impossible to find out who took what action are inherently incapable of ethical analysis or ethical action. Liability extends the concept of responsibility further to the area of laws. **Liability** is a feature of political systems in which a body of law is in place that permits individuals to recover the damages done to them by other actors, systems, or organizations. **Due process** is a related feature of law-governed societies: It means a process in which laws are known and understood and there is an ability to appeal to higher authorities to ensure that the laws were applied correctly.

These basic concepts form the underpinning of an ethical analysis of information systems and those who manage them. First, as we discussed in Chapter 3, information

---

responsibility Accepting the potential costs, duties, and obligations for the decisions one makes.

accountability The mechanisms for assessing responsibility for decisions made and actions taken.

liability The existence of laws that permit individuals to recover the damages done to them by other actors, systems, or organizations.

due process A process in which laws are well known and understood and there is an ability to appeal to higher authorities to ensure that laws are applied correctly.

technologies are filtered through social institutions, organizations, and individuals. Systems do not have "impacts" all by themselves. Whatever information system impacts exist are a product of institutional, organizational, and individual actions and behaviors. Second, responsibility for the consequences of technology falls clearly on the institutions, organizations, and individual managers who choose to use the technology. Using information technology in a "socially responsible" manner means that you can and will be held accountable for the consequences of your actions. Third, in an ethical political society, individuals and others can recover damages done them through a set of laws characterized by due process.

ETHICAL ANALYSIS

When confronted with a situation that seems to present ethical issues, how should you analyze and reason about the situation? Here's a five-step process that should help.

- *Identify and describe clearly the facts.* Find out who did what to whom, and where, when, and how. You will be surprised in many instances how wrong the initially reported facts typically are, and often you will find that simply getting the facts straight helps define the solution. It also helps to get the opposing parties involved in an ethical dilemma to agree on the facts.
- *Define the conflict or dilemma and identify the higher-order values involved.* Ethical, social, and political issues always reference higher values. The parties to a dispute all claim to be pursuing higher values (e.g., freedom, privacy, protection of property, and the free enterprise system).

  Typically, an ethical issue involves a dilemma: two diametrically opposed courses of action that support worthwhile values. In the Pizza Pizza opening case, you have two competing and opposing values: a company's need to keep costs low and workers' needs to have well-paying jobs.
- *Identify the stakeholders.* Every ethical, social, and political issue has stakeholders: players in the game who have an interest in the outcome, who have invested in the situation, and usually who have vocal opinions. Find out who these groups are and what they want. This will be useful later when designing a solution.
- *Identify the options that you can reasonably take.* You may find that none of the options satisfies all the interests involved, but that some options do a better job than others. Arriving at a "good" or ethical solution may not always be a "balancing" of consequences to stakeholders.
- *Identify the potential consequences of your options.* Some options may be ethically correct but disastrous from other points of view. Other options may work in this one instance but not be generalizable to other similar instances. Always ask yourself, "What if I choose this option consistently over time?"

Once your analysis is completed, what ethical principles or rules should you use to make a decision? What higher-order values should inform your judgment?

CANDIDATE ETHICAL PRINCIPLES

While you are the only one who can decide which among many ethical principles you will follow and how you will give priority to them, it is helpful to consider some ethical principles with deep roots in many cultures that have survived throughout recorded history.

1. Do unto others as you would have them do unto you (the Golden Rule). Putting yourself into the situation of others, and thinking of yourself as the object of the decision, can help you think about "fairness" in decision making.
2. If an action is not right for everyone to take, then it is not right for anyone (**Immanuel Kant's Categorical Imperative**). Ask yourself, "If everyone did this, could the organization, or society, survive?"

Immanuel Kant's Categorical Imperative A principle which states that if an action is not right for everyone to take, it is not right for anyone.

Descartes' rule of change A principle which states that if an action cannot be taken repeatedly, then it is not right to be taken at any time.

Utilitarian Principle Principle that one should take the action that achieves the higher or greater value.

Risk Aversion Principle Principle that one should take the action that produces the least harm or incurs the least cost.

ethical "no free lunch" rule Assumption that all tangible and intangible objects are owned by someone else unless there is a specific declaration otherwise and that the creator wants compensation for this work.

3. If an action cannot be taken repeatedly, then it is not right to be taken at any time (**Descartes' rule of change**). This is the slippery-slope rule: An action may bring about a small change now that is acceptable, but repeated action would bring unacceptable changes in the long run. In the vernacular, it might be stated as "once started down a slippery path you may not be able to stop."

4. Take the action that achieves the higher or greater value (the **Utilitarian Principle**). This rule assumes that you can prioritize values in a rank order and understand the consequences of various courses of action.

5. Take the action that produces the least harm, or the least potential cost (**Risk Aversion Principle**). Some actions have extremely high failure costs of very low probability (e.g., building a nuclear generating facility in an urban area), or extremely high failure costs of moderate probability (speeding and automobile accidents). Avoid these high failure cost actions, with greater attention obviously to high failure cost potential of moderate to high probability.

6. Assume that virtually all tangible and intangible objects are owned by someone unless there is a specific declaration otherwise. (This is the **ethical "no free lunch" rule**.) If something created by someone else is useful to you, it has value and you should assume that its creator wants compensation for his or her work.

These ethical rules have too many logical and substantive exceptions to be absolute guides to action. Nevertheless, actions that do not easily pass these rules deserve some very close attention and a great deal of caution if only because the appearance of unethical behavior may do as much harm to you and your company as actual unethical behavior.

PROFESSIONAL CODES OF CONDUCT

When groups of people claim to be professionals, they take on special rights and obligations based on their special claims to knowledge, wisdom, and respect. Professional codes of conduct are promulgated by associations of professionals like the American Medical Association (AMA), the American Bar Association (ABA), and the American Society of Mechanical Engineers (ASME). These professional groups take responsibility for the partial regulation of their professions by determining entrance qualifications and competence. Codes of ethics are promises by the profession to regulate themselves in the general interest of society. In return, professionals seek to raise both the pay and the respect given their profession.

U.S. professional computer societies such as the Data Processing Management Association (DPMA), the ICP (Institute for Certification of Computer Professionals, the ITAA (Information Technology Association of America), and the Association of Computing Machinery (ACM) have drafted codes of ethics (Oz, 1992). Table 4.1 describes the code of professional conduct with moral imperatives of the ACM, the oldest of these societies.

Extensions to these moral imperatives state that ACM professions should consider the health, privacy, and general welfare of the public in the performance of their work and that professionals should express their professional opinion to their employer regarding any adverse consequences to the public (see Oz, 1994).

SOME REAL-WORLD ETHICAL DILEMMAS

The recent ethical problems described in the following paragraphs illustrate a wide range of issues. Some of these issues are obvious ethical dilemmas. Others represent some type of breach of ethics. In either instance, there are rarely any easy solutions.

Continental Can: Based in Norwalk, Connecticut, Continental Can Co. developed a human resources database with files on all of its employees. Besides the typical employee data, the system included the capability to "red flag" employees nearing retire-

Table 4.1 Association of Computing Machinery Code of Professional Conduct

Recognition of professional status by the public depends not only on skill and dedication but also on adherence to a recognized code of professional conduct.

General Moral Imperatives

Contribute to society and human well-being

Avoid harm to others

Be honest and trustworthy

Honor property rights including copyrights and patents

Give proper credit for intellectual property

Access computing resources only when authorized

Respect the privacy of others

Source: The Association of Computing Machinery, New York, New York, 1993.

---

ment or approaching the age at which a pension would be vested in the individual. Throughout the 1980s, when the red flag went up, management would fire the person even after decades of loyal service. In 1991 a federal district court in Newark, New Jersey, awarded ex-employees $445 million for wrongful dismissal (McPartlin, June 22, 1992).

Technological Threats at AT&T: In March 1992, four months before entering into contract negotiations with the Communications Workers of America (CWA) and the International Brotherhood of Electrical Workers (IBEW), AT&T announced that it was introducing technology that would replace one-third of its 18,000 long distance operators by 1994. AT&T is using voice recognition software to reduce the need for human operators by allowing computers to recognize customers' responses to a series of computerized questions. New algorithms called "word spotting" allow the computer to recognize speech that is halting, stuttering, paused, or ungrammatical.

AT&T claims that the new technology will permit it to eliminate 3000 to 6000 operator jobs nationwide, 200 to 400 management positions, and 31 offices in 21 states. Long distance operators earn anywhere from $10,300 to $27,100 a year, with benefits adding another third of the cost. AT&T claims that not all workers will be dismissed and that many will be retrained for other positions.

Communications Workers of America officials expressed outrage at AT&T's announcement, branding it an "intimidation tactic" to combat union demands for higher wages and better working conditions (Ramirez, March 4, 1992).

E-mail Privacy at EPSON: In March 1990, e-mail administrator Alana Shoars filed a suit in Los Angeles Superior Court alleging wrongful termination, defamation, and invasion of privacy by her former employer, Epson America Inc. of Torrance, California. She sought $1 million in damages. In July 1990, Shoars filed a class-action suit seeking $75 million for 700 Epson employees and approximately 1,800 outsiders whose e-mail may have been monitored. Shoars contends that she was fired because she questioned the company's policy of monitoring and printing employees' e-mail messages. Epson claims that Shoars was fired because she opened an MCI:Mail account without permission. Many firms claim that they have every right to monitor the electronic mail of their employees because they own the facilities, intend their use to be for business purposes only, and create the facility for a business purpose (Bjerklie, 1994; Rifkin, 1991).

In each instance, you can find competing values at work, with groups lined up on either side of a debate. A close analysis of the facts can sometimes produce compromised solutions that give each side "half a loaf." Try to apply some of the principles of ethical analysis described earlier to each of these cases. What is the right thing to do?

4.3 THE MORAL DIMENSIONS OF INFORMATION SYSTEMS

In this section, we take a closer look at the five moral dimensions of information systems first described in Figure 4.1. In each dimension we identify the ethical, social, and political levels of analysis and illustrate with real-world examples the values involved, the stakeholders, and the options chosen.

INFORMATION RIGHTS: PRIVACY AND FREEDOM IN AN INFORMATION SOCIETY

privacy The claim of individuals to be left alone, free from surveillance by or interference from other individuals, organizations, or the state.

Privacy is the claim of individuals to be left alone, free from surveillance by or interference from other individuals or organizations, including the state. Claims to privacy are also involved at the workplace: Millions of employees are subject to electronic and other forms of high-tech surveillance. Information technology and systems threaten individual claims to privacy by making the invasion of privacy cheap, profitable, and effective.

The claim to privacy is protected in the U.S., Canadian, and German constitutions in a variety of different ways, and in other countries through various statutes. In the United States, the claim to privacy is protected primarily by the First Amendment guarantees of freedom of speech and association, the Fourth Amendment protections against unreasonable search and seizure of one's personal documents or home, and the guarantee of due process.

Most American and European privacy law is based on a regime called Fair Information Practices (FIP) first set forth in a report written in 1973 by a federal government advisory committee (U.S. Department of Health, Education, and Welfare, 1973). **Fair Information Practices** (FIP) is a set of principles governing the collection and use of information about individuals. The five fair information practices principles are shown in Table 4.2.

Fair Information Practices (FIP) A set of principles originally set forth in 1973 that governs the collection and use of information about individuals and forms the basis of most U.S. and European privacy law.

FIP principles are based on the notion of a "mutuality of interest" among the record holder and the individual. The individual has an interest in engaging in a transaction, and the recordkeeper—usually a business or government agency—requires information about the individual to support the transaction. Once the information is gathered, the individual maintains an interest in the record, and the record may not be used to support other activities without the individual's consent.

Fair Information Practices form the basis of 13 federal statutes listed in Table 4.3 that set forth the conditions for handling information about individuals in such areas as credit reporting, education, financial records, newspaper records, cable communications, electronic communications, and even video rentals. The Privacy Act of 1974 is the most important of these laws, regulating the federal government's collection, use, and disclosure of information. Most of the federal privacy laws apply only to the federal government. Only credit, banking, cable, and video rental industries have been regulated by federal privacy law.

In the United States, privacy law is enforced by individuals who must sue agencies or companies in court in order to recover damages. European countries and Canada de-

Table 4.2 Fair Information Practices Principles

1. There should be no personal record systems whose existence is secret.

2. Individuals have rights of access, inspection, review, and amendment to systems that contain information about them.

3. There must be no use of personal information for purposes other than those for which it was gathered without prior consent.

4. Managers of systems are responsible and can be held accountable, and liable for the damage done by systems, for their reliability and security.

5. Governments have the right to intervene in the information relationships among private parties.

Table 4.3 Federal Privacy Laws in the United States

(1) General Federal Privacy Laws

Freedom of Information Act, 1968 as Amended (5 USC 552)

Privacy Act of 1974 as Amended (5 USC 552a)

Electronic Communications Privacy Act of 1986

Computer Matching and Privacy Protection Act of 1988

Computer Security Act of 1987

Federal Managers Financial Integrity Act of 1982

(2) Privacy Laws Affecting Private Institutions

Fair Credit Reporting Act, 1970

Family Educational Rights and Privacy Act of 1978

Right to Financial Privacy Act of 1978

Privacy Protection Act of 1980

Cable Communications Policy Act of 1984

Electronic Communications Privacy Act of 1986

Video Privacy Protection Act of 1988

---

fine privacy in a similar manner to that in the United States, but they have chosen to enforce their privacy laws by creating Privacy Commissions or Data Protection Agencies to pursue complaints brought by citizens.

Ethical Issues

The ethical privacy issue in this information age is as follows: Under what conditions should I (you) invade the privacy of others? What legitimates intruding into others' lives through unobtrusive surveillance, through market research, or by whatever means? Do we have to inform people that we are eavesdropping? Do we have to inform people that we are using credit history information for employment screening purposes?

Social Issues

The social issue of privacy concerns the development of "expectations of privacy," as well as public attitudes. In what areas of life should we as a society encourage people to think they are "in private territory" as opposed to public view? For instance, should we as a society encourage people to develop expectations of privacy when using electronic mail, cellular telephones, bulletin boards, the postal system, the workplace, the street? Should expectations of privacy be extended to criminal conspirators?

Political Issues

The political issue of privacy concerns the development of statutes that govern the relations between record keepers and individuals. Should we permit the FBI to prevent the commercial development of encrypted telephone transmissions so its agents can eavesdrop at will (Denning et al., 1993)? Should a law be passed to require direct marketing firms to obtain the consent of individuals before using their names in mass marketing (a consensus database)? Should e-mail privacy—regardless of who owns the equipment—be protected in law? In general, large organizations of all kinds—public and private—are reluctant to give up the advantages that come from the unfettered flow of information on individuals. Civil liberties and other private groups have been the strongest voices supporting restraints on large organizations' information-gathering activities.

PROPERTY RIGHTS: INTELLECTUAL PROPERTY

intellectual property Intangible property created by individuals or corporations that is subject to protections under trade secret, copyright, and patent law.

Contemporary information systems have severely challenged existing law and social practice that protect private intellectual property. **Intellectual property** is considered to be intangible property created by individuals or corporations. Information technology has made it difficult to protect intellectual property because computerized information can be so easily copied or distributed on networks. Intellectual property is subject to a variety of protections under three different legal traditions: trade secret, copyright, and patent law (Graham, 1984).

Trade Secrets

trade secret Any intellectual work or product used for a business purpose that can be classified as belonging to that business provided it is not based on information in the public domain.

Any intellectual work product—a formula, device, pattern, or compilation of data—used for a business purpose can be classified as a **trade secret**, provided it is not based on information in the public domain. Trade secrets have their basis in state law, not federal law, and protections vary from state to state. In general, trade secret laws grant a monopoly on the ideas behind a work product, but it can be a very tenuous monopoly.

Software that contains novel or unique elements, procedures, or compilations can be included as a trade secret. Trade secret law protects the actual ideas in a work product and not just their manifestation. In order to make this claim, the creator or owner must take care to bind employees and customers with nondisclosure agreements and to prevent the secret from falling into the public domain.

The limitation of trade secret protection is that while virtually all software programs of any complexity contain unique elements of some sort, it is difficult to prevent the ideas in the work from falling into the public domain when the software is widely distributed.

Copyright

copyright A statutory grant that protects creators of intellectual property against copying by others for any purpose for a period of 28 years.

Copyright is a statutory grant that protects creators of intellectual property against copying by others for any purpose for a period of 28 years. Since the first Federal Copyright Act of 1790, and the creation of the copyright office to register copyrights and enforce copyright law, Congress has extended copyright protection to books, periodicals, lectures, dramas, musical compositions, maps, drawings, artwork of any kind, and motion pictures. Since the earliest days, the congressional intent behind copyright laws has been to encourage creativity and authorship by ensuring that creative people receive the financial and other benefits of their work.

In the mid-1960s the Copyright Office began registering software programs, and in 1980 Congress passed the Computer Software Copyright Act, which clearly provides protection for software programs. It also sets forth the rights of the purchaser to use the software while the creator retains legal title.

Copyright protection is explicit and clear-cut: It protects against copying of entire programs or their parts. Damages and relief are readily obtained for infringement. The drawback to copyright protection is that the underlying ideas are not protected, only their manifestation in a work. A competitor can use your software, understand how it works, and build his or her own software that follows the same concepts without infringing on a copyright.

"Look and feel" copyright infringement lawsuits are precisely about the distinction between an idea and its expression. For instance, in the early 1990s Apple Computer sued Microsoft Corporation and Hewlett-Packard Inc. for infringement of the expression of Apple's Macintosh interface. Among other claims, Apple claimed that the defendants copied the expression of overlapping windows. The defendants counterclaimed that the idea of overlapping windows can be expressed in only a single way and therefore was not protectable under the "merger" doctrine of copyright law. When ideas and their expression merge, the expression cannot be copyrighted. In general, courts appear to be following the reasoning of a 1989 case—*Brown Bag Software* vs. *Symantec*—in which the court dissected the elements of software alleged to be infringing. The court found that neither similar concept, function, general functional features (e.g., drop-down menus), or colors are protectable by copyright law (*Brown Bag* vs. *Symantec Corp.*, 1992).

Patents

A **patent** grants the owner an exclusive monopoly on the ideas behind an invention for 17 years. The congressional intent behind patent law was to ensure that inventors of new machines, devices, or methods receive the full financial and other rewards of their labor and yet still make widespread use of the invention possible by providing detailed diagrams for those wishing to use the idea under license from the owner of the patent. The granting of a patent is determined by the Patent Office and relies on court rulings.

The key concepts in patent law are originality, novelty, and invention. The Patent Office did not accept applications for software patents routinely until a 1981 Supreme Court decision which held that computer programs could be a part of a patentable process. Since then, hundreds of patents have been granted, and thousands await consideration.

The strength of patent protection is that it grants a monopoly on the underlying concepts and ideas of software. The difficulty is passing stringent criteria of non-obviousness (e.g., the work must reflect some special understanding and contribution), originality, and novelty, as well as years of waiting to receive protection.

Contemporary information technologies, especially software, pose a severe challenge to existing intellectual property regimes and therefore create significant ethical, social, and political issues. Digital media differ from books, periodicals, and other media in terms of ease of replication; ease of transmission; ease of alteration; difficulty classifying a software work as a program, book, or even music; compactness—making theft easy and making difficulties in establishing uniqueness. (See Samuelson, October 1991.) Publishers worry that even traditional hard-copy books themselves can no longer be protected because it has become so easy to distribute published material over the Internet (Carvajal, 1996).

> **patent** A legal document that grants the owner an exclusive monopoly on the ideas behind an invention for 17 years; designed to ensure that inventors of new machines or methods are rewarded for their labor while making widespread use of their inventions.

Ethical Issues

The central ethical issue posed to individuals concerns copying software: Should I (you) copy for our own use a piece of software protected by trade secret, copyright, and/or patent law? In the information age, it is so easy to obtain perfect, functional copies of software that the software companies themselves have abandoned software protection schemes to increase market penetration, and enforcement of the law is rare. However, if everyone copied software, very little new software would be produced because creators could not benefit from the results of their work.

Social Issues

Several property-related social issues are raised by new information technology. Most experts agree that the current intellectual property laws are breaking down in the information age. The ease with which software can be copied contributes to making us a society of lawbreakers. In 1990, the Software Publishers Association (SPA) estimates it lost $2.4 billion or half the total of $5.7 billion in software sales, and copied software is routinely found in both personal and business settings (Markoff, July 27, 1992). These routine thefts threaten significantly to reduce the speed with which new information technologies can be and will be introduced and thereby threaten further advances in productivity and social well-being.

Political Issues

The main property-related political issue concerns the creation of new property protection measures to protect investments made by creators of new software. Apple, Microsoft, and 900 other hardware and software firms formed the Software Publishers

Window on Organizations

A CORPORATE SOFTWARE CODE OF ETHICS

This code of ethics is to state our organization's policy concerning software duplication. All employees shall use software only in accordance with the license agreement. Unless otherwise provided in the license, any duplication of licensed software except for backup and archival purposes is a violation of the law. Any unauthorized duplication of copyrighted computer software violates the law and is contrary to the organization's standards of conduct. The following points are to be followed in order to comply with software license agreements.

1. We will use all software in accordance with our license agreements.
2. Legitimate software will promptly be provided to all employees who need it. No employee of the company will make any unauthorized copies of any software under any circumstances. Anyone found copying software other than for backup purposes is subject to termination.
3. We will not tolerate the use of any unauthorized copies of software in our company. Any person illegally reproducing software can be subject to civil and criminal penalties including fines and imprisonment. We do not condone illegal copying of software under any circumstances and anyone who makes, uses, or otherwise acquires unauthorized software shall be appropriately disciplined.
4. No employee shall give software to any outsiders (including clients, customers, and others).

To Think About: Try to find out your university's policy regarding software. Is there a software code of ethics on campus? If an employee finds routine copying of software in a firm, should he or she (a) call the firm's legal counsel or (b) call SPA on its anti-piracy hotline? Are there any circumstances in which software copying should be allowed?

5. Any employee who determines that there may be a misuse of software within the company shall notify their Department Manager or legal counsel.
6. All software used by the organization on company computers will be properly purchased through appropriate procedures.

I have read the company's software code of ethics. I am fully aware of our software policies and agree to abide by those policies.

Source: *Software Management Guide: A Guide for Software Asset Management,* version 1.0. Courtesy of Software Publishers Association, 1992.

Association (SPA) to lobby for new protection laws and to enforce existing laws. The SPA has developed a model Software Code of Ethics, which is described in the first Window on Organizations.

Allied against SPA are a host of groups and millions of individuals who resist efforts to strengthen anti-piracy laws and instead encourage situations where software can be copied. These groups believe that software should be free, that anti-piracy laws cannot in any event be enforced in the digital age, or that software should be paid for on a voluntary basis (shareware software). According to these groups, the greater social benefit results from the free distribution of software, and the "benefits" of software should accrue to the creators in the form of greater prestige, perhaps, but not in the form of profits.

ACCOUNTABILITY, LIABILITY, AND CONTROL

Along with privacy and property laws, new information technologies are challenging existing liability law and social practices for holding individuals and institutions accountable. If a person is injured by a machine controlled in part by software, who should be held accountable and therefore held liable? Should a public bulletin board or an electronic service like Prodigy or CompuServe permit the transmission of pornographic or offensive material (as broadcasters), or should they be held harmless against any liability for what users transmit (as is true of common carriers like the telephone system)? What about the Internet? If you outsource your information processing, can you hold the external vendor liable for injuries done to your customers? Try some real-world examples.

Some Recent Liability Problems

On March 13, 1993, a blizzard hit the east coast of the United States, knocking out an EDS (Electronic Data Systems Inc.) computer center in Clifton, New Jersey. The center operated 5,200 automatic teller machines in 12 different networks across the country involving more than one million card holders. In the two weeks required to recover operations, EDS informed its customers to use alternative ATM networks operated by other banks or computer centers and offered to cover more than $50 million in cash withdrawals. Because the alternative networks did not have access to the actual customer account balances, EDS is at substantial risk of fraud. Cash withdrawals were limited to $100 per day per customer to reduce the exposure. Most service was restored by March 26. Although EDS had a disaster recovery plan, it did not have a dedicated backup facility. Who is liable for any economic harm caused individuals or businesses that could not access their full account balances in this period (Joes, 1993)?

In April 1990, a computer system at Shell Pipeline Corporation failed to detect a human operator error. As a result, 93,000 barrels of crude oil were shipped to the wrong trader. The error cost $2 million because the trader sold oil that should not have been delivered to him. A court ruled later that Shell Pipeline was liable for the loss of the oil because the error was due to a human operator who entered erroneous information into the system. Shell was held liable for not developing a system that would prevent the possibility of misdeliveries (King, 1992). Whom would you have held liable—Shell Pipeline? The trader for not being more careful about deliveries? The human operator who made the error?

These cases point out the difficulties faced by information systems executives who ultimately are responsible for the harm done by systems developed by their staffs. In general, insofar as computer software is part of a machine, and the machine injures someone physically or economically, the producer of the software and the operator can be held liable for damages. Insofar as the software acts more like a book, storing and displaying information, courts have been reluctant to hold authors, publishers, and booksellers liable for content (the exception being instances of fraud or defamation), and hence courts have been wary of holding software authors liable for "book-like" software.

In general, it is very difficult (if not impossible) to hold software producers liable for their software products when those products are considered like books, regardless of the physical or economic harm that results. Historically, print publishers, books, and periodicals have not been held liable because of fears that liability claims would interfere with First Amendment rights guaranteeing freedom of expression.

What about "software as service"? Automatic teller machines are a service provided to bank customers. Should this service fail, customers will be inconvenienced and perhaps harmed economically if they cannot access their funds in a timely manner. Should liability protections be extended to software publishers and operators of defective financial, accounting, simulation, or marketing systems?

Software is very different from books. Software users may develop expectations of infallibility about software; software is less easily inspected than a book and more difficult to compare with other software products for quality; and software claims actually to perform a task rather than describe a task like a book. People come to depend on services essentially based on software. Given the centrality of software to everyday life, the chances are excellent that liability law will extend its reach to include software even when it merely provides an information service.

Telephone systems have not been held liable for the messages transmitted because they are regulated "common carriers." In return for their monopoly on telephone service, they must provide access to all, at reasonable rates, and achieve acceptable reliability. But broadcasters and cable television systems are subject to a wide variety of federal and local constraints on content and facilities.

Liability and accountability are also at the heart of debates over the responsibility and freedoms of computer bulletin boards and networks. The second Window on

Window on Organizations

LIABILITY ON THE INTERNET

How exposed is an organization with an Internet site to liability suits? How can it protect itself from such suits? We cannot answer this question with any certainty because telecommunications liability is a newly developing field. However, companies linked to the Internet may have exposure for such areas as libel, copyright infringement, pornography, and fraud.

When will your organization be held liable for content on its World Wide Web site? Clearly the Web site owner can be held liable for objectionable content if that content was posted by its own organization, whether or not management authorized it. For example, if an employee posts libelous material without authorization, the company may still be responsible. However, responsibility may not end there. On-line services such as Prodigy and CompuServe and many Web sites may be liable for postings by their customers or visitors. A court recently awarded Stratton Oakmont, a New York investment bank, $200 million from Prodigy after determining that a Prodigy subscriber posted libelous statements. The court compared Prodigy to a publisher, which has editorial control over content, because Prodigy screens all postings for unacceptable words. This ruling would probably have held CompuServe blameless for subscribers' statements because it does not screen messages before posting and so would be considered like a bookstore, which has no editorial control.

Many companies fear being held responsible for content on someone else's site. Some Web sites contain *hot buttons*—electronic links to other sites. Some believe that the site with the hot button can be held liable for content on the screen that the consumer reaches using that hot button. For this reason, AMR Corporation (parent to American Airlines) prohibits any hot link on its site.

Another major question is jurisdiction—can a viewer of content in one jurisdiction sue an owner for content located in a different jurisdiction? For example, can a viewer in New York sue a Web site located in California if that site contains pornographic materials? Amateur Action, a computer bulletin board in Milpitis, California, was convicted under Tennessee state

> **To Think About:** What management, organization, and technology issues should be addressed by companies trying to prevent libelous or offensive material from being distributed through the Internet?

pornography laws, which have tougher standards than those of California.

The global reach of the Internet adds new challenges. A scathing on-line message that may be protected under the First Amendment in the United States could be considered libelous in Great Britain, Canada, or Australia, which have more restrictions on free speech.

Companies can take some protective steps, such as seeking legal advice prior to establishing a Web site; adopting clear and well-publicized guidelines that limit what employees can post; enforcing guidelines by punishing offenders; and posting disclaimer notices on the site. For example, *Penthouse* magazine's Web site warns visitors of potentially offensive adult materials; it also warns visitors not to proceed if they are "accessing . . . from any country or locality where adult material is specifically prohibited by law," and the site lists 25 such countries.

Sources: Kate Maddox and Clinton Wilder, "Net Liability," *Information Week*, January 8, 1996; Mitch Betts, Ellis Booker, and Gary H. Anthes, "On-line Boundaries Unclear," *Computerworld*, June 5, 1995.

Organizations describes recent lawsuits seeking to establish liability of bulletin board providers and users of the Internet.

Ethical Issues

The central liability-related ethical issue raised by new information technologies is whether or not individuals and organizations that create, produce, and sell systems (both hardware and software) are morally responsible for the consequences of their use. (See Johnson and Mulvey, 1995.) If so, under what conditions? What liabilities (and responsibilities) should the user assume, and what should the provider assume?

Social Issues

The central liability-related social issue concerns the expectations that society should allow to develop around service-providing information systems. Should individuals and organizations be held strictly liable for system services they provide? If organizations are held strictly liable, what impact will this have on the development of new system services? Can society permit networks and bulletin boards to post libelous, inaccurate, and misleading information that will harm many persons? Or should information service companies become self-regulating, self-censoring?

Political Issues

The leading liability-related political issue is the debate between information providers of all kinds (from software developers to network service providers) who want to be relieved of liability insofar as possible (thereby maximizing their profits), and service users—individuals, organizations, communities—who want organizations to be held responsible for providing high-quality system services (thereby maximizing the quality of service). Service providers argue that they will withdraw from the marketplace if they are held liable, while service users argue that only by holding providers liable can we guarantee a high level of service and compensate injured parties. Should legislation impose liability or restrict liability on service providers? This fundamental cleavage is at the heart of numerous political and judicial conflicts.

SYSTEM QUALITY: DATA QUALITY AND SYSTEM ERRORS

The debate over liability and accountability for unintentional consequences of system use raises a related but independent moral dimension: What is an acceptable, technologically feasible level of system quality (see Chapter 14)? At what point should system managers say, "Stop testing, we've done all we can to perfect this software. Ship it."? Individuals and organizations may be held responsible for avoidable consequences—foreseeable consequences—which they have a duty to perceive and correct. And there is a gray area: Some system errors are foreseeable and correctable only at very great expense, an expense so great that pursuing this level of perfection is not feasible economically—no one could afford the product. For example, although software companies try to debug their products before releasing them for sale, they knowingly ship buggy products because the time and cost to fix all minor errors would prevent these products from ever being released (Rigdon, 1995). What if the product were not offered on the marketplace—would social welfare as a whole not advance and perhaps even decline? Carrying this further, just what is the responsibility of a producer of computer services—should the producer withdraw the product that can never be perfect, warn the user, or forget about the risk (let the buyer beware)?

Three principal sources of poor system performance are software bugs and errors, hardware or facility failures due to natural or other causes, and poor input data quality. Chapter 14 shows why zero defects in software code of any complexity cannot be achieved and the seriousness of remaining bugs cannot be estimated. Hence, there is a technological barrier to perfect software, and users must be aware of the potential for catastrophic failure. The software industry has not yet arrived at testing standards for producing software of acceptable but not perfect performance (Collins et al., 1994).

While software bugs and facility catastrophe are likely to be widely reported in the press, by far the most common source of business system failure is data quality. A total of 70% of IS executives in a recent survey reported data corruption as a source of business delay, 69% said their corporate data accuracy was unacceptable, and 44% said no systems were in place to check database information quality (Wilson, 1992). Table 4.4 describes some of these data quality problems.

Ethical Issues

The central quality-related ethical issue raised by information systems is: At what point should I (or you) release software or services for consumption by others? At what point can you conclude that your software or service achieves an economically and technologically adequate level of quality? What are you obliged to know about the quality of your software, its procedures for testing, and its operational characteristics?

| Table 4.4 | Illustrative Reported Data Quality Problems |

- An airline inadvertently corrupted its database of passenger reservations while installing new software, and for months planes took off with half loads.

- A manufacturer attempted to reorganize its customer files by customer number only to discover that the sales staff had been entering a new customer number for each sale because of special incentives for opening new accounts. One customer was entered 7,000 times. The company scrapped the software project after spending $1 million.

- J. P. Morgan, a New York bank, discovered that 40% of the data in its credit-risk management database was incomplete, necessitating double-checking by users.

- Several studies have established that 5–12% of bar code sales at retail grocery and merchandise chains are erroneous and that the ratio of overcharges to undercharges runs as high as 5:1, with 4:1 as a norm. The problem tends to be human error in keeping shelf prices accurate and corporate policy that fails to allocate sufficient resources to price checking, auditing, and development of error-free policies. The cause of the high overcharge has not yet been determined, but the pattern is disturbing, suggesting intentional behavior.

Sources: William M. Bulkeley, "Databases Plagued by a Reign of Error," *The Wall Street Journal* (May 26, 1992); Doug Bartholomew, "The Price Is Wrong," *Information Week* (September 14, 1992).

Social Issues

The leading quality-related social issue once again deals with expectations: Do we want as a society to encourage people to believe that systems are infallible, that data errors are impossible? Or do we instead want a society where people are openly skeptical and questioning of the output of machines, where people are at least informed of the risk? By heightening awareness of system failure, do we inhibit the development of all systems that in the end contribute to social well-being?

Political Issues

The leading quality-related political issue concerns the laws of responsibility and accountability. Should Congress establish or direct the National Institute of Science and Technology (NIST) to develop quality standards (software, hardware, data quality) and impose those standards on industry? Or should industry associations be encouraged to develop industry-wide standards of quality? Or should Congress wait for the marketplace to punish poor system quality, recognizing that in some instances this will not work (e.g., if all retail grocers maintain poor quality systems, then customers have no alternatives)?

QUALITY OF LIFE: EQUITY, ACCESS, BOUNDARIES

The negative social costs of introducing information technologies and systems are beginning to mount along with the power of the technology. Many of these negative social consequences are not violations of individual rights, nor are they property crimes. Nevertheless, these negative consequences can be extremely harmful to individuals, societies, and political institutions. Computers and information technologies potentially can destroy valuable elements of our culture and society even while they bring us benefits. If there is a balance of good and bad consequences to the use of information systems, whom do we hold responsible for the bad consequences? In the following paragraphs, we briefly examine just some of the negative social consequences of systems, considering individual, social responses, and political responses.

Balancing Power: Center Versus Periphery

One of the earliest fears of the computer age was that huge, centralized mainframe computers would centralize power at corporate headquarters and in the nation's capital, resulting in a "Big Brother" society as suggested in George Orwell's novel *1984*. The shift toward highly decentralized computing in the 1990s and the decentralization of decision making to lower organizational levels has reduced fears of power centralization in institutions. Yet much of the "empowerment" described in popular business magazines is trivial. Lower-level employees may be empowered to make minor decisions, but the key policy decisions may be as centralized as in the past.

Rapidity of Change: Reduced Response Time to Competition

Information systems have helped to create much more efficient national and international markets. The now more efficient global marketplace has reduced the normal social buffers that permitted businesses many years to adjust to competition. "Time-based competition" has an ugly side: The business you work for may not have enough time to respond to global competitors and may be wiped out in a year, along with your job. We stand the risk of developing a "just-in-time society" with "just-in-time jobs" and "just-in-time" workplaces, families, and vacations.

Maintaining Boundaries: Family, Work, Leisure

Parts of this book were produced on trains, planes, as well as on family "vacations," and what otherwise might have been "family" time. The danger to ubiquitous computing, telecommuting, nomad computing, and the "do anything anywhere" computing environment is that it might actually come to pass. If so, the traditional boundaries that separate work from family and just plain leisure will be weakened. The advent of information systems, coupled with the growth of knowledge work occupations, means that more and more people will be working when traditionally they would have been playing or communicating with family and friends. The "work umbrella" now extends far beyond the eight-hour day.

Weakening these institutions poses clear-cut risks. Family and friends historically have provided powerful support mechanisms for individuals, and they act as balance points in a society by preserving "private life," providing a place for one to collect one's thoughts, think in ways contrary to one's employer, and to dream.

Dependence and Vulnerability

Our businesses, governments, schools, and private associations like houses of worship are incredibly dependent now on information systems and therefore highly vulnerable.

While people may enjoy the convenience of working at home, the "do anything anywhere" computing environment can blur the traditional boundaries between work and family time.

Table 4.5	The Largest Information System Catastrophes		
Date	Event	Location	Number of Data Centers Affected
8/14/87	Flood	Chicago	64
5/8/88	Network outage	Hinsdale, Ill.	175
5/11/88	Pakistani virus	nationwide	90+
11/2/88	Internet virus	nationwide	500+
10/17/89	Earthquake	San Francisco	90
8/13/90	Power outage	New York	320
4/13/92	Flood	Chicago	400
5/1/92	Riot	Los Angeles	50
8/24/92	Hurricane Andrew	southeast	150
3/15/93	Blizzard	east coast	50

Sources: "Days of Infamy: The 10 Worst IT Disasters," *Information Week*, January 10, 1994; "The Largest System Catastrophes," *Information Week*, March 8, 1993.

Table 4.5 lists the biggest system disasters culled from a list of more than 300 begun in 1987. With systems now as ubiquitous as the telephone system, it is startling to remember that there are no regulatory or standard-setting forces in place similar to telephone, electrical, radio, television, or other public utility technologies. The absence of standards and the critical nature of some system applications will probably call forth demands for national standards, perhaps regulatory oversight.

Computer Crime and Abuse

Many new technologies in the industrial era have created new opportunities for committing crime. Technologies, including computers, create new valuable things to steal, new ways to steal them, and new ways to harm others. **Computer crime** can be defined as the commission of illegal acts through the use of a computer or against a computer system. Computers or computer systems can be the object of the crime (destroying a company's computer center or a company's computer files) as well as the instrument of a crime (stealing computer lists by illegally gaining access to a computer system using a home microcomputer). Simply accessing a computer system without authorization, or intent to do harm, even by accident, is now a federal crime. **Computer abuse** is the commission of acts involving a computer that may not be illegal but are considered unethical.

computer crime The commission of illegal acts through the use of a computer or against a computer system.

computer abuse The commission of acts involving a computer that may not be illegal but are considered unethical.

No one knows the magnitude of the computer crime problem—how many systems are invaded, how many people engage in the practice, or what is the total economic damage. Many companies are reluctant to report computer crimes because they may involve employees. The most economically damaging kinds of computer crime are introducing viruses, theft of services, disruption of computer systems, and theft of telecommunications services. Computer crime has been estimated to cost more than $1 billion in the United States, and an additional billion dollars if corporate and cellular phone theft is included.

Computer viruses (see Chapter 14) have grown exponentially during the past decade: More than 1,000 viruses have been documented. The average corporate loss for a bad virus outbreak is $250,000, and the probability of a large corporation's experiencing a significant computer virus infection in a single year is 50% according to some experts. While many firms now use anti-virus software, the proliferation of computer networks will surely increase the probability of infections.

The following list describes some illustrative computer crimes.

- "Hacker" Robert T. Morris, a computer science student at Cornell University, unleashed a computer virus over the Internet network on November 2, 1988, jamming thousands of machines in tens of networks throughout the system. He was convicted under the Computer Fraud and Abuse Act and given three years' probation, a $10,000 fine, and 400 hours of community service.
- In July 1992, a Federal grand jury indicted a national network of 1,000 hackers calling themselves MOD—Masters of Deception. Theirs was one of the largest thefts of computer information and services in history. The hackers were charged with computer tampering, computer fraud, wire fraud, illegal wiretapping, and conspiracy. The group broke into more than 25 of the largest corporate computer systems in the United States, including Equifax, Inc. (a credit reporting firm with 170 million records), Southwestern Bell Corporation, New York Telephone, and Pacific Bell. The group stole and resold credit reports, credit card numbers, and other personal information. The firms blamed their own lax security and a philosophy of "openness" for not detecting the hackers themselves, all of whom were under 22 years of age. The hackers all pled guilty. Their convicted leader, Mark Abene, spent 10 months in prison (Gabriel, 1995; Tabor, 1992).
- At AT&T's British headquarters in London, three technicians set up their company in 1992, assigned it a 900 number, and then programmed AT&T computers to dial the number often. The loss amounted to just under $500,000 before the fraud was accidentally detected.

In general, it is employees—insiders—who have inflicted the most injurious computer crimes because they have the knowledge, access, and frequently a job-related motive to commit such crimes.

Congress responded to the threat of computer crime in 1986 with the Computer Fraud and Abuse Act. This act makes it illegal to access a computer system without authorization. Most of the states have similar laws, and nations in Europe have similar legislation. Other existing legislation covering wiretapping, fraud, and conspiracy by any means, regardless of the technology employed, is adequate to cover computer crimes committed so far.

Employment: Trickle-Down Technology and Reengineering Job Loss

Reengineering work (see Chapter 10) is typically hailed in the information systems community as a major benefit of new information technology. It is much less frequently noted that redesigning business processes could potentially cause millions of middle-level managers and clerical workers to lose their jobs. One economist has raised the possibility that we will create a society run by a small "high tech elite of corporate professionals . . . in a nation of the permanently unemployed" (Rifkin, 1993). Some have estimated that if reengineering were seriously undertaken by the Fortune 1000 companies, about 25% of the U.S. labor force could be displaced. Reengineering has been seriously used at only 15% of American service and manufacturing companies, and the average reduction in employment in downsizing companies is 10% in a year. However, the effects of reengineering may be growing, leaving management with a serious ethical dilemma, as the first Window on Management illustrates.

Economists are much more sanguine about the potential job losses. They believe that relieving bright, educated workers from reengineered jobs will result in these workers' moving to better jobs in fast-growth industries. Left out of this equation are blue-collar workers and older, less well-educated middle managers. It is not clear that these groups can be retrained easily for high-quality (high-paying) jobs. Careful planning and sensitivity to employee needs can help companies redesign work to minimize job losses.

Equity and Access: Increasing Racial and Social Class Cleavages

Does everyone have an equal opportunity to participate in the digital age? Will the social, economic, and cultural gaps that exist in American and other societies be reduced

> **Window on Management**
>
> ## WHITHER THE DOWNSIZED SOCIETY?
>
> One impact of "leaner and meaner," more competitive organizations may be large-scale unemployment, even during a period of robust economic growth. The choice corporate managements have been facing is often productivity versus employment, and frequently the enabling tool is information technology.
>
> Pacific Bell (PacBell), a regional telephone unit of Pacific Telesis Group, has found a simple piece of technology that will save $2 million a day. Until recently PacBell had to send out a truck for every customer telephone outage report in order to determine whether the outage was in telephone lines it owned or in lines owned by the customer. Twenty thousand of these reports per day, costing $140 per truck, resulted in the discovery that the problem was in the customers' lines, not PacBell's line. Eliminating these unnecessary trips would save millions. The solution? PacBell is installing a $10 circuit box at every point where PacBell's lines join a customer's line. PacBell can send a test signal to the circuit box to determine which line is faulty. PacBell no longer needs to dispatch a $140 truck (unless it is a company line problem). While one result is a savings for the company of an estimated $2 million per day, another result is the loss of thousands of line repair and truck maintenance jobs.
>
> Aetna Insurance is eliminating 4,000 jobs of a total workforce of 42,000, through automation of the policy-issuing function. Between installing automated teller machines (ATMs) and bank-by-phone computers, banks have reduced the number of tellers from 480,000 in 1983 to 301,000 in 1994. Computer and telecommunications technology are being used to read customer meters, eliminating many meter-reader jobs. All told, the evidence indicates that the work force of the 500 largest manufacturing companies in the United States has dropped by one-third since 1979 (a loss of more than 5 million jobs).
>
> **To Think About:** Does management have any obligation to maintain jobs and the skills of its current employees when considering downsizing through technology-based productivity increases? If so, what criteria should it use in making such decisions?
>
> No one doubts that higher productivity is critical to the survival of many companies. Nonetheless, the trend toward job reduction raises serious questions. Most of the workers whose positions are eliminated through technology will need other jobs—jobs that may not be immediately available. How do these millions of people survive between jobs? How will the economy survive if the total number of jobs is reduced or if high-paying skilled jobs are replaced by low-paying service jobs? What is the responsibility of management and the government for replacing these lost jobs and for building the skills of our citizens so that the economy can continue to thrive and serve all the people?
>
> Sources: A. M. Rosenthal, "The Real Revolution," *The New York Times* (January 6, 1995); Marc Levinson, "Thanks. You're Fired," *Newsweek* (May 23, 1994); Joan E. Rigdon, "Technological Gains Are Cutting Costs, and Jobs, in Services," *The Wall Street Journal* (February 24, 1994).

by information systems technology? Or will the cleavages be increased, permitting the "better off" to become still better off? When and if computing becomes ubiquitous, will it include the poor as well as the rich?

The answers to these questions are clearly not known, as the differential impact of systems technology on various groups in society has not been well studied. What is known is that information and knowledge, and access to these resources through educational institutions and public libraries, are inequitably distributed. Access to computers is distributed inequitably along racial and social class lines, as are many other information resources. If this situation is left uncorrected, we could end up creating a society of information haves, computer literate and skilled, versus a large group of information have-nots, computer illiterate and unskilled.

Health Risks: RSI, CVS, and Technostress

repetitive stress injury (RSI)
Occupational disease that occurs when muscle groups are forced through many of the same, repetitive actions with high-impact loads or thousands of repetitions with low-impact loads.

The most important occupational disease today is **repetitive stress injury (RSI)**, representing 56% of all workplace maladies. RSI occurs when muscle groups are forced through the same repetitive actions often with high-impact loads (like tennis) or tens of thousands of repetitions under low-impact loads (like working at a computer keyboard).

The single largest source of RSI is computer keyboards. Forty-six million Americans use computers at work, and 185,000 cases of RSI are reported each year, according to

Repetitive stress injury (RSI) is the leading occupational disease today. The single largest cause of RSI is computer keyboard work.

the National Center for Health Statistics. The most common kind of computer-related RSI is **carpal tunnel syndrome (CTS),** in which pressure on the median nerve through the wrist's bony structure, called a "carpal tunnel," produces pain. The pressure is caused by constant repetition of keystrokes: In a single shift, a word processor may perform 23,000 keystrokes. Symptoms of carpal tunnel syndrome include numbness, shooting pain, inability to grasp objects, and tingling. So far, 1.89 million workers have been diagnosed with carpal tunnel syndrome.

RSI is avoidable. Designing workstations for a neutral wrist position (using a wrist rest to support the wrist), proper monitor stands, and footrests all contribute to proper posture and reduced RSI. New ergonomically correct keyboards are also an option, although their efficacy has yet to be clearly established. These measures should be backed up by frequent rest breaks, rotation of employees to different jobs, and moving toward voice or scanner data entry. RSI presents a serious challenge to management, as the second Window on Management illustrates.

RSI is not the only occupational illness caused by computers: back and neck pain, leg stress, and foot pain also result from poor ergonomic designs of workstations (see Tables 4.6 and 4.7).

Computer vision syndrome (CVS) refers to any eye strain condition related to computer display screen use. Its symptoms are headaches, blurred vision, and dry and irritated eyes. The symptoms are usually temporary (Furger, 1993).

The newest computer-related malady is **technostress,** defined as a computer use–induced stress whose symptoms are irritation, hostility toward humans, impatience, and

carpal tunnel syndrome (CTS) Type of RSI in which pressure on the median nerve through the wrist's bony carpal tunnel structure produces pain.

computer vision syndrome (CVS) Eye strain condition related to computer display screen use, with symptoms including headaches, blurred vision, and dry, irritated eyes.

technostress Stress induced by computer use whose symptoms include irritation, hostility toward humans, impatience, and enervation.

Table 4.6 OSHA Ergonomic Risk Factors

Intermittent keying

Intensive keying

Neck twisting/bending

Wrist bending

Prolonged mouse use

Prolonged sitting

Sitting without solid foot support

Lighting (poor illumination or glare)

Source: Mary E. Thyfault, "OSHA Clamps Down," *InformationWeek* (November 21, 1994).

Window on Management

MANAGING RSI

In December 1994, Chase Manhattan Bank N.A. announced a $2 million comprehensive program meant to prevent strain injuries (RSI) despite the lack of any signs of a rise in workers' compensation cases from RSI. The Chase RSI prevention program will include a 90-minute training session on ergonomics for all of its 34,000 employees worldwide. Employees will all be given adjustable chairs and will be offered the option to be given a telephone operator headset, an anti-glare screen for each computer, and a chair support. Chase is also experimenting with the Microsoft Corp. Natural Keyboard, which Microsoft claims was designed after extensive ergonomic and usability research).

Other corporate programs have been established to address the issue of RSI. For example, Levi Strauss & Co., the San Francisco-based clothing manufacturer, has set up a cross-department office ergonomics team that meets monthly to implement ergonomic strategy. The team even publishes an ergonomics newsletter.

Why all of this activity? One answer is the threat of lawsuits. The most serious lawsuits have been product liability cases filed against the manufacturers of computer equipment, particularly keyboard producers. Such lawsuits tend to focus on the failure of manufacturers to warn users of potential dangers in the use of their products.

In a few cases employees are suing their employers for their failure to carry workers' compensation that covers RSI-afflicted workers. Most employers, however, are shielded from any lawsuits because state workmen's compensation laws remove liability from companies and pay workers directly for lost income. The effect of all of the lawsuits is uncertain. Although several thousand suits have been filed, very few of them have made their way through the courts to a decision.

Despite all of this activity, the actual risk posed by computer technology is unclear. Some experts claim that RSI is caused by

To Think About: *If you were a corporate vice president with responsibility for corporate safety, what policies would you recommend to your CEO regarding RSI? Explain your recommendations.*

one factor, the keyboard. Others think that it is a combination of factors. Despite its decision to place warnings on its keyboards, Compaq Computer claims that there are no scientific studies proving a link between keyboards and hand and arm disorders such as CTS.

What about solutions? Many manufacturers are now producing ergonomic products such as keyboards, arm rests, and wrist splints. For instance, more than 20 manufacturers are producing wrist braces. Lexmark International has just introduced another ergonomic keyboard, the Select-Ease Keyboard, which is split down the middle. The user is able to set each half of the keyboard at the appropriate, comfortable angle needed for that hand. A recent survey of large corporations concluded that 92% of such companies include wrist braces in their safety programs.

Sources: Linda Himelstein, "The Asbestos Case of the 1990s?" *Business Week* (January 6, 1995); Mitch Betts, "Jury's Still Out on Worth of Stress-Injury Gadgets," *Computerworld* (June 6, 1994); Edward Cone, "Cause and Effect," *Information Week* (June 27, 1994); "Keyboard Injuries, Who Should Pay?" *Information Week* (June 27, 1994).

---

enervation. The problem according to experts is that humans working continually with computers come to expect other humans and human institutions to behave like computers, providing instant response, attentiveness, and with an absence of emotion. Computer-intense workers are irritated when put on hold during a phone call, become incensed or alarmed when their PCs take a few seconds longer to perform a task, lack

Table 4.7 Computer-Related Diseases

Disease/Risk	Incidence
RSI	185,000 new cases a year
Other joint diseases	Unknown
Computer vision syndrome	10 million cases a year
Miscarriage	Unknown. Related to manufacturing chemicals
Technostress	5–10 million cases
VDT radiation	Unknown impacts

empathy for humans, and seek out friends who mirror the characteristics of their machines. Technostress is thought to be related to high levels of job turnover in the computer industry, high levels of early retirement from computer-intense occupations, and elevated levels of drug and alcohol abuse.

The incidence of technostress is not known but is thought to be in the millions in the United States and growing rapidly. Although frequently denied as a problem by management, computer-related jobs now top the list of stressful occupations based on health statistics in several industrialized countries. The costs worldwide of stress are put at $200 billion.

To date the role of radiation from computer display screens in occupational disease has not been proven. Video display terminals (VDTs) emit non-ionizing electric and magnetic fields at low frequencies. These rays enter the body and have unknown effects on enzymes, molecules, chromosomes, and cell membranes. Early studies suggesting a link between low-level EMFs (electromagnetic fields) and miscarriages have been contradicted by one later, superior study published in 1991 (Schnorr, 1991; Stevens, 1991). Longer-term studies are investigating low-level EMFs and birth defects, stress, low birth weight, and other diseases. All manufacturers have reduced display screen emissions since the early years of the 1980s, and European countries like Sweden have adopted very stiff radiation emission standards.

The computer has become a part of our lives—personally as well as socially, culturally, and politically. It is unlikely that the issues and our choices will become easier as information technology continues to transform our world. The development of a national electronic superhighway described in the Window on Technology suggests that all the ethical and social issues we have described will be heightened further as we move into the first digital century.

MANAGEMENT ACTIONS: A CORPORATE CODE OF ETHICS

Many corporations have developed far-reaching corporate IS codes of ethics—among them Federal Express, IBM, American Express, and Merck and Co. But most firms have not developed these codes of ethics, which leaves them at the mercy of fate and their employees in the dark about expected correct behavior. There is some dispute concerning a general code of ethics (about 40% of the American Fortune 500 firms have such codes) versus a specific information systems code of ethics (about 40% of Fortune 500 firms). As managers, you should strive to develop an IS-specific set of ethical standards for each of the five moral dimensions.

- *Information rights and obligations.* A code should cover topics like employee e-mail privacy, workplace monitoring, treatment of corporate information, and policies on customer information.
- *Property rights and obligations.* A code should cover topics like software licenses, ownership of firm data and facilities, ownership of software created by employees on company hardware, and software copyrights. Specific guidelines for contractual relationships with third parties should be covered as well.
- *Accountability and control.* The code should specify a single individual responsible for all information systems, and underneath this individual should be others who are responsible for individual rights, the protection of property rights, system quality, and quality of life (e.g., job design, ergonomics, employee satisfaction). Responsibilities for control of systems, audits, and management should be clearly defined. The potential liabilities of systems officers, and the corporation, should be detailed in a separate document.
- *System quality.* The code should describe the general levels of data quality and system error that can be tolerated, with detailed specifications left to specific projects. The code should require that all systems attempt to estimate data quality and system error probabilities.

Window on Technology

THE COMING OF A NATIONAL DIGITAL SUPERHIGHWAY RAISES MANY ETHICAL AND SOCIAL ISSUES

In 1989, Congress passed the High Performance Computing Act, which provided $3 billion to spur the development of supercomputer centers in the United States and a very high-capacity network called the National Research Education Network (NREN) to connect universities and research centers. Vice President Al Gore and President Bill Clinton then suggested a much larger-scale national computing network to connect individuals, businesses, libraries, research centers, and universities. The proposed national computing network would be a network of networks similar to the Internet, capable of delivering data, voice, and video images rapidly to the household.

Here are just some projected benefits: Students could do research using the Library of Congress, or any library in the country, with full text retrieval possible; medical care would improve because patient records could be transferred anywhere they were needed; remote diagnosis by faraway specialists would be possible; scientists and engineers around the world could cooperate on the design of new products; working at home would be common because there would be as much information at home as in the office.

Briefly, the social impact of a national supernetwork is likely to be as great as that of the building of the transcontinental railway and the interstate highway system combined. The national computing network requires rewiring America with high-capacity fiberoptic cable to the household or neighborhood switch (from which ordinary twisted wire can be used to transmit into individual households); new hardware switches and/or upgrading the existing telephone system; and new software. The cost: hundreds of billions of dollars.

Who should build the network (and pay for it)? Owners of existing networks—like AT&T and other long distance companies—want the government to stay out and instead want to evolve the telephone network and existing technologies. Critics charge that the phone companies will never invest the money needed or they might charge so much that universities, libraries, and homeowners could not afford to use the network.

To Think About: Who should build the national computing network? Is it in the interests of U.S. citizens and taxpayers to fund this network?

The Clinton administration and public interest groups think that the private sector should build the information highway but want to make sure that everyone can use the services. Their feeling is that the new services, including picture telephones, two-way television, and links to Library of Congress archives, should be available to "virtually everyone," just as basic telephone service is now.

Universal service was not much of a problem when the telephone service was run by regulated monopolies such as AT&T. Regulations allowed carriers to charge higher rates to business customers to subsidize rural and poor residential customers who couldn't afford to pay the actual cost of their service. Now the telecommunications industry is becoming deregulated. But telecommunications companies would have trouble subsidizing money-losing network service to poor and rural customers if other companies were fiercely competing for their profitable customers. How can builders of the information highway avoid creating a society of information "haves" and "have-nots"?

Sources: Mark Lewyn, "The Information Age Isn't Just for the Elite," *Business Week* (January 10, 1994); Computer Systems Policy Project, "Perspectives on the National Information Infrastructure" (January 12, 1993); Telecommunications Policy Roundtable, 1994.

- *Quality of life*. The code should state that the purpose of systems is to improve the quality of life for customers and for employees by achieving high levels of product quality, customer service, and employee satisfaction and human dignity through proper ergonomics, job and work-flow design, and human resource development.

Management Challenges

1. Understanding the moral risks of new technology. Rapid technological change means that the choices facing individuals also rapidly change. The balance of risk and reward, the probabilities of apprehension for wrongful acts—all these change as well. In this environment it will be important for management to conduct an ethical and social impact analysis of new technologies. One might take each of the moral dimensions described in this chapter and briefly speculate on how a new technology will affect each dimension. There will be no right answers for how to behave, but there should be considered management judgment on the moral risks of new technology.

2. Establishing corporate ethics policies that include IS issues. As managers you will be responsible for developing corporate ethics policies and for enforcing them and explaining them to employees. Historically the IS area is the last to be consulted, and much more attention has been paid to financial integrity and personnel policies. But from what you now know after reading this chapter, it is clear that your corporation should have an ethics policy in the IS area covering such issues as privacy, property, accountability, system quality, and quality of life. The challenge will be in educating non-IS managers in the need for these policies, as well as educating your work force.

Summary

1. Understand the relationship among ethical, social, and political issues raised by information systems. Ethical, social, and political issues are closely related in an information society. Ethical issues confront individuals who must choose a course of action, often in a situation where two or more ethical principles are in conflict (a dilemma). Social issues spring from ethical issues. Societies must develop expectations in individuals about the correct course of action, and social issues then are debates about the kinds of situations and expectations that societies should develop so that individuals behave correctly. Political issues spring from social conflict and have to do largely with laws that prescribe behavior and seek to use the law to create situations in which individuals behave correctly.

2. Identify the main moral dimensions of an information society. Five main moral dimensions tie together ethical, social, and political issues in an information society. These moral dimensions are information rights and obligations, property rights, accountability and control, system quality, and quality of life.

3. Employ an ethical analysis to difficult situations. An ethical analysis is a five-step methodology for analyzing a situation. The method involves identifying the facts, values, stakeholders, options, and consequences of actions. Once this process is completed, you can begin to consider what ethical principle you should apply to a situation in order to arrive at a judgment.

4. Understand specific ethical principles for conduct. Six ethical principles are available to judge your own conduct (and that of others). These principles are derived independently from several cultures and from religious and intellectual traditions. They are not hard-and-fast rules and may not apply in all situations. The principles are the Golden Rule, Immanuel Kant's Categorical Imperative, Descartes' rule of change, the Utilitarian Principle, the Risk Aversion Principle, and the ethical "no free lunch" rule.

5. Develop corporate policies for ethical conduct. For each of the five moral dimensions, corporations should develop an ethics policy statement to assist individuals and to encourage the correct decisions. The policy areas are as follows. Individual information rights: Spell out corporate privacy and due process policies. Property rights: Clarify how the corporation will treat property rights of software owners. Accountability and control: Clarify who is responsible and accountable for information. System quality: Identify methodologies and quality standards to achieve. Quality of life: Identify corporate policies on family, computer crime, decision making, vulnerability, job loss, and health risks.

Key Terms

Ethics	Descartes' rule of change	Trade secret	Carpal tunnel syndrome (CTS)
Information rights	Utilitarian Principle	Copyright	Computer vision syndrome (CVS)
Responsibility	Risk Aversion Principle	Patent	
Accountability	Ethical "no free lunch" rule	Computer crime	Technostress
Liability	Privacy	Computer abuse	
Due process	Fair Information Practices (FIP)	Repetitive stress injury (RSI)	
Immanuel Kant's Categorical Imperative	Intellectual property		

Review Questions

1. In what ways are ethical, social, and political issues connected? Give some examples.
2. What are the key technological trends that heighten ethical concerns?
3. What are the differences between responsibility, accountability, and liability?
4. What are the five steps in an ethical analysis?
5. Identify six ethical principles.

6. What is a professional code of conduct?
7. What are meant by "privacy" and "fair information practices"?
8. What are the three different regimes that protect intellectual property rights?
9. Why is it so difficult to hold software services liable for failure or injury?
10. What is the most common cause of system quality problems?
11. Name four "quality of life" impacts of computers and information systems.
12. What is technostress, and how does one measure it?
13. Name three management actions that could reduce RSI (repetitive stress injury).

Discussion Questions

1. Why should anyone care about unemployment caused by reengineering? Won't these workers be rehired at some point in the future when business gets better?
2. If everyone copied software, there would be no real market for software products, and producers of software would go out of business. Is this really true? What ethical principle is being applied in this statement? Discuss.
3. Should producers of software-based services like ATMs be held liable for economic injuries suffered when their systems fail?

Group Projects

1. With three or four of your classmates, develop a corporate ethics code on privacy. Be sure to consider e-mail privacy and employee monitoring of work sites as well as hallways, entrances, and restrooms. You should also consider corporate use of information about employees concerning their off-job behavior (e.g., lifestyle, living arrangements, and so forth). Present your ethics code to the class.

2. With three or four of your classmates, interview managers of your university information systems department concerning university ethics policies in the systems area. Does your university have an ethics policy for students and for employees? What is it? You could also interview a local firm rather than university officials. Present your findings to the class.

Case Study

WHO IS RESPONSIBLE?

Hopper Specialty Co. Hopper Specialty is a retail vendor of industrial hardware located in Farmington, New Mexico. Working out of a small storefront, the company primarily serves the area's oil and gas drillers. The owner, Joe Hopper, nurtured the business during its first ten years (1978 to 1988) until it had become the largest distributor of industrial hardware in the northwest corner of the state. Oil and gas drills work 24 hours per day, and every minute a drill is shut down, the driller loses income—time truly is money. Therefore, drillers depend upon hardware dealers like Hopper Specialty to supply them with parts very quickly in order to minimize losses when problems occur. For example, Hopper Specialty's contract with its largest customer, BHP Mineral International Inc., contained a clause in which Hopper was required to fill 90% of any BHP parts order within 48 hours. As a result of these business conditions, in order to be competitive, Hopper Specialty must maintain a very large inventory of a wide range of products.

As the company grew, its inventory ballooned in size and became very comprehensive. Eventually Hopper decided he needed a computerized system to manage all of his inventory. In late 1987 he purchased a system called Warehouse Manager from NCR. The software promised to track thousands of items in inventory, keep prices current, warn when items were running low, generate invoices automatically, and even balance the monthly books—all at the touch of a few keystrokes. NCR promised support for the whole system, including hardware, the various software components, and terminals. Additionally, Hopper was impressed with the repeated statements by the NCR sales staff that the package was thoroughly tested and operating smoothly at more than 200 sites. NCR began installing the product in the spring of 1988.

In September of that year, when the installation was complete, the company turned the system on and problems immediately surfaced. The store clerks found that response times of 30 seconds to several minutes were common. In addition, the terminals would lock up 20 to 30 times per day. Delayed response times left Hopper's customers waiting in long lines. Moreover, employees soon discovered that the prices the system quoted were often in error. For example, an industrial hose that was supposed to be priced at $17 per foot was quoted on the system at $30 per foot. The company carried too many products for the clerks to know all the prices, causing Charles Brannig, Hopper Specialty's general manager, to observe that "our counter people didn't know it was the wrong price by looking at it." Moreover, the problem occurred erratically, so no one could know which prices might be wrong. Even more serious data problems occurred. The computer could indicate that the company had 50 units of an item that was actually out of stock with 50 on order. Or, it would show an item as out of stock and on order when in fact it was on the shelf. Again, where the errors would occur was unpredictable.

In early 1989 Hopper had his staff take six inventories within a two-month period, and every time, the computer data differed from actual count of inventory. Lines grew longer, with customers now even waiting on the sidewalk. The computer system was often down, causing the clerks to resort to hand writing the invoices.

Hopper remained in close touch with NCR throughout this ordeal. NCR representatives told him that his problems were isolated, that the system was running well elsewhere. They claimed that the source of the problem was employee inexperience.

One problem Hopper faced was that he had plenty of competition; his customers had alternatives if they were dissatisfied with Hopper Specialty's service. For example, just two doors down the street was Advance Supply & Pump Co., which began to advertise its excellent inventory and top-notch service. Hopper watched his customer base dwindle as many began to patronize his competition, forcing him to reduce his stock because he could no longer afford to carry such a large and extensive inventory. The result, of course, was that he often would not have the required item in stock and would have to turn away even more customers.

In early 1992, Hopper hired an outside accounting firm to try to make sense out of his accounting books. The accountants discovered that many numbers were missing from the company's computerized general ledger system—Warehouse Manager had randomly erased data. To save his business, Hopper was forced to put $350,000 of his own personal funds into it.

In April 1993, BHP canceled its contract, worth between $350,000 and $500,000 annually. Now Hopper no longer had a choice. He began to lay off employees, and those who remained found their health care benefits reduced. He also stopped using the computer system—the company's inventory was so low that it was no longer needed. Hopper decided to sue NCR. Hopper's suit stated that the company lost more than $4.2 million in profits because of the NCR system. As of this writing, the lawsuit has not been settled.

NCR. NCR was a $6 billion computer company headquartered in Dayton, Ohio. In 1991 the company was acquired by AT&T and was renamed AT&T Global Information Services (we refer to it as NCR throughout this case study). Overall it sold approximately 40 copies of Warehouse Manager from 1987 through 1992. More than two dozen of those sales ended with lawsuits being filed against NCR.

The Warehouse Manager application software was developed by Taylor Management Systems Inc. to run on Burroughs Corp. (now Unisys Corp.) computers. Taylor Management is now defunct. In 1987 copies of the software were running smoothly at more than 200 sites, all using Burroughs computers. The application could not run on NCR computers without being modified. In 1986 NCR licensed Warehouse Manager from Taylor, with Taylor assuming responsibility for converting the software to run under NCR computers. In April 1987, Warehouse Manager began to be installed on customers' NCR computers.

Trouble began immediately. In May 1987, Vogue Tyre & Rubber Co., an auto parts distributor in Skokie, Illinois, complained to NCR of "long delays, sloppy NCR service, inattention to detail, and 'Band-Aid' solutions to problems with its system." In August 1987, E. Kinast Distributors Inc., a Franklin Park, Illinois, wood-laminating company, complained to NCR that it hadn't been able to enter a single purchase order during the entire five weeks the system had been operating.

According to NCR internal documents, during that summer and autumn virtually every installation site complained. All indicated that the system response time slowed to a crawl during busy periods. They also all complained that if more than one user attempted to access Warehouse Manager simultaneously, all the terminals would lock up. All the users were then forced to log off the computer and then log back on again to be able to resume use. However, when logging back on, the users found that the data that had been saved were often inexplicably altered and invalid.

In December 1987, another problem was documented. John W. Shearer, president of Burgman Industries, a Jacksonville, Florida, supplier of heavy construction parts, complained that his company's general ledger was infected with inaccurate data from Warehouse Manager. For example, he reported one machine part that had cost the company $114 was priced for sale at 54 cents.

NCR's response was to tell virtually all of its customers that their problems were isolated, that the system was running smoothly everywhere else. Despite the denials of problems, however, NCR did keep a full record of all the complaints it received.

In January 1988, NCR temporarily suspended sales of Warehouse Manager in order to permit its engineers to eliminate the many critical bugs. NCR and Taylor began feuding over the cause of the problems. NCR blamed Taylor and its software; Taylor blamed the NCR hardware and its operating system. Eventually the two companies ended up in court over this issue as it related to the distribution of royalties.

In May 1988, NCR received two internal field reports which stated that Warehouse Manager had been "inadequately tested" prior to its release and "was performing unexpectedly badly in actual business settings." Nonetheless, in mid-1988 sales of the software package resumed. In 1992 NCR released a new version of the software. It did include improvements but was nonetheless still full of bugs. Later that year, NCR finally halted sales of Warehouse Manager for good.

As for the suits against NCR, the company claims (in a legal document) that it "had every reason to believe" that Taylor software worked on its computers. NCR has settled many of the lawsuits against it and has offered to settle them all on similar terms. However, all settlements include a provision binding all parties to secrecy. Publicly NCR denies responsibility and blames the flaws of Warehouse Manager on the software they licensed from Taylor Management. ■

Source: Milo Geyelin, "Doomsday Device," *The Wall Street Journal* (August 8, 1994).

Case Study Questions

1. What managerial, technological, and organizational factors allowed the NCR-Hopper case to develop?
2. Which of the six ethical principles apply here?
3. We have described five moral dimensions of the information age. Pick one of these dimensions and describe the ethical, social, and political aspects of this case. Include in your discussion the role of Joe Hopper.
4. Hopper Specialty was a successful and growing business prior to the installation of Warehouse Manager. Some believe that software can be responsible for a company's business failure. How do you assign responsibility for the drastic decline in Hopper Specialty's business? Explain your answer.
5. If you were a manager at Hopper Specialty Company, what would or could you have done to prevent the problems described here from occurring? What could NCR have done?

References

Anderson, Ronald E., Deborah G. Johnson, Donald Gotterbarn, and Judith Perrolle. "Using the New ACM Code of Ethics in Decision Making." *Communications of the ACM* 36, no. 2, February 1993.

Barlow, John Perry. "Electronic Frontier: Private Life in Cyberspace." *Communications of the ACM* 34, no. 8 (August 1991).

Bjerklie, David. "Does E-Mail Mean Everyone's Mail?" (January 3, 1994).

Brod, Craig. *Techno Stress—The Human Cost of the Computer Revolution*. Reading, MA: Addison-Wesley, 1982.

Brown Bag Software v. Symantec Corp. 960 F2D 1465 (Ninth Circuit, 1992).

Bulkeley, William M. "Databases Plagued by a Reign of Error." *The Wall Street Journal* (May 26, 1992).

Cafasso, Rosemary. "Rethinking Reengineering." *Computerworld* (March 15, 1993).

Caldwell, Bruce, with John Soat. "The Hidden Persuader." *Information Week* (November 19, 1990).

Carley, William M. "Rigging Computers for Fraud or Malice Is Often an Inside Job." *The Wall Street Journal* (August 27, 1992).

Carvajal, Dorren. "Book Publishers Worry about Threat of Internet." *The New York Times* (March 18, 1996).

Collins, W. Robert, Keith W. Miller, Bethany J. Spielman, and Phillip Wherry. "How Good Is Good Enough? An Ethical Analysis of Software Construction and Use." *Communications of the ACM* 37, no.1 (January 1994).

Computer Systems Policy Project. "Perspectives on the National Information Infrastructure." January 12, 1993.

Couger, J. Daniel. "Preparing IS Students to Deal with Ethical Issues." *MIS Quarterly* 13, no. 2 (June 1989).

Dejoie, Roy, George Fowler, and David Paradice, eds. *Ethical Issues in Information Systems*. Boston: Boyd & Fraser (1991).

Denning, Dorothy E. et al. "To Tap or Not to Tap." *Communications of the ACM* 36, no. 3 (March 1993).

"EMASS® Is Mobil's Mass Storage Solution." *Datamation* (September 15, 1993).

"Equifax Report on Consumers in the Information Age, A National Survey." Equifax Inc., 1992.

Feder, Barnaby J. "As Hand Injuries Mount, So Do the Lawsuits." *The New York Times* (June 8, 1992).

Furger, Roberta. "In Search of Relief for Tired, Aching Eyes." *PC World* (February 1993).

Gabriel, Trip. "Reprogramming a Convicted Hacker." *The New York Times* (January 14, 1995).

Graham, Robert L. "The Legal Protection of Computer Software." *Communications of the ACM* (May 1984).

Huff, Chuck, and C. Dianne Martin. "Computing Consequences: A Framework for Teaching Ethical Computing." *Communications of the ACM* 38, no. 12 (December 1995).

Joes, Kathryn. "EDS Set to Restore Cash-Machine Network." *The New York Times* (March 26, 1993).

Johnson, Deborah G., and John M. Mulvey. "Accountability and Computer Decision Systems." *Communications of the ACM* 38, no. 12 (December 1995).

King, Julia. "It's CYA Time." *Computerworld* (March 30, 1992).

Kling, Rob. "When Organizations Are Perpetrators: The Conditions of Computer Abuse and Computer Crime." In *Computerization & Controversy: Value Conflicts & Social Choices*, edited by Charles Dunlop and Rob Kling. New York: Academic Press (1991).

Laudon, Kenneth C. "Ethical Concepts and Information Technology." *Communications of the ACM* 38, no. 12 (December 1995).

Markoff, John. "Though Illegal, Copied Software Is Now Common." *The New York Times* (July 27, 1992).

———. "Computer Viruses: Just Uncommon Colds After All?" *The New York Times* (November 1, 1992).

Mason, Richard O. "Four Ethical Issues in the Information Age." *MIS Quarterly* 10, no. 1 (March 1986).

———. "Applying Ethics to Information Technology Issues." *Communications of the ACM* 38, no. 12 (December 1995).

McPartlin, John P. "Ten Years of Hard Labor." *Information Week* (March 29, 1993).

———. "The Terrors of Technostress." *InformationWeek* (July 30, 1990).

———. "Environmental Agency 'Held Hostage' by Outsourcer." *Information Week* (March 9, 1992).

———. "A Question of Complicity." *Information Week* (June 22, 1992).

Milberg, Sandra J., Sandra J. Burke, H. Jeff Smith, and Ernest A. Kallman. "Values, Personal Information Privacy, and Regulatory Approaches." *Communications of the ACM* 38, no. 12 (December 1995).

Mykytyn, Kathleen, Peter P. Mykytyn, Jr., and Craig W. Slinkman, "Expert Systems: A Question of Liability," *MIS Quarterly* 14, no. 1 (March 1990).

Neumann, Peter G. "Inside RISKS: Computers, Ethics and Values." *Communications of the ACM* 34, no. 7 (July 1991).

———. "Inside RISKS: Fraud by Computer." *Communications of the ACM* 35, no. 8 (August 1992).

Nissenbaum, Helen. "Computing and Accountability." *Communications of the ACM* 37, no. 1 (January 1994).

Office of the Mayor, New York City, "The Trillion Dollar Gamble." 1991.

Oz, Effy. "Ethical Standards for Information Systems Professionals." *MIS Quarterly* 16, no. 4 (December 1992).

———. *Ethics for the Information Age*. Dubuque, Iowa: W. C. Brown (1994).

———. "When Professional Standards Are Lax: The Confirm Failure and Its Lessons." *Communications of the ACM* 37, no. 10 (October 1994).

Pollack, Andrew. "San Francisco Law on VDTs Is Struck Down." *The New York Times* (February 14, 1992).

Ramirez, Anthony. "AT&T to Eliminate Many Operator Jobs." *The New York Times* (March 4, 1992).

Rifkin, Glenn. "The Ethics Gap." *Computerworld* (October 14, 1991).

———. "Watch Out for Trickle-Down Technology." *The New York Times* (March 16, 1993).

Rigdon, Joan E. "Frequent Glitches in New Software Bug Users." *The Wall Street Journal* (January 18, 1995).

Rotenberg, Marc. "Inside RISKS: Protecting Privacy." *Communications of the ACM* 35, no. 4 (April 1992).

———. "Communications Privacy: Implications for Network Design." *Communications of the ACM* 36, no. 8 (August 1993).

Samuelson, Pamela. "First Amendment Rights for Information Providers?" *Communications of the ACM* 34, no. 6 (June 1991).

———. "Digital Media and the Law." *Communications of the ACM* 34, no. 10 (October 1991).

———. "Updating the Copyright Look and Feel Lawsuits." *Communications of the ACM* 35, no. 9 (September 1992).

———. "Liability for Defective Electronic Information." *Communications of the ACM* 36, no. 1 (January 1993).

———. "The Ups and Downs of Look and Feel." *Communications of the ACM* 36, no. 4 (April 1993).

———. "Computer Programs and Copyright's Fair Use Doctrine." *Communications of the ACM* 36, no. 9 (September 1993).

———. "Copyright's Fair Use Doctrine and Digital Data." *Communications of the ACM* 37, no. 1 (January 1994).

———. "Self Plagiarism or Fair Use?" *Communications of the ACM* 37, no. 8 (August 1994).

Schnorr, Teresa M. "Miscarriage and VDT Exposure." *New England Journal of Medicine* (March 1991).

Sipior, Janice C., and Burke T. Ward. "The Ethical and Legal Quandary of Email Privacy." *Communications of the ACM* 38, no. 12 (December 1995).

Smith, H. Jeff. "Privacy Policies and Practices: Inside the Organizational Maze." *Communications of the ACM* 36, no. 12 (December 1993).

Sterling, Bruce. *The Hacker Crackdown: Law and Disorder on the Computer Frontier*. New York: Bantam Books (1992).

Stevens, William K. "Major U.S. Study Finds No Miscarriage Risk from Video Terminals." *The New York Times* (March 14, 1991).

Straub, Detmar W., Jr., and William D. Nance. "Discovering and Disciplining Computer Abuse in Organizations: A Field Study." *MIS Quarterly* 14, no. 1 (March 1990).

Straub, Detmar W., Jr., and Rosann Webb Collins. "Key Information Liability Issues Facing Managers: Software Piracy, Proprietary Databases, and Individual Rights to Privacy." *MIS Quarterly* 14, no. 2 (June 1990).

"Supercomputers Manage Holiday Stock." *The Wall Street Journal* (December 23, 1992).

Tabor, Mary W., with Anthony Ramirez. "Computer Savvy, with an Attitude." *The New York Times* (July 23, 1992).

The Telecommunications Policy Roundtable. "Renewing the Commitment to a Public Interest Telecommunications Policy." *Communications of the ACM* 37, no. 1 (January 1994).

U.S. Department of Health, Education, and Welfare. *Records, Computers and the Rights of Citizens*. Cambridge: MIT Press, 1973.

Weisband, Suzanne P., and Bruce A. Reinig. "Managing User Perceptions of Email Privacy." *Communications of the ACM* 38, no. 12 (December 1995).

Wilson, Linda. "Devil in Your Data." *Information Week* (August 31, 1992).

Wolinsky, Carol, and James Sylvester. "Privacy in the Telecommunications Age." *Communications of the ACM* 35, no. 2 (February 1992).

Chapter 5

Computers and Information Processing

EMI Tunes Its Information Technology

5.1 What Is a Computer System?
System Configuration
Bits and Bytes: How Computers Represent Data
Time and Size in the Computer World

5.2 The CPU and Primary Storage
Primary Storage
Types of Semiconductor Memory
Arithmetic-Logic Unit
Control Unit

5.3 The Evolution of Computer Hardware
Generations of Computer Hardware
What Is a Microprocessor? What Is a Chip?

5.4 Mainframes, Minicomputers, Microcomputers, Workstations, and Supercomputers
Mainframes, Minis, and Micros
Downsizing and Cooperative Processing
Window on Management:
Deutsche Bank Decides to Stay with Mainframes
Microcomputers and Workstations
Supercomputers and Parallel Processing
Window on Technology:
Parallel Processing Goes Commercial

5.5 Secondary Storage
Magnetic Tape
Magnetic Disk
Optical Disks

5.6 Input and Output Devices
Input Devices
Batch and On-Line Input and Processing
Output Devices

5.7 Information Technology Trends
Multimedia
Window on Organizations:
Multimedia Kiosks Educate the Public
Superchips
Fifth-Generation Computers

Management Challenges
Summary
Key Terms
Review Questions
Discussion Questions
Group Project
Case Study: Bar Codes Become a Strategic Business Weapon
References

EMI Tunes Its Information Technology

The music industry is known to lag behind many other industries in its strategic use of information systems, and the management at Thorn EMI PLC. of London decided to take advantage of that situation. EMI is the world's largest independent music group, with a major presence in a number of countries, including the United States, Canada, and Great Britain. Its stars range from Garth Brooks to Megadeth to Frank Sinatra. Since 1992 senior management has been selling off most of its nonmusic businesses, such as defense subsidiaries, in order to focus on its primary business, music. In shifting its focus, EMI management targeted a range of business functions. At the heart of the changes was a new emphasis upon planning and sales forecasting. Management decided to make better use of data collected at retail counters in order to more fully understand the tastes of the customers who purchase EMI products. The company could then use this information to forecast sales and link production to those forecasts, a common practice in many industries but not in the music field. Through proper planning and forecasting, the company could also significantly reduce inventory costs. Also central to the plan was improved management of the company's finances. All of this required a major redesign, first of EMI's business processes and then of its computer hardware technology, its telecommunications, and its application software.

EMI had actually not redesigned its North American information technology platform for 15 years. The existing technology was centered on an IBM 3090 mainframe in Los Angeles accessed by dumb terminals at more than two dozen locations. The various company sites were linked by a range of noncompatible public networks. The new technology infrastructure looks very different. The single mainframe has been replaced by five IBM AS/400 minicomputers in a data center in New York City. These computers are accessed by 900 Compaq 486 desktop microcomputers acting as minicomputer terminals and desktop computers, as well as working with other microcomputers through networking. EMI's many public networks were replaced by a single private network leased from AT&T that would not be subject to the public network traffic jams.

The AS/400 minicomputers now provide the processing power for EMI's financial, order entry, distribution, and royalties functions, which were previously handled by the IBM 3090 mainframe. But hardware is only part of any information systems solution. Data are critical as is the purchase of appropriate application software to support EMI's business goals. To make the data easier to access, three separate core systems were consolidated for management purposes. New software included an executive information system to support EMI's senior management. The company purchased planning and forecasting software from Demand Management Inc. of St. Louis, Missouri, and new software from Lawson Software in Minneapolis, Minnesota, to improve the management of corporate finances. Existing order entry and distribution systems were replaced by new ones from J. D. Edwards & Co. of Denver, Colorado. To support staff communications, it installed Lotus cc:Mail. Installation of the minicomputers was completed early in 1994, and the whole project will be completed in 1996. ∎

Sources: "City Analysts Believe Thorn EMI Set to Divide Itself in Two," *The Irish Times on the Web*, February 19, 1996 and Bruce Caldwell, "EMI Puts Processes in Tune," *Information Week*, October 17, 1994.

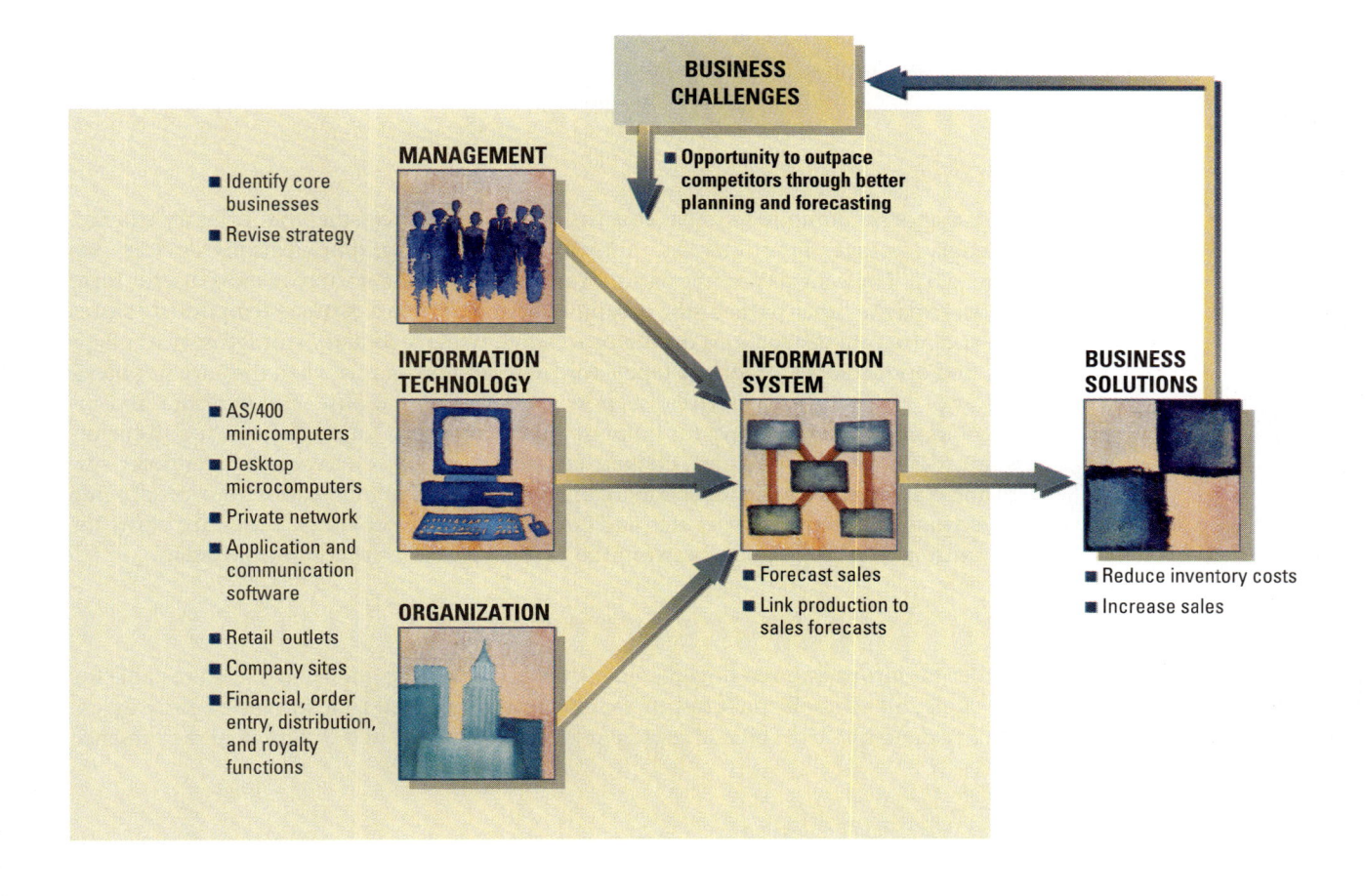

By shifting from one large mainframe computer to five midsize minicomputers, EMI was able to bring the right amount of computing power to its business operations. To implement this plan EMI's management not only had to understand the company's strategic goals and the changes to business functions necessary to achieve these goals but also needed to understand how much computer processing capacity was required by EMI's business and the performance criteria of various types of computers. They had to know why minicomputers were more appropriate for their centralized tasks rather than mainframes or supercomputers, and what role networked microcomputers could play rather than dumb terminals. Management also had to understand how the computer itself worked with related storage, input/output, and telecommunications technology.

In this chapter we describe the typical hardware configuration of a computer system, explaining how a computer works and how computer processing power and storage capacity are measured. We then compare the capabilities of various types of computers and related input, output, and storage devices.

Learning Objectives

After completing this chapter, you will be able to:

1. Identify the hardware components in a typical computer system.
2. Describe how information is represented and processed in a computer system.
3. Distinguish between generations of computer hardware.
4. Contrast the capabilities of mainframes, minicomputers, supercomputers, microcomputers, and workstations.
5. Describe the various media for storing data and programs in a computer system.
6. Compare the major input and output devices and approaches to input and processing.
7. Describe multimedia and future information technology trends.

5.1 WHAT IS A COMPUTER SYSTEM?

In order to understand how computers process data into information, you need to understand the components of a computer system and how computers work. No matter what their size, computers represent and process data using the same basic principles.

SYSTEM CONFIGURATION

A contemporary computer system consists of a central processing unit, primary storage, secondary storage, input devices, output devices, and communications devices (see Figure 5.1). The central processing unit manipulates raw data into a more useful form and controls the other parts of the computer system. Primary storage temporarily stores data and program instructions during processing, while secondary storage devices (magnetic and optical disks, magnetic tape) store data and programs when they are not being used in processing. Input devices, such as a keyboard or mouse, convert data and instructions into electronic form for input into the computer. Output devices, such as printers and video display terminals, convert electronic data produced by the computer system and display it in a form that people can understand. Communications devices provide connections between the computer and communications networks. Buses are paths for transmitting data and signals between the various parts of the computer system.

bit A binary digit representing the smallest unit of data in a computer system. It can only have one of two states, representing 0 or 1.

BITS AND BYTES: HOW COMPUTERS REPRESENT DATA

In order for information to flow through a computer system and be in a form suitable for processing, all symbols, pictures, or words must be reduced to a string of binary digits. A binary digit is called a **bit** and represents either a 0 or a 1. In the computer, the presence

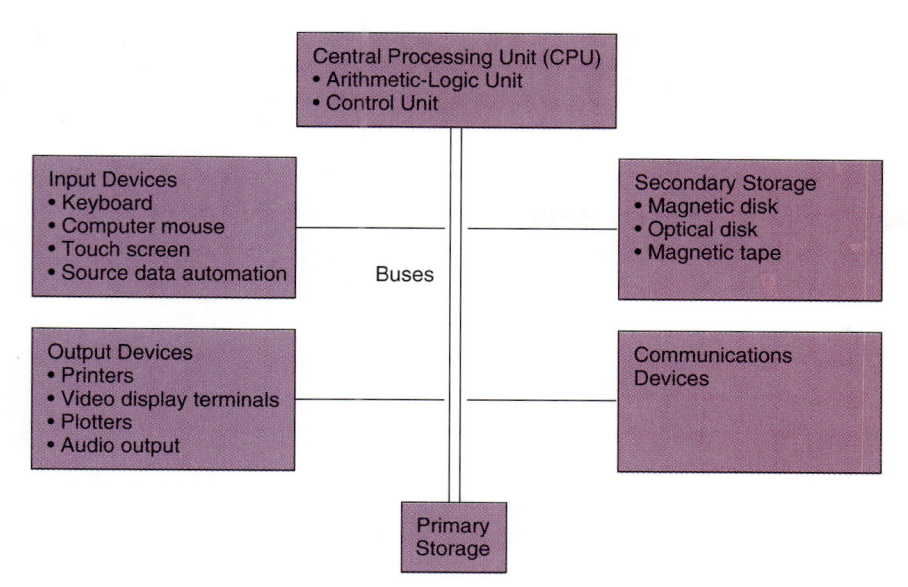

FIGURE 5.1
Hardware components of a computer system. A contemporary computer system can be categorized into six major components. The central processing unit manipulates data and controls the other parts of the computer system; primary storage temporarily stores data and program instructions during processing; secondary storage feeds data and instructions into the central processor and stores data for future use; input devices convert data and instructions for processing in the computer; output devices present data in a form that people can understand; and communications devices control the passing of information to and from communications networks.

of an electronic or magnetic signal means *one* and its absence signifies *zero*. Digital computers operate directly with binary digits, either singly or strung together to form bytes. A string of eight bits that the computer stores as a unit is called a **byte**. Each byte can be used to store a decimal number, a symbol, a character, or part of a picture (see Figure 5.2).

Figure 5.3 shows how decimal numbers are represented using *true binary digits*. Each position in a decimal number has a certain value. Any number in the decimal system (base 10) can be reduced to a binary number. The binary number system (base 2) can express any number as a power of the number 2. The table at the bottom of the figure shows how the translation from binary to decimal works. By using a binary number system a computer can express all numbers as groups of zeroes and ones. True binary cannot be used by a computer because, in addition to representing numbers, a computer must represent alphabetic characters and many other symbols used in natural language, such as $ and &. This requirement led manufacturers of computer hardware to develop standard *binary codes*.

byte A string of bits, usually eight, used to store one number or character in a computer system.

FIGURE 5.2
Bits and bytes. Bits are represented by either a 0 or 1. A string of 8 bits constitutes a byte, which represents a character. The computer's representation for the name *Alice* is a series of five bytes, where each byte represents one character (or letter) in the name.

5.1   What Is A Computer System?

FIGURE 5.3
True binary digits. Each decimal number has a certain value that can be expressed as a binary number. The binary number system can express any number as a power of the number 2.

$$10100, \text{ which is equal to: } \begin{aligned} 0 \times 2^0 &= 0 \\ 0 \times 2^1 &= 0 \\ 1 \times 2^2 &= 4 \\ 0 \times 2^3 &= 0 \\ 1 \times 2^4 &= \underline{16} \\ & 20 \end{aligned}$$

Place	5	4	3	2	1
Power of 2	2^4	2^3	2^2	2^1	2^0
Decimal value	16	8	4	2	1

EBCDIC (Extended Binary Coded Decimal Interchange Code) Binary code representing every number, alphabetic character, or special character with 8 bits, used primarily in IBM and other mainframe computers.

ASCII (American Standard Code for Information Interchange) A 7- or 8-bit binary code used in data transmission, microcomputers, and some large computers.

parity An extra bit built into the EBCDIC and ASCII codes used as a check bit to ensure accuracy.

pixel The smallest unit of data for defining an image in the computer. The computer reduces a picture to a grid of pixels. The term *pixel* comes from *picture element*.

millisecond One-thousandth of a second.

There are two common codes: EBCDIC and ASCII, which are illustrated in Table 5.1. The first is the **Extended Binary Coded Decimal Interchange Code** (**EBCDIC**—pronounced *ib-si-dick*). This binary code, developed by IBM in the 1950s, represents every number, alphabetic character, or special character with 8 bits. EBCDIC can be used to code up to 256 different characters in one byte (2 to the eighth power equals 256).

ASCII, which stands for the **American Standard Code for Information Interchange,** was developed by the American National Standards Institute (ANSI) to provide a standard code that could be used by many different manufacturers in order to make machinery compatible. ASCII was originally designed as a 7-bit code, but most computers use 8-bit versions. EBCDIC is used in IBM and other mainframe computers, whereas ASCII is used in data transmission, microcomputers, and some larger computers.

In actual use, EBCDIC and ASCII also contain an extra ninth **parity** or check bit. Bits can be accidentally or mistakenly changed from *on* to *off,* creating errors when data are transferred from one hardware device to another or during environmental disturbances. Parity bits are used to assist in detecting these errors. Computers are built as either *even parity* or *odd parity.* Assuming an even-parity machine, the computer expects the number of bits turned on in a byte always to be even. (If the machine were designed as an odd-parity machine, the number of bits turned on would always be odd.) When the number of bits in a byte is even, the parity bit is turned off. If the number of bits in an even-parity machine in a byte is odd, the parity bit is turned on to make the total number of *on* bits even. All computer hardware contains automatic parity checking to ensure the stability of data over time.

How can a computer represent a picture? The computer stores a picture by creating a grid overlay of the picture. In this grid or matrix, the computer measures the light or color in each box or cell, called a **pixel** (picture element). The computer then stores this information on each pixel. A high-resolution computer terminal has a 1024×768 VGA standard grid, creating more than 700,000 pixels. Whether pictures or text are stored, it is through this process of reduction that a modern computer is able to operate in a complex environment.

TIME AND SIZE IN THE COMPUTER WORLD

Table 5.2 presents some key levels of time and size that are useful in describing the speed and capacity of modern computer systems.

Processing Speed

Modern secondary storage devices generally operate at the speeds of **milliseconds** (thousandths of a second). For instance, a typical microcomputer could find your student record on a magnetic disk in about 15 milliseconds. It would take many seconds to find your name on a much slower tape system. (The reasons for this difference are discussed later

Table 5.1 EBCDIC and ASCII Codes

Character	EBCDIC Binary	Character	ASCII-8-Binary
A	1100 0001	A	1010 0001
B	1100 0010	B	1010 0010
C	1100 0011	C	1010 0011
D	1100 0100	D	1010 0100
E	1100 0101	E	1010 0101
F	1100 0110	F	1010 0110
G	1100 0111	G	1010 0111
H	1100 1000	H	1010 1000
I	1100 1001	I	1010 1001
J	1101 0001	J	1010 1010
K	1101 0010	K	1010 1011
L	1101 0011	L	1010 1100
M	1101 0100	M	1010 1101
N	1101 0101	N	1010 1110
O	1101 0110	O	1010 1111
P	1101 0111	P	1011 0000
Q	1101 1000	Q	1011 0001
R	1101 1001	R	1011 0010
S	1110 0010	S	1011 0011
T	1110 0011	T	1011 0100
U	1110 0100	U	1011 0101
V	1110 0101	V	1011 0110
W	1110 0110	W	1011 0111
X	1110 0111	X	1011 1000
Y	1110 1000	Y	1011 1001
Z	1110 1001	Z	1011 1010
0	1111 0000	0	0101 0000
1	1111 0001	1	0101 0001
2	1111 0010	2	0101 0010
3	1111 0011	3	0101 0011
4	1111 0100	4	0101 0100
5	1111 0101	5	0101 0101
6	1111 0110	6	0101 0110
7	1111 0111	7	0101 0111
8	1111 1000	8	0101 1000
9	1111 1001	9	0101 1001

Table 5.2	Size and Time in the Computer World		
Time			
Second	1		Time required to find a single record on a tape
Millisecond	1/1000 second		Time needed to find a single name on a disk, 1 to 2 milliseconds
Microsecond	1/1,000,000 second		IBM microcomputer instruction speed, .1 microseconds per instruction
Nanosecond	1/1,000,000,000 second		Mainframe instruction speed, one instruction each 15 nanoseconds
Picosecond	1/1,000,000,000,000 second		Speed of experimental devices
Size			
Byte	String of 8 bits		Amount of computer storage for 1 character or number
Kilobyte	1000 bytes*		Microcomputer primary memory, 640 kilobytes
Megabyte	1,000,000 bytes		Microcomputer hard disk storage 340 megabytes; mainframe primary memory 200+ megabytes
Gigabyte	1,000,000,000 bytes		External storage disk and tape
Terabyte	1,000,000,000,000 bytes		Social security programs and records

*Actually 1024 storage positions

microsecond One-millionth of a second.

nanosecond One-billionth of a second.

in this chapter.) A middle-range microcomputer can execute approximately 10 million program instructions per second, or .1 **microseconds** per instruction. The central processing unit in contemporary mainframe computers can execute over 200 million instructions per second (200 MIPS). At this speed the central processor is operating at speeds of **nanoseconds** (billionths of a second), or one instruction for every 15 nanoseconds.

Storage/Memory Size

Size, like speed, is an important consideration in a system. Information is stored in a computer in the form of 0s and 1s (binary digits, or bits), which are strung together to form bytes. One byte can be used to store one character, such as the letter *A*. A thousand bytes (actually 1024 storage positions) is called a **kilobyte**. Small microcomputers used to have internal primary memories of 640 kilobytes. A large microcomputer today can store 32 megabytes of information in primary memory. Each **megabyte** is approximately one million bytes. This means, theoretically, that the machine can store up to 32 million alphabetic letters or numbers. Modern secondary storage devices, such as hard disk drives in a microcomputer or disk packs in a large mainframe, store millions of bytes of information. A microcomputer may have a 500-megabyte disk, whereas a large mainframe may have many disk drives, each capable of holding 8 gigabytes. A **gigabyte** is approximately one billion bytes. Some large organizations, like the Social Security Administration or the Internal Revenue Service, have a total storage capacity adding up all their disk drive capacities measured in trillions of bytes. And if all of their records were added together, including those stored on punched cards, paper records, and tapes, the total would be at the terabyte (thousands of billions of bytes) level of information storage.

kilobyte One thousand bytes (actually 1024 storage positions). Used as a measure of microcomputer storage capacity.

megabyte Approximately one million bytes. Unit of computer storage capacity.

gigabyte Approximately one billion bytes. Unit of computer storage capacity.

Problems of Coordination in Computer Hardware

The vast differences in the size and speed of the major elements of computer systems introduce problems of coordination. For instance, while central processing units operate at the level of microseconds, and in some cases nanoseconds, ordinary printers operate at the level of only a few hundred to a few thousand characters per second. This means that the central processing unit can process information far faster than a printer can print it out. For this reason, additional memory and storage devices must be placed between the central processing unit and the printer so that the central processing unit is not needlessly held back from processing more information as it waits for the printer to print it out.

5.2 THE CPU AND PRIMARY STORAGE

The **central processing unit (CPU)** is the part of the computer system where the manipulation of symbols, numbers, and letter occurs, and it controls the other parts of the computer system. The CPU consists of a control unit and an arithmetic-logic unit (see Figure 5.4). Located near the CPU is **primary storage** (sometimes called *primary memory* or *main memory*), where data and program instructions are stored temporarily during processing. Three kinds of buses link the CPU, primary storage, and the other devices in the computer system. The data bus moves data to and from primary storage. The address bus transmits signals for locating a given address in primary storage. The control bus transmits signals specifying whether to read or write data to or from a given primary storage address, input device, or output device. The characteristics of the CPU and primary storage are very important in determining the speed and capabilities of a computer.

central processing unit (CPU) Area of the computer system that manipulates symbols, numbers, and letters, and controls the other parts of the computer system.

primary storage Part of the computer that temporarily stores program instructions and data being used by the instructions.

PRIMARY STORAGE

Primary storage has three functions. It stores all or part of the program that is being executed. Primary storage also stores the operating system programs that manage the operation of the computer. (These programs are discussed in Chapter 6.) Finally, the primary storage area holds data that are being used by the program. Data and programs are placed in primary storage before processing, between processing steps, and after processing has ended, prior to being returned to secondary storage or released as output.

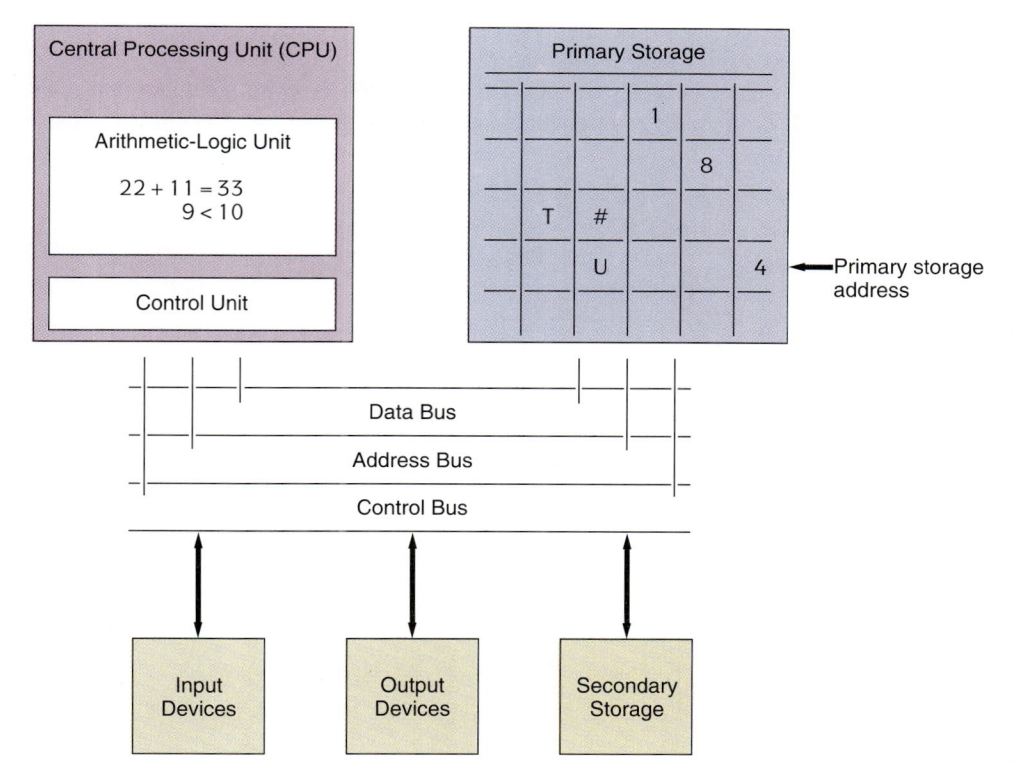

FIGURE 5.4
The CPU and primary storage. The CPU contains an arithmetic-logic unit and a control unit. Data and instructions are stored in unique addresses in primary storage that the CPU can access during processing. The data bus, address bus, and control bus transmit signals between the central processing unit, primary storage, and other devices in the computer system.

How is it possible for an electronic device such as primary storage to actually store information? How is it possible to retrieve this information from a known location in memory? Figure 5.5 illustrates primary storage in an electronic digital computer. Internal primary storage is often called **RAM**, or **random access memory**. It is called RAM because it can directly access any randomly chosen location in the same amount of time. The advantage of electronic information storage is the ability to store information in a precise known location in memory and to retrieve it from that same location.

Figure 5.5 shows that primary memory is divided into storage locations called *bytes*. Each location contains a set of eight binary switches or devices, each of which can store one bit of information. The set of eight bits found in each storage location is sufficient to store one letter, one digit, or one special symbol (such as $) using either EBCDIC or ASCII. Each byte has a unique address—similar to a mailbox, indicating where it is located in RAM. The computer can remember where the data in all of the bytes are located simply by keeping track of these addresses.

Most of the information used by a computer application is stored on secondary storage devices such as disks and tapes, located outside of the primary storage area. In order for the computer to do work on information, information must be transferred into primary memory for processing. Therefore, data are continually being read into and written out of the primary storage area during the execution of a program.

TYPES OF SEMICONDUCTOR MEMORY

Primary storage is actually composed of **semiconductors**. A semiconductor is an integrated circuit made by printing thousands and even millions of tiny transistors on a small silicon chip. There are several different kinds of semiconductor memory used in primary storage. RAM, or random access memory, is used for short-term storage of data or program instructions. RAM is volatile: Its contents will be lost when the computer's electric supply is disrupted by a power outage or when the computer is turned off. **ROM** or **read-only memory**, can only be read from; it cannot be written to. ROM chips come from the manufacturer with programs already *burned in*, or stored. ROM is used in general-purpose computers to store important or frequently used programs (such as computing routines for calculating the square roots of numbers). Other uses for ROM chips are the storage of manufacturer-specific microcodes such as the Basic Input Output System (BIOS) chip used on an IBM Personal System/2 microcomputer, which controls the handling of data within the machine.

There are two other subclasses of ROM chips: **PROM**, or **programmable read-only memory**, and **EPROM**, or **erasable programmable read-only memory**. PROM chips are used

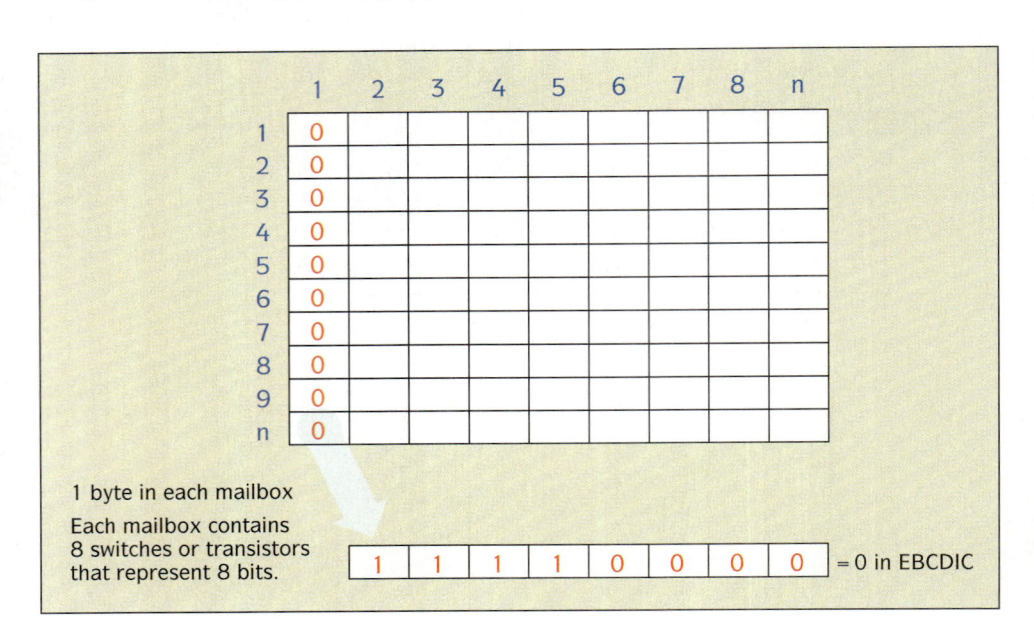

RAM (random access memory) Primary storage of data or program instructions that can directly access any randomly chosen location in the same amount of time.

semiconductor An integrated circuit made by printing thousands and even millions of tiny transistors on a small silicon chip.

ROM (read-only memory) Semiconductor memory chips that contain program instructions. These chips can only be read from; they cannot be written to.

PROM (programmable read-only memory) Subclass of ROM chip used in control devices because it can be programmed once.

EPROM (erasable programmable read-only memory) Subclass of ROM chip that can be erased and reprogrammed many times.

FIGURE 5.5
Primary storage in the computer. Primary storage can be visualized as a matrix. Each byte represents a mailbox with a unique address. In this example, mailbox [n,1] contains 8 bits representing the number 0 (as coded in EBCDIC).

	1	2	3	4	5	6	7	8	n
1	0								
2	0								
3	0								
4	0								
5	0								
6	0								
7	0								
8	0								
9	0								
n	0								

1 byte in each mailbox

Each mailbox contains 8 switches or transistors that represent 8 bits.

| 1 | 1 | 1 | 1 | 0 | 0 | 0 | 0 | = 0 in EBCDIC

by manufacturers as control devices in their products. They can be programmed once. In this way, manufacturers avoid the expense of having a specialized chip manufactured for the control of small motors, for instance; instead, they can program into a PROM chip the specific program for their product. PROM chips, therefore, can be made universally for many manufacturers in large production runs. EPROM chips are used for device control, such as in robots, where the program may have to be changed on a routine basis. With EPROM chips, the program can be erased and reprogrammed.

ARITHMETIC-LOGIC UNIT

The **arithmetic-logic unit (ALU)** performs the principal logical and arithmetic operations of the computer. It adds, subtracts, multiplies, and divides, determining whether a number is positive, negative, or zero. In addition to performing arithmetic functions, an ALU must be able to determine when one quantity is greater than or less than another and when two quantities are equal. The ALU can perform logical operations on the binary codes for letters as well as numbers.

arithmetic-logic unit (ALU) Component of the CPU that performs the principal logical and arithmetic operations of the computer.

CONTROL UNIT

The **control unit** coordinates and controls the other parts of the computer system. It reads a stored program, one instruction at a time, and directs other components of the computer system to perform the tasks required by the program. The series of operations required to process a single machine instruction is called the **machine cycle**. As illustrated in Figure 5.6, the machine cycle has two parts: an instruction cycle and an execution cycle.

control unit Component of the CPU that controls and coordinates the other parts of the computer system.

machine cycle Series of operations required to process a single machine instruction.

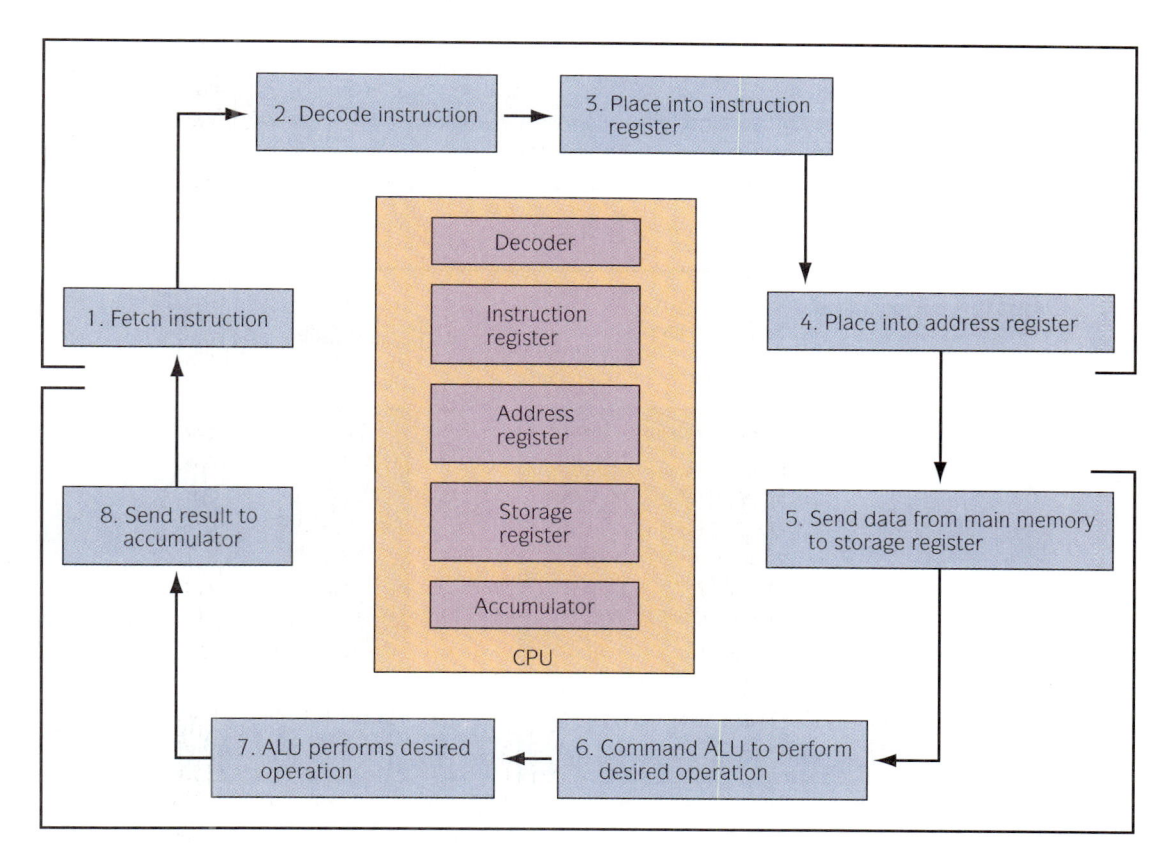

FIGURE 5.6
The various steps in the machine cycle. The machine cycle has two main stages of operation: the instruction cycle (I-cycle) and the execution cycle (E-cycle). There are several steps within each cycle required to process a single machine instruction in the CPU.

During the instruction cycle, the control unit retrieves one program instruction from primary storage and decodes it. It places the part of the instruction telling the ALU what to do next in a special instruction register and places the part specifying the address of the data to be used in the operation into an address register. (A register is a special temporary storage location in the ALU or control unit that acts like a high-speed staging area for program instructions or data being transferred from primary storage to the CPU for processing.)

During the execution cycle, the control unit locates the required data in primary storage, places it in a storage register, instructs the ALU to perform the desired operation, temporarily stores the result of the operation in an accumulator, and finally places the result in primary memory. As the execution of each instruction is completed, the control unit advances to and reads the next instruction of the program.

5.3 THE EVOLUTION OF COMPUTER HARDWARE

computer generations Major transitions in computer hardware; each generation is distinguished by a different technology for the components that do the processing.

There have been four major stages, or **computer generations**, in the evolution of computer hardware, each distinguished by a different technology for the components that do the computer's processing work. Each generation has dramatically expanded computer processing power and storage capabilities while simultaneously lowering costs (see Figure 5.7). For instance, the cost of performing 100,000 calculations plunged from several dollars in the 1950s to less than $0.025 in the 1980s and approximately $.00004 in 1995. These generational changes in computer hardware have been accompanied by generational changes in computer software (see Chapter 6) that have made computers increasingly more powerful, inexpensive, and easy to use.

GENERATIONS OF COMPUTER HARDWARE

The first and second generations of computer hardware were based on vacuum tube and transistor technology, whereas the third and fourth generations were based on semiconductor technology.

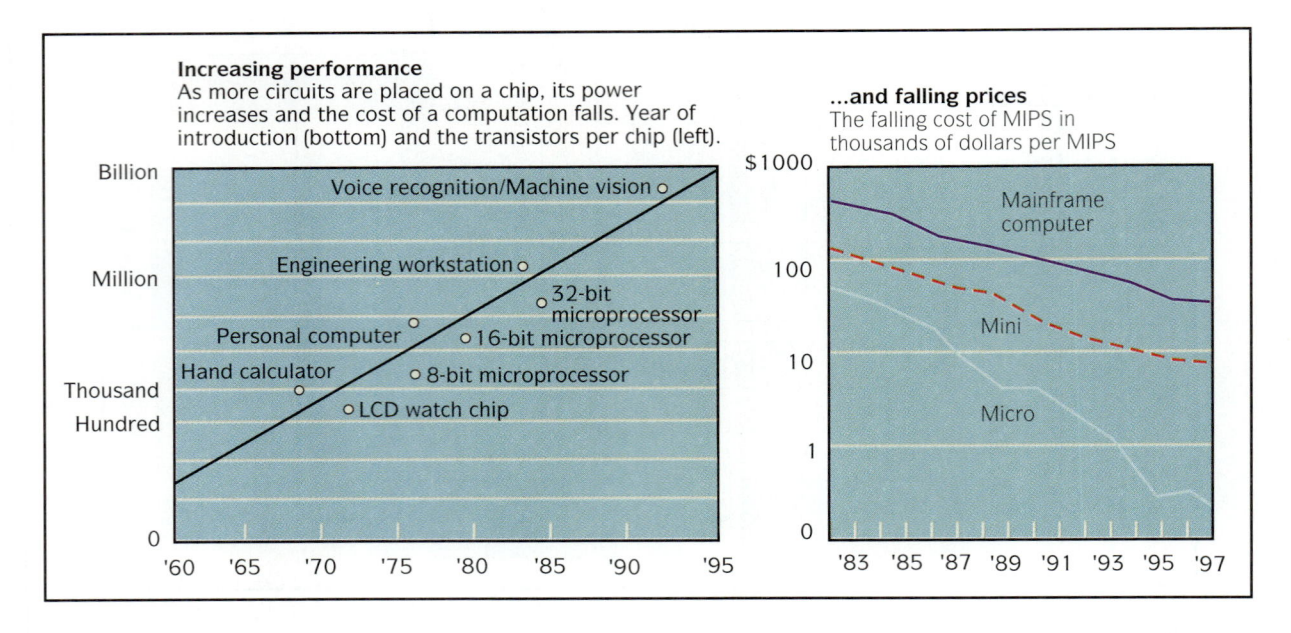

FIGURE 5.7
Increasing performance and falling prices of computers. MIPS: millions of instructions per second. *Adapted from "More Power for Less Money," The New York Times, September 12, 1988. Reprinted by permission of NYT Graphics.*

First Generation: Vacuum Tube Technology, 1946–1956

The first generation of computers relied on vacuum tubes to store and process information. These tubes consumed a great deal of power, were short-lived, and generated a great deal of heat. Colossal in size, first-generation computers had extremely limited memory and processing capability and were used for very limited scientific and engineering work. The maximum main memory size was approximately 2000 bytes (2 kilobytes), with a speed of 10 kiloinstructions per second. Rotating magnetic drums were used for internal storage and punched cards for external storage. Jobs such as running programs or printing output had to be coordinated manually.

Second Generation: Transistors, 1957–1963

In the second computer generation, transistors replaced vacuum tubes as the devices for storing and processing information. Transistors were much more stable and reliable than vacuum tubes, they generated less heat, and they consumed less power. However, each transistor had to be individually made and wired into a printed circuit board—a slow, tedious process. Magnetic core memory was the primary storage technology of this period. It was composed of small magnetic doughnuts (about 1 mm in diameter), which could be polarized in one of two directions to represent a bit of data. Wires were strung along and through these cores to both write and read data. This system had to be assembled by hand and, therefore, was very expensive. Second-generation computers had up to 32 kilobytes of RAM memory and speeds reaching 200,000 to 300,000 instructions per second. The enhanced processing power and memory of second-generation computers enabled them to be used more widely for scientific work and for such business tasks as automating payroll and billing.

Third Generation: Integrated Circuits, 1964–1979

Third-generation computers relied on integrated circuits, which were made by printing hundreds and later thousands of tiny transistors on small silicon chips. These devices were called *semiconductors*. Computer memories expanded to 2 megabytes of RAM memory, and speeds accelerated to 5 MIPS. Third-generation computer technology introduced software that could be used by people without extensive technical training, making it possible for computers to enlarge their role in business.

Fourth Generation: Very Large-Scale Integrated Circuits, 1980–Present

The fourth generation extends from 1980 to the present. Computers in this period use very large-scale integrated circuits (VLSIC), which are packed with hundreds of thousands—even millions—of circuits per chip. Costs have fallen to the point where desktop computers are inexpensive and widely available for use in business and everyday life. The power of a computer that once took up a large room can now reside on a small desktop. Computer memory sizes have mushroomed to over two gigabytes in large commercial machines; processing speeds have exceeded 200 MIPS. In Section 5.7, we discuss the next generation of hardware trends.

VLSIC technology has fueled a growing movement toward microminiaturization—the proliferation of computers that are so small, fast, and cheap that they have become ubiquitous. For instance, many of the intelligent features that have made automobiles, stereos, toys, watches, cameras, and other equipment easier to use are based on microprocessors.

WHAT IS A MICROPROCESSOR? WHAT IS A CHIP?

Very large-scale integrated circuit technology, with hundreds of thousands (or even millions) of transistors on a single chip (see Figure 5.8), integrates the computer's memory, logic, and control on a single chip; hence the name **microprocessor,** or *computer on a chip.* Some popular chips are shown in Table 5.3. Chips are measured in several ways.

microprocessor Very large-scale integrated circuit technology that integrates the computer's memory, logic, and control on a single chip.

FIGURE 5.8
The Pentium microprocessor contains more than 3 million transistors and provides mainframe- and supercomputer-like processing capabilities.

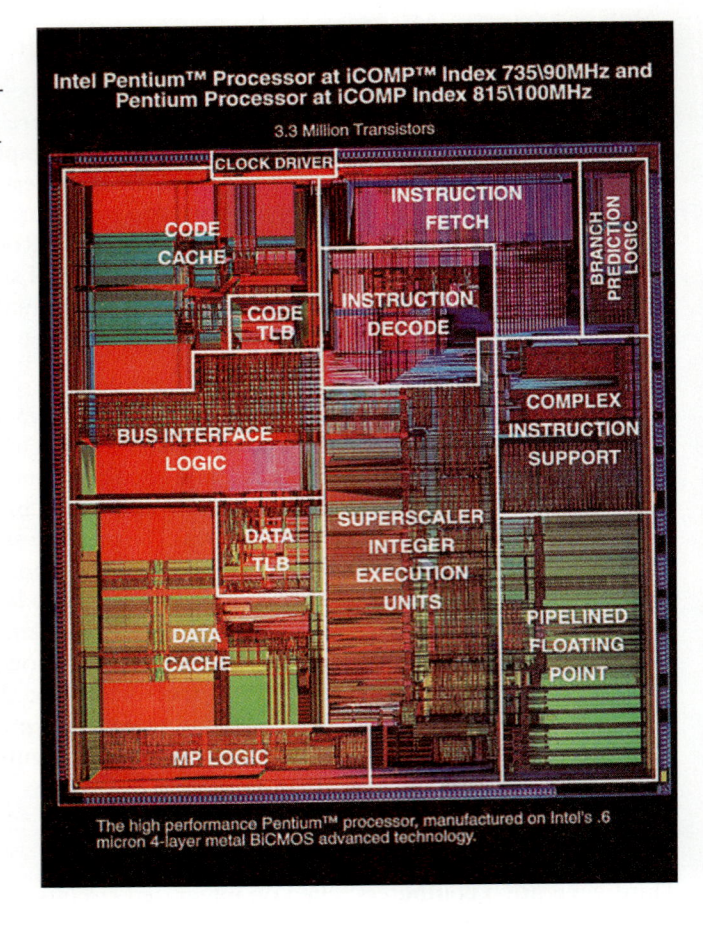

You will often see chips labeled as 8-bit, 16-bit, or 32-bit devices. These labels refer to the **word length,** or the number of bits that can be processed at one time by the machine. An 8-bit chip can process 8 bits, or 1 byte, of information in a single machine cycle. A 32-bit chip can process 32 bits or 4 bytes in a single cycle. The larger the word length, the greater the speed of the computer.

A second factor affecting chip speed is cycle speed. Every event in a computer must be sequenced so that one step logically follows another. The control unit sets a beat to the chip. This beat is established by an internal clock and is measured in **megahertz** (abbreviated MHz, which stands for millions of cycles per second). The Intel 8088 chip, for instance, originally had a clock speed of 4.47 megahertz, whereas the Intel 80486 chip has a clock speed that ranges from 20 to 100 megahertz.

A third factor affecting speed is the **data bus width.** The data bus acts as a highway between the CPU, primary storage, and other devices, determining how much data can be moved at one time. The 8088 chip used in the original IBM personal computer, for example, had a 16-bit word length but only an 8-bit data bus width. This meant that data were processed within the CPU chip itself in 16-bit chunks but could only be moved 8 bits at a time between the CPU, primary storage and external devices. On the other hand, the 80486 chip, used in IBM Personal System/2 microcomputers, has both a 32-bit word length and a 32-bit data bus width. Obviously, in order to get a computer to execute more instructions per second and work through programs or handle users expeditiously, it is necessary to increase the word length of the processor, the data bus width, or the cycle speed—or all three.

Microprocessors can be made faster by using **reduced instruction set computing (RISC)** in their design. Some instructions that a computer uses to process data are actually embedded in the chip circuitry. Conventional chips, based on complex instruction set computing, have several hundred or more instructions hard-wired into their cir-

word length The number of bits that can be processed at one time by a computer. The larger the word length, the greater the speed of the computer.

megahertz A measure of cycle speed, or the pacing of events in a computer; one megahertz equals one million cycles per second.

data bus width The number of bits that can be moved at one time between the CPU, primary storage, and the other devices of a computer.

reduced instruction set computing (RISC) Technology used to enhance the speed of microprocessors by embedding only the most frequently used instructions on a chip.

Table 5.3	Common Microprocessors				
Microprocessor Chip	Microcomputer Manufacturers	Word Length	Data Bus Width	Clock Speed (MHz)	Used in
80486	Intel	32	32	20–100	Microcomputers, workstations
68040	Motorola	32	32	25–40	Mac Quadras
Pentium	Intel	32	64	60–200	High-end workstations, microcomputers
PowerPC 601	IBM, Apple, Motorola	32	64	50–100	Workstations, microcomputers
PowerPC 620	IBM, Apple, Motorola	64	128	100–150	High-end workstations

cuitry, and usually take several clock cycles to execute a single instruction. In many instances, only 20 percent of these instructions are needed for 80 percent of the computer's tasks. If the little-used instructions are eliminated, the remaining instructions can execute much faster.

Reduced instruction set (RISC) computers have only the most frequently used instructions embedded in them. A RISC CPU can execute most instructions in a single machine cycle and sometimes multiple instructions at the same time. RISC is most appropriate for scientific and workstation computing, where there are repetitive arithmetic and logical operations on data or applications calling for three-dimensional image rendering.

Champions of RISC claim that a microcomputer or workstation with RISC technology can offer the performance of much larger computers costing ten times as much. But critics believe that gains in RISC processing speed may be offset by difficulties created by dropping complex instruction set computing. Programs written for conventional processors cannot automatically be transferred to RISC machines; new software is required. Many RISC suppliers are adding more instructions to appeal to a greater number of customers, and designers of conventional microprocessors are streamlining their chips to execute instructions more rapidly.

5.4 MAINFRAMES, MINICOMPUTERS, MICROCOMPUTERS, WORKSTATIONS, AND SUPERCOMPUTERS

Computers represent and process data the same way, but there are different classifications. We can use size and processing speed to categorize contemporary computers as mainframes, minicomputers, microcomputers, workstations, and supercomputers.

MAINFRAMES, MINIS, AND MICROS

A **mainframe** is the largest computer, a powerhouse with massive memory and extremely rapid processing power. It is used for very large commercial, scientific, or military applications where a computer must handle massive amounts of data or many complicated processes. A **minicomputer** is a mid-range computer, about the size of an office desk, often used in universities, factories, or research laboratories. A **microcomputer** is one that can be placed on a desktop or carried from room to room. Microcomputers are used as personal machines as well as in business. A **workstation** also fits on a desktop but has more powerful mathematical and graphics processing capability than a

mainframe Largest category of computer, classified as having 50 megabytes to over 1 gigabyte of RAM.

minicomputer Middle-range computer with about 10 megabytes to over 1 gigabyte of RAM.

microcomputer Desktop or portable computer classified with 640 kilobytes to 64 megabytes of RAM.

workstation Desktop computer with powerful graphics and mathematical capabilities and the ability to perform several tasks at once.

supercomputer Highly sophisticated and powerful computer that can perform very complex computations extremely rapidly.

distributed processing The distribution of computer processing work among multiple computers linked by a communication network.

centralized processing Processing that is accomplished by one large central computer.

downsizing The process of transferring applications from large computers to smaller ones.

microcomputer and can perform more complicated tasks at the same time than can a microcomputer. Workstations are used for scientific, engineering, and design work that requires powerful graphics or computational capabilities. A **supercomputer** is a highly sophisticated and powerful machine that is used for tasks requiring extremely rapid and complex calculations with hundreds of thousands of variable factors. Supercomputers have traditionally been used in scientific and military work, but they are starting to be used in business as well. The problem with this classification scheme is that the capacity of the machines changes so rapidly. A microcomputer today has the computing power of a mainframe from the 1980s or the minicomputer of a few years ago. Powerful microcomputers have sophisticated graphics and processing capabilities similar to workstations. Microcomputers still cannot perform as many tasks at once as mainframes, minicomputers, or workstations (see the discussion of operating systems in Chapter 6); nor can they be used by as many people simultaneously as these larger machines. Even these distinctions will become less pronounced in the future. In another decade, desktop micros might very well have the power and processing speed of today's supercomputers.

Generally, however, mainframes can be classified as having 50 megabytes to over 1 gigabyte of RAM; minicomputers, 10 megabytes to over 1 gigabyte of RAM; microcomputers, 640 kilobytes to 64 megabytes of RAM, and workstations, 8 to 300 megabytes of RAM. Figure 5.9 illustrates some of the capabilities of microcomputers and workstations.

Microcomputers have become so powerful that they are no longer confined to personal information systems. Micros can operate either as individual stand-alone machines with isolated processing power or as part of a departmental or companywide network of intelligent devices. They may be linked to other micros, telecommunications devices, workstations, or larger computers.

In either case, microcomputers are starting to do some of the work formerly performed by larger computers in business. Chapter 8 describes how microcomputers can be linked with other micros, printers, intelligent copy machines, and telephones to provide processing power and to coordinate the work-flow without relying on mainframes. Micros can also be linked to minicomputers and mainframes, forming company wide information networks that share hardware, software, and data resources. The use of multiple computers linked by a communication network for processing is called **distributed processing**. In contrast with **centralized processing,** in which all processing is accomplished by one large central computer, distributed processing distributes the processing work among various microcomputers, minicomputers, and mainframes linked together.

DOWNSIZING AND COOPERATIVE PROCESSING

In some firms microcomputers have actually replaced mainframes and minicomputers. The process of transferring applications from large computers to smaller ones is called **downsizing**. Downsizing has many advantages. The cost per MIPS on a mainframe is almost 100 times greater than on a microcomputer; a megabyte of mainframe memory costs about 10 times more than the same amount of memory on a micro. For some applications micros may also be easier for nontechnical specialists to use and maintain.

The decision to downsize involves many factors beside the cost of computer hardware, including the need for new software, training, and perhaps new organizational procedures. As the Window on Management illustrates, there are many applications where mainframes remain the most appropriate technology platform.

Another computing pattern divides processing work for transaction-based applications among mainframes and microcomputers. Each type of computer is assigned the functions it performs best, and each shares processing (and perhaps data) over a communications link. For example, the microcomputer might be used for data entry and

FIGURE 5.9
Workstations (top) are often used for sophisticated CAD/CAM applications. The IBM PS/2 (bottom) is a microcomputer capable of powerful applications processing.

validation, whereas the mainframe would be responsible for file input and output. This division of labor is called **cooperative processing**. Microcomputers are utilized because they can provide the same processing power much more economically than a mainframe or because they are superior at some tasks, such as at providing screen presentations for the user interface. Figure 5.10 illustrates cooperative processing.

cooperative processing Type of processing that divides the processing work for transaction-based applications among mainframes and microcomputers.

5.4 Mainframes, Minicomputers, Microcomputers, Workstations, and Supercomputers

Window on Management

DEUTSCHE BANK DECIDES TO STAY WITH MAINFRAMES

Deutsche Bank, headquartered in Frankfurt, is the largest bank in Germany and the second largest in Europe. It runs approximately 220 applications on its computers. Deutsche Bank's single biggest application, its branch banking system, generates by itself about 100 million transactions per month. Its financial applications serve about 1000 users and generate up to 12 million transactions per month. Its data processing department has more than 1000 employees, half of whom are writing new applications. This is a giant information systems unit by anyone's standards.

Germany is one of the few industrialized countries to place no restrictions on the scope of the financial services its banks are allowed to offer. The resultant competition for new products is great, and their staffs must be constantly developing large numbers of new applications just to stay competitive.

Given the size of their information systems budgets, the cost of information systems can have a major effect on a bank's bottom line. Banks usually focus heavily on reducing IS costs. Given that downsizing to networked smaller computers is widely believed to result in large cost savings while also improving computer service, why has Deutsche Bank not gone this route? Deutsche Bank IS management did examine the question of downsizing very carefully, stimulated both by the recession that hit Europe in the early 1990s and the tremendous interest in downsizing throughout the information systems field. The bank does use workstations for certain functions, such as equity trading, but relies primarily on mainframes for its heavy processing work. Mathias Junger, Deutsche Bank's manager of capacity planning, gives one major reason why the bank has not downsized. After careful study, he concluded that downsizing will not result in lower costs than operating with mainframes. "Downsizing might be cheaper on the hardware [side], but not when you take networking, support and re-education of users into account," he claims. Another fundamental reason banks like Deutsche have not downsized is that banks have to be able to serve their millions of customers at the cash point. "They can't afford to let response times drop. Otherwise, customers will go to another bank." He adds that to achieve the fastest retrieval times for the massive amounts of data maintained by large banks, the data must be stored on mainframes.

> **To Think About:** How was computer processing power related to Deutsche Bank's business strategy? What other management, organizational, and technical factors might have contributed to management's decision not to downsize?

To examine the performance of its mainframes, Deutsche Bank turned to software from BGS Systems of Waltham, Massachusetts. BGS focuses on software to manage the performance of computers, particularly large computers, and on capacity planning for medium to large data centers. Deutsche Bank is now using a full set of BGS tools to both monitor its mainframe performance in order to tune its mainframes and to improve that performance. In addition, the bank uses BGS tools to analyze and tune the performance of other critical computer system elements such as the mainframe DASD, cache, and response time. The bank is now better able to predict future needs and to plan for upgrades more effectively. With proper monitoring and tuning, mainframes become cost effective compared to the alternatives. With the help of such software to make better use of their investments in mainframes, banks not only will not be downsizing, but in the coming years will actually be consolidating their mainframes into fewer but larger machines. Mainframes provide much better data security than do minicomputers and microcomputers, a factor of prime importance to bank managements.

Sources: "IBM Wins Big at Deutsche Bank," *Wall Street and Technology* 14, no. 7 (July 1996) and George Black, "Deutsche Bank Gives BGS Tools Good Marks for Performance," *Software Magazine,* August 1994.

FIGURE 5.10
Cooperative processing. In cooperative processing, an application is divided into tasks that run on more than one type of computer. This example shows the tasks that a microcomputer is best at performing, the tasks that a mainframe computer is best at performing, and those tasks that each type is able to perform.

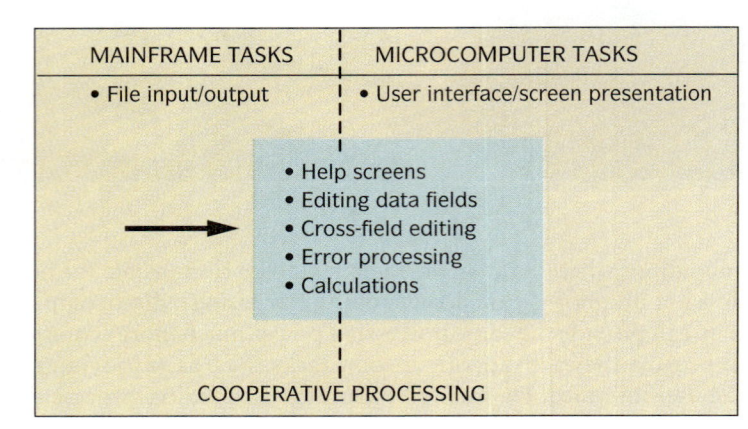

MAINFRAME TASKS	MICROCOMPUTER TASKS
• File input/output	• User interface/screen presentation

- Help screens
- Editing data fields
- Cross-field editing
- Error processing
- Calculations

COOPERATIVE PROCESSING

MICROCOMPUTERS AND WORKSTATIONS

What distinguishes a microcomputer from a workstation? Workstations have more powerful graphics and mathematical processing capabilities than microcomputers, and can easily perform several tasks at the same time. They are typically used by scientists, engineers, and other knowledge workers but are spreading to the financial industry because they have the computing power to simultaneously analyze portfolios, process securities trades, and provide financial data and news services (see Chapter 12).

Workstations are especially useful for computer-aided design (CAD) and for complex simulations and modeling. They can represent fully rendered multiple views of a physical object, such as an airplane wing, rotate the object three-dimensionally, and present design history and cost factors.

Powerful high-end microcomputers have many of the same capabilities as low-end workstations. As microcomputers become increasingly graphics oriented, the distinctions between the two types of computers are likely to blur further. Moreover, workstations themselves have increased in power, so that the most sophisticated workstations have some of the capabilities of earlier mainframes and supercomputers (Thomborson, 1993).

SUPERCOMPUTERS AND PARALLEL PROCESSING

A supercomputer is an especially sophisticated and powerful type of computer that is used primarily for extremely rapid and complex computations with hundreds or thousands of variable factors. Supercomputers have traditionally been used for classified weapons research, weather forecasting, and petroleum and engineering applications, all of which use complex mathematical models and simulations. Although extremely expensive, supercomputers are beginning to be employed in business, as the Window on Technology demonstrates.

Supercomputers can perform complex and massive computations almost instantaneously because they can perform billions and even hundreds of billions of calculations per second—many times faster than the largest mainframes. Supercomputers do not process one instruction at a time but instead rely on **parallel processing**. As illustrated in Figure 5.11, multiple processing units (CPUs) break down a problem into smaller

parallel processing Type of processing in which more than one instruction can be processed at a time by breaking down a problem into smaller parts and processing them simultaneously with multiple processors.

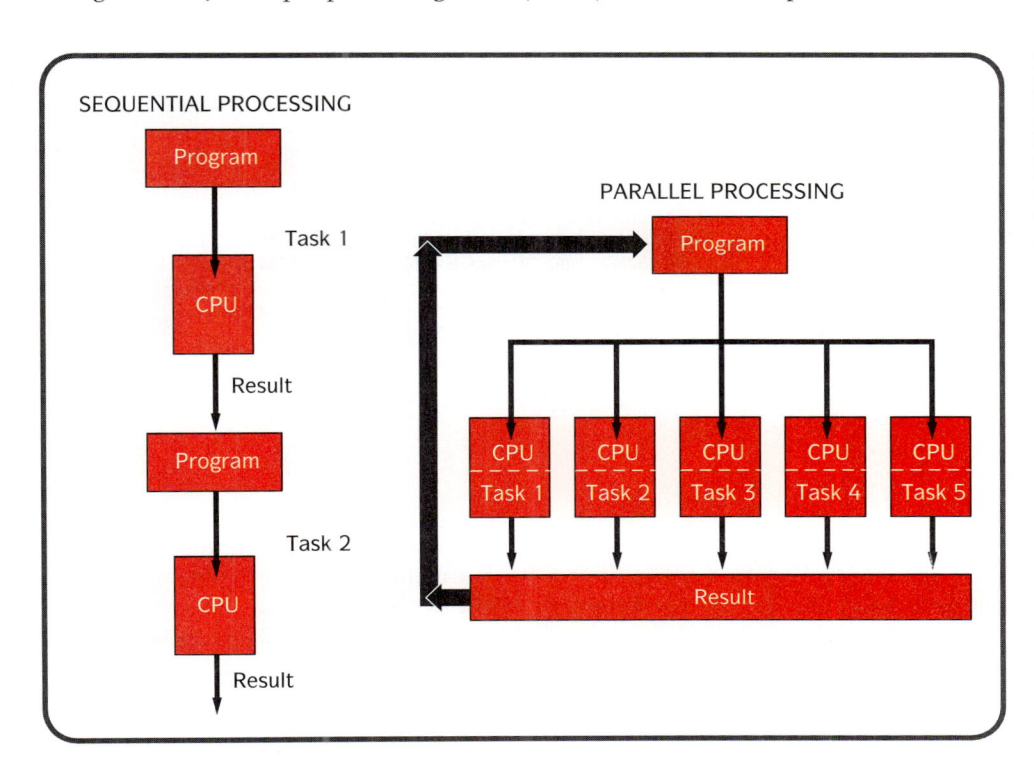

FIGURE 5.11
Sequential and parallel processing. During sequential processing, each task is assigned to one CPU that processes one instruction at a time. In parallel processing, multiple tasks are assigned to multiple processing units to expedite the result.

Window on Technology

PARALLEL PROCESSING GOES COMMERCIAL

Parallel processing computers—often known as *supercomputers*—have long been viewed as tools exclusively for scientists and engineers. Now, their great power is fast resulting in their finding new roles as commercial computers.

Parallel processors have not been widely used for commercial applications until recently primarily for two related reasons. First, they have been difficult to cost-justify for commonplace commercial uses. In addition, few corporate or IS managers have envisioned any uses for so much intense computing power—what would they do with them? Technology has progressed, resulting in the lowering of prices, while management has responded to the growing power of computers with new ideas on how the power might be used.

Wal-Mart Stores, Inc., the Bentonville, Arkansas, discounting giant and largest retailer in the United States, processes 20 million point-of-sale updates daily in its 2100 stores, storing trillions of bytes of data used to keep their inventory up to date and to spot sales trends. Wal-Mart needs supercomputers to process approximately 2300 queries per day against this massive collection of data. Trimark Investment Management, a Toronto, Canada, mutual funds company, has seen its account base shoot up from 250,000 customers in 1992 to 800,000 two years later. To post its accounts at the end of 1992, its more traditional IBM System 38 required 18 to 24 hours of processing. Today the company would not even be able to post the data for more than triple the number of customers the 1992 way—the computer simply could not handle all that data. However, in 1994, using a Pyramid Technology Niles 150 with six processors, Trimark posted all the customers in eight hours.

The SABRE Group, the reservation and ticketing organization that is owned by American Airlines but also services 52 other carriers plus a large number of travel agencies, uses an IBM Parallel Enterprise Server (PES) to price its tickets. SABRE processes a massive amount of data, normally handling about 3000 messages per second. SABRE's parallel processors have successfully processed a peak load of 4100 messages per second. Financial firms are starting to use supercomputers for derivatives pricing and portfolio optimization, which require numerous elements of computational analysis. For example, Atlantic Portfolio Analytics and Management in Orlando, Florida, uses a Cray EL98 supercomputer to keep track of and evaluate a portfolio of more than 600,000 securities. Companies are turning to parallel processing computers to improve customer service. Because parallel pro-

> **To Think About:** How is selection of parallel processor technology related to the business strategies of the firms described here? What management, organization, and technology criteria would you use in deciding whether to purchase a parallel processor?

cessing computers can search large databases so rapidly, companies are finding they can answer customer queries much more rapidly than with single-processor technology. Perhaps the applications that generate the most intense interest have come to be known as data mining (see Chapter 2). Organizations mine data—search through and analyze massive pools of data—to find hidden but useful information. For example, retail companies of all types, including Wal-Mart, are now analyzing huge databases to identify changing buying patterns and customer tastes, information that can then be used to support marketing or to drive the new product development process. Others are mining data to determine the consequences of a particular action. Max D. Hopper, chairman of the SABRE Group AA, Inc., offers an example of just such an application: "If Dallas–Fort Worth has a severe weather problem that affects 50 arriving or departing flights with 5000 passengers, the [parallel processing] technology has the power to let us see the impact on every flight, including aircraft, crew, maintenance and passengers." It might take a large mainframe several days or a week to come up with the answer, yet a parallel processing computer might deliver results within a few hours.

Sources: Dean Tomasula, "Entering a Parallel Universe," *Wall Street and Technology* 14, no. 4 (April 1996); Michael Alexander, "Mine for Gold with Parallel Systems," *Datamation*, November 15, 1994; Willie Schatz, "Out of the Lab, Into the Office," *Information Week*, May 16, 1994; and Craig Stedman, "Sabre Parallel Systems Reduce Transaction Costs," *Computerworld*, November 17, 1994.

---

parts and work on it simultaneously. Some experimental supercomputers use up to 64,000 processors. Getting a group of processors to attack the same problem at once is easier said than done. It requires rethinking of the problems and special software that can divide problems among different processors in the most efficient possible way, providing the needed data, and reassembling the many subtasks to reach an appropriate solution.

5.5 SECONDARY STORAGE

In addition to primary storage, where information and programs are stored for immediate processing, modern computer systems use other types of storage in order to accomplish their tasks. Information systems need to store information outside of the computer in a nonvolatile state (not requiring electrical power) and to store volumes of data too large to fit into a computer of any size today (such as a large payroll or the U.S. census). The relatively long-term storage of data outside the CPU and primary storage is called **secondary storage**.

Primary storage is where the fastest, most expensive technology is used. As shown in Table 5.4, there are actually three different kinds of primary memory: register, cache, and RAM. **Register** is the fastest and most expensive memory, where small amounts of data and instructions reside for thousandths of a second just prior to use, followed by **cache** memory (for high-speed storage of frequently used instructions and data) and RAM memory for large amounts of data. Access to information stored in primary memory is electronic and occurs almost at the speed of light. Secondary storage is nonvolatile and retains data even when the computer is turned off. There are many kinds of secondary storage; the most common are magnetic tape, magnetic disk, and optical disk. These media can transfer large bodies of data rapidly to the CPU. But since secondary storage requires mechanical movement to gain access to the data, in contrast to primary storage, it is relatively slow.

secondary storage Relatively long-term, nonvolatile storage of data outside the CPU and primary storage.

register Temporary storage location in the ALU or control unit where small amounts of data and instructions reside for thousandths of a second just before use.

cache High-speed storage of frequently used instructions and data.

MAGNETIC TAPE

Magnetic tape is an older device that is still important for secondary storage of large volumes of information. It is used primarily in mainframe batch applications and for archiving data. Generally, magnetic tape for large systems comes in 14-inch reels that are up to 2400 feet long and 0.5 inches wide. It is very similar to home cassette recording tape, but of higher quality. Figure 5.12 shows how information appears on magnetic tape using an EBCDIC coding scheme. Each byte of data utilizes one column across the width of the tape. Each column is composed of eight bits plus one check parity bit. Information can be stored on magnetic tape at different densities. Low density is 1600 bytes per inch (bpi), and densities of up to 6250 bpi are common. Tape cartridges with much higher density and storage capacity are starting to replace reel-to-reel tapes in mainframe and minicomputer systems. Microcomputers and some minicomputers use small tape cartridges resembling home audiocassettes to store information.

The principal advantages of magnetic tape are that it is very inexpensive, that it is relatively stable, and that it can store very large volumes of information. Moreover,

magnetic tape Inexpensive and relatively stable secondary storage medium in which large volumes of information are stored sequentially by means of magnetized and nonmagnetized spots on tape.

Table 5.4 Data Storage Devices in a Microcomputer

Type of Memory	Total Storage Capacity	Access Time
	Primary Storage	
Register	1 kilobyte	.01 microseconds
Cache	1 kilobyte	.1 microseconds
RAM	16 megabytes	.5 microseconds
	Secondary Storage	
Hard disk	800 megabytes	15 milliseconds
High-density diskette (3.5")	2.8 megabytes	200 milliseconds
Optical disk	660 megabytes	200–500 milliseconds
Magnetic tape (1/4" streaming tape backup)	40 megabytes	1–2 seconds

FIGURE 5.12
Magnetic tape storage. Data can be stored on nine-track magnetic tape, which is a stable and inexpensive medium. However, data are stored sequentially and, therefore, access and retrieval may be slow.

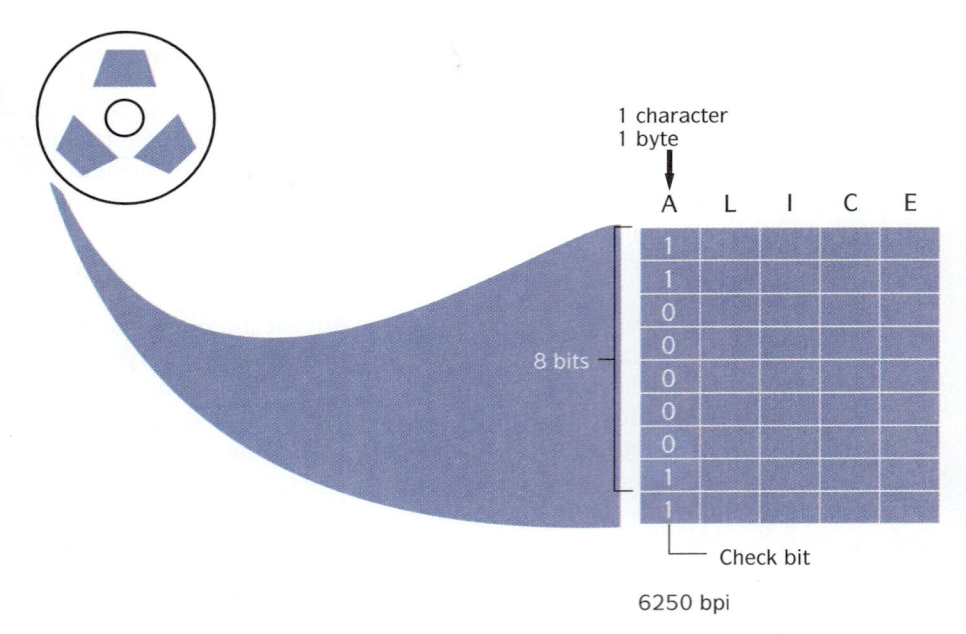

magnetic tape can be used over and over again, although it does age with time and computer users must handle it carefully.

The principal disadvantages of magnetic tape are that it stores data sequentially and is relatively slow compared to the speed of other secondary storage media. In order to find an individual record stored on magnetic tape, such as your professor's employment record, the tape must be read from the beginning up to the location of the desired record. Hence, magnetic tape is not a good medium when it is necessary to find information rapidly (such as for an airline reservation system). Tape can also be damaged and is labor intensive to mount and dismount. Tape represents a fading technology, but it continues to exist in changing forms.

MAGNETIC DISK

magnetic disk A secondary storage medium in which data are stored by means of magnetized spots on a hard or floppy disk.

hard disk Magnetic disk resembling a thin steel platter with an iron oxide coating; used in large computer systems and in many microcomputers.

cylinder Represents circular tracks on the same vertical line within a disk pack.

track Concentric circle on the surface area of a disk on which data are stored as magnetized spots; each track can store thousands of bytes.

The most widely used secondary storage medium today is **magnetic disk.** There are two kinds of magnetic disks: floppy disks (used in microcomputers) and hard disks (used on commercial disk drives and microcomputers). **Hard disks** are thin steel platters with an iron oxide coating. In larger systems, multiple hard disks are mounted together on a vertical shaft. Figure 5.13 illustrates a commercial hard disk pack for a large system. It has 11 disks, each with two surfaces, top and bottom. However, although there are 11 disks, no information is recorded on the top or bottom surfaces; thus, there are only 20 recording surfaces on the disk pack. On each surface, data are stored on tracks. The disk pack is generally sealed from the environment and rotates at a speed of about 3500 rpm, creating an air-stream speed of about 50 mph at the disk surface.

Information is recorded on or read from the disk by read/write heads, which literally fly over the spinning disks. Unlike a home stereo, the heads never actually touch the disk (which would destroy the data and cause the system to crash) but hover a few thousandths of an inch above it. A smoke particle or a human hair is sufficient to crash the head into the disk.

The read/write heads move horizontally (from left to right) to any of 200 positions called **cylinders.** At any one of these cylinders, the read/write heads can read or write information to any of 20 different concentric circles on the disk surface areas (called **tracks**). The cylinder represents the circular tracks on the same vertical line within the disk pack. Read/write heads are directed to a specific record using an address consisting of the cylinder number, the recording surface number, and the data record number.

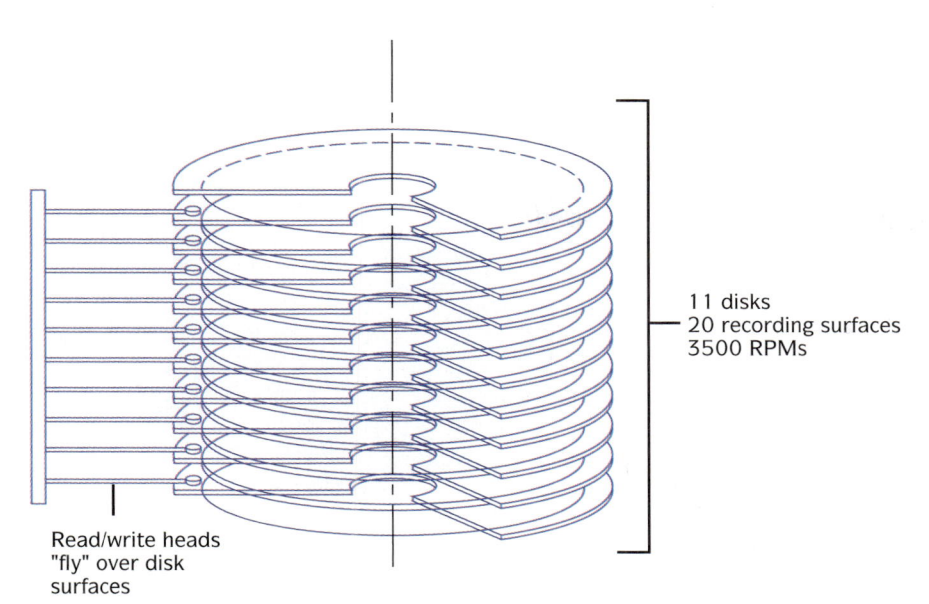

FIGURE 5.13
Disk pack storage. Large systems often rely on disk packs, which provide reliable storage for large amounts of data with quick access and retrieval. A typical removable disk pack system contains 11 two-sided disks.

11 disks
20 recording surfaces
3500 RPMs

Read/write heads "fly" over disk surfaces

The speed of access to data on a disk is a function of the rotational speed of the disk and the speed of the access arms. The read/write heads must position themselves, and the disk pack must rotate until the proper information is located. More advanced and expensive disks have access speeds of 1.5–10 milliseconds and capacities of up to 7.5 gigabytes per unit.

Each track contains several records. In general, 20,000 bytes of information can be stored on each track at densities of up to 12,000 bpi. If there are 20 such tracks and 200 cylinders in a disk pack, the total capacity of the illustrated disk pack is 80 megabytes. As noted previously, advanced commercial disks for large systems have much higher storage capacities over 1 billion bytes.

The entire disk pack is housed in a disk drive or disk unit. Large mainframe or minicomputer systems have multiple disk drives because they require immense disk storage capacity. Disk drive performance can be further enhanced by using a disk technology called **RAID (Redundant Array of Inexpensive Disks)**. RAID devices package more than a hundred 5.25-inch disk drives, a controller chip, and specialized software into a single large unit. While traditional disk drives deliver data from the disk drive along a single path, RAID delivers data over multiple paths simultaneously, accelerating disk access time. Smaller RAID systems provide 10 to 20 gigabytes of storage capacity, while larger systems provide over 700 gigabytes. RAID is potentially more reliable than standard disk drives because other drives are available to deliver data if one drive fails.

Microcomputers usually contain hard disks, which can store over 1.2 gigabytes, but 340 to 520 megabytes are the most common size. Microcomputers also use **floppy disks**, which are flat, 5.25-inch or 3.5-inch disks of polyester film with a magnetic coating. These disks have a storage capacity ranging from 360K to 2.8 megabytes and a much slower access rate than hard disks. Floppy disks and cartridges and packs of multiple disks use a **sector** method of storing data. As illustrated in Figure 5.14, the disk surface is divided into pie-shaped pieces, the actual number depending on the disk system used. (Some disks use eight sectors, others nine.) In most types of floppy disks, each sector has the same storage capacity (data are recorded more densely on the inner disk tracks). Each sector is assigned a unique number. Data can be located using an address consisting of the sector number and an individual data record number.

Magnetic disks on both large and small computers have several important advantages over magnetic tape. First, they permit direct access to individual records. Each record can be given a precise physical address in terms of cylinders and tracks, and the read/write head can be directed to go to that address and access the information in

RAID (Redundant Array of Inexpensive Disks) Disk storage technology to boost disk performance by packaging more than 100 smaller disk drives with a controller chip and specialized software in a single large unit to deliver data over multiple paths simultaneously.

floppy disk Removable magnetic disk primarily used with microcomputers. The two most common standard sizes are 3.5-inch and 5.25-inch disks that are made of polyester film with a magnetic coating.

sector Method of storing data on a floppy disk in which the disk is divided into pie-shaped pieces or sectors. Each sector is assigned a unique number so that data can be located using the sector number.

FIGURE 5.14
The sector method of storing data. Each track of a disk can be divided into sectors. Disk storage location can be identified by sector and data record number.

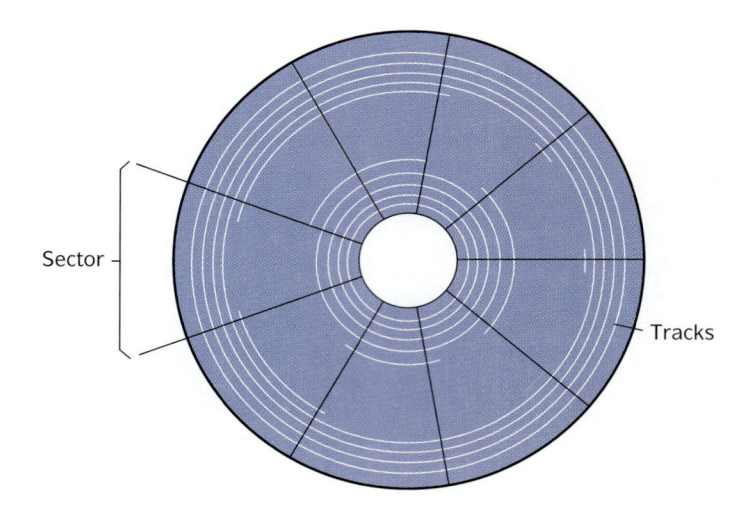

about 10 to 60 milliseconds. This means that the computer system does not have to search the entire file, as in a tape file, in order to find the person's record. Disk storage is often referred to as a **direct access storage device (DASD)**.

For on-line systems requiring direct access, disk technology provides the only practical means of storage today. Records can be easily and rapidly retrieved.

DASD is, however, more expensive than magnetic tape. Moreover, updating information stored on a disk destroys the old information because the old data on the disk are written over if changes are made. (In contrast, changes to data made on magnetic tape are made on a different reel of tape so that the old version of the tape can be retained and recovered.) Therefore, it becomes more difficult to back up and audit the transactions recorded on a disk.

In addition, disks can crash. The disk drives themselves are susceptible to environmental disturbances; even smoke particles can disrupt the movement of read/write heads over the disk surface. Therefore, the environment must be relatively pure and stable. That is why disk drives are sealed in a clean room.

direct access storage device (DASD) Refers to magnetic disk technology that permits the CPU to locate a record directly, in contrast to sequential tape storage that must search the entire file.

OPTICAL DISKS

optical disk Secondary storage device on which data are recorded and read by laser beams rather than by magnetic means.

Optical disks, also called compact disks or laser optical disks, store data at densities many times greater than those of magnetic disks and are available for both microcomputers and large computers. Data are recorded on optical disks when a laser device burns microscopic pits in the reflective layer of a spiral track. Binary information is encoded by the length of these pits and the space between them. Optical disks can thus store massive quantities of data, including not only text but also pictures, sound, and full motion video, in a highly compact form. The optical disk is read by having a low-power laser beam from an optical head scan the disk (see Figure 5.15).

The most common optical disk system used with microcomputers is called **CD-ROM (compact disk read-only memory)**. A 4.75-inch compact disk can store up to 660 megabytes, nearly 300 times more than a high-density floppy disk. Optical disks are most appropriate for applications where enormous quantities of unchanging data must be stored compactly for easy retrieval, or for storing graphic images and sound. CD-ROM is also less vulnerable than floppy disks to magnetism, dirt, or rough handling.

CD-ROM (compact disk read-only memory) Read-only optical disk storage used for imaging, reference, and database applications with massive amounts of data and for multimedia.

CD-ROM is read-only storage. No new data can be written to it; it can only be read. CD-ROM has been most widely used for reference materials with massive amounts of data, such as encyclopedias, directories, or on-line databases and for storing multimedia applications that combine text, sound, and images (see Section 5.7). For example, financial databases from Dow Jones or Dun and Bradstreet are available on CD-ROM. The U.S. Department of Defense has initiated a system of networks and

How a CD-ROM Drive Works

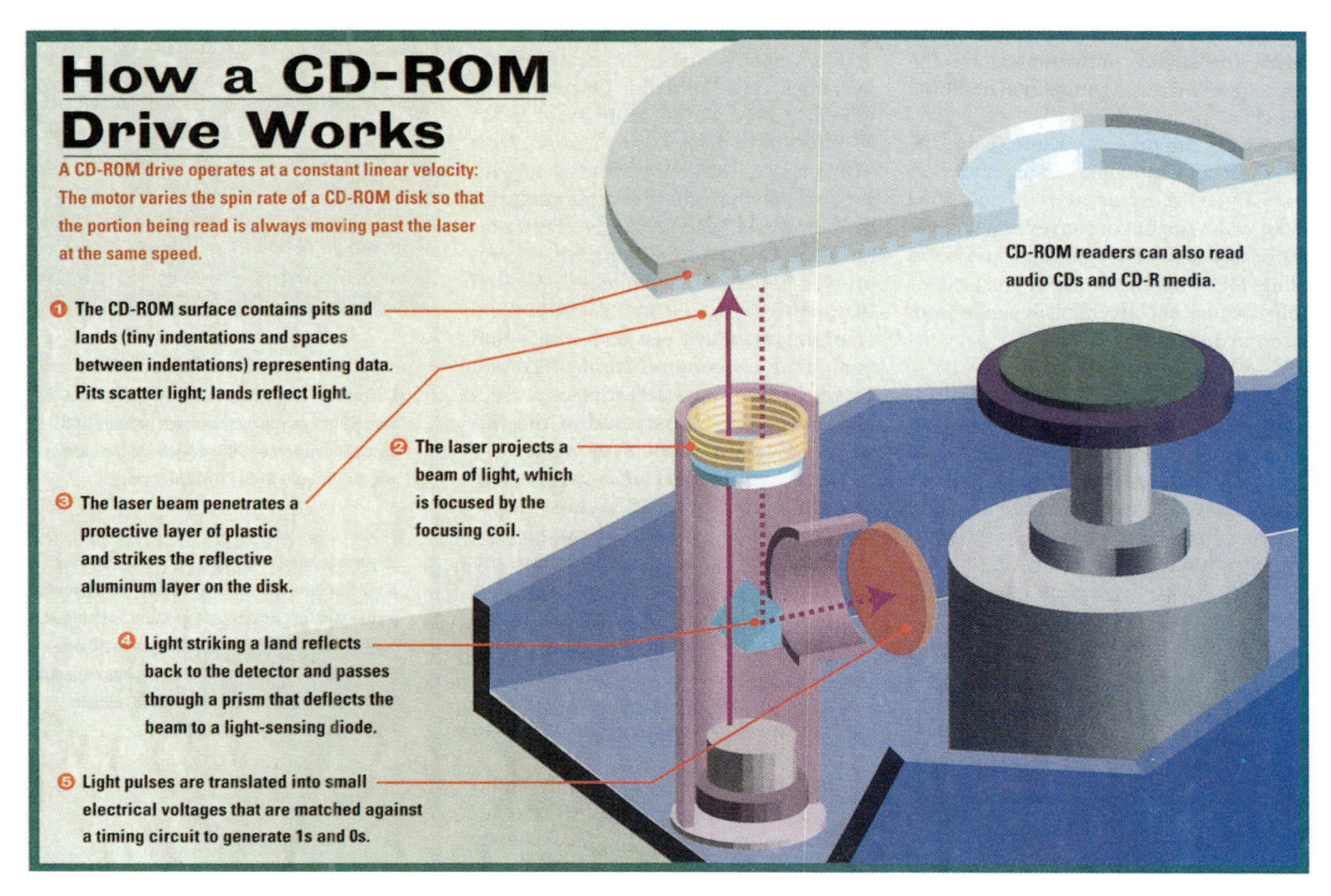

A CD-ROM drive operates at a constant linear velocity: The motor varies the spin rate of a CD-ROM disk so that the portion being read is always moving past the laser at the same speed.

① The CD-ROM surface contains pits and lands (tiny indentations and spaces between indentations) representing data. Pits scatter light; lands reflect light.

② The laser projects a beam of light, which is focused by the focusing coil.

③ The laser beam penetrates a protective layer of plastic and strikes the reflective aluminum layer on the disk.

④ Light striking a land reflects back to the detector and passes through a prism that deflects the beam to a light-sensing diode.

⑤ Light pulses are translated into small electrical voltages that are matched against a timing circuit to generate 1s and 0s.

CD-ROM readers can also read audio CDs and CD-R media.

FIGURE 5.15
How a CD-ROM drive works. A low-powered laser beam reads the pattern of pits and spaces representing data on the surface of the CD-ROM for translation into 0s and 1s. *Reprinted from* PC Magazine *July 1994. Copyright © 1994 Ziff-Davis Publishing Company. Reprinted by permission.*

Because a single CD-ROM can store vast quantities of data, the technology is often used for storing images, sound, and video, as well as text.

optical imaging to reduce the mountains of paper generated by technical design information and administrative data for weapons systems.

WORM (write once/read many) optical disk systems allow users to record data only once on an optical disk. Once written, the data cannot be erased, but can be read indefinitely. WORM has been used as an alternative to microfilm for archiving digitized document images. The disadvantages of CD-ROM and WORM optical disks are that their contents cannot easily be erased and written over, as can be done with magnetic disks, and that the access speed is slower than that of magnetic disks.

Rewritable **magneto-optical disks** are starting to become cost effective for data storage. The disk surface is coated with a magnetic material that can change magnetic polarity only when heated. To record data a high-powered laser beam heats tiny spots in the magnetic medium that allows it to accept magnetic patterns. Data can be read by shining a lower-powered laser beam at the magnetic layer and reading the reflected light. The magneto-optical disk is erasable and can be written on nearly a million times. The access speed of optical disks, while slower than that of a magnetic disk, is continuing to improve, making the optical disk a very attractive storage technology in coming years.

CD-ROM storage is likely to become more popular and more powerful in years to come. Consumer electronics companies such as Sony, Philips Electronics, Time Warner, and Toshiba are developing high-capacity compact disks that can store over 4 billion bytes of data, enough to hold two to three hours of high-resolution digital video with stereo sound. Such digital videodisks would contain 15 times more data than current CD-ROMs and would work with computers of all sizes as well as video and video-game players (Markoff, 1995).

WORM (write once/read many) Optical disk system that allows users to record data only once; data cannot be erased but can be read indefinitely.

magneto-optical disk Optical disk system that is erasable. Data are recorded by a high-powered laser beam that heats tiny spots in the magnetic media.

5.6 INPUT AND OUTPUT DEVICES

Human beings interact with computer systems largely through input and output devices. Advances in information systems rely not only on the speed and capacity of the CPU but also on the speed, capacity, and design of the input and output devices. Input/output devices are often called peripheral devices.

INPUT DEVICES

The traditional method of data entry has been by keyboarding. Today, most data are entered directly into the computer using a data entry terminal and they are processed on-line. For instance, on-line airline reservation and customer information systems have reservation clerks or salespeople enter transactions directly while dealing with the customer, and their systems are updated immediately.

Some batch applications developed during an earlier era in computing might still use keypunching to obtain input. Data entry clerks use a keypunch machine to code characters on an 80-column card, designating each character with a unique punch in a specific location on the card. An electromechanical card reader senses the holes and solid parts of the cards. A single card could store up to 80 bytes of information (80 columns). Key-to-tape or key-to-disk machines allowed data to be keyed directly onto magnetic tape or disk for later computer processing.

The Computer Mouse

The point-and-click actions of the **computer mouse** have made it an increasingly popular alternative to keyboard and text-based commands. A mouse is a handheld device that is usually connected to the computer by a cable. The computer user moves the mouse around on a desktop to control the position of the cursor on a video display screen. Once the cursor is in the desired position, the user can push a button on the mouse to select a command. The mouse can also be used to "draw" images on the screen.

computer mouse Handheld input device whose movement on the desktop controls the position of the cursor on the computer display screen.

Touch Screens

Touch screens are easy to use and are appealing to people who can't use traditional keyboards. Users can enter limited amounts of data by touching the surface of a sensitized video display monitor with a finger or a pointer. With colorful graphics, sound, and simple menus, touch screens allow the user to make selections by touching specified parts of the screen. Touch screens are proliferating in retail stores, restaurants, shopping malls, and even in some schools. For instance, music stores can install Intouch, touch screen–equipped kiosks produced by Muze Inc. of Brooklyn, to sell audio compact disks. Customers can use the touch screen to select 30-second samples of songs before making up their minds. Having listened to one song, a customer can again touch the screen to bring up lists of other songs by the same musicians.

touch screen Input device technology that permits the entering or selecting of commands and data by touching the surface of a sensitized video display monitor with a finger or a pointer.

Source Data Automation

Source data automation captures data in computer-readable form at the time and place they are created. Point-of-sale systems, optical bar-code scanners used in supermarkets, and other optical character recognition devices are examples of source data automation. One of the advantages of source data automation is that the many errors that occur when people use keyboards to enter data are almost eliminated. Bar-code scanners make fewer than 1 error in 10,000 transactions, whereas skilled keypunchers make about 1 error for every 1000 keystrokes.

The principal source data automation technologies are magnetic ink character recognition, optical character recognition, pen-based input, digital scanners, voice input, and sensors.

Magnetic ink character recognition (MICR) technology is used primarily in check processing for the banking industry. The bottom portion of a typical check contains characters that are preprinted using a special ink. Characters identify the bank, checking account, and check number. An MICR reader translates the characters on checks that have been cashed and sent to the bank for processing into digital form for the computer. The amount of the check, which is written in ordinary ink, must be keyed in by hand.

Optical character recognition (OCR) devices translate specially designed marks, characters, and codes into digital form. The most widely used optical code is the **bar code,** which is used in point-of-sale systems in supermarkets and retail stores. Bar codes are also used in hospitals, libraries, military operations, and transportation facilities. The codes can include time, date, and location data in addition to identification data; the information makes them useful for analyzing the movement of items and determining what has happened to them during production or other processes. (The discussion of the United Parcel Service in Chapter 1 and the case concluding this chapter show how valuable bar codes can be for this purpose.)

Handwriting-recognition devices such as pen-based tablets, notebooks, and notepads are promising new input technologies, especially for people working in the sales or service areas or for those who have traditionally shunned computer keyboards. These **pen-based input** devices usually consist of a flat-screen display table and a pen-like stylus.

With pen-based input, users print directly onto the tablet-sized screen. The screen is fitted with a transparent grid of fine wires that detects the presence of the special stylus, which emits a faint signal from its tip. The screen can also interpret tapping and flicking gestures made with the stylus.

Pen-based input devices transform the letters and numbers written by users on the tablet into digital form, where they can be stored or processed and analyzed. For instance, the United Parcel Service replaced its drivers' familiar clipboard with a battery-powered Delivery Information Acquisition Device (DIAD) to capture signatures (see the Chapter 1 Window on Technology) along with other information required for pickup and delivery. This technology requires special pattern-recognition software to accept pen-based input instead of keyboard input. At present, most pen-based systems cannot recognize freehand writing very well.

source data automation Input technology that captures data in computer-readable form at the time and place the data are created.

magnetic ink character recognition (MICR) Input technology that translates characters written in magnetic ink into digital codes for processing.

optical character recognition (OCR) Form of source data automation in which optical scanning devices read specially designed data off source documents and translate the data into digital form for the computer.

bar code Form of OCR technology widely used in supermarkets and retail stores in which identification data are coded into a series of bars.

pen-based input Input devices such as tablets, notebooks, and notepads consisting of a flat-screen display tablet and a pen-like stylus that digitizes handwriting.

digital scanners Input devices that translate images such as pictures or documents into digital form for processing.

voice input devices Technology that converts the spoken word into digital form for processing.

sensors Devices that collect data directly from the environment for input into a computer system.

Digital scanners translate images such as pictures or documents into digital form and are an essential component of image processing systems. **Voice input devices** convert spoken words into digital form. Voice-recognition software compares the electrical patterns produced by the speaker's voice to a set of prerecorded patterns. If the patterns match, the input is accepted. Most voice systems still have limited vocabularies of several hundred to several thousand words and can accept only very simple commands. For instance, some branches of the U.S. Postal Service are using voice-recognition systems to make sorting packages and envelopes more efficient. In one application, users can speak out ZIP codes instead of keying them in, so that both hands can manipulate a package.

Sensors are devices that collect data directly from the environment for input into a computer system. For instance, sensors are being used in General Motors cars with on-board computers and screens that display the map of the surrounding area and the driver's route. Sensors in each wheel and a magnetic compass supply information to the computer for determining the car's location.

BATCH AND ON-LINE INPUT AND PROCESSING

The manner in which data are input into the computer affects how the data can be processed. Information systems collect and process information in one of two ways: through batch or through on-line processing. In **batch processing,** transactions such as orders or payroll time cards are accumulated and stored in a group or batch until the time when, because of some reporting cycle, it is efficient or necessary to process them. This was the only method of processing until the early 1960s, and it is still used today in older systems or some systems with massive volumes of transactions. In **on-line processing,** which is now very common, the user enters transactions into a device that is directly connected to the computer system. The transactions are usually processed immediately.

batch processing A method of collecting and processing data in which transactions are accumulated and stored until a specified time when it is convenient or necessary to process them as a group.

on-line processing A method of collecting and processing data in which transactions are entered directly into the computer system and processed immediately.

transaction file In batch systems, a file in which all transactions are accumulated to await processing.

master file A file that contains all permanent information and is updated during processing by transaction data.

The demands of the business determine the type of processing. If the user needs periodic or occasional reports or output, as in payroll or end-of-the-year reports, batch processing is most efficient. If the user needs immediate information and processing, as in an airline or hotel reservation system, then the system should use on-line processing.

Figure 5.16 compares batch and on-line processing. Batch systems often use tape as a storage medium, whereas on-line processing systems use disk storage, which permits immediate access to specific items of information. In batch systems, transactions are accumulated in a **transaction file,** which contains all the transactions for a particular time period. Periodically this file is used to update a **master file,** which contains permanent information on entities. (An example is a payroll master file with employee earnings and deductions data. It is updated with weekly time-card transactions.) Adding the transaction data to the existing master file creates a new master file. In on-line processing, transactions are entered into the system immediately and the system usually responds immediately. The master file is updated continually. In on-line processing, there is a direct connection to the computer for input and output.

OUTPUT DEVICES

video display terminal (VDT) A screen, also referred to as a cathode ray tube (CRT). Provides a visual image of both user input and computer output. Displays text or graphics as either color or monochrome images.

bit mapping The technology that allows each pixel on the screen to be addressed and manipulated by the computer.

The major data output devices are *cathode ray tube (CRT)* terminals (sometimes called **video display terminals** or **VDTs),** and printers.

The CRT is probably the most popular form of information output in modern computer systems. It works much like a television picture tube, with an electronic gun shooting a beam of electrons to illuminate the pixels on the screen. The more pixels per screen, the higher the resolution. CRT monitors can be classified as monochrome or color and by their display capabilities. Some display only text, whereas others display both text and graphics. Typical CRTs display 80 columns and 24 lines of text data. Display devices for graphics often utilize **bit mapping.** Bit mapping allows each pixel on the screen to be addressed and manipulated by the computer (as opposed to blocks of pixels in character addressable displays). This requires more computer memory but permits finer detail and the ability to produce any kind of image on the display screen.

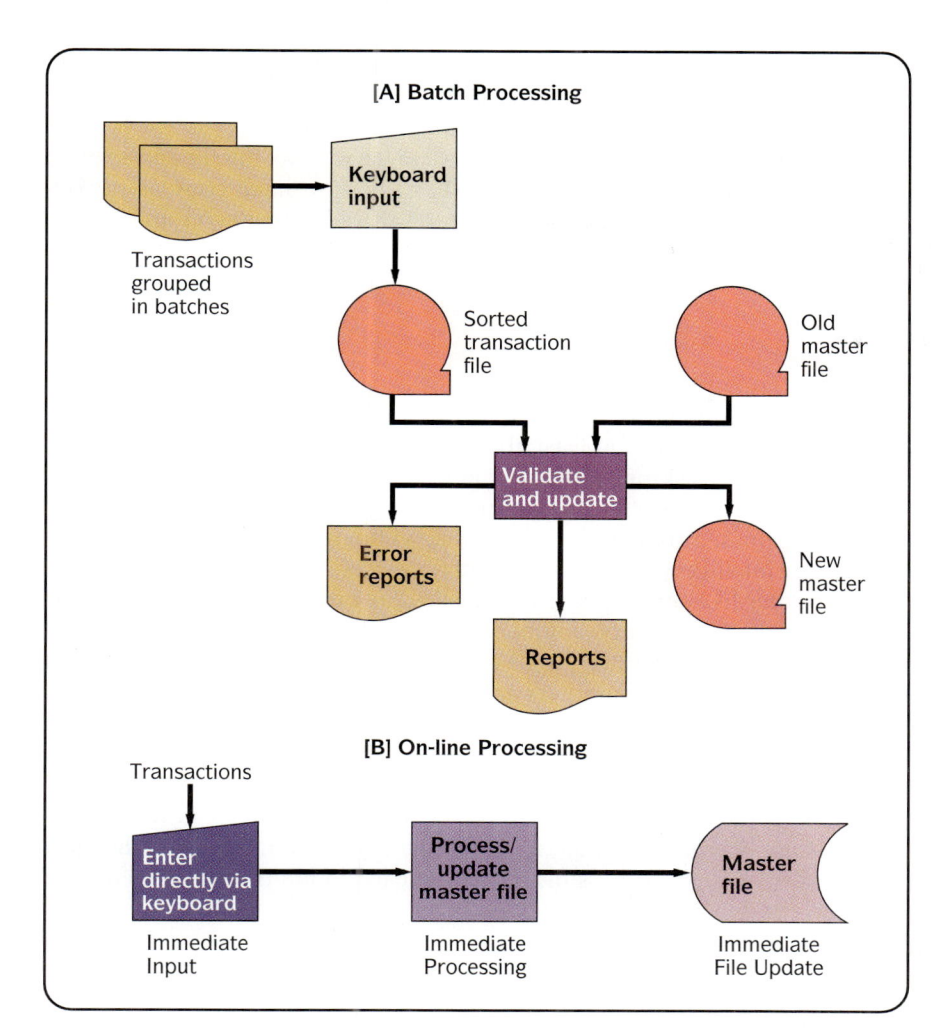

FIGURE 5.16

A comparison of batch and on-line processing. In batch processing, transactions are accumulated and stored in a group. Since batches are processed on a regular interval basis, such as daily, weekly, or monthly, information in the system will not always be up to date. A typical batch-processing job is payroll preparation. In on-line processing, transactions are input immediately and usually processed immediately. Information in the system is generally up to date. A typical on-line application is an airline reservation system.

Special-purpose graphics terminals used in CAD/CAM and commercial art have very high-resolution capabilities (1280 × 1024 pixels).

Printers

Printers produce a printed hard copy of information output. They include impact printers (a standard typewriter or a dot matrix) and nonimpact printers (laser, inkjet, and thermal transfer printers). Most printers print one character at a time, but some commercial printers print an entire line or page at a time. Line printers capable of printing an entire line of output in a single step can print up to 3000 lines per minute. Page printers print an entire page at a time, outputting 20,000 lines per minute. Printers working with microcomputers typically provide dot-matrix print at a speed of 60 to over 400 characters per second. Much slower letter-quality printers operate in the 10 to 50 characters-per-second range. In general, impact printers are slower than nonimpact printers. Laser printers for microcomputers can print 4 to 8 pages per minute. Laser printers in large computer centers can print more than 100 pages per minute. Dot-matrix printer quality is generally much lower than letter quality and is used for less important documents and spreadsheets.

printer A computer output device that provides paper hardcopy output in the form of text or graphics.

Other Devices

Microfilm and microfiche have been used to compactly store output as microscopic filmed images, and they are used mainly by insurance companies or other firms that need to output and store large numbers of documents. These media are cumbersome to search through and will be replaced by optical disk technology.

plotter Output device using multicolored pens to draw high-quality graphic documents.

voice output device A converter of digital output data into spoken words.

High-quality graphic documents can be created using **plotters** with multicolored pens to draw (rather than print) computer output. Plotters are much slower than printers, but are useful for outputting large-size charts, maps, or drawings.

A **voice output device** converts digital output data back into intelligible speech. Sounds are prerecorded, coded, and stored on disk, to be translated back as spoken words. For instance, when you call for information on the telephone, you may hear a computerized voice respond with the telephone number you requested.

5.7 INFORMATION TECHNOLOGY TRENDS

Over the last 30 years, computing costs have dropped by a factor of 10 each decade and capacity has increased by a factor of at least 100 each decade. Today's microprocessors can put a mainframe on a desktop, and eventually into a briefcase or shirt pocket. Chapter 9 shows how the traditional mainframe is being supplanted by networks of powerful desktop machines, although the mainframe will never be eliminated. The future will see even more intelligence built into everyday devices, with mainframe and perhaps even supercomputer-like computing power packed in a pocket- or notebook-sized computer. Pen, notebook, and palmtop computers will be as pervasive as handheld calculators. Computers on a chip will help guide automobiles, military weapons, robots, and everyday household devices. Computers and related information technologies will blend data, images, and sound, sending them coursing through vast networks that can process all of them with equal ease. Potentially, computer technology could be so powerful and integrated into daily experiences it would appear essentially invisible to the user (Weiser, 1993). People will increasingly interact with the computer in more intuitive and effortless ways—through writing, speech, touch, eye movement, and other gestures. We can see how this might be possible through the use of multimedia, superchips, and fifth-generation computers.

MULTIMEDIA

multimedia Technologies that facilitate the integration of two or more types of media such as text, graphics, sound, voice, full-motion video, or animation into a computer-based application.

Multimedia is defined as the technologies that facilitate the integration of two or more types of media, such as text, graphics, sound, voice, full-motion video, still video, or animation into a computer-based application. From the 1990s through the twenty-first century, multimedia will be the foundation of new consumer products and services, such as electronic books and newspapers, electronic classroom presentation technologies, full-motion video conferencing, imaging, graphics design tools, and video and voice mail.

By pressing a button, a person using a computer can call up a screenful of text; another button might bring up related video images. Still another might bring up related talk or music. For instance, Bell Canada, which provides residential and business telephone services across Canada, uses a multimedia application to help diagnose and repair problems on the network. The application contains hundreds of repair manuals that have been scanned, digitized, and made available on-line to technicians and network analysts as they work on repairing off-site network components. Each multimedia workstation can display maps of the network, sound alarms when problems occur on specific equipment, and fax maps on-line to repair personnel who have trouble locating their appointments. A voice-message annotation feature lets users click on an icon to hear new information or additional comments on specific diagnostic or repair cases (DePompa, 1993).

Multimedia systems combine the elements of today's personal computers (a computer, printer, keyboard, and mouse) with two new elements: audio (sound) and video (pictures). Figure 5.17 illustrates some of the hardware components that would be required to create and run multimedia applications. Today's microcomputers can be converted to multimedia systems by purchasing special expansion boards. By the year 2000, computers will come with built-in multimedia capabilities.

One of the principal applications of multimedia today is for interactive corporate training.

FIGURE 5.17
Multimedia applications require specially configured systems. This figure illustrates 11 components in a system used to develop a multimedia application. (1) CPU and primary storage: a minimum 80486 chip and 8 megabytes RAM. (2) Monitor: color monitor supporting super-high resolutions from 640 × 480 to 1280 × 1024; minimum 17″ screen. (3) CD-ROM: drive with 280 millisecond access time and 150 kilobits/second data transfer rate. (4) Hard disk: minimum 300 megabytes with 15 millisecond access time. (5) Stereo speakers. (6) Microphone for voice input. (7) Mouse. (8) Video input device or video board connected to a VCR or laser video disk player. (9) Sound card. (10) Video card. (11) Video compression card. Adapter cards integrate sound and video into the computer and digitally compress full-motion video. Adapted with permission from `J. William Semich, "Multimedia Tools for Development Pros,"DATAMATION MAGZINE copyright, *August 15, 1992.,* Cahners Publishing Company, a division of Reed Elsevier Inc. DATAMATION MAGAZINE is a trademark of Cahners Publishing Company, a division of Reed Elsevier Inc. All rights reserved."

5.7 Information Technology Trends

The marriage of text, graphics, sound, and video data into a single application has been made possible by the advances in microprocessor and storage technologies described in this chapter. A simple multimedia system consists of a personal computer with a 32-bit microprocessor and a CD-ROM disk. A five-inch optical disk holding more than 600 megabytes of information can store an hour of music, several thousand full-color pictures, several minutes of video or animation, and millions of words.

The possibilities of this technology are endless, but the most promising business applications appear to be in training and presentations. For training, multimedia is appealing because it is interactive and permits two-way communication (Lambert, 1990). People can use multimedia training sessions any time of the day, at their own pace. Instructors can easily integrate words, sounds, pictures, and both live and animated video to produce lessons that capture students' imaginations. For example, the multimedia training material used by the salespeople at Marion Merrell Dow Pharmaceutical allows users to display an index of a video glossary by clicking a button during the presentation of a selected topic. The last term used is highlighted. The user can view the glossary clip, return to the presentation, and be quizzed by the system (Williamson, 1994).

When multimedia is coupled with the telecommunications technologies described in Chapters 8 and 9, people will be able to capture, store, manipulate, and transmit photos and other document images and possibly full motion video on a network as easily as they do with text. The Window on Organizations focuses on kiosks, a rapidly emerging use of multimedia coupled with telecommunications, including the Internet.

The most difficult element to incorporate into multimedia information systems has been full-motion video, because so much data must be brought under the digital control of the computer. The process of actually integrating video with other kinds of data requires special software or compression boards with dedicated video processing chips. The massive amounts of data in each video image must be digitally encoded, stored, and manipulated electronically, using techniques that compress the digital data.

Soon all computers, regardless of size, will have built-in multimedia capabilities combining existing text and numbers with music, full-motion and still-frame video (snapshots), animation, voice messages, telephone, and fax capabilities.

SUPERCHIPS

Semiconductor researchers have continued to find means of packaging circuits more densely, so that millions of transistors can be packed onto a fingernail-sized silicon wafer. Intel's P6 microprocessor squeezes 5.5 million transistors on a postage-stamp size silicon pad and can achieve twice the processing speed of the Pentium. The most powerful microprocessors—such as the P6, Pentium, and PowerPC chips and Digital Equipment Corporation's Alpha chip—package mainframe and even supercomputer-like capabilities on a single chip.

In addition to improving their design, microprocessors have been made to perform faster by shrinking the distance between transistors. This process gives the electrical current less distance to travel. One step in fashioning microprocessors is to etch lines in silicon wafers that form the outlines of circuits. The narrower the lines forming transistors, the larger the number of transistors that can be squeezed onto a single chip, and the faster these circuits will operate. Figure 5.18 shows that line widths have shrunk from the diameter of a hair to less than one micron and should reach one-fifth of a micron by the year 2000. The lower part of the figure shows the number of transistors on some prominent microprocessors and memory chips. Since the number of transistors that can fit economically onto a single silicon chip is doubling every 18 months, between 50 and 100 million transistors could soon conceivably be squeezed onto a single microprocessor. There are physical limits to this approach that may soon be reached, but researchers are experimenting with new materials to increase microprocessor speed.

Window on Organizations

MULTIMEDIA KIOSKS EDUCATE THE PUBLIC

Multimedia kiosks have been used widely in airports, hotels, and retail stores to deliver public information. Now they have started to educate millions of citizens who are becoming rulers of their country for the first time. In the April, 1994 South African elections, millions of South African blacks who had never been allowed to vote before were able to vote. That in itself was a political revolution. But to complicate the situation further, many of these new voters were illiterate. In addition, they were faced with a daunting ballot, having to select candidates from among 19 political parties. One method used to help educate these first-time voters was to place multimedia kiosks in locations throughout the country.

The Voter Education Kiosks were developed by Sandenbergh Pavon Ltd., a multimedia company located in Johannesburg, South Africa. The kiosks disseminated basic information on when and where to vote, and why the citizen should vote, as well as basic information on the candidates and parties. According to Sandenbergh Pavon director Margot Sandenbergh, they "tried to make the kiosk as graphical and simple as possible, since many illiterate people will be voting for the first time." The basic technology used in the kiosks was Intel Corporation's 486-based PCs using 14-inch color monitors. Using touch screens and political party symbols, new voters were able to listen to mission statements from each of the political parties and view digital video messages from the candidates. The kiosks even explained the role of the independent election observers from the United Nations and other organizations. A total of 30 kiosks were set up and rotated among 70 different sites around the country. According to Sandenbergh, well over one million people used the kiosks by the time the election took place.

The kiosk presentations were flexible and easily altered, which became an asset in a newly emerging democracy with

> **To Think About:** Why are multimedia kiosks so appropriate for public information delivery and the task of educating new voters?

late-breaking political changes. For example, because the Inkatha Freedom Party had originally refused to participate in the elections, it was not represented in kiosk presentations. When the party agreed to compete at the last minute, its information had to be added quickly.

Other countries are experimenting with interactive kiosks to provide the public with information using the Internet. Companies or public agencies could develop multimedia applications that could be stored at a single site and linked through the Internet with kiosks in many different locations, or they could deliver information from many locations around the world to individual kiosks. For example, sports fans would be able to use kiosks at San Francisco's 3Com Park to access sports information, the White House, and even the Louvre Museum in Paris.

Sources: Mary Hayes, "The Internet at Your Fingertips," *Information Week,* February 12, 1996; and Mitch Betts, "Multimedia Kiosks Provide Voter Education in South Africa Election," *Computerworld,* May 9, 1994.

FIFTH-GENERATION COMPUTERS

Conventional computers are based on the Von Neumann architecture, which processes information serially, one instruction at a time. In the future, more computers will use parallel processing and massively parallel processing to blend voice, images, and massive pools of data from diverse sources, using artificial intelligence and intricate mathematical models.

Massively parallel computers, illustrated in Figure 5.19, have huge networks of processor chips interwoven in complex and flexible ways. As opposed to parallel processing, where small numbers of powerful but expensive specialized chips are linked together, massively parallel machines chain hundreds or even thousands of inexpensive, commonly used chips to attack large computing problems, attaining supercomputer speeds. For instance, Wal-Mart Stores uses a massively parallel machine to sift through an inventory and sales trend database with 1.8 trillion bytes of data. Massively parallel systems are said to have cost and speed advantages over conventional computers because they can take advantage of off-the-shelf chips. They may be able to accomplish processing work for one-tenth to one-twentieth the cost of traditional mainframes or supercomputers.

massively parallel computers
Computers that use hundreds or thousands of processing chips to attack large computing problems simultaneously.

FIGURE 5.18
The shrinking size and growth in number of transistors. *Reprinted by permission of Intel Corporation.*

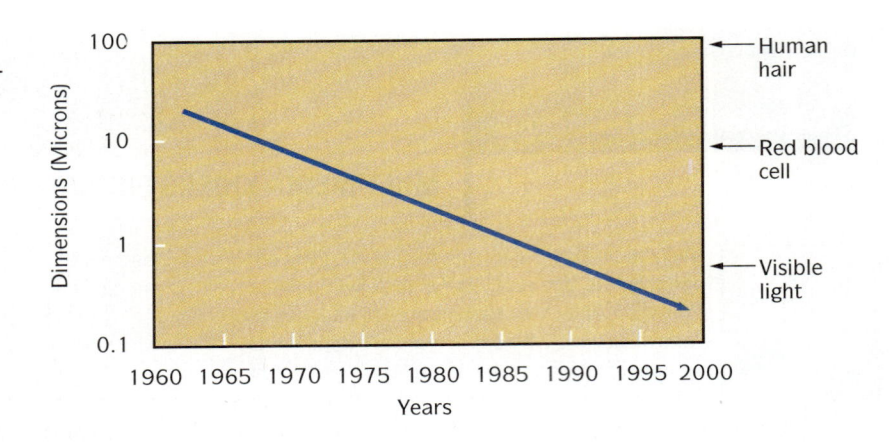

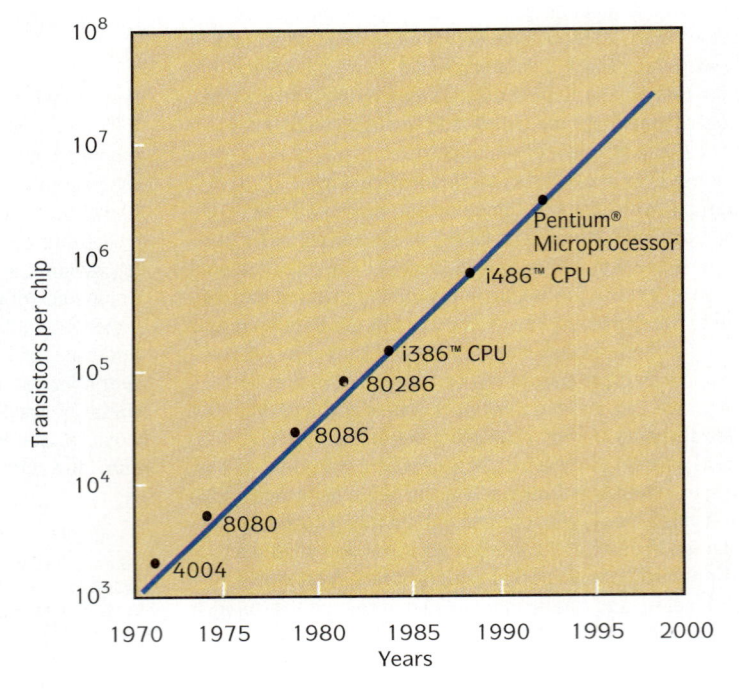

FIGURE 5.19
Computer architecture. A comparison of traditional serial processing, parallel processing, and massively parallel processing. *From John Markoff, "Foray into Mainstream for Parallel Computing,"* The New York Times, *June 15, 1992. Reprinted by permission of NYT Graphics.*

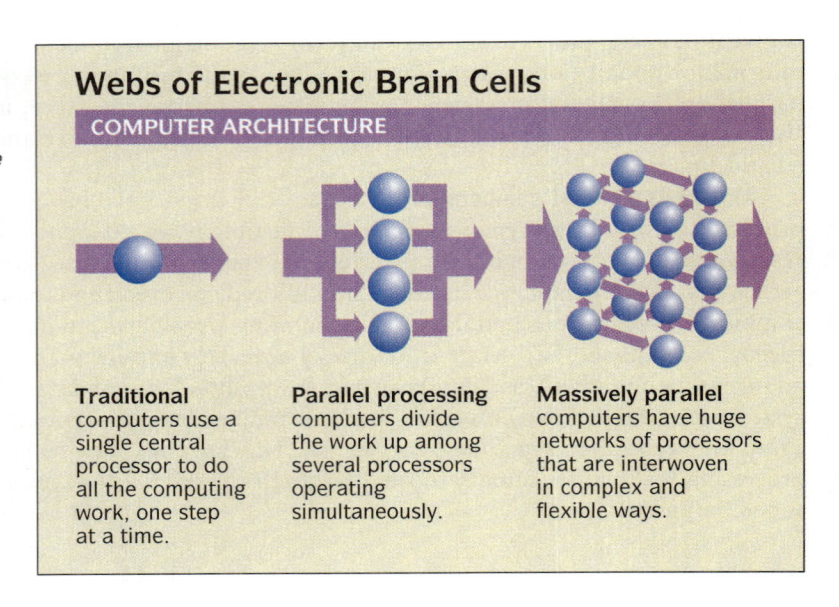

Today's supercomputers can perform hundreds of billions of calculations per second. Now supercomputer makers are racing to harness tens of thousands of microprocessors and memory chips together to create super-supercomputers that can perform more than a trillion mathematical calculations each second—a teraflop. The term *teraflop* comes from the Greek *teras*, which for mathematicians means one trillion, and *flop*, an acronym for floating point operations per second. (A floating point operation is a basic computer arithmetic operation, such as addition, on numbers that include a decimal point.) In the twenty-first century, teraflop machines could support projects such as mapping the surface of planets, designing new computers, or testing the aerodynamics of supersonic airplanes, where trillions of calculations would be required.

Management Challenges

1. Keeping abreast of technological change. Because the technology is growing in power so rapidly and is changing basic patterns of information processing, managers must keep abreast of changes in the field. This requires time and resources. In medium to large firms, a person or small group must be assigned the task of tracking new technological developments and encouraging prototypes within the firm.

2. Making wise purchasing decisions. Soon after having made an investment in information technology, managers find the completed system is obsolete and too expensive, given the power and lower cost of new technology. In this environment it is very difficult to keep one's own systems up to date. A rather considerable amount of time must be spent anticipating and planning for technological change.

3. Training the information systems staff and all employees. In the transition from mainframe computing to desktops, enormous changes in perspective, skills, and attitudes are required on the part of an organization's information systems staff. Typically, staff members must be completely retrained every five years. All employees likewise will require extensive retraining simply to keep abreast of new ways of doing business with new information technologies.

Summary

1. Identify the hardware components in a typical computer system. The modern computer system has six major components: a central processing unit (CPU), primary storage, input devices, output devices, secondary storage, and communications devices.

2. Describe how information is represented and processed in a computer system. Digital computers store and process information in the form of binary digits called *bits*. A string of 8 bits is called a *byte*. There are several coding schemes for arranging binary digits into characters. The most common are EBCDIC and ASCII. The CPU is the center of the computer, where the manipulation of symbols, numbers, and letters occurs. The CPU has two components: an arithmetic-logic unit and a control unit. The arithmetic-logic unit performs arithmetic and logical operations on data, while the control unit controls and coordinates the other components of the computer.

The CPU is closely tied to primary memory, or primary storage, which stores data and program instructions temporarily before and after processing.

Several different kinds of semiconductor memory chips are used with primary storage: RAM (random access memory) is used for short-term storage of data and program instructions, while ROM (read-only memory) permanently stores important program instructions. Other memory devices include PROM (programmable read-only memory) and EPROM (erasable programmable read-only memory).

3. Distinguish between generations of computer hardware. Computer technology has gone through four generations, from vacuum tubes to transistors, integrated circuits, and very large-scale integrated circuits, each dramatically increasing computer processing power while shrinking the size of computing hardware.

4. Contrast the capabilities of mainframes, minicomputers, microcomputers, workstations, and supercomputers. Depending on their size and processing power, computers are categorized as mainframes, minicomputers, microcomputers, workstations, or supercomputers. Mainframes are the largest computers with 50 megabytes to over 1 gigabyte of RAM; minicomputers are mid-range machines with 10 megabytes to over 1 gigabyte of RAM; microcomputers are desktop or laptop machines with 640 kilobytes to 64 megabytes of RAM; workstations are desktop machines with powerful mathematical and graphic capabilities and 8 to 300 megabytes of RAM and supercomputers are sophisticated, powerful computers that can perform massive and complex computations because they use parallel processing. The capabilities of microprocessors used in these computers can be gauged by their word length, data bus width, and cycle speed. Because of continuing advances in microprocessor technology, the distinctions between these various types of computers are constantly changing. Microcomputers are now powerful enough to perform much of the work that was formerly limited to mainframes and minicomputers.

5. **Describe the various media for storing data and programs in a computer system.** The principal forms of secondary storage are magnetic tape, magnetic disk, and optical disk. Tape stores records in sequence and can only be used in batch processing. Disk permits direct access to specific records and is much faster than tape. Disk technology is used in on-line processing. Optical disks can store vast amounts of data compactly. CD-ROM disk systems can only be read from, but rewritable optical disk systems are becoming available.

6. **Compare the major input and output devices and approaches to input and processing.** The principal input devices are keyboards, computer mice, touch screens, magnetic ink and optical character recognition, pen-based instruments, digital scanners, sensors, and voice input. The principal output devices are video display terminals, printers, plotters, voice output devices, and microfilm and microfiche. In batch processing, transactions are accumulated and stored in a group until the time when it is efficient or necessary to process them. In on-line processing, the user enters transactions into a device that is directly connected to the computer system. The transactions are usually processed immediately.

7. **Describe multimedia and future information technology trends.** Multimedia integrates two or more types of media, such as text, graphics, sound, voice, full-motion video, still video, and/or animation into a computer-based application. The future will see steady and impressive progress toward faster chips at lower cost and microprocessors with the power of today's mainframes or supercomputers. Hardware using massively parallel processing will be utilized more widely, and computers and related information technologies will be able to blend data, images, and sound.

Key Terms

Bit	PROM (programmable read-only memory)	Parallel processing	Source data automation
Byte	EPROM (erasable programmable read-only memory)	Secondary storage	Magnetic ink character recognition (MICR)
EBCDIC (Extended Binary Coded Decimal Interchange Code)	Arithmetic-logic unit (ALU)	Register	Optical character recognition (OCR)
ASCII (American Standard Code for Information Interchange)	Control unit	Cache	Bar code
	Machine cycle	Magnetic tape	Pen-based input
Parity	Computer generations	Magnetic disk	Digital scanners
Pixel	Microprocessor	Hard disk	Voice input device
Millisecond	Word length	Cylinder	Sensors
Microsecond	Megahertz	Track	Batch processing
Nanosecond	Data bus width	RAID (Redundant Array of Inexpensive Disks)	On-line processing
Kilobyte	Reduced instruction set computing (RISC)	Floppy disk	Transaction file
Megabyte	Mainframe	Sector	Master file
Gigabyte	Minicomputer	Direct access storage device (DASD)	Video display terminal (VDT)
Central processing unit (CPU)	Microcomputer	Optical disk	Bit mapping
Primary storage	Workstation	CD-ROM (compact disk read-only memory)	Printer
RAM (random access memory)	Supercomputer	WORM (write once/read many)	Plotter
Semiconductor	Distributed processing	Magneto-optical disk	Voice output device
ROM (read-only memory)	Centralized processing	Computer mouse	Multimedia
	Downsizing	Touch screen	Massively parallel computers
	Cooperative processing		

Review Questions

1. What are the components of a contemporary computer system?
2. Distinguish between a bit and a byte.
3. What are ASCII and EBCDIC, and why are they used? Why can true binary not be used in a computer as a machine language?
4. Name and define the principal measures of computer time and storage capacity.
5. What problems of coordination exist in a computing environment and why?
6. Name the major components of the CPU and the function of each.

7. Describe how information is stored in primary memory.
8. What are the four different types of semiconductor memory, and when are they used?
9. Describe the major generations of computers and the characteristics of each.
10. Name and describe the factors affecting the speed and performance of a microprocessor.
11. What are downsizing and cooperative processing?
12. What is the difference between primary and secondary storage?
13. List the most important secondary storage media. What are the strengths and limitations of each?
14. List and describe the major input devices.
15. What is the difference between batch and on-line processing? Diagram the difference.
16. List and describe the major output devices.
17. Distinguish between serial, parallel, and massively parallel processing.
18. What is multimedia? What technologies are involved?

Discussion Questions

1. What is the difference between a mainframe, a minicomputer, and a microcomputer? Between a mainframe and a supercomputer? Between a microcomputer and a workstation? Why are these distinctions disappearing?
2. How are the capabilities of an information system affected by its input, output, and storage devices?
3. A firm would like to introduce computers into its order entry process but feels that it should wait for a new generation of machines to be developed. After all, any machine bought now will be quickly out of date and less expensive a few years from now. Discuss.

Group Project

It has been predicted that notebook computers will be available that have 20 times the power of a current personal computer, with a touch-sensitive color screen that one can write on or draw on with a stylus or type on when a program displays a keyboard. Each will have a small compact, rewritable, removable CD-ROM disk that can store the equivalent of a set of encyclopedias. In addition, the computers will have elementary voice-recognition capabilities, including the ability to record sound and give voice responses to questions. The computer will be able to carry on a dialogue by voice, graphics, typed words, and displayed video graphics. Thus, computers will be about the size of a thick pad of letter paper and just as portable and convenient, but with the intelligence of a computer and the multimedia capabilities of a television set. Such a computer is expected to cost about $2000. Form a group with three or four of your classmates and develop an analysis of the impacts such developments would have on university education. Explain why you think the impact will or will not occur.

Case Study

BAR CODES BECOME A STRATEGIC BUSINESS WEAPON

According to most business analysts, video rental stores will soon be joining the dinosaurs—they too will be extinct. Instead, they will be replaced by the new, interactive, fiber-optic cable and telephone systems that will be in our homes in the near future. These systems will allow customers to call up any movie they wish at any time. So why is Wayne Bailey optimistic that his Aurora, Colorado, video store business, Accurate Inventory Management (AIM), will thrive? Bailey believes that it will take many years and many hundreds of billions of dollars in technology investments before the cable business will be able to replace video stores. In the meantime, he is betting on other technology to cause his company to flourish. One key to his planned, prosperous future is the computer input device he is using—bar code scanners.

Bailey is using scanners as part of a larger business plan both to service his customers better and more efficiently and to expand his enterprise into new, related areas. First, he has redefined the business he is in from movie rentals to entertainment rentals. When video games became popular, he began renting them. Then, he moved into music video rentals, followed most recently by rentals of multimedia CD-ROM titles. Bailey also decided to market his inventory management skills and his computerized video rental technology, to retail merchants such as grocery stores renting videos, managing their video rental businesses for them better than they ever could themselves. Next, he realized that video rental companies are constantly buying and selling their inventory (primarily movies, based upon their local demand). He decided to establish a national bulletin board where their videos could be bought and sold. AIM makes its money from this bulletin board by charging all users $28 per hour of connect time. AIM and Bailey have been successful in all these new businesses.

Before implementing bar coding, Bailey had to decide what to bar code. He chose not only to bar code the rental items (such as videos and CD-ROMs), but also to bar code the customers themselves, issuing a bar-coded card customers present when renting. Thus, all the checkout counter clerk needs to do is to scan the bar code on both the customer card and the item or items being rented, and the computer has all the data needed, instantly and accurately. Next, Bailey had to decide what information he wanted the bar codes to carry. The codes can contain whatever information the user decides needs to be recorded. For example, AIM bar codes for their inventory items might include the item type (movie, CD-ROM, music), the category (adventure, comedy, horror), name (*Star Wars, Crooklyn, Frankenstein*), and copy number.

Next Bailey needed to determine how to produce and affix the bar codes. Many products come with bar codes on their labels (such as prepackaged items in grocery stores). However, AIM wants to determine the data to be carried and will have to design, produce, and affix its own bar codes or go to outside specialists to do the job. Bailey originally chose to produce his own bar codes, but he quickly found that his dot-matrix printer did not produce bar codes with the clarity needed to be read accurately by bar code scanners. His checkout clerks ended up spending a great deal of time typing in information when the scanner failed, resulting in long customer waiting lines and, of course, a great many data errors. Bailey soon turned to a professional organization to print the bar codes for him.

The next choice Bailey had to make was the scanner to be used. He selected charge-coupled devices (CCDs), which his clerks found easier to use and which can read the bar code from several inches away. While more expensive, they proved to save money both because clerks were more productive and because they resulted in more accurate data—the cost of the whole system would be wasted if the data were inaccurate.

Finally, Bailey had to select or develop application software. The software needed to collect and store the data, and to secure the data from intrusions into the privacy of AIM's customers. Moreover, the application software functionality would need to support the business goals and practices of the organization.

What did Bailey want from the data collected by scanner? First, he wanted high-quality customer service. By using bar coding technology, his clerks are able to process customers quickly and accurately, keeping checkout lines small. Second, he was looking for productivity. This was achieved partially by speeding up the checkout process. The system always knows exactly which products are out, which are on the shelves, how many of each item AIM owns, as well as the turnover rate of each item. By keeping a tight control over inventory, it keeps inventory costs low. Every time an item is checked out or in, the system is automatically updated, so AIM can see how much each item is earning.

AIM also uses the data to increase business from existing customers. Because the computer shows which products are rented by whom, AIM is able to determine the tastes of its customers and then to target advertising mailings accordingly, sending literature on children's films, for example, to families that rent a large number of children's films. The company is also able to identify which customers have not rented for a long period of time (currently AIM uses a six months' threshold) so it can attempt to reactivate dormant customers.

Perhaps the most important use of the data, however, is AIM's market trend analysis. By having complete, up-to-date data on what items are renting and what are not, AIM is able to keep in constant touch with customer tastes. Staff spot rental trends very early and respond in time to take advantage of them. Their analyses tell them when to sell items that are no longer needed and when to purchase additional copies of items. Using computer modeling software, AIM is even able to predict with a high degree of accuracy how many copies of a new item staff need to purchase. For example, their model projected they would need 88 copies of *The Firm* when it was first released. At a purchase price of $70 each, it was important not to overbuy copies of this film. Five weeks after the release of the film, an update of the model showed that they actually could have used 89 copies, indicating the original estimate had been excellent.

Given that AIM is a small business, cost was a key factor in adopting bar coding technology. Costs were low. AIM has found that one 486 microcomputer is powerful enough to handle all of its functions, including its own checkout and analyses functions, the same services for the 150 other video outlets serviced, and the nationwide bulletin board for buying and selling its inventories. The scanners cost $200 to $300 each but only require occasional maintenance. The technology is mature enough so as not to require updating of software and hardware so that the costs are very little beyond the initial investment. Payback was very quick, making this a viable technology, even for a small business.

With bar coding technology and imaginative management, the company has been able to prosper, grow, and even branch out in a market that is often considered to be difficult. ∎

Source: Tony Seideman, "The Dream Beam," *Profit,* September–October 1994.

Case Study Questions

1. What are the advantages and disadvantages of using bar coding as the input technology over other input technologies?
2. How was the use of bar coding for input technology related to AIM's business strategy?
3. It has been observed that the challenging part of using bar codes is not collecting bar code data but designing the information systems and the business practices to use the information. Do you agree? Why or why not?
4. What management, organization, and technology changes did AIM institute in order to make bar coding effective? For each of these changes, indicate whether or not they were critical to the success of the technology and the company.
5. In what ways does bar coding improve customer service and so customer satisfaction?

References

Bell, Gordon. "The Future of High Performance Computers in Science and Engineering." *Communications of the ACM* 32, no. 9 (September 1989).

Bell, Gordon. "Ultracomputers: A Teraflop Before Its Time." *Communications of the ACM* 35, no. 8 (August 1992).

Burgess, Brad, Nasr Ullah, Peter Van Overen, and Deene Ogden. "The PowerPC 603 Microprocessor." *Communications of the ACM* 37, no. 6 (June 1994).

Camp, W. J., S. J. Plimpton, B. A. Hendrickson, and R. W. Leland. "Massively Parallel Methods for Engineering and Science Problems." *Communications of the ACM* 37, no. 4 (April 1994).

De Pompa, Barbara. "Multimedia Isn't the Message." *Information Week* (July 19, 1993).

Demasco, Patrick W., and Kathleen F. McCoy. "Generating Text from Compressed Input: An Intelligent Interface for People with Severe Motor Impairments." *Communications of the ACM* 35, no. 5 (May 1992).

Emmett, Arielle. "Simulations on Trial." *Technology Review* (May–June 1994).

Fitzmaurice, George W. "Situated Information Spaces and Spatially Aware Palmtop Computers." *Communications of the ACM* 36, no. 7 (July 1993).

Hills, W. Daniel, and Lewis W. Tucker. "The CM-5 Connection Machine. A Scalable Supercomputer." *Communications of the ACM* 36, no. 11 (November 1993).

Jenkins, Avery. "The Right Time for RAID." *Computerworld* (March 14, 1994).

Lambert, Craig. "The Electronic Tutor." *Harvard Magazine* (November–December 1990).

Markoff, John. "Foray into Mainstream for Parallel Computing." *The New York Times* (June 15, 1992).

Markoff, John. "Battle for Influence over Insatiable Disks." *The New York Times* (January 11, 1995).

Mel, Bartlett W., Stephen M. Omohundro, Arch D. Robison, Steven S. Skiena, Kurt H. Thearling, Luke T. Young, and Stephen Wolfram. "Tablet: Personal Computer in the Year 2000." *Communications of the ACM* 31, no. 6 (June 1988).

Nelson, Neal. "The Reality of RISC." *Computerworld* (March 22, 1993).

Peled, Abraham. "The Next Computer Revolution." *Scientific American* 257, no. 4 (October 1987).

Port, Otis et al. "Wonder Chips." *Business Week* (July 4, 1994).

Press, Larry. "Compuvision or Teleputer?" *Communications of the ACM* 33, no. 3 (September 1990).

Press, Larry. "Personal Computing: Dynabook Revisited—Portable Computers Past, Present, and Future." *Communications of the ACM* 35 no. 3 (March 1992).

Smarr, Larry, and Charles E. Catlett, "Metacomputing." *Communications of the ACM* 35, no. 6 (June 1992).

Thomborson, Clark D. "Does Your Workstation Computation Belong to a Vector Supercomputer?" *Communications of the ACM* 36, no. 11 (November 1993).

Thompson, Tom. "The Macintosh at 10." *Byte* (February 1994).

Thompson, Tom, and Bob Ryan. "PowerPC 620 Soars." *Byte* (November 1994).

Weiser, Mark. "Some Computer Science Issues in Ubiquitous Computing." *Communications of the ACM* 36, no. 7 (July 1993).

Williamson, Miday. "High-Tech Training." *Byte* (December 1994).

Wood, Elizabeth. "Multimedia Comes Down to Earth." *Computerworld* (August 1, 1994).

Chapter 6

Information Systems Software

Sand Dollar Saves Many Dollars Through Mailing Software

6.1 What Is Software?
Software Programs
Major Types of Software

6.2 System Software
Functions of the Operating System
Multiprogramming, Virtual Storage, Time Sharing, and Multiprocessing
Language Translation and Utility Software
Graphical User Interfaces
Microcomputer Operating Systems
Selecting a Microcomputer Operating System
Window on Management:
NASA Selects Operating Systems

6.3 Application Software
Generations of Programming Languages
Popular Programming Languages
Fourth-Generation Languages
Window on Organizations:
Bell Quebec Repairs Its Pay Phones by Magic

6.4 New Software Tools and Approaches
Object-Oriented Programming

Window on Technology:
Power Short-Circuits in Object-Oriented Development
Java and the Software Revolution

Management Challenges
Summary
Key Terms
Review Questions
Discussion Questions
Group Project
Case Study: A Geographic Information System Adds Zest to Sonny's Bar-B-Q
References

Sand Dollar Saves Many Dollars Through Mailing Software

The resort business relies heavily upon mailings of sales literature to attract clients. So it is no surprise that Sand Dollar Management Co.'s director of new-product development, Pat Simpson, decided to computerize her whole mailing list function. Sand Dollar, with 1993 sales of $20 million, manages resort property on Hilton Head Island, South Carolina. In the past this small company purchased mailing lists of potential customers, hired office temps to type labels and paste the labels on the stuffed envelopes, and mailed them. The whole process was costly and often required several weeks to be completed. Now, using computerized mailing software, Simpson saves her company more than $80,000 annually.

Savings start with the mailing lists Sand Dollar receives, which now can be sent on computer disk and printed on labels or envelopes, eliminating the need for the office temps. The software also checks for duplicates, eliminating the cost of duplicate mailings. Computerized mailing lists can also be stored on the computer and reused, reducing the cost of mailing list purchases. Sand Dollar's software can also be used to check its mailing list against the United States Postal Service's (USPS) National Change of Address file, which is updated quarterly and lists all reported new addresses.

The largest saving from the software, however, comes from the fact that the software bar codes the labels and sorts them by ZIP code. Because this makes it much cheaper for the USPS to process the mail, they offer large discounts for sorted, bar-coded mail. Sand Dollar receives a USPS discount of $50,000 annually.

The software has other benefits as well. For example, Sand Dollar also uses it to capture and maintain valuable personal customer data it then uses in its marketing efforts. Moreover, the software was low cost, making it easy for a small business to adopt it. In fact, although Sand Dollar did purchase a new computer to run its new mailing software, an older computer could have run it had the company not been ready to finance a new computer. ■

Source: Mel Mandell, "Smart Mailing Techniques Deliver Postage Savings," *Profit*, May–June 1994.

In the last twenty-five years, public media have paid a great deal of attention to advances in computer hardware. But without the software to utilize the expanding capabilities of the hardware, the "computer revolution" would have been stillborn. The many businesses that rely heavily upon mailing lists, like Sand Dollar described in the opening vignette, had the names and addresses they needed and could easily have had access to computer hardware to process the addresses. What prevented them from reducing their mailing costs while more effectively reaching potential customers was the lack of appropriate software.

The usefulness of computer hardware depends a great deal on available software and the ability of management to evaluate, monitor, and control the utilization of software in the organization. This chapter shows how software turns computer hardware into useful information systems, describes the major types of software, provides criteria for selecting software, and presents new approaches to software development.

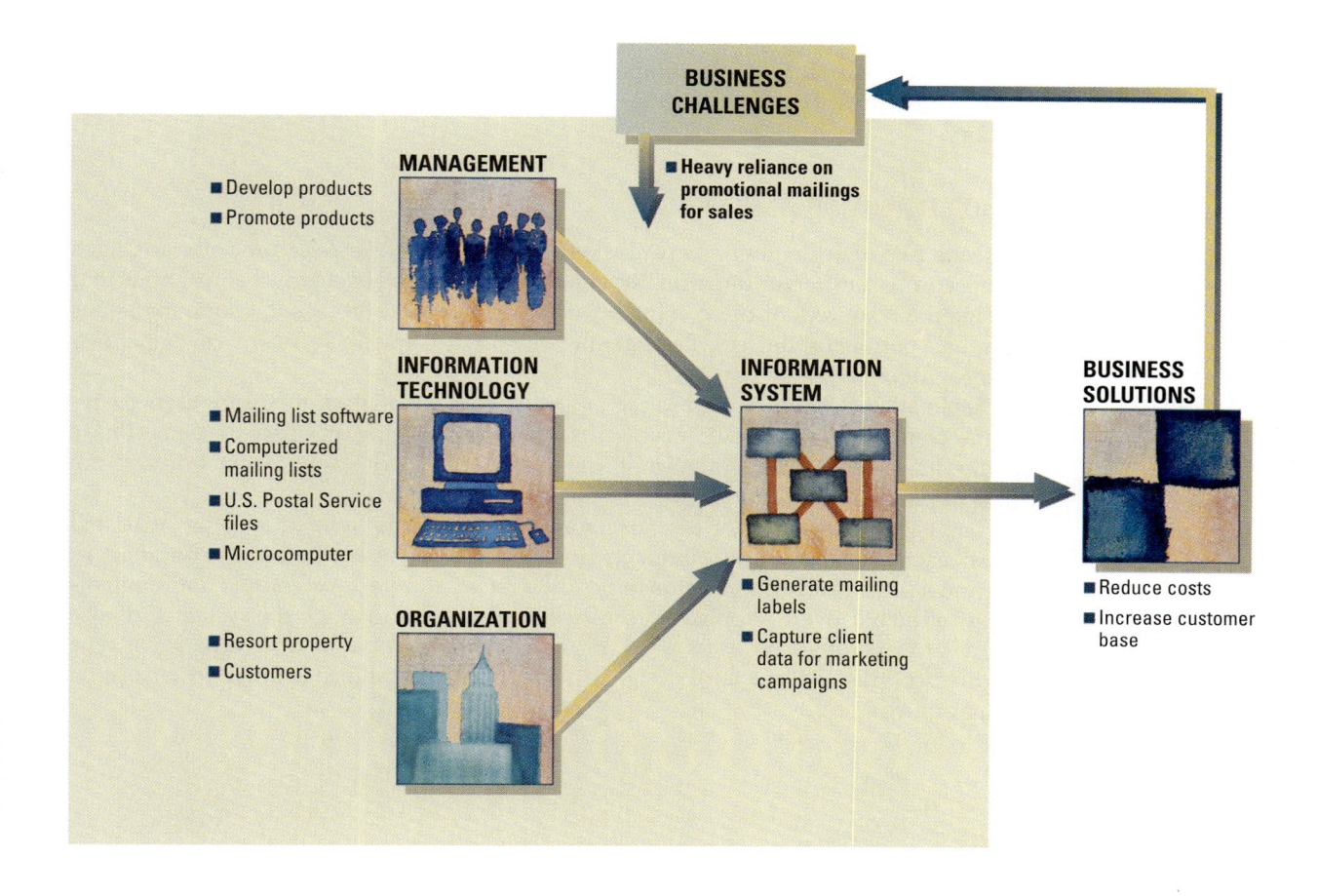

> **Learning Objectives**
>
> *After completing this chapter, you will be able to:*
>
> 1. Describe the major types of software.
> 2. Describe the function of system software and compare leading microcomputer operating systems.
> 3. Explain how software has evolved and how it will continue to develop.
> 4. Compare strengths and limitations of the major application programming languages and software tools.
> 5. Describe new approaches to software development.

6.1 WHAT IS SOFTWARE?

software The detailed instructions that control the operation of a computer system.

Software is the detailed instructions that control the operation of a computer system. Without software, computer hardware could not perform the tasks we associate with computers. The functions of software are to (1) manage the computer resources of the organization; (2) provide tools for human beings to take advantage of these resources; and (3) act as an intermediary between organizations and stored information. Selecting appropriate software for the organization is a key management decision.

SOFTWARE PROGRAMS

program A series of statements or instructions to the computer.

stored program concept The idea that a program cannot be executed unless it is stored in a computer's primary storage along with required data.

A software **program** is a series of statements or instructions to the computer. The process of writing or coding programs is termed *programming,* and individuals who specialize in this task are called programmers.

The **stored program concept** means that a program must be stored in the computer's primary storage along with the required data in order to execute, or have its instructions performed by the computer. Once a program has finished executing, the computer hardware can be used for another task when a new program is loaded into memory.

MAJOR TYPES OF SOFTWARE

system software Generalized programs that manage the resources of the computer, such as the central processor, communications links, and peripheral devices.

application software Programs written for a specific business application in order to perform functions specified by end users.

There are two major types of software: system software and application software. Each kind performs a different function. **System software** is a set of generalized programs that manage the resources of the computer, such as the central processor, communications links, and peripheral devices. Programmers who write system software are called *system programmers.*

Application software describes the programs that are written for or by users to apply the computer to a specific task. Software for processing an order or generating a mailing list is application software. Programmers who write application software are called *application programmers.*

The types of software are interrelated and can be thought of as a set of nested boxes, each of which must interact closely with the other boxes surrounding it. Figure 6.1 illustrates this relationship. The system software surrounds and controls access to the hardware. Application software must work through the system software in order to operate. End users work primarily with application software. Each type of software must be specially designed to a specific machine in order to ensure its compatibility.

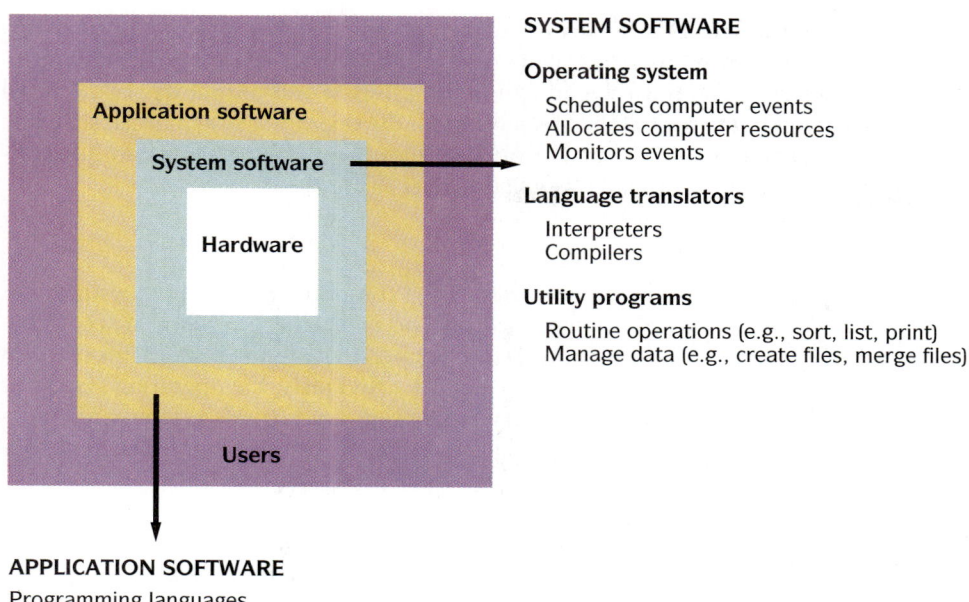

SYSTEM SOFTWARE

Operating system
  Schedules computer events
  Allocates computer resources
  Monitors events

Language translators
  Interpreters
  Compilers

Utility programs
  Routine operations (e.g., sort, list, print)
  Manage data (e.g., create files, merge files)

APPLICATION SOFTWARE
Programming languages
Assembly language
FORTRAN
COBOL
PL/1
BASIC
PASCAL
C
"Fourth-generation" languages

FIGURE 6.1
The major types of software. The relationship between the system software, application software, and users can be illustrated by a series of nested boxes. System software—consisting of operating systems, language translators, and utility programs—controls access to the hardware. Application software, such as the programming languages and "fourth-generation" languages must work through the system software to operate. The user interacts primarily with the application software.

6.2 SYSTEM SOFTWARE

System software coordinates the various parts of the computer system and mediates between application software and computer hardware. The system software that manages and controls the activities of the computer is called the **operating system.** Other system software consists of computer language translation programs that convert programming languages into machine language and utility programs that perform common processing tasks.

operating system The system software that manages and controls the activities of the computer.

FUNCTIONS OF THE OPERATING SYSTEM

One way to look at the operating system is as the system's chief manager. Operating system software decides which computer resources will be used, which programs will be run, and the order in which activities will take place.

An operating system performs three functions. It allocates and assigns system resources; it schedules the use of computer resources and computer jobs; and it monitors computer system activities.

Allocation and Assignment

The operating system allocates resources to the application jobs in the execution queue. It provides locations in primary memory for data and programs and controls the input and output devices such as printers, terminals, and telecommunication links.

Scheduling

Thousands of pieces of work can be going on in a computer simultaneously. The operating system decides when to schedule the jobs that have been submitted and when to coordinate the scheduling in various areas of the computer so that different parts of different jobs can be worked on at the same time. For instance, while a program is executing, the operating system is scheduling the use of input and output devices. Not all jobs are performed in the order they are submitted; the operating system must schedule these jobs according to organizational priorities. On-line order processing may have priority over a job to generate mailing lists and labels.

Monitoring

The operating system monitors the activities of the computer system. It keeps track of each computer job and may also keep track of who is using the system, of what programs have been run, and of any unauthorized attempts to access the system. Information system security is discussed in detail in Chapter 14. Obviously, the operating system of a major mainframe computer is itself a very large program. For this reason, only parts of the operating system are actually stored in the primary storage area. Most of the operating system is stored in a copy on a disk, to which primary storage has very rapid access. Whenever parts of the operating system are required by a given application, they are transferred from the disk and loaded into primary storage. The device on which a complete operating system is stored is called the **system residence device.**

system residence device The secondary storage device on which a complete operating system is stored.

MULTIPROGRAMMING, VIRTUAL STORAGE, TIME SHARING, AND MULTIPROCESSING

How is it possible for 1000 or more users sitting at remote terminals to use a computer information system simultaneously if, as we stated in the previous chapter, most computers can execute only one instruction from one program at a time? How can computers run thousands of programs? The answer is that the computer has a series of specialized operating system capabilities.

Multiprogramming

multiprogramming A method of executing two or more programs concurrently using the same computer. The CPU executes only one program but can service the input/output needs of others at the same time.

The most important operating system capability for sharing computer resources is **multiprogramming.** Multiprogramming permits multiple programs to share a computer system's resources at any one time through concurrent use of a CPU. By concurrent use, we mean that only one program is actually using the CPU at any given moment but that the input/output needs of other programs can be serviced at the same time. Two or more programs are active at the same time, but they do not use the same computer resources simultaneously. With multiprogramming, a group of programs takes turns using the processor.

Figure 6.2 shows how three programs in a multiprogramming environment can be stored in primary storage. The first program executes until an input/output event is read in the program. The operating system then directs a channel (a small processor limited to input and output functions) to read the input and move the output to an output device. The CPU moves to the second program until an input/output statement occurs. At

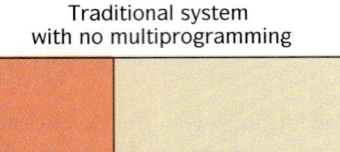

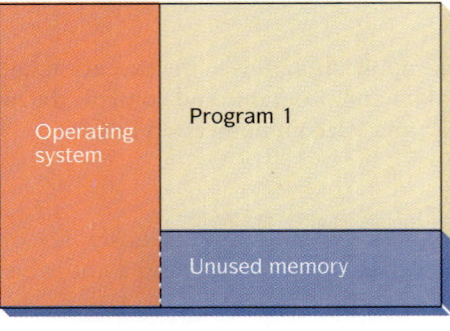

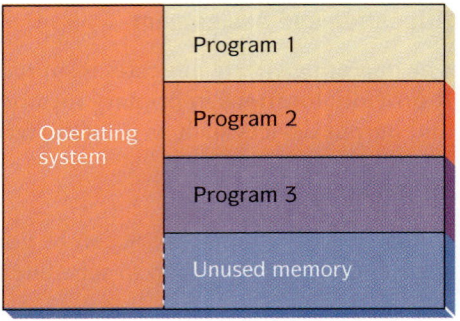

FIGURE 6.2
Single-program execution versus multiprogramming. In multiprogramming, the computer can be used much more efficiently because a number of programs can be executing concurrently. Several complete programs are loaded into memory. This memory management aspect of the operating system greatly increases throughput by better management of high-speed memory and input/output devices.

166   CHAPTER 6   Information Systems Software

this point, the CPU switches to the execution of the third program, and so forth, until eventually all three programs have been executed. Notice that the interruptions in processing are caused by events that take place in the programs themselves. In this manner, many different programs can be executing at the same time, although different resources within the CPU are actually being utilized.

The first operating systems executed only one program at a time. Before multiprogramming, whenever a program read data off a tape or disk or wrote data to a printer, the entire CPU came to a stop. This was a very inefficient way to use the computer. With multiprogramming, the CPU utilization rate is much higher.

Multitasking

Multitasking refers to multiprogramming on single-user operating systems such as those in microcomputers. One person can run two or more programs concurrently on a single computer. For example, a sales representative could write a letter to prospective clients with a word processing program while simultaneously using a database program to search for all sales contacts in a particular city or geographic area. Instead of terminating his or her session with the word processing program, returning to the operating system, and then initiating a session with the database program, multitasking allows the sales representative to display both programs on the computer screen and work with them at the same time.

multitasking The multiprogramming capability of primarily single-user operating systems, such as those for microcomputers.

Virtual Storage

Virtual storage handles programs more efficiently because the computer divides the programs into small fixed- or variable-length portions, storing only a small portion of the program in primary memory at one time. If only two or three large programs can be read into memory, a certain part of main memory generally remains underutilized because the programs add up to less than the total amount of primary storage space available. Given the limited size of primary memory, only a small number of programs can reside in primary storage at any given time.

Only a few statements of a program actually execute at any given moment. Virtual storage breaks a program into a number of fixed-length portions called **pages** or into variable-length portions called *segments*. Each of these portions is relatively small (a page is approximately 2 to 4 kilobytes). This permits a very large number of programs to reside in primary memory, inasmuch as only one page of each program is actually located there (see Figure 6.3).

virtual storage A way of handling programs more efficiently by the computer by dividing the programs into small fixed- or variable-length portions with only a small portion stored in primary memory at one time.

page A small fixed-length section of a program, which can be easily stored in primary storage and quickly accessed from secondary storage.

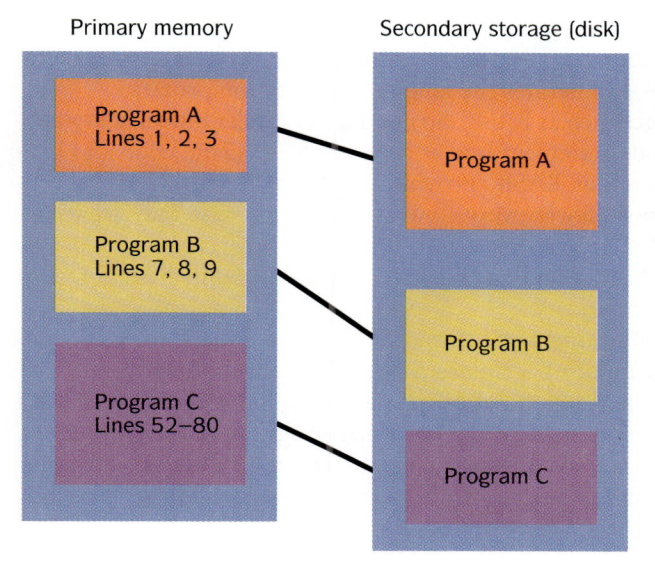

FIGURE 6.3
Virtual storage. Virtual storage is based on the fact that in general, only a few statements in a program can actually be utilized at any given moment. In virtual storage, programs are broken down into small sections called pages. Individual program pages are read into memory only when needed. The rest of the program is stored on disk until it is required. In this way, very large programs can be executed by small machines, or a large number of programs can be executed concurrently by a single machine.

All other program pages are stored on a peripheral disk unit until they are ready for execution. Virtual storage provides a number of advantages. First, the central processor is utilized more fully. Many more programs can be in primary storage because only one page of each program actually resides there. Second, programmers no longer have to worry about the size of the primary storage area. With virtual storage, programs can be of infinite length and small machines can execute a program of any size (admittedly, small machines will take longer than big machines to execute a large program).

Time Sharing

Time sharing is an operating system capability that allows many users to share computer processing resources simultaneously. It differs from multiprogramming in that the CPU spends a fixed amount of time on one program before moving on to another. In a time-sharing environment, thousands of users are each allocated a tiny slice of computer time (2 milliseconds). In this time slot, each user is free to perform any required operations; at the end of this period, another user is given a 2-millisecond time slice of the CPU. This arrangement permits many users to be connected to a CPU simultaneously, with each receiving only a tiny amount of CPU time. But since the CPU is operating at the nanosecond level, a CPU can accomplish a great deal of work in 2 milliseconds.

Multiprocessing

Multiprocessing is an operating system capability that links together two or more CPUs to work in parallel in a single computer system. The operating system can assign multiple CPUs to execute different instructions from the same program or from different programs simultaneously, dividing the work between the CPUs. While multiprogramming uses concurrent processing with one CPU, multiprocessing uses simultaneous processing with multiple CPUs.

LANGUAGE TRANSLATION AND UTILITY SOFTWARE

When computers execute programs written in languages such as COBOL, FORTRAN, or C, the computer must convert these human-readable instructions into a form it can understand. System software includes special language translator programs that translate higher-level language programs written in programming languages such as BASIC, COBOL, and FORTRAN into machine language that the computer can execute. This type of system software is called a *compiler* or *interpreter*. The program in the high-level language before translation into machine language is called **source code**. A **compiler** translates source code into machine code called **object code**. Just before execution by the computer, the object code modules are joined together with other object code modules in a process called *linkage editing*. The resulting load module is what is actually executed by the computer. Figure 6.4 illustrates the language translation process.

Some programming languages such as BASIC do not use a compiler but an **interpreter**, which translates each source code statement one at a time into machine code and executes it. Interpreter languages such as BASIC provide immediate feedback to the programmer if a mistake is made, but they are very slow to execute because they are translated one statement at a time.

An assembler is similar to a compiler, but it is used to translate only assembly language (see Section 6.3) into machine code.

System software includes **utility programs** for routine, repetitive tasks, such as copying, clearing primary storage, computing a square root, or sorting. If you have worked on a computer and have performed such functions as setting up new files, deleting old files, or formatting diskettes, you have worked with utility programs. Utility programs are prewritten programs that are stored so that they can be shared by all users of a computer system and can be rapidly used in many different information system applications when requested.

---

time sharing The sharing of computer resources by many users simultaneously by having the CPU spend a fixed amount of time on each user's program before proceeding to the next.

multiprocessing An operating system feature for executing two or more instructions simultaneously in a single computer system by using multiple central processing units.

source code Program instructions written in a high-level language that must be translated into machine language in order to be executed by the computer.

compiler Special system software that translates a higher-level language into machine language for execution by the computer.

object code Program instructions that have been translated into machine language so that they can be executed by the computer.

interpreter A special translator of source code into machine code that translates each source code statement into machine code and executes it, one at a time.

utility program System software consisting of programs for routine, repetitive tasks, which can be shared by many users.

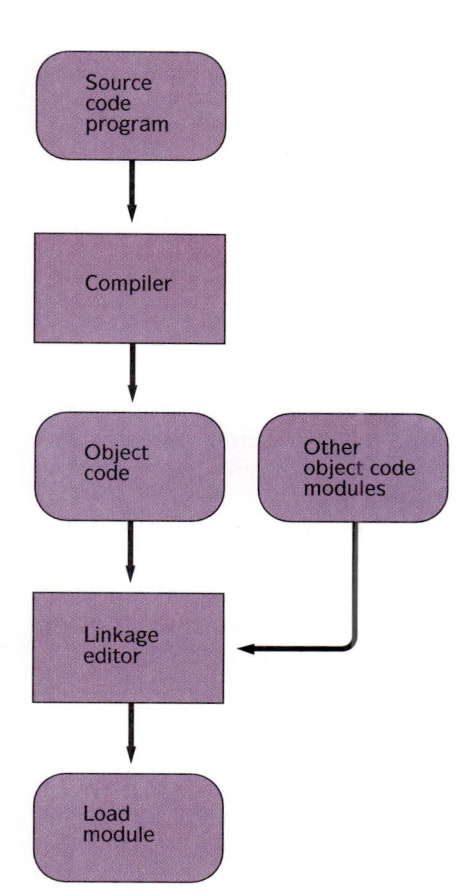

FIGURE 6.4

The language translation process. The source code, the program in a high-level language, is translated by the compiler into object code so that the instructions can be "understood" by the machine. These are grouped into modules. Prior to execution, the object code modules are joined together by the linkage editor to create the load module. It is the load module that is actually executed by the computer.

GRAPHICAL USER INTERFACES

Whenever users interact with a computer, even a microcomputer, the interaction is controlled by an operating system. The user interface is the part of an information system that users interact with. Users communicate with an operating system through the user interface of that operating system. Early microcomputer operating systems were command-driven, but the **graphical user interface**, often called a **GUI**, makes extensive use of icons, buttons, bars, and boxes to perform the same task. It has become the dominant model for the user interface of microcomputer operating systems.

Older microcomputer operating systems, such as DOS, described on the following page, are command-driven, requiring the user to type in text-based commands using a keyboard. For example, to perform a task such as deleting a file named DATAFILE, the user must type in a command such as *DELETE C:\DATAFILE*. Users need to remember these commands and their syntax to work with the computer effectively. An operating system with a graphical user interface uses graphical symbols called *icons* to depict programs, files, and activities. Commands can be activated by rolling a mouse to move a cursor about the screen and clicking a button on the mouse to make selections. Icons are symbolic pictures and they are also used in GUIs to represent programs and files. For example, a file could be deleted by moving the cursor to a Trash icon. Many graphical user interfaces use a system of pull-down menus to help users select commands and pop-up boxes to help users select among various command options. Windowing features allow users to create, stack, size, and move around various boxes of information.

Proponents of graphical user interfaces claim that they save learning time because computing novices do not have to learn different arcane commands for each application. Common functions such as getting help, saving files, or printing output are performed the same way. A complex series of commands can be issued simply by linking icons. Graphical user interfaces can promote superior screen and print output communicated

graphical user interface (GUI) The part of an operating system that users interact with that uses graphic icons and the computer mouse to issue commands and make selections.

6.2 System Software

through graphics. On the other hand, GUIs may not always simplify complex tasks if the user has to spend too much time first pointing to icons and then selecting operations to perform on those icons (Morse and Reynolds, 1993). Graphical symbols themselves are not always easy to understand unless the GUI is well designed. Existing GUIs are modeled after an office desktop, with files, documents, and actions based on typical office behavior, making them less useful for nonoffice applications in control rooms or processing plants (Mandelkern, 1993).

MICROCOMPUTER OPERATING SYSTEMS

Like any other software, microcomputer software is based on specific operating systems and computer hardware. A software package written for one microcomputer operating system generally cannot run on another. The microcomputer operating systems themselves have distinctive features—such as whether they support multitasking or graphics work—that determine the types of applications they are suited for.

Multitasking is one of the principal strengths of operating systems such as IBM's OS/2 (Operating System/2) for the IBM Personal System/2 line of microcomputers or UNIX. PC-DOS and MS-DOS, the older operating system for IBM personal computers and IBM-PC clones, do not allow multitasking, although the Microsoft Corporation markets Windows software to create a multitasking environment for DOS programs.

Table 6.1 compares the leading microcomputer operating systems—Windows 95, Windows NT, OS/2, UNIX, the Macintosh operating system, and DOS. **DOS** was the most popular operating system for 16-bit microcomputers. It is still used today with microcomputers based on the IBM microcomputer standard because so much available application software has been written for systems using DOS. (PC-DOS is used exclusively with IBM microcomputers. MS-DOS, developed by Microsoft, is used with other 16-bit microcomputers that function like the IBM microcomputer.) DOS itself does not support multitasking and limits the size of a program in memory to 640 K.

DOS is command-driven, but it can present a graphical user interface by using Microsoft **Windows,** a highly popular graphical user interface shell that runs in conjunction with the DOS operating system. Windows supports multitasking and some

DOS Operating system for 16-bit microcomputers based on the IBM personal computer standard.

Windows A graphical user interface shell that runs in conjunction with the DOS microcomputer operating system. Supports multitasking and some forms of networking.

Table 6.1	Leading Microcomputer Operating Systems
Operating System	**Features**
DOS	Operating system for IBM (PC-DOS) and IBM-compatible (MS-DOS) microcomputers. Limits program use of memory to 640 K.
Windows 95	32-bit operating system with a streamlined graphical user interface. Has multitasking and powerful networking capabilities.
Windows NT	32-bit operating system for microcomputers and workstations not limited to Intel microprocessors. Supports multitasking, multiprocessing, and networking.
OS/2 (Operating System/2)	Operating system for the IBM Personal System/2 line of microcomputers. Can take advantage of the 32-bit microprocessor. Supports multitasking and networking.
UNIX (XENIX)	Used for powerful microcomputers, workstations, and minicomputers. Supports multitasking, multi-user processing, and networking. Is portable to different models of computer hardware.
System 7	Operating system for the Macintosh computer. Supports multitasking and has powerful graphics and multimedia capabilities.

forms of networking but shares the memory limitations of DOS. It is not considered to run very efficiently in a multitasking environment. Early versions of Windows had some problems with application crashing when multiple programs competed for the same memory space. Windows requires a minimum 386 or 486 microprocessor, 4–8 megabytes of RAM, and 80 megabytes of hard disk storage.

Microsoft's **Windows 95** is a 32-bit operating system designed to remedy many of the deficiencies of Windows sitting atop DOS. A 32-bit operating system can run faster than DOS (which could only address data in 16-bit chunks) because it can address data in 32-bit chunks. Windows 95 provides a streamlined graphical user interface that arranges icons to provide instant access to common tasks. It can support software written for DOS and Windows but it can also run programs that take up more than 640 K of memory. Windows 95 features multitasking, multithreading (the ability to manage multiple independent tasks simultaneously), and powerful networking capabilities, including the capability to integrate fax, e-mail, and scheduling programs. This operating system requires a fast 386 or 486 microprocessor, 8 megabytes of RAM, and 24–48 megabytes of hard disk storage.

Windows NT is another operating system developed by Microsoft with features that make it appropriate for critical applications in large networked organizations. Windows NT uses the same graphical user interface as Windows, but it has powerful multitasking and memory management capabilities. Windows NT can support existing software written for DOS and Windows, and it can provide mainframe-like computing power for new applications with massive memory and file requirements. It can address data in 32-bit chunks if required and can even support multiprocessing with multiple CPUs. Unlike OS/2, Windows NT is not tied to computer hardware based on Intel microprocessors. A company might choose Windows NT if it values flexibility and wants to use an operating system that can run different types of applications on a variety of computer hardware platforms using a common interface that is familiar to users. Windows NT operates best on microcomputers or workstations with the minimum processing capacity of an 80486 microprocessor and requires 16 megabytes of RAM and a 100-megabyte hard disk.

Windows 95 A 32-bit operating system, with a streamlined graphical user interface that can support software written for DOS and Windows but can also run programs that take up more than 640 K of memory. Features multitasking, multithreading, and powerful networking capabilities.

Windows NT Powerful operating system developed by Microsoft for use with 32-bit microcomputers and workstations based on Intel and other microprocessors. Supports networking, multitasking, and multiprocessing.

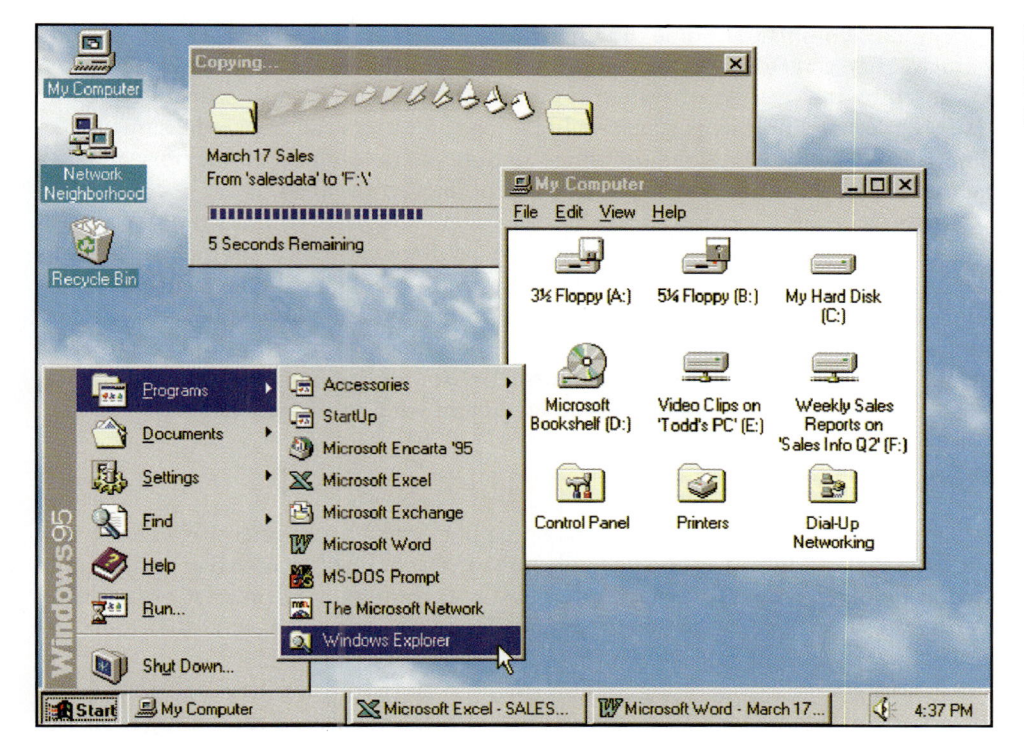

Microsoft's Windows 95 is a powerful operating system with networking capabilities and a streamlined graphical user interface.

OS/2 Powerful operating system used with the 32-bit IBM/Personal System/2 microcomputer workstations that supports multitasking, networking, and more memory-intensive applications than DOS.

OS/2 is a robust operating system that is used with 32-bit IBM Personal System/2 microcomputers or IBM-compatible microcomputers with Intel microprocessors. OS/2 is being used for more complex memory-intensive applications or those that require networking, multitasking, or large programs. OS/2 supports multitasking, accommodates larger applications, allows applications to be run simultaneously, supports networked multimedia and pen computing applications, and is a much more protected operating system. One application that crashes is less likely to bring the whole operating system and other applications down with it. This operating system requires powerful computer hardware—a minimum 80386 or 80486 microprocessor, 4 megabytes of RAM, and 60-megabyte hard disk. OS/2 provides powerful desktop computers with mainframe operating system–like capabilities, such as multitasking and supporting multiple users in networks. Credit Industriel et Commercial de Paris, a major French bank, adopted OS/2 for its networked branch office systems because its stability and support for multitasking made it suitable for serious financial applications (Greenbaum, 1994).

OS/2 has its own graphical user interface, which resembles the graphical user interface for the Macintosh computer. It provides users with a consistent graphical user interface across applications. OS/2 supports DOS applications and can run Windows and DOS applications at the same time in its own resizable windows. The latest version of OS/2 is called OS/2 Warp.

UNIX Operating system for microcomputers, minicomputers, and mainframes, which is machine-independent and supports multi-user processing, multitasking, and networking.

UNIX was developed at Bell Laboratories in 1969 to help scientific researchers share data and programs while keeping other information private. It is an interactive, multi-user, multitasking operating system. Many people can use UNIX simultaneously to perform the same kind of task, or one user can run many tasks on UNIX concurrently. UNIX was developed to connect various machines together and is highly supportive of communications and networking.

UNIX was initially designed for minicomputers but now has versions for microcomputers, workstations, and mainframes. UNIX can run on many different kinds of computers and can be easily customized. It can also store and manage a large number of files. At present, UNIX is primarily used for workstations, minicomputers, and inexpensive multi-user environments in small businesses, but its use in large businesses is growing because of its machine-independence. Application programs that run under UNIX can be ported from one computer to run on a different computer with little modification.

UNIX is accused of being unfriendly to users. It is powerful but very complex. It has a legion of commands, some of which are very cryptic and terse. A typing error on a command line can easily destroy important files. UNIX cannot respond well to problems caused by the overuse of system resources such as jobs or disk space. UNIX also poses some security problems, since multiple jobs and users can access the same file simultaneously. Finally, UNIX requires huge amounts of random access memory and disk capacity, limiting its usefulness for less powerful microcomputers.

System 7 Operating system for the Macintosh computer that supports multitasking and has powerful graphics and multimedia capabilities.

System 7, the latest version of Macintosh system software, features multitasking as well as powerful graphics capabilities and a mouse-driven graphical user interface (illustrated in Figure 6.5). An extension of this operating system called QuickTime™ allows Macintosh users to integrate video clips, stereo sound, and animated sequences with conventional text and graphics software. (Recall the discussion of multimedia in Chapter 5.) System 7 has some features that make it attractive for global applications. For instance, it provides system-level support for Asian languages with large character sets.

SELECTING A MICROCOMPUTER OPERATING SYSTEM

How should a firm go about choosing the operating system for its microcomputer-based applications? Should the decision be made only on the basis of technical merits? Should companies look at other issues such as ease of use, training, and the cost of hardware and software that use the operating system? This brief survey suggests that there are many factors to consider.

If a firm wants an operating system for its mainstream business applications, it needs an operating system that is compatible with the software required by these ap-

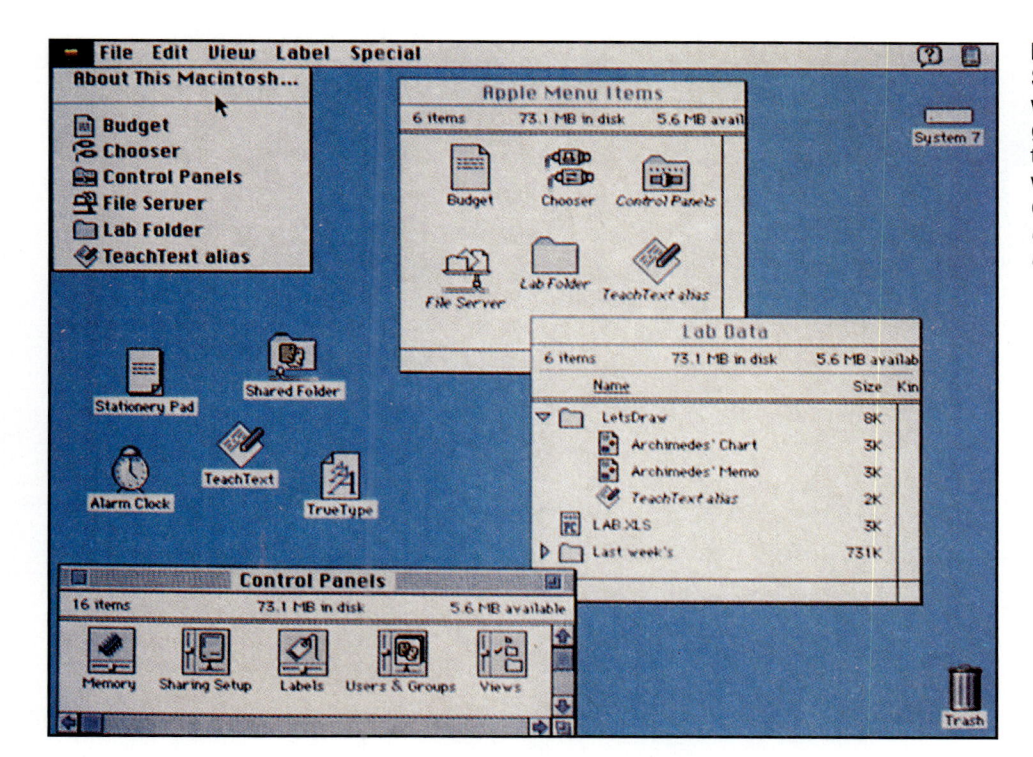

FIGURE 6.5
System 7—Macintosh system software. System 7 supports powerful graphics capabilities as well as multitasking. Users can view multiple windows and make selections by clicking on icons in pull-down menus.
Courtesy of John Greenleigh/Apple Computer, Inc.

plications. The operating system should be easy to use and install. The user interface features of the operating system should be easy to learn. Mission-critical applications have special operating system requirements, since businesses depend on them for their continuing operation and survival. For such applications an operating system that provides reliable support for multitasking and memory management is essential. The operating system should be able to run multiple applications quickly without having the system crash because applications are contending for the same memory space. Mission-critical applications typically have large volumes of transactions to process and require operating systems that can handle large complex software programs and massive files.

The Window on Management shows how NASA selected its operating systems based on its individual business requirements.

6.3 APPLICATION SOFTWARE

Application software is primarily concerned with accomplishing the tasks of end users. Many different languages can be used to develop application software. Each has different strengths and drawbacks.

GENERATIONS OF PROGRAMMING LANGUAGES

To communicate with the first generation of computers, programmers had to write programs in **machine language**—the 0s and 1s of binary code. End users who wanted applications had to work with specialized programmers who could understand, think, and work directly in the machine language of a particular computer. Programming in 0s and 1s (reducing all statements such as add, subtract, and divide into a series of 0s and 1s) made early programming a slow, labor-intensive process.

As computer hardware improved and processing speed and memory size increased, computer languages changed from machine language to languages that were easier for humans to understand. Generations of programming languages developed to correspond with the generations of computer hardware. Figure 6.6 shows the development of programming languages over the last 50 years as the capabilities of hardware have

machine language A programming language consisting of the 1s and 0s of binary code.

Window on Management

NASA SELECTS OPERATING SYSTEMS

NASA's Marshall Space Flight Center Space Sciences Laboratory in Huntsville, Alabama, found that selecting an operating system became an important management issue. The center, famous for building jet propulsion systems for the space shuttle, has a staff of 3500 employees, all of whom are connected to a network. The staff includes 2500 scientists and 1000 administrators (including managers and clerical personnel). The scientists run powerful applications such as 32-bit computer-aided design (CAD) programs and so require powerful workstations. The administrators need much less power because they mainly run word processors. They use 386, 486, and Pentium PCs and Macintosh machines.

Management's business goals were to improve communication among the scientists and administrators without investing in new hardware. Their specific concerns in selecting an operating system included the following:

1. All computers had to be networked together.
2. Workers (both administrators and scientists) had to see and access a coworker's files, and be able to collaborate with coworkers on those files.
3. File names had to be understandable to administrators and scientists alike.
4. A common operating system was needed to reduce the high cost of supporting different types of hardware. The system had to meet the computing needs of both administrators and scientists.
5. The facility had to keep its computer hardware budget low.

Management settled on two related operating systems, Windows 95 and Windows NT. Windows NT replaced the laboratory's previous software for managing the computer storing files and programs used on the network. Individual user computers were upgraded to Windows 95. The two Microsoft operating systems work well together and enable all NASA's computers and servers to be networked. Windows 95 runs powerful 32-bit

To Think About: Why is the selection of an operating system an important business management decision?

applications, such as CAD, as well as less powerful administrative programs. Both share a common, easy-to-use graphical user interface. Through Windows 95's Network Neighborhood facility, users can locate which computer a file is on, click on that file, and drag a copy of it to their own hard drive, where they can work on it.

The Windows 95 file-naming facility allows file names to be 250 characters long versus only a paltry eight characters for previous DOS, Windows, or UNIX file names. As a result, file names can now be written in understandable English. In addition, with such long names, a single, across-the-board file-naming convention can be established. Users could continue to use their existing, varied computer equipment, and they would all be supported by a common operating system, making that support much easier and less expensive than in the past.

Windows 95 is powerful enough to run the scientific programs while requiring minimal memory so that it can run on the less powerful administrators' computers. NASA did not need to purchase new computers and could even save hardware costs by using its older, retired computers again.

Source: Bronwyn Fryer, "NASA Rockets Into Win95," *Information Week*, August 21, 1995.

---

increased. The major trend is to increase the ease with which users can interact with the hardware and software.

Machine language was the first-generation programming language. The second generation of programming languages occurred in the early 1950s with the development of assembly language. Instead of using 0s and 1s, programmers could now substitute language-like acronyms and words such as *add, sub* (subtract), and *load* in programming statements. A language translator called a *compiler* converted the English-like statements into machine language.

When the third hardware generation was underway, programming languages entered their third generation as well. From the mid-1950s to the 1970s, the first higher-level languages emerged. These languages permitted mathematicians for the first time to work with computers through the use of languages such as FORTRAN (FORmula TRANslator program). Mathematicians were now able to define variables with statements such as $Z = A + B$. The software translated these definitions and mathematical statements into a series of 0s and 1s. COBOL (COmmon Business Oriented Language) permitted the use of English statements such as *print* and *sort* to be used by programmers, who did not have to think in terms of 0s and 1s.

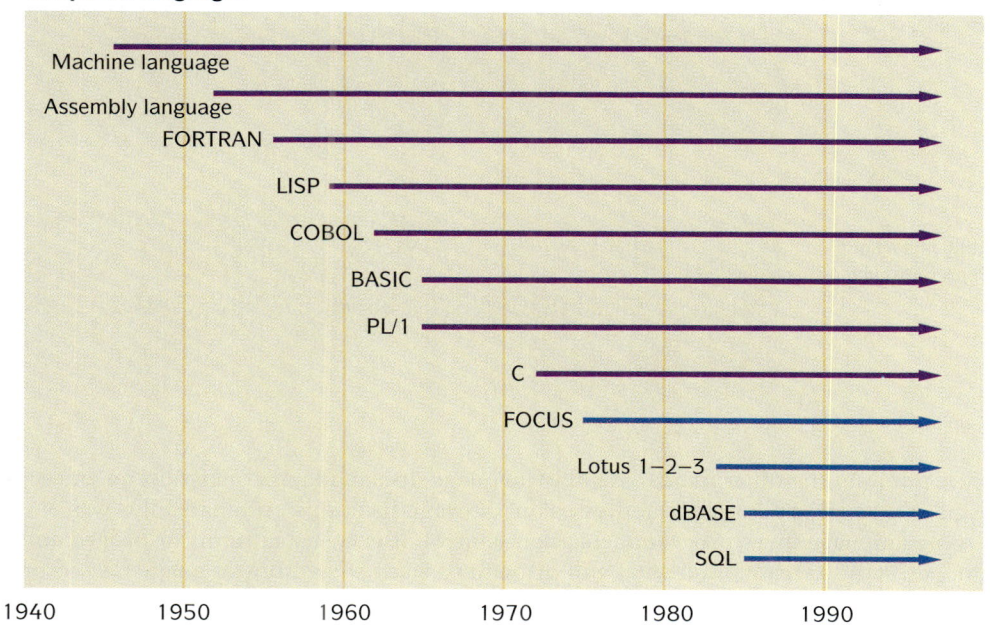

FIGURE 6.6
Generations of programming languages. As the capabilities of hardware increased, programming languages developed from the first generation of machine and second generation of assembly languages of the 1950s to 1960, through the third generation high-level languages such as FORTRAN and COBOL developed in the 1960s and 1970s, to the fourth-generation languages.

A. Generations
- First Generation
- Second Generation
- Third Generation
- Fourth Generation

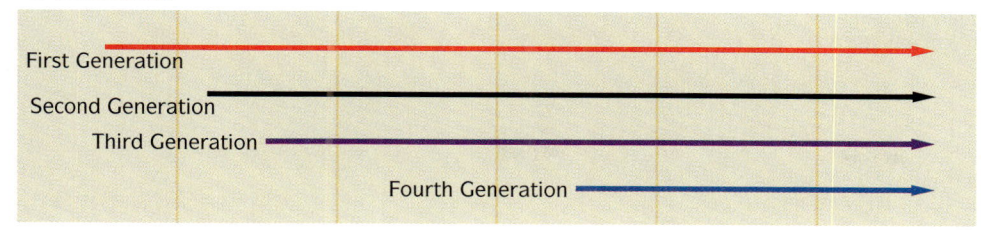

B. Specific languages
- Machine language
- Assembly language
- FORTRAN
- LISP
- COBOL
- BASIC
- PL/1
- C
- FOCUS
- Lotus 1–2–3
- dBASE
- SQL

1940   1950   1960   1970   1980   1990

These **high-level languages** are so called because each statement in FORTRAN or COBOL generates multiple statements at the machine-language level. The use of these higher-level languages requires much faster, more efficient compilers to translate higher-level languages into machine codes.

Fourth-generation computer languages emerged in the late 1970s, and their development is still in progress. These languages dramatically reduce programming time and make software tasks so easy that nontechnical computer users can develop applications without the help of professional programmers. Fourth-generation tools also include prewritten application software packages that can be used directly by end users. Using the software package Lotus 1–2–3, for instance, users can create their own financial spreadsheets and manipulate data without programmer intervention. Such sophistication by nonspecialists using FORTRAN would have been impossible in the 1960s and 1970s.

high-level language Programming languages where each source code statement generates multiple statements at the machine-language level.

POPULAR PROGRAMMING LANGUAGES

Most managers need not be expert programmers, but they should understand how to evaluate software applications and to select programming languages that are appropriate for their organization's objectives. We will now briefly describe the more popular high-level languages.

Assembly Language

Many programmers still prefer to write programs in assembly language because this language gives them close control over the hardware and very efficient execution. Like machine language, **assembly language** (Figure 6.7) is designed for a specific machine and specific microprocessors. Each operation in assembly corresponds to a machine

assembly language A programming language developed in the 1950s that resembles machine language but substitutes mnemonics for numeric codes.

6.3 Application Software   175

FIGURE 6.7
Assembly language. This sample assembly language command adds the contents of register 3 to register 5 and stores the result in register 5.

AR 5, 3

FIGURE 6.8
FORTRAN. This sample FORTRAN program code is part of a program to compute sales figures for a particular item.

READ (5,100) ID, QUANT, PRICE
TOTAL = QUANT * PRICE

FIGURE 6.9
COBOL. This sample COBOL program code is part of a routine to compute total sales figures for a particular item.

MULTIPLY QUANT-SOLD BY UNIT-PRICE GIVING SALES-TOTAL.

operation. On the other hand, assembly language does make use of certain mnemonics (e.g., *load, sum*) and assigns addresses and storage locations automatically. While assembly language gives programmers great control, it is costly in terms of programmer time, difficult to read and debug, and difficult to learn. Assembly language is used primarily today in system software.

FORTRAN

FORTRAN (FORmula TRANslator)
A programming language developed in 1956 for scientific and mathematical applications.

FORTRAN (FORmula TRANslator) (Figure 6.8) was developed in 1956 to provide an easier way of writing scientific and engineering applications. FORTRAN is especially useful in processing numeric data. Many kinds of business applications can be written in FORTRAN, it is relatively easy to learn, and contemporary versions (e.g., FORTRAN 77) provide sophisticated structures for controlling program logic. FORTRAN is not very good at providing input/output efficiency or in printing and working with lists. The syntax is very strict and keying errors are common, making the programs difficult to debug.

COBOL

COBOL (COmmon Business Oriented Language) The predominant programming language for business applications because it can process large data files with alphanumeric characters.

COBOL (COmmon Business Oriented Language) (Figure 6.9) came into use in the early 1960s. It was originally developed by a committee representing both government and industry because the Defense Department wished to create a common administrative language for internal and external software. Rear Admiral Grace M. Hopper was a key committee member who played a major role in COBOL development. COBOL was designed with business administration in mind, for processing large data files with alphanumeric characters (mixed alphabetic and numeric data), and for performing repetitive tasks like payroll. Its primary data structures are records, files, tables, and lists. The weakness of COBOL is a result of its virtue. It is poor at complex mathematical calculations. Also, there are many versions of COBOL, and not all are compatible with each other.

BASIC (Beginners All-purpose Symbolic Instruction Code) A general-purpose programming language used with microcomputers and for teaching programming.

BASIC

BASIC (Beginners All-purpose Symbolic Instruction Code) was developed in 1964 by John Kemeny and Thomas Kurtz to teach students at Dartmouth College how to use computers. Today it is a popular programming language on college campuses and for microcomputers. BASIC can do almost all computer processing tasks from inventory to mathematical calculations. It is easy to use, demonstrates computer capabilities well, and requires only a small interpreter. The weakness of BASIC is that it does few tasks well even though it does them all. It has no sophisticated program logic control or data structures, which makes it difficult to use in teaching good programming practices. Different versions of BASIC programs often cannot be moved from one machine to another.

PL/1

PL/1 (Programming Language 1) was developed by IBM in 1964. It is the most powerful general-purpose programming language because it can handle mathematical and business applications with ease, is highly efficient in input/output activities, and can handle large volumes of data.

Unfortunately, the huge volume of COBOL and FORTRAN programs written in the private sector at great cost cannot simply be jettisoned when a newer, more powerful language comes along. PL/1 has not succeeded largely because programmers trained in COBOL could not be convinced to learn an entirely new language, and business organizations could not be convinced to spend millions of dollars rewriting their software. PL/1 is, moreover, somewhat difficult to learn in its entirety.

> **PL/1 (Programming Language 1)** A programming language developed by IBM in 1964 for business and scientific applications.

Pascal

Named after Blaise Pascal, the seventeenth-century mathematician and philosopher, **Pascal** was developed by the Swiss computer science professor Niklaus Wirth of Zurich in the late 1960s. Pascal programs can be compiled using minimal computer memory, so they can be used on microcomputers. With sophisticated structures to control program logic and a simple, powerful set of commands, Pascal is used primarily in computer science courses to teach sound programming practices. The language is weak at file handling and input/output and is not easy for beginners to use.

> **Pascal** A programming language used on microcomputers and to teach sound programming practices in computer science courses.

Ada

Ada was developed in 1980 to provide the United States Defense Department with a structured programming language to serve as the standard for all of its applications. Ada was named after Ada, Countess of Lovelace, a nineteenth-century mathematician whose father was the English poet Lord Byron. The Countess is sometimes called the first programmer because she developed the mathematical tables for an early calculating machine. This language was initially conceived for weapons systems, where software is developed on a processor and then imbedded into the weapon. It was explicitly designed so that it could be uniformly executed in diverse hardware environments. The language also promotes structured software design. U.S. government experts hope Ada will produce more cost-effective software because it facilitates more clearly structured code than COBOL.

Ada is used in nonmilitary government applications as well. The language can also be used for general business applications since it can operate on microcomputers and is portable across different brands of computer hardware.

> **Ada** A programming language that is portable across different brands of hardware; is used for both military and nonmilitary applications.

C

C was developed at AT&T's Bell Labs in the early 1970s and is the language in which much of the UNIX operating system is written. C combines some of the tight control and efficiency of execution features of assembly language with machine portability. In other words, it can work on a variety of computers rather than on just one. Much commercial microcomputer software has been written in C, but C is gaining support for some minicomputer and mainframe applications. C is unlikely to dislodge COBOL for mainframe business applications, but it will be used increasingly for commercial microcomputer software and for scientific and technical applications.

> **C** A powerful programming language with tight control and efficiency of execution; is portable across different microprocessors and is used primarily with microcomputers.

LISP and Prolog

LISP (designating LISt Processor) and Prolog are widely used in artificial intelligence. LISP was created in the late 1950s by M.I.T. mathematician John McCarthy and is oriented toward putting symbols such as operations, variables, and data values into meaningful lists. LISP is better at manipulating symbols than at ordinary number crunching.

Prolog, introduced around 1970, is also well suited to symbol manipulation and can run on general-purpose computers, whereas LISP usually runs best on machines configured especially to run LISP programs.

FOURTH-GENERATION LANGUAGES

fourth-generation language A programming language that can be employed directly by end users or less skilled programmers to develop computer applications more rapidly than conventional programming languages.

Fourth-generation languages consist of a variety of software tools that enable end users to develop software applications with minimal or no technical assistance or that enhance the productivity of professional programmers. Fourth-generation languages tend to be nonprocedural or less procedural than conventional programming languages. Procedural languages require specification of the sequence of steps, or procedures, that tell the computer what to do and how to do it. Nonprocedural languages need only to specify what has to be accomplished rather than provide details about how to carry out the task. Thus, a nonprocedural language can accomplish the same task with fewer steps and lines of program code than a procedural language.

There are seven categories of fourth-generation languages: query languages, report generators, graphics languages, application generators, very high-level programming languages, application software packages, and microcomputer tools. Figure 6.10 illustrates the spectrum of these tools and some commercially available products in each category.

Query Languages

query language A high-level computer language used to retrieve specific information from databases or files.

Query languages are high-level languages for retrieving data stored in databases or files. They are usually interactive, on-line, and capable of supporting requests for information that are not predefined. They are often tied to database management systems (see Chapter 7) and microcomputer tools (see the following discussion). Query languages can search a database or file, using simple or complex selection criteria to display information relating to multiple records. Available query language tools have different kinds of syntax and structure, some being closer to natural language than others (Vassiliou, 1984–1985). Some support updating of data as well as retrieval. An example of a typical ad hoc query is "List all employees in the payroll department." Figure 6.11 illustrates how two different query languages, Query-by-Example and FOCUS, express this request.

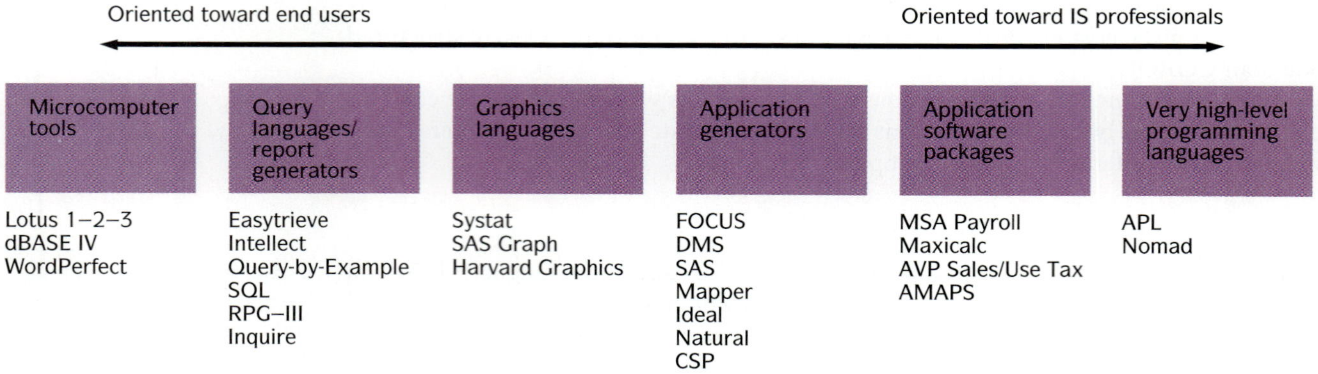

Oriented toward end users ← → Oriented toward IS professionals

Microcomputer tools	Query languages/ report generators	Graphics languages	Application generators	Application software packages	Very high-level programming languages
Lotus 1–2–3	Easytrieve	Systat	FOCUS	MSA Payroll	APL
dBASE IV	Intellect	SAS Graph	DMS	Maxicalc	Nomad
WordPerfect	Query-by-Example	Harvard Graphics	SAS	AVP Sales/Use Tax	
	SQL		Mapper	AMAPS	
	RPG–III		Ideal		
	Inquire		Natural		
			CSP		

FIGURE 6.10
Fourth-generation languages. The spectrum of major categories of fourth-generation languages and commercially available products in each category is illustrated. Tools range from those that are simple and designated primarily for end users to complex tools designed for information systems professionals.

Report Generators

Report generators are facilities for creating customized reports. They extract data from files or databases and create reports in many formats. Report generators generally provide more control over the way data are formatted, organized, and displayed than query languages. The more powerful report generators can manipulate data with complex calculations and logic before they are output. Some report generators are extensions of database or query languages. The more complex and powerful report generators may not be suitable for end users without some assistance from professional information systems specialists.

report generator Software that creates customized reports in a wide range of formats that are not routinely produced by an information system.

Graphics Languages

Graphics languages retrieve data from files or databases and display them in graphic format. Users can ask for data and specify how they are to be charted. Some graphics software can perform arithmetic or logical operations on data as well. SAS, Harvard Graphics, and Lotus Freelance Graphics are popular graphics tools.

graphics language A computer language that displays data from files or databases in graphic format.

Application Generators

Application generators contain preprogrammed modules that can generate entire applications, greatly speeding development. A user can specify what needs to be done, and the application generator will create the appropriate code for input, validation, update, processing, and reporting. Most full-function application generators consist of a comprehensive, integrated set of development tools: a database management system, data dictionary, query language, screen painter, graphics generator, report generator, decision support/modeling tools, security facilities, and a high-level programming language. For unique requirements that cannot be met with generalized modules, most application generators contain *user exits* where custom-programmed routines can be inserted. Some application generators are interactive, enabling users sitting at a terminal to define inputs, files, processing, and reports by responding to questions on-line.

application generator Software that can generate entire information system applications; the user needs only to specify what needs to be done, and the application generator creates the appropriate program code.

Very High-Level Programming Languages

Very high-level programming languages are designed to generate program code with fewer instructions than conventional languages such as COBOL or FORTRAN. Programs and applications based on these languages can be developed in much shorter periods of time. Simple features of these languages can be employed by end users. However, these languages are designed primarily as productivity tools for professional programmers. APL and Nomad2 are examples of these languages. The Window on Organizations illustrates how a Canadian telephone company used one such language, Magic, to solve a serious problem it faced.

very high-level programming language A programming language that uses fewer instructions than conventional languages. Used primarily as a professional programmer productivity tool.

Query: "List all employees in the Payroll department."

Using Query-by-Example:

EMPLOYEE	EMPLOYEE #	NAME	DEPARTMENT
		P.	PAYROLL

Using FOCUS:
> > TABLE FILE EMPDEPT
> PRINT EMP_NAME IF DEPT EQ 'PAYROLL'
> END

FIGURE 6.11
Query languages. This figure illustrates how the simple query, "List all employees in the Payroll department," would be handled by the two different query languages: Query-by-Example and FOCUS.

Window on Organizations

BELL QUEBEC REPAIRS ITS PAY PHONES BY MAGIC

How would you react if, when you called your telephone company to report an out-of-order pay phone, you were put on hold? That was a small piece of the problem faced in 1993 by Montreal-based Bell Quebec, a division of Bell Canada. These Good Samaritan customers were put on hold because the agent had to go to another telephone line to contact the repair department to determine if someone else had already reported the problem. When a technician did finally arrive at the out-of-order phone, he or she often found coins in the coin box, forcing the repairperson first to report that fact to the accounting department. Repair of the telephone then had to wait until a collector had collected those coins.

Bell Quebec did have a telephone monitoring system that polled each of the pay phones periodically to see if they were working. However, the polling system itself was a nightmare. The data were transmitted to a headquarters mainframe computer where they were accumulated and then printed once a day in six-inch-thick paper reports. Workers then had to manually ferret out the out-of-order telephones so that technicians could be dispatched to repair them.

Today, agents who take repair calls now enter the pay phone's telephone number into the computer and the telephone's repair history immediately pops up, showing the current status, including whether or not a repair truck has been dispatched, and the other information the agent needs. Previous systems were developed in isolation. Within Bell Quebec, installation and support, repair services, marketing, and accounting all had stand-alone systems that shared no information and stored their own, often conflicting data. To make matters worse, each of the isolated systems operated on different hardware, including IBM, Hewlett-Packard (HP), and Amdahl mainframes; Sequent, Tandem, and DEC VAX minicomputers; HP9000s; Sun workstations; and various PCs and PC local-area networks. Operating systems included MVS, VMS, HP-UX, and SunOS.

Claude Prouix, Bell Quebec's general manager of operator and public telecommunications services, decided in late 1992 that something had to be done. His staff immediately began to look at a range of outside solutions. The approach it finally selected was to contract for Magic Software. Magic Software Enterprises Ltd. is an Israeli-based company that offers a fourth-generation tool for table-based programming. With Magic, Bell

> **To Think About:** How was the use of Magic related to Bell Quebec's business needs? What were the organizational implications of the installation of Magic? Suggest other uses for this type of fourth-generation language.

Quebec quickly built an information backbone shared by all the departmental systems, collected from all the relevant departments, and stored in one common data repository. With the data in a central location, queries quickly produced the information needed at each stage of the pay phone maintenance process. According to David Wegman, chief operating officer of Magic Software Enterprises, prior to building the information backbone, Bell Quebec had "great systems for collecting mountains of data that nobody could use." Now, however, Magic had become "data-central, able to reach out and grab the data everywhere it existed. It became . . . a central data manipulation tool."

Magic works with no program coding by its users. Instead, users define their needs through visual programming (see this chapter's Window on Technology) and filling in tables. Central to Magic is its data dictionary that looks much like a spreadsheet. Using it, Bell Quebec staff can update information on a telephone number in this one place and all changes needed by the underlying systems will automatically be made, meaning no programming work for Bell Quebec staff. Also important to Bell Quebec, Magic runs on many platforms. Magic programs written on a DOS PC were moved to the Sun, VAX, and HP9000 without modification of any kind.

Source: Connie Winkler, "Bell Quebec Tries Magic to Put Pay Phones in Working Order," *Software Magazine*, January 1995.

Application Software Packages

software package A prewritten, precoded, commercially available set of programs that eliminates the need to write software programs for certain functions.

A **software package** is a prewritten, precoded, commercially available set of programs that eliminates the need for individuals or organizations to write their own software programs for certain functions. There are software packages for system software, but the vast majority of package software is application software.

Application software packages consist of prewritten application software that is marketed commercially. These packages are available for major business applications on mainframes, minicomputers, and microcomputers. They contain customization features so that they can be tailored somewhat to an organization's unique requirements. Although application packages for large complex systems must be installed by technical specialists, many application packages, especially those for microcomputers, are

Sophisticated graphics software tools such as those from Systat Inc. can present data in the form of three-dimensional charts.

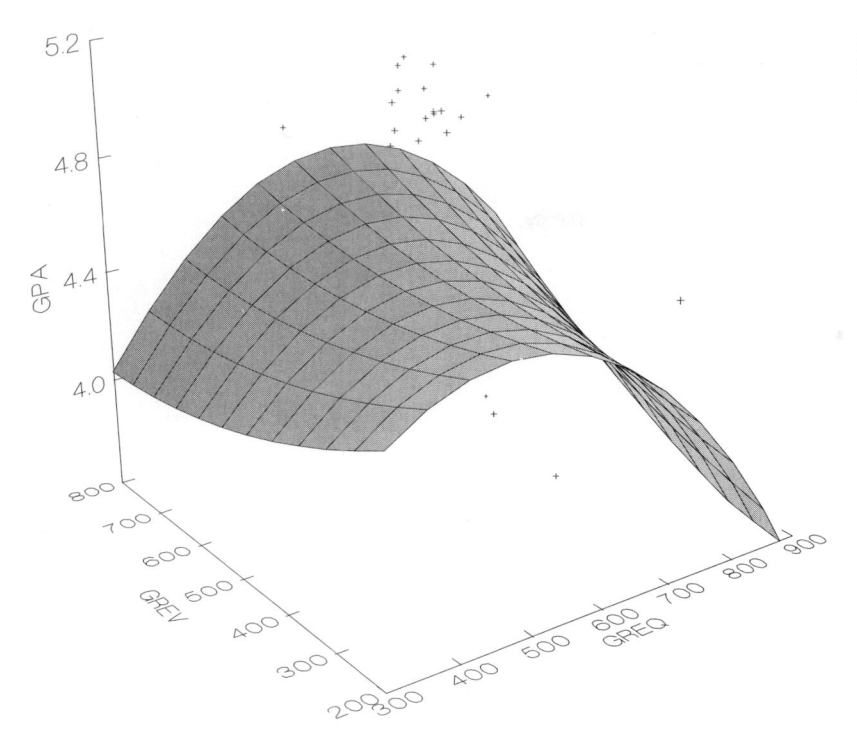

marketed directly to end users. Systems development based on application packages is discussed in Chapter 11.

Microcomputer Tools

Some of the most popular and productivity-promoting fourth-generation tools are the general-purpose application packages that have been developed for microcomputers, especially word processing, spreadsheet, data management, graphics, and integrated software packages.

WORD PROCESSING SOFTWARE. **Word processing software** stores text data electronically as a computer file rather than on paper. The word processing software allows the user to make changes in the document electronically in memory. This eliminates the need to retype an entire page in order to incorporate corrections. The software has formatting options to make changes in line spacing, margins, character size, and column width. Microsoft Word and WordPerfect are popular word processing packages. Figure 6.12 illustrates a Microsoft Word screen for Windows displaying text, graphics, and major menu options.

Most word processing software has advanced features that automate other writing tasks: spelling checkers, style checkers (to analyze grammar and punctuation), thesaurus programs, and mail merge programs (which link letters or other text documents with names and addresses in a mailing list).

word processing software Software that handles electronic storage, editing, formatting, and printing of documents.

SPREADSHEETS. Electronic **spreadsheet** software provides computerized versions of traditional financial modeling tools such as the accountant's columnar pad, pencil, and calculator. An electronic spreadsheet is organized into a grid of columns and rows. The power of the electronic spreadsheet is evident when one changes a value or values, because all other related values on the spreadsheet will be automatically recomputed.

Spreadsheets are valuable for applications where numerous calculations with pieces of data must be related to each other. Spreadsheets are also useful for applications that require modeling and what-if analysis. After the user has constructed a set of mathematical relationships, the spreadsheet can be recalculated instantaneously using a

spreadsheet Software displaying data in a grid of columns and rows, with the capability of easily recalculating numerical data.

FIGURE 6.12
Text and some of the options available in Microsoft Word for Windows. Word processors provide many easy-to-use options to create and output a text document to meet a user's specifications. *Courtesy of Microsoft.*

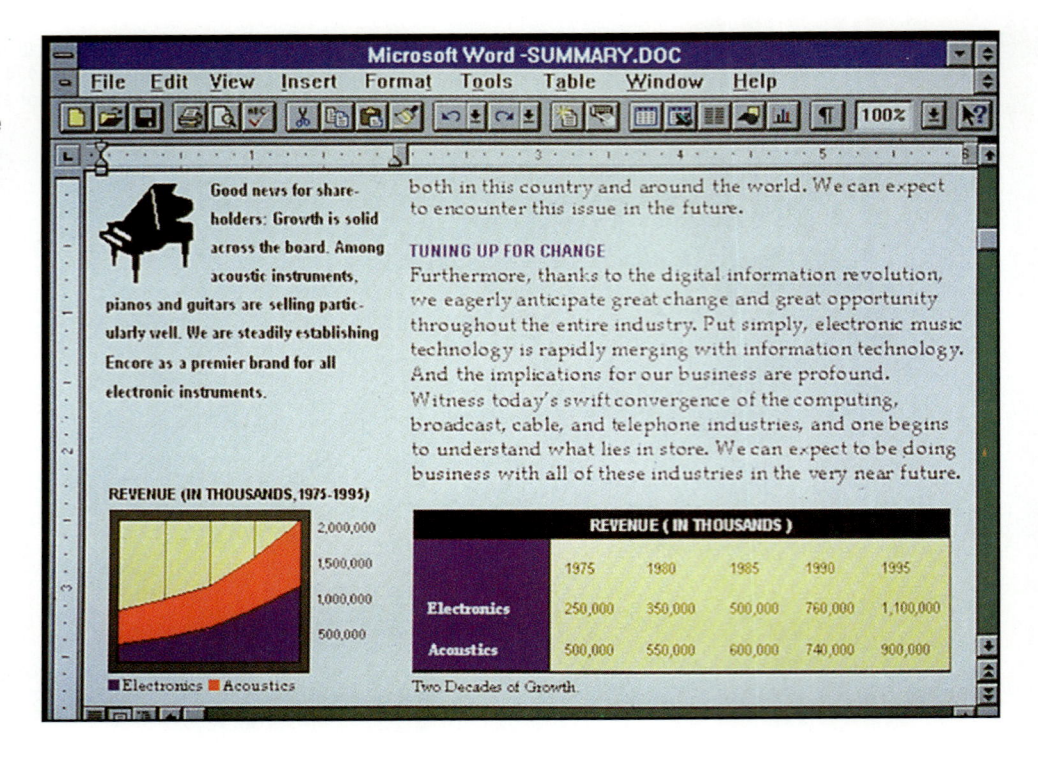

different set of assumptions. A number of alternatives can easily be evaluated by changing one or two pieces of data without having to rekey in the rest of the worksheet. Many spreadsheet packages include graphics functions that can present data in the form of line graphs, bar graphs, or pie charts. The most popular spreadsheet packages are Microsoft Excel and Lotus 1–2–3.

Figure 6.13 illustrates the output from a spreadsheet for a breakeven analysis and its accompanying graph.

DATA MANAGEMENT SOFTWARE. While spreadsheet programs are powerful tools for manipulating quantitative data, **data management software** is more suitable for creating and manipulating lists and for combining information from different files. Microcomputer database management packages have programming features and easy-to-learn menus that enable nonspecialists to build small information systems.

Data management software typically has facilities for creating files and databases and for storing, modifying, and manipulating data for reports and queries. A detailed treatment of data management software and database management systems can be found in Chapter 7. Popular database management software for the personal computer includes Microsoft Access, Paradox, and dBASE IV. Figure 6.14 shows a screen from Microsoft Access for Windows illustrating some of its capabilities.

INTEGRATED SOFTWARE PACKAGES. **Integrated software packages** combine the functions of the most important microcomputer software packages, such as word processing, spreadsheets, graphics, and data management. This integration provides a more general-purpose software tool and eliminates redundant data entry and data maintenance. For example, the breakeven analysis spreadsheet illustrated in Figure 6.13 could

data management software
Software used for creating and manipulating lists, creating files and databases to store data, and combining information for reports.

integrated software package A software package that provides two or more applications, such as word processing and spreadsheets, providing for easy transfer of data between them.

Total fixed cost	19,000.00
Variable cost per unit	3.00
Average sales price	17.00
Contribution margin	14.00
Breakeven point	1,357

Custom Neckties Pro Forma Income Statement

Units sold	0.00	679	1,357	2,036	2,714
Revenue	0	11,536	23,071	34,607	46,143
Fixed cost	19,000	19,000	19,000	19,000	19,000
Variable cost	0	2,036	4,071	6,107	8,143
Total cost	19,000	21,036	23,071	25,107	27,143
Profit/Loss	(19,000)	(9,500)	0	9,500	19,000

FIGURE 6.13
Spreadsheet software. Spreadsheet software organizes data into columns and rows for analysis and manipulation. Contemporary spreadsheet software provides graphing abilities for clear visual representation of the data in the spreadsheets. This sample breakeven analysis is represented as numbers in a spreadsheet as well as a line graph for easy interpretation.

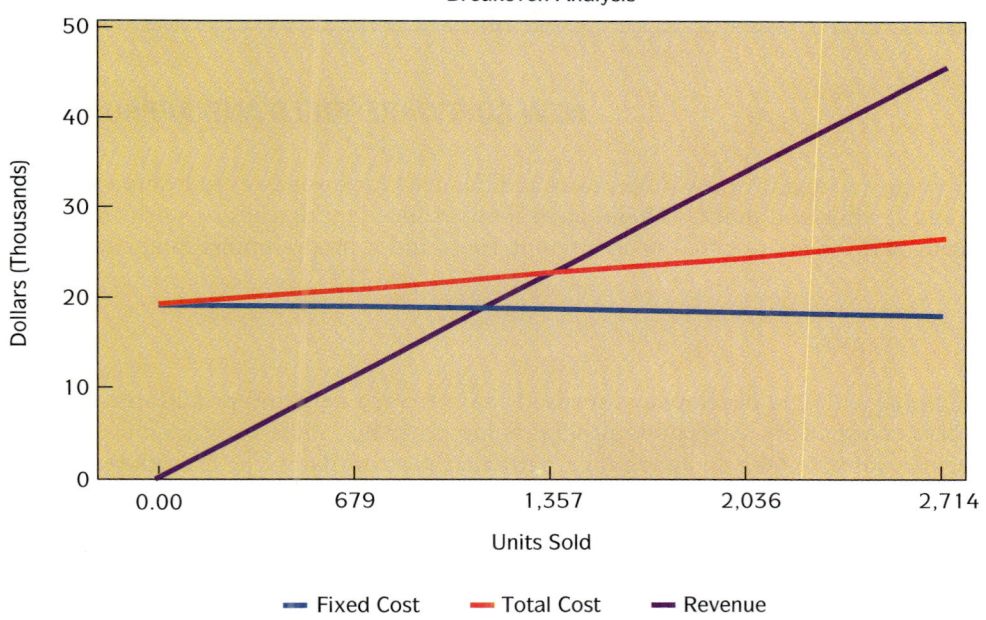

be reformatted into a polished report with word processing software without separately keying the data into both programs. Integrated packages are a compromise. While they can do many things well, they generally do not have the same power and depth as single-purpose packages.

As Chapter 11 will discuss, fourth-generation tools are applicable only to specific areas of application development. Nevertheless, fourth-generation tools have provided many productivity and cost-cutting benefits for businesses.

FIGURE 6.14
Data management software. This screen from Microsoft Access for Windows illustrates some of its powerful capabilities for managing text and graphic data.

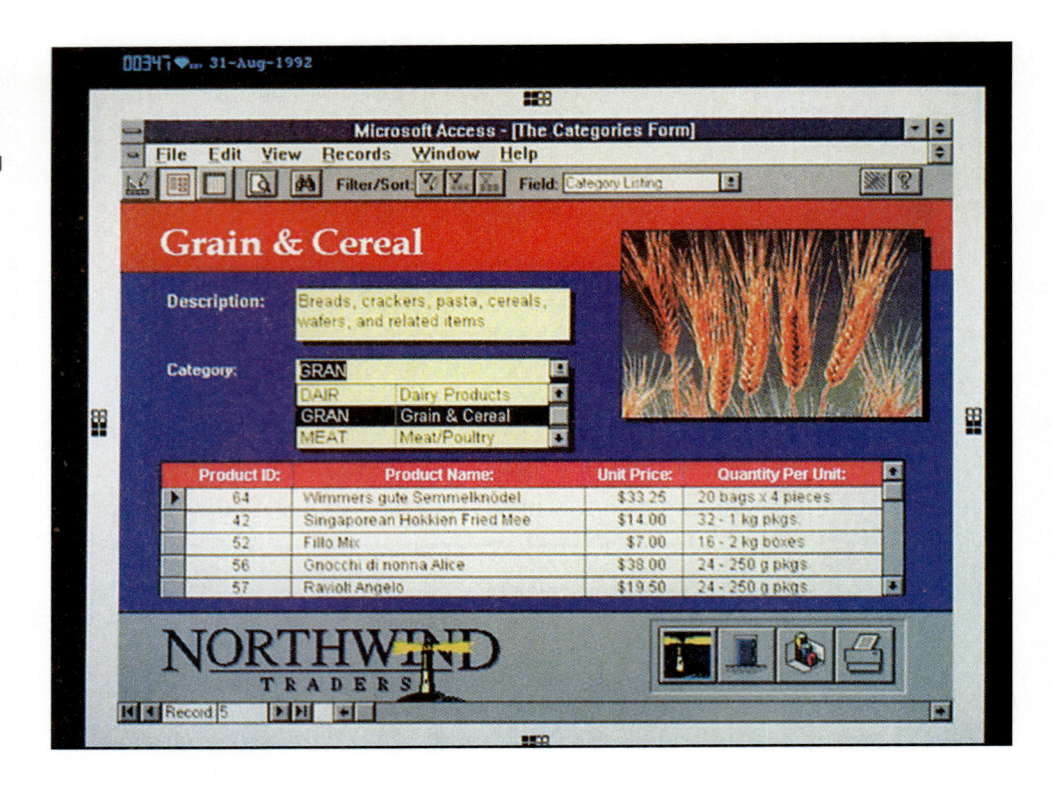

6.4 NEW SOFTWARE TOOLS AND APPROACHES

A growing backlog of software projects and the need for businesses to fashion systems that are flexible and quick to build have spawned new approaches to software development with object-oriented programming tools and a programming language called Java.

OBJECT-ORIENTED PROGRAMMING

Traditional software development methods have treated data and procedures as independent components. A separate programming procedure must be written every time someone wants to take an action on a particular piece of data. The procedures act on data that the program passes to them.

What Makes Object-Oriented Programming Different?

object-oriented programming
An approach to software development that combines data and procedures into a single object.

Object-oriented programming combines data and the specific procedures that operate on those data into one *object*. The object combines data and program code. Instead of passing data to procedures, programs send a message for an object to perform a procedure that is already embedded into it. (Procedures are termed *methods* in object-oriented languages.) The same message may be sent to many different objects, but each will implement that message differently.

For example, an object-oriented financial application might have Customer objects sending debit and credit messages to Account objects. The Account objects in turn might maintain Cash-on-Hand, Accounts-Payable, and Accounts-Receivable objects.

An object's data are hidden from other parts of the program and can only be manipulated from inside the object. The method for manipulating the object's data can be changed internally without affecting other parts of the program. Programmers can focus on what they want an object to do, and the object decides how to do it.

Because an object's data are encapsulated from other parts of the system, each object is an independent software building block that can be used in many different sys-

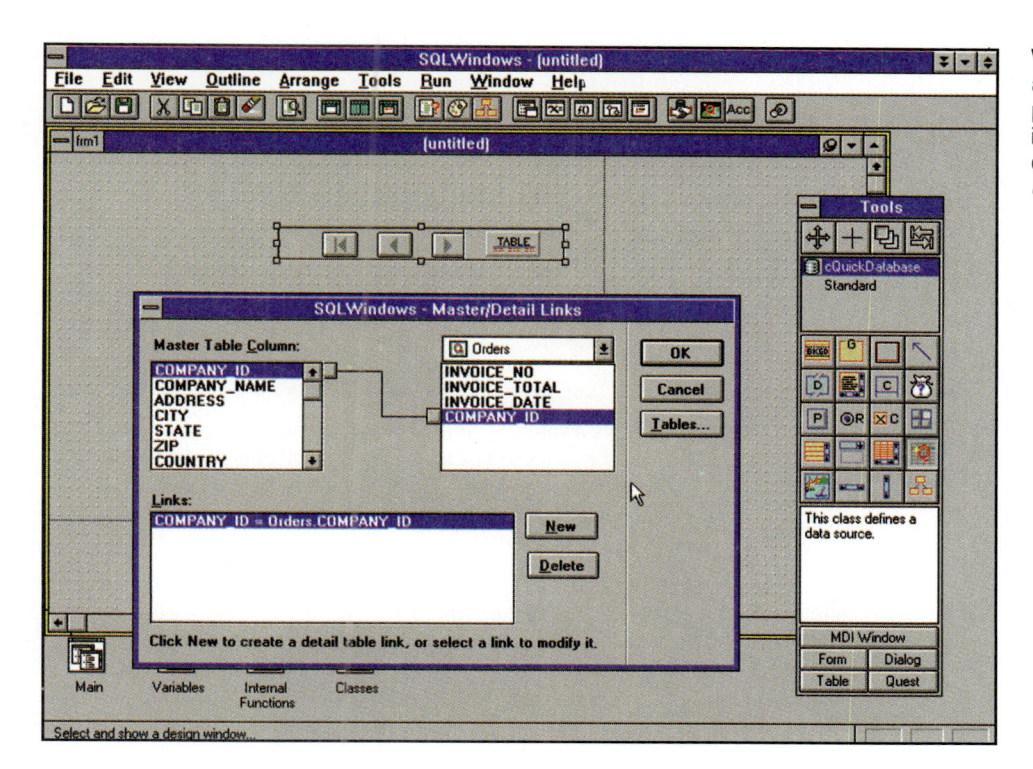

With visual programming tools such as SQL Windows, working software programs can be created by drawing, pointing, and clicking instead of writing program code. *Source: Courtesy of the Gupta Corporation.*

tems without changing the program code. Thus, object-oriented programming is expected to reduce the time and cost of writing software by producing reusable program code or software *chips* that can be reused in other related systems. Future software work can draw upon a library of reusable objects, and productivity gains from object-oriented technology could be magnified if objects were stored in reusable software libraries.

Object-oriented programming has spawned a new programming technology known as **visual programming**. With visual programming, programmers do not write code. Rather, they use a mouse to select and move around programming objects, copying an object from a library into a specific location in a program, or drawing a line to connect two or more objects. The Window on Technology more fully describes *drag-and-drop*, one visual programming method.

visual programming The construction of software programs by selecting and arranging programming objects rather than by writing program code.

Object-Oriented Programming Concepts

Object-oriented programming is based on the concepts of class and inheritance. Program code is not written separately for every object but for classes, or general categories of similar objects. Objects belonging to a certain class have the features of that class. Classes of objects in turn can inherit all the structure and behaviors of a more general class and then add variables and behaviors unique to each object. New classes of objects are created by choosing an existing class and specifying how the new class differs from the existing class, instead of starting from scratch each time.

Classes are organized hierarchically into superclasses and subclasses. For example, a *car* class might have a *vehicle* class for a superclass, so that it would inherit all the methods and data previously defined for *vehicle*. The design of the *car* class would only need to describe how cars differ from vehicles. A banking application could define a Savings-Account object that is very much like a Bank-Account object with a few minor differences. Savings-Account inherits all of the Bank-Account's state and methods and then adds a few extras.

We can see how class and **inheritance** work in Figure 6.15, which illustrates a tree of classes concerning employees and how they are paid. Employee is the common ancestor of the other four classes. Contractor and Paid weekly are subclasses of Employee, while Hourly and Salaried are subclasses of Paid weekly. The variables for the class are

class The feature of object-oriented programming so that all objects belonging to a certain class have all of the features of that class.

inheritance The feature of object-oriented programming in which a specific class of objects receives the features of a more general class.

6.4 New Software Tools and Approaches 185

Window on Technology

POWER SHORT-CIRCUITS IN OBJECT-ORIENTED DEVELOPMENT

Ontario Hydro, the Toronto-based and government-owned utility, faces an enormous task in maintaining its 69 hydroelectric power stations, eight fossil-fuel generators, and five nuclear power plants. It is the Northern hemisphere's biggest electric utility, servicing one of the most electricity-intensive economies of any high-population state or province. Whenever an unscheduled shutdown of a plant does occur, it can cost the company as much as $1 million a day. It also can affect the 8 million customers served by this $8.3 billion (Canadian) power utility. Mike Benjamin, an Ontario Hydro project manager, had an idea for an information system that would reduce unscheduled shutdowns by assisting on-site maintenance staff in their performance of plant component predictive maintenance. Much of the information the staff required to enable it to predict problems was already available, but in scattered existing systems. Benjamin launched a project that combined data from a hodgepodge of existing systems—from simulation packages to commercial databases and artificial intelligence—running on various computers so that all operators could monitor operations and even predict equipment failure. To build the system rapidly, Benjamin first developed a pilot system using object-oriented technology. Ontario Hydro plans to roll it out to all of its plants. This system won't prevent shutdowns, but it should decrease the frequency of shutdowns and the amount of downtime.

The key software tool Ontario Hydro used to program the objects was Xshell from Expersoft Corp. of San Diego, California, which relies on a programming technique known as drag-and-drop. Drag-and-drop is a visually oriented and easy-to-use object-oriented programming method that is gaining popularity. It relies on ORBs (or object request brokers) that are hidden to the programmer but are the elements that allow objects to communicate with each other. Microcomputer users who work under Microsoft's Windows (or Apple Macintosh computer users) are familiar with two functions of ORBs. If you copy data from one Windows application to another, such as from Microsoft's Excel spreadsheet into WordPerfect's word processor, the tool that makes this transfer of data possible is an ORB called OLE (Microsoft's Object Linking and Embedding). All the user needs to do is highlight the data to be copied from the first application, click the copy command with the mouse, move the cursor to the appropriate place in the other application, click the paste command, and the data are there. Similarly, many Windows users easily customize their button bars in many of their applications. They do so by pointing the mouse at the button they want to add

> **To Think About:** How was object-oriented development related to Ontario Hydro's business needs? What management, technology, and organization factors would you consider before making a recommendation to use object-oriented development?

to the bar and dragging it to the bar. In fact, a Windows application button is nothing more than an object.

Benjamin's pilot system, which was developed on a Sun Microsystems workstation, is a database of plant component data that Ontario Hydro operators need if they are to do predictive and preventive maintenance. To program it, he first had to convert the relevant sections of the various Ontario Hydro applications into objects. Then, all Benjamin had to do to create the pilot application (or any future application) was to click and drag each of the needed objects to the appropriate place in the new program and then drop them there by releasing the mouse button.

While object-oriented programming is proving effective and so is expanding in use, that expansion is slowed by two technical problems. One is the use of ORBs. While programmers should not have to concern themselves with ORBs, the problem is that no ORB standard yet exists. Software developers do not have one ORB they can use to communicate with all their software applications.

A second technical problem is the difficulties being encountered in the use of object libraries for the reuse of objects. Reuse of code is one of the major benefits of object-oriented programming, but reuse turns out to be difficult to learn to do.

The time and cost to start using the technology is another major hurdle companies must overcome. Object-oriented startup requires a long-range commitment by management and a significant investment in hardware, software, and retraining.

Sources: "Don't Water Down Ontario Hydro Privatization," *The Wall Street Journal*, March 15, 1996; Emily Kay, "Code That's Ready to Go," *Information Week*, August 22, 1994; Lamont Wood, "The Future of Object Systems," *Information Week*, November 21, 1994.

---

in the top half of the box, and the methods are in the bottom half. Shaded items in each box are inherited from some ancestor class. (For example, by following the tree upward, we can see that Name and Title in the Contractor, Paid weekly, Hourly, and Salaried subclasses are inherited from the Employee superclass [ancestor class].) Unshaded methods, or class variables, are unique to a specific class and they override, or redefine, existing methods. When a subclass overrides an inherited method, its object still responds to the same message, but it executes its definition of the method rather than its ancestor's. Whereas Print is a method inherited from some superclass, the method

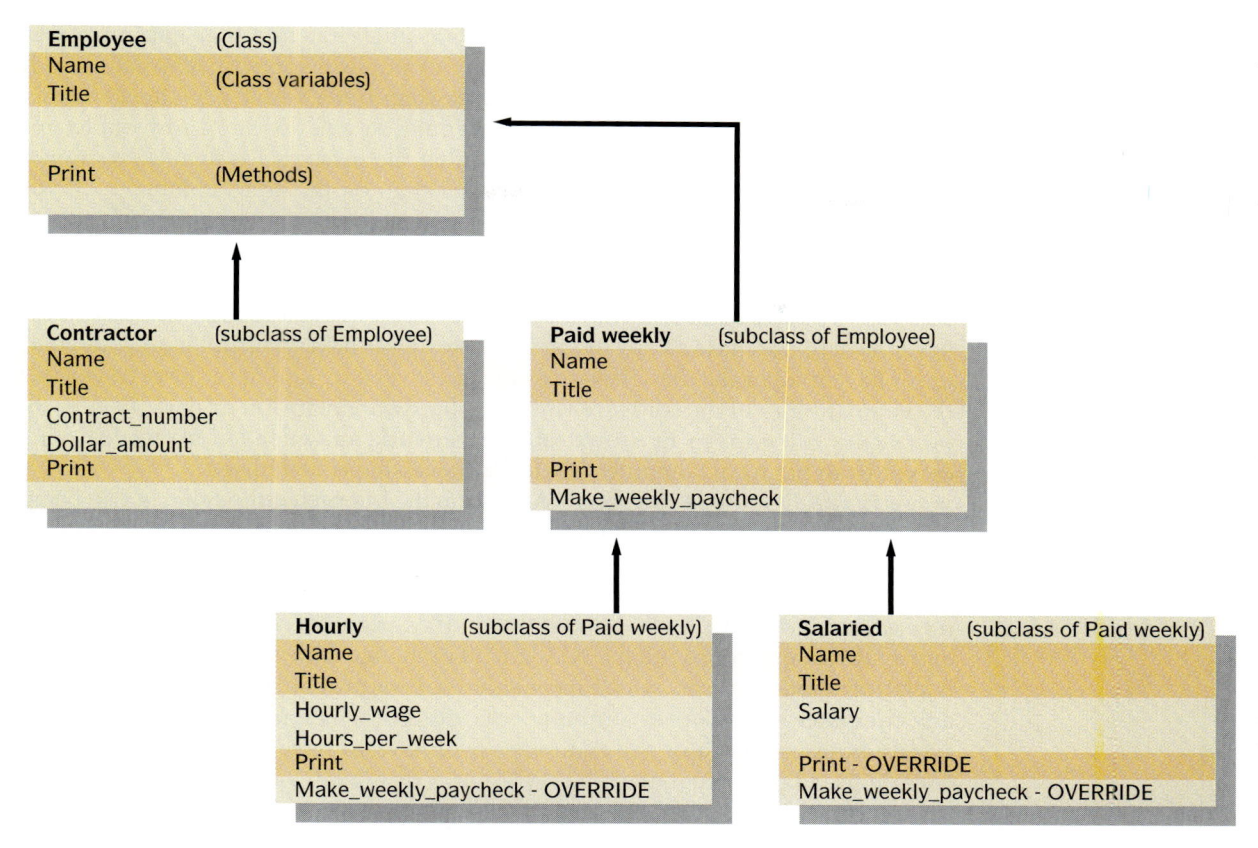

FIGURE 6.15
Class, subclasses, inheritance, and overriding. This figure illustrates how a message's method can come from the class itself or an ancestor class. Class variables and methods are shaded when they are inherited from above. *Hypercard 2.2 © 1987-1991, 1993 Apple Computer, Inc. Apple ®, the Apple logo and Hypercard ® are registered trademarks of Apple Computer, Inc. Used with permission. All rights reserved.*

Make_weekly_paycheck is specific to the Paid weekly class, and Make_weekly_paycheck-OVERRIDE is specific to the Hourly class. The Salaried class uses its own Print-OVERRIDE method.

JAVA AND THE SOFTWARE REVOLUTION

Java is a programming language named after the many cups of coffee its Sun Microsystems developers drank along the way. It has the potential to revolutionize both computer software and hardware.

Traditional application software packages address a single, general function and includes all of its subfunctions in one package. For example, a popular word processor includes not only the functions we all would use—such as setting margins, indenting, line spacing, and bolding—but also the ability to use automatic bullets and numbering, to use footnotes or endnotes, to insert graphics, to merge documents with mailing lists, to check grammar or spelling, and many more special features. Few people use any more than a small subset of the many functions contained in each of these packages, and no one uses more than a few functions at a time. Such software requires a computer with a large amount of storage, memory, and processing power to execute. The software must be run on the specific platform for which it was designed, such as a Microsoft Windows operating system running on an Intel-type microprocessor.

The Technology of Java

Technically, Java is an object-oriented language, combining the data with the specific functions for processing that data. Java is designed so that its users can build small

Java An object-oriented programming language that can deliver only the software functionality needed for a particular task as a small applet downloaded from a network; can run on any computer and operating system.

applets—tiny Java programs that execute one small function that until now were obtained only as part of larger applications. For example, if you wished to access and modify data on an employee's dependents, rather than run a whole personnel system in order to be able to modify that data, you would be able to run a tiny applet for that specific function only. Now, if you assume that the personnel system is programmed in Java applets and resides on a network rather than on the user's computer, all you (the user) would need to do on the network would be to ask for dependent data on a specific individual. The data would arrive with whatever processing functionality you need. When you are finished, you would save the data through the network, and the data and software would disappear from your personal computer. Note that with this system you never have to purchase a copy of the software, never have to install it on your computer, never have to upgrade the software to the latest version, and never have to worry about the compatibility of the software with your hardware platform or data. Java enables all processing software to be stored on the network, downloaded as needed, and then erased from the local computer when the processing is completed.

Java was developed specifically for use on the Internet, although it is also being used as a general-purpose programming language in other areas. Any computer that adheres to Internet technology standards is able to access the network and communicate with any other connected computer, regardless of the specific hardware and software used on each computer. An Apple Macintosh, an IBM personal computer running Windows, and a DEC computer running UNIX can all exchange data with each other. Hence, Java is platform-independent, which means that a Java program could be transferred from any computer to any other computer regardless of which microprocessor or operating system both use. Both of the computers will have to have either an operating system containing a Java virtual machine (JVM) or a very small virtual computer control unit (CPU). Java is also a very robust language that is able to handle text, data, graphics, sound, and video, all within one program if needed.

Because Java was designed for use on networks, security was given high priority by the Sun developers. Sun claims that no Java program can penetrate the rest of your computer, making it safe from viruses and other types of damage that might occur when downloading more conventional programs off a network. The language has other network-specific facilities built in.

How Java Is Changing the Way Software Is Developed and Used

It will take years before we see a large number of full-blown applications available through networks in the manner promised by Java. When Java software development does catch on, software developers will no longer need to create separate versions for the UNIX, Microsoft Windows, Macintosh, IBM mainframe, and other environments—one version will run on all of them.

Java will change the way software is distributed. If the model proves effective, more work than ever will be done through networks. Functionality will be stored with data on the network and both will be downloaded only as needed. Many users will no longer purchase software packages to run on their personal computers, eliminating many software wholesale and retail organizations. As software improvements are completed, they will immediately be installed on the network and so become available to everyone instantly. Table 6.2 summarizes the impact that Java could have on software development and use.

Management and Organizational Benefits of Java

Java and Java-like systems promise many potential benefits for organizations. These benefits include the following:

- Companies will no longer need to purchase hundreds or thousands of copies of commercial software to run on individual computers. Instead they will purchase one network copy made of Java applets; the way such software is paid for may

Table 6.2	The Promise of Java	
	Today	Five Years from Now
Hardware/software independence	Application software must run on the specific hardware and operating system for which it was written.	Platform-independent applications will run on any computer and operating system.
Program size	Giant applications with more functionality than needed and which require large, powerful computers to run	Small applets, which deliver only the functionality needed and which run on small computers
Software distribution	Vast, costly distribution chain including packaging, wholesalers, retailers, advertising, and catalogue companies with users needing to upgrade every two years	Distribution chain eliminated; software comes to desktop from network as needed with latest upgrades

also change dramatically—companies could be charged for each usage much as companies are charged today for telephone or photocopying service.

- Companies will no longer need to purchase such powerful personal computers for most employees. If most computers will only download applets when needed and do not need to store the software on their computers, this cost can be reduced to $500 for a network device, including a monitor, that has far less memory and storage.

- Organizations will have less need to set IT standards (software, hardware, telecommunications), because all development can now be done without concern for the platform on which it will be run.

- Companies will have better control over both data and software—both major corporate investments—because both will be controlled at the center on network computers. Upgrades will occur on one machine instead of on thousands.

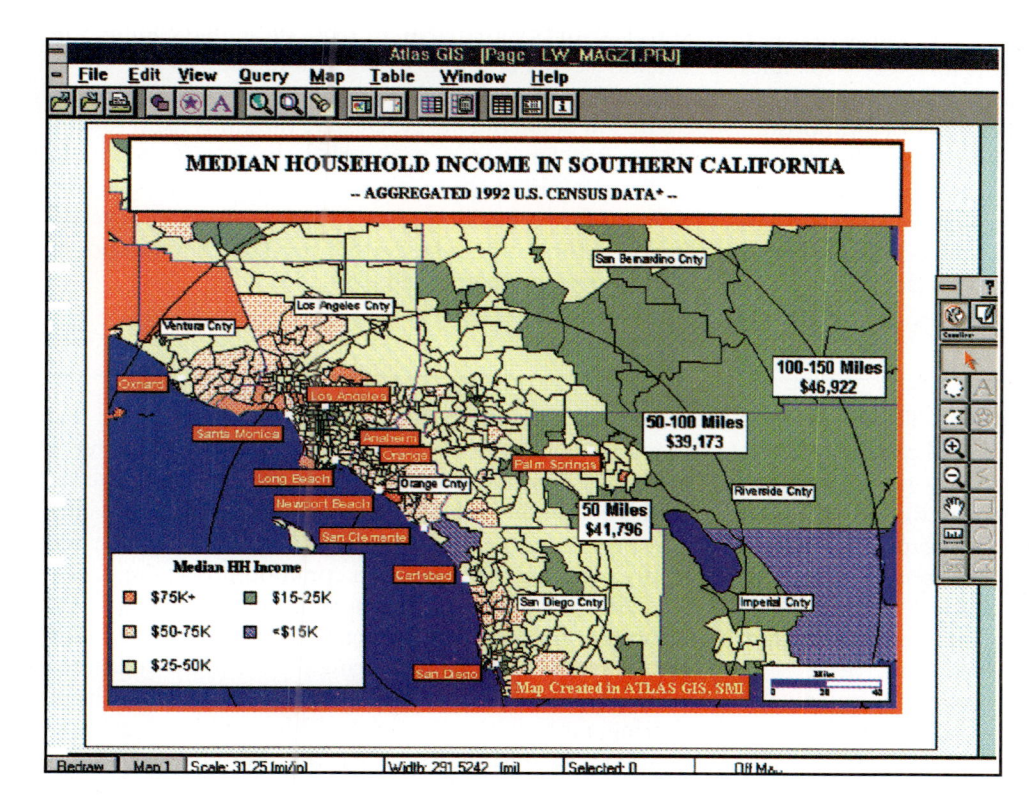

Geographic information system (GIS) software presents and analyzes data geographically, tying business data to points, lines, and areas on a map.

6.4 New Software Tools and Approaches

Citibank's automatic teller machines required nearly 800,000 lines of program code. Creating large, complex pieces of software remains a major management challenge.

Management Challenges

1. Increasing complexity and software errors. While much of the software of the next decade will be rapidly generated on desktops for smaller systems and applications, a great deal of what software will be asked to do remains far-reaching and sophisticated, requiring programs that are large and complex. Citibank's automatic teller machine application required 780,000 lines of program code, written by hundreds of people, each working on small portions of the program. Large and complex systems tend to be error-prone, with software errors or bugs that may not be revealed for years until exhaustive testing and actual use. AT&T, for instance, found 300 errors for every 1000 lines of code in its large programs. Researchers do not know if the number of bugs grows exponentially or proportionately to the number of lines of code, nor can they tell for certain whether all segments of a complex piece of software will always work in total harmony. The process of designing and testing software that is bug-free is a serious quality control and management problem (see Chapter 14).

2. The application backlog. Advances in computer software have not kept pace with the breathtaking productivity gains in computer hardware. Developing software has become a major preoccupation for organizations. A great deal of software must be intricately crafted. Moreover, the software itself is only one component of a complete information system that must be carefully designed and coordinated with other people, as well as with organizational and hardware components. Managerial, procedural, and policy issues must be carefully researched and evaluated apart from the actual coding. The software crisis is actually part of a larger systems analysis, design, and implementation issue, which will be treated in detail in Part IV. Despite the gains from fourth-generation languages, personal desktop software tools, and object-oriented programming, many businesses continue to face a backlog of two to three years in developing the information systems they need, or they will not be able to develop them at all.

Summary

1. Describe the major types of software. The major types of software are system software and application software. Each serves a different purpose. System software manages the computer resources and mediates between application software and computer hardware. Application software is used by application programmers and some end users to develop systems and specific business applications. Application software works through system software, which controls access to computer hardware.

2. Describe the functions of system software and compare leading microcomputer operating systems. System software coordinates the various parts of the computer system and mediates between application software and computer hardware. The system software that manages and controls the activities of the computer is called the operating system. Other system software includes computer language translation programs that convert programming languages into machine language and utility programs that perform common processing tasks.

The operating system acts as the chief manager of the information system, allocating, assigning, and scheduling system resources and monitoring the use of the computer. Multiprogramming, multitasking, virtual storage, time sharing, and multiprocessing, enable system resources to be used more efficiently so that the computer can attack many problems at the same time.

Multiprogramming (multitasking in microcomputer environments) allows multiple programs to use the computer's resources concurrently. Virtual storage splits up programs into pages so that main memory can be utilized more efficiently. Time sharing enables many users to share computer resources simultaneously by allocating each user a tiny slice of computing time. Multiprocessing is the use of two or more CPUs linked together working in tandem to perform a task.

In order to be executed by the computer, a software program must be translated into machine language via special language translation software—a compiler, an assembler, or an interpreter.

Microcomputer operating systems are starting to develop sophisticated capabilities such as multitasking and support for multiple users on networks. Leading microcomputer operating systems include Windows 95, Windows NT, OS/2, UNIX, System 7, and DOS. Microcomputer operating systems with graphical user interfaces are gaining popularity over command-driven operating systems. Windows is a popular graphical user interface shell for the DOS operating system.

3. Explain how software has evolved and how it will continue to develop. Software has evolved along with hardware. The general trend is toward user-friendly high-level languages that both increase professional programmer productivity and make it possible for complete amateurs to use information systems. There have been four generations of software development: (1) machine language; (2) symbolic languages such as assembly language; (3) high-level languages such as FORTRAN and COBOL; and (4) fourth-generation languages, which are less procedural and closer to natural language than earlier generations of software. Software is starting to incorporate both sound and graphics and to support multimedia applications.

4. Compare strengths and limitations of the major application programming languages and software tools. The most popular conventional programming languages are assembly language, FORTRAN, COBOL, BASIC, PL/1, Pascal, C, and Ada. Conventional programming languages make more efficient use of computer resources than fourth-generation languages and each is designed to solve specific types of problems.

Fourth-generation languages include query languages, report generators, graphics languages, application generators, very high-level programming languages, application software packages, and microcomputer tools. They are less procedural than conventional programming languages and enable end users to perform many software tasks that previously required technical specialists.

5. Describe new approaches to software development. Object-oriented programming combines data and procedures into one *object*, which can act as an independent software building block. Each object can be used in many different systems without changing program code.

Java is an object-oriented programming language designed to operate from the Internet. It can deliver only the software functionality needed for a particular task as a small *applet* that is downloaded from a network. Java can run on any computer and operating system and could potentially eliminate the need for many powerful desktop computers.

Key Terms

Software	Interpreter	COBOL (COmmon Business Oriented Language)	Very high-level programming language
Program	Utility program	BASIC (Beginners All-purpose Symbolic Instruction Code)	Software package
Stored program concept	Graphical user interface (GUI)		Word processing software
System software	DOS		Spreadsheet
Application software	Windows	PL/1 (Programming Language 1)	Data management software
Operating system	Windows 95	Pascal	Integrated software package
System residence device	Windows NT	Ada	Object-oriented programming
Multiprogramming	OS/2	C	Visual programming
Multitasking	UNIX	Fourth-generation language	Class
Virtual storage	System 7	Query language	Inheritance
Page	Machine language	Report generator	Java
Time sharing	High-level language	Graphics language	
Multiprocessing	Assembly language	Application generator	
Source code	FORTRAN (FORmula TRANslator)		
Compiler			
Object code			

Review Questions

1. What are the major types of software? How do they differ in terms of users and uses?

2. What is the operating system of a computer? What does it do?

3. Describe multiprogramming, virtual storage, time sharing, and multiprocessing. Why are they important for the operation of an information system?
4. Define multitasking.
5. What is the difference between an assembler, a compiler, and an interpreter?
6. Define graphical user interfaces.
7. Compare the major microcomputer operating systems.
8. What are the major generations of software and approximately when were they developed?
9. What is a high-level language? Name three high-level languages. Describe their strengths and weaknesses.
10. Define fourth-generation languages and list the seven categories of fourth-generation tools.
11. What is the difference between fourth-generation languages and conventional programming languages?
12. What is the difference between an application generator and an application software package? Between a report generator and a query language?
13. Name and describe the most important microcomputer software tools.
14. What is object-oriented programming? How does it differ from conventional software development?
15. What is Java? How could it change the way software is created and used?

Discussion Questions

1. What factors should be considered in selecting microcomputer software?
2. Your firm wishes to develop a system that will process sales orders and update inventory. The programmers in your information systems department wish to use assembly language to write the programs for this system. Is this a good idea? Discuss.
3. Several authorities have claimed that fourth-generation languages will soon replace conventional programming languages such as COBOL for implementing the vast majority of information system applications. Discuss.

Group Project

Is Windows NT better than Windows 95? Your instructor will divide the class into two groups to discuss this question from both a technical and business standpoint. Use articles from computer magazines to help prepare your group's analysis.

Case Study

A GEOGRAPHIC INFORMATION SYSTEM ADDS ZEST TO SONNY'S BAR-B-Q

Sonny's Bar-B-Q is a chain of 83 southern United States barbecue restaurants of which eight are company owned. The company generated about $100 million in revenues in 1994. The income came from fees of $25,000 each for about 11 new franchises, royalties of 2.5 percent of each franchisee's gross income, and the income from company-owned restaurants.

The first Sonny's was established in 1968 in Gainesville, Florida, as a low-priced barbecue restaurant, delivering quality food at 50 percent of the price of many of its competitors. Sonny's has expanded slowly ever since.

Sonny's has a well-thought-out growth plan for the company to meet their growth target of 100 new franchises over the next few years. First, franchisees must be qualified to run a barbecue restaurant. Second, the company will expand only into regions where barbecued food is very common but where the number of barbecue restaurants is small. Third, the company is trying to grow in concentric circles expanding out from Florida. To date they have established restaurants in Georgia, Alabama, South Carolina, and Tennessee. Fourth, new Sonny's sites are selected very carefully to generate the most revenue from the least number of people and the smallest area.

No Sonny's is closer than seven miles from any other Sonny's. The company looks at a range of factors when determining the suitability of a given territory, including traffic count, median age, household income, total population, and population distribution.

Locating the data Sonny's requires in order to evaluate potential new territories is not a problem. The problem Sonny's did face, however, was how to obtain and analyze this data at a reasonable price. Sonny's also faced the problem of interpreting the data—reading and understanding mountains of statistics in numeric form. To solve these problems the company turned to a type of software that has been growing in popularity over the last few years, geographic information systems (GIS).

Geographic information systems (GIS) presents masses of data by overlaying the data onto maps.

Geographic interfaces can make certain problems easier to analyze. For example, Johanna Dairies of Union, New Jersey, has been able to save $800,000 per year by using a GIS to help it plan its delivery routes. It is making available customer orders and locations through a GIS that displays customer locations on digital street maps. The user is able to zoom in on sections of the city to actually see the customer locations. With this information, Johanna was able to plan more efficient delivery routes in which delivery trucks traveled much shorter distances. As a result Johanna Dairies was able to reduce the number of delivery routes from 60 to 52 at an average annual saving of $100,000 per delivery route.

A not-for-profit consumer watchdog organization named Environmental Systems Research Institute, Inc. (ESRI), located in Redlands, California, is using GIS to monitor the effectiveness of certain federal lending laws in 16 cities throughout the United States. What they have found—demonstrated with great clarity by the graphic displays of the software—is that lending institutions that are federally regulated commit a far larger percentage of their funds to minority neighborhoods than do unregulated institutions. Police forces are now using GIS to pinpoint high crime areas in order to better deploy their police officers. They are also using GIS to alert them to changes in crime patterns. For example, if a neighborhood normally has four to eight break-ins a month, the software can be set to issue an alert whenever the monthly total of such crimes in that neighborhood rises above nine.

While a GIS interface is simple and makes the data easy to grasp, a company that turns to GIS software must do a great deal of preparation prior to actually using it. GIS has four basic components users must prepare. They need to select the demographic data required, develop search-and-retrieve software to collect the required data, select the maps to be displayed, and then acquire a GIS system which will bring the data and maps together as needed.

Sonny's growth plan told them the data they would need. The traffic data had to be located locally. The U.S. census data turned out to be readily available on CD-ROM and to be relatively inexpensive. Sonny's also had to purchase the maps it needs. Map data can be rather expensive, depending partially upon the detail the user requires. Digital street maps for the entire United States can be purchased for about $15,000. To search the census data, Sonny's purchased PSearch-USA from Tetrad Computer Applications in Bellingham, Washington. It also purchased MapInfo geographic information software to do the geographic analysis and display the data. Of course, the company must have hardware capable of running the software efficiently. Sonny's is using 486 PCs.

The whole system cost Sonny's about $30,000, including the data. The MapInfo geographic information system application cost $1295. Digital street maps of the United States were $15,000, plus an additional $3995 for ZIP-code boundaries; ZIP plus-four codes cost $10,000. Tetrad's census data for a state ranges from $300 to $600; for the entire country the cost is $2000. Tetrad's PCensus and PSearch-USA search-and-retrieve software each cost $250.

For GIS to be successful, the appropriate business functions must be altered to integrate the GIS software, which, in the case of Sonny's, is the marketing and sales departments. Sonny's had no problem with these aspects—funding, developing, and integrating—because Robert Yarmuth, CEO of Sonny's, views GIS as significant for supporting his style of quick decision making.

Sonny's uses MapInfo to display population data, including eating habits for a targeted area. The company can bring up a map of a region and, using a mouse, outline the area in which it is interested. The computer will then display the selected population data superimposed on the map. Sonny's does plan to use the software to develop demographic models of successful franchises and then use the software to search for areas that fit the model. The company has one key success to point to already. One Florida county was franchised with the expectation that they could fit four restaurants in the area successfully. However, the software indicated that the county could safely absorb eight Sonny's. Ultimately they decided to open seven franchises. The unexpected additional three franchises brought in a total of $75,000 in franchise fees alone, more than covering the total cost of the GIS installation. ■

Sources: Tony Seideman, "You Gotta Know the Territory," *Profit*, November–December 1994; Vera Tweed, "The Graphic Detail," *Information Week*, August 29, 1994; David Forrest, "Seeing Data in New Ways," *Computerworld*, June 29, 1993; Rick Tetzeli, "Mapping for Dollars," *Fortune*, October 18, 1993.

Case Study Questions

1. Use the competitive forces and value chain models to evaluate Sonny's business strategy. How does Sonny's use of software support that strategy?

2. Analyze the benefits obtained from Sonny's geographic information system (GIS) applications.

3. What kinds of problems can software solve for Sonny's and what kinds of problems will it not solve?

4. Name businesses for which your answer to question 3 might be different, and explain why.
5. What other applications can you suggest for geographic information systems?
6. As a manager in your company, how would you determine whether to use such software in your firm?

References

Abdel-Hamid, Tarek K. "The Economics of Software Quality Assurance: A Simulation-Based Case Study." *MIS Quarterly* 12, no. 3 (September 1988).

Apte, Uday, Chetan S. Sankar, Meru Thakur, and Joel E. Turner. "Reusability-Based Strategy for Development of Information Systems: Implementation Experience of a Bank." *MIS Quarterly* 14, no. 4 (December 1990).

Barrett, Jim, Kevin Knight, Inderject Man, and Elaine Rich. "Knowledge and Natural Language Processing." *Communications of the ACM* 33, no. 8 (August 1990).

Bochenski, Barbara. "GUI Builders Pay Price for User Productivity." *Software Magazine* (April 1992).

Borning, Alan, "Computer System Reliability and Nuclear War." *Communications of the ACM* 30, no. 2 (February 1987).

Cortese, Amy with John Verity, Kathy Rebello, and Rob Hof. "The Software Revolution." *Business Week* (December 4, 1995).

Flynn, Jim and Bill Clarke. "How Java Makes Network-Centric Computing Real." *Datamation* (March 1, 1996).

Freedman, David H. "Programming Without Tears." *High Technology* (April 1986).

Greenbaum, Joshua. "The Evolution Revolution." *Information Week* (March 14, 1994).

Haavind, Robert. "Software's New Object Lesson," *Technology Review* (February/March 1992).

Jalics, Paul J. "Cobol on a PC: A New Perspective on a Language and Its Performance." *Communications of the ACM* 30, no. 2 (February 1987).

Joyce, Edward J. "Reusable Software: Passage to Productivity?" *Datamation* (September 15, 1988).

Kim, Chai, and Stu Westin. "Software Maintainability: Perceptions of EDP Professionals." *MIS Quarterly* 12, no. 2 (June 1988).

Korson, Timothy D. and Vijay K. Vaishnavi. "Managing Emerging Software Technologies: A Technology Transfer Framework." *Communications of the ACM* 35, no. 9 (September 1992).

Korson, Tim and John D. McGregor. "Understanding Object-Oriented: A Unifying Paradigm." *Communications of the ACM* 33 no. 9 (September 1990).

Layer, D. Kevin and Chris Richardson. "LISP Systems in the 1990s." *Communications of the ACM* 34, no. 9 (September 1991).

Littlewood, Bev and Lorenzo Strigini. "The Risks of Software." *Scientific American* 267, no. 5 (November 1992).

Mandelkern, David. "Graphical User Interfaces: The Next Generation." *Communications of the ACM* 36, no. 4 (April 1993).

Monarchi, David E. and Gretchen I. Puhr. "A Research Typology for Object-Oriented Analysis and Design." *Communications of the ACM* 35, no. 9 (September 1992).

Morse, Alan and George Reynolds. "Overcoming Current Growth Limits in UI Development." *Communications of the ACM* 36, no. 4 (April 1993).

Mukhopadhyay, Tridas, Stephen S. Vicinanza, and Michael J. Prietula. "Examining the Feasibility of a Case-Based Reasoning Model for Software Effort Estimation," *MIS Quarterly* 16, no. 2 (June 1992).

Nance, Barry. "Windows NT and OS/2 Compared." *Byte*, June 1992.

Nerson, Jean-Marc. "Applying Object-Oriented Analysis and Design." *Communications of the ACM* 35, no. 9 (September 1992).

Nielsen, Jakob. "Noncommand User Interfaces." *Communications of the ACM* 36, no. 4 (April 1993).

Pancake, Cherri M. "The Promise and the Cost of Object Technology: A Five-Year Forecast." *Communications of the ACM* 38, no. 10 (October 1995).

Schonberg, Edmond, Mark Gerhardt, and Charlene Hayden. "A Technical Tour of Ada," *Communications of the ACM* 35, no. 11 (November 1992).

Semich, Bill and David Fisco. "Java: Internet Toy or Enterprise Tool?" *Datamation* (March 1, 1996).

Swanson, Kent, Dave McComb, Jill Smith, and Don McCubbrey. "The Application Software Factory: Applying Total Quality Techniques to Systems Development." *MIS Quarterly* 15, no. 4 (December 1991).

Vassiliou, Yannis, "On the Interactive Use of Databases: Query Languages." *Journal of Management Information Systems* 1 (Winter 1984–1985).

White, George M. "Natural Language Understanding and Speech." *Communications of the ACM* 33, no. 8 (August 1990).

Wiederhold, Gio, Peter Wegner, and Stefano Ceri. "Toward Megaprogramming." *Communications of the ACM* 35, no. 11 (November 1992).

Wilkes, Maurice V. "The Long-Term Future of Operating Systems." *Communications of the ACM* 35, no. 11 (November 1992).

Chapter 7

Managing Data Resources

A Land Title System That Makes a Difference

7.1 Organizing Data in a Traditional File Environment
File Organization Terms and Concepts
Accessing Records from Computer Files
Problems with the Traditional File Environment

7.2 A Modern Database Environment
Database Management Systems (DBMS)
Logical and Physical Views of Data
Advantages of Database Management Systems

7.3 Designing Databases
Hierarchical Data Model
Network Data Model
Relational Data Model
Advantages and Disadvantages of the Three Database Models
Window on Organizations:
Denmark Runs on DB2
Creating a Database

7.4 Database Trends
Distributed Processing and Distributed Databases
Object-Oriented and Hypermedia Databases
Window on Technology:
Volkswagen Opts for an Object-Oriented Database
Multidimensional Databases
Data Warehousing
Window on Management:
Linking Databases to the Internet

7.5 Management Requirements for Database Systems
Data Administration
Data Planning and Modeling Methodology
Database Technology and Management
Users

Management Challenges
Summary
Key Terms
Review Questions
Discussion Questions
Group Project
Case Study: Can Migration to a Relational Database Management System Help a German Home Loan Lender?
References

A Land Title System That Makes a Difference

Queensland, Australia's "Sunshine State," has been undergoing strong business growth for a number of years. As a result the Queensland Department of Lands has been very busy, with no letup in sight. The Department tracks and administers all Queensland land transactions. With an annual operating budget of $100 million (U.S. $75 million), it employs 1500 people in its 34 offices. In the past all land title transfer registration had to go through three of those offices (Brisbane, Rockhampton, and Townsville), which also stored all certificates of title in leather-bound volumes. As business boomed the Department had to continually increase its staff in order manually to handle the daily workload of registering, filing, and searching through titles. Moreover, the whole system was slow—land title transfer registration took several weeks to complete, and title searches required that photocopies and faxes be sent between the three registration offices and the office where a lawyer or other interested party wanted to search a specific title (users now conduct about 55,000 searches a month).

In the early 1990s management saw no end in sight to the staff growth to handle the increase or to the concomitant rise in costs. It decided to automate the manual title registration and search processes to bring the growing costs to an end. Any new information system would have to store the title certificates on-line and make them available for title searches at all the offices. The system would have to store older documents as well as new titles.

The new system, Automated Titles System (ATS), was completed in 1995 at a cost of A$13 million (U.S. $9.75 million). Title certificate data are now available on-line, with older certificates stored through document imaging technology. The registration process had to be redesigned so that a title registration, which used to be handled by a number of people, is now essentially completed by one person. The redesign still restricted the final step in the new process to only five centers, however, because that step requires specially trained, highly skilled staff, an expense too costly to implement at all the offices. The users of the ATS did have to undergo training. Today, land title transfers take only a few days while lawyers, real estate agents, bankers, and Department clerks can undertake on-line title searches at all the 34 offices or, for a fee, from their own computers in their own company offices. The new system is able to handle up to 300 concurrent users.

To accomplish the Department's goals, ATS uses a relational database that is able to store all needed data from a vast number of registration certificates—at present it holds 25 gigabytes of data. Moreover, its relational database management system is flexible enough to accommodate rapid growth of data without any problems. In the relational database, the user-friendly database interface software makes it easy for all to search the database and quickly retrieve the data they need. ∎

Source: Keith Power, "Australian Agency Breaks New Ground," *International Software Magazine*, February 1996.

The Automated Titles System illustrates how much the effective use of information depends on how data are stored, organized, and accessed. Proper delivery of information not only depends on the capabilities of computer hardware and software but also on the organization's ability to manage data as an important resource.

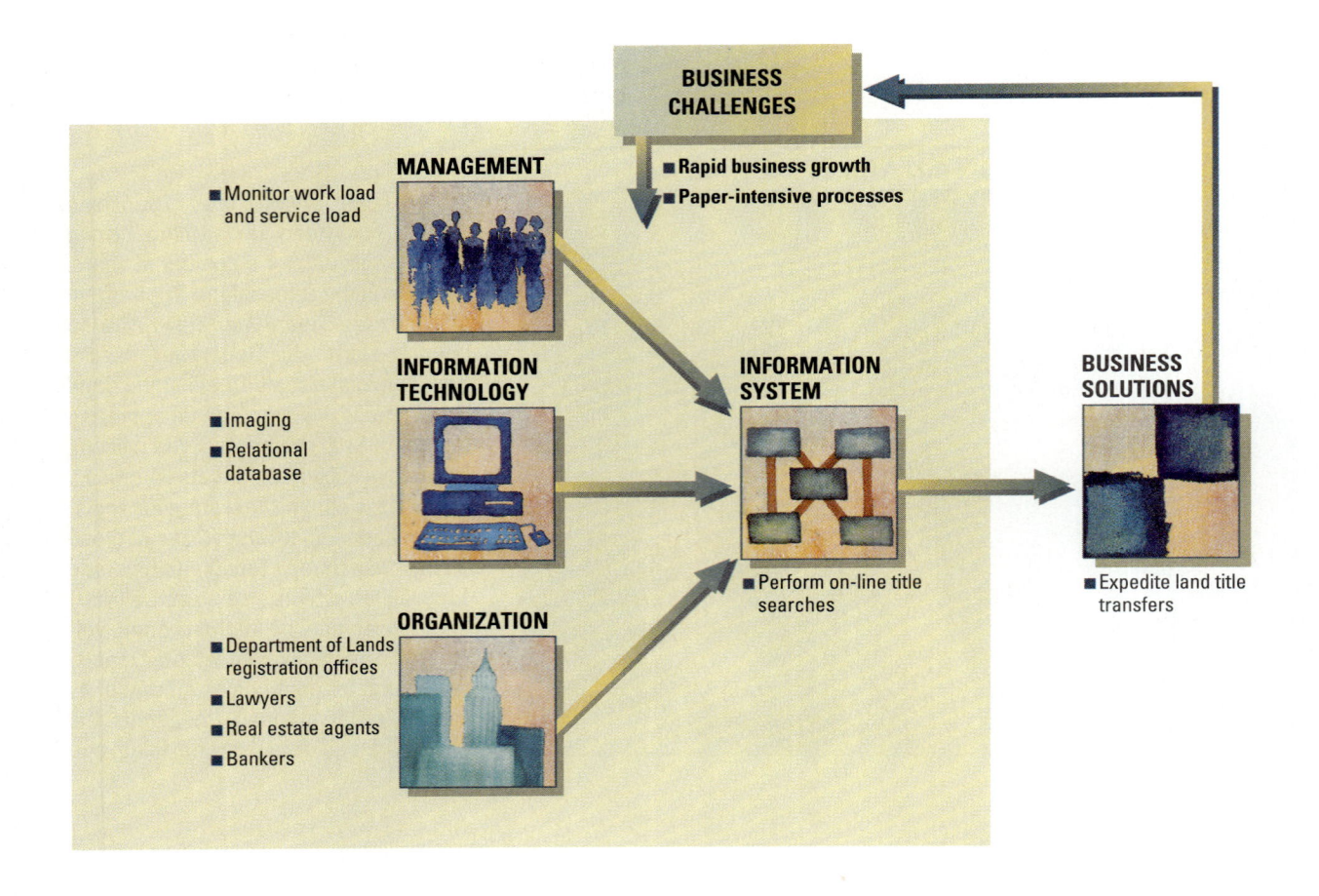

This chapter examines the managerial and organizational requirements as well as the technologies for managing data as a resource. First we describe the traditional file management technologies that have been used for arranging and accessing data on physical storage media and the problems they have created for organizations. Then we describe the technology of database management systems, which can overcome many of the drawbacks of traditional file management. We end the chapter with a discussion of the managerial and organizational requirements for successful implementation of database management systems.

> **Learning Objectives**
>
> *After completing this chapter, you will be able to:*
>
> 1. Describe traditional file organization and management techniques.
> 2. Explain the problems of the traditional file environment.
> 3. Describe how a database management system organizes information.
> 4. Identify the three principal database models.
> 5. Discuss new database trends.
> 6. Explain the managerial and organizational requirements for creating a database environment.

7.1 ORGANIZING DATA IN A TRADITIONAL FILE ENVIRONMENT

An effective information system provides users with timely, accurate, and relevant information. This information is stored in computer files. When the files are properly arranged and maintained, users can easily access and retrieve the information they need.

You can appreciate the importance of file management if you have ever written a term paper using 3 × 5 index cards. No matter how efficient your storage device (a metal box or a rubber band), if you organize the cards randomly your term paper will have little or no organization. Given enough time, you could put the cards in order, but your system would be more efficient if you set up your organizational scheme early on. If your scheme is flexible enough and well documented, you can extend it to account for any changes in your viewpoint as you write your paper.

The same need for file organization applies to firms. Well-managed, carefully arranged files make it easy to obtain data for business decisions, whereas poorly managed files lead to chaos in information processing, high costs, poor performance, and little, if any flexibility. Despite the use of excellent hardware and software, many organizations have inefficient information systems because of poor file management. In this section we describe the traditional methods that organizations have used to arrange data in computer files. We also discuss the problems with these methods.

FILE ORGANIZATION TERMS AND CONCEPTS

A computer system organizes data in a hierarchy that starts with bits and bytes and progresses to fields, records, files, and databases (see Figure 7.1). A *bit* represents the smallest unit of data a computer can handle. A group of bits, called a *byte*, represents a single character, which can be a letter, a number, or another symbol. A grouping of characters into a word, a group of words, or a complete number (such as a person's name or age), is called a **field**. A group of related fields, such as the student's name, the course taken, the date, and the grade make up a **record**; a group of records of the same type is called a **file**. For instance, all of the student records in Figure 7.1 could constitute a course file. A group of related files make up a database. The student course file illustrated in Figure 7.1 could be grouped with files on students' personal histories and financial backgrounds to create a student database.

field A grouping of characters into a word, a group of words, or a complete number, such as a person's name or age.

record A group of related fields.

file A group of records of the same type.

FIGURE 7.1
The data hierarchy. A computer system organizes data in a hierarchy that starts with the bit, which represents either a 0 or a 1. Bits can be grouped to form a byte to represent one character, number, or symbol. Bytes can be grouped to form a field, and related fields can be grouped to form a record. Related records can be collected to form a file, and related files can be organized into a database.

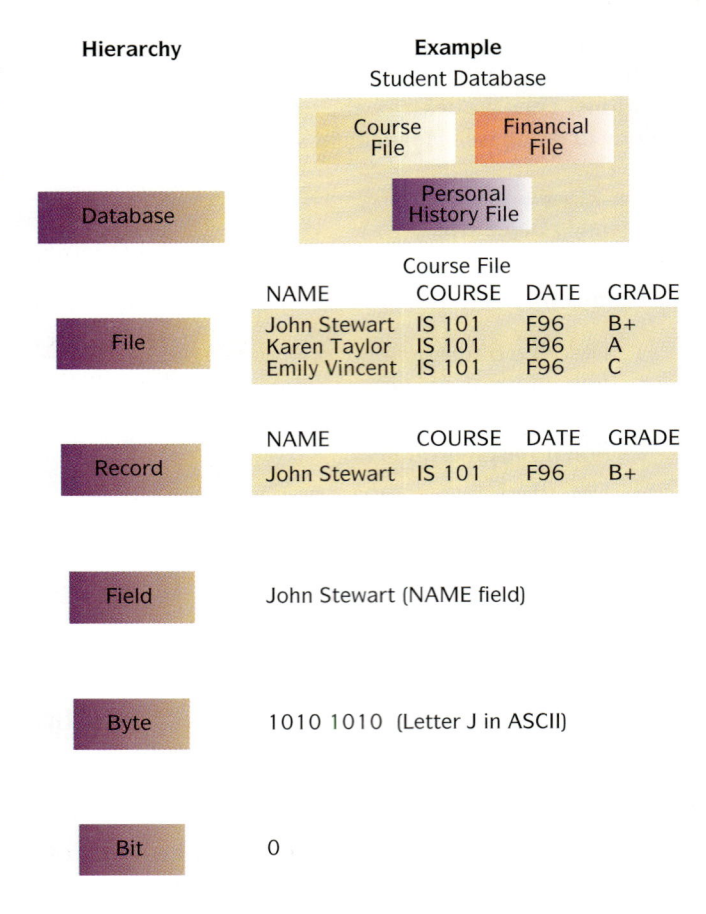

Hierarchy	Example
	Student Database
Database	Course File / Financial File / Personal History File
File	Course File NAME — COURSE — DATE — GRADE John Stewart — IS 101 — F96 — B+ Karen Taylor — IS 101 — F96 — A Emily Vincent — IS 101 — F96 — C
Record	NAME — COURSE — DATE — GRADE John Stewart — IS 101 — F96 — B+
Field	John Stewart (NAME field)
Byte	1010 1010 (Letter J in ASCII)
Bit	0

entity A person, place, thing, or event about which information must be kept.

attribute A piece of information describing a particular entity.

key field A field in a record that uniquely identifies instances of that record so that it can be retrieved, updated, or sorted.

A record describes an entity. An **entity** is a person, place, thing, or event on which we maintain information. An order is a typical entity in a sales order file, which maintains information on a firm's sales orders. Each characteristic or quality describing a particular entity is called an **attribute.** For example, order number, order date, order amount, item number, and item quantity would each be an attribute of the entity order. The specific values that these attributes can have can be found in the fields of the record describing the entity *order* (see Figure 7.2).

Every record in a file should contain at least one field that uniquely identifies that record so that the record can be retrieved, updated, or sorted. This identifier field is called a **key field.** An example of a key field is the order number for the order record illustrated in Figure 7.2 or an employee number or social security number for a personnel record (containing employee data such as the employee's name, age, address, job title, and so forth).

FIGURE 7.2
Entities and attributes. This record describes the entity called ORDER and its attributes. The specific values for order number, order date, item number, quantity, and amount for this particular order are the fields for this record. Order number is the key field because each order is assigned a unique identification number.

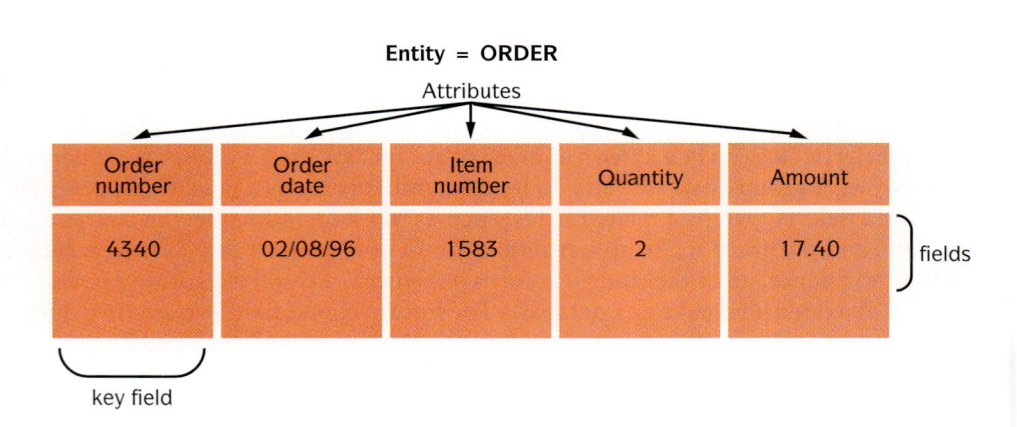

Entity = ORDER
Attributes

Order number	Order date	Item number	Quantity	Amount
4340	02/08/96	1583	2	17.40

} fields

key field (Order number)

ACCESSING RECORDS FROM COMPUTER FILES

Computer systems store files on secondary storage devices. Records can be arranged in several ways on storage media, and the arrangement determines the manner in which individual records can be accessed or retrieved. One way to organize records is sequentially. In **sequential file organization,** data records must be retrieved in the same physical sequence in which they are stored. In contrast, **direct** or **random file organization** allows users to access records in any sequence they desire, without regard to actual physical order on the storage media.

Sequential file organization is the only file organization method that can be used on magnetic tape. This file organization method is no longer popular, but some organizations still use it for batch processing applications in which they access and process each record sequentially. A typical application using sequential files is payroll, where all employees in a firm must be paid one by one and issued a check. Direct or random file organization is utilized with magnetic disk technology (although records can be stored sequentially on disk if desired). Most computer applications today utilize some method of direct file organization.

The Indexed Sequential Access Method

Although records may be stored sequentially on direct access storage devices, individual records can be accessed directly using the **indexed sequential access method (ISAM).** This access method relies on an index of key fields to locate individual records. An **index** to a file is similar to the index of a book, as it lists the key field of each record and where that record is physically located in storage to expedite location of that record. Figure 7.3 shows how a series of indexes identifies the location of a specific record. Records are stored on disk in their key sequence. A cylinder index shows the highest value of the key field that can be found on a specific cylinder. A track index shows the highest value of the key field that can be found on a specific track. To locate a specific record, the

sequential file organization A method of storing data records in which the records must be retrieved in the same physical sequence in which they are stored.

direct or **random file organization** A method of storing data records in a file so that they can be accessed in any sequence without regard to their actual physical order on the storage media.

indexed sequential access method (ISAM) A file access method to directly access records organized sequentially using an index of key fields.

index A table or list that relates record keys to physical locations on direct access files.

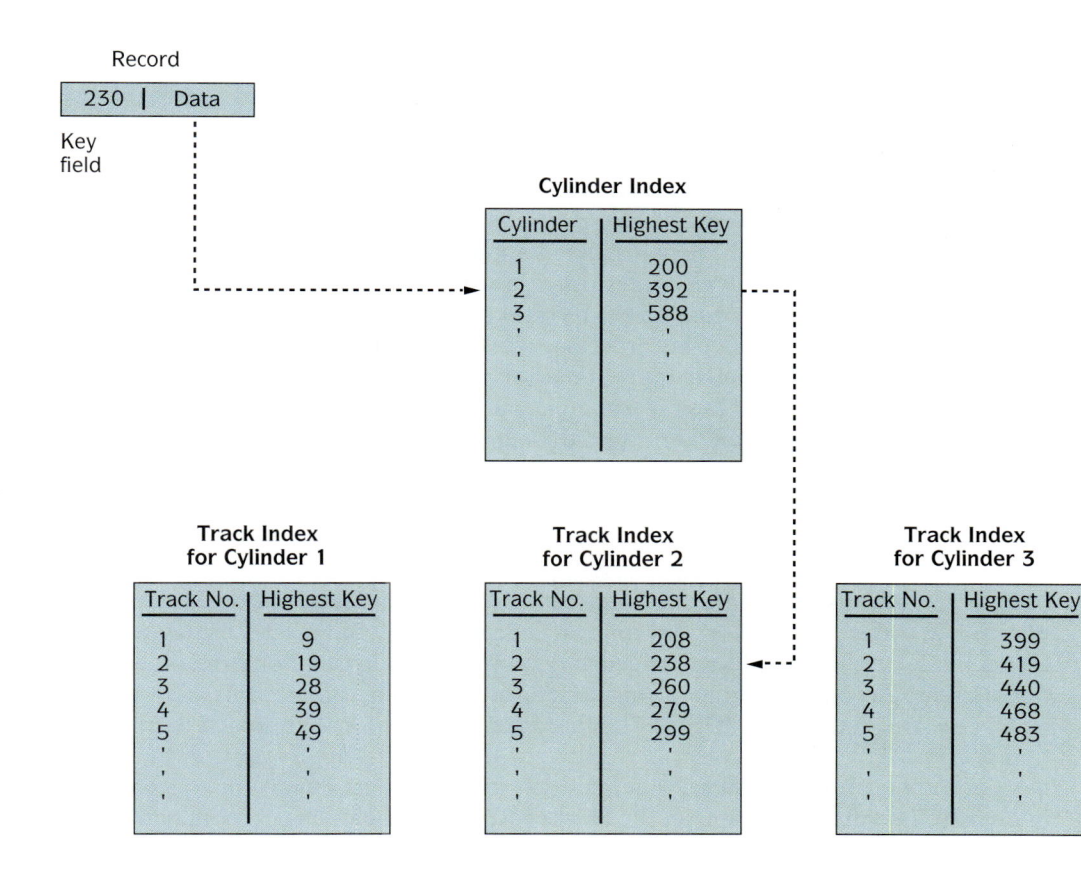

Record

| 230 | Data |

Key field

Cylinder Index

Cylinder	Highest Key
1	200
2	392
3	588
.	.
.	.

Track Index for Cylinder 1

Track No.	Highest Key
1	9
2	19
3	28
4	39
5	49
.	.
.	.

Track Index for Cylinder 2

Track No.	Highest Key
1	208
2	238
3	260
4	279
5	299
.	.
.	.

Track Index for Cylinder 3

Track No.	Highest Key
1	399
2	419
3	440
4	468
5	483
.	.
.	.

FIGURE 7.3
The indexed sequential access method (ISAM). To find a record with a key field of 230, the cylinder index would be searched to find the correct cylinder (in this case, cylinder 2). The track index for cylinder 2 would then be searched to find the correct track. Since the highest key on track 2 of cylinder 2 is 238 and the highest key on track 1 of cylinder 2 is 208, track 2 must contain the record. Track 2 of cylinder 2 would then be read to find the record with key 230.

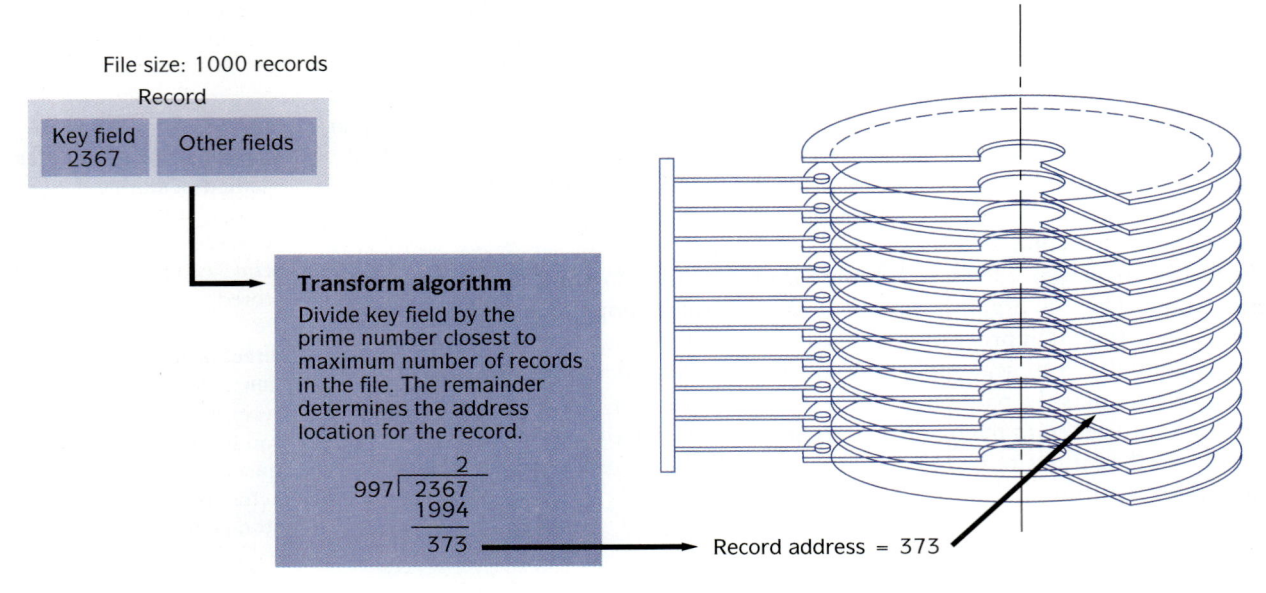

FIGURE 7.4
The direct file access method. Records are not stored sequentially on the disk but are arranged according to the results of some mathematical computation. Here, the transform algorithm divides the value in the key field by the prime number closest to the maximum number of records in the file (in this case, the prime number is 997). The remainder designates the storage location for that particular record.

cylinder index and then the track index are searched to locate the cylinder and track containing the record. The track itself is then sequentially read to find the record. If a file is very large, the cylinder index might be broken down into parts and a master index created to help locate each part of the cylinder index. ISAM is employed in applications that require sequential processing of large numbers of records but that occasionally require direct access of individual records.

Direct File Access Method

direct file access method A method of accessing records by mathematically transforming the key fields into the specific addresses for the records.

transform algorithm A mathematical formula used to translate a record's key field directly into the record's physical storage location.

The **direct file access method** is used with direct file organization. This method employs a key field to locate the physical address of a record. However, the process is accomplished using a mathematical formula called a **transform algorithm** to translate the key field directly into the record's physical storage location on disk. The algorithm performs some mathematical computation on the record key, and the result of that calculation is the record's physical address. This process is illustrated in Figure 7.4.

This access method is most appropriate for applications where individual records must be located directly and rapidly for immediate processing only. A few records in the file need to be retrieved at one time, and the required records are found in no particular sequence. An example might be an on-line hotel reservation system.

PROBLEMS WITH THE TRADITIONAL FILE ENVIRONMENT

Most organizations began information processing on a small scale, automating one application at a time. Systems tended to grow independently, and not according to some grand plan. Each functional area tended to develop systems in isolation from other functional areas. Accounting, finance, manufacturing, and marketing all developed their own systems and data files. Figure 7.5 illustrates the traditional approach to information processing.

Each application, of course, required its own files and its own computer program in order to operate. For example, the Human Resources functional area might have a

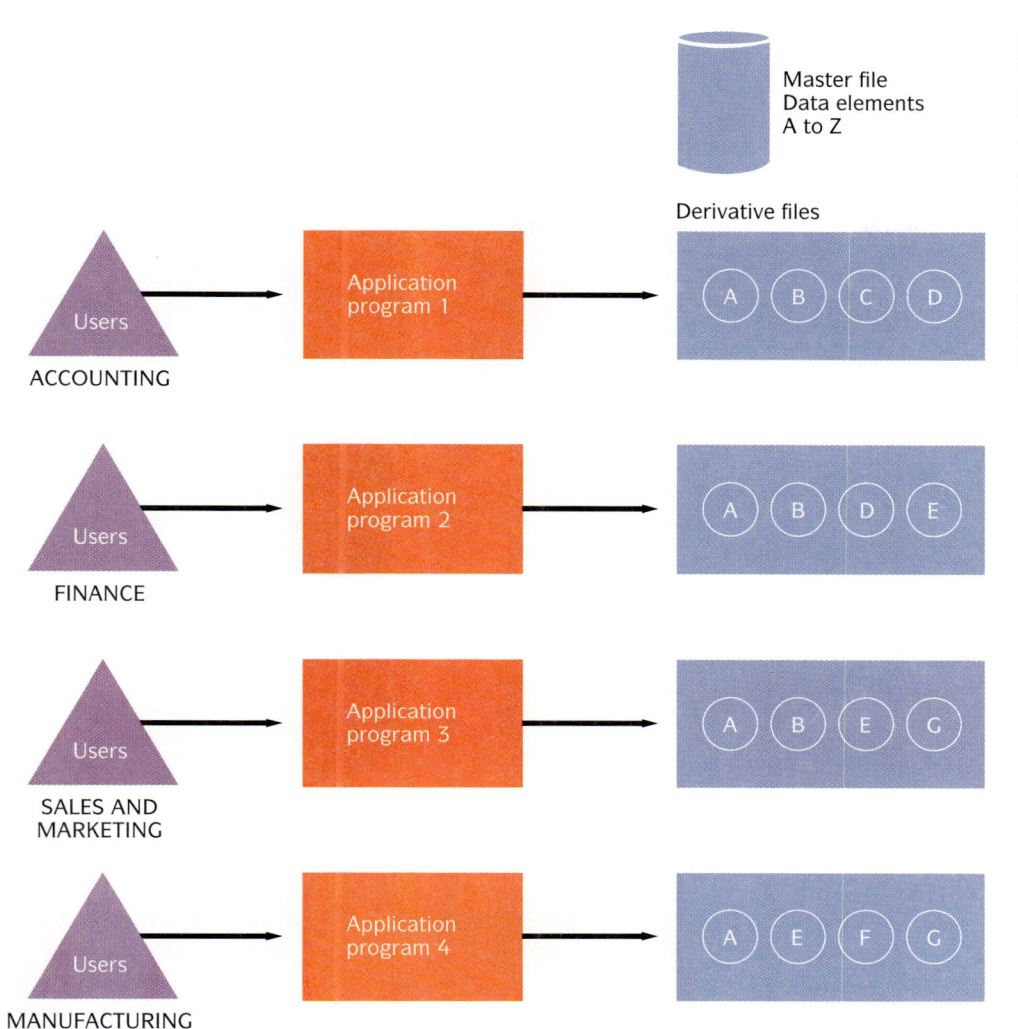

FIGURE 7.5
Traditional file processing. The use of a traditional approach to file processing encourages each functional area in a corporation to develop specialized applications. Each application requires a unique data file that is likely to be a subset of the master file. These subsets of the master file lead to data redundancy, processing inflexibility, and wasted storage resources.

personnel master file, a payroll file, a medical insurance file, a pension file, a mailing list file, and so forth until tens, perhaps hundreds, of files and programs existed.

In the company as a whole, this process led to multiple master files created, maintained, and operated by separate divisions or departments. Figure 7.6 shows three separate master files: customer, personnel, and sales. Creating a simple report such as that listed in this example, sales personnel by annual sales and by principal customers, required a complex matching program that read each of the three files, copied pertinent records, and recombined the records into an intermediate file. This intermediate file had to be sorted in the desired sequence (sales personnel ranked by highest sales) before a final report could be printed.

There are names for this situation: the **traditional file environment**; the *flat file organization* (because most of the data are organized in flat files); and the *data file approach* (because the data and business logic are tied to specific files and related programs). By any name, the situation results in growing inefficiency and complexity.

As this process goes on for five or ten years, the firm becomes tied up in knots of its own creation. The organization is saddled with hundreds of programs and applications, with no one who knows what they do, what data they use, and who is using the data. There is no central listing of data files, data elements, or definitions of data. The organization is collecting the same information in far too many files. The resulting problems are data redundancy, program-data dependence, inflexibility, poor data security, and inability to share data among applications.

traditional file environment A way of collecting and maintaining data in an organization that leads to each functional area or division creating and maintaining its own data files and programs.

7.1 Organizing Data in a Traditional File Environment

FIGURE 7.6
Creating a report using traditional file processing. In this example, three separate files—customer, personnel, and sales—have been created and are maintained by each respective division or department. In order to create a simple report consisting of a list of sales personnel by annual sales and principal customers, the three files had to be read, and an intermediate file had to be created. This required writing several programs. The table in the figure shows the information selected from each file.

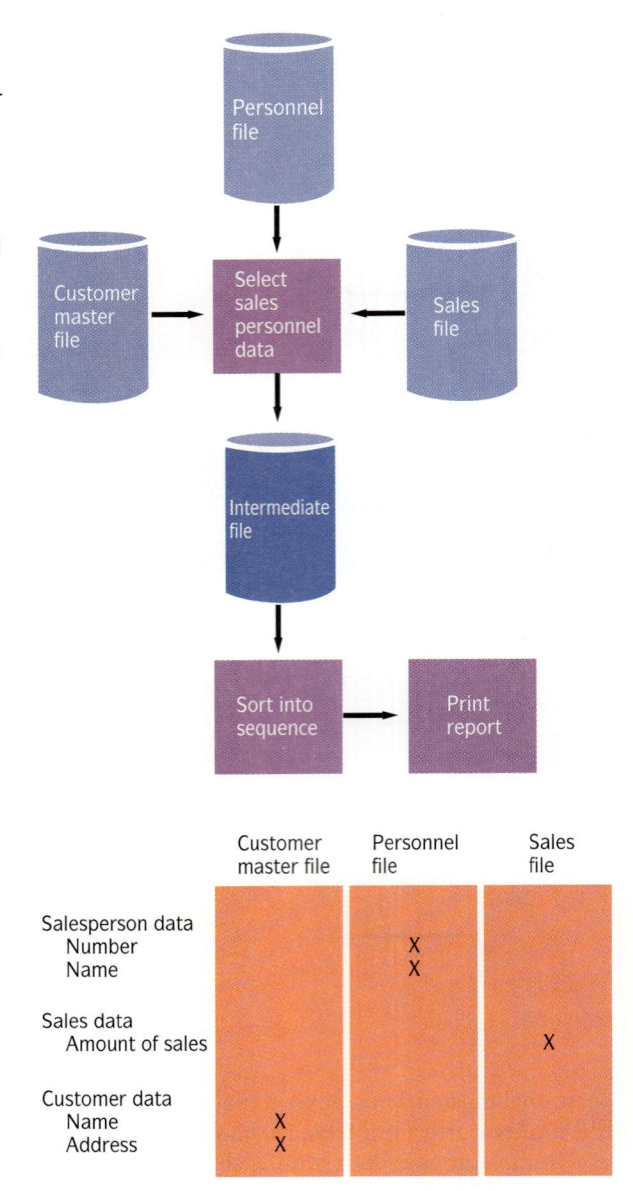

	Customer master file	Personnel file	Sales file
Salesperson data			
Number		X	
Name		X	
Sales data			
Amount of sales			X
Customer data			
Name	X		
Address	X		

Data Redundancy and Confusion

data redundancy The presence of duplicate data in multiple data files.

Data redundancy is the presence of duplicate data in multiple data files. Data redundancy occurs when different divisions, functional areas, and groups in an organization independently collect the same piece of information. For instance, within the commercial loans division of a bank, the marketing and credit information functions might collect the same customer information. Because it is collected and maintained in so many different places, the same data item may have different meanings in different parts of the organization. Simple data items like the fiscal year, employee identification, and product code can take on different meanings as programmers and analysts work in isolation on different applications.

Program-Data Dependence

program-data dependence The close relationship between data stored in files and the software programs that update and maintain those files. Any change in data organization or format requires a change in all the programs associated with those files.

Program-data dependence is the tight relationship between data stored in files and the specific programs required to update and maintain those files. Every computer program has to describe the location and nature of the data with which it works. In a traditional file environment, any change in data requires a change in all of the programs that access the data. Changes, for instance, in tax rates or ZIP-code length require changes in programs. Such programming changes may cost millions of dollars to implement in each program that requires the revised data.

Lack of Flexibility

A traditional file system can deliver routine scheduled reports after extensive programming efforts, but it cannot deliver ad hoc reports or respond to unanticipated information requirements in a timely fashion. The information required by ad hoc requests is somewhere in the system but too expensive to retrieve. Several programmers would have to work for weeks to put together the required data items in a new file.

Poor Security

Because there is little control or management of data, access to and dissemination of information are virtually out of control. What limits on access exist tend to be the result of habit and tradition, as well as of the sheer difficulty of finding information.

Lack of Data Sharing and Availability

The lack of control over access to data in this confused environment does not make it easy for people to obtain information. Because pieces of information in different files and different parts of the organization cannot be related to one another, it is virtually impossible for information to be shared or accessed in a timely manner.

7.2 A MODERN DATABASE ENVIRONMENT

Database technology can cut through many of the problems created by traditional file organization. A more rigorous definition of a **database** is a collection of data organized to serve many applications efficiently by centralizing the data and minimizing redundant data. Rather than storing data in separate files for each application, data are stored physically to appear to users as being stored in only one location. A single database services multiple applications. For example, instead of a corporation storing employee data in separate information systems and separate files for personnel, payroll, and benefits, the corporation could create a single common Human Resources database. Figure 7.7 illustrates the database concept.

database A collection of data organized to service many applications at the same time by storing and managing data so that they appear to be in one location.

DATABASE MANAGEMENT SYSTEMS (DBMS)

A **database management system (DBMS)** is simply the software that permits an organization to centralize data, manage them efficiently, and provide access to the stored data by application programs. As illustrated in Figure 7.8, the DBMS acts as an interface between application programs and the physical data files. When the application program calls for a data item such as gross pay, the DBMS finds this item in the database and presents it to the application program. Using traditional data files the programmer would have to define the data and then tell the computer where they are. A DBMS eliminates most of the data definition statements found in traditional programs.

A database management system has three components:

- A data definition language
- A data manipulation language
- A data dictionary

The **data definition language** is the formal language used by programmers to specify the content and structure of the database. The data definition language defines each data element as it appears in the database before that data element is translated into the forms required by application programs.

database management system (DBMS) Special software to create and maintain a database and enable individual business applications to extract the data they need without having to create separate files or data definitions in their computer programs.

data definition language The component of a database management system that defines each data element as it appears in the database.

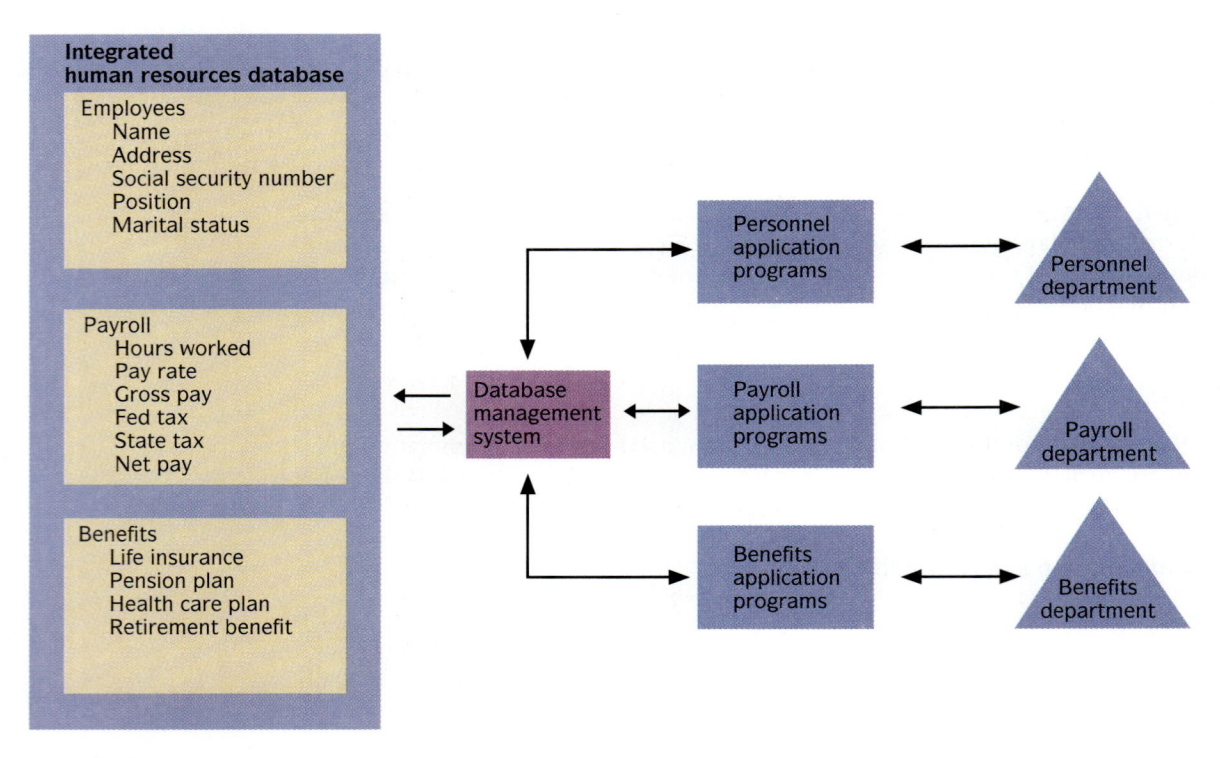

FIGURE 7.7
The contemporary database environment. A single Human Resources database serves multiple applications and also allows a corporation easily to draw together all of the information on various applications. The database management system acts as the interface between the application programs and the data.

data manipulation language A language associated with a database management system that is employed by end users and programmers to manipulate data in the database.

Structured Query Language (SQL) The emerging standard data manipulation language for relational database management systems.

Most DBMS have a specialized language called a **data manipulation language** that is used in conjunction with some conventional third- or fourth-generation programming languages to manipulate the data in the database. This language contains commands that permit end users and programming specialists to extract data from the database to satisfy information requests and develop applications. The most prominent data manipulation language today is **SQL,** or **Structured Query Language**. Complex programming tasks cannot be performed efficiently with typical data manipulation languages. However, most mainframe DBMSs are compatible with COBOL, FORTRAN, and other third-generation programming languages, permitting greater processing efficiency and flexibility.

The third element of a DBMS is a **data dictionary.** This is an automated or manual file that stores definitions of data elements and data characteristics such as usage, phys-

FIGURE 7.8
Elements of a database management system. In an ideal database environment, application programs work through a database management system to obtain data from the database. This diagram illustrates a database management system with an active data dictionary that not only records definitions of the contents of the database but also allows changes in data size and format to be automatically utilized by the application programs.

204   CHAPTER 7   Managing Data Resources

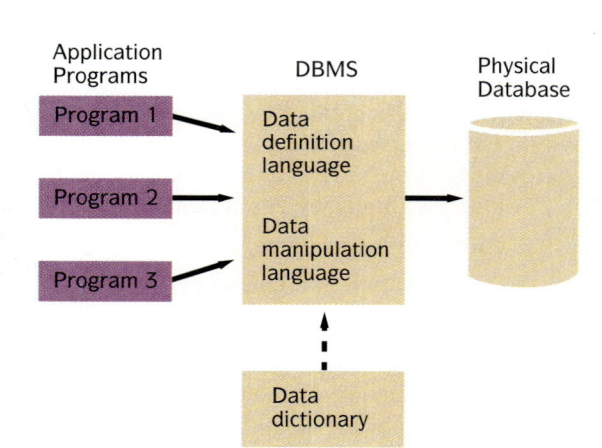

ical representation, ownership (who in the organization is responsible for maintaining the data), authorization, and security. Many data dictionaries can produce lists and reports of data utilization, groupings, program locations, and so on. Figure 7.9 illustrates a sample data dictionary report that shows the size, format, meaning, and uses of a data element in a Human Resources database. A **data element** represents a field. Besides listing the standard name (AMT-PAY-BASE), the dictionary lists the names that reference this element in specific systems and identifies the individuals, business functions, programs, and reports that use this data element.

By creating an inventory of all the pieces of data contained in the database, the data dictionary serves as an important data management tool. For instance, business users could consult the dictionary to find out exactly what pieces of data are maintained for the sales or marketing function or even to determine all of the information maintained by the entire enterprise. The dictionary could supply business users with the name, format, and specifications required to access data for reports. Technical staff could use the dictionary to determine what data elements and files must be changed if a program is changed.

Most data dictionaries are entirely passive; they simply report. More advanced types are active; changes in the dictionary can be automatically utilized by related programs. For instance, to change ZIP codes from five to nine digits, one could simply enter the change in the dictionary without having to modify and recompile all application programs using ZIP codes.

data dictionary An automated or manual tool for storing and organizing information about the data maintained in a database.

data element A field.

```
NAME:   AMT-PAY-BASE
FOCUS NAME:  BASEPAY
PC NAME:     SALARY

DESCRIPTION:  EMPLOYEE'S ANNUAL SALARY

SIZE: 9 BYTES
TYPE: N        (NUMERIC)
DATE CHANGED: 01/01/85
OWNERSHIP: COMPENSATION
UPDATE SECURITY: SITE PERSONNEL
ACCESS SECURITY:  MANAGER, COMPENSATION PLANNING AND RESEARCH
                  MANAGER, JOB EVALUATION SYSTEMS
                  MANAGER, HUMAN RESOURCES PLANNING
                  MANAGER, SITE EQUAL OPPORTUNITY AFFAIRS
                  MANAGER, SITE BENEFITS
                  MANAGER, CLAIMS PAYING SYSTEMS
                  MANAGER, QUALIFIED PLANS
                  MANAGER, SITE EMPLOYMENT/EEO
BUSINESS FUNCTIONS USED BY:  COMPENSATION
                             HR PLANNING
                             EMPLOYMENT
                             INSURANCE
                             PENSION
                             ISP

PROGRAMS USING:  PI01000
                 PI02000
                 PI03000
                 PI04000
                 PI05000

REPORTS USING:   REPORT 124 (SALARY INCREASE TRACKING REPORT)
                 REPORT 448 (GROUP INSURANCE AUDIT REPORT)
                 REPORT 452 (SALARY REVIEW LISTING)
                 PENSION REFERENCE LISTING
```

FIGURE 7.9
Sample data dictionary report. The sample data dictionary report for a Human Resources database provides helpful information such as the size of the data element, which programs and reports use it, and which group in the organization is the owner responsible for maintaining it. The report also shows some of the other names that the organization uses for this piece of data.

With a database program that permits users to share and integrate employee health statistics, the Epidemiology group of Texaco Inc. can track unusual patterns of employee disease.

In an ideal database environment, the data in the database are defined once and consistently, and used for all applications whose data reside in the database. Application programs (which are written using a combination of the data manipulation language of the DBMS and a conventional language such as COBOL) request data elements from the database. Data elements called for by the application programs are found and delivered by the DBMS. The programmer does not have to specify in detail how or where the data are to be found.

LOGICAL AND PHYSICAL VIEWS OF DATA

Perhaps the greatest difference between a DBMS and traditional file organization is that the DBMS separates the logical and physical views of the data, relieving the programmer or end user from the task of understanding where and how the data are actually stored.

The database concept distinguishes between *logical* and *physical* views of data. The **logical view** presents data as they would be perceived by end users or business specialists, whereas the **physical view** shows how data are actually organized and structured on physical storage media.

logical view A representation of data as they would appear to an application programmer or end user.

physical view The representation of data as they would be actually organized on physical storage media.

Suppose, for example, that a professor of information systems wanted to know at the beginning of the semester how students performed in the prerequisite computer literacy course (Computer Literacy 101) and what their current majors are. Using a database supported by the registrar, the professor would need something like the report shown in Figure 7.10.

Ideally, for such a simple report, the professor could sit at an office terminal connected to the registrar's database and write a small application program using the data manipulation language to create this report. The professor first would create the desired logical view of the data (Figure 7.10) for the application program. The DBMS would then assemble the requested data elements, which may reside in several different files and disk locations. For instance, the student major information may be located in a file called *Student*, whereas the grade data may be located in a file called *Course*. Wherever they are located, the DBMS would pull these pieces of information together and present them to the professor according to the logical view requested.

206   CHAPTER 7   Managing Data Resources

Student Name	ID No.	Major	Grade in Computer Literacy 101
Lind	468	Finance	A-
Pinckus	332	Marketing	B+
Williams	097	Economics	C+
Laughlin	765	Finance	A
Orlando	324	Statistics	B

FIGURE 7.10
The report required by the professor. The report requires data elements that may come from different files but it can easily be pulled together with a database management system if the data are organized into a database.

```
SELECT Stud_name, Stud.stud_id, Major, Grade
FROM Student, Course
WHERE Stud.stud_id = Course.stud_id
AND Course_id = "CL101"
```

FIGURE 7.11
The query used by the professor. This example shows how Structured Query Language (SQL) commands could be used to deliver the data required by the professor. These commands join two files, the student file (Student) and the course file (Course), and extract the specified pieces of information on each student from the combined file.

The query using the data manipulation language constructed by the professor might look something like Figure 7.11. Several DBMSs working on both mainframes and microcomputers permit this kind of interactive report creation.

ADVANTAGES OF DATABASE MANAGEMENT SYSTEMS

The preceding discussion illustrates the advantages of a DBMS:

- Complexity of the organization's information system environment can be reduced by central management of data, access, utilization, and security.
- Data redundancy and inconsistency can be reduced by eliminating all of the isolated files in which the same data elements are repeated.
- Data confusion can be eliminated by providing central control of data creation and definitions.
- Program-data dependence can be reduced by separating the logical view of data from its physical arrangement.
- Program development and maintenance costs can be radically reduced.
- Flexibility of information systems can be greatly enhanced by permitting rapid and inexpensive ad hoc queries of very large pools of information.
- Access and availability of information can be increased.

Given all of these benefits of DBMS, one might expect all organizations to change immediately to a database form of information management. But it is not that easy, as we will see later.

7.3 DESIGNING DATABASES

There are alternative ways of organizing data and representing relationships among data in a database. Conventional DBMSs use one of three principal logical database models for keeping track of entities, attributes, and relationships. The three principal logical database models are hierarchical, network, and relational. Each logical model has certain processing advantages and certain business advantages.

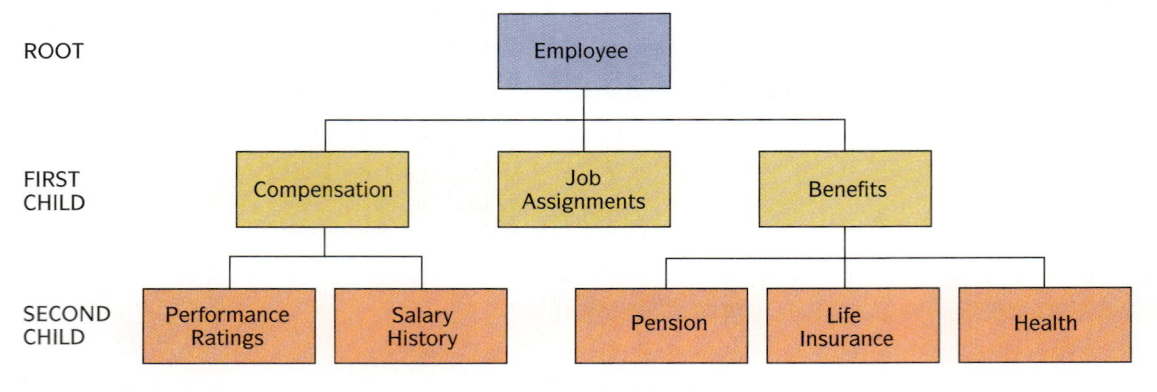

FIGURE 7.12
A hierarchical database for a human resources system. The hierarchical database model looks like an organizational chart or a family tree. It has a single root segment (Employee) connected to lower-level segments (Compensation, Job Assignments, and Benefits). Each subordinate segment, in turn, connects to other subordinate segments. Here, Compensation connects to Performance Ratings and Salary History. Benefits connects to Pension, Life Insurance, and Health Care. Each subordinate segment is the child of the segment directly above it.

HIERARCHICAL DATA MODEL

hierarchical data model One type of logical database model that organizes data in a treelike structure. A record is subdivided into segments that are connected to each other in one-to-many parent-child relationships.

The earliest DBMS were hierarchical. The **hierarchical data model** presents data to users in a treelike structure. The most common hierarchical DBMS is IBM's IMS (Information Management System). Within each record, data elements are organized into pieces of records called segments. To the user, each record looks like an organization chart with one top-level segment called the *root*. An upper segment is connected logically to a lower segment in a parent-child relationship. A parent segment can have more than one child, but a child can have only one parent.

Figure 7.12 shows a hierarchical structure that might be used for a human resources database. The root segment is Employee, which contains basic employee information such as name, address, and identification number. Immediately below it are three child segments: Compensation (containing salary and promotion data), Job Assignments (containing data about job positions and departments), and Benefits (containing data about beneficiaries and various benefit options). The Compensation segment has two children below it: Performance Ratings (containing data about employees' job performance evaluations) and Salary History (containing historical data about employees' past salaries). Below the Benefits segment are child segments for Pension, Life Insurance, and Health Care, containing data about these various benefit plans.

pointer A special type of data element attached to a record that shows the absolute or relative address of another record.

Behind the logical view of data are a number of physical links and devices to tie the information together into a logical whole. In a hierarchical DBMS the data are physically linked to one another by a series of **pointers** that form chains of related data segments. Pointers are data elements attached to the ends of record segments on the disk directing the system to related records. In our example, the end of the Employee segment would contain a series of pointers to all of the Compensation, Job Assignments, and Benefits segments. In turn, at the end of the Compensation and Benefits segments are pointers to their respective child segments.

NETWORK DATA MODEL

network data model A logical database model that is useful for depicting many-to-many relationships.

The **network data model** is a variation of the hierarchical data model. Indeed, databases can be translated from hierarchical to network and vice versa in order to optimize processing speed and convenience. Whereas hierarchical structures depict one-to-many relationships, network structures depict data logically as many-to-many relationships. In other words, parents can have multiple children, and a child can have more than one parent.

A typical many-to-many relationship in which a network DBMS excels in performance is the student-course relationship (see Figure 7.13). There are many courses in a

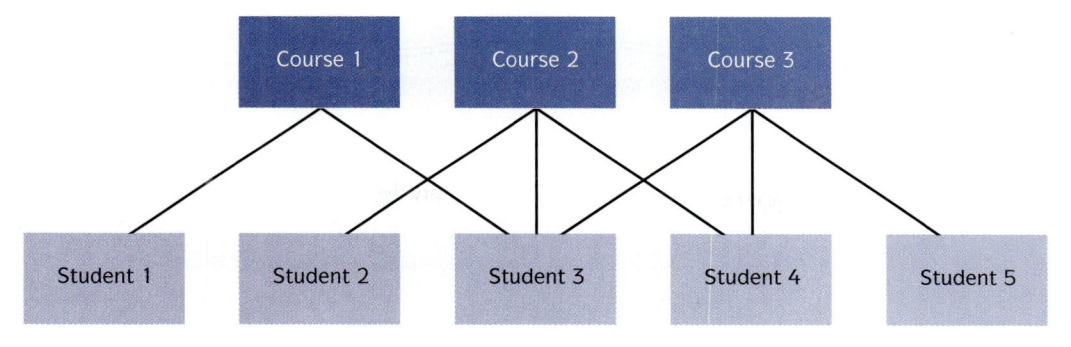

FIGURE 7.13
The network data model. This illustration of a network data model showing the relationship the students in a university have to the courses they take represents an example of logical many-to-many relationships. The network model reduces the redundancy of data representation through the increased use of pointers.

university and many students. A student takes many courses and a course has many students. The data in Figure 7.13 could be structured hierarchically. But this could result in considerable redundancy and a slowed response to certain types of information queries; the same student would be listed on the disk for each class he or she was taking instead of just once. Network structures reduce redundancy and, in certain situations (where many-to-many relationships are involved), respond more quickly. However, there is a price for this reduction in redundancy and increased speed: The number of pointers in network structures rapidly increases, making maintenance and operation potentially more complicated.

RELATIONAL DATA MODEL

The **relational data model,** the most recent of these three database models, overcomes some of the limitations of the other two models. The relational model represents all data in the database as simple two-dimensional tables called relations. The tables appear similar to flat files, but the information in more than one file can be easily extracted and combined. Sometimes the tables are referred to as files.

Figure 7.14 shows a supplier table, a part table, and an order table. In each table the rows are unique records and the columns are fields. Another term for a row or record in a relation is a **tuple.** Often a user needs information from a number of relations to produce a report. Here is the strength of the relational model: It can relate data in any one file or table to data in another file or table *as long as both tables share a common data element.*

To demonstrate, suppose we wanted to find in the relational database in Figure 7.14 the names and addresses of suppliers who could provide us with part number 137 or part number 152. We would need information from two tables: the supplier table and the part table. Note that these two files have a shared data element: SUPPLIER-NUMBER.

In a relational database, three basic operations are used to develop useful sets of data: select, project, and join. The *select* operation creates a subset consisting of all records in the file that meet stated criteria. *Select* creates, in other words, a subset of rows that meet certain criteria. In our example, we want to select records (rows) from the part table where the part number equals 137 or 152. The *join* operation combines relational tables to provide the user with more information than is available in individual tables. In our example we want to join the now shortened part table (only parts numbered 137 or 152 will be presented) and the supplier table into a single new result table.

The *project* operation creates a subset consisting of columns in a table, permitting the user to create new tables that contain only the information required. In our example, we want to extract from the new result table only the following columns: PART-NUMBER, SUPPLIER-NUMBER, SUPPLIER-NAME, and SUPPLIER-ADDRESS.

relational data model A type of logical database model that treats data as if they were stored in two-dimensional tables. It can relate data stored in one table to data in another as long as the two tables share a common data element.

tuple A row or record in a relational database.

7.3 Designing Databases

Table (Relation)				Columns (Fields)			
ORDER	ORDER-NUMBER	ORDER-DATE	DELIVERY-DATE	PART-NUMBER	PART-AMOUNT	ORDER-TOTAL	
	1634	02/02/96	02/22/96	152	2	144.50	Rows (Records, Tuples)
	1635	02/12/96	02/29/96	137	3	79.70	
	1636	02/13/96	03/01/96	145	1	24.30	

	PART-NUMBER	PART-DESCRIPTION	UNIT-PRICE	SUPPLIER-NUMBER
PART	137	Door latch	26.25	4058
	145	Door handle	22.50	2038
	152	Compressor	70.00	1125

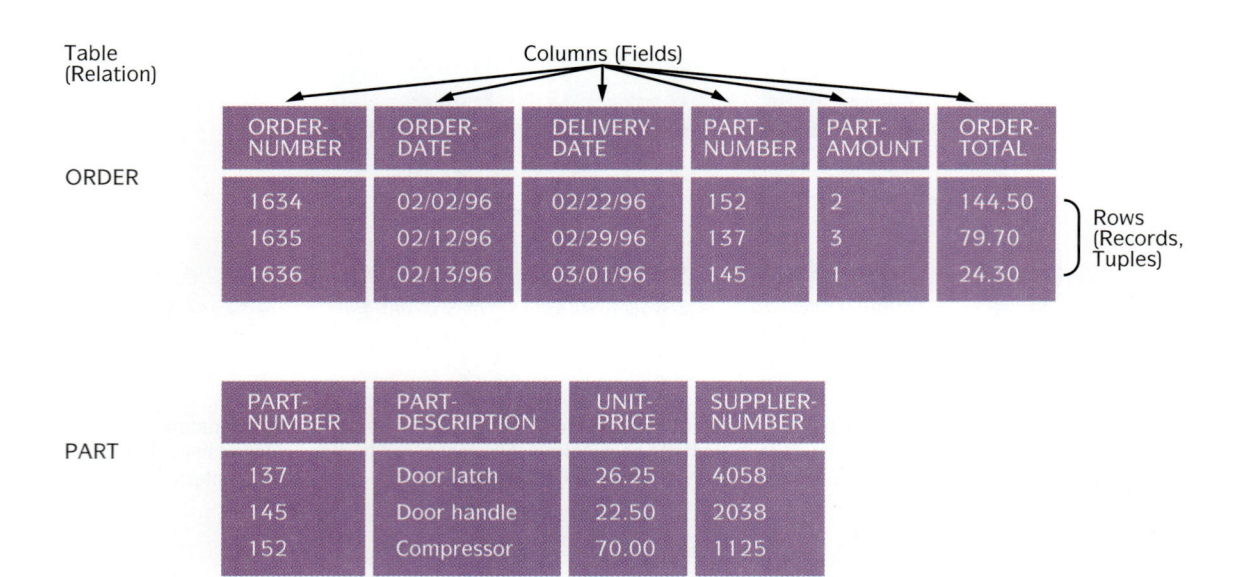

	SUPPLIER-NUMBER	SUPPLIER-NAME	SUPPLIER-ADDRESS
SUPPLIER	1125	CBM Inc.	44 Winslow, Gary IN 44950
	2038	Ace Inc.	Rte. 101, Essex NJ 07763
	4058	Bryant Corp.	51 Elm, Rochester NY 11349

FIGURE 7.14
The relational data model. Each table is a *relation* and each row or record is a *tuple*. Each column corresponds to a field. These relations can easily be combined and extracted in order to access data and produce reports, provided that any two share a common data element. In this example, the ORDER file shares the data element "PART-NUMBER" with the PART file. The PART and SUPPLIER files share the data element "SUPPLIER-NUMBER."

Leading mainframe relational database management systems include IBM's DB2 and Oracle from the Oracle Corporation. Microsoft Access and dBASE IV and Paradox from Borland International Inc. are examples of microcomputer relational database management systems.

ADVANTAGES AND DISADVANTAGES OF THE THREE DATABASE MODELS

The principal advantage of the hierarchical and network database models is processing efficiency. For instance, a hierarchical model is appropriate for airline reservation transaction processing systems, which must handle millions of structured routine requests each day for reservation information.

Hierarchical and network structures have several disadvantages. All of the access paths, directories, and indices must be specified in advance. Once specified, they are not easily changed without a major programming effort. Therefore, these designs have low flexibility. For instance, if you queried the Human Resources database illustrated in Figure 7.12 to find out the names of the employees with the job title of Administrative Assistant, you would discover that there is no way that the system can find the answer in a reasonable amount of time. This path through the data was not specified in advance.

Both hierarchical and network systems are programming-intensive, time-consuming, difficult to install, and difficult to remedy if design errors occur. They do not support ad hoc, English language–like inquiries for information.

Window on Organizations

DENMARK RUNS ON DB2

One could say that the country of Denmark runs on IBM's DB2 relational database management system. That's because DB2 supports virtually all of Denmark's major public service systems. All of these systems use data from Denmark's central population register, which is stored in a DB2 database. If the register were unavailable, most other systems couldn't operate, and the entire population of Denmark would be affected.

Everyone born in Denmark receives a social security number at birth. This event is registered in the system, as are all Danish marriages, divorces, deaths, and maintenance arrangements for children. When children go to kindergarten, their records are administered through the system. Citizens receive their social security payments and pay their local taxes through the system. (The system even includes all addresses and details of citizen properties and property values, as well as changes of ownership and occupation.) All of these public service applications are administered by Kommunedata, a nonprofit company jointly owned by Denmark's nine counties and 273 local governments.

Kommunedata, which is headquartered in Ballerup, runs more than 60 of Denmark's public service applications on four large mainframes at regional sites throughout the country. All of the transactions for these systems rely on DB2. The DB2 database handles over 500,000 transactions each day.

Denmark maintains an extensive welfare state, so the efficiency of its public service systems is critical. Its Social Democrat-led coalition government is trying to defend the welfare state against calls for budget cuts. Government users of the system believe that having a single source of information keeps overhead costs, and therefore income tax rates, to a minimum. There's less bureaucratic red tape, too, because citizens have to fill out fewer forms.

The response time of Denmark's public systems is highly dependent on the design of the DB2 database and how programs are written. The database had to be carefully designed to support multiple systems from the same source of data. Database analysts review all SQL code before it is used. Kommunedata committed to DB2 as the underlying database management system in 1988.

> **To Think About:** What are the benefits of using DB2 for Denmark's public service systems? What are the drawbacks? Was Kommunedata's selection of DB2 a sound management decision? What management, organization, and technology factors had to be addressed?

In choosing DB2 over competing database management systems, Kommunedata believed that DB2 offered the best opportunity to achieve substantial long-term cost savings through data sharing and data reuse. However, by the end of 1990, Kommunedata's study of DB2 benefits failed to show any gains. At that point the company had only developed a few DB2-based applications because users feared excessive costs from the mainframe CPU time required for DB2. The experience of the few programmers who worked in DB2 was not widely shared. Kommunedata made too much of its initial retraining investment.

Since then, significant benefits have emerged. Kommunedata's management decided it had overestimated the amount of extra CPU time required by DB2. At that point the company converted more of its old flat-file systems to DB2. It retrained most of its 500 systems developers to use DB2. By 1994, Kommunedata found that the savings in systems development costs, especially by using a data dictionary when analyzing the data required by various applications, more than offset the cost of extra CPU time.

Source: George Black, "Denmark's Dependency on DB2 Pays Off in Development Time," *Software Magazine*, February 1994.

The strengths of relational DBMS are great flexibility in regard to ad hoc queries, power to combine information from different sources, simplicity of design and maintenance, and the ability to add new data and records without disturbing existing programs and applications. However, these systems are somewhat slower because they typically require many accesses to the data stored on disk to carry out the select, join, and project commands. Selecting one part number from among millions, one record at a time, can take a long time. Of course the database can be indexed and tuned to speed up prespecified queries. Relational systems do not have the large number of pointers carried by hierarchical systems.

With improvements in performance and reliability, relational databases are starting to be used for some large transaction-oriented applications, as illustrated in the Window on Organizations.

Table 7.1	Comparison of Database Alternatives			
Type of Database	Processing Efficiency	Flexibility	End-User Friendliness	Programming Complexity
Hierarchical	High	Low	Low	High
Network	Medium–high	Low–medium	Low–moderate	High
Relational	Lower but improving	High	High	Low

Large relational databases may be designed to have some data redundancy in order to make retrieval of data more efficient. The same data element may be stored in multiple tables. Updating redundant data elements is not automatic in many relational DBMS. For example, changing the employee status field in one table will not automatically change it in all tables. Special arrangements are required to ensure that all copies of the same data element are updated together.

Hierarchical databases remain the workhorse for intensive high-volume transaction processing. Banks, insurance companies, and other high-volume users continue to use reliable hierarchical databases such as IBM's IMS, developed in 1969. Many organizations have converted to DB2, IBM's relational DBMS for new applications, while retaining IMS for traditional transaction processing. For example, Dallas-based Texas Instruments depends on IMS for its heavy processing requirements. Texas Instruments bases its complete operations, including inventory, accounting, and manufacturing, on IMS. The firm has built up a huge library of IMS applications over 20 years, and a complete conversion to DB2 would take 10 more years. As relational products acquire more muscle, firms will shift away completely from hierarchical DBMS, but this will happen over a long period of time. Table 7.1 compares the characteristics of the different database models.

CREATING A DATABASE

In order to create a database, one must go through two design exercises: a conceptual design and a physical design. The conceptual design of a database is an abstract model of the database from a business perspective, whereas the physical design shows how the database is actually arranged on direct access storage devices. Physical database design is performed by database specialists, whereas logical design requires a detailed description of the business information needs of actual end users of the database. Ideally, database design will be part of an overall organizational data planning effort (see Chapter 10).

The conceptual database design describes how the data elements in the database are to be grouped. The design process identifies relationships among data elements and the most efficient way of grouping data elements together to meet information requirements. The process also identifies redundant data elements and the groupings of data elements required for specific application programs. Groups of data are organized, refined, and streamlined until an overall logical view of the relationships among all of the data elements in the database emerges.

entity-relationship diagram A methodology for documenting databases illustrating the relationship between various entities in the database.

Database designers document the conceptual data model with an **entity-relationship diagram,** illustrated in Figure 7.15. The boxes represent entities and the diamonds represent relationships. The *1* or *M* on either side of the diamond represents the relationship among entities as either one-to-one, one-to-many, or many-to-many. Figure 7.15 shows that the entity ORDER can have only one PART and a PART can only have one SUPPLIER. Many parts can be provided by the same supplier. The attributes for each entity are listed next to the entity and the key field is underlined.

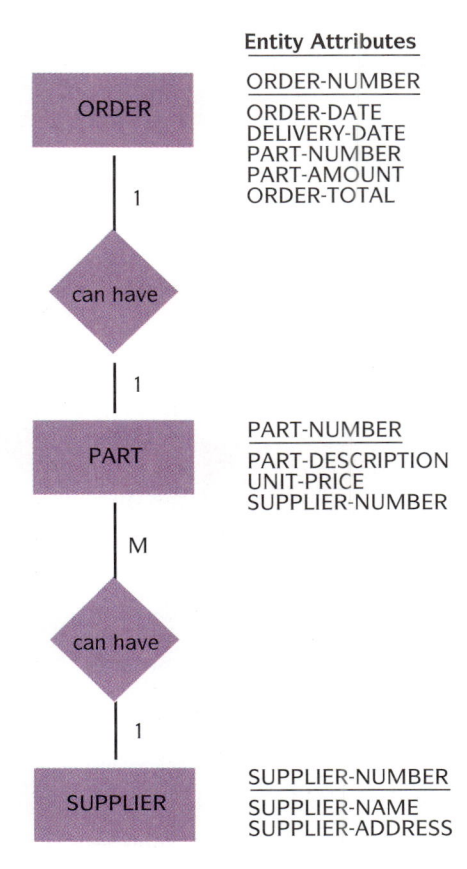

FIGURE 7.15
An entity-relationship diagram. This diagram shows the relationships between the entities ORDER, PART, and SUPPLIER that were used to develop the relational database illustrated in Figure 7.14.

Entity Attributes:

ORDER
- ORDER-NUMBER
- ORDER-DATE
- DELIVERY-DATE
- PART-NUMBER
- PART-AMOUNT
- ORDER-TOTAL

ORDER can have (1:1) PART

PART
- PART-NUMBER
- PART-DESCRIPTION
- UNIT-PRICE
- SUPPLIER-NUMBER

PART can have (M:1) SUPPLIER

SUPPLIER
- SUPPLIER-NUMBER
- SUPPLIER-NAME
- SUPPLIER-ADDRESS

7.4 DATABASE TRENDS

Recent database trends include the growth of distributed databases and the emergence of object-oriented and hypermedia databases.

DISTRIBUTED PROCESSING AND DISTRIBUTED DATABASES

Information processing became more distributed with the growth of powerful telecommunications networks and the decline in computer hardware costs. Instead of relying on a single centralized mainframe computer to provide service to remote terminals, organizations began to install minicomputers and microcomputers at remote sites. These distributed processors directly serve local and regional branch offices and factories and are generally linked together in networks. The dispersion and use of computers among multiple geographically or functionally separate locations so that local computers handle local processing needs is called **distributed processing**. Chapters 8 and 9 will describe the various network arrangements for distributed processing.

It is only a short step from distributed processing to distributed databases. Although early distributed systems worked with a single centralized database, over time the smaller local systems began to store local databases as well. It soon became obvious that the central database could be entirely distributed to local processors as long as some mechanism existed to provide proper updating, integrity of data, sharing of data, and central administrative controls.

A **distributed database** is one that is stored in more than one physical location. Parts of the database are stored physically in one location and other parts are stored and maintained in other locations. There are two main ways of distributing a database (see Figure 7.16). The central database (see Figure 7.16a) can be partitioned so that each remote processor has the necessary data on customers to serve its local area. Changes in

distributed processing The distribution of computer processing among multiple geographically or functionally separate locations linked by a communications network.

distributed database A database that is stored in more than one physical location. Parts or copies of the database are physically stored in one location, and other parts or copies are stored and maintained in other locations.

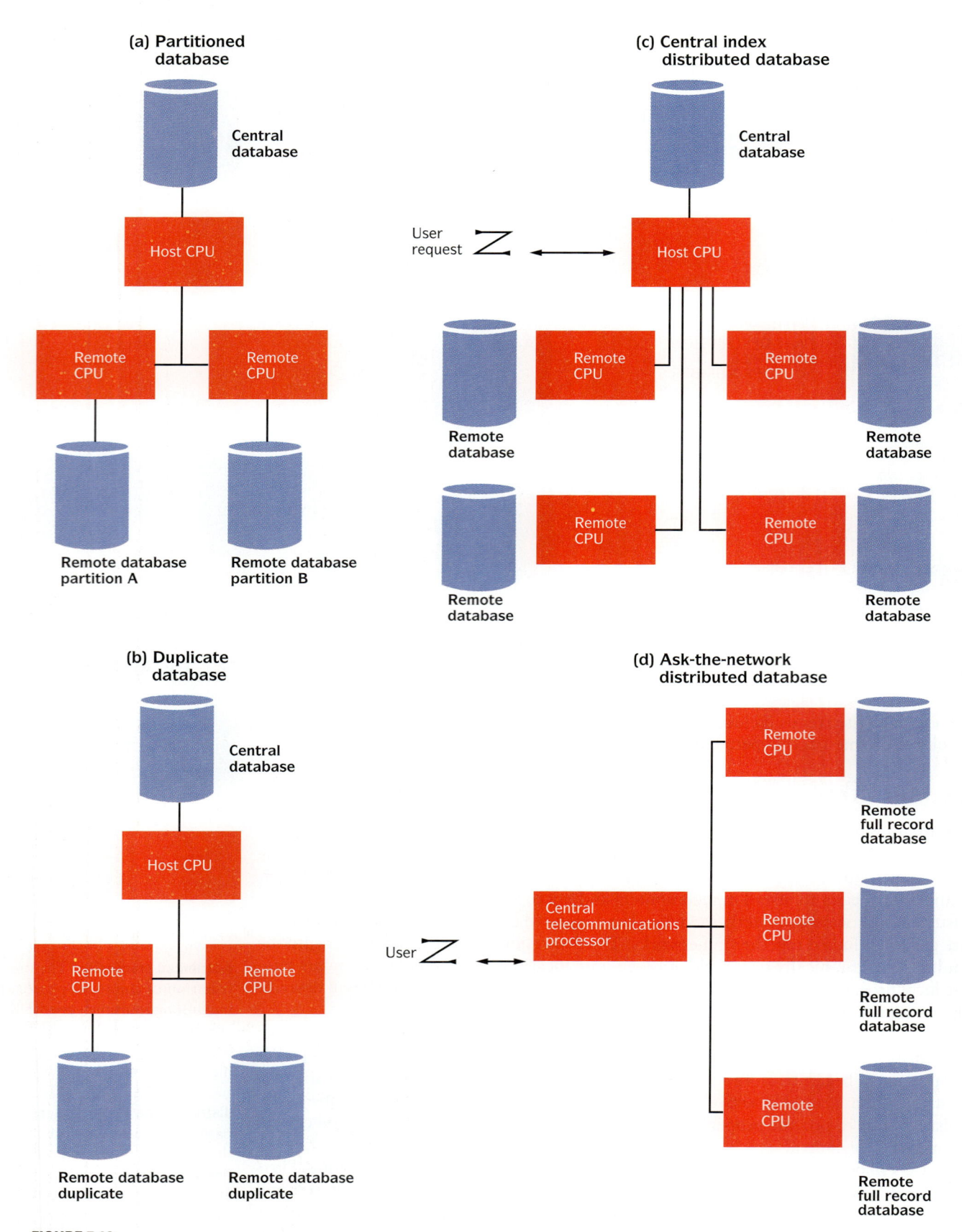

FIGURE 7.16
Distributed databases. There are alternative ways of distributing a database. The central database can be partitioned (a) so that each remote processor has the necessary data to serve its own local needs. The central database can also be duplicated (b) at all remote locations. In the central index distributed database (c) complete records are stored locally and can be located using a central name index. In an ask-the-network distributed database (d), the network polls its remote processors to locate a record and transfers the complete record to whatever processor requests it.

local files can be justified with the central database on a batch basis, often at night. Another strategy is to replicate the central database (Figure 7.16b) at all remote locations. This strategy also requires updating of the central database on off hours.

Still another possibility—one used by very large databases like the FBI's National Crime Information Center—is to maintain only a central name index and to store complete records locally (Figure 7.16c). A query to the central name index identifies a location where the full record can be found. Here there is no central database and no updating costs. National Westminster Bank in London uses a similar approach to maintain all of its customer account information in two massive fragmented DB2 databases. Specially developed software allows each of its 22,000 users to access the data on either database with a global catalog of where the data are stored. Another variation is an ask-the-network scheme (Figure 7.16d). There is no central index of names in this design. Instead, all remote processors are polled to find a complete record. The complete record is then transferred to whatever processor requests it (Laudon, 1986).

Both distributed processing and distributed databases have benefits and drawbacks. Distributed systems reduce the vulnerability of a single, massive central site. They permit increases in systems' power by purchasing smaller, less expensive minicomputers. Finally, they increase service and responsiveness to local users. Distributed systems, however, are dependent on high-quality telecommunications lines, which themselves are vulnerable. Moreover, local databases can sometimes depart from central data standards and definitions, and pose security problems by widely distributing access to sensitive data. The economies of distribution can be lost when remote sites buy more computing power than they need.

Despite these drawbacks, distributed processing is growing rapidly. With the advent of microcomputers and powerful telecommunications systems, more and more information services will be distributed. For large national organizations working in several regions, the question is no longer whether to distribute but how to distribute in such a way as to minimize costs and improve responsiveness without sacrificing data and system integrity.

OBJECT-ORIENTED AND HYPERMEDIA DATABASES

Conventional database management systems were designed for homogeneous data that can be easily structured into predefined data fields and records. But many applications today and in the future will require databases that can store and retrieve not only structured

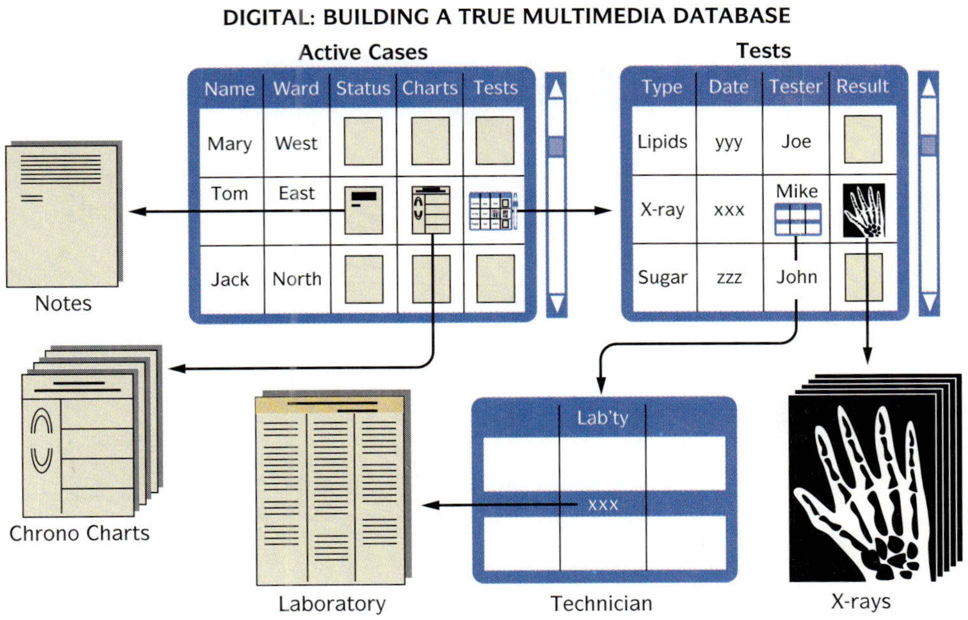

FIGURE 7.17
An object-oriented multimedia database. Medical data on patients in a hospital might likely be stored in a multimedia database such as this one. Doctors could access patient files including vital medical images to generate the reports and derive the information they need to deliver quality health care quickly. *Reprinted by permission of Digital Equipment Corporation.*

Object-oriented database management systems can store graphic, audio, video, and text data along with procedures.

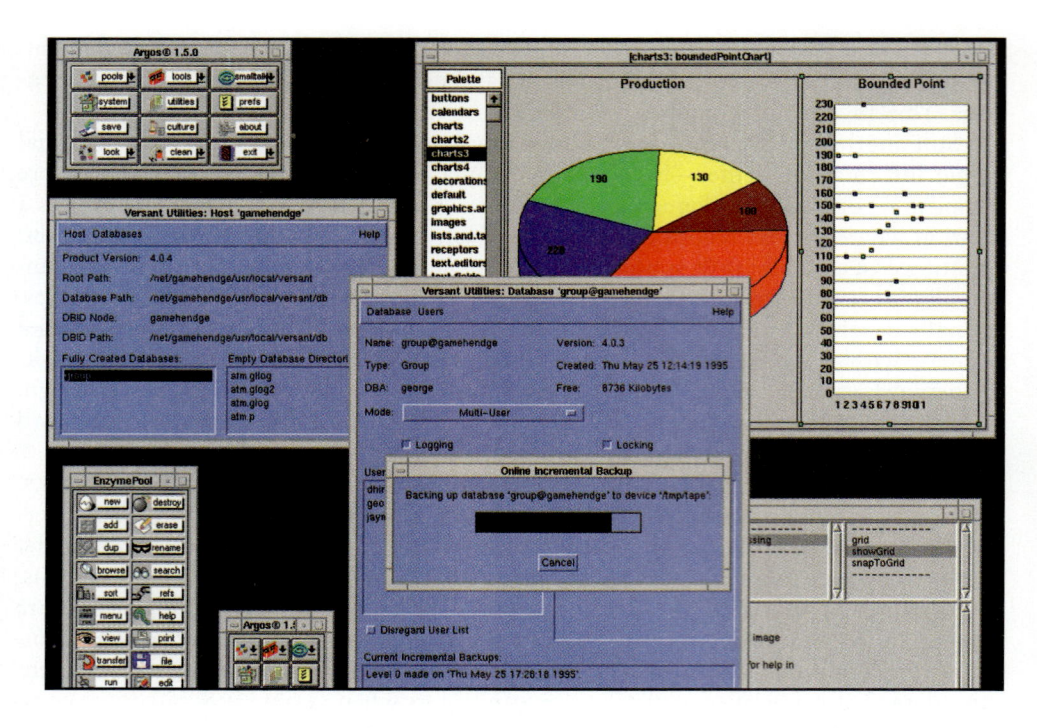

object-oriented database An approach to data management that stores both data and the procedures acting on the data as objects that can be automatically retrieved and shared; the objects can contain multimedia.

hypermedia database An approach to data management that organizes data as a network of nodes linked in any pattern established by the user; the nodes can contain text, graphics, sound, full-motion video, or executable programs.

numbers and characters but also drawings, images, photographs, voice, and full-motion video (see Figure 7.17). Conventional DBMS are not well suited to handling graphics-based or multimedia applications. For instance, design data in a CAD database consist of complex relationships among many types of data. Manipulating these kinds of data in a relational system requires extensive programming to translate these complex data structures into tables and rows. An **object-oriented database,** on the other hand, stores the data and procedures as objects that can be automatically retrieved and shared. The Window on Technology describes how firms can benefit from these new capabilities.

The **hypermedia database** approach to information management transcends some of the limitations of traditional database methods by storing chunks of information in the form of nodes connected by links established by the user (see Figure 7.18). The nodes can contain text, graphics, sound, full-motion video, or executable computer programs. Searching for information does not have to follow a predetermined organization scheme. Instead, one can branch instantly to related information in any kind of relationship established by the author. The relationship between records is less structured than in a traditional DBMS.

In most systems each node can be displayed on a screen. The screen also displays the links between the node depicted and other nodes in the database. Figure 7.19 illus-

FIGURE 7.18
Hypermedia. In a hypermedia database, the user can choose his or her own path to move from node to node. Each node can contain text, graphics, sound, full-motion video, or executable programs.

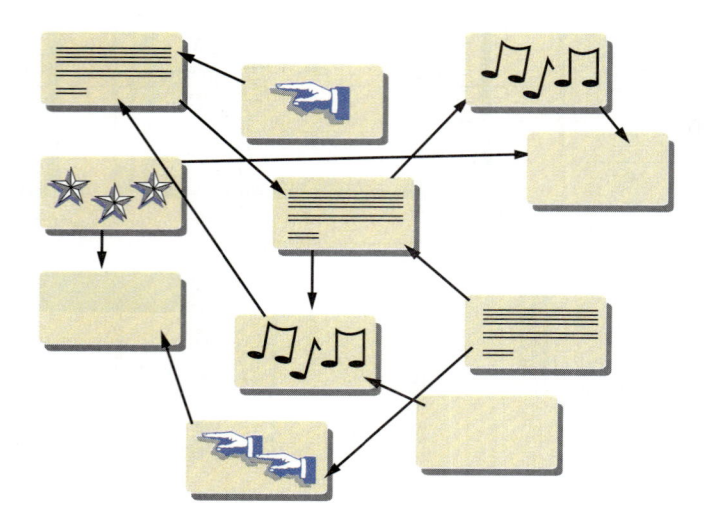

Window on Technology

VOLKSWAGEN OPTS FOR AN OBJECT-ORIENTED DATABASE

Volkswagen has the highest sales in Europe of any automobile, and yet in 1992 it was the highest-cost high-volume car maker in the world, with a profit of only about $26 per unit. Volkswagen management needed to find ways to cut costs. One Volkswagen subsidiary, EuroMarketing Systems, came up with an idea to build a system that all VW distributors can use to track cars, from the building of them through selling and maintenance, all the way to recycling them later on. The project, named EuroElan, is targeted to 110,000 users worldwide and will link dealerships and factories to allow all to better track every Volkswagen automobile throughout its useful life. The project is being financed by the wholesalers themselves.

The database must be able to hold and process an enormous amount of data. For every automobile Volkswagen produces, the dealers want to be able to determine where in the manufacturing process it is and to which dealer it will be delivered. After it is produced, they want to be able to find out which dealer currently has it. After it is sold, they want to identify the purchaser of the automobile and the dealer maintenance performed on the car. Ultimately, they even want to know the final disposition of the car at the end of its useful life. When database design was complete, the team found that the database would contain more than 700 relational tables. They also found that the data to be stored needed to include unstructured, binary data such as automobile images. In selecting a database management system, the most fundamental criterion was the ability of the DBMS to handle all of the types of data, and to do so quickly and with efficiency.

The project team found that relational databases (RDBMSs) such as Ingress (from the ASK Group, Inc.) handled relatively simple queries well but that they slowed dramatically when the queries became more complicated. They also found that when using RDBMSs they were unable to do queries on the unstructured binary fields. Object-oriented databases (OODBs), they discovered, handle complex queries much more quickly than RDBMSs, and they also allow for queries on binary objects. Thus they selected OODB as the underlying technology. The specific OODB they selected on which to build EuroElan was Versant from Versant Object Technology Corp. One reason they chose Versant was that the company promised to provide techniques to

> **To Think About:** Analyze Volkswagen using the competitive forces and value chain models. Did the use of object-oriented database technology enhance its competitive position? What management, organization, and technology issues did the selection of the Versant object-oriented database address?

allow Volkswagen to access existing data currently stored in RDBMSs. The project team also received positive feedback from other global companies currently using the product.

The contract between Volkswagen and Versant was for $2.6 million. The total cost of the project after the signing of the contract had already reached $8 million. Volkswagen management believes the project will help to reduce costs by reducing the size of automobile and parts inventories. In addition, they believe customer service quality will rise while costs will go down. They point out that today when a customer asks for a specific car (such as a black Volkswagen Jetta with a sunroof, antilock brakes, and no air conditioning), the customer might have to wait a long time while the dealer does a telephone search to many of the 10,000 Volkswagen dealers worldwide in order to find the automobile. When EuroElan becomes operational, the search of the database will take only moments.

Versant (and OODBs in general) did present one major problem that Volkswagen will have to address—security. RDBMSs include better security features than do Versant and other OODBs.

Source: Kim S. Nash, "Users Scout for Right Object DBMS Fit," *Computerworld*, January 10, 1994.

---

trates sample nodes from Apple Corporation's HyperCard, which is based on the hypermedia concept. The node for Sugar City, Montana, is linked to a node for the state of Montana and to a node showing a map of the entire United States. The node for the state of Montana illustrated in Figure 7.19 is linked to nodes for each of the cities illustrated on the map; to a node for the map of the entire United States; and to a node to return to the Home card, the first node in the HyperCard system. HyperCard is used primarily for small, single-user applications. Massive, multi-user hypermedia databases are starting to be constructed for business and military applications (Carmel et al., 1989).

MULTIDIMENSIONAL DATABASES

Sometimes managers need to analyze data in ways that can't be represented by traditional database models. For example, a company selling four different products—apples, bananas, oranges, and pears—in three regions—East, West, and Central—might

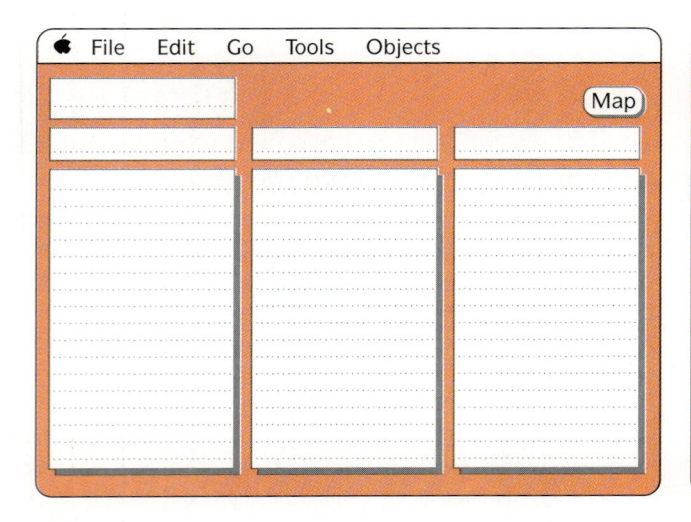

FIGURE 7.19
HyperCard. HyperCard programs are constructed as if they were stacks of individual cards, each of which can be linked to one or more other cards in any way the user chooses. The links do not have to follow the structured formulas of conventional databases or lists. HyperCard programs can contain digitized sound, drawings, and video images, as well as text. *Hypercard 2.2 © 1987-1991, 1993 Apple Computer Inc. Apple ®, the Apple logo and Hypercard ® are registered trademarks of Apple Computer, Inc. Used with permission. All rights reserved.*

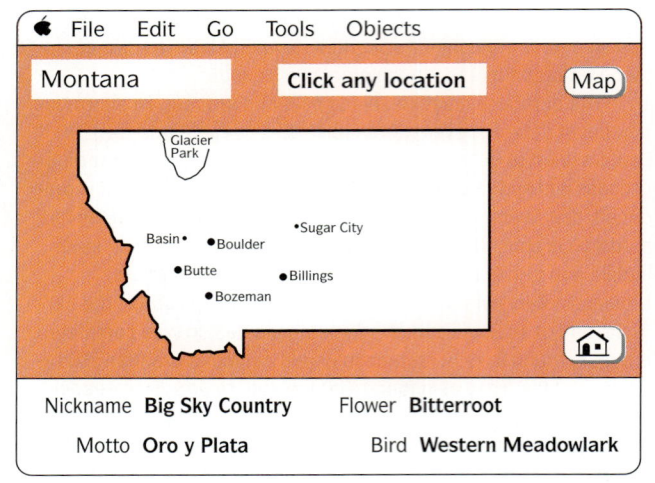

multidimensional database model A database model that represents relationships between data as a multidimensional structure, which can be visualized as cubes of data and cubes within cubes of data; it can create complex views of data for sophisticated reporting and analysis.

want to know actual sales by product for each region and might also want to compare them to projected sales. This analysis requires a multidimensional view of data. Such data could be combined into a single entity by using a multidimensional database model.

A **multidimensional database model** represents relationships between data as a multidimensional structure, which can be visualized as cubes of data and cubes within cubes of data. Each side of the cube is considered a dimension of data. Figure 7.20 shows a multidimensional model that could be created to represent products, regions, actual sales, and projected sales. A matrix of actual sales can be stacked on top of a matrix of projected sales to form a cube with six faces. If you rotate the cube 90 degrees horizontally, the face showing will be product versus actual and projected sales. If you rotate the cube 90 degrees vertically, you can see region versus actual and projected sales. If you rotate 180 degrees from the original view, you can see projected sales and product versus region. Cubes can be nested within cubes to build complex views of data.

DATA WAREHOUSING

Decision makers need concise, reliable information about current operations, trends, and changes. What has been immediately available at most firms is current data only (historical data was available through special IS reports that took a long time to produce). Data are often fragmented in separate operational systems such as sales or payroll so that different managers make decisions from incomplete knowledge bases. Data warehousing addresses this problem by integrating key operational data from around the company in a form that is consistent, reliable, and easily available for reporting.

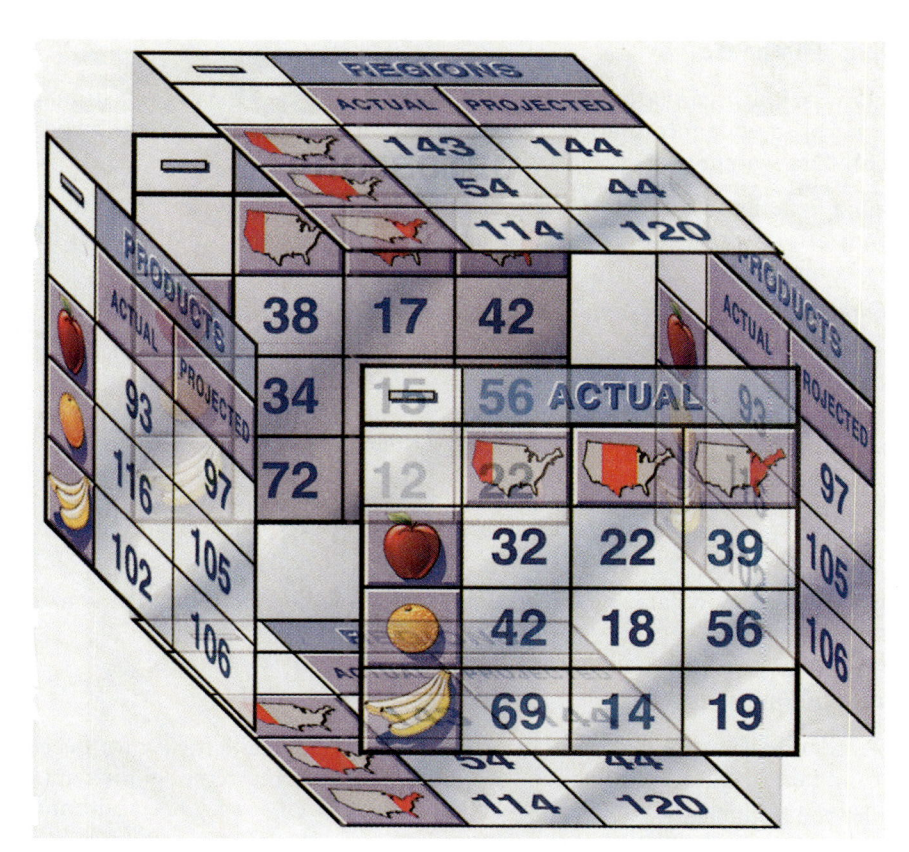

FIGURE 7.20
Only one view can be seen at a time on a two-dimensional computer monitor, in this case the original view, or product versus region. But if you rotate the cube 90 degrees horizontally, the face showing will be product versus actual and projected sales. If you rotate the cube 90 degrees vertically, you're looking at region versus actual and projected sales. Rotate 180 degrees from the original view, and you have projected sales, product versus region. And views can be nested within views to build complex, yet useful data matrices. Reproduced with permission from *Mike Ricciuti, "Winning the Competitive Game,"* DATAMATION MAGAZINE, copyright, *February 15, 1994,* Calmers Publishing Company, a division of Reed Elsevier Inc. DATAMATION MAGAZINE is a trademark of Cahners Publishing Company, a division of Reed Elsevier Inc. All rights reserved."

What Is a Data Warehouse?

A **data warehouse** is a database, with tools, that stores current and historical data of potential interest to managers throughout the company. The data originate in many core operational systems and are copied into the data warehouse database as often as needed—hourly, daily, weekly, monthly. The data are standardized and consolidated so that they can be used across the enterprise for management analysis and decision making. The data are available for anyone to access as needed but cannot be altered. A data warehouse system includes a range of ad hoc and standardized query tools, analytical tools, and graphical reporting facilities. These systems can perform high-level analysis of patterns or trends, but they can also drill down into more detail where needed. Table 7.2 shows how data warehouse data differ from operational data.

data warehouse A database, with reporting and query tools, that stores current and historical data extracted from various operational systems and consolidated for management reporting and analysis.

Table 7.2

Operational Data	Data Warehouse Data
Isolated data stored in and used by isolated legacy systems	Enterprise-wide integrated data collected from legacy systems
Contains current operational data	Contains recent data as well as historical data
Data are stored on multiple platforms	Data are stored on a single platform
Individual fields (such as customer number) may be inconsistent across the enterprise	A single, agreed-upon definition exists for every field stored in the system
Data are organized from an operational or functional view—such as sales, production, purchasing, payroll, order processing	Data are organized around major business informational subjects—such as customer or product
Data are volatile to support operations within a company	Data are stabilized for decision making

Building a Data Warehouse

Building a data warehouse can be a very difficult process because of the organizational obstacles to enterprise-wide information management that we have already described. Most successful data warehousing projects include the following steps:

1. Defining the mission and business objectives for the data warehouse at a high level of the organization, and mapping those objectives to the mission and objectives of the whole organization
2. Identifying data from all operational databases required for the data warehouse
3. Defining the data items by standardizing data names and meanings across the company. It is usually too big a job to make these data items consistent in existing operational systems. Instead, the project needs to identify any problems and eliminate inconsistencies as data are copied from the legacy systems into the data warehouse.
4. Designing the database
5. Developing a policy for archiving older data so storage space does not become too large and so queries don't become too slow
6. Extracting the production data, cleaning them up, and loading them into the warehouse databases

Benefits of a Data Warehouse

Data warehouses not only offer improved information, but they make it easy for decision makers to obtain it. They even include the ability to model and remodel the data. These systems also enable decision makers to access data as often as they need without affecting the processing performance of the operational systems.

For example, financial controllers at Philips Electronics, Sunnyvale, California, were wasting enormous amounts of time tracking product information from around the world. The firm's data warehouse helped it integrate sales, returns, and marketing expense data.

Victoria's Secret Stores had been spending too much time trying to locate information and not enough time analyzing it. Through data warehousing, the lingerie chain learned that its system of allocating merchandise to its 678 shops, based on a mathematical store average, was wrong. For example, an average store sells equal pieces of black and ivory lingerie, but Miami-area consumers buy ivory designs by a margin of 10 to 1. Geographic demand patterns also showed that some stores did not need to discount merchandise. Data warehousing gave this firm a more precise understanding of customer behavior (Goldberg and Vijayan, 1996).

The Window on Management explores another promising database trend, the linking of internal corporate databases to the Internet. The interactive features of the Internet's World Wide Web can provide an easy-to-use user interface to these databases for inside and outside the organization.

7.5 MANAGEMENT REQUIREMENTS FOR DATABASE SYSTEMS

Much more is required for the development of database systems than simply selecting a logical database model. Indeed, this selection may be among the last decisions. The database is an organizational discipline, a method, rather than a tool or technology. It requires organizational and conceptual change.

Without management support and understanding, database efforts fail. The critical elements in a database environment are (1) data administration, (2) data planning and modeling methodology, (3) database technology and management, and (4) users. This environment is depicted in Figure 7.21 and will now be described.

Window on Management

LINKING DATABASES TO THE INTERNET

United Parcel Service (UPS) delivers more than 3 billion parcels per year to most places in the world. The company is already so automated that it can tell customers who call where their package is and, if it has been delivered, who received it. What more can UPS do?

For one, they can use the Internet to reduce costs by eliminating even the telephone call for those customers who are Internet users. Inquiries by telephone cause customers to be put on hold during busy hours. Then the customer has to wait while the UPS customer service representative checks the package tracking database for the information before then verbally relaying it to the customer, a time-consuming and expensive method of giving and getting the information. UPS must pay for toll-free support lines and the customer service payroll. Why not just eliminate the person in the middle and give the customer direct access to the same database the customer service rep would use? That is exactly what UPS has done by linking its site on the World Wide Web of the Internet to its internal databases.

UPS first established an Internet Web site (*http://www.ups.com*) and then linked some of its corporate databases to that site. All a customer needs do now is access her local network (if it is connected to the Internet), jump to the UPS Web site, and enter the package's UPS tracking number. Very quickly the status of the package is displayed on her screen. The same Web site enables customers to calculate the transit time between two ZIP codes and to obtain the price of shipping a package by entering the package's weight, destination, and place of origin. By using the Internet, UPS does not need to distribute its own software to each customer to enable them to access their package tracking database—Web

To Think About: What are the management benefits of giving customers direct access to customer databases via the Internet? Can you suggest companies in other industries that might make use of the Internet the way UPS has?

browsers are free or low cost and run on any platform. And the Internet is almost universally accessible now.

What are the gains for UPS? In February, 1996, with the UPS service still new, the Web site was already responding to 5000 inquiries per day. That is 5000 inquiries that did not have to go through a customer service rep. UPS management does not expect to eliminate the telephone as a way of answering the questions that can be answered through the Web. Just reducing the calls a few thousand per day will help cut costs, and they hope to see the numbers increase. In addition, they see this Web service as a way to improve customer service. According to Steven Height, a UPS network development manager, the Web site is "a faster, more responsive mechanism for customers."

Source: Lynda Radosevich, "Outside In and Inside Out," *Computerworld Client/Server Journal*, February, 1996.

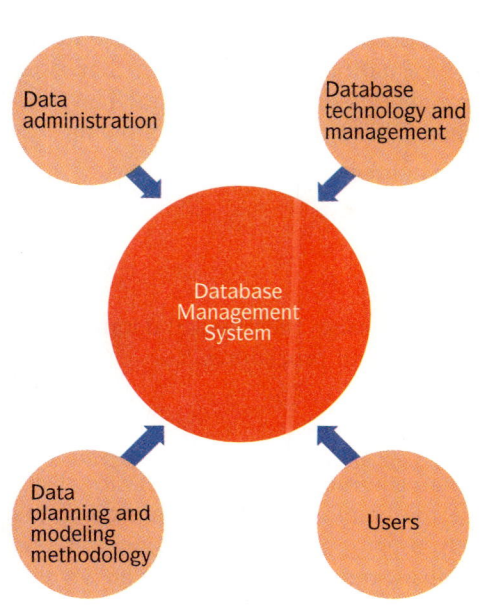

FIGURE 7.21
Key organizational elements in the database environment. For a database management system to flourish in any organization, data administration functions and data planning and modeling methodologies must be coordinated with database technology and management. Resources must be devoted to train end users to use databases properly.

DATA ADMINISTRATION

Database systems require that the organization recognize the strategic role of information and begin actively to manage and plan for information as a corporate resource. This means that the organization must develop a **data administration** function with the power to define information requirements for the entire company and with direct access to senior management. The chief information officer (CIO) or vice president of information becomes the primary advocate in the organization for database systems.

Data administration is responsible for the specific policies and procedures through which data can be managed as an organizational resource. These responsibilities include developing information policy, planning for data, overseeing logical database design and data dictionary development, and monitoring the usage of data by information system specialists and end-user groups.

The fundamental principle of data administration is that all data are the property of the organization as a whole. Data cannot belong exclusively to any one business area or organizational unit. All data are to be made available to any group that requires them to fulfill its mission. An organization needs to formulate an **information policy** that specifies its rules for sharing, disseminating, acquiring, standardizing, classifying, and inventorying information throughout the organization. Information policy lays out specific procedures and accountabilities, specifying which organizational units share information; where information can be distributed; and who has responsibility for updating and maintaining the information. Although data administration is a very important organizational function, it has proven very challenging to implement.

data administration A special organizational function for managing the organization's data resources, concerned with information policy, data planning, maintenance of data dictionaries, and data quality standards.

information policy Formal rules governing the maintenance, distribution, and use of information in an organization.

DATA PLANNING AND MODELING METHODOLOGY

Because the organizational interests served by the DBMS are much broader than those in the traditional file environment, the organization requires enterprise-wide planning for data. Enterprise analysis, which addresses the information requirements of the entire organization (as opposed to the requirements of individual applications), is needed to develop databases. The purpose of enterprise analysis is to identify the key entities, attributes, and relationships that constitute the organization's data. These techniques are described in greater detail in Chapter 10.

DATABASE TECHNOLOGY AND MANAGEMENT

Databases require new software and a new staff specially trained in DBMS techniques as well as new management structures. Most corporations develop a database design and management group within the corporate information system division that is responsible for the more technical and operational aspects of managing data. The functions it performs are called **database administration**. This group does the following:

- Defines and organizes database structure and content
- Develops security procedures to safeguard the database
- Develops database documentation
- Maintains the database management software

In close cooperation with users, the design group establishes the physical database, the logical relations among elements, and the access rules and procedures.

database administration Refers to the more technical and operational aspects of managing data, including physical database design and maintenance.

USERS

A database serves a wider community of users than traditional systems. Relational systems with fourth-generation query languages permit employees who are not computer specialists to access large databases. In addition, users include trained computer specialists. In order to optimize access for nonspecialists, more resources must be devoted to training end users. Professional systems workers must be retrained in the DBMS language, DBMS application development procedures, and new software practices.

Management Challenges

Hierarchical database technology first became commercially available in the late 1960s. Since then, more sophisticated database models have appeared. Nevertheless, progress in creating a true database environment in organizations has been much slower than anticipated. Why? Three challenges stand out.

1. Organizational obstacles to a database environment. Implementing a database requires widespread organizational change in the role of information (and information managers), the allocation of power at senior levels, the ownership and sharing of information, and patterns of organizational agreement. A DBMS challenges the existing arrangements in an organization and for that reason often generates political resistance. In a traditional file environment, each department constructed files and programs to fulfill its specific needs. Now, with a database, files and programs must be built that take into account the full organization's interest in data. Although the organization has spent the money on the hardware and software for a database environment, it may not reap the benefits it should because it is unwilling to make the requisite organizational changes.

2. Cost/benefit considerations. The costs of moving to a database environment are tangible, up front, and large in the short term (three years). Most firms buy a commercial DBMS package and related hardware. The software alone can cost one-half million dollars for a full-function package with all options. New hardware may cost an additional $1 million to $2 million annually.

Unfortunately, the benefits of the DBMS are often intangible, back-loaded, and long term (five years). The systems that the DBMS seeks to replace generally work, although they are inefficient. For all of these reasons, and despite the clear advantages of the DBMS, the short-term costs of developing a DBMS often appear to be nearly as great as the benefits. The obvious long-term benefits of the DBMS tend to be severely discounted by managers, especially those unfamiliar with (and perhaps unfriendly to) systems. Moreover, it may not be cost-effective to build organization-wide databases that integrate all of the organization's data (Goodhue et al., September 1992).

3. Organizational placement of the data management function. Many organizations, seeking to avoid large commitments and organizational change, begin (and end) by buying a DBMS package and placing it in the hands of a low-level database group in the information systems department. Generally this leads to a piecemeal approach to database use; that is, small database systems will be developed for various divisions, functional areas, departments, and offices. Eventually this results in incompatible databases throughout the company and fails to address the key organizational issue: What is the role of information and who will manage it for the organization as a whole? Senior management must be persuaded to implement a data administration function and data planning methodology at the highest corporate level.

Summary

1. Describe traditional file organization and management techniques. In a traditional file environment, data records are organized using either a sequential file organization or a direct or random file organization. Records in a sequential file can be accessed sequentially or they can be accessed directly if the sequential file is on disk and uses an indexed sequential access method. Records on a file with direct file organization can be accessed directly without an index.

2. Explain the problems of the traditional file environment. By allowing different functional areas and groups in the organization to maintain their own files independently, the traditional file environment creates problems such as data redundancy and inconsistency, program-data dependence, inflexibility, poor security, and lack of data sharing and availability.

3. Describe how a database management system organizes information. Database management systems (DBMS) are the software that permits centralization of data and data management. A DBMS includes a data definition language, a data manipulation language, and a data dictionary capability. The most important feature of the DBMS is its ability to separate the logical and physical views of data. The user works with a logical view of data. The DBMS software translates user queries into queries that can be applied to the physical view of the data. The DBMS retrieves information so that the user does not have to be concerned with its physical location. This feature separates programs from data and from the management of data.

4. Identify the three principal database models. There are three principal logical database models: hierarchical, network, and relational. Each has unique advantages and disadvantages. Hierarchical systems, which support one-to-many relationships, are low in flexibility but high in processing speed and efficiency. Network systems support many-to-many relationships. Relational systems are relatively slow but are very flexible for supporting ad hoc requests for information and for combining information from different sources. The choice depends on the business requirements.

5. Discuss new database trends. It is no longer necessary for data to be centralized in a single, massive database. A complete database or portions of the database can be distributed to more than one location to increase responsiveness and reduce vulnerability and costs. There are two major types of distributed databases: *replicated databases* and *partitioned databases*. Object-oriented, hypermedia, and multidimensional databases may be alternatives to traditional database structures for certain types of applications. Object-oriented and hypermedia databases can store graphics and other types of data in addition to conventional text data to support multimedia applications. Hypermedia databases allow data to be stored in nodes linked together in any pattern established by the user. A multidimensional database represents relationships among data as a multidimensional structure, which can be visualized as cubes of data and cubes within cubes of data, allowing for more sophisticated data analysis. Data can be more conveniently analyzed across the enterprise by using a data warehouse, in which current and historical data are extracted from many different operational systems and consolidated for management decision making.

6. Explain the managerial and organizational requirements for creating a database environment. Development of a database environment requires much more than selection of technology. It requires a change in the corporation's attitude toward information. The organization must develop a data administration function and a data planning methodology. The database environment has developed more slowly than was originally anticipated. There is political resistance in organizations to many key database concepts, especially to sharing of information that has been controlled exclusively by one organizational group. There are difficult cost/benefit questions in database management. Often, to avoid raising difficult questions, database use begins and ends as a small effort isolated in the information systems department.

Key Terms

Field	**Index**	**Structured Query Language (SQL)**	**Entity-relationship diagram**
Record	**Direct file access method**	**Data dictionary**	**Distributed processing**
File	**Transform algorithm**	**Data element**	**Distributed database**
Entity	**Traditional file environment**	**Logical view**	**Object-oriented database**
Attribute	**Data redundancy**	**Physical view**	**Hypermedia database**
Key field	**Program-data dependence**	**Hierarchical data model**	**Multidimensional database model**
Sequential file organization	**Database**	**Pointer**	**Data warehouse**
Direct or random file organization	**Database management system (DBMS)**	**Network data model**	**Data administration**
Indexed sequential access method (ISAM)	**Data definition language**	**Relational data model**	**Information policy**
	Data manipulation language	**Tuple**	**Database administration**

Review Questions

1. Why is file management important for overall system performance?
2. Describe how indexes and key fields enable a program to access specific records in a file.
3. Define and describe the indexed sequential access method and the direct file access method.
4. List and describe some of the problems of the traditional file environment.
5. Define a database and a database management system.
6. Name and briefly describe the three components of a DBMS.
7. What is the difference between a logical and a physical view of data?
8. List some of the benefits of a DBMS.
9. Describe the three principal database models and the advantages and disadvantages of each.
10. What is a distributed database, and how does it differ from distributed data processing?
11. What are object-oriented hypermedia, and multidimensional databases? How do they differ from a traditional database?
12. What is a data warehouse? How can it benefit organizations?
13. What are the four key elements of a database environment? Describe each briefly.
14. Describe and briefly comment on the major management challenges in building a database environment.

Discussion Questions

1. It has been said that you do not need database management software to have a database environment. Discuss.
2. As an information system manager, you are concerned that the percentage of your staff working on maintenance of existing programs is growing and the

percentage working on new applications is declining. How could a database environment change this trend?

3. To what extent should end users be involved in the selection of a database management system and in database design?

Group Project

Form a group with half of your classmates. Consider two strategies for building a database environment. One strategy recommends that a small group be created in the information systems department to begin exploring database applications throughout the firm. The other strategy recommends the creation of a vice president of information and subsequent development of important database applications. Debate the costs and benefits of each strategy with the other group.

Case Study

CAN MIGRATION TO A RELATIONAL DATABASE MANAGEMENT SYSTEM HELP A GERMAN HOME LOAN LENDER?

Will moving to new database technology help a company stay competitive? Officials at BHW Bausparkasse AG thought so and gave that as the reason they moved from the IDMS database management system to the DB2 database management system. BHW, which is headquartered in Hameln, Germany, is the second-largest building society (home loan association) in Germany. They had used IDMS from Computer Associates (CA) of Islandia, New York (a network database management system), for many years with upward of 2000 programs accessing it. The 1991 decision to move to IBM's DB2, a relational database management system (RDBMS), was therefore a major strategic move.

BHW was founded in 1928 and by the 1990s was offering not only mortgages but also banking, real estate, and life insurance services. Its basic business data was stored in the IDMS DBMS. It required 55 gigabytes of storage to hold its 440 separate databases encompassing about 12,000 data elements—a gigantic system by any standards. To service its nearly 3 million customers and 12 million contracts, BHW found that its 2500 employees accessed IDMS on average about 33 million times per day, a very well-used system. Any improvement in its performance was bound to have a major and positive impact on the company.

To remain competitive, home loan companies such as BHW must be able to read the market and quickly provide customers with new financial products and services. According to Harry Gehlen, project manager for the database reengineering project, IDMS was not modern enough to allow BHW to react rapidly to customer needs. IDMS was a network DBMS, and BHW needed to move into the world of relational databases. For example, BHW wanted to develop an executive information system (EIS), an application that really only works well using a RDBMS. In addition Gehlen sees his company adding object-oriented databases next and then moving to distributed technology. He hopes that BHW will be able to establish total independence of its data from its application software. He believes that all these moves would be too complex to be done directly from a network DBMS. He concludes that a move to a RDBMS is a proper migration path to these other newer technologies.

BHW managers had looked at the possibility of moving to an RDBMS as early as 1987 but rejected the idea at that earlier date because they did not find any RDBMS that could meet their needs. What they did do was migrate from their longtime Unisys Corp. mainframe to IBM mainframes, thus positioning themselves very well to take advantage of RDBMS technology as it matured. By 1991 they determined that DB2 would serve their needs. However, because they had always been pleased with CA's IDMS, they also looked at its announced release, version 12. They rejected it for several reasons. First, version 12 was only announced, not actually released (software purchasers tend to be very wary of *vaporware*). Second, BHW required that any RDBMS it purchases must include standard SQL, but again, while CA had announced that its new product would be SQL compliant, CA indicated no shipping date. Third, the BHW IS staff did not find what they considered an adequate contact for their project at CA's European headquarters at Daarmstadt, Germany, and so they became very concerned about future product support should they convert to version 12. They also reasoned that a move to any relational database, whether it be DB2, IDMS, or some other product, would take about the same amount of time, so that they would gain nothing by staying with IDMS. Thus, they made the decision to purchase DB2.

Mario Pelleschi, senior vice president of CA's European operation, disputes Gehlen's version, and particularly the last point. He claims that his product has all the functionality of DB2, and that BHW could have converted to version 12 much more quickly and inexpensively because it would not need to rewrite programs or convert the databases. Gehlen countered that BHW "wanted to have a secure system which will be maintained for many years, and Computer Associates didn't seem to be the right partner for us in the future." This seemed to indicate that the real basis for the decision to go with DB2 was the vendor rather than the product.

The conversion project lasted only about 10 months and used highly automated tools. Before converting to DB2, Gehlen decided that they needed to convert the 2000 older VS COBOL programs into the more up-to-date COBOL Ansi 85, a task for which good automated tools were available. In the process, the team also identified programs which were no longer being used and eliminated them. His team also analyzed the IDMS data and prepared an automated conversion tool to use to convert the data to DB2. Once the data were converted, they found they were able to use the upgraded programs to access and update both the DB2 and IDMS databases, enabling them to work with either one, as needed. They set up a pilot project to convert three applications to DB2. This pilot lasted four months, and Gehlen used this time to educate his IS staff on DB2. In early 1993 they began to convert programs on a mass basis.

The project was not only successfully completed, but the team also had a positive surprise. They had expected that performance would decline in the conversion from IDMS, a network database, to DB2, a relational database. However, according to Gehlen, "performance went up by a factor of three to five," thus giving BHW a clear jump in productivity. ■

Source: Elke Gronert, "German Financial Institution Comes Home to Database," *Software Magazine*, March 1994.

Case Study Questions

1. Analyze BHW from the standpoint of the competitive forces and value chain models.
2. To what extent is selecting a database management system an important business decision? Did BHW's selection of DB2 enhance its competitive position?
3. From what you have learned in this case study, was a relational database management system the best choice for BHW Bausparkasse AG? Why or why not?
4. In the case study, Harry Gehlen is cited as the source for future plans to move BHW into object-oriented and distributed technologies. Comment on the appropriateness of using him as the source.
5. What management, organization, and technology factors should be considered when selecting a database management system?

References

Belkin, Nicholas J. and W. Bruce Croft. "Information Filtering and Information Retrieval: Two Sides of the Same Coin?" *Communications of the ACM* 35, no. 12 (November 1992).

Butterworth, Paul, Allen Otis, and Jacob Stein, "The GemStone Object Database Management System." *Communications of the ACM* 34, no. 10 (October 1991).

Carmel, Erran, William K. McHenry, and Yeshayahu Cohen. "Building Large, Dynamic Hypertexts: How Do We Link Intelligently?" *Journal of Management Information Systems* 6, no. 2 (Fall 1989).

Date, C.J. *An Introduction to Database Systems*. 5th ed. Reading, MA: Addison-Wesley, 1990.

Everest, G.C. *Database Management: Objectives, System Functions, and Administration*. New York: McGraw-Hill Book Company, 1985.

Fiori, Rich. "The Information Warehouse." *Relational Database Journal* (January–February 1995).

Fryer, Bronwyn. "Zeneca Takes its Medicine," *Information Week* (March 18, 1996).

Goldberg, Michael and Jaikumar Vijayan. "Data 'Wearhouse' Gains." *Computerworld* (April 8, 1996).

Goldstein, R.C., and J.B. McCririck. "What Do Data Administrators Really Do?" *Datamation* 26 (August 1980).

Goodhue, Dale L., Judith A. Quillard, and John F. Rockart. "Managing the Data Resource: A Contingency Perspective." *MIS Quarterly* (September 1988).

Goodhue, Dale L., Laurie J. Kirsch, Judith A. Quillard, and Michael D. Wybo. "Strategic Data Planning: Lessons from the Field." *MIS Quarterly* 16, no. 1 (March 1992).

Goodhue, Dale L., Michael D. Wybo, and Laurie J. Kirsch. "The Impact of Data Integration on the Costs and Benefits of Information Systems." *MIS Quarterly* 16, no. 3 (September 1992).

Grover, Varun, and James Teng. "How Effective Is Data Resource Management?" *Journal of Information Systems Management* (Summer 1991).

Hackathorn, Richard. "Data Warehousing Energizes Your Enterprise." *Datamation* (February 1, 1995).

Kahn, Beverly K. "Some Realities of Data Administration." *Communications of the ACM* 26 (October 1983).

Kahn, Beverly, and Linda Garceau. "The Database Administration Function." *Journal of Management Information Systems* 1 (Spring 1985).

Kent, William. "A Simple Guide to Five Normal Forms in Relational Database Theory." *Communications of the ACM* 26, no. 2 (February 1983).

King, John L., and Kenneth Kraemer. "Information Resource Management Cannot Work." *Information and Management* (1988).

Kroenke, David. *Database Processing.* 4th ed. New York: Macmillan Publishing Company, 1992.

Laudon, Kenneth C. *Dossier Society: Value Choices in the Design of National Information Systems.* New York: Columbia University Press, 1986.

Madnick, Stuart E., and Richard Y. Wang. "Evolution Towards Strategic Application of Databases through Composite Information Systems." *Journal of Management Information Systems* 5, no. 3 (Winter 1988–1989).

March, Salvatore T., and Young-Gul Kim. "Information Resource Management: A Metadata Perspective." *Journal of Management Information Systems* 5, no. 3 (Winter 1988–1989).

Martin, James. *Managing the Data-Base Environment.* Englewood Cliffs, NJ: Prentice-Hall, 1983.

Ricciuti, Mike. "Winning the Competitive Game," *Datamation* (February 15, 1994).

Silberschatz, Avi, Michael Stonebraker, and Jeff Ullman, eds. "Database Systems: Achievements and Opportunities." *Communications of the ACM* 34, no. 10 (October 1991).

Smith, John B., and Stephen F. Weiss. "Hypertext." *Communications of the ACM* 31, no. 7 (July 1988).

Chapter 8

Telecommunications

Networks Promote Global Trade

8.1 The Telecommunications Revolution
The Marriage of Computers and Communications
The Information Superhighway
Window on Organizations:
Telephone Companies Face an Expansive Future

8.2 Components and Functions of a Telecommunications System
Telecommunications System Components
Types of Signals: Analog and Digital
Types of Communications Channels
Characteristics of Communications Channels
Communications Processors
Telecommunications Software

8.3 Types of Telecommunications Networks
Network Topologies
Private Branch Exchanges and Local-Area Networks (LANs)
Wide-Area Networks (WANs)
Value-Added Networks (VANs)

8.4 How Organizations Use Telecommunications for Competitive Advantage
Facilitating Applications
Window on Management:
Monitoring Employees on Networks: Unethical or Good Business?

Window on Technology:
Intelligent Agents: Network Valets
Electronic Data Interchange
Groupware

8.5 Management Issues and Decisions
The Telecommunications Plan
Implementing the Plan

Management Challenges
Summary
Key Terms
Review Questions
Discussion Questions
Group Project
Case Study: Goodyear Automates Its Sales Force
References

Networks Promote Global Trade

By establishing a global electronic trading network, the United Nations is attempting to address some of the problems faced by small and medium-sized businesses in developing countries as they become involved with world trade. The goal of the network is to stimulate growth in international trade by helping small businesses or firms in countries without adequate foreign trade support services find information that would help them enter global markets. A pilot version of the network, known as the Global Trade Point Network, was established in late 1994 with a messaging service that companies can use to locate trade leads, negotiate business transactions, and make shipping and payment arrangements. "Trade points" have been established in Dar es Salaam;

Tanzania; Columbus, Ohio; and about 50 other sites around the world. They act as gateways into the network and as sites to store data being made available to network users. Users in many countries can access the trade points through their national telecommunications infrastructures. Those in countries that do not have adequate infrastructures can travel to any of the trade points to utilize the network. The electronic traffic on the network uses a range of existing telecommunications networks, including General Electric Information Systems (GEIS), AT&T's EasyLink, and the Internet (see Chapter 9).

The network will quickly be adding other services. Several trade points, including one in Bangkok, Thailand, are making electronic data interchange services for exchanging business transactions available based upon the United Nation's Edifact EDI standard. The United States Department of Commerce, whose Foreign and Commercial service has joined the pilot in its overseas offices, is making accessible through the network the National Trade Database which contains import/export guides, foreign trade indices, and other foreign trade data. The Bankers Association of Foreign Trade is establishing Trade Point databases that will bring traders together with businesses that finance international trade. The trade association also will help businesses obtain letters of credit if they are operating in countries where the local currency cannot readily be used in international trade. A number of American manufacturers, such as cylinder and industrial equipment producer Worthington Industries, are making product catalogs available on-line. The network enables such catalogs to list printed product information, show product pictures, and even show short, animated product demonstrations. Plans exist to expand these services and to add others, such as a database of trade leads, data on customs regulations, information on freight forwarders, and listings of international trade insurance companies.

Small and medium-sized businesses are finding that other networks have been established that are targeted to support them as well. For example, the more than 150,000 users of IndustryNet are often able to locate needed supplies quickly and easily via IndustryNet's catalogs on the World Wide Web. IndustryNet is planning for on-line purchase ordering. (Businesses can currently place orders via e-mail.) Companies such as Livingston Products, Inc., a small diversified manufacturer in Wheeling, Illinois, use IndustryNet to enhance their bargaining power by comparing various suppliers' selections and prices. Small-business users are particularly pleased with this service, and not only because it saves time and effort. They also point out that although large suppliers often will not deal with small businesses, transactions occur through this network without the supplier knowing the size of the purchaser, so smaller businesses are put on an equal footing with their larger competitors. Without such networks, only large

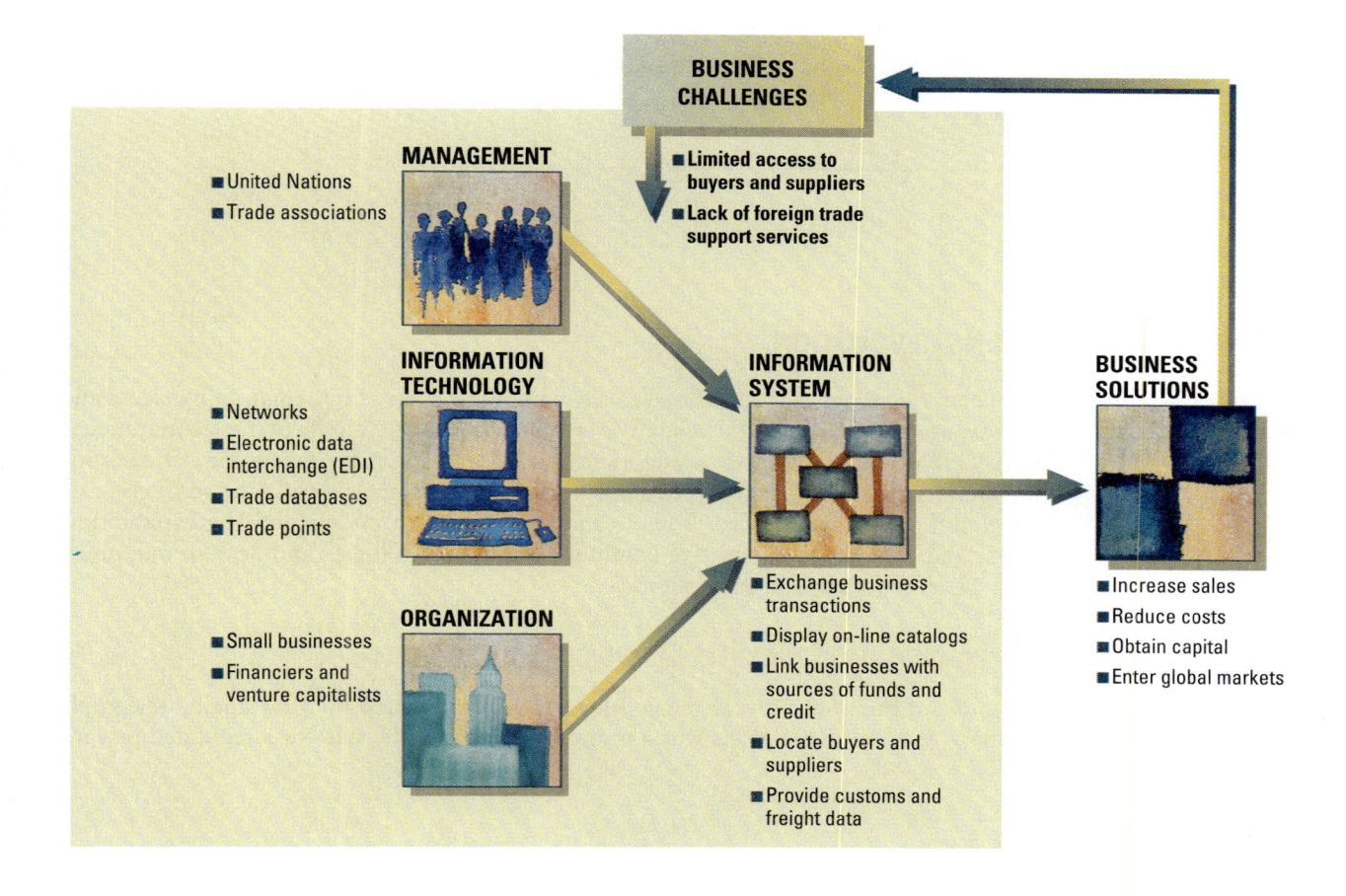

BUSINESS CHALLENGES
- Limited access to buyers and suppliers
- Lack of foreign trade support services

MANAGEMENT
- United Nations
- Trade associations

INFORMATION TECHNOLOGY
- Networks
- Electronic data interchange (EDI)
- Trade databases
- Trade points

ORGANIZATION
- Small businesses
- Financiers and venture capitalists

INFORMATION SYSTEM
- Exchange business transactions
- Display on-line catalogs
- Link businesses with sources of funds and credit
- Locate buyers and suppliers
- Provide customs and freight data

BUSINESS SOLUTIONS
- Increase sales
- Reduce costs
- Obtain capital
- Enter global markets

manufacturers could link their computers directly to those of their suppliers and distributors.

Even startup companies are finding on-line services to aid them. A number of new services have been established to facilitate bringing together entrepreneurs with venture capitalists. For example, American Venture Capital Exchange, an on-line service based in Portland, Oregon, lists entrepreneurial companies seeking investors at a flat fee of $150 each for six months. Potential investors pay $95 for 12 months of access. Ken Hamilton of Western Call & Decoy produces decoys and game calls for hunters and is a satisfied user of the exchange. After trying to raise investment funds through more traditional methods, he turned to the Venture Capital network, and within several months he found a venture capitalist who invested $110,000 in startup funds. ∎

Sources: Kate Maddox, Mitch Wagner and Clinton Wilder, "Making Money on the Web," *Information Week,* September 4, 1995; Timothy L. O'Brien, "Entrepreneurs Raise Funds Through On-line Computer Services," *The Wall Street Journal,* June 2, 1994; and Lynda Radosevich, "United Nations Launches Worldwide Network," *Computerworld,* October 24, 1994.

Many companies, large and small from all over the world, are finding they can benefit from telecommunications to locate suppliers and buyers, to negotiate contracts with them, and to service their trades. In fact, the uses of telecommunications are multiplying for research, customer support, and even for organizational coordination and control. Many of the technical advances in computing and information systems, such as on-line processing and providing direct access to data, would be impossible without telecommunications technology.

Telecommunications has become so essential to the conduct of business life that managers will be making telecommunications-related decisions throughout their careers. This chapter describes the components of telecommunications systems, showing how they can be arranged to create various types of telecommunications networks and network-based applications that can increase the efficiency and competitiveness of an organization. It provides a method for determining the organization's telecommunications requirements.

Learning Objectives

After completing this chapter, you will be able to:

1. Describe the basic components of a telecommunications system.
2. Measure the capacity of telecommunications channels and evaluate transmission media.
3. Describe the three basic network topologies.
4. Classify the various types of telecommunications networks.
5. Identify telecommunications applications that can provide competitive advantages to organizations.
6. Explain the criteria used in planning for telecommunications systems.

8.1 THE TELECOMMUNICATIONS REVOLUTION

telecommunications The communication of information by electronic means, usually over some distance.

Telecommunications can be defined as the communication of information by electronic means, usually over some distance. We are currently in the middle of a telecommunications revolution that has two components: rapid changes in the technology of communications and equally important changes in the ownership, control, and marketing of telecommunications services. Today's managers need to understand the capabilities, costs, and benefits of alternative communications technologies and how to maximize their benefits for their organizations.

THE MARRIAGE OF COMPUTERS AND COMMUNICATIONS

For most of the last 120 years since Alexander Bell invented the first singing telegraph in 1876, telecommunications was a monopoly of either the state or a regulated private firm. In the United States, American Telephone and Telegraph (AT&T) was the largest regulated monopoly, providing virtually all telecommunications services. In Europe and in the rest of the world, there is a state post, telephone, and telegraph authority (PTT). In the United States the monopoly ended in 1984, when the Justice Department forced AT&T to give up its monopoly and allow competing firms to sell telecommunications services and equipment.

The end of AT&T's monopoly widened the market for new telecommunications technologies and devices, from cheaper long-distance service to telephone answering equipment, cellular telephones, and private satellite services. AT&T itself started marketing computing services and computing equipment.

Changes in the telecommunications industry were accompanied by changes in telecommunications technology. Previously, telecommunications meant voice transmission over telephone lines. Today, much telecommunications transmission is digital data transmission, using computers to transmit data from one location to another. On-line information systems and remote access to information would be impossible without telecommunications. Table 8.1 shows some of the common tasks performed by computer systems that would be impossible without advanced telecommunications.

THE INFORMATION SUPERHIGHWAY

Deregulation and the marriage of computers and communications has also made it possible for the telephone companies to expand from traditional voice communications into new information services, such as providing transmission of news reports, stock reports, television programs, and movies. The Window on Organizations describes how the telecommunications revolution has allowed the telephone companies created by the breakup of AT&T to move into the information service business.

The efforts described in the Window on Organizations are laying the foundation for the **information superhighway,** a vast web of high-speed digital telecommunications

information superhighway
High-speed digital telecommunications networks that are national or worldwide in scope and accessible by the general public rather than restricted to use by members of a specific organization or set of organizations such as a corporation.

Table 8.1 Common Tasks Performed by Computer Systems Requiring Telecommunications

Application	Example	Requirements
Business		
On-line data entry	Inventory control	Transactions occurring several times/second, direct response required
On-line text retrieval	Hospital information systems; library systems	Response required in real time; high character volumes
Inquiry/response	Point-of-sale system; airline reservation system; credit checking	Transactions several times/second; instant response within seconds
Administrative message switching	Electronic mail	Short response and delivery times (minutes to hours)
Process control	Computer aided manufacturing (CAM); numeric control of machine tools	Continuous input transactions and on-line responses required
Intercomputer data exchange	International transfer of bank funds	Infrequent but high-volume bursts of information; transfer of large data blocks; on-line immediate response
Home		
Inquiry response	Home banking; shopping; ordering	On-line transactions collected with high frequency
Text retrieval	Home education	High-volume, rapid transmission
Special entertainment	Sports; polling and political participation	High-capacity video and data capabilities

Window on Organizations

TELEPHONE COMPANIES FACE AN EXPANSIVE FUTURE

On February 8, 1996, President Clinton signed the Telecommunications Act of 1996, the most extensive deregulation of telecommunications to date. The law freed telephone companies, broadcasters, and cable operators to enter each other's markets. Already local telephone companies are entering the long-distance phone business; long-distance and cable companies, such as AT&T and Time-Warner, are entering the local telephone business; and telephone companies are beginning to sell cable TV services over their phone lines. How will this change the landscape for the telephone companies?

Telephone companies already bundle services. For example, AT&T offers a package combining long-distance and cellular phone service, Internet access, and satellite TV in all 50 U.S. states, and it will soon add local phone service in some areas. Sprint joined three cable companies to offer combined long-distance, wireless, local, and entertainment services. Earlier federal court rulings allowed the telephone companies to own information services, so that they could deliver movies and television to homes as well as telephone calls.

The new freedom will change many phone company practices. For instance, telephone companies will likely cease subsidizing low residential telephone rates with high business rates. Many practices will occur because federal government rules will supersede state and local regulations, creating greater standardization nationwide.

One outcome will be the expansion of the information superhighway. This is very expensive—fiber-optic and wireless networks are costly to build. However, once built, the cost per user and per transaction will drop dramatically, resulting in an explosion of business. In areas where communications, computer, and entertainment industries overlap, 400,000 jobs were created in 1995 alone, 20 percent of all jobs created that year in the United States. Local phone companies appear well placed to profit from this because they are very profitable, with 12 percent after-tax margins, and so have the funds to invest. Long-distance

> **To Think About:** How has the business strategy of telephone companies changed as the result of deregulation? What are some of the obstacles the telephone companies now face?

companies have one advantage—their high-speed fiber-optic and cellular networks.

Europe has lagged behind the United States in deregulation, and European markets remain closed to competition in public telephone services. However, worldwide competition is forcing great changes so that by January, 1998, twenty European countries will be open to telecommunications competition. Meanwhile, competition is already intense for corporate network and mobile phone services. Also, companies are joining forces to build networks to challenge existing monopolies. For example, Bell Atlantic, France Télécom, and Deutsche Telekom have joined to fight Telecom Italia's monopoly. Beginning July, 1996, cable companies, railways, and utilities are being freed to lease their phone lines to anyone, again challenging national monopolies.

Sources: Gail Edmondson and Karen Lowry Miller, "Europe's Markets Are Getting Rewired, Too," *Business Week,* April 8, 1996; Bryan Gruley and Albert R. Karr, "Telecom Vote Signals Competitive Free-for-All," *The Wall Street Journal,* February 2, 1996; Catherine Arnst and Michael Mandel, "The Coming Telescramble," *Business Week,* April 8, 1995.

---

networks delivering information, education, and entertainment services to offices and homes. The networks comprising the highway are national or worldwide in scope and accessible by the general public rather than restricted to use by members of a specific organization or set of organizations such as a corporation. Some analysts believe the information superhighway will have as profound an impact on economic and social life in the twenty-first century as railroads and interstate highways did in the past.

The press has stressed the home entertainment implications of this technology, extolling movies on demand with VCR-like forward and reverse controls. This technology has also been touted for its ability to offer an almost unlimited number of cable television channels—the standard number quoted is 500. Users will be able to read newspapers and magazines via these networks, and many predict the decline of paper-based news media as a result. The technology will make possible interactive communications between the televised programs and the viewers at home. While all of this is indeed an important aspect of the information superhighway, the concept is much broader and richer than indicated in these popular press reports. It involves new ways to obtain and disseminate information that virtually eliminate the barriers of time and place. The business implications of this new superhighway are only now beginning to emerge. The most well known and easily the largest implementation of the information superhighway is the Internet.

Another aspect of the information superhighway is the national computing network proposed by the U.S. federal government described in the Window on Technology in Chapter 4. The Clinton administration envisions this network linking universities, research centers, libraries, hospitals, and other institutions that need to exchange vast amounts of information while being accessible in homes and schools.

8.2 COMPONENTS AND FUNCTIONS OF A TELECOMMUNICATIONS SYSTEM

A **telecommunications system** is a collection of compatible hardware and software arranged to communicate information from one location to another. Figure 8.1 illustrates the components of a typical telecommunications system. Telecommunications systems can transmit text, graphic images, voice, or video information. This section describes the major components of telecommunications systems. Subsequent sections describe how the components can be arranged into various types of networks.

telecommunications system A collection of compatible hardware and software arranged to communicate information from one location to another.

TELECOMMUNICATIONS SYSTEM COMPONENTS

The essential components of a telecommunications system are these:

1. Computers to process information
2. Terminals or any input/output devices that send or receive data
3. Communications channels, the links by which data or voice are transmitted between sending and receiving devices in a network. Communications channels use various

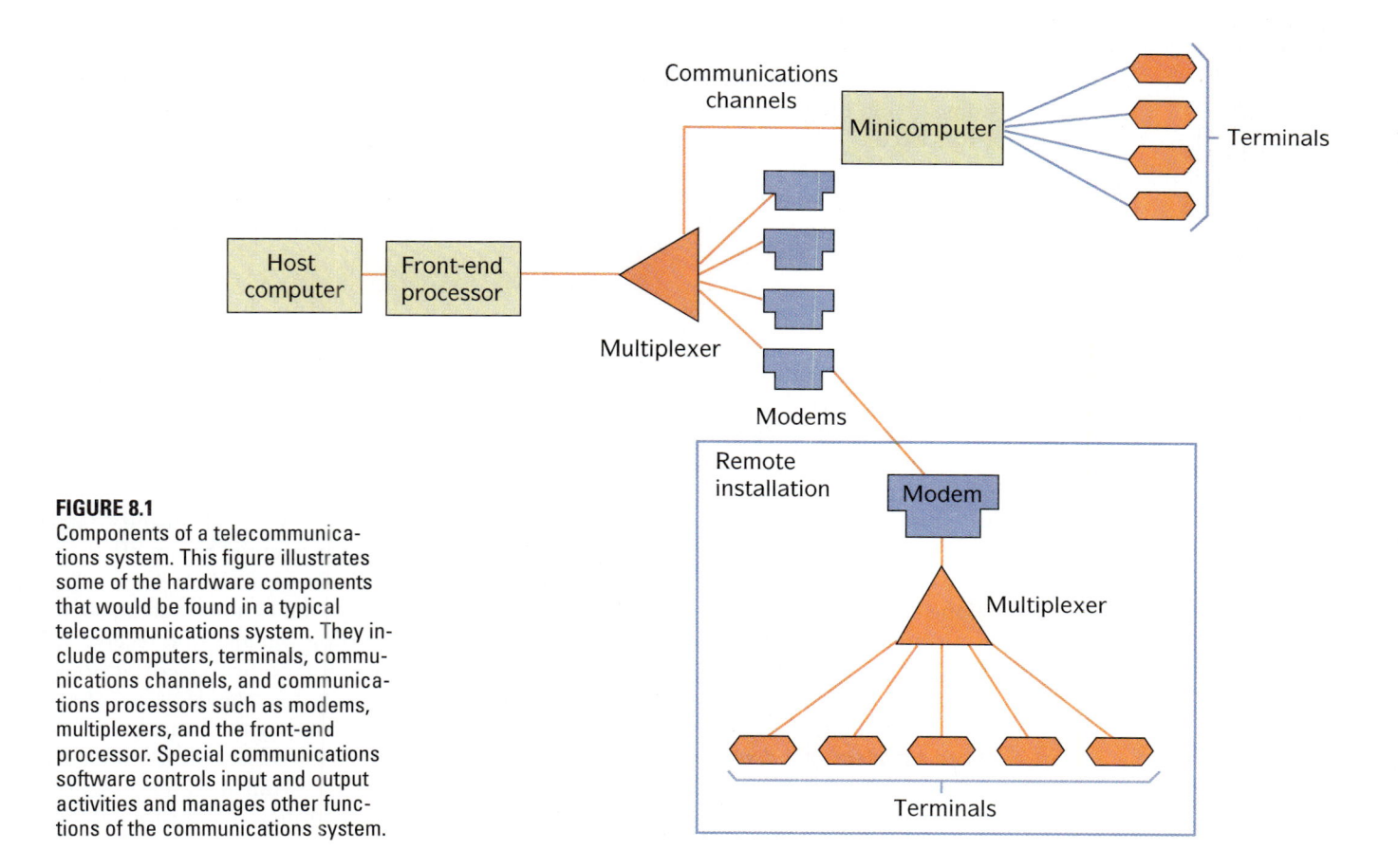

FIGURE 8.1
Components of a telecommunications system. This figure illustrates some of the hardware components that would be found in a typical telecommunications system. They include computers, terminals, communications channels, and communications processors such as modems, multiplexers, and the front-end processor. Special communications software controls input and output activities and manages other functions of the communications system.

8.2 Components and Functions of a Telecommunications System   233

communications media, such as telephone lines, fiber-optic cables, coaxial cables, and wireless transmission.

4. Communications processors, such as modems, multiplexers, controllers, and front-end processors, which provide support functions for data transmission and reception
5. Communications software that controls input and output activities and manages other functions of the communications network

Functions of Telecommunications Systems

In order to send and receive information from one place to another, a telecommunications system must perform a number of separate functions, which are largely invisible to the people using the system. A telecommunications system transmits information, establishes the interface between the sender and the receiver, routes messages along the most efficient paths, performs elementary processing of the information to ensure that the right message gets to the right receiver, performs editorial tasks on the data (such as checking for errors and rearranging the format), and converts messages from one speed (say, the speed of a computer) into the speed of a communications line or from one format to another. Lastly, the telecommunications system controls the flow of information. Many of these tasks are accomplished by computer.

Protocols

protocol A set of rules and procedures that govern transmission between the components in a network.

A telecommunications network typically contains diverse hardware and software components that need to work together to transmit information. Different components in a network can communicate by adhering to a common set of rules that enable them to talk to each other. This set of rules and procedures governing transmission between two points in a network is called a **protocol**. Each device in a network must be able to interpret the other device's protocol.

The principal functions of protocols in a telecommunications network are to identify each device in the communication path, to secure the attention of the other device, to verify correct receipt of the transmitted message, to verify that a message requires retransmission because it cannot be correctly interpreted, and to perform recovery when errors occur.

Although business, government, and the computer industry recognize the need for common communications standards, the industry has yet to put a universal standard into effect. Chapter 9 discusses the question of telecommunications standards in greater detail.

TYPES OF SIGNALS: ANALOG AND DIGITAL

Information travels through a telecommunications system in the form of electromagnetic signals. Signals are represented in two ways: There are analog and digital signals. An **analog signal** is represented by a continuous waveform that passes through a communications medium. Analog signals are used to handle voice communications and to reflect variations in pitch.

analog signal A continuous waveform that passes through a communications medium. Used for voice communications.

digital signal A discrete waveform that transmits data coded into two discrete states as 1-bits and 0-bits, which are represented as on–off electrical pulses; used for data communications.

modem A device for translating digital signals into analog signals and vice versa.

A **digital signal** is a discrete, rather than a continuous, waveform. It transmits data coded into two discrete states: 1-bits and 0-bits, which are represented as on–off electrical pulses. Most computers communicate with digital signals, as do many local telephone companies and some larger networks. But if a telecommunications system, such as a traditional telephone network, is set up to process analog signals—the receivers, transmitters, amplifiers, and so forth—a digital signal cannot be processed without some alterations. All digital signals must be translated into analog signals before they can be transmitted in an analog system. The device that performs this translation is called a **modem**. (*Modem* is an abbreviation for MOdulation/DEModulation.) A modem translates the digital signals of a computer into analog form for transmission over ordinary telephone lines, or it translates analog signals back into digital form for reception by a computer (see Figure 8.2).

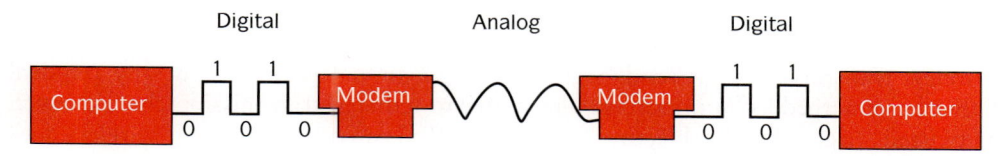

FIGURE 8.2
Functions of the modem. A modem is a device that translates digital signals from a computer into analog form so that they can be transmitted over analog telephone lines. The modem is also used to translate analog signals back into digital form for the receiving computer.

TYPES OF COMMUNICATIONS CHANNELS

Communications **channels** are the means by which data are transmitted from one device in a network to another. A channel can utilize different kinds of telecommunications transmission media: twisted wire, coaxial cable, fiber optics, terrestrial microwave, satellite, and wireless transmission. Each has certain advantages and limitations. High-speed transmission media are more expensive in general, but they can handle higher volumes (which reduces the cost per bit). For instance, the cost per bit of data can be lower via satellite link than via leased telephone line if a firm uses the satellite link 100 percent of the time. There is also a wide range of speeds possible for any given medium depending on the software and hardware configuration.

channels The links by which data or voice are transmitted between sending and receiving devices in a network.

Twisted Wire

Twisted wire consists of strands of copper wire twisted in pairs and is the oldest transmission medium. Most of the telephone system in a building relies on twisted wires installed for analog communication. Most buildings have additional cables installed for future expansion, and so there are usually a number of twisted-pair cables unused in every office of every building. These unused cables can be used for digital communications. Although it is low in cost and is already in place, **twisted wire** is relatively slow for transmitting data, and high-speed transmission causes interference called *crosstalk*. On the other hand, new software and hardware have raised the capacity of existing twisted-wire cables up to 10 megabits per second, which is often adequate for connecting microcomputers and other office devices.

twisted wire A transmission medium consisting of pairs of twisted copper wires. Used to transmit analog phone conversations but can be used for data transmission.

Coaxial Cable

Coaxial cable, like that used for cable television, consists of thickly insulated copper wire, which can transmit a larger volume of data than twisted wire can. It is often used in place of twisted wire for important links in a telecommunications network because it is a faster, more interference-free transmission medium, with speeds of up to 200 megabits per second. However, coaxial cable is thick, is hard to wire in many buildings, and cannot support analog phone conversations. It must be moved when computers and other devices are moved.

coaxial cable A transmission medium consisting of thickly insulated copper wire. Can transmit large volumes of data quickly.

Fiber Optics

Fiber-optic cable consists of thousands of strands of clear glass fiber, each the thickness of a human hair, which are bound into cables. Data are transformed into pulses of light, which are sent through the fiber-optic cable by a laser device at a rate of 500 kilobits to several billion bits per second. On the one hand, fiber-optic cable is considerably faster, lighter, and more durable than wire media and is well suited to systems requiring transfers of large volumes of data. On the other hand, fiber-optic cable is more difficult to work with, more expensive, and harder to install. It is best used as the backbone of a network and not for connecting isolated devices to a backbone. In most networks fiber-optic cable is used as the high-speed trunk line, while twisted wire and coaxial cable are used to connect the trunk line to individual devices.

fiber-optic cable A fast, light, and durable transmission medium consisting of thin strands of clear glass fiber bound into cables. Data are transmitted as light pulses.

Wireless Transmission

Wireless transmission that sends signals through air or space without any physical tether has emerged as an important alternative to tethered transmission channels such as twisted wire, coaxial cable, and fiber optics. Today, common uses of wireless data transmission include pagers, cellular telephones, microwave transmissions, communication satellites, mobile data networks, personal communications services, personal digital assistants, and even television remote controls.

The wireless transmission medium is the *electromagnetic spectrum*, illustrated in Figure 8.3. Some types of wireless transmission, such as microwave or infrared, by nature occupy specific spectrum frequency ranges (measured in megahertz). Other types of wireless transmissions are actually functional uses, such as cellular telephones and paging devices, that have been assigned a specific range of frequencies by national regulatory agencies and international agreements. Each frequency range has its own strengths and limitations, and these have helped determine the specific function or data communications niche assigned to it.

microwave A high-volume, long-distance, point-to-point transmission in which high-frequency radio signals are transmitted through the atmosphere from one terrestrial transmission station to another.

satellite The transmission of data using orbiting satellites to serve as relay stations for transmitting microwave signals over very long distances.

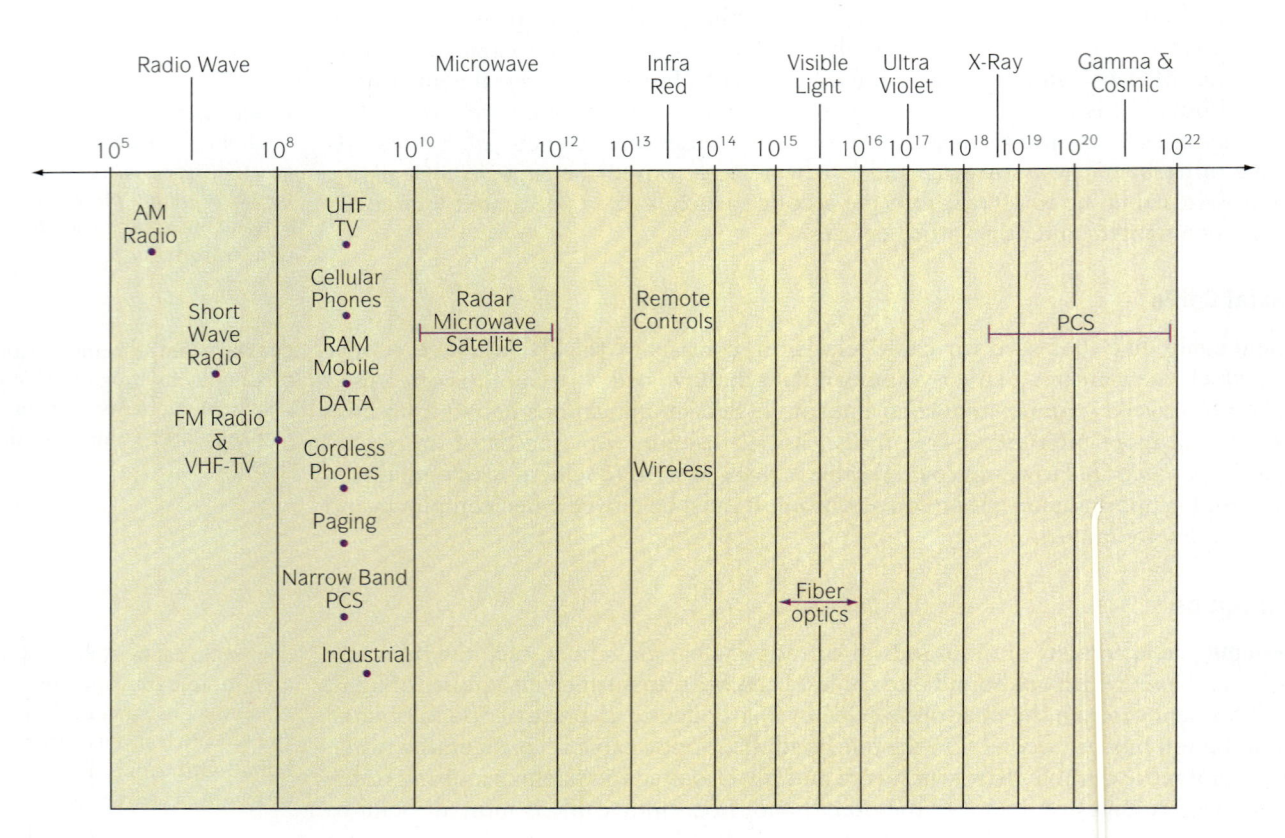

Microwave systems, both terrestrial and celestial, transmit high-frequency radio signals through the atmosphere and are widely used for high-volume, long-distance, point-to-point communication. Because microwave signals follow a straight line and do not bend with the curvature of the earth, long-distance terrestrial transmission systems require that transmission stations be positioned 25 to 30 miles apart, adding to the expense of microwave.

This problem can be solved by bouncing microwave signals off **satellites,** enabling them to serve as relay stations for microwave signals transmitted from terrestrial stations. Communication satellites are cost effective for transmitting large quantities of data over long distances. Satellites are typically used for communications in large, geo-

FIGURE 8.3
Frequency ranges for communications media and devices. Each telecommunications transmission medium or device occupies a different frequency range, measured in megahertz, on the electromagnetic spectrum.

graphically dispersed organizations that would be difficult to tie together through cabling media or terrestrial microwave. For instance, the Rite Aid pharmacy chain uses a satellite network to provide instant two-way communications between its stores and its corporate mainframe in Camp Hill, Pennsylvania. Each store has a server (a powerful microcomputer dedicated to storing data and programs—see Section 8.3) which supports cash registers, pharmacy terminals, and the manager's terminal and tracks inventory. The server can communicate with the central mainframe via satellite to post sales and to fill prescriptions stored in the mainframe database (see Figure 8.4).

Conventional communication satellites move in stationary orbits approximately 22,000 miles above the earth. A newer satellite medium, the **low-orbit satellite,** is beginning to be deployed. These satellites travel much closer to the earth and so are able to pick up signals from weak transmitters. They also consume less power and cost less to launch than conventional satellites. With such wireless networks, business persons will be able to travel virtually anywhere in the world and have access to full communication capabilities, regardless of the adequacy of the telecommunications infrastructure of the country they are in.

low-orbit satellite Satellites that travel much closer to the earth than traditional satellites and so are able to pick up signals from weak transmitters while consuming less power.

Other wireless transmission technologies have recently been developed and are being used in situations requiring mobile computing power. **Paging systems** have been in common use for several decades, originally just beeping when the user receives a message and requiring the user to telephone an office to learn what the message is. Today, paging devices can receive short alphanumeric messages that the user reads on the pager's screen. Paging is useful for communicating with mobile workers such as repair crews; one-way paging can also provide an inexpensive way of communicating with workers in offices. For example, Ethos Corporation in Boulder, Colorado, markets mortgage-processing software that uses a paging system that can deliver daily changes

paging system A wireless transmission technology in which the pager beeps when the user receives a message; used to transmit short alphanumeric messages.

More than 3000 Amoco dealers use the ARSTA (Amoco Retail Systems Technology Architecture) satellite communications network to speed communications, transfer data, and reduce costs.

FIGURE 8.4
Satellite transmission at Rite Aid. Satellites help the Rite Aid pharmacy chain transmit data between its 2960 stores and its corporate mainframe in Camp Hill, Pennsylvania. *Adapted from Jean S. Bozman, "UNIX PCs Strengthen Pharmacy Chain," Computerworld, August 1, 1994. Copyright 1994 by Computerworld, Inc., Framingham, MA 01701. Reprinted from Computerworld. Reprinted by permission.*

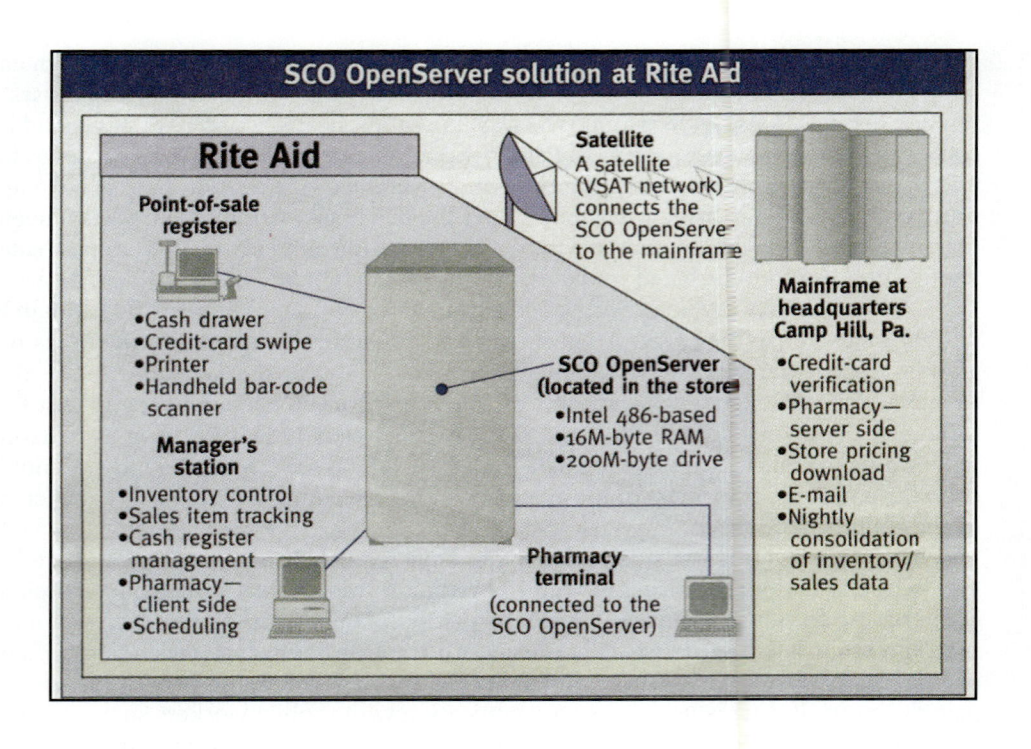

SCO OpenServer solution at Rite Aid

Rite Aid

Point-of-sale register
- Cash drawer
- Credit-card swipe
- Printer
- Handheld bar-code scanner

Manager's station
- Inventory control
- Sales item tracking
- Cash register management
- Pharmacy—client side
- Scheduling

SCO OpenServer (located in the store)
- Intel 486-based
- 16M-byte RAM
- 200M-byte drive

Pharmacy terminal (connected to the SCO OpenServer)

Satellite
A satellite (VSAT network) connects the SCO OpenServer to the mainframe

Mainframe at headquarters Camp Hill, Pa.
- Credit-card verification
- Pharmacy—server side
- Store pricing download
- E-mail
- Nightly consolidation of inventory/sales data

---

in mortgage rates to thousands of real estate brokers. The data transmitted through the paging network can be downloaded and manipulated, saving brokers approximately one and a half hours of work each week.

Cellular telephones (sometimes called mobile telephones) work by using radio waves to communicate with radio antennas (towers) placed within adjacent geographic areas called *cells*. A telephone message is transmitted to the local cell by the cellular telephone and then is handed off from antenna to antenna—cell to cell—until it reaches the cell of its destination, where it is transmitted to the receiving telephone. As a cellular signal travels from one cell into another, a computer that monitors signals from the cells switches the conversation to a radio channel assigned to the next cell. The radio antenna cells normally cover eight-mile hexagonal cells, although their radius is smaller in densely populated localities. While the cellular telephone infrastructure has primarily been used for voice transmission, recent developments have made it capable of two-way digital data transmission. The breakthrough came in the form of a transmission stan-

cellular telephone A device that transmits voice or data, using radio waves to communicate with radio antennas placed within adjacent geographic areas called *cells*.

Pagers are increasingly used for wireless transmission of brief messages in China and throughout the globe.

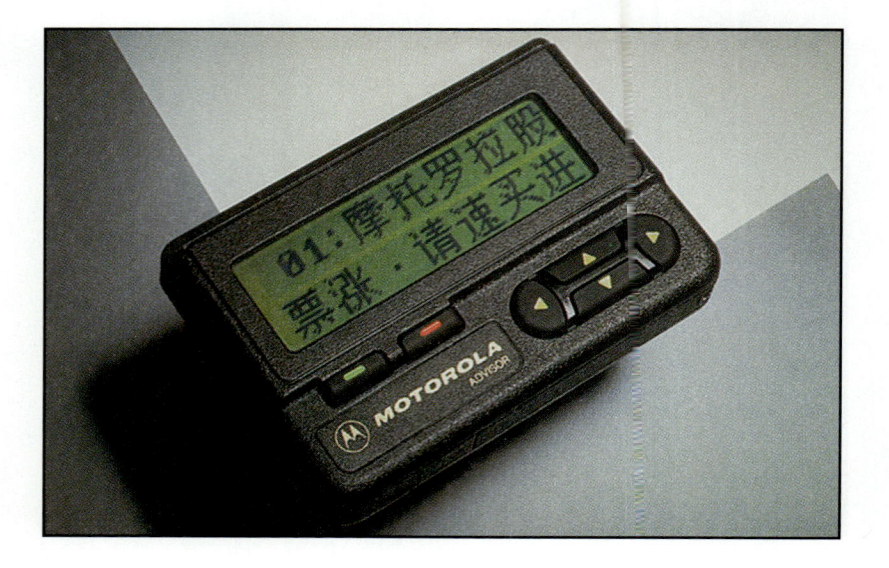

dard called Cellular Digital Packet Data (CDPD), with the support of such telecommunications giants as AT&T, Bell Atlantic, Nynex, Sprint, and McCaw Cellular. CDPD uses the pauses in voice communication, when the transmission channel is idle, filling them with packets of data.

Wireless networks explicitly designed for two-way transmission of data files are called **mobile data networks**. These radio-based networks transmit data to and from handheld computers. Another type of mobile data network is based upon a series of radio towers constructed specifically to transmit text and data. RAM Mobile Data (jointly owned by Ram Broadcasting and Bell South) and Ardis (jointly owned by IBM and Motorola) are two publicly available networks that use such media for national two-way data transmission. Mastercard uses the RAM Mobile Data network for wireless credit-card verification terminals at county fairs or merchants' sidewalk kiosks. Otis Elevators uses the Ardis network to dispatch repair technicians around the country from a single office in Connecticut and to receive their reports. Value-added companies are now beginning to offer services built upon those mobile data networks. For instance, RadioMail has introduced a wireless fax service at only 99 cents per domestic page. The cellular telephone network is also starting to be used for this purpose.

Wireless support is becoming more common in both computer hardware and software. Portable computers, using either internal or external wireless modems, can now be linked to wireless networks. IBM ThinkPad notebooks, for example, can include the hardware and software for wireless communications.

One new wireless cellular technology that should soon be available for both voice and data is called **personal communication services (PCS)**. PCS uses lower-power, higher-frequency radio waves than does cellular technology. Because of the lower power, PCS cells are much smaller and so must be more numerous and closer together. The higher-frequency signals enable PCS devices to be used in many places where cellular telephones are not effective, such as in tunnels and inside office buildings. Moreover, because PCS telephones need less power, they can be much smaller (shirt-pocket size) and less expensive than cellular telephones. According to some estimates PCS networks will offer better service and quality than existing cellular telephones while being 20 times more efficient. Also, because they operate at higher, less-crowded frequencies than cellular telephones (see Figure 8.3), they will have the bandwidth to offer video and multimedia communication.

mobile data networks Wireless networks that enable two-way transmission of data files cheaply and efficiently.

personal communication services (PCS) A new wireless cellular technology that uses lower-power, higher-frequency radio waves than does cellular technology and so can be used with smaller-sized telephones inside buildings and tunnels.

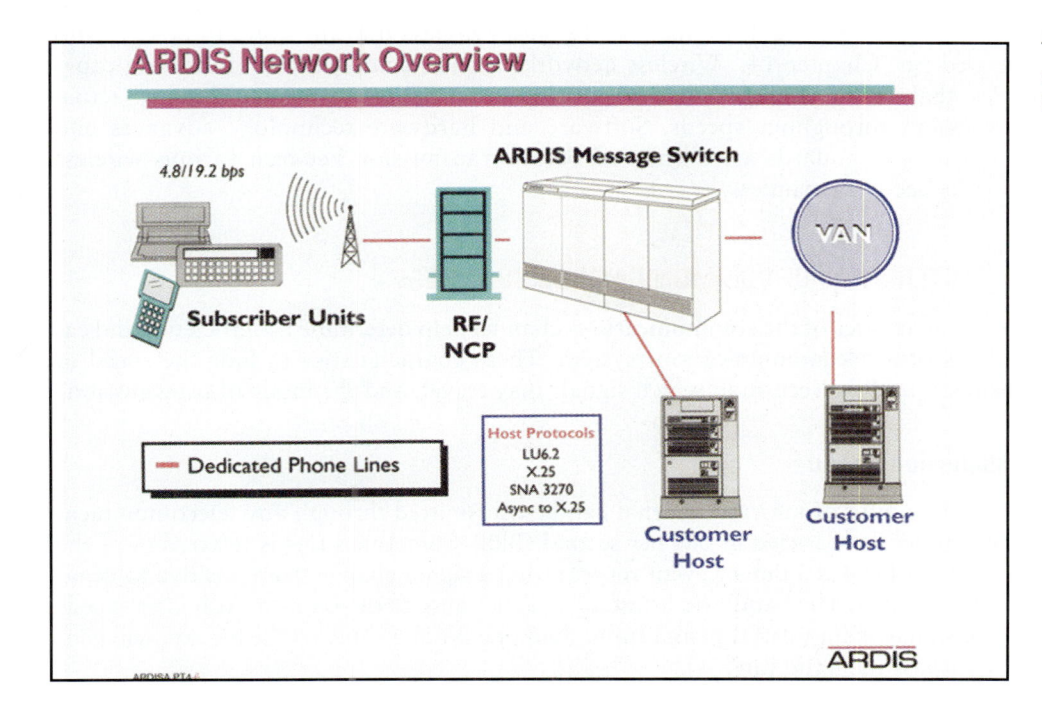

This schematic diagram shows a network overview of the Ardis wireless data transmission system.

personal digital assistants (PDA) Small, pen-based, handheld computers with built-in wireless telecommunications capable of entirely digital communications transmission.

Personal digital assistants (PDA) are small, pen-based, handheld computers capable of entirely digital communications transmission. They have built-in wireless telecommunications capabilities as well as work organization software. A well-known example is the one-pound Apple Newton MessagePad. It can be equipped with a special card that allows it to function as a pager, and when hooked to a cigarette package–sized modem, it will transmit e-mail, faxes, documents for printing, and data to other computers. The Newton also includes an electronic scheduler, calendar, and notepad software and is able to accept handwriting input entered through its special stylus.

JC Penney Co., the fourth-largest retailer in the United States with 1200 retail stores and a large catalog business, provides an example of a mundane but very practical use of wireless technology. The company operates three warehouses nationwide with a combined storage area of 3.3 million square feet. Receiving and storing the goods and later locating, pulling, and shipping them consumes a great deal of time and effort and is very costly. JC Penney has made both processes more efficient, faster, and less expensive through the use of computers and wireless telecommunications, as illustrated in Figure 8.5. As shipments arrive the goods are immediately bar coded. Wireless handheld scanners then transmit the data on each box to a warehouse computer, which immediately assigns a storage location and wirelessly transmits this data to the forklift operator. The company selected wireless scanners to be used in receiving in order to free the warehouse workers from the inconvenience and potential dangers of strapped-on wired scanners. Later, when goods are to be picked and placed on a conveyor belt that brings them to the shipping dock, the forklift operator is sent a picking list with location data by wireless transmission. Scanners used to read and transmit data on goods on the conveyor belt are wired. (Because these scanners are stationary—the goods pass under them—the designers found no gain in using wireless technology for this task.) JC Penney claims a 23-percent improvement in accuracy as a result of the system, as well as enhanced productivity. The company also expects the system to eliminate the expensive twice-yearly inventory warehouse shutdowns.

While wireless telecommunications holds great potential for the expansion of communication worldwide, the technology does have limitations as well. Wireless transmission is highly error prone because it is susceptible to many kinds of environmental disturbance, from magnetic interference from the sun to automobile ignition emissions. Bandwidth and energy supply in wireless devices require careful management from both hardware and software standpoints (Imielinski and Badrinath, 1994). Security and privacy will be more difficult to maintain because wireless transmission can be easily intercepted (see Chapter 14). Wireless networks require complex error-correcting capabilities that result in repeated transmission of message segments, slowing actual transmission throughput speeds. Software and hardware technology advances and agreement on standards are all needed before transmission between various wireless networks becomes seamless.

CHARACTERISTICS OF COMMUNICATIONS CHANNELS

The characteristics of the communications channel help determine the efficiency and capabilities of a telecommunications system. These characteristics include the speed of transmission, the direction in which signals may travel, and the mode of transmission.

Transmission Speed

The total amount of information that can be transmitted through any telecommunications channel is measured in bits per second (BPS). Sometimes this is referred to as the *baud rate*. A **baud** is a binary event representing a signal change from positive to negative or vice versa. The baud rate is not always the same as the bit rate. At higher speeds a single signal change can transmit more than one bit at a time, so the bit rate will generally surpass the baud rate.

baud A change in signal from positive to negative or vice versa that is used as a measure of transmission speed.

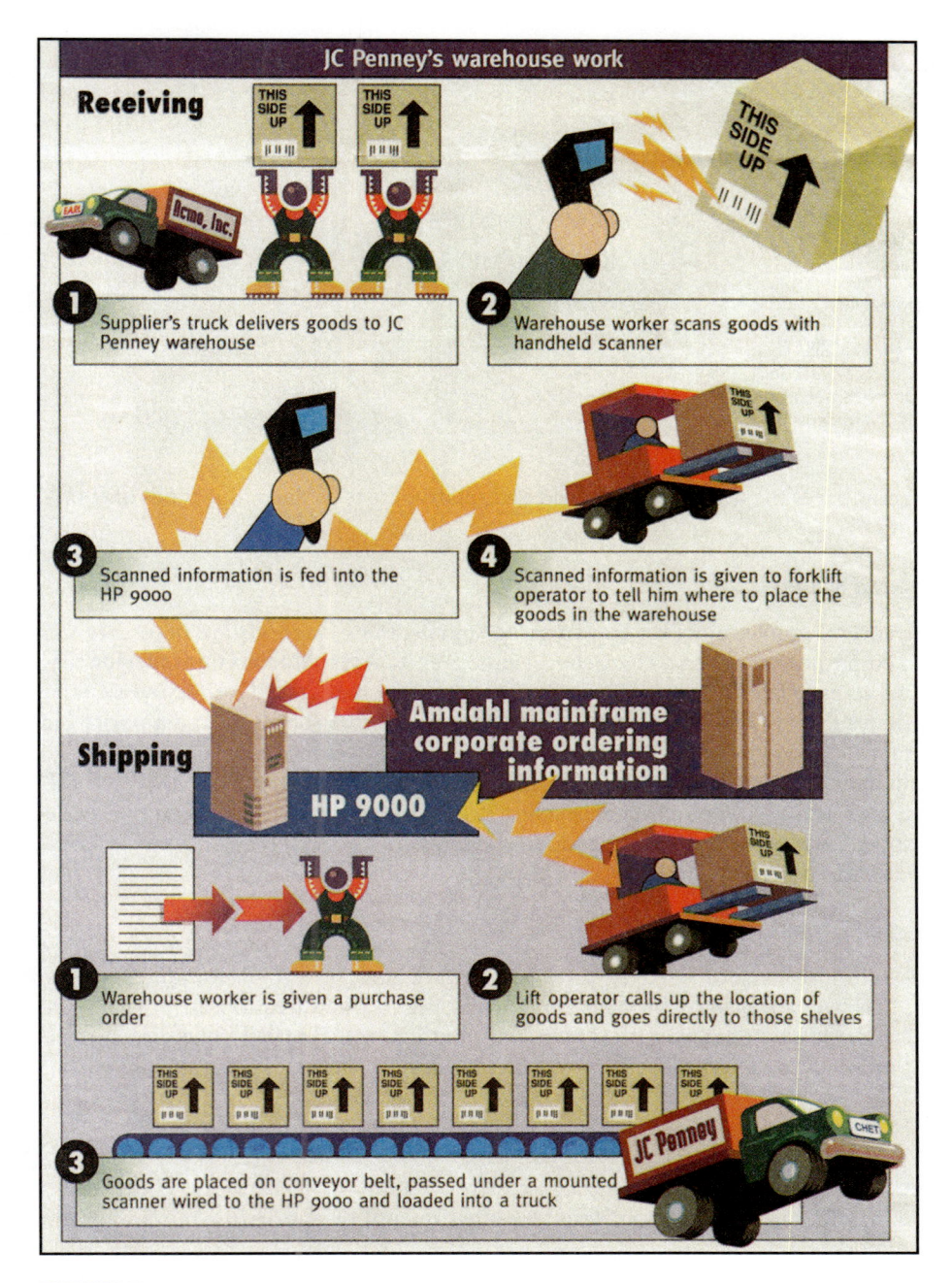

FIGURE 8.5
Wireless transmission at JC Penney's. JC Penney uses wireless handheld scanners to locate goods for shipping and receiving at its three massive warehouses throughout the U.S. *Adapted from Mark Halper, "JC Penney Warehouses Do Away with Paper,"* Computerworld, *September 12, 1994. Copyright 1994 by Computerworld, Inc., Framingham, MA 01701. Reprinted from* Computerworld. *Reprinted by permission.*

Since one signal change, or cycle, is required to transmit one or several bits per second, the transmission capacity of each type of telecommunications medium is a function of its frequency, the number of cycles per second that can be sent through that medium measured in *hertz* (see Chapter 5). The range of frequencies that can be accommodated on a particular telecommunications channel is called its **bandwidth**. The bandwidth is the difference between the highest and lowest frequencies that can be accommodated on a single channel. The greater the range of frequencies, the greater the bandwidth and the greater the channel's telecommunications transmission capacity.

bandwidth The capacity of a communications channel as measured by the difference between the highest and lowest frequencies that can be transmitted by that channel.

Table 8.2	Typical Speeds and Cost of Telecommunications Transmission Media	
Medium	Speed	Cost
Twisted wire	300 BPS–10 MBPS	Low
Microwave	256 KBPS–100 MBPS	
Satellite	256 KBPS–100 MBPS	
Coaxial cable	56 KBPS–200 MBPS	
Fiber-optic cable	500 KBPS–10 GBPS	High

BPS = bits per second
KBPS = kilobits per second
MBPS = megabits per second
GBPS = gigabits per second

Table 8.2 compares the transmission speed and relative costs of the major types of transmissions media.

Transmission Modes

There are several conventions for transmitting signals; these methods are necessary for devices to communicate when a character begins or ends. **Asynchronous transmission** (often referred to as *start–stop transmission*) transmits one character at a time over a line, each character framed by control bits—a start bit, one or two stop bits, and a parity bit (see Chapter 5). Asynchronous transmission is used for low-speed transmission.

Synchronous transmission transmits groups of characters simultaneously, with the beginning and ending of a block of characters determined by the timing circuitry of the sending and receiving devices. Synchronous transmission is used for transmitting large volumes of data at high speeds.

Transmission Direction

Transmission must also consider the direction of data flow over a telecommunications network. In **simplex transmission** data can travel only in one direction at all times. In **half-duplex transmission** data can flow two ways but can travel in only one direction at a time. In **full-duplex transmission** data can be sent in both directions simultaneously.

COMMUNICATIONS PROCESSORS

Communications processors, such as front-end processors, concentrators, controllers, multiplexers, and modems, support data transmission and reception in a telecommunications network.

The **front-end processor** is a small computer (often a programmable minicomputer) dedicated to communications management and is attached to the main, or host, computer in a computer system. The front-end processor performs special processing related to communications such as error control, formatting, editing, controlling, routing, and speed and signal conversion. It takes some of the load off the host computer. The front-end processor is largely responsible for collecting and processing input and output data to and from terminals and grouping characters into complete messages for submission to the CPU of the host computer.

A **concentrator** is a programmable telecommunications computer that collects and temporarily stores messages from terminals until enough messages are ready to be sent economically. The concentrator bursts signals to the host computer.

A **controller,** which is often a specialized minicomputer, supervises communications traffic between the CPU and peripheral devices such as terminals and printers. The controller manages messages from these devices and communicates them to the CPU. It also routes output from the CPU to the appropriate peripheral device.

---

asynchronous transmission The low-speed transmission of one character at a time.

synchronous transmission The high-speed simultaneous transmission of large blocks of data.

simplex transmission A transmission in which data can travel in only one direction at all times.

half-duplex transmission A transmission in which data can flow two ways but in only one direction at a time.

full-duplex transmission A transmission in which data can travel in both directions simultaneously.

communications processors Hardware that supports data transmission and reception in a telecommunications network.

front-end processor A small computer managing communications for the host computer in a network.

concentrator Telecommunications computer that collects and temporarily stores messages from terminals for batch transmission to the host computer.

controller A specialized computer that supervises communications traffic between the CPU and the peripheral devices in a telecommunications system.

A **multiplexer** is a device that enables a single communications channel to carry data transmissions from multiple sources simultaneously. The multiplexer divides the communications channel so that it can be shared by multiple transmission devices. The multiplexer may divide a high-speed channel into multiple channels of slower speed or may assign each transmission source a very small slice of time for using the high-speed channel.

multiplexer A device that enables a single communications channel to carry data transmissions from multiple sources simultaneously.

TELECOMMUNICATIONS SOFTWARE

Special **telecommunications software** is required to control and support the activities of a telecommunications network. This software resides in the host computer, front-end processor, and other processors in the network. The principal functions of telecommunications software are network control, access control, transmission control, error detection/correction, and security.

Network control software routes messages, polls network terminals, determines transmission priorities, maintains a log of network activity, and checks for errors. Access control software establishes connections between terminals and computers in the network, establishing transmission speed, mode, and direction. Transmission control software enables computers and terminals to send and receive data, programs, commands, and messages. Error-control software detects and corrects errors, then retransmits the corrected data. Security-control software monitors utilization, log ons, passwords, and various authorization procedures to prevent unauthorized access to a network. More detail on security software can be found in Chapter 14.

telecommunications software Special software for controlling and supporting the activities of a telecommunications network.

8.3 TYPES OF TELECOMMUNICATIONS NETWORKS

A number of different ways exist to organize telecommunications components to form a network and hence provide multiple ways of classifying networks. Networks can be classified by their shape, or **topology**. Networks can also be classified by their geographic scope and the type of services provided. Wide-area networks, for example, encompass a relatively wide geographic area, from several miles to thousands of miles, whereas local networks link local resources such as computers and terminals in the same department or building of a firm. This section will describe the various ways of looking at networks.

topology The shape or configuration of a network.

NETWORK TOPOLOGIES

One way of describing networks is by their shape, or topology. As illustrated in Figures 8.6 to 8.8, the three most common topologies are the star, bus, and ring.

The Star Network

The **star network** (see Figure 8.6) consists of a central host computer connected to a number of smaller computers or terminals. This topology is useful for applications where some processing must be centralized and some can be performed locally. One problem with the star network is its vulnerability. All communication between points in the network must pass through the central computer. Because the central computer is the traffic controller for the other computers and terminals in the network, communication in the network will come to a standstill if the host computer stops functioning.

star network A network topology in which all computers and other devices are connected to a central host computer. All communications between network devices must pass through the host computer.

The Bus Network

The **bus network** (see Figure 8.7) links a number of computers by a single circuit made of twisted wire, coaxial cable, or fiber-optic cable. All of the signals are broadcast in both directions to the entire network, with special software to identify which components receive each message (there is no central host computer to control the network). If one of the computers in the network fails, none of the other components in the network is

bus network Network topology linking a number of computers by a single circuit with all messages broadcast to the entire network.

FIGURE 8.6
A star network topology. In a star network configuration a central host computer acts as a traffic controller for all the other components of the network. All communication between the smaller computers, terminals, and printers must first pass through the central computer.

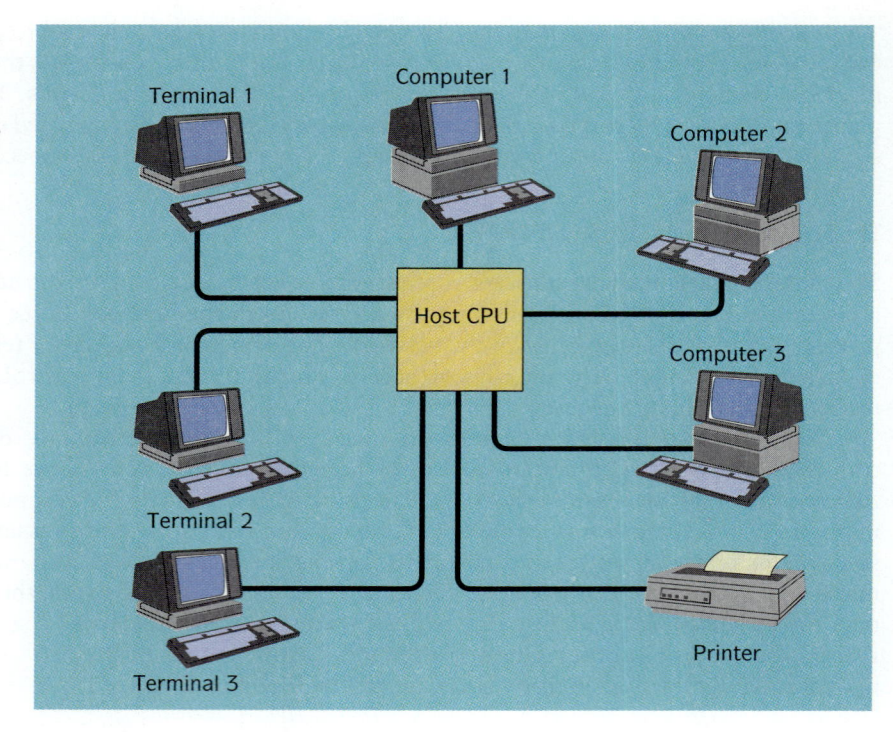

FIGURE 8.7
A bus network topology. This topology allows for all messages to be broadcast to the entire network through a single circuit. There is no central host, and messages can travel in both directions along the cable.

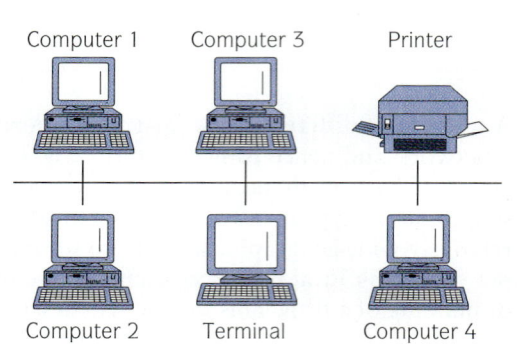

affected. This topology is commonly used for local-area networks (LANs), discussed in the following section.

The Ring Network

ring network A network topology in which all computers are linked by a closed loop in a manner that passes data in one direction from one computer to another.

Like the bus network, the **ring network** (see Figure 8.8) does not rely on a central host computer and will not necessarily break down if one of the component computers malfunctions. Each computer in the network can communicate directly with any other computer, and each processes its own applications independently. However, in ring topology, the connecting wire, cable, or optical fiber forms a closed loop. Data are passed along the ring from one computer to another and always flow in one direction.

The token ring network is a variant of the ring network. In the token ring network all of the devices on the network communicate using a signal, or token. The token is a predefined packet of data, which includes data indicating the sender, receiver, and whether the packet is in use. The tokens may contain a message or be empty.

A token moves from device to device in the network, and each device examines the token as it passes by. If the token contains data and is meant for that device, the device accepts the data and marks the packet as empty. If a computer wants to send a message, it finds an available token; supplies sender, receiver, and message data; loads the message onto the token; and marks it as used. If no message is pending, the token passes unchanged. The token ring configuration is most useful for transmitting large

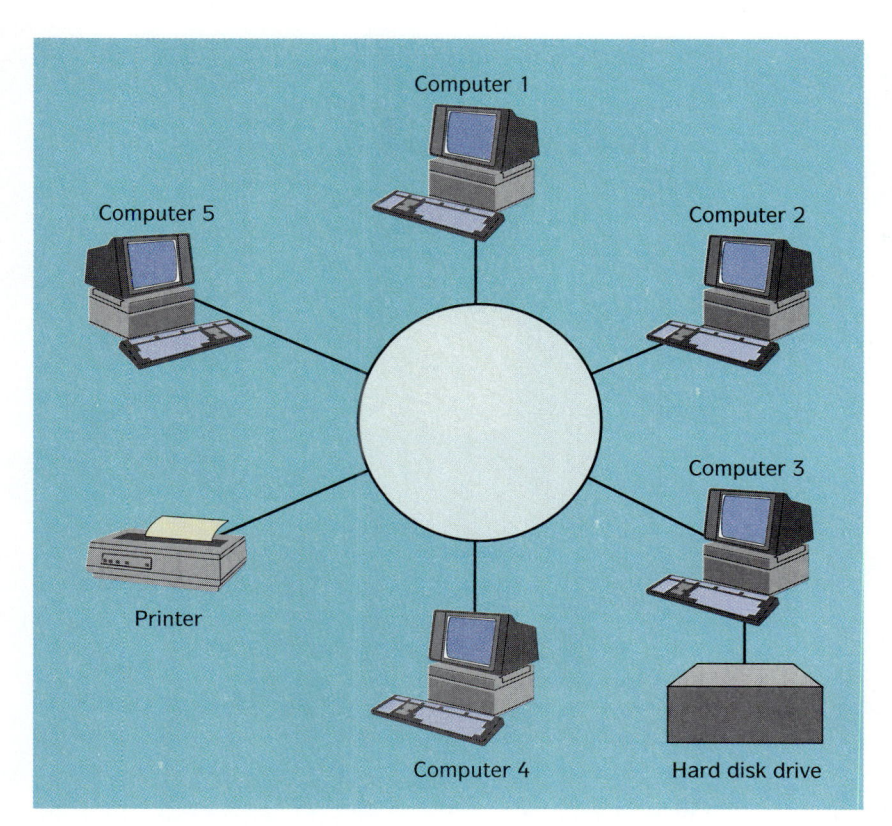

FIGURE 8.8
A ring network topology. In a ring network configuration, messages are transmitted from computer to computer, flowing in a single direction through a closed loop. Each computer operates independently so that if one fails, communication through the network is not interrupted.

volumes of data between microcomputers or for transmission between micros and a larger computer.

PRIVATE BRANCH EXCHANGES AND LOCAL-AREA NETWORKS (LANS)

Networks may be classified by geographic scope into local networks and wide-area networks. Local networks consist of private branch exchanges and local-area networks.

Private Branch Exchanges

A **private branch exchange (PBX)** is a special-purpose computer designed for handling and switching office telephone calls at a company site. Today's PBXs can carry both voice and data to create local networks.

While the first PBXs performed limited switching functions, they can now store, transfer, hold, and redial telephone calls. PBXs can also be used to switch digital information among computers and office devices. For instance, you can write a letter on a microcomputer in your office, send it to the printer, then dial up the local copying machine and have multiple copies of your letter created. All of this activity is possible with a digital PBX connecting smart machines in the advanced office. Figure 8.9 illustrates a PBX system.

The advantage of digital PBXs over other local networking options is that they utilize existing telephone lines and do not require special wiring. A phone jack can be found almost anywhere in the office building. Equipment can therefore be moved when necessary with little worry about having to rewire the building. A hard-wired computer terminal or microcomputer connected to a mainframe with coaxial cable must be rewired at considerable cost each time it is moved. A microcomputer connected to a network by telephone can simply be plugged or unplugged anywhere in the building, utilizing the existing telephone lines. PBXs are also supported by commercial vendors such as the local telephone company, so that the organization does not need special expertise to manage them.

private branch exchange (PBX)
A central switching system that handles a firm's voice and digital communications.

8.3 Types of Telecommunications Networks 245

FIGURE 8.9
A PBX system. A PBX can switch digital information among telephones and among computers, copiers, printers, fax machines, and other devices to create a local network based on ordinary telephone wiring.

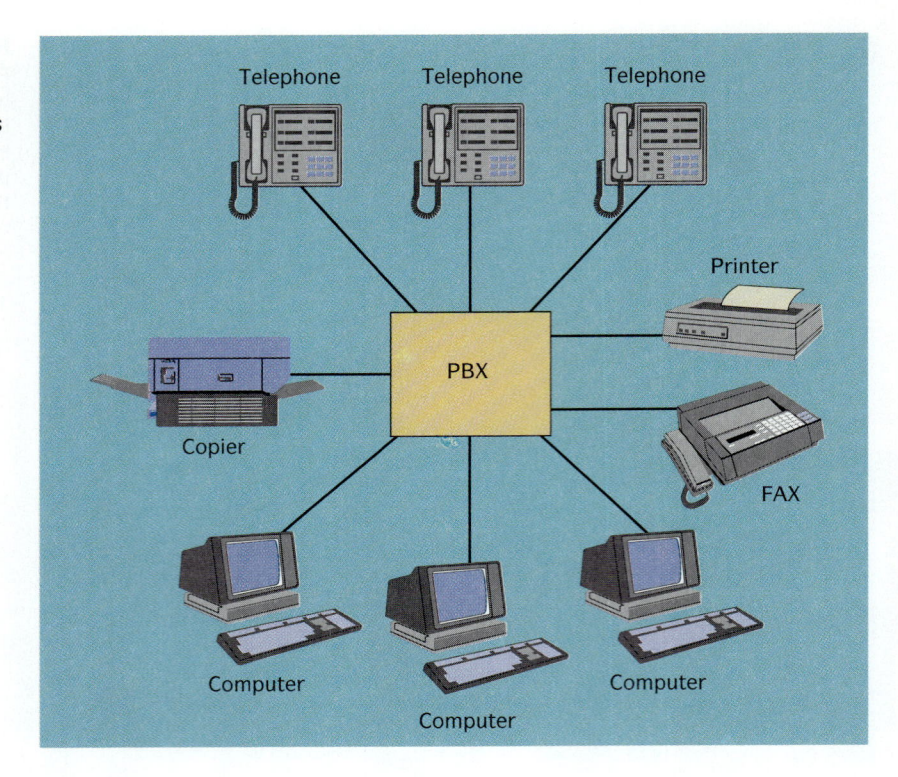

The geographic scope of PBXs is limited, usually to several hundred feet, although the PBX can be connected to other PBX networks or to packet-switched networks (see the discussion of value-added networks in this section) to encompass a larger geographic area. The primary disadvantage of PBXs is that they are limited to telephone lines and that they cannot easily handle very large volumes of data.

Local-Area Networks

local-area network (LAN) A telecommunications network that requires its own dedicated channels and that encompasses a limited distance, usually one building or several buildings in close proximity.

A **local-area network (LAN)** encompasses a limited distance, usually one building or several buildings in close proximity. Most LANs connect devices located within a 2000-foot radius and have been widely used to link microcomputers. LANs require their own communications channels.

LANs generally have higher transmission capacities than PBXs, using bus or ring topologies and a high bandwidth. A very fast PBX can have a maximum transmission capacity of over 2 megabits per second. LANs typically transmit at a rate of 256 kilobits per second to over 100 megabits per second. They are recommended for applications requiring high volumes of data and high transmission speeds. For instance, because a picture consumes so many bits of information, an organization might require a LAN for video transmissions and graphics.

LANs are totally controlled, maintained, and operated by end users. This produces the advantage of allowing user control, but it also means that the user must know a great deal about telecommunications applications and networking.

LANs allow organizations to share expensive hardware and software. For instance, several microcomputers can share a single printer by being tied together in a LAN. LANs can promote productivity because users are no longer dependent upon a centralized computer system (which can fail) or upon the availability of a single peripheral device such as a printer. Finally, there are many new applications—such as electronic mail, graphics, video teleconferencing, and on-line applications—requiring high-capacity networks.

The most common use of LANs is for linking personal computers within a building or office to share information and expensive peripheral devices such as laser printers. Another popular application of LANs is in factories, in which they link computers and computer-controlled machines.

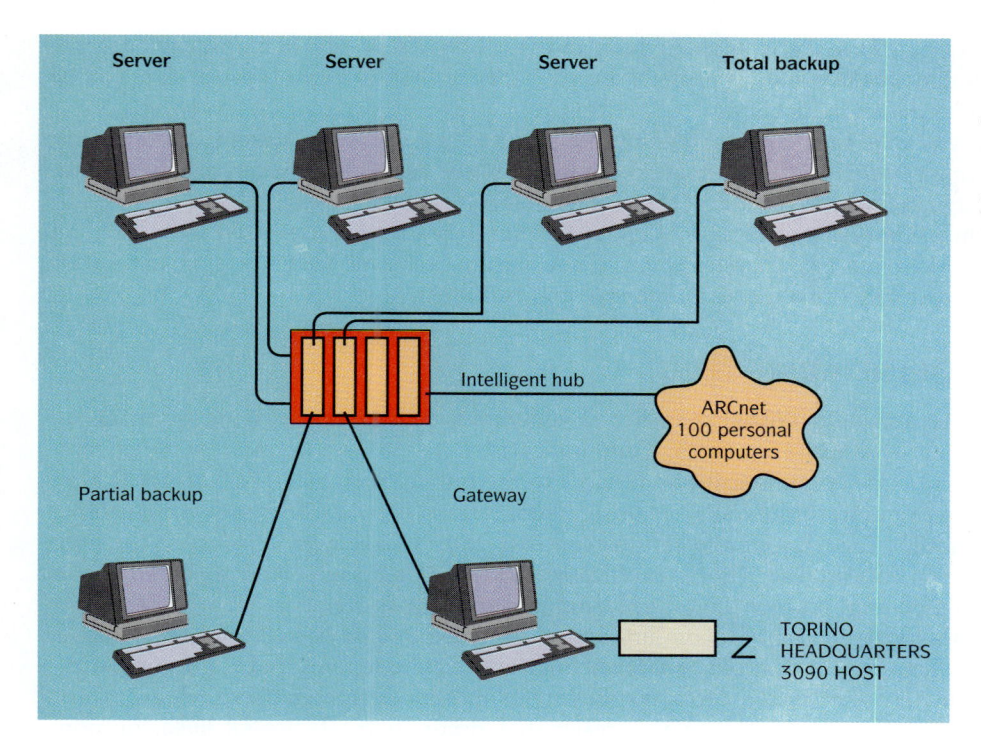

FIGURE 8.10
Michelin Milan's LAN. The Milan division of Michelin Italia chose ARCnet as the technology for connecting the devices in its 100-seat local-area network for several reasons, including the floor plan of the Michelin building and the need for a star topology to allow upgrades to the network.

Figure 8.10 illustrates a LAN employed by the Milan division of Michelin Italia, the Italian branch of the Michelin Corporation. The corporation is noted for its tires and guides to hotels and restaurants. Michelin Italia Milan's staff uses the LAN primarily for electronic filing, word processing, and graphics applications. This LAN consists of one hundred personal computer workstations that are attached to three Compaq 386/20 file servers, each equipped with 300-megabyte hard disks. The network also contains an Epson 286 PC and an Olivetti M290 PC for backup, and an Olivetti M290 PC serving as a gateway. The entire network and important files are backed up every night.

The **file server** acts as a librarian, storing various programs and data files for network users. The server determines who gets access to what and in what sequence. Servers may be powerful microcomputers with large hard disk capacity, workstations, minicomputers, or mainframes, although specialized computers are now available for this purpose. The server typically contains the LAN's **network operating system,** which manages the server and routes and manages communications on the network.

The network **gateway** connects the LAN to public networks, such as the telephone network, or to other corporate networks so that the LAN can exchange information with networks external to it. A gateway is generally a communications processor that can connect dissimilar networks by translating from one set of protocols to another. (A bridge connects two networks of the same type. A router is used to route messages through several connected LANs or to a wide-area network.)

The gateway illustrated in Figure 8.10 connects Michelin Italia's Milan division to Michelin Italia's 3090 IBM mainframe host computer in its Torino headquarters. Application software, such as word processing, works with the network operating system to keep data traffic flowing smoothly.

LAN technology consists of cabling (twisted wire, coaxial, or fiber-optic cable) or wireless technology that links individual computer devices, network interface cards (which are special adapters serving as interfaces to the cable), and software to control LAN activities. The LAN network interface card specifies the data transmission rate, the size of message units, the addressing information attached to each message, and network topology (Ethernet utilizes a bus topology, for example).

LAN technologies for physically connecting devices employ either a baseband or a broadband channel technology. **Baseband** products provide a single path for transmit-

file server The computer in a network that stores various programs and data files for users of the network. Determines access and availability in the network.

network operating system Special software that manages the file server in a LAN and routes and manages communications on the network.

gateway A communications processor that connects dissimilar networks by providing the translation from one set of protocols to another.

baseband LAN channel technology that provides a single path for transmitting either text, graphics, voice, or video data at one time.

8.3 Types of Telecommunications Networks   *247*

broadband LAN channel technology that provides several paths for transmitting text, graphics, voice, or video data so that different types of data can be transmitted simultaneously.

ting text, graphics, voice, or video data, and only one type of data at a time can be transmitted. **Broadband** products provide several paths so that different types of data can be transmitted simultaneously.

LAN capabilities are also defined by the network operating system. The network operating system can reside on every computer in the network, or it can reside on a single designated file server for all the applications on the network.

The primary disadvantages of LANs are that they are more expensive to install than PBXs and are more inflexible, requiring new wiring each time the LAN is moved. LANs require specially trained staff to manage and run them.

WIDE-AREA NETWORKS (WANS)

wide-area network (WAN) Telecommunications network that spans a large geographical distance. May consist of a variety of cable, satellite, and microwave technologies.

Wide-area networks (WANs) span broad geographical distances, ranging from several miles to across entire continents. Common carriers (companies licensed by the government to provide communications services to the public, such as AT&T or MCI) typically determine transmission rates or interconnections between lines, but the customer is responsible for telecommunications contents and management. It is up to the individual firm to establish the most efficient routing of messages, and to handle error checking, editing, protocols, and telecommunications management.

switched lines Telephone lines that a person can access from his or her terminal to transmit data to another computer, the call being routed or switched through paths to the designated destination.

WANs may consist of a combination of switched and dedicated lines, microwave, and satellite communications. **Switched lines** are telephone lines that a person can access from his or her terminal to transmit data to another computer, the call being routed or switched through paths to the designated destination. **Dedicated lines,** or nonswitched lines, are continuously available for transmission and the lessee typically pays a flat rate for total access to the line. The lines can be leased or purchased from common carriers or private communications media vendors. Dedicated lines are often conditioned to transmit data at higher speeds than switched lines and are more appropriate for higher-volume transmissions. Switched lines, on the other hand, are less expensive and more appropriate for low-volume applications requiring only occasional transmission.

dedicated lines Telephone lines that are continuously available for transmission by a lessee. Typically conditioned to transmit data at high speeds for high-volume applications.

Individual business firms may maintain their own wide-area networks. Figure 8.11 illustrates a wide-area network used by the Burlington Northern Railroad to help keep its trains moving. The WAN carries traffic controls from dispatch offices to various rail locations, relaying information to make trains stop and start. But private wide-area networks are expensive to maintain, or firms may not have the resources to manage their

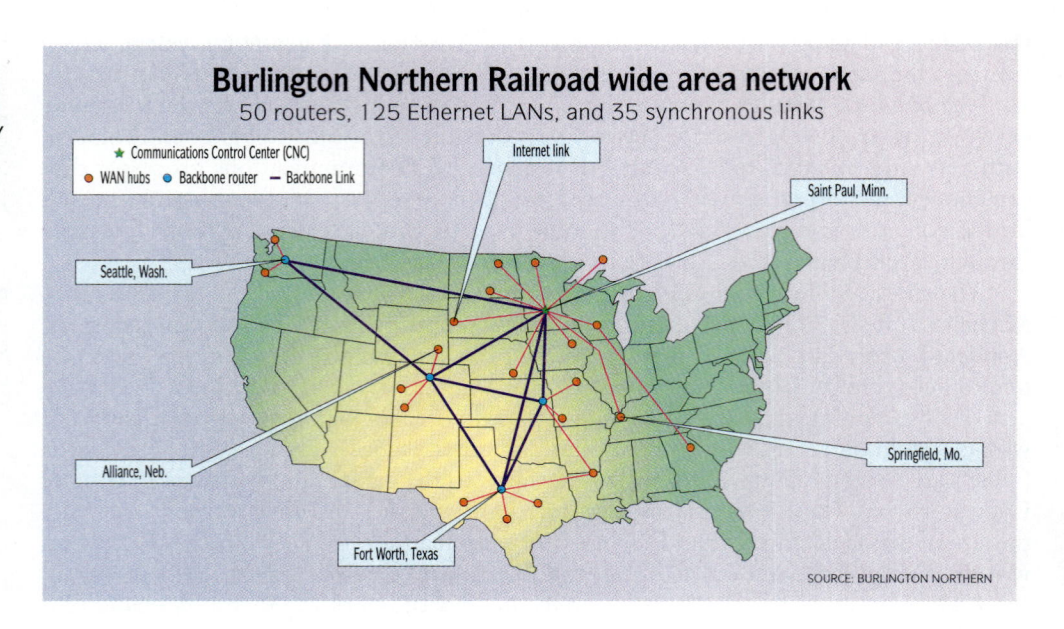

FIGURE 8.11
Burlington Northern's WAN plays a critical role in keeping its trains moving. *Source: Adapted from Peggy Wallace, "Burlington Northern Puts Down WAN Tracks," illustrator G. Boren,* Infoworld, *December 20, 1993.*

own wide-area networks. In such instances, companies may choose to use commercial network services to communicate over vast distances.

VALUE-ADDED NETWORKS (VANS)

Value-added networks are an alternative to firms designing and managing their own networks. **Value-added networks (VANs)** are private, multipath, data-only, third-party-managed networks that can provide economies in the cost of service and in network management because they are used by multiple organizations. The value-added network is set up by a firm that is in charge of managing the network. That firm sells subscriptions to other firms wishing to use the network. Subscribers pay only for the amount of data they transmit plus a subscription fee. The network may utilize twisted-pair lines, satellite links, and other communications channels leased by the value-added carrier.

The term *value added* refers to the extra value added to communications by the telecommunications and computing services these networks provide to clients. Customers do not have to invest in network equipment and software or perform their own error checking, editing, routing, and protocol conversion. Subscribers may achieve savings in line charges and transmission costs because the costs of using the network are shared among many users. The resulting costs may be lower than if the clients had leased their own lines or satellite services. VANs are attractive for firms such as Continental Grain because they provide special services such as electronic mail and access to foreign telecommunications systems.

Continental Grain switched from a private network to GE Information Services' (GEIS) value-added network to link its 175 domestic locations with its 45 branch locations in South America, the Far East, and Europe. Continental found that switching to the value-added network reduced costs and reduced operational problems associated with networks. International VANs such as GEIS have representatives with language skills and knowledge of various countries' telecommunications administrations. The

value-added network (VAN) Private, multipath, data-only, third-party-managed networks that are used by multiple organizations on a subscription basis.

Department stores such as Marshall Fields, a unit of Dayton Hudson, use electronic commerce services to track inventory from the warehouses to the truck and into its stores.

FIGURE 8.12
Packet switched networks and packet communications. Data are grouped into small packets, framed by identifying information, which are transmitted independently via various communication channels to maximize the potential of the paths in a network.

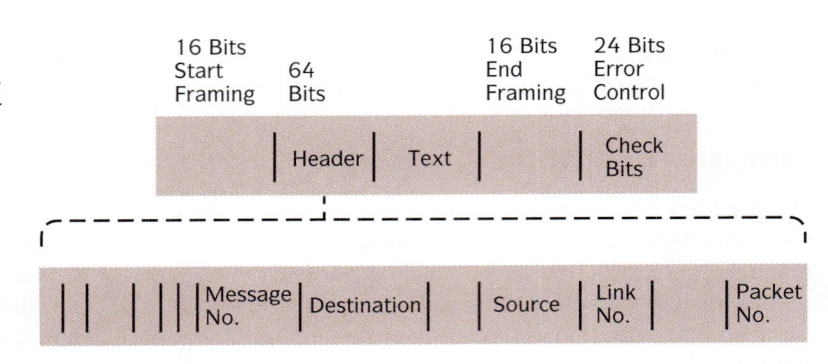

```
16 Bits       64        16 Bits    24 Bits
Start        Bits       End        Error
Framing                 Framing    Control

        | Header | Text |         | Check Bits |

  | | | | | Message No. | Destination | Source | Link No. | Packet No. |
```

VANs have already leased lines from foreign telecommunications authorities or can arrange access to local networks and equipment abroad.

The leading international value-added networks provide casual or intermittent users international services on a dial-up basis and can provide a private network using dedicated circuits for customers requiring a full-time network. (Maintaining a private network may be most cost-effective for organizations with a high communications volume.)

Another way value-added networks provide economies is through **packet switching**. Packet switching breaks up a lengthy block of text into small, fixed bundles of data (often 128 bytes each) called *packets* (see Figure 8.12). The VAN gathers information from many users, divides it into small packets, and continuously uses various communications channels to send the packets. Each packet travels independently through the network (this contrasts to one firm using a leased line, for example, for one hour and then not using it for three or four hours). Packets of data originating at one source can be routed through different paths in the network, and then may be reassembled into the original message when they reach their destination. Packet switching enables communications facilities to be utilized more fully by more users.

packet switching Technology that breaks blocks of text into small, fixed bundles of data and routes them in the most economical way through any available communications channel.

Frame relay is a faster and less expensive variant of packet switching. Frame relay is a shared network service that packages data into frames that are similar to packets. Frame relay, however, does not perform error correction. This is because so many of today's digital lines are cleaner than in the past and networks are more adept at correcting transmission problems. Frame relay can communicate at transmission speeds up to 1.544 megabits per second. Frame relay is essentially used for transmitting data. It is not recommended for any transmissions that are sensitive to varying delay, such as voice or digital video traffic, and it cannot easily control network congestion. Frame relay works successfully only over reliable lines that do not require frequent retransmission because of error.

frame relay A shared network service technology that packages data into bundles for transmission but does not use error-correction routines. Cheaper and faster than packet switching.

Most corporations today use separate networks for voice, private-line services, and data, each of which is supported by a different technology. An emerging networking technology called **asynchronous transfer mode (ATM)** may overcome some of these problems because it can seamlessly and dynamically switch voice, data, images, and video between users. ATM also promises to tie LANs and wide-area networks together more easily (LANs are generally based on lower-speed protocols, whereas WANs operate at higher speeds). ATM technology parcels information into uniform cells, each with 53 groups of eight bytes, eliminating the need for protocol conversion. It can pass data between computers from different vendors and permits data to be transmitted at any speed the network handles (Vetter, 1995). ATM currently requires fiber-optic cable, but it can transmit up to 2.5 GBPS.

asynchronous transfer mode (ATM) A networking technology that parcels information into 8-byte cells, allowing data to be transmitted between computers from different vendors at any speed.

8.4 HOW ORGANIZATIONS USE TELECOMMUNICATIONS FOR COMPETITIVE ADVANTAGE

Baxter International, described in Chapter 2, realized the strategic significance of telecommunications. The company placed its own computer terminals in hospital supply rooms and provided a direct telecommunications link with its central headquarters via a VAN. Customers could dial up a local VAN node and send their orders directly to the company. Since then, many other corporations have realized the strategic potential of networked computer systems.

Telecommunications has helped eliminate barriers of geography and time, enabling organizations to accelerate the pace of production, to speed decision making, to forge new products, to move into new markets, and to create new relationships with customers. Many of the strategic applications described in Chapter 2 would not be possible without telecommunications. Firms that fail to consider telecommunications in their strategic plans will fall behind (Keen, 1986).

FACILITATING APPLICATIONS

Some of the leading telecommunications applications for communication, coordination, and speeding the flow of transactions, messages, and information throughout business firms are electronic mail, voice mail, facsimile machines (fax), digital information services, teleconferencing, dataconferencing, videoconferencing, electronic data interchange, and groupware.

Electronic Mail

Electronic mail, or **e-mail,** is the computer-to-computer exchange of messages. A person can use a microcomputer attached to a modem or a terminal to send notes and even lengthier documents just by typing in the name of the message's recipient. Many organizations operate their own internal electronic mail systems, but communications companies such as GTE, Telenet, MCI, and AT&T offer these services, as do commercial online information services such as America Online, CompuServe, and Prodigy and public networks on the Internet (see Chapter 9). E-mail eliminates telephone tag and costly long-distance telephone charges, expediting communication between different parts of the organization. Nestlé SA, the Swiss-based multinational food corporation, installed an electronic mail system to connect its 60,000 employees in 80 countries. Nestlé's European units can use the electronic mail system to share information about production schedules and inventory levels to ship excess products from one country to another.

electronic mail (e-mail) The computer-to-computer exchange of messages.

CompuServe gives subscribers access to extensive information, including news reports, travel, weather, education, and financial services—directly from their desktop computers in their homes or offices.

Window on Management

MONITORING EMPLOYEES ON NETWORKS: UNETHICAL OR GOOD BUSINESS?

Should managers monitor employees using networks? Is it unethical? Or is it just good business? While many view monitoring employee e-mail as unethical and even an illegal invasion of privacy, many companies consider it to be legitimate. They claim they need to know that the business facilities they own are being used to further their business goals. Some also argue that they need to be able to search electronic mail messages for evidence of illegal activities, racial discrimination, or sexual harassment. Others argue that the company needs access to business information stored in e-mail files just the same as if it were stored in paper file cabinets.

E-mail privacy within a company is not covered by U.S. federal law. The Electronic Communications Privacy Act of 1986 only prohibits interception or disclosure of e-mail messages by parties outside the company where the messages were sent without a proper warrant. Lawsuits have so far failed to limit the right of companies to monitor e-mail. For example, when Alana Shoars, a former e-mail administrator at Epson America Inc. discovered that her supervisor was copying and reading employees' e-mail, she sued in the Los Angeles, California, courts, alleging invasion of privacy. Later she filed a class action suit in the name of 700 Epson employees and 1800 outsiders also charging privacy invasion. Both cases were dismissed on the grounds that e-mail does not fall within the state's wiretapping laws.

Despite the lack of legal restrictions, many observers see electronic mail privacy as serious. Michael Godwin, legal adviser for the Electronic Frontier Foundation, recommends that employers who intend to monitor e-mail establish a stated policy to that effect. Various companies have such policies, including Nordstrom, Eastman Kodak, and Federal Express, all of which claim the right to intercept and read employee e-mail. General Motors and Hallmark Cards have policies that grant employees greater privacy.

To Think About: *Do you believe management should have the right to monitor employee e-mail and Internet usage? Why or why not? Describe the problems such monitoring might present to management.*

The Internet presents different issues—the use of company facilities not only for nonbusiness purposes but also for illegal uses such as retrieving pornography. Some employers take a tough stance. Sixty-four employees at Sandia Labs in Albuquerque, New Mexico, were disciplined for reading pornography at work on company time—or on their own time. Many were suspended without pay. Other firms, including Eli Lilly, publish a clear policy and then leave it to individual managers to enforce it if they so choose. Many, however, take a middle-of-the-road position. At Chicago's WMS Industries, the IS department logs the amount of time each employee spends on the Net and sends such reports to managers to use as they wish.

Sources: Alice LaPlante, "Firms Spell Out Appropriate Use of Internet for Employees," *Computerworld,* February 5, 1996; "Does E-Mail Mean Everyone's Mail?" *Information Week,* January 3, 1994; and David Bjerklie, "E-Mail: The Boss Is Watching," *Technology Review,* April 1993.

E-mail systems present security problems because without adequate protection, electronic eavesdroppers can read the mail as it moves through a network. We discuss such security problems in Chapter 14. The Window on Management looks at the privacy of e-mail messages from a different perspective, examining whether monitoring employees using e-mail, the Internet, and other network facilities is ethical.

Voice Mail

voice mail A system for digitizing a spoken message and transmitting it over a network.

A **voice mail** system digitizes the spoken message of the sender, transmits it over a network, and stores the message on disk for later retrieval. When the recipient is ready to listen, the messages are reconverted to audio form. Various store-and-forward capabilities notify recipients that messages are waiting. Recipients have the option of saving these messages for future use, deleting them, or routing them to other parties.

Facsimile Machines (fax)

facsimile (fax) A machine that digitizes and transmits documents with both text and graphics over telephone lines.

Facsimile (fax) machines can transmit documents containing both text and graphics over ordinary telephone lines. A sending fax machine scans and digitizes the document im-

Table 8.3 Commercial Digital Information Services

Provider	Type of Service
America Online	General interest/business information
CompuServe	General interest/business information
Prodigy	General interest/business information
Dow Jones News Retrieval	Business/financial information
Quotron	Financial information
Dialog	Business/scientific/technical information
Lexis	Legal research
Nexis	News/business information

age. The digitized document is then transmitted over a network and reproduced in hard copy form by a receiving fax machine. The process results in a duplicate, or facsimile, of the original.

Digital Information Services

Powerful and far-reaching digital electronic services now enable networked microcomputer and workstation users to obtain information from outside the firm instantaneously without leaving their desks. Stock prices, historical references to periodicals, industrial supplies catalogs, legal research, news articles, reference works, weather forecasts, and travel information are just some of the electronic databases that can be accessed on-line. Many of these services have capabilities for electronic mail, electronic bulletin boards, and for on-line discussion groups, shopping, and travel reservations. Table 8.3 describes the leading commercial digital information services. An extension of the Windows 95 operating system will let users use Microsoft Network, Microsoft's on-line information service featuring interactive publishing tools. In the following chapter we describe the capabilities of the Internet, a publicly available network of networks offering access to many thousands of databases throughout the world.

Today, the sheer abundance of networks and on-line information services has created problems of information overload. Individuals and organizations may be inundated with too much useless information, such as unsolicited e-mail, while valuable information remains hard to find. One solution is to use intelligent agent software. **Intelligent agents** are "smart" programs that can carry out specific, repetitive, and predictable tasks for an individual user, business process, or software application. They can be programmed to make decisions based on the user's personal preferences—for example, to delete junk e-mail, schedule appointments, or travel over interconnected networks to find the cheapest airfare to California. The agent can be likened to a personal assistant collaborating with the user in the same work environment. It can help the user by performing tasks on the user's behalf; training or teaching the user; hiding the complexity of difficult tasks; helping the user collaborate with other users; or monitoring events and procedures (Maes, 1994). The Window on Technology describes some of the capabilities of intelligent agent software and its implications for networking and electronic commerce.

intelligent agents Software programs that can carry out specific, repetitive, and predictable tasks for individuals, organizations, or software applications.

Teleconferencing, Dataconferencing, and Videoconferencing

People can meet electronically—even though they are hundreds or thousands of miles apart—by using teleconferencing, dataconferencing, or videoconferencing. **Teleconferencing** allows a group of people to confer simultaneously via telephone or via electronic mail group communication software. Teleconferencing that includes the ability of two or

teleconferencing The ability to confer with a group of people simultaneously using the telephone or electronic mail group communication software.

8.4 How Organizations Use Telecommunications for Competitive Advantage

Window on Technology

INTELLIGENT AGENTS: NETWORK VALETS

What a dream—an electronic valet that searches networks for the information you need while you—and your computer—are left free to pursue other tasks! That dream recently came true with the release of intelligent agent technology from General Magic of Mountain View, California. Intelligent agents (see Figure 8.13) can move around interconnected networks, including the Internet, from computer to computer, performing tasks you assign, making as many stops as needed until the tasks are completed. For example, you can give a General Magic agent the brand name and model number of a television set you want to purchase and then send the agent off to buy it for you. That intelligent agent would travel through your network, stop at all the on-line stores, checking prices and availability, then determine which visited store sells it at the lowest price, return there, purchase the TV, and report the results to you. All the while, you and your computer are free to do other work. Some of the many uses envisioned for these agents include (1) filtering your e-mail (weeding out the junk mail) and sorting the rest; (2) monitoring a flight you need to meet and notifying you if it is late; and (3) monitoring your customer's computer and launching an

> **To Think About:** How can intelligent agents benefit organizations? What organization, management, and technical factors should be considered in determining whether or not to use intelligent agents?

order on your computer to produce and ship more product when the customer's stock falls to a certain level.

DHL Worldwide Express, the delivery service based in Redwood City, California, and Brussels, Belgium, uses an agent-based package tracking application to communicate with more than 3000 U.S. customers daily. Using prerecorded phrases, an agent asks touch-tone callers to DHL's toll-free number to punch in their airbill number. If the package has been successfully delivered, the agent responds with the time, date, and name of the person who signed for it. If not, the agent transfers the caller to a human operator for more assistance.

Scores of companies are working on software agents for tasks such as searching World Wide Web sites or other databases and reporting back to the user's pager, e-mail address, or personal Web page. Agent software developed by Verity Inc. of Mountain View, California, can weigh information by its importance to the user and choose the method of notifying the user based on that ranking.

While intelligent agent technology can make people more efficient and well-informed, it raises some serious technical, social, and legal concerns. Should agents be authorized to execute financial transactions without any human intervention? Should employers be able to create agents that count employees' keystrokes, monitor their telephone calls, or note how often they access important computer files? Can the boss demand to see an employee's agents to see how well he or she handled delegated responsibilities? How can we be sure that agents won't clog networks or damage another party's agents or computer systems?

FIGURE 8.13
Intelligent agents. Intelligent agent software cuts down on the number of transmissions that must be sent over a network to complete a transaction—such as a purchase or travel reservation between two distant parties—by sending an electronic agent across a network. Data are transmitted only once each way: when the buyer launches the intelligent agent and when the agent completes its task and reports back the results. *Adapted from: Peter Wayner, "Agents Away," Byte (May 1994). Reprinted with permission from BYTE Magazine, © by McGraw-Hill, Inc., New York, NY. All rights reserved.*

Sources: G. Christian Hill, "Cyberslaves," *The Wall Street Journal*, June 17, 1996; Dan Richman, "Let Your Agent Handle It," *Information Week*, April 17, 1995; G. Christian Hill, "Electronic 'Agents' Bring Virtual Shopping a Bit Closer to Reality," *The Wall Street Journal*, September 27, 1994; Peter Wayner, "Agents Away," *Byte*, May 1994.

more people at distant locations to work on the same document or data simultaneously is called **dataconferencing**. With dataconferencing, two or more users at distant locations are able to edit and directly modify data (text, such as word processing documents; numeric, such as spreadsheets; and graphic) files simultaneously. Teleconferencing that also has the capability to let participants see each other face-to-face over video screens is termed *video teleconferencing*, or **videoconferencing**.

These various forms of electronic conferencing are growing in popularity because they save travel time and cost. Legal firms might use videoconferencing to take depositions and to convene meetings between lawyers in different branch offices. For example, the firm of Howrey & Simon with 300 lawyers in Los Angeles has several expensive teleconferencing rooms that are busy almost constantly, linking them with their staff counterparts in Washington, DC. Designers and engineers use videoconferencing for remote collaboration. The cosmetics manufacturer Estée Lauder is using desktop videoconferencing to enable staff in Manhattan and Melville, Long Island, to view products under design along with the talking heads of meeting participants. Hospitals, universities, and even corporate researchers are using videoconferencing to fill in personnel expertise gaps (Brandel, 1995; Frye, 1995). Electronic conferencing is even useful in supporting telecommuting, enabling home workers to meet with or collaborate with their counterparts working in the office or elsewhere.

Videoconferencing has usually required special video conference rooms and videocameras, microphones, television monitors, and a computer equipped with a codec device that converts video images and analog sound waves into digital signals and compresses them for transfer over communications channels. Another codec on the receiving end reconverts the digital signals back into analog for display on the receiving monitor. Microcomputer-based desktop videoconferencing systems where users can see each other and simultaneously work on the same document are reducing videoconferencing costs so that more organizations can benefit from this technology.

dataconferencing Teleconferencing in which two or more users are able to edit and directly modify data files simultaneously.

videoconferencing Teleconferencing with the capability of participants to see each other over video screens.

ELECTRONIC DATA INTERCHANGE

Electronic data interchange (EDI) is the direct computer-to-computer exchange between two organizations of standard business transaction documents such as invoices, bills of lading, or purchase orders. EDI saves money and time because transactions can be transmitted from one information system to another through a telecommunications network, eliminating the printing and handling of paper at one end and the inputting of data at the other. EDI may also provide strategic benefits by helping a firm lock in customers, making it easier for customers or distributors to order from them rather than from competitors.

EDI differs from electronic mail in that it transmits an actual structured transaction (with distinct fields such as the transaction date, transaction amount, sender's name, and recipient's name) as opposed to an unstructured text message such as a letter.

Figure 8.14 illustrates how EDI operates at the Cummins Engine Company. Cummins implemented EDI to automate purchasing, shipping, and payment transactions with its customers. Cummins transmits price updates and shipping notices directly to its customers' computer system. Customers in turn transmit material releases, reports on receiving discrepancies, and payment and remittance data directly to Cummins's computer system. EDI has replaced paper for these transactions.

EDI lowers routine transaction processing costs and turnaround time because there is less need to transfer data from hard copy forms into computer-ready transactions. EDI reduces transcription errors and associated costs that occur when data are entered and printed out many times. Chapter 2 has shown how EDI can also curb inventory costs by minimizing the amount of time components are in inventory. Organizations can most fully benefit from EDI when they integrate the data supplied by EDI with applications such as accounts payable, inventory control, shipping, and production planning (Premkumar, Ramamurthy, and Nilakanta, 1994). However, to use EDI successfully,

electronic data interchange (EDI) The direct computer-to-computer exchange between two organizations of standard business transaction documents.

FIGURE 8.14
How EDI works at Cummins Engine Company. Cummins Engine Company uses EDI to automate price, shipping, receiving, and payment transactions with its customers. Cummins's price updates and shipping notices are entered by the appropriate departments directly into Cummins's computer system, which transmits them to its customers' computer systems. Customers' material releases, receiving reports, and payment data are also transmitted directly through the computer systems back to Cummins. *Source: From Robert Knight "EDI Hitting Stride in Data Entry" Software Magazine, February 1992. Copyright Sentry Technology Group. Reprinted by permission.*

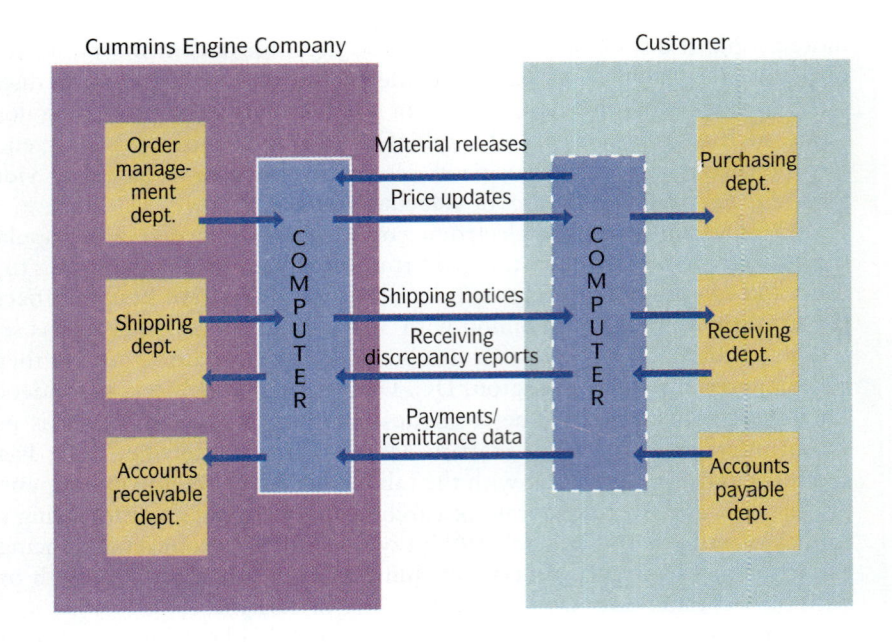

companies must standardize the form of the transactions they use with other firms and comply with legal requirements for verifying that the transactions are authentic.

As intelligent agent technology and commercial networks open new electronic marketplaces, they will lead to more flexible forms of EDI in which exchange of purchase and sale transactions are not limited to the computer systems of two organizations.

GROUPWARE

groupware Software and networking that recognizes the significance of groups in offices by providing functions and services that support the collaborative activities of work groups.

Groupware provides functions and services to support the collaborative activities of work groups. Groupware includes software for information sharing, electronic meetings, scheduling, and e-mail, and a network to connect the members of the group as they work on their own desktop computers, often in widely scattered locations. The groupware definition of groups is fluid, allowing users to define the work groups, with multiple group definitions allowed. For example, a manager may define a group of only those people who work for him. A group may be established for all employees dealing with a specific customer. A company wide group may be established. Of course, an individual will belong to as many of those groups as is appropriate. Table 8.4 describes the capabilities of groupware.

Groupware enhances collaboration by allowing the exchange of ideas (in the form of electronic messages) on a given topic. All the messages on that topic will be saved in a group, stamped with the date, time, and author. Any group member can review the ideas of others at any time and add ideas of his or her own. Similarly, individuals can

Table 8.4	Groupware Capabilities
Group writing and commenting	
Electronic mail distribution	
Scheduling meetings and appointments	
Shared files and databases	
Shared time lines and plans	
Electronic meetings	

256 CHAPTER 8 Telecommunications

post a document for other members of the group to comment upon or edit. Members of a group can post requests for help from the group, and any member of the group can respond and can view the responses of other members of the group. Finally, if a group so chooses, the members of that group can store their work notes on the groupware so that all others in the group can see what progress is being made, what problems occur, and what activities are planned.

The leading groupware product has been Lotus Notes from the Lotus Development Corporation. The Microsoft Corporation has developed Microsoft Exchange for this purpose and the Internet can be used for many groupware functions (see Chapters 9 and 12).

The Emergency Operations Center of Pacific Gas and Electric (PG&E) uses Lotus Notes groupware to receive damage reports and repair requests from 150 offices throughout the 93,000 square miles in Northern California. While management in San Francisco may use the database to view a chronological list of outages, the local offices will use it to produce a listing of outages that still need repairing. When the San Francisco earthquake hit in October 1989, PG&E found the system to be quite effective in facilitating the management of the many repairs urgently needed. The database was also the source for information supplied to the press on the types of outages that had occurred. Chapter 12 provides more detail on how organizations are using groupware to coordinate and distribute knowledge.

8.5 MANAGEMENT ISSUES AND DECISIONS

The starting point for rational planning of telecommunications is to forget about the features of systems and instead to try to understand the requirements of one's organization. A telecommunications plan is more likely to succeed if it advances the key business goals of the company. Cutting costs and installing advanced systems for their own sake is rarely a sufficient reason to justify large telecommunications projects.

THE TELECOMMUNICATIONS PLAN

Telecommunications has enormous potential for enhancing a firm's strategic position, but managers need to determine exactly how the firm's competitive position could be enhanced by telecommunications technology. Managers need to ask how telecommunications can reduce costs by increasing the *scale* and *scope* of operations without additional management costs; they need to determine if telecommunications technology can help them *differentiate* products and services; or if telecommunications technology can improve the firm's *cost structure* by eliminating intermediaries such as distributors or by accelerating business processes.

There are steps to implement a strategic telecommunications plan. First, start with an audit of the communications functions in your firm. What are your voice, data, video, equipment, staffing, and management capabilities? Then identify priorities for improvement.

Second, you must know the long-range business plans of your firm. Your plan should include an analysis of precisely how telecommunications will contribute to the specific five-year goals of the firm and to its longer-range strategies (e.g., cost reduction, distribution enhancement).

Third, identify critical areas where telecommunications currently does or can have the potential to make a large difference in performance. In insurance, these may be systems that give field representatives quick access to policy and rate information; in retailing, inventory control and market penetration; and in industrial products, rapid, efficient distribution and transportation.

IMPLEMENTING THE PLAN

Once an organization has developed a business telecommunications plan, it must determine the initial scope of the telecommunications project. Managers should take eight factors into account when choosing a telecommunications network.

The first and most important factor is *distance*. If communication will be largely local and entirely internal to the organization's buildings and social networks, there is little or no need for VANs, leased lines, or long-distance communications.

Along with distance, one must consider the *range of services* the network must support, such as electronic mail, EDI, internally generated transactions, voice mail, videoconferencing, or imaging, and whether these services must be integrated in the same network.

A third factor to consider is *security*. The most secure means of long-distance communications is through lines that are owned by the organization. The next-most secure form of telecommunications is through dedicated leased lines. VANs that slice up corporate information into small packets are among the least secure modes. Finally, ordinary telephone lines, which can be tapped at several locations, are even less secure than VANs.

A fourth factor to consider is whether *multiple access* is required throughout the organization or whether it can be limited to one or two nodes within the organization. A multiple-access system requirement suggests that there will be perhaps several thousand users throughout the corporation; therefore, a commonly available technology such as installed telephone wire and the related technology of a PBX is recommended. However, if access is restricted to fewer than 100 high-intensity users, a more advanced, higher-speed technology like a fiber optic or broadband LAN system may be recommended.

A fifth and most difficult factor to judge is *utilization*. There are two aspects of utilization that must be considered when developing a telecommunications network: the frequency and the volume of communications. Together, these two factors determine the total load on the telecommunications system. On the one hand, high-frequency, high-volume communications suggest the need for high-speed LANs for local communication and leased lines for long-distance communication. On the other hand, low-frequency, low-volume communications suggest dial-up, voice-grade telephone circuits operating through a traditional modem.

A sixth factor is *cost*. How much does each telecommunications option cost? Total costs should include costs for development, operations, maintenance, expansion, and overhead. Which cost components are fixed? Which are variable? Are there any hidden costs to anticipate? It is wise to recall the *thruway effect*. The easier it is to use a communications path, the more people will want to use it. Most telecommunications planners estimate future needs on the high side and still often underestimate the actual need. Underestimating the cost of telecommunications projects or uncontrollable telecommunications costs are principal causes of network failure.

Seventh, you must consider the difficulties of *installing* the telecommunications system. Are the organization's buildings properly constructed to install fiber optics? In some instances, buildings have inadequate wiring channels underneath the floors, which makes installation of fiber-optic cable extremely difficult.

Eighth, you must consider how much *connectivity* would be required to make all of the components in a network communicate with each other or to tie together multiple networks. There are so many different standards for hardware, software, and communication systems that it may be very difficult to get all of the components of a network to talk to each other or to distribute information from one network to another. Chapter 9 treats connectivity issues in greater detail. Table 8.5 summarizes these implementation factors.

Table 8.5	Implementation Factors in Telecommunications Systems
Distance	
Range of services	
Security	
Multiple access	
Utilization	
Cost	
Installation	
Connectivity	

Management Challenges

1. Managing LANs. While local-area networks appear to be flexible and inexpensive ways of delivering computing power to new areas of the organization, they must be carefully administered and monitored. LANs are especially vulnerable to network disruption, loss of essential data, access by unauthorized users, and infection from computer viruses (see Chapters 9 and 14). Dealing with these problems, or even installing popular applications such as spreadsheets or data management software on a network, requires special technical expertise that is not normally available in end-user departments and is in very short supply.

2. Compatibility and standards. There is such a bewildering array of hardware, software, and network standards that managers may have trouble choosing the right telecommunications platform for the firm's information architecture. Telecommunications systems based on one standard may not be able to be linked to telecommunications based on another without additional equipment, expense, and management overhead. Networks that meet today's requirements may lack the connectivity for domestic or global expansion in the future. The compatibility and standards challenge is such a serious management challenge that an entire section of the following chapter is devoted to connectivity issues.

Summary

1. Describe the basic components of a telecommunications system. A telecommunications system is a set of compatible devices that are used to develop a network for communication from one location to another by electronic means. The essential components of a telecommunications system are computers, terminals, or other input/output devices, communications channels, communications processors (such as modems, multiplexers, controllers, and front-end processors), and telecommunications software. Different components of a telecommunications network can communicate with each other with a common set of rules termed *protocols*.

Data are transmitted throughout a telecommunications network using either analog signals or digital signals. A modem is a device that translates from analog to digital and vice versa.

2. Measure the capacity of telecommunications channels and evaluate transmission media. The capacity of a telecommunications channel is determined by the range of frequencies it can accommodate. The higher the range of frequencies, called *bandwidth*, the higher the capacity (measured in bits per second). The principal transmission media are twisted copper telephone wire, coaxial copper cable, fiber-optic cable, and wireless transmission utilizing microwave, satellite, low frequency radio, or infrared waves.

Transmission media use either synchronous or asynchronous transmission modes for determining where a character begins or ends and when data are transmitted from one computer to another. Three different transmission modes governing the direction of data flow over a transmission medium are simplex, half-duplex, and full-duplex transmission.

3. Describe the three basic network topologies. The three common network topologies are the *star* network, the *bus* network, and the *ring* network. In a star network, all communications must pass through a central computer. The bus network links a number of devices to a single channel and broadcasts all of the signals to the entire network, with special software to identify which components receive each message. In a ring network, each computer in the network can communicate directly with any other computer but the channel is a closed loop. Data are passed along the ring from one computer to another.

4. Classify the various types of telecommunications networks. Networks can be classified by their shape or configuration or by their geographic scope and type of services provided. *Local-area networks* (LANs) and *private branch exchanges* (PBXs) are used to link offices and buildings in close proximity. *Wide-area networks* (WANs) span a broad geographical distance, ranging from several miles to entire continents and are private networks that are independently managed. *Value-added networks* (VANs) also encompass a wide geographic area but are managed by a third party, which sells the services of the network to other companies.

5. Identify telecommunications applications that can provide competitive advantages to organizations. Using information systems for strategic advantage increasingly depends on telecommunications technology and applications such as electronic mail, voice mail, fax, digital information services, teleconferencing, dataconferencing, videoconferencing, electronic data interchange (EDI), and groupware. Electronic data interchange (EDI) is the direct computer-to-computer exchange between two organizations of standard business transaction documents such as invoices, bills of lading, and purchase orders. Groupware allows people working in groups to collaborate and share information.

6. Explain the criteria used in planning for telecommunications systems. Firms should develop strategic telecommunications plans to ensure that their telecommunications systems serve business objectives and operations. Important factors to consider are distance, range of services, security, access, utilization, cost, installation, and connectivity.

Key Terms

Telecommunications
Information superhighway
Telecommunications system
Protocol
Analog signal
Digital signal
Modem
Channels
Twisted wire
Coaxial cable
Fiber-optic cable
Microwave
Satellite
Low-orbit satellites
Paging systems
Cellular telephone

Mobile data networks
Personal communication services (PCS)
Personal digital assistants (PDA)
Baud
Bandwidth
Asynchronous transmission
Synchronous transmission
Simplex transmission
Half-duplex transmission
Full-duplex transmission
Communications processors
Front-end processor
Concentrator
Controller

Multiplexer
Telecommunications software
Topology
Star network
Bus network
Ring network
Private branch exchange (PBX)
Local-area network (LAN)
File server
Network operating system
Gateway
Baseband
Broadband
Wide-area network (WAN)
Switched lines

Dedicated lines
Value-added network (VAN)
Packet switching
Frame relay
Asynchronous transfer mode (ATM)
Electronic mail (e-mail)
Voice mail
Facsimile (fax)
Intelligent agent
Teleconferencing
Dataconferencing
Videoconferencing
Electronic data interchange (EDI)
Groupware

Review Questions

1. What is the significance of telecommunications deregulation for managers and organizations?
2. What is a telecommunications system? What are the principal functions of all telecommunications systems?
3. Name and briefly describe each of the components of a telecommunications system.
4. Distinguish between an analog and a digital signal.
5. Name the different types of telecommunications transmission media and compare them in terms of speed and cost.
6. What is the relationship between bandwidth and the transmission capacity of a channel?
7. What is the difference between synchronous and asynchronous transmission? Between half-duplex, duplex, and simplex transmission?
8. Name and briefly describe the different kinds of communications processors.
9. Name and briefly describe the three principal network topologies.
10. Distinguish between a PBX and a LAN.
11. Define a wide-area network (WAN).

12. Define the following:
    - Modem
    - Baud
    - File server
    - Value-added network (VAN)
    - Packet switching
    - Asynchronous transfer mode (ATM)
13. Name and describe the telecommunications applications that can provide strategic benefits to businesses.
14. What are the principal factors to consider when developing a telecommunications plan?

Discussion Questions

1. Your firm has just decided to build a new headquarters building in a suburban setting. You have been assigned to work with an architect on plans for making the new building intelligent—that is, capable of supporting the computing and telecommunications needs of the business. What factors should you consider?
2. Your boss has just read in a leading business magazine that local-area networks are the wave of the future. You are directed to explore how the firm can use these LANs. What words of caution and what factors should the boss consider?
3. You are an electronic parts distributor for television repair shops throughout the country. You would like to edge out regional competitors and improve service. How could you use computers and telecommunications systems to achieve these goals?
4. If a channel has capacity of 1200 bits per second, approximately how long would it take to transmit this book? (Assume that there are 250 words per page and spaces do not count as characters. Do not include graphics.)

Group Project

With a group of two or three of your fellow students, describe in detail the various ways that telecommunications technology can provide a firm with competitive advantage. Use the companies described in Chapter 2 or other chapters you have read about so far to illustrate the points you make, or select examples of other companies using telecommunications from business or computer magazines. Present your findings to the class.

Case Study

GOODYEAR AUTOMATES ITS SALES FORCE

Goodyear Tire & Rubber Co., of Akron, Ohio, manufactures tires and rubber products for automobiles, trucks, and heavy equipment, and sells its products throughout the world. At the end of 1994 it had 16 percent of the world's market for tires. Its sales were growing at an annual rate of 4.2 percent versus an industry average of 2.5 percent.

The picture was very different in 1991. At that time the company was heavily debt-laden and was losing money rapidly. It had a 14 percent share of the world's tire market. In June of that year Stanley C. Gault became the chief executive officer (CEO) of Goodyear. Gault had previously been the senior vice president of General Electric followed by a turn as CEO of Rubbermaid. During his stewardship of Rubbermaid, he led the transformation of the company from a little-known maker of household cleaning items into a $3-billion-a-year maker of 4000 different products. Given this record, he was brought to Goodyear to turn the company around.

Gault accomplished the turnaround through a series of policies. He quickly sold off Goodyear's nontire businesses, freeing the company to focus its core skills. He engineered a sharp reduction in staff, led the development of a range of new products, and expanded sales by changing its distribution policy. He also issued new stock which helped to reduce its immense debt. By 1993 Goodyear's debt had been drastically reduced. Moreover, not only had the company returned to profitability, but its profit of $388 million that year was more than all other tire makers in the world combined.

The change in distribution channels was a major shift in policy. Historically the company had sold exclusively through independents, many of them selling only Goodyear products. In 1992 Gault initiated a policy to begin selling tires through large retailers in addition to independents, starting with Sears, Roebuck & Co., the largest tire retailer in the United States. The following year, he announced that Goodyear would also begin selling its tires to Wal-Mart Stores, the nation's largest retailer, and to Discount Tire, a major tire discounter.

Not surprisingly, this move to major retailers generated a great deal of antagonism among independent Goodyear dealers. In early 1995 the company revamped its sales organization. This move was preceded several years earlier by a sales force automation (SFA) development project to automate Goodyear's sales and marketing systems.

Widespread interest in automating sales forces is a 1990s phenomenon. A number of technological developments contributed to the growing popularity of SFA, including lightweight portable computers with multimedia capabilities and graphical user interfaces, the proliferation of LANs and WANs, and integration of databases distributed throughout the enterprise, thus enabling easy access to a wide range of enterprise data. The popularity of such fourth-generation tools as spreadsheets and word processors have made SFA systems easier to use and more productive, as has the spreading use of electronic mail.

Observers believe these systems offer a range of benefits to organizations. Their most basic benefit is that they can increase the productivity of the sales staff. This has been a driving force both because of the intensified competitive environment putting pressure on sales staffs, and because of the business need to keep costs low (in some cases downsized sales forces are expected to increase sales). Traditionally, many salespersons had spent a significant amount of time prior to a sales call collecting information from various computers and via telephone (see Figure 8.15 to obtain a picture of the sales process). For example, a study demonstrated that the sales staff of Deere Power, a maker of diesel engines and other heavy equipment, often spent a full day collecting data before a sales call. Studies indicate that the average sales call now costs about $250, up from only $80 as recently as 1975.

Efficiencies can be achieved in a variety of ways, as illustrated in Figure 8.16. First, these systems can help salespersons to select the best sales prospects. Moreover, with an SFA system, the salesperson can quickly load

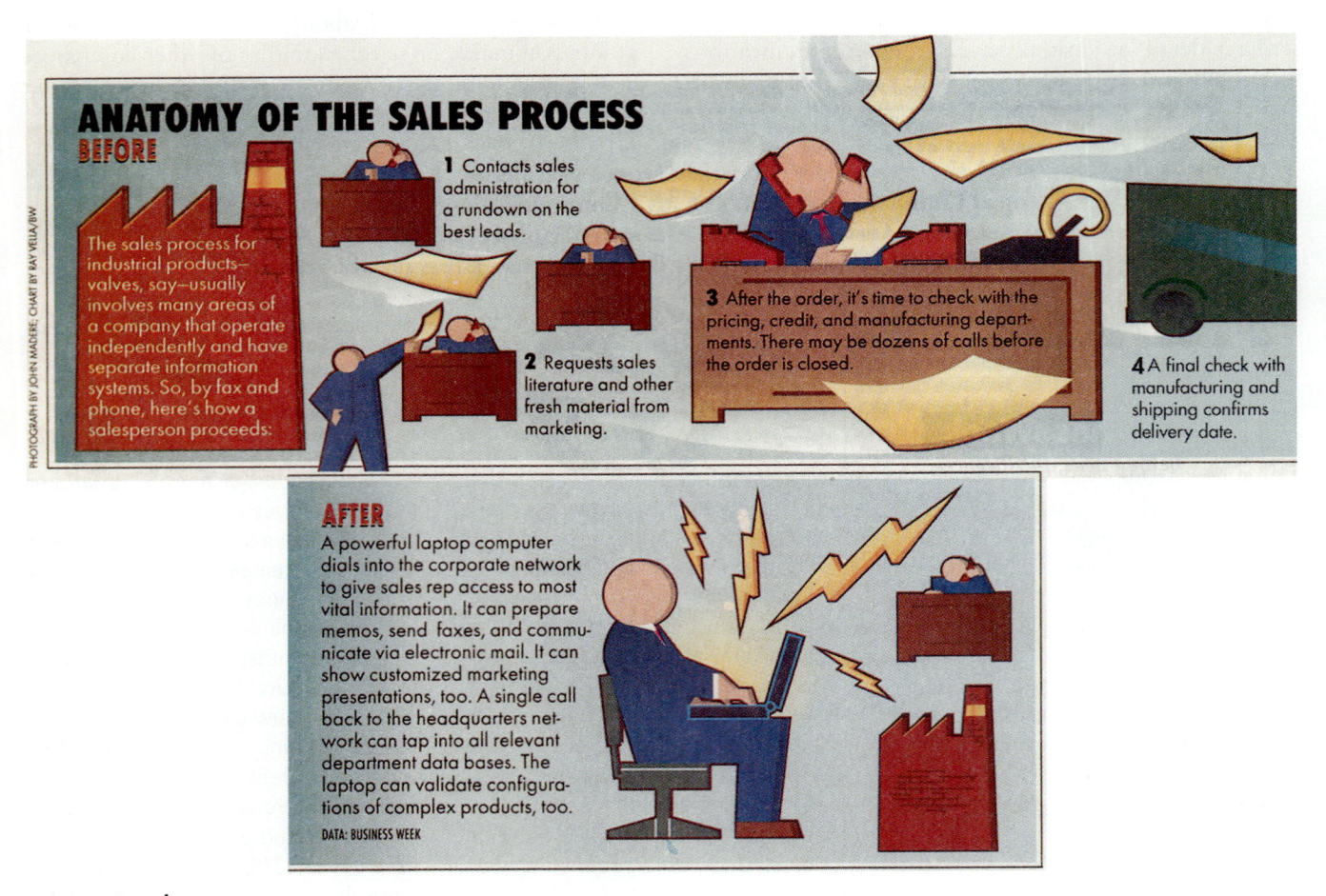

FIGURE 8.15
The sales process before and after automation. Laptop computers and corporate networks can radically streamline the sales process and give sales representatives new capabilities. *Adapted from: "Anatomy of the Sales Process,"* Business Week, *October 25, 1993.*

onto his or her laptop computer all the latest data needed for that day's calls. In addition to customer and product information, the computer will carry production and product availability data, order forms, pricing information, an electronic calendar and a tickler file, word processing integrated with mail-merge capabilities and reporting facilities, and even access to e-mail. Studies also show that the average sales rep traditionally spends 9 to 11 minutes per day per account on paperwork, offering immense room for savings through the use of the software on the laptop. For example, with an SFA system, the sales staff will no longer need to write product descriptions, add up orders, call in about production status, or check the order for errors, leaving them more time for selling. Many systems even electronically transmit the orders to the organization.

Automated systems also can result in higher quality sales calls. While the salesperson will actually be in the customer's office, she or he is able to respond as if the customer had come into the salesperson's own office. The salesperson not only will be able to talk about the product and show catalog pictures (stored on the computer) but also might be able to show short video clips. The computer files will include up-to-date production data, allowing the salesperson to respond immediately to a customer's timing requests. Moreover, because the salesperson's computer carries all that data, the salesperson does not need to tie up the client's telephone trying to get cost or production data prior to closing a sale.

SFAs usually offer the ability to forecast sales, to calculate commissions, and to adjust sales quotas, all while in the field. They also support team selling which is particularly valuable for large corporate accounts. They have proven to be valuable in generating new sales. For example, they aid in closing the sale on the spot because of the availability of production data and access to full pricing data so that the sales rep is able to respond immediately to a competitor's price. Companies have also found that after the installation of a sales force system, their current customer attrition rate drops.

Problems do exist with sales force automation systems. First, studies indicate that a new system costs from $7500 to $15,000 per salesperson to develop. Once in place, they usually cost $2500 to $3500 per salesperson per year for maintenance and support. SFAs can be expensive, resulting in multimillion-dollar systems. Moreover, some com-

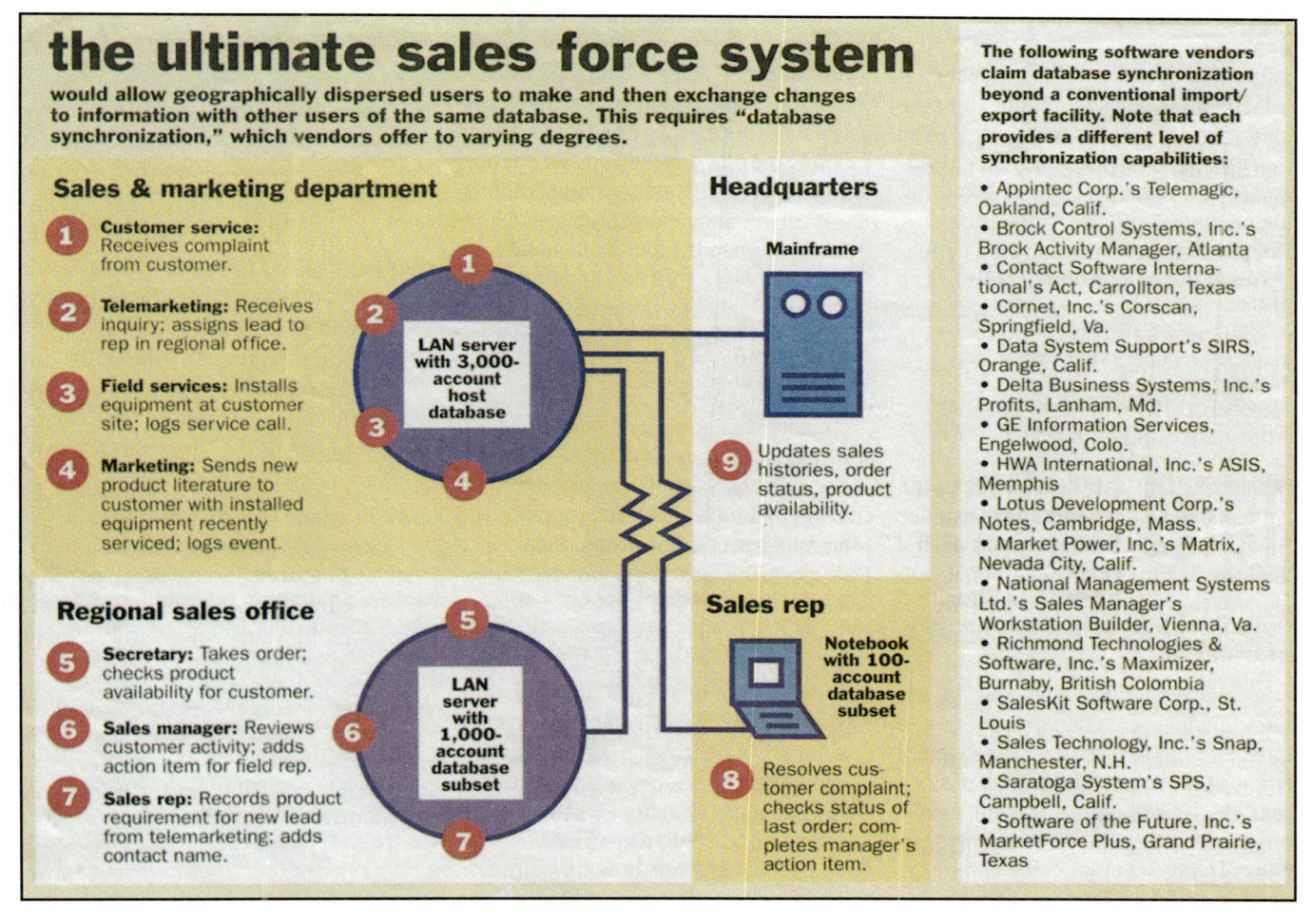

the ultimate sales force system

would allow geographically dispersed users to make and then exchange changes to information with other users of the same database. This requires "database synchronization," which vendors offer to varying degrees.

Sales & marketing department

1. **Customer service:** Receives complaint from customer.
2. **Telemarketing:** Receives inquiry; assigns lead to rep in regional office.
3. **Field services:** Installs equipment at customer site; logs service call.
4. **Marketing:** Sends new product literature to customer with installed equipment recently serviced; logs event.

LAN server with 3,000-account host database

Regional sales office

5. **Secretary:** Takes order; checks product availability for customer.
6. **Sales manager:** Reviews customer activity; adds action item for field rep.
7. **Sales rep:** Records product requirement for new lead from telemarketing; adds contact name.

LAN server with 1,000-account database subset

Headquarters

Mainframe

9. Updates sales histories, order status, product availability.

Sales rep

Notebook with 100-account database subset

8. Resolves customer complaint; checks status of last order; completes manager's action item.

The following software vendors claim database synchronization beyond a conventional import/export facility. Note that each provides a different level of synchronization capabilities:

- Appintec Corp.'s Telemagic, Oakland, Calif.
- Brock Control Systems, Inc.'s Brock Activity Manager, Atlanta
- Contact Software International's Act, Carrollton, Texas
- Cornet, Inc.'s Corscan, Springfield, Va.
- Data System Support's SIRS, Orange, Calif.
- Delta Business Systems, Inc.'s Profits, Lanham, Md.
- GE Information Services, Englewood, Colo.
- HWA International, Inc.'s ASIS, Memphis
- Lotus Development Corp.'s Notes, Cambridge, Mass.
- Market Power, Inc.'s Matrix, Nevada City, Calif.
- National Management Systems Ltd.'s Sales Manager's Workstation Builder, Vienna, Va.
- Richmond Technologies & Software, Inc.'s Maximizer, Burnaby, British Colombia
- SalesKit Software Corp., St. Louis
- Sales Technology, Inc.'s Snap, Manchester, N.H.
- Saratoga System's SPS, Campbell, Calif.
- Software of the Future, Inc.'s MarketForce Plus, Grand Prairie, Texas

FIGURE 8.16
The power of sales force automation. If properly designed to take advantage of powerful networks, databases, and desktop computers, automated sales force systems can deliver a wide range of capabilities. *From:* "The Hardest Sell," Computerworld, *September 20, 1993.*

panies install them without redesigning the sales function and other related functions. Without changing the way the sales staff works and the way the organization both supports the sales staff and makes use of sales data, that company will probably benefit very little from the new, expensive system. Applications that cut down on administrative time for sales reps don't automatically translate into more sales. Another key problem is the failure of top salespersons to use the system. Sales persons' strengths include individualism, a strong memory, and their people skills, and many reject the idea that carrying a laptop computer can help them.

Goodyear's North American tire division, with more than 500 sales staff, covers all the United States, from Maine to Hawaii, from Florida to Alaska. The sales force automation project began in early 1992. The major goal of the project was to boost the efficiency of marketing and sales departments, to make them more effective, and to boost customer relations (especially with the independent dealers). Management believed that the sales staff put in too much *windshield time* (hours spent traveling between home, office, and customers). Document communication was by regular mail, overnight delivery, and fax. The division management seldom was able to talk with the sales staff—after all, the division covered five time zones—and so they felt out of touch. The previous system tracked orders and deliveries on Goodyear's Amdahl mainframe running custom COBOL applications. As with many older mainframe systems, Goodyear's had very poor reporting and analysis features and was difficult to use. Moreover, it had no repository for institutional memory. When salespeople left, they took everything about the customer with them. Goodyear did expect to improve customer service and customer satisfaction. Management wanted the system to support their sales reps in assisting dealers with everything from advertising and sales, to business trends, cutting customer expenses, and running special events and promotions. They planned a system that would replace inadequate or absent technologies with an integrated sales and marketing system that would also work well with Goodyear's suite of financial applications.

Goodyear equipped its sales staff with laptop microcomputers, fax modems, and application and communication software. The core application of Goodyear's sales force automation system, dubbed Samis (Sales And Marketing Information System) is SPS. SPS distributes customer records to sales staffers, engineers, and technicians. The system also uses Metaphor, an IBM data access tool that extracts data from Samis and integrates it with the old COBOL executive information system (EIS). For communications software Goodyear used Advantis Passport.

With the new system, the sales person is able to download data from Goodyear's mainframe DB2 database in the morning into his or her laptop microcomputer, carry all the data needed that day in the laptop so that sales person will not normally need to go on-line during the day, and then upload any new data (orders, customer-contact reports, e-mail) in the evening. Samis also contains software to lighten the paperwork load. The sales staff can generate mailings to targeted customers; store small, useful details about the Goodyear dealer; and analyze data on shifts in consumer demand and in buying habits for the customer. The system supports key word searches in the DB2 database, enabling the sales staff in one area to learn about and monitor sales programs and promotions in other areas. Samis also supports the customers directly. For example, according to Jim McDonough, a Goodyear franchisee and owner of the Millburn, New Jersey, Tire & Auto Service, "We go on-line all the time to track my accruals." Finally, the system is much more than a laptop system. Middle management uses the system to communicate with the 26 sales offices and corporation management.

Goodyear's marketing department tracks how its staff uses the sales force automation system. According to Al Eastwood, Goodyear's VP responsible for replacement sales to franchisees and independent dealers, the company believes Samis is a worthwhile investment, even though its benefits can't be quantified. "How did you run your business before you could pick up a phone?" he asks. ∎

Source: Zachary Schiller, "And Fix That Flat Before You Go, Stanley," *Business Week*, January 16, 1995; Timothy Middleton, "Tire Maker Burns Rubber," *Information Week*, October 31, 1994; Jack Falvey, "The Hottest Thing in Sales Since the Electric Fork," *The Wall Street Journal*, January 10, 1994; Michael Fitzgerald, "Users Trying Again with Sales Force Automation," *Computerworld*, November 28, 1994; and John W. Verity, "Taking a Laptop on Call," *Business Week*, October 25, 1993.

Case Study Questions

1. What problems did Goodyear face, and what competitive strategy did the company follow to address these problems?

2. How did sales force automation fit in with and contribute to its strategy? How did the fact that the Samis system was networked support Goodyear's strategy?

3. Evaluate both the benefits and shortcomings of the Samis system. How could it have better supported the company's strategic goals?

4. Evaluate the role of Samis in addressing the disgruntled small dealers and franchisees. Was this a successful move? Was Goodyear's overall strategy successful? Explain your answer.

5. What management, organization, and technology issues had to be addressed when Goodyear implemented sales force automation?

References

Berst, Jesse. "Deciphering Lotus' Notes." *Computerworld* (May 18, 1992).

Brandel, Mary. "Videoconferencing Slowly Goes Desktop." *Computerworld* (February 20, 1995).

Dertouzos, Michael. "Building the Information Marketplace." *Technology Review* (January 1991).

Donovan, John J. "Beyond Chief Information Officer to Network Manager." *Harvard Business Review* (September–October 1988).

Etzioni, Oren and Daniel Weld. "A Softbot-Based Interface to the Internet." *Communications of the ACM* 37, no. 7 (July 1994).

Frye, Colleen. "Talking Heads: Coming to a Desktop Near You." *Software Magazine* (May 1995).

Gilder, George. "Into the Telecosm." *Harvard Business Review* (March–April 1991).

Grief, Irene. "Desktop Agents in Group-Enabled Projects." *Communications of the ACM* 37, no. 7 (July 1994).

Grover, Varun and Martin D. Goslar. "Initiation, Adoption, and Implementation of Telecommunications Technologies in U.S. Organizations." *Journal of Management Information Systems* 10, no. 1 (Summer 1993).

Hall, Wayne A., and Robert E. McCauley. "Planning and Managing a Corporate Network Utility." *MIS Quarterly* (December 1987).

Hammer, Michael, and Glenn Mangurian. "The Changing Value of Communications Technology." *Sloan Management Review* (Winter 1987).

Hansen, James V. and Ned C. Hill. "Control and Audit of Electronic Data Interchange." *MIS Quarterly* 13, no. 4 (December 1989).

Imielinski, Tomasz and B.R. Badrinath. "Mobile Wireless Computing: Challenges in Data Management." *Communications of the ACM* 37, no. 10 (October 1994).

Johansen, Robert. "Groupware: Future Directions and Wild Cards." *Journal of Organizational Computing* 1, no. 2 (April–June 1991).

Keen, Peter G.W. *Competing in Time*. Cambridge, MA: Ballinger Publishing Company, 1986.

Keen, Peter G.W. *Shaping the Future: Business Design Through Information Technology*. Cambridge, MA: Harvard Business School Press, 1991.

Keen, Peter G.W. and J. Michael Cummins. *Networks in Action: Business Choices and Telecommunications Decisions*. Belmont, California: Wadsworth Publishing Company, 1994.

Kim, B.G. and P. Wang. "ATM Network: Goals and Challenges." *Communications of the ACM* 38, no. 2 (February 1995).

Maes, Pattie. "Agents that Reduce Work and Information Overload." *Communications of the ACM* 37, no. 7 (July 1994).

Orlikowski, Wanda J. "Learning from Notes: Organizational Issues in Groupware Implementation." Sloan Working Paper no. 3428, Cambridge, MA: Sloan School of Management, Massachusetts Institute of Technology.

Press, Lawrence. "Lotus Notes (Groupware) in Context." *Journal of Organizational Computing* 2, no. 3 and 4 (1992b).

Premkumar, G., K. Ramamurthy, and Sree Nilakanta. "Implementation of Electronic Data Interchange: An Innovation Diffusion Perspective." *Journal of Management Information Systems* 11, no. 2 (Fall 1994).

Railing, Larry, and Tom Housel. "A Network Infrastructure to Contain Costs and Enable Fast Response." *MIS Quarterly* 14, no. 4 (December 1990).

Roche, Edward M. *Telecommunications and Business Strategy*. Chicago: The Dryden Press, 1991.

Rochester, Jack B. "Networking Management: The Key to Better Customer Service." *I/S Analyzer* 27, no. 12 (December 1989).

Rowe, Stanford H. II. *Business Telecommunications*. New York: Macmillan, 1991.

Schultz, Brad. "The Evolution of ARPANET." *Datamation* (August 1, 1988).

Selker, Ted. "Coach: A Teaching Agent that Learns." *Communications of the ACM* 37, no. 7 (July 1994).

Stahl, Stephanie and John Swenson. "Groupware Grows Up." *Information Week* (March 4, 1996).

Torkzadeh, Gholamreza, and Weidong Xia. "Managing Telecommunications Strategy by Steering Committee." *MIS Quarterly* 16, no. 2 (June 1992).

Vetter, Ronald J. "ATM Concepts, Architectures, and Protocols." *Communications of the ACM* 38, no. 2 (February 1995).

Chapter 9

Enterprise Networking and the Internet

Michigan Transportation Department Reinvents Itself with Networked Computers

9.1 Enterprise Networking
The Client/Server Model of Computing
Business Drivers of Enterprise Networking
Electronic Commerce

9.2 The Internet
Internet Capabilities
Internet Benefits to Organizations
Window on Organizations:
The Internet Becomes the Middleman

Window on Technology:
The Internet for EDI?
Intranets
Internet Challenges

9.3 Connectivity and Standards
Models of Connectivity for Networks
Other Networking Standards
Operating System Standards: The Open Systems Movement

9.4 Implementing Enterprise Networking
Problems Posed by Enterprise Networking
Some Solutions

Window on Management:
Bass Beer Serves a Client/Server Environment

Management Challenges
Summary
Key Terms
Review Questions
Discussion Questions
Group Project
Case Study: Unilever Tries to Unify World Operations
References

Michigan Transportation Department Reinvents Itself with Networked Computers

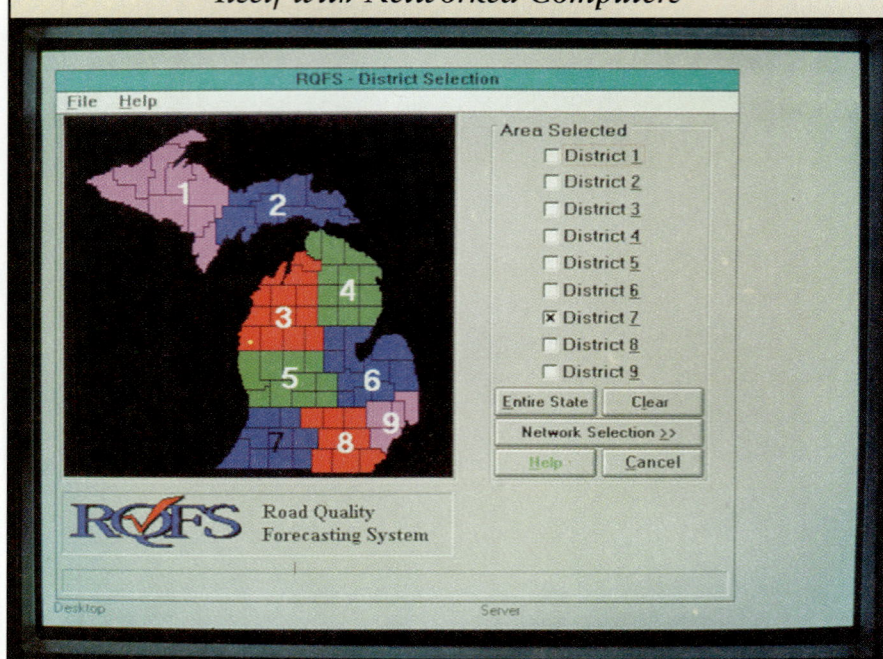

Managing all public transportation for the state of Michigan is a big business, with big business challenges. With 3600 employees and an annual budget exceeding $1 billion, the Michigan Department of Transportation (MDOT) had difficulty meeting its customers' needs. When the state legislature, for example, asked how a proposed gasoline tax increase would benefit the transportation system, MDOT had no idea. It couldn't just pull the numbers together using its old mainframe-based information systems.

MDOT management knew it had to reinvent the department. It asked fundamental questions, such as "Why are we in business? What is our mission?" It wanted MDOT to be able to examine all of the state's transportation needs, not just highways. It realized that MDOT had to communicate a lot better within the department in order to communicate better with its customers. So MDOT started moving toward more networked systems based on microcomputers and workstations and unplugging its mainframe. They began implementing systems based on client/server computing to provide staff members with more immediate access to the data they needed.

Using client/server technology, MDOT developed a strategic Road Quality and Forecasting System that furnishes project managers and pavement engineers with a graphical view of Michigan's roadway infrastructure and upcoming maintenance needs. Engineers using micros can select a geographic area and try out various maintenance strategies at their desktops. They can ask the system for the costs and expected lifespan of various improvements on any number of miles of road. The system instantly shows what Michgan's road network will look like in 10, 20, or 30 years.

Another client/server application called the Financial Obligation System allows anyone working on a project to access job information using a desktop micro. The network transmits the project manager's funding requests directly to MDOT's program control section. The system checks information automatically before routing it to an accountant, who makes spending decisions on-line. The accountant then routes the requests digitally to the federal highway office in Washington, D.C., which has communications links to MDOT. Before this system was implemented, the requisition and approval process used to average four to six weeks. The time lag put MDOT in a financial bind. MDOT had no way of knowing what its federal account balances were. Managers would sometimes have to proceed without approval and pay bills out of the state coffer until the federal funds came in. Now the process can be completed in only 24 hours.

By redesigning its information systems using networks and client/server computing, the Michigan Department of Transportation was able to reduce its work force by 20 percent while increasing the number of programs it handled. ■

Source: "Michigan Department of Transportation" in "Business Solutions from the New Computer Industry," Intel Corporation, 1994.

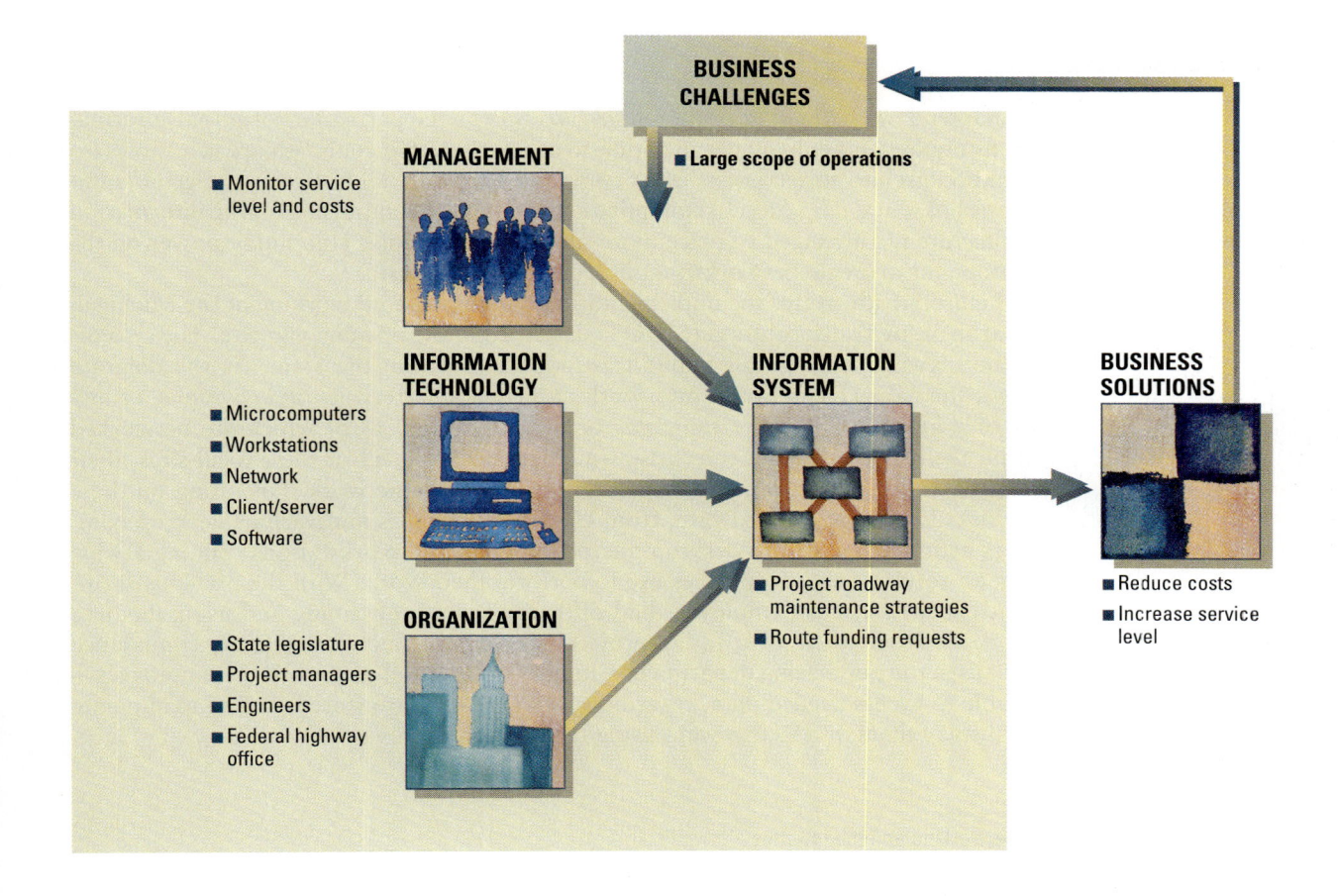

The Michigan Department of Transportation is one of many organizations that has rearranged its hardware, software, and communications capabilities into an enterprise-wide networked architecture. In the process, it transformed itself into a more efficient, effective organization. Instead of relying fundamentally on large centralized mainframe computers for processing, MDOT distributed computing power and information to powerful microcomputers and workstations on the desktop at many different locations. It divided the computer processing for various applications among desktop and larger computers. MDOT tied all of its computers together into a companywide network and developed communications links to other organizations.

By putting more control of computer processing on the desktop and linking mainframes, minicomputers and smaller networks into a companywide network, enterprise networking can help organizations achieve new levels of competitiveness and productivity. However, achieving these goals requires an understanding of how to make disparate hardware, software, and communications devices work together.

This chapter examines enterprise networking and the ways in which it is transforming organizations and fueling electronic commerce. It also examines the Internet, which links networks from many different organizations so that they can share information with each other. The key to creating networks where users can share data throughout the organization is connectivity. This chapter describes the connectivity models organizations use to link their systems and the standards that make such linkages possible.

Despite the benefits of linking networks, enterprise networking has created new management problems. We describe the problems and their solutions so that organizations can maximize the benefits of this new information architecture.

Learning Objectives

After completing this chapter, you will be able to:

1. Describe the characteristics of enterprise networking and explain how it is changing organizations.
2. Describe the client/server model of computing.
3. Identify the capabilities of the Internet and describe both the benefits it offers organizations and the problems it presents to them.
4. Describe important standards used for linking hardware, software, and networks to achieve connectivity.
5. Identify problems posed by enterprise networking and recommend solutions.

9.1 ENTERPRISE NETWORKING

enterprise networking An arrangement of the organization's hardware, software, telecommunications, and data resources to put more computing power on the desktop and create a companywide network linking many smaller networks.

In Chapter 1 we defined *information architecture* as the particular form that information technology takes in an organization to achieve selected goals. An organization's information architecture consists of its computer hardware and software, telecommunications links, and data files. In **enterprise networking** the components of the information architecture are arranged to place more of the organization's computing power on the desktop and to create networks that link entire enterprises.

Figure 9.1 illustrates the implementation of enterprise networking at the Michigan Department of Transportation (MDOT) described in the opening vignette. The systems on the network manage all public transportation within the state. As the diagram shows, the MDOT employees may work at its headquarters, its main campus, or any one of a number of remote campuses or district offices, all of which are networked within their own site. The enterprise-wide network links all of these local sites, their workers, and their information, together into one large network. Operating on these networks is a range of hardware, from Unisys mainframes and various desktop computers acting as servers, to desktop microcomputers and workstations running a wide range of software that employees use to perform their work. With the previous mainframe-centered system, employees had difficulty in both obtaining and using the data they needed to do their jobs. Today, project managers, engineers, regulatory compliance specialists, the purchasing department—in fact, virtually all of the MDOT employees—are able to access needed data, regardless of where they are stored, and to manipulate and display them in effective ways using the tools they prefer.

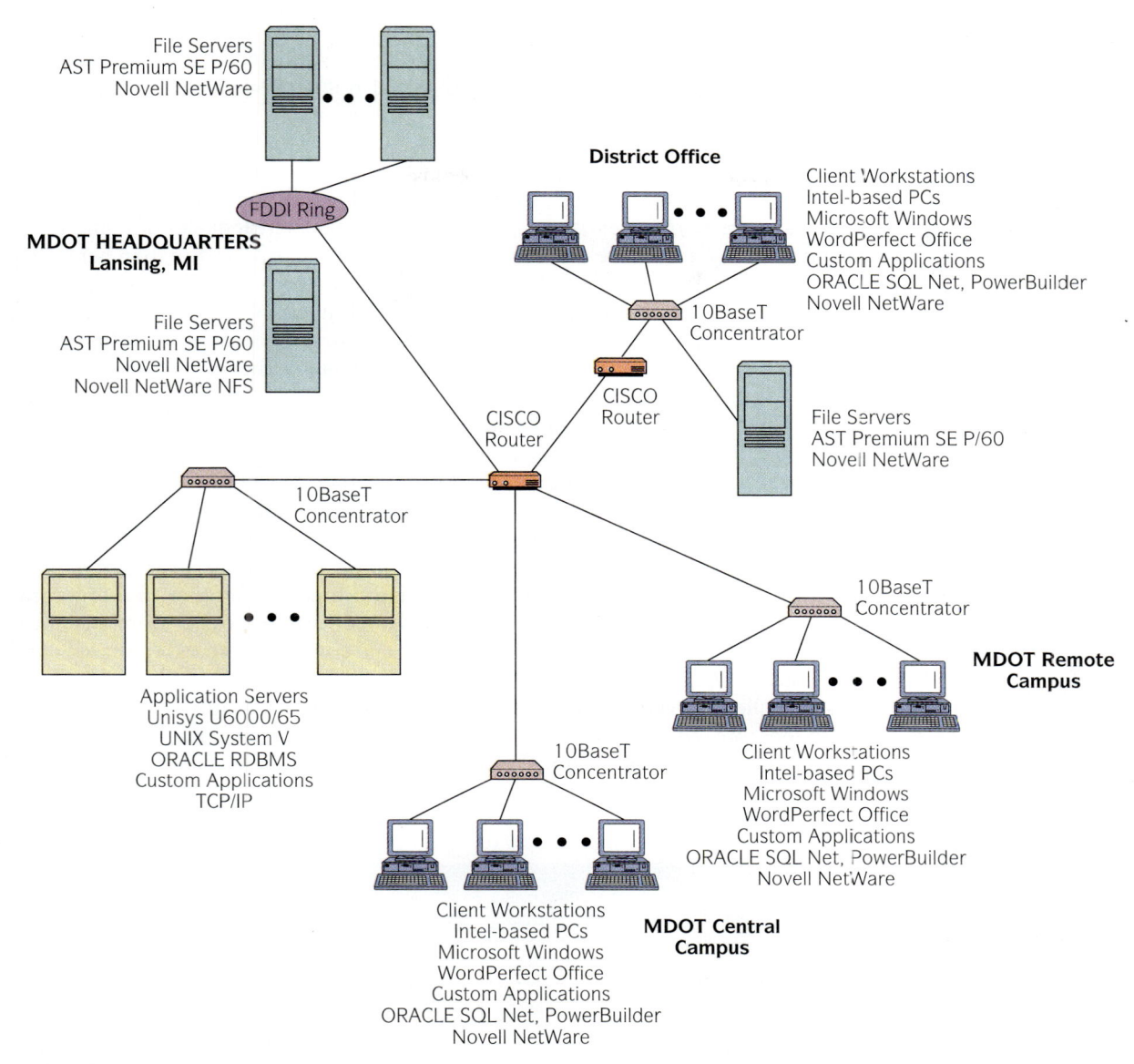

FIGURE 9.1
Enterprise networking at the Michigan Department of Transportation. MDOT's enterprise-wide network links desktop workstations and file servers at remote sites, district offices, and the MDOT headquarters. *Adapted from "Business Solutions from the New Computer Industry," Intel Corporation, 1994. Reprinted by permission.*

In earlier information systems, mainframes and minicomputers from the same computer manufacturer, using proprietary operating systems, were responsible for most of the firm's information processing. Microcomputers and workstations were used independently by individual users or were linked into small localized networks. By adopting an enterprise-wide information architecture, Michigan's Department of Transportation now uses a mixture of computer hardware supplied by different hardware vendors. Much of the organization's computer processing takes place on desktops. The role of the mainframes and minicomputers is diminished and more specialized. Large, complex databases that need central storage are found on mainframes, minis, or specialized file servers, while smaller databases and parts of large databases are loaded on microcomputers and workstations.

The system is a network. In fact, for all but the smallest organizations, the system is composed of multiple networks. A high-capacity backbone network connects many

internetworking The linking of separate networks, each of which retains its own identity, into an interconnected network.

client/server model A model for computing that splits the processing between clients and servers on a network, assigning functions to the machine most able to perform the function.

client The user point-of-entry for the required function. Normally a desktop computer, workstation, or laptop computer, the user generally interacts directly only with the client.

local area networks and devices. The backbone may be connected to many external networks like the Internet. The linking of separate networks (each of which retains its own identity) into an interconnected network is called **internetworking**.

THE CLIENT/SERVER MODEL OF COMPUTING

In enterprise networking, the primary way of delivering computing power to the desktop is known as the *client/server model*. In the **client/server model** of computing, data and processing power are distributed out into the enterprise rather than being centrally controlled. Client/server computing splits processing between *clients* and *servers*. Both are on the network, but each machine is assigned functions it is best suited to perform. Ideally, the user will experience the network as a single system with all functions, both client and server, integrated and accessible. The **client** is the user point-of-entry for the required function and is normally a desktop computer, workstation, or laptop computer. The user generally interacts directly only with the client portion of the application, typically through a graphical user interface. He or she typically uses it to input data and query a database to retrieve data. Once the data have been retrieved, the user can analyze and report on them, using fourth-generation packages such as spreadsheets, word processors, and graphics applications available on the client machine on his or her own desktop. The **server** satisfies some or all of the user's request for data and/or functionality and might be a supercomputer, mainframe, or another desktop computer. Servers store and process shared data and also perform back-end functions not visible to users, such as managing peripheral devices and controlling access to shared databases (see Figure 9.2).

The client/server model requires that application programs be written as two or more separate software components that run on different machines but that appear to operate as a single application. The exact division of tasks depends on the requirements of each application, including its processing needs, the number of users, and the avail-

FIGURE 9.2
The client/server model of computing. In the client/server model, computer processing is split between client machines and server machines, with each machine handling those tasks for which it is best suited. Users interface with the client machines. Client/server machines afford great customization and processing power.

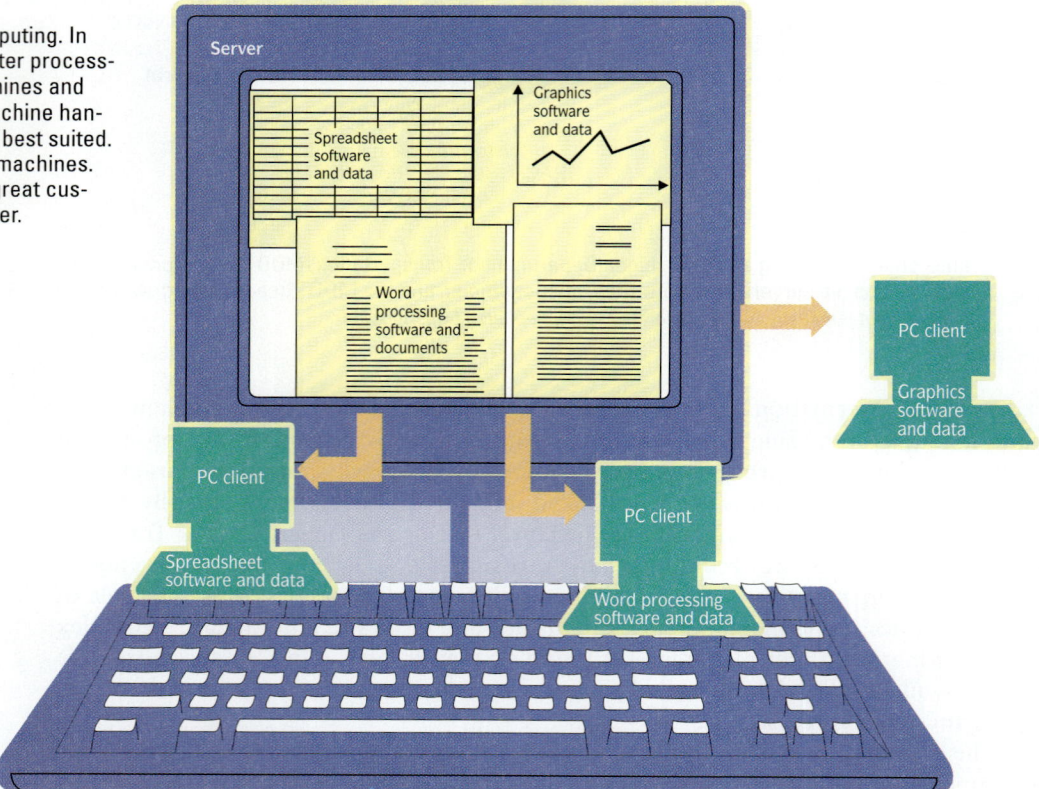

able resources. In the Michigan Department of Transportation network, the clients are fully functional microcomputers and the servers are specialized mainframes, workstations, and microcomputers.

The client/server model does have limitations. It is difficult to write software that divides processing among clients and servers, although more and more client/server software is commercially available. A specific server can get bogged down quickly when too many users simultaneously want service. Microcomputers with independent processing power are more difficult to coordinate and administer on a network. We explore management issues raised by client/server computing and enterprise networking in Section 9.4.

server A computer that satisfies some or all of a user's request for data and/or functionality, such as storing and processing shared data and performing back-end functions not visible to users, such as managing peripheral devices and controlling access to shared databases. It might be a supercomputer, mainframe, or desktop computer.

BUSINESS DRIVERS OF ENTERPRISE NETWORKING

Organizations have adopted enterprise networking and client/server computing for compelling business reasons, including the need to reduce costs, maintain global competitiveness and take advantage of new technologies. Chapters 5 and 8 have shown that the enhanced power of microprocessors coupled with falling prices and reliable and accessible communications mechanisms make it both technically and economically feasible to transfer computing resources to client/server-based networks. Today's desktop machines provide capabilities lacking in traditional mainframes—graphical user interfaces, productivity-promoting software such as spreadsheets and word processors, access to on-line information services, and interactive audiovisual computing involving multiple media such as sound, moving pictures, and text.

Enterprise networking and client/server computing intuitively reflect the new business environment of flattening organizations and decentralized management better than traditional mainframe systems. A client/server infrastructure is more decentralized and able to deliver more information at all organizational levels. The person using a networked desktop computer has more control over her or his own work. Networked computers also allow teams to work closely together, even when members of those teams are hundreds or thousands of miles apart.

In addition, a networked platform is flexible enough to support a nimble organization because it can be transformed rapidly in response to changing competitive needs of the current marketplace. In many instances, adding a few hundred—or even a few thousand—staff members to a network can be done in several weeks or months without degradation of service. Adding that many to a mainframe computer might require a major upgrade project that would consume a year or more.

For instance, Richmond Savings, the $1.1 billion (Canadian) full-service bank of Richmond, British Columbia, has been running all of its systems on networked workstations since 1988. The system performs virtually all of the normal banking functions, including automatic payroll deposits, ATMs, even touch-tone balance inquiries. According to management, the system makes the bank more nimble. For example, it added a touch-tone bill-payment subsystem in 1994 with no degradation of service, although it handles as many as 4000 bills per month. Because of the system, the bank staff was able to change from narrow departmental specialists to full personal bankers who are able to handle all tasks (Celko, 1994).

ELECTRONIC COMMERCE

Enterprise networking and internetworking are enabling companies to build a new business model in which they are directly linked to customers and suppliers as well as to other parts of their organizations. We have described various information technologies that are transforming the way products are produced, marketed, shipped, and sold. Companies are using WANs, VANs, the Internet, electronic data interchange (EDI), e-mail, shared databases, digital image processing, bar coding, and interactive software to replace telephone calls and traditional paper-based procedures for product design, marketing, ordering, delivery, and payment. Trading partners can directly communicate with each other, bypassing middlemen and inefficient multilayered procedures.

FIGURE 9.3
Electronic Commerce Technologies. The technology business partners use to communicate depends on the stage of their business deal. *Source: Gartner Group, Inc., Stamford, Conn.*

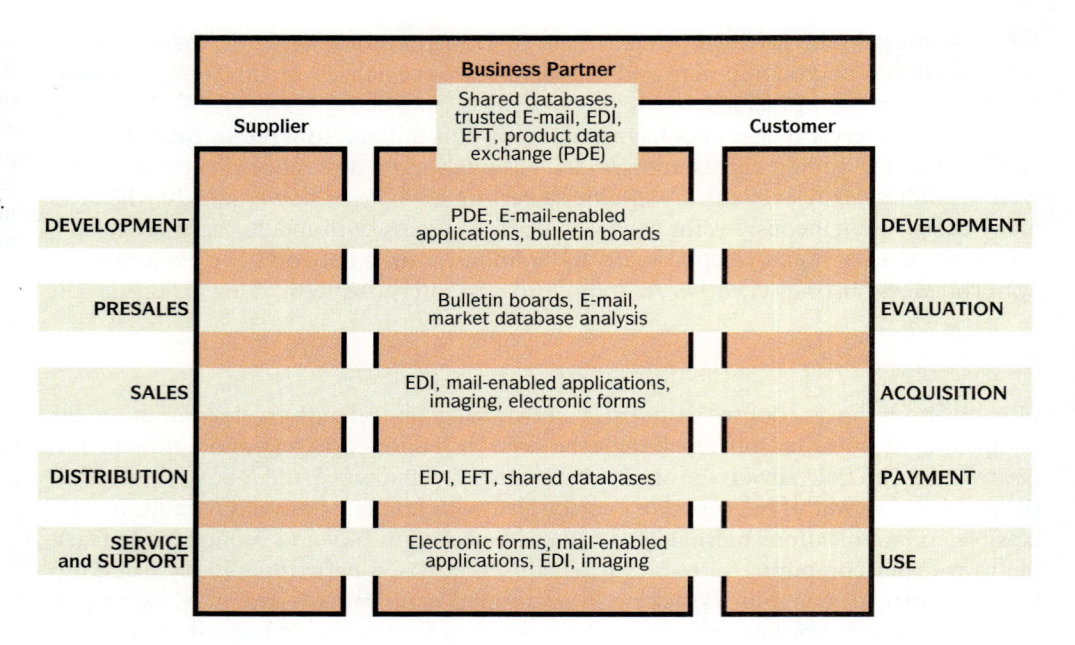

	Business Partner	
Supplier	Shared databases, trusted E-mail, EDI, EFT, product data exchange (PDE)	Customer
DEVELOPMENT	PDE, E-mail-enabled applications, bulletin boards	DEVELOPMENT
PRESALES	Bulletin boards, E-mail, market database analysis	EVALUATION
SALES	EDI, mail-enabled applications, imaging, electronic forms	ACQUISITION
DISTRIBUTION	EDI, EFT, shared databases	PAYMENT
SERVICE and SUPPORT	Electronic forms, mail-enabled applications, EDI, imaging	USE

Payment for purchases can take place through credit cards, electronic funds transfer, or digital cash transactions. *Electronic funds transfer* is the transfer of money from one bank's computer to another bank's computer. *Digital cash* is money transactions that move through a multiplicity of networks instead of the traditional banking system. Businesses can bypass banks and move digital cash directly to customers and suppliers. Technologies to authenticate and encrypt digital payment transactions are employed (see Chapter 14).

These tight inter-enterprise connections are the foundations of electronic commerce. **Electronic commerce** is the process of doing business electronically, involving the automation of various business-to-business transactions. By reducing clerical procedures and eliminating paper handling, electronic commerce can accelerate ordering, delivery, and payment for goods and services while reducing operating and inventory costs. Electronic commerce requires careful management of the firm's various divisions, production sites, and sales offices, as well as close partnering relationships with customers, suppliers, banks, and other trading partners. Figure 9.3 shows the information technologies that can be used to support various steps in electronic commerce. As time goes on, these steps will be increasingly automated.

electronic commerce The process of doing business electronically, involving the automation of various business-to-business transactions.

9.2 THE INTERNET

An increasingly important way that both public and private organizations are networking internally and with other organizations is through the Internet. The Internet is perhaps the most well known—and the largest—implementation of internetworking, linking over one hundred thousand individual networks all over the world. The Internet has a range of capabilities that organizations are using to exchange information internally or to communicate externally with other organizations. This giant network of networks is becoming a major catalyst for electronic commerce.

The Internet began as a United States Department of Defense network to link scientists and university professors around the world. Even today individuals cannot directly connect to the Net, although anyone with a computer and a modem and the willingness to pay a small monthly usage fee can access it through one of the many service providers that are popping up everywhere. Individuals can also access it through such popular on-line services as CompuServe, Prodigy, and America Online and through networks established by such giants as Microsoft and AT&T. Popular operating systems such as Windows 95 now include a built-in Internet gateway.

One of the most puzzling aspects of the Internet is that no one owns it and it has no formal management organization. To join the Internet, an existing network need only to pay a small registration fee and agree to certain standards based on the TCP/IP reference model (Transmission Control Protocol/Internet Protocol, described in Section 9.3). Costs are low because the Internet owns nothing and so has no real costs to offset. Each organization, of course, pays for its own networks and its own telephone bills, but those costs usually exist independent of the Internet. Regional Internet companies have been established to which member networks forward all transmissions. These Internet companies route and forward all traffic, and the cost is still only that of a local telephone call. The result of all this is that the cost of e-mail and other Internet connections tend to be far lower than equivalent voice, postal, or overnight delivery costs, making the Net a very inexpensive communications medium. It is also a very fast method of communication, with messages arriving anywhere in the world in a matter of seconds, or a minute or two at most.

The value of the Internet lies precisely in its ability to easily and inexpensively connect so many diverse people from so many places all over the globe. Anyone who has an Internet address can log onto a computer and reach virtually every other computer on the network, regardless of location, computer type, or operating system. We will now briefly describe the most important Internet capabilities.

INTERNET CAPABILITIES

The Internet is based upon client/server technology. Users of the Net control what they do through client applications, using graphical user interfaces or character-based products that control all functions. All the data, including e-mail messages, databases, and Web sites are stored on servers. Servers dedicated to the Internet, or even to specific Internet functions, are the heart of the information on the Net (see Figure 9.4).

Major Internet capabilities include e-mail, Usenet newsgroups, chatting, Telnet, gophers, Archie, WAIS, FTP, and the World Wide Web. Table 9.1 lists these capabilities and describes the functions they support.

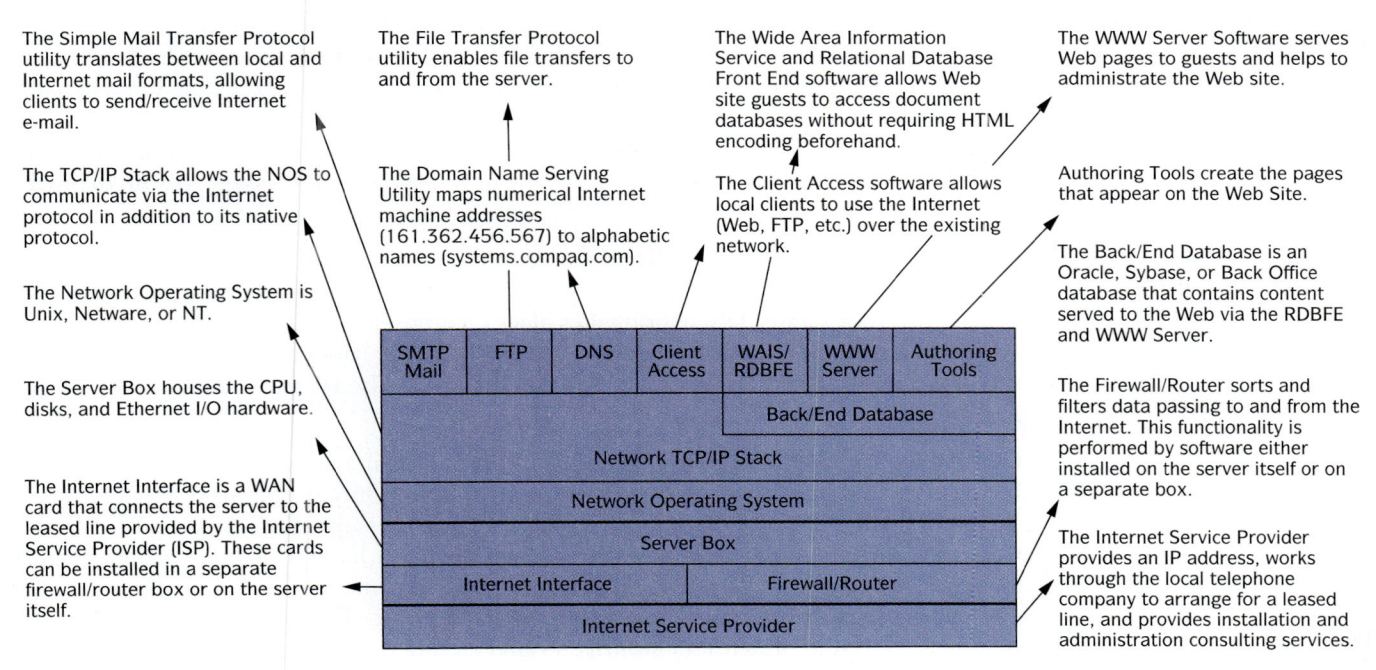

The Simple Mail Transfer Protocol utility translates between local and Internet mail formats, allowing clients to send/receive Internet e-mail.

The TCP/IP Stack allows the NOS to communicate via the Internet protocol in addition to its native protocol.

The Network Operating System is Unix, Netware, or NT.

The Server Box houses the CPU, disks, and Ethernet I/O hardware.

The Internet Interface is a WAN card that connects the server to the leased line provided by the Internet Service Provider (ISP). These cards can be installed in a separate firewall/router box or on the server itself.

The File Transfer Protocol utility enables file transfers to and from the server.

The Domain Name Serving Utility maps numerical Internet machine addresses (161.362.456.567) to alphabetic names (systems.compaq.com).

The Wide Area Information Service and Relational Database Front End software allows Web site guests to access document databases without requiring HTML encoding beforehand.

The Client Access software allows local clients to use the Internet (Web, FTP, etc.) over the existing network.

The WWW Server Software serves Web pages to guests and helps to administrate the Web site.

Authoring Tools create the pages that appear on the Web Site.

The Back/End Database is an Oracle, Sybase, or Back Office database that contains content served to the Web via the RDBFE and WWW Server.

The Firewall/Router sorts and filters data passing to and from the Internet. This functionality is performed by software either installed on the server itself or on a separate box.

The Internet Service Provider provides an IP address, works through the local telephone company to arrange for a leased line, and provides installation and administration consulting services.

SMTP Mail	FTP	DNS	Client Access	WAIS/ RDBFE	WWW Server	Authoring Tools
				Back/End Database		
Network TCP/IP Stack						
Network Operating System						
Server Box						
Internet Interface				Firewall/Router		
Internet Service Provider						

FIGURE 9.4
Components of an Internet Server *Source: Compaq*

Table 9.1 Major Internet Capabilities

Capability	Functions Supported
E-mail	Person-to-person messaging; document sharing
Usenet newsgroups	Discussion groups on electronic bulletin boards
Chatting	Interactive conversations
Telnet	Log on to one computer system and do work on another
Gophers	Locate textual information using a hierarchy of menus
Archie	Search database of documents, software and data files available for downloading
WAIS	Locate files in databases using keywords
FTP	Transfer files from computer to computer
World Wide Web	Retrieve, format, and display information (including text, audio, graphics, and video) using hypertext links

People-to-People Communications

Internet communication capabilities include E-mail, Usenet Newsgroups, Chatting, and Telnet.

ELECTRONIC MAIL (E-MAIL). The Net has become the most important e-mail system in the world because it connects so many people from all over the world, creating a productivity gain that observers have compared to Gutenberg's development of movable type in the fifteenth century. Private individuals typically use Internet e-mail facilities to keep in touch with friends. Organizations use it to facilitate communication among employees and among offices, to communicate with customers and suppliers, and to keep in touch with the outside world.

Researchers use this facility to share ideas, information, even documents. E-mail over the Net has also made possible many collaborative research and writing projects, even though the participants were thousands of miles apart. Dr. Brendan McKay, a scientist and member of the faculty of the Australian National University in Canberra, carries out his research in collaboration with Dr. Stanislaw Radziszowsky at the Rochester Institute of Technology in Rochester, New York. The two have exchanged more than 1000 messages in three years, working together much as they would if they were only a few miles apart. With proper software, the user will find it easy to attach documents and files when sending a message to someone or to broadcast a message to a predefined group. Figure 9.5 illustrates the components of an Internet e-mail address.

Usenet Forums in which people share information and ideas on a defined topic through large electronic bulletin boards where anyone can post messages on the topic for others to see and respond to.

USENET NEWSGROUPS (FORUMS). **Usenet** newsgroups are worldwide discussion groups in which people share information and ideas on a defined topic such as colorimetry or rock bands. Discussion takes place on large electronic bulletin boards where anyone can post messages on the topic for others to read. More than 10,000 such newsgroups exist on almost every conceivable topic. Each Usenet site is financed and administered independently.

chatting Live, interactive conversations over a public network.

CHATTING. **Chatting** allows people who are simultaneously connected to the Internet to hold live, interactive written conversations. Only people who happen to be signed on at the same time are able to chat because messages are not stored for later viewing as they are on Usenet newsgroups. On the other hand, this function can be an effective business tool if people who can benefit from interactive conversations set an appointed time to meet and talk about a particular topic. The limitation of this is that the topic is open to all without security so that intruders can also participate.

Telnet A network tool that allows someone to log onto one computer system while doing work on another.

TELNET. We have included **Telnet** in this section even though it actually serves a different purpose—allowing someone to be on one computer system while doing work on

ggalileo@univpisa.edu.it

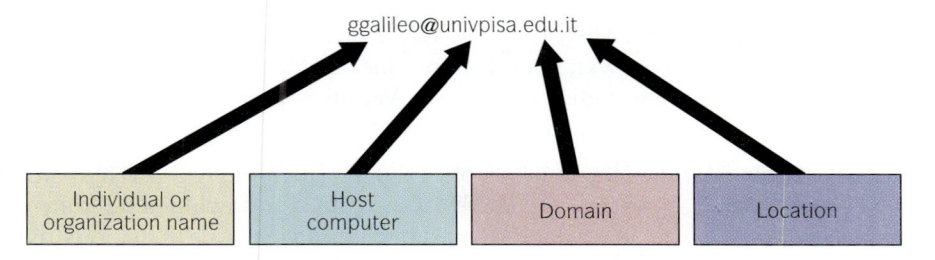

| Individual or organization name | Host computer | Domain | Location |

FIGURE 9.5
Analysis of an Internet Address. The portion of the address to the left of the @ symbol in Net e-mail addresses is the name or identifier of the specific individual or organization. To the right is the computer address. The address may end in either a country indicator (such as *ja,* for Japan) or with a function indicator such as *com* for a commercial organization or *edu* for an educational institution. All e-mail addresses end with a country indicator except those in the United States, which does not use one. In English, the e-mail address of physicist and astronomer Galileo Galilei would be translated as *G. Galileo at the University of Pisa, educational institution, Italy.*

another. Telnet is the protocol that establishes an error-free, rapid link between the two computers, allowing you, for example, to log-in to your business computer from a remote computer when you are on the road or working from home. You can also log-in to and use third-party computers that have been made accessible to the public, such as using the catalogue of the United States Library of Congress. Telnet will use the computer address you supply to locate the computer you want to reach and connect you to it.

Information Retrieval on the Internet

Information retrieval is a second basic Internet function. Many hundreds of library catalogues are on-line through the Internet, including those of such giants as the Library of Congress, the University of California, and Harvard University. In addition, users are able to search many thousands of databases that have been opened to the public by corporations, governments, and nonprofit organizations. Individuals can gather information on almost any conceivable topic stored in these databases and libraries. For example teachers interested in finding information on hyperactive children can quickly search computer databases and locate many articles, papers, books, and even conference reports from universities and other organizations all over the world. They can then download the information for their reading and use at their leisure. Many use the Internet to locate and download some of the free, quality computer software that has been made available by developers on computers all over the world.

Because the Internet is a voluntary, decentralized effort with no central listing of participants or sites—much less a listing of the data located at all those sites—the major challenge is finding what you need from among the vast storehouses of data found in databases and libraries all over the world. Here we will introduce four major methods of accessing computers and locating the files you need. We will discuss a fifth method—search engines—in the section on the World Wide Web.

GOPHERS. A **gopher** is a computer client tool that enables the user to locate textual information stored on Internet gopher servers through a series of easy-to-use, hierarchical menus. The Internet has thousands of gopher server sites throughout the world. Each gopher site contains its own system of menus listing subject-matter topics, local files, and other relevant gopher sites. One gopher site might have as many as several thousand listings within various levels of its menus. When you use gopher software to search a specific topic and select a related item from a menu, the server will automatically transfer you to the appropriate file on that server or to the selected server wherever in the world it is located. Once on the distant server, the process continues—you are presented with more menus of files and other gopher site servers that might interest you. You thus can move from site to site, narrowing your search as you go, locating in-

gopher A character-oriented tool for locating data on the Internet that enables the user to locate textual information stored on Internet servers through a series of easy-to-use, hierarchical menus.

formation that you want anywhere in the world. When you do find information or files you want, you are free to browse, read them on-line, or download them onto your own computer for more leisurely reading or printing. Veronica is an additional capability for searching for text that appears in gopher menus.

Archie A tool for locating data on the Internet that keyword searches a database of documents, software, and data files available for downloading from servers around the world.

ARCHIE. **Archie** addresses the same problem differently through a search of an actual database of documents, software, and data files available for downloading from servers around the world. While no individual Archie database can list more than a very tiny percentage of the files in the world, clicking on a relevant listing from one Archie server will bring you to another computer system where other relevant files are stored. There, the Archie server may have yet other relevant references, allowing you to continue your search for pertinent files, moving from database to database, library to library, until you locate what you need. Archie database searches use subject key words that you enter, such as *Beijing, telecommuting, polymers,* or *inflation,* resulting in a list of sites that contain files on that topic. Through Archie you are even able to search the catalogues of more than 300 on-line college, university, and government libraries around the world. Of course, once you find files you want, you may use a file transfer program to download them.

WAIS A tool for locating data on the Internet that requires the name of the databases to be searched based upon key words.

WAIS. **WAIS** (Wide Area Information Servers) is yet a third way to handle the problem of locating files around the world. WAIS is the most thorough way to locate a specific file, but it requires that you know the name of the databases you want searched. Once you specify database names and key identifying words, WAIS searches for the key words in all the files in those databases. When the search has been completed, you will be given a menu listing all the files that contain your key words.

File Transfer Protocol (FTP) A tool for retrieving and transferring files from a remote computer.

FTP. **File Transfer Protocol (FTP)** is used to access a remote computer and retrieve files from it. While you can retrieve files using capabilities already described, FTP is a quick and easy method if you know the remote computer site where the file is stored. Once you have logged on to the remote computer, you can move around directories that have been made accessible for FTP to search for the file(s) you want to retrieve. Once located, FTP makes transfer of the file to your own computer very easy.

The World Wide Web

World Wide Web A set of standards for storing, retrieving, formatting, and displaying information using a client/server architecture, graphical user interfaces, and a hypertext language that enables dynamic links to other documents.

The **World Wide Web** (the Web), is at the heart of the explosion in the business use of the Net. The Web is a universally accepted set of standards for storing, retrieving, formatting, and displaying information using a client/server architecture. It was originally developed to allow collaborators in remote sites to share their ideas about all aspects of a common project. If the Web was used for two independent projects and later relationships were found between the projects, information could flow smoothly between the projects without making major changes (Berners-Lee et al., 1994).

While the other methods of locating information on the Net are primarily character-based, the Web combines text, hypermedia, graphics, and sound. Together they can handle all types of digital communication while making it easy to link resources that are half-a-world apart. The Web uses graphical user interfaces for easy viewing. It is based upon a hypertext language called **Hypertext Markup Language (HTML)** that formats documents and incorporates dynamic links to other documents and pictures stored in the same or remote computers. Using these links, all the user need do is point at a highlighted key word or graphic, click on it, and immediately be transported to another document—maybe on another computer somewhere else in the world. The user is free to jump from place to place, following his or her own logic and interests. The Web thus provides a very flexible and powerful platform for distributing information.

Hypertext Markup Language (HTML) A programming tool that uses hypertext to establish dynamic links to other documents stored in the same or remote computers.

browser A software tool that supports graphics and hyperlinks and is needed to navigate the Web.

To access a Web site, the user must use a special software tool known as a Web **browser,** which is programmed according to HTML standards. Because the standard is universally accepted, anyone using a browser can access any of the millions of Web sites anywhere in the world. Browsers use hypertext's point-and-click ability to enable the user easily to navigate (or *surf*)—move from site to site on the Web—to another desired site. Browsers also include an arrow or Back button to enable the user to retrace his

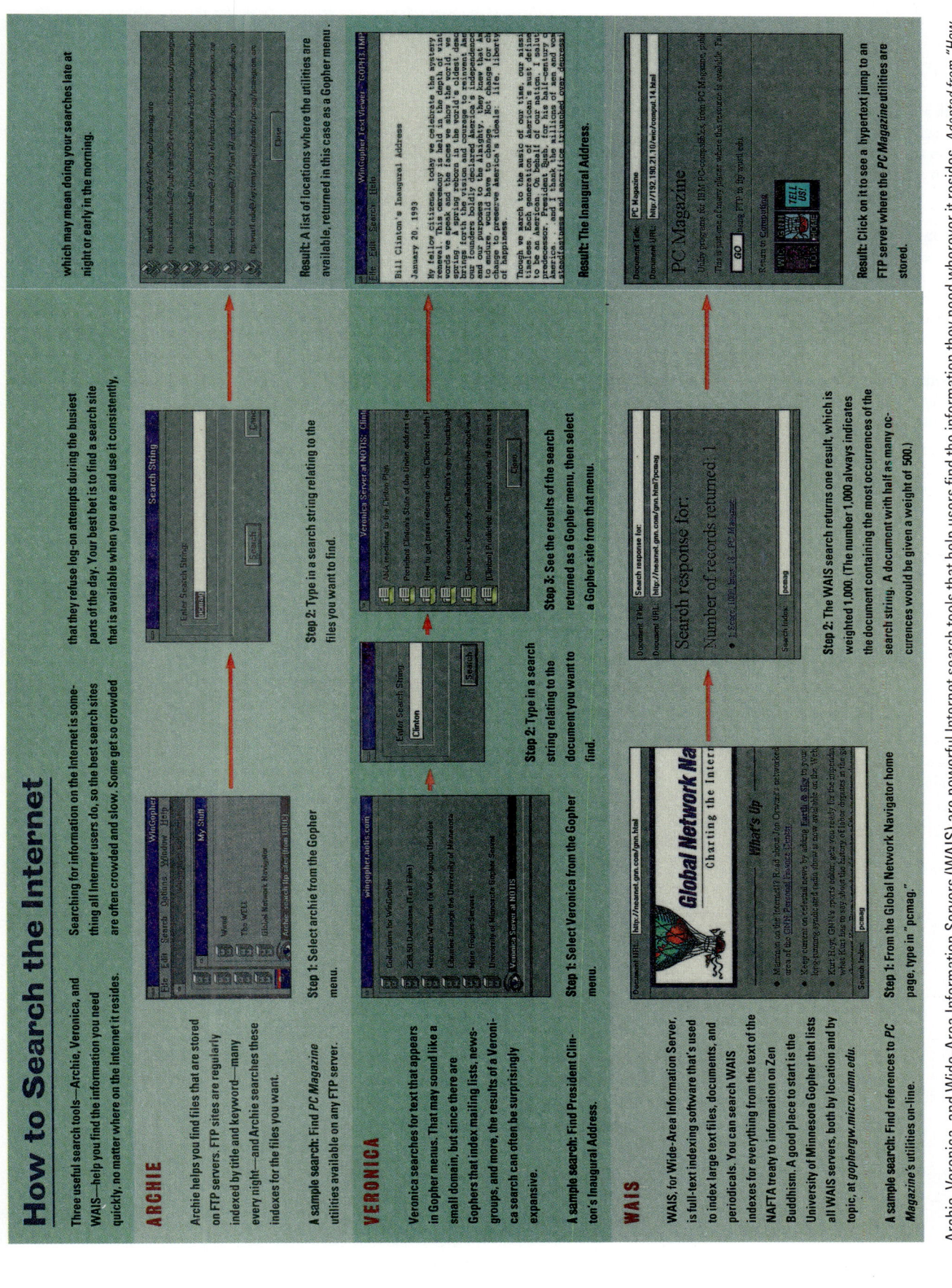

How to Search the Internet

Three useful search tools—Archie, Veronica, and WAIS—help you find the information you need quickly, no matter where on the Internet it resides.

Searching for information on the Internet is something all Internet users do, so the best search sites are often crowded and slow. Some get so crowded that they refuse log-on attempts during the busiest parts of the day. Your best bet is to find a search site that is available when you are and use it consistently, which may mean doing your searches late at night or early in the morning.

ARCHIE

Archie helps you find files that are stored on FTP servers. FTP sites are regularly indexed by title and keyword—many every night—and Archie searches these indexes for the files you want.

A sample search: Find *PC Magazine* utilities available on any FTP server.

Step 1: Select archie from the Gopher menu.

Step 2: Type in a search string relating to the files you want to find.

Result: A list of locations where the utilities are available, returned in this case as a Gopher menu.

VERONICA

Veronica searches for text that appears in Gopher menus. That may sound like a small domain, but since there are Gophers that index everything from the text of the NAFTA treaty to information on Zen Buddhism. A good place to start is the University of Minnesota Gopher that lists all WAIS servers, both by location and by topic, at *gophergw.micro.umn.edu*.

A sample search: Find President Clinton's Inaugural Address.

Step 1: Select Veronica from the Gopher menu.

Step 2: Type in a search string relating to the document you want to find.

Step 3: See the results of the search returned as a Gopher menu, then select a Gopher site from that menu.

Result: The Inaugural Address.

WAIS

WAIS, for Wide-Area Information Server, is full-text indexing software that's used to index large text files, documents, and periodicals. You can search WAIS indexes for everything from the text of the NAFTA treaty to information on Zen Buddhism. A good place to start is the University of Minnesota Gopher that lists all WAIS servers, both by location and by topic, at *gophergw.micro.umn.edu*.

A sample search: Find references to *PC Magazine*'s utilities on-line.

Step 1: From the Global Network Navigator home page, type in "pcmag."

Step 2: The WAIS search returns one result, which is weighted 1,000. (The number 1,000 always indicates the document containing the most occurrences of the search string. A document with half as many occurrences would be given a weight of 500.)

Result: Click on it to see a hypertext jump to an FTP server where the *PC Magazine* utilities are stored.

Archie, Veronica, and Wide-Area Information Servers (WAIS) are powerful Internet search tools that help users find the information they need wherever it resides. *Adapted from "How to Search the Internet," PC Magazine, October 11, 1994. Reprinted with permission.*

steps, navigating back, site by site. Netscape software from Netscape Communications Inc. is the most popular Web browser. Mosaic, developed by the National Center for Supercomputing Applications at the University of Illinois, Urbana-Champaign campus, is available for free.

The existence of the Web has spawned a large number of **search engines,** which are used like gophers, Archie, and WAIS to locate specific sites or information on the Net. Most of these search engines primarily search Web sites. Some search engines, such as Yahoo, are organized according to topic (business, education, government) and others, such as Alta Vista, can search most of the sites according to key words.

Those who offer information through the Web must first establish a **home page**—a text and graphical screen display that usually welcomes the user and introduces the organization that has established the page. For most organizations the home page will lead the user to other pages, with all the pages of a company being known as a **Web site.** For a corporation to establish a presence on the Web, therefore, it must set up a Web site of one or more pages. Most Web pages offer a way to contact the organization or individual. Figure 9.6 illustrates both the structural and navigational architecture of a Web site, showing how it can be used to access information supplied by *Datamation* magazine.

search engine A tool for locating specific sites or information on the Internet. Primarily used to search the World Wide Web.

home page A World Wide Web text and graphical screen display that welcomes the user and introduces the organization that has established the page.

Web site All of the World Wide Web pages maintained by an organization.

INTERNET BENEFITS TO ORGANIZATIONS

Organizations are deriving many benefits from the Internet, including reducing communications costs, enhancing communication and coordination, accelerating the distribution of knowledge, and facilitating electronic commerce.

Reducing Communications Costs

Prior to the Net, to realize the communications benefits described below, organizations had to build their own wide-area networks or subscribe to a value-added network service. Employing the Internet, while far from cost-free, is certainly more cost-effective for many organizations than building their own network or paying VAN subscription fees. Moreover, companies are finding that by using the Net to fulfill a range of their communication needs, they are lowering other communication costs, including their network management expenses and their telephone and fax costs. For instance, one estimate is that a direct mailing or faxing to 1200 customers within the United States can cost $1200 to $1600, whereas the same coverage through the Net can cost only about $10. Adding 600 more recipients who are spread through six other countries would increase the cost only another $10.

Each time Federal Express clients use FedEx's Web site to track the status of their packages instead of inquiring by telephone, FedEx saves $8, amounting to $2 million in savings each year (Cortese, 1996). While all companies can benefit from lower costs, small businesses find reduced communication costs particularly beneficial because it sometimes enables them to compete with larger companies in markets that would otherwise be closed to them.

Enhancing Communication and Coordination

As organizations expand and globalization continues, the need to coordinate activities in far-flung locations is becoming more critical. The Internet has become an important instrument for that coordination. Cygnus Support, a software developer with only 125 employees in offices in both Mountain View, California, and Somerville, Massachusetts, originally turned to the Internet to link its offices inexpensively via e-mail. Later, Cygnus established an internal Web site to keep employees informed about company developments. Through the Web employees are able to see a company calendar, the employee policy manual, company financial data, even the number of customer problems and the speed of their resolution. The site is also an important tool to help manage the large number of telecommuters that work for the company.

The Internet has made it easier and less expensive for companies to coordinate small staffs when opening new markets or working in isolated places because they do not have

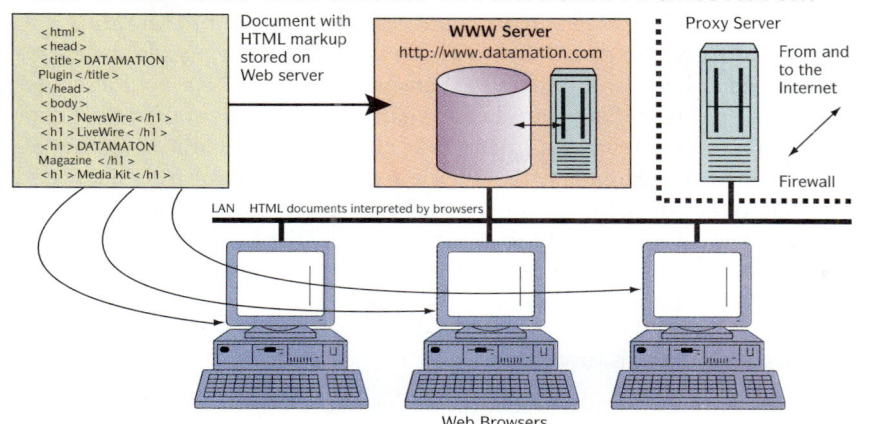

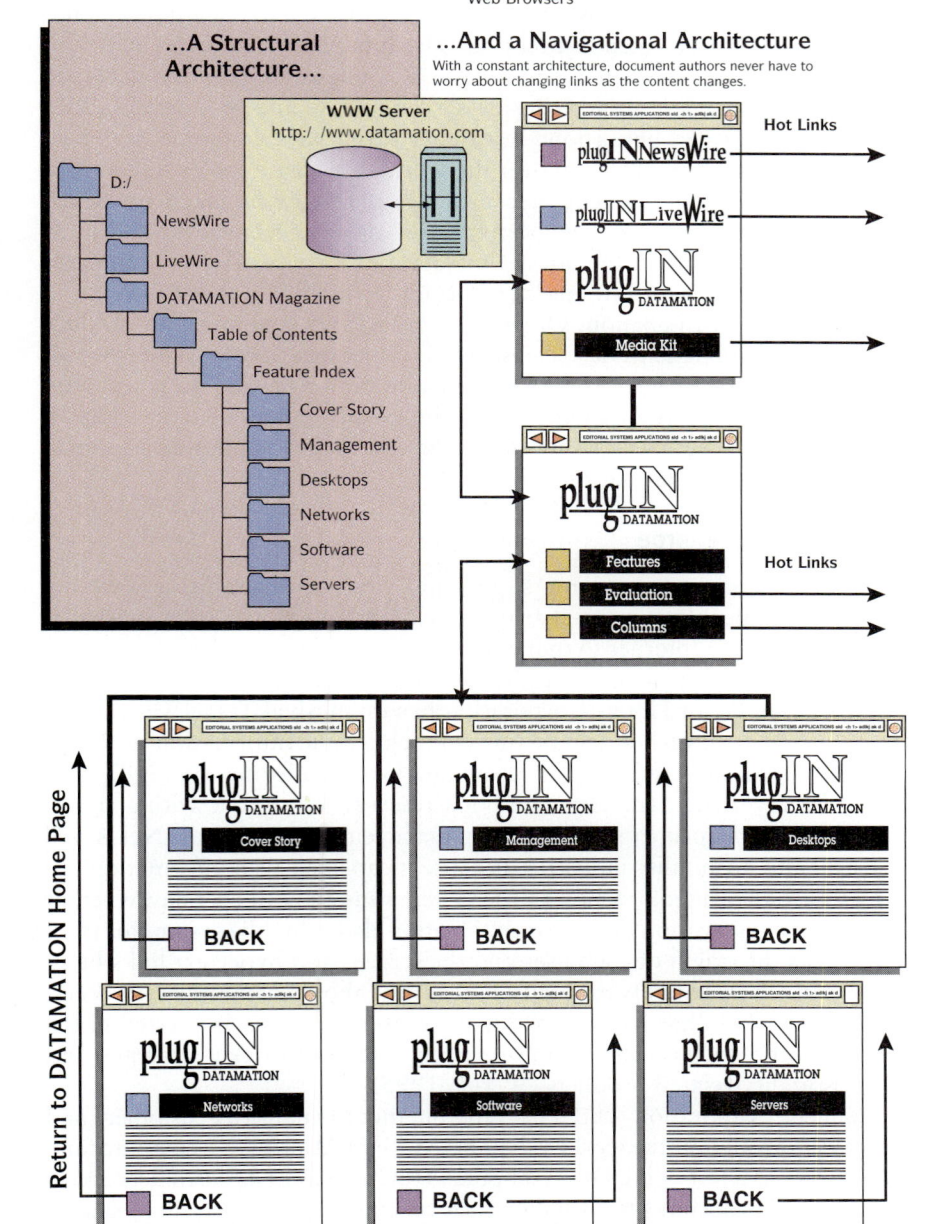

FIGURE 9.6

World Wide Web architecture. Organizations such as *Datamation* magazine can store magazine pages or other information on servers that can be accessed through the World Wide Web all over the globe. Through hypertext links users can easily move from page to page or select the features and topics they want to see. Adapted with permission from *"The World Wide Web Needs: A Functional Architecture . . . A Structural Architecture . . . and a Navigational Architecture,"* DATAMATION MAGAZINE, copyright, *March 1, 1995, p. 41,* Cahners Publishing Company, a division of Reed Elsevier Inc. DATAMATION MAGAZINE is a trademark of Cahners Publishing Company, a division of Reed Elsevier Inc. All rights reserved."

9.2 The Internet

to build their own networks. Schlumberger Ltd., the New York and Paris oil-drilling equipment and electronics producer, operates in 85 countries, and in most of them their employees are in remote locations. To install their own network for so few people at each remote location would have been prohibitively expensive. Using the Net, Schlumberger engineers in Dubai (on the Persian Gulf) can check e-mail and effectively stay in close contact with management at a very low cost. In addition, the field staff is able to follow research projects as easily as can personnel within the United States. Schlumberger has found that since it converted to the Net from its own network, the overall communications costs are down 2 percent, despite a major increase in network and IT infrastructure spending. The main reason for these savings is the dramatic drop in voice traffic and in overnight delivery service charges (complete documents can be attached to the e-mail messages).

Accelerating the Distribution of Knowledge

In today's information economy, rapid access to knowledge is critical to the success of many companies. Yet new knowledge is expanding so swiftly that keeping up is an immense task that requires management's attention. The Internet system helps with this problem. Organizations are using e-mail and access to databases to gain easy access to information resources in such key areas as business, science, law, and government. With blinding speed the Internet can link a lone researcher sitting at a computer screen to mountains of data (including graphics) all over the world, otherwise too expensive and too difficult to tap. For example, scientists can obtain photographs taken by NASA space probes within an hour after they've been released. It has become easy and inexpensive for corporations to obtain the latest United States Department of Commerce statistics, current weather data, or laws of legal entities from all over the globe.

Entek Manufacturing, of Lebanon, Oregon, manufactures equipment to produce plastic sheeting for automobile batteries. The sheeting sometimes develops microscopic holes as a result of the high temperatures of today's automobile motors. Engineer Ron Cordell needed to find a material for patching these holes and so presented his problem on a polymer forum on the Net. Several hours later an Australian responded via e-mail with the name of an adhesive that did the job.

Facilitating Electronic Commerce

The Internet has enormous potential for supporting electronic commerce, offering global connectivity, flexible information-sharing, and low transaction costs. Companies large and small are using the Internet to make product information, ordering, and customer support immediately available and to help buyers and sellers make contact. For example, Chicago-based Hyatt Hotels Corporation has established TravelWeb, a Web site that offers to prospective vacationers pictures and electronic information on 16 resort hotels in the United States and the Caribbean and similar information on 87 nonresort hotels in North America. Travelers can book reservations on-line with a credit-card number if they have the proper security. Hyatt management believes the Net is well suited for the travel and hospitality industries because it can keep Web information up-to-date more readily than printed brochures. The system runs 24 hours per day, whether or not a specific hotel's reservation desk is open. Hyatt is also using the system for market research. It tracks the origin of each user and the screens and hypertext links he or she uses. By analyzing these data Hyatt learns a great deal about customer preferences. For instance, the hotel chain has found that Japanese users are most interested in the golf facilities of a resort, which is valuable information in shaping market strategies and for developing hospitality-related products (Wilder, 1995).

Digital Equipment Corporation (DEC) uses the Internet to enable its customers and software developers from all over the world to log-on to its DEC Alpha AXP computer and run their own software as a test of the DEC computer. DEC also gives its customers access to more than 3000 on-line documents, including sales brochures and technical manuals.

Companies find that through e-mail they can answer customer questions very rapidly, and usually at lower cost, than by staffing a telephone system. Dell Computer has established a Dell newsgroup on the Net and other on-line services to receive and

Window on Organizations

THE INTERNET BECOMES THE MIDDLEMAN

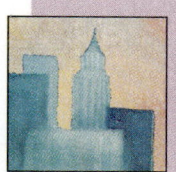

The World Wide Web performs one function exceedingly well—putting people in direct touch with each other. Professionals such as brokers, dealers, and agents—the middlemen in many marketplace transactions—may be threatened.

Many believe that travel agents will be needed less and less as people make their own airline and hotel reservations through the Web. A site called Travelocity will offer live chat forums with travel experts, searchable restaurant and entertainment listings, and even luggage for sale—features that can't be found at the average travel agency. Will travel agents disappear? Observers say no. Travel agents offering reliable, personal service will survive and thrive.

Real estate will be affected. Real estate agents charge the seller a commission, often 6 percent of the sale price ($12,000 on a $200,000 home), a powerful incentive for sellers to seek other avenues to advertise their properties. Real estate listings on the Web can include pictures and floor plans as well as descriptive information. These Web sites typically charge the seller a small fee, in some cases, as little as $15 per month, for the listing. Buyers view listings for free. Some sites, such as Properties OnLine (http://propol.com/pol/) include listings from anywhere and rely on powerful search engines to help visitors locate what they want. Others, such as BayNet World, Inc. (http://www.baynet.com) focus on a specific area, in this case the San Francisco Bay area. The more traditional real estate firms, such as Coldwell Banker (http://coldwellbanker.com) are also establishing a presence on the Web, trying to capture part of the cyberspace business. However, they still charge commissions.

In businesses impacted by the Internet, middlemen will have to adjust their services to fit the new business model or create new services based on the model. So many real estate sites have appeared on the Internet (about 40,000 by early 1996)

> **To Think About:** How is the Internet changing the business model of these organizations? Suggest and discuss how other organizations might be affected by the Web.

that a new type of middleman has emerged to sort them out. Entrepreneur Jerry Caviston set up a Web-based service called Matchpoint, which operates a customized search engine for locating homes for sale on-line. The service is free to prospective buyers, making its profit by charging realtors a small fee for each listing.

Not all middlemen will disappear because there are services that the Web simply can't replicate, particularly in the purchase of physical goods. Web-based dealers such as Auto-by-Tel (http://www.autobytel.com/) and DealerNet (http://www.dealernet.com/) enable people to search for particular models and makes of cars offered by participating dealers, but people can't just pick up a car and drive it away. They need to test-drive the car and have it checked by a mechanic, functions that can best be performed by the auto dealers.

Sources: Elizabeth Baatz, "Will the Web Cut Your Job?" *Webmaster,* May/June 1996; Mary Brandel, "The Exchange," *Computerworld,* April 29, 1996.

---

handle customer complaints and questions. They answer about 90 percent of the questions within 24 hours. Dell also does market research for free through these newsgroups rather than paying a professional for the same information. Recently, for example, Dell gathered customer reaction to a potential change in the color of desktop cases. Its Internet presence is important enough to Dell that it assigns a staff of seven people, who are active 24 hours a day, keeping up with any mention of Dell and the other computer producers in the newsgroups and answering questions on-line.

The Internet is also performing electronic marketplace functions, directly connecting buyers and sellers. By bypassing intermediaries such as distributors or retail outlets, purchase transaction costs can be reduced. The Window on Organizations describes how the Internet is supplanting traditional middlemen in some industries and creating new opportunities for others. For Internet-based commerce, distributors with warehouses of goods may be replaced by intermediaries specializing in helping Internet users efficiently obtain product and price information. The Internet is also promoting commerce internationally by facilitating cross-border transactions and information flows (Quelch and Klein, 1996).

Once the Internet becomes secure enough to conduct on-line purchase transactions, the Net will vastly expand the electronic marketplace, reducing transaction costs (see Chapters 2 and 3). The Window on Technology explores some of the issues that companies must consider if they plan to use the Internet for electronic data interchange (EDI).

Window on Technology

THE INTERNET FOR EDI?

Is EDI over the Internet possible and appropriate? The answer is not only that it *is* possible, but that it is just beginning to be done—and its appropriateness depends upon who is answering the question. Lawrence Livermore National Laboratory in Livermore, California, is piloting Internet EDI with BankAmerica Corp. of San Francisco. The lab purchases $300 million annually in goods and services and has about 1000 vendors, six of which are participating in the pilot. When the pilot is completed, the lab hopes to begin using Net-based EDI with many of its vendors, while the bank plans to offer this service to many of its customers.

Why use the Net? Boosters see two main advantages. First, it will reduce EDI costs. Currently, most EDI is processed through a number of VANs. One estimate indicates that 125,000 EDI messages monthly over a VAN would cost $50,000 to $100,000, whereas the same volume over the Net would cost about $10,000. The main reason for the difference is that VANs charge by volume whereas the Internet charge is fixed, regardless of volume. A second benefit is that use of the Net should expand the number of EDI partners because small companies that cannot afford use of a VAN can afford the Net. More partners means not only lowered transaction costs for those partners, but it also means more competition as more vendors can bid for a company's business. The Net has other benefits as well. For example, an EDI transaction over the Net usually brings a response in ten minutes or less, whereas in using a VAN, a response can take hours to overnight, because VAN-based transactions are batched and transmitted only every so often, often at night during low-traffic hours.

Then why not use the Net for EDI? First, Internet security and reliability have not been proven. Secure electronic payment

> **To Think About:** What management, organization, and technology issues should be addressed in order for the Internet to be used effectively for EDI?

systems for the Internet are starting to be developed. However, many companies are waiting for more proof that they actually work as intended. Second, VANs charge more but they also add services. For example, Wright Patterson Air Force Base wants a VAN because it filters and directs EDI messages automatically. VANs also will recover data in case of a computer crash. Net detractors also claim that the projected savings are not even real. They state that transmission costs are no more than 15 percent of total EDI costs, with support and maintenance absorbing the rest. Without VAN-based EDI, a live person will have to direct Wright Patterson's transactions to the appropriate receiving computer system, and that person's time adds cost. Using VANs, the transaction doesn't even have to appear on a computer screen.

Sources: Richard Adhikari, "EDI Heads for the Net," *InformationWeek,* May 6, 1996; Colleen Frye, "EDI Users Explore Internet as Tool of Trade," *Software Magazine,* December 1995.

INTRANETS

intranet An internal network based on World Wide Web technology.

firewall A security system with specialized software to prevent outsiders from invading private networks.

Many organizations are starting to build internal networks called *intranets* based on Web technology. An **intranet** is an internal organizational network that is modeled upon the Web. It uses the existing company network infrastructure, but the software is the software developed for the World Wide Web. The difference between the Web and an intranet is that while the Web is open to anyone, the intranet is private and is protected from public visits by **firewalls**—security systems with specialized software to prevent outsiders from invading private networks. Intranets have spread very rapidly in the past several years.

Intranet Technology

Intranets require no special hardware and so are run over any existing network infrastructure. Intranet software technology is the same as that of the World Wide Web. Intranets use HTML to program Web pages and to establish dynamic, point-and-click hypertext links to other sites. The Web browsers used for intranets are the same as those being used on the Web, with the Netscape browser currently the most popular. Even the Web server software is the same.

Whereas most companies, particularly the larger ones, must support a multiplicity of computer platforms that cannot communicate with each other, Internet technology

A DAY IN THE LIFE OF THE CORPORATE WEB AT US WEST

■ At this Baby Bell, 15,000 employees rely on the company's intranet, Global Village, all day long. Typically, they log on to the home page shown below and select one of five icons. Then they point and click to information stored on computers around the company. The web relays the data back to their desktop PC.

LAB
11 A.M.: A project manager clicks on to the lab page to check out software being designed for a new service she wants to offer. She can test-drive the program from her desktop computer.

GATE
4 P.M.: An engineer researching the design of a new network component gets on to the global Internet via this "gateway" built into the home page. He visits World Wide Web sites belonging to possible suppliers, then clicks back to the internal web and updates his colleagues via E-mail.

VIRTUAL ROOM
9 P.M.: After tucking in the kids, a busy exec logs on to the corporate web via his home PC. He catches up on E-mail and checks out his team's project page for tomorrow's schedule. Finally, he looks over the volunteer page. After deciding to help paint a neighborhood center on Sunday, he signs off.

MODELS
1 P.M.: Squirrels are wreaking havoc on phone lines in Golden, Colorado. Repair technicians in Golden and supervisors at Denver HQ use the web to share a map of the damage and the results of trials of new materials for insulating wires. Together, they explore different strategies for repelling the critters.

LIBRARY
7:30 A.M.: A sales consultant in the Denver office begins his day by checking what's going on around the company. He pulls up *News of the Day*, an internal newsletter. Today's items include an update on winter storms that have knocked out company telephone lines in the Midwest. He also checks US West's stock price.

FIGURE 9.7
The US West intranet. Companies are finding many uses for internal networks based on World Wide Web technology. *From Alison L. Sprout, "The Internet Inside Your Company" in* Fortune, *November 27, 1995. © 1995 Time Inc. All rights reserved. Reprinted by permission. Graphic reprinted by permission of US West Communications.*

overcomes these platform differences, uniting all computers into a single, virtually seamless network system. Web software presents users with a uniform interface, reducing the user training requirements. With standard Web search engines, users can easily locate information on an organization's network, even if it happens to be stored halfway around the world. Companies can connect their intranet to company databases just as is done with the Web, enabling employees to take actions central to a company's operations. For instance, through the US West intranet, the company's customer representatives are able to turn on customer services such as call waiting through the intranet while the customer is still on the telephone. In the past customers had to wait hours or even days (see Figure 9.7).

For companies with an installed network infrastructure, intranets are very inexpensive to build and to run. Existing networks usually require no additional work to run an intranet. All an organization needs to do is to install Web software on its existing networks, develop some home pages, connect up any databases, and do some user training. Software costs are exceedingly low. Programming Web pages is quick and easy; some employees are programming their own Web pages. In addition, intranet networks cost very little to maintain, other than the cost of maintaining the infrastructure itself.

Benefits and Limitations of Intranets

Companies are using their intranets in many ways. They are making customer profiles, product inventories, policy manuals, and company telephone directories available to their employees. Made available in this way, these documents are always up-to-date, eliminating paper, printing, and distributing costs. Some companies are using their intranets for virtual conferencing. Intranets are simple, cost-effective communication tools.

Earlier, we described how Cygnus Support uses its intranet for organizational communication and coordination. Silicon Graphics installed an intranet to connect its 7200 employees, enabling them to create reports from corporate databases, using easy point-and-click technology. In addition to documents, the intranet delivers video and audio material to employees. Compaq Computers employees use their intranet to reallocate funds in their 401(k) savings plans. Mitre Corporation of Bedford, Massachusetts, uses its intranet for virtual conferencing, discussion groups, and even for news feed. The animation division of DreamWorks SKG—the entertainment production company founded by Steven Spielberg, Jeffrey Katzenberg, and David Geffen—has set up its own divisional intranet to track the daily status of projects, including animation objects, and to coordinate movie scenes. The intranet will also support the production of live-action films, music, TV shows, and digital media products.

Intranets do have important limitations. They cannot replace such complex business programs as payrolls, accounting, manufacturing, and marketing systems because Web systems are too slow for high-speed transaction processing. Although companies use intranets to support group work (see Chapter 12), they still lack the functionality of specialized groupware systems such as Lotus Notes. Since Web technology is designed for open communications, appropriate security measures are required (see Chapter 14). Effective intranets require careful management planning (*I/S Analyzer*, May 1996).

INTERNET CHALLENGES

The Internet presents challenges to the business user, largely stemming from the fact that most of the technology and functions are relatively immature.

Security

The Internet is a highway that carries a great deal of personal and organizational information and data, much of it sensitive or proprietary— for example, profit reports, product development information, pricing data, marketing plans, sales contacts, and scientific research data. Electronic links tend to be exposed to attacks from both thieves and vandals. Internet hackers have found ways to steal passwords and use them to break into computer systems at sites all over the world. The lack of security is one reason that the Net, while being widely used to facilitate transactions, is still only in limited use to consummate transactions. We explore this issue in greater detail in Chapter 14.

Technology Problems

Several technology problems still exist. A number of incompatible ways exist to access the Net, allowing specific users to perform certain functions but not others. For example, no single method of e-mailing graphics files exists, and so many people cannot mail graphic documents to each other. We discuss standards in greater detail in Section 9.3.

To make extensive use of the Internet, some companies need more expensive telecommunications connections, workstations, or higher-speed computers that can handle transmission of bandwidth-hungry graphics. To establish a presence on the World Wide Web, they may require an information systems specialist with skills related specifically to the Internet. Individuals and organizations in less-developed countries with poor telephone lines, limited hardware and software capacity, or government controls on communications will not be able to take full advantage of Internet resources (Goodman, Press, Ruth, and Rutkowski, 1994).

Users are suffering psychological burnout as they struggle with their inability to absorb and use the Internet's vast resources. Technology to filter out extraneous information while allowing people to access the specific information they need will be highly valued.

Legal Issues

Laws governing electronic commerce are mostly nonexistent or currently being written. Legislatures, courts, and international agreements will have to settle such still open questions as the legality and force of e-mail contracts (including the role of electronic signatures), and the application of copyright laws to electronically copied documents. For instance, if a product is offered for sale in Australia via a server in Japan and the purchaser lives in Hungary, whose law applies? Until these and other critical legal questions are resolved, doing business on the Internet will bring a level of unreliability that many will find unacceptable.

9.3 CONNECTIVITY AND STANDARDS

Telecommunications and networks are most likely to increase productivity and competitive advantage when digitized information can move through a seamless web of electronic networks, connecting different kinds of machines, databases, functional divisions, departments, and work groups. They require **connectivity**—the ability of computers and computer-based devices to communicate with one another and share information in a meaningful way without human intervention. Internet technology and Java software provides some of this connectivity, but the Internet cannot be used as a foundation for all of the organization's information systems. Most organizations will still require their own proprietary networks. They will need to develop their own connectivity solutions to make different kinds of hardware, software, and communications systems work together.

Open systems promote connectivity because they enable disparate equipment and services to work together. **Open systems** are built upon public, nonproprietary operating systems; user interfaces; application standards; and networking protocols. In open systems, software can operate on different hardware platforms and, in that sense, can be portable. Java software (described in Chapter 6) is an open system. The UNIX operating system supports open systems because it can operate on many different kinds of computer hardware. However, there are different versions of UNIX, and no one version has been accepted as an open systems standard.

Achieving connectivity requires standards for networking, operating systems, and user interfaces. This section describes the most important standards that are being used today.

connectivity A measure of how well computers and computer-based devices communicate and share information with one another without human intervention.

open systems Software systems that can operate on different hardware platforms because they are built on public nonproprietary operating systems, user interfaces, application standards, and networking protocols.

MODELS OF CONNECTIVITY FOR NETWORKS

Because of the many interests involved in connectivity and standard setting, there are different models for achieving connectivity in telecommunications networks. A **reference model** is a generic framework for thinking about a problem. It is a logical breakdown of some activity (such as communications) into a number of distinct steps or parts. Specific protocols are required in order to implement a reference model. A **protocol** is a statement that explains how a specific task, such as transferring data, will be performed. Reference models and protocols become **standards** when they are approved by important standard-setting groups or when industry builds or buys products that support the models and protocols.

Network connectivity can also be achieved without reference models or protocols by using gateways. Firms develop gateways between two disparate networks when it is impossible or too costly to integrate them by complying with reference models or standards. However, gateways are expensive to build and maintain, and they can be slow and inefficient. We now describe the most important models of network connectivity.

reference model A generic framework for thinking about a problem.

protocol A statement that explains how a specific task will be performed.

standard Approved reference models and protocols as determined by standard-setting groups for building or developing products or services.

FIGURE 9.8
The Transmission Control Protocol/Internet Protocol (TCP/IP) reference model. This figure illustrates the five layers of the TCP/IP reference model for communications.

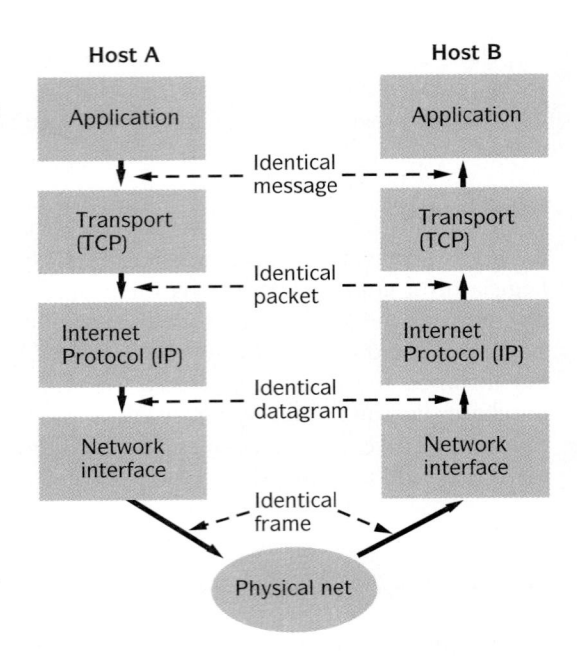

Transmission Control Protocol/Internet Protocol (TCP/IP) A U.S. Department of Defense reference model for linking different types of computers and networks.

The **Transmission Control Protocol/Internet Protocol (TCP/IP)** model was developed by the U.S. Department of Defense in 1972 and is used in the Internet. Its purpose was to help scientists link disparate computers. Because it is one of the oldest communications reference models (and is the model on which the Internet is based), TCP/IP is widely used. Figure 9.8 shows that TCP/IP has a five-layer reference model.

1. **Application:** Provides end-user functionality by translating the messages into the user/host software for screen presentation.
2. **Transmission Control Protocol (TCP):** Performs transport, breaking application data from the end user down into TCP packets called *datagrams*. Each packet consists of a header with the address of the sending host computer, information for putting the data back together, and information for making sure the packets don't become corrupted.
3. **Internet Protocol (IP):** The Internet Protocol receives datagrams from TCP and breaks the packets down further. An IP packet contains a header with address information and carries TCP information and data. IP routes the individual datagrams from the sender to the recipient. IP packets are not very reliable, but the TCP level can keep resending them until the correct IP packets get through.
4. **Network interface:** Handles addressing issues, usually in the operating system, as well as the interface between the initiating computer and the network.
5. **Physical net:** Defines basic electrical transmission characteristic for sending the actual signal along communications networks.

Two different computers using TCP/IP would be able to communicate, even if they were based on different hardware and software platforms. Data sent from one computer to the other would pass downward through all five layers, starting with the application layer of the sending computer and passing through the physical net. Once the data reach the recipient host computer, they travel up the layers. The TCP level would assemble the data into a format the receiving host computer can use. If the receiving computer found a damaged packet, it would ask the sending computer to retransmit it. This process would be reversed when the receiving computer responds.

Open Systems Interconnect (OSI) International reference model for linking different types of computers and networks.

Open Systems Interconnect (OSI) model is an international reference model developed by the International Standards Organization for linking different types of computers and networks. It was designed to support global networks with large volumes of transaction processing. OSI enables a computer connected to a network to communicate with any other computer on the same network or a different network, regardless of the

---

286   CHAPTER 9   Enterprise Networking and the Internet

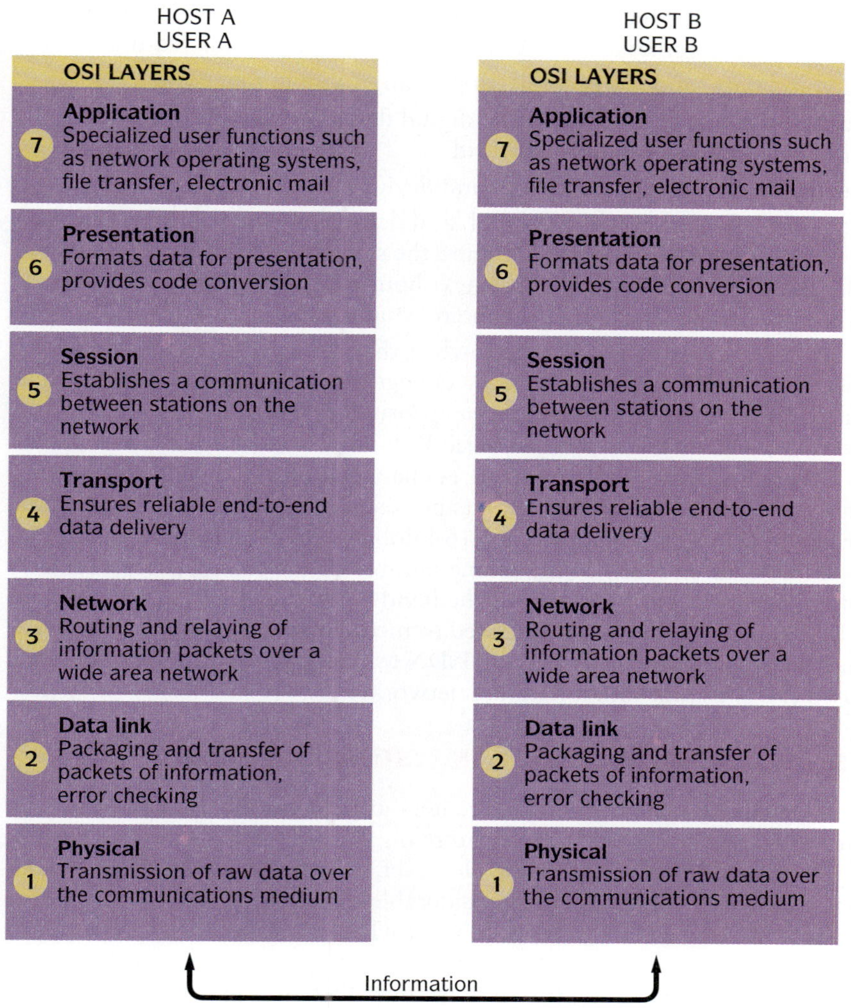

FIGURE 9.9
The Open Systems Interconnect (OSI) reference model. The figure illustrates the seven layers defining the communication functions for the flow of information over an OSI network.

HOST A / USER A — OSI LAYERS
7. **Application** — Specialized user functions such as network operating systems, file transfer, electronic mail
6. **Presentation** — Formats data for presentation, provides code conversion
5. **Session** — Establishes a communication between stations on the network
4. **Transport** — Ensures reliable end-to-end data delivery
3. **Network** — Routing and relaying of information packets over a wide area network
2. **Data link** — Packaging and transfer of packets of information, error checking
1. **Physical** — Transmission of raw data over the communications medium

HOST B / USER B — OSI LAYERS
7. **Application** — Specialized user functions such as network operating systems, file transfer, electronic mail
6. **Presentation** — Formats data for presentation, provides code conversion
5. **Session** — Establishes a communication between stations on the network
4. **Transport** — Ensures reliable end-to-end data delivery
3. **Network** — Routing and relaying of information packets over a wide area network
2. **Data link** — Packaging and transfer of packets of information, error checking
1. **Physical** — Transmission of raw data over the communications medium

Information

manufacturer, by establishing communication rules that permit the exchange of information between dissimilar systems.

The OSI model divides the telecommunications process into seven layers (see Figure 9.9). Each layer in the OSI model deals with a specific aspect of the communications process. Two different computers using OSI standards would each have software and hardware that correspond to each layer of the OSI model.

For example, if an officer at a local bank wanted information about a particular client's checking account that was stored in the bank's central host computer, he or she would enter the instructions to retrieve the client's account records into his or her terminal under control of layer 7, the application layer. The presentation layer (layer 6) would change this input data into a format for transmission. Layer 5 (the session layer) initiates the session. Layer 4 (the transport layer) checks the quality of the information traveling from user to host node. Layers 3 and 2 (the network and data link layers) transmit the data through layer 1 (the physical layer). When the message reaches the host computer, control moves up the layers back to the user, reversing the sequence.

OTHER NETWORKING STANDARDS

Standards have also been developed for transmitting digital data over public switched networks. **Integrated Services Digital Network (ISDN)** is an international digital public switched network standard for transmitting voice, data, image, and video over phone lines. ISDN was developed in the late 1970s by the CCITT (Consultative Committee on

Integrated Services Digital Network (ISDN) An international standard for transmitting voice, image, video, and data to support a wide range of service over public telephone lines.

9.3 Connectivity and Standards   **287**

International Telegraphy and Telephony), an international standards body representing over 150 countries. ISDN combines in one single service the following features:

- Complete voice, data, and video connection to anywhere in the world
- Complete digital connection to any other digital device in the world, from one next door to one halfway around the world
- Simultaneous use of voice, video, and digital devices
- User-controlled definition of video, digital, and data lines. You can use a line for digital personal service this hour, reconfigure the same phone line as an incoming 800 WATS line the next hour, and in the next hour redefine the line as a video line carrying pictures of a group videoconferencing session.

Modems are not used with ISDN except when they are needed to link up with a non-ISDN user. With some simple technology changes, ordinary twisted copper telephone wire can be more fully utilized without expensive recabling.

There are two levels of ISDN service: Basic Rate ISDN and Primary Rate ISDN. Basic Rate ISDN serves a single desktop with three channels. Two channels are B (bearer) channels with a capacity to transmit 64 kilobits per second of digital data (voice, data, video). A third delta channel (D channel) is a 16-kilobit-per-second channel for signaling and control information (such as the phone number of the calling party). Primary Rate ISDN offers 1.5 MBPS of bandwidth. The bandwidth is divided into 23 B channels and one D channel. This service is intended to meet the telecommunications needs of large users. Plans are under way to increase ISDN transmission capacity and to stitch together isolated ISDN islands into a national network.

OPERATING SYSTEM STANDARDS: THE OPEN SYSTEMS MOVEMENT

The battle over operating system standards centers around UNIX. UNIX is the only nonproprietary operating system that can operate on all computers—from microcomputers to mainframes, irrespective of vendor. However, the effort to make UNIX the operating system standard has encountered considerable opposition. Hardware vendors have split into two warring camps over the issue of what version of UNIX to support, led by IBM and DEC on one side and AT&T and Sun Corporation on the other.

Table 9.2 summarizes the standards we have described and lists other important standards for graphical user interfaces, electronic mail, packet switching, and electronic

Table 9.2 Standards for Achieving Connectivity

Area	Standard or Reference Model	Description
Networking	TCP/IP, OSI	Computer-to-computer communications
Digital public switched network transmission	ISDN	Transmission of voice, video, and data over public telephone lines
Fiber-optic transmission	FDDI	100 MBPS data transmission over dual fiber optical ring
Electronic mail	X.400	Permits e-mail systems operating on different hardware to communicate
Packet switching	X.25	Permits different international and national networks to communicate
EDI	X.12 Edifact (Europe)	Standardized transaction format
Graphical user interface	X Windows	High-level graphics description for standardized window management
Operating system	UNIX	Software portable to different hardware platforms

data interchange. Any manager wishing to achieve some measure of connectivity in his or her organization should try to use them when designing networks, purchasing hardware and software, or developing information system applications.

9.4 IMPLEMENTING ENTERPRISE NETWORKING

Implementing enterprise networking has created problems as well as opportunities for organizations. Managers need to address these problems as they design and build networks for their organizations.

PROBLEMS POSED BY ENTERPRISE NETWORKING

We have already described the connectivity problems created by incompatible network components and standards. Four additional problems stand out: (1) loss of management control over information systems; (2) the need for organizational change; (3) the hidden costs of client/server computing; and (4) the difficulty of ensuring network reliability and security (see Table 9.3).

Loss of Management Control over Information Systems

Managing both information systems technology and corporate data are proving much more difficult in a distributed environment because of the lack of a single central point where needed management can occur. Desktop computing and networks have empowered end users to become independent sources of computing power capable of collecting, storing, and disseminating data and software. Data and software are no longer confined to the mainframe and the management of the traditional information systems department.

Under enterprise networking it becomes increasingly difficult to determine where data are located and to ensure that the same piece of information, such as a product number, is used consistently throughout the organization. User-developed applications may combine incompatible pieces of hardware and software. Yet observers worry that excess centralization and management of information resources will stifle the independence and creativity of end users and reduce their ability to define their own information needs. The dilemma posed by enterprise networking is one of central management control versus end-user creativity and productivity.

Organizational Change Requirements

Decentralization also results in changes in corporate culture and organizational structure. While enterprise-wide computing is an opportunity to reengineer the organization into a more effective unit, it will only create problems or chaos if the underlying organizational issues are not fully addressed.

Hidden Costs of Client/Server Computing

Many companies have found that the savings they expected from client/server computing did not materialize because of unexpected costs. Hardware acquisition savings resulting

Table 9.3 Problems Posed by Enterprise Networking

Connectivity problems

Loss of management control over systems

Organizational change requirements

Hidden costs of client/server computing

Network reliability and security

FIGURE 9.10

Cost breakdowns for client/server computing. Labor costs, by far the largest cost component in client/server computing, are frequently underestimated when organizations downsize. *Adapted from Julia King and Rosemary Cafasso "Client/Server Trimmings,"* Computerworld, *December 19, 1994. Copyright 1994 by Computerworld, Inc., Framingham, MA 01701. Reprinted from* Computerworld. *Reprinted by permission.*

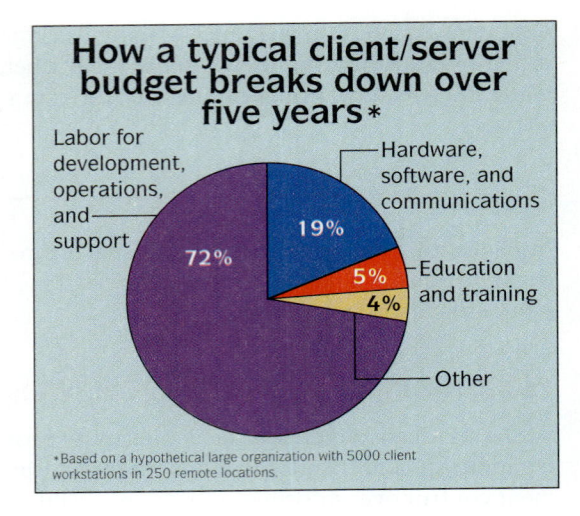

How a typical client/server budget breaks down over five years*

- Labor for development, operations, and support — 72%
- Hardware, software, and communications — 19%
- Education and training — 5%
- Other — 4%

*Based on a hypothetical large organization with 5000 client workstations in 250 remote locations.

from significantly lower costs of MIPS on microcomputers are often offset by high annual operating costs for additional labor and time required for network and system management. Forrester Research estimated that the costs of running a large microcomputer network can run 300 percent higher than supporting the same number of users in a mainframe network (Laberis, 1994).

The most difficult to evaluate and control are the hidden costs that accompany a decentralized client/server system. These systems can result in lowered knowledge worker productivity. Professional employees, many being paid $100,000 per year or more, must spend their own time performing such tasks as network maintenance, data backup, technical problem solving, and hardware, software, and software-update installations. As illustrated in Figure 9.10, the Gartner consulting group of Stanford, Connecticut, after a five-year study, concluded that each client/server user cost $40–50,000 to support over the five-year period, an amount far in excess of the cost of supporting a mainframe terminal user. The largest cost component is labor for development, operations, and support.

Network Reliability and Security

Network technology is still immature and highly complex. The networks themselves have dense layers of interacting technology, and the applications too are often intricately layered. Enterprise networking is highly sensitive to different versions of operating systems and network management software, with some applications requiring specific versions of each. It is difficult to make all of the components of large heterogeneous networks work together as smoothly as management envisions (see Figure 9.11). **Downtime** (periods of time in which the system is not operational) remains much more frequent in client/server systems than in established mainframe systems and should be considered carefully before one takes essential applications off the mainframe.

Tools for managing distributed networks are still in their infancy. Adequate, easy-to-use tools are lacking for such vital system functions as system configuration, tuning, system-wide backup and recovery, security, upgrading both system and application software, capacity planning, and the pinpointing of bottlenecks. Performance monitoring tools for client/server networks (for instance, monitoring CPU usage) are also not as well-developed or sophisticated as the tools that are available for mainframes or minicomputers.

Security is of paramount importance in organizations where information systems make extensive use of networks. Networks present end users, hackers, and thieves with many points of access and opportunities to steal or modify data in networks. Moreover, because users may simultaneously access several different computers (their client plus

downtime Periods of time during which an information system is not operational.

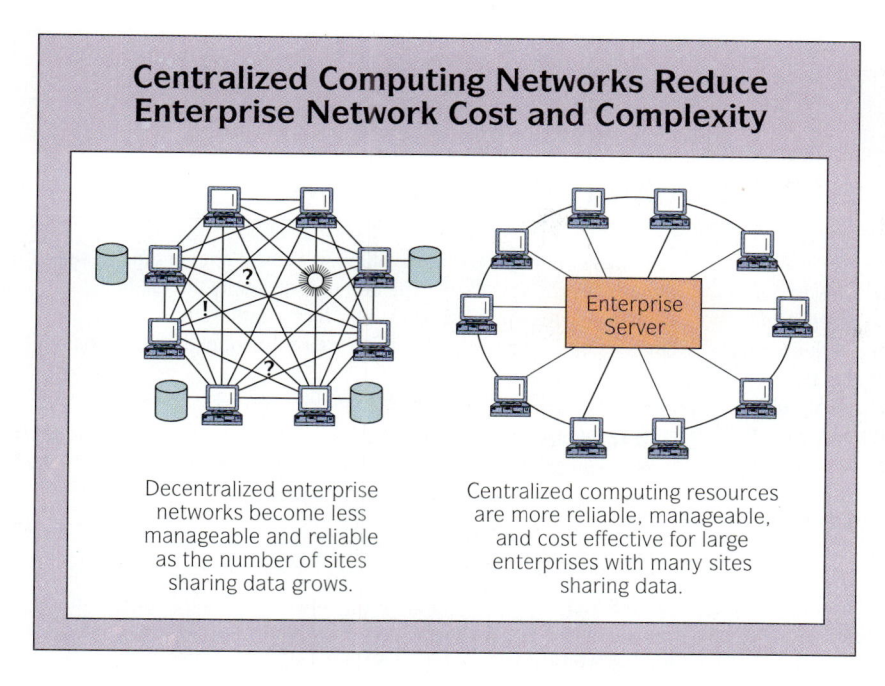

FIGURE 9.11

Increasing network complexity and decentralized computing. As more and more new sites are added to a decentralized network, complexity increases because there are so many diverse components to manage and coordinate. Adapted with permission form *"Managing the Costs of Enterprise Computing,"* DATAMATION MAGAZINE, Copyright, March 15, 1994, from a special report prepared by IBM. Copyright 1994 by International Business Machines Corporation and reprinted by their permission and Cahners Publishing Company, a division of Reed Elsevier Inc. DATAMATION MAGAZINE is a trademark of Cahners Publishing Company, a division of Reed Elsevier Inc. All rights reserved."

Centralized Computing Networks Reduce Enterprise Network Cost and Complexity

Decentralized enterprise networks become less manageable and reliable as the number of sites sharing data grows.

Centralized computing resources are more reliable, manageable, and cost effective for large enterprises with many sites sharing data.

one or more servers) with different security systems, access can become overly complex and interfere with the user's productivity. We discuss these issues in greater detail in Chapter 14.

SOME SOLUTIONS

Organizations can counteract problems created by enterprise networking by planning for and managing the business and organizational changes, increasing end-user training, asserting data administration disciplines, and considering connectivity and cost controls when planning their information architecture.

Managing the Change

To gain the full benefit of any new technology, organizations must carefully plan for and manage the change. Business processes need to be reengineered to insure that the organization fully benefits from the new technology (see Chapter 10). The company's information architecture must be redrawn to shape the new client/server environment. Management must address the organizational issues that arise from shifts in staffing, function, power, and organizational culture. Data models must be developed, training be given, network support assigned, and network management tools acquired. The Window on Management describes how one large, multinational corporation managed its downsizing project.

Education and Training

A well-developed training program can help end users overcome problems resulting from the lack of management support and understanding of desktop computing (Westin et al., 1985; Bikson et al., 1988). Technical specialists will need training in client/server development and network support methods. Figure 9.10 shows that firms should expect to spend at least 5 percent of their client/server budgets on training.

Data Administration Disciplines

The role of data administration (see Chapter 7) becomes even more important when networks link many different applications and business areas. Organizations must systematically identify where their data are located, which groups are responsible for maintaining

Window on Management

BASS BEER SERVES A CLIENT/SERVER ENVIRONMENT

Bass PLC, located in Burton-on-Trent, Staffordshire, England, is the leading brewer in the United Kingdom. It is also a large and diversified multinational corporation. Its divisions include Bass Brewers, Bass Taverns, Bass Soft Drinks, Bass Leisure, and Holiday Inn Worldwide. In 1988 Bass concluded that it needed more cost-effective systems based on client/server technology. Profits were threatened from a beginning recession that was expected to decrease leisure activity spending and from the cost of conforming to new government regulations.

Bass systems had been primarily IBM and Unisys Corp. mainframe-based using dumb terminals. Individual operating units had their own information technology and their own technology policies. Many systems could not communicate with each other, even though Bass does an unusually large amount of internal trading (such as Holiday Inns purchasing all its beverages from within the Bass organization). Information technology skills were spread very unevenly throughout the organization. Bass units were purchasing from many different technology suppliers.

Bass management created a central Information Technology steering committee with representation from each of the Bass businesses. Management goals included (1) taking advantage of bulk purchasing of information technology; (2) setting corporate-wide hardware and software standards; (3) creating long-term business partnerships with leading suppliers of information technology; and (4) establishing a system that not only connected the whole corporation but did so in a seamless way. An individual had to be able to go to any workstation in a Bass location and with a single password have seamless access to any service on any machine in the network.

Bass management was willing to commit a lot of time to setting worldwide standards. The standards specify the leading suppliers with whom Bass has long-term partnerships. Bass now limits its business units to working with four suppliers: IBM and Unisys for hardware; Novell for networking; and Microsoft Corp. for desktop software. The steering committee reserved for itself the job of overseeing information technology purchases for all the Bass units.

To Think About: How well did Bass's information systems support its business strategy? How important are standards at Bass? Why? How much connectivity is there at Bass?

Bass has successfully made the move from mainframes to client/server computing. Their LANs connect more than 200 IBM AS/400 minicomputers and 4500 PCs, all linked in a client/server environment. To develop more internal expertise on the technology, Bass launched a program to get members of their information technology department certified as either Novell NetWare engineers or Microsoft experts.

The move to a client/server environment resulted in a drop in information technology staff from 1300 to 850. Half of the remaining 850 were actually new to the company, having been hired well into the client/server project. Many of the employees who left Bass had mainframe expertise, whereas most of the new employees are skilled in networking and desktop software.

Sources: "Fermenting a New Formula," *Computerworld Client/Server Journal,* June 1995; and George Black, "Bass Brews Up Hearty Client/Server Strategy," *Software Magazine,* May 1994.

---

each piece of data, and which individuals and groups are allowed to access and use that data. They need to develop specific policies and procedures to ensure that their data are accurate, available only to authorized users, and properly backed up.

Planning for Connectivity

Senior management must take a long-term view of the firm's information architecture and must make sure that its systems have the right degree of connectivity for its current and future information needs. Clearly, complete connectivity is usually not needed in most corporations. On the one hand, it is very expensive to develop gateway solutions one at a time. On the other hand, it is usually too expensive to achieve systemic connectivity for older applications. It is far more sensible to identify classes of connectivity problems and general solutions.

A longer-term strategy accepts the reality of today's incompatible systems but maintains a vision of the future, where connectivity is an important goal. Procurement strategy then should focus on new systems and follow the simple rule that, from today, systems will be developed only if (1) they support connectivity standards developed by the firm, and (2) they build upon existing networks and user applications in a seamless fashion. Management can establish policies to keep networks as homogeneous as possible, limiting the number of hardware, software, and network operating systems from different vendors.

Management Challenges

1. Enterprise networking and use of the Internet require a complete change of mindset. Companies must consider a different organizational structure, a different support structure for information systems, and different procedures of managing employees and desktop processing functions. To implement networked computing successfully, companies must examine and perhaps redesign an entire business process rather than throw new technology at existing business practices and hope that it will stick.

2. Connectivity and standards are very difficult to enforce, even when a firm's connectivity needs are well understood. Firms are reluctant to abandon their existing, albeit incompatible, systems because these systems represented such large investments. Corporate culture and competing interest groups within the firm often resist change. Business practices tend to favor short-term efforts over the long-term planning that is essential for creating an open systems environment.

3. Resolving the centralization vs. decentralization debate. Since the growth of minicomputers in the 1970s, a long-standing issue among IS managers and CEOs has been the question of centralization. Should processing power and data be distributed to departments and divisions, or should they be concentrated at a central location? The new architecture facilitates decentralization, but this may not always be in the organization's best interest. Managers need to make sure that the commitment to systems centralization or decentralization actually serves organizational objectives.

Summary

1. Describe the characteristics of enterprise networking and explain how it is changing organizations. Enterprise-wide computing architecture has produced a mixed environment composed mostly of networked desktop workstations and microcomputers. Although it often contains minicomputers and mainframes, computing power tends to take place on the desktop. The system is a network or multiple networks connecting many local area networks and devices. Enterprise networking provides flexibility for organizations trying to coordinate their activities without excess centralization because it can help eliminate layers of bureaucracy and invest lower-level line workers with more responsibility and authority. It also allows organizations to link directly with customers and suppliers, facilitating electronic commerce.

2. Describe the client/server model of computing. The client/server model splits computer processing between *clients* and *servers,* connected via a network. Each function of an application is assigned to the machine best suited to perform it. Clients are the user point-of-entry to the computer functionality they require and are usually a workstation, desktop, or laptop computer with a graphical user interface. The server, which may be anything from a supercomputer to a microcomputer, stores and processes shared data. The user generally interacts only with the client portion of the application. The exact division of tasks between client and server depends on the nature of the application.

3. Identify the capabilities of the Internet and describe both the benefits it offers organizations and the problems it presents to them. The Internet is used for communications, including e-mail; public forums on thousands of topics; and live, interactive conversations. It is also used for information retrieval from hundreds of libraries and thousands of library, corporate, government, and nonprofit databases from around the world. It has also developed into an effective way for individuals and organizations to offer information and products through a web of graphical user interfaces and easy-to-use links worldwide. Major Internet capabilities include e-mail, Usenet, chatting, Telnet, Gophers, Archie, WAIS, FTP, and the World Wide Web.

Organizations benefit from the Internet in a number of ways. Many use the Net to reduce their communications costs when they coordinate organizational activities and communicate with employees. Researchers and knowledge workers are finding the Internet a quick, low-cost way to both gather and disperse knowledge. The Internet facilitates electronic commerce, creating new opportunities for marketing, sales, and customer support and eliminating middlemen in buy and sell transactions. Organizations are building internal networks, called *intranets,* based on Internet technology for cost-effective communication and information sharing.

The Internet presents many problems to the business user, largely stemming from the fact that most of the technology is relatively new. Security is difficult because the Net offers spies, thieves, and hackers out to do damage many potential entry points. The rapid growth of Net popularity and the rapid expansion of the transmission of data-intensive graphics, sound, and video applications has created inadequate bandwidth. No adequate system has yet developed to allow individuals to effortlessly search through such immense amounts of data located anywhere in the world. Laws governing electronic commerce are mostly nonexistent or still in the process of being written, making it difficult to use public networks such as the Net to consummate legal contracts, for example.

4. Describe important standards used for linking hardware, software, and networks to achieve connectivity. Connectivity is a measure of how well computers and computer-based devices can communicate with one another and share information in a meaningful way without human intervention. It is essential in enterprise networking where different hardware, software, and network components must work together to transfer information seamlessly from one part of the organization to another.

There are several different models for achieving connectivity in networks. Public standards like OSI and TCP/IP are recognized as important reference models for network connectivity. Each divides the communications process into layers. TCP/IP is widely used in the United States, whereas OSI is favored in Europe. ISDN is an emerging standard for digital transmission over twisted-pair telephone lines. UNIX is an operating system standard that can be used to create open systems.

5. Identify problems posed by enterprise networking and recommend solutions. Problems posed by enterprise-wide computing include (1) loss of management control over systems; (2) the need to carefully manage organizational change; (3) difficulty of ensuring network reliability and security; (4) connectivity; and (5) controlling the hidden costs of client/server computing.

Solutions include planning for and managing the business and organizational changes associated with enterprise-wide computing, increasing end-user training, asserting data administration disciplines, and considering connectivity and cost controls when planning information architecture. While many corporations have assumed connectivity as a strategic goal, a more reasonable strategy would move incrementally toward greater connectivity while not giving up the vision of connectivity.

Key Terms

Enterprise networking	Gopher	Home page	Transmission Control Protocol/Internet Protocol (TCP/IP)
Internetworking	Archie	Web site	
Client/server model	WAIS	Intranet	
Client	File Transfer Protocol (FTP)	Firewall	Open Systems Interconnect (OSI)
Server	World Wide Web	Connectivity	
Electronic commerce	Hypertext markup language (HTML)	Open systems	Integrated Services Digital Network (ISDN)
Usenet		Reference model	
Chatting	Browser	Protocol	Downtime
Telnet	Search engine	Standard	

Review Questions

1. Define *enterprise networking*. List five of its characteristics. How is it related to internetworking?
2. What is *client/server computing*? What is the difference between the client and the server? What are the different roles each fulfills?
3. What is *electronic commerce*? How is it enhanced by enterprise networking and the Internet?
4. What is *the Internet*? What are its principal functions and capabilities?
5. Describe the role of the following in the World Wide Web: hypertext markup language, Web browsers, search engines.
6. Describe four ways in which the Internet can benefit many organizations.
7. Define and describe *intranets*. How can they benefit organizations?
8. Describe three basic problems of the Internet.
9. What is *connectivity*? Why is it a goal for enterprise networking?
10. Describe the two major models for network connectivity.
11. Describe ISDN and explain why it is important.
12. Why is UNIX important to connectivity?
13. Give four examples of problems posed by enterprise networking.
14. What are some solutions to the problems raised in the previous question?

Discussion Questions

1. Should all organizations use the Internet? Why or why not?
2. The Internet and Java will eliminate connectivity problems. Discuss.
3. Is there any point in maintaining an information systems department when most of the computing power of the corporation resides on a desktop?
4. Your employer has just announced a new strategic program to achieve complete connectivity of your firm's information systems in five years. What are some of the difficulties and potential dangers of such a policy?

Group Project

Form a group with three or four of your classmates. Locate a business, using a popular business magazine, or find a local business that could benefit from using the Internet. Develop an Internet strategy for that business, explaining what Internet capabilities should be used, technical requirements, and how the Internet could change the company's business model. Present your findings to the class.

Case Study

UNILEVER TRIES TO UNIFY WORLD OPERATIONS

The sun never sets on the worldwide holdings of Unilever, one of the world's largest multinational corporations. The sprawling conglomerate has more than 1000 different product brands, 300,000 employees, and more than 300 operating divisions located in 75 countries. Its holdings include T.J. Lipton, Calvin Klein Cosmetics, and Lever Brothers. Unilever's largest core business is food products. Profits have seesawed, increasing in 1992, falling in 1993, rising in 1994, and dropping 2.5% in 1995.

Unilever maintains two equally powerful cochairmen—Morris Tabaksblat in Rotterdam and Niall FitzGerald in London. FitzGerald and Tabaksblat are trying to make their octopus-like organization a nimble player in today's hypercompetitive global marketplace. Unilever is constantly mired in battles over soap, ice cream, shampoo, margarine, and sauces with fierce competitors such as Procter & Gamble, Nestlé, Colgate-Palmolive, and Snapple. Unilever needs to fend off these rivals while dealing with slow-growing populations in its mainstay markets and huge increases in its advertising and promotion costs.

As profits in developed markets stagnate, Unilever is shifting its weight to Asia, Latin America, and Central Europe. FitzGerald and Tabaksblat are trying to pare down Unilever's broad array of products and sell off underperforming units. Management also wants more efficiency by building plants that serve entire continents instead of just one country. It wants to be able to roll out the best products globally in the shortest period of time.

FitzGerald and Tabaksblat have delegated the job of developing products and marketing strategies for an entire region. This means that Thailand might be the detergent expert for Southeast Asia and that the Philippines would handle manufacturing. In Europe, the Frankfurt office would oversee skin care, while the Paris office would be in charge of shampoo. In other words, one country develops new products and creates marketing campaigns for the whole region. In the past, Unilever stressed geographic decentralization. While maintaining a measure of centralized control, it allowed country managers to meet the needs of local markets in different countries.

The firm tries to *Unileverize* its managers with a common organizational culture that transcends national boundaries. Managers are trained at Unilever's international management training college near London and are assigned job positions in various countries throughout their careers.

The senior management of this London- and Rotterdam-based firm believed that with so many companies under one roof, Unilever was "drowning in technology." Unilever had many redundant systems as well as many systems that were poorly conceived and poorly implemented. Management handed

Michael Johnson, Unilever's head of information technology, the responsibility of standardizing the behemoth's multitudinous hardware and software systems around an open systems architecture and bringing them together in a global network.

Unilever's old laissez-faire approach toward information systems had left it with a polyglot mix of hardware and software. Despite the official corporate policy of only using IBM, Hewlett-Packard, or DEC hardware, the firm had drastic incompatibility problems. The systems of various operating units had mushroomed out of control. To make his plan work, Johnson had to convince his three designated hardware vendors to cooperate on a cross-vendor software architecture.

The challenge for global firms is to provide companywide information in a consistent, common format while allowing local units to perform effectively. Unilever wanted to pursue this goal by providing a common foundation for disparate far-flung operations without hamstringing its businesses.

Johnson moved quickly. In June 1990 he started focusing on applications portability. He told Unilever's three primary hardware suppliers—IBM, DEC, and Hewlett-Packard—that he wanted to be able to build an application and port it anywhere in the world within ten days. He especially wanted to build "competitive-edge applications" in one place, send them to other Unilever companies, and install them instantly as if the recipients had developed them themselves.

Johnson enlisted Unilever's key hardware and software vendors to agree upon an open systems architecture for the firm that could serve as the foundation for a global network. Unilever chose the suite of standards built around the Open Software Foundation's Applications Environment Specification (AES) for systems and software throughout the corporation. AES is a massive suite of standards that includes elements of the OSF/1 operating system, the Motif graphical user interface, OSF's Distributed Computing Environment, SQL (Structured Query Language), and Posix. (Posix establishes a standard interface between an applications program and an operating system, rather than requiring a specific operating system.)

With this base environment, Johnson added important software and database standards. Unilever chose Oracle and Sybase Inc.'s database management systems, Lotus 1-2-3 spreadsheet software, and WordPerfect word processing software. Oracle's SQL Forms and Unify Corporation's Uniface applications environments were selected as front-end software development standards.

Johnson and his team decided to use AES's distributed client/server capabilities as the foundation for Unilever's global data network. Unilever chose Sprint International to manage its pan-European data network. Eventually Unilever hopes its software tools and global network will provide the technology to manage group projects around the world. FitzGerald and Tabaksblat can use a sophisticated e-mail system to help them monitor Unilever's new operating regions.

Unilever believes its move to open systems has not stifled local technology innovation. For instance, Quest International, a Unilever food ingredients and fragrance company based in England and the Netherlands, is using AES standards to develop its critical applications. Quest is relatively small (its 1991 revenue was $842 million) and it could move quickly to new standards.

While Johnson has taken a strong position about standards and open systems, he does not want to disrupt the company's operations during implementation. He realizes that he will not be able to make all of Unilever's operations switch to open systems overnight. Unilever inherited hundreds of proprietary applications that Johnson wants to leave in place until his staff figures out how to make them communicate among computers. While Unilever's companywide open systems model excludes proprietary systems such as those using IBM's AS/400 minicomputer environment, it is too costly to shut down these machines right away. Johnson is letting companies with AS/400 computers delay the changeover while mandating that all new software purchased or developed for the AS/400 computers must be portable to RISC (reduced instruction set computing) machines that are compatible with AES standards. ∎

Sources: Tara Parker-Pope, "Unilever Plans a Long-Overdue Pruning," *The Wall Street Journal*, September 3, 1996; Joshua Greenbaum, "Unilever's Unifying Theme," *Information Week*, March 2, 1992; and Floris A. Maljers, "Inside Unilever: The Evolving Transnational Company," *Harvard Business Review*, September–October 1992.

Case Study Questions

1. Analyze Unilever's problems using the competitive forces and value chain models. How well did Unilever's information systems support its business strategy?

2. What problems did Unilever's systems have? How serious were Unilever's connectivity problems? What management, technology, and organization factors were responsible for these problems?

3. How would you characterize Unilever's strategy for dealing with connectivity problems? Do you agree with this strategy?

4. How much connectivity should there be at a firm like Unilever? Would you recommend a five-year systems plan for Unilever to achieve a higher level of connectivity? If so, describe your plan.

References

Applegate, Lynda, "Paving the Information Superhighway: Introduction to the Internet." Harvard Business School 9-195-202 (October 6, 1995).

Berg, Lynn. "The SCOOP on Client/Server Costs." *Computerworld* (November 16, 1992).

Benjamin, Robert and Rolf Wigand. "Electronic Markets and Virtual Value Chains on the Information Superhighway." *Sloan Management Review* (Winter 1995).

Berners-Lee, Tim, Robert Cailliau, Ari Luotonen, Henrik Frystyk Nielsen, and Arthur Secret. "The World-Wide Web." *Communications of the ACM* 37, no. 8 (August 1994).

Bikson, Tora K., J. D. Eveland, and Barbara A. Gutek. "Flexible Interactive Technologies for Multi-Person Tasks: Current Problems and Future Prospects." Rand Corporation (December 1988).

Bikson, Tora K., Cathleen Stasz, and Donald A. Mankin. "Computer-Mediated Work: Individual and Organizational Impact on One Corporate Headquarters." Rand Corporation (1985).

Bowman, C. Mic, Peter B. Danzig, Udi Manger, and Michael F. Schwartz. "Scalable Internet Resource Discovery: Research Problems and Approaches." *Communications of the ACM* 37, no. 8 (August 1994.)

Celko, Joe. "Everything You Know Is Wrong." *Datamation* (January 21, 1994).

Chabrow, Eric R. "On-Line Employment." *Information Week* (January 23, 1995).

Cortese, Amy. "Here Comes the Intranet." *Business Week* (February 26, 1996).

Dearth, Jeffrey and Arnold King, "Negotiating the Internet." *Information Week* (January 9, 1995).

De Pompa, Barbara. "More Power at Your Fingertips." *Information Week* (December 30, 1991).

Dion, William R. "Client/Server Computing." *Personal Workstation* (May 1990).

Fisher, Sharon. "TCP/IP." *Computerworld* (October 7, 1991).

Flynn, Laurie. "Browsers Make Navigating the World Wide Net a Snap." *The New York Times* (January 29, 1995).

Goldman, Kevin. "Ad Agencies Slowly Set Up Shop at New Address on the Internet." *The Wall Street Journal* (December 29, 1994).

Goodman, S.E., L.I. Press, S.R. Ruth, and A.M. Rutkowski. "The Global Diffusion of the Internet: Patterns and Problems." *Communications of the ACM* 37, no. 8 (August 1994).

Guimaraes, Tom. "Personal Computing Trends and Problems: An Empirical Study." *MIS Quarterly* (June 1986).

Horwitt, Elisabeth. "Intranet Intricacies." *Computerworld Client/Server Journal* (February 1996).

"How to Use Intranets to Support Business Applications." *I/S Analyzer Case Studies* 35, no. 5 (May 1996).

Huff, Sid, Malcolm C. Munro, and Barbara H. Martin. "Growth Stages of End User Computing." *Communications of the ACM* (May 1988).

Johnson, Jim. "A Survival Guide for Administrators." *Software Magazine* (December 1992).

Kantor, Andrew. "The Best of the Lot." *Internet World* (January 1995).

King, Julia and Rosemary Cafasso. "Client/Server trimmings." *Computerworld* (December 19, 1994).

Laberis, Bill. "Pull the Plug on Computer Hype." *The Wall Street Journal* (April 25, 1994).

Laudon, Kenneth C. "From PCs to Managerial Workstations." In Matthias Jarke, *Managers, Micros, and Mainframes*. New York: John Wiley (1986).

Lee, Denis M. "Usage Pattern and Sources of Assistance for Personal Computer Users." *MIS Quarterly* (December 1986).

Lee, Sunro and Richard P. Leifer. "A Framework for Linking the Structure of Information Systems with Organizational Requirements for Information Sharing." *Journal of Management Information Systems* 8, no. 4 (Spring 1992).

Leiner, Barry M. "Internet Technology." *Communications of the ACM* 37, no. 8 (August 1994).

Lewis, Peter H. "Getting Down to Business on the Net." *The New York Times* (June 19, 1994).

Maglitta, Joseph and Ellis Booker. "Seller Beware." *Computerworld* (October 24, 1994).

Markoff, John. "Commerce Comes to the Internet." *The New York Times* (April 13, 1994).

Meeker, Mary and Chris DePuy. *The Internet Report*. New York: Morgan Stanley & Co. (1996).

Mossberg, Walter S. "Before You Cruise the Internet, Get the Right Road Map." *The Wall Street Journal* (January 19, 1995).

"Plans and Policies for Client/Server Technology." *I/S Analyzer* 30, no. 4 (April 1992).

Pyburn, Philip J. "Managing Personal Computer Use: The Role of Corporate Management Information Systems." *Journal of Management Information Systems* (Winter 1986–87).

Quelch, John A. and Lisa R. Klein. "The Internet and International Marketing." *Sloan Management Review* (Spring 1996).

Richard, Eric. "Anatomy of the World-Wide Web." *Internet World* (April 1995).

Richardson, Gary L., Brad M. Jackson, and Gary W. Dickson. "A Principles-Based Enterprise Architecture: Lessons from Texaco and Star Enterprise." *MIS Quarterly* 14, no. 4 (December 1990).

Semich, J. William. "The World Wide Web: Internet Boomtown?" *Datamation* (January 15, 1995).

Sinha, Alok. "Client-Server Computing." *Communications of the ACM* 35, no. 7 (July 1992).

Smarr, Larry, and Charles E. Catlett. "Metacomputing." *Communications of the ACM* 35, no. 6 (June 1992).

Sprout, Alison L. "The Internet Inside Your Company." *Fortune* (November 27, 1995).

Tash, Jeffrey B., and Paul Korzeniowski. "Theory Meets Reality for New Breed of APPs." *Software Magazine* (May 1992).

Tetzeli, Rick. "The INTERNET and Your Business," *Fortune* (March 7, 1994).

Ubois, Jeffrey. "CFOs in Cyberspace." *CFO* (February, 1995).

United States General Accounting Office. "FTS 2000: An Overview of the Federal Government's New Telecommunications System." *GAO/IMTEC-90-17FS* (February 1990).

Vacca, John R. "Mosaic: Beyond Net Surfing." *Byte* (January 1995).

Verity, John W. with Robert D. Hof. "The Internet: How It Will Change the Way You Do Business." *Business Week* (November 14, 1994).

Westin, Alan F., Heather A. Schwader, Michael A. Baker, and Sheila Lehman. *The Changing Workplace*. New York: Knowledge Industries, 1985.

Wilder, Clinton. "The Internet Pioneers." *Information Week* (January 9, 1995).

Withers, Suzanne. "The Trader and the Internet." *Technical Analysis of Stocks & Commodities* (March 1995).

Xeniakis, John J. "Moving to Mission Critical." *CFO*, September 1994.

Chapter 10

Redesigning the Organization with Information Systems

New Zealand Designs for Paperless Tax Returns

10.1 Systems as Planned Organizational Change
Linking Information Systems to the Business Plan
Establishing Organizational Information Requirements
Systems Development and Organizational Change
Window on Technology:
Redesigning with the Internet
Business Reengineering

10.2 Overview of Systems Development
Systems Analysis
Systems Design
Completing the Systems Development Process
Window on Organizations:
Europcar Struggles to Migrate Its Systems

10.3 System Implementation: Managing Change
Implementation Success and Failure
Managing Implementation
Window on Management:
Hoechst Heads Off a Reengineering Disaster
Designing for the Organization

10.4 Understanding the Business Value of Information Systems
Capital Budgeting Models
Nonfinancial and Strategic Considerations

Management Challenges
Summary
Key Terms
Review Questions
Discussion Questions
Group Project
Case Study: Curing Chaos at Methodist Hospital
References

New Zealand Designs for Paperless Tax Returns

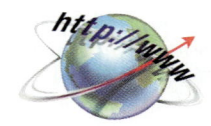

Since the mid-1980s New Zealand has been moving away from being one of the most highly regulated economies in the world. Its government agencies now have to be more flexible and responsive. Beset by constant changes in New Zealand's tax collection management, the New Zealand Inland Revenue Department (IRD) relied on an inflexible 20-year-old mainframe-oriented system.

So in 1990 IRD decided to modernize its information systems and redesign its business processes. It enlisted Andersen Consulting to help it build a new $300 million information system that would automate tax filing for the country's citizens. The system's objectives were to improve efficiency, generate additional revenue, and reduce the Revenue Department's staff requirements.

The new system, dubbed Future Inland Revenue Systems and Technology (FIRST), allows taxpayers to either mail their income tax forms to a regional tax office or transmit them electronically to the Revenue Department's computer. Tax forms that previously took three or four months to process by hand can now be completed in 14 days. Such service improvements have enabled the Revenue Department to cut its staff from 7000 to 5200. By 1997 the revenue department hopes to eliminate paper tax forms, queries, and correspondence altogether.

The systems analysis process identified redundant and paper-intensive office functions. Each of the district offices of the Revenue Department was a mirror of the other. The new system design eliminated superfluous tasks. The system-building team developed new client/server software programs for functions such as client registration and tax return generation. The Revenue Department decided to implement the new system slowly to allow time for user training and to minimize organizational disruptions.

After a 12-month study the Revenue Department's Information Technology Group began building the new system. It installed a nationwide network of 240 UNIX file servers, 500 microcomputers, and about 800 terminal devices and developed client/server applications for 40 district offices and 4 regional centers. Individual transactions would be processed on microcomputers or by using terminals in the district offices, while larger applications, such as corporate management systems, remained on the agency's two mainframes. The system handles about 2 million machine transaction inquiries per day.

Although the total cost of FIRST is expected to exceed $300 million, its efficiencies have already produced savings to offset more than 90 percent of this amount. ■

Sources: Randal Jackson, "Inland Revenue Department," *Computerworld: The Global 100*, May 1, 1995; and John McMullen, "Taxation without Vexation," *Information Week*, March 22, 1993.

New Zealand's automated tax filing system illustrates the many factors at work in the development of a new information system. Building the new system entailed analyzing the agency's problems with existing information systems, assessing people's information needs, selecting appropriate technology, and redesigning procedures and jobs. Management had to monitor the system-building effort and evaluate its benefits and costs. The new information system represented a process of planned organizational change.

This chapter describes how new information systems are conceived, built, and installed, with special attention to the issues of organizational design and organizational change. It describes the core systems development activities and the organizational change process of implementing a new information system. The chapter explains how to establish the business value of information systems and how to ensure that new systems are linked to the organization's business plan and information requirements.

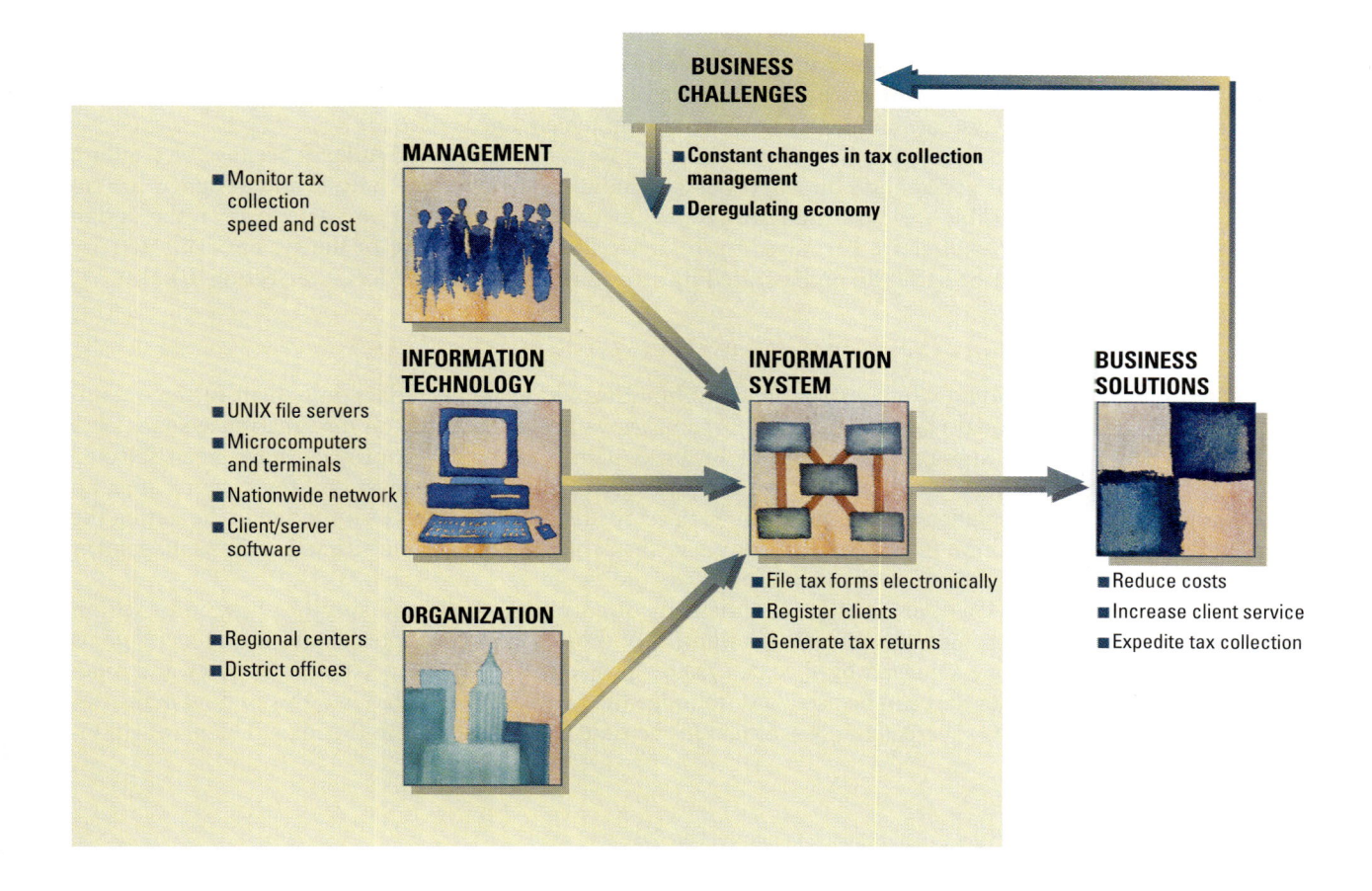

BUSINESS CHALLENGES

MANAGEMENT
- Monitor tax collection speed and cost

- Constant changes in tax collection management
- Deregulating economy

INFORMATION TECHNOLOGY
- UNIX file servers
- Microcomputers and terminals
- Nationwide network
- Client/server software

ORGANIZATION
- Regional centers
- District offices

INFORMATION SYSTEM
- File tax forms electronically
- Register clients
- Generate tax returns

BUSINESS SOLUTIONS
- Reduce costs
- Increase client service
- Expedite tax collection

> **Learning Objectives**
>
> *After completing this chapter, you will be able to:*
>
> 1. Show how building new systems can produce organizational change.
> 2. Explain how the organization can develop information systems that fit its business plan.
> 3. Identify the core activities in the systems development process.
> 4. Explain the organizational change requirements for building successful systems.
> 5. Describe various models for determining the business value of information systems.

10.1 SYSTEMS AS PLANNED ORGANIZATIONAL CHANGE

This text has emphasized that an information system is a sociotechnical entity, an arrangement of both technical and social elements. The introduction of a new information system involves much more than new hardware and software. It also includes changes in jobs, skills, management, and organization. In the sociotechnical philosophy, one cannot install new technology without considering the people who must work with it (Bostrom and Heinen, 1977). When we design a new information system, we are redesigning the organization.

One of the most important things to know about building a new information system is that this process is one kind of planned organizational change. System builders must understand how a system will affect the organization as a whole, focusing particularly on organizational conflict and changes in the locus of decision making. Builders must also consider how the nature of work groups will change under the impact of the new system. Builders determine how much change is needed.

Systems can be technical successes but organizational failures because of a failure in the social and political process of building the system. Analysts and designers are responsible for ensuring that key members of the organization participate in the design process and are permitted to influence the ultimate shape of the system. This activity must be carefully orchestrated by information system builders (see Section 10.3).

LINKING INFORMATION SYSTEMS TO THE BUSINESS PLAN

Deciding which new systems to build should be an essential component of the organizational planning process. Organizations need to develop an information systems plan that supports their overall business plan. Once specific projects have been selected within the overall context of a strategic plan for the business and the systems area, an **information systems plan** can be developed. The plan serves as a road map indicating the direction of systems development, the rationale, the current situation, the management strategy, the implementation plan, and the budget (see Table 10.1).

The plan contains a statement of corporate goals and specifies how information technology supports the attainment of those goals. The report shows how general goals will be achieved by specific systems projects. It lays out specific target dates and milestones that can be used later to judge the progress of the plan in terms of how many objectives were actually attained in the time frame specified in the plan. The plan will in-

information systems plan A road map indicating the direction of systems development: the rationale, the current situation, the management strategy, the implementation plan, and the budget.

Table 10.1 Information Systems Plan

1. **Purpose of the Plan**
   Overview of plan contents
   Changes in firm's current situation
   Firm's strategic plan
   Current business organization
   Management strategy

2. **Strategic Business Plan**
   Current situation
   Current business organization
   Changing environments
   Major goals of the business plan

3. **Current Systems**
   Major systems supporting business functions
   Major current capabilities
      Hardware
      Software
      Database
      Telecommunications
   Difficulties meeting business requirements
   Anticipated future demands

4. **New Developments**
   New system projects
      Project descriptions
      Business rationale
   New capabilities required
      Hardware
      Software
      Database
      Telecommunications

5. **Management Strategy**
   Acquisition plans
   Milestones and timing
   Organizational realignment
   Internal reorganization
   Management controls
   Major training initiatives
   Personnel strategy

6. **Implementation Plan**
   Detailed implementation plan
   Anticipated difficulties in implementation
   Progress reports

7. **Budget Requirements**
   Requirements
   Potential savings
   Financing
   Acquisition cycle

---

dicate the key management decisions concerning hardware acquisition; telecommunications; centralization/decentralization of authority, data, and hardware; and required organizational change. Organizational changes are also usually described, including management and employee training requirements; recruiting efforts; and changes in authority, structure, or management practice.

ESTABLISHING ORGANIZATIONAL INFORMATION REQUIREMENTS

In order to develop an effective information systems plan, the organization must have a clear understanding of both its long- and short-term information requirements. Two principal methodologies for establishing the essential information requirements of the organization as a whole are enterprise analysis and critical success factors.

Enterprise Analysis (Business Systems Planning)

Enterprise analysis (also called *business systems planning*) argues that the information requirements of a firm can only be understood by looking at the entire organization in terms of organizational units, functions, processes, and data elements. Enterprise analysis can help identify the key entities and attributes of the organization's data. This method starts with the notion that the information requirements of a firm or a division can be specified only with a thorough understanding of the entire organization. This method was developed by IBM in the 1960s explicitly for establishing the relationship among large system development projects (Zachman, 1982).

The central method used in the enterprise analysis approach is to take a large sample of managers and ask them how they use information, where they get the information, what their environment is like, what their objectives are, how they make decisions, and what their data needs are.

enterprise analysis An analysis of organization-wide information requirements by looking at the entire organization in terms of organizational units, functions, processes, and data elements; helps identify the key entities and attributes in the organization's data.

Logical application groups	Processes \ Data classes	Actuarial estimates	Agency plans	Budget	Program regs./policy	Admin. regs./policy	Labor agreements	Data standards	Procedures	Automated systems documentation	Educational media	Public agreements	Intergovernmental agreements	Grants	External	Exchange control	Administrative accounts	Program expenditures	Audit reports	Organization/position	Employee identification	Recruitment/placement	Complaints/grievances	Training resources	Security	Equipment utilization	Space utilization	Supplies utilization	Workload schedules	Work measurement	Enumeration I.D.	Enumeration control	Earnings	Employer I.D.	Earnings control	Claims characteristics	Claims control	Decisions	Payment	Collection/waiver	Notice	Inquiries control	Quality appraisal
PLANNING	Develop agency plans	C	C	C	U	U									U																												
PLANNING	Administer agency budget	C	C	C	U	U						U	U	U		U	U	U		U	U					U	U	U		U		U			U		U			U		U	U
PLANNING	Formulate program policies	U	U		C				U						U				U				U															U					U
PLANNING	Formulate admin. policies		U		U	C	C		U						U				U	U			U																				
PLANNING	Formulate data policies		U	U		U		C	U	U															U	U	U	U															
PLANNING	Design work processes		U		U	U			C	C		U	U						U																			U					U
GENERAL MANAGEMENT	Manage public affairs		U		U	U			U		C	C	C																														
GENERAL MANAGEMENT	Manage intrgovt. affairs	U	U		U	U			U		U		C	C	C															U	U		U	U		U			U				
GENERAL MANAGEMENT	Exchange data				U				U			U	U	U	U	C	U	U												U													
GENERAL MANAGEMENT	Maintain admin. accounts			U		U			U			U	U				C				U					U	U	U								U			U				
GENERAL MANAGEMENT	Maintain prog. accounts			U	U				U			U	U					C														U			U		U	U	U	U		U	
GENERAL MANAGEMENT	Conduct audits				U	U			U	U							U	U	C		U								U														
GENERAL MANAGEMENT	Establish organizations			U		U			U											C	U								U	U													U
GENERAL MANAGEMENT	Manage human resources			U		U	U		U											C	C	C	C	C																			
GENERAL MANAGEMENT	Provide security				U	U		U	U	U															C	C	C	C		U													
GENERAL MANAGEMENT	Manage equipment			U		U		U	U	U															C	C	C	C															
GENERAL MANAGEMENT	Manage facilities			U		U			U																U	U	C																
GENERAL MANAGEMENT	Manage supplies			U		U			U																C	U	U	C															
GENERAL MANAGEMENT	Manage workloads	U		U	U	U			U							U										U	U	U	C	C		U			U		U					U	U
PROGRAM ADMIN.	Issue social security nos.								U				U		U																C	C											
PROGRAM ADMIN.	Maintain earnings								U				U	U	U																U		C	C	C	U							
PROGRAM ADMIN.	Collect claims information				U	U			U						U																U	U				C	C	U	U	U			
PROGRAM ADMIN.	Determine elig/entlmt.								U																						U	U	U			U		C	U	U			
PROGRAM ADMIN.	Compute payments				U				U									U													U		U			U		U	C	C			
PROGRAM ADMIN.	Administer debt mgmt.				U				U									U																					U	C			
SUPPORT	Generate notices								U						U																U		U			U		U	U	U	C		
SUPPORT	Respond to prog. inquiries				U				U		U																				U		U	U		U		U	U	U	U	C	
SUPPORT	Provide quality assessment				U	U			U	U																					U		U			U		U			U		C

KEY
C = creators of data U = users of data

FIGURE 10.1
Process/data class matrix. This chart depicts which data classes are required to support particular organizational processes and which processes are the creators and users of data.

The results of this large survey of managers are aggregated into sub-units, functions, processes, and data matrices. Data elements are organized into *logical application groups*—groups of data elements that support related sets of organizational processes. Figure 10.1 is an output of enterprise analysis conducted by the Social Security Administration as part of a massive systems redevelopment effort. It shows what information is required to support a particular process, which processes create the data, and which use them. The shaded boxes in the figure indicate a logical application group. In this case, actuarial estimates, agency plans, and budget data are created in the planning process, suggesting that an information system should be built to support planning.

The weakness of enterprise analysis is that it produces an enormous amount of data that is expensive to collect and difficult to analyze. Most of the interviews are conducted with senior or middle managers, with little effort to collect information from clerical workers and supervisory managers. Moreover, the questions frequently focus not on the critical objectives of management and where information is needed, but rather on what *existing* information is used. The result is a tendency to automate whatever exists. But in many instances, entirely new approaches to how business is conducted are needed, and these needs are not addressed.

Strategic Analysis or Critical Success Factors

The strategic analysis, or critical success factor, approach argues that the information requirements of an organization are determined by a small number of **critical success factors (CSFs)** of managers. If these goals can be attained, the success of the firm or organization is assured (Rockart, 1979; Rockart and Treacy, 1982).

CSFs are shaped by the industry, the firm, the manager, and the broader environment. This broader focus, in comparison to that of previous methods, accounts for the description of this technique as *strategic*. An important premise of the strategic analysis approach is that there is a small number of objectives that managers can easily identify and information systems can focus on.

The principal method used in CSF analysis is personal interviews—three or four—with a number of top managers to identify their goals and the resulting CSFs. These personal CSFs are aggregated to develop a picture of the firm's CSFs. Then systems are built to deliver information on these CSFs. (See Table 10.2 for an example of CSFs. For the method of developing CSFs in an organization, see Figure 10.2.)

The strength of the CSF method is that it produces a smaller data set to analyze than does enterprise analysis. Only top managers are interviewed, and the questions focus on a small number of CSFs rather than a broad inquiry into what information is used or needed. This method can be tailored to the structure of each industry, with different competitive strategies producing different information systems. Therefore, this method produces systems that are more custom-tailored to an organization.

A unique strength of the CSF method is that it takes into account the changing environment with which organizations and managers must deal. This method explicitly asks managers to look at the environment and consider how their analysis of it shapes their information needs. It is especially suitable for top management and for the development of DSS and ESS. Unlike enterprise analysis, the CSF method focuses organizational attention on how information should be handled.

The weakness of this method is that the aggregation process and the analysis of the data are art forms. There is no particularly rigorous way in which individual CSFs can be aggregated into a clear company pattern. Second, there is often confusion among interviewees (and interviewers) between *individual* and *organizational* CSFs. They are not necessarily the same. What can be critical to a manager may not be important for the organization. Moreover, this method is clearly biased toward top managers because they are the ones (generally the only ones) interviewed. Last, it should be noted that this method does not necessarily overcome the impact of a changing environment or changes in managers. Environments and managers change rapidly, and information systems must adjust accordingly. The use of CSFs to develop a system does not mitigate these factors.

critical success factors (CSFs)
A small number of easily identifiable operational goals shaped by the industry, the firm, the manager, and the broader environment that are believed to assure the success of an organization. Used to determine the information requirements of an organization.

Table 10.2 Critical Success Factors and Organizational Goals

Example	Goals	CSF

Profit concern	Earnings/share
	Return on investment
	Market share
	New product
		Automotive industry
		  Styling
		  Quality dealer system
		  Cost control
		  Energy standards

Nonprofit	Excellent health care Meeting government regulations Future health needs	Regional integration with other hospitals Efficient use of resources Improved monitoring of regulations

Source: Rockart (1979).

FIGURE 10.2
Using CSFs to develop systems. The CSF approach relies on interviews with key managers to identify their CSFs. Individual CSFs are aggregated to develop CSFs for the entire firm. Systems can then be built to deliver information on these CSFs.

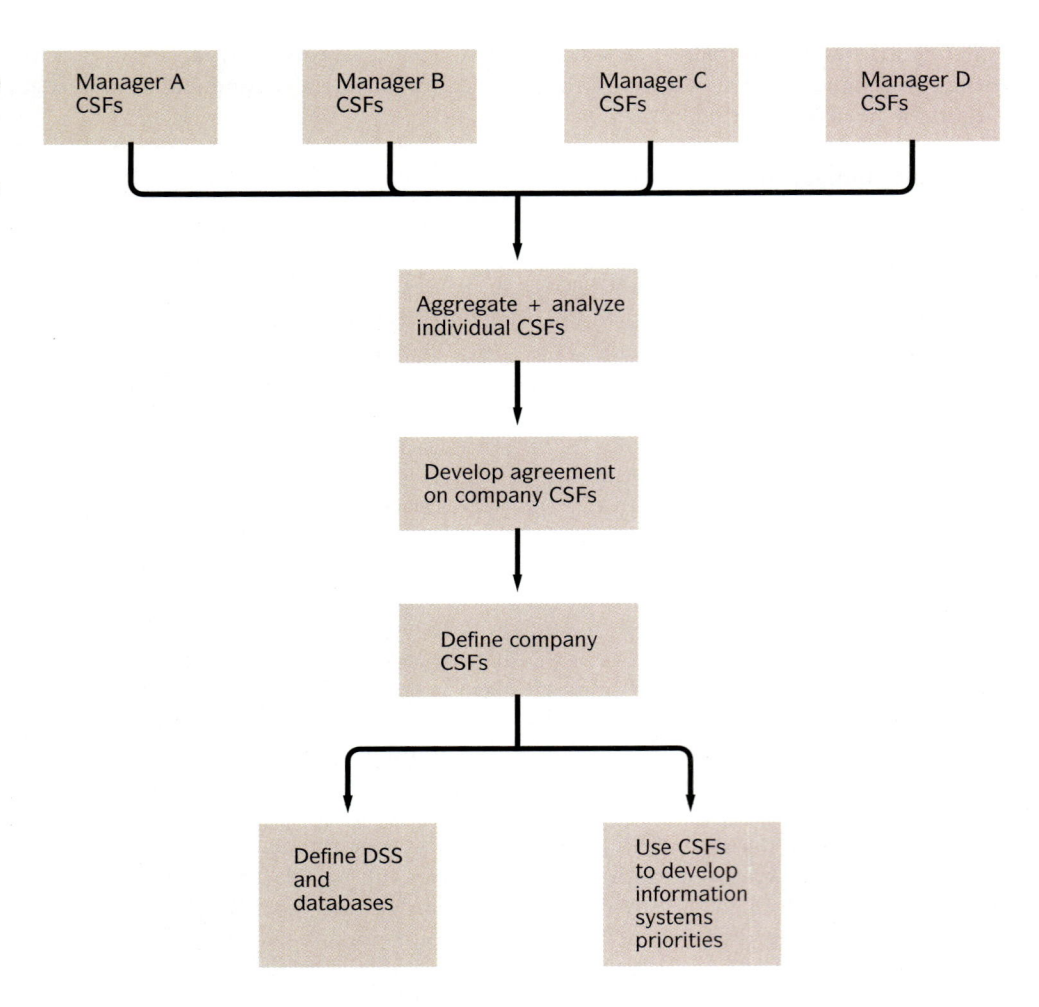

Manager A CSFs → Manager B CSFs → Manager C CSFs → Manager D CSFs → Aggregate + analyze individual CSFs → Develop agreement on company CSFs → Define company CSFs → Define DSS and databases / Use CSFs to develop information systems priorities

SYSTEMS DEVELOPMENT AND ORGANIZATIONAL CHANGE

New information systems can be powerful instruments for organizational change, enabling organizations to redesign their structure, scope, power relationships, workflows, products, and services. Table 10.3 describes some of the ways that information technology is being used to transform organizations.

The Spectrum of Organizational Change

Information technology can promote various degrees of organizational change, ranging from incremental to far-reaching. Figure 10.3 shows four kinds of structural organizational change that are enabled by information technology: (1) automation, (2) rationalization, (3) reengineering, and (4) paradigm shifts. Each carries different rewards and risks.

The most common form of IT enabled organizational change is **automation**. The first applications of information technology involved assisting employees to perform their tasks more efficiently and effectively. Calculating paychecks and payroll registers, giving bank tellers instant access to customer deposit records, and developing a nationwide network of airline reservation terminals for airline reservation agents are all examples of early automation.

A deeper form of organizational change—one that follows quickly from early automation—is **rationalization of procedures**. Automation frequently reveals new bottlenecks in production and makes the existing arrangement of procedures and structures painfully cumbersome. Rationalization of procedures is the streamlining of standard operating procedures, eliminating obvious bottlenecks, so that automation can make

automation Using the computer to speed up the performance of existing tasks.

rationalization of procedures The streamlining of standard operating procedures, eliminating obvious bottlenecks, so that automation makes operating procedures more efficient.

Table 10.3	How Information Technology Can Transform Organizations
Information Technology	Organizational Change
Global networks	International division of labor: The operations of a firm are no longer determined by location; the global reach of firms is extended; costs of global coordination decline. Transaction costs decline.
Enterprise networks	Collaborative work and teamwork: The organization of work can now be coordinated across divisional boundaries; a customer and product orientation emerges; widely dispersed task forces become the dominant work group. The costs of management (agency costs) decline. Business processes are changed.
Distributed computing	Empowerment: Individuals and work groups now have the information and knowledge to act. Business processes are redesigned, streamlined. Management costs decline. Hierarchy and centralization decline.
Portable computing	Virtual organizations: Work is no longer tied to geographic location. Knowledge and information can be delivered anywhere they are needed, anytime. Work becomes portable. Organizational costs decline as real estate is less essential for business.
Graphical user interfaces	Accessibility: Everyone in the organization—even senior executives—can access information and knowledge; work-flows can be automated, contributed to by all from remote locations. Organizational costs decline as work-flows move from paper to digital image, documents, and voice.

operating procedures more efficient. For example, the New Zealand Inland Revenue Department's system is effective not just because it utilizes state-of-the-art computer technology but also because its design allows the IRD to operate more efficiently. The procedures of IRD or of any organization, must be rationally structured to achieve this result. Before the IRD could automate its tax filing system, it had to have identification numbers for all taxpayers and standard rules for calculating and submitting tax payments in either paper or electronic form. Without a certain amount of rationalization

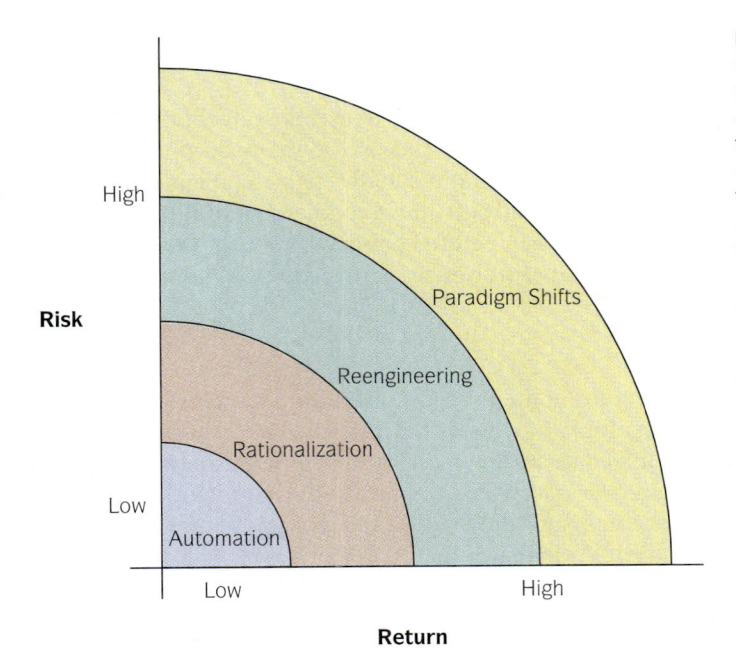

FIGURE 10.3
Organizational change carries risks and rewards. The most common forms of organizational change are automation and rationalization. These relatively slow-moving and slow-changing strategies present modest returns but little risk. Faster and more comprehensive change—like reengineering and paradigm shifts—carry high rewards but offer a substantial chance of failure.

in the Inland Revenue Department's organization, its computer technology would have been useless.

A more powerful type of organizational change is **business reengineering,** in which business processes are analyzed, simplified, and redesigned. Reengineering involves radically rethinking the flow of work and the business procedures used to produce products and services, with a mind to radically reduce the costs of business. A **business process** is a set of logically related tasks performed to achieve a defined business outcome. Some examples of business processes are developing a new product, ordering goods from a supplier, or processing and paying an insurance claim. Using information technology, organizations can rethink and streamline their business processes to improve speed, service, and quality. Business reengineering reorganizes work-flows, combining steps to cut waste and eliminating repetitive, paper-intensive tasks (sometimes the new design eliminates jobs as well). It is much more ambitious than rationalization of procedures, requiring a new vision of how the process is to be organized.

An widely-cited example of business reengineering is Ford Motor Company's *invoiceless processing.* Ford employed more than 500 people in its North American Accounts Payable organization. The accounts payable clerks spent most of their time resolving discrepancies between purchase orders, receiving documents, and invoices. Ford reengineered its accounts payable process, instituting a system wherein the purchasing department enters a purchase order into an on-line database that can be checked by the receiving department when the ordered items arrive. If the received goods match the purchase order, the system automatically generates a check for accounts payable to send to the vendor. There is no need for vendors to send invoices. After reengineering, Ford was able to reduce headcount in accounts payable by 75 percent and produce more accurate financial information (Hammer and Champy, 1993).

Rationalizing procedures and redesigning business processes are limited to specific parts of a business. New information systems can ultimately affect the design of the entire organization, by actually transforming how the organization carries out its business or even the nature of the business itself. For instance, Schneider National (described in Chapter 3) used new information systems to create a competitive on-demand shipping service and to develop a new sideline business managing the logistics for other companies. Baxter International's stockless inventory system (described in Chapter 2) transformed Baxter into a working partner with hospitals and into a manager of its customers' supplies. This still more radical form of business change is called a **paradigm shift.** A paradigm shift involves rethinking the nature of the business and the nature of the organization itself.

The Window on Technology illustrates how Internet technology can be used for making these organizational changes.

Paradigm shifts and reengineering often fail because extensive organizational change is so difficult to orchestrate (see Section 10.3). Why then do so many corporations entertain such radical change? Because the rewards are equally high (see Figure 10.3). In many instances firms seeking paradigm shifts and pursuing reengineering strategies achieve stunning, order-of-magnitude increases in their returns on investment (or productivity). Some of these success stories, and some failure stories, are included throughout this book.

BUSINESS REENGINEERING

Many companies today are focusing on building new information systems where they can perform business reengineering. Table 10.4 describes various ways that information technology can streamline and consolidate business processes. If the business process is first redesigned before computing power is applied, organizations can potentially obtain very large payoffs from their investments in information technology. Figure 10.4 illustrates how business process redesign worked at Banc One Mortgage, an Indianapolis-based subsidiary of Banc One Corporation in Columbus, Ohio. Banc One, the twelfth-largest bank in the United States, has expanded by aggressively pursuing acquisitions. In 1992 the company expected to move from handling 33,000 loans per year to 300,000

---

business reengineering The radical redesign of business processes, combining steps to cut waste and eliminating repetitive, paper-intensive tasks in order to improve cost, quality, service, and to maximize the benefits of information technology.

business process A set of logically related tasks performed to achieve a defined business outcome.

paradigm shift Radical reconceptualization of the nature of the business and the nature of the organization.

Window on Technology

REDESIGNING WITH THE INTERNET

Many businesses are using the Internet to redesign their work-flows, products, and services. Here are a few examples:

New York-based **J.P. Morgan & Co.** (*http://www.jpmorgan.com/*), one of the most prestigious banks in the world, turned to the Internet because its IT vendors took too long providing technical help. David Spector, vice president of corporate technology, decided the quickest way to report problems to vendors and get back software modifications was through the Net. Spector claims that problems that used to take days to fix are now remedied in hours or minutes. Word of the Net quickly spread, and now Morgan employees worldwide use it to gather information such as corporate financial or government census data. Later Morgan decided to become a Web information provider. It established a service, known as RiskMetrics, that provides daily risk measurement data on more than 300 financial instruments, including complex financial derivatives, government bonds, and mortgage refinance and mortgage purchase indices. Morgan claims that thousands of investors access its site each day. "The goal is to establish ourselves as a leader in providing information," says Spector. "Being positioned as experts is good for our business."

Trane Co. (*http://www.trane.com/*), the LaCrosse, Wisconsin, heating and air-conditioning manufacturer, reengineered its business to reduce the time to manufacture a custom-designed commercial air-conditioning system from 36 days to 6 days. The company wanted "dramatic improvements in customer service and double revenues." Nonetheless, its paperwork still took 46 days using its mainframe-based network. To shrink its office cycles, the company installed desktop computers at its 120 locations—sales offices, warehouses, corporate offices—connecting them via the Net. In addition, sales staff were issued laptops. Now Trane staff, vendors, collaborators, and customers exchange sales bids and all other documents instantly. Using the Net, rather than installing their own wide-area network, cut setup costs by at least 25 percent.

> **To Think About:** How are these companies using the Internet for organizational design? What types of organizational change are taking place?

RoweCom (*http://www.rowe.com*) facilitates library and research institute purchases of journal subscriptions. Richard Rowe was paying $2 million annually for leased lines. Now he uses the Net, saving his clients 7–9 percent on purchases. Through software developed by RoweCom, customers enter journal orders directly on the Internet. (Traditional subscription agencies act as intermediaries for these transactions.) The orders are then transmitted via the Internet to Banc One. The bank in turn collects the funds, forwards the subscription to the publisher and pays the customer. Setup costs were also much lower because they used the Net. Development and complete testing by RoweCom and Banc One took only a few months, rather than several years as is common for such an operation.

Sources: L. Buchonon, "A Subscription for Change," *Webmaster*, January/February, 1996; Clinton Wilder, "The Internet Pioneers," *Information Week*, January 9, 1995; and "ANS Builds Virtual Private Data Network to Support Business Transformation at Trane," *ANS Update*, November, 1994.

---

loans per year. To forestall a blizzard of paperwork, Banc One redesigned the mortgage application process so that it required fewer steps and paper forms to complete and reduced the time to process a mortgage to only two days.

In the past, a mortgage applicant filled out a paper loan application. The bank entered the application transaction into its computer system. Specialists such as credit analysts and underwriters from eight different departments accessed and evaluated the application individually. If the loan application was approved, the closing was scheduled. After the closing, bank specialists dealing with insurance or funds in escrow serviced the loan. This desk-to-desk assembly-line approach took 17 days.

Banc One Mortgage replaced the sequential desk-to-desk approach with a speedier *work cell* or team approach. Now, loan originators in the field enter the mortgage application directly into laptop computers. Software checks the application transaction to make sure that all of the information is correct and complete. The loan originators transmit the loan applications using a dial-up network to regional production centers. Instead of working on the application individually, the credit analysts, loan underwriters, and other specialists convene electronically, working as a team to approve the mortgage.

Table 10.4 — IT Capabilities and Their Organizational Impacts

Capability	Organizational Impact/Benefit
Transactional	IT can transform unstructured processes into routinized transactions.
Geographical	IT can transfer information with rapidity and ease across large distances, making processes independent of geography.
Automational	IT can replace or reduce human labor in a process.
Analytical	IT can bring complex analytical methods to bear on a process.
Informational	IT can bring vast amounts of detailed information into a process.
Sequential	IT can enable changes in the sequence of tasks in a process, often allowing multiple tasks to be worked on simultaneously.
Knowledge management	IT allows the capture and dissemination of knowledge and expertise to improve the process.
Tracking	IT allows the detailed tracking of task status, inputs, and outputs.
Disintermediation	IT can be used to connect two parties within a process that would otherwise communicate through an intermediary (internal or external).

Source: Thomas H. Davenport and James E. Short, "The New Industrial Engineering: Information Technology and Business Process Redesign," *Sloan Management Review* 11, Summer 1990.

After closing, another team of specialists sets up the loan for servicing. The entire loan application process takes only two days. Loan information is also easier to access than before, when the loan application could be in eight or nine different departments. Loan originators can also dial into the bank's network to obtain information on mortgage loan costs or to check the status of a loan for the customer.

FIGURE 10.4
Redesigning mortgage processing at Banc One. By redesigning their mortgage processing system and the mortgage application process, Banc One will be able to handle the increased paperwork as they move from processing 33,000 loans per year to processing 300,000 loans per year. *Adapted from Mitch Betts, "Banc One Mortgage Melts Paper Blizzard,"* Computerworld, *December 14, 1992. Copyright 1994 by Computerworld, Inc., Framingham, MA 01701. Reprinted from* Computerworld. *Reprinted by permission.*

Shifting from a traditional approach helped BANC ONE Mortgage slash processing time from 17 days to two

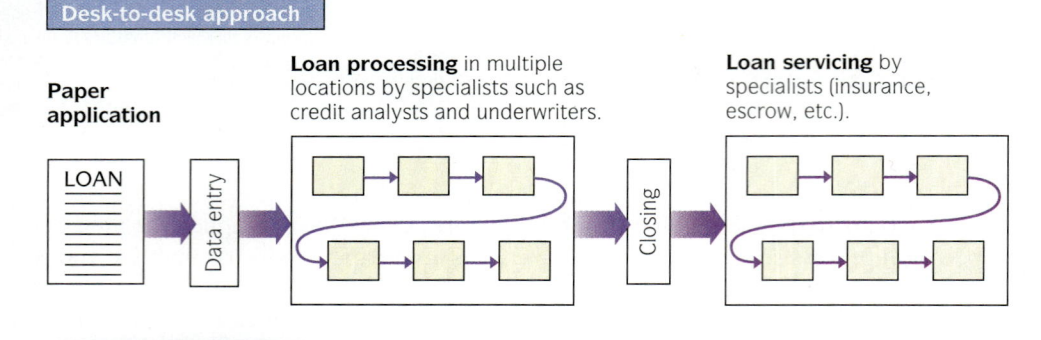

BEFORE Desk-to-desk approach

Paper application → Data entry → Loan processing in multiple locations by specialists such as credit analysts and underwriters. → Closing → Loan servicing by specialists (insurance, escrow, etc.).

AFTER Work-cell approach

Application on laptop computer → Dial-up network → Regional production center: Teams process open applications. → Closing → Servicing: Specialists work together as a team.

Reengineered mortgage processing at Banc One. Mortgage loan applications entered via laptop computers can now be evaluated by many people simultaneously, expediting the mortgage application process.

By redesigning its entire approach to mortgage processing, Banc One achieved remarkable efficiencies. Instead of automating the way it had always done mortgage processing, it completely rethought the entire mortgage application process.

Work-Flow Management

To streamline the paperwork in its mortgage application process, Banc One turned to work-flow and document management software. By using this software to store and process documents electronically, organizations can redesign their work-flow so that documents can be worked on simultaneously or moved more easily and efficiently from one location to another. The process of streamlining business procedures so that documents can be moved easily and efficiently from one location to another is called **work-flow management.** Work-flow and document management software automates processes such as routing documents to different locations, securing approvals, scheduling, and generating reports. Two or more people can work simultaneously on the same document, allowing much quicker completion time. Work need not be delayed because a file is out or a document is in transit. And with a properly designed indexing system, users will be able to retrieve files in many different ways, based on the content of the document. Chapter 2 describes how the United Services Automobile Association (USAA) developed a document imaging system to obtain such benefits.

work-flow management The process of streamlining business procedures so that documents can be moved easily and efficiently from one location to another.

Steps in Effective Reengineering

To reengineer effectively, senior management needs to develop a broad strategic vision that calls for redesigned business processes. For example, Odense Shipyard's management looked for breakthroughs to lower costs and accelerate product development that would enable the firm to become the market leader in producing double-hulled tanker ships. Companies should identify a few core business processes to be redesigned, focusing on those with the greatest potential payback (Davenport and Short, 1990).

Table 10.5	New Process Design Options with Information Technology		
Assumption	Technology	Option	Examples
Field personnel need offices to receive, store, and transmit information.	Wireless communications	Personnel can send and receive information wherever they are.	Chiat/Day Ernst & Young
Information can appear only in one place at one time.	Shared databases	People can collaborate on the same project from scattered locations; information can be used simultaneously wherever it is needed.	Odense Shipyards Banc One
People are needed to ascertain where things are located.	Automatic identification and tracking technology	Things can tell people where they are.	United Parcel Service Schneider National
Businesses need reserve inventory to prevent stockouts.	Telecommunications networks and EDI	Just-in-time delivery and stockless supply.	Wal-Mart Baxter International

Management must understand and measure the performance of existing processes as a baseline. If, for example, the objective of process redesign is to reduce time and cost in developing a new product or filling an order, the organization needs to measure the time and cost consumed by the unchanged process. For example, before reengineering, it cost C.R. England & Sons Inc. $5.10 to send an invoice; after processes were reengineered the cost per invoice dropped to 15 cents (Davidson, 1993).

The conventional method of designing systems establishes the information requirements of a business function or process and then determines how they can be supported by information technology. However information technology can create new design options for various processes because it can be used to challenge longstanding assumptions about work arrangements that used to inhibit organizations. Table 10.5 provides examples of innovations that have overcome these assumptions using companies discussed in the text. Information technology should be allowed to influence process design from the start.

Following these steps does not automatically guarantee that reengineering will always be successful. In point of fact, the majority of reengineering projects do not achieve breakthrough gains in business performance, with reengineering failure rates estimated as high as 70 percent (Hammer and Stanton, 1995; King, 1994; Moad, 1993). Problems with reengineering are part of the larger problem of orchestrating organizational change, a problem that attends the introduction of all new innovations, including information systems. Managing change is neither simple nor intuitive. A reengineered business process or a new information system inevitably affects jobs, skill requirements, workflows, and reporting relationships. Fear of these changes breeds resistance, confusion, and even conscious efforts to undermine the change effort. We examine these organizational change issues more carefully in Section 10.3.

10.2 OVERVIEW OF SYSTEMS DEVELOPMENT

Whatever their scope and objectives, new information systems are an outgrowth of a process of organizational problem solving. A new information system is built as a solution to some type of problem or set of problems the organization perceives it is facing. The problem may be one where managers and employees realize that the organization is not performing as well as expected, or it may come from the realization that the organization should take advantage of new opportunities to perform more successfully.

Review the diagrams at the beginning of each chapter of this text. They show an information system that is a solution to a particular set of business challenges or problems. The resulting information system is an outgrowth of a series of events called *sys-*

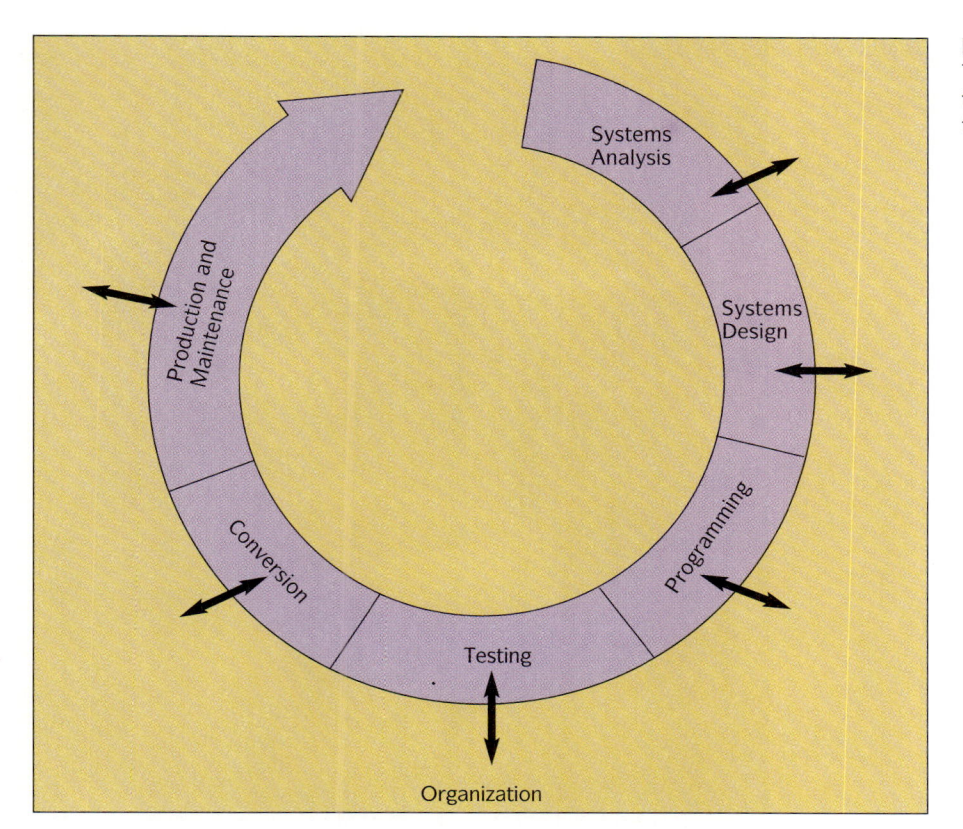

FIGURE 10.5
The systems development process. Each of the core systems development activities entails interaction with the organization.

tems development. **Systems development** refers to all the activities that go into producing an information systems solution to an organizational problem or opportunity. Systems development is a structured kind of problem solving with distinct activities. These activities consist of systems analysis, systems design, programming, testing, conversion, and production and maintenance.

Figure 10.5 illustrates the systems development process. The systems development activities depicted here usually take place in sequential order. But some of the activities may need to be repeated or some may be taking place simultaneously, depending on the approach to system building that is being employed (see Chapter 11). Note also that each activity involves interaction with the organization. Members of the organization participate in these activities and the systems development process creates organizational changes.

systems development The activities that go into producing an information systems solution to an organizational problem or opportunity.

SYSTEMS ANALYSIS

Systems analysis is the analysis of the problem that the organization will try to solve with an information system. It consists of defining the problem, identifying its causes, specifying the solution, and identifying the information requirements that must be met by a system solution.

The systems analyst creates a road map of the existing organization and systems, identifying the primary owners and users of data in the organization. These stakeholders have a direct interest in the information affected by the new system. In addition to these organizational aspects, the analyst also briefly describes the existing hardware and software that serve the organization.

From this organizational analysis, the systems analyst details the problems of existing systems. By examining documents, work papers, and procedures; observing system operations; and interviewing key users of the systems, the analyst can identify the problem areas and objectives to be achieved by a solution. Often the solution requires building a new information system or improving an existing one.

systems analysis The analysis of a problem that the organization will try to solve with an information system.

10.2 Overview of Systems Development

Building successful information systems requires close co-operation among end users and information systems specialists throughout the systems development process.

Feasibility

feasibility study As part of the systems analysis process, the way to determine whether the solution is achievable, given the organization's resources and constraints.

technical feasibility Determines whether a proposed solution can be implemented with the available hardware, software, and technical resources.

economic feasibility Determines whether the benefits of a proposed solution outweigh the costs.

In addition to suggesting a solution, systems analysis involves a **feasibility study** to determine whether that solution is feasible, or achievable, given the organization's resources and constraints. Three major areas of feasibility must be addressed:

1. **Technical feasibility**: whether the proposed solution can be implemented with the available hardware, software, and technical resources.
2. **Economic feasibility**: whether the benefits of the proposed solution outweigh the costs. We explore this topic in greater detail in Section 10.4, Understanding the Business Value of Information Systems.
3. **Operational feasibility**: whether the proposed solution is desirable within the existing managerial and organizational framework.

Normally the systems analysis process will identify several alternative solutions that can be pursued by the organization. The process will then assess the feasibility of each. A written systems proposal report will describe the costs and benefits, advantages and disadvantages of each alternative. It is then up to management to determine which mix of costs, benefits, technical features, and organizational impacts represents the most desirable alternative.

Establishing Information Requirements

Perhaps the most difficult task of the systems analyst is to define the specific information requirements that must be met by the system solution selected. At the most basic level, the **information requirements** of a new system involve identifying who needs what information, where, when, and how. Requirements analysis carefully defines the objectives of the new or modified system and develops a detailed description of the functions that the new system must perform. Requirements must consider economic, technical, and time constraints, as well as the goals, procedures, and decision processes of the organization. Faulty requirements analysis is a leading cause of systems failure and high systems development costs. A system designed around the wrong set of requirements will either have to be discarded because of poor performance or will need to be heavily revised. Therefore, the importance of requirements analysis cannot be underestimated.

Developing requirements specifications may involve considerable research and revision. To derive information systems requirements, analysts may be forced to work and rework requirements statements in cooperation with users. There are also alternative approaches to eliciting requirements that help minimize these problems (see Chapter 11).

In many instances, building a new system creates an opportunity to redefine how the organization conducts its daily business. Some problems do not require an information system solution but instead need an adjustment in management, additional training, or refinement of existing organizational procedures. If the problem is information-related, systems analysis may still be required to diagnose the problem and arrive at the proper solution.

operational feasibility Determines whether a proposed solution is desirable within the existing managerial and organizational framework.

information requirements A detailed statement of the information needs that a new system must satisfy; identifies who needs what information, and when, where, and how the information is needed.

SYSTEMS DESIGN

While systems analysis describes what a system should do to meet information requirements, **systems design** shows how the system will fulfill this objective. The design of an information system is the overall plan or model for that system. Like the blueprint of a building or house, it consists of all the specifications that give the system its form and structure.

The systems designer details the system specifications that will deliver the functions identified during systems analysis. These specifications should address all of the managerial, organizational, and technological components of the system solution. Table 10.6 lists the types of specifications that would be produced during systems design.

systems design Details how a system will meet the information requirements as determined by the systems analysis.

Logical and Physical Design

The design for an information system can be broken down into logical and physical design specifications. **Logical design** lays out the components of the system and their relationship to each other as they would appear to users. It shows what the system solution will do as opposed to how it is actually implemented physically. It describes inputs and outputs, processing functions to be performed, business procedures, data models, and controls. (Controls specify standards for acceptable performance and methods for measuring actual performance in relation to these standards. They are described in detail in Chapter 14.)

Physical design is the process of translating the abstract logical model into the specific technical design for the new system. It produces the actual specifications for hardware, software, physical databases, input/output media, manual procedures, and specific controls. Physical design provides the remaining specifications that transform the abstract logical design plan into a functioning system of people and machines.

Like houses or buildings, information systems may have many possible designs. They may be centralized or distributed, on-line or batch, partially manual, or heavily automated. Each design represents a unique blend of all of the technical and organizational factors that shape an information system. What makes one design superior to others is the ease and efficiency with which it fulfills user requirements within a specific set of technical, organizational, financial, and time constraints.

logical design Lays out the components of the information system and their relationship to each other as they would appear to users.

physical design The process of translating the abstract logical model into the specific technical design for the new system.

Table 10.6 Design Specifications

Output
  Medium
  Content
  Timing
	Controls
	  Input controls (characters, limit, reasonableness)
	  Processing controls (consistency, record counts)
	  Output controls (totals, samples of output)
	  Procedural controls (passwords, special forms)

Input
  Origins
  Flow
  Data entry
	Security
	  Access controls
	  Catastrophe plans
	  Audit trails

User interface
  Simplicity
  Efficiency
  Logic
  Feedback
  Errors
	Documentation
	  Operations documentation
	  Systems documents
	  User documentation

Database design
  Logical data relations
  Volume and speed requirements
  File organization and design
  Record specifications
	Conversion
	  Transfer files
	  Initiate new procedures
	  Select testing method
	  Cut over to new system

Processing
  Computations
  Program modules
  Required reports
  Timing of outputs
	Training
	  Select training techniques
	  Develop training modules
	  Identify training facilities

Manual procedures
  What activities
  Who performs them
  When
  How
  Where
	Organizational changes
	  Task redesign
	  Job design
	  Process design
	  Office and organization structure design
	  Reporting relationships

The Role of End Users

User information requirements drive the entire system-building effort. Users must have sufficient control over the design process to ensure that the system reflects their business priorities and information needs, not the biases of the technical staff. Working on design increases users' understanding and acceptance of the system, reducing problems caused by power transfers, intergroup conflict, and unfamiliarity with new system functions and procedures. As we describe later in this chapter, insufficient user involvement in the design effort is a major cause of system failure.

The nature and level of user participation in design vary from system to system. There is less need for user involvement in systems with simple or straightforward requirements than in those with requirements that are elaborate, complex, or vaguely defined. Less structured systems need more user participation to define requirements and may necessitate many versions of design before specifications can be finalized. Different levels of user involvement in design are reflected in different systems development methods. Chapter 11 describes how user involvement varies with each development approach.

COMPLETING THE SYSTEMS DEVELOPMENT PROCESS

The remaining steps in the systems development process translate the solution specifications established during systems analysis and design into a fully operational information system. These concluding steps consist of programming, testing, conversion, production, and maintenance.

Programming

The process of translating design specifications into software for the computer constitutes a smaller portion of the systems development cycle than design and, perhaps, the testing activities. But it is here, in providing the actual instructions for the machine, that the heart of the system takes shape. During the **programming** stage, system specifications that were prepared during the design stage are translated into program code. On the basis of detailed design documents for files, transaction and report layouts, and other design details, specifications for each program in the system are prepared.

programming The process of translating the system specifications prepared during the design stage into program code.

Testing

Exhaustive and thorough **testing** must be conducted to ascertain whether the system produces the right results. Testing answers the question, "Will the system produce the desired results under known conditions?"

The amount of time needed to answer this question has been traditionally underrated in systems project planning (see Chapter 14). As much as 50 percent of the entire software development budget can be expended in testing. Testing is also time-consuming: Test data must be carefully prepared, results reviewed, and corrections made in the system. In some instances parts of the system may have to be redesigned. Yet the risks of glossing over this step are enormous.

testing The exhaustive and thorough process that determines whether the system produces the desired results under known conditions.

Testing an information system can be broken down into three types of activities:

Unit testing, or program testing, consists of testing each program separately in the system. While it is widely believed that the purpose of such testing is to guarantee that programs are error-free, this goal is realistically impossible. Testing should be viewed instead as a means of locating errors in programs, focusing on finding all the ways to make a program fail. Once pinpointed, problems can be corrected.

unit testing The process of testing each program separately in the system. Sometimes called *program testing*.

System testing tests the functioning of the information system as a whole. It tries to determine if discrete modules will function together as planned and whether discrepancies exist between the way the system actually works and the way it was conceived. Among the areas examined are performance time, capacity for file storage and handling peak loads, recovery and restart capabilities, and manual procedures.

system testing Tests the functioning of the information system as a whole in order to determine if discrete modules will function together as planned.

Acceptance testing provides the final certification that the system is ready to be used in a production setting. Systems tests are evaluated by users and reviewed by management. When all parties are satisfied that the new system meets their standards, the system is formally accepted for installation.

acceptance testing Provides the final certification that the system is ready to be used in a production setting.

It is essential that all aspects of testing be carefully thought out and that they be as comprehensive as possible. To ensure this, the development team works with users to devise a systematic test plan. The **test plan** includes all of the preparations for the series of tests previously described.

test plan Prepared by the development team in conjunction with the users; it includes all of the preparations for the series of tests to be performed on the system.

Figure 10.6 shows an example of a test plan. The general condition being tested is a record change. The documentation consists of a series of test-plan screens maintained on a database (perhaps a microcomputer database) that is ideally suited to this kind of application.

Conversion

Conversion is the process of changing from the old system to the new system. It answers the question, "Will the new system work under real conditions?" Four main conversion strategies can be employed: the parallel strategy, the direct cutover strategy, the pilot study strategy, and the phased approach strategy.

conversion The process of changing from the old system to the new system.

In a **parallel strategy** both the old system and its potential replacement are run together for a time until everyone is assured that the new one functions correctly. This is the safest conversion approach because, in the event of errors or processing disruptions,

parallel strategy A safe and conservative conversion approach where both the old system and its potential replacement are run together for a time until everyone is assured that the new one functions correctly.

FIGURE 10.6
A sample test plan to test a record change. When developing a test plan, it is imperative to include the various conditions to be tested, the requirements for each condition tested, and the expected results. Test plans require input from both end users and information system specialists.

Procedure	Address and Maintenance "Record Change Series"		Test Series 2		
Prepared By:		Date:	Version:		
Test Ref.	Condition Tested	Special Requirements	Expected Results	Output On	Next Screen
2	Change records				
2.1	Change existing record	Key field	Not allowed		
2.2	Change nonexistent record	Other fields	"Invalid key" message		
2.3	Change deleted record	Deleted record must be available	"Deleted" message		
2.4	Make second record	Change 2.1 above	OK if valid	Transaction file	V45
2.5	Insert record		OK if valid	Transaction file	V45
2.6	Abort during change	Abort 2.5	No change	Transaction file	V45

the old system can still be used as a backup. However, this approach is very expensive, and additional staff or resources may be required to run the extra system.

The **direct cutover** strategy replaces the old system entirely with the new system on an appointed day. At first glance, this strategy seems less costly than parallel conversion strategy. However, it is a very risky approach that can potentially be more costly than parallel activities if serious problems with the new system are found. There is no other system to fall back on. Dislocations, disruptions, and the cost of corrections may be enormous.

The **pilot study** strategy introduces the new system to only a limited area of the organization, such as a single department or operating unit. When this pilot version is complete and working smoothly, it is installed throughout the rest of the organization, either simultaneously or in stages.

The **phased approach** strategy introduces the new system in stages, either by functions or by organizational units. If, for example, the system is introduced by functions, a new payroll system might begin with hourly workers who are paid weekly, followed six months later by adding salaried employees (who are paid monthly) to the system. If the system is introduced by organizational units, corporate headquarters might be converted first, followed by outlying operating units four months later.

A formal **conversion plan** provides a schedule of all the activities required to install the new system. The most time-consuming activity is usually the conversion of data (see the Window on Organizations). Data from the old system must be transferred to the new system, either manually or through special conversion software programs. The converted data then must be carefully verified for accuracy and completeness.

Moving from an old system to a new one requires that end users be trained to use the new system. Detailed **documentation** showing how the system works from both a technical and end-user standpoint is finalized during conversion time for use in training and everyday operations. Lack of proper training and documentation contributes to system failure, so this portion of the systems development process is very important.

Production and Maintenance

After the new system is installed and conversion is complete, the system is said to be in **production.** During this stage the system will be reviewed by both users and technical specialists to determine how well it has met its original objectives and to decide whether any revisions or modifications are in order. Changes in hardware, software, documentation,

direct cutover A risky conversion approach where the new system completely replaces the old one on an appointed day.

pilot study A strategy to introduce the new system to a limited area of the organization until it is proven to be fully functional; only then can the conversion to the new system across the entire organization take place.

phased approach Introduces the new system in stages either by functions or by organizational units.

conversion plan Provides a schedule of all activities required to install a new system.

documentation Descriptions of how an information system works from either a technical or end-user standpoint.

production The stage after the new system is installed and the conversion is complete; during this time the system is reviewed by users and technical specialists to determine how well it has met its original goals.

> **Window on Organizations**
>
> ## EUROPCAR STRUGGLES TO MIGRATE ITS SYSTEMS
>
> Paris-based Europcar Interrent, Europe's number one European-based auto rental agency, had grown over the years partly by acquiring local companies. Europcar did not fully integrate the newly acquired units. Instead, the firm allowed them mostly to continue business operations as they had done in the past, only under the new corporate name. Europcar's inheritance problems were magnified by the mass of differing laws, cultures, and languages resulting from the many countries in which it operates. Management determined it had no choice but to make changes if Europcar were to continue to be competitive once European economic integration accelerated beginning in 1993.
>
> The problem Europcar faced was the many different computer systems in nine different countries residing on 55 different mainframe and minicomputers, each with its own software and data sets. Robert Verasdonck, Europcar's corporate director of information systems, decided to convert these systems into a single, client/server-based platform with data residing in a relational database to service all the local Europcar units. The new system would consolidate reservations, billing, and fleet management for the company's business across Europe.
>
> Some of the problems were technical. For example, there were too many data sources for a single automated conversion tool to handle. Up to 40 engineers were assigned to manually convert and migrate the data.
>
> The technical problems only reflected the underlying business problems—Europcar had not standardized its business policies and practices across the company as it acquired new organizations. Each of the 55 systems reflected the information needs, business practices, customer preferences, and corporate cultures of the local unit it was serving. The systems also represented disparate local business operations such as local rates, local products, local contracts (Austria levies a tax on mileage on cars driven within the country but does not tax driving outside the country), and local accounting practices. Verasdonck quickly realized that creating a single unified system was impossible without first addressing the business issue of organizational unity. Before it could convert the data and programs, the company would first need to develop corporate standards and operating procedures. The new, unified system had to blend a wide range of languages, currencies, and corporate cultures into a single business entity.
>
> > **To Think About:** It has been said that the significance of conversion in systems development has been underestimated. Do you agree? What management, organization, and technology issues did Europcar have to address when converting its systems?
>
> Even establishing corporate standards is usually not adequate, however. In the complex environment of Europcar, standard data formats will not work if they are not accepted and supported locally. Building that support and educating the users became a key task of Verasdonck. In December, 1993, at a meeting of local management, he discovered that local managers wanted to undertake the educational process as quickly as possible. The new system was to be used by some 3000 employees at 800 offices across Europe. Verasdonck launched a crash training program, establishing 37 training centers throughout Europe that together were capable of training 225 users each week.
>
> The new system, dubbed Greenway, went fully operational in February, 1995, and can handle up to 4000 users simultaneously. It incorporates five Sequent 2000/790 computers running Oracle databases, which can be accessed throughout Europe from 960 Europcar offices equipped with microcomputers.
>
> Verasdonck now plans to convert all of Europcar's remaining franchises in Africa, Asia, Australia, South America, and the Caribbean to the new system, adding even more local customs, laws, languages, and operating procedure problems.
>
> *Sources:* Pierre Berger and Cara A. Cunningham, "Europcar Drives Rocky Road to Unix," *Computerworld,* March 6, 1995; Joshua Greenbaum, "Under Repair," *Information Week,* October 3, 1994; and "A Bumpy Road for Europcar," *Information Week,* February 7, 1994.

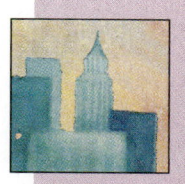

or procedures to a production system to correct errors, meet new requirements, or improve processing efficiency are termed **maintenance**.

Studies of maintenance have examined the amount of time required for various maintenance tasks (Lientz and Swanson, 1980). Approximately 20 percent of the time is devoted to debugging or correcting emergency production problems; another 20 percent is concerned with changes in data, files, reports, hardware, or system software. But 60 percent of all maintenance work consists of making user enhancements, improving documentation, and recoding system components for greater processing efficiency. The amount of work in the third category of maintenance problems could be reduced significantly through better systems analysis and design practices. Table 10.7 summarizes the systems development activities.

maintenance Changes in hardware, software, documentation, or procedures to a production system to correct errors, meet new requirements, or improve processing efficiency.

Table 10.7	Systems Development
Core Activity	**Description**
Systems analysis	Identify problem(s) Specify solution Establish information requirements
Systems design	Create logical design specifications Create physical design specifications Manage technical realization of system
Programming	Translate design specifications into program code
Testing	Unit test Systems test Acceptance test
Conversion	Plan conversion Prepare documentation Train users and technical staff
Production and maintenance	Operate the system Evaluate the system Modify the system

Systems differ in terms of their size, technological complexity, and in terms of the organizational problems they are meant to solve. Because there are different kinds of systems, a number of methods have been developed to build systems. We describe these various methods in the next chapter.

10.3 SYSTEM IMPLEMENTATION: MANAGING CHANGE

The introduction or alteration of an information system has a powerful behavioral and organizational impact. It transforms the way various individuals and groups perform and interact. Changes in the way information is defined, accessed, and used to manage the resources of the organization often lead to new distributions of authority and power (Lucas, 1975). This internal organizational change breeds resistance and opposition and can lead to the demise of an otherwise good system.

A very large percentage of information systems fail to deliver benefits or to solve the problems for which they were intended because the process of organizational change associated with system-building was not properly addressed. Successful system-building requires careful planning and change management. We now turn to the problem of change management by examining patterns of implementation.

IMPLEMENTATION SUCCESS AND FAILURE

implementation All of the organizational activities working toward the adoption, management, and routinization of an innovation.

change agent The individual acting as the catalyst during the change process to ensure successful organizational adaptation to a new system or innovation.

In the context of change management, **implementation** refers to all of the organizational activities working toward the adoption, management, and routinization of an innovation such as a new information system. In the implementation process, the systems analyst is a **change agent**. The analyst not only develops technical solutions but redefines the configurations, interactions, job activities, and power relationships of various organizational groups. The analyst is the catalyst for the entire change process and is responsible for ensuring that the changes created by a new system are accepted by all parties involved. The change agent communicates with users, mediates between competing interest groups, and ensures that the organizational adjustment to such changes is complete.

Whether system implementations are successful or not depend largely on managerial and organizational factors. The role of users, the degree of management support, the manner in which the systems project handles complexity and risk, and the management of the implementation process itself all have a profound impact on system outcome.

User Involvement and Influence

Heavy user involvement in the design and operation of information systems afford them more opportunities to mold the system according to their priorities and business requirements. In addition, they are more likely to react positively to the completed system because they have been active participants in the change process.

Communication problems between end users and designers are a major reason why user requirements are not properly incorporated into information systems and why users are driven out of the implementation process. Users and information system specialists tend to have different backgrounds, interests, and priorities and often pursue different goals. This is referred to as the **user-designer communications gap**. These differences are manifested in divergent organizational loyalties, approaches to problem solving, and vocabularies. Information system specialists, for example, often have a highly technical or machine orientation to problem solving. They look for elegant and sophisticated technical solutions in which hardware and software efficiency is optimized at the expense of ease of use or organizational effectiveness. Users, on the other hand, prefer systems that are oriented to solving business problems or facilitating organizational tasks. Often the orientations of both groups are so at odds that they appear to speak in different tongues. These differences are illustrated in Table 10.8, which depicts the typical concerns of end users and technical specialists (information system designers) regarding the development of a new information system.

> **user-designer communications gap** The difference in backgrounds, interests, and priorities that impede communication and problem solving among end users and information systems specialists.

Management Support

If an information systems project has the backing and approval of management at various levels, it is more likely to be perceived positively by both users and the technical information services staff. Both groups will feel that their participation in the development process will receive higher-level attention, priority, and reward. Management backing also ensures that a systems project will receive sufficient funding and resources to be successful. Furthermore, all of the changes in work habits and procedures and any organizational realignments associated with a new system depend on management backing to be enforced effectively.

Level of Complexity and Risk

Systems differ dramatically in their size, scope, level of complexity, and organizational and technical components. Some systems development projects are more likely to fail because they carry a much higher level of risk than others. Researchers have identified three key dimensions that influence the level of project risk (McFarlan, 1981).

Table 10.8 The User-Designer Communications Gap

User Concerns	Designer Concerns
Will the system deliver the information I need for my work?	How much disk storage space will the master file consume?
How quickly can I access the data?	How many lines of program code will it take to perform this function?
How easily can I retrieve the data?	How can we cut down on CPU time when we run the system?
How much clerical support will I need to enter data into the system?	What is the most efficient way of storing this piece of data?
How will the operation of the system fit into my daily business schedule?	What database management system should we use?

Table 10.9	Dimensions of Project Risk		
Project Structure	Project Technology Level	Project Size	Degree of Risk
High	Low	Large	Low
High	Low	Small	Very low
High	High	Large	Medium
High	High	Small	Medium-low
Low	Low	Large	Low
Low	Low	Small	Very low
Low	High	Large	Very high
Low	High	Small	High

PROJECT SIZE. The larger the project—as indicated by the dollars spent, the size of the implementation staff, the time allocated to implementation, and the number of organizational units affected—the greater the risk.

PROJECT STRUCTURE. Projects that are more highly structured run a much lower risk than those whose requirements are relatively undefined, fluid, and constantly changing; when requirements are clear and straightforward, outputs and processes can be easily defined. Users in highly structured projects tend to know exactly what they want and what the system should do; there is a much lower possibility of their changing their minds.

EXPERIENCE WITH TECHNOLOGY. The project risk will rise if the project team and the information system staff are unfamiliar with the hardware, system software, application software, or database management system proposed for the project.

These dimensions of project risk will be present in different combinations for each implementation effort. Table 10.9 shows that eight different combinations are possible, each with a different degree of risk. The higher the level of risk, the more likely it is that the implementation effort will fail.

Management of the Implementation Process

The conflicts and uncertainties inherent in any implementation effort will be magnified when an implementation project is poorly managed and organized. Under poor management basic elements of success may be omitted. Training to ensure that end users are comfortable with the new system and fully understand its potential uses is often sacrificed, in part because the budget is strained toward the end of a project. A systems development project without proper management will most likely suffer vast cost overruns, major time slippages, and technical performances that fall significantly below the estimated level.

How badly are projects managed? On average, private-sector projects are underestimated by one-half in terms of budget and time required to deliver the complete system promised in the system plan. A very large number of projects are delivered with missing functionality (promised for delivery in later versions). Government projects suffer about the same failure level, sometimes worse (Laudon, 1989; Helms and Weiss, 1986).

MANAGING IMPLEMENTATION

Not all aspects of the implementation process can be easily controlled or planned (Alter and Ginzberg, 1978). However, the chances for system success can be increased by anticipating potential implementation problems and applying appropriate corrective strategies. Strategies have also been devised for ensuring that users play an appropriate role throughout the implementation period and for managing the organizational change process. Various project management, requirements gathering, and planning methodologies have been developed for specific categories of problems.

Increasing User Involvement

The level of user involvement should vary depending upon both the development methodology being used and the risk level of the project. Tools to involve users—**external integration tools**—consist of ways to link the work of the implementation team to users at all organizational levels. For example, users can be made active members or leaders of systems development project teams or placed in charge of system training and installation.

external integration tools Project management technique that links the work of the implementation team to that of users at all organizational levels.

Overcoming User Resistance

Systems development is not an entirely rational process. Users leading design activities have used their position to further private interests and to gain power rather than to promote organizational objectives (Franz and Robey, 1984). Participation in implementation activities may not be enough to overcome the problem of user resistance. The implementation process demands organizational change. Such change may be resisted because different users may be affected by the system in different ways. While some users may welcome a new system because it brings changes they perceive as beneficial to them, others may resist these changes because they believe the shifts are detrimental to their interests (Joshi, 1991).

If use of a system is voluntary, users may tend to avoid it. If use is mandatory, resistance will take the form of increased error rates, disruptions, turnover, and even sabotage. Implementation strategy must address the issue of counterimplementation (Keen, 1981). **Counterimplementation** is a deliberate strategy to thwart the implementation of an information system or an innovation in an organization.

counterimplementation A deliberate strategy to thwart the implementation of an information system or an innovation in an organization.

Strategies to overcome user resistance include user participation (to elicit commitment as well as to improve design), user education (training), management coercion (edicts, policies), and user incentives. User resistance can be addressed through changes to the new system, such as improved human factors (user/system interface). Finally, users will be more cooperative if organizational problems are solved prior to introducing the new system.

Managing Technical Complexity

Projects with *high levels of technology* benefit from **internal integration tools**. The success of such projects depends on how well their technical complexity can be managed. Project leaders need both heavy technical and administrative experience. They must be able to anticipate problems and develop smooth working relationships among a predominantly technical team. Team members should be highly experienced. Team meetings should take place frequently, with routine distribution of meeting minutes concerning key design decisions. Essential technical skills or expertise not available internally should be secured from outside the organization.

internal integration tools Project management technique that ensures that the implementation team operates as a cohesive unit.

Formal Planning and Control Tools

Large projects will benefit from appropriate use of **formal planning and control tools**. With project management techniques such as PERT (Program Evaluation and Review Technique) or Gantt charts, a detailed plan can be developed. (PERT lists the specific activities that make up a project, their duration, and the activities that must be completed before a specific activity can start. A Gantt chart such as that illustrated in Figure 10.7 visually represents the sequence and timing of different tasks in a development project, as well as their resource requirements.) Tasks can be defined and resources budgeted.

formal planning tools Project management technique that structures and sequences tasks; budgeting time, money, and technical resources required to complete the tasks.

formal control tools Project management technique that helps monitor the progress toward completion of a task and fulfillment of goals.

HRIS COMBINED PLAN-HR	Da	Who	1995 Oct	Nov	Dec	1996 Jan	Feb	Mar	Apr	May	Jun	Jul	Aug	Sep	Oct	Nov	Dec	1997 Jan	Feb	Mar	Apr
DATA ADMINISTRATION SECURITY																					
QMF security review/setup	20	EF TP																			
Security orientation	2	EF JV																			
QMF security maintenance	35	TP GL																			
Data entry sec. profiles	4	EF TP																			
Data entry sec. views est.	12	EF TP																			
Data entry security profiles	65	EF TP																			
DATA DICTIONARY																					
Orientation sessions	1	EF																			
Data dictionary design	32	EF WV																			
DD prod. coordn-query	20	GL																			
DD prod. coord-live	40	EF GL																			
Data dictionary cleanup	35	EF GL																			
Data dictionary maint.	35	EF GL																			
PROCEDURES REVISION DESIGN PREP																					
Work flows (old)	10	PK JL																			
Payroll data flows	31	JL PK																			
HRIS P/R model	11	PK JL																			
P/R interface orient. mtg.	6	PK JL																			
P/R interface coordn. I	15	PK																			
P/R interface coordn.	8	PK																			
Benefits interfaces (old)	5	JL																			
Ben. interfaces new flow	8	JL																			
Ben. communication strategy	3	PK JL																			
New work flow model	15	PK JL																			
Posn. data entry flows	14	WV JL																			
RESOURCE SUMMARY																					
Edith Farrell	5.0	EF	2	21	24	24	23	22	22	27	34	34	29	26	28	19	14	4	3		
Woody Holand	5.0	WH	5	17	20	19	12	10	14	10	2										
Charles Pierce	5.0	CP		5	11	20	13	9	10	7	6	8	4	4	4	4	4				9
Ted Leurs	5.0	TL		12	17	17	19	17	14	12	15	16	2	1	1	1	1				
Toni Cox	5.0	TC	1	11	10	11	11	12	19	19	21	21	21	17	17	12	9	3	2		
Patricia Clark	5.0	PC	7	23	30	34	27	25	15	24	25	16	11	13	17	10	3				
Jane Lawton	5.0	JL	1	9	16	21	19	21	21	20	17	15	14	12	14	8	5				6
David Holloway	5.0	DH	4	4	5	5	5	2	7	5	4	16	2								
Diane O'Neill	5.0	DO	6	14	17	16	13	11	9	4											
Joan Albert	5.0	JA	5	6			7	6	2	1				5	5	1					
Marie Marcus	5.0	MM	15	7	2	1	1														
Don Stevens	5.0	DS	4	4	5	4	5	1													
Casual	5.0	CASL		3	4	3			4	7	9	5	3	2							
Kathy Manley	5.0	KM		1	5	16	20	19	22	19	20	18	20	19	11	2					
Anna Borden	5.0	AB					9	10	16	15	11	12	19	10	7	1					
Gail Loring	5.0	GL		3	6	5	9	10	17	18	17	10	13	10	10	7	17	14	13	3	1
UNASSIGNED	0.0	X												9	236	225	230	216	178	9	7
Co-op	5.0	CO	6	4					2	3	4	4	2	4	16						
Casual	5.0	CAUL								3	3	3									
TOTAL DAYS			49	147	176	196	194	174	193	195	190	181	140	125	358	288	284	237	196	12	23

FIGURE 10.7
Formal planning and control tools help to manage information systems projects successfully. The Gantt chart in this figure was produced by a commercially available project management software package. It shows the task, man-days, and initials of each responsible person, as well as the start and finish dates for each task. The resource summary provides a good manager with the total man-days for each month and for each person working on the project to successfully manage the project. The project described here is a data administration project.

These project management techniques can help managers identify bottlenecks and determine the impact problems will have on project completion times. Standard control techniques can be used to chart project progress against budgets and target dates, so that deviations can be spotted and the implementation team can make adjustments to meet their original schedule. Periodic formal status reports against the plan will show the extent of progress.

Window on Management

HOECHST HEADS OFF A REENGINEERING DISASTER

Hoechst Celanese Corporation of Somerville, New Jersey, desperately needed a new order system. Its German parent corporation, Hoechst International, had suffered heavy losses in 1993. To boost competitiveness in an increasingly competitive global marketplace, management wanted to expedite orders, reduce errors, and reduce huge inventory overstock caused by sales forecasts that were only 60-percent accurate.

Hoechst Celanese makes 45,000-pound bales of material for clothing, carpets, home furnishings, and auto parts. In December, 1994, it proudly rolled out a new order commitment system for faster and more accurate bulk deliveries to its manufacturing plants in the United States, Mexico, and Canada. The system integrates all customer information, including order placement, inventory, and shipping, using EDI and client/server technology. It provides a real-time view of production scheduling along with just-in-time manufacturing and automatic replenishment of customer inventories. This highly-acclaimed achievement was the culmination of a two-year reengineering effort that almost failed.

In early 1994 Jen Helke, the fulfillment manager at Hoechst's polyester unit, was assigned to make the new order commitment process operational at the company's Spartanburg, South Carolina, factory. She had to fight to get involved in the reengineering project. By the time she arrived the system was in final testing. Helke had trouble getting answers to simple questions such as why certain display screens were created the way they were. The reengineering team appeared too busy or uninterested to explain.

Management had focused so much on building the reengineering team that it forgot to build ways to let newcomers in. The team discussed ethnic differences, mission statements, and thinking styles. In January, 1994, after interviewing more than one hundred workers in order processing, manufacturing, credit, warehousing, and sales, they were ready to begin implementation.

At that point Helke joined the team and started asking questions. She didn't understand how the team made its decisions yet had no documentation. Team members had trouble going back to justify what they had done. Helke discovered that people did not

> **To Think About:** Describe the management problems that had to be addressed by this reengineering effort. What were the causes of these problems? What strategies were used to solve these problems? How successful were they?

feel any ownership of the system; they felt that it had been handed to them without their input. The order entry workers, stressed by having to learn a difficult new system, complained about the reengineering effort.

In February, 1994, fifteen people, including the entire order fulfillment group, key customer service representatives, Helke, and the reengineering team, left work early for a half-day site retreat. As people laid their issues on the table, there were tears, accusations, anger, and lack of trust. The customer service representatives took matters very personally. "Why did you let them do this to us?" they asked Helke.

Eventually the meeting worked out a mutually agreeable rollout plan. Teams from the reengineering, corporate information systems, and business groups fine-tuned the system the rest of the year, eliminating data communications bugs and speeding database access. Although the system is running smoothly, personality conflicts still remain.

Source: Joseph Maglitta, "Too Darn Tight," *Computerworld,* January 16, 1995.

Controlling Risk Factors

One way implementation can be improved is by adjusting the project management strategy to the level of risk inherent in each project. In order to control the risk, projects with relatively *little structure* may involve users fully at all stages, whereas more formal projects may need to adjust user involvement according to the project phase. There may be situations in which user participation is not appropriate. For example, some users may react negatively to a new design even though its overall benefits outweigh its drawbacks. Some individuals may stand to lose power as a result of design decisions (Robey and Markus, 1984). In this instance, participation in design may actually exacerbate resentment and resistance.

Projects using complex, new technology are riskier and require more emphasis upon internal integration tools. Large projects can reduce risk by an increased use of formal planning and control tools.

The Window on Management illustrates how some of the implementation strategies described here were applied to head off a potential reengineering disaster.

DESIGNING FOR THE ORGANIZATION

The systems development process must explicitly address the ways in which the organization will change when the new system is installed. In addition to procedural changes, transformations in job functions, organizational structure, power relationships, and behavior will all have to be carefully planned. For example, Figure 10.8 illustrates the organizational dimensions that would need to be addressed for planning and implementing office automation systems.

Although systems analysis and design activities are supposed to include an organizational impact analysis, this area has traditionally been neglected. An **organizational impact analysis** explains how a proposed system will affect organizational structure, attitudes, decision making, and operations. To integrate information systems successfully with the organization, thorough and fully documented organizational impact assessments must be given more attention in the development effort.

organizational impact analysis
Study of the way a proposed system will affect organizational structure, attitudes, decision making, and operations.

Allowing for the Human Factor

The quality of information systems should be evaluated in terms of user criteria rather than just the technical criteria of the information systems staff. For example, a project objective might be that data entry clerks be able to learn the procedures and codes for four new on-line data entry screens in a half-day training session.

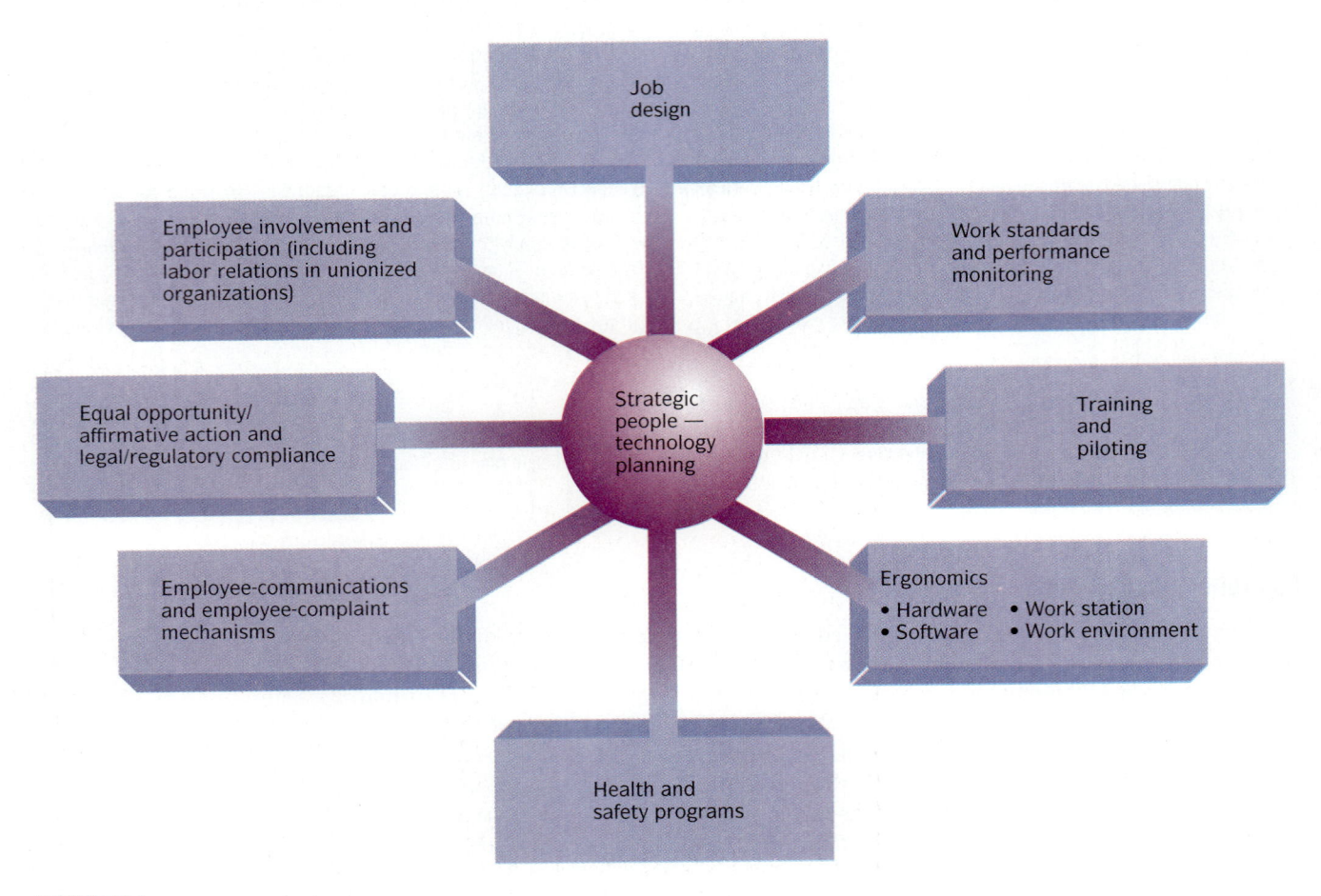

FIGURE 10.8
Key human organizational factors for office automation planning and implementation. For successful implementation the planner must consider ergonomics, job design, work standards, health and safety, training, employee communications, employee participation, and legal/regulatory factors. *Reprinted with permission of G.K. Hall & Co., an imprint of Simon & Schuster Macmillan, from* The Changing Workplace *by Alan F. Westin, et al.. Copyright © 1985 by G.K. Hall & Co.*

Good GUI meets bad GUI

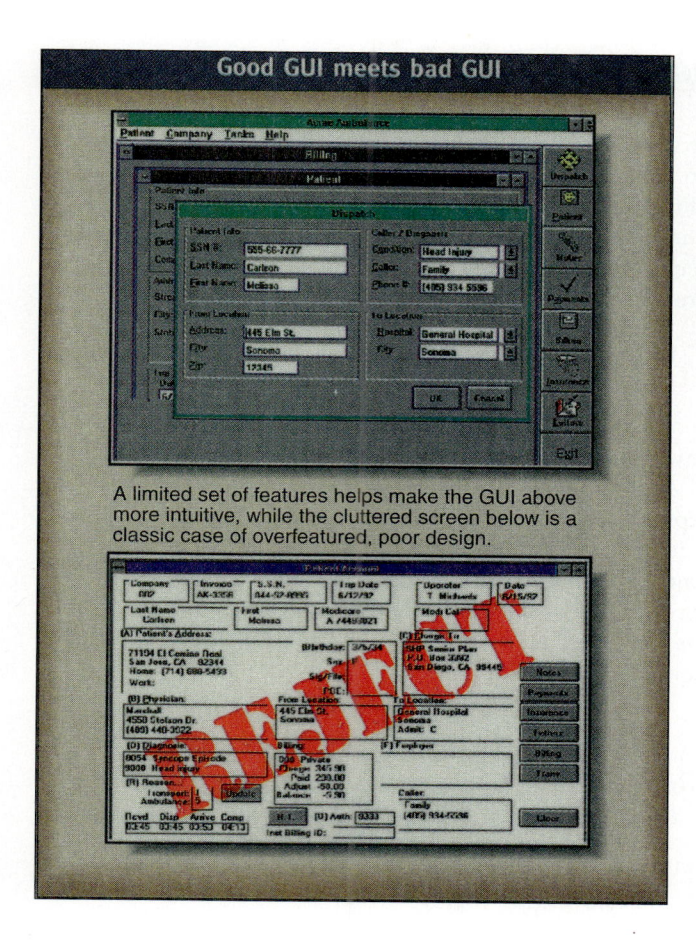

A well designed GUI, such as the top illustration, can make a system easy to use, whereas one that is cluttered, over featured, and poorly designed will add to users' frustrations. *Adapted from William Brandel and Lynda Radosovich, "GUIs Still a Sticky Issue,"* Computerworld, *August 1, 1994. Copyright 1994 by CW Publishing, Inc. Framingham, MA 01701. Reprinted from* Computerworld.

A limited set of features helps make the GUI above more intuitive, while the cluttered screen below is a classic case of overfeatured, poor design.

Areas where users interface with the system should be carefully designed, with sensitivity to ergonomic issues. **Ergonomics** refers to the interaction of people and machines in the work environment. It considers the design of jobs, health issues, and the end-user interface of information systems. The impact of the application system on the work environment and job dimensions must be carefully assessed. One noteworthy study of 620 Social Security Administration claims representatives showed that the representatives with on-line access to claims data experienced greater stress than those with serial access to the data via teletype. Even though the on-line interface was more rapid and direct than teletype, it created much more frustration. Claims representatives with on-line access could interface with a larger number of clients per day, which changed the dimensions of their jobs. The restructuring of work—involving tasks, quality of working life, and performance—had a more profound impact than the nature of the technology itself (Turner, 1984).

Management and organizational researchers have suggested a *sociotechnical* approach to information systems design and organizational change. **Sociotechnical design** aims to produce information systems that blend technical efficiency with sensitivity to organizational and human needs, leading to high job satisfaction (Mumford and Weir, 1979). The sociotechnical design process emphasizes participation by individuals most affected by a new system. The design plan establishes human objectives for the system that lead to increased job satisfaction. Designers set forth separate sets of technical and social design solutions. The social design plans explore different work group structures, allocation of tasks, and the design of individual jobs. The design solution that best fulfills both technical and social objectives is selected for the final design.

ergonomics The interaction of people and machines in the work environment, including the design of jobs, health issues, and the end-user interface of information systems.

sociotechnical design Design to produce information systems that blend technical efficiency with sensitivity to organizational and human needs.

10.4 UNDERSTANDING THE BUSINESS VALUE OF INFORMATION SYSTEMS

Information systems can have several different values for business firms. A consistently strong information technology infrastructure can, over the longer term, play an important strategic role in the life of the firm. Looked at less grandly, information systems can permit firms simply to survive. The value of systems from a financial view comes down to one question: Does a particular information system investment produce sufficient returns to justify its costs? There are many issues to consider with this approach.

CAPITAL BUDGETING MODELS

Capital budgeting models are one of several techniques used to measure the value of investing in long-term capital investment projects. The process of analyzing and selecting various proposals for capital expenditures is called **capital budgeting**. Firms invest in capital projects in order to expand production to meet anticipated demand, or to modernize production equipment in order to reduce costs. Information systems are considered long-term capital investment projects.

capital budgeting The process of analyzing and selecting various proposals for capital expenditures.

Alternative methods are available to compare different projects with one another, and to make a decision about the investment. Two that are widely used are the cost-benefit ratio and the net present value.

Cost-Benefit Ratio

A simple method for calculating the returns from a capital expenditure is to calculate the **cost-benefit ratio,** which is the ratio of benefits to costs. The formula is as follows:

cost-benefit ratio A method for calculating the returns from a capital expenditure by dividing the total benefits by total costs.

$$\frac{\text{Total benefits}}{\text{Total costs}} = \text{Cost-benefit ratio}$$

Table 10.10 lists some of the more common costs and benefits of systems. **Tangible benefits** can be quantified and assigned a monetary value. **Intangible benefits,** such as more efficient customer service or enhanced decision making, cannot be immediately quantified but may lead to quantifiable gains in the long run.

tangible benefits Benefits that can be quantified and assigned monetary value; they include lower operational costs and increased cashflows.

Some firms establish a minimum cost-benefit ratio that must be attained by capital projects, looking primarily at tangible benefits.

Net Present Value

intangible benefits Benefits that are not easily quantified; they might include more efficient customer service or enhanced decision making.

Evaluating a capital project requires that the cost of an investment be compared with the net cash inflows that occur many years later as the investment produces returns. But these two kinds of inflows are not directly comparable because of the time value of money. Money you have been promised to receive 3, 4, and 5 years from now is not worth as much as money received today. Money received in the future has to be discounted by some appropriate percentage rate—usually the prevailing interest rate, or sometimes the cost of capital. **Present value** is the value in current dollars of a payment or stream of payments to be received in the future. It can be calculated by using the following formula:

present value The value, in current dollars, of a payment or stream of payments to be received in the future.

$$\text{Payment} \times \frac{1 - (1 + \text{interest})^{-n}}{\text{Interest}} = \text{Present value}$$

Thus, in order to compare the investment (made in today's dollars) with future savings or earnings, you need to discount the earnings to their present value and then calculate the net present value of the investment. The **net present value** is the amount of money an investment is worth, taking into account its cost, earnings, and the time value of money. The formula for net present value is as follows:

net present value The amount of money an investment is worth, taking into account its cost, earnings, and the time value of money.

Present value of expected cash flows − Initial investment cost = Net present value

Table 10.10 Costs and Benefits of Information Systems

Costs	Benefits
Hardware	**Tangible** (cost savings)
	Increased productivity
Telecommunications	Low operational costs
	Reduced work force
Software	Lower computer expenses
	Lower outside vendor costs
Services	Lower clerical and professional costs
	Reduced rate of growth in expenses
Personnel	Reduced facility costs
	Intangible
	Improved asset utilization
	Improved resource control
	Improved organizational planning
	Increased organizational flexibility
	More timely information
	More information
	Increased organizational learning
	Legal requirements attained
	Enhanced employee goodwill
	Increased job satisfaction
	Improved decision making
	Improved operations
	Higher client satisfaction
	Better corporate image

Limitations of Financial Models

Financial models assume that all relevant alternatives have been examined, that all costs and benefits are known, and that these costs and benefits can be expressed in a common metric, specifically, money. However, financial models do not express the risks and uncertainty of their own cost and benefit estimates. Costs and benefits do not occur in the same time frame—costs tend to be up front and tangible, while benefits tend to be back-loaded and intangible. Inflation may affect costs and benefits differently. Technology—especially information technology—can change during the course of the project, causing estimates to vary greatly. Intangible benefits are difficult to quantify.

The difficulties of measuring intangible benefits give financial models an *application bias:* Transaction and clerical systems that displace labor and save space always produce more measurable, tangible benefits than management information systems, decision-support systems, or computer-supported collaborative work systems (see Chapter 12).

NONFINANCIAL AND STRATEGIC CONSIDERATIONS

Other methods of selecting and evaluating information system investments involve nonfinancial and strategic considerations. When the firm has several alternative investments to select from, it can employ portfolio analysis and scoring models. Several of these methods can be used in combination.

Portfolio Analysis

Rather than using capital budgeting, a second way of selecting among alternative projects is to consider the firm as having a portfolio of potential applications. Each application carries risks and benefits. The portfolio can be described as having a certain profile of risk and benefit to the firm (see Figure 10.9). While there is no ideal profile for

FIGURE 10.9
A system portfolio. Companies should examine their portfolio of projects in terms of potential benefits and likely risks. Certain kinds of projects should be avoided altogether and others developed rapidly. There is no ideal mix. Companies in different industries have different profiles.

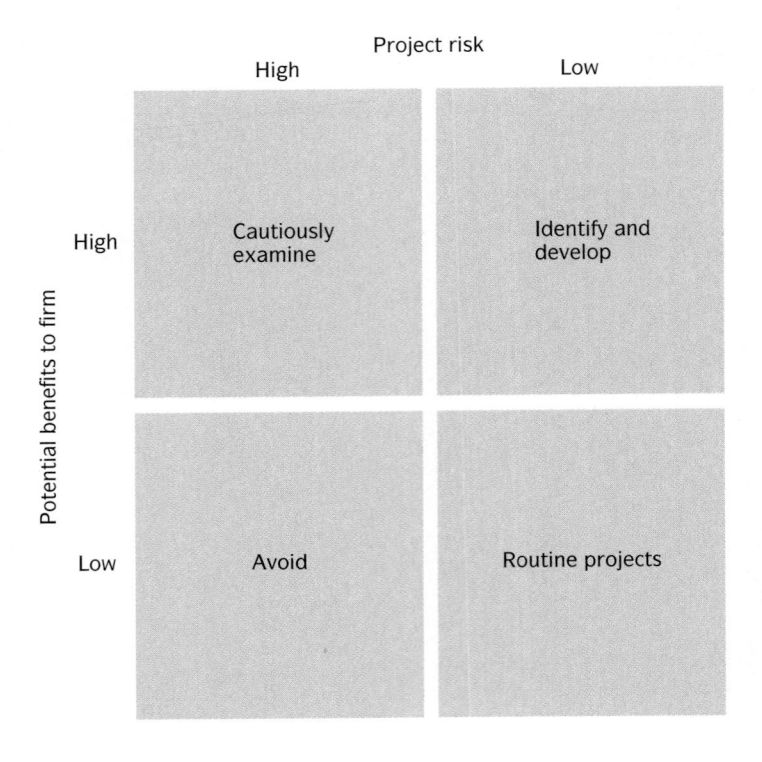

	Project risk	
	High	Low
Potential benefits to firm High	Cautiously examine	Identify and develop
Low	Avoid	Routine projects

all firms, information-intensive industries (e.g., finance) should have a few high-risk–high-benefit projects to ensure that they stay current with technology. Firms in non-information-intensive industries should focus on high-benefit–low-risk projects.

Some of the major risks in system-building are that benefits may not be obtained; system-building may exceed the organization's budget and time frame; or the system does not perform as expected. Risks are not necessarily bad. They are tolerable as long as the benefits are commensurate.

portfolio analysis An analysis of the portfolio of potential applications within a firm to determine the risks and benefits and select among alternatives for information systems.

Once strategic analyses have determined the overall direction of system development, a **portfolio analysis** can be used to select alternatives. Obviously, one can begin by focusing on systems of high benefit and low risk. These promise early returns and low risks. Second, high-benefit–high-risk systems should be examined. Low-benefit–high-risk systems should be totally avoided, and low-benefit–low-risk systems should be re-examined for the possibility of rebuilding and replacing them with more desirable systems having higher benefits.

Scoring Models

scoring models A quick method for deciding among alternative systems based on a system of ratings for selected objectives.

A quick, and sometimes compelling, method for arriving at a decision on alternative systems is a **scoring model.** Scoring models give alternative systems a single score based on the extent to which they meet selected objectives (the method is similar to the *objective attained* model) (Matlin, 1989; Buss, 1983).

In Table 10.11 the firm must decide among three alternative office automation systems (a mainframe system, a minicomputer system, and a microcomputer-based system). Column 1 lists the criteria that decision makers may apply to the systems. These criteria are usually the result of lengthy discussions among the decision-making group. Often the most important outcome of a scoring model is not the score but simply agreement on the criteria used to judge a system (Ginzberg, 1979; Nolan, 1982).

Column 2 lists the weights that decision makers attach to the decision criterion. The scoring model helps to bring about agreement among participants concerning the rank of the criteria.

Columns 3 to 5 use a 1-to-5 scale (lowest to highest) to express the judgments of participants on the *relative* merits of each system. For example, concerning the per-

Table 10.11 Scoring Model Used to Choose Among Alternative Office Automation Systems*

Criterion	Weight		Central Mainframe		Department Minicomputer		Individual PCs
Percentage of user needs met	0.40	2	0.8	3	1.2	4	1.6
Cost of the initial purchase	0.20	1	0.2	3	0.6	4	0.8
Financing	0.10	1	0.1	3	0.3	4	0.4
Ease of maintenance	0.10	2	0.2	3	0.3	4	0.4
Chances of success	0.20	3	0.6	4	0.8	4	0.8
Final score			1.9		3.2		4.0

Scale: 1 = low, 5 = high.
*One of the major uses of scoring models is in identifying the criteria of selection and their relative weights. In this instance an office automation system based on PCs appears preferable.

centage of user needs that each system meets, a score of 1 for a system argues that this system when compared to others being considered will be low in meeting user needs.

As with all objective techniques, there are many qualitative judgments involved in using the scoring model. This model requires experts who understand the issues and the technology. It is appropriate to cycle through the scoring model several times, changing the criteria and weights, to see how sensitive the outcome is to reasonable changes in criteria. Scoring models are used most commonly to confirm, to rationalize, and to support decisions, rather than being the final arbiters of system selection.

Management Challenges

1. Major risks and uncertainties in systems development. Information systems development has major risks and uncertainties that make it difficult for the systems to achieve their goals. Sometimes the cost of achieving them is too high. One problem is the difficulty of establishing information requirements, both for individual end users and for the organization as a whole. The requirements may be too complex or subject to change. Another problem is that the time and cost factors to develop an information system can be very difficult to analyze, especially in large projects. This chapter has described some ways of dealing with these risks and uncertainties, but the issues remain major management challenges.

2. Determining benefits of a system when they are largely intangible. As the sophistication of systems grows, they produce fewer tangible and more intangible benefits. By definition, there is no solid method for pricing intangible benefits, but organizations could lose important opportunities if they only use strict financial criteria for determining information systems benefits. On the other hand, organizations could make very poor investment decisions if they overestimate intangible benefits.

3. Managing change. Although building a new information system is a process of planned organizational change, this does not mean that change can always be planned or controlled. Individuals and groups in organizations have varying interests and may resist changes in procedures, job relationships, and technologies.

Summary

1. Show how building new systems can produce organizational change. Building a new information system is a form of planned organizational change that involves many different people in the organization. Because information systems are sociotechnical entities, a change in information systems involves changes in work, management, and the organization. Four kinds of technology-enabled change are (1) automation, (2) rationalization of procedures, (3) business reengineering, and (4) paradigm shift, with far-reaching changes carrying the greatests risks and rewards. Many organizations are attempting business reengineering to redesign work-flows and business processes in the hope of achieving dramatic productivity breakthroughs.

2. **Explain how the organization can develop information systems that fit its business plan.** Organizations should develop an information systems plan that describes how information technology supports the attainment of their goals. The plan indicates the direction of systems development, the rationale, implementation strategy, and budget. Enterprise analysis and critical success factors (CSFs) can be used to elicit organization-wide information requirements that must be addressed by the plan.

3. **Identify the core activities in the systems development process.** The core activities in systems development are systems analysis, systems design, programming, testing, conversion, production, and maintenance. Systems analysis is the study and analysis of problems of existing systems and the identification of requirements for their solution. Systems design provides the specifications for an information system solution, showing how its technical and organizational components fit together.

4. **Explain the organizational change requirements for building successful systems.** From an organizational and behavioral standpoint, the major causes of information system failure are (1) insufficient or improper user participation in the systems development process, (2) lack of management support, (3) poor management of the implementation process, and (4) high levels of complexity and risk in systems development projects.

Implementation is the entire process of organizational change surrounding the introduction of a new information system. One can better understand system success and failure by examining different patterns of implementation. Especially important is the relationship between participants in the implementation process, notably the interactions between system designers and users. The success of organizational change can be determined by how well information systems specialists, end users, and decision makers deal with key issues at various stages in implementation.

Management support and control of the implementation process are essential, as are mechanisms for dealing with the level of risk in each new systems project. The level of risk in a systems development project is determined by three key dimensions: (1) project size, (2) project structure, and (3) experience with technology. The risk level of each project will determine the appropriate mix of external integration tools, internal integration tools, formal planning tools, and formal control tools to be applied.

Appropriate strategies can be applied to ensure the correct level of user participation in the systems development process and to minimize user resistance. Information system design and the entire implementation process should be managed as planned organizational change. Sociotechnical design emphasizes the participation of the individuals most affected by a new system and aims for an optimal blend of social and technical design solutions.

5. **Describe various models for determining the business value of information systems.** Capital budgeting models such as the cost/benefit ratio and net present value are widely used financial models for determining the business value of information systems. Portfolio analysis and scoring models include nonfinancial considerations and can be used to evaluate alternative information systems projects.

Key Terms

Information systems plan
Enterprise analysis
Critical success factors (CSFs)
Automation
Rationalization of procedures
Business process
Business reengineering
Paradigm shift
Workflow management
Systems development
Systems analysis
Feasibility study
Technical feasibility

Economic feasibility
Operational feasibility
Information requirements
Systems design
Logical design
Physical design
Programming
Testing
Unit testing
System testing
Acceptance testing
Test plan
Conversion
Parallel strategy
Direct cutover

Pilot study
Phased approach
Conversion plan
Documentation
Production
Maintenance
Implementation
Change agent
User-designer communications gap
External integration tools
Counterimplementation
Internal integration tools
Formal planning and control tools

Organizational impact analysis
Ergonomics
Sociotechnical design
Capital budgeting
Tangible benefits
Intangible benefits
Cost-benefit ratio
Present value
Net present value
Portfolio analysis
Scoring models

Review Questions

1. Why can a new information system be considered planned organizational change?
2. What are the major categories of an information systems plan?
3. How can enterprise analysis and critical success factors be used to establish organization-wide information system requirements?
4. Describe each of the four kinds of organizational change that can be promoted with information technology.
5. What is *business reengineering*? What steps are required to make it effective?
6. What is the difference between *systems analysis* and *systems design*?
7. What is *feasibility*? Name and describe each of the three major areas of feasibility for information systems.
8. What are *information requirements*? Why are they difficult to determine correctly?
9. What is the difference between the *logical design* and the *physical design* of an information system?
10. Why is the testing stage of systems development so important? Name and describe the three stages of testing for an information system.
11. What is *conversion*? Why is it important to have a detailed conversion plan?
12. What role do programming, production, and maintenance play in systems development?
13. What is *implementation*? How is it related to information system success or failure?
14. Describe the ways that implementation can be managed to make the organizational change process more successful.
15. Name and describe the principal capital budgeting methods used to evaluate information systems projects. What are their limitations?
16. Describe how portfolio analysis and scoring models can be used to establish the worth of systems.

Discussion Questions

1. Information systems often have to be redesigned after testing. Discuss.
2. Which conversion strategy would you use for the following? Why?
   - A system to track stock purchase and sale transactions
   - A process control system at a chemical plant
   - A system to record attendance at a 2000-student high school
   - A corporate accounting system that will consolidate general ledger data from ten different operating units
3. Discuss the roles of users and information processing specialists in the following systems development activities:
   - Systems analysis
   - Determination of information requirements
   - Assessment of feasibility
   - Design
   - Testing
   - Conversion
4. A prominent MIS researcher has observed that "The reason most information systems have failed is that we have ignored organizational behavior problems in the design and operation of computer-based information systems." Discuss.

Group Project

With three or four of your classmates, read the following case or a description of another system in this text. Prepare a report describing (on the basis of the information provided) some of the design specifications that might be appropriate for the Information Exchange Platform or the system you select. Present your findings to the class.

Case Study

CURING CHAOS AT METHODIST HOSPITAL

Methodist Hospital is a large teaching hospital in Indianapolis, Indiana. In 1990 it had about 43,000 patient admissions, served 250,000 outpatients, and handled 80,000 emergency room visits. During the 1970s the hospital had purchased a mainframe-based turnkey billing and patient records system. A turnkey system is delivered to a customer as a complete hardware and software configuration. The client simply has to *turn the key* to begin the system. Since then, the hospital's information systems department has spent most of its time maintaining the old system and working on a five- to seven-year application backlog. User departments such as the hospital laboratory and emergency room became frustrated because their computing needs could not be satisfied. So they bought their own systems, none of which communicated with the others.

When Walter Zerrenner took over as Methodist Hospital's chief information officer in 1989, he found three strategic information systems plans sitting on a shelf. There was never any time to implement them. The plans were developed without any user input, so no one outside the information systems department was committed to them.

Zerrenner brought in a team from Andersen Consulting in Chicago to assess the state of the hospital's information systems department as well as user attitudes toward the department. The assessment turned up 3 incompatible wide-area networks, more than 20 incompatible local area networks, and more than 100 different information systems throughout the hospital.

Information systems in different departments in Methodist Hospital use different identification codes for the same patients. Patients had to register separately in each department, often answering the same questions over and over again. The mainframe patient management system showed that lab tests were scheduled but did not display the results. The results of the tests were stored on a separate departmental system in the lab. The only place to find complete information on a patient was in a paper file.

The mainframe patient management system could only be accessed from terminals located within the hospital. Physicians complained that they could not use microcomputers in their offices to dial into the system for patient information. The system only kept information on patients who were formally admitted to the hospital. Even that information was available on-line for only five days after a patient's discharge. If a discharged patient had unforeseen complications, his or her medical records could only be found in manual paper files. Additionally, the mainframe patient management system did not handle outpatients or people who merely came in for tests. Yet most users liked the way the mainframe system worked. Dr. Chris Steffy, a resident in internal medicine, believed it was more efficient and richer in functions than other systems he had used.

Zerrenner formed a 25-member information systems planning committee with representatives from all of the hospital's major departments, including a contingent of physicians and nurses. Zerrenner and the planning committee identified three options for an improved patient information system: (1) scrap the existing systems; (2) try to make all of the existing systems communicate with each other; and (3) establish a centralized database for the data collected by individual departments.

The first solution meant walking away from the hospital's enormous investment in existing systems, which did work well for individual departments. The second solution appeared to be a logistical nightmare, because the information systems department would have had to create a separate interface for every departmental system. Physicians would have had to sit at terminals and sign on and off each individual system. The third solution seemed the only reasonable choice. The database could obtain information from each departmental system and make it commonly available.

Zerrenner built a working model of the new system, called the Information Exchange Platform (IXP), for users to evaluate. People were encouraged to sit down at a workstation, sign on with a password, and use a mouse to move around sample windows, viewing patient data, graphing the results, or sending the data via e-mail to another physician for consultation. The system uses the Sybase relational database management system running on an IBM RS/6000 file server. From the prototype, the development team created a pilot system. The pilot features a patient care application that provides physicians with patient information generated by hospital procedures and an application that allows a person to access the laboratory computer system, the radiology computer system, and the physician office system on IXP microcomputer workstations.

The Information Exchange Platform was never designed to capture all of the data from individual departments. A second committee, a broad-based information systems steering committee formed by Zerrenner, is determining what information is needed by multiple departments. The project has adopted an 80/20 rule, focusing on the most important information that is used 80 percent of the time. Most of that information consists of lab, radiology, patient demographics, and electrocardiogram interpretations. ■

Sources: Scott D. Palmer, "A Plan That Cured Chaos," *Datamation,* January 1, 1993; and E.W. Martin, "Methodist Hospital of Indiana, Inc." in Martin, De Hayes, Hoffer, and Perkins, *Managing Information Technology* (New York: Macmillan Publishing, 1994).

Case Study Questions

1. Prepare a report analyzing the problems with Methodist Hospital's systems. Describe the problems and their causes. What management, organization, and technology factors were responsible?
2. If you were the systems analyst for this project, list five questions you would ask during interviews to elicit the information needed for your systems analysis report.
3. Do you agree that the Information Exchange Platform was the best solution for Methodist Hospital? Why or why not? What would you recommend? Why?
4. Evaluate the approach to systems building that was used for the IXP project.
5. Describe the role of end users and technical specialists in analyzing the problem and in developing the solution.
6. What conversion strategy would you use when the Information Exchange Platform is completed?
7. Why could it be said that the Information Exchange Platform is only one part of the solution for Methodist Hospital?

References

Ahituv, Niv, and Seev Neumann. "A Flexible Approach to Information System Development." *MIS Quarterly* (June 1984).

Alter, Steven, and Michael Ginzberg. "Managing Uncertainty in MIS Implementation." *Sloan Management Review* 20 (Fall 1978).

Bacon, C. James. "The Uses of Decision Criteria in Selecting Information Systems/Technology Investments." *MIS Quarterly* 16, no. 3 (September 1992).

Barki, Henri, and Jon Hartwick. "User Participation, Conflict and Conflict Resolution: The Mediating Roles of Influence." *Information Systems Research* 5, no. 4 (December 1994).

Baroudi, Jack, Margrethe H. Olsen, and Blake Ives. "An Empirical Study of the Impact of User Involvement on System Usage and Information Satisfaction." *Communications of the ACM* 29, no. 3 (March 1986).

Beath, Cynthia Mathis, and Wanda J. Orlikowski. "The Contradictory Structure of Systems Development Methodologies: Deconstructing the IS-User Relationship in Information Engineering." *Information Systems Research* 5, no. 4 (December 1994).

Bikson, Tora K., Cathleen Stasz, and D.A. Mankin. "Computer Mediated Work. Individual and Organizational Impact in One Corporate Headquarters." Santa Monica, CA: Rand Corporation, 1985.

Bostrom, R.P., and J.S. Heinen. "MIS Problems and Failures: A Socio-Technical Perspective; Part I: The Causes." *MIS Quarterly* 1 (September 1977); "Part II: The Application of Socio-Technical Theory." *MIS Quarterly* 1 (December 1977).

Bullen, Christine, and John F. Rockart. "A Primer on Critical Success Factors." Cambridge, MA: Center for Information Systems Research, Sloan School of Management, 1981.

Buss, Martin D. J. "How to Rank Computer Projects." *Harvard Business Review* (January 1983).

Cerveny, Robert P., Edward J. Garrity, and G. Lawrence Sanders. "A Problem-Solving Perspective on Systems Development." *Journal of Management Information Systems* 6, no. 4 (Spring 1990).

Clement, Andrew, and Peter Van den Besselaar. "A Retrospective Look at PD Projects." *Communications of the ACM* 36, no. 4 (June 1993).

Cooper, Randolph B., and Zmud, Robert W. "Information Technology Implementation Research: A Technological Diffusion Approach." *Management Science* 36, no. 2 (February 1990).

Davenport, Thomas H., and James E. Short. "The New Industrial Engineering: Information Technology and Business Process Redesign." *Sloan Management Review* 31, no. 4 (Summer 1990).

Davidson, W.H. "Beyond Engineering: The Three Phases of Business Transformation." *IBM Systems Journal* 32, no.1 (1993).

Davis, Fred R. "Perceived Usefulness, Ease of Use, and User Acceptance of Information Technology." *MIS Quarterly* 13, no. 3 (September 1989).

Davis, Gordon B. "Determining Management Information Needs: A Comparison of Methods." *MIS Quarterly* 1 (June 1977).

Davis, Gordon B. "Information Analysis for Information System Development." *Systems Analysis and Design: A Foundation for the 1980's*. Ed. W.W. Cotterman, J.D. Cougar, N.L. Enger, and F. Harold. New York: Wiley, 1981.

Davis, Gordon B. "Strategies for Information Requirements Determination." *IBM Systems Journal* 1 (1982).

Dennis, Alan R., Robert M. Daniels, Jr., Glenda Hayes, and Jay F. Nunamaker, Jr. "Methodology-Driven Use of Automated Support in Business Process Re-Engineering." *Journal of Management Information Systems* 10, no. 3 (Winter 1993–94).

Doll, William J. "Avenues for Top Management Involvement in Successful MIS Development." *MIS Quarterly* (March 1985).

Dos Santos, Brian. "Justifying Investments in New Information Technologies." *Journal of Management Information Systems* 7, no. 4 (Spring 1991).

Ein-Dor, Philip, and Eli Segev. "Strategic Planning for Management Information Systems." *Management Science* 24, no. 15 (1978).

El Sawy, Omar, and Burt Nanus. "Toward the Design of Robust Information Systems." *Journal of Management Information Systems* 5, no. 4 (Spring 1989).

Emery, James C. "Cost/Benefit Analysis of Information Systems." Chicago: Society for Management Information Systems Workshop Report No. 1, 1971.

Flatten, Per O., Donald J. McCubbrey, P. Declan O'Riordan, and Keith Burgess. *Foundations of Business Systems*, 2nd ed. Fort Worth, TX: The Dryden Press, 1992.

Franz, Charles, and Daniel Robey. "An Investigation of User-Led System Design: Rational and Political Perspectives." *Communications of the ACM* 27 (December 1984).

Gerlach, James H. and Feng-Yang Kuo. "Understanding Human-Computer Interaction for Information Systems Design." *MIS Quarterly* 15, no. 4 (December 1991).

Ginzberg, Michael J., "Improving MIS Project Selection." *Omega, Internal Journal of Management Science* 6, no. 1 (1979).

Goodhue, Dale L., Laurie J. Kirsch, Judith A. Quillard, and Michael D. Wybo. "Strategic Data Planning: Lessons from the Field." *MIS Quarterly* 16, no. 1 (March 1992).

Gould, John D., and Clayton Lewis. "Designing for Usability: Key Principles and What Designers Think." *Communications of the ACM* 28 (March 1985).

Grudnitski, Gary. "Eliciting Decision Makers' Information Requirements." *Journal of Management Information Systems* (Summer 1984).

Hammer, Michael. "Reengineering Work: Don't Automate, Obliterate." *Harvard Business Review* (July–August 1990).

Hammer, Michael, and James Champy. *Reengineering the Corporation*. New York: HarperCollins Publishers, 1993.

Hammer, Michael, and Steven A. Stanton. *The Reengineering Revolution*. New York: HarperCollins, 1995.

Helms, Glenn L., and Ira R. Weiss. "The Cost of Internally Developed Applications: Analysis of Problems and Cost Control Methods." *Journal of Management Information Systems* (Fall 1986).

Hirscheim, R.A. "User Experience with and Assessment of Participative Systems Design." *MIS Quarterly* (December 1985).

Ives, Blake, Margrethe H. Olson, and Jack J. Baroudi. "The Measurement of User Information Satisfaction." *Communications of the ACM* 26 (October 1983).

Joshi, Kailash. "A Model of Users' Perspective on Change: The Case of Information Systems Technology Implementation." *MIS Quarterly*, 15, no. 2 (June 1991).

Keen, Peter W. "Information Systems and Organizational Change." *Communications of the ACM* 24 (January 1981).

Kendall, Kenneth E., and Julie E. Kendall. *Systems Analysis and Design*. 3/e. Englewood Cliffs, NJ: Prentice-Hall, 1995.

King, Julia. "Reengineering Slammed." *Computerworld* (June 13, 1994).

King, William R. "Alternative Designs in Information System Development." *MIS Quarterly* (December 1982).

Kolb, D.A., and A.L. Frohman. "An Organization Development Approach to Consulting." *Sloan Management Review* 12 (Fall 1970).

Laudon, Kenneth C. "CIOs Beware: Very Large-Scale Systems." Center for Research on Information Systems, New York University Stern School of Business, working paper, 1989.

Lederer, Albert L., Rajesh Mirani, Boon Siong Neo, Carol Pollard, Jayesh Prasad, and K. Ramamurthy. "Information System Cost Estimating: A Management Perspective." *MIS Quarterly* 14, no. 2 (June 1990).

Lederer, Albert, and Jayesh Prasad. "Nine Management Guidelines for Better Cost Estimating." *Communications of the ACM* 35, no. 2 (February 1992).

Lientz, Bennett P., and E. Burton Swanson. *Software Maintenance Management*. Reading, MA: Addison-Wesley, 1980.

Lucas, Henry C., Jr. *Implementation: The Key to Successful Information Systems*. New York: Columbia University Press, 1981.

Lucas, Henry C., Jr. *Why Information Systems Fail*. New York: Columbia University Press, 1975.

Mahmood, Mo Adam, and Gary J. Mann. "Measuring the Organizational Impact of Information Technology Investment." *Journal of Management Information Systems* 10, no. 1 (Summer 1993).

Markus, M.L. "Power, Politics and MIS Implementation." *Communications of the ACM* 26 (June 1983).

Markus, M. Lynne, and Mark Keil. "If We Build It, They Will Come: Designing Information Systems That People Want to Use." *Sloan Management Review* (Summer 1994).

Matlin, Gerald. "What Is the Value of Investment in Information Systems?" *MIS Quarterly* 13, no. 3 (September 1989).

McFarlan, F. Warren. "Portfolio Approach to Information Systems." *Harvard Business Review* (September–October 1981).

Moad, Jeff. "Does Reengineering Really Work?" *Datamation* (August, 1993).

Mumford, Enid, and Mary Weir. *Computer Systems in Work Design: The ETHICS Method*. New York: Wiley, 1979.

Nolan, Richard L. "Managing Information Systems by Committee." *Harvard Business Review* (July-August 1982).

Parker, M.M. "Enterprise Information Analysis: Cost-Benefit Analysis and the Data-Managed System." *IBM Systems Journal* 21 (1982), pp. 108–123.

Premkumar, G., and William R. King. "Organizational Characteristics and Information Systems Planning: An Empirical Study." *Information Systems Research* 5, no. 2 (June 1994).

Raghunathan, Bhanu, and T.S. Raghunathan. "Adaptation of a Planning System Success Model to Information Systems Planning." *Information Systems Research* 5, no. 3 (September 1994).

Robey, Daniel, and M. Lynne Markus. "Rituals in Information System Design." *MIS Quarterly* (March 1984).

Rockart, John F. "Chief Executives Define Their Own Data Needs." *Harvard Business Review* (March–April 1979).

Rockart, John F., and Michael E. Treacy. "The CEO Goes on Line." *Harvard Business Review* (January–February 1982).

Shank, Michael E., Andrew C. Boynton, and Robert W. Zmud. "Critical Success Factor Analysis as a Methodology for MIS Planning." *MIS Quarterly* (June 1985).

Swanson, E. Burton. *Information System Implementation*. Homewood, IL: Richard D. Irwin Inc., 1988.

Tait, Peter, and Iris Vessey. "The Effect of User Involvement on System Success: A Contingency Approach." *MIS Quarterly* 12, no. 1 (March 1988).

Tornatsky, Louis G., J.D. Eveland, M.G. Boylan, W.A. Hetzner, E.C. Johnson, D. Roitman, and J. Schneider. *The Process of Technological Innovation: Reviewing the Literature*. Washington, DC: National Science Foundation, 1983.

Turner, Jon A. "Computer Mediated Work: The Interplay Between Technology and Structured Jobs." *Communications of the ACM* 27 (December 1984).

Vessey, Iris, and Sue Conger. "Learning to Specify Information Requirements: The Relationship between Application and Methodology." *Journal of Management Information Systems* 10, no. 2 (Fall 1993).

Vitalari, Nicholas P. "Knowledge as a Basis for Expertise in Systems Analysis: Empirical Study." *MIS Quarterly* (September 1985).

Westin, Alan F., Heather A. Schweder, Michael A. Baker, and Sheila Lehman. *The Changing Workplace*. White Plains, NY, and London: Knowledge Industry Publications, Inc., 1985.

Yin, Robert K. "Life Histories of Innovations: How New Practices Become Routinized." *Public Administration Review* (January/February 1981).

Zachman, J.A. "Business Systems Planning and Business Information Control Study: A Comparison." *IBM Systems Journal* 21 (1982).

Zmud, Robert W., William P. Anthony, and Ralph M. Stair, Jr. "The Use of Mental Imagery to Facilitate Information Identification in Requirements Analysis." *Journal of Management Information Systems* 9, no. 4 (Spring 1993).

Chapter 11

Approaches to Systems-Building

ClubCorp Serves Its Members with a Rapid Method of Developing Applications

11.1 The Traditional Systems Lifecycle
Stages of the Systems Lifecycle
Limitations of the Lifecycle Approach

11.2 Alternative System-Building Approaches
Prototyping
Application Software Packages
Window on Technology
Can Saab Find Happiness with a Manufacturing Package from a Tiny, Unknown Vendor?

End-User Development
Outsourcing
Window on Management
Ford Europe Makes Its Outsourcing Contractors Part of Its Team

11.3 System-Building Methodologies
Structured Methodologies
Object-Oriented Software Development
Computer-Aided Software Engineering (CASE)
Window on Organizations
Air Canada Overhauls Its Web Site
Software Reengineering

Management Challenges
Summary
Key Terms
Review Questions
Discussion Questions
Group Project
Case Study: Can a German Software Giant Provide Client/Server Solutions?
References

ClubCorp Serves Its Members with a Rapid Method of Developing Applications

Competition for members is fierce among private clubs. With average annual membership fees nearing $3000, the elimination by the United States federal government of most individual federal income tax deductions for club dues, and growing competition from luxury hotels, club membership actually declined slightly during the early 1990s. The problem faced by $1.2 billion ClubCorp International Inc. was how to keep its members and attract new ones. The competitive strategy ClubCorp chose to follow was that of product differentiation, setting itself apart with a higher level of service than other hospitality providers.

To better serve its members, ClubCorp developed a new information system that would track member interests and link that information to reservations, allowing the clubs to offer more personal service based upon recognition of their members. For example, when the Ft. Lauderdale Tower Club member and investment banker Paul Sallarulo called and made a luncheon reservation for himself and his secretary, Linda Nobilski, the computer system indicated that Nobilski likes flowers and candy. When the pair arrived for lunch, the club had peach-colored roses and chocolate-covered cherries waiting. The new system also carries a digitalized photograph of each member, so that the staff can view the pictures of members with reservations and so be able to greet each one personally. The system is used by the receptionists, food and beverage managers, chefs, and maitre d's to personalize all service. In addition, when a member from a club travels to another ClubCorp club in a different city, that member's computer file is transmitted to the other club so that it, too, can provide this same kind of personalized service.

When ClubCorp decided to develop its new system, it needed to create the system as quickly as possible while controlling the cost of the system. The company chose to use a rapid applications development method that took only 15 weeks to complete, as opposed to an estimated one year using more traditional methods. Cost was held to $167,000, partly as a result of the shorter time needed for development. The higher speed and lower cost were achieved by a combination of factors. An object-oriented development tool was used and the system was built through prototyping. Also, ClubCorp went to an outside development consulting group, IBM Consulting Group's Southwest Rapid Solutions Services in Dallas, Texas, who are experts in this type of development. Finally, one key feature of their approach was the emphasis upon the central role of the prospective business users of the new system. Dan Barth, ClubCorp's CIO, likes to tell the story of the "sexy, glitzy, and Star Wars-like" reservation screen the information systems developers created, which they presented to prospective users with great pride. When the users tried it, one asked a simple question: Why can't the reservation screen look just like the reservation sheets we are already using? The glitzy screen was, of course, abandoned, in favor of the more familiar and appropriate design suggested by the user. In the final system, users are presented with 11 file folder tabs (with functional labels such as *Reservations*) as a main menu. Each tabbed file folder will bring up a familiar looking screen to allow the user to retrieve and enter needed information.

The rapidly developed system has apparently been a success. Users appear to be happy with the system and are providing club members improved service. Members are responding to the higher level of service, evidenced by the increase in membership applications—the Tower Club list of prospective members has doubled in size in the year since the system has been in place. ■

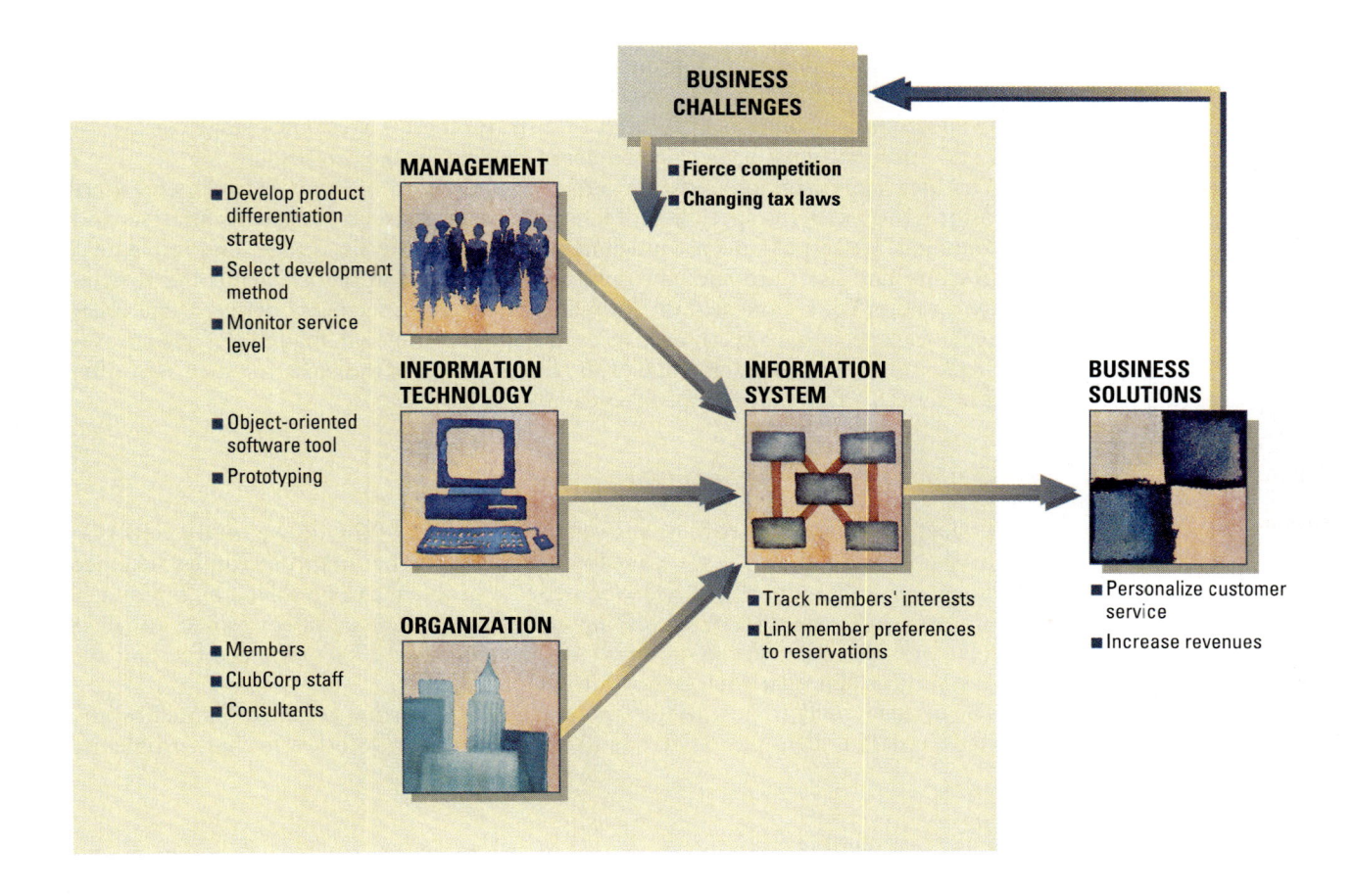

MANAGEMENT
- Develop product differentiation strategy
- Select development method
- Monitor service level

INFORMATION TECHNOLOGY
- Object-oriented software tool
- Prototyping

ORGANIZATION
- Members
- ClubCorp staff
- Consultants

BUSINESS CHALLENGES
- Fierce competition
- Changing tax laws

INFORMATION SYSTEM
- Track members' interests
- Link member preferences to reservations

BUSINESS SOLUTIONS
- Personalize customer service
- Increase revenues

Sources: Eric R. Chabrow, "Member of the RAD Club," *Information Week*, November 21, 1994; and David S. Linthicum, "RADical Development," *PC Magazine*, November 8, 1994.

Like ClubCorp, many organizations are examining alternative methods of building new information systems. While they are designing and building some applications entirely on their own, they are also turning to software packages, external consultants, and other strategies to reduce time, cost, and inefficiency. They are also experimenting with alternative tools to document, analyze, design, and implement systems.

There is no one approach that can be used for all situations and types of systems. Each of these approaches has advantages and disadvantages, and each provides managers with a range of choices. This chapter describes and compares the various system-building approaches and methodologies so that managers know how to choose among them.

> **Learning Objectives**
>
> *After completing this chapter, you will be able to:*
>
> 1. Distinguish between the various system-building alternatives: the traditional systems lifecycle, prototyping, application software packages, end-user development, and outsourcing.
> 2. Understand the strengths and limitations of each approach.
> 3. Describe the solutions to the management problems created by these approaches.
> 4. Describe the various tools and methodologies used for systems development.

11.1 THE TRADITIONAL SYSTEMS LIFECYCLE

systems lifecycle A traditional methodology for developing an information system that partitions the systems development process into six formal stages that must be completed sequentially with a very formal division of labor between end users and information systems specialists.

The **systems lifecycle** is the oldest method for building information systems and is still used today for medium or large complex systems projects. This methodology assumes that an information system has a lifecycle similar to that of any living organism, with a beginning, middle, and end. The lifecycle for an information system has six stages: (1) project definition, (2) systems study, (3) design, (4) programming, (5) installation, and (6) post-implementation. Figure 11.1 illustrates these stages. Each stage consists of basic activities that must be performed before the next stage can begin.

The lifecycle methodology has a very formal division of labor between end users and information systems specialists. Technical specialists such as systems analysts and programmers are responsible for much of the systems analysis, design, and implementation work; end users are limited to providing information requirements and reviewing the work of the technical staff. Formal sign-offs or agreements between end users and technical specialists are required as each stage is completed. Figure 11.1 also shows the product or output of each stage of the lifecycle that is the basis for such sign-offs. We now describe the stages of the lifecycle in detail.

project definition A stage in the systems lifecycle that determines whether or not the organization has a problem and whether or not the problem can be solved by launching a system project.

STAGES OF THE SYSTEMS LIFECYCLE

The **project definition** stage tries to answer the questions, "Why do we need a new system project?" and "What do we want to accomplish?" This stage determines whether the organization has a problem and whether that problem can be solved by building a new information system or by modifying an existing one. If a system project is called for, this stage identifies its general objectives, specifies the scope of the project, and develops a project plan that can be shown to management.

systems study A stage in the systems lifecycle that analyzes the problems of existing systems, defines the objectives to be attained by a solution, and evaluates various solution alternatives.

The **systems study** stage analyzes the problems of existing systems (manual or automated) in detail, identifies objectives to be attained by a solution to these problems,

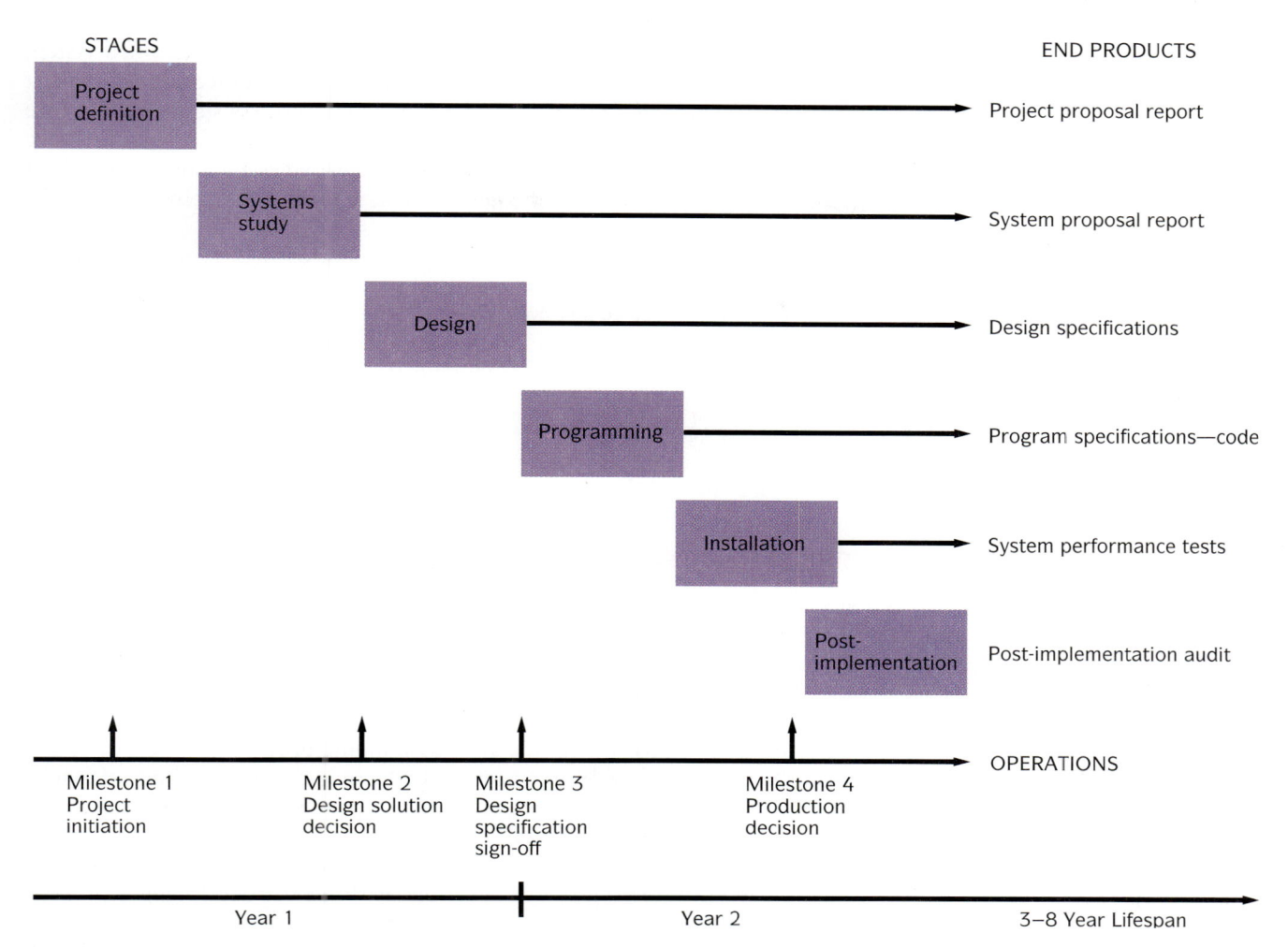

FIGURE 11.1
The lifecycle methodology for systems development. The lifecycle methodology divides systems development into six formal stages with specifics for milestones and end products at each stage. A typical medium-sized development project requires two years to deliver and has an expected life span of three to eight years.

and describes alternative solutions. The systems study stage examines the feasibility of each solution alternative for review by management.

Systems study requires extensive information gathering and research; sifting through documents, reports, and work papers produced by existing systems; observing how these systems work; polling users with questionnaires; and conducting interviews. All of the information gathered during the systems study phase will be used to determine information system requirements. Finally, the systems study stage describes in detail the remaining lifecycle activities and the tasks for each phase.

The **design** stage produces the logical and physical design specifications for the solution. Because the lifecycle emphasizes formal specifications and paperwork, many of the design and documentation tools described in Section 11.3, such as data flow diagrams, program structure charts, or system flowcharts, are likely to be utilized.

The **programming** stage translates the design specifications produced during the design stage into software program code. Systems analysts work with programmers to prepare specifications for each program in the system. Programmers write customized program code, typically using a conventional third-generation programming language such as COBOL or FORTRAN or a high-productivity fourth-generation language. Since large systems have many programs with hundreds of thousands of lines of program code, entire teams of programmers may be required.

design A stage in the systems lifecycle that produces the logical and physical design specifications for the systems solution.

programming A stage in the systems lifecycle that translates the design specifications produced during the design stage into software program code.

11.1 The Traditional Systems Lifecycle

installation A stage in the systems lifecycle consisting of testing, training, and conversion; the final steps required to put a system into operation.

post-implementation The final stage of the systems lifecycle in which the system is used and evaluated while in production and is modified to make improvements or meet new requirements.

The **installation** stage consists of the final steps to put the new or modified system into operation: testing, training, and conversion. The software is tested to make sure it performs properly from both a technical and a functional business standpoint. (More detail on testing can be found in Chapter 10.) Business and technical specialists are trained to use the new system. A formal conversion plan provides a detailed schedule of all of the activities required to install the new system, and the old system is converted to the new one.

The **post-implementation** stage consists of using and evaluating the system after it is installed and is in production. Users and technical specialists will go through a formal postimplementation audit that determines how well the new system has met its original objectives and whether any revisions or modifications are required. After the system has been fine-tuned it will need to be maintained while it is in production to correct errors, meet requirements, or improve processing efficiency. Over time, the system may require so much maintenance to remain efficient and meet user objectives that it will come to the end of its useful lifespan. Once the system's lifecycle comes to an end, a completely new system is called for and the cycle may begin again.

LIMITATIONS OF THE LIFECYCLE APPROACH

The systems lifecycle is still used for building large transaction processing systems (TPS) and management information systems (MIS) where requirements are highly structured and well defined (Ahituv and Neumann, 1984). It will also remain appropriate for complex technical systems such as space launches, air traffic control, and refinery operations. Such applications need a rigorous and formal requirements analysis, predefined specifications, and tight controls over the systems-building process.

However, the systems lifecycle approach is costly, time-consuming, and inflexible. Volumes of new documents must be generated and steps repeated if requirements and specifications need to be revised. The lifecycle approach is inflexible and discourages change. Because of the time and cost to repeat the sequence of lifecycle activities, the methodology encourages freezing of specifications early in the development process. The lifecycle method is ill-suited to decision-oriented applications. Decision makers may need to experiment with concrete systems to clarify the kinds of decisions they wish to make. Formal specification of requirements may inhibit system-builders from exploring and discovering the problem structure (Fraser, et al., 1994). Likewise, the lifecycle approach is not suitable for many small desktop systems, which tend to be less structured and more individualized.

11.2 ALTERNATIVE SYSTEM-BUILDING APPROACHES

Some of the problems of the traditional systems lifecycle can be solved by alternative system-building approaches. These approaches include prototyping, application software packages, end-user development, and outsourcing.

prototyping The process of building an experimental system quickly and inexpensively for demonstration and evaluation so that users can better determine information requirements.

prototype The preliminary working version of an information system for demonstration and evaluation purposes.

PROTOTYPING

Prototyping consists of building an experimental system rapidly and inexpensively for end users to evaluate. By interacting with the prototype, users can get a better idea of their information requirements. The prototype endorsed by the users can be used as a template to create the final system.

The **prototype** is a working version of an information system or part of the system, but it is meant to be only a preliminary model. Once operational, the prototype will be further refined until it conforms precisely to users' requirements. Once the design has been finalized, the prototype can be converted to a polished production system.

The process of building a preliminary design, trying it out, refining it, and trying again has been called an **iterative** process of systems development because the steps required to build a system can be repeated over and over again. Prototyping is more explicitly iterative than the conventional lifecycle, and it actively promotes system design changes. It has been said that prototyping replaces unplanned rework with planned iteration, with each version more accurately reflecting users' requirements.

iterative A process of repeating the steps to build a system over and over again.

Steps in Prototyping

Figure 11.2 shows a four-step model of the prototyping process, which consists of the following:

STEP 1. *Identify the user's basic requirements.* The system designer (usually an information systems specialist) works with the user only long enough to capture his or her basic information needs.

STEP 2. *Develop an initial prototype.* The system designer creates a working prototype quickly, most likely using the fourth-generation software tools described in Chapter 6 that speed application development. Some features of computer-aided software engineering (CASE) tools described later in this chapter can be used for prototyping as can multimedia software tools that present users with interactive storyboards that sketch out the tasks of the proposed system for evaluation and modification (Madsen and Aiken, 1993).

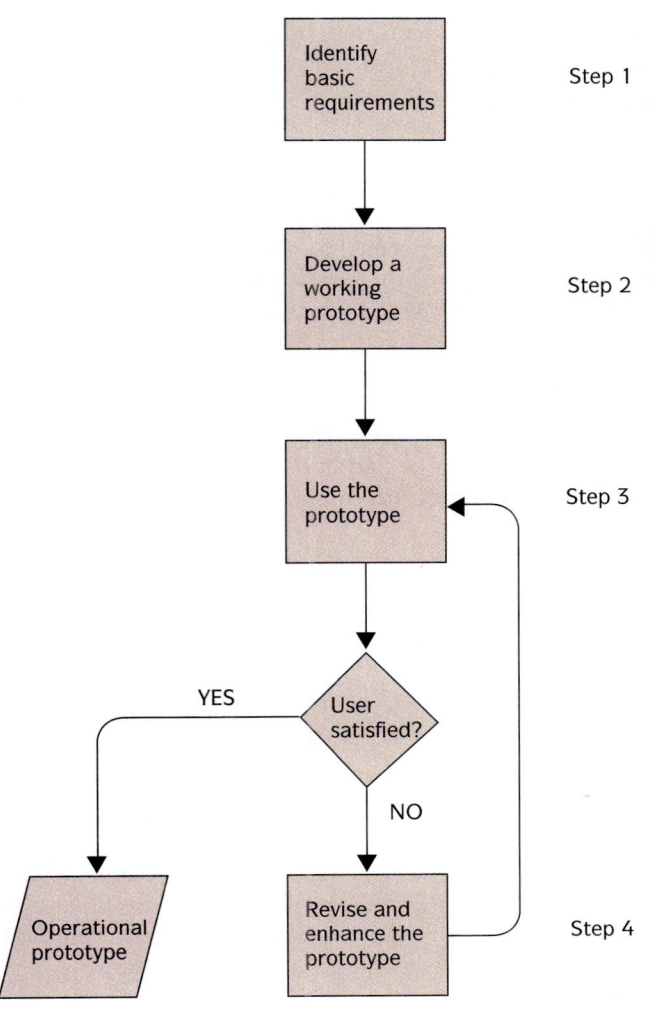

FIGURE 11.2
The prototyping process. The process of developing a prototype can be broken down into four steps. Because a prototype can be developed quickly and inexpensively, the developers can go through several iterations, repeating steps 3 and 4, in order to refine and enhance the prototype before arriving at the final operational one.

STEP 3. *Use the prototype.* The user is encouraged to work with the system in order to determine how well the prototype meets his or her needs and to make suggestions for improving the prototype.

STEP 4. *Revise and enhance the prototype.* The system builder notes all changes requested by the user and refines the prototype accordingly. After the prototype has been revised, the cycle returns to step 3. Steps 3 and 4 are repeated until the user is satisfied.

When no more iterations are required, the approved prototype then becomes an operational prototype that furnishes the final specifications for the application. Sometimes the prototype itself is adopted as the production version of the system.

Advantages and Disadvantages of Prototyping

Prototyping is most useful when there is some uncertainty about requirements or design solutions. For example, a major securities firm requests consolidated information to analyze the performance of its account executives. But what should the measures of performance be? Can the information be extracted from the personnel system alone, or must data from client billings be incorporated as well? What items should be compared on reports? Users may not be initially able to see how the system will work.

Prototyping is especially valuable for the design of the **end-user interface** of an information system (the part of the system that end users interact with, such as on-line display and data-entry screens or reports). The prototype enables users to react immediately to the parts of the system they will be dealing with. Figure 11.3 illustrates the prototyping process for an on-line calendar for retail securities brokers. The first version of the screen was built according to user-supplied specifications for a calendar to track appointments and activities. But when users actually worked with the calendar screen, they suggested adding labels for month and year to the screen and a box to indicate whether the appointment had been met or an activity completed. The brokers also found that they wanted to access information that was maintained in the system about clients with whom they had appointments. The system designer added a link enabling brokers to move directly from the calendar screen to client records.

Prototyping encourages intense end-user involvement throughout the systems development lifecycle (Cerveny et al., 1986). Prototyping is more likely to produce systems that fulfill user requirements. For instance, when the DuPont Company used prototyping to build its systems, it produced more than 400 new programs with no failures (Arthur, 1992).

Prototyping is better suited for smaller applications. Large systems would have to be subdivided so that prototypes would be built one part at a time (Alavi, 1984), which may not be possible without a thorough requirements analysis using the conventional approach.

Rapid prototyping can gloss over essential steps in systems development. Once finished, if the prototype works reasonably well, management may not see the need for reprogramming, redesign, or full documentation and testing. Some of these hastily constructed systems may not easily accommodate large quantities of data or a large number of users in a production environment.

APPLICATION SOFTWARE PACKAGES

Another alternative strategy is to develop an information system by purchasing an application software package. As introduced in Chapter 6, an **application software package** is a set of prewritten, precoded application software programs that are commercially available for sale or lease. Application software packages may range from a simple task (e.g., printing address labels from a database on a microcomputer) to more than 400 program modules with 500,000 lines of code for a complex mainframe system.

Packages have flourished because there are many applications that are common to all business organizations—for example, payroll, accounts receivable, general ledger, or

---

end-user interface The part of an information system through which the end user interacts with the system, such as on-line screens and commands.

application software package A set of prewritten, precoded application software programs that are commercially available for sale or lease.

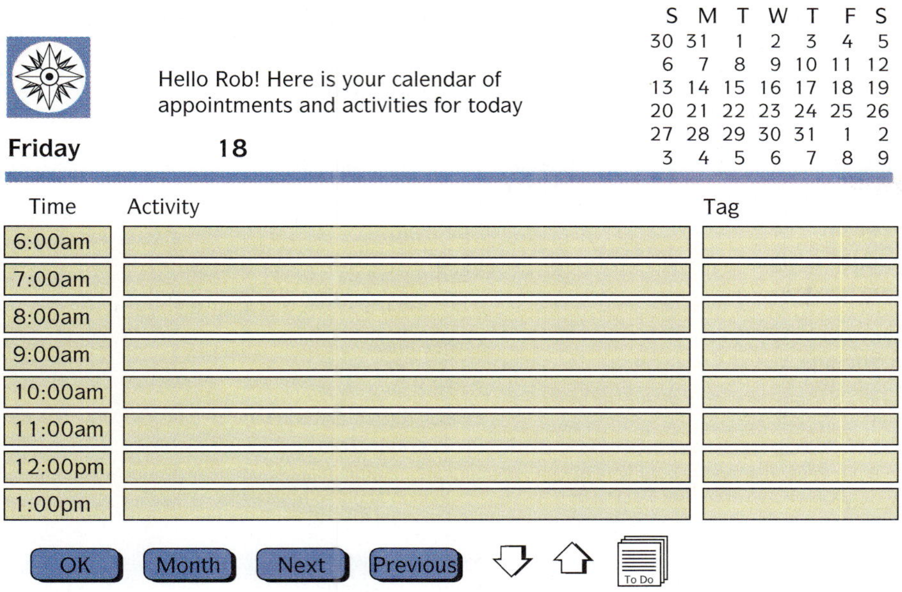

FIGURE 11.3
Prototyping a portfolio management application. This figure illustrates the process of prototyping one screen for the Financial Manager, a client and portfolio management application for securities brokers. Figure 11.3a shows an early version of the on-line appointment screen. Based on the special needs of a client, Fig. 11.3b has two enhancements: a *done* indicator to show whether the task has been completed and a link to reference information maintained by the system on the client with whom the broker has an appointment.

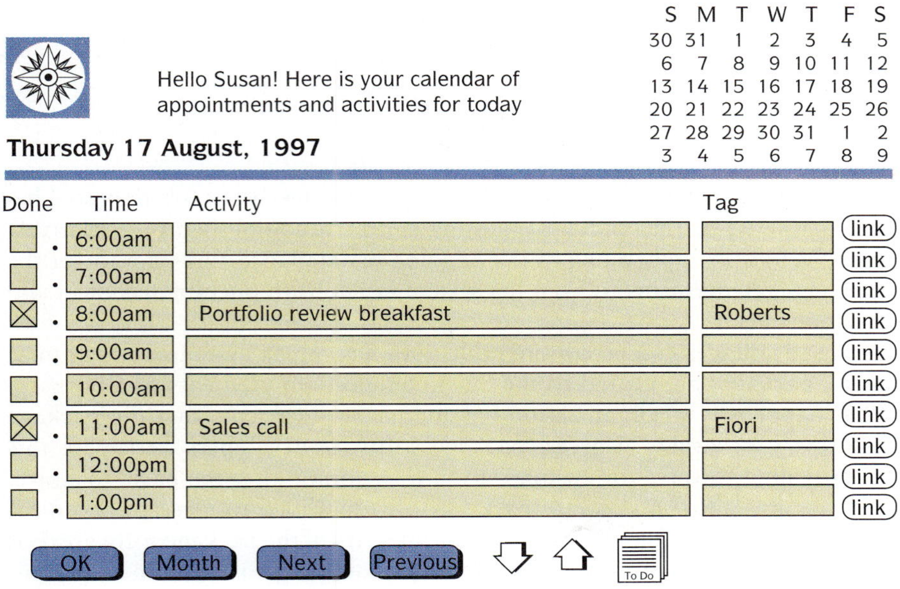

inventory control. For such universal functions with standard procedures, a generalized system will fulfill the requirements of many organizations. Table 11.1 provides examples of applications for which packages are commercially available.

When an appropriate software package is available, it is not necessary for a company to write its own programs; the prewritten, predesigned, pretested software package can fulfill the requirements and can be substituted instead. Since the package vendor has already done most of the design, programming, and testing, the time frame and costs for developing a new system should be considerably reduced.

Advantages and Disadvantages of Software Packages

Using other development strategies, design activities may easily consume up to 50 percent or more of the development effort. However, with packages, most of the design

Table 11.1	Examples of Applications for Which Application Packages Are Available
Accounts payable	Installment loans
Accounts receivable	Inventory control
Architectural design	
Banking systems	Job costing
Bond and stock management	Job scheduling
	Library systems
Check processing	Life insurance
Computer-aided design	
Construction costing	Mailing labels
	Mathematical/statistical modeling
Data management systems	Order entry
Document imaging	
Electrical engineering	Payroll
Education	Performance measurement
E-mail	Process control
Financial control	Real estate management
Forecasting and modeling	Route scheduling
Forms design	Sales and distribution
General ledger	Savings systems
Government purchasing	Stock management
Graphics	Tax accounting
Health care	Utilities control
Health insurance	Word processing
Hotel management	
Human resources	

work has been accomplished in advance. Software package programs are pretested before they are marketed so that purchaser testing can be accomplished in a relatively shorter period. Vendors supply much of the ongoing maintenance and support for the system, supplying enhancements to keep the system in line with ongoing technical and business developments.

Package disadvantages can be considerable with a complex system. To maximize market appeal, packages are geared to the most common requirements of all organizations. What happens if an organization has unique requirements that the package does not address? To varying degrees, package software developers anticipate this problem by providing features for customization that do not alter the basic software. **Customization** features allow a software package to be modified to meet an organization's unique requirements without destroying the integrity of the package software. For instance, the package may allocate parts of its files or databases to maintain an organization's own unique pieces of data. Some packages have a modular design that allows clients to select only the software functions with the processing they need from an array of options. Ultimately, required customization and additional programming may become so expensive and time-consuming that they eliminate many advantages of the package. Figure 11.4 shows how package costs in relation to total implementation costs rise with the degree of customization. The initial purchase price of the package can be deceptive because of these hidden implementation costs.

customization The modification of a software package to meet an organization's unique requirements without destroying the integrity of the package software.

Selecting Software Packages

Application software packages must be thoroughly evaluated before they can be used as the foundation of a new information system. The most important evaluation criteria are the functions provided by the package, flexibility, user-friendliness, hardware and software resources, database requirements, installation and maintenance effort, documentation, vendor quality, and cost. The package evaluation process is often based on

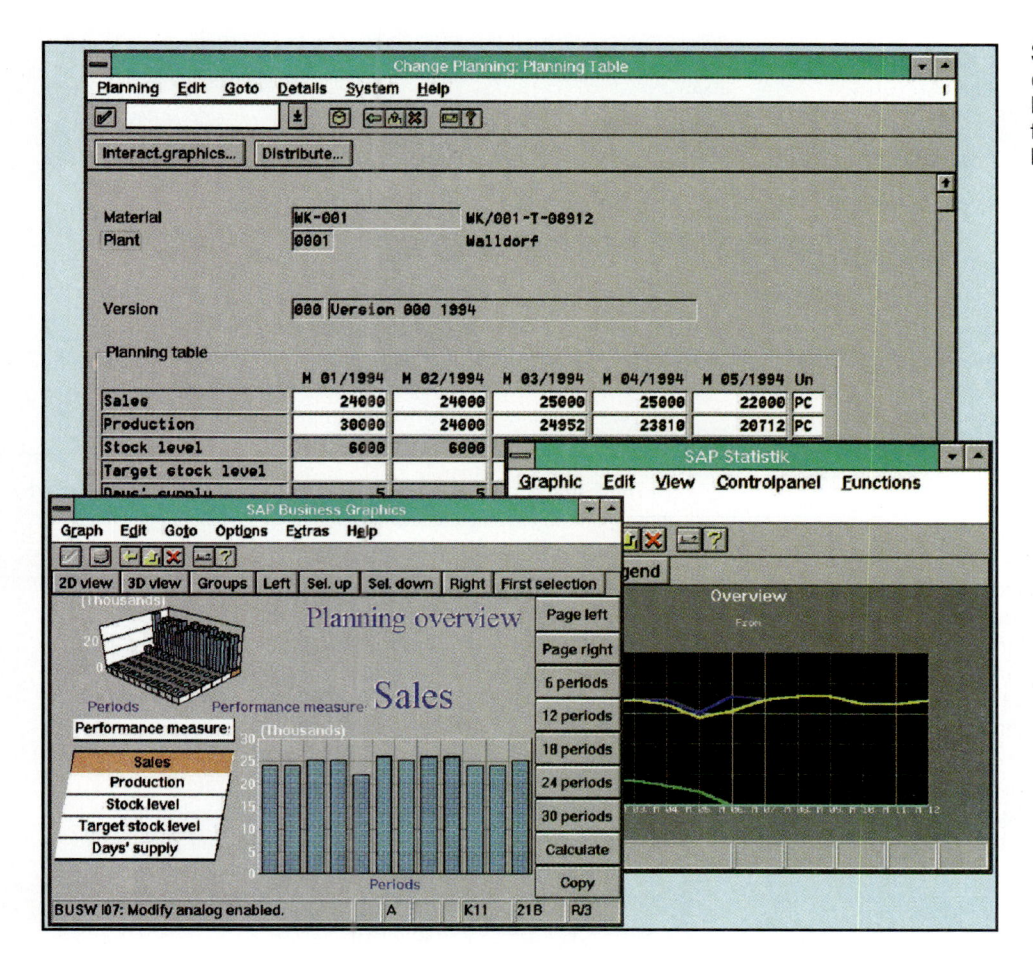

SAP's R/3 software package runs in client/server environments and can be customized to accommodate different languages, currencies, tax laws, and accounting practices.

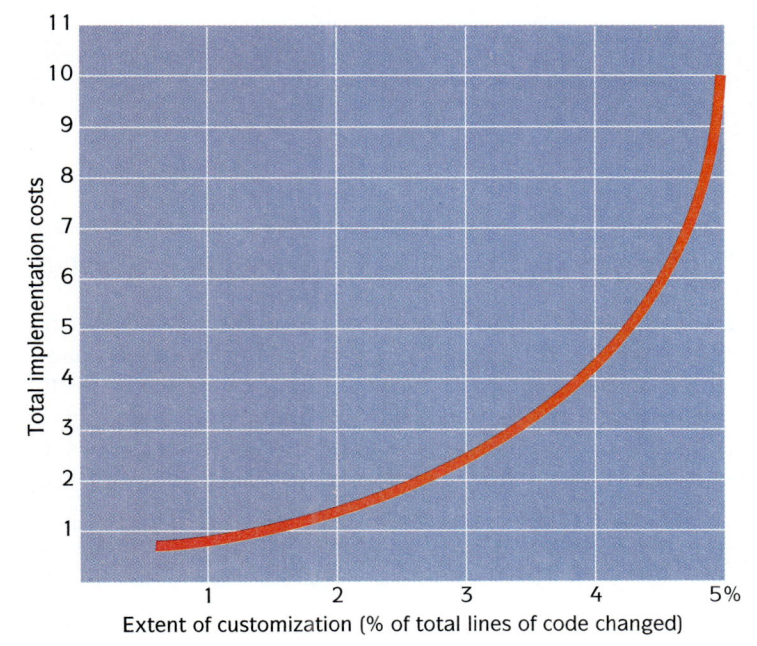

FIGURE 11.4
The effects of customizing a software package on total implementation costs. As the modifications to a software package rise, so does the cost of implementing the package. Sometimes the savings promised by the package are whittled away by excessive changes. As the number of lines of program code changed approaches 5 percent of the total lines in the package, the costs of implementation rise fivefold.

11.2 Alternative System-Building Approaches   *345*

Window on Technology

CAN SAAB FIND HAPPINESS WITH A MANUFACTURING PACKAGE FROM A TINY, UNKNOWN VENDOR?

Should a company select a critical application package from a small, unknown vendor? Saab-Scania, the truck manufacturing arm of the Swedish automobile company Saab, was faced with this question. With headquarters in Sodertalje, Sweden, and production plants in Sweden, France, the Netherlands, and Brazil, Scania produces 140 trucks per day, making it the second-largest truck manufacturer in the world. Scania has long used computers to help keep production lines moving fast while maintaining the lowest possible parts inventory.

Scania was becoming locked into outdated, proprietary systems. Its computer system was a Sperry Univac using a proprietary operating system and running a manufacturing application designed for that hardware and operating system. With this technology platform, Saab could not continue to build new programs onto the system. Management decided to move into a relational database environment to give additional flexibility to add new tables or fields as their production needs changed.

Scania already used Digital Equipment Corporation (DEC) VAX/VMS hardware and operating systems in its commercial systems. A great deal of new software and technology were being developed for the VAX and its VMS operating system. In addition the DEC VAX is a popular platform for running the UNIX operating system and the many applications being developed for UNIX. Scania opted for a DEC VAX platform.

Scania determined its other main requirement was for a package that would be flexible enough to support its well-established production methods. The company examined seven well-known packages and found all of them too inflexible. The company would have had to adapt its work practices to accommodate such software and it did not want to make major package modifications. Ultimately Saab turned to Computer-Integrated Interactive Manufacturing (CIIM) from unknown Avalon Software Inc. of Tucson, Arizona.

Why CIIM? First, although it would require some modification, it was far more flexible than other packages. Scania hoped

> **To Think About:** Was the selection of CIIM a wise decision? What management, organization, and technology issues did Scania have to address when selecting a software package?

to use about 80 percent of the package without modification. Second, the software's broad functionality includes production planning, shop floor control, production engineering, transport data monitoring, handling of bills of material and order processing, determining manpower requirements, monitoring production efficiency and quality control—essentially, all of the functions Scania was seeking. Third, CIIM was based on Oracle RDBMS, the largest independent vendor of relational database management systems. Fourth, the software would run on the VAX under either VMS or UNIX. Fifth, CIIM was written using Oracle's computer-aided software engineering (CASE) tools (see the discussion of CASE in Section 11.3).

Avalon and CIIM did present several problems. Its 1993 revenues were only $9 million. At the time Scania signed the contract, Avalon had no major installations in Europe. But so far Scania has been satisfied. It took Scania only about a year to get the system up and running (including translating the user prompts into Swedish). Scania has been able to cut the time between order and delivery by 50 percent, down to only five days.

Source: George Black, "Saab Story Ends Well Thanks to CIIM on RDBMS," *Software Magazine*, June 1994.

Request for Proposal (RFP) A detailed list of questions submitted to vendors of packaged software or other computer services to determine if the vendor's product can meet the organization's specific requirements.

a **Request for Proposal (RFP),** which is a detailed list of questions submitted to vendors of packaged software.

The Window on Technology examines the issue of vendor quality when other requirements lead the potential purchaser of the package to a small, unknown company.

When a system is developed using an application software package, systems analysis will include a package evaluation effort. Design activities will focus on matching requirements to package features. Instead of tailoring the system design specifications directly to user requirements, the design effort will consist of trying to mold user requirements to conform to the features of the package.

When a software package solution is selected, the organization no longer has total control over the system design process. At best, packages can meet only 70 percent of most organizations' requirements. If the package cannot adapt to the organization, the organization will have to adapt to the package and change its procedures.

END-USER DEVELOPMENT

In many organizations end users are developing a growing percentage of information systems with little or no formal assistance from technical specialists. This phenomenon is called **end-user development**. End-user development has been made possible by the special fourth-generation software tools introduced in Chapter 6. With fourth-generation languages, graphics languages, and microcomputer tools, end-users can access data, create reports, and develop entire information systems on their own, with little or no help from professional systems analysts or programmers. Many of these end-user developed systems can be created much more rapidly than with the traditional systems lifecycle. Figure 11.5 illustrates the concept of end-user development.

end-user development The development of information systems by end users with little or no formal assistance from technical specialists.

End-User Computing Tools: Strengths and Limitations

Many organizations have reported appreciable gains in application development productivity by using fourth-generation tools. Productivity enhancements based on conventional programming languages, such as structured programming (see Section 11.3), have resulted in a maximum productivity improvement of only 25 percent (Jones, 1979). In contrast, some studies of organizations developing applications with fourth-generation tools have reported productivity gains of 300 to 500 percent (Green, 1984–85; Harel, 1985). Fourth-generation tools have new capabilities, such as graphics, spreadsheets, modeling, and ad hoc information retrieval, that meet important business needs.

Unfortunately, fourth-generation tools still cannot replace conventional tools for some business applications because their capabilities remain limited. Fourth-generation processing is relatively inefficient, processing individual transactions too slowly and at too high a cost to make these systems suitable for very large transaction processing systems. Slow response time and computer performance degradation often result when very large files are used.

Most fourth-generation tools are more nonprocedural than conventional programming languages. They thus cannot easily handle applications with extensive procedural logic and updating requirements, such as systems used for the design of nuclear

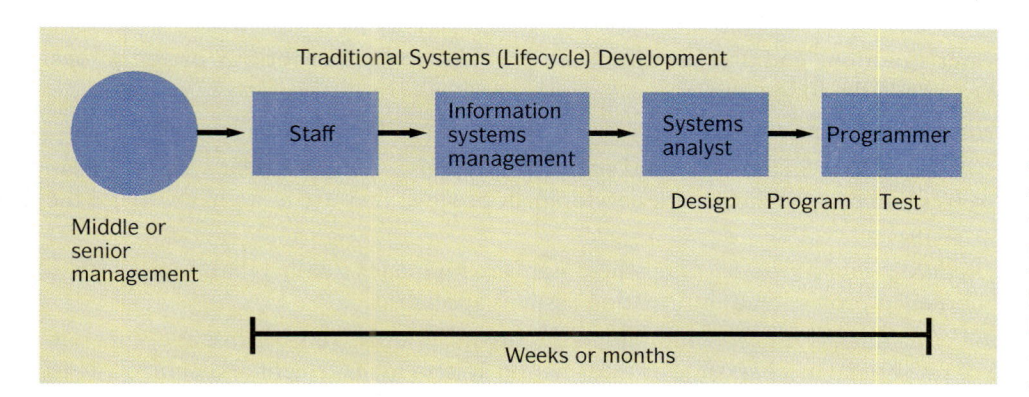

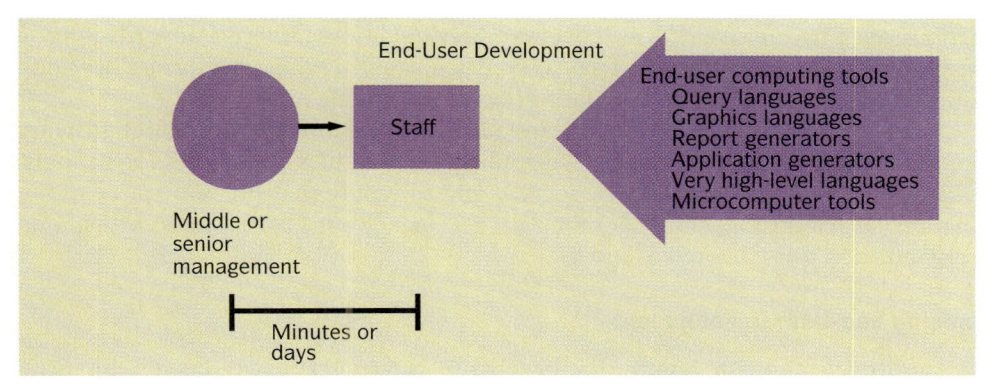

FIGURE 11.5
End-user versus system lifecycle development. End users can access computerized information directly or develop information systems with little or no formal technical assistance. On the whole, end-user developed systems can be completed more rapidly than those developed through the conventional systems lifecycle. *From* Applications Development without Programmers, *by Martin, James, © 1982. Reprinted by permission of Prentice-Hall, Inc., Upper Saddle River, NJ.*

Features such as the easy-to-use graphical interface and natural language capabilities of Esperant's query software allow end users to develop some applications on their own.

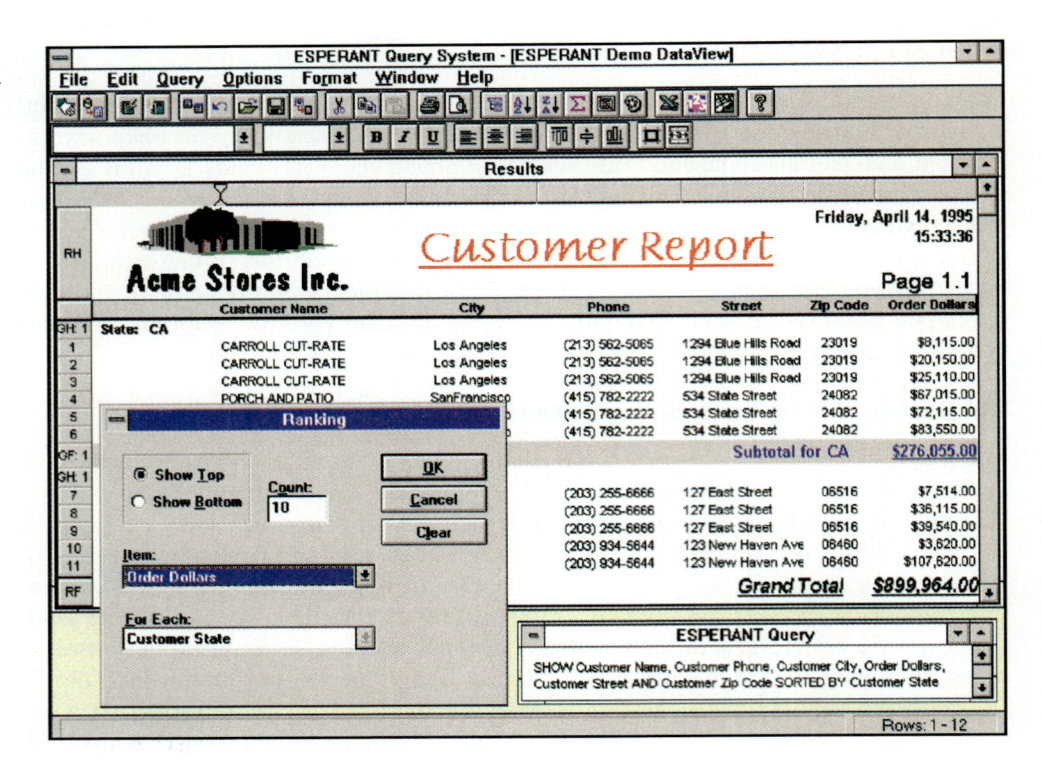

reactors, optimal production scheduling, or tracking daily trades of stocks, bonds, and other securities that require complex processing and often the matching of multiple files. Fourth-generation tools make their greatest contribution to the programming and detail design aspects of the systems development process but have little impact on other system-building activities.

Management Benefits and Problems

Without question, end-user development provides many benefits to organizations. These include the following:

- *Improved requirements determination* as users specify their own business needs.
- *Increased user involvement and satisfaction.* As users develop their systems themselves and control the system development process, they are more likely to use the system.
- *Reduced application backlog* when users are no longer totally reliant upon overburdened professional information systems specialists.

At the same time, end-user computing poses organizational risks because it occurs outside of traditional mechanisms for information system management and control. Most organizations have not yet developed strategies to ensure that end-user-developed applications meet organizational objectives or meet quality assurance standards appropriate to their function. When systems are created rapidly, without a formal development methodology, testing and documentation may be inadequate.

Control over data can be lost in systems outside the traditional information systems department. When users create their own applications and files, it becomes increasingly difficult to determine where data are located and to ensure that the same piece of information (such as product number or annual earnings) is used consistently throughout the organization (see Chapters 7 and 9).

Managing End-User Development

How can organizations maximize the benefits of end-user applications development while keeping it under management control? A number of strategies have been suggested.

Retail staff receive instruction in this New Jersey computer management class. An important function of information centers is to make end users feel proficient with computers.

One way both to facilitate and manage end-user application development is to set up an information center. The **information center** is a special facility that provides training and support for end-user computing. Information centers feature hardware, software, and technical specialists that supply end users with tools, training, and expert advice so that they can create information system applications on their own. With information center tools, users can create their own computer reports, spreadsheets, or graphics, or extract data for decision making and analysis with minimal technical assistance. Information-center consultants are available to instruct users and to assist in the development of more complex applications.

Information centers provide many management benefits. They can help end users find tools and applications that will make them more productive. They prevent the creation of redundant applications. They promote data sharing and minimize integrity problems (see Chapter 7). They ensure that the applications developed by end users meet audit, data quality, and security standards. They can help establish and enforce standards for hardware and software so that end users do not introduce many disparate and incompatible technologies into the firm (Fuller and Swanson, 1992; see Chapter 9). The information center will assist users with only hardware and software that have been approved by management.

In addition to using information centers, managers can pursue other strategies to ensure that end-user computing serves larger organizational goals (see Alavi, Nelson, and Weiss, 1987–88; Rockart and Flannery, 1983). Management should control the development of end-user applications by incorporating them into its strategic systems plans. Management should also develop controls on critical end-user development, such as insisting on cost justification of end-user information system projects and establishing hardware, software, and quality standards for user-developed applications.

information center A special facility within an organization that provides training and support for end-user computing.

OUTSOURCING

If a firm does not want to use its own internal resources to build and operate information systems, it can hire an external organization that specializes in providing these services to do the work. The process of turning over an organization's computer center operations, telecommunications networks, or applications development to external vendors of these services is called **outsourcing**. In firms where the cost of the information systems function has risen rapidly, managers are turning to outsourcing to control these costs.

Outsourcing is becoming popular because some organizations perceive it as being more cost-effective than maintaining their own computer center and information systems staff. The provider of outsourcing services can benefit from economies of scale (the same knowledge, skills, and capacity can be shared with many different customers) and

outsourcing The practice of contracting computer center operations, telecommunications networks, or applications development to external vendors.

11.2 Alternative System-Building Approaches

is likely to charge competitive prices for information systems services. Outsourcing allows a company with fluctuating needs for computer processing to pay for only what it uses rather than to build its own computer center to stand underutilized when there is no peak load. Some firms outsource because their internal information systems staff cannot keep pace with technological change or because they want to free up scarce and costly talent for activities with higher payback.

But not all organizations benefit from outsourcing, and the disadvantages of outsourcing can create serious problems for organizations if they are not well understood and managed (Earl, 1996). When a firm farms out the responsibility for developing and operating its information systems to another organization, it can lose control over its information systems function. Outsourcing can place the vendor in an advantageous position where the client has to accept whatever the vendor does and whatever fees the vendor charges. This dependency could eventually result in higher costs or loss of control over technological direction. Trade secrets or proprietary information may leak out to competitors because a firm's information systems are being run or developed by outsiders. This could be especially harmful if a firm allows an outsourcer to develop or to operate applications that give it some type of competitive advantage.

When to Use Outsourcing

If systems development and operations functions are well managed and productive, there may not be much immediate benefit in using an external vendor. However, there are a number of circumstances under which outsourcing makes a great deal of sense if it is used selectively.

- *When there is limited opportunity for the firm to distinguish itself competitively through a particular information systems application or series of applications.* Figure 11.6 illustrates a matrix that could help firms determine appropriate applications for outsourcing. Applications such as payroll or cafeteria accounting, for which the firm obtains little competitive advantage from excellence, are strong candidates for outsourcing. If carefully developed, applications such as airline reservations or plant scheduling could provide a firm with a distinct advantage over competitors. The firm could lose profits, customers, or market share if such systems have problems. Applications where the rewards for excellence are high and where the penalties for failure are high should probably be developed and operated internally.

- *When the predictability of uninterrupted information systems service is not very important.* For instance, airline reservations or catalogue shopping systems are too crit-

FIGURE 11.6
Rewards and penalties of outsourcing. This reward/penalty matrix shows that those applications with low reward for excellence and low penalty for problems are good candidates for outsourcing. *From Paul Clermont, "Outsourcing without Guilt,"* Computerworld, *September 9, 1991. Copyright 1991 by Computerworld, Inc., Framingham, MA 01701. Reprinted from* Computerworld. *Reprinted by permission.*

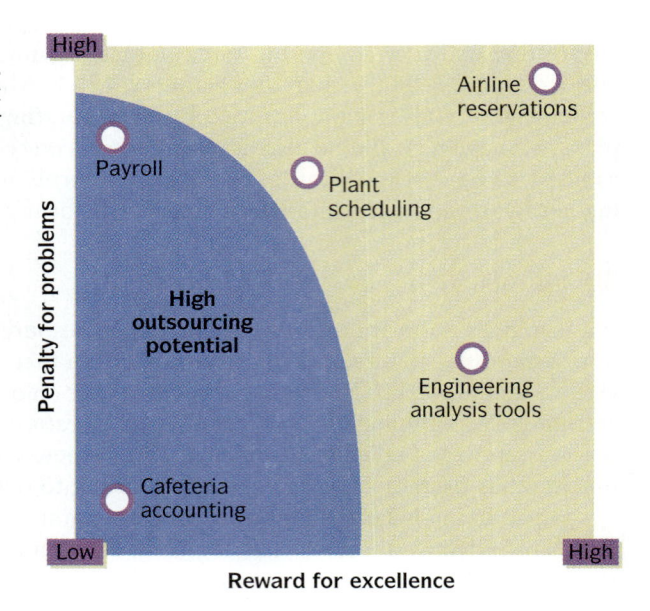

Window on Management

FORD EUROPE MAKES ITS OUTSOURCING CONTRACTORS PART OF ITS TEAM

When Ford of Europe recently outsourced the computer functions that support its giant Parts and Services Operations, it went against all conventional wisdom. That wisdom says that companies should not outsource critical, strategic functions. Ford views its parts and services unit as strategic, in which continuity of computer service is central. Why then did Ford outsource? And how did Ford deal with the need to make the outsourcing contractor committed to its team?

Ford of Europe is a $2.4 billion Ford division based in Cologne, Germany, with major computer centers in Cologne, Daventry, England, and Valencia, Spain. In February, 1994, Ford signed a five-year outsourcing contract with Computer Sciences Corp. (CSC) of El Segundo, California, to run these computer centers and to develop new applications for Ford.

Ford's aim is to improve the efficiency of its parts and services operations in order to improve service throughout Europe. Its first goal was to give service centers access to an up-to-the-minute picture of what parts are in stock locally, and if out of stock, which other service centers would have the needed parts. A new system, the Dealer Computer Architecture Strategy, has reduced the average time needed to locate a part from 20 minutes to about 2 seconds. Ford intends to make similar improvements in other functions within the parts and service area.

CSC employees will be given access to Ford's privileged, proprietary information, and they will have to work as if they are full members of the Ford organization and team. Ford tried to structure the agreement so that CSC employees would act with the same loyalty and care for Ford's future as Ford employees. Ford insisted that CSC not work with the parts and services func-

To Think About: Did outsourcing Ford's Parts and Services function support its business strategy? Why or why not? Do you believe Ford faced any risks by doing this? If so, do you think they have successfully dealt with those risks? Again, why or why not?

tion of another automobile manufacturer. Language establishing the requirement of exclusivity was inserted into the agreement. CSC agreed to give up parts and service work in the automotive industry in order to gain and hold this lucrative contract with Ford. Although CSC remains free to seek work with Ford competitors in areas other than parts and service, it would check with Ford first.

The size of the Ford-CSC contract—approximately $100 million over five years—is another incentive to draw CSC into the Ford team. To further sweeten the deal, Ford allowed CSC to use Ford's three computer centers to process work of CSC's other customers (as long as they are not part of the automotive industry).

Source: Mark Halper, "Ford Drives Exclusive Outsourcing Deal," *Computerworld*, February 21, 1994.

---

ical to be trusted outside. If these systems failed to operate for a few days or even a few hours, they could close down the business (see Chapter 2). On the other hand, a system to process employee insurance claims could be more easily outsourced because uninterrupted processing of claims is not critical to the survival of the firm.

- *When the firm's existing information system capabilities are limited, ineffective, or technically inferior.* Some organizations use outsourcers as an easy way to revamp their information systems technology. For instance, they might use an outsourcer to help them make the transition from traditional mainframe-based computing to a distributed client/server computing environment. On the other hand, outsourcing new technology projects can be risky because the organization may lack the expertise to negotiate a sound contract and may remain too dependent on the vendor after implementation (Lacity, Willcocks, and Feeny, 1996).

Despite the conventional wisdom on when to outsource, companies sometimes do outsource strategic functions, as we see with Ford of Europe in the Window on Management.

Organizations need to manage the outsourcer as they would manage their own internal information systems department by setting priorities, ensuring that the right people are brought in, and guaranteeing that information systems are running smoothly. They should establish criteria for evaluating the outsourcing vendor. Firms should design outsourcing contracts carefully so that the outsourcing services can be adjusted if the nature of the business changes.

Table 11.2 Comparison of Systems-Development Approaches

Approach	Features	Advantages	Disadvantages
Systems lifecycle	Sequential step-by-step formal process Written specification and approvals Limited role of users	Necessary for large complex systems and projects	Slow and expensive Discourages changes Massive paperwork to manage
Prototyping	Requirements specified dynamically with experimental system Rapid, informal, and iterative process Users continually interact with the prototype	Rapid and inexpensive Useful when requirements uncertain or when end-user interface is important Promotes user participation	Inappropriate for large, complex systems Can gloss over steps in analysis, documentation, and testing
Application software package	Commercial software eliminates need for internally developed software programs	Design, programming, installation, and maintenance work reduced Can save time and cost when developing common business applications Reduces need for internal information systems resources	May not meet organization's unique requirements May not perform many business functions well Extensive customization raises development costs
End-user development	Systems created by end users using fourth-generation software tools Rapid and informal Minimal role of information systems specialists	Users control systems-building Saves development time and cost Reduces application backlog	Can lead to proliferation of uncontrolled information systems Systems do not always meet quality assurance standards
Outsourcing	Systems built and sometimes operated by external vendor	Can reduce or control costs Can produce systems when internal resources not available or technically deficient	Loss of control over the information systems function Dependence on the technical direction and prosperity of external vendors

Table 11.2 compares the advantages and disadvantages of each of the system-building alternatives described in this chapter.

11.3 SYSTEM-BUILDING METHODOLOGIES

development methodology A collection of methods, one or more for every activity within every phase of a development project.

Various tools and development methodologies have been employed to help system builders document, analyze, design, and implement information systems. A **development methodology** is a collection of methods, one or more for every activity within every phase of a systems development project. Some development methodologies are suited to specific technologies, while others reflect different philosophies of systems development. The most widely-used methodologies and tools include the traditional structured methodologies, object-oriented software development, computer-aided software engineering (CASE), and software reengineering.

STRUCTURED METHODOLOGIES

structured Refers to the fact that techniques are instructions that are carefully drawn up, often step-by-step, with each step building upon a previous one.

Structured methodologies have been used to document, analyze, and design information systems since the 1970s and remain an important methodological approach. **Structured** refers to the fact that the techniques are step-by-step, with each step building upon the previous one. Structured methodologies are top-down, progressing from the highest, most abstract level to the lowest level of detail—from the general to the specific. For example, the highest level of a top-down description of a human resources system would show the main human resources functions: personnel, benefits, compensation, and Equal Employment Opportunity (EEO). Each of these would be broken down into the next layer. Benefits, for instance, might include pension, employee savings, health care, and insurance. Each of these layers in turn would be broken down until the lowest level of detail could be depicted.

The traditional structured methodologies are process-oriented rather than data-oriented. While data descriptions are part of the methods, the methodologies focus on how the data are transformed rather than on the data themselves. These methodologies are largely linear—each phase must be completed before the next one can begin. Structured methodologies include structured analysis, structured design, and the use of flowcharts.

Structured Analysis

Structured analysis is widely used to define system inputs, processes, and outputs. It offers a logical graphic model of information flow, partitioning a system into modules that show manageable levels of detail. It rigorously specifies the processes or transformations that occur within each module and the interfaces that exist between them. Its primary tool is the **data flow diagram (DFD)**, a graphic representation of a system's component processes and the interfaces (flow of data) between them.

Figure 11.7 shows a simple data flow diagram for a mail-in university course registration system. The rounded boxes represent processes, which portray the transformation of data. The square box represents an external entity, which is an originator or receiver of information located outside the boundaries of the system being modeled. The open rectangles represent data stores, which are either manual or automated inventories of data. The arrows represent data flows, which show the movement between

structured analysis A method for defining system inputs, processes, and outputs and for partitioning systems into subsystems or modules that show a logical graphic model of information flow.

data flow diagram (DFD) A primary tool in structured analysis that graphically illustrates the system's component processes and the flow of data between them.

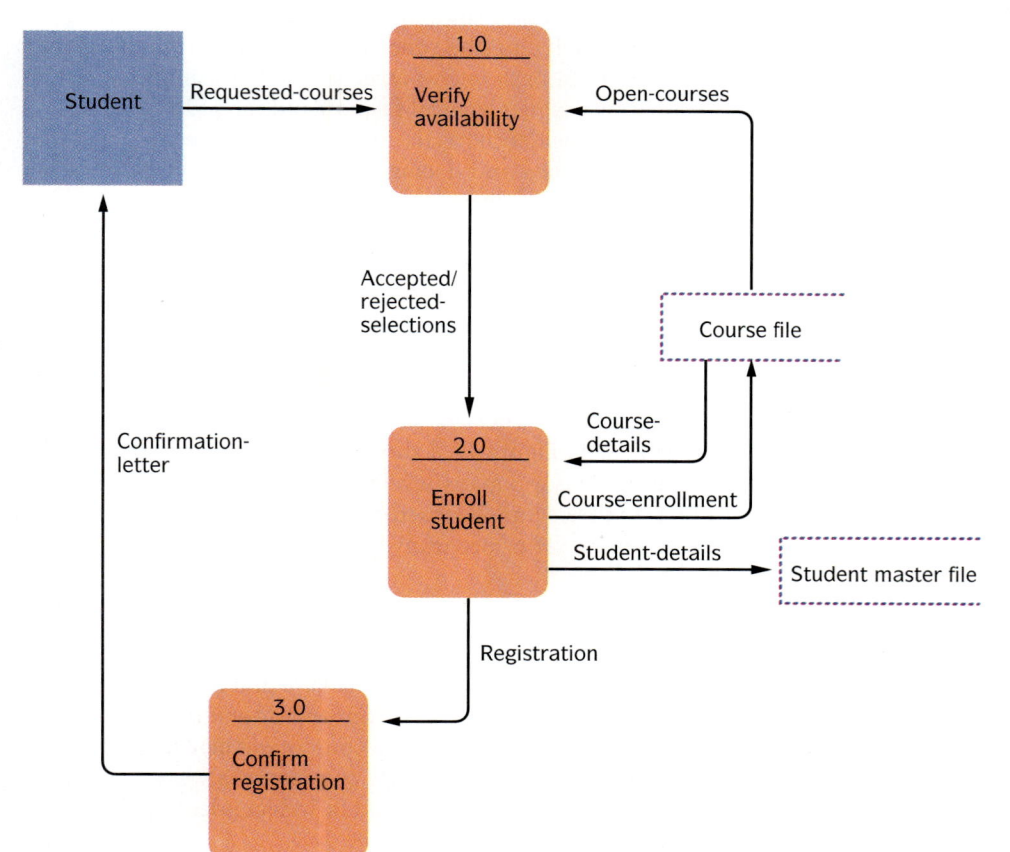

FIGURE 11.7
Data flow diagram for mail-in university registration system. The system has three processes: Verify availability (1.0), Enroll student (2.0), and Confirm registration (3.0). The name and content of each of the data flows appear adjacent to each arrow. There is one external entity in this system: the student. There are two data stores: the student master file and the course file.

processes, external entities, and data stores. They always contain packets of data, with the name or content of each data flow listed beside the arrow.

This data flow diagram shows that students submit registration forms with their name, identification number, and the numbers of the courses they wish to take. In process 1.0 the system verifies that each course selected is still open by referencing the university's course file. The file distinguishes courses that are still open from those that have been canceled or filled. Process 1.0 then determines which of the student's selections can be accepted or rejected. Process 2.0 enrolls the student in the courses for which he or she has been accepted. It updates the university's course file with the student's name and identification number and recalculates the class size. If maximum enrollment has been reached, the course number is flagged as closed. Process 2.0 also updates the university's student master file with information about new students or changes in address. Process 3.0 then sends each student applicant a confirmation-of-registration letter listing the courses for which he or she is registered and noting the course selections that could not be fulfilled.

The diagrams can be used to depict higher-level processes as well as lower-level details. Through leveled data flow diagrams, a complex process can be broken down into successive levels of detail. An entire system can be divided into subsystems with a high-level data flow diagram. Each subsystem, in turn, can be divided into additional subsystems with second-level data flow diagrams, and the lower-level subsystems can be broken down again until the lowest level of detail has been reached.

Another tool for structured analysis is a data dictionary, which contains information about individual pieces of data and data groupings within a system (see Chapter 7). The data dictionary defines the contents of data flows and data stores so that system builders understand exactly what pieces of data they contain. **Process specifications** describe the transformation occurring within the lowest level of the data flow diagrams. They express the logic for each process.

process specifications Describes the logic of the processes occurring within the lowest levels of the data flow diagrams.

Structured Design

Structured design encompasses a set of design rules and techniques that promotes program clarity and simplicity, thereby reducing the time and effort required for coding, debugging, and maintenance. The main principle of structured design is that a system should be designed from the top down in hierarchical fashion and refined to greater levels of detail. The design should first consider the main function of a program or system, then break this function into subfunctions and decompose each subfunction until the lowest level of detail has been reached. The lowest-level modules describe the actual processing that will occur. In this manner all high-level logic and the design model are developed before detailed program code is written. If structured analysis has been performed, the structured specification document can serve as input to the design process. Our earlier human resources top-down description is also a good overview example of structured design.

structured design Software design discipline, encompassing a set of design rules and techniques for designing a system from the top down in a hierarchical fashion.

As the design is formulated, it is documented in a structure chart. The **structure chart** is a top-down chart, showing each level of design, its relationship to other levels, and its place in the overall design structure. Figure 11.8 shows a structure chart that can be used for a payroll system. If a design has too many levels to fit onto one structure chart, it can be broken down further on more detailed structure charts. A structure chart may document one program, one system (a set of programs), or part of one program.

structure chart System documentation showing each level of design, the relationship among the levels, and the overall place in the design structure; can document one program, one system, or part of one program.

Structured Programming

Structured programming extends the principles governing structured design to the writing of programs to make software programs easier to understand and modify. It is based upon the principle of modularization, which follows from top-down analysis and design. Each of the boxes in the structure chart represents a component **module** that is usually directly related to a bottom-level design module. It constitutes a logical unit that performs one or several functions. Ideally, modules should be independent of each other

structured programming A discipline for organizing and coding programs that simplifies the control paths so that the programs can be easily understood and modified. Uses the basic control structures and modules that have only one entry point and one exit point.

module A logical unit of a program that performs one or several functions.

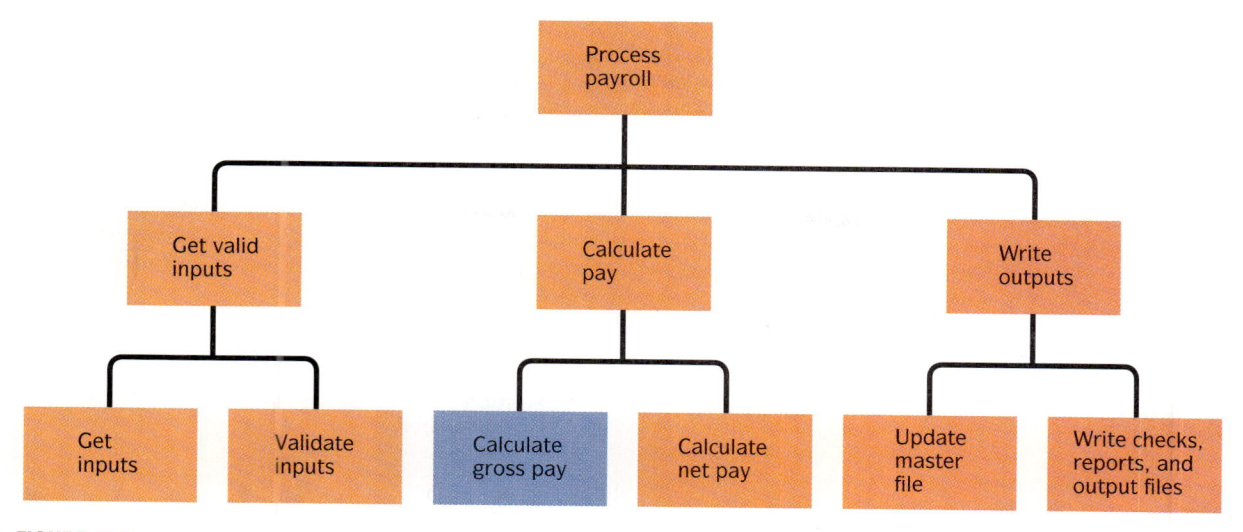

FIGURE 11.8
High-level structure chart for a payroll system. This structure chart shows the highest or most abstract level of design for a payroll system, providing an overview of the entire system.

and should have only one entry to and exit from their parent modules. They should share data with as few other modules as possible. Each module should be kept to a manageable size. An individual should be able to read and understand the program code for the module and easily keep track of its functions.

Proponents of structured programming have shown that any program can be written using three basic control constructs, or instruction patterns: (1) simple sequence, (2) selection, and (3) iteration. These control constructs are illustrated in Figure 11.9.

The **sequence construct** executes statements in the order in which they appear, with control passing unconditionally from one statement to the next. The program will execute statement A and then statement B.

The **selection construct** tests a condition and executes one of the two alternative instructions based on the results of the test. Condition R is tested. If R is true, statement C is executed. If R is false, statement D is executed. Control then passes to the next statement.

The **iteration construct** repeats a segment of code as long as a conditional test remains true. Condition S is tested. If S is true, statement E is executed and control returns to the test of S. If S is false, E is skipped and control passes to the next statement.

Flowcharts

Flowcharting is an old design tool that is still in use. **System flowcharts** detail the flow of data throughout an entire information system. Program flowcharts describe the processes taking place within an individual program in the system and the sequence in which they must be executed. Flowcharting is no longer recommended for program design because it does not provide top-down modular structure as effectively as other techniques. However, system flowcharts may still be used to document physical design specifications because they can show all inputs, major files, processing, and outputs for a system and they can document manual procedures.

Using specialized symbols and flow lines, the system flowchart traces the flow of information and work in a system, the sequence of processing steps, and the physical media on which data are input, output, and stored. Figure 11.10 shows the basic symbols for system flowcharting. The plain rectangle is a general symbol. Flow lines show the sequence of steps and the direction of information flow. Arrows are employed to show direction if it is not apparent in the diagram. Figure 11.11 illustrates a high-level system flowchart for a payroll system.

sequence construct The sequential single steps or actions in the logic of a program that do not depend on the existence of any condition.

selection construct The logic pattern in programming where a stated condition determines which of two or more actions can be taken, depending on which satisfies the stated condition.

iteration construct The logic pattern in programming where certain actions are repeated while a specified condition occurs or until a certain condition is met.

system flowchart A graphic design tool that depicts the physical media and sequence of processing steps used in an entire information system.

FIGURE 11.9
Basic control constructs. The three basic control constructs used in structured programming are sequence, selection, and iteration.

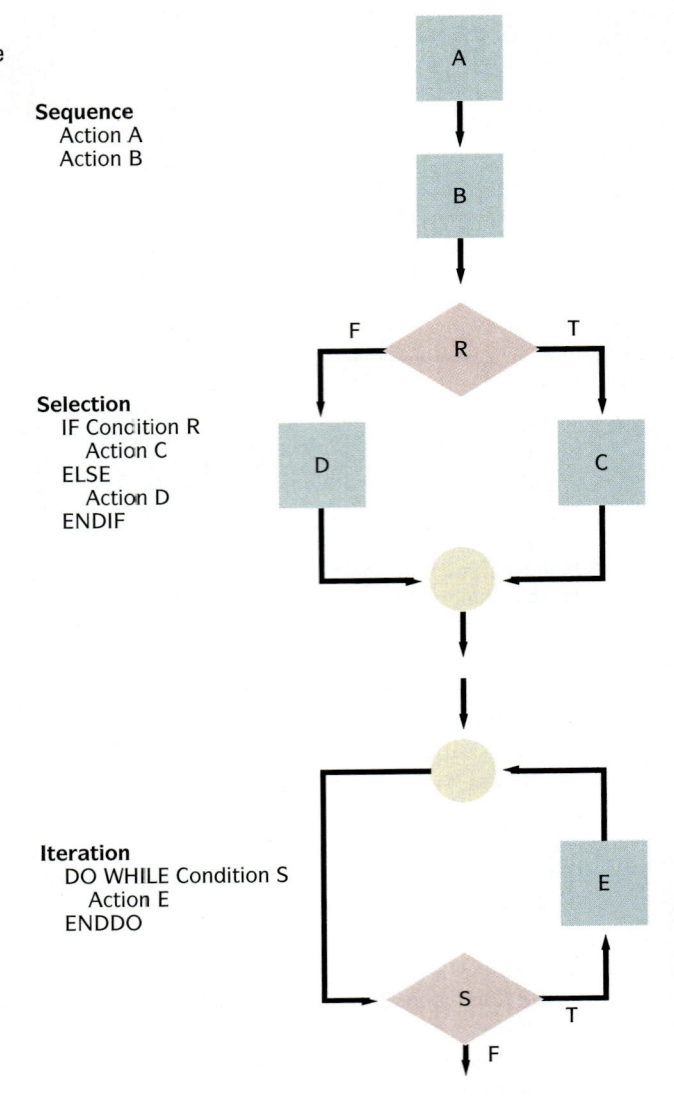

Sequence
  Action A
  Action B

Selection
  IF Condition R
    Action C
  ELSE
    Action D
  ENDIF

Iteration
  DO WHILE Condition S
    Action E
  ENDDO

Limitations of Traditional Methods

While traditional methods are valuable, they can be inflexible and time-consuming. Completion of structured analysis is required before design can begin, and programming must await the completed deliverables from design. A change in specifications requires that first the analysis documents and then the design documents must be modified before the programs can be changed to reflect the new requirement. Structured methodologies are function-oriented, focusing on the processes that transform the data. Yet business management has come to understand that most information systems must be data-oriented. Consequently, system builders are turning to object-oriented software development, computer-aided software engineering (CASE), and software reengineering to deal with these issues.

object-oriented software development An approach to software development that de-emphasizes procedures and shifts the focus from modeling business processes and data to combining data and procedures to create objects.

OBJECT-ORIENTED SOFTWARE DEVELOPMENT

In Chapter 6 we explained that object-oriented programming combines data and the specific procedures that operate on those data into one object. Object-oriented programming is part of a larger approach to systems development called *object-oriented software development*. **Object-oriented software development** differs from traditional

Input/Output	Processing	Storage
Input/output	Process	Magnetic tape
Punched card	Preparation	On-line storage (magnetic disk)
Document	Collate	Database (magnetic disk)
Punched tape	Manual operation	
On-line input	Sort	**Telecommunications**
On-line display	Auxiliary operation	Telecommunications link
Keying operation	Merge	

FIGURE 11.10
Basic system flowchart symbols. Use these symbols and interconnecting lines to show the sequence of processing taking place within a system and the physical media used in each step.

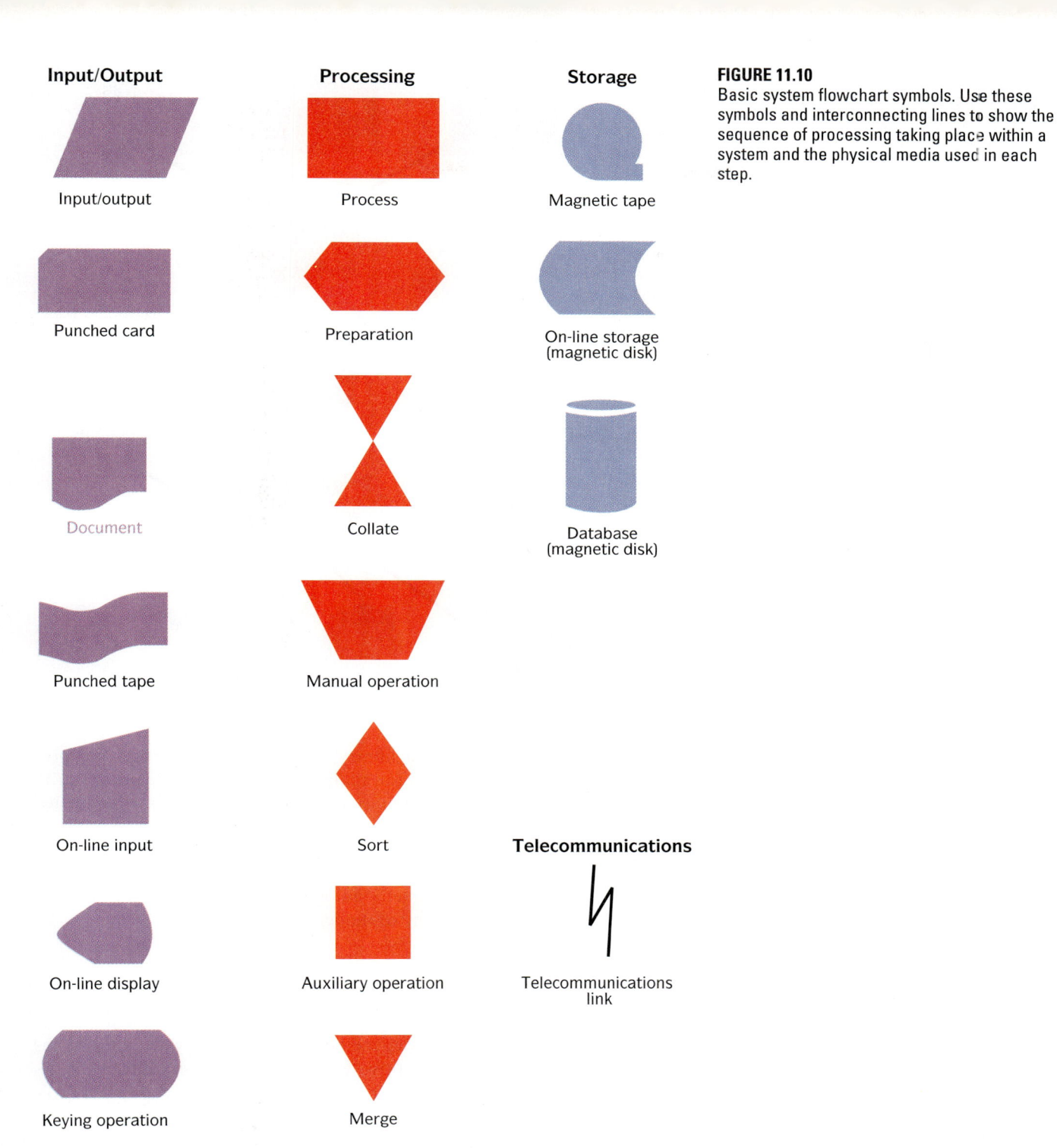

methodologies by shifting the focus from separately modeling business processes and data to combining data and procedures into unified objects. The system is viewed as a collection of classes and objects and relationships among them. The objects are defined, programmed, documented, and saved as building blocks for future applications.

Because objects are easily reusable, object-oriented software development directly addresses the issue of reusability and is expected to reduce the time and cost of writing software. Of course, no organization will see savings from reusability until it builds up

11.3 System-Building Methodologies

FIGURE 11.11
System flowchart for a payroll system. This is a high-level system flowchart for a batch payroll system. Only the most important processes and files are illustrated. Data are input from two sources: time cards and payroll-related data (such as salary increases) passed from the human resources system. The data are first edited and validated against the existing payroll master file before the payroll master is updated. The update process produces an updated payroll master file, various payroll reports (such as the payroll register and hours register), checks, a direct deposit tape, and a file of payment data that must be passed to the organization's general ledger system. The direct deposit tape is sent to the automated clearinghouse that serves the banks offering direct deposit services to employees.

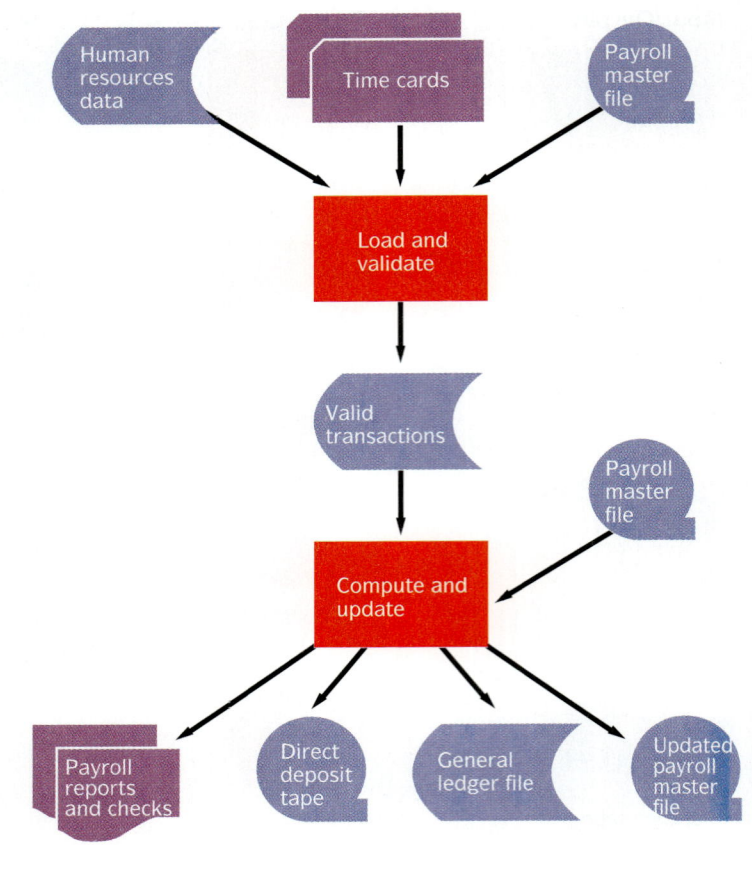

a library of objects to draw upon. Once a library of objects exists, design and programming often can begin without waiting for analysis documents (see Figure 11.12). In theory, design and programming can begin as soon as requirements are completed through the use of iterations of rapid prototyping.

Although the demand for training in object-oriented techniques and programming tools is exploding, object-oriented software development is still in its infancy. No agreed-upon object-oriented development methodology yet exists. Information systems specialists must learn a completely new way of modeling a system.

COMPUTER-AIDED SOFTWARE ENGINEERING (CASE)

computer-aided software engineering (CASE) The automation of step-by-step methodologies for software and systems development to reduce the amount of repetitive work the developer needs to do.

Computer-aided software engineering (CASE)—sometimes called *computer-aided systems engineering*—is the automation of step-by-step methodologies for software and systems development to reduce the amount of repetitive work the developer needs to do. Its adoption can free the developer for more creative problem-solving tasks. CASE tools also facilitate creation of clear documentation and the coordination of team development efforts. Team members can share their work more easily by accessing each other's files to review or modify what has been done. Systems developed with CASE and the newer methodologies have been found to be more reliable and require repairs less often (Dekleva, 1992). Many CASE tools are microcomputer based, with powerful graphical capabilities.

CASE tools provide automated graphics facilities for producing charts and diagrams, screen and report generators, data dictionaries, extensive reporting facilities, analysis and checking tools, code generators, and documentation generators. Most CASE tools are based on one or more of the popular structured methodologies. Some are starting to support object-oriented development. In general, CASE tools try to increase productivity and quality by doing the following:

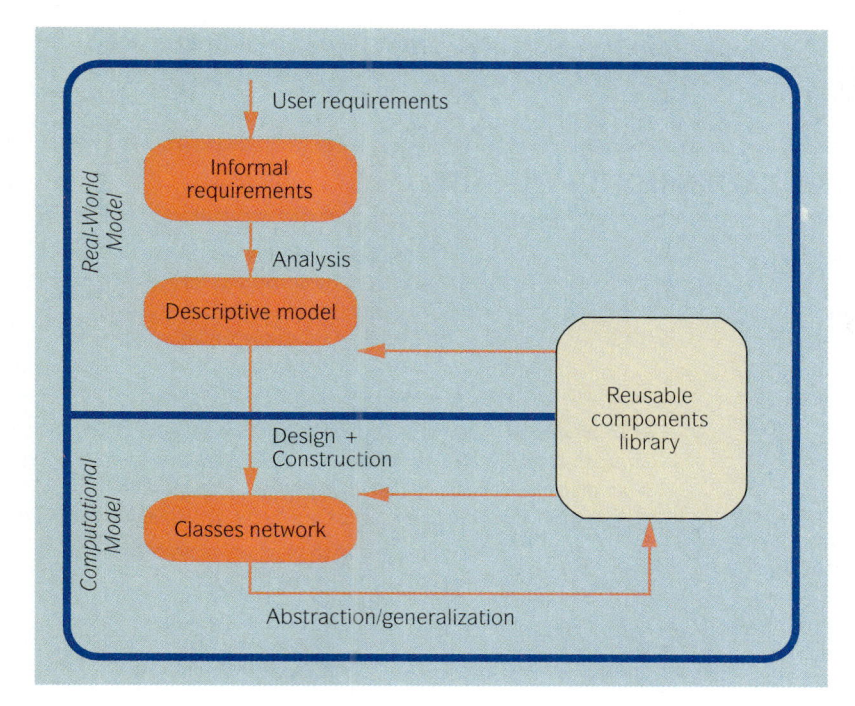

FIGURE 11.12
The object-oriented software lifecycle. *Source:* Jean-Marc Nerson, "Applying Object-Oriented Analysis and Design," Communications of the ACM *35(9): 64 (September 1992).*

- Enforce a standard development methodology and design discipline.
- Improve communication between users and technical specialists.
- Organize and correlate design components and provide rapid access to them via a design repository.
- Automate tedious and error-prone portions of analysis and design.
- Automate code generation, testing, and control rollout.

Case Tools

Many CASE tools have been classified in terms of whether they support activities at the front end or the back end of the systems development process. Front-end CASE tools focus on capturing analysis and design information in the early stages of systems development, whereas back-end CASE tools address coding, testing, and maintenance activities. Back-end tools help convert specifications automatically into program code.

The Window on Organizations shows how one company is using CASE tools to overhaul its World Wide Web site on the Internet.

CASE tools automatically tie data elements to the processes where they are used. If a data flow diagram is changed from one process to another, the elements in the data dictionary would be altered automatically to reflect the change in the diagram. CASE tools also contain features for validating design diagrams and specifications. CASE tools thus support iterative design by automating revisions and changes and providing prototyping facilities.

A CASE information repository stores all the information defined by the analysts during the project. The repository includes data flow diagrams, structure charts, entity-relationship diagrams (see Figure 11.13), data definitions, process specifications, screen and report formats, notes and comments, and test results.

The Challenge of Using CASE

To be used effectively, CASE tools require organizational discipline. Every member of a development project must adhere to a common set of naming conventions, standards, and development methodology. The best CASE tools enforce common methods and

Window on Organizations

AIR CANADA OVERHAULS ITS WEB SITE

Many airlines have set up shop on the Internet, creating World Wide Web sites where travellers can check flight schedules and review their frequent flyer points. Some are adding features to allow people to make reservations and purchase tickets through the Web. Air Canada felt that it was being left behind because its World Wide Web site could not do these things. So it embarked on an ambitious systems development project to make its Web site competitive with those of the larger airlines.

Air Canada's goal is to offer customers more ways of obtaining flight, frequent flier, and destination information. A key feature of its Web site overhaul will be the ability to make reservations on the Internet by linking the Web site to the company's internal databases. Air Canada engineers and systems development consultants are working on linking legacy applications developed with computer-aided software engineering (CASE) to the World Wide Web site so that reservation or frequent flyer information can be accessed or updated through the Web interface. The airline has used Texas Instrument's (TI) CASE tools for six years.

Most of the legacy applications that must be linked to the Web are mainframe-based. Texas Instruments has promised that the project can be completed "in days, not months or years." Although development time may be short, more time will be required to test and refine the new applications. While the Web site makeover is going on, Air Canada will periodically deactivate it to test and rework it. Ultimately, Air Canada would like its Web site to provide as many services to customers as its interactive telephone reservation system and provide them in a superior manner. According to Dan Ivanov, Air Canada's manager of information technology, voice applications are limited because customers "can't flip back and forth easily between menus." Those things are very easy using the graphical point-and-click World Wide Web.

On the other hand, Ivanov believes that the Web won't ever fully replace its traditional reservation system because the response time to place a reservation using the company's internal network is much faster. Ivanov also noted that Web-based ticketing and reservations are creating labor issues: Canadian travel agents are protesting plans to let Web customers bypass them for such services.

To Think About: How is use of the World Wide Web related to Air Canada's business strategy? How could CASE tools help in the effort to overhaul its Web site? What management, organization, and technology issues had to be addressed by the Web makeover project?

Source: Kim S. Nash, "Air Canada Says Web Is the Ticket," *Computerworld*, May 20, 1996.

---

standards, which may discourage their use in situations where organizational discipline is lacking.

CASE is not a magic cure-all. It does not enable systems to be designed automatically or ensure that business requirements are met. Systems designers still have to understand what a firm's business needs are and how the business works. Systems analysis and design are still dependent upon the analytical skills of the analyst/designer.

SOFTWARE REENGINEERING

software reengineering A methodology that addresses the problem of aging software by salvaging and upgrading it so that the users can avoid a long and expensive replacement project.

Software reengineering is a methodology that addresses the problem of aging software. A great deal of the software that organizations use was written without the benefit of a methodology such as structured analysis, design, and programming. Such software is difficult to maintain or update. However, the software serves the organization well enough to continue to be used, if only it could be more easily maintained. The purpose of software reengineering is to salvage such software by upgrading it so that users can avoid a long and expensive replacement project. In essence, developers use reengineering to extract design and programming intelligence from existing systems, thereby creating new systems without starting from scratch. Reengineering involves three steps: (1) reverse engineering, (2) revision of design and program specifications, and (3) forward engineering.

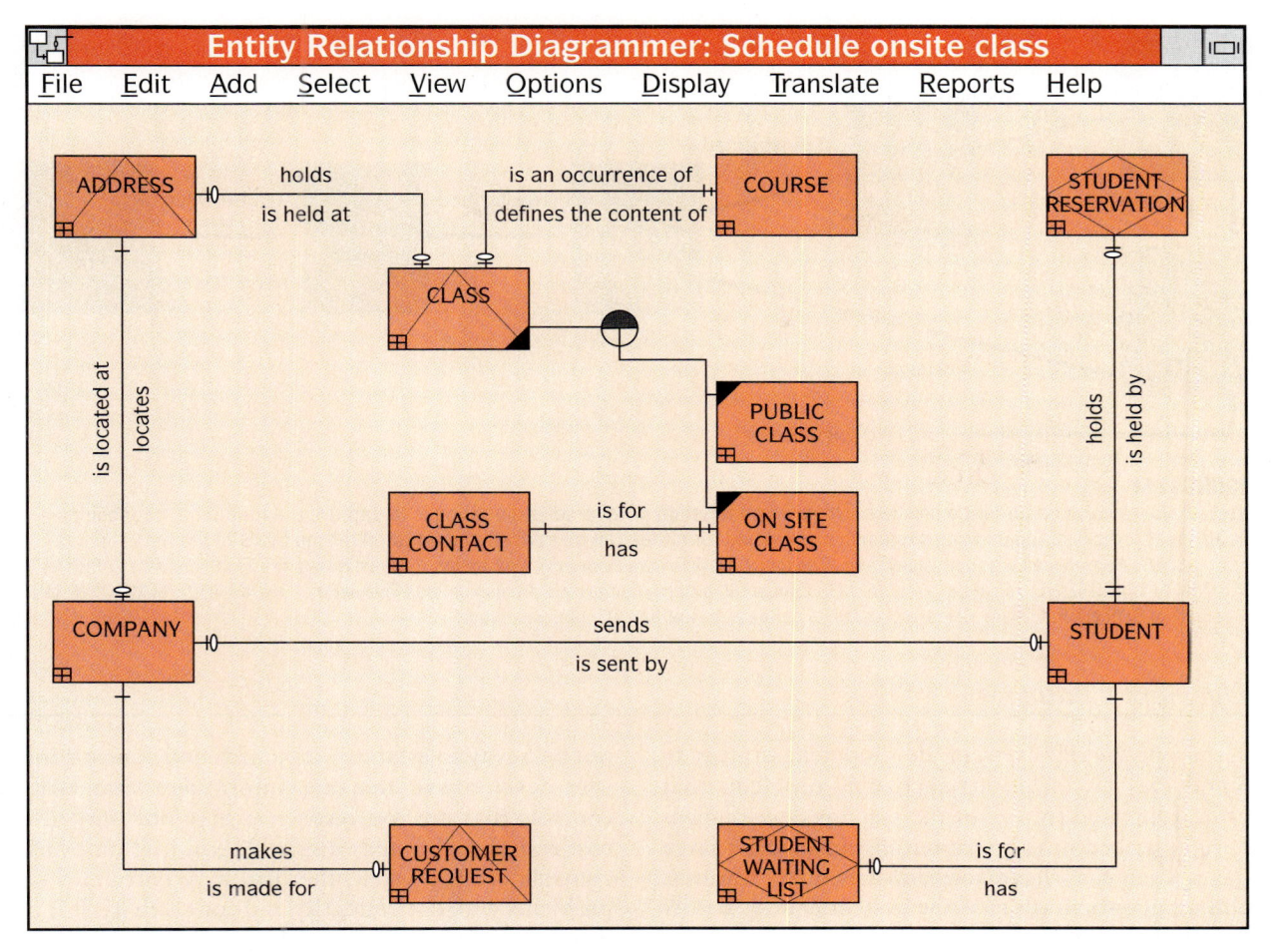

FIGURE 11.13
The entity relationship diagrammer in Sterling Software's KEY:Enterprise helps systems designers build a logical data model by documenting the types of entities found in an organization and how they relate. This CASE tool can display an entity-relationship diagram for the entire entity model or for a context-sensitive view. This figure, for example, displays only the entities and relationships relevant to the process of scheduling a class. *Reprinted by permission of Sterling Software, Inc.*

Reverse engineering entails extracting the underlying business specifications from existing systems. Older, nonstructured systems do not have structured documentation of the business functions the system is intended to support. Nor do they have adequate documentation of either the system design or the programs. Reverse engineering tools read and analyze the program's existing code, file, and database descriptions and produce structured documentation of the system. The output will show design-level components, such as entities, attributes, and processes. With structured documentation to work from, the project team can then revise the design and specifications to meet current business requirements. In the final step, **forward engineering**, the revised specifications are used to generate new, structured code for a structured and now maintainable system. In Figure 11.14, you can follow the reengineering process. Note that CASE tools can be used in the forward engineering step.

Although software reengineering can reduce system development and maintenance costs, it is a very complex undertaking. Additional research and analysis are usually required to determine all of the business rules and data requirements for the new system (Aiken, Muntz, and Richards, 1994).

reverse engineering The process of converting existing programs, files, and database descriptions into corresponding design-level components that can then be used to create new applications.

forward engineering The final step in reengineering when the revised specifications are used to generate new, structured program code for a structured and maintainable system.

11.3 System-Building Methodologies

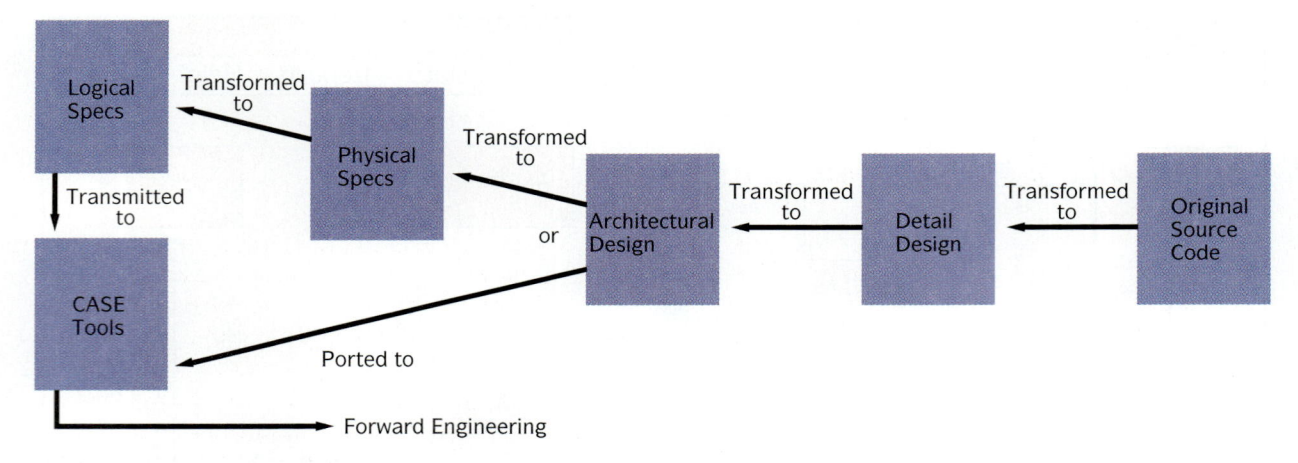

FIGURE 11.14
Steps in the reverse engineering process. The primary function of reverse engineering is to capture the functional capabilities—the process logic—of the existing system in a simplified form that can be revised and updated for the basis of the new replacement system. Reproduced with permission from *Thomas J. McCabe and Eldonna S. Williamson, "Tips on Reengineering Redundant Software,"* DATAMATION MAGAZINE, copyright, *April 15, 1992,* Cahners Publishing Company, a division of Reed Elsevier Inc. DATAMATION MAGAZINE is a trademark of Cahners Publishing Company, a division of Reed Elsevier Inc. All rights reserved."

Management Challenges

1. Determining the right systems development strategy to use. Sometimes organizations encounter problems that cannot be addressed by any of the systems development strategies described in this chapter. For instance, a large complex system may have some unstructured features. The ultimate configuration of the system cannot be decided beforehand because information requirements or the appropriate technology are uncertain. Alternatively, a proposed system calls for major organizational as well as technical changes. In such instances a firm may need to pursue a strategy of phased commitment in which systems projects are broken down into smaller portions and developed piece by piece in phases, or a firm may need to postpone the project altogether.

2. Controlling information systems development outside the information systems department. There may not be a way to establish standards and controls for end-user development that are appropriate. Standards and controls that are too restrictive may not only generate user resistance but may also stifle end-user innovation. If controls are too weak, the firm may encounter serious problems with data integrity and connectivity. It is not always possible to find the perfect balance.

3. Enforcing a standard methodology. Although structured methodologies have been available for twenty-five years, very few organizations have been able to enforce them. It is impossible to use CASE or object-oriented methods effectively unless all participants in system-building adopt a common development methodology as well as common development tools. Methodologies are organizational disciplines.

Summary

1. Distinguish between the various system-building alternatives: the traditional systems lifecycle, prototyping, application software packages, end-user development, and outsourcing. The traditional systems lifecycle—the oldest method for building systems—breaks the development of an information system into six formal stages: (1) project definition, (2) systems study, (3) design, (4) programming, (5) installation, and (6) post-implementation. The stages must proceed sequentially, have defined outputs, and require formal approval before the next stage can commence.

Prototyping consists of building an experimental system rapidly and inexpensively for end users to interact with and evaluate. The prototype is refined and enhanced until users are satisfied that it includes all of their requirements and can be used as a template to create the final system.

Developing an information system using an application software package eliminates the need for writing software programs when developing an information system. Using a software package cuts down on the amount of design, testing, installation, and maintenance work required to build a system.

End-user development is the development of information systems by end users, either alone or with minimal assistance from information systems specialists. End-user-developed systems can be created rapidly and informally using fourth-generation software tools.

Outsourcing consists of using an external vendor to build (or operate) a firm's information systems. The system may be custom-built or may use a software package. In either case, the work is done by the vendor rather than by the organization's internal information systems staff.

2. Understand the strengths and limitations of each approach. The traditional system lifecycle is still useful for large projects that need formal specifications and tight management control over each stage of system-building. However, the traditional method is very rigid and costly for developing a system, and is not well suited for unstructured, decision-oriented applications where requirements cannot be immediately visualized.

Prototyping encourages end-user involvement in systems development and iteration of design until specifications are captured accurately. The rapid creation of prototypes can result in systems that have not been completely tested or documented or that are technically inadequate for a production environment.

Application software packages are helpful if a firm does not have the internal information systems staff or financial resources to custom-develop a system. To meet an organization's unique requirements, packages may require extensive modifications that can substantially raise development costs. A package may not be a feasible solution if implementation necessitates extensive customization and changes in the organization's procedures.

The primary benefits of end-user development are improved requirements determination, reduced application backlog, and increased end-user participation in, and control of, the systems development process. However, end-user development, in conjunction with distributed computing, has introduced new organizational risks by propagating information systems and data resources that do not necessarily meet quality assurance standards and that are not easily controlled by traditional means.

Outsourcing can save application development costs or allow firms to develop applications without an internal information systems staff, but it can also make firms lose control over their information systems and make them too dependent on external vendors.

3. Describe the solutions to the management problems created by these approaches. Organizations can overcome some of the limitations of using software packages by performing a thorough requirements analysis and using rigorous package selection procedures to determine the extent to which a package will satisfy its requirements. The organization can customize the package or modify its procedures to ensure a better fit with the package.

Information centers help promote and control end-user development. They provide end users with appropriate hardware, software, and technical expertise to create their own applications and encourage adherence to application development standards. Organizations can also develop new policies and procedures concerning system development standards, training, data administration, and controls to manage end-user computing effectively.

Organizations can benefit from outsourcing by only outsourcing part of their information systems, by thoroughly understanding which information systems functions are appropriate to outsource, by designing outsourcing contracts carefully, and by trying to build a working partnership with the outsourcing vendor.

4. Describe the various tools and methodologies used for systems development. Structured analysis highlights the flow of data and the processes through which data are transformed. Its principal tool is the data flow diagram. Structured design and programming are software design disciplines that produce reliable, well-documented software with a simple, clear structure that is easy for others to understand and maintain. System flowcharts are useful for documenting the physical aspects of system design.

Computer-aided software engineering (CASE) automates methodologies for systems development. It promotes standards and improves coordination and consistency during systems development. CASE tools help system builders build a better model of a system and facilitate revision of design specifications to correct errors. Object-oriented software development is expected to reduce the time and cost of writing software and of making maintenance changes because it models a system as a series of reusable objects that combine both data and procedures. Software reengineering helps system builders reconfigure aging software to conform to structured design principles, making it easier to maintain.

Key Terms

Systems lifecycle	**End-user interface**	**Structured analysis**	**System flowcharts**
Project definition	**Application software**	**Data flow diagram (DFD)**	**Object-oriented software**
Systems study	**package**	**Process specifications**	**development**
Design	**Customization**	**Structured design**	**Computer-aided software**
Programming	**Request for Proposal (RFP)**	**Structure chart**	**engineering (CASE)**
Installation	**End-user development**	**Structured programming**	**Software reengineering**
Post-implementation	**Information center**	**Module**	**Reverse engineering**
Prototyping	**Outsourcing**	**Sequence construct**	**Forward engineering**
Prototype	**Development methodology**	**Selection construct**	
Iterative	**Structured**	**Iteration construct**	

Review Questions

1. What is the traditional systems lifecycle? Describe each of its steps.
2. What are the advantages and disadvantages of building an information system using the traditional systems lifecycle?
3. What do we mean by *information system prototyping*? What are its benefits and limitations?
4. List and describe the steps in the prototyping process.
5. What is an *application software package*? What are the advantages and disadvantages of developing information systems based on software packages?
6. What do we mean by *end-user development*? What are its advantages and disadvantages?
7. What is an *information center*? How can information centers solve some of the management problems created by end-user development?
8. Name some policies and procedures for managing end-user development.
9. What is *outsourcing*? Under what circumstances should it be used for building information systems?
10. What is *structured analysis*? What is the role of the data flow diagram in structured analysis?
11. What are the principles of structured design? How is it related to structured programming?
12. Describe the use of system flowcharts.
13. What is the difference between object-oriented software development and traditional structured methodologies?
14. What is *CASE*? How can it help system builders?
15. What are *software reengineering* and *reverse engineering*? How can they help system builders?

Discussion Questions

1. A widely-cited research report found that prototyping facilitated communication between users and information system designers but that designers who used prototyping had difficulty controlling and managing the design process. Discuss.
2. Some have said that the best way to avoid using professional programmers is to install an application software package. Discuss.
3. What theories describing the impact of information systems on organizations could be applied to describe outsourcing?

Group Project

With a group of your classmates, obtain product information or attend a demonstration for a microcomputer application software package such as DacEasy Accounting/Payroll, Quicken, Managing Your Money, or Microsoft Profit for Windows. Write an analysis of the strengths and limitations of the package you select. Present your findings to the class.

Case Study

CAN A GERMAN SOFTWARE GIANT PROVIDE CLIENT/SERVER SOLUTIONS?

SAP A.G., based in Walldorf, Germany, is Europe's largest vendor of software running on IBM mainframe computers and is an emerging leader in software packages for client/server environments. Among its clients are the Dow Chemical Company, E.I. du Pont de Nemours & Company, Chevron Corporation, Apple Computer, IBM, Intel, and the Exxon Corporation.

SAP sells integrated software applications for a wide range of business functions, including human resources, plant management, and manufacturing. The software modules are integrated so that they can automatically share data between them, and they have their own common database management system. The programs come in twelve different languages. Specific versions are tailored to accommodate different currencies, tax laws, and accounting practices. Managers can generate reports in their own local languages and currencies yet have the same reports generated in the language and currency that are used as the corporate standard by top management. SAP's R/2 System runs on IBM-compatible mainframes, and its R/3 system runs in a client/server environment.

Businesses appreciate the multinational flavor of the software, especially its ability to overcome language and currency barriers fluently and to connect divisions and operating units spread around the world. Marion Merrel Dow Inc. is using SAP software for its financial and sales-and-service departments because it believes that no other available packages can handle its global business needs.

Despite being a standard software package, SAP software can be customized by approximately 10 percent to handle multinational currencies and accounting practices. SAP makes this flexibility one of its key selling points. SAP has also benefited from two strategic moves. It developed R/3 to take advantage of open systems with client/server architecture, and it began promoting the package as a platform for business reengineering.

R/3 is an integrated, client/server, distributed system with a graphical user interface that runs on smaller and cheaper hardware than R/2. (R/2 runs on Siemens, IBM, and IBM-compatible mainframes; R/3 operates on a wide range of computers, including Unix-based machines, Power PC-enabled IBM AS/400 minicomputers, and other file servers.) The back-end server and front-end client portions of R/3 can run on a number of different operating systems, including five variations of UNIX, Digital Equipment Corporation's VAX/VMS operating system, and Hewlett-Packard's MPE operating system. Versions for OS/2, Windows NT, and other operating systems have been developed as well. R/3 offers a number of options for its graphical user interface: Presentation Manager under OS/2, Motif under UNIX, and Microsoft Windows.

The R/3 package includes integrated financial accounting, production planning, sales and distribution, cost-center accounting, order-costing, materials management, human resources, quality assurance, fixed assets management, plant maintenance, and project planning applications. Users do not have to shut down one application to move to another; they can just click on a menu choice. R/3 also provides word processing, filing systems, e-mail, and other office support functions.

R/3 can be configured to run on a single hardware platform, or it can be partitioned to run on separate machines (in whatever combination users choose) in order to minimize network traffic and place data where users need it the most. For instance, a firm could put the data used most frequently by its accounting department on a file server located close to the accounting department to minimize network traffic. A central data dictionary keeps track of data and its location to maintain the integrity of distributed data. SAP will sell clients a blueprint of R/3's information, data, and function models and software tools to facilitate custom development and integration of existing applications into R/3.

The management of SAP America, Inc. (the Lester, Pennsylvania, subsidiary of SAP A.G.), thinks that the most important feature of R/3 may be the way it helps organizations automate their business processes. By adopting the system design offered by the package, companies can evaluate and streamline their business processes. The promise of reengineering was what initially attracted the Eastman Kodak Company to SAP software. Kodak launched a pilot project in 1991 that installed SAP programs to redefine the job of order taking. The SAP package lets order takers make immediate decisions about granting customers credit and lets them access production data on-line so that they can tell customers exactly when their orders will be available for shipment. The project resulted in a 70-percent reduction in the amount of time it took to deliver products; response time to customers was also cut in half. These results prompted Kodak to use SAP software as the global architecture for all of its core systems.

The intricate and sophisticated features of SAP software deeply affect the infrastructure of a corporation. Installing SAP's fully integrated suite of software modules with all the business alterations required is a complex process with many interdependent options, which can overwhelm smaller firms lacking the resources of top-tier large corporations.

Unfortunately, SAP has lagged in product support. SAP has a large internal staff to support its software packages, but it also uses legions of consultants from large consulting firms such as Price Waterhouse, Andersen Consulting, EDS Corporation, and Coopers & Lybrand as well as smaller consulting firms. These external consultants work with SAP clients to install the SAP packages. Because SAP is growing so fast, there is a worldwide shortage of SAP experts with experience implementing R/3. The Gartner Group, a Stamford, Connecticut, research firm, estimates that there are 18,000 R/3 consultants and integrators worldwide, but only 500 have worked on more than two R/3 implementations from start to finish.

One reason for the shortage of experienced SAP consultants is that it can take years for even experienced technologists to understand all of the complexities and methodologies of SAP software. It takes about three years, or two or three installations of the package, before a consultant becomes an expert in the software. (R/3 was built with SAP's own internally-developed programming language called *Abap*. Users need to work with Abap to modify or extend the SAP software package.) SAP pairs one or more of its seasoned eight- to ten-year German veterans with less experienced U.S. consultants at each installation. But according to Greg Staszko, a partner at the Cincinnati branch of Deloitte & Touche (a leading accounting and consulting firm), the SAP experts tend to be troubleshooters or product experts, rather than business consultants, so clients do not necessarily get the best advice on how to integrate the software into their business operations most efficiently and painlessly. The perception remains among some U.S. companies that even an on-site SAP expert who knows the financial accounting module cannot correct a bug in the sales and distribution module.

To augment the ranks of qualified consultants, SAP built a world training headquarters in Walldorf, costing an estimated $50 to $60 million. It recruited more consultants by signing agreements with new consulting firms, such as Cap Gemini America and Coopers & Lybrand, and de-emphasized its relationship with firms such as Computer Sciences Corporation and KPMG Peat Marwick, which it felt have not worked out well. Other product support includes using Intel Corporation's ProShare videoconferencing software to provide customers with face-to-face advice and inviting customers to send project teams to SAP for training prior to implementation. ■

Sources: Emily Kay, "Desperately Seeking SAP Support," *Datamation*, February 15, 1996; Rosemary Cafasso, "SAP American Plans Improvements for R/3 Package," *Computerworld*, June 6, 1994; Doug Bartholomew, "SAP America: R/3 + R/3 = ?," *Information Week,* January 10, 1994; and "An American Beachhead," *Information Week*, March 9, 1992; and Mike Ricciuti and J. William Semich, "SAP's Client/Server Battle Plan," *Datamation*, March 15, 1993.

Case Study Questions

1. What advantages and disadvantages of application software packages are illustrated by SAP?
2. Analyze the specific strengths and weaknesses of SAP software packages.
3. If you were the manager of a corporation looking for new business application software, would you choose SAP? Would you choose another package? Why or why not? What management, organization, and technology factors would you consider?

References

Ahituv, Niv and Seev Neumann. "A Flexible Approach to Information System Development." *MIS Quarterly* (June 1984).

Aiken, Peter, Alice Muntz, and Russ Richards. "DOD Legacy Systems: Reverse Engineering Data Requirements." *Communications of the ACM* 37, no. 5 (May 1994).

Alavi, Maryam. "An Assessment of the Prototyping Approach to Information System Development." *Communications of the ACM* 27 (June 1984).

Alavi, Maryam, R. Ryan Nelson, and Ira R. Weiss. "Strategies for End-User Computing: An Integrative Framework." *Journal of Management Information Systems* 4, no. 3 (Winter 1987–88).

Anderson, Evan A. "Choice Models for the Evaluation and Selection of Software Packages." *Journal of Management Information Systems* 6, no.4 (Spring 1990).

Arthur, Lowell Jay. "Quick and Dirty." *Computerworld* (December 14, 1992).

Bersoff, Edward H. and Alan M. Davis. "Impacts of Life Cycle Models on Software Configuration Management." *Communications of the ACM* 34, no. 8, August 1991.

Blum, Bruce I. "A Taxonomy of Software Development Methods." *Communications of the ACM* 37, no. 11 (November 1994).

Booch, Grady. *Object Oriented Design with Applications*. Redwood City, California: Benjamin Cummings (1991).

Caldwell, Bruce. "Blue Cross, in Intensive Care, Beeps EDS." *Information Week* (January 27, 1992).

Carr, Houston H. "Information Centers: The IBM Model vs. Practice." *MIS Quarterly* (September 1987).

Cerveny, Robert P., Edward J. Garrity, and G. Lawrence Sanders. "The Application of Prototyping to Systems Development: A Rationale and Model." *Journal of Management Information Systems* 3 (Fall 1986).

Christoff, Kurt A. "Building a Fourth-Generation Environment." *Datamation* (September 1985).

Clermont, Paul. "Outsourcing Without Guilt." *Computerworld* (September 9, 1991).

Coad, Peter, with Edward Yourdon. *Object-Oriented Analysis*. Englewood Cliffs, NJ: Prentice-Hall (1989).

Cotterman, William W., and Kuldeep Kumar. "User Cube: A Taxonomy of End Users." *Communications of the ACM* 32, no. 11 (November 1989).

Davis, Sid A., and Robert P. Bostrum. "Training End Users: An Experimental Investigation of the Role of the Computer Interface and Training Methods." *MIS Quarterly* 17, no. 1 (March 1993).

Dekleva, Sasa M. "The Influence of Information Systems Development Approach on Maintenance." *MIS Quarterly* 16, no. 3 (September 1992).

DeMarco, Tom. *Structured Analysis and System Specification*. New York: Yourdon Press (1978).

Dijkstra, E. "Structured Programming," in *Classics in Software Engineering,* ed. Edward Nash Yourdon. New York: Yourdon Press (1979).

Earl, Michael J. "The Risks of Outsourcing IT." *Sloan Management Review* (Spring 1996).

Flatten, Per O., Donald J. McCubbrey, P. Declan O'Riordan, and Keith Burgess. *Foundations of Business Systems*, 2nd ed. Fort Worth, TX: The Dryden Press (1992).

Fraser, Martin D., Kuldeep Kumar, and Vijay K. Vaishnavi. "Strategies for Incorporating Formal Specifications in Software Development." *Communications of the ACM* 37, no. 10 (October 1994).

Fuller, Mary K., and E. Burton Swanson. "Information Centers as Organizational Innovation." *Journal of Management Information Systems* 9, no. 1 (Summer 1992).

Gane, Chris, and Trish Sarson. *Structured Systems Analysis: Tools and Techniques*. Englewood Cliffs, NJ: Prentice-Hall (1979).

Gould, John D., and Clayton Lewis. "Designing for Usability: Key Principles and What Designers Think." *Communications of the ACM* 28 (March 1985).

Grant, F.J. "The Downside of 4GLs." *Datamation* (July 1985).

Green, Jesse. "Productivity in the Fourth Generation." *Journal of Management Information Systems* 1 (Winter 1984–85).

Harel, Elie C., and Ephraim R. McLean. "The Effects of Using a Nonprocedural Computer Language on Programmer Productivity." *MIS Quarterly* (June 1985).

Harrison, Allison W., and R. Kelly Rainer, Jr. "The Influence of Individual Differences on Skill in End-User Computing." *Journal of Management Information Systems* 9, no. 1 (Summer 1992).

Henderson-Sellers, Brian, and Julian M. Edwards. "The Object-Oriented Systems Life Cycle." *Communications of the ACM* 33, no. 9 (September 1990).

Holtzblatt, Laren and Hugh Beyer. "Making Customer-Centered Design Work for Teams." *Communications of the ACM* 36, no. 10 (October 1993).

Huff, Sid L., Malcolm C. Munro, and Barbara H. Martin. "Growth Stages of End User Computing." *Communications of the ACM* 31, no. 5 (May 1988).

Janson, Marius, and L. Douglas Smith. "Prototyping for Systems Development: A Critical Appraisal." *MIS Quarterly* 9 (December 1985).

Jenkins, A. Milton. "Prototyping: A Methodology for the Design and Development of Application Systems." *Spectrum* 2 (April 1985).

Johnson, Richard T. "The Infocenter Experiences." *Datamation* (January 1984).

Jones, T.C. "The Limits of Programming Productivity." Guide and Share Application Development Symposium, Proceedings. New York: Share 1979.

Korson, Tim, and McGregor, John D. "Understanding Object Oriented: A Unifying Paradigm." *Communications of the ACM* 33, no. 9 (September 1990).

Kozar, Kenneth A., and John M. Mahlum. "A User-Generated Information System: An Innovative Development Approach." *MIS Quarterly* (June 1987).

Kraushaar, James M., and Larry E. Shirland. "A Prototyping Method for Applications Development by End Users and Information Systems Specialists." *MIS Quarterly* (September 1985).

Lacity, Mary C., Leslie P. Willcocks, and David Feeny. "The Value of Selective IT Outsourcing." *Sloan Management Review* (Spring 1996).

Livingston, Dennis. "Outsourcing: Look Beyond the Price Tag." *Datamation* (November 15, 1992).

Loh, Lawrence, and N. Venkatraman. "Determinants of Information Technology Outsourcing." *Journal of Management Information Systems* 9, no. 1 (Summer 1992).

Loh, Lawrence, and N. Venkatraman. "Diffusion of Information Technology Outsourcing: Influence Sources and the Kodak Effect." *Information Systems Research* 3, no. 4 (December 1992).

Livingston, Dennis. "Outsourcing: Look Beyond the Price Tag." *Datamation* (November 15, 1992).

Lucas, Henry C., Eric J. Walton, and Michael J. Ginzberg. "Implementing Packaged Software." *MIS Quarterly* (December 1988).

Madsen, Kim Halskov, and Peter H. Aiken. "Experience Using Cooperative Interactive Storyboard Prototyping." *Communications of the ACM* 36, no. 4 (June 1993).

Martin, James. *Application Development without Programmers.* Englewood Cliffs, NJ: Prentice-Hall (1982).

Martin, J., and C. McClure. "Buying Software Off the Rack." *Harvard Business Review* (November–December 1983).

Martin, James, and Carma McClure. *Structured Techniques: The Basis of CASE.* Englewood Cliffs, NJ: Prentice-Hall (1988).

Mason, R.E.A., and T.T. Carey. "Prototyping Interactive Information Systems." *Communications of the ACM* 26 (May 1983).

Matos, Victor M., and Paul J. Jalics. "An Experimental Analysis of the Performance of Fourth-Generation Tools on PCs." *Communications of the ACM* 32, no. 11 (November 1989).

Mazzucchelli, Louis. "Structured Analysis Can Streamline Software Design." *Computerworld* (December 9, 1985).

McIntyre, Scott C., and Lexis F. Higgins, "Object-Oriented Analysis and Design: Methodology and Application." *Journal of Management Information Systems* 5, no. 1 (Summer 1988).

McMullen, John. "Developing a Role for End Users." *Information Week* (June 15, 1992).

Moran, Robert. "The Case Against CASE." *Information Week* (February 17, 1992).

Nerson, Jean-Marc. "Applying Object-Oriented Analysis and Design." *Communications of the ACM* 35, no. 9 (September 1992).

Norman, Ronald J., and Jay F. Nunamaker, Jr., "CASE Productivity Perceptions of Software Engineering Professionals." *Communications of the ACM* 32, no. 9 (September 1989).

Rivard, Suzanne, and Sid L. Huff. "Factors of Success for End-User Computing." *Communications of the ACM* 31, no. 5 (May 1988).

Roche, Edward M. *Managing Information Technology in Multinational Corporations.* New York: Macmillan Publishing Company, 1992.

Rockart, John F., and Lauren S. Flannery. "The Management of End-User Computing." *Communications of the ACM* 26, no. 10 (October 1983).

Schatz, Willie. "Bailoutsourcing." *Computerworld* (January 25, 1993).

Timmreck, Eric M. "Performance Measurement: Vendor Specifications and Benchmarks." In *The Information Systems Handbook*, ed. F. Warren McFarlan and Richard C. Nolan. Homewood, IL: Dow-Jones-Richard D. Irwin, 1975.

Trauth, Eileen M., and Elliot Cole. "The Organizational Interface: A Method for Supporting End Users of Packaged Software." *MIS Quarterly* 16, no. 1 (March 1992).

White, Clinton E., and David P. Christy. "The Information Center Concept: A Normative Model and a Study of Six Installations." *MIS Quarterly* (December 1987).

Willis, T. Hillman, and Debbie B. Tesch. "An Assessment of Systems Development Methodologies." *Journal of Information Technology Management* 2, no. 2 (1991).

Vessey, Iris, and Sue A. Conger. "Requirements Specification: Learning Object, Process, and Data Methodologies." *Communications of the ACM* 37, no. 5 (May 1994).

Yourdon, Edward, and L.L. Constantine, *Structured Design.* New York: Yourdon Press (1978).

Zahniser, Richard A. "Design by Walking Around." *Communications of the ACM* 36, no. 10 (October 1993).

Chapter 12

Managing Knowledge

The Electronic Hospital

12.1 Knowledge Management in the Organization
Information Systems and Knowledge Management
Knowledge Work and Productivity

12.2 Information and Knowledge Work Systems
Distributing Knowledge: Office Information Systems
Creating Knowledge: Knowledge Work Systems
Window on Technology
Flying High with CAD
Sharing Knowledge: Group Collaboration Systems
Group Collaboration Via the Internet

12.3 Artificial Intelligence
What Is Artificial Intelligence?
Why Business Is Interested in Artificial Intelligence
Capturing Knowledge: Expert Systems
Organizational Intelligence: Case-Based Reasoning
Window on Management
Enabling Reuse of Designs Through Artificial Intelligence

12.4 Other Intelligent Techniques
Neural Networks

Window on Organizations
The Neural Network Approach to Stock Picking
Fuzzy Logic
Genetic Algorithms

Management Challenges
Summary
Key Terms
Review Questions
Discussion Questions
Group Project
Case Study: Designing the Paperless Airplane
References

The Electronic Hospital

A massive amount of new medical information is constantly being generated, and doctors need access to this information to provide quality medical care. More and more, medical professionals are turning to on-line medical databases to diagnose unusual and unfamiliar symptoms. Collins Kellogg, an internist in Watertown, New York, was baffled when one of his patients turned deep red on one side of his body and chalk white on the other whenever he exercised. Using an on-line medical database, Dr. Kellogg quickly identified the problem as Harlequin's syndrome, a rare nervous disorder that can be cured by a neurosurgeon.

These databases enable doctors to keep up with the enormous amount of new medical research that is being published daily. William Tierney, professor of medicine at Indiana University School of Medicine, consulted the popular Medline database when a woman was admitted to the school hospital with an inflamed and severely painful pancreas but showing none of the normal causes for this condition. Triggering a search with key words that included *pancreas* as well as the name of a new arthritis drug she was taking, English-language abstracts of two Japanese and two French medical journal articles were identified that reported a link between the drug and the inflammation. Dr. Tierney removed the woman from the drug and she quickly improved. Not only did the search take only a few minutes, but Dr. Tierney would not have been able to find these articles in any other way both because of the language problem and the impossibility of an individual keeping up with the 3700 journals that are stored in the Medline database. Aside from identifying rare conditions, the use of these databases has resulted in a reduction of unnecessary procedures and so a lowering of hospital costs and a shortening of hospital stays. In addition to general medical databases like Medline, a number of databases now exist that focus on such specialties as cancer, AIDS, and medical ethics.

Television and telecommunications technologies have combined to improve medical care while reducing costs by bringing medical expertise back into the home and into other places where medical knowledge is required. Through the growth of telemedicine, doctors are able to see patients in their home without ever leaving the hospital. The Emory University Health Communications Project has developed a point-to-point video system known as Picasso that enables doctors to examine patients remotely. The system uses a television camera, computer software, and telecommunications transmission to send pictures from the patient to a doctor waiting in the hospital. Picasso systems cost only $5000 and a portable version in an oversized briefcase runs about $11,000. With such equipment, paramedics can actually do house calls rather than just rush the patient to the hospital for treatment. Not only does this save the time of the doctor, but studies have shown that 85 percent of patients transported to a hospital by paramedics do not actually need hospitalization at that time, so Picasso is reducing unneeded hospitalization and patient inconvenience as well. ■

Sources: Michael Fitzgerald, "Pictures Tell the Story to Atlanta Doctors," *Computerworld*, September 26, 1994; Fred Guterl, "The Doctor Will See You Now—Just Not in Person," *Business Week*, October 3, 1994; and Ron Winslow, "More Doctors Are Adding On-Line Tools to Their Kits," *The Wall Street Journal*, October 7, 1994.

Collaborating and communicating with other experts and sharing ideas and information are essential requirements not only for medical institutions, but for businesses today as well. In an information economy, capturing and distributing intelligence and knowledge and enhancing group collaboration have become vital to organizational innovation and survival.

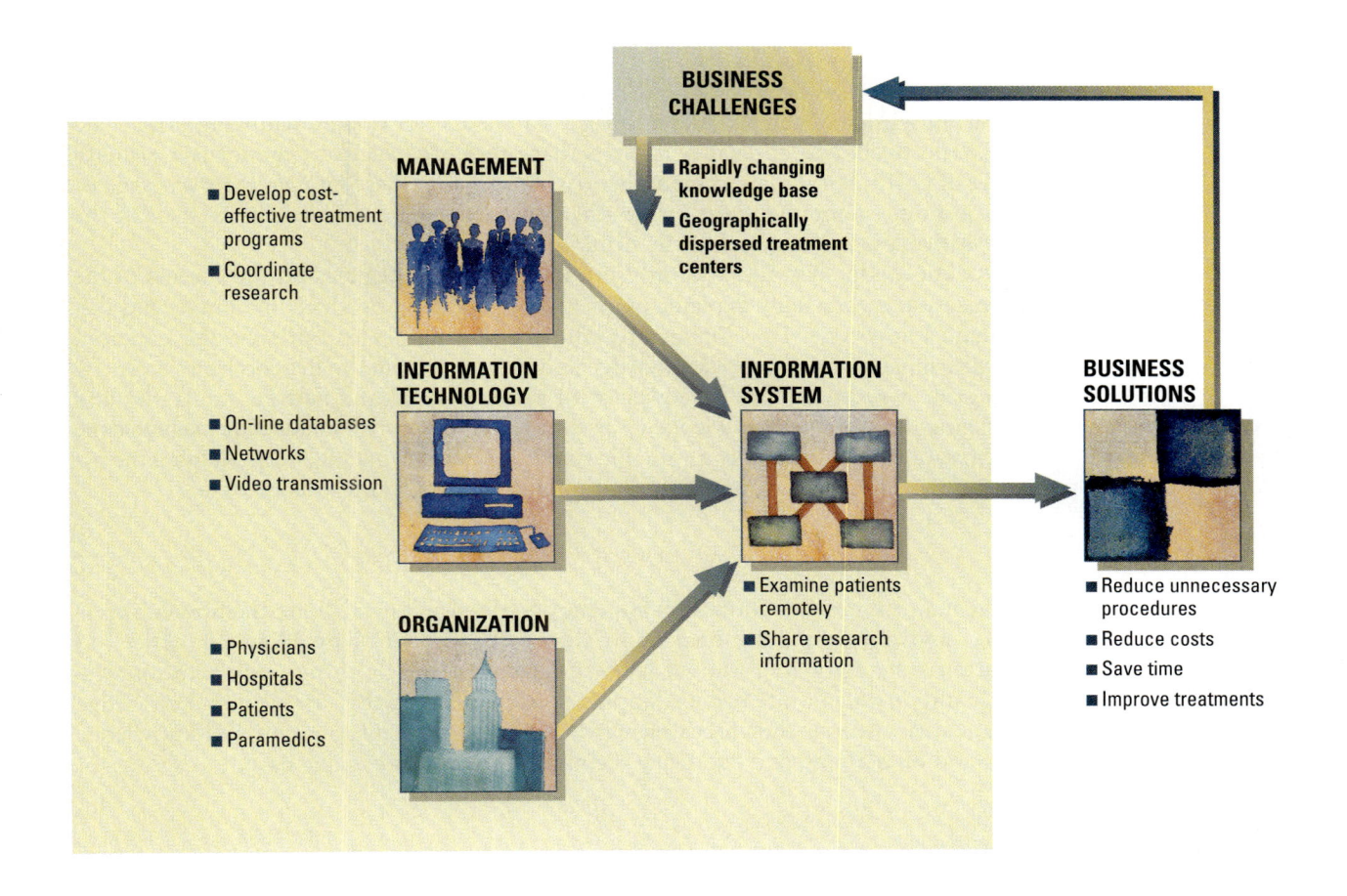

BUSINESS CHALLENGES
- Rapidly changing knowledge base
- Geographically dispersed treatment centers

MANAGEMENT
- Develop cost-effective treatment programs
- Coordinate research

INFORMATION TECHNOLOGY
- On-line databases
- Networks
- Video transmission

ORGANIZATION
- Physicians
- Hospitals
- Patients
- Paramedics

INFORMATION SYSTEM
- Examine patients remotely
- Share research information

BUSINESS SOLUTIONS
- Reduce unnecessary procedures
- Reduce costs
- Save time
- Improve treatments

This chapter examines information system applications specifically designed to help organizations achieve these goals. First, we examine information systems for supporting information and knowledge work. Then we look at the ways that organizations can use artificial intelligence technologies for capturing and storing knowledge and expertise.

> **Learning Objectives**
>
> *After completing this chapter, you will be able to:*
>
> 1. Explain the importance of knowledge management in contemporary organizations.
> 2. Describe the applications that are most useful for distributing, creating, and sharing knowledge in the firm.
> 3. Define artificial intelligence.
> 4. Explain how organizations can use expert systems and case-based reasoning to capture knowledge.
> 5. Describe how organizations can use neural networks and other intelligent techniques to improve their knowledge base.

12.1 KNOWLEDGE MANAGEMENT IN THE ORGANIZATION

Chapter 1 described the emergence of the information economy, in which the major source of wealth and prosperity is the production and distribution of information and knowledge. For example, 70 percent of the U.S. labor force now consists of knowledge and information workers, and 75 percent of the gross domestic product of the United States comes from the knowledge and information sectors, such as finance and publishing. Knowledge-intensive technology is vital to these information-intense sectors but also plays a major role in more traditional industrial sectors such as the automobile and mining industries.

In an information economy, knowledge and core competencies—the two or three things that an organization does best—are key organizational assets. Producing unique products or services or producing them at lower cost than competitors is based on superior knowledge of the production process and superior design. Knowing how to do things effectively and efficiently in ways that other organizations cannot is a primary source of profit. Some management theorists believe that these *knowledge assets* are just as important—if not more important—than physical and financial assets in ensuring the competitiveness and survival of the firm.

As knowledge becomes a central productive and strategic asset, the success of the organization increasingly depends on its ability to gather, produce, maintain, and disseminate knowledge. Developing procedures and routines to optimize the creation, flow, learning, and sharing of knowledge and information in the firm becomes a central management responsibility. The process of systematically and actively managing and leveraging the stores of knowledge in an organization is called **knowledge management**. Information systems can play a valuable role in knowledge management, helping the organization optimize its flow of information and capture its knowledge base.

knowledge management The process of systematically and actively managing and leveraging the stores of knowledge in an organization.

INFORMATION SYSTEMS AND KNOWLEDGE MANAGEMENT

All the major types of information systems described so far facilitate the flow of information and have organizational knowledge embedded in them. However, office automation systems (OAS), knowledge work systems (KWS), group collaboration systems, and artificial intelligence applications are especially useful for knowledge management because they focus primarily on supporting information and knowledge work and on defining and capturing the organization's knowledge base.

Figure 12.1 illustrates the array of information systems specifically designed to support knowledge management. Office automation systems (OAS) help disseminate and coordinate the flow of information in the organization. Knowledge work systems (KWS) support the activities of highly skilled knowledge workers and professionals as they create new knowledge and try to integrate it into the firm. Group collaboration and support systems support the creation and sharing of knowledge among people working in groups. Artificial intelligence systems provide organizations and managers with codified knowledge that can be reused by others in the organization.

KNOWLEDGE WORK AND PRODUCTIVITY

In information economies, organizational productivity depends on increasing the productivity of information and knowledge workers. Consequently, companies have made massive investments in information technology to support information work. (Since 1989 more than 50 percent of all capital investment in the United States has been for information technology, with most of that information technology investment going directly into offices.) Office automation and professional work systems have been the fastest-growing information system applications for over a decade.

Although information technology has increased productivity in manufacturing, the extent to which computers have enhanced the productivity of information workers is under debate. Some studies show that investment in information technology has not led to any appreciable growth in productivity among office workers and that the average white-collar productivity gain from 1980 to 1990 has only been 0.28 percent annually (Roach, 1988). Other studies suggest that information technology investments are starting to generate a productivity payback (Brynjolfsson and Hitt, 1993). It is too early to tell whether these gains are short-term or represent a genuine turnaround in service sector productivity.

Productivity changes among information workers are difficult to measure because of the problems of identifying suitable units of output for information work (Panko, 1991). How does one measure the output of a law office? Should one measure productivity by examining the number of forms completed per employee (a measure of physical unit productivity), or by examining the amount of revenue produced per employee (a measure of financial unit productivity) in an information- and knowledge-intense industry?

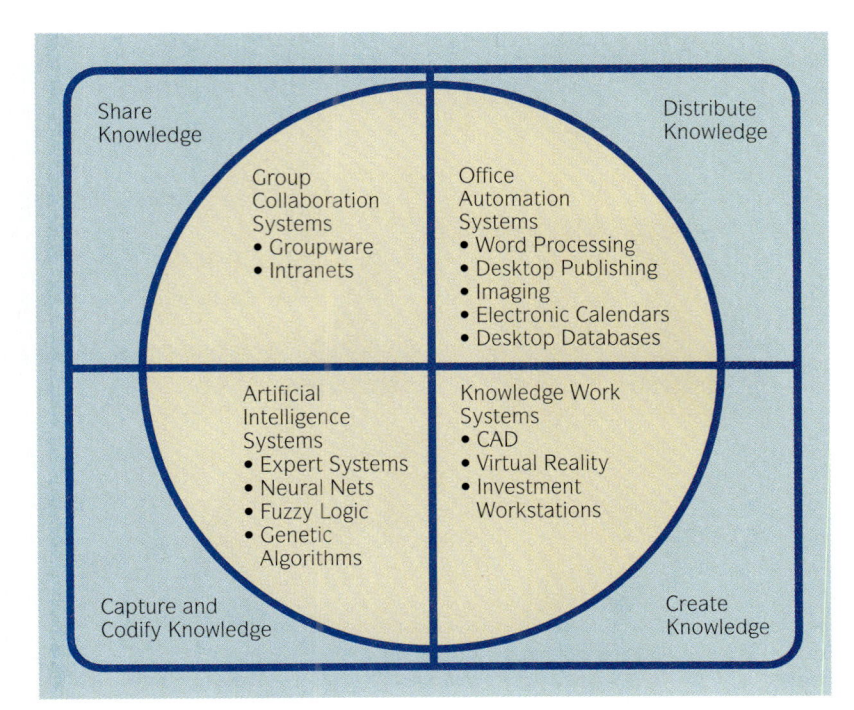

FIGURE 12.1
A number of contemporary information systems are designed to give close-in support to information workers at many levels in the organization.

Introduction of information technology doesn't automatically guarantee productivity. Desktop computers, e-mail, and fax applications can actually generate more drafts, memos, spreadsheets, and messages—*increasing* bureaucratic red tape and paperwork. Firms are more likely to produce high returns on information technology investments if they rethink their procedures, processes, and business goals.

12.2 INFORMATION AND KNOWLEDGE WORK SYSTEMS

information work Work that primarily consists of creating or processing information.

data workers People such as secretaries or bookkeepers who primarily process and disseminate the organization's paperwork.

knowledge workers People such as engineers, scientists, or architects who design products or services or create new knowledge for the organization.

Information work is work that consists primarily of creating or processing information. It is carried out by information workers who are usually divided into two subcategories: **data workers,** who primarily process and disseminate information; and **knowledge workers,** who primarily create new knowledge and information.

Examples of data workers include secretaries, sales personnel, accountants, and draftsmen. Researchers, designers, architects, writers, and judges are examples of knowledge workers. Data workers can usually be distinguished from knowledge workers because knowledge workers usually have higher levels of education and membership in professional organizations. In addition, knowledge workers exercise independent judgment as a routine aspect of their work. Data and knowledge workers have different information requirements and different systems to support them.

DISTRIBUTING KNOWLEDGE: OFFICE INFORMATION SYSTEMS

Most data work and a great deal of knowledge work takes place in offices, including most of the work done by managers. The office plays a major role in coordinating the flow of information throughout the entire organization. The office has three basic functions (see Figure 12.2):

- Managing and coordinating the work of data and knowledge workers
- Connecting the work of the local information workers with all levels and functions of the whole organization
- Connecting the organization to the external world, including customers, suppliers, government regulators, and external auditors

Office workers span a very broad range of workers—professionals, managers, sales, and clerical workers working alone or in groups. Their major activities include the following:

FIGURE 12.2
The three major roles of offices. Offices perform three major roles. [1] They coordinate the work of local professionals and information workers. [2] They coordinate work in the organization across levels and functions. [3] They couple the organization to the external environment.

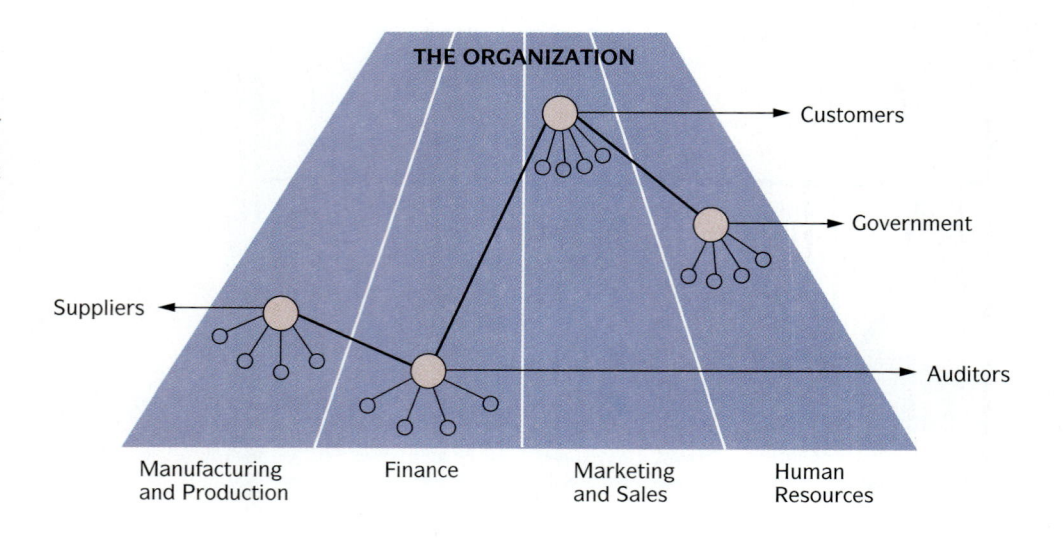

- Managing documents, including document creation, storage, retrieval, and dissemination
- Scheduling, for both individuals and groups
- Communicating, including initiating, receiving, and managing voice, digital, and document-based communications for both individuals and groups
- Managing data, such as on employees, customers, and vendors

These activities can be supported by office automation systems (see Table 12.1). **Office automation systems (OAS)** can be defined as any application of information technology that intends to increase productivity of information workers in the office. Fifteen years ago *office automation* meant only the creation, processing, and management of documents. Today professional knowledge and information work remains highly document-centered. However, digital image processing—words and documents—is also at the core of today's systems, as are high-speed digital communications services. Because office work involves many people jointly engaged in projects, contemporary office automation systems have powerful group assistance tools like networked digital calendars. An ideal contemporary office automation system would involve a seamless network of digital machines linking professional, clerical, and managerial work groups and running a variety of types of software.

While word processing and desktop publishing address the creation and presentation of documents, they only exacerbate the existing paper avalanche problem. For instance, Ultramar Oil, a Long Beach, California, oil refinery, maintains about 20,000 material safety data sheets in huge notebooks; if an emergency chemical spill occurs, employees must manually search these notebooks for the appropriate sheet or sheets that contain the life-saving and damage-control information they urgently need. Work-flow problems arising from paper handling are enormous.

One way to reduce problems stemming from paper-based work-flow is to employ document imaging systems. **Document imaging systems** are systems that convert documents and images into digital form so that they can be stored and accessed by the computer. Such systems store, retrieve, and manipulate a digitized image of a document, allowing the document itself to be discarded. The system must contain a scanner that converts the document image into a bit-mapped image, storing that image as a graphic. With imaging systems the document will originally be stored on a magnetic disk, where it can be retrieved instantly. When it ceases to be active, it will be transferred to an optical disk, where it will be stored for as many months or years as is needed. Optical disks, kept on-line in a **jukebox** (a device for storing and retrieving many optical disks) require up to a minute to retrieve the document automatically. A typical large jukebox will hold more than 10,000,000 pages (an 8 1/2" × 11" document usually requires about 50 kilobytes of storage after data compression).

An imaging system also requires an **index server** to contain the indexes that will allow users to identify and retrieve the document when needed. Once the document has been scanned, index data are entered so that the document can be retrieved in a variety of ways, depending upon the application. For example, the index may contain the

office automation systems (OAS) Computer systems, such as word processing, voice-mail systems, and video conferencing systems, that are designed to increase the productivity of information workers in the office.

document imaging systems Systems that convert documents and images into digital form so that they can be stored and accessed by the computer.

jukebox A device for storing and retrieving many optical disks.

index server In imaging systems, a device that stores the indexes that allow a user to identify and retrieve a specific document.

Table 12.1 Typical Office Automation Systems

Office Activity	Technology
Managing documents	Word processing; desktop publishing; document imaging; work-flow managers
Scheduling	Electronic calendars; groupware
Communicating	E-mail; voice mail; digital answering systems; groupware
Managing data	Desktop databases; spreadsheets; user-friendly interfaces to mainframe databases

document scan date, the customer name and number, the document type, and some subject information. Finally, the system must include retrieval equipment, primarily workstations capable of handling graphics, although printers are usually included. USAA's imaging system in Chapter 2 illustrates the kinds of benefits imaging technology can provide.

To achieve the large productivity gains promised by imaging technology, organizations must redesign their work-flow. In the past, the existence of only one copy of the document largely shaped work-flow. Work had to be performed serially; two people could not work on the same document at the same time. Significant staff time had to be devoted to filing and retrieving documents. Once a document has been stored electronically, work-flow management can change the traditional methods of working with documents (see Chapter 10).

CREATING KNOWLEDGE: KNOWLEDGE WORK SYSTEMS

Knowledge work is that portion of information work that creates new knowledge and information. For example, knowledge workers create new products or find ways to improve existing ones. Knowledge work is segmented into many highly specialized fields, and each field has a different collection of **knowledge work systems (KWS)** that are specialized to support workers in that field. Knowledge workers perform three key roles that are critical to the organization and to the managers who work within the organization:

- Keeping the organization up-to-date in knowledge as it develops in the external world—in technology, science, social thought, and the arts
- Serving as internal consultants on the areas of their knowledge, the changes taking place, and the opportunities
- Acting as change agents evaluating, initiating, and promoting change projects

Knowledge workers and data workers have somewhat different information systems support needs. Most knowledge workers rely upon office automation systems such as word processors, voice-mail systems, and calendaring systems, but they also require more specialized knowledge work systems. Knowledge work systems are specifically designed to promote the creation of new knowledge and ensure that new knowledge and technical expertise are properly integrated into the business.

Requirements of Knowledge Work Systems

Knowledge work systems have special characteristics that reflect the special needs of knowledge workers. First, knowledge work systems must give knowledge workers the specialized tools they need, such as powerful graphics, analytical tools, and communications and document management tools. These systems require great computing power in order to handle rapidly the sophisticated graphics or complex calculations necessary to such knowledge workers as scientific researchers, product designers, and financial analysts. Because knowledge workers are so focused on knowledge in the external world, these systems must also give the worker quick and easy access to external databases.

A user-friendly interface is very important to a knowledge worker's system. User-friendly interfaces save time by allowing the user to perform the needed tasks and get to the required information without having to spend a lot of time learning how to use the computer. Saving time is more important for knowledge workers than for most other employees because knowledge workers are highly paid—wasting a knowledge worker's time is simply too expensive. Figure 12.3 summarizes the requirements of knowledge work systems.

Knowledge workstations are often designed and optimized for the specific tasks to be performed so that a design engineer will require a different workstation than does a lawyer. Design engineers need graphics with enough power to handle three-dimensional computer-aided design (CAD) systems. On the other hand, financial analysts are more interested in having access to a myriad of external databases and in optical disk technology so that they can access massive amounts of financial data very quickly.

---

knowledge work systems (KWS) Information systems that aid knowledge workers in the creation and integration of new knowledge in the organization.

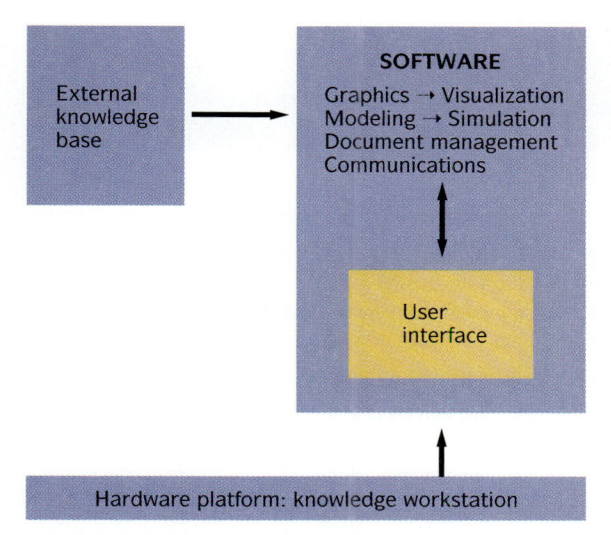

FIGURE 12.3
Requirements of knowledge work systems. Knowledge work systems require strong links to external knowledge bases in addition to specialized hardware and software.

Examples of Knowledge Work Systems

Major knowledge work applications include computer-aided design (CAD) systems, virtual reality systems for simulation and modeling, and financial workstations. **Computer-aided design (CAD)** automates the creation and revision of designs, using computers and sophisticated graphics software. Using a more traditional design methodology, each new design modification requires a mold to be made and a prototype to be physically tested. That process has to be repeated many times over, which is a very expensive and time-consuming process. Using a CAD workstation, the designer only needs to make a physical prototype toward the end of the design process because the design can be easily tested and changed on the computer. The ability of the CAD software to provide design specifications for the tooling and the manufacturing process also saves a great deal of time and money while producing a manufacturing process with far fewer problems. The chapter-end Case Study explores the benefits of CAD in more detail.

The Window on Technology describes how the new Hong Kong airport is being designed with CAD software.

Virtual reality systems have visualization, rendering, and simulation capabilities that go far beyond those of conventional CAD systems. They use interactive graphics software to create computer-generated simulations that are so close to reality that users believe they are participating in a real-world situation.

Virtual reality is interactivity in such a way that the user actually feels immersed in the world that the computer creates. To enter the virtual world, the user dons special clothing, headgear, and equipment, depending upon the application. The clothing contains sensors that record the user's movements and immediately transmit that information back to the computer. For instance, to walk through a virtual reality simulation of a house, you would need garb that monitors the movement of your feet, hands, and head. You would also need goggles that contain video screens and sometimes audio attachments and feeling gloves so that you can be immersed in the computer feedback.

Virtual reality is just starting to provide benefits in educational, scientific, and business work. Matsushita Electric Works in Japan has put virtual reality to work in its department stores. The stores sell kitchen appliances and cabinets. To promote these products Matsushita has created an application it calls Virtual Kitchen. The prospective buyers bring their kitchen layouts to the department store, where trained staff enters a copy of the design into the computer. The customers then don the appropriate equipment and suddenly find themselves in their own kitchen. Now they can try out the appliances in various sizes, colors, and locations. They can test new cabinets, opening and closing the cabinet doors and drawers. They can place their existing table and chairs into the picture so the scene will be very realistic. They can walk around and discover the feel and

computer-aided design (CAD)
Information system that automates the creation and revision of designs using sophisticated graphics software.

virtual reality systems
Interactive graphics software and hardware that create computer-generated simulations that provide sensations that emulate real-world activities.

Window on Technology

FLYING HIGH WITH CAD

Hong Kong's Kai Tak airport, third-busiest international airport in the world for passengers and second busiest for freight, reached its absolute capacity in 1994. To meet predicted traffic through the year 2040, Hong Kong's Provisional Airport Authority contracted to build the Chek Lap Kok Airport at a cost of $16 billion on land that will be reclaimed on a nearby island.

The new airport will be connected to Hong Kong by a 1500-yard bridge, the second-largest suspension bridge in the world. It will include a highway, a rail link, and a complete town for 20,000 employees. It is one of the largest infrastructure projects in the world.

Designing the airport has been a massive undertaking involving a number of design firms and sophisticated ways to link the designers and their designs. The runway design had to take into account local topology, the urban surroundings, prevalent wind patterns, and criteria from the International Civil Aviation Authority. The designers had to assume that the airport would be able to accommodate 900-passenger jets that are now only on the drawing boards. The Mott Consortium in charge of the project must keep track of a multidisciplinary team of more than 200 professionals handling architectural design, structural design, civil engineering, and production of specialized airport systems.

The client required all 10,000 design and construction drawings to be produced using CAD software. To integrate the work, the consortium purchased UNIX workstations and microcomputers for each technician and linked them into a LAN. The consortium decided to use CAD software from Intergraph Corp. because it was especially well suited for large projects. When run on a UNIX workstation, Intergraph can process large amounts of data very quickly. It also has file reference capabilities to coordinate the work of various design groups.

The team defined fifteen aspects of design, such as vertical structure, horizontal structure, signage, and interior planning, to

> **To Think About:** Do you think this project could be attempted without CAD technology? Why or why not?

store in separate files. With the file reference capability, designers can overlay files to create composite drawings and they can see what changes have been made to the various aspects of design.

Other facets of the project—including land reclamation, the bridge, the highway, the railway systems, and an analysis of the town and its infrastructure—are being designed by other companies using a wide array of specialized CAD programs. Each team is very dependent upon the output of work by other teams. To integrate the work, the Mott Consortium uses an optical jukebox holding 54 read-only optical disks of 650 Mb each. Finished drawings are archived to the optical disks, where they are immediately available to all via a network. Each drawing has a version number so that it can be updated later if needed. When updates occur that might affect the work of other teams, earlier versions of the same document are marked with a warning.

So far, the airport project has been proceeding on time and under budget.

Sources: Edward A. Gargan, "Reshaping Hong Kong's Face," *The New York Times,* October 27, 1995; Anna Foley, "Design Firm Flies Through the Airport Project with CAD," *Computerworld,* September 5, 1994; and Ross Milburn, "Flying High," *Computer Graphics World,* February, 1993.

---

ambiance of the new kitchen. With this technology the customer is able to buy with a great deal more confidence. Matsushita is able to make many more on-the-spot sales.

At General Electric's Research and Development Center in Schenectady, New York, GE scientists are working with a group of surgeons from Boston's Brigham and Women's Hospital to develop a virtual reality system to be used in surgery. One of their stated goals is to be able to superimpose a 3-D image of the patient onto the patient and then to operate on the image and the patient at the same time. The surgeon's actions on the large virtual image would be duplicated by computer-controlled instruments on the patient.

While these are futuristic hopes, the GE research team is making progress. Currently, for example, they are able to use a magnetic resonance imaging (MRI) machine to make two-dimensional-slice pictures of a volunteer's brain. Using virtual reality goggles, and with those MRI images as input, they are able to view the virtual brain with superb, three-dimensional reality. They can peel off layers of the image to reveal the parts below. They have used these images to put a special cap on a volunteer, project the image of his own brain on the cap, and then sketch onto the cap the surgical pathway through the brain's furrows to a spot where they might need to perform surgery. While the process of operating on the image itself is still a long way off, the team does hope that within the next several years they will be able to create a virtual image that surgeons can have beside the operating table so that they can consult it during the operation (Naj, 1993).

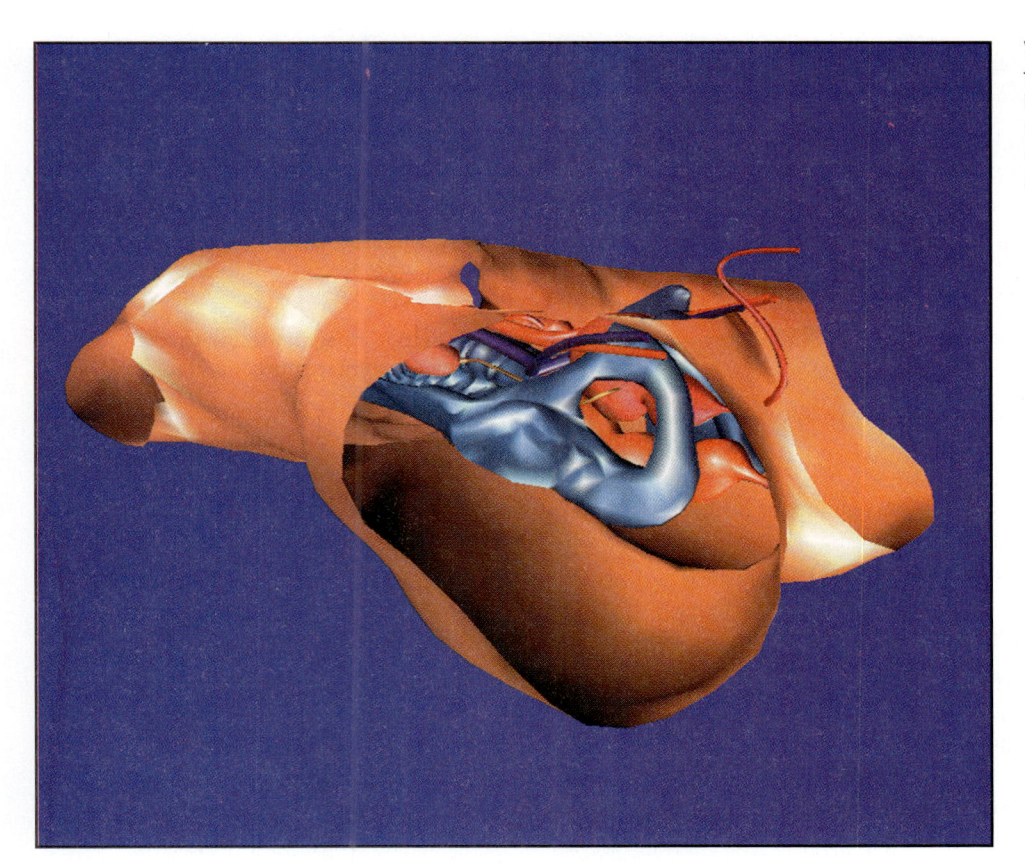

Virtual reality helps medical schools teach anatomy and surgery by simulating the workings of the human body, allowing students the options of 3-D viewing and unlimited removal and repositioning of tissues.

The financial industry is using specialized **investment workstations** to leverage the knowledge and time of its traders and portfolio managers. New York-based Chancellor Capital Management, Inc., developed its own investment workstations to help it manage $25 billion in assets for 300 clients. The workstations integrate the wide range of data required by portfolio managers from the firm's investment management systems and its portfolio accounting systems and make them available with the touch of a button. By providing one-stop information faster and with fewer errors, the workstations streamline Chancellor's entire investment process from stock selection to updating accounting records.

Previously, Chancellor's data were stored separately in its accounting, trading, research, and analytical systems. That not only meant a loss of data integrity, but also an increase in the difficulty the professional staff had in locating and accessing data. The professional staff had to use separate systems to access data on differing areas of investment.

Chancellor built software bridges between these systems with one feeding the other, thus reducing data integrity problems while making access easy. It installed a new user interface so that users have one very friendly screen with a number of windows on it. Different users have different windows, depending upon their own needs. The user can move from one window to another with ease, noting a market trend in one window, checking a second window to determine the state of his or her assets, then to a third window to check analysts' reports on stocks he or she is interested in, and finally moving to a fourth window to execute the trades decided upon. In the past, each of these moves would have required the user to log-off one system and on to another, a process that is not only time-wasting but frustrating as well (Michaels, February 1993).

Table 12.2 summarizes the major types of knowledge work systems.

investment workstation
Powerful desktop computer for financial specialists, which is optimized to access and manipulate massive amounts of financial data.

SHARING KNOWLEDGE: GROUP COLLABORATION SYSTEMS

While many knowledge and information work applications have been designed for individuals working alone, organizations have an increasing need to support people working in groups. Chapters 8 and 9 have introduced key technologies that can be used

Table 12.2	Examples of Knowledge Work Systems
Knowledge Work System	Function in Organization
CAD/CAM (Computer-aided design/ computer-aided manufacturing)	Provides engineers, designers, and factory managers with precise control over industrial design and manufacturing
Virtual reality systems	Provide drug designers, architects, engineers, and medical workers with precise, photo-realistic simulations of objects
Investment workstations	High-end PCs used in financial sector to analyze trading situations instantaneously and facilitate portfolio management

for group coordination and collaboration: e-mail, teleconferencing, dataconferencing, videoconferencing, groupware, and the Internet. Groupware and the Internet are especially valuable for this purpose.

Groupware

groupware Software that recognizes the significance of groups in offices by providing functions and services that support the collaborative activities of work groups.

Groupware consists of specialized software designed to promote information-sharing. Groupware systems allow groups of people to work together on documents, schedule meetings, route electronic forms, access shared folders, develop shared databases, and send e-mail. Information-intensive companies such as consulting firms and law firms have found groupware a valuable tool for leveraging their knowledge assets.

For example, Ernst & Young, one of the Big Six accounting firms, hopes to improve its worldwide competitiveness by using Lotus Notes to create a communications infrastructure. In the past, Ernst & Young could not respond quickly to worldwide business opportunities because its international offices were often unaware of activities in the other branches and even in branches in the same country. The company's offices in the United States, the United Kingdom, Canada, the Netherlands, and Australia are linking Lotus Notes to Oracle relational databases, eliminating the need for multiple copies of files. Employees' desktop computers are tied into local-area networks (LANs) that are connected regionally into a private wide-area network (WAN). Figure 12.4 illustrates the infrastructure created for the company's offices in the United Kingdom, so that staff can work together on projects that require regional teamwork. The Eastern regional offices share an Oracle database containing staff demographic data that helps Ernst & Young put together the best team for a specific job. Managers from these offices are building a shared client and prospect database to help employees stay abreast of developments in other offices. Using Lotus Notes, employees can share a diary, which may be more effective than posting notices on bulletin boards (Black, 1995).

Groupware is becoming popular in traditional manufacturing companies because it promotes information-sharing and coordination across the sales and production functions. For instance, Howmet, a manufacturer of jet aircraft and industrial gas turbine engine components, uses Lotus Notes for information-sharing among geographically dispersed sales and production units. Howmet casts engine parts based on client specifications; its sales force must coordinate orders with factories in the United States, the United Kingdom, France, and Japan. Using groupware reduces the time to exchange this information and resolve the sales staff's questions about orders. Instead of spending so much time collecting information, Howmet's sales and marketing managers can use that time to analyze it for competitive advantage (McCune, 1996).

GROUP COLLABORATION VIA THE INTERNET

Chapter 9 has described the multiple ways in which organizations can use the Internet for group collaboration and coordination, especially the Internet capabilities for e-mail,

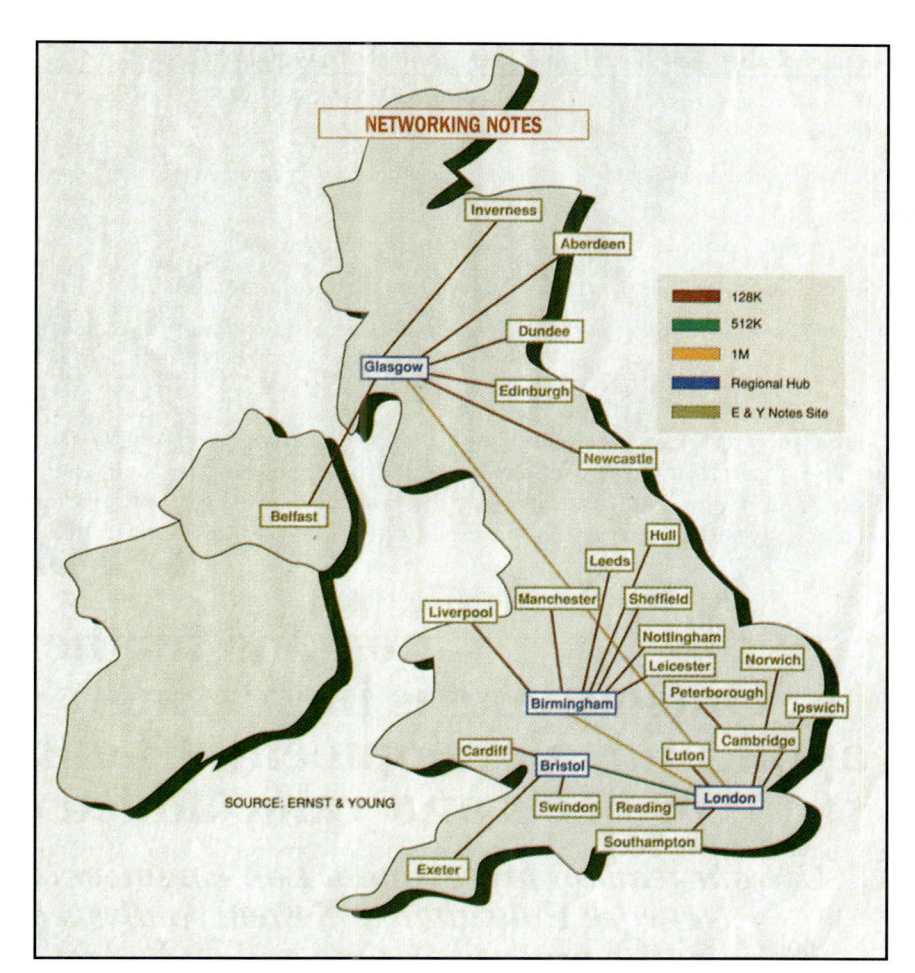

FIGURE 12.4

Ernst & Young's knowledge work infrastructure. Ernst & Young is developing a network linking its offices in the United Kingdom to speed up the pace of collaboration using groupware and other communications tools. *Adapted from George Black, "Taking Notes, Big Sixer Aims for Head of the Class," Software Magazine, March 1995, page 108. Copyright Sentry Technology Group. Reprinted by permission.*

discussion groups, and intranets for information-sharing on the World Wide Web. (The Web allows collaborators in remote sites to display and exchange information that includes text, graphics, and sound about a common project or related projects using hypermedia links.) For simple tasks such as sharing documents or document publishing, the Web is much less expensive to use than proprietary products such as Lotus Notes. Some companies may find their communication needs satisfied by Web-based intranets.

However, proprietary groupware software such as Notes has important capabilities that can't yet be matched by Web technology. Notes is more flexible when documents have to be changed, updated, or edited on the fly. It can track revisions to a document as it moves through a collaborative editing process. Internal Notes-based networks are more secure than intranets (Web sites are more likely to crash or to have their servers overloaded when there are many requests for data). Notes is thus more appropriate for applications involving production and publication of documents by many authors, those with information requiring frequent updating and document tracking, and those that need high security and replication.

In contrast, the Web is best suited for applications with a central repository, a small number of authors, and relatively static information; Web documents can't be easily updated every hour. However Web capabilities for work-flow and document management are continuing to improve. Table 12.3 compares the capabilities for group collaboration of Lotus Notes and the World Wide Web.

Notes and other groupware products are being enhanced so that they can be integrated with the Internet. Notes can act as a Web server, providing an easy route for companies to take their document-based data to the Internet or an intranet. Notes clients can act as Web browsers. Notes servers and data can be accessed by Web browsers as well as by Notes clients; Notes databases can contain HTML pages as well as Notes documents.

Table 12.3 Group Collaboration Capabilities: Groupware vs. the World Wide Web	
Uses for Lotus Notes Groupware Collaboration Tools	Uses for the World Wide Web Collaboration Tools
Documents with many collaborating authors	Publishing documents completed by only one author
Data that require frequent updating	Data that are relatively static
Applications with data at multiple sites	Applications with one central source of data
Applications with high security requirements	Applications where content must be secure but the Web server can be accessed by anyone

Group collaboration technologies alone cannot promote information-sharing if team members do not feel it is in their interest to share, especially in organizations that encourage competition among employees. This technology can best enhance the work of a group if the applications are properly designed to fit the organization's needs and work practices.

12.3 ARTIFICIAL INTELLIGENCE

Organizations are using artificial intelligence technology to capture individual and collective knowledge and to codify and extend their knowledge base.

WHAT IS ARTIFICIAL INTELLIGENCE?

artificial intelligence The effort to develop computer-based systems that can behave like humans, with the ability to learn languages, accomplish physical tasks, use a perceptual apparatus, and emulate human expertise and decision making.

Artificial intelligence can be defined as the effort to develop computer-based systems (both hardware and software) that behave as humans. Such systems would be able to learn natural languages, accomplish coordinated physical tasks (robotics), utilize a perceptual apparatus that informs their physical behavior and language (visual and oral perception systems), and emulate human expertise and decision making (expert systems). Such systems would also exhibit logic, reasoning, intuition, and the just-plain common-sense qualities that we associate with human beings. Figure 12.5 illustrates the elements of the artificial intelligence family. Another important element is *intelligent machines*, the physical hardware that performs these tasks.

Successful artificial intelligence systems are based on human expertise, knowledge, and selected reasoning patterns but they do not exhibit the intelligence of human beings. Existing artificial intelligence systems do not come up with new and novel solutions to problems. Existing systems extend the powers of experts but in no way substitute for them or capture much of their intelligence. Briefly, existing systems lack the common sense and generality of naturally intelligent machines like human beings.

Human intelligence is vastly complex and much broader than computer or information systems. A key factor that distinguishes human beings from other animals is their ability to develop associations and to use metaphors and analogies such as *like* and *as*. Using metaphor and analogy, humans create new rules, apply old rules to new situations, and at times act intuitively and/or instinctively without rules. Much of what we call *common sense* or *generality* in humans resides in the ability to create metaphor and analogy.

FIGURE 12.5
The artificial intelligence family. The field of AI currently includes many initiatives: natural language, robotics, perceptive systems, expert systems, and intelligent machines.

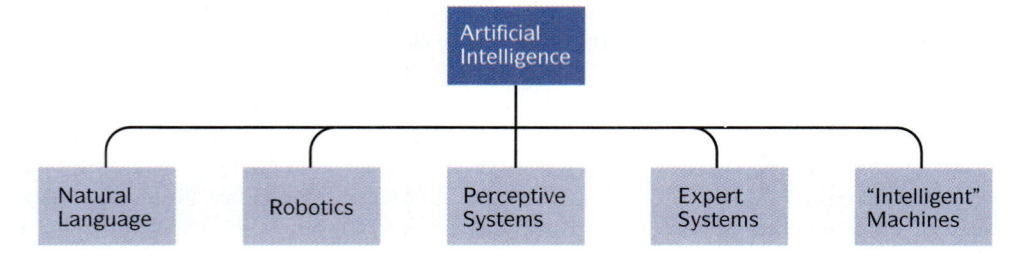

Human intelligence also includes a unique ability to impose a conceptual apparatus on the surrounding world. Meta-concepts such as *cause-and-effect* and *time,* and concepts of a lower order such as *breakfast, dinner,* and *lunch,* are all imposed by human beings on the world around them. Thinking in terms of these concepts and acting on them are central characteristics of intelligent human behavior.

WHY BUSINESS IS INTERESTED IN ARTIFICIAL INTELLIGENCE

Although artificial intelligence applications are much more limited than human intelligence, they are of great interest to business for the following reasons:

- To preserve expertise that might be lost through the retirement, resignation, or death of an acknowledged expert
- To store information in an active form—to create an organizational knowledge base—that many employees can examine, much like an electronic textbook or manual, so that others may learn rules of thumb not found in textbooks
- To create a mechanism that is not subject to human feelings such as fatigue and worry. This may be especially useful when jobs may be environmentally, physically, or mentally dangerous to humans. These systems may also be useful advisors in times of crisis.
- To eliminate routine and unsatisfying jobs held by people
- To enhance the organization's knowledge base by suggesting solutions to specific problems that are too massive and complex to be analyzed by human beings in a short period of time

CAPTURING KNOWLEDGE: EXPERT SYSTEMS

In limited areas of expertise, such as diagnosing a car's ignition system or classifying biological specimens, the rules of thumb used by real-world experts can be understood, codified, and placed in a machine. Information systems that solve problems by capturing knowledge for a very specific and limited domain of human expertise are called **expert systems.** An expert system can assist decision making by asking relevant questions and explaining the reasons for adopting certain actions.

Expert systems lack the breadth of knowledge and the understanding of fundamental principles of a human expert. They are quite narrow, shallow, and brittle. They typically perform very limited tasks that can be performed by professionals in a few minutes or hours. Problems that cannot be solved by human experts in the same short period of time are far too difficult for an expert system. But by capturing human expertise in limited areas, expert systems can provide benefits, helping organizations make higher-quality decisions with fewer people.

expert system Knowledge-intensive computer program that captures the expertise of a human in limited domains of knowledge.

How Expert Systems Work

Human knowledge must be modeled or represented in a way that a computer can deal with it. The model of human knowledge used by expert systems is called the **knowledge base.** Three ways have been devised to represent human knowledge and expertise: (1) rules, (2) semantic nets, and (3) frames.

A standard structured programming construct (see Chapter 11) is the IF–THEN construct, in which a *condition* is evaluated. If the condition is true, an *action* is taken. For instance,

IF INCOME>$45,000 (condition)
THEN PRINT NAME AND ADDRESS (action)

A series of these rules can be a knowledge base. Any reader who has written computer programs knows that virtually all traditional computer programs contain IF–THEN statements. The difference between a traditional program and a **rule-based expert system** program is one of degree and magnitude. AI programs can easily have 200 to 10,000

knowledge base Model of human knowledge that is used by expert systems.

rule-based expert system An AI program that has a large number of interconnected and nested IF–THEN statements, or rules, that are the basis for the knowledge in the system.

12.3 Artificial Intelligence

rules, far more than traditional programs, which may have 50 to 100 IF–THEN statements. Moreover, in an AI program the rules tend to be interconnected and nested to a far larger degree than in traditional programs, as shown in Figure 12.6. Hence the complexity of the rules in a rule-based expert system is considerable.

Could you represent the knowledge in the *Encyclopedia Britannica* this way? Probably not, because the **rule base** would be too large, and not all the knowledge in the encyclopedia can be represented in the form of IF–THEN rules. In general, expert systems can be efficiently used only in those situations where the domain of knowledge is highly restricted (such as in granting credit) and involves no more than a few thousand rules.

Semantic nets can be used to represent knowledge when the knowledge base is composed of easily identified chunks or objects of interrelated characteristics. Semantic nets can be much more efficient than rules. They use the property of inheritance to organize and classify objects. A condition such as "IS A" ties objects together—"IS A" is a pointer to all objects of a specific class. For instance, Figure 12.7 shows a semantic net that is used to classify kinds of automobiles. All specific automobiles in the lower part of the diagram inherit characteristics of the general categories of the automobiles above them. Insurance companies can use such a semantic net to classify cars into rating classes.

Knowledge **frames** also organize knowledge into chunks, but the relationships are based on shared characteristics rather than a hierarchy. This approach is grounded in the belief that humans use frames, or concepts, to make rapid sense out of perceptions. For instance, when a person is told, "Look for a tank and shoot when you see one," experts believe that humans invoke a concept, or frame, of what a tank should look like. Anything that does not fit this concept of a tank is ignored. In a similar fashion, AI re-

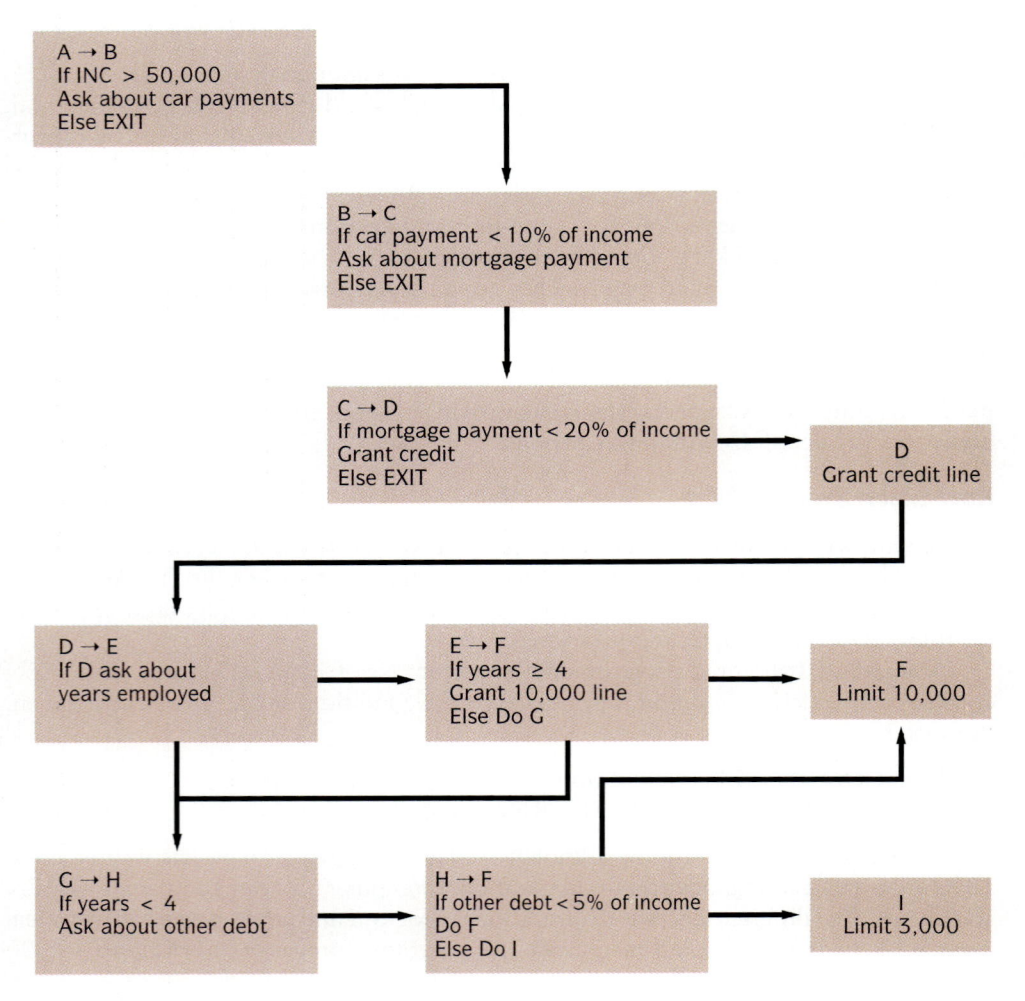

rule base The collection of knowledge in an AI system that is represented in the form of IF–THEN rules.

semantic nets Expert systems that use the property of inheritance to organize and classify knowledge when the knowledge base is composed of easily identifiable chunks or objects of interrelated characteristics.

frames A method of organizing expert system knowledge into chunks; the relationships are based on shared characteristics determined by the user rather than a hierarchy.

FIGURE 12.6
Rules in an AI program. An expert system contains a number of rules to be followed when utilized. The rules themselves are interconnected; the number of outcomes is known in advance and is limited; there are multiple paths to the same outcome; and the system can consider multiple rules at a single time. The rules illustrated are for simple credit-granting expert systems.

A → B
If INC > 50,000
Ask about car payments
Else EXIT

B → C
If car payment < 10% of income
Ask about mortgage payment
Else EXIT

C → D
If mortgage payment < 20% of income
Grant credit
Else EXIT

D
Grant credit line

D → E
If D ask about years employed

E → F
If years ≥ 4
Grant 10,000 line
Else Do G

F
Limit 10,000

G → H
If years < 4
Ask about other debt

H → F
If other debt < 5% of income
Do F
Else Do I

I
Limit 3,000

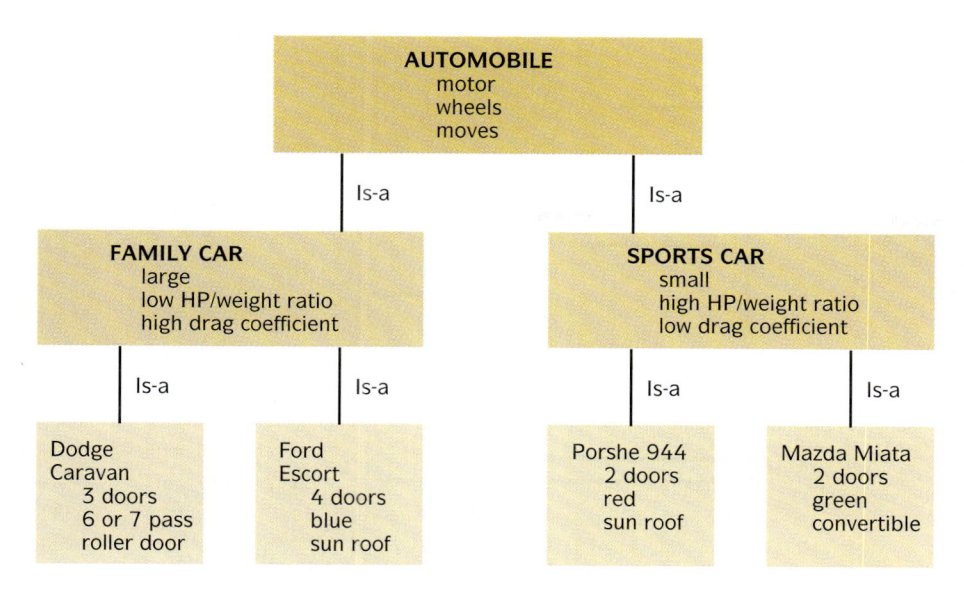

FIGURE 12.7
Semantic nets to model knowledge. Knowledge can be organized into semantic nets with inheritance. All lower levels inherit the characteristics of those objects above. For example, a Dodge Caravan inherits the characteristics of Family Car as well as Automobile. The link among levels is crucial; in this case, the link is *is-a*. In other instances it could be *produces, looks like,* and so forth.

searchers can organize a vast array of information into frames. The computer is then instructed to search the database of frames and list connections to other frames of interest. The user can then follow the various pathways pointed to by the system.

Figure 12.8 shows a part of a knowledge base organized by frames. A "CAR" is defined by characteristics or slots in a frame as a vehicle, with four wheels, a gas or diesel motor, and an action like rolling or moving. This frame could be related to just about any other object in the database that shares any of these characteristics, such as the tank frame.

The **AI shell** is the programming environment of an expert system. In the early years of expert systems, computer scientists used specialized programming languages such as Lisp or Prolog that could process lists of rules efficiently. Today a growing number of

AI shell The programming environment of an expert system.

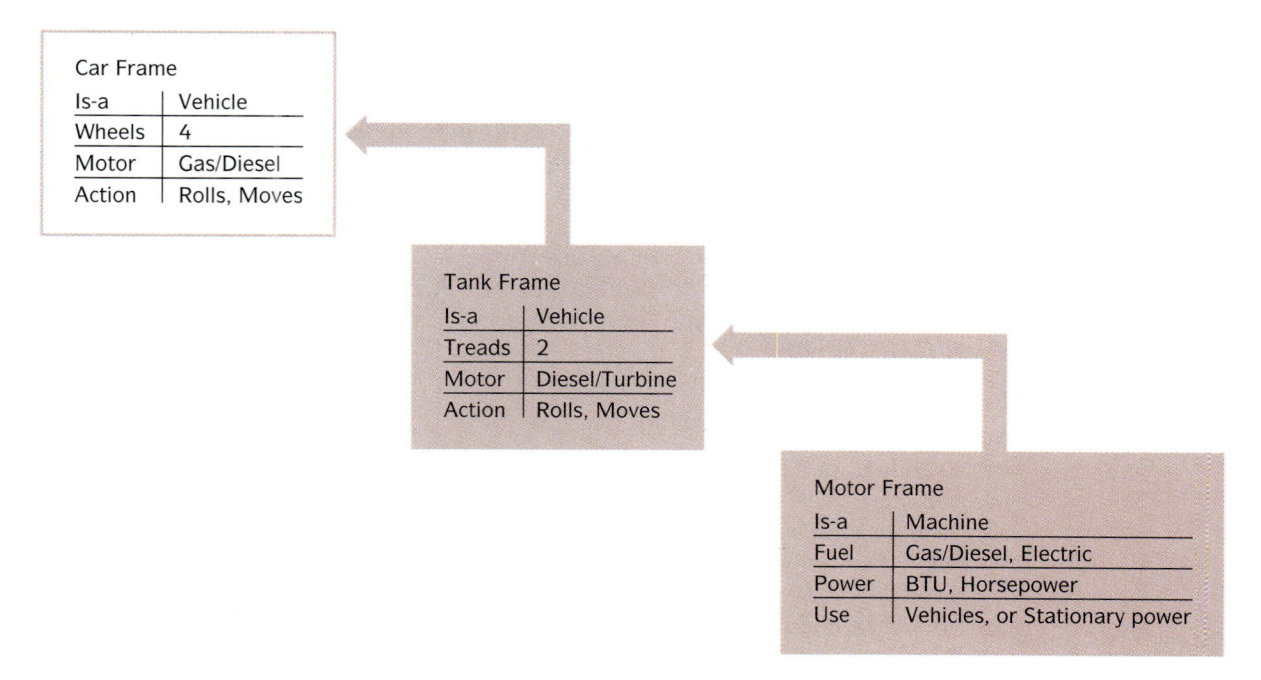

FIGURE 12.8
Frames to model knowledge. Knowledge and information can be organized into frames in a manner similar to semantic nets. Frames capture the relevant characteristics of the objects of interest. This approach is based on the belief that humans use *frames* or *concepts* to narrow the range of possibilities when scanning incoming information in order to make rapid sense out of perceptions.

12.3 Artificial Intelligence   383

Income Rules

```
If Inc > $100,000     →  If life ins.            →  If sales rep or term ins. or
  then life ins.           then send sales rep         FinAdv
                                                       then search dbase

If Inc > $50,000      →  If term ins.                                               other accounts
  then term ins.           then send brochure
                                                                                  If not on dbase
                                                                                    then add prospect file
```

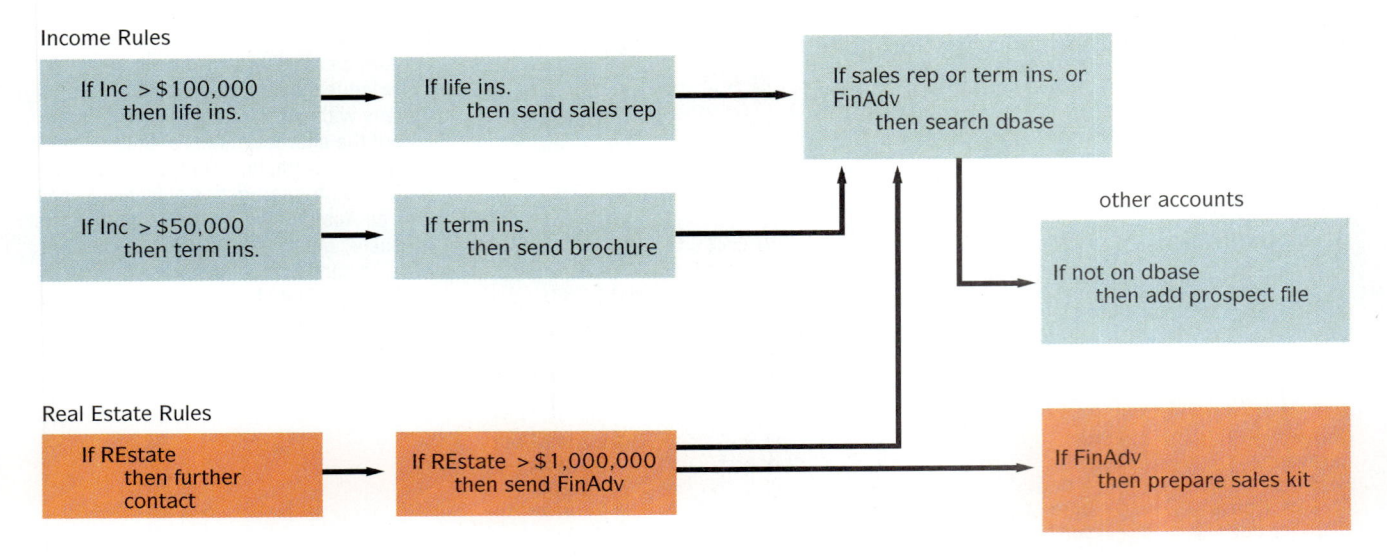

Real Estate Rules

```
If REstate            →  If REstate > $1,000,000                                  If FinAdv
  then further             then send FinAdv                                         then prepare sales kit
  contact
```

FIGURE 12.9
Inference engines in expert systems. An inference engine works by searching through the rules and firing those rules that are triggered by facts gathered and entered by the user. Basically, a collection of rules is similar to a series of nested IF statements in a traditional software program; however, the magnitude of the statements and degree of nesting are much greater in an expert system.

---

expert systems use AI shells that are user-friendly development environments. AI shells can quickly generate user-interface screens, capture the knowledge base, and manage the strategies for searching the rule base.

inference engine The strategy used to search through the rule base in an expert system; can be forward or backward chaining.

The strategy used to search through the rule base is called the **inference engine**. Two strategies are commonly used: forward chaining and backward chaining (see Figure 12.9).

In **forward chaining** the inference engine begins with the information entered by the user and searches the rule base to arrive at a conclusion. The strategy is to fire, or carry out, the action of the rule when a condition is true. In Figure 12.9, beginning on the left, if the user enters a client with income greater than $100,000, the engine will fire all rules in sequence from left to right. If the user then enters information indicating that the same client owns real estate, another pass of the rule base will occur and more rules will fire. Processing continues until no more rules can be fired.

forward chaining A strategy for searching the rule base in an expert system that begins with the information entered by the user and searches the rule base to arrive at a conclusion.

In **backward chaining** the strategy for searching the rule base starts with a hypothesis and proceeds by asking the user questions about selected facts until the hypothesis is either confirmed or disproved. In our example in Figure 12.9, ask the question, "Should we add this person to the prospect database?" Begin on the right of the diagram and work toward the left. You can see that the person should be added to the database if a sales rep is sent, term insurance is granted, or a financial advisor will be sent to visit the client.

backward chaining A strategy for searching the rule base in an expert system that acts like a problem solver by beginning with a hypothesis and seeking out more information until the hypothesis is either proved or disproved.

Building an Expert System

Building an expert system is similar to building other information systems, although building expert systems is an iterative process with each phase possibly requiring several iterations before a full system is developed. Typically the environment in which an expert system operates is continually changing so that the expert system must also continually change. Some expert systems, especially large ones, are so complex that in a few years the maintenance costs will equal the development costs.

knowledge engineer A specialist who elicits information and expertise from other professionals and translates it into a set of rules, frames, or semantic nets for an expert system.

An AI development team is composed of one or more experts, who have a thorough command over the knowledge base, and one or more **knowledge engineers,** who can translate the knowledge (as described by the expert) into a set of rules, frames, or semantic nets. A knowledge engineer is similar to a traditional systems analyst but has special expertise in eliciting information and expertise from other professionals.

Examples of Successful Expert Systems

There is no accepted definition of a *successful* expert system. What is successful to an academic ("It works!") may not be successful to a corporation ("It cost a million dollars!"). The following are examples of expert systems that provide organizations with an array of benefits, including reduced errors, reduced cost, reduced training time, improved decisions, and improved quality and service.

Countrywide Funding Corp. in Pasadena, California, are loan underwriters with about 400 underwriters in 150 offices around the country. The company developed a microcomputer-based expert system in 1992 to make preliminary creditworthiness decisions on loan requests. The company had experienced rapid, continuing growth and wanted the system to help ensure consistent and high-quality loan decisions.

CLUES (Countrywide's Loan Underwriting Expert System) has about 400 rules. Countrywide tested the system by having every loan application handled by a human underwriter also fed to CLUES. The system was refined until it agreed with the underwriter in 95 percent of the cases. However, Countrywide will not rely on CLUES to reject loans, because the expert system cannot be programmed to handle exceptional situations such as those involving a self-employed person or complex financial schemes. An underwriter will review all rejected loans and will make the final decision. CLUES has other benefits. Traditionally, an underwriter could handle six or seven applications a day. Using CLUES, the same underwriter can evaluate at least sixteen per day (Nash, 1993).

The Digital Equipment Corporation (DEC) and Carnegie-Mellon University developed XCON in the late 1970s to configure VAX computers on a daily basis. The system configures customer orders and guides the assembly of those orders at the customer site. XCON has been used for major functions such as sales and marketing, manufacturing and production, and field service, and played a strategic role at DEC (Sviokla, June 1990; Barker and O'Conner, 1989). It is estimated that XCON and related systems saved DEC approximately $40 million per year. XCON started out with 250 rules but has expanded to about 10,000.

Problems with Expert Systems

Although expert systems lack the robust and general intelligence of human beings, they can provide benefits to organizations if their limitations are well understood. Only certain classes of problems can be solved using expert systems. Virtually all successful expert systems deal with problems of classification in which there are relatively few alternative outcomes and in which these possible outcomes are all known in advance. Many expert systems require large, lengthy, and expensive development efforts. Hiring or training more experts may be less expensive than building an expert system.

The knowledge base of expert systems is fragile and brittle; they cannot learn or change over time. In fast-moving fields such as medicine or the computer sciences, keeping the knowledge base up to date is a critical problem.

Expert systems can only represent limited forms of knowledge. IF–THEN knowledge exists primarily in textbooks. There are no adequate representations for deep causal models or temporal trends. No expert system, for instance, can write a textbook on information systems or engage in other creative activities not explicitly foreseen by system designers. Many experts cannot express their knowledge using an IF–THEN format. Expert systems cannot yet replicate knowledge that is intuitive, based on analogy and on a sense of things.

Contrary to early promises, expert systems do best in automating lower-level clerical functions. They can provide electronic check lists for lower-level employees in service bureaucracies such as banking, insurance, sales, and welfare agencies. The applicability of expert systems to managerial problems is very limited. Managerial problems generally involve drawing facts and interpretations from divergent sources, evaluating the facts, and comparing one interpretation of the facts with another, and do not involve analysis or simple classification. Expert systems based on the prior knowledge of a few known alternatives are unsuitable to the problems managers face on a daily basis.

ORGANIZATIONAL INTELLIGENCE: CASE-BASED REASONING

Expert systems primarily capture the knowledge of individual experts. But organizations also have collective knowledge and expertise which they have built up over the years. This organizational knowledge can be captured and stored using case-based reasoning. In **case-based reasoning (CBR)**, descriptions of past experiences of human specialists, represented as cases, are stored in a database for later retrieval when the user encounters a new case with similar parameters. The system searches for stored cases similar to the new one, finds the closest fit, and applies the solutions of the old case to the new case. Successful solutions are tagged to the new case and both are stored together with the other cases in the knowledge base. Unsuccessful solutions are also appended to the case database along with explanations as to why the solutions didn't work (see Figure 12.10).

Expert systems work by applying a set of IF–THEN–ELSE rules against a knowledge base, both of which are extracted from human experts. Case-based reasoning, in contrast, represents knowledge as a series of cases and this knowledge base is continuously expanded and refined by users.

For example, let us examine Compaq Computer of Houston, Texas, a company that operates in a highly competitive, customer service-oriented business environment and is daily flooded with customer phone calls crying for help. Keeping those customers sat-

case-based reasoning (CBR)
Artificial intelligence technology that represents knowledge as a database of cases.

FIGURE 12.10
How case-based reasoning works. Case-based reasoning represents knowledge as a database of past cases and their solutions. The system uses a 6-step process to generate solutions to new problems encountered by the user.

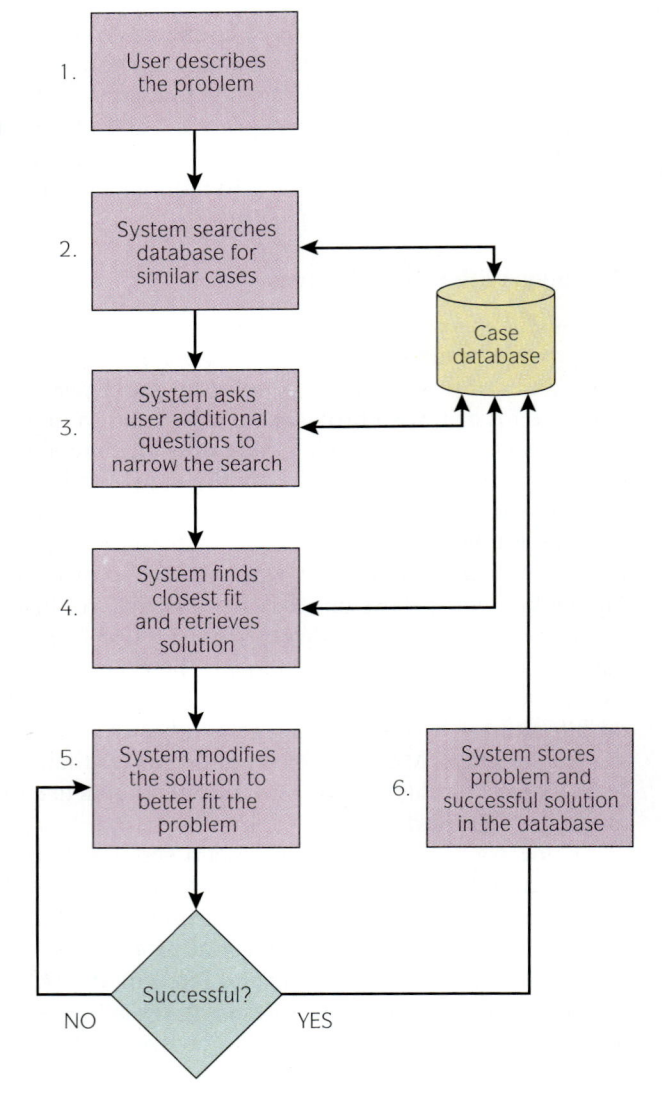

isfied requires Compaq to spend millions of dollars annually to maintain large, technically skilled, customer-support staffs. When customers call with problems, they first must describe the problem to the customer service staff, and then wait on hold while customer service transfers the call to an appropriate technician. The customer then describes the problem all over again while the technician tries to come up with an answer—all in all, a most frustrating experience. To improve customer service while reining in costs, Compaq began giving away expensive case-based reasoning software to customers purchasing their Pagemarq printer.

The software knowledge base is a series of several hundred actual cases of Pagemarq printer problems—actual war stories about smudged copies, printer memory problems, jammed printers—all the typical problems people face with laser printers. Trained CBR staff entered case descriptions in textual format into the CBR system. They entered certain key words necessary to categorize the problem (such as *smudge, smear, lines, streaks, paper jam*). They also entered a series of questions that might need to be asked to allow the software to further narrow the problem. Finally, solutions were also attached to each case.

With the Compaq-supplied CBR system running on their computer, owners no longer need to call Compaq's service department. Instead they run the software and describe the problem to the software. The system swiftly searches actual cases, discarding unrelated ones, selecting related ones. If necessary to further narrow the search results, the software will ask the user for more information. In the end, one or more cases relevant to the specific problem are displayed, along with their solutions. Now, customers can solve most of their own problems quickly without even a telephone call while Compaq saves $10 million to $20 million annually in customer support costs.

The Window on Management shows how another company, Loma Engineering, used CBR to cut its product development time while also reducing development costs.

12.4 OTHER INTELLIGENT TECHNIQUES

Organizations are starting to utilize other intelligent computing techniques to extend their knowledge base by providing solutions to specific problems that are too massive or complex to be handled by people with limited time and resources. Neural networks, fuzzy logic, and genetic algorithms are developing into promising business applications.

NEURAL NETWORKS

There has been an exciting resurgence of interest in bottom-up approaches to artificial intelligence in which machines are designed to imitate the physical thought process of the biological brain. Figure 12.11 shows two neurons from a leech's brain. The soma, or nerve cell, at the center acts like a switch, stimulating other neurons and being stimulated in turn. Emanating from the neuron is an axon, which is an electrically active link to the dendrites of other neurons. Axons and dendrites are the "wires" that electrically connect neurons to one another. The junction of the two is called a *synapse*. This simple biological model is the metaphor for the development of neural networks. **Neural networks** consist of hardware or software that attempts to emulate the processing patterns of the biological brain.

neural network Hardware or software that attempts to emulate the processing patterns of the biological brain.

The human brain has about 100 billion (10^{11}) neurons, each having about 1000 dendrites, which form 100,000 billion (10^{14}) synapses. The brain's neurons operate in parallel, and the human brain can accomplish about 10^{16} or ten million billion interconnections per second. This far exceeds the capacity of any known machine or any machine now planned or ever likely to be built with current technology.

But far more complex networks of neurons have been simulated on computers. Figure 12.12 shows an artificial neural network with two neurons. The resistors in the circuits are variable and can be used to *teach* the network. When the network makes a

Window on Management

ENABLING REUSE OF DESIGNS THROUGH ARTIFICIAL INTELLIGENCE

Loma Engineering Ltd. of Farnsborough, England, produces customized equipment used by pharmaceutical and food manufacturing companies to inspect their products during the production cycle. Companies buy Loma equipment to verify the quality, weight, count, and purity of their products during manufacturing. The problem Loma management faced was the cost and time needed to customize and individualize every piece of equipment they sold. Every piece must be designed to the individual customer's specifications. Not only does each food and drug product require individual approaches to testing, but the equipment also needs to be customized according to the product safety laws and electrical requirements of the country of manufacture. Despite the fact that most machines were very similar to previously produced pieces of equipment, Loma engineers were custom designing each item essentially from scratch.

Management knew that their engineers could save a great deal of time, and thereby reduce costs, if they could reuse previous designs by modifying them to fit the newly ordered products rather than designing each item from scratch. The issue was the engineers' ability to locate existing designs of similar products. The only way Loma could reuse designs would be if an engineer could remember and trace a similar job—quite a task when thousands of units are produced in its Farnsborough factory each year. Loma needed to find a better way to search and retrieve relevant designs. Management believed that a computer program would result in a major reduction in engineering time and costs.

After much searching, Loma turned to CBR Express, case-based reasoning software from Inference Corp. of El Segundo, California. The software stores Loma's experience with product configurations in a database. Engineers can match the specifications for their current order against previous designs stored as cases in the database. At various stages the system lists a number of likely configurations and the probability of the configuration being the right one. When a match or matches (identical or very similar designs) are located, the engineer can use it as the basis for the design of the newly ordered product. New cases (designs) are then appended to the database for future use.

CBR Express has been a success for Loma. Whereas in the past the design of a Loma 6000 check-weigher product required 12 to 14 weeks, using the CBR system Loma has cut two to three weeks from that time. Moreover, before CBR Express was installed, 100 percent of new Loma orders required an engineer; now only 25 percent of new orders require an engineer to design them.

To Think About: How did case-based reasoning support Loma's business strategy? What organizational and management problems would Loma likely have faced when it adapted case-based reasoning technology?

Source: Connie Winkler, "Redrawing Design Process Cuts Repetition at Loma," *Software Magazine,* April, 1994.

---

mistake (i.e., chooses the wrong pathway through the network and arrives at a false conclusion), resistance can be raised on some circuits, forcing other neurons to fire. If this learning process continues for thousands of cycles, the machine *learns* the correct response. The neurons are highly interconnected and operate in parallel.

The Difference Between Neural Networks and Expert Systems

What is different about neural networks? Whereas expert systems seek to emulate or model a human expert's way of solving a set of problems, neural network builders claim that they do not model human intelligence, do not program solutions, and do not aim to solve specific problems per se. Instead, neural network designers seek to put intelligence into the hardware in the form of a generalized capability to learn. In contrast, the expert system is highly specific to a given problem and cannot be easily retrained.

Take a simple problem like identifying a cat. An expert system approach would interview hundreds of people to understand how humans recognize cats, resulting in a large set of rules, or frames, programmed into an expert system. In contrast, a trainable neural network would be brought to the test site, connected to the television, and started out on the process of learning. Every time a cat was not correctly perceived, the system's interconnections would be adjusted. When cats were correctly perceived, the system would be left alone and another object scanned.

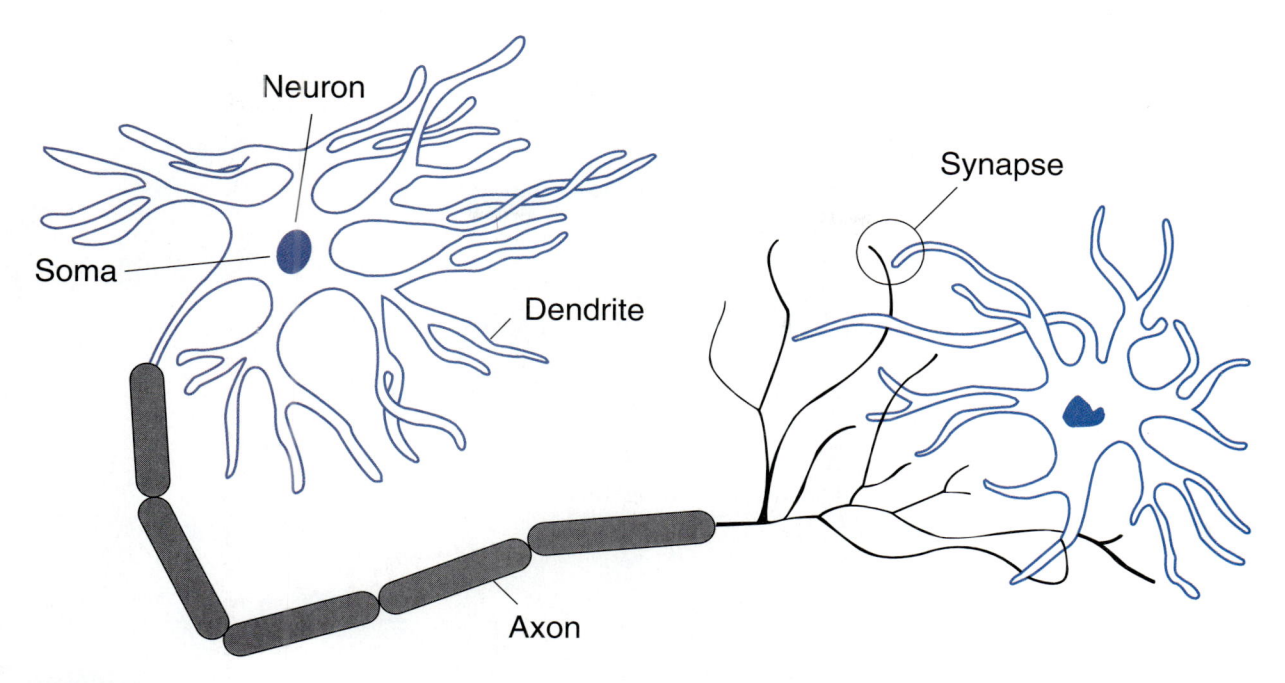

FIGURE 12.11
Biological neurons of a leech. Simple biological models, like the neurons of a leech, have influenced the development of artificial or computational neural networks in which the biological cells are replaced by transistors or entire processors. *Source: Defense Advanced Research Projects Agency (DARPA), 1988. Unclassified. Hereinafter "DARPA, 1988."*

The pattern-recognition power of neural networks is starting to be harnessed by medicine. Papnet is a system to distinguish between normal and abnormal cells when examining Pap smears for cervical cancer, with far greater accuracy than visual examination by technicians. The computer is not able to make the final decision and so the technician will review the selected abnormal cells. Using Papnet a technician requires one-fifth the time to review a smear while attaining perhaps ten times the accuracy of the existing manual method. Mellon Bank in Pittsburgh, Pennsylvania, is using a neural network to help detect credit-card fraud. The network was taught to recognize irregular pattens in charge-card purchases and to evaluate potentially fraudulent transac-

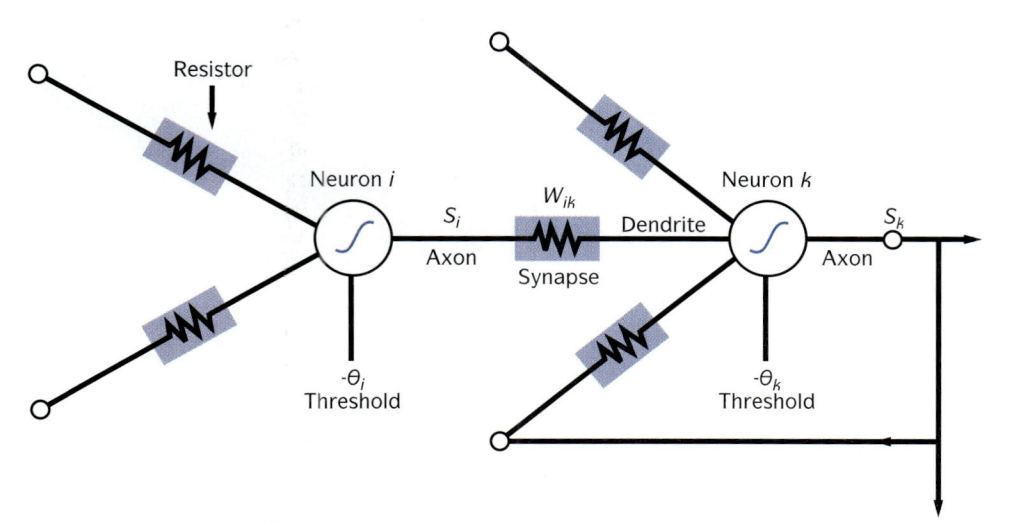

FIGURE 12.12
Artificial neural network with two neurons. In artificial neurons, the biological neurons become processing elements (switches), the axons and dendrites become wires, and the synapses become variable resistors that carry weighted inputs (currents) that represent data. *Source: DARPA, 1988.*

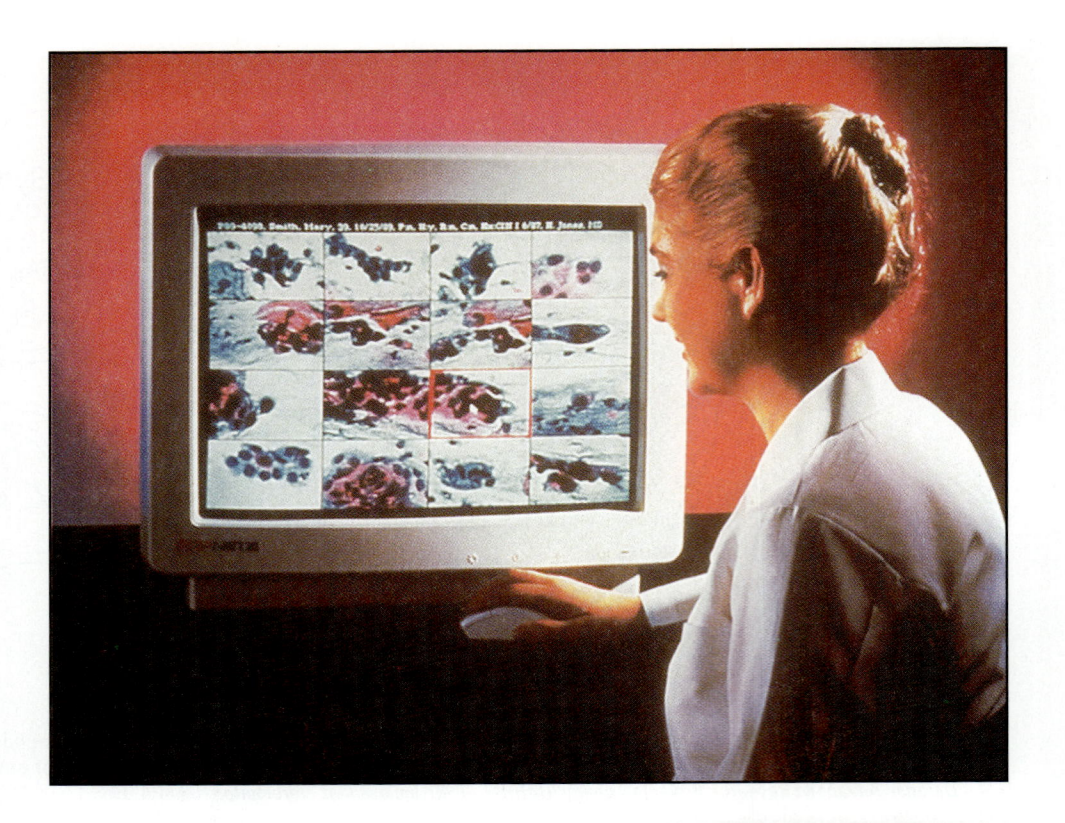

Because they can identify complex relationships and patterns in vast quantities of data, neural networks are starting to be used for evaluating certain cancer screening tests and for stock picking.

tions. The Window on Organizations illustrates a use of neural networks to improve stock selection.

Neural nets cannot always guarantee a completely certain solution, arrive at the same solution again with the same input data, or always guarantee the *best* solution (Trippi and Turban, 1989–90). In most current applications, neural networks are best used as aids to human decision makers instead of substitutes for them.

Window on Organizations

THE NEURAL NETWORK APPROACH TO STOCK PICKING

Fidelity Disciplined Equity has stood out as one of the top-performing mutual funds. This fund is managed by Brad Lewis, who uses a neural network to help him pick his stocks. Lewis's system, which runs on a 90-megahertz desktop computer, uses massive amounts of data to select stocks. Fidelity Disciplined Equity attempts to mirror the S&P 500 stock index in terms of the industry weightings of that index, but Lewis's goal is to outperform the index every year and, hopefully, every quarter. Lewis is very clear that his neural network is only part of his system for stock selection, but it is essential. The selection process begins every Friday afternoon when his desktop starts processing the data on 2800 stocks. It runs the whole weekend to project the expected return of those stocks over the following nine months. It examines a wide range of data, including each stock's projected price-earnings ratio for the next 12 months, the price-to-cash flow, insider buys and sells, and economic environment factors such as the yield curve and industrial production rates-of-change. After examining seven to ten years of data on a particular stock, the neural network finds patterns on its own, defining the quantifiable factors that contribute to the stock's performance.

For example, the neural network system might find that over the past ten years General Electric is a buy when the yield curve is accelerating upward. The analyst may not have thought of this relationship and so would not be looking for it. However, the neural network will find it if it is there.

When the weekend run is completed, Lewis has a list of stock buy-and-sell recommendations. He claims that he neither knows nor cares why the computer makes specific recommendations. However, he does not blindly follow the neural network recommendation. He first optimizes the list to make certain his portfolio approximately reflects the industry balance of the S&P 500 and to balance the number of shares owned on each stock.

To Think About: What do you consider to be the strengths and weaknesses of using neural networks for investment? Would you use it to aid yourself in making investment decisions, and why?

Asked if he countermands the computer and makes subjective decisions about buying and selling, he answers that he used to do so a lot. But as he gained experience with the system and became more confident about its results, he has come to trust it and so makes subjective decisions only rarely. Lewis also notes that there are factors affecting stock performance that the computer can't identify. The price of certain types of stocks can be driven up by investing fads. For instance, when hype surrounding the information superhighway drove up telecommunications stock prices in the fall of 1993, Lewis's neural network discarded telecommunications stocks because their prices were high relative to other measures such as earnings. The performance of the fund suffered because Lewis had programmed the network to discard stocks that were too expensive.

Sources: "Fidelity Disciplined Equity Fund," *Fidelity Focus,* Winter 1995; and Fred W. Frailey, "Brad Lewis," *Kiplinger's Personal Finance Magazine,* October 1994.

FUZZY LOGIC

Traditional computer programs require precision—on–off, yes–no, right–wrong. However, we human beings do not experience the world this way. We might all agree that +120 degrees is hot and −40 degrees is cold; but is 75 degrees hot, warm, comfortable, or cool? The answer depends on many factors: the wind, the humidity, the individual experiencing the temperature, one's clothing, and one's expectations. Many of our activities are also inexact. Tractor-trailer drivers would find it nearly impossible to back their rig into a space precisely specified to less than an inch on all sides. Fuzzy logic, a relatively new, rule-based development in AI, tolerates imprecision and even uses it to solve problems we could not have solved before. **Fuzzy logic** consists of a variety of concepts and techniques for representing and inferring knowledge that is imprecise, uncertain, or unreliable. Fuzzy logic can create rules that use approximate or subjective values and incomplete or ambiguous data. By expressing logic with some carefully defined imprecision, fuzzy logic is closer to the way people actually think than traditional IF–THEN rules.

Ford Motor Co. has developed a fuzzy logic application that backs a simulated tractor-trailer into a parking space. The application uses the following three rules:

fuzzy logic Rule-based AI that tolerates imprecision by using nonspecific terms called *membership functions* to solve problems.

Auto-focusing camcorders employ a focus algorithm based on fuzzy logic. The camera examines three focus points and then uses fuzzy logic to determine the one spot that has the highest probability of being the main subject.

IF the truck is *near* jackknifing, THEN *reduce* the steering angle.

IF the truck is *far away* from the dock, THEN steer *toward* the dock.

IF the truck is *near* the dock, THEN point the trailer *directly at* the dock.

This logic makes sense to us as human beings, for it represents how we think as we back that truck into its berth.

How does the computer make sense of this programming? The answer is relatively simple. The terms (known as *membership functions*) are imprecisely defined so that, for example, in Figure 12.13 *cool* is between 50 degrees and 70 degrees, although the temperature is most clearly cool between about 60 degrees and 67 degrees. Note that *cool*

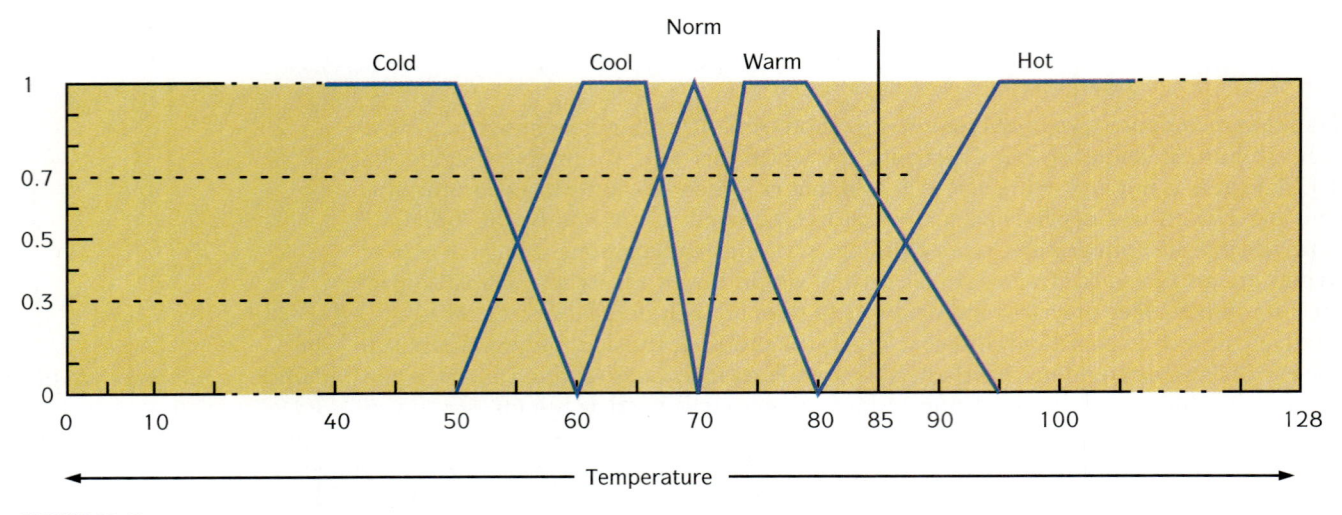

FIGURE 12.13
Implementing fuzzy logic rules in hardware. The membership functions for the input called *temperature* are in the logic of the thermostat to control the room temperature. Membership functions help translate linguistic expressions such as *warm* into numbers that can be manipulated by the computer. *Source: James M. Sibigtroth, "Implementing Fuzzy Expert Rules in Hardware,"* AI Expert, *April 1992.*

392   CHAPTER **12**   Managing Knowledge

is overlapped by *cold* or *norm*. To control the room environment using this logic, the programmer would develop similarly imprecise definitions for humidity and other factors such as outdoor wind and temperature. The rules might include one that says *If the temperature is cool or cold and the humidity is low while the outdoor wind is high and the outdoor temperature is low, raise the heat and humidity in the room.* The computer would combine the membership function readings in a weighted manner and, using all the rules, raise and lower the temperature and humidity.

Fuzzy logic is widely used in Japan and is gaining popularity in the United States. Its popularity has occurred partially because managers find they can use it to reduce costs and shorten development time. Fuzzy logic code requires few IF–THEN rules, making it simpler than traditional code. The rules required in the trucking example on page 392, plus its term definitions, might require hundreds of IF–THEN statements to implement in traditional logic. Compact code requires less computer capacity, allowing Sanyo Fisher USA to implement camcorder controls without adding expensive memory to their product.

Fuzzy logic also allows us to solve problems not previously solvable, thus improving product quality. In Japan, Sendai's subway system uses fuzzy logic controls to accelerate so smoothly that standing passengers need not hold on. Mitsubishi Heavy Industries in Tokyo has been able to reduce the power consumption of its air conditioners by 20 percent through implementing control programs in fuzzy logic. The autofocus device in our cameras is only possible because of fuzzy logic.

Management has also found it useful for decision making and organizational control. A Wall Street firm had a system developed that selects companies for potential acquisition, using the language stock traders understand. Recently a system has been developed to detect possible fraud in medical claims submitted by health care providers anywhere in the United States.

GENETIC ALGORITHMS

Genetic algorithms (also referred to as *adaptive computation*) refer to a variety of problem-solving techniques that are conceptually based on the method that living organisms use to adapt to their environment—the process of evolution. They are programmed to work the way populations solve problems—by changing and reorganizing their component parts using processes such as reproduction, mutation, and natural selection. Thus, genetic algorithms promote the *evolution* of solutions to particular problems, controlling the generation, variation, adaptation, and selection of possible solutions using genetically based processes. As solutions alter and combine, the worst ones are discarded and the better ones survive to go on and produce even better solutions. Genetic algorithms *breed* programs that solve problems even when no person can fully understand their structure (Holland, 1992).

Genetic algorithms originated in the work of John H. Holland, a professor of psychology and computer science at the University of Michigan, who devised a *genetic code* of binary digits that could be used to represent any type of computer program with a *1* representing *true* and a *0* representing *false*. With a long enough string of digits, any object can be represented by the right combination of digits. The genetic algorithm provides methods of searching all possible combinations of digits to identify the right string representing the best possible structure for the problem.

In one method, one first randomly generates a population of strings consisting of combinations of binary digits. Each string corresponds to one of the variables in the problem. One applies a test for fitness, ranking the strings in the population according to their level of desirability as possible solutions. Once the initial population is evaluated for fitness, the algorithm then produces the next generation of strings (consisting of strings that survived the fitness test plus offspring strings produced from mating pairs of strings) and tests their fitness. The process continues until a solution is reached (see Figure 12.14).

genetic algorithms Problem-solving methods that promote the evolution of solutions to specified problems using the model of living organisms adapting to their environment.

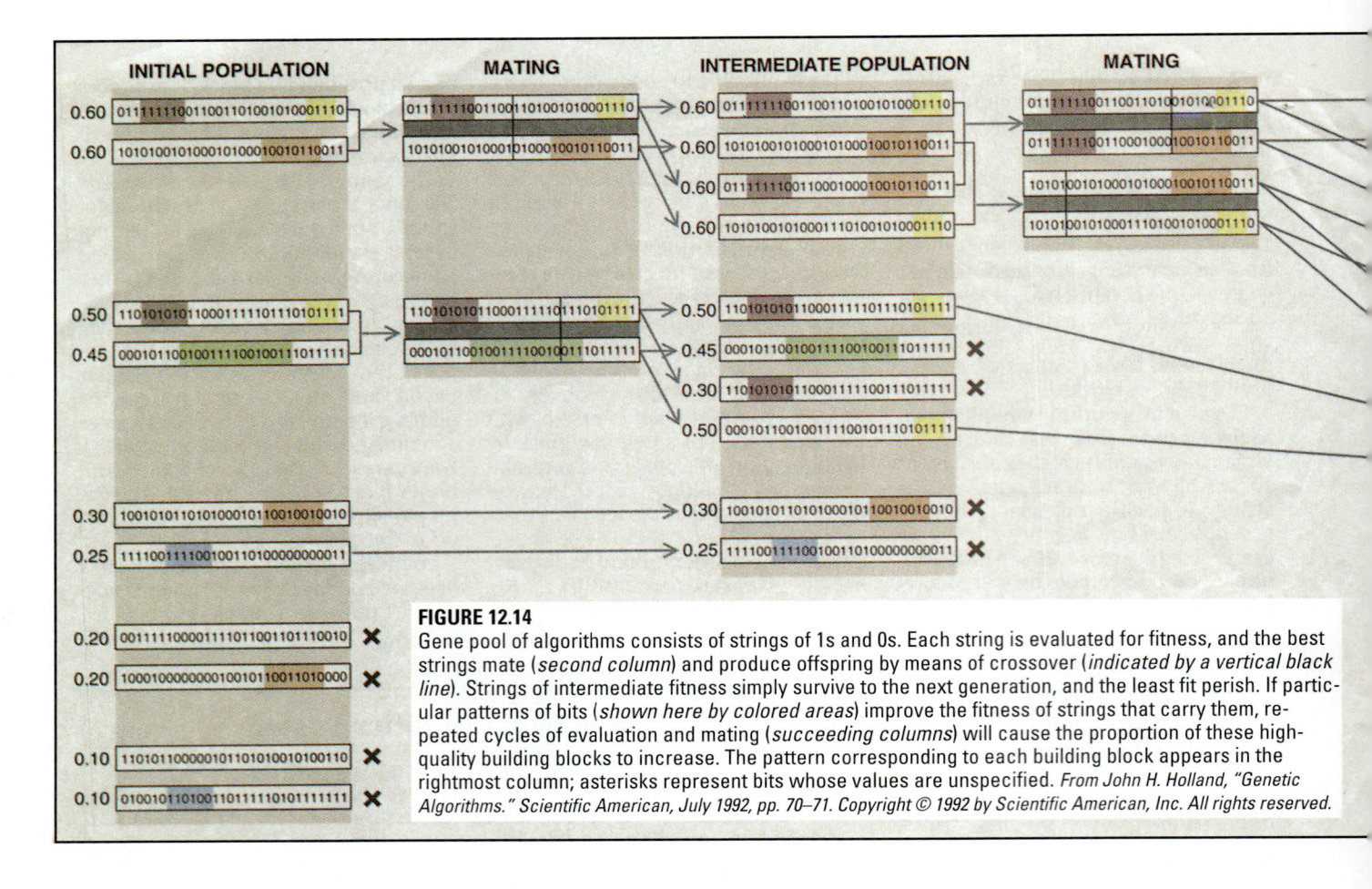

FIGURE 12.14
Gene pool of algorithms consists of strings of 1s and 0s. Each string is evaluated for fitness, and the best strings mate (*second column*) and produce offspring by means of crossover (*indicated by a vertical black line*). Strings of intermediate fitness simply survive to the next generation, and the least fit perish. If particular patterns of bits (*shown here by colored areas*) improve the fitness of strings that carry them, repeated cycles of evaluation and mating (*succeeding columns*) will cause the proportion of these high-quality building blocks to increase. The pattern corresponding to each building block appears in the rightmost column; asterisks represent bits whose values are unspecified. *From John H. Holland, "Genetic Algorithms." Scientific American, July 1992, pp. 70–71. Copyright © 1992 by Scientific American, Inc. All rights reserved.*

Like neural networks, genetic algorithms are ideal applications for massively parallel computers. Each processor can be assigned a single string. Thus, the entire population of a genetic algorithm can be processed in parallel, offering growing potential for solving problems of enormous complexity.

Solutions to certain types of problems in areas of optimization, product design, and the monitoring of industrial systems are especially appropriate for genetic algorithms. Many business problems require optimization because they deal with issues such as minimization of costs, maximization of profits, most efficient scheduling, and use of resources. If these situations are very dynamic and complex, involving hundreds of variables or hundreds of formulas, genetic algorithms are suitable for solving them because they can attack a solution from many directions at once.

Commercial applications of genetic algorithms are emerging. Engineers at General Electric use a genetic algorithm to help them design jet turbine aircraft engines, a complex problem involving about 100 variables and 50 constraint equations. The engineers evaluate design changes on a workstation that runs a simulation of the engine in operation. Because each design change requires a new simulation to test its effectiveness, the designers can spend weeks on solutions that may or may not be optimal. Using an expert system reduced the time to produce a satisfactory design from several weeks to several days but would produce solutions only up to a point. Further improvements required simultaneous changes in large numbers of variables. At that point GE introduced a genetic algorithm that took the initial population of designs produced by the expert system and generated a design that contained three times the number of improvements over the best previous version in a period of only two days. Other organizations using genetic algorithms include the Coors Brewing Company, which uses genetic algorithms for scheduling the fulfillment and shipment of orders, and the U.S. Navy, which uses genetic algorithms for scheduling F-16 tryouts (Burtka, 1993).

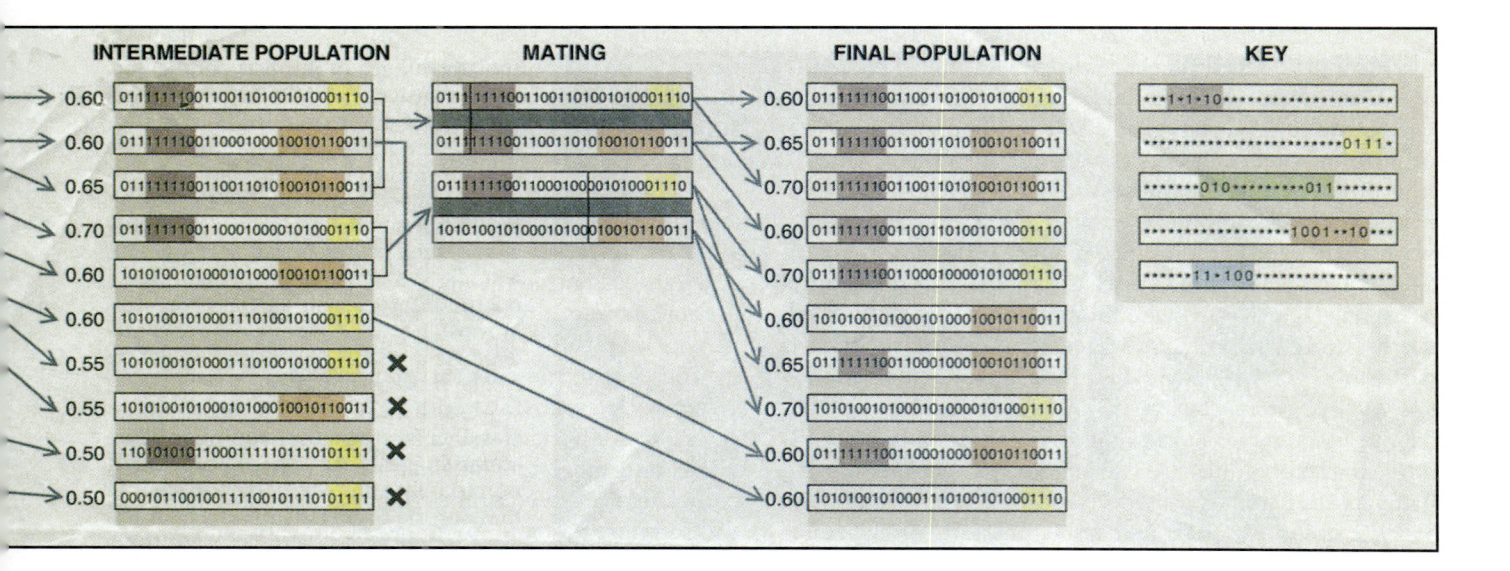

Management Challenges

1. Designing information systems that truly enhance the productivity of knowledge workers. Information systems that truly enhance the productivity of knowledge workers may be difficult to build because the manner in which information technology can enhance higher-level tasks such as those performed by managers and professionals (i.e., scientists or engineers) is not always clearly understood (Sheng et al. 1989/90). High-level knowledge workers may resist the introduction of any new technology, or they may resist knowledge work systems because such systems diminish personal control and creativity. For instance, some architects may resist using computer-aided architectural rendering systems because they fear that the computer-generated representations of buildings cannot convey the individual artistry and imagination of hand-drawn renderings.

2. Creating robust expert systems. Expert systems must be changed every time there is a change in the organizational environment. Every time there is a change in the rules used by experts, they have to be reprogrammed. It is difficult to provide expert systems with the flexibility of human experts. Many thousands of businesses have undertaken experimental projects in expert systems, but only a small percentage have created expert systems that can actually be used on a production basis.

3. Determining appropriate applications for artificial intelligence. Finding suitable applications for artificial intelligence techniques is not easy. Some parts of business processes are rule-based, others are based on patterns, and still others are based on exhaustive searching of manual files for the proverbial needle in the haystack. Identifying the business process, identifying the right technique, and determining how to build the system requires a focused effort.

Summary

1. Explain the importance of knowledge management in contemporary organizations. Knowledge management is the process of systematically and actively managing and leveraging the stores of knowledge in an organization. Knowledge is a central productive and strategic asset in an information economy. Information systems can play a valuable role in knowledge management, helping the organization optimize its flow of information and capture its knowledge base. Office automation systems (OAS), knowledge work systems (KWS), group collaboration systems, and artificial intelligence applications are especially useful for knowledge management because they focus primarily on supporting information and knowledge work and on defining and codifying the organization's knowledge base.

2. Describe the applications that are most useful for distributing, creating, and sharing knowledge in the firm. Offices coordinate information work in the organization, link the work of diverse groups in the organization, and couple the organization to its external environment. Office automation systems (OAS) support these functions by automating document management, communications, scheduling, and data management. Word processing, desktop publishing, and digital imaging systems support document management activities. Electronic mail systems and groupware support communications activities. Electronic calendar applications and groupware support scheduling activities. Desktop data management systems support data management activities.

Knowledge work systems (KWS) support the creation of new knowledge and its integration into the organization. KWS require easy access to an external knowledge base; powerful computer hardware that can support software with intensive graphics, analysis, document management, and communications capabilities; and a friendly user interface. Knowledge work systems often run on workstations that are customized for the work they must perform. Computer-aided design (CAD) systems and virtual reality systems that create interactive simulations that behave like the real world require graphics and powerful modeling capabilities. Knowledge work systems for financial professionals provide access to external databases and the ability to analyze massive amounts of financial data very quickly.

Groupware is special software to support information-intensive activities where people work collaboratively in groups. Intranets based on the World Wide Web can perform many group collaboration and support functions.

3. Define artificial intelligence. Artificial intelligence is the development of computer-based systems that behave like humans. There are five members of the artificial intelligence family tree: (1) natural language, (2) robotics, (3) perceptive systems, (4) expert systems, and (5) intelligent machines. Artificial intelligence lacks the flexibility, breadth, and generality of human intelligence but it can be used to capture and codify organizational knowledge.

4. Explain how organizations can use expert systems and case-based reasoning to capture knowledge. Expert systems are knowledge-intensive computer programs that solve problems that heretofore required human expertise. The systems capture a limited domain of human knowledge using rules, frames, or semantic nets. The strategy to search through the knowledge base, called the *inference engine*, can use either forward or backward chaining. Expert systems are most useful for problems of classification or diagnosis. Case-based reasoning represents organizational knowledge as a database of cases that can be continually expanded and refined. When the user encounters a new case, the system searches for similar cases, finds the closest fit, and applies the solutions of the old case to the new case. The new case is stored together with successful solutions in the case database.

5. Describe how organizations can use neural networks and other intelligent techniques to improve their knowledge base. Neural networks consist of hardware and software that attempt to mimic the thought processes of the human brain. Neural networks are notable for their ability to learn without programming and to recognize patterns that cannot be easily described by humans. They are being used in science, medicine, and business primarily to discriminate patterns in massive amounts of data.

Fuzzy logic is a software technology that expresses logic with some carefully defined imprecision so that it is closer to the way people actually think than traditional IF–THEN rules. Fuzzy logic has been used for controlling physical devices and is starting to be used for limited decision-making applications. Genetic algorithms develop solutions to particular problems using genetically based processes such as fitness, crossover, and mutation to breed solutions. Genetic algorithms are starting to be applied to problems involving optimization, product design, and monitoring industrial systems.

Key Terms

Knowledge management	**Knowledge work systems (KWS)**	**Knowledge base**	**Knowledge engineer**
Information work		**Rule-based expert system**	**Case-based reasoning (CBR)**
Data workers	**Computer-aided design (CAD)**	**Rule base**	
Knowledge workers		**Semantic nets**	**Neural network**
Office automation systems (OAS)	**Virtual reality systems**	**Frames**	**Fuzzy logic**
	Investment workstation	**AI shell**	**Genetic algorithms**
Document imaging systems	**Groupware**	**Inference engine**	
Jukebox	**Artificial intelligence**	**Forward chaining**	
Index server	**Expert system**	**Backward chaining**	

Review Questions

1. What is *knowledge management?* List and briefly describe the information systems that support it.
2. What is the relationship between information work and productivity in contemporary organizations?
3. Describe the roles of the office in organizations. What are the major activities that take place in offices?
4. What are the principal types of information systems that support information worker activities of the office?
5. What are the generic requirements of knowledge work systems? Why?
6. Describe how the following systems support knowledge work: computer-aided design (CAD), virtual reality, investment workstations.

7. How does groupware support information work? Describe its capabilities and the Internet capabilities for collaborative work.
8. What is *artificial intelligence*? Why is it of interest to business?
9. What is the difference between artificial intelligence and natural or human intelligence?
10. Define an *expert system* and describe how it can help organizations use their knowledge assets.
11. Define and describe the role of the following in expert systems: rule base, frames, semantic nets, inference engine.
12. What is *case-based reasoning*? How does it differ from an expert system?
13. Describe three problems of expert systems.
14. Describe a neural network. What kinds of tasks would a neural network be good at?
15. Define and describe *fuzzy logic*. What kinds of applications is it suited for?
16. What are genetic algorithms? How can they help organizations solve problems? What kinds of problems are they suited for?

Discussion Questions

1. A famous person has declared that artificial intelligence will lead to a fundamental redistribution of knowledge because all people will be able to have their own knowledge-based system, giving them access to knowledge that heretofore only experts have possessed. Discuss.
2. The CEO, in an effort to cut middle-management costs, has just announced a major effort to use artificial intelligence and expert systems to assist managers and, if possible, through attrition, to reduce the total cost of management. Discuss.
3. Describe some information system applications that would benefit from using fuzzy logic.

Group Project

With a group of classmates, find a task in an organization (near your college or university) that requires some intelligence to perform and that might be suitable for an expert system. Describe as many of the rules required to perform this task as possible. Interview and observe the person performing this task. Consider changing the task in order to simplify the system. Report your findings to the class.

Case Study

DESIGNING THE PAPERLESS AIRPLANE

The Boeing Company of Seattle is the single largest exporter in the United States and the number one commercial aircraft producer in the world, with 55 to 60 percent of the world market since the 1970s. The company is now entering the mid-long-range twin-engine widebody market just after European competitor Airbus Industrie opened the market in late 1994.

Airbus's new A330 widebody twin-jet plane went into service in November, 1994. In late 1994 Airbus announced a new four-engine double-decker plane, the A3XX, priced at about $200 million. This plane will carry 570 passengers up to 8400 miles, with operating costs projected to be 20 percent lower than Boeing's competing 747-400.

Although Airbus, McDonnell Douglas, and Japanese companies have become troubling sources of competition, Boeing's major competition may be its own old aircraft that are still in use. The cost of new planes has risen so dramatically that airlines are often choosing to refurbish older ones to make them last longer rather than placing orders for new aircraft.

Boeing has developed a multifaceted strategy to respond to these problems. The fundamental component of this strategy is to cut costs and prices. The company reduced its work force by one-third over a six-year period. At the same time the company is making design changes so that new planes will be significantly cheaper to operate than are existing planes. Boeing plans to use the lowered costs to drop new-plane prices so dramatically that it becomes cheaper for an airline to purchase and operate a new plane rather than to refurbish and operate an aging one. Management established a goal of reducing production costs by 25 percent between 1992 and 1998. They also intend to radically reduce the time needed to build a plane, for example, lowering the production time of 747s and 767s from 18 months in 1992 down to eight months in 1996. Reducing production time would result in major cost savings, for example, by reducing inventory expenses.

A second strategic decision was to hold tight and not attempt to compete directly with the Airbus A3XX. Many airlines today prefer to fly smaller planes direct from point of departure to destination, such as Cincinnati to Zurich. By using smaller airplanes and avoiding hubs such as New York's Kennedy Airport, the airlines avoid both slot congestion and the high cost of flying in and out of such hubs.

A third element of Boeing's strategy is to upgrade its existing aircraft lines. Boeing has invested $2.5 billion to upgrade its 737 short-haul line, and management is considering extensive redesign of the 747 in order to make it a reasonable competitor of the A3XX.

Finally, the company is introducing a new aircraft line—the 777—to compete in, and hopefully to dominate, the twin-engine widebody market that is just opening. The 777 class are medium-sized, widebody, twinjet, commercial passenger aircraft, carrying between 300 and 440 people. They are designed to fly with only two pilots, thus reducing the cost of operations. They use only two engines, which are the largest, most powerful aircraft engines ever built, achieving from 74,000 to 100,000 pounds of thrust each. Using only two engines reduces operating costs by saving on fuel, maintenance, and spare parts. Boeing claims that altogether the 777 will cost 25 percent less to operate than older Boeing models.

The planes use a number of new, lightweight, cost-effective structural materials, such as a new composite material for the floors and a new aluminum alloy used in wing skin that also improves corrosion and fatigue resistance. As a result of the lighter materials and fewer engines, a 777 weighs about 500,000 pounds, compared to 800,000 pounds for a four-engine 747. The planes will use a fly-by-wire flight-control system in which aircraft control and maneuver commands are transmitted to the elevators, rudder ailerons, and flaps as electrical signals flowing through electrical wires rather than by mechanical steel cables. Fly-by-wire control systems are easier to construct, lighter weight, and require fewer spare parts, and less maintenance.

The 777s are priced between $116 and $140 million. Industry analysts estimate that it will take about 300 aircraft and four years for Boeing to break even. They warn that if sales are slow, if this process is stretched out over twenty years, Boeing will never make a profit on the planes.

Boeing management opted to reengineer the whole design and production process for the 777. One major innovation was their decision to involve customers in design and testing. Four buyers—United, ANA, British Airways, and Japan Airlines—each kept a team of two to four engineers on site to work with the Boeing project team during the design, building, and testing phases. One of the results was that eighty items that in past lines had been optional equipment were made standard in response to users' requests, including satellite communications and global position systems.

Because during fabrication each airplane has to be individually configured to match customer specification, making optional equipment standard reduces variability during design and production of an order. The results are a lower cost of production and redesign and, ultimately, a lower sale price. In addition, other vital changes were made in response to customer requests. For example, the length of the wingspan of the 777 is far greater than previous Boeing planes. The users wanted the wingspan to be no greater than those of DC-10s and 767s so that the 777s would fit in existing airport gate and taxiway spaces. To accommodate this request, Boeing changed the wing design to incorporate a hinge that allows the wingtip to fold once the plane is on the runway, a feature that has long been common on military aircraft. Another issue raised by the customers involved the wing fuel intake panel. The 777 wing has a sharp upward sweep, resulting in the fuel intake panel being 31 inches higher than it is on 747s. At that location it was too high for current airport fuel trucks. Boeing agreed to move the intake panels closer to the aircraft body, where they would be at an appropriate height for existing fuel trucks.

One key change involves the move to paperless design—the *paperless airplane*. Boeing had to fight a paper war to design its airplanes. The final design of the Boeing 747 consisted of 75,000 engineering drawings, a typical amount for such a job. But the original design is only the opening battle of the paper war. The specific problem that propelled Boeing to move to paperless design was the need to repeatedly copy and reuse these designs. Every order for a plane or group of planes is customized according to the customer's requirement so that, for example, the seating arrangements and the electronic equipment will differ from order to order. In such situations Boeing designers long ago realized that they would save a great deal of time and work if they reused existing designs rather than design the customized configuration from scratch. However, the process of design customization was manual and took more than 1000 engineers a year of full-time work to complete. To reuse old, stored paper-aircraft configurations and parts designs, the engineers first needed to laboriously search through immense numbers of paper drawings to find appropriate designs to reuse for the configuration ordered. They then laboriously copied the old designs to use as a starting point for the new ones. Inevitably, errors crept in to the new designs—large numbers of errors, given the large numbers of design sheets—because of unavoidable copying mistakes. The thousands of engineers who manually worked on these designs rarely compared notes. Planes were built in fits and starts, filling warehouses with piles of paper and years of wasted byproducts.

Another problem with manual design was that the staff needed to create life-size mockups in plywood and plastic in order to make sure the pipes and wires that run through the plane are placed properly and do not interfere with other necessary equipment. They also needed to verify the accuracy of part specifications. This was a slow, expensive, laborious process. At production time, errors would again occur when part numbers of specifications were manually copied and at times miscopied onto order sheets, resulting in many wrong or mis-sized parts arriving. All of these challenges resulted in Boeing's decision to turn to a computer-aided design (CAD) system and to a team approach to designing and building the 777.

In addition to involving customers in the design process, Boeing established *design-build teams* that brought together designers and fabricators from a range of specialties throughout the whole process. In this way changes that used to have to be made after production began are now made during design because of the presence of production staff on the design team, saving a great deal of time and cost. Boeing's primary aim in turning to a CAD system was to reduce the possibility of human error.

Boeing's CAD system is gigantic, employing nine IBM mainframes, a Cray supercomputer, and 2200 workstations, and ultimately storing 3500 billion bits of information. The hardware alone cost hundreds of millions of dollars. It is one of the world's largest networks. Fiber-optic links connect Boeing's Seattle-area plants with a plant in Wichita, Kansas, which is constructing the flight deck for the 777, and with plants in Japan that are building most of the 777's fuselage. Boeing engineers calculate that their system has exchanged more than 1.5 trillion bytes of production data with Japan alone.

The amount of data on the network is so vast—more than 600 databases in different software languages—that information is sometimes hard for users to find. Some engineers need four kinds of computers on their desks to obtain the information they need. Analysts have likened the network to the Tower of Babel.

Boeing purchased three-dimensional graphics software called Catia, developed by France's Dassault Systems, a unit of Dassault Aviation SA. *Catia* stands for *computer aided three-dimensional interactive application*. The system enables engineers to call up any of the 777's three million parts, modify them, fit them into the surrounding structure, and put them back into the plane's "electronic box" so that other engineers can make their own adjustments.

For instance, an engineer designing the rib of the aircraft's wing might find that the wing spar abutting the rib overlaps it by 11/100ths of an inch. He or she could move the computer icon to the intruding spar, and the system would call up the name and telephone number of the designer for that piece. In the past, the clash would trigger a new pile of paperwork. With the new CAD system, engineers can alter the rib's design to fit snugly against the spar in 30 minutes. Boeing officials claim they could use the system to redesign large pieces of an airplane's fuselage in a matter of weeks. The system has cut the time spent reworking 777 parts by more than 90 percent, compared to the paper-based approach for earlier models.

The team set a specific goal of reducing engineering changes and ill-fitting components by 50 percent compared to the last major Boeing design project (767s). CAD software enables engineers to test how all parts fit together without having to build models and without having to solve most problems during the assembly of the first aircraft at which time extensive redesign of the aircraft and of individual parts is very costly and time consuming. The designs stored in the CAD software system can be used to generate parts orders and fabrication specifications automatically without all the errors that result from hand copying. Finally, by electronically storing aircraft configurations and parts designs, those designs can quickly and easily be located, copied, and used as the basis for designing new plane orders. CAD technology helped Boeing break from the traditional method of building the whole plane sequentially. Boeing moved to parallel production, building selected sections of the plane simultaneously.

Boeing put in more engineering time on the project than originally planned because the software proved somewhat slow and complicated to manipulate. Some engineers had trouble making the transition from working two-dimensionally on paper to working three-dimensionally on the computer screen. Boeing is working with IBM and Dassault to improve the CAD system for advanced versions of the 777. Boeing management believes the ease with which the parts are going together will make up for the increased front-end costs.

The preliminary results have certainly been promising. The airplane was designed entirely on the computer screen, and it was assembled without first building mockups. Using electronic pre-assembly, many of the space conflicts were solved before any physical production took place. The value of electronic design software was proven, for example, when the wing flaps were designed and electronically tested in mid-1992 wholly on the computer. Later, in 1994, the actual tests on a live aircraft showed that the wing flaps worked perfectly.

The accuracy of the CAD design system is clear. In the past, the typical horizontal or vertical variances of any part was 3/8 to 1/2 inch. Using the CAD system to design the parts, the average variance was reduced to 23/1000 of an inch vertically and 11/1000 of an inch horizontally. The company reports that it exceeded its goal of cutting overall engineering design errors by 50 percent. Boeing has announced that the time to design and build a 777 order has already been reduced to 10 months compared to the 18 months initially required for 747 and 767 orders. Total cost to design and bring the 777 to production was $4 billion.

One final issue Boeing faced was that of testing and receiving governmental approval for operation from the United States Federal Aviation Administration (FAA). Standard certification testing has not been a problem. The main testing hurdle Boeing faced was the need to achieve ETOPS certification. ETOPS stands for Extended-range Twinjet Operations, and ETOPS approval is granted by the FAA. It is needed before commercial long-range flights over water can occur. It is required for two-engine planes (four-engine planes are less vulnerable to problems from engine failure, because the failure of one or two engines will leave two or three still operating).

In the past ETOPS approval has come only after the plane has been in service two years so its performance could be evaluated under actual operational conditions. Boeing wanted approval for the 777 earlier than that to prevent Airbus from garnering too large a portion of the twin-engine widebody market.

To obtain ETOPS approval at the same time the 777 aircraft went into service in the spring, 1995, Boeing engaged in a far more extensive than normal testing program, working closely with the FAA. Boeing management asserted that the computerized design of the airplane, along with the heavy testing regimen, justified an early award. On May 30, 1995, the FAA granted unprecedented approval for the 777 to begin over-water flights without two years of in-service tests.

Boeing made its first delivery of 777s on time to United Airlines on May 15, 1995, and the 777 commenced commercial service the following month. Since then Boeing booked over 200 orders for the new aircraft, with very strong demand from Asian carriers. United complained that the 777 had too many mechanical problems that had disrupted departures twice as often as expected. Expectations for immediate reliability were high because Boeing management had so heavily promoted the advanced testing performed on the 777. Some FAA officials subsequently revealed that the pressure for early ETOPS certification led top-level officials to overrule safety concerns about a design flaw in the engine fan blades that might severely destabilize the plane. ■

Sources: Jeff Cole and Michael J. McCarthy, "United Warns Boeing that Performance of New 777 Is 'Major Disappointment,'" *The Wall Street Journal*, March 6, 1996; Christina Del Valle and Michael Schroeder, "Did the FAA Go Easy on Boeing?" *Business Week*, January 29, 1996; John Holusha, "Can Boeing's New Baby Fly Financially?" *The New York Times*, March 27, 1994; Bill Richards, "The Future is Now," *The Wall Street Journal*, November 14, 1994; Howard Banks, "Superjumbo," *Forbes*, October 24, 1994; Shawn Tully, "Why to Go for Stretch Targets," *Fortune*, November 4, 1994; Boeing News Release, "Boeing 777 Designers Take B-Market to New Level," Boeing Commercial Airplane Group, March 2, 1995; "Boeing 777 Sets New Standards in Aircraft Design," Boeing Commercial Airplane Group (no date).

Case Study Questions

1. Analyze Boeing's competitive position using the competitive forces and value chain models.
2. What is Boeing's competitive business strategy? In what ways do you consider their strategy sound? Risky? Explain your answers.
3. Describe how the Boeing 777 line fits in with this strategy.
4. What role do knowledge work systems play in Boeing's business strategy? Evaluate the significance of that role.
5. How well does the knowledge work system function as a factor in Boeing's business strategy?
6. What management, organization, and technology problems do you think the use of the knowledge work software presented to Boeing? What steps do you think they did take, or should have taken, to deal with these problems?

References

Allen, Bradley P. "Case-Based Reasoning: Business Applications." *Communications of the ACM* 37, no. 3 (March 1994).

Amaravadi, Chandra S., Olivia R. Liu Sheng, Joey F. George, and Jay F. Nunamaker, Jr. "AEI: A Knowledge-Based Approach to Integrated Office Systems." *Journal of Management Information Systems* 9, no. 1 (Summer 1992).

Applegate, Linda. "Technology Support for Cooperative Work: A Framework for Studying Introduction and Assimilation in Organizations." *Journal of Organizational Computing* 1, no. 1 (January–March 1991).

Asakawa, Kazuo, and Hideyuki Takagi. "Neural Networks in Japan." *Communications of the ACM* 37, no. 3 (March 1994).

Bansal, Arun, Robert J. Kauffman, and Rob R. Weitz. "The Modeling Performance of Regression and Neural Networks." *Journal of Management Information Systems* 10, no. 1 (Summer 1993).

Barker, Virginia E., and Dennis E. O'Connor. "Expert Systems for Configuration at Digital: XCON and Beyond." *Communications of the ACM* (March 1989).

Bair, James H. "A Layered Model of Organizations: Communication Processes and Performance." *Journal of Organizational Computing* 1, no. 2 (April–June 1991).

Bikson, Tora K., J.D. Eveland, and Barbara A. Gutek. "Flexible Interactive Technologies for Multi-Person Tasks: Current Problems and Future Prospects." Rand Corporation (December 1988).

Black, George. "Taking Notes, Big Sixer Aims for Head of the Class." *Software Magazine* (March 1995).

Blanning, Robert W., David R. King, James R. Marsden, and Ann C. Seror. "Intelligent Models of Human

Organizations: The State of the Art." *Journal of Organizational Computing* 2, no. 2 (1992).

Bobrow, D.G., S. Mittal, and M.J. Stefik. "Expert Systems: Perils and Promise." *Communications of the ACM* 29 (September 1986).

Bohn, Roger E. "Measuring and Managing Technological Knowledge." *Sloan Management Review* (Fall 1994).

Braden, Barbara, Jerome Kanter, and David Kopcso. "Developing an Expert Systems Strategy." *MIS Quarterly* 13, no. 4 (December 1989).

Brynjolfsson, Erik. "The Productivity Paradox of Information Technology." *Communications of the ACM* 36, no. 12 (December 1993).

Brynjolfsson, Erik, and Lorin Hitt. "New Evidence on the Returns to Information Systems." MIT Sloan School of Management, October 1993.

Burtka, Michael. "Generic Algorithms." *The Stern Information Systems Review* 1, no. 1 (Spring 1993).

Busch, Elizabeth, Matti Hamalainen, Clyde W. Holsapple, Yongmoo Suh, and Andrew B. Whinston. "Issues and Obstacles in the Development of Team Support Systems." *Journal of Organizational Computing* 1, no. 2 (April–June 1991).

Byrd, Terry Anthony. "Implementation and Use of Expert Systems in Organizations: Perceptions of Knowledge Engineers." *Journal of Management Information Systems* 8, no. 4 (Spring 1992).

Carlson, David A., and Sudha Ram. "A Knowledge Representation for Modeling Organizational Productivity." *Journal of Organizational Computing* 2, no. 2 (1992).

Churchland, Paul M., and Patricia Smith Churchland. "Could a Machine Think?" *Scientific American* (January 1990).

Clifford, James, Henry C. Lucas, Jr., and Rajan Srikanth. "Integrating Mathematical and Symbolic Models through AESOP: An Expert for Stock Options Pricing." *Information Systems Research* 3, no. 4 (December 1992).

Cox, Earl. "Applications of Fuzzy System Models." *AI Expert* (October 1992).

Cox, Earl. "Solving Problems with Fuzzy Logic." *AI Expert* (March 1992).

Creecy, Robert H., Brij M. Masand, Stephen J. Smith, and Davis L. Waltz. "Trading MIPS and Memory for Knowledge Engineering." *Communications of the ACM* 35, no. 8 (August 1992).

Dhar, Vasant. "Plausibility and Scope of Expert Systems in Management." *Journal of Management Information Systems* (Summer 1987).

El Najdawi, M.K. and Anthony C. Stylianou. "Expert Support Systems: Integrating AI Technologies." *Communications of the ACM* 36, no. 12 (December 1993).

Feigenbaum, Edward A. "The Art of Artificial Intelligence: Themes and Case Studies in Knowledge Engineering." *Proceedings of the IJCAI* (1977).

Feigenbaum, Edward A., and Pamela McCorduck. *The Fifth Generation: Artificial Intelligence and Japan's Computer Challenge to the World*. Reading, MA: Addison-Wesley (1985).

Gelernter, David. "The Metamorphosis of Information Management." *Scientific American* (August 1989).

Gill, Philip J. "A False Rivalry Revealed." *Information Week* (May 20, 1996).

Giuliao, Vincent E. "The Mechanization of Office Work." *Scientific American* (September 1982).

Goldberg, David E. "Genetic and Evolutionary Algorithms Come of Age." *Communications of the ACM* 37, no. 3 (March 1994).

Griggs, Kenneth. "Visual Aids that Model Organizations." *Journal of Organizational Computing* 2, no. 2 (1992).

Hayes-Roth, Frederick. "Knowledge-Based Expert Systems." *Spectrum IEEE* (October 1987).

Hayes-Roth, Frederick, and Neil Jacobstein. "The State of Knowledge-Based Systems." *Communications of the ACM* 37, no. 3 (March 1994).

Hinton, Gregory. "How Neural Networks Learn from Experience." *Scientific American* (September 1992).

Holland, John H. "Genetic Algorithms." *Scientific American* (July 1992).

"How Organizations Use Groupware to Improve a Wide Range of Business Processes." *I/S Analyzer* 35, no. 2 (February 1996).

Jacobs, Paul S., and Lisa F. Rau. "SCISOR: Extracting Information from On-line News." *Communications of the ACM* 33, no. 11 (November 1990).

Johansen, Robert. "Groupware: Future Directions and Wild Cards." *Journal of Organizational Computing* 1, no. 2 (April–June 1991).

Kanade, Takeo, Michael L. Reed, and Lee E. Weiss. "New Technologies and Applications in Robotics." *Communications of the ACM* 37 no. 3 (March 1994).

Lee, Soonchul. "The Impact of Office Information Systems on Power and Influence." *Journal of Management Information Systems* 8, no. 2 (Fall 1991).

Leonard-Barton, Dorothy, and John J. Sviokla. "Putting Expert Systems to Work." *Harvard Business Review* (March–April 1988).

Liker, Jeffrey K., Mitchell Fleischer, Mitsuo Nagamachi, and Michael S. Zonnevylle. "Designers and Their Machines: CAD Use and Support in the U.S. and Japan." *Communications of the ACM* 35, no. 2 (February 1992).

Lin, Frank C., and Mei Lin. "Neural Networks in the Financial Industry." *AI Expert* (February 1993).

Mann, Marina M., Richard L. Rudman, Thomas A. Jenckes, and Barbara C. McNurlin. "EPRINET: Leveraging Knowledge in the Electronic Industry." *MIS Quarterly* 15, no. 3 (September 1991).

Marsden, James R., David E. Pingry, and Ming-Chian Ken Wang. "Intelligent Information and Organization Structures: An Integrated Design Approach." *Journal of Organizational Computing* 2, no. 2 (1992).

McCarthy, John. "Generality in Artificial Intelligence." *Communications of the ACM* (December 1987).

McCune, Jenny C. "All Together Now." *Beyond Computing* (May 1996).

Meador, C. Lawrence, and Ed G. Mahler. "Choosing an Expert System Game Plan," *Datamation* (August 1, 1990).

Meyer, Marc H., and Kathleen Foley Curley. "An Applied Framework for Classifying the Complexity of Knowledge-Based Systems." *MIS Quarterly* 15, no. 4 (December 1991).

Michaels, Jenna. "Managing Technology." *Wall Street & Technology* (February 1993).

Motiwalla, Luvai, and Jay F. Nunamaker, Jr. "Mail-Man: A Knowledge-Based Mail Assistant for Managers." *Journal of Organizational Computing* 2, no. 2 (1992).

Munakata, Toshinori, and Yashvant Jani. "Fuzzy Systems: An Overview." *Communications of the ACM* 37, no. 3 (March 1994).

Mykytyn, Kathleen, Peter P. Mykytyn, Jr., and Craig W. Stinkman. "Expert Systems: A Question of Liability." *MIS Quarterly* 14, no. 1 (March 1990).

Naj, Amal Kumar. "Virtual Reality Isn't a Fantasy for Surgeons." *The Wall Street Journal* (March 3, 1993).

Nash, Jim. "Expert Systems: A New Partnership." *AI Expert* (December 1992).

Nash, Jim. "State of the Market, Art, Union, and Technology." *AI Expert* (January 1993).

Newquist, Harvey P. "AI at American Express." *AI Expert* (January 1993).

Newquist, Harvey P. "Virtual Reality's Commercial Reality." *Computerworld* (March 30, 1992).

Panko, Raymond R. "Is Office Productivity Stagnant?" *MIS Quarterly* 15, no. 2 (June 1991).

Porat, Marc. *The Information Economy: Definition and Measurement*. Washington, DC: U.S. Department of Commerce, Office of Telecommunications (May 1977).

Press, Lawrence. "Systems for Finding People." *Journal of Organizational Computing* 2, no. 3 and 4 (1992a).

Press, Lawrence. "Lotus Notes (Groupware) in Context." *Journal of Organizational Computing* 2, no. 3 and 4 (1992b).

Roach, Stephen S. "Industrialization of the Information Economy." New York: Morgan Stanley and Co. (1984).

Roach, Stephen S. "Making Technology Work." New York: Morgan Stanley and Co. (1993).

Roach, Stephen S. "Services Under Siege—The Restructuring Imperative." *Harvard Business Review* (September–October 1991).

Roach, Stephen S. "Technology and the Service Sector." *Technological Forecasting and Social Change* 34, no. 4 (December 1988).

Ruhleder, Karen, and John Leslie King. "Computer Support for Work Across Space, Time, and Social Worlds." *Journal of Organizational Computing* 1, no. 4 (1991).

Rumelhart, David E., Bernard Widrow, and Michael A. Lehr. "The Basic Ideas in Neural Networks." *Communications of the ACM* 37 no. 3 (March 1994).

Schatz, Bruce R. "Building an Electronic Community System." *Journal of Management Information Systems* 8, no. 3 (Winter 1991–1992).

Searle, John R. "Is the Brain's Mind a Computer Program?" *Scientific American* (January 1990).

Self, Kevin. "Designing with Fuzzy Logic." *Spectrum IEEE* (November 1990).

Sheng, Olivia R. Liu, Luvai F. Motiwalla, Jay F. Nunamaker, Jr., and Douglas R. Vogel. "A Framework to Support Managerial Activities Using Office Information Systems." *Journal of Management Information Systems* 6, no. 3 (Winter 1989–90).

Sibigtroth, James M. "Implementing Fuzzy Expert Rules in Hardware." *AI Expert* (April 1992).

Simon, H. A., and A. Newell. "Heuristic Problem Solving: The Next Advance in Operations Research." *Operations Research* 6 (January–February 1958).

Sproull, Lee, and Sara Kiesler. *Connections: New Ways of Working in the Networked Organization*. Cambridge, MA: MIT Press, 1992.

Starbuck, William H. "Learning by Knowledge-Intensive Firms." *Journal of Management Studies* 29, no. 6 (November 1992).

Stein, Eric W. "A Method to Identify Candidates for Knowledge Acquisition." *Journal of Management Information Systems* 9, no. 2 (Fall 1992).

Storey, Veda C., and Robert C. Goldstein, "Knowledge-Based Approaches to Database Design," *MIS Quarterly* 17, no. 1 (March 1993).

Sylianou, Anthony C., Gregory R. Madey, and Robert D. Smith. "Selection Criteria for Expert System Shells: A Socio-Technical Framework." *Communications of the ACM* 35, no. 10 (October 1992).

Sviokla, John J. "An Examination of the Impact of Expert Systems on the Firm: The Case of XCON." *MIS Quarterly* 14, no. 5 (June 1990).

Sviokla, John J. "Expert Systems and Their Impact on the Firm: The Effects of PlanPower Use on the Information Processing Capacity of the Financial Collaborative." *Journal of Management Information Systems* 6, no. 3 (Winter 1989–90).

Tam, Kar Yan. "Automated Construction of Knowledge-Bases from Examples." *Information Systems Research* 1, no. 2 (June 1990).

Tank, David W., and John J. Hopfield. "Collective Computation in Neuronlike Circuits." *Scientific American* (October 1987).

Trippi, Robert, and Efraim Turban. "The Impact of Parallel and Neural Computing on Managerial Decision Making." *Journal of Management Information Systems* 6, no. 3 (Winter 1989–1990).

Turban, Efraim, and Paul R. Watkins. "Integrating Expert Systems and Decision Support Systems." *MIS Quarterly* (June 1986).

Wallich, Paul. "Silicon Babies." *Scientific American* (December 1991).

Waltz, David L. "Artificial Intelligence." *Scientific American* (December 1982).

Weitzel, John R., and Larry Kerschberg. "Developing Knowledge Based Systems: Reorganizing the System Development Life Cycle." *Communications of the ACM* (April 1989).

Weizenbaum, Joseph. *Computer Power and Human Reason—From Judgment to Calculation*. San Francisco: Freeman (1976).

White, George M. "Natural Language Understanding and Speech Recognition." *Communications of the ACM* 33, no. 8 (August 1990).

Widrow, Bernard, David E. Rumelhart, and Michael A. Lehr. "Neural Networks: Applications in Industry, Business and Science." *Communications of the ACM* 27, no. 3 (March 1994).

Zadeh, Lotfi A. "Fuzzy Logic, Neural Networks, and Soft Computing." *Communications of the ACM* 37, no. 3 (March 1994).

Zadeh, Lotfi A. "The Calculus of Fuzzy If/Then Rules." *AI Expert* (March 1992).

Chapter 13

Enhancing Management Decision Making

The Ideal Investment Portfolio:
What Does the System Say?

13.1 Decision-Support Systems (DSS)
What Are Decision-Support Systems?
Examples of DSS Applications
Components of DSS
Window on Management
Practicing Decision Making
Building DSS

13.2 Group Decision-Support Systems (GDSS)
What Is a GDSS?

Window on Organizations
The Hohenheim CATeam Room
Characteristics of GDSS
GDSS Software Tools
How GDSS Can Enhance Group Decision Making

13.3 Executive Support Systems (ESS)
The Role of ESS in the Organization
Developing ESS
Window on Technology
Fighting Infoglut

Benefits of ESS
Examples of ESS

Management Challenges
Summary
Key Terms
Review Questions
Discussion Questions
Group Project
Case Study: Zeneca Searches for Decisions
References

The Ideal Investment Portfolio: What Does the System Say?

Redstone Advisors is a $550 million money management firm specializing in taxable and tax-exempt fixed income investments. It must track and analyze complex financial instruments under rapidly changing market conditions. Redstone has monthly policy meetings to determine how its investment portfolios will be constructed. The meetings establish general guidelines for the portfolios, such as the percentage of cash, the weight of each sector, and the average duration of the portfolios (that is, the average number of years for the underlying bonds to reach maturity). The firm then makes trades to bring its portfolios into line with the established guidelines.

To help its traders make buy and sell decisions, Redstone uses a LAN-based portfolio management system called PORTIA supplied by Thomson Financial Services in Boston and

London. Redstone analysts enter proposed trades into PORTIA. The system has a what-if capability; when they enter the proposed trades PORTIA tells them what the portfolio will look like. The traders can keep experimenting with different trades until the simulated portfolio matches the investment guidelines. They can even examine the portfolio from many angles using multiple currencies—their system's base currency, the currency of a particular security, or a currency for the selected portfolio. The system allows users to examine the impact of various currencies on investment performance. With this information they then make the trades. Once the actual trades have been entered into PORTIA, the change is instantly reflected in a portfolio's cash balances and holdings. According to Marc Vincent, Redstone's management director, the ability to perform what-if analysis and to know exact portfolio holdings and cash balances improves productivity and decision making. ■

Sources: "Fixed Income Money Manager Boosts Efficiency with Flexible, Comprehensive System," *Wall Street and Technology* 12, no. 6 (May 1994); and Sheila O'Henry, "The Portfolio Management and Accounting Supermarket," *Wall Street and Technology* 11, no. 5 (November 1993).

With the ability to perform complex calculations and to create what-if scenarios, Redstone's portfolio management system is a classic example of a decision-support system. Decision-support systems (DSS) provide powerful analytic capabilities for supporting managers during the process of arriving at a decision.

Most of the information systems described throughout this text help people make decisions in one way or another, but DSS are part of a special category of information systems that are explicitly designed to enhance managerial decision making. Other systems in this category are group decision-support systems (GDSS), which support decision making in groups and executive support systems (ESS), which provide information for making strategic-level decisions. This chapter describes the characteristics of each of these types of information systems and shows how each actually enhances the managerial decision-making process.

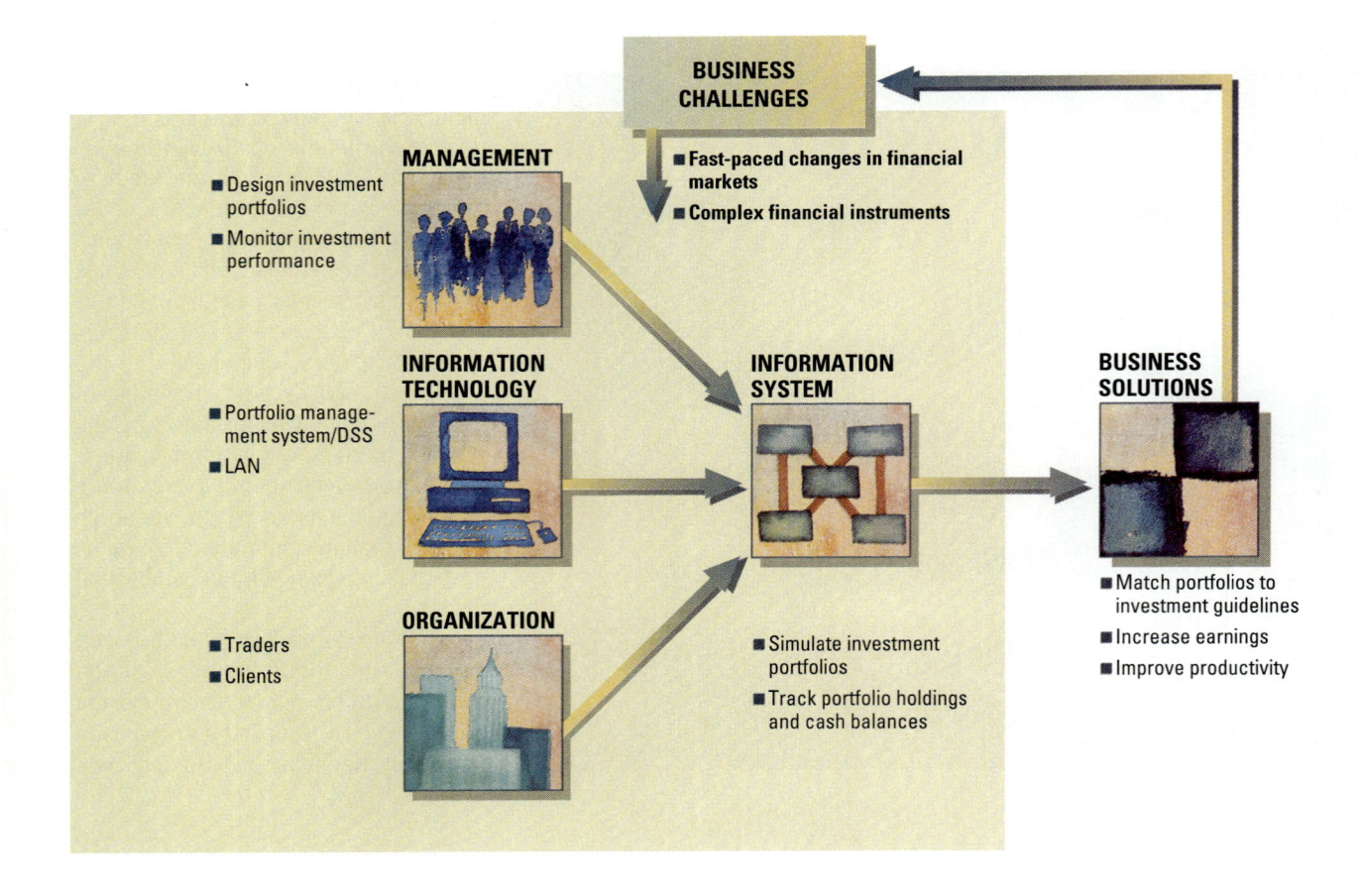

BUSINESS CHALLENGES
- Fast-paced changes in financial markets
- Complex financial instruments

MANAGEMENT
- Design investment portfolios
- Monitor investment performance

INFORMATION TECHNOLOGY
- Portfolio management system/DSS
- LAN

ORGANIZATION
- Traders
- Clients

INFORMATION SYSTEM
- Simulate investment portfolios
- Track portfolio holdings and cash balances

BUSINESS SOLUTIONS
- Match portfolios to investment guidelines
- Increase earnings
- Improve productivity

> **Learning Objectives**
>
> *After completing this chapter, you will be able to:*
>
> 1. Define a decision-support system (DSS) and a group decision-support system (GDSS).
> 2. Describe the components of decision-support systems and group decision-support systems.
> 3. Explain how decision-support systems and group decision-support systems can enhance decision making.
> 4. Describe the capabilities of executive support systems (ESS).
> 5. Describe the benefits of executive support systems.

13.1 DECISION-SUPPORT SYSTEMS (DSS)

In the 1970s a number of companies began developing information systems that were quite different from traditional MIS systems. These new systems were smaller, interactive, and designed to help end users utilize data and models to discuss and decide (not solve) semi-structured and unstructured problems (Henderson and Schilling, 1985). By the late 1980s these early efforts to assist individual decision making were extended to groups and entire organizations.

WHAT ARE DECISION-SUPPORT SYSTEMS?

These systems are called *decision-support systems* (DSS). As we noted in Chapter 2, **decision-support systems (DSS)** assist management decision making by combining data, sophisticated analytical models, and user-friendly software into a single powerful system that can support semi-structured or unstructured decision making. The DSS is under user control from early inception to final implementation and daily use. Figure 13.1 is a schematic diagram of a DSS.

In Figure 13.1 the relationships between DSS and the organization's existing TPS, KWS, and MIS are left deliberately vague. In some cases DSS are linked closely to existing corporate information flows. Often, however, DSS are isolated from major organizational information systems. DSS tend to be stand-alone systems, developed by end-user divisions or groups not under central IS control, although it is obviously better if they are integrated into organizational systems when this is a functional requirement (Hogue, 1985).

decision-support system (DSS) Computer system at the management level of an organization that combines data, sophisticated analytical models, and user-friendly software to support semi-structured and unstructured decision making.

DSS as a Philosophy

Stated simply, the philosophy of DSS is to give users the tools necessary to analyze important blocks of data, using easily controlled sophisticated models in a flexible manner. DSS are designed to deliver capabilities, not simply to respond to information needs (Keen and Morton, 1982; Sprague and Carlson, 1982).

DSS are tightly focused on a specific decision or classes of decisions such as routing, queuing, evaluating, and so forth. Table 13.1 summarizes the differences between DSS and MIS. In philosophy, DSS promises end-user control of data, tools, and sessions. MIS is still largely dominated by professionals: Users receive information from a professional staff of analysts, designers, and programmers. In terms of objectives, MIS focuses on structured information flows to middle managers. DSS is aimed at top managers and middle managers, with emphasis on change, flexibility, and a quick response; with DSS there is less of an effort to link users to structured information flows and a correspondingly greater emphasis on models, assumptions, and display graphics. Both

FIGURE 13.1
Overview of a decision-support system (DSS). The DSS is often isolated from the corporation's transaction processing systems (TPS), knowledge work systems (KWS), and management information systems (MIS). The main components of the DSS are the model base, the DSS database, and the DSS software system and user interface.

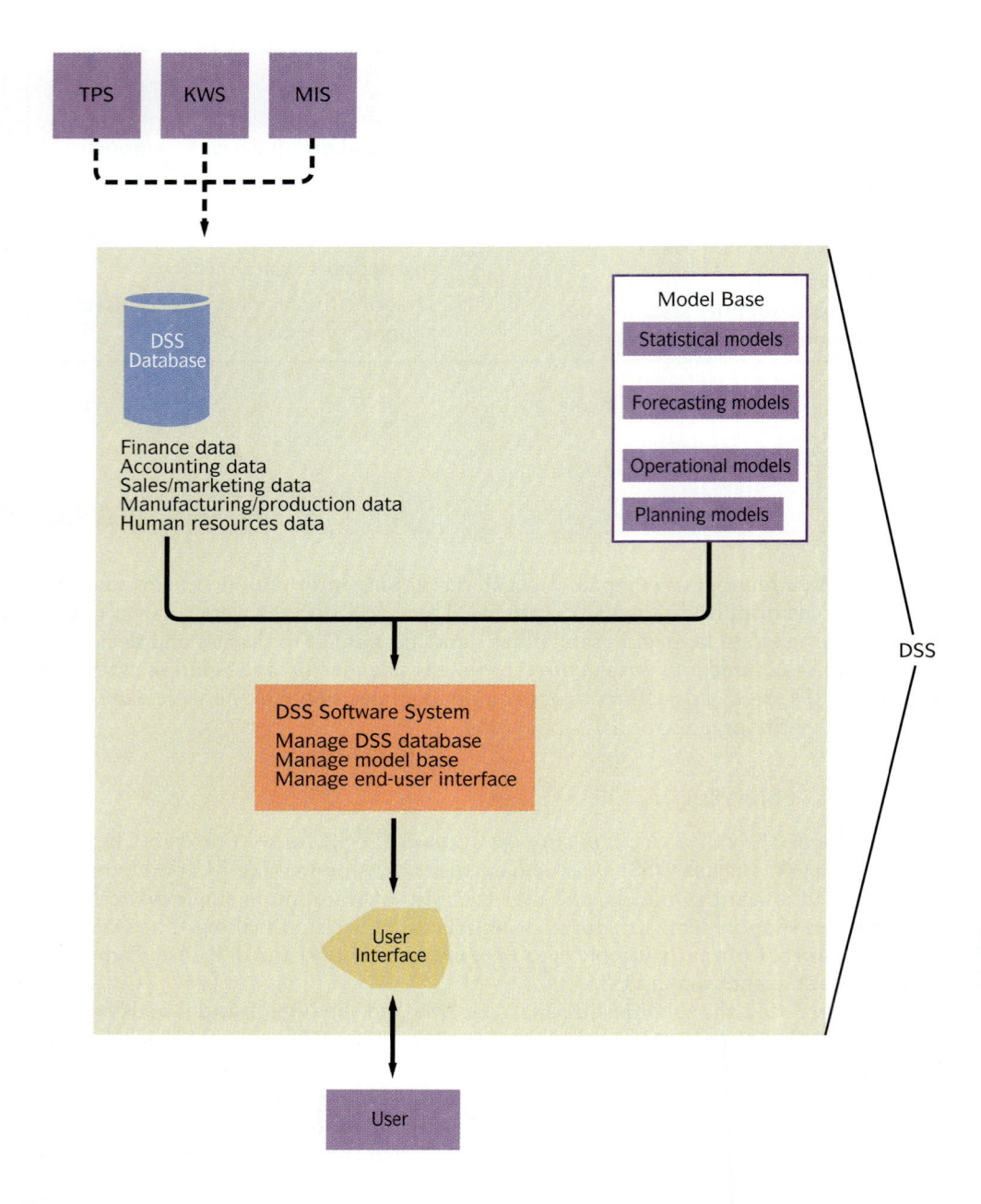

DSS and MIS rely on professional analysis and design. However, whereas MIS usually follows a traditional systems development methodology, freezing information requirements before design and throughout the lifecycle, DSS systems are consciously iterative, are never frozen, and in a sense are never finished.

Table 13.1	Differences between DSS and MIS	
Dimension	**DSS**	**MIS**
Philosophy	Provide integrated tools, data, models, and language to users	Provide structured information to end users
Systems analysis	Establish what tools are used in the decision process	Identify information requirements
Design	Iterative process	Deliver system based on frozen requirements

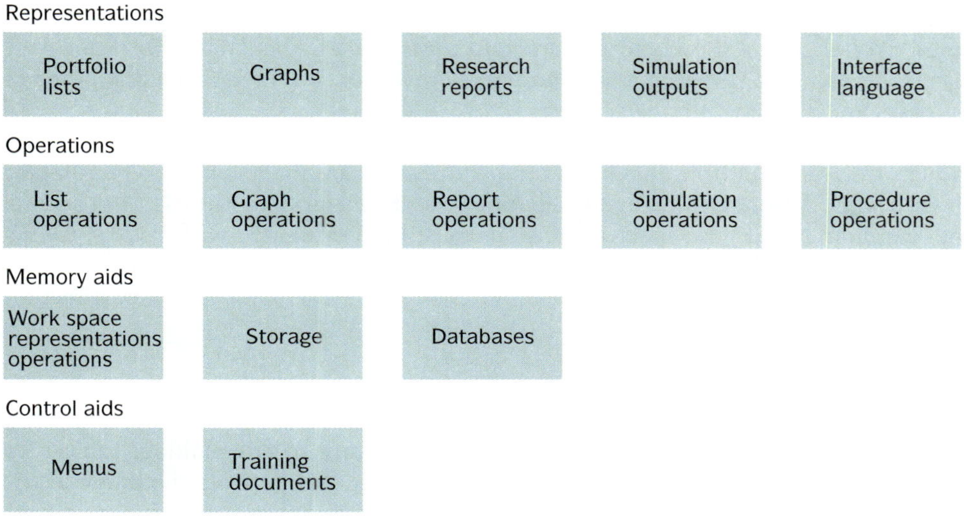

FIGURE 13.2
DSS approach to investment decisions. In a DSS approach to systems, the emphasis is on providing capabilities to answer questions and reach decisions. The four core capabilities are representations, operations, memory aids, and control aids. *From* Building Effective Decision Support Systems *by Sprague/Carlson, © 1982. Adapted by permission of Prentice-Hall, Inc., Upper Saddle River, NJ.*

Representations: Portfolio lists | Graphs | Research reports | Simulation outputs | Interface language

Operations: List operations | Graph operations | Report operations | Simulation operations | Procedure operations

Memory aids: Work space representations operations | Storage | Databases

Control aids: Menus | Training documents

Figure 13.2 shows how a DSS would support stock investment decisions. In this figure a DSS is portrayed as a set of capabilities that would be useful in a number of decision processes used in making investment decisions. Making such decisions requires reviewing portfolios, individual company research data, and stock data (the databases).

Four core DSS capabilities are portrayed in Figure 13.2, and all DSS can be characterized in this manner (Sprague and Carlson, 1982):

- **Representations:** Conceptualizations of information used in making decisions, such as graphs, charts, lists, reports, and symbols to control operations.
- **Operations:** Logical and mathematical manipulations of data, such as gathering information, generating lists, preparing reports, assigning risks and values, generating statistics, and simulating alternatives.
- **Memory aids:** Databases, views of data, work spaces, libraries, links among work spaces and libraries, and other capabilities to refresh and update memory.
- **Control aids:** Capabilities that allow the user to control the activities of the DSS. They include a software language permitting user control of representations, operations, and memory that features menus, function keys, conventions, training, help commands, and tutorials.

In essence, a DSS is a decision-making scratch pad that can be applied to problems with quantifiable dimensions that provide criteria for the evaluation of alternative solutions. The DSS helps the decision maker identify the best alternative.

Characteristics of DSS: What It Means to Support Decisions

Chapter 3 introduces the distinction between structured, unstructured, and semistructured decisions. Structured problems are repetitive and routine, for which known algorithms provide solutions. Unstructured problems are novel and nonroutine, for which there are no algorithms for solutions. One can discuss, decide, and ruminate about unstructured problems, but they are not solved in the sense that one finds an answer to an equation (Henderson and Schilling, 1985). Semi-structured problems fall between structured and unstructured problems. DSS are designed to support semi-structured and unstructured problem analysis.

Chapter 3 also introduces Simon's description of decision making, which consists of four stages: intelligence, design, choice, and implementation. DSS is intended to help design and evaluate alternatives and monitor the adoption or implementation process.

A well-designed DSS can be used at many levels of the organization. Senior management can use a financial DSS to forecast the availability of corporate funds for investment by division. Middle managers within divisions can use these estimates and the

representations In DSS, conceptualizations of information in the form of graphs, charts, lists, reports, and symbols to control operations.

operations In DSS, logical and mathematical manipulations of data.

memory aids In DSS, capabilities to update and refresh memory, including databases, views of data, work spaces, and libraries.

control aids Capabilities that allow the user to control the activities and functions of the DSS.

same system and data to make decisions about allocating division funds to projects. Capital project managers within divisions, in turn, can use this system to begin their projects, reporting to the system (and ultimately to senior managers) on a regular basis about how much money has been spent.

As noted in Chapter 3, it is a mistake to think that decisions are made only by individuals in large organizations. In fact, most decisions are made collectively. Chapter 3 describes the rational, bureaucratic, political, and garbage-can models of organizational decision making. Frequently, decisions must be coordinated with several groups before being finalized. In large organizations decision making is inherently a group process, and DSS can be designed to facilitate group decision making. The next section of this chapter deals with this issue.

EXAMPLES OF DSS APPLICATIONS

There are many ways in which DSS can be used to support decision making. Table 13.2 lists examples of DSS in well-known U.S. organizations. To illustrate the range of capabilities of DSS, we will now describe some recent DSS applications.

The Advanced Planning System—A Manufacturing DSS

To support most kinds of manufacturing, companies use a type of software known as *manufacturing resources planning* (MRPII). The typical MRPII system includes such applications as master production scheduling, purchasing, material requirements planning, and even general ledger. While they are useful as far as they go, MRPII packages usually run on a mainframe so that they can process massive amounts of data. As a result, they are too large and slow to be used for what-if simulations and too procedural to be modified into decision-support software. A Canadian company, Carp Systems International, of Kanata, Ontario, sells the Advanced Planning System (APS) to give the user DSS functionality using the data from existing MRPII systems.

APS allows a range of what-if processing by pulling the relevant data from the manufacturing software and performing calculations based upon user-defined variables. Pitney Bowes, the $3.3 billion business equipment manufacturer, uses the software to simulate supply changes. Pitney Bowes carries enough manufacturing inventory to satisfy demand for 30 days. Using APS, the firm asked to see the impact if it would reduce the inventory to 15 days. APS responded with an answer within five minutes, including an estimate of what Pitney Bowes would save. Similarly, Sikorsky Aircraft of Stratford,

Table 13.2 Examples of DSS Systems

American Airlines	Price and route selection
Champlin Petroleum	Corporate planning and forecasting
Equico Capital Corporation	Investment evaluation
Frito-Lay, Inc.	Price, advertising, and promotion selection
General Dynamics	Price evaluation
Juniper Lumber	Production optimization
Kmart	Price evaluation
National Gypsum	Corporate planning and forecasting
Southern Railway	Train dispatching and routing
Texas Oil and Gas Corporation	Evaluation of potential drilling sites
United Airlines	Flight scheduling
U.S. Department of Defense	Defense contract analysis

Connecticut, claims that over a three-year period the company has been able to use this software to help halve its inventory even while its sales doubled.

APS is a complex piece of software costing from $150,000 to $1 million and requiring intensive computing power. It runs on an IBM RS/6000 workstation. As with any other software, users caution that APS (and similar packages) are only as good as the data. If the data are out of date or wrong, APS only allows the user to do wrong things more quickly (Rifkin, 1992).

Yasuda Models Financial Investment Decisions

Yasuda Fire and Marine Insurance Co. of Tokyo found itself evolving ever more into a financial services firm as it was issuing an increasing number of savings-oriented insurance policies. These policies have a wide range of maturities and fluctuating interest rates. Yasuda had been using a computer model to help guide its managers in financial investment decisions, but it was no longer adequate for management decision making. It could not handle the many complex factors involved with financial markets, nor could it address the numerous government regulations regarding these investments. Management decided to develop a new decision-support system that would more effectively guide Yasuda's investment managers as they invest their portfolios of assets.

Yasuda turned to Frank Russell Co., a Tacoma, Washington, investment consulting firm, to help its managers develop the new DSS. Together they produced the Russell/Yasuda model, a more complex and realistic description of the financial markets that also took into consideration government regulations for minimum capital reserves. Older models could search for only a single answer; they had no ability to optimize their response. The new Russell/Yasuda model searches for the best possible results before issuing an optimized investment strategy. Depending on the number of scenarios, the system can arrive at a solution in one to three hours.

The DSS tells Yasuda investment managers how to invest their portfolio of assets in order to meet multiple and conflicting objectives. The firm can thus produce a high income to pay the annual interest on savings-type policies while still maximizing profits. The outcome has been very positive. After one year of using the model, Yasuda's income was up $26 million over what the old model would have produced. Yasuda is now able to pay bonuses on its savings-oriented policies that are larger than those its competitors can pay without sacrificing the longer-term goal of maximizing profits. As a result Yasuda has for now gained a real competitive advantage in its ability not only to retain existing customers but also to attract new ones (Betts, 1993).

The Egyptian Cabinet DSS

The Egyptian Cabinet is composed of the Prime Minister, thirty-two other ministers, and four ministerial-level committees with their staffs. Decision making here involves questions of survival: balance of payments, deficit management, public sector performance, economic growth, and national defense.

Decision making at these high levels of governments, or corporations, is often portrayed as a rational decision process. But in fact, decision making involves managing issues that are forced on decision makers with varying and shifting priorities. The issues are themselves complex, poorly defined, interdependent, and related to many features of society. Information is voluminous but unreliable and qualitative.

In 1985 the Egyptian Cabinet developed a three-person Information and Decision Support Center (IDSC) to assist its own decision-making process (Figure 13.3). Today, 150 people work full-time providing DSS services to the Cabinet on critical issues. The IDSC system is based upon a network of 110 microcomputers connected to a mainframe. Software includes standard desktop packages for database management, spreadsheet software, and FOCUS, a fourth-generation language and application generator, all of which have been fully converted to Arabic form. The electronic mail system is bilingual (Arabic/English).

FIGURE 13.3
The cabinet decision-making process with IDSC. *Reprinted by special permission from* MIS Quarterly, *Volume 12, Number 4, December 1988. Copyright 1988 by the Society for Information Management and the Management Information Systems Research Center at the University of Minnesota.*

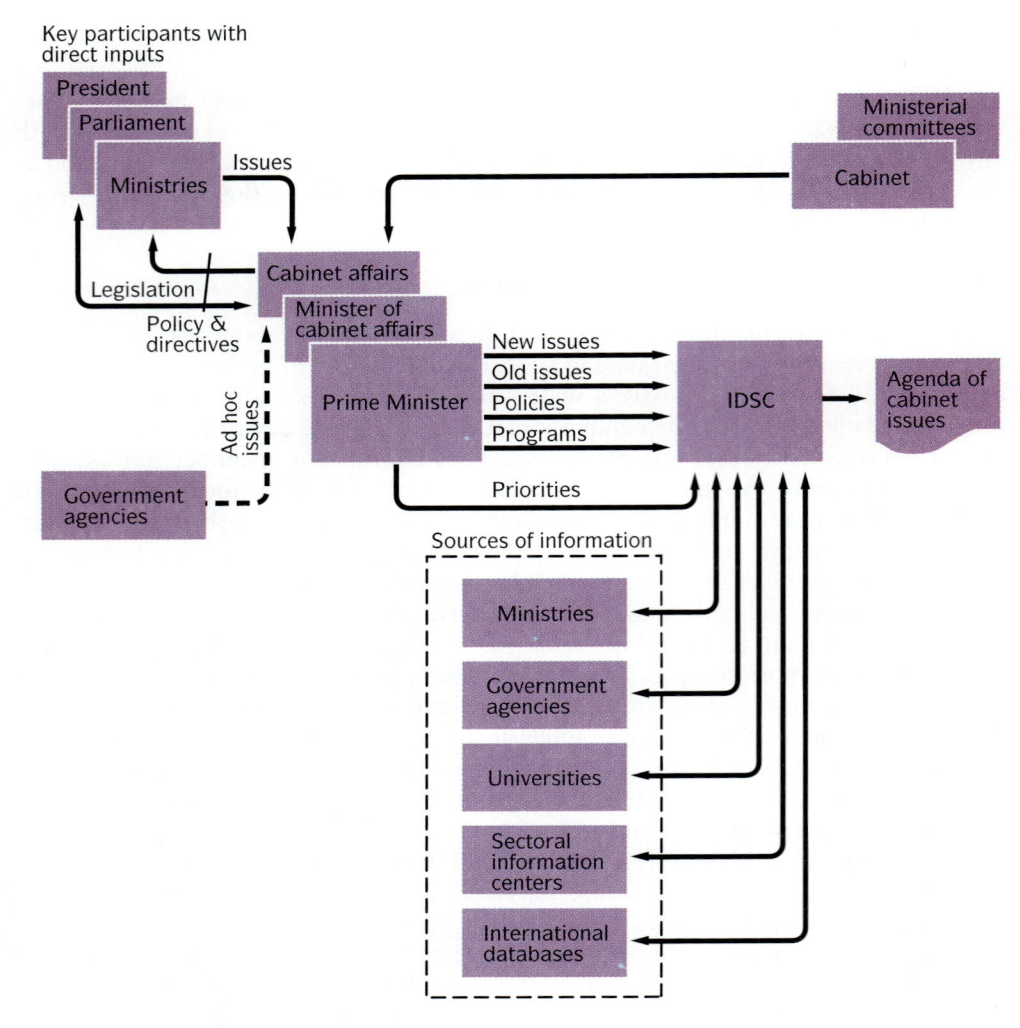

One of the first uses of IDSC was to develop a new tariff structure to replace an inconsistent and complex structure that was thought to be impeding economic growth. The goal of the policy set forth by the Cabinet was to create a consistent, simple tariff structure; increase revenues to the treasury; and promote economic growth without harming poor citizens. A microcomputer-based DSS model of the proposed new tariff structure was built, using a prototyping methodology.

The Ministry of Industry, hoping to increase local production of auto parts, supported new tariffs on imported auto parts. This was supported as well by the Ministry of Economy, which supported local production. But the policy was opposed by the Ministry of Finance because it would reduce customs revenue.

The DSS was walked around, back and forth, from one ministry to another, making adjustments to the proposed tariffs, playing what-if games to see the impact of tariff changes on revenue and local employment. After one month of intensive effort, agreement was reached on the new tariff policy. Builders of the DSS felt the system reduced conflict by clarifying the trade-offs and potential impacts of tariff changes. While early estimates of higher tariffs claimed $250 million in increased revenues would result, the DSS predicted $25 million. By 1987 the actual increased revenue was $28 million (El Sherif and El Sawy, 1988).

DSS can also be used as training instruments to teach managers how to make better decisions. Ford Motor Company is using simulation software that lets managers practice making decisions before they are faced with real-world decision making on the job (see the Window on Management).

Window on Management

PRACTICING DECISION MAKING

Designing, building, and marketing a new automobile model requires thousands of decisions made by hundreds of employees, and Ford wants to improve their decision-making skills. During the early years of the 1990s, more than 100 engineers, planners, and marketing and financial experts who are members of Ford's new product development team have attended a two-day seminar during which they use a business simulator for practice in decision making. The goal for the seminar is to integrate decision-making learning into ongoing education at Ford. The overall strategic goal for Ford is to re-architect its core business processes so that employees will be able to do more with less while doing it faster. Managers involved in product development who know how to make the very best choices each and every time would bring the company closer to this objective.

The simulator was developed by the Center for Organizational Learning at the Sloan School of Management at M.I.T. in Cambridge, Massachusetts, using the Strategy Support Simulation System from MicroWorlds, Inc., also in Cambridge. It is actually a game with a number of interacting variables of time, cost, and quality. It is intended to help managers understand the dynamic complexities of the issues they confront and the long-term

> **To Think About:** Do you think decision-making skills can be taught? Why? Suggest other possible methods for teaching decision making. How can using simulation systems such as those described help promote a firm's business strategy?

implications of their decisions. Using the simulator, managers are able to make decisions they might avoid making in the real world, experimenting with new ways to solve problems. The game is always played by a team of two or three managers or engineers, never by individuals alone.

The simulator resembles a what-if tool, such as those found in popular spreadsheets. However, the simulator is much more complex, with more dynamic relationships among the many elements of the simulation model. Currently it uses generic automobile design and production process data rather than live Ford data. The student might choose a function in which to invest capital, such as marketing or training. The software will then simulate its financial performance impact over a ten-year period. The student can then play with various elements, simulating marketplace interventions, such as speeding up development time or reducing expenditures on production tooling.

Source: Ellis Booker, "Have You Driven a *Simulated* Ford Lately?" *Computerworld*, July 4, 1994. Copyright ©1994 by Computerworld, Inc., Framingham, MA 01701. Reprinted from *Computerworld* by permission.

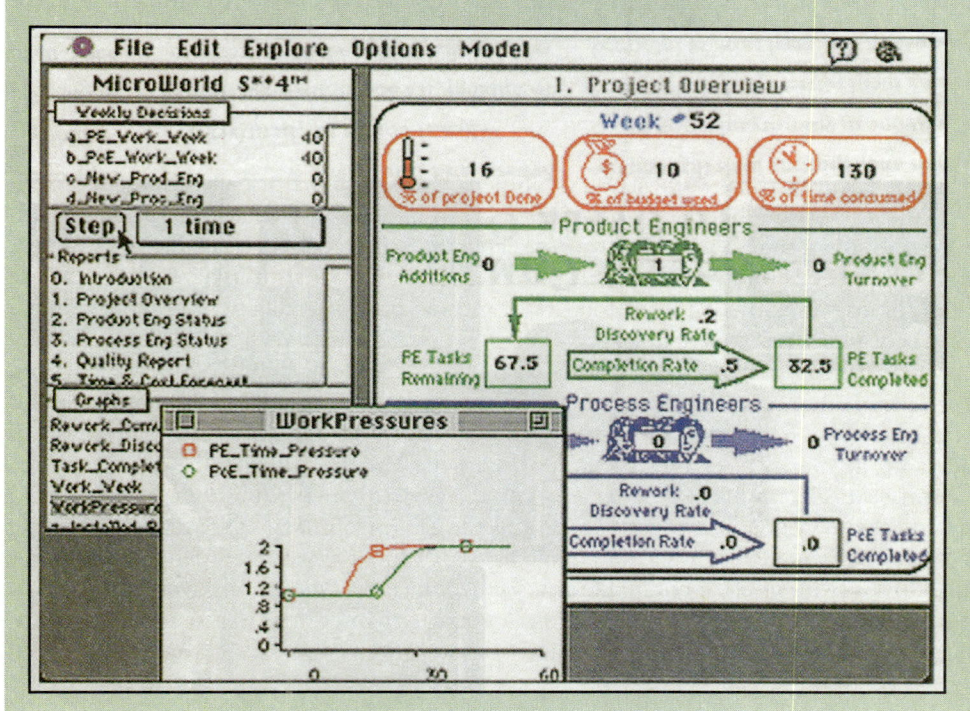

COMPONENTS OF DSS

Review Figure 13.1 again. It shows that a decision-support system has three basic components—a database, a model base, and the DSS software system. The **DSS database** is a collection of current or historical data from a number of applications or groups, organized for easy access by a range of applications. The DSS database management system protects the integrity of the data while controlling the processing that keeps the data

DSS database A collection of current or historical data from a number of applications or groups.

current; it also saves historical data. DSS use organizational data (from such systems as production and sales) so that individuals and groups are able to make decisions based upon actual conditions. The data are usually extracted from relevant databases and stored specifically for use by the DSS.

A **model base** is a collection of mathematical and analytical models that can easily be made accessible to the DSS user. A **model** is an abstract representation that illustrates the components or relationships of a phenomenon. A model can be a physical model (such as a model airplane), a mathematical model (such as an equation), or a verbal model (such as a description of a procedure to write up an order). Each decision-support system is built for a specific set of purposes and will make different collections of models available depending upon those purposes.

Optimization models, often using linear programming, determine optimal resource allocation to maximize or minimize specified variables such as cost or time. The Advanced Planning System (discussed earlier) uses such software to determine the effect that filling a new order will have upon meeting target dates for existing orders. A classic use of optimization models is to determine the proper mix of products within a given market to maximize profits.

Forecasting models are often used to forecast sales. The user of this type of model might supply a range of historical data to project future conditions and the sales that might result from those conditions. The decision maker could then vary those future conditions (entering, for example, a rise in raw materials costs or the entry of a new, low-priced competitor in the market) to determine how these new conditions might affect sales. Companies often use this software to attempt to predict the actions of competitors. Model libraries exist for specific functions, such as financial and risk analysis models.

Among the most widely used models are **sensitivity analysis** models that ask what-if questions repeatedly to determine the impact of changes in one or more factors on outcomes. What-if analysis—working forward from known or assumed conditions—allows the user to vary certain values to test results in order to better predict outcomes if changes occur in those values. What happens if we raise the price by 5 percent or increase the advertising budget by $100,000? What happens if we keep the price and advertising budget the same? Desktop spreadsheet software, such as Lotus 1-2-3 or Microsoft Excel, is often used for this purpose. Backwards sensitivity analysis software is used for goal seeking: If I want to sell one million product units next year, how much must I reduce the price of the product?

The third component of DSS is the **DSS software system**. The DSS software system permits easy interaction between the users of the system and the DSS database and model base. The DSS software system manages the creation, storage, and retrieval of models in the model base and integrates them with the data in the DSS database. The DSS software system also provides a graphic, easy to use, flexible user interface that supports the dialogue between the user and the DSS. DSS users are usually corporate executives or managers. Often they have little or no computer experience and no patience for learning to use a complex tool, so the interface must be relatively intuitive. In order to mimic a typical way of working, a good user interface should allow the manager to move back and forth between activities at will.

BUILDING DSS

Building a DSS is different from building a TPS or MIS system. Developing TPS or MIS results in systems that represent a response to a specific set of information needs. Development of DSS systems focuses on identifying a problem and a set of capabilities that users consider helpful in arriving at decisions about that problem. DSS generally use smaller amounts of data, do not need on-line transaction data, involve a smaller number of important users, and tend to employ more sophisticated analytic models than other systems. Because DSS are customized to specific users and specific classes of decisions, they require much greater user participation to develop. In addition, they must be flexible and must evolve as the sophistication of users grows.

Factors in DSS Success and Failure

As experience with DSS has grown, a number of factors have been identified as important to their success and failure. The success factors are not very different from those of MIS and other systems. Several studies have noted that user training, involvement, and experience; top management's support; length of use; and novelty of the application were the most important factors in DSS success. Success is defined as perceived improvements in decision making and overall satisfaction with the DSS (Alavi and Joachimsthaler, 1992; Sanders and Courtney, 1985).

A smaller study of 34 DSS found that DSS orientation toward top management (assistance with making important decisions) and return on investment are the most important factors in the approval process for DSS (Meador and Keen, 1984; King, 1983). Organizations need support for upper management decision making, which requires custom-built, flexible, and easy-to-use systems that address important organizational problems.

13.2 GROUP DECISION-SUPPORT SYSTEMS (GDSS)

The early work in DSS focused largely on supporting individual decision making. However, because so much work is accomplished in groups within organizations, during the late 1980s system developers and scholars began to focus on how computers can support group and organizational decision making. A new category of systems developed, known as *group decision-support systems* (GDSS).

WHAT IS A GDSS?

A **group decision-support system (GDSS)** is an interactive computer-based system to facilitate the solution of unstructured problems by a set of decision makers working together as a group (DeSanctis and Gallupe, 1987). GDSS were developed in response to growing concern over the quality and effectiveness of meetings. The underlying problems in group decision making have been the explosion of decision-maker meetings, the growing length of those meetings, and the increased number of attendees. Estimates on the amount of a manager's time spent in meetings range from 35 to 70 percent.

Meeting facilitators, organizational development professionals, and information systems scholars have been focusing on this issue and have identified a number of discrete meeting elements that need to be addressed (Grobowski et al., 1990; Kraemer and King, 1988; Nunamaker et al., 1991). Among these elements are the following:

1. *Improved pre-planning,* to make meetings more effective and efficient.
2. *Increased participation,* so that all attendees will be able to contribute fully even if the number of attendees is large. Free riding (attending the meeting but not contributing) must also be addressed.
3. *Open, collaborative meeting atmosphere,* in which attendees from various organizational levels feel able to contribute freely. Lower-level attendees must be able to participate without fear of being judged by their management; higher-status participants must be able to participate without having their presence or ideas dominate the meeting and result in unwanted conformity.
4. *Criticism-free idea generation,* enabling attendees to contribute without undue fear of feeling personally criticized.
5. *Evaluation objectivity,* creating an atmosphere where an idea will be evaluated on its merits rather than on the basis of the source of the idea.

group decision-support system (GDSS) An interactive computer-based system to facilitate the solution to unstructured problems by a set of decision makers working together as a group.

Window on Organizations

THE HOHENHEIM CATEAM ROOM

How does the physical environment of a group decision-support system meeting room affect the work of a GDSS-supported group? How do ergonomics affect the decision-making process? These are some of the questions that were explored by information systems researchers at the University of Hohenheim, in Stuttgart, Germany. Their methodology? Do the research and design their own GDSS room—the Computer Aided Team Room, known as the CATeam Room.

The information systems specialists worked with interior and furniture design architects from the State Academy of the Arts in Stuttgart. Realizing that people's sense of privacy and their social interactions can be affected by their level of physical comfort and the design of their meeting environment, the team looked into alternative designs for meeting rooms. In their quest for a meeting room design that would enhance group work, the team consulted specialists in psychology and ergonomics and visited GDSS research laboratories in the United States.

One of the principal questions addressed by the project was the relationship of seating arrangements in the GDSS meeting room to meeting interactions. The team started with a set of basic rules that demanded a maximum of twelve participants in a meeting (a limitation set because of the small size of the room they had available). The table they endorsed at the end included built-in computer equipment that could automatically be stored inside the table at the push of a button so that the room could be used for traditional non-GDSS meetings. The table also is modular, allowing flexibility. For example, the room could be rearranged into a U-shape for a teaching situation. The team also wanted seating arrangements that would create a friendly teamwork atmosphere. While their principles did not include a speci-

> **To Think About:** 1. This chapter listed ten specific meeting elements that need to be addressed to improve decision-making meetings. Which of these elements are addressed by the CATeam ergonomic design, and in what ways might the design improve meetings?
> 2. Do you believe that the physical placement of the computer is adequate for guaranteeing the privacy of an attendee's work? Can you think of ways that privacy could be further protected?

fication for participant equality, that proved, in the end, to be the deciding factor for the table setup. This issue is particularly important because meeting attendees often come from a range of different organizational levels, creating an initial atmosphere of inequality.

The final decision for table shape called for a table called a *Roundabout* (see Figure 13.4). At a round table everyone is equal, and the arrangement is democratic. Face-to-face contact is equally possible with anyone at the table. A GDSS requires a computer projection screen so that all can view the common screens together (as well as independently on their own PCs).

FIGURE 13.4
The Roundabout Table Model. The system that the CATeam researchers at the University of Hohenheim settled upon as the final design for a GDSS room table was the Roundabout table. With this design everybody is equal, and face-to-face contact is equally possible with all participants at the table.

> To support the Roundabout solution, the CATeam project decided to use two common screens opposite each other. That way everyone would be able to view a screen easily and comfortably without attendees having to turn around or otherwise disturb the symmetry of the arrangement.
>
> The placement of the computer equipment within the table also contributed to an environment of equality. When in use, the computer screen is placed slightly below table level. The team saw two advantages to this arrangement. First, no computer equipment would interfere with the attendees' eye-to-eye contact with other attendees. Second, an attendee's monitor can only be viewed by the closest neighbor, if at all. They believe that privacy, and therefore anonymity, are protected.
>
> The Roundabout design was selected for display by the jury of the 1989 "Anno 2000 Office Design Competition" in Milan.
>
> Source: Henrik Lewe and Helmut Krcmar, "The Design Process for a Computer-Supported Cooperative Work Research Laboratory: The Hohenheim CATeam Room," *Journal of Management Information Systems*, Winter 1991–92. Helmut Krcmar, Henrik Lewe, and Gerhard Schwabe: *Empirical CATeam Research of Meetings*. Working Paper no. 38 of the Information Systems Department, University of Hohenheim, Germany, 1993.

6. *Idea organization and evaluation,* which require keeping the focus on the meeting objectives, finding efficient ways to organize the many ideas that can be generated in a brainstorming session, and evaluating those ideas not only on their merits but also within appropriate time constraints.
7. *Setting priorities and making decisions,* which require finding ways to encompass the thinking of all the attendees in making these judgments.
8. *Documentation of meetings* so that attendees will have as complete and organized a record of the meeting as may be needed to continue the work of the project.
9. *Access to external information,* which will allow significant, factual disagreements to be settled in a timely fashion, thus enabling the meeting to continue and be productive.
10. *Preservation of organizational memory,* so that those who do not attend the meeting can also work on the project. Often a project will include teams at different locations who will need to understand the content of a meeting at only one of the affected sites.

One response to the problems of group decision making has been the adoption of new methods of organizing and running meetings. Techniques such as facilitated meetings, brainstorming, and criticism-free idea generation have become popular and are now accepted as standard. Another response has been the application of technology to the problems resulting in the emergence of group decision-support systems.

CHARACTERISTICS OF GDSS

How can information technology help groups to arrive at decisions? Scholars have identified at least three basic elements of GDSS: hardware, software, and people. *Hardware* refers first to the conference facility itself, including the room, the tables, and the chairs. Such a facility must be physically laid out in a manner that supports group collaboration. It must also include some electronic hardware, such as electronic display boards, as well as audiovisual and computer equipment. The Window on Organizations examines one important aspect of the physical setup—the ergonomics of the meeting room design.

A wide range of *software tools,* including tools for organizing ideas, gathering information, ranking and setting priorities, and other aspects of collaborative work are now being used to support decision-making meetings. We describe these tools on the following page. *People* refers not only to the participants but also to a trained facilitator and often to a staff that supports the hardware and software. Together these elements have led to the creation of a range of different kinds of GDSS, from simple electronic boardrooms to elaborate collaboration laboratories. In a collaboration laboratory, individuals work on their own desktop microcomputers. Their input is integrated on a file server and is viewable on a common screen at the front of the room; in most systems the integrated input is also viewable on the individual participant's screen. See Figure 13.5 for an illustration of an actual GDSS collaborative meeting room.

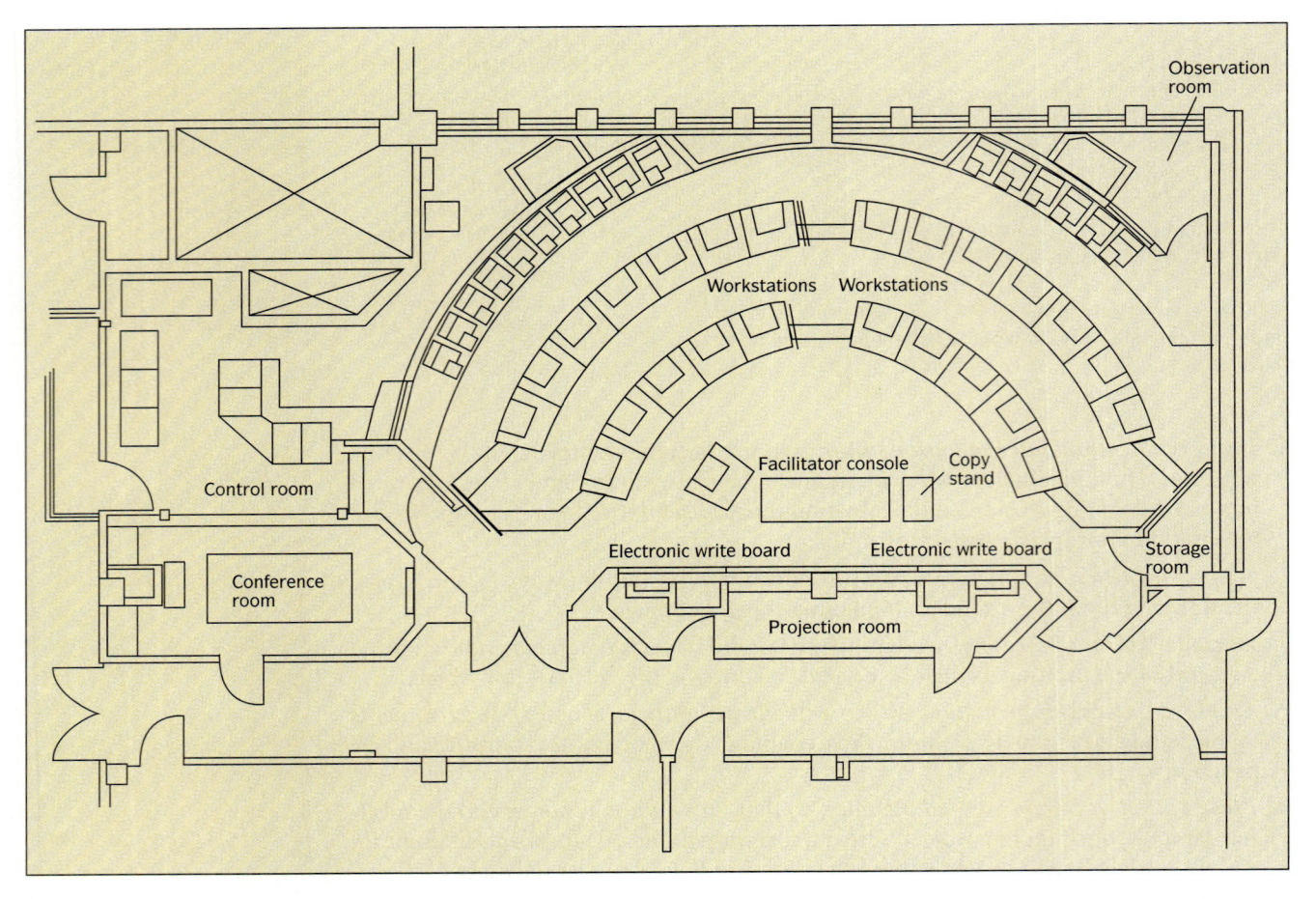

FIGURE 13.5
Illustration of PLEXSYS decision room. The large group room was opened in 1987, with 24 IBM PS/2 workstations. A gallery holds 18 observers. The room has 38 audio pickup microphones and 6 video cameras with stereo audio. Two large-screen electronic displays and projectors permit playing of videotapes, discs, 35 mm slides, and computer graphics presentations. *Reprinted by special permission from the MIS Quarterly, Volume 12, Number 4, December 1988. Copyright 1988 by the Society for Information Management and the Management Information Systems Research Center at the University of Minnesota.*

GDSS SOFTWARE TOOLS

Some of the features of the groupware tools for collaborative work described in Chapters 8 and 12 can be used to support group decision making. But GDSS are considered more explicitly decision-oriented and task-oriented than groupware, as they focus on helping a group solve a problem or reach a decision (Dennis et al., 1988). Groupware is considered more communication-oriented. Specific GDSS software tools include the following:

- *Electronic questionnaires* aid the organizers in pre-meeting planning by identifying issues of concern and by helping to ensure that key planning information is not overlooked.
- *Electronic brainstorming tools* allow individuals simultaneously and anonymously to contribute ideas on the topics of the meeting.
- *Idea organizers* facilitate the organized integration and synthesis of ideas generated during brainstorming.
- *Questionnaire tools* support the facilitators and group leaders as they gather information before and during the process of setting priorities.
- *Tools for voting or setting priorities* make available a range of methods from simple voting, to ranking in order, to a range of weighted techniques for setting priorities or voting.

- *Stakeholder identification and analysis tools* use structured approaches to evaluate the impact of an emerging proposal upon the organization, and to identify stakeholders and evaluate the potential impact of those stakeholders upon the proposed project.
- *Policy formation tools* provide structured support for developing agreement on the wording of policy statements.
- *Group dictionaries* document group agreement on definitions of words and terms central to the project.

Additional tools are available, such as group outlining and writing tools, software that stores and reads project files, and software that allows the attendees to view internal operational data stored by the organization's production computer systems.

Overview of a GDSS Meeting

An **electronic meeting system (EMS)** is a type of collaborative GDSS that uses information technology to make group meetings more productive by facilitating communication as well as decision making. It supports any activity where people come together, whether at the same place at the same time or in different places at different times (Dennis et al., 1988; Nunamaker et al., 1991). IBM has a number of EMS installed at various sites. Each attendee has a workstation. The workstations are networked and are connected to the facilitator's console that serves as both the facilitator's workstation and control panel and the meeting's file server. All data that the attendees forward from their workstations to the group are collected and saved on the file server. The facilitator is able to project computer images onto the projection screen at the front of the room. The facilitator also has an overhead projector available. Whiteboards are visible on either side of the projection screen. Many electronic meeting rooms are arranged in a semicircle and are tiered in legislative style to accommodate a larger number of attendees.

The facilitator controls the use of tools during the meeting, often selecting from a large tool box that is part of the organization's GDSS. Tool selection is part of the pre-meeting planning process. Which tools are selected depends upon the subject matter, the goals of the meeting, and the facilitation methodology the facilitator will use.

Each attendee has full control over his or her own microcomputer. An attendee is able to view the agenda (and other planning documents), look at the integrated screen (or screens as the session moves on), use ordinary desktop microcomputer tools (such

electronic meeting system (EMS) A collaborative GDSS that uses information technology to make group meetings more productive by facilitating communication as well as decision making. Supports meetings at the same place and time or in different places and times.

The Ventana Corporation demonstrates the features of its GroupSystems for Windows electronic meeting software, which helps people create, share, record, organize, and evaluate ideas in meetings, between offices, or around the world.

13.2 Group Decision-Support Systems (GDSS) 417

FIGURE 13.6

Group system tools. The sequence of activities and collaborative support tools used in an electronic meeting system (EMS) facilitates communication among attendees and generates a full record of the meeting. *Source: Adapted from Nunamaker, Dennis, Valacich, Vogel, and George, "Electronic Meeting Systems to Support Group Work," Communications of the ACM, July 1991.*

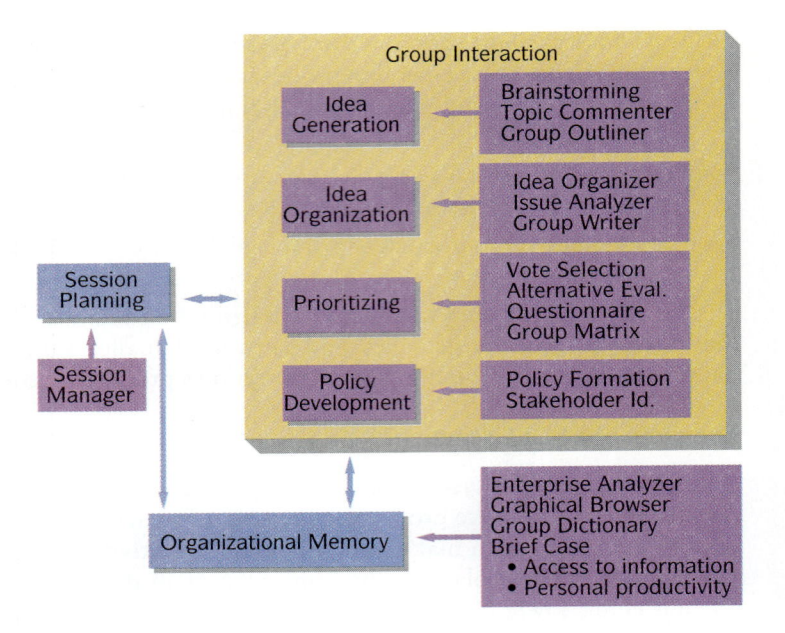

Group Interaction

- Idea Generation — Brainstorming, Topic Commenter, Group Outliner
- Idea Organization — Idea Organizer, Issue Analyzer, Group Writer
- Prioritizing — Vote Selection, Alternative Eval., Questionnaire, Group Matrix
- Policy Development — Policy Formation, Stakeholder Id.

Session Planning ↔ Session Manager

Organizational Memory — Enterprise Analyzer, Graphical Browser, Group Dictionary, Brief Case
- Access to information
- Personal productivity

as a word processor or a spreadsheet), tap into production data that have been made available, or work on the screen associated with the current meeting step and tool (such as a brainstorming screen). However, no one can view anyone else's screens, so an individual's work is confidential until he or she releases it to the file server for integration with the work of others. All input to the file server is anonymous—at each step everyone's input to the file server (brainstorming ideas, idea evaluation and criticism, comments, voting, etc.) can be seen by all attendees on the integrated screens, but no information is available to identify the source of specific inputs. Attendees enter their data simultaneously rather than in round-robin fashion as is done in meetings that have little or no electronic systems support.

Figure 13.6 shows the sequence of activities at a typical EMS meeting. For each activity it also indicates the type of tools and the output of those tools. During the meeting all input to the integrated screens is saved on the file server. As a result, when the meeting is completed, a full record of the meeting (both raw material and resultant output) is available to the attendees and can be made available to anyone else with a need for access.

HOW GDSS CAN ENHANCE GROUP DECISION MAKING

GDSS are still relatively new, so firm conclusions are not yet possible. Nonetheless, scholars and business specialists have studied these systems, and the systems are now being used more widely, so that we are able at least to understand their potential benefits and even evaluate some of the tools. We look again at how GDSS affect the ten group meeting issues raised earlier.

1. *Improved pre-planning.* Electronic questionnaires, supplemented by word processors, outlining software, and other desktop PC software, can structure planning, thereby improving it. The availability of the planning information at the actual meeting also can serve to enhance the quality of the meeting. Experts seem to feel that these tools add significance and emphasis to meeting pre-planning.

2. *Increased participation.* Studies show that in traditional decision-making meetings without GDSS support the optimal meeting size is three to five attendees. Beyond that size the meeting process begins to break down. Using GDSS software, studies show the meeting size can increase while productivity also increases. One reason for this is that attendees contribute simultaneously rather than one at a time and can thus make more efficient use of the meeting time. Free riding is apparently

decreased too, perhaps because the one or two individuals who are not working will stand out when everyone else in the room is busy at workstations. Interviews of GDSS meeting attendees indicate that the quality of participation is higher than in traditional meetings.

3. *Open, collaborative meeting atmosphere.* GDSS contribute to a more collaborative atmosphere in several ways. First, anonymity of input is essentially guaranteed. An individual need not be afraid of being judged by his or her boss for contributing a possibly offbeat idea. Anonymity also reduces or eliminates the deadening effect that often occurs when high-status individuals contribute. Even the numbing pressures of social cues are reduced or eliminated.

4. *Criticism-free idea generation.* Anonymity ensures that attendees can contribute without fear of being personally criticized or of having their ideas rejected because of the identity of the contributor. Several studies show that interactive GDSS meetings generate more ideas and more satisfaction with those ideas than verbally interactive meetings (Nunamaker et al., 1991). GDSS can help reduce unproductive interpersonal conflict (Miranda and Bostrum, 1993–94).

5. *Evaluation objectivity.* Anonymity prevents criticism of the source of the ideas, thus supporting an atmosphere in which attendees focus on evaluating the ideas themselves. The same anonymity allows participants to detach themselves from their own ideas and so are able to view them from a critical perspective. Evidence suggests that evaluation in an anonymous atmosphere increases the free flow of critical feedback and even stimulates the generation of new ideas during the evaluation process.

6. *Idea organization and evaluation.* GDSS software tools used for this purpose are structured and are based on methodology. They usually allow individuals each to organize and then submit their results to the group (still anonymously). The group then iteratively modifies and develops the organized ideas until a document is completed. Attendees have generally viewed this approach as productive.

7. *Setting priorities and making decisions.* Anonymity helps lower-level participants have their positions taken into consideration along with the higher-level attendees.

8. *Documentation of meetings.* Evidence at IBM indicates that post-meeting use of the data is crucial. Attendees use the data to continue their dialogues after the meetings, to discuss the ideas with those who did not attend, and even to make presentations (Grobowski et al., 1990). Some tools even enable the user to zoom in to more detail on specific information.

9. *Access to external information.* Often a great deal of meeting time is devoted to factual disagreements. More experience with GDSS will indicate whether or not GDSS technology reduces this problem.

10. *Preservation of organizational memory.* Specific tools have been developed to facilitate access to the data generated during a GDSS meeting, allowing nonattendees to locate needed information after the meeting. The documentation of a meeting by one group at one site has also successfully been used as input to another meeting on the same project at another site.

Experience to date suggests that GDSS meetings can be more productive, make more efficient use of time, and produce the desired results in fewer meetings. One problem with understanding the value of GDSS is their complexity. A GDSS can be configured in an almost infinite variety of ways. In addition, the effectiveness of the tools will partially depend upon the effectiveness of the facilitator, the quality of the planning, the cooperation of the attendees, and the appropriateness of tools for different types of meetings.

Researchers have noted that the design of an electronic meeting system is only one of a number of contingencies that affect the outcome of group meetings. Other factors, including the nature of the group, the task, the cultural setting, and the context also affect the process of group meetings and meeting outcomes (Dennis et al., 1988; Nunamaker et al., 1991; Watson, Ho, and Raman, 1994). Figure 13.7 graphically illustrates these relationships.

FIGURE 13.7
The research model for electronic meetings. For effective group meetings, include the nature of the group, the task to be accomplished, and the context of the meeting in the design of the EMS. *Reprinted by special permission from* MIS Quarterly, *Volume 12, Number 4, December 1988. Copyright 1988 by the Society for Information Management and the Management Information Systems Research Center at the University of Minnesota.*

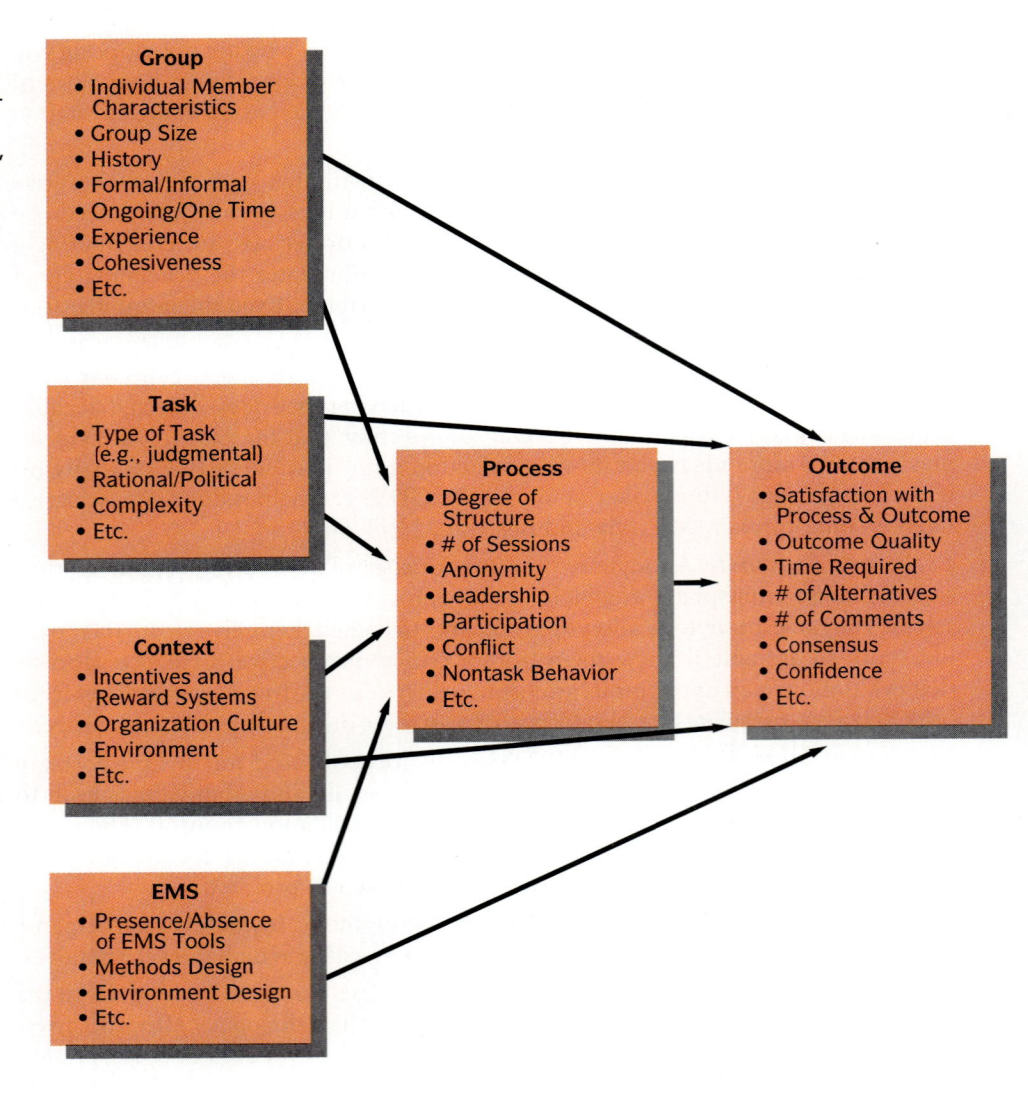

Group
- Individual Member Characteristics
- Group Size
- History
- Formal/Informal
- Ongoing/One Time
- Experience
- Cohesiveness
- Etc.

Task
- Type of Task (e.g., judgmental)
- Rational/Political
- Complexity
- Etc.

Context
- Incentives and Reward Systems
- Organization Culture
- Environment
- Etc.

EMS
- Presence/Absence of EMS Tools
- Methods Design
- Environment Design
- Etc.

Process
- Degree of Structure
- # of Sessions
- Anonymity
- Leadership
- Participation
- Conflict
- Nontask Behavior
- Etc.

Outcome
- Satisfaction with Process & Outcome
- Outcome Quality
- Time Required
- # of Alternatives
- # of Comments
- Consensus
- Confidence
- Etc.

13.3 EXECUTIVE SUPPORT SYSTEMS (ESS)

executive support system (ESS) An information system at the strategic level of an organization designed to address unstructured decision making through advanced graphics and communications.

briefing books On-line data in the form of fixed-format reports for executives; part of early ESS.

drill down The ability to move from summary data down to lower and lower levels of detail.

We have described how DSS and GDSS help managers make unstructured and semi-structured decisions. **Executive support systems (ESS)** also help managers with unstructured problems, focusing on the information needs of senior management. Combining data from both internal and external sources, ESS create a generalized computing and communications environment that can be focused and applied to a changing array of problems. ESS help senior executives monitor organizational performance, track activities of competitors, spot problems, identify opportunities, and forecast trends.

THE ROLE OF ESS IN THE ORGANIZATION

Prior to ESS it was common for executives to receive numerous fixed-format reports, often hundreds of pages every month (or even every week). The first systems developed specifically for executives in the early 1980s were mainframe systems designed to replace that paper, delivering the same data to the executive in days rather than in weeks. Executives had access to the same data, only it was on-line in the form of reports. Such systems were known as senior management **briefing books**. Using a briefing book, executives usually could **drill down** (move from a piece of summary data down to lower and lower levels of detail). Briefing books did not spread widely through the executive suites. The data that could be provided by briefing books were limited and the briefing books were too inflexible.

By the late 1980s ways were found to bring together data from throughout the organization and allow the manager to select, access, and tailor them easily as needed. Today, an ESS is apt to include a range of easy-to-use desktop analytical tools. Use of the systems has migrated down several organizational levels so that the executive and his or her subordinates are able to look at the same data in the same way.

Today's systems try to avoid the problem of data overload so common in paper reports because the data can be filtered or viewed in graphic format (if the user so chooses). Systems have maintained the ability to drill down (even starting from a graph).

One limitation in ESS is that they use data from systems designed for very different purposes. Often data that are critical to the senior executive are simply not there. For example, sales data coming from an order entry transaction processing system are not linked to marketing information, a linkage the executive would find useful. External data are now much more available in many ESS systems. Executives need a wide range of external data, from current stock market news to competitor information, industry trends, and even projected legislative action. Through their ESS, many managers have access to news services, financial market databases, economic information, and whatever other public data they may require.

ESS today include tools for modeling and analysis. For example, many ESS use Lotus 1-2-3, Excel, or other spreadsheets as the heart of their analytical tool base. With only a minimum of experience, most managers find they can use these common software packages to create graphic comparisons of data by time, region, product, price range, and so on. Costlier systems include more sophisticated specialty analytical software. (While DSS use such tools primarily for modeling and analysis in a fairly narrow range of decision situations, ESS use them primarily to provide status information about organizational performance.)

DEVELOPING ESS

ESS are executive systems, and executives create special development problems (we introduced this topic in Section 13.1). Because executives' needs change so rapidly, most executive support systems are developed through prototyping. A major difficulty for developers is that high-level executives expect success the first time. Developers must be certain that the system will work before they demonstrate it to the user. In addition, the initial system prototype must be one that the executive can learn very rapidly. Finally, if the executive finds that the ESS offers no added value, he or she will reject it.

One area that merits special attention is the determination of executive information requirements. ESS need to have some facility for environmental scanning. A key information requirement of managers at the strategic level is the capability to detect signals of problems in the organizational environment that indicate strategic threats and opportunities (Walls et al., 1992). The ESS needs to be designed so that both external and internal sources of information can be used for environmental scanning purposes. The Critical Success Factor methodology for determining information requirements (see Chapter 10) is recommended for this purpose.

The Window on Technology shows how technologies can be used to design filtering mechanisms so that managers receive only the essential information from the environment that they actually need, including information from the Internet.

Because ESS could potentially give top executives the capability of examining other managers' work without their knowledge, there may be some resistance to ESS at lower levels of the organization. Implementation of ESS should be carefully managed to neutralize such opposition (see Chapter 10).

Cost justification presents a different type of problem with ESS. Since much of an executive's work is unstructured, how does one quantify benefits for a system that primarily supports such unstructured work? An ESS is often justified in advance by the

Window on Technology

FIGHTING INFOGLUT

"Be careful what you wish for. You just might get it." Managers have long wished for more information, and now, with voice mail, the Internet, e-mail, faxes, and news feeds—in addition to newspapers, magazines, radio, and television—they've got it. With the glut of information—*infoglut*—they are being overwhelmed. Greg Lobdell, a product management director at Microsoft, receives 300 e-mail messages daily. At one minute per message, he would need six hours per day just to read them. Eric Sachs, vice president at Wolf Communications, in Houston, Texas, reports answering 60 e-mail messages per day as well as monitoring six news services and participating in several on-line forums. Thankfully, solutions are being developed to deal with this infoglut.

Consolidating incoming information into a single format and place is one key to reducing overload, and tools do exist for that purpose. Microsoft's Windows 95 integrates e-mail, voice mail, fax, and information service feeds into one integrated mailbox. However, integration only makes the information easier to handle—it does not reduce the volume. Not all e-mail must be read—junk mail also comes in electronic form. Groupware software and e-mail systems often both include a filtering facility to cut the volume. These products are usually rule-based, enabling the system to filter out messages that do not meet a set of criteria either in its SUBJECT field or in the body of the message. More sophisticated software can now be programmed to automatically forward a specific message to another person, again based upon criteria specified by the user. Systems sometimes include a *delegate* facility, which directs e-mail to a delegate mailbox where an assistant can handle it, even responding as if the answer had come from the boss.

News filtering has been around for a long time—individuals and companies used to hire clipping services to read through a

To Think About: Discuss the management and organizational issues involved in determining whether to give employees access to e-mail, the Internet, and other sources of electronic information.

specific set of journals and clip and forward articles on specific topics of interest to them. However, today news is available in electronic form (the complete *Wall Street Journal* is now available through the Web at *http://interactive.wsj.com*). Individual Inc., of Burlington, Massachusetts, will deliver via e-mail a summary of news events to corporate customers. Individual also produces software to filter the news and organize it for the customer. Another approach that is just beginning to be tried is the use of software agents that travel through a network, including the Internet, searching databases for specific requested information (see Chapter 8). Such software will reduce infoglut by returning with only the information the user requests, saving him the time and energy of having to cull out the information himself.

No one claims that these products will solve the information glut problem. That will also require nonelectronic approaches, perhaps even rethinking our approach to information. In the meantime, they do help.

Source: John Foley, "Infoglut," *Information Week,* October 30, 1995.

Commander EIS provides executives with easy-to-use graphics, communications, and financial analysis tools for scanning the external environment and for analyzing the performance of their firm.

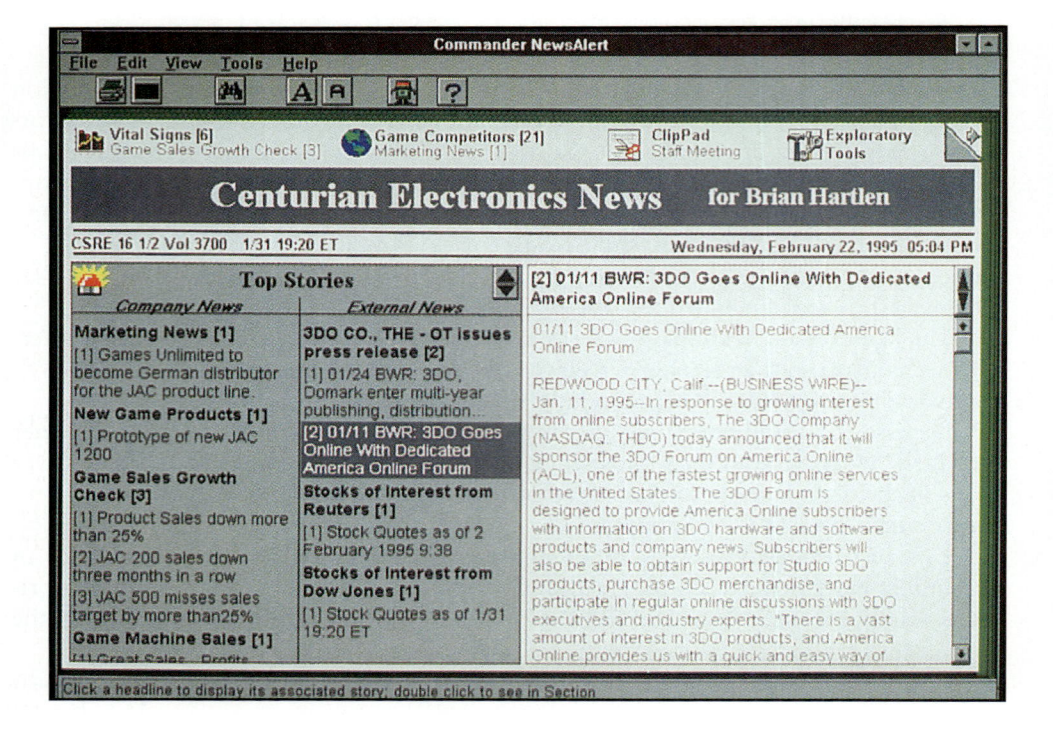

intuitive feeling that it will pay for itself (Watson et al., 1991). If ESS benefits can ever be quantified, it is only after the system is operational.

BENEFITS OF ESS

Much of the value of ESS is found in their flexibility. These systems put data and tools in the hands of executives without addressing specific problems or imposing solutions. Executives are free to shape the problems as they need, using the system as an extension of their own thinking processes. These are not decision-making systems; they are tools to aid executives in making decisions.

The most visible benefit of ESS is their ability to analyze, compare, and highlight trends. The easy use of graphics allows the user to look at more data in less time with greater clarity and insight than paper-based systems can provide. In the past, executives obtained the same information by taking up days and weeks of their staffs' valuable time. By using ESS those staffs and the executives themselves are freed up for the more creative analysis and decision making in their jobs. ESS capabilities for drilling down and highlighting trends may also enhance the quality of such analysis and decision making (Leidner and Elam, 1993–94).

Executives are using ESS to monitor performance more successfully in their own areas of responsibility. Some are also using these systems to monitor key performance indicators. The timeliness and availability of the data result in needed actions being identified and taken earlier. Problems can be handled before they become too damaging; opportunities can also be identified earlier as well.

ESS can and do change the workings of organizations. Immediate access to so much data allows executives to better monitor activities of lower units reporting to them. That very monitoring ability often allows decision making to be decentralized and to take place at lower operating levels. Executives are often willing to push decision making further down into the organization as long as they can be assured that all is going well. ESS can enable them to get that assurance. A well-designed ESS could dramatically improve management performance and increase upper management's span of control.

EXAMPLES OF ESS

To illustrate the various ways in which ESS can enhance management decision making, we now describe three executive support systems: one for private industry and two for the public sector. These systems were developed for very different reasons and serve their organizations in different ways.

Pratt & Whitney

Pratt & Whitney is a multibillion-dollar corporation located in East Hartford, Connecticut, whose Commercial Engine Business (CEB) produces jet engines. The firm's executives view customer service and product performance as the heart of their business and, therefore, as the heart of their strategic plan to expand their market share. Pratt & Whitney purchased Commander EIS, a leading ESS package from Comshare. Commander EIS features colorful presentations and a pictorial menu that can be learned intuitively, with variances and exceptions highlighted in color. Users can access data with a touch screen, a mouse, or a keyboard, and they can zoom in for deeper levels of detail either by navigating on their own or by following predefined paths.

Implementation began with a prototype built for the president of CEB, Selwyn Berson. Commander EIS allows Berson to track key quality and reliability measures for each jet engine model by customer. The data are shown from existing production systems and provide information on reliability, spare engine and parts availability, and deliveries. Using this system CEB is able to answer customers' questions regarding repair status and can project how long repairs will take. Berson and others are able to drill down to determine reasons for repairs on specific engines. They also are capable of drilling down to specific data on service to an individual customer. Thus, CEB executives are able to determine where quality improvements need to be made in terms of both customer service and engine quality. CEB's ESS is helping them to meet their strategic plan objective ("The New Role," January 1992).

The United States General Services Administration

The General Services Administration (GSA) manages the vast real estate holdings of the United States government. The organization needed to find ways to optimize the use of the government's multibillion-dollar inventory of 16,000 properties worldwide. Yet GSA managers facing this challenge had no system that would support them by making easily available to them the 4 gigabytes of data stored in their computers. Analysis of the data was nearly impossible. GSA's response was GAMIS (Glenn Asset Management Information System), an executive support system based primarily on Lotus Notes that literally puts the needed data and analysis at the fingertips of the GSA's nontechnical managers.

The main purpose of the system was to give management quick and easy views of the organization's assets. Managers now can easily use ad hoc queries and perform what-if analysis, receiving the results on screen, in graphics format when desired. After indicating a specific office building, for example, the user will be offered 13 choices of data on that building, such as who occupies it, its financials, information on the congressional district it is in (if it is in the United States), and even a scanned photograph of the building. The data can be accessed via geographic information system (GIS) software from MapInfo Corp. (see Chapter 6). Through this software interface, the user begins with a national map and drills down into regional and city maps that show detail on location and type of property. Another click of the mouse and the user will pull up all the data on that piece of property. Users can limit the data at the outset, specifying, for example, that they want to look only at Justice Department properties with more than 50,000 square feet of floor space. All of the data are available to about 100 GSA employees in Washington, while about 50 employees in each of the ten regions have access to all of the data for their own region.

With GAMIS, nontechnical managers can access and analyze gigabytes of information that were formerly available only via printouts and custom programming. The system has received high marks from many officials. Observers have also praised the system because it was built from off-the-shelf software, making it quick and inexpensive to develop, providing high returns with minimum investments (Anthes, 1994).

New York State Office of General Services

The New York State Office of General Services (OGS) is responsible for servicing other state agencies throughout New York. Its services include (but are not limited to) design and construction, maintenance of state buildings, food and laundry services to both correctional facilities and health-related institutions, statewide vehicle management, and centralized printing. With this diversity of services, an annual budget well over $500 million, and more than 4000 employees, executive oversight was a nightmare. OGS felt no pressure to improve efficiency or stay within its budget. That changed in 1986 when a new administrative head of the agency was appointed. He decided that the organization had to operate in a more efficient, effective, and responsive manner. He also wanted to avoid year-end deficits. These objectives required better management at the top.

The first module of a new OGS ESS was implemented in 1988. The system allows the executives to monitor status by program, comparing budget to actual expenditures and showing estimated expenditures through the remainder of the fiscal year. Management can drill down to see specific details in any category. For example, users are able to view a single expense category by month across organizations, or view several months of expenses for a given unit. Because the raw data are there, the executives can drill down to the source. The system includes exception reporting so that budget problems are highlighted and detected early. Executives are also using the system to compare budgetary control by units to spot personnel performance problems.

The system uses ordinary microcomputers networked with the agency's mainframe and off-the-shelf, standard, inexpensive software tools. The total cost was less than $100,000. The system is menu-driven and very easy to use. New users are trained through a 30-minute demonstration, and experience has shown that this is all that they need. This ESS is helping the Office of General Services enhance management control (Mohan et al., 1990).

Management Challenges

1. **Building information systems that can actually fulfill executive information requirements.** Even with the use of Critical Success Factors and other information requirements determination methods, it may still be difficult to establish information requirements for ESS and DSS serving senior management. Chapter 3 has already described why certain aspects of senior management decision making cannot be supported by information systems because the decisions are too unstructured and fluid. Even if a problem can be addressed by an information system, senior management may not understand its true information needs. For instance, senior managers may not agree on the firm's critical success factors, or the critical success factors they describe may be inappropriate or outdated if the firm is confronting a crisis requiring a major strategic change.

2. **Integrating DSS and ESS with existing systems in the business.** Even if system builders know the information requirements for DSS or ESS and use data warehousing tools, it may be extremely difficult to fulfill them using data from the firm's existing information systems. Various MIS or TPS may define important pieces of data, such as the time period covered by fiscal year, in different ways. It may not be possible to reconcile data from incompatible internal systems for analysis by managers. A significant amount of organizational change may be required before the firm can build and install effective DSS and ESS.

Summary

1. **Define a decision-support system (DSS) and a group decision-support system (GDSS).** A decision-support system (DSS) is an interactive system under user control that combines data, sophisticated analytical models, and user-friendly software into a single powerful system that can support semi-structured or unstructured decision making. A group decision-support system (GDSS) is an interactive computer-based system to facilitate the solution of unstructured problems by a set of decision makers working together as a group rather than individually.

2. **Describe the components of decision-support systems and group decision-support systems.** The components of a DSS are the DSS database, the model base, and the DSS software system. The DSS database is a collection of current or historical data from a number of applications or groups that can be used for analysis. The model base is a collection of mathematical and analytical models that are used for analyzing the data in the database. The DSS software system allows users to interact with the DSS database and model base directly.

Group decision-support systems (GDSS) have hardware, software, and people components. Hardware components consist of the conference room facilities, including seating arrangements and computer and other electronic hardware. Software components include tools for organizing ideas, gathering information, ranking and setting priorities, and documenting meeting sessions. People components include participants, a trained facilitator, and staff to support the hardware and software.

3. **Explain how decision-support systems and group decision-support systems can enhance decision making.** Both DSS and GDSS support steps in the process of arriving at decisions. DSS provides results of model-based analysis that help managers design and evaluate alternatives and monitor the progress of the solution that was adopted. GDSS help decision makers meeting together to arrive at a decision more efficiently and are especially useful for increasing the productivity of meetings larger than four or five people. However, the effectiveness of GDSS is contingent upon the nature of the group, the task, and the context of the meeting.

4. **Describe the capabilities of executive support systems (ESS).** Executive support systems (ESS) help managers with unstructured problems that occur at the strategic level of management. ESS provide data from both internal and external sources and provide a generalized computing and communications environment that can be focused and applied to a changing array of problems. ESS help senior executives spot problems, identify opportunities, and forecast trends. They can filter out extraneous details for high-level overviews, or they can drill down to provide senior managers with detailed transaction data if required.

5. **Describe the benefits of executive support systems.** ESS help senior managers analyze, compare, and highlight trends so that they more easily may monitor organizational performance or identify strategic problems and opportunities. ESS may increase the span of control of senior management and allow decision making to be decentralized and to take place at lower operating levels.

Key Terms

Decision-support system (DSS)	Control aids	DSS software system	Executive support system (ESS)
Representations	DSS database	Group decision-support system (GDSS)	Briefing books
Operations	Model base	Electronic meeting system (EMS)	Drill down
Memory aids	Model		
	Sensitivity analysis		

Review Questions

1. What is a *decision-support system* (DSS)? How does it differ from a *management information system* (MIS)?
2. What are the four capabilities of a DSS?
3. How can DSS support unstructured or semi-structured decision making?
4. What are the three basic components of a DSS? Briefly describe each.
5. In what ways is building decision-support systems different from building traditional MIS systems?
6. What is a *group decision-support system* (GDSS)? How does it differ from a DSS?
7. What are the three underlying problems in group decision making that have led to the development of GDSS?
8. Describe the three elements of a GDSS.
9. Name five GDSS software tools.
10. What is an *electronic meeting system* (EMS)?
11. For each of the three underlying problems in group decision making referred to in question 7, describe one or two ways GDSS can contribute to a solution.
12. Define and describe the capabilities of an *executive support system*.
13. Define *briefing books*. Explain why they were not adequate to support executive decision making.
14. In what ways is building executive support systems different from building traditional MIS systems?
15. What are the benefits of ESS? How do they enhance managerial decision making?

Discussion Questions

1. Some have argued that all information systems support decision making. The argument holds that conceptually a DSS is just a good MIS. Discuss.
2. What kinds of skills must you, as an end user of systems, have in order to participate in the design and use of a DSS?
3. Identify an organization with which you are familiar. Identify specific areas where DSS could help decision making and describe the DSS you would recommend.

Group Project

With three or four of your classmates, identify several groups in your university that could benefit from a GDSS. Design a GDSS for one of those groups, describing its hardware, software, and people elements. Present your findings to the class.

Case Study

ZENECA SEARCHES FOR DECISIONS

Staying competitive in the pharmaceuticals business requires a great deal of information. With $1.3 billion in annual sales and 12,600 employees, Zeneca Pharmaceuticals of Wilmington, Delaware must compete against much larger drug companies and dozens of successful products if it is to grow. In today's health care market, price is a key factor as governments, insurance companies, and patients all are exerting great pressure on pharmaceutical companies, HMOs, and all types of health care companies to lower their prices. To the deliverers of healthcare services, lower prices mean they must have lower costs. While remaining profitable, Zeneca must be able to compete with lower costs, while being more aggressive, creative, and innovative than its competitors in marketing its products.

Zeneca has no shortage of data. In the early 1990s its IBM mainframe already held 6 million records which were the source of the 6-inch thick reports that were distributed monthly to 200 marketing and sales managers. The paper reports contained current and historical details about customers, products, contracts, drug pricing, and sales. Given their size, they required great patience and perseverance to locate and identify specific information needed by a user. According to senior systems engineer Keith Magay, "It could take as long as two days for a manager to find the pertinent data" because of the size of the paper reports. Once the needed data were located (if they were), they were still paper-based, static data, difficult to use and analyze.

Yet use of marketing and sales data is vital to Zeneca if it is to compete successfully. For example Zeneca's prostate cancer treatment drug, Zolodex, has been outsold by its more expensive competitor, Lupron. Given the pressures on their customers to lower costs, one would expect that Zolodex would be the leader rather than Lupron. But Zeneca managers were only able to find out which drug was selling the most through analysis of their stored data, and that was a most daunting task when it was delivered in monthly paper reports.

To address the problem, Zeneca management decided to build a decision-support system which would enable managers to mine the data quickly. The system, known as ZICS (Zeneca Integrated Contracting System), draws its data from multiple mainframe databases as if those databases were a single data warehouse. Marketing and sales managers gain access to the data through their desktop computers or portable laptops. They can easily obtain information on account types, customers, product classes, contract terms, prescription drug pricing, and sales and contract histories.

The system itself is very sophisticated, using a new technology known as OLAP (on-line analytical processing) that enables users to analyze multiple factors simultaneously. Zeneca business managers can obtain a multidimensional view of data to manipulate product and customer information. Because the system is interactive and supports complex many-to-many comparisons, users can find indirect correlations that would otherwise not be visible. The analysis takes place on-line and interactively. Users can view the data from several perspectives, including by product, by account type, or by broad market segment. A manager might tap into the system to see how much of a given prescription drug an HMO purchased over six months. He or she could click on a cell for the account name, then click on other cells to view the time period and sales information, then click on still other cells to view the products. The manager could use menu-based navigational tools to shop around for better data comparisons.

In 1995, using this system, managers at Zeneca did discover that Zolodex was being outsold by Lupron. Sales managers were then able to pull together sales data by customer so they would be able to demonstrate to their customers how many tens of thousands of dollars they could save by purchasing Zolodex rather than Lupron. According to Bob Bogle, Zeneca's vice-president of information systems, "With this kind of system, we can analyze large volumes of data in ways that let us reach intelligent competitive decisions." The company intends to use the data to help its staff demonstrate to customers how a contract with Zeneca can increase the customer's profit. ZICS cost Zeneca only about $30,000 to build, although they also had to pay $200,000 for the underlying DSS software. However, that software can be used as the basis for other decision-support systems, and ZICS has garnered such glowing reports from its users that the company plans to build others in 1996, including one to serve their 27 corporate account managers and another to support the company's 50 national managers. ■

Source: Bronwyn Fryer, "Zeneca Take Its Medicine," *Information Week*, March 18, 1996.

Case Study Questions

1. What problems did Zeneca face in trying to make good decisions?
2. What was Zeneca's business strategy and how was decision making related to it?
3. What kinds of decisions did the decision-support system support?
4. What management, organization, and technology issues had to be addressed when building the new system?

References

Alavi, Maryam, and Erich A. Joachimsthaler. "Revisiting DSS Implementation Research: A Meta-Analysis of the Literature and Suggestions for Researchers." *MIS Quarterly* 16, no. 1 (March 1992).

Anthes, Gary H. "Notes System Sends Federal Property Data Nationwide." *Computerworld* (August 8, 1994).

Betts, Mitch. "Insurer's Financial Model Spawns Profits." *Computerworld* (July 5, 1993).

Bonzcek, R. H., C. W. Holsapple, and A. B. Whinston. "Representing Modeling Knowledge with First Order Predicate Calculus." *Operations Research* 1 (1982).

Chidambaram, Laku, Robert P. Bostrum, and Bayard E. Wynne. "A Longitudinal Study of the Impact of Group Decision Support Systems on Group Development." *Journal of Management Information Systems* 7, no. 3 (Winter 1990–91).

Dennis, Alan R., Joey F. George, Len M. Jessup, Jay F. Nunamaker, and Douglas R. Vogel. "Information Technology to Support Electronic Meetings." *MIS Quarterly* 12, no. 4 (December 1988).

Dennis, Alan R., Jay F. Nunamaker, Jr., and Douglas R. Vogel. "A Comparison of Laboratory and Field Research in the Study of Electronic Meeting Systems." *Journal of Management Information Systems* 7, no. 3 (Winter 1990–91).

DeSanctis, Geraldine, and R. Brent Gallupe. "A Foundation for the Study of Group Decision Support Systems." *Management Science* 33, no. 5 (May 1987).

DeSanctis, Geraldine, Marshall Scott Poole, Howard Lewis, and George Desharnias. "Computing in Quality Team Meetings." *Journal of Management Information Systems* 8, no. 3 (Winter 1991–92).

Easton, George K., Joey F. George, Jay F. Nunamaker, Jr., and Mark O. Pendergast. "Two Different Electronic Meeting Systems." *Journal of Management Information Systems* 7, no. 3 (Winter 1990–91).

El Sawy, Omar. "Personal Information Systems for Strategic Scanning in Turbulent Environments." *MIS Quarterly* 9, no. 1 (March 1985).

El Sherif, Hisham, and Omar A. El Sawy. "Issue-Based Decision Support Systems for the Egyptian Cabinet." *MIS Quarterly* 12, no. 4 (December 1988).

Gallupe, R. Brent, Geraldine DeSanctis, and Gary W. Dickson. "Computer-Based Support for Group Problem-Finding: An Experimental Investigation." *MIS Quarterly* 12, no. 2 (June 1988).

Ginzberg, Michael J., W. R. Reitman, and E. A. Stohr, eds. *Decision Support Systems,* New York: North Holland (1982).

Gopal, Abhijit, Robert P. Bostrum, and Wynne W. Chin. "Applying Adaptive Structuration Theory to Investigate the Process of Group Support Systems Use." *Journal of Management Information Systems* 9, no. 3 (Winter 1992–93).

Grobowski, Ron, Chris McGoff, Doug Vogel, Ben Martz, and Jay Nunamaker. "Implementing Electronic Meeting Systems at IBM: Lessons Learned and Success Factors." *MIS Quarterly* 14, no. 4 (December 1990).

Henderson, John C., and David A. Schilling. "Design and Implementation of Decision Support Systems in the Public Sector." *MIS Quarterly* (June 1985).

Hiltz, Starr Roxanne, Kenneth Johnson, and Murray Turoff. "Group Decision Support: Designated Human Leaders and Statistical Feedback." *Journal of Management Information Systems* 8, no. 2 (Fall 1991).

Ho, T. H., and K. S. Raman. "The Effect of GDSS on Small Group Meetings," *Journal of Management Information Systems* 8, no. 2 (Fall 1991).

Hogue, Jack T. "Decision Support Systems and the Traditional Computer Information System Function: An Examination of Relationships During DSS Application Development." *Journal of Management Information Systems* (Summer 1985).

Hogue, Jack T. "A Framework for the Examination of Management Involvement in Decision Support Systems." *Journal of Management Information Systems* 4, no. 1 (Summer 1987).

Houdeshel, George, and Hugh J. Watson. "The Management Information and Decision Support (MIDS) System at Lockheed, Georgia." *MIS Quarterly* 11, no. 2 (March 1987).

Jessup, Leonard M., Terry Connolly, and Jolene Galegher. "The Effects of Anonymity on GDSS Group Process with an Idea-Generating Task." *MIS Quarterly* 14, no. 3 (September 1990).

Jones, Jack William, Carol Saunders, and Raymond McLeod, Jr. "Media Usage and Velocity in Executive Information Acquisition: An Exploratory Study." *European Journal of Information Systems* 2 (1993).

Keen, Peter G. W., and M. S. Scott Morton. *Decision Support Systems: An Organizational Perspective.* Reading, MA: Addison-Wesley (1982).

King, John. "Successful Implementation of Large Scale Decision Support Systems: Computerized Models in U.S. Economic Policy Making." *Systems Objectives Solutions* (November 1983).

Kraemer, Kenneth L., and John Leslie King. "Computer-Based Systems for Cooperative Work and Group Decision Making." *ACM Computing Surveys* 20, no. 2 (June 1988).

Laudon, Kenneth C. *Communications Technology and Democratic Participation.* New York: Praeger (1977).

Le Blanc, Louis A., and Kenneth A. Kozar. "An Empirical Investigation of the Relationship Between DSS Usage and System Performance." *MIS Quarterly* 14, no. 3 (September 1990).

Leidner, Dorothy E., and Joyce L. Elam, "Executive Information Systems: Their Impact on Executive Decision Making." *Journal of Management Information Systems* 10, no. 3 (Winter 1993–94).

Lewe, Henrik, and Helmut Krcmar. "A Computer-Supported Cooperative Work Research Laboratory." *Journal of Management Information Systems* 8, no. 3 (Winter 1991–92).

McLeod, Poppy Lauretta, and Jeffry R. Liker. "Electronic Meeting Systems: Evidence from a Low Structure Environment." *Information Systems Research* 3, no. 3 (September 1992).

Meador, Charles L., and Peter G. W. Keen. "Setting Priorities for DSS Development." *MIS Quarterly* (June 1984).

Miranda, Shalia M., and Robert P. Bostrum. "The Impact of Group Support Systems on Group Conflict and Conflict Management." *Journal of Management Information Systems* 10, no. 3 (Winter 1993–94).

Mohan, Lakshmi, William K. Holstein, and Robert B. Adams. "EIS: It Can Work in the Public Sector." *MIS Quarterly* 14, no. 4 (December 1990).

"The New Role for 'Executive Information Systems.'" *I/S Analyzer* (January 1992).

Nunamaker, J. F., Alan R. Dennis, Joseph S. Valacich, Douglas R. Vogel, and Joey F. George. "Electronic Meeting Systems to Support Group Work." *Communications of the ACM* 34, no. 7 (July 1991).

Panko, Raymond R. "Managerial Communication Patterns." *Journal of Organizational Computing* 2, no. 1 (1992).

Post, Brad Quinn. "A Business Case Framework for Group Support Technology." *Journal of Management Information Systems* 9, no. 3 (Winter 1992–93).

Rifkin, Glenn. "'What-If' Software for Manufacturers." *The New York Times* (October 18, 1992).

Rockart, John F., and David W. DeLong. "Executive Support Systems and the Nature of Work." Working Paper: Management in the 1990s, Sloan School of Management (April 1986).

Rockart, John F., and David W. DeLong. *Executive Support Systems: The Emergence of Top Management Computer Use*. Homewood, IL: Dow-Jones Irwin (1988).

Sambamurthy, V., and Marshall Scott Poole. "The Effects of Variations in Capabilities of GDSS Designs on Management of Cognitive Conflict in Groups." *Information Systems Research* 3, no. 3 (September 1992).

Sanders, G. Lawrence, and James F. Courtney. "A Field Study of Organizational Factors Influencing DSS Success." *MIS Quarterly* (March 1985).

Silver, Mark S. "Decision Support Systems: Directed and Nondirected Change." *Information Systems Research* 1, no. 1 (March 1990).

Sprague, R. H., and E. D. Carlson. *Building Effective Decision Support Systems*. Englewood Cliffs, NJ: Prentice-Hall (1982).

Stefik, Mark, Gregg Foster, Daniel C. Bobrow, Kenneth Kahn, Stan Lanning, and Luch Suchman. "Beyond the Chalkboard: Computer Support for Collaboration and Problem Solving in Meetings." *Communications of the ACM* (January 1987).

Turban, Efraim. *Decision Support and Expert Systems: Management Support Systems*. New York: Macmillan (1993).

Turoff, Murray. "Computer-Mediated Communication Requirements for Group Support." *Journal of Organizational Computing* 1, no. 1 (January–March 1991).

Tyran, Craig K., Alan R. Dennis, Douglas R. Vogel, and J. F. Nunamaker, Jr. "The Application of Electronic Meeting Technology to Support Senior Management." *MIS Quarterly* 16, no. 3 (September 1992).

Vogel, Douglas R., Jay F. Nunamaker, William Benjamin Martz, Jr., Ronald Grobowski, and Christopher McGoff. "Electronic Meeting System Experience at IBM." *Journal of Management Information Systems* 6, no. 3 (Winter 1989–90).

Volonino, Linda, and Hugh J. Watson. "The Strategic Business Objectives Method for EIS Development." *Journal of Management Information Systems* 7, no. 3 (Winter 1990–91).

Walls, Joseph G., George R. Widmeyer, and Omar A. El Sawy. "Building an Information System Design Theory for Vigilant EIS." *Information Systems Research* 3, no. 1 (March 1992).

Watson, Richard T., Geraldine DeSanctis, and Marshall Scott Poole. "Using a GDSS to Facilitate Group Consensus: Some Intended and Unintended Consequences." *MIS Quarterly* 12, no. 3 (September 1988).

Watson, Richard T., Teck Hua Ho, and K. S. Raman. "Culture: A Fourth Dimension of Group Support Systems." *Communications of the ACM* 37, no. 10 (October 1994).

Watson, Hugh J., Astrid Lipp, Pamela Z. Jackson, Abdelhafid Dahmani, and William B. Fredenberger. "Organizational Support for Decision Support Systems." *Journal of Management Information Systems* 5, no. 4 (Spring 1989).

Watson, Hugh J., R. Kelly Rainer, Jr., and Chang E. Koh. "Executive Information Systems: A Framework for Development and a Survey of Current Practices." *MIS Quarterly* 15, no. 1 (March 1991).

Chapter 14

Controlling Information Systems

Broadcast Storms Bring Swissair Network to a Halt

14.1 System Vulnerability and Abuse
Why Systems Are Vulnerable
Window on Organizations
Uprooting the Internet Hackers
Concerns for System Builders and Users
Window on Management
Client/Server Disaster Planning
System Quality Problems: Software and Data

14.2 Creating a Control Environment
General Controls
Application Controls
Developing a Control Structure: Costs and Benefits
The Role of Auditing in the Control Process

14.3 Ensuring System Quality
Software Quality Assurance
Window on Technology
British Customs Tests Its GUIs
Data Quality Audits

Management Challenges
Summary
Key Terms
Review Questions
Discussion Questions
Group Project
Case Study: Can We Trust Mutual Fund Pricing?
References

Broadcast Storms Bring Swissair Network to a Halt

Like most airlines, Swissair is heavily dependent upon its network for making reservations and so for generating revenue. In North America the network that connected Swissair's ten offices was periodically bombarded by broadcasting storms. These storms will flood a network with unneeded data packets, slowing the network to a crawl and requiring that it be brought down to be fixed. Broadcasting storms can be caused by misconfigured software or by faulty hardware. This problem occurred regularly at Swissair and brought the computer down for up to three hours per week for repair, making the company's reservations and ticketing network unavailable about 1 percent of the time.

Such a small amount of time—1 percent—did not seem insignificant to Swissair. The downtime totaled about four days per year—four days of lost customers, lost revenue, and lost profit opportunities. In January 1995 the airline consolidated its two New York-area offices into a new North American headquarters office in Melville, Long Island, New York. Given their broadcast storm problem, they took the opportunity of the move to install a new, failsafe reservations and ticketing network to eliminate the unnecessary downtime problem. The new network is based upon a fiber-optic communications backbone designed to handle network glitches. The network can be managed with intelligent workstations. The airline now has a 99.8 percent network availability 24 hours per day. The 0.2 percent downtime is less than one day per year and is needed mainly for planned network maintenance. ■

Source: Thomas Hoffman, "Swissair Bullet-Proofs New Network," *Computerworld*, April 24, 1995.

Vulnerability to network disruptions is but one of many problems that organizations relying on computer-based information systems may face. Hardware and software failures, natural disasters, employee errors, and use by unauthorized people may prevent information systems from running properly or running at all.

Computer systems play such a critical role in business, government, and daily life that organizations must take special steps to protect their information systems and ensure that they are accurate and reliable. Swissair took these steps; other companies suffer because they do not. This chapter describes how information systems can be *controlled* so that they serve the purposes for which they are intended.

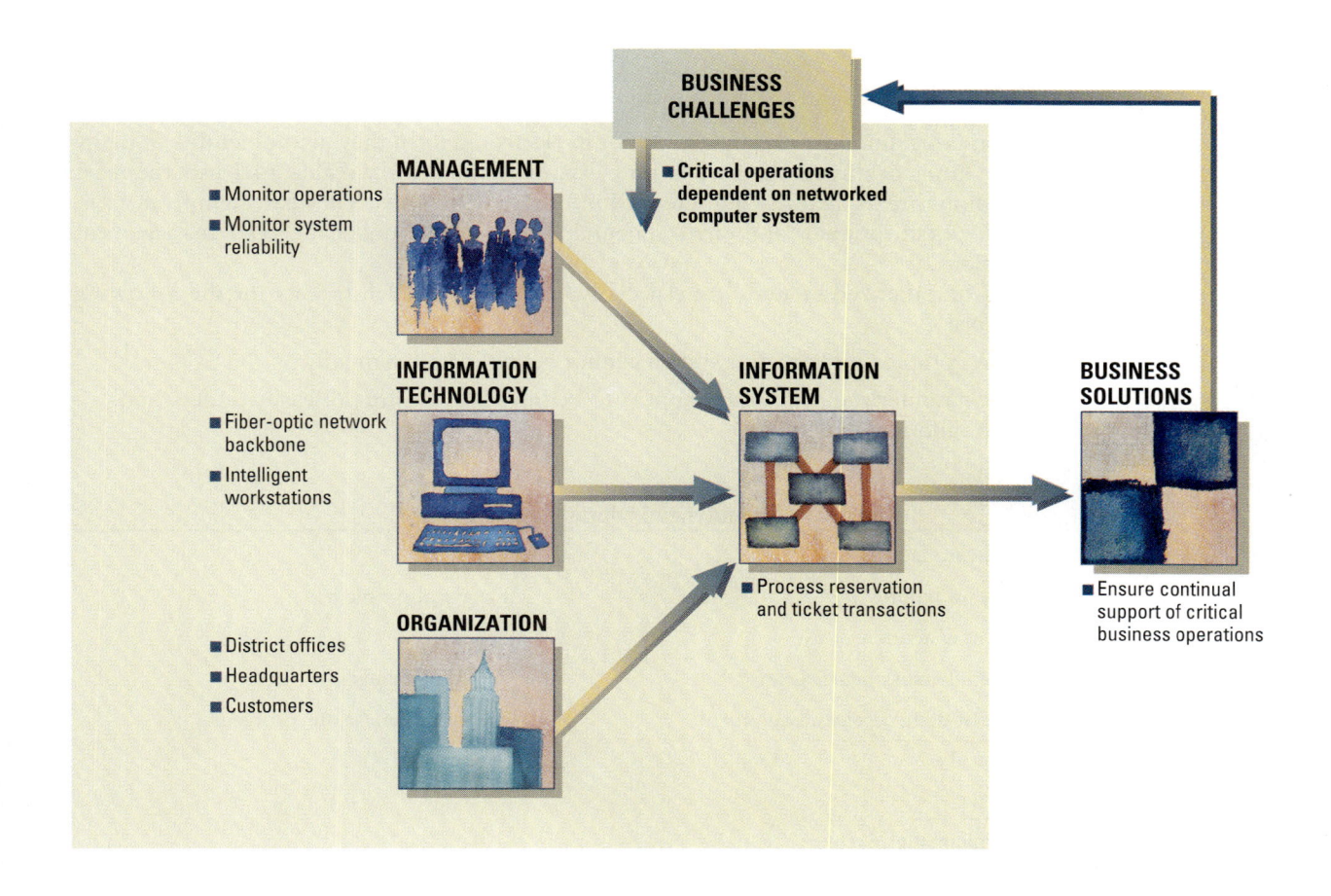

BUSINESS CHALLENGES

MANAGEMENT
- Monitor operations
- Monitor system reliability

■ Critical operations dependent on networked computer system

INFORMATION TECHNOLOGY
- Fiber-optic network backbone
- Intelligent workstations

INFORMATION SYSTEM
■ Process reservation and ticket transactions

BUSINESS SOLUTIONS
■ Ensure continual support of critical business operations

ORGANIZATION
- District offices
- Headquarters
- Customers

> **Learning Objectives**
>
> *After completing this chapter, you will be able to:*
>
> 1. Show why information systems are so vulnerable to destruction, error, abuse, and system quality problems.
> 2. Describe general controls and application controls for information systems.
> 3. Identify the factors that must be considered when developing the controls for information systems.
> 4. Describe the most important software quality assurance techniques.
> 5. Explain the importance of auditing information systems and safeguarding data quality.

14.1 SYSTEM VULNERABILITY AND ABUSE

Before computer automation, data about individuals or organizations were maintained and secured as paper records dispersed in separate business or organizational units. Information systems concentrate data in computer files that can potentially be accessed more easily by large numbers of people and by groups outside the organization. Consequently, automated data are more susceptible to destruction, fraud, error, and misuse.

When computer systems fail to run or work as required, firms that depend heavily on computers experience a serious loss of business function. A 1992 survey of 450 Fortune 1000 firms found that unplanned disruptions in computer service cost U.S. businesses $4 billion a year and result in at least 37 million hours of lost worker productivity (McPartlin, 1992). The longer computer systems are down, the more serious the consequences for the firm. Some firms relying on computers to process their critical business transactions might experience a total loss of business function if they lose computer capability for more than a few days.

WHY SYSTEMS ARE VULNERABLE

When large amounts of data are stored in electronic form they are vulnerable to many more kinds of threats than when they exist in manual form. Table 14.1 lists the most common threats against computerized information systems. They can stem from technical, organizational, and environmental factors compounded by poor management decisions.

Computerized systems are especially vulnerable to such threats for the following reasons:

- A complex information system cannot be replicated manually.
- Computerized procedures appear to be invisible and are not easily understood or audited.

Table 14.1 Threats to Computerized Information Systems

Hardware failure	Fire
Software failure	Electrical problems
Personnel actions	User errors
Terminal access penetration	Program changes
Theft of data, services, equipment	Telecommunications problems

- Although the chances of disaster in automated systems are no greater than in manual systems, the effect of a disaster can be much more extensive. In some cases all of the system's records can be destroyed and lost forever.
- On-line information systems are directly accessible by many individuals. Legitimate users may gain easy access to computer data that they are not authorized to view. Unauthorized individuals can also gain access to such systems.

Advances in telecommunications and computer software have magnified these vulnerabilities. Through telecommunications networks, information systems in different locations can be interconnected. The potential for unauthorized access, abuse, or fraud is not limited to a single location but can occur at any access point in the network.

Additionally, more complex and diverse hardware, software, organizational, and personnel arrangements are required for telecommunications networks, creating new areas and opportunities for penetration and manipulation. Wireless networks using radio-based technology are even more vulnerable to penetration because radio frequency bands are easy to scan. The vulnerabilities of telecommunications networks are illustrated in Figure 14.1.

Hackers and Computer Viruses

The efforts of hackers to penetrate computer networks have been widely publicized. A **hacker** is a person who gains unauthorized access to a computer network for profit, criminal mischief, or personal pleasure. The potential damage from intruders is frightening. In July 1992 a Federal grand jury in Manhattan indicted five computer hackers who belonged to a group called the Masters of Deception. They were charged with breaking into the information systems of three regional telephone companies, numerous credit bureaus, and BankAmerica Corporation, stealing telephone service and selling information on how to obtain credit reports. The Window on Organizations describes problems created by hackers for organizations that use the Internet.

hacker A person who gains unauthorized access to a computer network for profit, criminal mischief, or personal pleasure.

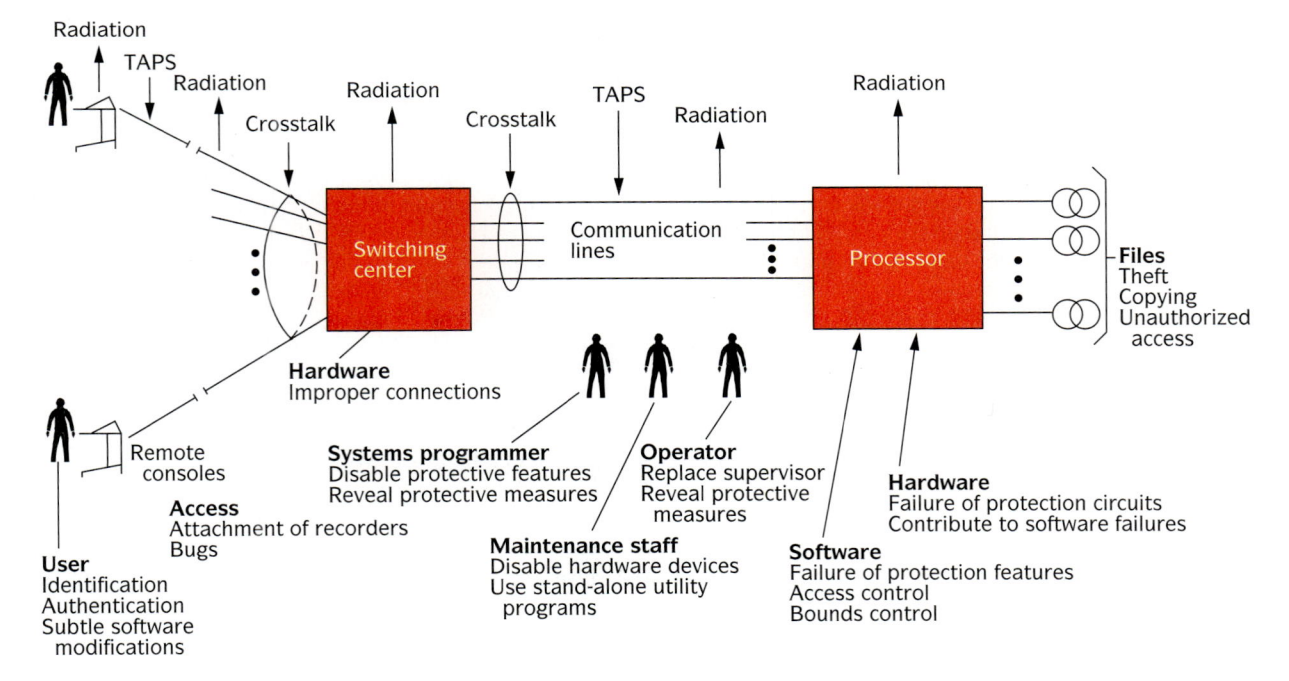

FIGURE 14.1
Telecommunications network vulnerabilities. Telecommunications networks are highly vulnerable to natural failure of hardware and software and to misuse by programmers, computer operators, maintenance staff, and end users. It is possible to tap communications lines and illegally intercept data. High-speed transmission over twisted wire communications channels causes interference called *crosstalk*. Radiation can disrupt a network at various points as well.

Window on Organizations

UPROOTING THE INTERNET HACKERS

Many businesses are afraid to use the Internet. Why? They fear that unwanted intruders—hackers, who use the latest technology—will use the Internet to break into their computer systems. The Internet Society, in Reston, Virginia, estimates that about 30,000 organizations that would link up to the Internet have not done so due to security concerns.

In October, 1993, a group of hackers broke into the computer of Panix (Public Access Network Corp.), a commercial seller of access to the Internet. The hackers had embedded a program in the Panix computer that collected passwords from users of the Panix system. With those passwords, the hackers were then able to access other computers connected to the Internet, to steal both data and more passwords. The security of the whole system had been compromised.

In October, 1994, newspapers revealed that a group of hackers had stolen valuable copies of new software from such companies as Microsoft and IBM kept at Florida State University. The thieves quietly made the software available for free to people through the Internet. Most of the recipients of the free software were not from the United States, highlighting the worldwide nature of the problem.

Concerns mounted in September, 1994, when it was revealed that the underlying software formula for a data encryption system belonging to RSA Data Security Inc., of Redwood City, California, was being distributed on the Internet. Data encryption, where data are scrambled into a coded form for transmission over a communications network, is viewed as one effective protection against data thieves. Even if hackers could steal encrypted data as it travels through the Internet (or any other network), it would be meaningless gibberish if the thieves did not have the encryption key to unscramble it. RSA's encryption software has become a kind of encryption standard. Now that its coding has been circulated on the Internet, data transmitted using RSA software are no longer secure.

A report issued on May 22, 1996, by the U.S. General Accounting Office warned that computer hackers cruising the Internet pose a serious and growing threat to national security, with Pentagon computers suffering as many as 250,000 "attacks" in 1995, most made through the Internet. In about 65 percent of those efforts, hackers were able to gain entry into a computer network.

What can businesses do? One rule of good security is to require system users to change their passwords often. This will not

> **To Think About:** In light of these security problems, under what circumstances might you recommend that your organization use the Internet? What management, organization, and technology issues would you consider?

stop password stealing altogether, but it would tighten a key loophole. Some companies are achieving a measure of security by installing firewalls. An Internet *firewall* is a range of devices that operate between networks, such as routers and gateways. They contain specialized software with user-defined rules for blocking certain services or kinds of traffic between the public Internet and a private corporate network. Some of these devices are being used to route all communications through a third-party computer, allowing no one directly into the home computer. Other firewalls allow the user of the firewall to list all applications and computer user log-ons that are allowed to send messages to the computer being protected. If a message arrives from a source not on the firewall table, it is simply rejected.

One organization exists for the purpose of addressing security on the Internet. CERT (the Computer Emergency Response Team at the Software Engineering Institute of Carnegie-Mellon University) helps both to determine who is breaking in to the Internet, and to devise solutions to the method used for the break-in. With the increase in break-ins, the United States Defense Department's Advanced Research Projects Agency (ARPA) is planning to add funding to CERT in order to double their staff.

Sources: Philip Sherman, "Report Warns of Security Threats Posed by Computer Hackers," *The New York Times,* May 23, 1996; David Bernstein, "Insulate Against Internet Intruders," *Datamation,* October 1, 1994; John Markoff, "A Dose of Computer Insecurity," *The New York Times,* October 30, 1993; and Joseph C. Panettiere, "Guardian of the Net," *Information Week,* May 23, 1994.

---

computer virus Rogue software programs that are difficult to detect and which spread rapidly through computer systems, destroying data or disrupting processing and memory systems.

Most recently, alarm has risen over hackers propagating **computer viruses,** rogue software programs that spread rampantly from system to system, clogging computer memory or destroying programs or data. More than 2100 viruses are known to exist, with 50 or more new viruses created each month. (Figure 14.2 describes the characteristics of the most common viruses found to date.) The most notorious virus outbreak occurred in November 1988, when Robert Morris, a brilliant computer science student, introduced a program through a Cornell University terminal that spread uncontrollably throughout the Internet. Morris intended his program to reside quietly on Internet computers, but it echoed throughout the network in minutes, tying up computer memory and storage space as it copied and recopied itself hundreds of thousands of times.

FIGURE 14.2
Frequently occurring computer viruses. From "Frequently Occurring Viruses," Wall Street Journal, *August 29, 1994.* Reprinted by permission of Wall Street Journal, © 1994 Dow Jones & Company, Inc. All rights reserved worldwide.

COMPUTERS
Frequently Occurring Computer Viruses

VIRUS NAME	FREQUENCY AS % OF ALL INCIDENTS	WHAT IT DOES
FORM	34.7%	Makes a clicking sound with each keystroke, but only on the 18th of the month. Has a hidden, obscene reference to someone named Corinne.
JOSHI	6.4	Freezes your PC once a year, on Jan. 5, until the phrase "Happy Birthday Joshi" is typed on the keyboard.
STONED	4.0	Once the most common virus, it sometimes displays on-screen "Your PC is now Stoned."
CANSU	3.4	One out of every eight times the PC is switched on, it displays a V-shaped symbol on the screen.
MICHELANGELO	3.3	Very nasty. It wipes out most of your data on March 6, the artist's birthday.
MONKEY-2	2.7	Mysterious. Hides in memory and infects every disk it contacts, making some unusable.
GREEN CATERPILLAR	1.6	Most effective in color, it unleashes a little worm that crawls around the screen rearranging characters, changing their color.

Source: IBM

The virus was quickly detected, but hundreds of computer centers in research institutions, universities, and military bases had to shut down. Estimates of the number of systems actually infected ranged from 6,000 to 250,000. A virus that was not intended to harm caused upwards of $100 million in lost machine time, lost access, and direct labor costs for recovery and cleanup.

In addition to spreading via computer networks, viruses can invade computerized information systems from "infected" diskettes from an outside source, through infected machines, or even from on-line electronic bulletin boards. The potential for massive damage and loss from future computer viruses remains (see Figure 14.3). A survey conducted by the National Computer Security Association (NCSA) and Dataquest, Inc. found that the average virus attack affected 142 PCs and took 2.4 days to eradicate, with many taking more than five days to correct. The study estimated that viruses cost U.S. businesses $2 million in 1994 alone (Anthes, 1993).

Organizations can use antivirus software and screening procedures to reduce the chances of infection. **Antivirus software** is special software designed to check computer systems and disks for the presence of various computer viruses. Often the software can eliminate the virus from the infected area. However, most antivirus software is only effective against viruses already known when the software is written—to protect their systems, management must continually update their antivirus software.

antivirus software Software designed to detect, and often eliminate, computer viruses from an information system.

CONCERNS FOR SYSTEM BUILDERS AND USERS

The heightened vulnerability of automated data has created special concerns for the builders and users of information systems. These concerns include disaster, security, and administrative error.

Disaster

Computer hardware, programs, data files, and other equipment can be destroyed by fires, power failures, or other disasters. It may take many years and millions of dollars to reconstruct destroyed data files and computer programs. If an organization needs

FIGURE 14.3

From Gary H. Anthes, "Viruses Continue to Wreak Havoc at Many U.S. Companies," Computerworld, *June 28, 1993 (Data from Dataquest, San Jose, Calif.). Copyright 1994 by Computerworld, Inc., Framingham, MA 01701. Reprinted from* Computerworld. *Reprinted by permission.*

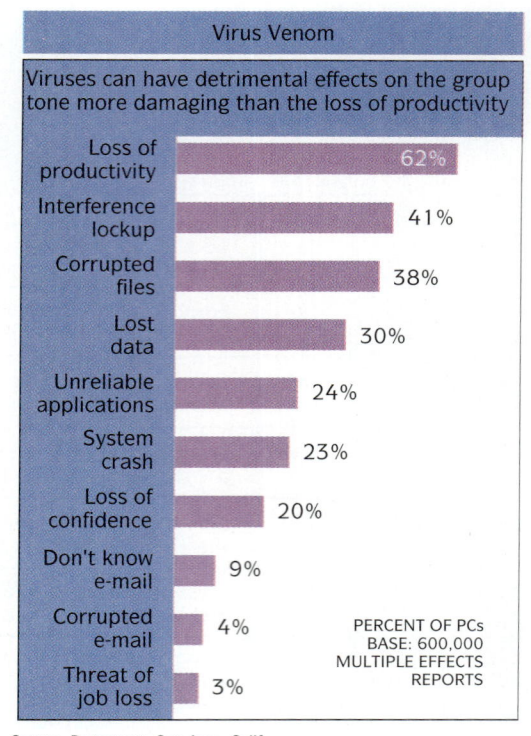

Virus Venom

Viruses can have detrimental effects on the group tone more damaging than the loss of productivity

Effect	Percent
Loss of productivity	62%
Interference lockup	41%
Corrupted files	38%
Lost data	30%
Unreliable applications	24%
System crash	23%
Loss of confidence	20%
Don't know e-mail	9%
Corrupted e-mail	4%
Threat of job loss	3%

PERCENT OF PCs
BASE: 600,000
MULTIPLE EFFECTS REPORTS

Source: Dataquest, San Jose, Calif.

Companies can detect and eliminate computer viruses in their systems by regularly using anti-virus software.

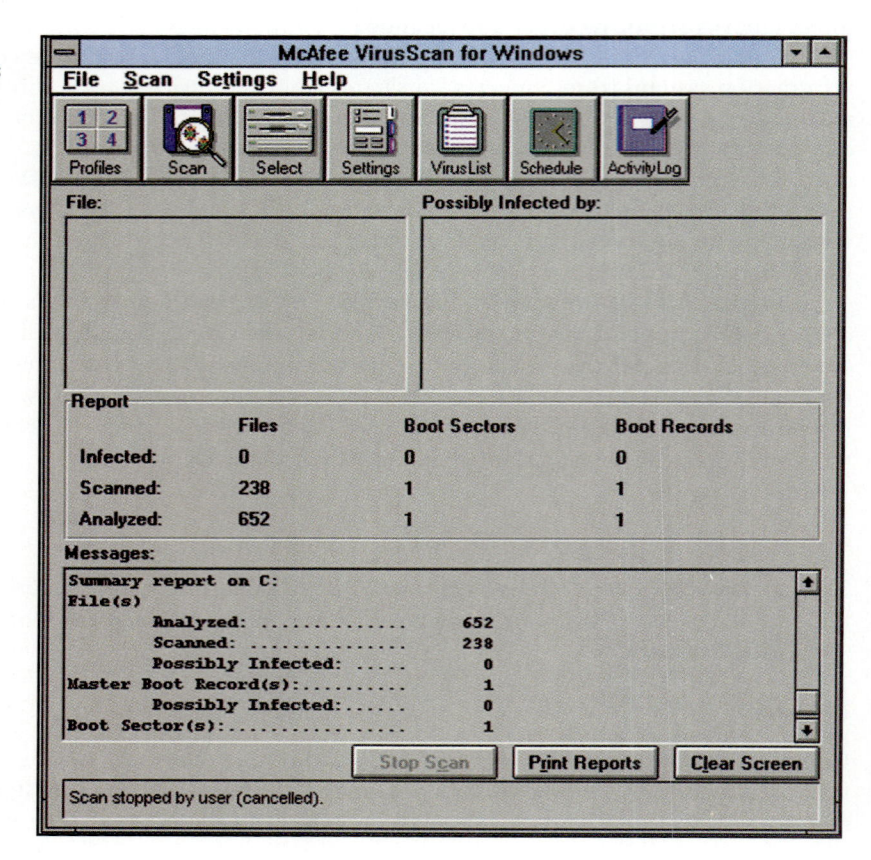

McAfee VirusScan for Windows

File   Scan   Settings   Help

Profiles | Scan | Select | Settings | VirusList | Schedule | ActivityLog

File:

Possibly Infected by:

Report

	Files	Boot Sectors	Boot Records
Infected:	0	0	0
Scanned:	238	1	1
Analyzed:	652	1	1

Messages:

```
Summary report on C:
File(s)
        Analyzed: ............  652
        Scanned: .............  238
        Possibly Infected: ....    0
Master Boot Record(s):.........    1
        Possibly Infected:.....    0
Boot Sector(s):................    1
```

Stop Scan | Print Reports | Clear Screen

Scan stopped by user (cancelled).

them to function on a day-to-day basis, it will no longer be able to operate. This is why companies such as Visa USA Inc. employ elaborate emergency backup facilities. Visa USA Inc. has duplicate mainframes, duplicate network pathways, duplicate terminals, and duplicate power supplies. Visa even uses a duplicate data center in McLean, Virginia, to handle half of its transactions and to serve as an emergency backup to its primary data center in San Mateo, California.

Fault-tolerant computer systems contain extra hardware, software, and power supply components that can back the system up and keep it running to prevent system failure. Fault-tolerant computers contain extra memory chips, processors, and disk storage devices. They can use special software routines or self-checking logic built into their circuitry to detect hardware failures and automatically switch to a backup device. Parts from these computers can be removed and repaired without disruption to the computer system. Their increased reliability is the reason the European Community banks are using fault-tolerant computer systems to clear cross-border transaction trading in the unified European currency, the European Currency Unit (ECU).

Fault-tolerant technology is used by firms for critical applications with heavy on-line transaction processing requirements. In **on-line transaction processing,** transactions entered on-line are immediately processed by the computer. Multitudinous changes to databases, reporting, or requests for information occur each instant.

Rather than build their own backup facilities, many firms contract with disaster recovery firms, such as Comdisco Disaster Recovery Services in Rosemont, Illinois, and Sungard Recovery Services headquartered in Wayne, Pennsylvania. These disaster recovery firms provide *hot sites* housing spare computers at various locations around the country where subscribing firms can run their critical applications in an emergency. Disaster recovery services now offer backup for client/server systems as well as traditional mainframe applications (see the Window on Management).

fault-tolerant computer systems Systems that contain extra hardware, software, and power supply components that can back the system up and keep it running to prevent system failure.

on-line transaction processing Transaction processing mode in which transactions entered on-line are immediately processed by the computer.

Security

Security refers to the policies, procedures, and technical measures used to prevent unauthorized access or alteration, theft, and physical damage to record systems. Security can be promoted with an array of techniques and tools to safeguard computer hardware, software, communications networks, and data. We have already discussed disaster protection measures. Other tools and techniques for promoting security will be discussed in subsequent sections.

security Policies, procedures, and technical measures used to prevent unauthorized access, alteration, theft, or physical damage to information systems.

Errors

Computers can also serve as instruments of error, severely disrupting or destroying an organization's record keeping and operations. For instance, a computer operator at the Exxon Corporation inadvertently erased valuable records about the 1989 grounding of the Exxon Valdez and the Alaskan oil spill, which were stored on magnetic tape. Errors in automated systems can occur at many points in the processing cycle: through data entry, program error, computer operations, and hardware. Figure 14.4 illustrates all of the points in a typical processing cycle where errors can occur.

SYSTEM QUALITY PROBLEMS: SOFTWARE AND DATA

In addition to disasters, viruses, and security breaches, defective software and data pose a constant threat to information systems, causing untold losses in productivity. An undiscovered error in a company's credit software or erroneous financial data can result in millions of dollars of losses. Several years ago, a hidden software problem in AT&T's long distance system brought down that system, bringing the New York-based financial exchanges to a halt and interfering with billions of dollars of business around the country for a number of hours. Modern passenger and commercial vehicles are increasingly dependent upon computer programs for critical functions. A hidden software defect in a braking system could result in the loss of lives.

Window on Management

CLIENT/SERVER DISASTER PLANNING

Is it less important to back up client/server systems than it is to back up mainframe-based systems? Apparently many managers seem to think so. A recent survey of 200 large U.S. corporations relying upon client/server systems found that two-thirds have no disaster recovery plan for data stored away from their central computers. However, disasters do not discriminate based on infrastructure type—fires and earthquakes play no favorites. Cedar Sinai Medical Center in Los Angeles found that out when the Northridge earthquake of January, 1994, knocked out half of its network.

Cedar Sinai's Dennis Martin, manager of computer resource administration, indicated after the earthquake that they had anchored most of their systems at their central location but not at the remote locations. They now plan to tie them down and to install uninterruptible power supplies at the outlying sites also. In contrast, the network of ITT Gilfillan, a radar manufacturer located in Van Nuys—the town right next to Northridge—survived with few problems, partly because they were already backing up their off-site server data. Backup of client/server systems has become important enough that all three of the leading mainframe disaster recovery services (SunGard, Comdisco, and IBM) are now offering client/server recovery options.

Most experts agree that client/server disaster recovery is much more complex than in a mainframe environment. Planning

To Think About: What management, organization, and technology issues should be addressed in a disaster recovery plan?

and testing, which are critical to a mainframe disaster recovery program, become even more critical within a distributed environment. They recommend that the organization begin with a business analysis to determine what must be backed up. The analysis should identify which managers and technical employees are critical to a rapid recovery from a disaster and what they would need (in programs, data, and equipment) to bring the system back. SunGard offers planning software called Comprehensive Business Recovery (CBR) to store such information and to provide model recovery procedures and plans. Testing also is key. Testing will build team skills so that disaster recovery will actually work if a disaster occurs. In addition, testing will allow the organization to find and solve problems. Procedures for client/server backup and disaster recovery must be enforced, which requires the backing of management.

Determining whether to rely on an outside, third-party service or to do it themselves internally can be a complex issue. Almost every client/server implementation is a unique multivendor combination of hardware and software. Disaster recovery services can't keep a single system available to be shared by many users, as they can with mainframe computer hot sites. A client/server hot site set up for a company is only useful to that specific company. Many small companies do not use an outside service because they are viewed as expensive.

Sources: Barbara Mary Hanna, "When Disasters Strike Distributed Systems," *Software Magazine,* September 1995, and Barbara DePompa, "Averting a Complete Disaster," *Information Week,* July 15, 1996 and "Date With Disaster," *Information Week,* May 2, 1994.

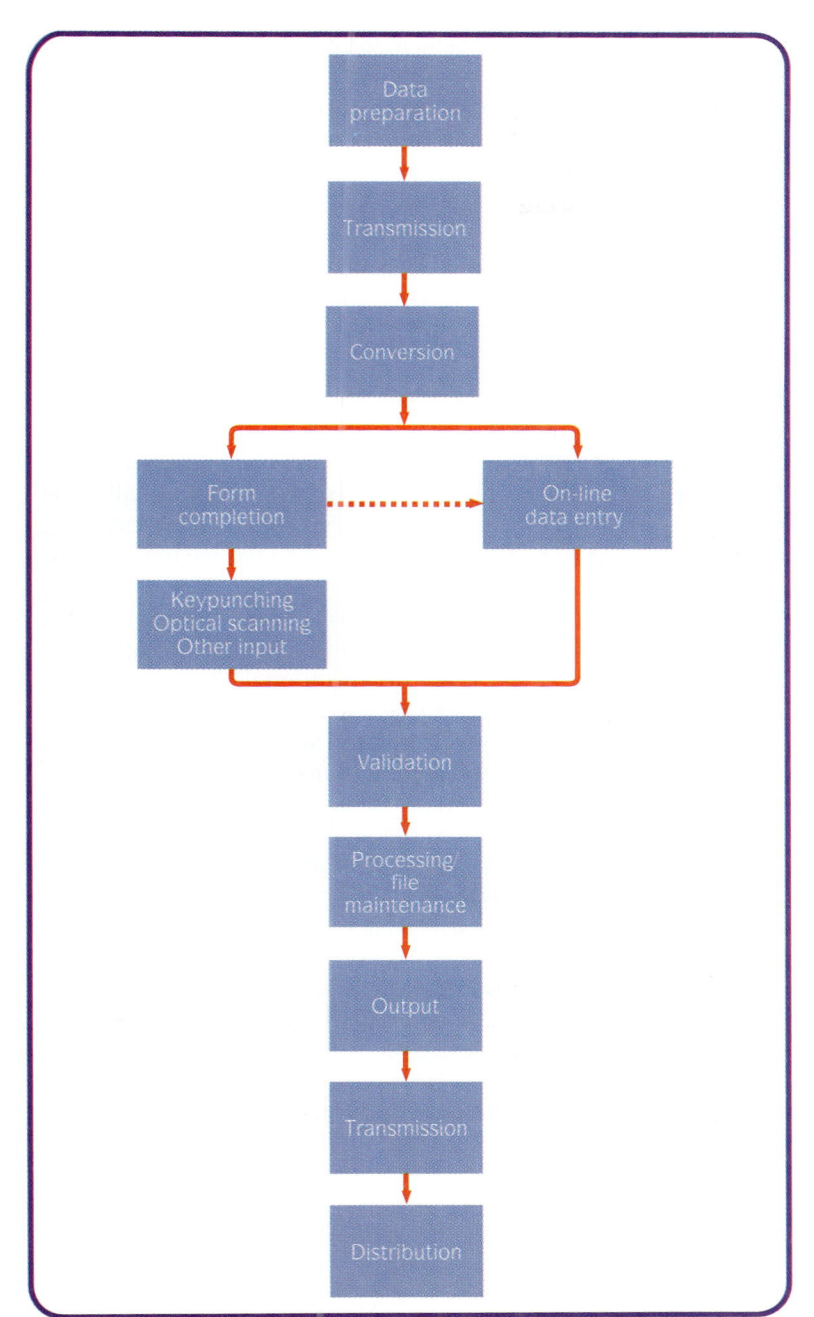

FIGURE 14.4
Points in the processing cycle where errors can occur. Each of the points illustrated in this figure represents a control point where special automated and/or manual procedures should be established to reduce the risk of errors during processing.

```
Data preparation
      ↓
Transmission
      ↓
Conversion
      ↓
   ┌──┴──┐
   ↓     ↓
Form    On-line
completion  data entry
   ↓     
Keypunching
Optical scanning
Other input
   ↓     ↓
   └──┬──┘
      ↓
Validation
      ↓
Processing/
file
maintenance
      ↓
Output
      ↓
Transmission
      ↓
Distribution
```

Bugs and Defects

A major problem with software is the presence of hidden **bugs** or program code defects. Studies have shown that it is virtually impossible to eliminate all bugs from large programs. The main source of bugs is the complexity of decision-making code. Even a relatively small program of several hundred lines will contain tens of decisions leading to hundreds or even thousands of different paths. Important programs within most corporations are usually much larger, containing tens of thousands or even millions of lines of code, each with many times the choices and paths of the smaller programs. Such complexity is difficult to document and design—designers document some reactions wrongly or fail to consider some possibilities. Studies show that about 60 percent of errors discovered during testing are a result of specifications in the design documentation that were missing, ambiguous, in error, or in conflict.

bugs Program code defects or errors

Zero defects, a goal of the total quality management movement, cannot be achieved in larger programs. Complete testing is simply not possible. Fully testing programs that contain thousands of choices and millions of paths would require thousands of years. Eliminating software bugs is an exercise in diminishing returns, because it would take proportionately longer testing to detect and eliminate obscure residual bugs (Littlewood and Strigini, 1993). Even without rigorous testing, one could not know for sure that a piece of software was dependable until the product proved itself after much operational use. The message? We cannot eliminate all bugs, and we cannot know with certainty the seriousness of the bugs that do remain.

The Maintenance Nightmare

Another reason that systems are unreliable is that computer software has traditionally been a nightmare to maintain. Maintenance, the process of modifying a system in production use, is the most expensive phase of the systems development process. In one-fifth of information systems departments, 85 percent of personnel hours are allocated to maintenance, leaving little time for new systems development. In most organizations nearly half of information systems staff time is spent in the maintenance of existing systems.

Why are maintenance costs so high? One major reason is organizational change. The firm may experience large internal changes in structure or leadership, or change may come from its surrounding environment. These organizational changes affect information requirements. Another reason appears to be software complexity, as measured by the number and size of interrelated software programs and subprograms and the complexity of the flow of program logic between them (Banker, Datar, Kemerer, and Zweig, 1993). A third common cause of long-term maintenance problems is faulty systems analysis and design, especially information requirements analysis. Some studies of large TPS systems by TRW, Inc., have found that a majority of system errors—64 percent—result from early analysis errors (Mazzucchelli, 1985).

Figure 14.5 illustrates the cost of correcting errors based on the experience of consultants reported in the literature.

If errors are detected early, during analysis and design, the cost to the systems development effort is small. But if they are not discovered until after programming, testing, or conversion has been completed, the costs can soar astronomically. A minor logic error, for example, that could take one hour to correct during the analysis and design stage could take 10, 40, and 90 times as long to correct during programming, conversion, and post-implementation, respectively.

FIGURE 14.5
The cost of errors over the systems development cycle. The most common, most severe, and most expensive system errors develop in the early design stages. They involve faulty requirements analysis. Errors in program logic or syntax are much less common, less severe, and less costly to repair than design errors.
Source: Alberts, 1976.

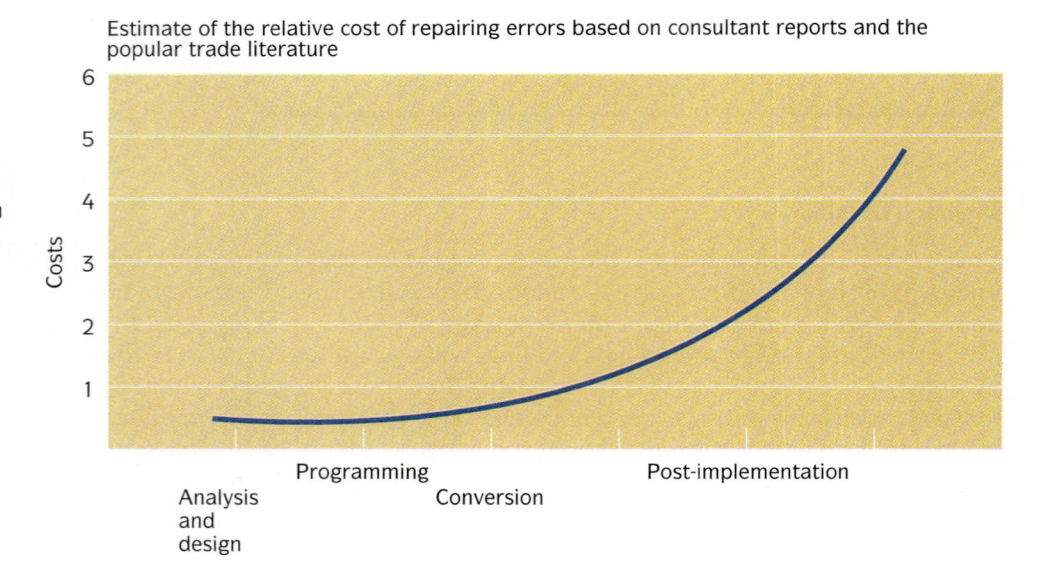

Data Quality Problems

Chapter 4 has pointed out that the most common source of information system failure is poor data quality. Data that are inaccurate, untimely, or inconsistent with other sources of information can create serious operational and financial problems for businesses. When bad data go unnoticed, they can lead to bad decisions, product recalls, and even financial losses. For instance, Geer DuBois, a New York advertising agency, lost a $2.5-million-a-year account after the agency's billing system failed to credit the client for a six-figure payment. Even though Geer DuBois repaid the client with interest, the client decided to use another advertising firm. First Financial Management Corporation of Atlanta had to restate its earnings for the first nine months of the year because a subsidiary had lost track of some records after changing its accounting system (Wilson 1992).

Data quality problems plague the public sector as well. A study of the FBI's computerized criminal record systems found a total of 54.1 percent of the records in the National Crime Information Center System to be inaccurate, ambiguous, or incomplete, and 74.3 percent of the records in the FBI's semi-automated Identification Division system exhibited significant quality problems. A summary analysis of the FBI's automated Wanted-Persons File also found that 11.2 percent of the warrants were invalid. A study by the FBI itself found that 6 percent of the warrants in state files were invalid and that 12,000 invalid warrants are sent out nationally each day.

The FBI has taken some steps to correct these problems, but low levels of data quality in these systems have disturbing implications. In addition to their use in law enforcement, computerized criminal history records are increasingly being used to screen employees in both the public and private sectors. This is the fastest growing use of these records in some states. Many of these records are incomplete and show arrests but no court disposition; that is, they show charges without proof of conviction or guilt. Many individuals may be denied employment unjustifiably because these records overstate their criminality. These criminal record systems are not limited to violent felons. They contain the records of 36 million people, about one-third of the labor force. Inaccurate and potentially damaging information is being maintained on many law-abiding citizens. The level of data quality in these systems threatens citizens' constitutional right to due process and impairs the efficiency and effectiveness of any law enforcement programs in which these records are used (Laudon, 1986a).

In the following sections we examine how organizations can deal with data and software quality problems as well as other threats to information systems.

14.2 CREATING A CONTROL ENVIRONMENT

To minimize errors, disaster, computer crime, and breaches of security, special policies and procedures must be incorporated into the design and implementation of information systems. The combination of manual and automated measures that safeguard information systems and ensure that they perform according to management standards is termed *controls*. **Controls** consist of all the methods, policies, and organizational procedures that ensure the safety of the organization's assets, the accuracy and reliability of its accounting records, and operational adherence to management standards.

In the past, the control of information systems was treated as an afterthought, addressed only toward the end of implementation, just before the system was installed. Today, however, organizations are so critically dependent on information systems that vulnerabilities and control issues must be identified as early as possible. The control of an information system must be an integral part of its design. Users and builders of systems must pay close attention to controls throughout the system's life span.

Computer systems are controlled by a combination of general controls and application controls.

controls All of the methods, policies, and procedures that ensure protection of the organization's assets, accuracy and reliability of its records, and operational adherence to management standards.

general controls Overall controls that establish a framework for controlling the design, security, and use of computer programs throughout an organization.

application controls Specific controls unique to each computerized application.

General controls are those that control the design, security, and use of computer programs and the security of data files in general throughout the organization. On the whole, general controls apply to all computerized applications and consist of a combination of system software and manual procedures that create an overall control environment.

Application controls are specific controls unique to each computerized application, such as payroll, accounts receivable, and order processing. They consist of both controls applied from the user functional area of a particular system and from programmed procedures.

GENERAL CONTROLS

General controls are overall controls that ensure the effective operation of programmed procedures. They apply to all application areas. General controls include the following:

- Controls over the system implementation process
- Software controls
- Physical hardware controls
- Computer operations controls
- Data security controls
- Administrative disciplines, standards, and procedures

Implementation Controls

implementation controls The audit of the systems development process at various points to make sure that it is properly controlled and managed.

Implementation controls audit the systems development process at various points to ensure that the process is properly controlled and managed. The systems development audit should look for the presence of formal review points at various stages of development that enable users and management to approve or disapprove the implementation.

The systems development audit should also examine the level of user involvement at each stage of implementation and check for the use of a formal cost/benefit methodology in establishing system feasibility. The audit should also look for the use of controls and quality assurance techniques for program development, conversion, and testing and for complete and thorough system, user, and operations documentation.

Software Controls

software controls Controls to ensure the security and reliability of software.

program security controls Controls designed to prevent unauthorized changes to programs in systems that are already in production.

Controls are essential for the various categories of software used in computer systems. **Software controls** monitor the use of system software and prevent unauthorized access of software programs, system software, and computer programs. System software is an important control area because it performs overall control functions for the programs that directly process data and data files. **Program security controls** are designed to prevent unauthorized changes to programs in systems that are already in production.

Hardware Controls

hardware controls Controls to ensure the physical security and correct performance of computer hardware.

Hardware controls ensure that computer hardware is physically secure and check for equipment malfunction. Computer hardware should be physically secured so that it can be accessed only by authorized individuals. Computer equipment should be specially protected against fires and extremes of temperature and humidity. Organizations that are critically dependent on their computers must also make provisions for emergency backup in case of power failure.

Many kinds of computer hardware also contain mechanisms that check for equipment malfunction. Parity checks detect equipment malfunctions responsible for altering bits within bytes during processing. Validity checks monitor the structure of on–off bits within bytes to make sure that it is valid for the character set of a particular computer machine. Echo checks verify that a hardware device is performance ready. Chapter 5 discusses computer hardware in detail.

Computer Operations Controls

Computer operations controls apply to the work of the computer department and help ensure that programmed procedures are consistently and correctly applied to the storage and processing of data. They include controls over the setup of computer processing jobs, operations software, and computer operations, and backup and recovery procedures for processing that ends abnormally.

Instructions for running computer jobs should be fully documented, reviewed, and approved by a responsible official. Controls over operations software include manual procedures designed to both prevent and detect error.

System software can maintain a system log detailing all activity during processing. This log can be printed for review so that hardware malfunctions, abnormal endings, and operator actions can be investigated. Specific instructions for backup and recovery can be developed so that in the event of a hardware or software failure, the recovery process for production programs, system software, and data files does not create erroneous changes in the system.

computer operations controls Procedures to ensure that programmed procedures are consistently and correctly applied to data storage and processing.

Data Security Controls

Data security controls ensure that valuable business data files on either disk or tape are not subject to unauthorized access, change, or destruction. Such controls are required for data files when they are in use and when they are being held for storage.

When data can be input on-line through a terminal, entry of unauthorized input must be prevented. For example, a credit note could be altered to match a sales invoice on file. In such situations, security can be developed on several levels:

- Terminals can be physically restricted so that they are available only to authorized individuals.
- System software can include the use of passwords assigned only to authorized individuals. No one can log on to the system without a valid password.
- Additional sets of passwords and security restrictions can be developed for specific systems and applications. For example, data security software can limit access to specific files, such as the files for the accounts receivable system. It can restrict the type of access so that only individuals authorized to update these specific files will have the ability to do so. All others will only be able to read the files or will be denied access altogether.

data security controls Controls to ensure that data files on either disk or tape are not subject to unauthorized access, change, or destruction.

Systems that allow on-line inquiry and reporting must have data files secured. Figure 14.6 illustrates the security allowed for two sets of users of an on-line personnel database with sensitive information such as employees' salaries, benefits, and medical histories. One set of users consists of all employees who perform clerical functions such as inputting employee data into the system. All individuals with this type of profile can update the system but can neither read nor update sensitive fields such as salary, medical history, or earnings data. Another profile applies to a divisional manager, who cannot update the system but who can read all employee data fields for his or her division, including medical history and salary. These profiles would be established and maintained by a data security system. The data security system illustrated in Figure 14.6 provides very fine-grained security restrictions, such as allowing authorized personnel users to inquire about all employee information except in confidential fields such as salary or medical history.

Data files on disk or tape can be secured in lockable storage areas. Usage logs and library records can be maintained for each removable storage device if it is labeled and assigned a unique identity number.

Administrative Controls

Administrative controls are formalized standards, rules, procedures, and control disciplines to ensure that the organization's general and application controls are properly ex-

administrative controls Formalized standards, rules, procedures, and disciplines to ensure that the organization's controls are properly executed and enforced.

FIGURE 14.6
Security profiles for a personnel system. These two examples represent two security profiles or data security patterns that might be found in a personnel system. Depending upon the security profile, a user would have certain restrictions on access to various systems, locations, or data in an organization.

SECURITY PROFILE 1

User: Personnel Dept. Clerk

Location: Division 1

Employee Identification
Codes with This Profile: 00753, 27834, 37665, 44116

Data Field Restrictions	Type of Access
All employee data for Division 1 only	Read and Update
• Medical history data	None
• Salary	None
• Pensionable earnings	None

SECURITY PROFILE 2

User: Divisional Personnel Manager

Location: Division 1

Employee Identification
Codes with This Profile: 27321

Data Field Restrictions	Type of Access
All employee data for Division 1 only	Read Only

ecuted and enforced. The most important administrative controls are (1) segregation of functions, (2) written policies and procedures, and (3) supervision.

Segregation of functions means that job functions should be designed to minimize the risk of errors or fraudulent manipulation of the organization's assets. The individuals responsible for operating systems should not be the same ones who can initiate transactions that change the assets held in these systems. A typical arrangement is to have the organization's information systems department responsible for data and program files and end users responsible for initiating transactions such as payments or checks.

Written policies and procedures establish formal standards for controlling information system operations. Procedures must be formalized in writing and authorized by the appropriate level of management. Accountabilities and responsibilities must be clearly specified.

Supervision of personnel involved in control procedures ensures that the controls for an information system are performing as intended. Without adequate supervision, the best-designed set of controls may be bypassed, short-circuited, or neglected.

Weakness in each of these general controls can have a widespread effect on programmed procedures and data throughout the organization. Table 14.2 summarizes the effect of weaknesses in major general control areas.

APPLICATION CONTROLS

Application controls are specific controls within each separate computer application, such as payroll or order processing. They include both automated and manual procedures that ensure that only authorized data are completely and accurately processed by that application. The controls for each application should encompass the whole sequence of processing.

segregation of functions The principle of internal control to divide responsibilities and assign tasks among people so that job functions do not overlap, to minimize the risk of errors and fraudulent manipulation of the organization's assets.

Table 14.2 Effect of Weakness in General Controls

Weakness	Impact
Implementation controls	New systems or systems that have been modified will have errors or fail to function as required.
Software controls (program security)	Unauthorized changes can be made in processing. The organization may not be sure of which programs or systems have been changed.
Software controls (system software)	These controls may not have a direct effect on individual applications. Since other general controls depend heavily on system software, a weakness in this area impairs the other general controls.
Physical hardware controls	Hardware may have serious malfunctions or may break down altogether, introducing numerous errors or destroying computerized records.
Computer operations controls	Random errors may occur in a system. (Most processing will be correct, but occasionally it may not be.)
Data file security controls	Unauthorized changes can be made in data stored in computer systems or unauthorized individuals can access sensitive information.
Administrative controls	All of the other controls may not be properly executed or enforced.

Not all of the application controls discussed here are used in every information system. Some systems require more of these controls than others, depending on the importance of the data and the nature of the application.

Application controls can be classified as (1) input controls, (2) processing controls, and (3) output controls.

Input Controls

Input controls check data for accuracy and completeness when they enter the system. There are specific input controls for input authorization, data conversion, data editing, and error handling.

Input authorization: Input must be properly authorized, recorded, and monitored as source documents flow to the computer. For example, formal procedures can be set up to authorize only selected members of the sales department to prepare sales transactions for an order entry system.

Data conversion: Input must be properly converted into computer transactions, with no errors as it is transcribed from one form to another. Transcription errors can be eliminated or reduced by keying input transactions directly into computer terminals or by using some form of source data automation.

Batch control totals can be established beforehand for transactions grouped in batches. These totals can range from a simple document count to totals for quantity fields such as total sales amount (for the batch). Computer programs count the batch totals from transactions input. Batches that do not balance are rejected. On-line, real-time systems can also utilize batch controls by creating control totals to reconcile with hard copy documents that feed input.

Edit checks: Various programmed routines can be performed to edit input data for errors before they are processed. Transactions that do not meet edit criteria will be

input controls The procedures to check data for accuracy and completeness when they enter the system, including input authorization, batch control totals, and edits.

input authorization The proper authorization, recording, and monitoring of source documents as they enter the computer system.

data conversion The process of properly transcribing data from one form into another form for computer transactions.

batch control totals A type of input control that requires counting batches or any quantity field in a batch of transactions prior to processing for comparison and reconciliation after processing.

edit checks Routines performed to verify input data and correct errors prior to processing.

Table 14.3 Important Edit Techniques

Edit Technique	Description	Example
Reasonableness checks	To be accepted, data must fall within certain limits set in advance, or they will be rejected.	If an order transaction is for 20,000 units and the largest order on record was 50 units, the transaction will be rejected.
Format checks	Characteristics of the contents (letter/digit), length, and sign of individual data fields are checked by the system.	A nine-position Social Security number should not contain any alphabetic characters.
Existence checks	The computer compares input reference data to tables or master files to make sure that valid codes are being used.	An employee can have a Fair Labor Standards Act code of only 1, 2, 3, 4, or 5. All other values for this field will be rejected.
Dependency checks	The computer checks whether a *logical* relationship is maintained between data for the *same* transaction. When it is not, the transaction is rejected.	A car loan initiation transaction should show a logical relationship between the size of the loan, the number of loan repayments, and the size of each installment.
Check digit	An extra reference number called a *check digit* follows an identification code and bears a mathematical relationship to the other digits. This extra digit is input with the data, recomputed by the computer, and the result compared with the one input.	See the check digit in Figure 14.7 for a product code using the Modulus 11 check digit system.

rejected. The edit routines can produce lists of errors to be corrected later. The most important types of edit techniques are summarized in Table 14.3.

Processing Controls

processing controls The routines for establishing that data are complete and accurate during updating.

run control totals The procedures for controlling completeness of computer updating by generating control totals that reconcile totals before and after processing.

computer matching The processing control that matches input data to information held on master files.

Processing controls establish that data are complete and accurate during updating. The major processing controls are run control totals, computer matching, and programmed edit checks.

Run control totals reconcile the input control totals with the totals of items that have updated the file. Updating can be controlled by generating control totals during processing. The totals, such as total transactions processed or totals for critical quantities, can be compared manually or by computer. Discrepancies are noted for investigation.

Computer matching matches the input data with information held on master or suspense files, with unmatched items noted for investigation. Most matching occurs during input, but under some circumstances it may be required to ensure completeness of updating. For example, a matching program might match employee time cards with a payroll master file and report missing or duplicate time cards.

Most edit checking occurs at the time data are input. However, certain applications require some type of reasonableness or dependency check during updating. For example, consistency checks might be utilized by a utility company to compare a customer's electric bill with previous bills. If the bill was 500 percent higher this month compared to last month, the bill would not be processed until the meter was rechecked.

Product Code:	2	9	7	4	3
Weight:	6	5	4	3	2
Multiply each product code number by weight:	12	45	28	12	6
Sum results:	12 + 45 + 28 + 12 + 6 = 103				
Divide the sum by modulus:	103/11 = 9 with remainder of 4				
Subtract remainder from modulus number to obtain check digit:	11 – 4 = 7				
Add check digit to original product code to obtain new code:	297437				

FIGURE 14.7
Check digit for a product code. This is a product code with the last position as a check digit, as developed by the Modulus 11 check digit system, the most common check digit method. The check digit is 7 and is derived by the steps listed in this figure. Errors in the transcription or transposition of this product code can be detected by a computer program that replicates the same procedure for deriving the check digit. If a data entry person mistakenly keys in the product number as 29753, the program will read the first five digits and carry out the Modulus 11 process. It will derive a check digit of 4. When this is compared to the original check digit on the last position of the product code, the program will find that the check digits do not match and that an error has occurred.

Output Controls

Output controls ensure that the results of computer processing are accurate, complete, and properly distributed. Typical output controls include the following:

- Balancing output totals with input and processing totals
- Reviews of the computer processing logs to determine that all of the correct computer jobs executed properly for processing
- Formal procedures and documentation specifying authorized recipients of output reports, checks, or other critical documents

output controls Measures that ensure that the results of computer processing are accurate, complete, and properly distributed.

DEVELOPING A CONTROL STRUCTURE: COSTS AND BENEFITS

Information systems can make exhaustive use of all the control mechanisms previously discussed. But they may be so expensive to build and so complicated to use that the system is economically or operationally unfeasible. Some cost/benefit analysis must be performed to determine which control mechanisms provide the most effective safeguards without sacrificing operational efficiency or cost.

One of the criteria that determine how much control is built into a system is the *importance of its data*. Major financial and accounting systems, for example, such as a payroll system or one that tracks purchases and sales on the stock exchange, must have higher standards of controls than a *tickler* system to track dental patients and remind them that their six-month checkup is due. For instance, Swissair invested in additional hardware and software to increase its network reliability because it was running critical reservation and ticketing applications (see the chapter-opening vignette).

Standing data, the data that are permanent and that affect transactions flowing into and out of a system (e.g., codes for existing products or cost centers), require closer monitoring than individual transactions. A single error in transaction data will affect only that transaction, while a standing data error may affect many or all transactions each time the file is processed.

The cost effectiveness of controls will also be influenced by the efficiency, complexity, and expense of each control technique. For example, complete one-for-one checking may be time-consuming and operationally impossible for a system that processes hundreds of thousands of utilities payments daily. But it might be possible to use this technique to verify only critical data such as dollar amounts and account numbers, while ignoring names and addresses.

A third consideration is the *level of risk* if a specific activity or process is not properly controlled. System builders can undertake a **risk assessment,** determining the likely

standing data The data that are permanent and which affect transactions flowing into and out of a system.

risk assessment Determining the potential frequency of the occurrence of a problem and the potential damage if the problem were to occur. Used to determine the cost/benefit of a control.

Table 14.4	On-Line Order Processing Risk Assessment		
Exposure	Probability of Occurrence (%)	Loss Range/ Average ($)	Expected Annual Loss ($)
Power failure	30	5000–200,000 (102,500)	30,750
Embezzlement	5	1000–50,000 (25,500)	1,275
User error	98	200–40,000 (20,100)	19,698

This chart shows the results of a risk assessment of three selected areas of an on-line order processing system. The likelihood of each exposure occurring over a one-year period is expressed as a percentage. The next column shows the highest and lowest possible loss that could be expected each time the exposure occurred and an average loss calculated by adding the highest and lowest figures together and dividing by 2. The expected annual loss for each exposure can be determined by multiplying the average loss by its probability of occurrence.

frequency of a problem and the potential damage if it were to occur. For example, if an event is likely to occur no more than once a year, with a maximum of $1000 loss to the organization, it would not be feasible to spend $20,000 on the design and maintenance of a control to protect against that event. However, if that same event could occur at least once a day, with a potential loss of more than $300,000 a year, $100,000 spent on a control might be entirely appropriate.

Table 14.4 illustrates sample results of a risk assessment for an on-line order processing system that processes 30,000 orders per day. The probability of a power failure occurring in a one-year period is 30 percent. Loss of order transactions while power is down could range from $5000 to $200,000 for each occurrence, depending on how long processing was halted. The probability of embezzlement occurring over a yearly period is about 5 percent, with potential losses ranging from $1000 to $50,000 for each occurrence. User errors have a 98 percent chance of occurring over a yearly period, with losses ranging from $200 to $40,000 for each occurrence. The average loss for each event can be weighted by multiplying it by the probability of its occurrence annually to determine the expected annual loss. Once the risks have been assessed, system builders can concentrate on the control points with the greatest vulnerability and potential loss. In this case, controls should focus on ways to minimize the risk of power failures and user errors.

In some situations, organizations may not know the precise probability of threats occurring to their information systems, and they may not be able to quantify the impact of events that disrupt their information systems. In these instances, management may choose to describe risks and their likely impact in a qualitative manner (Rainer, Snyder, and Carr, 1991).

To decide which controls to use, information system builders must examine various control techniques in relation to each other and to their relative cost-effectiveness. A control weakness at one point may be offset by a strong control at another. It may not be cost-effective to build tight controls at every point in the processing cycle if the areas of greatest risk are secure or if compensating controls exist elsewhere. The combination of all of the controls developed for a particular application will determine its overall control structure.

THE ROLE OF AUDITING IN THE CONTROL PROCESS

How does management know that information system controls are effective? To answer this question, organizations must conduct comprehensive and systematic *audits*. An **MIS audit** identifies all of the controls that govern individual information systems and assesses their effectiveness. To accomplish this, the auditor must acquire a thorough understanding of operations, physical facilities, telecommunications, control systems, data

MIS audit Identifies all the controls that govern individual information systems and assesses their effectiveness.

| Function: Personal Loans | Prepared by: J. Ericson | Received by: T. Barrow |
| Location: Peoria, Ill. | Preparation date: June 16, 1996 | Review date: June 28, 1996 |

Nature of Weakness and Impact	Chance for Substantial Error		Effect on Audit Procedures	Notification to Management	
	Yes/No	Justification	Required Amendment	Date of Report	Mangement Response
Loan repayment records are not reconciled to borrower's records during processing.	Yes	Without a detection control, errors in individual client balances may remain undetected.	Confirm a sample of loans.	5/10/96	Interest Rate Compare Report provides this control.
There are no regular audits of computer-generated data (interest charges).	Yes	Without a regular audit or reasonableness check, widespread miscalculations could result before errors are detected.		5/10/96	Periodic audits of loans will be instituted.
Programs can be put into production libraries to meet target deadlines without final approval from the Standards and Controls group.	No	All programs require management authorization. The Standards and Controls group controls access to all production systems, and assigns such cases to a temporary production status.			

FIGURE 14.8
Sample auditor's list of control weaknesses. This chart is a sample page from a list of control weaknesses that an auditor might find in a loan system in a local commercial bank. This form helps auditors record and evaluate control weaknesses and shows the result of discussing those weaknesses with management, as well as any corrective actions taken by management.

security objectives, organizational structure, personnel, manual procedures, and individual applications.

The auditor usually interviews key individuals who use and operate a specific information system concerning their activities and procedures. Application controls, overall integrity controls, and control disciplines are examined. The auditor should trace the flow of sample transactions through the system and perform tests, using, if appropriate, automated audit software.

The audit lists and ranks all control weaknesses and estimates the probability of their occurrence. It then assesses the financial and organizational impact of each threat. Figure 14.8 is a sample auditor's listing of control weaknesses for a loan system. It includes a section for notifying management of such weaknesses and for management's response. Management is expected to devise a plan for countering significant weaknesses in controls.

14.3 ENSURING SYSTEM QUALITY

Organizations can improve system quality by using software quality assurance techniques and by improving the quality of their data.

SOFTWARE QUALITY ASSURANCE

Solutions to software quality problems include using an appropriate systems development methodology; proper resource allocation during systems development; the use of metrics; attention to testing; and the use of quality tools.

Methodologies

Chapter 11 has already described widely used systems development methodologies. The primary function of a development methodology is to provide discipline to the entire development process. A good development methodology establishes organization-wide standards for requirements gathering, design, programming, and testing. To produce quality software, organizations must select an appropriate methodology and then enforce its use. The methodology should call for systems requirement and specification documents that are complete, detailed, accurate, and documented in a format the user community can understand before they approve it. Specifications must also include agreed upon measures of system quality so that the system can be evaluated objectively while it is being developed and once it is completed.

Resource Allocation During Systems Development

resource allocation The determination of how costs, time, and personnel are assigned to different activities of a systems development project.

Views on **resource allocation** during systems development have changed significantly over the years. Resource allocation determines the way the costs, time, and personnel are assigned to different phases of the project. In earlier times, developers focused on programming, with only about 1 percent of the time and costs of a project being devoted to systems analysis (determining specifications). More time should be spent in specifications and systems analysis, decreasing the proportion of programming time and reducing the need for so much maintenance time. Figure 14.9 illustrates the shift in resources to earlier in the project cycle, although the ideal allocation of time for analysis and design should be greater. Current literature suggests that about one-quarter of a project's time and cost should be expended in specifications and analysis, with perhaps 50 percent of its resources being allocated to design and programming. Installation and post-implementation ideally should require only one-quarter of the project's resources.

Software Metrics

software metrics The objective assessments of the software used in a system in the form of quantified measurements.

Software metrics can play a vital role in increasing system quality. **Software metrics** are objective assessments of the system in the form of quantified measurements. Ongoing use of metrics allows the IS department and the user jointly to measure the performance of the system and identify problems as they occur. Examples of software metrics include the number of transactions that can be processed in a specified unit of time, on-line response time, the number of payroll checks printed per hour, and the number of known bugs per hundred lines of code. Unfortunately, most manifestations of quality are not so easy to define in metric terms. In those cases developers must find indirect measure-

FIGURE 14.9
Ideal and actual software development costs. Ideally, relatively balanced amounts of time are allowed for analysis, design, programming, and installation. About 8% of costs are allocated ideally to analysis and design, 60% to programming and installation, and 32% to long-term maintenance. Actually, however, the early stages of analysis and design receive far fewer resources than is desirable. Programming and installation (including all important testing) also receive less time and fewer resources than is desirable, reflecting pressure to deliver a workable system as soon as possible. As a result, systems maintenance is far more expensive than is desirable—about 50% of the total software costs over the expected life span of the system. *Source: Alberts, 1976.*

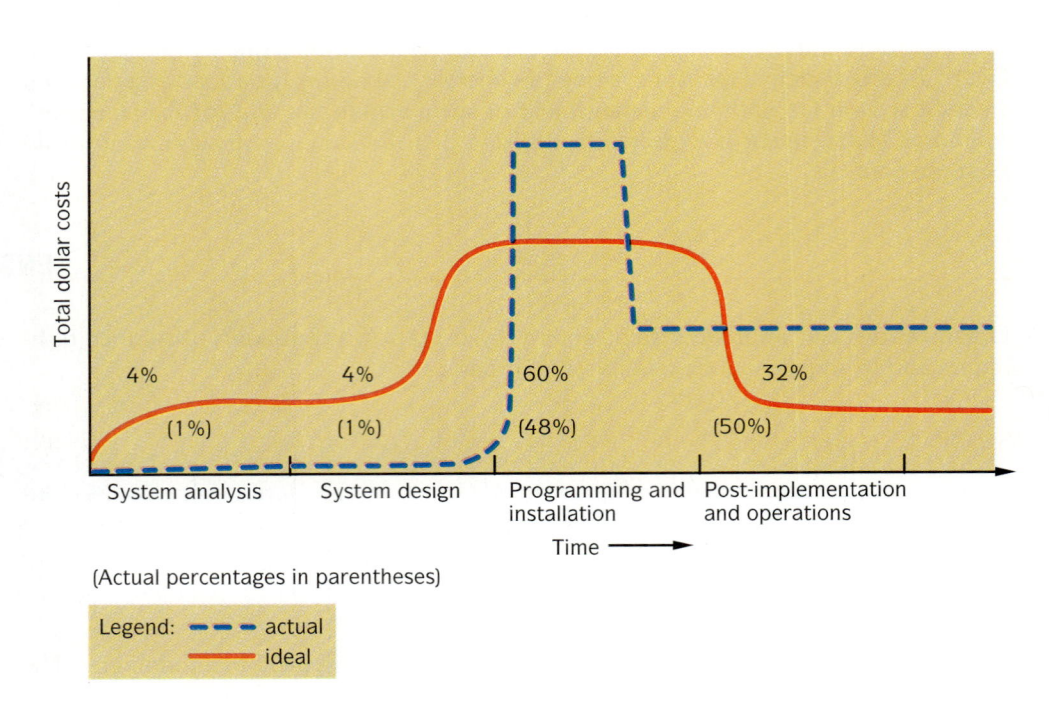

Window on Technology

BRITISH CUSTOMS TESTS ITS GUIS

The British Customs and Excise Department is responsible for managing the country's value-added tax (VAT). VAT is an indirect tax on all goods and services and is collected throughout Europe. Because so many goods and services are taxed and because specific taxes are changed frequently, managing the tax is a real challenge. In 1995 the department decided to move from a mainframe-based system to a more user-friendly, distributed client/server system with several hundred GUI (graphical user interface) screens. To aid in the enormous task of testing these screens, the department selected WinRunner from Mercury Interactive Corp., Santa Clara, California.

Selecting the proper testing tool was no easy task. Mike Trice, a consultant on the project, discovered more than six types of GUI testing tools. WinRunner is a capture/playback tool, capturing input and output needed for regression testing. This is the most popular type of tool today. Trice established specific requirements for the tool to be selected. First, the department needed a tool that would work with its software, Ingress 4GL. Trice also wanted a tool that enabled the project to use object names that were easily recognizable to users. "Otherwise," he said, "you just get gobbledygook" that nontechnicians will not understand. Finally, he needed a tool that supported UNIX as well as Windows. WinRunner did not meet one requirement: an integrated test manager. However, Trice was able to purchase another one that did the job, and Mercury even released its own test manager several months later.

Testing proved to be more difficult than the IS staff had imagined. The tool certainly helped, but testing with a tool still presented a number of problems. First, using such a tool effectively is not intuitive. It requires that the project team try it and

To Think About: Why was the testing process, including the selection of a GUI testing tool, an important business as well as technical decision for the Customs and Excise Department?

then establish a method for its use. Next, users use the same GUI screen differently because they can tailor the screen to specify window size and shape, location, color, and background. The project team could not test every scenario with every user. The team was not even able to test every microcomputer on the complex departmental network. Finally, not all aspects of a screen could be tested automatically. Some manual checking was required, even though it was time consuming. However, the tool did prove valuable, and Trice has no difficulty in recommending it to others if it meets their specific requirements. He says, for example, that the tool enables tests that could never have been carried out manually, such as simulating a network in which 300 users are accessing the database simultaneously.

Source: George Black, "British Government Puts New GUIs to the Test," *Software Magazine,* May 1995.

---

ments. For example, an objective measurement of a system's ease of use might be the number of calls for help the IS staff receives per month from system users.

For metrics to be successful, they must be carefully designed, formal, and objective. They must measure significant aspects of the system. In addition, metrics are of no value unless they are used consistently and users agree to the measurements in advance.

Testing

Early, regular, and thorough testing will contribute significantly to system quality. In general, software testing is often misunderstood. Many view testing as a way to prove the correctness of work they have done. In fact, we know that all sizable software is riddled with errors, and we must test to uncover these errors.

Testing begins at the design phase. Because no coding yet exists, the test normally used is a **walkthrough**—a review of a specification or design document by a small group of people carefully selected based on the skills needed for the particular objectives being tested. Once coding begins, coding walkthroughs also can be used to review program code. However, code must be tested by computer runs. When errors are discovered, the source is found and eliminated through a process called **debugging**.

Chapter 10 described the various stages of testing required to put an information system in operation—program testing, system testing, and acceptance testing. Testing will be successful only if planned properly. Tests must also be tailored to the technology being tested, as the Window on Technology describes.

walkthrough A review of a specification or design document by a small group of people carefully selected based on the skills needed for the particular objectives being tested.

debugging The process of discovering and eliminating the errors and defects—the bugs—in program code.

Quality Tools

Finally, system quality can be significantly enhanced by the use of quality tools. Many tools have been developed to address every aspect of the systems development process. Information systems professionals are using project management software to manage their projects. Products exist to document specifications and system design in text and graphic forms. Programming tools include data dictionaries, libraries to manage program modules, and tools that actually produce program code (see Chapters 6 and 11). Many types of tools exist to aid in the debugging process. The most recent set of tools automates much of the preparation for comprehensive testing.

DATA QUALITY AUDITS

Information system quality can also be improved by identifying and correcting faulty data. The analysis of data quality often begins with a **data quality audit,** which is a structured survey of the accuracy and level of completeness of the data in an information system. Data quality audits are accomplished by the following methods:

- Surveying end users for their perceptions of data quality
- Surveying entire data files
- Surveying samples from data files

Unless regular data quality audits are undertaken, organizations have no way of knowing to what extent their information systems contain inaccurate, incomplete, or ambiguous information. Some organizations, such as the Social Security Administration, have established data quality audit procedures. These procedures control payment and process quality by auditing a 20,000-case sample of beneficiary records each month. The FBI, on the other hand, did not conduct a comprehensive audit of its record systems until 1984. With few data quality controls, the FBI criminal record systems were found to have serious problems.

---

data quality audit A survey of files and samples of files for accuracy and completeness of data in an information system.

This data quality auditor is analyzing the quality of data for a client by conducting a survey of data files for accuracy in the information system.

Management Challenges

1. Controlling large distributed multi-user networks. No system is totally secure, but large, distributed multi-user networks are especially difficult to secure. Security becomes more problematic when networks are no longer confined to individual departments or groups or to centralized mainframe systems. It is very difficult to assert companywide control over networks using heterogeneous hardware, software, and communications components when thousands of workers can access networks from many remote locations.

2. Designing systems that are neither overcontrolled nor undercontrolled. The biggest threat to information systems is posed by authorized users, not outside intruders. Most security breaches and damage to information systems come from organizational insiders. If there are too many passwords and authorizations required to access an information system, the system will go unused. Controls that are effective but that do not prevent authorized individuals from using a system are difficult to design.

3. Applying quality assurance standards in large system projects. We have explained why the goal of zero defects in large, complex pieces of software is impossible to achieve. If the seriousness of remaining bugs cannot be ascertained, what constitutes an acceptable—if not perfect—performance? And even if meticulous design and exhaustive testing could eliminate all defects, software projects have time and budget constraints that often prevent management from devoting as much time to thorough testing as it should. Under these circumstances it will be difficult for managers either to define a standard for software quality or to enforce it.

Summary

1. Show why information systems are so vulnerable to destruction, error, abuse, and system quality problems. Organizations have become so dependent on computerized information systems that they must take special measures to ensure that these systems are properly controlled. With data easily concentrated into electronic form and many procedures invisible through automation, systems are vulnerable to destruction, misuse, error, fraud, and hardware or software failures. The effect of disaster in a computerized system can be greater than in manual systems because all of the records for a particular function or organization can be destroyed or lost. On-line systems and those utilizing telecommunications are especially vulnerable because data and files can be immediately and directly accessed through computer terminals or at many points in the telecommunications network. Computer viruses can spread rampantly from system to system, clogging computer memory or destroying programs and data. Software presents problems because of the high costs of correcting errors and because software bugs may be impossible to eliminate. Data quality can also severely impact system quality and performance.

2. Describe general controls and application controls for information systems. Controls consist of all the methods, policies, and organizational procedures that ensure the safety of the organization's assets, the accuracy and reliability of its accounting records, and adherence to management standards. There are two main categories of controls: general controls and application controls.

General controls handle the overall design, security, and use of computer programs and files for the organization as a whole. They include physical hardware controls, system software controls, data file security controls, computer operations controls, controls over the system implementation process, and administrative disciplines.

Application controls are those unique to specific computerized applications. They focus on the completeness and accuracy of input, updating and maintenance, and the validity of the information in the system. Application controls consist of (1) input controls, (2) processing controls, and (3) output controls.

3. Identify the factors that must be considered when developing the controls for information systems. To determine which controls are required, designers and users of systems must identify all of the control points and control weaknesses and perform risk assessment. They must also perform a cost/benefit analysis of controls and design controls that can effectively safeguard systems without making them unusable.

4. Describe the most important software quality assurance techniques. The quality and reliability of software can be improved by using a standard development methodology, software metrics, thorough testing procedures, quality tools, and by reallocating resources to put more emphasis on the analysis and design stages of systems development.

5. Explain the importance of auditing information systems and safeguarding data quality. Comprehensive and systematic MIS auditing can help organizations to determine the effectiveness of the controls in their information systems. Regular data quality audits should be conducted to help organizations ensure a high level of completeness and accuracy of the data stored in their systems.

Key Terms

Hacker	General controls	Segregation of functions	Standing data
Computer virus	Application controls	Input controls	Risk assessment
Antivirus software	Implementation controls	Input authorization	MIS audit
Fault-tolerant computer systems	Software controls	Data conversion	Resource allocation
	Program security controls	Batch control totals	Software metrics
On-line transaction processing	Hardware controls	Edit checks	Walkthrough
	Computer operations controls	Processing controls	Debugging
Security		Run control totals	Data quality audit
Bugs	Data security controls	Computer matching	
Controls	Administrative controls	Output controls	

Review Questions

1. Why are computer systems more vulnerable than manual systems to destruction, fraud, error, and misuse? Name some of the key areas where systems are most vulnerable.
2. Name some features of on-line information systems that make them difficult to control.
3. What are *fault-tolerant computer systems?* When should they be used?
4. How can bad software and data quality affect system performance and reliability? Describe two software quality problems.
5. What are *controls?* Distinguish between *general controls* and *application controls.*
6. Name and describe the principal general controls for computerized systems.
7. List and describe the principal application controls.
8. How does MIS auditing enhance the control process?
9. What is the function of risk assessment?
10. Name and describe four software quality assurance techniques.
11. Why are data quality audits essential?
12. What is security? List and describe controls that promote security for computer hardware, computer networks, computer software, and computerized data.

Discussion Questions

1. It has been said that controls and security should be among the first areas to be addressed by information system designers. Discuss.
2. The Young Professional Quarterly magazine publishing company receives thousands of subscription orders by mail each day. A document is created for each order. The order documents are batched in groups of thirty to fifty, and a header form is completed showing the total number of documents per batch. The documents are then keyed and verified by separate data entry clerks and processed each night. An edit/validation program rechecks the number of units in each batch. It prints valid and invalid batch reports and posts valid batches to a valid transaction file. The valid transaction file is fed to a series of programs that update Young Professional Quarterly's inventory, produce sales invoices, and feed the accounts receivable system. The Valid Batch Report is reconciled to the totals on the batch headers. Batches listed in the Invalid Batch Report are reviewed, corrected, and resubmitted. List and discuss the control weaknesses in this system and their impact. What corrective measures would you suggest?
3. Suppose you were asked to help design the controls for an information system. What pieces of information would you need?
4. Many organizations, such as Visa USA (cited earlier in this chapter) take elaborate precautions for backing up their computer systems. Why is this essential? What considerations must be addressed by a backup plan?

Group Project

Form a group with two or three other students. Select a system described in one of the *Window on* boxes or chapter-ending cases. Write a description of the system, its functions, and its value to the organization. Then write a description of both the general and application controls that should be used to protect the organization. Present your findings to the class.

Case Study

CAN WE TRUST MUTUAL FUND PRICING?

Few if any industries handle as much data as quickly as do the financial markets. With more than 10,000 financial instruments (stocks, bonds, mutual funds, futures, and others) trading daily and trading volume in the many hundreds of million of shares, keeping up with values is a Herculean task. The problem is compounded for the huge mutual fund industry because they not only need current information on the value of all the stocks, bonds, and other instruments they hold, but they must also calculate the value of their funds at the end of each trading day. Public confidence is fundamental to the survival of the mutual fund—after all, the investing public has placed more than $2 trillion of their money into the care of mutual funds. Imagine, then, the shock of investors worldwide when they found out that Fidelity Investments, the largest and one of the most respected mutual fund companies in the world, had deliberately released false data on the value of its funds at the close of trading on June 17, 1994.

Fidelity's problem arose from the need of mutual fund managers to report their funds' net asset value (NAV) to the National Association of Securities Dealers (NASD) by 5:30 PM of the trading day (all times cited are New York time). The NASD then passes the data to Lipper Analytical Services, who checks for extreme price movements (a simple form of data validation) and calculates each fund's total returns. By 6:15 PM Lipper forwards this data to the various news services, which in turn distribute them to subscribing newspapers. The deadline was set many years ago by the Associated Press (AP) and was necessary to give the newspapers enough lead time to get their type set for the morning editions. Given that the stock markets close at 4:00 PM and that financial data suppliers cannot get closing price data to the funds until 4:20 PM, the funds have only about 70 minutes to calculate their NAV and report it. (The basic calculation is the sum of the price of each financial instrument the fund owns multiplied by the number of shares.) It is a daily race against time with no spare room for unexpected problems.

A fund's alternative, if it cannot make the deadline, is to report *NA* (not available), something funds take great pains to avoid. When *NA* appears as a fund's price in the newspapers, many market observers claim investor confidence in that fund is eroded. Enough *NA*s and the whole industry could be hurt. Moreover, the next morning, when investors fail to find their fund valuations, they call the funds in large numbers, swamping the fund's customer service lines.

In the case of Fidelity on that Friday, when the 5:30 PM deadline arrived the firm did not have the NAV for 166 of its 208 funds. A low-level employee, not wanting to report *NA*, knowingly decided to transmit the prior day's prices as that day's closing prices. The employee apparently intended to correct the inaccurate numbers when accurate numbers became available. The inaccurate prices were only caught because that Friday was *triple-witching day*, the one day each quarter when three sets of market futures and options were expiring simultaneously. The markets are usually quite volatile on such days, and static fund prices would be surprising.

Fidelity was not punished. Although it is illegal for funds to report incorrect prices, funds are not normally penalized. In fact, inaccurate fund prices are reported every day, although usually not intentionally. According to a Lipper Analytical spokesperson, 30 to 40 fund prices out of the total of about 3800 funds will have to be repriced daily. On average another 20 to 25 do report *NA* daily. The requirement for speed is only one of the problems. Another is that the many new, exotic financial instruments such as mortgage-backed bonds, are difficult to price. In addition, closing prices can be more difficult to determine in this age of global markets—many securities are still being traded someplace else in the world when the New York markets close. Furthermore, many instruments, such as corporate bonds, are illiquid and may not have traded at the end of a particular day. In this case the actual value may have changed because bond prices in general may have risen or fallen, but the particular bond the fund owns will not have traded. One reason funds are seldom penalized for inaccuracies is the difficulties of calculating NAV. In addition, however, they also are not penalized because no apparatus exists for the NASD to verify the accuracy of NAV prices (aside from the one simple check Lipper does to identify extreme price movement).

In Fidelity's case, the problem that day resulted from an information systems software bug. Fidelity's closing stock prices are obtained from five different financial data suppliers, using state-of-the-art portfolio accounting software. On that day one of Fidelity's outside providers made a change in their software. They transmitted the correct data, but they changed the format, adding a couple of fields that had never been there before. Fidelity's programs, unable to handle the new data format, filled the data fields instead with all nines. At 5:00 PM when Fidelity employees discovered the problem, they had only a half hour to correct it, too little time to modify their own programs.

Many observers believe that investors normally are not hurt by these pricing errors. After all, the daily NAV feed to NASD is only for reporting to newspapers. Mutual funds do use their own internal numbers, which can be calculated at a somewhat more leisurely pace, to calculate actual buy and sell prices. However, others point out that the numbers reported in the newspapers are used by many mutual fund investors to help them make buy and sell decisions. Moreover, some stock brokers often use them to report on customer account values. Industry experts point out that NAV pricing problems are growing worse. Fund pricing errors are increasing as the number of funds multiply and also because fund holdings are a lot more complex than they used to be. ■

> **Sources:** Leslie Eaton, "Errors Seem on Rise in Figuring Fund Prices," *The New York Times*, June 14, 1994; Robert McGough, John R. Emshwiller, and Sara Calian, "Deliberate Mispricing at Fidelity Highlights Lax Controls on Quotes," *The Wall Street Journal*, June 23, 1994; Carrie R. Smith, "The Price is Right . . . Or Is It?" *Wall Street & Technology*, September, 1994.

Case Study Questions

1. Evaluate the importance of the mutual fund pricing problems described here to a firm such as Fidelity. Do they need to be addressed? Why?

2. Identify control weaknesses in the mutual fund NAV price-reporting process that allow for inaccurate prices to be reported in the newspapers. What management, organization, and technology factors were responsible for those weaknesses?

3. Design controls for the pricing process to deal with these problems.

4. What other changes to the overall pricing and reporting system might you make to help solve the problem of inaccurate pricing?

References

Abdel-Hamid, Tarek K. "The Economics of Software Quality Assurance: A Simulation-Based Case Study." *MIS Quarterly* (September 1988).

Alberts, David S. "The Economics of Software Quality Assurance." Washington, DC: National Computer Conference, 1976 Proceedings.

Anderson, Ross J. "Why Cryptosystems Fail." *Communications of the ACM* 37, no. 11 (November 1994).

Anthes, Gary H. "Viruses Continue to Wreak Havoc at Many U.S. Companies." *Computerworld* (June 28, 1993).

Banker, Rajiv D., Srikant M. Datar, Chris F. Kemerer, and Dani Zweig. "Software Complexity and Maintenance Costs." *Communications of the ACM* 36, no. 11 (November 1993).

Banker, Rajiv D., Robert J. Kaufmann, and Rachna Kumar. "An Empirical Test of Object-Based Output Measurement Metrics in a Computer-Aided Software Engineering (CASE) Environment." *Journal of Management Information Systems* 8, no. 3 (Winter 1991–92).

Banker, Rajiv D., and Chris F. Kemerer. "Performance Evaluation Metrics in Information Systems Development: A Principal-Agent Model." *Information Systems Research* 3, no. 4 (December 1992).

Boehm, Barry W. "Understanding and Controlling Software Costs." *IEEE Transactions on Software Engineering* 14, no. 10 (October 1988).

Boockholdt, J.L. "Implementing Security and Integrity in Micro-Mainframe Networks." *MIS Quarterly* 13, no. 2 (June 1989).

Borning, Alan. "Computer System Reliability and Nuclear War." *Communications of the ACM* 30, no. 2 (February 1987).

Bouldin, Barbara M. "What Are You Measuring? Why Are You Measuring It?" *Software Magazine* (August 1989).

Buss, Martin D.J., and Lynn M. Salerno. "Common Sense and Computer Security." *Harvard Business Review* (March–April 1984).

Charette, Ron. "Inside RISKS: Risks with Risk Analysis." *Communications of the ACM* 34, no. 5 (June 1991).

Chaum, David. "Security Without Identification: Transaction Systems to Make Big Brother Obsolete." *Communications of the ACM* 28 (October 1985).

Corbato, Fernando J. "On Building Systems that Will Fail." *Communications of the ACM* 34, No. 9 (September 1991).

Dekleva, Sasa M. "The Influence of Information Systems Development Approach on Maintenance." *MIS Quarterly* 16, no. 3 (September 1992).

DeMarco, Tom. *Structured Analysis and System Specification*. New York: Yourdon Press (1978).

Dijkstra, E. "Structured Programming," in *Classics in Software Engineering*, ed. Edward Nash Yourdon. New York: Yourdon Press (1979).

Flatten, Per O., Donald J. McCubbrey, P. Declan O'Riordan, and Keith Burgess. *Foundations of Business Systems*, 2nd ed. Fort Worth, TX: The Dryden Press (1992).

Gane, Chris, and Trish Sarson. *Structured Systems Analysis: Tools and Techniques*. Englewood Cliffs, NJ: Prentice-Hall (1979).

Halper, Stanley D., Glenn C. Davis, Jarlath P. O'Neill-Dunne, and Pamela R. Pfau. *Handbook of EDP Auditing*. Boston: Warren, Gorham, and Lamont (1985).

Hoffman, Lance. *Rogue Programs*. New York: Van Nostrand Reinhold (1990).

"Information Security and Privacy." *EDP Analyzer* (February 1986).

Kahane, Yehuda, Seev Neumann, and Charles S. Tapiero. "Computer Backup Pools, Disaster Recovery, and Default Risk." *Communications of the ACM* 31, no. 1 (January 1988).

Keyes, Jessica. "New Metrics Needed for New Generation." *Software Magazine* (May 1992).

King, Julia. "It's C.Y.A. Time." *Computerworld* (March 30, 1992).

Laudon, Kenneth C. "Data Quality and Due Process in Large Interorganizational Record Systems." *Communications of the ACM* 29 (January 1986a).

Laudon, Kenneth C. *Dossier Society: Value Choices in the Design of National Information Systems*. New York: Columbia University Press (1986b).

Lientz, Bennett P., and E. Burton Swanson. *Software Maintenance Management*. Reading, MA: Addison-Wesley (1980).

Littlewood, Bev, and Lorenzo Strigini. "The Risks of Software." *Scientific American* 267, no. 5 (November 1992).

Littlewood, Bev and Lorenzo Strigini. "Validation of Ultra-high Dependability for Software-based Systems." *Communications of the ACM* 36, no. 11 (November 1993).

Loch, Karen D., Houston H. Carr, and Merrill E. Warkentin. "Threats to Information Systems: Today's Reality, Yesterday's Understanding." *MIS Quarterly* 16, no. 2 (June 1992).

Maglitta, Joe, and John P. Mello, Jr. "The Enemy Within." *Computerworld* (December 7, 1992).

Martin, James, and Carma McClure. *Structured Techniques: The Basis of CASE*. Englewood Cliffs, NJ: Prentice-Hall (1988).

Mazzucchelli, Louis. "Structured Analysis Can Streamline Software Design." *Computerworld* (December 9, 1985).

McPartlin, John P. "The True Cost of Downtime." *Information Week* (August 3, 1992).

Needham, Roger M. "Denial of Service: An Example." *Communications of the ACM* 37, no. 11 (November 1994).

Neumann, Peter G. "Risks Considered Global(ly)." *Communications of the ACM* 35, no. 1 (January 1993).

Perrow, Charles. *Normal Accidents*. New York: Basic Books (1984).

Post, Gerald V., and J. David Diltz. "A Stochastic Dominance Approach to Risk Analysis of Computer Systems." *MIS Quarterly* (December 1986).

Putnam, L.H., and A. Fitzsimmons. "Estimating Software Costs." *Datamation* (September 1979, October 1979, and November 1979).

Rainer, Rex Kelley, Jr., Charles A. Snyder, and Houston H. Carr. "Risk Analysis for Information Technology." *Journal of Management Information Systems* 8, no. 1 (Summer 1991).

Rettig, Marc. "Software Teams." *Communications of the ACM* 33, no. 10 (October 1990).

Straub, Detmar W. "Controlling Computer Abuse: An Empirical Study of Effective Security Countermeasures." Curtis L. Carlson School of Management, University of Minnesota (July 20, 1987).

Swanson, Kent, Dave McComb, Jill Smith, and Don McCubbrey. "The Application Software Factory: Applying Total Quality Techniques to Systems Development." *MIS Quarterly* 15, no. 4 (December 1991).

Tate, Paul. "Risk! The Third Factor." *Datamation* (April 15, 1988).

Thyfault, Mary E., and Stephanie Stahl. "Weak Links." *Information Week* (August 10, 1992).

United States General Accounting Office. "Computer Security: DEA Is Not Adequately Protecting National Security Information." *GAO/IMTEC-92-31* (February 1992).

United States General Accounting Office. "Computer Security: Virus Highlights Need for Improved Internet Management." *GAO/IMTEC-89-57* (June 1989).

United States General Accounting Office. "Patriot Missile Defense: Software Problem Led to System Failure at Dharan, Saudi Arabia." *GAO/IMTEC-92-26* (February 1992).

Weber, Ron. *EDP Auditing: Conceptual Foundations and Practice*. 2nd ed. New York: McGraw-Hill (1988).

Wilson, Linda. "Devil in Your Data." *Information Week* (August 31, 1992).

Yourdon, Edward, and L.L. Constantine. *Structural Design*. New York: Yourdon Press (1978).

Chapter 15

Managing International Information Systems

Molex Goes Global

15.1 The Growth of International Information Systems
Developing the International Information Systems Infrastructure
The Global Environment: Business Drivers and Challenges
Window on Organizations
The 800-Pound Gorilla of Transnational Technological Change
State of the Art

15.2 Organizing International Information Systems
Global Strategies and Business Organization
Global Systems to Fit the Strategy
Reorganizing the Business

15.3 Managing Global Systems
A Typical Scenario: Disorganization on a Global Scale
Strategy: Divide, Conquer, Appease
Implementation Tactics: Cooptation
Wrapping Up: The Management Solution
Window on Management
Traveling Down the Road of International Technology Infrastructure Mergers

15.4 Technology Issues and Opportunities
Main Technical Issues
Window on Technology
Is the Internet a World Tool?
New Technical Opportunities

Management Challenges
Summary
Key Terms
Review Questions
Discussion Questions
Group Project
Case Study: Global Information Systems to Support Nestlé's Global Business Strategy
References

Molex Goes Global

When it comes to doing business around the world, Molex Corporation is a seasoned pro. This manufacturer of electrical connectors, headquartered in Lisle, Illinois, has been operating multinationally for more than 30 years. Molex runs 44 production plants in 21 countries and has sales offices in 35 nations.

Molex had been run using a decentralized international model. Each site operated independently. But new customer demands called for a global business model where the company could present a single face in every worldwide location. Molex needed to find ways to standardize the flow of information and information services across the corporation.

Management stipulated that all of the manufacturing and research and development centers around the world share cost data (to consolidate financial information), production statistics (to allocate manufacturing resources more efficiently), and engineering and quality data (to promote a single quality standard). Information systems had to provide one level of support and one uniform set of services from Illinois to Tokyo. Molex is linking disparate desktop computers and computer centers into a TCP/IP wide-area network backbone for global connectivity. It is contracting with a frame relay vendor for WAN services. Like Molex, many companies in a wide range of industries are searching for ways to link their multinational facilities into a single coherent information architecture. ∎

Source: Mark Mehler, "Networking the World," *Beyond Computing*, May 1996.

Molex is one of many business firms that are moving toward global forms of organization that transcend national boundaries. But Molex could not make this move unless it reorganized its information systems. Molex improved its network connectivity and standardized some of its information systems so that the same information could be used by disparate business units in different countries.

The changes Molex made are some of the changes in international information systems infrastructures—the basic systems needed to coordinate worldwide trade and other activities—that organizations need to consider if they want to operate across the globe. Such changes are not always easy to make. Information technology is both a powerful driver of the movement toward international business and a powerful servant. This chapter explores how to organize, manage, and control the development of international information systems.

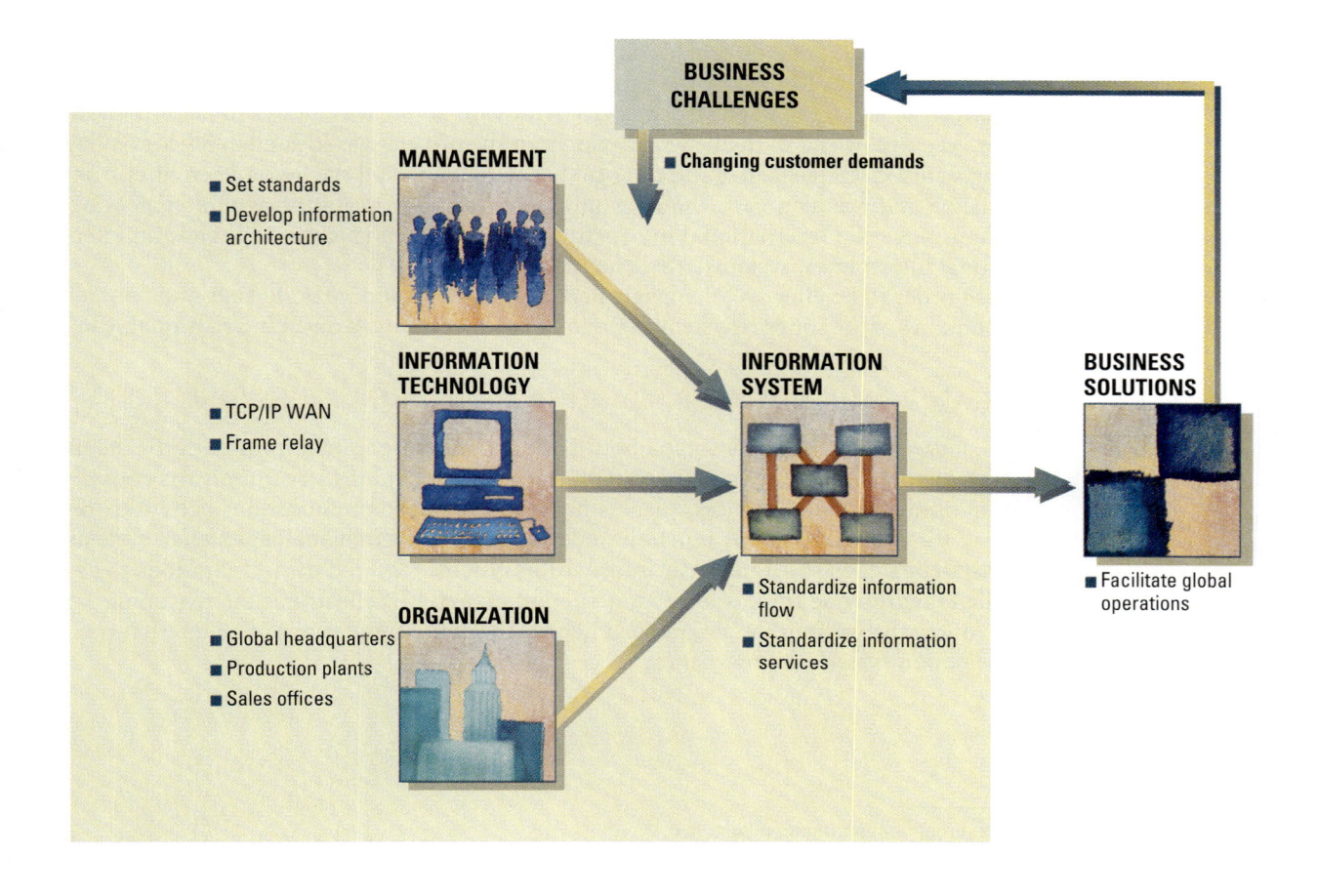

BUSINESS CHALLENGES
- Changing customer demands

MANAGEMENT
- Set standards
- Develop information architecture

INFORMATION TECHNOLOGY
- TCP/IP WAN
- Frame relay

ORGANIZATION
- Global headquarters
- Production plants
- Sales offices

INFORMATION SYSTEM
- Standardize information flow
- Standardize information services

BUSINESS SOLUTIONS
- Facilitate global operations

> **Learning Objectives**
>
> *After completing this chapter, you will be able to:*
>
> 1. Identify the major factors behind the growing internationalization of business.
> 2. Choose among several global strategies for developing business.
> 3. Understand how information systems support different global strategies.
> 4. Manage the development of international systems.
> 5. Understand the main technical alternatives in developing global systems.

15.1 THE GROWTH OF INTERNATIONAL INFORMATION SYSTEMS

We have already described two powerful worldwide changes driven by advances in information technology that have transformed the business environment and posed new challenges for management. One is the transformation of industrial economies and societies into knowledge- and information-based economies. The other is the emergence of a global economy and global world order.

The new world order will sweep away national corporations, national industries, and national economies controlled by domestic politicians. Much of the Fortune 500—the 500 largest U.S. corporations—will disappear in the next 50 years, mirroring past behavior of large firms since 1900. Many firms will be replaced by fast-moving networked corporations that transcend national boundaries. The growth of international trade has radically altered domestic economies around the globe. About $1 trillion worth of goods, services, and financial instruments—one fifth of the annual U.S. gross national product—changes hands each day in global trade.

Consider a laptop computer as an example: The CPU is likely to have been designed and built in the United States; the DRAM (or dynamic random access memory, which makes up the majority of primary storage in a computer) was designed in the United States but built in Malaysia; the screen was designed and assembled in Japan, using American patents; the keyboard was from Taiwan; and it was all assembled in Japan, where the case was also made. Management of the project was located in Silicon Valley along with marketing, sales, and finance that coordinated all the myriad activities from financing and production to shipping and sales efforts. None of this would be possible without powerful international information and telecommunication systems, an international information systems infrastructure.

In order to be effective, managers need a global perspective on business and an understanding of the support systems needed to conduct business on an international scale.

DEVELOPING THE INTERNATIONAL INFORMATION SYSTEMS INFRASTRUCTURE

This chapter describes how to go about building an international information systems infrastructure suitable for your international strategy. An infrastructure is the constellation of facilities and services, such as highways or telecommunications networks, required for organizations to function and prosper. An **international information systems infrastructure** consists of the basic information systems required by organizations to coordinate worldwide trade and other activities. Figure 15.1 illustrates the reasoning we will follow throughout the chapter and depicts the major dimensions of an international information systems infrastructure.

international information systems infrastructure: The basic information systems required by organizations to coordinate worldwide trade and other activities.

Arrow International, an international supplier of innovative medical devices, has international distributors as well as direct sales, manufacturing, and warehouse units throughout the globe. Businesses need an international information systems infrastructure to coordinate their worldwide activities.

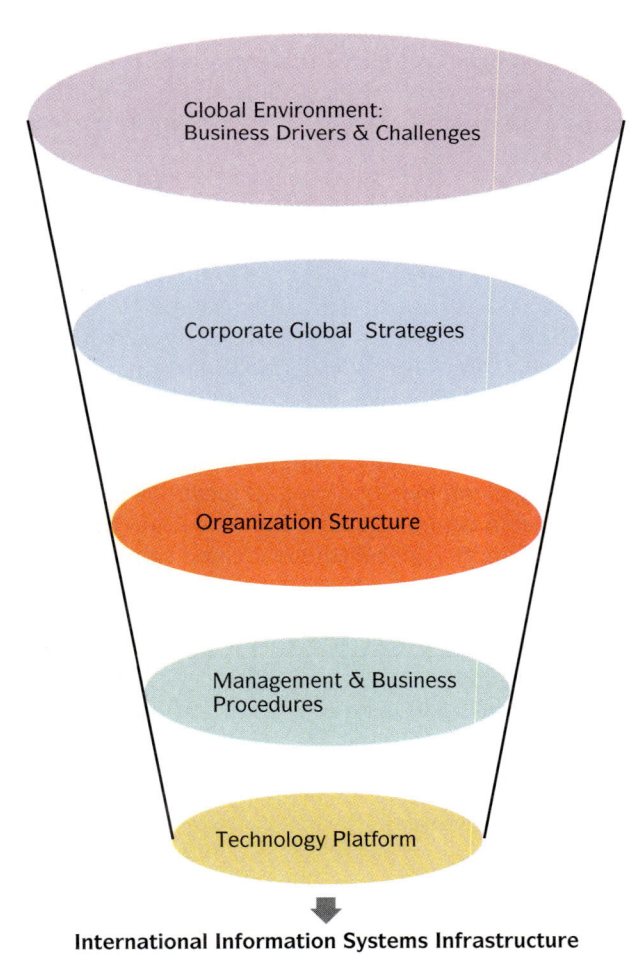

FIGURE 15.1
International information systems infrastructure. The major dimensions for developing an international information systems infrastructure are the global environment, the corporate global strategies, the structure of the organization, the management and business procedures, and the technology platform.

- Global Environment: Business Drivers & Challenges
- Corporate Global Strategies
- Organization Structure
- Management & Business Procedures
- Technology Platform

→ International Information Systems Infrastructure

15.1 The Growth of International Information Systems

business driver A force in the environment to which businesses must respond and that influences the direction of business.

The basic strategy to follow when building an international system is first to understand the global environment in which your firm is operating. This means understanding the overall market forces, or *business drivers,* that are pushing your industry toward global competition. A **business driver** is a force in the environment to which businesses must respond and that influences the direction of the business. Likewise, examine carefully the inhibitors or negative factors that create *management challenges*—factors that could scuttle the development of a global business. Once you have examined the global environment, you will need to consider a *corporate strategy for competing in that environment.* How will your firm respond? You could ignore the global market and focus on domestic competition only, sell to the globe from a domestic base, or organize production and distribution around the globe. There are many in-between choices.

Once you have developed a strategy, it is time to consider *how to structure your organization* so it can pursue the strategy. How will you accomplish a division of labor across a global environment? Where will production, administration, accounting, marketing, and human resource functions be located? Who will handle the systems function?

Once you have designed an international organization, you will have to consider the management issues in implementing your strategy and making the organization design come alive. Key here will be the design of business procedures. How can you discover and manage user requirements? How can you induce change in local units to conform to international requirements? How can you reengineer on a global scale, and how can you coordinate systems development?

The last issue to consider is the technology platform. Although changing technology is a key driving factor leading toward global markets, you need to have a corporate strategy and structure before you can rationally choose the right technology.

Once you have completed this process of reasoning, you will be well on your way toward an appropriate international information infrastructure capable of achieving your corporate goals. Let us begin by looking at the overall global environment.

THE GLOBAL ENVIRONMENT: BUSINESS DRIVERS AND CHALLENGES

Table 15.1 illustrates the business drivers in the global environment that are leading all industries toward global markets and competition.

The global business drivers can be divided into two groups: general cultural factors and specific business factors. There are easily recognized general cultural factors driving internationalization since World War II. Information, communication, and transportation technologies have created a *global village* in which communication (by telephone, television, radio, or computer network) around the globe is no more difficult and not much more expensive than communication down the block. Moving goods and services to and from geographically dispersed locations has fallen dramatically in cost.

global culture The development of common expectations, shared artifacts, and social norms among different cultures and peoples.

The development of global communications has created a global village in a second sense: There is now a **global culture** created by television and other globally-shared me-

Table 15.1 The Global Business Drivers

General Cultural Factors
   Global communication and transportation technologies
   Development of global culture
   Emergence of global social norms
   Political stability
   Global knowledge base

Specific Business Factors
   Global markets
   Global production and operations
   Global coordination
   Global work force
   Global economies of scale

dia like movies which permits different cultures and peoples to develop common expectations about right and wrong, desirable and undesirable, heroic and cowardly. A shared culture, with shared cultural artifacts like news programs and movies, permits the emergence of shared societal norms concerning proper attire, proper consumption, and good and bad government. The collapse of the Eastern bloc has speeded up the growth of a world culture enormously, increased support for capitalism and business, and reduced the level of cultural conflict considerably.

A last factor to consider is the growth of a global knowledge base. At the end of World War II, knowledge, education, science, and industrial skills were highly concentrated in North America, Europe, and Japan, with the rest of the world euphemistically called the *Third World*. This is no longer true. Latin America, China, Southern Asia, and Eastern Europe have developed powerful educational, industrial, and scientific centers, resulting in a much more democratically and widely dispersed knowledge base.

These general cultural factors leading toward internationalization result in four specific business globalization factors that affect most industries. The growth of powerful communications technologies and the emergence of world cultures creates the condition for *global markets*—global consumers interested in consuming similar products that are culturally approved. Coca-Cola, American tennis shoes (made in Korea but designed in Los Angeles), and *Dallas* (a TV show) can now be sold in Latin America, Africa, and Asia.

Responding to this demand, *global production and operations* have emerged with precise on-line coordination between far-flung production facilities and central headquarters thousands of miles away. At Sealand Transportation, a major global shipping company based in Newark, New Jersey, shipping managers in Newark can watch the loading of ships in Rotterdam on-line, check trim and ballast, and trace packages to specific ship locations as the activity proceeds. This is all possible through an international satellite link.

The new global markets and pressure toward global production and operation have called forth whole new capabilities for *global coordination* of all factors of production. Not just production but also accounting, marketing and sales, human resources, and systems development (all the major business functions) can now be coordinated on a global scale. Frito Lay, for instance, can develop a marketing salesforce automation system in the United States, and once provided, may try the same techniques and technologies in Spain. Micromarketing—marketing to very small geographic and social units—no longer means marketing to neighborhoods in the United States, but to neighborhoods throughout the world! In our laptop computer example (p. 460), design has become internationalized and coordinated through shared culture (defining what is good design) and dense communications networks. These new levels of global coordination permit for the first time in history the location of business activity according to comparative advantage. Design should be located where it is best accomplished, as should marketing, production, and finance.

Finally, global markets, production, and administration create the conditions for powerful, *sustained global economies of scale*. Production driven by worldwide global demand can be concentrated where it can be best accomplished, fixed resources can be allocated over larger production runs, and production runs in larger plants can be scheduled more efficiently and precisely estimated. Lower cost factors of production can be exploited wherever they emerge. The result is a powerful strategic advantage to firms that can organize globally. These general and specific business drivers have greatly enlarged world trade and commerce.

Not all industries are similarly affected by these trends. Clearly, manufacturing has been much more affected than services that still tend to be domestic—and highly inefficient. However, the localism of services is breaking down in telecommunications, entertainment, transportation, financial services, and general business services including law. Clearly those firms within an industry who can understand the internationalization of their industry and respond appropriately will reap enormous gains in productivity and stability.

| Table 15.2 | Challenges and Obstacles to Global Business Systems |

General
    Cultural particularism: regionalism, nationalism
    Social expectations: brand-name expectations; work hours
    Political laws: transborder data and privacy laws

Specific
    Standards: different EDI, e-mail, telecommunications standards
    Reliability: phone networks not reliable
    Speed: data transfer speeds differ, slower than U.S.
    Personnel: shortages of skilled consultants

Business Challenges

While the possibilities of globalization for business success are enormous, fundamental forces are operating to inhibit a global economy and to disrupt international business. Table 15.2 lists the most common and powerful challenges to the development of global systems.

At a cultural level, **particularism,** making judgments and taking action on the basis of narrow or personal characteristics, in all its forms (religious, nationalistic, ethnic, regionalism, geopolitical position) rejects the very concept of a shared global culture and rejects the penetration of domestic markets by foreign goods and services. Differences among cultures produce differences in social expectations, politics, and ultimately legal rules. In certain countries, like the United States, consumers expect domestic name-brand products to be built domestically and are disappointed to learn that much of what they thought of as domestically produced is in fact foreign made.

Different cultures produce different political regimes. Among the many different countries of the world there are different laws governing the movement of information, information privacy of their citizens, origins of software and hardware in systems, and radio and satellite telecommunications. Even the hours of business and the terms of business trade vary greatly across political cultures. These different legal regimes complicate global business and must be taken into account when building global systems.

For instance, European countries have very strict laws concerning transborder data flow and privacy. **Transborder data flow** is defined as the movement of information across international boundaries in any form. Some European countries prohibit the processing of financial information outside their boundaries or the movement of employee information to foreign countries. The European Commission (the highest planning body for the integration of Europe) is considering a Digital Services Data Protection Directive that would restrict the flow of any information to countries (like the United States) that do not meet strict European information laws on personal information. That means, for instance, that a French marketing manager may not be able to use his or her credit card in New York because the credit information cannot be forwarded to the United States, given its privacy laws. In response, most multinational firms develop information systems within each European country to avoid the cost and uncertainty of moving information across national boundaries.

Cultural and political differences profoundly affect organizations' standard operating procedures. A host of specific barriers arise from the general cultural differences, everything from different reliability of phone networks to the shortage of skilled consultants (see Steinbart and Nath, 1992). The Window on Organizations illustrates how such differences have affected attempts by corporations to spread information systems technology advances across international borders.

National laws and traditions have created disparate accounting practices in various countries, which impact the way profits and losses are analyzed. German companies generally do not recognize the profit from a venture until the project is completely finished and they have been paid. British firms, on the other hand, begin posting profits before a project is completed, when they are reasonably certain they will get the money.

particularism Making judgments and taking actions on the basis of narrow or personal characteristics.

transborder data flow The movement of information across international boundaries in any form.

Window on Organizations

THE 800-POUND GORILLA OF TRANSNATIONAL TECHNOLOGICAL CHANGE

How do you handle a major change in information technology in a multinational corporation? The answer is the same as the old vaudeville routine about how to handle an 800-pound gorilla: "Very carefully!" Organizational and technological changes that may be easily accepted within one country may be very difficult to institute across national boundaries, due to the peculiar characteristics of the national cultures involved.

Eric Singleton, information systems director for the Orange County (Florida) Property Appraiser's office, recently led his organization through a successful downsizing into client/server technology. Flushed with success, he embarked upon a European speaking tour to share his experiences. He spoke in Geneva, Switzerland; Birmingham, England; Paris, France; and Copenhagen, Denmark. Singleton returned home quite discouraged about the future of client/server technology in most of these countries. The problems were seldom technological, however. Instead, they were rooted in attitude and culture.

The most widespread attitude he encountered was unwillingness to overcome tradition. A Dutch government information systems director with 15 years experience in the United States proposed a downsizing project to dramatically improve the way his organization functioned. He was surprised to learn that if he were allowed to downsize the technology, he still could not improve the functioning of the business because he would not be allowed to do business reengineering. The current way of doing business, he was told, is more than 400 years old.

Another cultural difference Singleton met was the European tendency to show much more concern about the loss of employee jobs upon downsizing than American counterparts. Swedish businesses will not even consider laying off employees as a result of technological change. Government unemployment policy in Sweden and other countries is actually a disincentive to a company laying off employees.

Both language and culture can erect major hurdles. A major U.S. groupware software vendor wanted to market its product in

> **To Think About:** What management and organizational factors would you address in building a management reporting system for a multinational corporation doing business in Europe and Asia?

Japan. The vendor hired a professional translator to translate the application help messages and user's manual. Problems occurred because professional translators were unfamiliar with the vocabulary of the very specialized field of computer groupware. In the Japanese translation, the term *groupware* became *a device for a crowd*.

The cultural problems can be even greater than the language problems. A major function of groupware is to record the events of a meeting and to support the decision-making process during that meeting. But this function is irrelevant in Japan, where formal meetings merely ratify decisions already made before the meeting. Brainstorming is done informally after work, and negotiations take place privately, prior to any meeting. So that key function of a groupware application is not relevant to the Japanese business environment.

Sources: Kumiyo Nakakoji, "Crossing the Cultural Boundary," *Byte*, June 1994; Eric Singleton, "The Accidental IS Tourist," *Computerworld Client/Server Journal*; and Paul Tate, "Hands Across the Borders," *Information Week*, October 10, 1994.

Many European companies do not report per-share earnings, which is considered essential for U.S. and British firms.

These accounting practices are tightly intertwined with each country's legal system, business philosophy, and tax code. British, U.S., and Dutch firms share a predominantly Anglo-Saxon outlook that separates tax calculations from reports to shareholders to focus on showing shareholders how fast profits are growing. Continental European accounting practices are less oriented toward impressing investors, focusing on demonstrating compliance with strict rules, and minimizing tax liabilities. These diverging accounting practices make it difficult for large international companies with units in different countries to evaluate their performance.

Cultural differences can also affect the way organizations use information technology. For example, Japanese firms fax extensively but are reluctant to take advantage of the capabilities of e-mail. One explanation is that the Japanese view e-mail as poorly suited for much intragroup communication and depiction of the complex symbols used in the Japanese written language (Straub, 1994).

Language remains a significant barrier. Although English has become a kind of standard business language, this is truer at higher levels of companies and not throughout the middle and lower ranks. Software may have to be built with local language interfaces before a new information system can be successfully implemented.

Currency fluctuations can play havoc with planning models and projections. Although a great deal of progress has been made in developing a common currency for the European Economic Community, occasionally this regime breaks down, evidenced by the British pound fluctuation in 1992 and 1993, or the U.S. dollar fluctuating against the Japanese yen and stronger European currencies. A product that appears profitable in Mexico or Japan may actually produce a loss due to changes in foreign exchange rates.

These inhibiting factors must be taken into account when you are designing and building an international infrastructure for your business.

STATE OF THE ART

Where do firms now have international applications and where do they plan expansion in the future? Figure 15.2 indicates the state of the art in terms of current applications and likely future growth areas of international systems infrastructure.

One might think given the opportunities for achieving competitive advantages outlined above, and the interest in future applications, that most international companies have rationally developed marvelous international systems architectures. Nothing could be further from the truth. Most companies have inherited patchwork international systems from the distant past, often based on concepts of information processing developed in the 1960s—batch-oriented reporting from independent foreign divisions to corporate headquarters, with little on-line control and communication. At some point, corporations in this situation will face powerful competitive challenges in the marketplace from firms that have rationally designed truly international systems. Still other companies have recently built technology platforms for an international infrastructure but have nowhere to go with it because they lack global strategy. For instance, one survey of 100 global firms found that 52 percent never or rarely considered information systems when devising global strategies (Cox, 1991).

As it turns out, there are significant difficulties in building appropriate international infrastructures. The difficulties involve planning a system appropriate to the firm's global strategy, structuring the organization of systems and business units, solving implementation issues, and choosing the right technical platform. Let us examine these problems in greater detail.

FIGURE 15.2
Frequency and type of business entities supported by global systems and databases. Most current IT applications are relatively simple office systems involving budgeting, communications, and general ledger financial coordination. Most corporations have local human resource and equipment/facilities systems. In the future, global firms plan to expand product support, customer service, and supplier systems to global stature.
Source: Adapted from Blake Ives and Sirkka Jarvenpaa, "Wiring the Stateless Corporation: Empowering the Drivers and Overcoming the Barriers," SIM Network, September/October 1991, p. 4C.

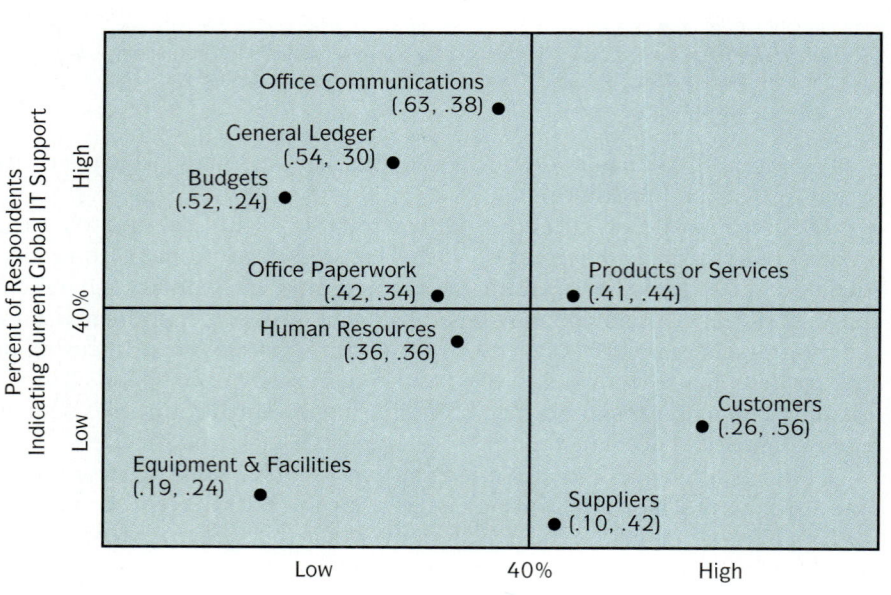

15.2 ORGANIZING INTERNATIONAL INFORMATION SYSTEMS

There are three organizational issues facing corporations seeking a global position: choosing a strategy, organizing the business, and organizing the systems management area. The first two are closely connected, so we will discuss them together.

GLOBAL STRATEGIES AND BUSINESS ORGANIZATION

There are four main global strategies that form the basis for global firms' organizational structure. These are domestic exporter, multinational, franchiser, and transnational. Each of these strategies is pursued with a specific business organizational structure (see Table 15.3). For simplicity's sake, we describe three kinds of organizational structure or governance: centralized (in the home country), decentralized (to local foreign units), and coordinated (all units participate as equals). There are other types of governance patterns observed in specific companies (e.g., authoritarian dominance by one unit, a confederacy of equals, a federal structure balancing power among strategic units, and so forth; see Keen, 1991).

The **domestic exporter** strategy is characterized by heavy centralization of corporate activities in the home country of origin. Nearly all international companies begin this way, and some move on to other forms. Production, finance/accounting, sales/marketing, human resources, and strategic management are set up to optimize resources in the home country. International sales are sometimes dispersed using agency agreements or subsidiaries, but even here foreign marketing is totally reliant on the domestic home base for marketing themes and strategies. Caterpillar Corporation and other heavy capital equipment manufacturers fall into this category of firm.

domestic exporter A strategy characterized by heavy centralization of corporate activities in the home country of origin.

The **multinational** strategy concentrates financial management and control out of a central home base while decentralizing production, sales, and marketing operations to units in other countries. The products and services on sale in different countries are adapted to suit local market conditions. The organization becomes a far-flung confederation of production and marketing facilities in different countries. Many financial service firms, along with a host of manufacturers such as General Motors, Chrysler, and Intel, fit this pattern.

multinational A global strategy that concentrates financial management and control out of a central home base while decentralizing production, sales, and marketing operations to units in other countries.

Franchisers are an interesting mix of old and new. On the one hand, the product is created, designed, financed, and initially produced in the home country, but for product-specific reasons must rely heavily on foreign personnel for further production, marketing, and human resources. Food franchisers such as McDonald's, Mrs. Fields Cookies, and Kentucky Fried Chicken fit this pattern. McDonald's created a new form of fast-food chain in the United States and continues to rely largely on the United States for inspiration of new products, strategic management, and financing. Nevertheless, because the product must be produced locally—it is perishable—extensive coordination and dispersal of production, local marketing, and local recruitment of personnel are required. Generally, foreign franchisees are clones of the mother country units, yet fully coordinated worldwide production that could optimize factors of production is not possible.

franchiser A firm where product is created, designed, financed, and initially produced in the home country, but for product-specific reasons must rely heavily on foreign personnel for further production, marketing, and human resources.

Table 15.3 Global Business Strategy and Structure

| | Strategy | | | |
Business Function	Domestic Exporter	Multinational	Franchiser	Transnational
Production	Centralized	Dispersed	Coordinated	Coordinated
Finance/Accounting	Centralized	Centralized	Centralized	Coordinated
Sales/Marketing	Mixed	Dispersed	Coordinated	Coordinated
Human Resources	Centralized	Centralized	Coordinated	Coordinated
Strategic Management	Centralized	Centralized	Centralized	Coordinated

McDonald's offers Chinese diners a full selection of burgers, fries, and drinks. McDonald's patrons in other countries will find the same choices available to them.

transnational Truly globally managed firms that have no national headquarters; value-added activities are managed from a global perspective without reference to national borders, optimizing sources of supply and demand and taking advantage of any local competitive advantage.

For instance, potatoes and beef can generally not be bought where they are cheapest on world markets but must be produced reasonably close to the area of consumption.

Transnational firms are the stateless, truly globally managed firms which may represent a larger part of international business in the future. Transnational firms have no single national headquarters but instead have many regional headquarters and perhaps a world headquarters. In a **transnational** strategy, nearly all of the value-adding activities are managed from a global perspective without reference to national borders, optimizing sources of supply and demand wherever they appear, and taking advantage of any local competitive advantages. Transnational firms take the globe, not the home country as their management frame of reference. The governance of these firms has been likened to a federal structure in which there is a strong central management core of decision making, but considerable dispersal of power and financial muscle throughout the global divisions. Few companies have actually attained transnational status, but Citicorp, Sony, Ford, and others are attempting this transition.

Information technology and improvements in global telecommunications are giving international firms more flexibility to shape their global strategies. Protectionism and a need to serve local markets better encourage companies to disperse production facilities and at least become multinational. At the same time, the drive to achieve economies of scale and take advantage of short-term local advantages moves transnationals toward a global management perspective and a concentration of power and authority. Hence, there are forces of decentralization and dispersal, as well as forces of centralization and global coordination (Ives and Jarvenpaa, 1991).

GLOBAL SYSTEMS TO FIT THE STRATEGY

The configuration, management, and development of systems tend to follow the global strategy chosen (Roche, 1992; Ives and Jarvenpaa, 1991). Figure 15.3 depicts the typical arrangements. By *systems* we mean the full range of activities involved in building information systems: conception and alignment with the strategic business plan, systems development, and ongoing operation. For the sake of simplicity, we consider four types of systems configuration. *Centralized systems* are those where systems development and operation occur totally at the domestic home base. *Duplicated systems* are those where development occurs totally at the home base but operations are handed

SYSTEM CONFIGURATION	STRATEGY			
	Domestic Exporter	Multinational	Franchiser	Transnational
Centralized	X			
Duplicated			X	
Decentralized	x	X	x	
Networked		x		X

FIGURE 15.3
Global strategy and systems configurations. The large **X**'s show the dominant pattern, and the small **x**'s show the emerging patterns. For instance, domestic exporters rely predominantly on centralized systems, but there is continual pressure and some development of decentralized systems in local marketing regions.

over to autonomous units in foreign locations. *Decentralized systems* are those where each foreign unit designs its own, totally unique solutions and systems. Last, *networked systems* are those in which systems development and operations occur in an integrated and coordinated fashion across all units. As can be seen in Figure 15.3, domestic exporters tend to have highly centralized systems in which a single domestic systems development staff develops worldwide applications. Multinationals offer a direct and striking contrast: Here foreign units devise their own systems solutions based on local needs with few if any applications in common with headquarters (the exceptions being financial reporting and some telecommunications applications). Franchisers have the simplest systems structure: Like the products they sell, franchisers develop a single system usually at the home base and then replicate it around the world. Each unit—no matter where it is located—has the same identical applications. Last, the most ambitious form of systems development is found in the transnational: Networked systems are those in which there is a solid, singular global environment for developing and operating systems. This usually presupposes a powerful telecommunications backbone, a culture of shared applications development, and a shared management culture that crosses cultural barriers. The networked systems structure is most visible in financial services where the homogeneity of the product, money, and money instruments seems to overcome cultural barriers.

REORGANIZING THE BUSINESS

How should a firm organize itself for doing business on an international scale? Developing a global company and an information systems support structure requires following these principles:

1. Organize value-adding activities along lines of comparative advantage. For instance, marketing/sales functions should be located where they can best be performed, for least cost and maximum impact; likewise with production, finance, human resources, and information systems.
2. Develop and operate systems units at each level of corporate activity—national, regional, and international. In order to serve local needs, there should be *host country systems units* of some magnitude. *Regional systems* units should handle telecommunications and systems development across national boundaries that take place within major geographic regions (European, Asian, American). *Transnational systems units*

should be established to create the linkages across major regional areas and coordinate the development and operation of international telecommunications and systems development (Roche, 1992).

3. Establish at world headquarters a single office responsible for development of international systems, a global chief information officer (CIO) position.

Many successful companies have devised organizational systems structures along these principles. The success of these companies relies not just on the proper organization of activities. A key ingredient is a management team that can understand the risks and benefits of international systems and that can devise strategies for overcoming the risks. We turn to these management topics next.

15.3 MANAGING GLOBAL SYSTEMS

The survey of 100 large global corporations described earlier found that CIOs believed the development and implementation of international systems were the most difficult problems they faced. Table 15.4 lists what these CIOs believed were the principal management problems posed by developing international systems.

It is interesting to note that these problems are the chief difficulties managers experience in developing ordinary domestic systems as well! But these are enormously complicated in the international environment.

A TYPICAL SCENARIO: DISORGANIZATION ON A GLOBAL SCALE

Let us look at a common scenario. A traditional multinational consumer goods company based in the United States and operating in Europe would like to expand into Asian markets and knows that it must develop a transnational strategy and a supportive information systems structure. Like most multinationals it has dispersed production and marketing to regional and national centers while maintaining a world headquarters and strategic management in the United States. Historically, it has allowed each of the subsidiary foreign divisions to develop its own systems. The only centrally coordinated system is financial controls and reporting. The central systems group in the United States focuses only on domestic functions and production. The result is a hodgepodge of hardware, software, and telecommunications. The mail systems between Europe and the United States are incompatible. Each production facility uses a different manufacturing resources planning system (or different version with local variations), and different marketing, sales, and human resource systems. The technology platforms are wildly different: Europe is using mostly UNIX-based file servers and IBM microcomputer clones on desktops. Communications between different sites are poor, given the high cost and low quality of European intercountry communications. The U.S. group is moving from an IBM mainframe environment centralized at headquarters to a highly distributed network architecture based on a national value-added network, with local sites developing their own local-area networks. The central systems group at head-

Table 15.4 Management Issues in Developing International Systems	
Agreeing on common user requirements	88%
Inducing procedural business changes	79
Coordinating applications development	77
Coordinating software releases	69
Encouraging local users to take on ownership	58

Source: Adapted from Butler Cox, *Globalization: The IT Challenge* (Sunnyvale, CA: Amdahl Executive Institute, 1991).

quarters was recently decimated and dispersed to the U.S. local sites in the hope of serving local needs better and reducing costs.

What do you recommend to the senior management leaders of this company who now want to pursue a transnational strategy and develop an information systems infrastructure to support a highly coordinated global systems environment? Consider the problems you face by reexamining Table 15.4. The foreign divisions will resist efforts to agree on common user requirements—they have never thought about much other than their own units' needs. The systems groups in American local sites, which have been recently enlarged and told to focus on local needs, will not easily accept guidance from anyone recommending a transnational strategy. It will be difficult to convince local managers anywhere in the world that they should change their business procedures to align with other units in the world, especially if this might interfere with their local performance. After all, local managers are rewarded in this company for meeting local objectives of their division or plant. Finally, it will be difficult to coordinate development of projects around the world in the absence of a powerful telecommunications network, or therefore difficult to encourage local users to take on ownership in the systems developed.

STRATEGY: DIVIDE, CONQUER, APPEASE

Figure 15.4 lays out the main dimensions of a solution. First, consider that not all systems should be coordinated on a transnational basis—only some core systems are truly worth sharing from a cost and feasibility point of view. **Core systems** are systems that support functions that are absolutely critical to the organization. Other systems should only be partially coordinated because they share key elements, but they do not have to be totally common across national boundaries. For such systems, a good deal of local

core systems Systems that support functions that are absolutely critical to the organization.

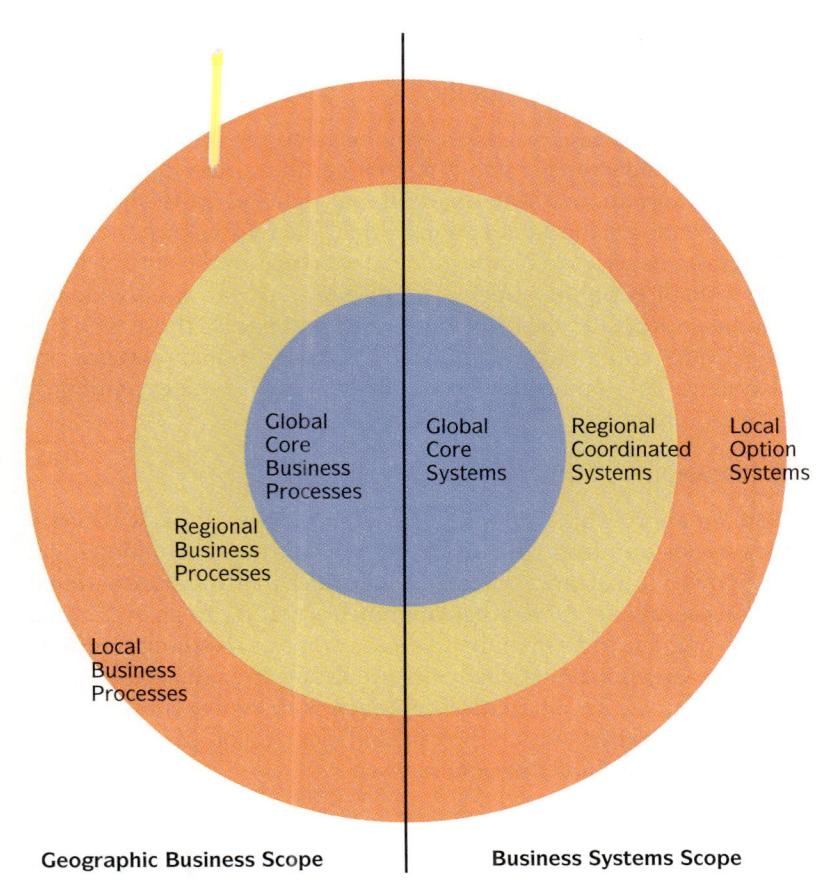

FIGURE 15.4
Agency and other coordination costs increase as the firm moves from local option systems toward regional and global systems. On the other hand, transaction costs of participating in global markets probably decrease as firms develop global systems. A sensible strategy is to reduce agency costs by developing only a few core global systems that are vital for global operations, leaving other systems in the hands of regional and local units. *From* Managing Information Technology in Multinational Corporations *by Roche, Edward M., © 1992. Reprinted by permission of Prentice-Hall, Inc., Upper Saddle River, NJ.*

variation is possible and desirable. A last group of systems are peripheral, truly provincial, and are needed to suit local requirements only.

Define the Core Business Processes

How do you identify *core systems?* The first step is to define a short list of truly critical core business processes. Business processes have been defined before in Chapter 10, which you should review. Briefly, **business processes** are sets of logically related tasks performed to achieve a defined business outcome, such as shipping out correct orders to customers or delivering innovative products to the market. Each business process typically involves many functional areas working together, effectively communicating and coordinating.

The way to identify these core business processes is to conduct a work-flow analysis. How are customer orders taken, what happens to them once they are taken, who fills the order, how are they shipped to the customers? What about suppliers? Do they have access to manufacturing resource planning systems so that supply is automatic? You should be able to identify and set priorities in a short list of ten business processes that are absolutely critical for the firm.

Next, can you identify centers of excellence for these processes? Is the customer order fulfillment superior in the United States, manufacturing process control superior in Germany, and human resources superior in Asia? You should be able to identify some areas of the company, for some lines of business, where a division or unit stands out in the performance of one or several business functions.

When you understand the business processes of a firm, you can rank order them. You can then decide which processes should be core applications, centrally coordinated, designed, and implemented around the globe, and which should be regional and local. At the same time, by identifying the critical business processes, the really important ones, you have gone a long way to defining a vision of the future that you should be working toward.

Identify the Core Systems to Coordinate Centrally

By identifying the critical core business processes, you begin to see opportunities for transnational systems. The second strategic step is to conquer the core systems and define these systems as truly transnational. The financial and political costs of defining and implementing transnational systems are extremely high. Therefore, keep the list to an absolute minimum, letting experience be the guide and erring on the side of minimalism. By dividing off a small group of systems as absolutely critical, you divide opposition to a transnational strategy. At the same time, you can appease those who oppose the central worldwide coordination implied by transnational systems by permitting peripheral systems development to go on unabated, with the exception of some technical platform requirements.

Choose an Approach: Incremental, Grand Design, Evolutionary

A third step is to choose an approach. Avoid piecemeal approaches. These will surely fail for lack of visibility, opposition from all who stand to lose from transnational development, and lack of power to convince senior management that the transnational systems are worth it. Likewise, avoid *grand design* approaches that try to do everything at once. These also tend to fail, due to an inability to focus resources. Nothing gets done properly, and opposition to organizational change is needlessly strengthened because the effort requires huge resources. An alternative approach is to evolve transnational applications from existing applications with a precise and clear vision of the transnational capabilities the organization should have in five years.

Make the Benefits Clear

What is in it for the company? One of the worst situations to avoid is to build global systems for the sake of building global systems. From the beginning, it is crucial that se-

---

business processes Sets of logically related tasks performed to achieve a defined business outcome; each business process typically involves many functional areas working together.

nior management at headquarters and foreign division managers clearly understand the benefits that will come to the company as well as to individual units. While each system offers unique benefits to a particular budget, the overall contribution of global systems lies in four areas.

Global systems—truly integrated, distributed, and transnational systems—contribute to superior management and coordination. A simple price tag cannot be put on the value of this contribution, and the benefit will not show up in any capital budgeting model. It is the ability to switch suppliers on a moment's notice from one region to another in a crisis, the ability to move production in response to natural disasters, and the ability to use excess capacity in one region to meet raging demand in another.

A second major contribution is vast improvement in production, operation, and supply and distribution. Imagine a global value chain, with global suppliers and a global distribution network. For the first time, senior managers can locate value-adding activities in regions where they are most economically performed.

Third, global systems mean global customers and global marketing. Fixed costs around the world can now be amortized over a much larger customer base. This will unleash new economies of scale at production facilities.

Last, global systems mean the ability to optimize the use of corporate funds over a much larger capital base. This means, for instance, that capital in a surplus region can be moved efficiently to expand production of capital-starved regions; that cash can be managed more effectively within the company and put to use more effectively.

These strategies will not by themselves create global systems. You will have to implement what you strategize and this is a whole new challenge.

IMPLEMENTATION TACTICS: COOPTATION

The overall tactic for dealing with resistant local units in a transnational company is cooptation. **Cooptation** is defined as bringing the opposition into the process of designing and implementing the solution without giving up control over the direction and nature of the change. As much as possible, raw power should be avoided. Minimally, however, local units must agree on a short list of transnational systems and raw power may be required to solidify the idea that transnational systems of some sort are truly required.

cooptation Bringing the opposition into the process of designing and implementing the solution without giving up control over the direction and nature of the change.

How should cooptation proceed? Several alternatives are possible. One alternative is to permit each country unit the opportunity to develop one transnational application first in its home territory, and then throughout the world. In this manner, each major country systems group is given a piece of the action in developing a transnational system, and local units feel a sense of ownership in the transnational effort. On the downside, this assumes the ability to develop high-quality systems is widely distributed, and that, say, the German team can successfully implement systems in France and Italy. This will not always be the case. Also, the transnational effort will have low visibility.

A second tactic is to develop new transnational centers of excellence, or a single center of excellence. There may be several centers around the globe that focus on specific business processes. These centers draw heavily from local national units, are based on multinational teams, and must report to worldwide management—their first line of responsibility is to the core applications. Centers of excellence perform the initial identification and specification of the business process, define the information requirements, perform the business and systems analysis, and accomplish all design and testing. Implementation, however, and pilot testing occur in World Pilot Regions where new applications are installed and tested first. Later, they are rolled out to other parts of the globe. This phased roll-out strategy is precisely how national applications are successfully developed.

WRAPPING UP: THE MANAGEMENT SOLUTION

We can now reconsider how to handle the most vexing problems facing managers developing the transnational information system infrastructures that were described in Table 15.4.

- *Agreeing on common user requirements:* Establishing a short list of the core business processes and core support systems will begin a process of rational comparison across the many divisions of the company, develop a common language for discussing the business, and naturally lead to an understanding of common elements (as well as the unique qualities that must remain local).

- *Inducing procedural business changes:* Your success as a change agent will depend on your legitimacy, your actual raw power, and your ability to involve users in the change design process. **Legitimacy** is defined as the extent to which your authority is accepted on grounds of competence, vision, or other qualities. The selection of a viable change strategy, which we have defined as evolutionary but with a vision, should assist you in convincing others that change is feasible and desirable. Involving people in change, assuring them that change is in the best interests of the company and their local units is a key tactic.

- *Coordinating applications development:* Choice of change strategy is critical for this problem. At the global level there is simply far too much complexity to attempt a grand design strategy of change. It is far easier to coordinate change by making small incremental steps toward a larger vision. Imagine a five-year plan of action rather than a two-year plan of action, and reduce the set of transnational systems to a bare minimum in order to reduce coordination costs.

- *Coordinating software releases:* Firms can institute procedures to ensure that all operating units convert to new software updates at the same time so that everyone's software is compatible.

- *Encouraging local users to take on ownership:* The key to this problem is to involve users in the creation of the design without giving up control over the development of the project to parochial interests. Recruiting a wide range of local individuals to transnational centers of excellence helps send the message that all significant groups are involved in the design and will have an influence.

Even with the proper organizational structure and appropriate management choices, it is still possible to stumble over technological issues. Choices of technology, platforms, networks, hardware, and software are the final elements in building transnational information system infrastructures. The Window on Management describes how two large multinational corporations are grappling with these problems as they merge their companies.

legitimacy The extent to which one's authority is accepted on grounds of competence, vision, or other qualities.

15.4 TECHNOLOGY ISSUES AND OPPORTUNITIES

Information technology is itself a powerful business driver encouraging the development of global systems, but it creates significant challenges for managers. Global systems presuppose that business firms develop a solid technical foundation and are willing to continually upgrade facilities.

MAIN TECHNICAL ISSUES

Hardware, software, and telecommunications pose special technical challenges in an international setting. The major hardware challenge is finding some way to standardize the firm's computer hardware platform when there is so much variation from operating unit to operating unit and from country to country. Figure 15.5 illustrates the diverse hardware platforms used by Citibank Asia-Pacific in various countries. (Citibank Asia-Pacific is starting to centralize some back-office applications, such as check and savings account processing, loan processing, and general ledger, and to consolidate computer centers.) Managers will need to think carefully about where to locate the firm's computer centers and about how to select hardware suppliers. The major global software challenge is finding applications that are user friendly and that truly enhance the pro-

Citibank Asia-Pacific's Conversion Schedule

Country	Conversion date
Australia	December '94
Guam	March '96
Hong Kong	April '95
India	October '97
Indonesia	November '96
Japan	No conversion
Malaysia	May '95
Pakistan	August '98
Philippines	June '96
Saudi Arabia	October '97
Singapore	March '95
South Korea	October '97
Taiwan	August '97
Thailand	August '96
Turkey	September '95
United Arab Emirates	January '97

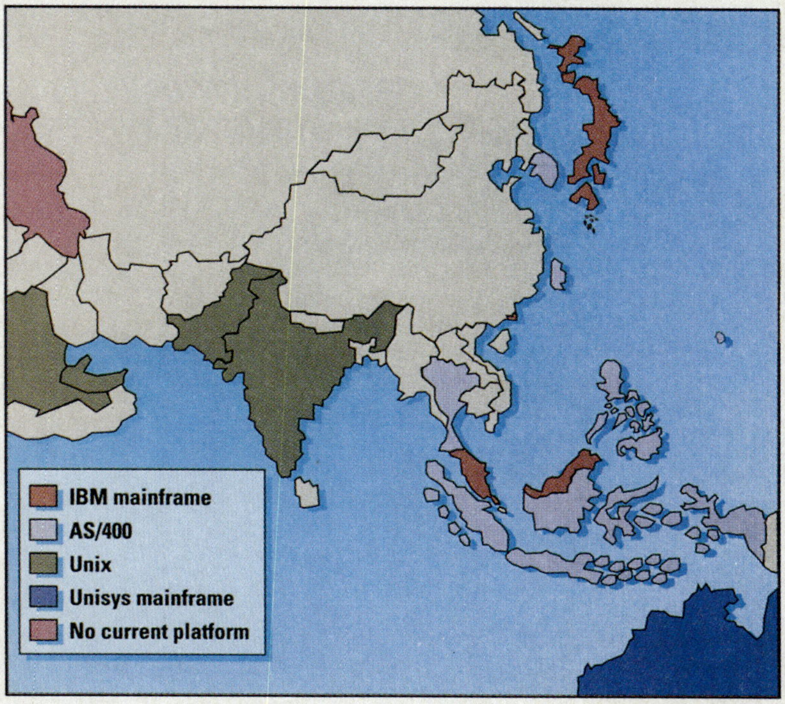

Legend:
- IBM mainframe
- AS/400
- Unix
- Unisys mainframe
- No current platform

FIGURE 15.5
Citibank Asia-Pacific's hardware platforms. Citibank Asia-Pacific uses different hardware platforms in the various countries where it operates. It is consolidating its computer centers and standardizing core back-office applications to run on software at its Singapore IBM mainframe. *Source: Adapted from Clinton Wilder, "Making Borders Disappear,"* InformationWeek, *February 27, 1995, page 44.*

ductivity of international work teams. The major telecommunications challenge is making data flow seamlessly across networks shaped by disparate national standards. Overcoming these challenges requires systems integration and connectivity on a global basis.

Hardware and Systems Integration

The development of transnational information system infrastructures based on the concept of core systems raises questions about how the new core systems will fit in with the existing suite of applications developed around the globe by different divisions, different people, and for different kinds of computing hardware. The goal is to develop global, distributed, and integrated systems. Briefly, these are the same problems faced by any large domestic systems development effort. However, the problems are more complex because of the international environment. For instance, in the United States, IBM Corp. and IBM operating systems have played the predominant role in building core systems for large organizations, whereas in Europe, UNIX was much more commonly used for large systems. How can the two be integrated in a common transnational system?

The correct solution will often depend on the history of the company's systems and the extent of commitment to proprietary systems. For instance, finance and insurance firms have typically relied almost exclusively on IBM proprietary equipment and architectures in the 1980s, and it would be extremely difficult and cost ineffective to

Window on Management

TRAVELING DOWN THE ROAD OF INTERNATIONAL TECHNOLOGY INFRASTRUCTURE MERGERS

How can two giants in the travel agency field, one American and one European, merge their information technology infrastructure? Carlson Travel Group is headquartered in Minnetonka, Minnesota, and does its main business primarily in the United States. Wagonlit Travel, a giant subsidiary of Accor Group of Paris, France, is strong mainly in Europe.

The drive to merge came from their large clients who wanted to be able to have all of their travel business handled by one agency, an agency that could service them anywhere in the world. One reason the big multinational corporations want to concentrate all their travel business with one agent is so that they can better control their own travel costs through access to all of their travel records. With appropriate data they not only can stay on top of the travel expenditure habits of their employees but also will be able to negotiate special rates with hotels, auto rental companies, and airlines. Hanna Murphy, travel manager in Siemens' San Jose, California, office, values the new merger because he can easily obtain worldwide information and go into global trend analysis.

The product of the merger, London-based Carlson Wagonlit Travel, laid out a five-year consolidation plan that began to take effect in July 1994. The reason the company will take so long to complete the merger is because of the difficulties of amalgamating two very different corporate cultures and technology infrastructures. The new company will have 4000 locations in 125 countries. Carlson has a highly centralized, IBM-mainframe technology infrastructure, an infrastructure made possible by the fact that its primary business is within one country. Wagonlit's technology infrastructure is more decentralized and operates over a wide range of disparate platforms, including IBM's AS/400 and Digital Equipment Corporation's (DEC) VAX. This decentralized infrastructure stems from their need to have a strong presence in a number of European countries each of which has different laws and procedures as well as individualized computerized reservation systems (CRSs).

The business plan gives Carlson control of all operations within the United States for the time being while Wagonlit has been given control over all European operations. A new company, Carlson Wagonlit Development, is based in London and is taking charge of developing business in Asia and Australia where the two companies currently have very little presence.

To Think About: What organization, management, and technology problems do you think the two companies are likely to experience as they merge and develop a common technology infrastructure?

Merging the two technology infrastructures has been made more difficult because of the lofty goals the new company has set—it expects to have a fully integrated company with standardized systems at the end of those five years. The new company must first select a worldwide architecture. It has already made certain architecture decisions. Eventually the new company will operate on a single open, distributed client/server architecture. The telecommunications choices made will have to supply fast, frame-relay service between all locations. The standard programming language will be either C or C++. The servers will use a variant of UNIX or Windows NT. Carlson and Wagonlit are also establishing a single central repository of object-oriented code (Carlson already has some object-oriented applications).

Data will be made available in a uniform way to both customers and employees. All offices will share a single CRS. Customer information needs will be addressed through a single information support system that customers will be able to access in order to monitor their own data.

The unified company will have to work fast to iron out kinks and consolidate its international infrastructure. Competitors such as Maritz are also trying to create worldwide networked information systems that customers can access. Maritz recently joined an alliance of 12 large international travel agencies, including Protravel in Paris and Jetset in Singapore, to build such systems.

Source: Linda Wilson with Joshua M. Greenbaum, "Travel Duo Charts Course," *Information Week,* August 22, 1994.

---

abandon that equipment and software. Newer firms and manufacturing firms generally find it much easier to adopt open UNIX systems for international systems. As we pointed out in previous chapters, open UNIX-based systems are far more cost-effective in the long run, provide more power at a cheaper price, and preserve options for future expansion.

Once a hardware platform is chosen, the question of standards has to be addressed. Just because all sites use the same hardware does not guarantee common, integrated systems. Some central authority in the firm has to establish data, as well as other technical standards, for sites to comply with. For instance, technical accounting terms such as the beginning and end of the fiscal year must be standardized (review our earlier discussion of the cultural challenges to building global businesses), as well as the acceptable interfaces between systems, communications speeds and architectures, and network software.

Connectivity

The heart of the international systems problem is telecommunications—linking together the systems and people of a global firm into a single integrated network just like the phone system but capable of voice, data, and image transmissions. However, integrated global networks are extremely difficult to create (see Figure 15.6). For example, many countries cannot even fulfill basic business telecommunications needs such as obtaining reliable circuits, coordinating among different carriers and the regional telecommunications authority, obtaining bills in a common currency standard, and obtaining standard agreements for the level of telecommunications service provided.

Despite moves toward economic unity, Europe remains a hodgepodge of disparate national technical standards and service levels. The problem is especially critical for banks or airlines that must move massive volumes of data around the world. Although most circuits leased by multinational corporations are fault-free more than 99.8 percent of the time, line quality and service vary widely from the north to the south of Europe. Network service is much more unreliable in southern Europe (Stahl, 1992).

Although the European Economic Community has endorsed EDIfact as the European electronic data interchange (EDI) standard, existing European standards for networking and EDI are very industry-specific and country-specific. Most European banks use the SWIFT (Society for Worldwide Interbank Financial Telecommunications)

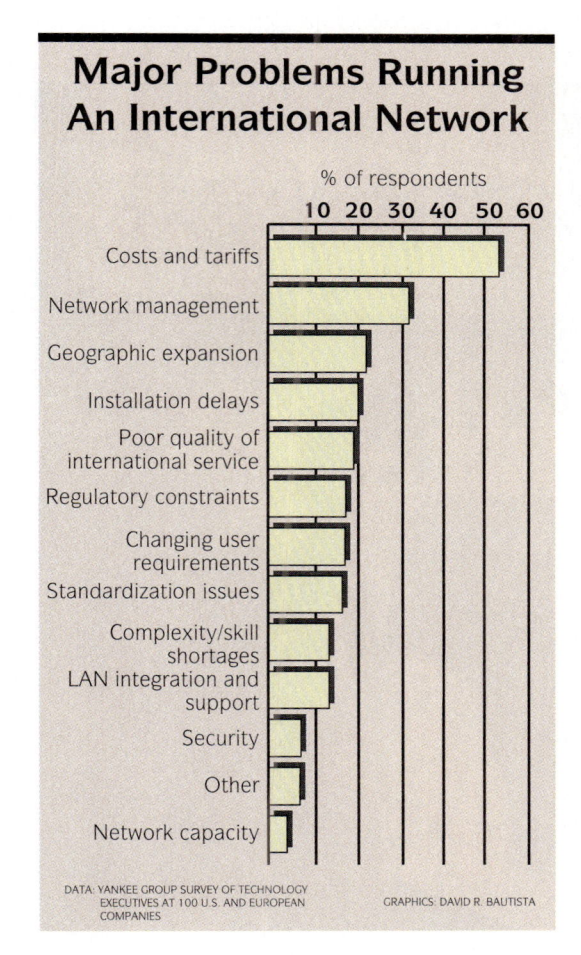

FIGURE 15.6
Problems of international networks. There are numerous hurdles to overcome before companies can successfully run networked systems that span many countries. *Source: Adapted from Mary E. Thyfault, "Virtual Europe," InformationWeek, November 14, 1994.*

protocol for international funds transfer, while automobile companies and food producers often use industry-specific or country-specific versions of standard protocols for EDI. Complicating matters further, the United States standard for EDI is ANSI (American National Standards Institute) X.12. Although the Open Systems Interconnect (OSI) reference model for linking networks is more popular in Europe than it is in the United States, it is not universally accepted. Various industry groups have standardized on other networking architectures, such as Transmission Control Protocol/Internet Protocol (TCP/IP); IBM's proprietary Systems Network Architecture (SNA); and Digital Equipment's proprietary network architecture, Decnet. Even standards such as ISDN (Integrated Services Digital Network) vary from country to country.

Firms have several options for providing international connectivity: Build their own international private network, rely on a network service based on the public switched networks throughout the world, or use the Internet and intranets.

One possibility is for the firm to put together its own private network based on leased lines from each country's PTT (Post, Telegraph, and Telephone authorities). Each country, however, has different restrictions on data exchange, technical standards, and acceptable vendors of equipment. These problems magnify in certain parts of the world. Despite such limitations, in Europe and the United States, reliance on PTTs still makes sense while these public networks expand services to compete with private providers.

The second major alternative to building one's own network is to use one of several expanding network services. With deregulation of telecommunications around the globe, private providers have sprung up to service business customers' data needs, along with some voice and image communications.

Although common in the United States, IVANs (International Value-Added Network Services) are expanding in both Europe and Asia. These private firms offer valued-added telecommunications capacity usually rented from local PTTs or international satellite

With limited information technology resources, Frank Russell Co., a financial firm, created a powerful global network to link its headquarters in Tacoma, Washington, with offices in New York City, Toronto, London, Sydney, Tokyo, and Zurich.

Window on Technology

IS THE INTERNET A WORLD TOOL?

The Internet offers global connectivity, but it is not yet truly a worldwide tool. What are the challenges to be overcome? The Net is most fully developed and employed in the United States. The rest of the world lags, and the problems are many and varied. Countries face high costs, government control, or government monitoring. Often an infrastructure doesn't exist, and many countries cannot afford to develop it.

The rich, developed country of Canada faces two unique problems. First, the nation tries to keep out telecommunications competition from U.S. giants in order to protect its distinct cultural identity from domination by the behemoth on its southern border. In addition, Canada is a vast country—second only to Russia in size—requiring an equally vast telecommunications infrastructure. With a relatively small population the per-capita cost is very high, with the cost of a high-grade telecommunications line being 5 to 8 times its U.S. equivalent. Finally, the government has maintained a monopoly in the expectation that it can achieve economies of scale and keep prices relatively low.

Western Europe faces both high transmission costs and the lack of a unified technology because it is not politically unified. Leased-line megabytes are about 25 times as expensive in Europe than in the United States. Most European telecommunications systems are still government monopolies, which accounts for the costs and the separate technologies. This situation will be ending over the next several years, hopefully bringing costs down while also establishing international standards. In addition, European countries have a native caution. Like Club Mediterranée, a Paris-based organization, they move slowly. The company allowed its American subsidiary to establish a Web site but stated emphatically that it is not yet time for its European units to do the same.

The rest of the world faces yet other problems, the largest of which is the lack of an infrastructure and the cost of installing one. In Vietnam more than half of its 74,000,000 people earn an annual income under $100, so the country must have outside support to finance an Internet infrastructure. In South Africa a slow (14.4 Kbps) modem costs more than a month's average wages. One organization, African Internet Development Action Team (http://www.africa.com/pages/aidat) is attempting to improve the situation on that continent. Where an infrastructure exists, as in China and Pakistan, it is often outdated, lacking digital circuits and has very noisy lines. Many countries monitor all transmissions. In Singapore the government's Censorship Section monitors all messages coming through its Internet services, causing most corporations to refuse to use such an insecure Net. In Haiti, although former President Jean-Bertrand Aristide does use the Net, 85 percent of his fellow Haitians can neither read nor write—the ultimate stumbling block to a successful Internet. Companies planning international operations through the Net still have much to contend with.

Source: Alix Christie, Montieth Illingworth, and Larry Lange, "One World?" *Information Week,* October 2, 1995.

To Think About: What management, organization, and technology issues should be addressed when considering whether to use the Internet for global communication and business applications?

---

authorities, and then resell it to corporate users. IVANs add value by providing protocol conversion, operating mailboxes and mail systems, and offering integrated billing that permits a firm to track its data communications costs. Currently these systems are limited to data transmissions, but in the future they will expand to voice and image.

The Window on Technology explores some of the hurdles that must be overcome when using the Internet option.

Software

Compatible hardware and communications provide a platform but not the total solution. Also critical to global core infrastructure is software. The development of core systems poses unique challenges for software: How will the old systems interface with the new? Entirely new interfaces must be built and tested if old systems are kept in local areas (which is common). These interfaces can be costly and messy to build. If new software must be created, another challenge is to build software that can be realistically used by multiple business units from different countries when these business units are accustomed to their unique procedures and definitions of data.

Aside from integrating the new with the old systems, there are problems of human interface design and functionality of systems. For instance, in order to be truly useful for enhancing productivity of a global work force, software interfaces must be easily

Lotus 1-2-3 screen displays and menu options in the user interface have been translated into Japanese to accommodate end users in East Asia.

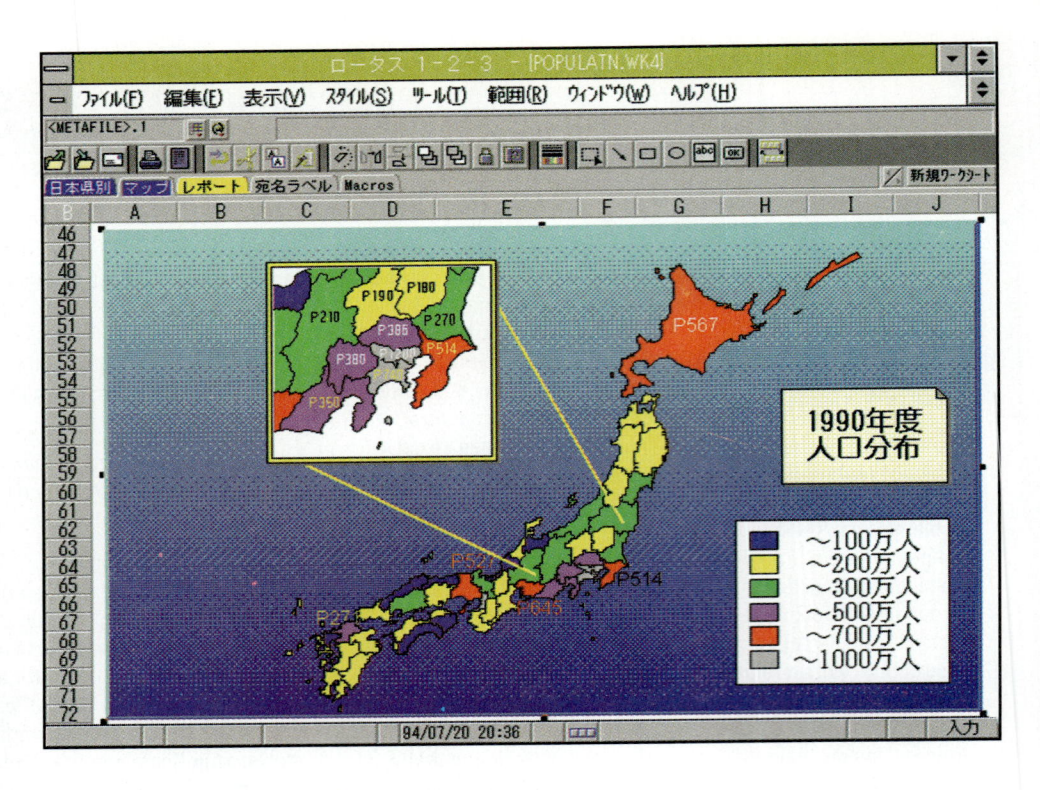

understood and mastered quickly. Graphical user interfaces are ideal for this but presuppose a common language—often English. When international systems involve knowledge workers only, English may be the assumed international standard. But as international systems penetrate deeper into management and clerical groups, a common language may not be assumed and human interfaces must be built to accommodate different languages and even conventions.

What are the most important software applications? While most international systems focus on basic transaction and MIS systems, there is an increasing emphasis on international collaborative work groups. *EDI*—electronic data interchange—is a common global transaction processing application used by manufacturing and distribution firms to connect units of the same company, as well as customers and suppliers on a global basis. *Groupware systems* such as electronic mail, videoconferencing, Lotus Notes, and other products supporting shared data files, notes, and electronic mail are much more important to knowledge- and data-based firms like advertising firms, research-based firms in medicine and engineering, and graphics and publishing firms. The Internet will be increasingly employed for such purposes.

NEW TECHNICAL OPPORTUNITIES

Major technical advances that should fall in price and gain in power over the next few years have importance to global networking and systems. After many years of stagnant development, PTTs in Europe and local Bell operating companies in the United States are finally moving ISDN (Integrated Services Digital Network) into the marketplace. Chapter 9 has described the benefits of using ISDN as an international standard for transmitting voice, images, and data over the public telephone network. ISDN will make networking services of all kinds as readily available as a phone jack in the wall.

Virtual private networks (VPNs) add features to the basic public telephone system that are usually available only to private networks. The basic idea of these services is that the local phone company provides each corporate user the ability to custom configure a network and use whatever portion of the public switched net is needed to do the job, charging only for services used. In a sense, the phone company becomes a digital net-

virtual private network (VPN) The ability to custom configure a network using a portion of the public switched network to create the illusion of a private network for a company.

work company, providing many features of a private network (including abbreviated dialing) for firms operating internationally. Firms using virtual private networks avoid the expense of leasing entire lines and many of the technical and maintenance problems of private networks. Throughout this text we have shown how the Internet facilitates global coordination, communication, and electronic commerce. As Internet technology becomes more widespread outside the United States, it will expand opportunities for international trade. The global connectivity and low cost of Internet technology will further remove obstacles of geography and time zones for companies seeking to expand operations and sell their wares abroad. Small companies may especially benefit (Quelch and Klein, 1996).

Finally, the variety of satellite systems described in Chapter 8 will revolutionize communications because they bypass existing ground-based systems. Thus, a salesperson in China could send an order confirmation request to the home office in London effortlessly and expect a reply instantly. The evolution of digital cellular phone and personal communications services will greatly increase the number of cellular communications units and wireless networks. These kinds of *communicate and compute anytime, anywhere* networks will be built throughout the next decade.

Management Challenges

1. The social and political role of stateless firms. It is one thing to talk about a stateless transnational firm, but the people who work in these firms do have states, cultures, and loyalties; the operating divisions of these firms do in fact reside in various nation-states with their own laws, politics, and cultures. It is unclear precisely how these stateless firms fit into the national cultures they must serve. In reality, so-called stateless firms have had to be very careful to show local populations that they do serve the interests of the state and broader culture.

2. The difficulties of managing change in a multicultural firm. While engineering change in a single corporation in a single nation can be difficult, costly, and long term, bringing about significant change in very large-scale global corporations can be daunting. Agreeing on core business processes in a transnational context, and then deciding on common systems, requires either extraordinary insight, a lengthy process of consensus building, or the exercise of sheer power.

3. Lines of business and global strategy. Firms will have to decide whether some or all of their lines of business should be managed on a global basis. There are some lines of business in which local variations are slight, and the possibility exists to reap large rewards by organizing globally. Microcomputers and power tools may fit this pattern, as well as industrial raw materials. Other consumer goods may be quite different by country or region. It is likely that firms with many lines of business will have to maintain a very mixed organizational structure.

Summary

1. Identify the major factors behind the growing internationalization of business. There are both general cultural factors as well as specific business factors to consider. The growth of cheap international communication and transportation has created a world culture with stable expectations or norms. Political stability and a growing global knowledge base that is widely shared contribute also to the world culture. These general factors create the conditions for global markets, global production, coordination, distribution, and global economies of scale.

2. Choose among several global strategies for developing business. There are four basic international strategies: domestic exporter, multinational, franchiser, and transnational. In a transnational strategy, all factors of production are coordinated on a global scale. However, the choice of strategy is a function of the type of business and product.

3. Understand how information systems support different global strategies. There is a connection between firm strategy and information system design. Transnational firms must develop networked system configurations and permit considerable decentralization of development and operations. Franchisers almost always duplicate systems across many countries and use centralized financial controls. Multinationals typically rely on decentralized independence among foreign units with some movement toward development of networks. Domestic exporters are typically centralized in domestic headquarters with some decentralized operations permitted.

4. Manage the development of international systems. Implementing a global system requires an implementation strategy. Typically, global systems have evolved without conscious plan. The remedy is to define a small subset of core business processes and focus on building systems that could support these processes. Tactically, you will have to coopt widely-dispersed foreign units to participate in the development and operation of these systems, being careful not to lose overall control.

5. **Understand the main technical alternatives in developing global systems.** The main hardware and telecommunications issues are systems integration and connectivity. The choices for integration are to go either with a proprietary architecture or with an open systems technology such as UNIX. Global networks are extremely difficult to build and operate. Some measure of connectivity may be achieved by relying on local PTT authorities to provide connections, building a system oneself, relying on private providers to supply communications capacity or using the Internet and intranets. Public authorities and PTTs are moving forward rapidly with ISDN and other digital services to compete with private companies. The main software issue concerns building interfaces to existing systems and providing much-needed group support software.

Key Terms

International information systems infrastructure	**Particularism**	**Franchiser**	**Cooptation**
Business driver	**Transborder data flow**	**Transnational**	**Legitimacy**
Global culture	**Domestic exporter**	**Core systems**	**Virtual private networks (VPN)**
	Multinational	**Business processes**	

Review Questions

1. What are the five major factors to consider when building an international information systems infrastructure?
2. Describe the five general cultural factors leading toward growth in global business and the four specific business factors. Describe the interconnection among these factors.
3. What is meant by a *global culture*?
4. What are the major challenges to the development of global systems?
5. Why have firms not planned for the development of international systems?
6. Describe the four main strategies for global business and organizational structure.
7. Describe the four different system configurations that can be used to support different global strategies.
8. What are the major management issues in developing international systems?
9. What are three principles to follow when organizing the firm for global business?
10. What are three steps of a management strategy for developing and implementing global systems?
11. What is meant by *cooptation,* and how can it be used to build global systems?
12. Describe the main technical issues facing global systems.
13. Describe three new technologies that can help firms develop global systems.

Discussion Questions

1. As a member of your company's global information systems group that oversees development of global core systems, what criteria would you use to determine if an application should be developed as a global application or as a peripheral local application?
2. As the CEO of a domestic exporter with large production facilities in the United States, you are considering moving toward a multinational model by creating production facilities in Europe and Asia. What strategy would you follow in building an international information infrastructure? What applications would you recommend be shared and global, and how would you implement the strategy?

Group Project

With a group of students, identify an area of emerging information technology and explore how this technology might be useful for supporting global business strategies. For instance, you might choose an area such as digital telecommunications (e.g., electronic mail, wireless communications, value-added networks) or collaborative workgroup software or new standards in operating systems or EDI or the Internet. It will be helpful to choose a business scenario to discuss the technology. You might choose, for instance, an automobile parts franchiser or a clothing franchise such as the Limited Express as example businesses. What applications would you make global, what core business processes would you choose, and how would the technology be helpful?

Case Study

GLOBAL INFORMATION SYSTEMS TO SUPPORT NESTLÉ'S GLOBAL BUSINESS STRATEGY

Nestlé SA, headquartered in Vesey, Switzerland, is a $43 billion (1993) food and pharmaceutical company that operates virtually all over the world. The corporation has close to 300 operating companies, with 80 information technology units to service its approximately 200,000 employees worldwide. This giant, diverse company even has three official languages: English, French, and Spanish. In the food area, although it is best known for its coffee, chocolate, and milk products, Nestlé is actually the manufacturer and/or purveyor of thousands of products. It has been an enormously successful company, increasing sales in 1993 by 5.5 percent, resulting in a 7 percent increase in earnings, reaching $2.2 billion.

In recent years Nestlé's global business strategy has changed in response to changing market conditions in Europe and the United States. These two giant markets have long accounted for a majority of Nestlé's sales and profits. Nonetheless, they are mature markets, where fierce competition is cutting into either Nestlé's market share or its profit margin (lowered profits in order to maintain market share). For example, in the United States in the first three years of the 1990s, they watched their coffee business lose a total of $100 million due to fierce price competition from Folgers Coffee (a Procter & Gamble brand). In Europe Nestlé's operating margin has fallen to 10.7 percent, below such major competitors as Kellogg, Heinz, and Hershey.

The question facing Nestlé management was this: What business strategy should they follow to compensate for the lower profit margins in the very countries where their major sales and profits have traditionally occurred? In the mature markets, Nestlé management has continued to make acquisitions such as Carnation, Stouffer's, Perrier, Hills Brothers, and Buitoni to improve their margin of profit through economies of scale. Nonetheless, their major strategy to counteract reduced profits and other market problems in Europe and the United States has been to emphasize accelerating the growth of both sales and profit in the less-developed countries.

Nestlé has long and vigorously pursued a globalization policy. Behind that policy is their strong commitment to a strategy of localization and regionalization. This localization and regionalization strategy involves the following five principles.

First, Nestlé leadership does not believe in trying to sell the same product worldwide. Rather, they buy or develop products that fit well in the local market and culture.

Second, Nestlé is committed to reliance upon local and regional staff to manage their interests. Thus, many national and regional managers in the Nestlé organization—at present, about 100—spend their whole careers in their own country and region. Their career paths never require them to do a stint in the home office or in a more advanced country to gain experience, as is the custom for so many managers in most American and European firms.

The third principle in the strategy of localization is Nestlé's patience and long-term perspective as they build their presence in a specific national market. For example, in their talks with Chinese officials, they persevered for 13 years before they were invited in to actually do business.

The fourth principle is their willingness to evaluate market possibilities on a regional basis. For example, Nestlé looks at Thailand, Vietnam, Laos, Cambodia, and the neighboring Chinese province of Yunnan as a single geographic and cultural region.

Fifth, Nestlé is committed to developing products from the less developed countries made from ingredients native to those countries, thereby supporting the local economy while keeping costs low.

Has Nestlé's globalization strategy been successful? By the end of 1993 at least 25 percent of their sales was coming from East and Southeast Asia and Latin America. That 25 percent equals more than all of General Mills' worldwide sales in the same year.

In some of the less-developed Asian countries, Nestlé is beginning to see some of the market maturation that has taken place in Europe and the United States, and Nestlé's response is an indication of their flexibility in working with local conditions. American-style supermarkets are appearing in large numbers in Taiwan, Malaysia, and Thailand. In Thailand supermarkets accounted for 8 percent of Nestlé's urban business five years ago; today it's 45 percent of the business. The problem for Nestlé is that supermarkets mean a serious reduction in profit margin. Nestlé Thailand's response? They overhauled their sales team. They nicknamed the new team the Red Hot Sales Force, staffed it with college graduates who were fluent in English, and gave the team members a great deal of training in increasing supermarket product sales and in techniques in building partnerships with supermarket managers.

What about Nestlé's information systems infrastructure? With 80 different information technology units, their information technology infrastructure has been described as a virtual Tower of Babel, with all types of hardware and software being used, including equipment from IBM, Hewlett-Packard, and

Digital Equipment Corporation (DEC) running both proprietary and open systems. Some of these systems were redundant. There was no way for developers to communicate with each other. Every time Nestlé makes another acquisition, this condition is made only worse.

Therefore, Nestlé has embarked upon a program to standardize and coordinate its information systems. The word *standardize* does not mean that everyone will do everything the same way. Rather, to Nestlé IS, standardization has several goals: First, standardization should promote communication between various units of the company, if for no other reason than that Vesey management needs to be able to communicate with its many units and to monitor and control their activities. Second, Nestlé's annual technology budget is more than 500 million Swiss francs, or about $350 million, and Manfred Kruger, assistant vice president of management services in Vesey, believes that IT standards will prove to be cost effective by eliminating redundancies and building more effective systems. The company has decided to move to a client/server environment internationally and, to that effect, has already established some standards, including Hewlett-Packard's HP-UX, IBM's AIX, and Digital Equipment Corporation's OSF/1 operating systems; Oracle Corporation's relational database management system; and Ernst & Young's Navigator Systems Series for development methodology and CASE tools. SAP's R/3 integrated material, distribution, and accounting application software package is mandatory in Europe, the United States, and Canada because it directly affects profitability and data-sharing (see the Chapter 11 ending case). However, the work of standardization has barely begun. They still need to establish standards in many other areas.

According to Jean-Claude Dispaux, Nestlé senior vice president and Kruger's boss, headquarters does have the power to enforce any standards they institute for all units of this global giant. All Nestlé really needs to do is block the IT budget of the noncomplying unit until it accepts the standards. However, this is rarely done. Nestlé prefers to push responsibility out to the countries. What Kruger does instead is to recommend standards. This approach reflects Kruger's personal philosophy that "nothing works if you don't get key players to agree." In addition, Kruger's experience has shown him that the staff in Vesey, Switzerland, is just too far away from most of the Nestlé locations to understand their problems. Previously, for example, when his organization had standardized on a specific microcomputer vendor, he heard a large outcry from the operating units. Ultimately his organization listened and replaced the recommended vendor with a list of recommended PCs from which the local units could select. For Nestlé, 100 percent standardization is not feasible.

The heart of Kruger's technology strategy is "a culture of working together" that reflects his belief that key players must agree. To develop a core application (whether in Vesey or elsewhere), IS gathers together a team representing a number of different organizations and the appropriate hardware and software technologies. The team will work to reach consensus on application requirements and development strategies. Once the application has been developed, it is sent to field organizations for adaptation. After modification to meet local needs, the appropriate version is deployed in various countries. For example, when corporate IS wanted to develop a lifecycle for corporate microcomputer development, Nestlé brought in 20 developers from eight countries. The result was a set of standards that have blended smoothly into different Nestlé units. ■

Sources: "Cross-border Confections," *Computerworld Client/Server Journal*, June 1995; Joshua Greenbaum, "Nestlé's Global Mix," *Information Week*, April 25, 1994; "Nestle Makes the Very Best . . . . Standard?" *Information Week*, August 23, 1993; and Carla Rappaport, "Nestlé's Brand Building Machine," *Fortune*, September 19, 1994.

Case Study Questions

1. What kind of global business strategy is Nestlé pursuing?
2. Do you think Nestlé's information systems strategy supports its global business strategy? How is it supportive? In what ways is it not supportive? What changes would you make to this strategy?
3. Do you think Kruger's approach to establishing and enforcing standards fits in well with Nestlé's global business strategy? Explain.
4. What management problems do you envision for Kruger's approach?
5. How do you think Nestlé should determine which new systems must conform to corporate information systems standards and which ones need not conform?

References

Cash, James I., F. Warren McFarlan, James L. McKenney, and Lynda M. Applegate. *Corporate Information Systems Management*, 3rd ed. Homewood, IL: Irwin (1992).

Chismar, William G., and Laku Chidambaram. "Telecommunications and the Structuring of U.S. Multinational Corporations." *International Information Systems* 1, no. 4 (October 1992).

Cox, Butler. *Globalization: The IT Challenge*. Sunnyvale, California: Amdahl Executive Institute (1991).

Deans, Candace P., and Michael J. Kane. *International Dimensions of Information Systems and Technology*. Boston, MA: PWS-Kent (1992).

Deans, Candace P., Kirk R. Karwan, Martin D. Goslar, David A. Ricks, and Brian Toyne. "Key International Issues in

U.S.-Based Multinational Corporations." *Journal of Management Information Systems* 7, no. 4 (Spring 1991).

Dutta, Amitava. "Telecommunications Infrastructure in Developing Nations." *International Information Systems* 1, no. 3 (July 1992).

Holland, Christopher, Geoff Lockett, and Ian Blackman. "Electronic Data Interchange Implementation: A Comparison of U.S. and European Cases." *International Information Systems* 1, no. 4 (October 1992).

Ives, Blake, and Sirkka Jarvenpaa. "Applications of Global Information Technology: Key Issues for Management." *MIS Quarterly* 15, no. 1 (March 1991).

Ives, Blake, and Sirkka Jarvenpaa. "Global Business Drivers: Aligning Information Technology to Global Business Strategy." *IBM Systems Journal* 32, no. 1 (1993).

Ives, Blake, and Sirkka Jarvenpaa. "Global Information Technology: Some Lessons from Practice." *International Information Systems* 1, no. 3 (July 1992).

Karin, Jahangir, and Benn R. Konsynski. "Globalization and Information Management Strategies." *Journal of Management Information Systems* 7 (Spring 1991).

Keen, Peter. *Shaping the Future*. Cambridge, MA: Harvard Business School Press (1991).

King, William R., and Vikram Sethi. "An Analysis of International Information Regimes." *International Information Systems* 1, no. 1 (January 1992).

Mannheim, Marvin L. "Global Information Technology: Issues and Strategic Opportunities." *International Information Systems* 1, no. 1 (January 1992).

Nelson, R. Ryan, Ira R. Weiss, and Kazumi Yamazaki. "Information Resource Management within Multinational Corporations: A Cross-Cultural Comparison of the U.S. and Japan." *International Information Systems* 1, no. 4 (October 1992).

Neumann, Seev. "Issues and Opportunities in International Information Systems." *International Information Systems* 1, no. 4 (October 1992).

Palvia, Shailendra, Prashant Palvia, and Ronald Zigli, eds. *The Global Issues of Information Technology Management*. Harrisburg, PA: Idea Group Publishing (1992).

Quelch, John A. and Lisa R. Klein. "The Internet and International Marketing." *Sloan Management Review* (Spring 1996).

Roche, Edward M. *Managing Information Technology in Multinational Corporations*. New York: Macmillan (1992).

Sadowsky, George. "Network Connectivity for Developing Countries." *Communications of the ACM* 36, no. 8 (August 1993).

Stahl, Stephanie. "Global Networks: The Headache Continues." *InformationWeek* (October 12, 1992).

Steinbart, Paul John, and Ravinder Nath. "Problems and Issues in the Management of International Data Networks." *MIS Quarterly* 16, no. 1 (March 1992).

Straub, Detmar W. "The Effect of Culture on IT Diffusion: E-Mail and FAX in Japan and the U.S." *Information Systems Research* 5, no. 1 (March 1994).

Tractinsky, Noan and Sirkka L. Jarvenpaa. "Information Systems Design Decisions in a Global Versus Domestic Context." *MIS Quarterly* 19, no. 4 (December 1995).

International Case Studies

*From Geelong and District Water Board to Barwon Water:
An Integrated IT Infrastructure*
Joel B. Barolsky and Peter Weill
University of Melbourne (Australia)

Ginormous Life Insurance Company
Len Fertuck
University of Toronto (Canada)

Kone Elevators
Tapio Reponen
**Turku School of Economics and
Business Administration (Finland)**

Festo Pneumatic
Helmut Krcmar and Bettina Schwarzer
University of Hohenheim (Germany)

Corning Telecommunications Division
**Andrew Boynton, University of North Carolina at Chapel Hill
and the International Institute for Management Development (Switzerland)
and Michael E. Shank, Renaissance Vision**

International Case Study 1

From Geelong and District Water Board to Barwon Water: An Integrated IT Infrastructure[1]

Joel B. Barolsky and Peter Weill, University of Melbourne (Australia)

Joe Adamski, the Geelong and District Water Board's (GDWB) Executive Manager Information Systems, clicked his mouse on the Phone Messages menu option. Two messages had been left. The first was from an IT manager of a large Sydney-based insurance company confirming an appointment to "visit the GDWB and to assess what the insurance company could learn from the GDWB's IT experience." The second was from the general manager of another large water board asking whether Adamski and his team could assist, on a consultancy basis, in their IT strategy formulation and implementation.

The site visit from the insurance company was the 35th such request the Board had received since the completion of the first stage of their IT infrastructure investment strategy in January 1992. These requests were a pleasant diversion, but the major focus of the GDWB's IT staff was to nurture and satisfy the increasing demands from the operational areas for building applications utilizing the newly installed IT infrastructure. The Water Board also faced the problem of balancing further in-house developments with external requests for consulting and demands from the GDWB's IT staff for new challenges and additional rewards.

ORGANIZATION BACKGROUND

The GDWB was constituted as a public utility of the Australian State of Victoria in July 1984, following an amalgamation of the Geelong Waterworks and Sewerage Trust and a number of other smaller regional water boards. The Board has the responsibility for the collection and distribution of water and the treatment and disposal of wastewater within a 1600-square-mile region in the southwest part of the State. In 1991 the permanent population serviced by the Board exceeded 200,000 people, this number growing significantly in the holiday periods with an influx of tourists.

The GDWB financed all its capital expenditure and operational expenditure through revenue received from its customers and through additional loan borrowings. Any profits generated were reinvested in the organization or used to pay off long-term debt. For the financial year 1990–91 the Board invested more than $35.3 million in capital works and spent more than $25 million in operating expenditure. Operating profit for the year 1990–91 exceeded $62.4 million on total assets of $292.5 million.

In 1992 the GDWB was headed by a Governing Board with a State Government-appointed chairperson and eight members, elected by the residents of the community, who each sat for a three-year term. Managerial and administrative responsibilities were delegated to the GDWB's Executive Group, which consists of the CEO and Executive Managers from each of the five operating divisions, namely Information Systems, Finance, Corporate Services, Engineering Development, and Engineering Operations. From 1981 to 1992 the number of GDWB employees across all divisions rose from 304 to 454.

The GDWB's head office, situated in the regional capital city of Geelong, housed most of the Board's customer service, administrative, engineering, IT, and other managerial staff. Complementing these activities, the GDWB operated five regional offices and a specialized 24-hour emergency contact service.

Commenting on the Board's competitive environment at the time, the GDWB's CEO, Geoff Vines, stated, "*Although the organization operated in a monopolistic situation there still were considerable pressures on us to perform efficiently. Firstly, and most importantly, our objective was to be self funding—our customers wouldn't tolerate indiscriminate rate increases as a result of our inefficiencies and we could not go cap in hand to the State Government. Secondly, the amalgamation trend of* water boards was continuing and the stronger the Board was, the less likely it would be a target of a takeover. And thirdly, we did in a sense compare ourselves with private sector organizations and in some ways with other water boards. We had limited resources and we have to make the most of them."

KEY PROBLEM AREAS

Relating the situation up until the mid-1980's, Vines said that the Board faced a major problem in collectively identifying its largest assets—the underground pipes, drains, pumps, sewers, and other facilities. He explained that most of these facilities were installed at least two or three meters below the surface and therefore it was almost impossible to gain immediate physical access to them. The exact specifications of each particular asset could only be ascertained through a thorough analysis of the original installation documentation and other geophysical surveys and maps of the area.

The limitations on identifying these underground facilities impacted operational performance in a number of key areas:

- Most of the maintenance work conducted by the Board was based on reactive responses to leaks and other faults in the systems. It was difficult to introduce a coordinated preventative maintenance program because it was not possible to accurately predict when a particular pipe or piece of equipment was nearing the end of its expected life span.
- Only a limited number of hard copies of this facility information could be kept. This significantly reduced the productivity of the engineering and operations staff, especially in remote areas where they had to request this information from the central record keeping systems. Backlogs and inaccuracies in filing also impacted efforts to repair, upgrade, or install new piping, pumps, and other equipment. On numerous occasions changes would be made to one set of plans without the same changes being recorded on the other copies of the same plans. Engineers designing improvements to existing facilities were often confronted with the problem of not being sure whether they were using the most up-to-date information of the facilities currently installed in the area concerned.
- The Board could not place realistic replacement values and depreciation charges on these underground assets.

With more than 100,000 rateable properties in its area of responsibility, the GDWB maintained a centralized paper filing system containing more than a billion pages of related property information. The documents, most of which were of different sizes, quality, and age, were divided into 95,000 different files and sorted chronologically within each file. Access to the documents was made difficult as larger documents were cumbersome to copy and older documents were beginning to disintegrate. Having just one physical storage area significantly increased the potential exposure to fire and other risks and limited the wider distribution and sharing of the information. In the early 1980s it was commonplace for a customer request for a statement of encumbrances placed at one of the GDWB's regional offices to take in excess of four weeks. The delays usually centered on finding the appropriate documents at the Property Services' central files, making the necessary copies, and transferring the documents back to the regional offices.

THE INFORMATION SYSTEMS DIVISION

In 1985 PA Consulting was commissioned to conduct a comprehensive review of the Board's strategy, management, operations structures, and systems. One of the recommendations made by the consultants was that the Board should institute a more systematic approach to strategic planning. A major outcome of the planning process that followed was to create a new division for computing services and to recruit a new manager for this new area who would report directly to the CEO. The EDP Division was created with the objectives of "satisfying the Board's Information System needs through the provision of integrated and secure corporate computer systems and communication network." Vines said that the Board needed a stand-alone information services group that could be used as a resource center for all users and that could add value to the work conducted by each functional group within the Board.

In April 1987 Joe Adamski was employed to fill the new position of EDP Manager (later changed to Executive Manager Information Systems). At the time of his arrival only a small part of the GDWB's work systems were computerized, the main components of which included the following:

- A low-end IBM System 38, primarily to run financial and other accounting software and some word processing applications. The System ran an in-house developed rate collection system which kept basic information on ratepayers including property details and consumption records
- Nineteen dumb terminals—none of the Board's regional offices had terminal access to the central computer systems
- A terminal link to the local university's DEC 20 computer to support the technical and laboratory services
- Four stand-alone PCs running some individual word processing packages as well as spreadsheet (Lotus 1-2-3), basic CAD, and database applications

Computer maintenance, support, and development was allocated to the Finance Division and delegated to an EDP supervisor (and three staff) who reported to the Finance Manager. Adamski noted, "*The computer set-up when I joined was pretty outdated and* inefficient. For example, the secretarial staff at Head Office were using the System 38's word processing facility and had to collect their dot-matrix printouts from the computer room situated on the ground floor of the five-story building. In the technical area, some water supply network analysis data was available through the use of the DEC 20 system; however, hard copy output had to be collected from the University, which was over five kilometers away. Most of the design engineers were using old drafting tables with rulers, erasers, and pencils as their only drafting tools."

Recognizing that some users required immediate solutions to problems they were facing, the Board purchased additional terminals, peripherals, and stand-alone microcomputers for the various areas thought to be in greatest need. Adamski said that these additional purchases further compounded some of the Board's computer-related problems. "We had a situation where we had at least four different CAD packages in use in different departments and we couldn't transfer data between them. There was a duplication of peripheral equipment with no sharing of printers, plotters, and other output devices. In addition, various managers began to complain that system expertise was too localized and that there was little compatibility between the various applications."

PLANNING THE NEW ROLE FOR *IT*

In July 1988 Adamski initiated a long-term computing strategy planning process with the establishment of a special planning project team with both IT and user representatives. The team embarked on a major program of interviews and discussion with all user areas within the Board. They investigated other similar public utilities across Australia to assess their IT strategies and infrastructures and made contact with various computer hardware and software vendors to determine the latest available technologies and indicative costs.

The Project Team developed a comprehensive corporate computing strategy that would provide, as Adamski put it, the "quantum leap forward in the Board's IT portfolio." Adamski said that central to the computing strategy that was devised was that there should be as much integration and flexibility as possible in all the Board's technical and administrative systems. "*Linked to this strategy was the notion that we should strive for an open-systems approach with all our applications. This meant that each system had to have publicly specifiable interfaces, or hooks so that each system could talk to each other. From the users' perspective an open systems approach meant that all the different applications looked pretty much the same and it was easy to cross over from one to the other. It also meant that if we weren't happy with one particular product within the portfolio or we wanted to add a new one, we could do it without too much disruption to the whole system.*"

He continued, "*A key decision was made that we should build on our existing IT investments. With this in mind we had to make sure that the new systems were able to use the data and communicate with the System 38. We wanted only one hardware platform using only one operating system and only one relational database management system (RDBMS). We also wanted only one homogenous network that was able to cater to a number of protocols and interfaces, such as the network system for the microcomputers, workstations, and the Internet connection. There also had to be a high degree of compatibility and interaction with all the data files and applications that were proposed. In view of this, we chose a UNIX platform with a client/server architecture.*"

In addition to specifying the software components of the system, the Project Team outlined the hardware that was necessary to run the new systems and the additional staff that needed to be hired. To achieve the stated computing strategies and benefits, the Team also recommended that implementation take place over three key stages, with a formal progress review instituted at the end of each stage.

APPROVAL

In February 1989 the corporate computing strategy planning process was completed and Adamski presented the key recommendations to the Governing Board. In his presentation Adamski stated that the infrastructure cost of implementing the strategy was estimated to be about $5 million for the entire project (excluding data capture costs) and that the project would take up to the end of 1995 for full commissioning.

Vines stated, "*From my perspective, the proposed IT strategy took into account the critical functions in the organization that needed to be supported, such as customer services, asset management and asset creation. These were fundamental components of the Board's corporate objectives and the computer strategy provided a means to realize these objectives and provide both short- and long-term benefits. There were some immediate short-term benefits, such as securing property services data that had no backup, and productivity gains in design and electronic mail. From a long-term perspective, I believe you can never really do an accurate rate-of-return calculation and base your decision solely on that. If you did you probably would never make such a large capital investment in IT. We did try to cost-justify all the new systems as best we could but we stressed that implementing IT strategy should be seen as providing long-term benefits for the entire organization that were not immediately measurable and would come to fruition many years later. Until all the information was captured and loaded on the IT facilities from the manual systems, the full benefits could not be realized.*"

Following an extensive and rigorous tendering process, it was decided that the Board should follow a multi-vendor solution, because no one vendor could provide a total solution. Sun Micro systems was selected as the major hardware vendor and was asked to act as prime contractors in implementation. As prime contractors Sun was paid one project fee and then negotiated separate contracts with all other suppliers.

IMPLEMENTATION

In April 1990 the implementation of the IT strategy commenced with the delivery of the Sun file servers and workstations and installation of a homogenous network throughout the Board. Adamski said that the implementation stage went surprisingly smoothly. *"We didn't fire anybody as a direct result of the new systems, but jobs were changed. There was some resistance to the new technology—most of it was born out of unfamiliarity and fear of not having the appropriate skills. Some people were very committed in doing things 'their way.' When some of these people started to perceive tangible productivity benefits, their perspectives started to change. We tried to counsel people as best we could and encourage them to experiment with the new systems. Most people eventually converted but there were still some objectors."*

Adamski added that while they were implementing the new systems it was important for the IS Division not to lose sight of its key objectives and role within the organization. *"We had to make sure that we didn't get carried away with the new whiz-bang technology and reduce our support and maintenance of the older, more conventional systems. For example, the Board went onto a new tariff system and we had to make significant changes to our rating system to accommodate this. Having an application generator in place significantly improved the systems upgrade time."*

In May 1992 the Board's computer facilities included 4 Sun file servers, 80 Sun workstations, 100 microcomputers, 40 terminals, and the IBM System 38 Model 700. By this time the IS Division had implemented the following components of the systems (see Figure 1 for a schematic of the systems).

1. A **Document Imaging Processing System (DIPS)** used for scanning, storing, and managing all documents on each property within the GDWB region, which were being kept in 95,000 separate paper files. This system was also used for the storage, backup, and retrieval of 25,000 engineering plans and drawings. DIPS gave designated Head Office departments and regional offices real-time access to all property documentation and allowed them to print out scanned images when required. The system had a sophisticated indexing system that facilitated easy retrieval of stored images by users and access by other programs. Figure 2 presents a copy of a property plan from DIPS.

2. A digital mapping **Facilities Information System (FIS)** that provided for the storage, management, and ongoing maintenance of all graphic

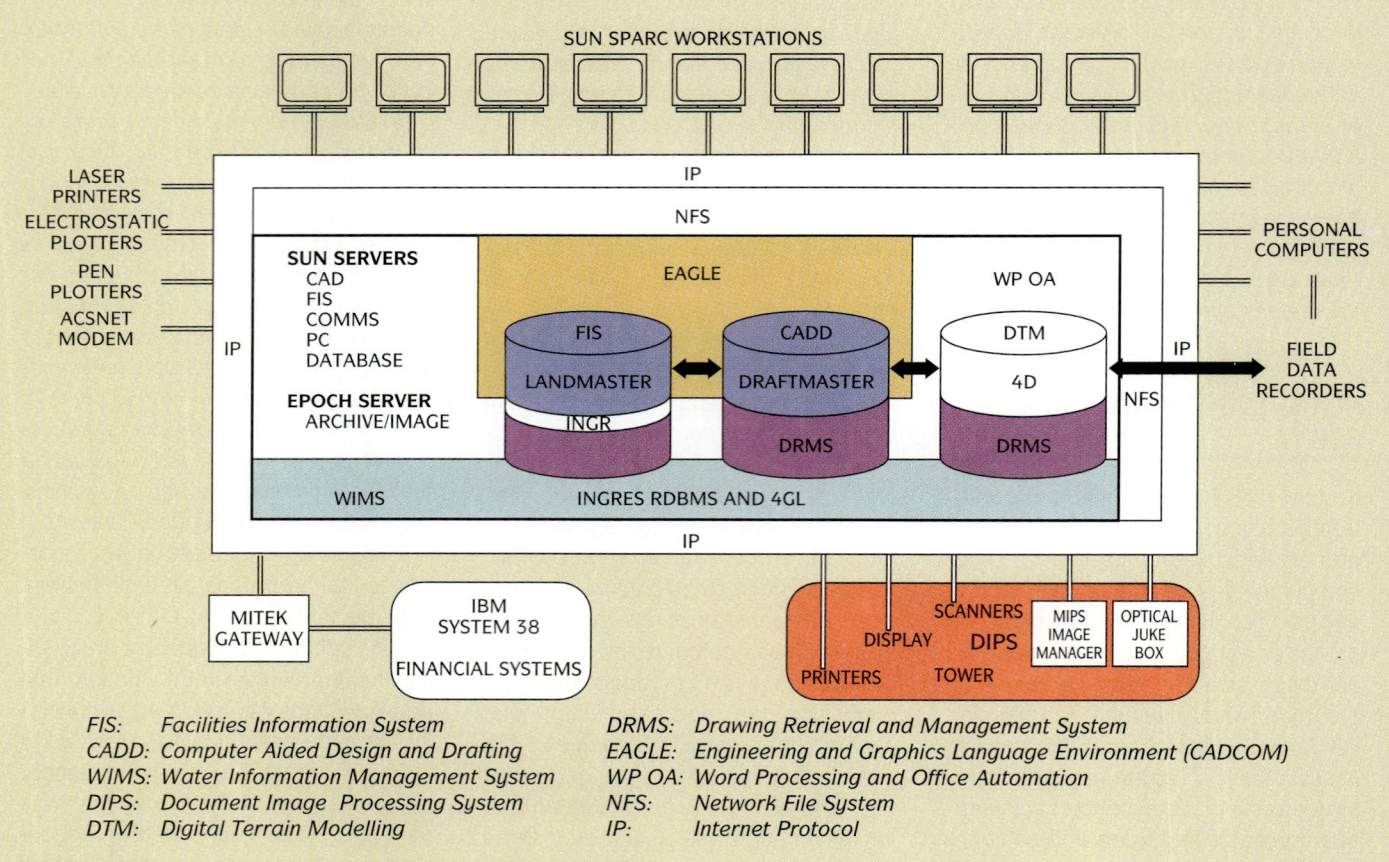

FIGURE 1
GDWB corporate computing system.

FIS: Facilities Information System
CADD: Computer Aided Design and Drafting
WIMS: Water Information Management System
DIPS: Document Image Processing System
DTM: Digital Terrain Modelling
DRMS: Drawing Retrieval and Management System
EAGLE: Engineering and Graphics Language Environment (CADCOM)
WP OA: Word Processing and Office Automation
NFS: Network File System
IP: Internet Protocol

FIGURE 2
Example of a building plan kept for each rateable property.

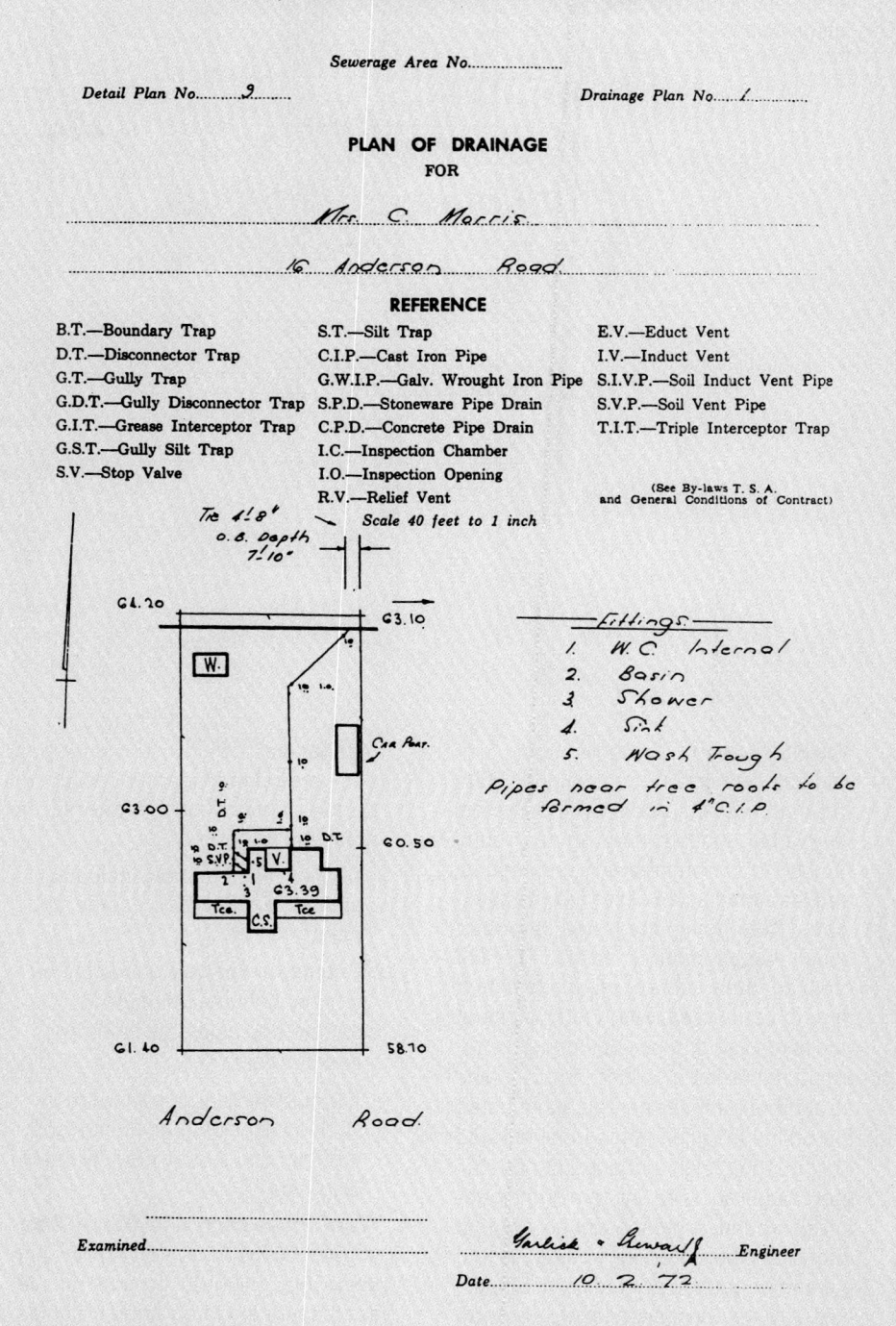

(map-related) and nongraphic information relating to water and wastewater services, property information, property boundaries, and easements throughout the Board's region. The FIS system provided a computerized, seamless geographic map covering the entire GDWB region. The system encompassed the storing of all maps in digital form and attaching map coordinates to each digital point. Every point on a digital map was linked to a unique X and Y coordinate, based on the standard Australian Mapping Grid system, and had a specific address linked to it. Once each point on a map was precisely addressed and identified, specific attributes were attached to it. These attributes were then used as methods of recording information or used as indexes for access to/by other programs; for example, sewer pipe details, property details, water consumption, vertical heights above sea level, and so on. The selected map area with all the related attributes and information was then displayed graphically in full color on a high-resolution workstation monitor (see Figure 3).

From Geelong and District Water Board to Barwon Water

FIGURE 3
Illustration of the type of information available on the Facilities Information System.

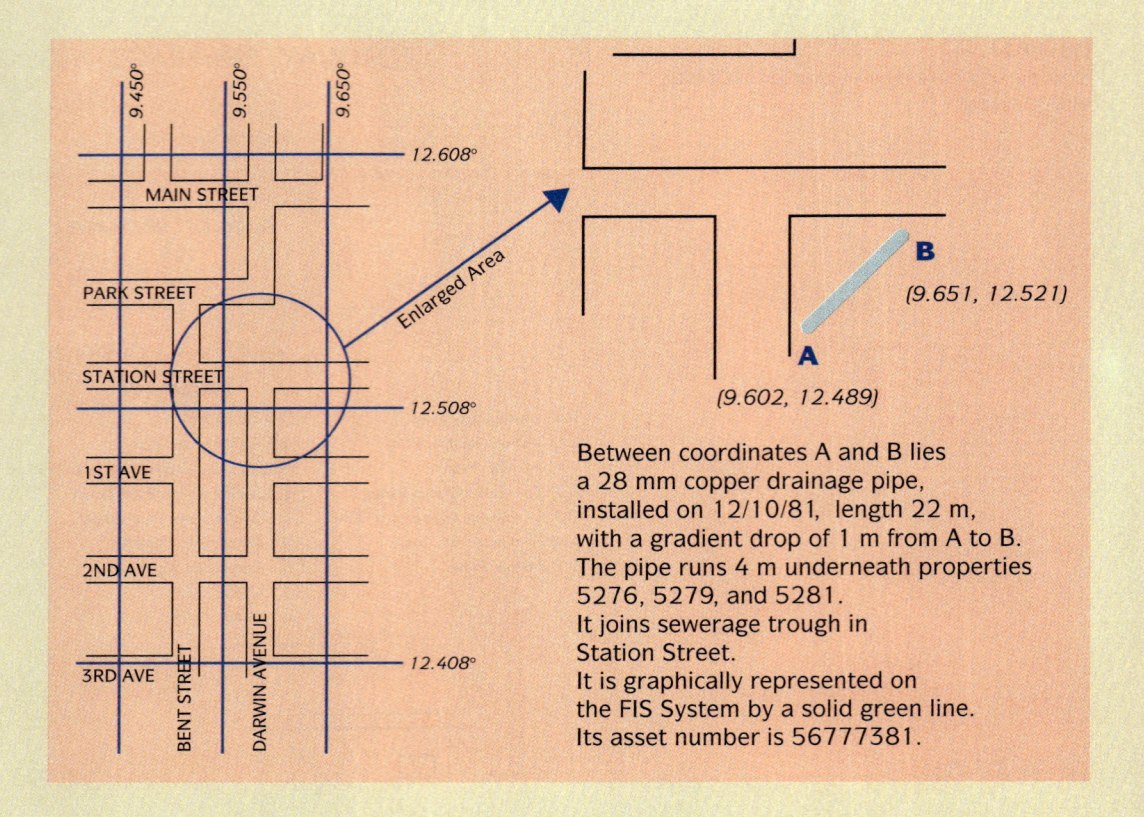

[Map showing streets: Main Street, Park Street, Station Street, 1st Ave, 2nd Ave, 3rd Ave, intersecting with Bent Street and Darwin Avenue. Coordinates shown: 9.450°, 9.550°, 9.650°, 12.608°, 12.508°, 12.408°. Enlarged area shows points A (9.602, 12.489) and B (9.651, 12.521).]

Between coordinates A and B lies a 28 mm copper drainage pipe, installed on 12/10/81, length 22 m, with a gradient drop of 1 m from A to B. The pipe runs 4 m underneath properties 5276, 5279, and 5281. It joins sewerage trough in Station Street. It is graphically represented on the FIS System by a solid green line. Its asset number is 56777381.

The FIS allowed cross-referencing to financial, rating, and consumption data (through indexing) held on the System 38. It also enabled each underground facility to be numbered, catalogued, and identified as an asset with its associated data being integrated into other asset management systems. The FIS enabled data stored on a particular map to be layered, with water pipes at one layer, sewer pipes at another, property boundaries at a third, future plans at another, and so on. This gave users the ability to recall maps in layers and to select the level and amount of detail they required. The system was centered around a mouse-driven graphic interface where the user zoomed in and out and/or panned around particular areas—at the broadest level, showing the whole of southern Victoria, and at the most detailed, the individual plumbing and drainage plan of one particular property (through cross-referencing to the DIPS system).

3. A **Computer Aided Design and Drafting (CADD)** system that provided an integrated programmable 3D environment for a range of civil, mechanical, electrical, surveying, and general engineering design and drafting applications. It offered the following features:
   - Display manipulation, including multiple angle views, zooms, and pans
   - Geometric analysis, including automatic calculation of areas, perimeters, moments of inertia, and centroids
   - Various customization features, such as user-defined menus and prompts and a user-friendly macro language
4. **Word Processing and Office Automation (WP/OA)** systems providing users the ability to prepare quality documentation integrating graphics, spreadsheets, mail merge, and databases, as well as other utilities such as electronic mail and phone message handling.
5. A **Relational Database Management System and a Fourth-Generation Language** as a base foundation for the development of new applications. Some of the RDBMS applications included the following:
   - A Drawing and Retrieval Management System (DRMS) to control the development, release, and revision of all CADD projects and files
   - A Water Information Management System (WIMS) used for the storage and management of hydrographic engineering and laboratory data, both current and historical

OUTCOMES

Vines said that one of the most important strategic outcomes of the changes introduced had been the way in which decision making at all levels within the organization had been enhanced. "*This improvement is largely due to the fact that people have now got ready access to information they have never had before. This information is especially useful in enhancing our ability to forward plan. The flow and reporting of financial information has also speeded up, and we now complete our final accounts up to two months earlier than we used to. In the areas that have come on-line* there has been a definite improvement in productivity and in customer service. The CADD system, for example, is greatly enhancing our ability to design and plan new facilities. The turnaround time, the accuracy of the plans, and the creativity of the designers have been improved dramatically. In many departments there has been a change in work practices—some of the mundane activities are handled by the computer, allowing more productive work to be carried out, like spending more time with customers. Our asset management and control also started to improve. There was greater integrity in the information kept, and having just one central shared record meant that updating with new data or changes to existing data was far more efficient."

Adamski added that the initial reaction by Board staff to the whole corporate computing strategy "ranged from scepticism to outright hostility." He continued, "By the end of 1991 I would say that there had been a general reversal in attitude. Managers started to queue outside my office asking if we could develop specific business applications for them. They had begun to appreciate what the technology could do and most often they suddenly perceived a whole range of opportunities and different ways in which they could operate. One manager asked me, for example, if we could use document imaging technology to eliminate the need for any physical paper flows within his office. Technically this was possible, but it was not really cost-justifiable and the corporate culture would not really have supported it. Putting together the IS Division budget is now a difficult balancing act with a whole range of options and demands from users. I now ask the users to justify the benefits to be derived from new application proposals, and I help out with the cost side. Cost/benefit justification usually drives the decisions as well as the fit with the existing IT and other corporate objectives. What also must be considered is that these objectives are not written in stone. They are flexible and can and should adjust to changes in both the internal and external environment."

A number of GDWB staff indicated that the new systems had enhanced their ability to fulfill their work responsibilities:

- A customer service officer at one of the Board's regional offices stated that the DIPS had enabled her to respond to customer requests for encumbrance statements within a matter of minutes instead of weeks. She added that a number of customers had sent letters to their office complimenting them on the improvements in the service they received. She said that the new DIPS system had flow-on benefits that weren't fully recognized. She cited a case where local architects were able to charge their clients less because they had more ready access to information from the GDWB.

- A maintenance manager declared that the FIS system had enabled his department to predict when pipes and drains should be replaced before they actually ruptured or broke down by examining their installation dates and the types of materials used. He said that this process over time started to shift the emphasis of his department's maintenance work from being reactive to being more preventative. He added that the system also enabled him to easily identify and contact the residents that would be affected by the work that the Board was going to do in a particular area. He said that the FIS enabled him to plot out with his mouse a particular area of a map on his screen. It would then pick up all the relevant properties in the area and identify the names and addresses of the current ratepayers residing in those properties.

- A secretary to a senior head office manager said that despite being a little daunted at first by the new word processing system, she felt that the system had helped her considerably. She said that besides the obvious benefits in being able to prepare and edit documents on a WYSIWYG screen, she also had the ability of viewing as well as integrating scanned property plans, correspondence, and other documents from the DIPS System.

Adamski said that one of the flow-on benefits from the FIS system in particular was that the Board had the potential of selling the information stored on the system to municipal councils and other public utilities, such as Telecom, the State Electricity Commission, and the Gas and Fuel Corporation. He added that they had also considered marketing the information to private organizations, such as building managers, architects, and property developers, and that the return from these sales could significantly reduce the overall costs in developing the FIS system.

THE FUTURE

Commenting on the future prospects for the Board's IS Division, Adamski said, "There are some very complex applications that we are developing, but we now have the skills, the tools, and the infrastructure to develop them cost-effectively and to ensure that they deliver results. I think one of the main reasons why we are in this fortuitous position is that we chose a UNIX platform with client/server processing and a strong networking backbone. It gives us the flexibility and integration that we set out to achieve and we will need in the future to realize both our long- and short-term objectives. It's a lot easier now to cost-justify requests for new applications. The challenges ahead lie in three areas. First, it's going to be difficult to consistently satisfy all our users' needs in that their expectations will be increasing all the time and they will become more demanding. We have to recognize these demands and at the same time keep investing in and maintaining our infrastructure. Secondly, we still have some way to go in developing a total corporate management information system. There are still some islands of data floating around and the challenge is to get it all integrated. And thirdly, as the most senior IT manager at the Board, I have to make sure that we retain our key IT staff and we compensate them adequately, both monetarily and in providing them stimulating and demanding work."

The Geelong and District Water Board changed its name to Barwon Water in February 1994. The name change reflected the change in the organization's governance structure with the appointment by the State Government of a professional, skills-based Governing Board to replace the community-elected members. This initiative was part of a broader Government strategy to commercialize state-owned utilities and to strive for greater efficiencies and productivity across the whole public service.

Four months after the name change, Geoff Vines retired and was replaced by Dennis Brockenshire as Barwon Water's Chief Executive. Brockenshire, formerly a senior manager with the State Electricity Commission, had considerable business and engineering experience relating to large-scale supply systems serving a large customer base. Commenting on Barwon Water's Information Technology (IT) infrastructure, Brockenshire stated, "*Barwon Water has made and continues to make a significant investment in IT. The organization has spent something in the region of $7 to $10 million in building its IT infrastructure and has recurrent costs of 3 percent of total expenditure. I want to make sure we get an appropriate return for this investment. It is critical that IT delivers real business benefits. Since I've come into this role, I have insisted that my line managers justify any new IT investment on the grounds of the business value it will create.*"

From the period 1992 to 1995, Barwon Water's Information Systems (IS) department had focused most of its efforts in capturing all the relevant mapping, customer, and facilities data for its key systems. Significant resources were allocated to utilize the existing IT infrastructure to improve customer service and to streamline work-flows. Improvements in security were also a major priority, given the confidential and private nature of information stored on the various databases and the listing of Barwon Water's home page on the World Wide Web. In terms of hardware and software, the IBM System 38 was replaced by a Sun Server running the Prophecy accounting package in a UNIX operating environment. The IS department had commenced work on an executive information system to assist with cost and performance measurement, particularly at the business unit level. This system would provide the core information to support a major benchmarking exercise in which Barwon Water compared its performance on key processes to other organizations, both within and external to the water industry.

Business processes were mapped and examined where steps could be eliminated or substituted by new IT applications. An interesting example of this was the introduction of a paperless encumbrance certificating system. In this system a solicitor handling a property matter could interact with Barwon Water via fax without the need to actually visit an office. All documents sent to and from Barwon Water, and those transferred within the organization, were accomplished entirely on the system with no need to print a hard copy. Processing times for these applications were reduced from an average of 10 days to a few hours.

A number of other efficiency gains were realized with the utilization of the IT infrastructure. The productivity of the engineering design staff increased by 20 to 50 percent for most drawings and by 90 percent for re-drawings. The systems' distributed computing design also reduced design cycles by enabling staff to share files and work on a common file to avoid duplicated effort. Overall staff numbers with Barwon Water had dropped to 400 by July 1995. Adamski said that while the total reduction in staff numbers could not be directly attributed to the new systems, there were several areas where staff had been made redundant or redeployed. He said that in many cases the systems freed up front-line service personnel to spend more time listening and being responsive to customer concerns.

Barwon Water continued to receive acclaim for its innovative IT systems. In 1994 it was awarded the Geelong Business Excellence Award in the Innovation Systems/Development of Technology category. It also received a nomination for the award for innovation by the Washington-based Smithsonian Institute.[2]

A major organizational restructuring in early 1995 saw Joe Adamski take over the responsibility for strategic planning as well as information systems. Adamski said that this restructure ensured that IT developments would be closely aligned with broader business objectives and strategies. As part of the restructuring, new business units were formed with the managers of these units made accountable for both revenue and cost items.

Commenting on future challenges, Adamski outlined his vision for Barwon Water as the computing center for the Greater Geelong region. "*Geelong and district covers 4000 square kilometers. Within this region there has recently been an amalgamation of councils into two supercouncils—the City of Greater Geelong and the Surf Coast Council. These two organizations serve the same customers as ourselves. We have articulated what we see as benefits of using common databases, mapping, and other information to serve these customers. Suggested benefits include a service shopfront where customers could pay rates, water tariffs, and apply for property approvals at the same place. These systems we now have in place at Barwon Water would be a good starting point in building this regional concept. Data is our most valuable asset and there is no point in duplicating it.*"[3]

---

[1]This case study was prepared by Joel B. Barolsky and Professor Peter Weill as part of the Infrastructure Study funded by IBM Consulting Group (International). It should be read in conjunction with the Geelong and District Water Board—Information Technology Management (CL298—1992) case. Both

these cases were written as the basis of discussion rather than to illustrate either effective or ineffective handling of a managerial situation. © 1995 Joel Barolsky, Peter Weill, Melbourne Business School Limited, The University of Melbourne.

[2] The original case study written by Barolsky and Weill on Geelong and District Water Board was awarded the Australian Computer Society prize for Best IT Case Study in 1993.

[3] "IT Manager Leads Corporate Plan to Water," *MIS,* April 1994, 41–46.

Case Study Questions

1. Describe the Geelong and District Water Board and the environment in which it operates. What problems did GDWB have before 1988? What were the management, organization, and technology factors that contributed to those problems?

2. Describe the role of information systems at GDWB and the GDWB's information system portfolio before July 1988.

3. Describe and critique the process of upgrading GDWB's information systems portfolio.

4. How did the water board justify its investments in new information system technology? What were the benefits?

International Case Study 2

Ginormous Life Insurance Company

Len Fertuck, University of Toronto (Canada)

Ginormous Life is an insurance company with a long tradition. The company has four divisions. Each operates its own computers. The IS group provides analysis, design, and programming services to all the divisions. The divisions are actuarial, marketing, operations, and investment, and they are all located at the corporate headquarters building. Marketing also has field offices in twenty cities across the country.

The Actuarial Division is responsible for the design and pricing of new kinds of policies. They use purchased industry data and weekly summaries of data obtained from the Operations Division. They have their own DEC minicomputer, running the UNIX operating system, to store data files. They do most of their analysis on microcomputers and Sun workstations, either on spreadsheets or with a specialized interactive language called *APL*.

The Marketing Division is responsible for selling policies to new customers and for follow-up of existing customers in case they need changes to their current insurance. All sales orders are sent to the Operations Division for data entry and billing. They use purchased external data for market research and weekly copies of data from operations for follow-ups. They have their own DEC VAX minicomputer with dumb terminals for clerks to enter sales data. There are also many microcomputers used to analyze market data using statistical packages such as SAS.

The Operations Division is responsible for processing all mission-critical financial transactions, including payroll. They record all new policies, send regular bills to customers, evaluate and pay all claims, and cancel lapsed policies. They have all their data and programs on a large IBM ES/9000 mainframe. The programs are often huge and complex because they must service not only the 15 products currently being sold, but also the 75 old kinds of policies that are no longer being sold but still have existing policy holders. Clerks use dumb terminals to enter and update data. Application programs are almost always written in COBOL. Some recent applications have used an SQL relational database to store data, but most use COBOL flat files. The average age of the transaction-processing programs is about ten years.

The Investment Division is responsible for investing premiums until they are needed to pay claims. Their data consists primarily of internal portfolio data and research data obtained by direct links to financial data services. They have a DEC minicomputer to store their data. The internal data are received by a weekly download of cash flows from the Operations Division. External data are obtained as needed. They use minicomputers to analyze data obtained from the mini or from commercial data services.

A controlling interest in Ginormous Life has recently been purchased by Financial Behemoth Corp. The management of Financial Behemoth has decided that the firm's efficiency and profitability must be improved. Their first move has been to put Dan D. Mann, a hotshot information systems specialist from Financial Behemoth, in charge of the Information Systems Division. He has been given the objective of modernizing and streamlining the computer facilities without any increase in budget.

In his first week on the job, Dan discovered that none of the staff of 200 information systems specialists knew anything about CASE tools, end-user computing, or LANs. All microcomputer applications have been purchased, and no one has experience in implementing microcomputer systems. There is no evidence of any formal Decision-Support Systems or Executive Information Systems in the organization. There have been a few tentative experiments with DB2, a relational database product, purchased from IBM, their mainframe vendor. Most managers say that "they do not need all those fancy Executive Information Systems." They would be happy if Information Systems would just provide basic reports on the financial performance of each product line and customer group.

There have been some problems with these systems. Maintenance is difficult and costly because almost every change to the data structure of applications in operations requires corresponding changes to applications in the other divisions. There has been a growing demand in other divisions for faster access to operations data. For instance, the Investment Division claims that they could make more profitable investments if they had continuous access to the cash position in operations. Marketing complains that they get calls from clients about claims and cannot answer them because they do not have current access to the status of the claim. Management wants current access to a wide variety of data in summary form so they can get a better understanding of the business. The IS group says that it would be difficult to provide access to data in operations because of security considerations. It is difficult to ensure that users do not make unauthorized changes to the COBOL files.

The IS group complains that they cannot deliver all the applications the users want because they are short-staffed. They spend 90 percent of their time maintaining the existing systems, most of which are in the COBOL language. The programmers are mostly old and experienced, and employee turnover is unusually low, so there is not likely to be much room for improvement by further training in programming. Morale is generally good despite the perception of overwork. Employees often remark that the company is a very pleasant and benevolent place to work. At least, they did until rumors of deregulation and foreign competition started to sweep the industry.

Dan began to look for ways to solve the many problems of the Information Systems Division. He solicited proposals from various vendors and consultants in the computer industry. After a preliminary review of the proposals, Dan was left with three broad options suggested by IBM, Oracle Corp., and Systemotion, a local consulting firm. The proposals are briefly described below.

IBM proposed an integrated solution using IBM hardware and software. The main elements of their proposal are as follows:

- **Data and applications will remain on a mainframe.** The IBM ES/9000 series of hardware running their proprietary operating system will provide mainframe services. Mainframe hardware capacity will have to be approximately doubled. AS/400 minicomputers running under the OS/400 operating system will replace DEC minicomputers. RS/6000 workstations running AIX, a flavor of the UNIX operating system, can be used for actuarial computations. All hardware will be interconnected with IBM's proprietary SNA network architecture. Microcomputers will run under the OS/2 operating system and the IBM LAN Server to support both Microsoft Windows applications and locally designed applications that communicate with mainframe databases.

- **A DB2 relational database will store all data on-line.** Users will be able to access any data they need through their terminals or through microcomputers that communicate with the mainframe.

- **Legacy systems will be converted using reengineering tools,** such as Design Recovery and Maintenance Workbench from Intersolve, Inc. Using these will provide the advantage that they will continue to use the COBOL code that the existing programmers are familiar with. New work will be done using CASE tools with code generators that produce COBOL code.

- **Proven technology.** The IBM systems are widely used by many customers and vendors. Many mission-critical application programs are available on the market that address a wide variety of business needs.

Oracle Corp. proposed that all systems be converted to use their Oracle database product and its associated screen and report generators. They said that such a conversion would have the following advantages:

- **Over 75 hardware platforms are supported.** This means that the company is no longer bound to stay with a single vendor. Oracle databases and application programs can be easily moved from one manufacturer's machine to another manufacturer's machine by a relatively simple export-and-import operation as long as applications are created with Oracle tools. Thus the most economical hardware platform can be used for the application. Oracle will also access data stored in an IBM DB2 database.

- **Integrated CASE tools and application generators.** Oracle has its own CASE tool and its own form and report generators. Databases designed with the Oracle CASE tool can be automatically created in an Oracle database using CASE*Generator. SQL*Forms, one of their application generation tools, can design and generate screens for a wide variety of terminals. The same design can be implemented on dumb terminals, a Macintosh, X Windows in UNIX, or Systems Application Architecture (SAA) in an IBM environment. Applications are created using graphic tools that eliminate the need for a language like COBOL. In fact, the programmer cannot see the underlying language that is being used for implementation. The designer works entirely with visual prototyping specifications. SQL*ReportWriter can generate reports in the same way.

- **Vertically integrated applications.** Oracle sells a number of common applications, such as accounting programs, that can be used as building blocks in developing a complete system. These applications could eliminate the need to redevelop some applications.

- **Distributed network support.** A wide variety of common network protocols such as SNA, DecNet, Novell, and TCP/IP are supported. Different parts of the database can be distributed to different machines on the network and accessed or updated by any application. Access can be controlled at the file, record, or field level for each user on the system. All data is stored on-line for instant access. The data can be stored on one machine and the applications can be run on a different machine, including a microcomputer or workstation, to provide a client/server environment. The ability to distribute a database allows a large database on an expensive mainframe to be distributed to a number of cheaper minicomputers.

Systemotion proposed a state-of-the-art system using the Sybase Object Oriented Relational Data Base Management System (OORDBMS) with applications implemented in a Microsoft Windows environment. This proposal offers the following advantages:

- **A modern object-oriented database.** Sybase is a relatively new entrant in the database field so it is able to exploit the benefits of an object-oriented approach without having to worry about a large number of legacy applications already coded in an older non-object-oriented version. This means that it is possible to include complex validation rules in the database rather than having to code them in the application code. This reduces application testing and speeds development as well as improving data integrity.

- **Client/server systems.** Since Sybase is object-oriented, it is a natural product for a client/server environment. It becomes particularly easy to install the database on a server (commonly one or more Hewlett-Packard or DEC minicomputers) and place the applications and entry screens on microcomputers or workstations like those from Sun Microsystems. Object-oriented applications can be easily built using graphic languages such as Power Builder or Visual Basic. The database can be easily extended to store graphics such as photos or scanned documents. This could allow business reengineering to reduce the paper burden that is common in insurance firms. The client applications would run on a LAN with Microsoft SQL Server, a networked relational DBMS server.

- **Open UNIX environment.** Many programs have been written for the UNIX operating system. UNIX can be run on many different hardware platforms and network communication systems. This openness will make it possible to integrate applications on a number of platforms while obtaining the cost benefits of downsizing to smaller platforms.

- **Easy integration with purchased Windows applications.** The object-oriented approach meshes well with the Windows environment that has a feature called Object Linking and Embedding (OLE), which permits direct reference from one Windows software product to another. Thus, it is quite easy to write a program that obtains data from a central database and brings it into a spreadsheet such as Excel, where it can be analyzed, manipulated, or graphed. The graph, in turn, can be embedded in a word processor report. If new data are downloaded into the spreadsheet, the graph will automatically be updated whenever the report is opened in the word processor. This makes it easy to satisfy management needs for information within the word-processing or spreadsheet environment they are familiar with. It also makes it relatively easy to create customized management and executive information systems. In addition, many functions can be performed directly by purchased Windows programs to eliminate the need to design, build, and maintain many applications.

Dan is not sure which approach to take for the future of Ginormous Life. He appreciates that whichever route he follows, the technology will have an enormous impact on the kinds of applications his staff will be able to produce in the future and the way in which they will produce them. He is concerned about industry trends toward downsizing and distribution of systems. While this trend may eventually prove to be more efficient, his staff does not have much experience with the new technologies that would be required. He is uncertain about whether there would be a sufficient payoff to justify the organizational turmoil that would result from a major change in direction.

Dan must prepare a strategy for the renewal of the Information Systems Division over the next three years. As his assistant, he has asked you to address the following questions.

Case Study Questions

1. Prepare a list of factors or issues that must be considered in developing a strategy and selecting a technology platform for Ginormous.

2. Analyze how each of the three proposals performs on each factor or issue. If you find issues that a proposal fails to address, advise Dan as to the significance of the omission and how you think the proposal might be modified to address that issue.

3. Advise Dan on special criteria, if any, that he might need to apply when evaluating a proposal for a companywide information strategy coming from a technology vendor. Explain your reasoning.

4. Assuming Dan were to make his decision without seeking further information from the proposers, recommend to him which proposal he should accept and your reason for selecting that proposal.

5. Based upon your advice in the previous question, state the order in which each component of the new technology should be introduced and the reason for selecting the order.

International Case Study 3

Kone Elevators

Tapio Reponen, Turku School of Economics and Business Administration (Finland)

Elevators are products that are made according to customer specification. Each building is different, and the products have to fit the building's structure and framework. However, the elevator components can often be selected from a range of standard components either in predefined sets (preengineered, standard elevators) or in custom-made combinations (nonstandard elevators). The following description illustrates how information systems can support the process of elevator sales, order, and delivery at Kone Elevators, an international elevator manufacturer with headquarters in Helsinki, Finland.

"Kone Lifts, good morning. Larry Liftagain speaking. How can I help you?"

"Good morning. This is Mr. Beaver from Bayswater Builders. I would like to have a quotation for a lift for our new project, please."

The preengineered elevator sale is usually handled by the salesman himself, using tools, materials, and procedures provided by sales support, engineering, and manufacturing. If the salesman needs additional information or if the equipment is outside the preengineered range, he contacts the engineering department for further calculations and specifications.

Larry's sales tool kit consists of his PC with its tendering system, traffic analysis and simulation programs, price and material lists, and his sales guide and technical information binders. He also needs tools to communicate with his own back-up in sales support and in engineering. This is possible either by electronic mail and messaging systems or by conventional phone and fax. Finally, he will enter the order received in the Order book and project management system, where the elevator will be managed and followed up from the specification throughout material order, installation, and testing to final handover to the customer. After customer handover the data is transferred to the maintenance and call-out system for the guarantee period and often beyond.

Tender Enquiry

"Yes, Mr. Beaver, we will be pleased to provide you with a quotation, but I'll need some information from you to specify the type of the lift. What type of building are we dealing with?"

"A small office building, with six floors."

"How many occupants will there be on each floor? Have you reserved any space for the lift shaft and the machine room? Is the machine room on the top or at the bottom of the building?"

Tender Preparation

Larry has obtained all the data that he needs: the customer details, building drawings, and the specification request from the architect or consultant. He inputs these to the tendering system. The elevator type, load, travel height, and number of stops provide the basic range and specification. The further items to be specified are the door type, width, height, control features, elevator car interior, signals, and push buttons on the car and landings. The specification is made by selecting from a predefined list of items. If the item combinations are restricted or not allowed, a message will be displayed. If the customer requests a feature that does not appear on the standard list, it can either be added as a local item, which will be purchased from a subcontractor, or the salesman can ask for a specification from the Kone factory.

Based on the items selected, the basic tender price is calculated. The price includes the value of materials, which can be partly from a Kone factory and partly from local subcontractors; the installation and labor cost; elevator service during the guarantee period; and any adjustable items for market area or building customer type, possibly indexing and discounts included.

The tender documents will be produced by combining the selected values and parameters to predefined letter and text blocks in word processing. The tender letters and technical description of the items tendered can be modified by the salesman if required to suit this particular customer and project.

Tender Follow-Up and Negotiation

"Good morning, Larry! Nice Monday! The sun is shining and the sky is blue! What's up this week?"

"Good morning, boss! I just printed out my action list for this week. The first thing I'll do is to follow up a tender I sent to Bayswater Builders last week. Then I have another three outstanding tenders that I need to track. The project we tendered in Brighton is due to be decided this week and I'm 90-percent sure we're going to get it."

When the tenders are registered in the salesman's system, the follow-up and updating of data can take place in an organized way. During the negotiations the elevator specifications often change, alternative options are submitted to the customer, the price is negotiated, and the schedules and installation programs are agreed on. All changes and modifications are done by changing parameters in the original tender. Different versions are saved and the full tender history is available for sales managers and salesmen themselves, if required.

Order Booking

"Good afternoon, Mr. Liftagain, this is Mr. Beaver from Bayswater Builders. At our meeting this morning we decided to give the lift order to Kone, for the price and specifications agreed in your revised quotation on Friday. I will send you the letter of instruction confirming this. When can you give me the detailed schedule and the final drawings?"

The order was received, but this is just the start for the next phase of the job: the implementation. The order is transferred from the tendering system to the order book; job numbers are opened; the customer details, commercial details, cost budget estimate, elevator specification, and project schedule are entered.

Interface to Other Systems

Information about the new order is sent automatically to the financial department, which will open job numbers in the accounting systems. The new elevators will appear in order book reports for the sales and branch managers and other authorized users.

The factory will be informed about the new order received. This can take place at order booking or in cases where the drawings and completion of specification are handled locally by the salesman, the complete order is sent to the factory at no-return point—just in time for the manufacture.

Drawings

After the tender and specification have been agreed on, the production of layout and design drawings starts. These drawings are produced either by the salesman or by the engineering department when technical expertise and advanced CAD systems are required. The salesman's drawing system can be a parameter-driven PC CAD, which fills the building and elevator dimensions into predefined layout sheets. This enables the salesman to submit standard drawings to the architect and builder in a few minutes or hours, sometimes even in their office.

Installation Planning and Scheduling

"Hi Larry, this is Bob! Listen, I noticed on my capacity plan that you've booked a new order with Bayswater Builders—well done! When you're ready with the specs (= technical specifications), can you arrange the handover to Peter, who I've appointed as supervisor. He will also make the detailed installation plan and coordinate the deliveries from the factory, as usual. I can see in his labor plan that he has two men available in September for the installation work. The estimated hours proposed by the computer say we will take three weeks to complete, so we can achieve the handover to customer on October 1 as planned."

Factory Order

When the drawings have been approved, the remaining items of the specification have been agreed on, and the car interior and landing features designed, the salesman fills in the order form and specification for the factory. When the order form is in electronic format, the system checks whether the components, options, and combinations are allowed, the dimensions are within acceptable limits, and all mandatory items have been specified. The completed order is sent electronically to the supplying factory. The order consists of the material list, order header and customer details, contact person, delivery groups, and required schedule.

The order confirmation is received, including confirmed transfer price, delivery groups, and schedules.

Any items that are purchased locally from subcontractors are specified. Prices and schedules are agreed and monitored.

Site and Installation Activities

"Good morning, gentlemen, welcome to our Monday site meeting. The building works are progressing on schedule and the lift installation is due to start next week. We have the Installation Supervisor Peter Jones from Kone Lifts here to agree on the next stages. Peter, can you tell us about your program?"

"Good morning, all. The lift installation is due to start next Monday and to continue for 3 weeks. I have two men working on site and I will be visiting twice a week. The materials will arrive in two shipments. The first one, consisting of the shaft and machine room equipment, will arrive next Monday. The doors, car finishes, and signal equipment will arrive the following Monday. I have spoken to your transport manager and he has arranged for your truck driver to assist in moving the equipment from the truck to the area assigned by the site manager. The installation work will progress in 11 steps—here is the step-by-step plan— starting from unloading and distributing the material, installing the machine room equipment, and ending at commissioning and testing. The time allowed for each activity you can see in this schedule. My guys will be filling time sheets and progress reports every week, which will be used for the payroll and monitoring of site progress. . . ."

Handover

"Hello, Mr. Beaver. How are you? You have a nice group of lifts in here, completed all on time, as planned. Let's take a closer look.... So, everything is in order, we have received your interim payments, and the final invoice will be sent to you today. I would like to introduce you to our Maintenance Manager, Paul Simon. He and his guys will be looking after your lifts for the next twelve months, as per our contract. If you have any further projects, please don't hesitate to contact us."

This is a typical successful elevator order-delivery process, which demonstrates all parts of the process. Selling is not always so easy and becomes more complicated and harder all the time.

KONE ELEVATORS

Kone Elevators is the third-largest elevator manufacturer in the world, the market share being around 15 percent, compared to Otis Elevators' (in the U.S.) 25 percent and Shindler's (in Switzerland) 19 percent. The company employs more than 17,000 people worldwide, fewer than one in ten of whom are Finnish. The primary strategic objective, since the late 1960s, has been the creation of a multinational elevator and escalator company via the acquisition of national elevator companies in various countries.

Kone Oy was founded in 1910, and the first elevator was delivered eight years later. In 1968 Kone expanded from the Finnish domestic market into Scandinavia by acquiring the Swedish company ASEA, tripling elevator deliveries in the process. The second step in intensive acquisition took place in 1975, when Kone acquired the Westinghouse elevator and escalator business in Europe, thus doubling sales.

The 1980s saw Kone's breakthrough in North America, and in Europe expansion continued when two leading Italian elevator companies, Sabiem and Fiam, joined the organization in 1985 and 1986, respectively. During 1987, joint-venture operations for elevator production were started in Australia, India, and Turkey.

On two occasions the company has absorbed nonprofitable operations as large or even larger than itself and turned them into profitable ones. Profitability has been restored through using the same business concept in all units.

Each acquisition constitutes a separate case. Kone has tried to handle them very flexibly with their own schedules, measures, and models. Following acquisition the role of each new unit has been thought over, and some of its operations have been standardized with other units of the corporation. Sometimes the changes have taken several years, and there have been some cultural differences. Although Kone has a similar business concept in each unit, it's been realized in different ways in different countries. On occasion, tough measures have had to be used in order to remove obstacles to company reorganization.

Kone has learned several cultural lessons. For instance, in Italy you have to agree on everything with top management. Direct contacts with different functions such as accounting failed to work if the decisions had not been made first at the top level. Implementing new models and systems therefore took more time than expected. In Germany the thinking was quite functional; users thought that it was the task of the systems specialists from Finland to implement new systems without bothering them.

Kone is now a global company whose operations have been organized into five areas: Europe North, Central, and South; Asia-Pacific; and the Americas. Each area is headed by a full-time Area Director. The sales of new elevators and installations are organized by local companies in each country. Within each area there is one Engineering Center for product engineering and design and tailoring to customer orders. The Engineering Center compiles and delivers market-specific elevators from Kone standard components to local customers.

Component manufacturing is organized globally so that in Europe, for example, there are more than ten component factories in different countries. The elevator components are transported to the Logistics Center, which is located with the Engineering Center. The Engineering and Logistics Centers are the area service centers of the elevator delivery process. On-site elevator installation is carried out in each country by the local organization. A locally competitive product, an elevator that meets customer requirements, is developed in each area, but Kone's standard components are used in all areas.

Kone Elevators is now organized in the following way:

- Sales and installations—separate companies in each country
- Engineering and logistics—one unit within each geographical area
- Components production—a global operation

COMPETITION IN THE ELEVATOR BUSINESS

The elevator business is a highly competitive one, with overcapacity in production. The demand for new elevators and industrial cranes is on the decline in all markets except the Far East. The downturn in the construction industry seems set to last, because in many countries there is overproduction of both office space and flats. In such a situation the competition for market shares is fierce, and there is a great deal of pressure on price levels.

The business in elevator modernization, maintenance, and repair continues to grow and form an increasingly significant proportion of the sales industry. In this line of business there is a structural, permanent-looking change happening to which companies must adapt. The focus in building new elevators must be shifted toward maintenance. In this competitive situation the maintenance of customer service is extremely important.

Kone Elevators aims at competitive success through a decentralized business concept, the aim of which is to combine economies of scale and local flexibility. The key element in Kone strategy is the global logistics system, which is based on common basic system modules that can be modified and localized to suit local users' needs. The global logistics system informs every person involved in the process of the tasks they need to perform in order to get the elevator delivered and installed on time. The system makes it possible to schedule and record major activities, such as orders to the Engineering Center, component orders released, installations programmed, elevators shipped, and installations completed. Each elevator order can be tracked down on screens or reports at the main points of the process. With this system Kone salesmen can give more reliable and quicker responses to customer requirements.

With this global mode of operation Kone has been successful in a very difficult competitive situation. A combination of good customer service and cost effectiveness has been achieved. However, the structural change in competition offers new challenges to Kone's management in terms of how to adapt the company to the changing environment.

Director of Information Systems Markku Rajaniemi stated from his Helsinki headquarters that,

"During the 80s many medium-sized elevator companies disappeared from the market, mostly through acquisition. Small companies survived by flexibility and low cost; big companies developed their products and activities and utilized economies of scale; while mid-sized companies were caught in between and got eaten up by the big ones. Kone has also grown by acquiring typically medium-sized companies with small resources for developing activities and low economies of scale. We organized the activities so that local companies can benefit from Kone development activities and scale advantages.

Our competitiveness is very much based on our systems to manage the global logistics where orders, components, and products are moving between countries. We try to combine global scale and local flexibility with our three-level management (global, area, and country)."

INFORMATION TECHNOLOGY IN KONE ELEVATORS

Kone Elevators has a decentralized data processing setup, with around 200 medium-sized computers (HP9000, AS400) and with around 200 Local Area Networks (NOVELL). The main operating systems are UNIX, OS400, OSF-UX, and DOS. In international data transmission different services from multiple network operators are used. The transmission protocols are TCP/IP and SNA Routers.

Kone's information technology strategy is roughly as follows:

The main corporate activities are research and testing of new technologies, updating Elevators Headquarters IT on corporate technical standards, and negotiating and managing frame agreements with corporatewide hardware and software suppliers. Development, management, and support of Kone's international telecommunications network is an important task.

Elevator Headquarters concentrates on developing and updating technical standards and the application architecture, developing the Kone Elevators application portfolio in line with business needs and priorities, and organizing support and maintenance of portfolio applications. Providing Kone units with adequate support in general and specific IT issues is also important.

Company IT activities involve defining business requirements and analyzing business benefits, procuring hardware and software in line with Kone's technical standards, and managing implementation projects. They also include running local computer operations and the development and maintenance of local applications and adaptations. Managing the migration of the local infrastructure toward harmonization constitutes an important task.

Kone Elevators has a common applications architecture, which maps out the main applications in a unit, describes their functionality, and defines their interfaces. It also describes the underlying common data structure and how the various applications access data. The applications architecture is a vital communication vehicle in developing, implementing, and maintaining systems applications.

The technical standard defines the hardware, software, and telecommunications solutions applicable in the units. Deviations from these standards are allowed only after consultation with headquarters' IT function.

Altogether this is a very coordinated decentralized solution. Units have to work within a given frame, but they take care of their own operations. Within the framework there is some flexibility for individual solutions.

In the units, coordination has been experienced as mainly positive, although some complaints have been made about the fact that matters had been defined in too great detail. Personnel in the information systems function are, however, of the opinion that the input of coordination has even been limited, so that the function's resources would just suffice to provide sufficient support to the local unit.

At Kone Elevators there are around one hundred IS professionals who are mainly decentralized in different units. The objective of the IS function is to obtain software that is as complete as possible, in order for its own software production to be as limited as possible. Total IS costs are around 2 percent of sales, an average level in manufacturing.

The applications are divided into three different areas:

- Management systems (e.g., management accounting and budgeting)
- Operations support (e.g., logistic systems)
- Resource management (e.g., personnel administration, supplier control, and customer service)

Kone has concentrated on internal systems. It has not invested much on external links. They have thought that it is enough to have information less frequently, but in a reliable and consistent form. Recently, however, there has been discussion on how to improve the quality of market information, but there are no ongoing projects.

References

Annual Report, Kone, 1992.

Hurskainen, Jorma. "Business Process Approach to Global Logistics Case: Kone Elevators," in *Joining the Global Roll*. Jahnukainen and Vepsäläinen (eds). Helsinki: 1992. pp. 86–102.

Rajaniemi, Markku. "Process Development in Perspective." Ibid. pp. 132–38.

Interviews: Ulla Mäkelä and Markku Rajaniemi, Kone Elevators.

Case Study Questions

1. What kind of global strategy is Kone Elevators pursuing?
2. Evaluate Kone's information systems in light of this strategy. How well do they support it?
3. Evaluate Kone's strategy for managing its international information systems infrastructure.
4. How easy would it have been for Kone to implement the order-delivery system described at the beginning of this case on an international basis? What management, organization, and technology issues had to be addressed?
5. How strategic is the order-delivery system described here for a firm such as Kone? Why?

Festo Pneumatic

Helmut Krcmar and Bettina Schwarzer, University of Hohenheim (Germany)

Festo, a medium-sized German company headquartered in Esslingen, with 3500 employees around the world, is one of the world market leaders in the field of pneumatics and device control. The company was founded in 1925 and opened its first subsidiary, in Italy, in 1956. By now Festo has branches in 187 countries, offering full service for its products around the world (see Figure 1). Festo has four major product groups: Festo Electronic, which offers products and services for electronic device control; Festo Tooltechnic, offering electronic and air-pressure tools for crafts and industry; Festo Didactic, which provides courses for all kinds of device control; and finally, Festo Pneumatic, which manufactures valves and cylinders and provides complete solutions for device control.

The major group is Festo Pneumatic, which specializes in the design and manufacturing of valves and cylinders, offering 35,000 components and 4000 products by catalogue. It also provides custom-made solutions for device control in which cylinders are combined with other Festo components according to specific customer requirements. This combined approach of manufacturing components and offering complete solutions distinguishes Festo from most of its competitors in the pneumatic business. All products are designed and produced in Germany. Only in the case of special made-to-order cylinders does production take place in the subsidiaries to meet customer requirements. Of the products manufactured in Germany, 55 percent are exported.

Festo Pneumatic has 35 subsidiaries and more than 100 branch offices selling its products. In general, all pneumatic products are designed and manufactured in Germany; therefore, the same product is available around the world. As parts are shipped all over the world from the German production site and warehouse, all orders have to be processed centrally. Processing a workload of about 200–300 orders with an average of 4 items per order from each of the major subsidiaries daily, Festo Pneumatic is dependent on a global computer system.

Even though Festo is a fairly small company with only 1000 employees abroad, it is highly internationalized and continuously expanding its international engagements, now turning to Eastern Europe. The subsidiaries are independent companies but are dependent on the German headquarters because they neither design nor manufacture products. Festo Pneumatic Germany views its subsidiaries as *shops* for selling the company's products in foreign markets. Not only in the business area but also in the field of information systems, Festo pursues a centralized approach. Hardware and software are selected in the corporate headquarters, which also provides systems support. The major advantage of this approach is cost savings; detailed knowledge of the systems can be centralized in one place. Any changes in the system only have to be made in one place and are then taken to all subsidiaries. This not only reduces costs but also guarantees that the system is the same everywhere.

In 1976, confronted with continuing international growth and an increasing workload, Festo Pneumatic decided to implement a common system in the headquarters and the subsidiaries to be able to handle and improve order processing, logistics, and production on an international basis. The goals pursued with the system were *high quality of customer service* and *minimized stock levels*. To match the structure of their international operations Festo decided to implement one common system for all subsidiaries, as they had exactly the same information-processing requirements in their data exchange with the headquarters. Because there was no standardized software package available at that time, a system was developed in-house starting in 1976. Development took place in the headquarters and, beginning in 1978, the system was introduced in the subsidiaries.

Due to the lack of standardized software packages at that time and the high costs of in-house development, most competitors did not have sophisticated systems in place when Festo introduced its first integrated system. At that time the rationale for systems development was not strategic advantage—the idea of strategic information systems was not yet known—but simply to make order processing on an international basis more efficient. Still, Festo realized that the new system

FIGURE 1
Festo corporate organization.

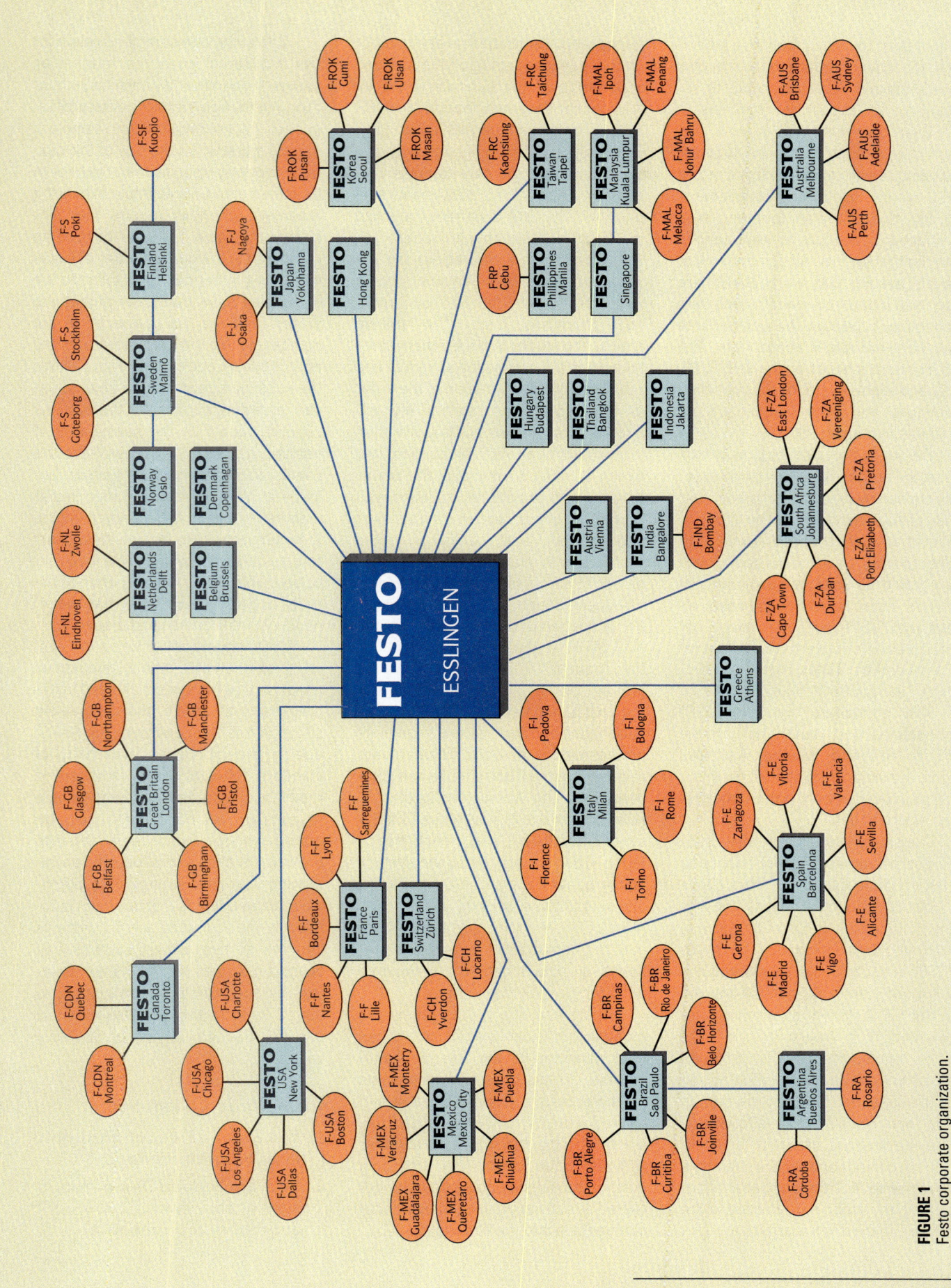

505

helped them to gain competitive advantage; the time for order processing was shortened and Festo was able to respond quicker to customer requests.

Over the years the system has been continuously improved to meet changing requirements. Festo's current FIP-2 system, used for order processing, logistics, and manufacturing, was developed based on its experiences with the first system. All components of the old system that worked well are also used in the new system, with new technology replacing the components that were no longer appropriate. The FIP-2 system is based on the COBOL 85, RPG, and High-Level RPG programming languages and uses TurboImage for database management.

Before systems development took place, the hardware platform was carefully chosen by experts after a one-year study of different vendors. The main criterion for hardware selection was scalability, to make sure that the same hardware could be used in subsidiaries of different sizes. Festo headquarters always used IBM computers but it selected Hewlett-Packard computers for its subsidiaries. Today Festo's 24 subsidiary headquarters run the system on HP 3000 computers with the RISC-technology-based operating system MPE/iX. No matter whether 4 or 4000 people are using the system at the same time, all users can work in the same systems environment.

Customers order in the subsidiaries' branches by either telephone or fax (in some cases there are shops for over-the-counter sales). Festo's branch offices in various countries use microcomputers linked directly to an HP 3000 in each subsidiary's headquarters for order entry. An order is entered into the FIP-2 system on a microcomputer and then transmitted to subsidiary headquarters either immediately or once a day, depending on the type of connection between the branch office and subsidiary headquarters. There the order is checked for availability of components in the country's own warehouse. If the components are available, the order is processed in the country. Otherwise, the orders are collected and transmitted every hour or once a day (depending on the size and importance of the subsidiary) via an X.25 packet-switched network to an HP 3000 in Festo headquarters in Germany. The HP 3000 at German headquarters in turn transforms the data to make processing on an IBM 3090 mainframe possible. The IBM mainframe is linked to Festo's German branches, so German orders are entered directly into this system. The IBM combines orders from abroad with the German orders and processes them. The system checks the stocks in the German warehouse and the production schedule and returns with a confirmation of the order to the subsidiaries, stating the expected date of delivery. Data are then transmitted to an AEG 80-30 computer, which is used to manage the warehouse. Festo reports no problems with these linkages on either a national or international level, although some problems may arise when transmitting data to and from technologically underdeveloped countries such as Brazil.

If the components are in stock, the AEG 80-30 in the warehouse handles the request. A warehouse note is printed, giving information on where the components are to be found in the warehouse and how many components are needed for the order. The parts are removed from the warehouse and commissioned: The worker enters the *finished* status into the system and a delivery note, the bill, and a confirmation of the order are printed by the system. These papers are put into the packet and sent to the subsidiary either on the road or by air. The subsidiary either puts the components in its own warehouse or puts together the required parts for the individual orders.

Apart from the orders processed together, customer-specific orders can be transmitted to the German headquarters. In this case, all components for the order are packed together and marked in the German warehouse. They are delivered to the subsidiary together with the other parts. After checking them in the subsidiary they can be delivered directly to the customer without putting them into the warehouse.

Designing one common system for use in different countries was not as easy as it sounds and caused a number of problems. Apart from the different languages that are required, for example in printed material for the use of the customer, country-specific features have to be implemented. For example, in Italy the revenue authorities require that bills sent to the same customer have to be numbered in the correct order of issue, whereas in other countries the revenue authorities have their own numbering system and are not interested in the number of the bill. If special features are only needed in one country, Festo allows the subsidiary to make the changes itself, providing support for the systems support people in the subsidiaries if needed. If several countries have the same requirements, the changes are made at headquarters and then implemented abroad. In making the changes at headquarters, so far only headquarters systems personnel have been involved. This policy is being changed in order to gain advantage of the knowledge available in the subsidiaries.

Whereas in former times the system provided Festo with a competitive advantage as the system allowed faster processing of orders, the competitive situation has changed over the years, due to the increasing availability of standard software. Today, software is readily available, and in order to be able to compete, all companies use integrated systems. Festo has adapted to the new situation and is focusing on improving customer service. One potential area for benefits that has been identified is incorporating expert systems into the system. Expert systems can support the sales people in their meetings by suggesting system configurations. Thereby the ordering process can be speeded up and qualitatively improved.

Case Study Questions

1. What kind of global strategy is Festo Pneumatic pursuing?
2. Evaluate Festo's FIP-2 system in light of this strategy. How well does this system support it?

3. Evaluate Festo Pneumatic's strategy for managing its international information systems infrastructure.

4. How much competitive advantage does Festo's FIP-2 system provide?

5. What problems did Festo have implementing its order processing, logistics, and production system? What management, organization, and technology issues had to be addressed?

6. Festo's order processing, logistics, and production system is custom-developed. In this particular instance, is it an advantage or disadvantage to have custom-built software?

Corning Telecommunications Division (A): The Flexible Manufacturing Systems Project

Andrew Boynton, University of North Carolina at Chapel Hill and the International Institute for Management Development (Switzerland)
Michael E. Shank, Renaissance Vision

Driving across the Gibson Bridge toward his office in July 1990, Bob McAdoo, senior vice president and head of manufacturing for the Telecommunications division of Corning, Inc., thought about the appropriations request he would be discussing with his staff on Friday morning. The division was requesting $5 million for a new planning and scheduling system plus a reconfigured information system to cope with manufacturing changes at its Wilmington, North Carolina, plant, where Corning made optical waveguides. Such a sum was not an incidental capital investment. Moreover, exactly what they would be getting for the money was hard to say. The budget for hardware and packaged software was dwarfed by the costs of design work and consultants. The consultants would be designing a system that had never been built before, and after problems with the last systems-development project, ATLAS, the idea of breaking new ground in software was troubling. (ATLAS, even though it was a well-understood business data system, had been two years late and millions over budget.) In addition, no one could tell McAdoo if the proposed Flexible Manufacturing System (FMS) would work once it was designed, written, and implemented. All they would say is that they "didn't think the plant could continue to work without it."

OPTICAL WAVEGUIDES

Optical waveguides are glass fibers that allow communication by light rather than electricity. One-fifth thinner than a human hair, the core of these fibers can carry more than 16,000 simultaneous phone conversations (compared with 24 for copper wire). Unlike copper, optical fiber can also carry information in both directions (sending and receiving) simultaneously. Fibers can transmit light more than 100 miles without regeneration and operate 20,000 feet under water with a 40-year life. Despite their close resemblance to fishing line when coated, fibers can withstand 1 million pounds per square inch of tensile stress. Optical fiber can also carry more information much faster than copper wire. Fiber's carrying capacity of 1.8 billion bits per second can transmit the Encyclopedia Britannica and the Bible around the earth together in less than 2 seconds.

Optical fibers behave like light-pipes. Because of their differences in composition, the refractive index of the core is higher than that of the outer coat (cladding). As a result, light rays traveling through the core will be reflected back into the core if they stray from a straight line and bounce into the core/cladding interface. Consequently, light stays in the core even when the fiber is bent.

The two types of fiber were multimode and single mode. Multimode was primarily used for local building-to-building and intrabuilding wiring, where its comparatively large core size contributed to reduced installation costs. Multimode was available in several glass and coating designs, which when combined with various optical performance levels, resulted in a wide and increasing variety of stock-keeping units (SKUs).

Single-mode fiber was used primarily by telephone companies. Initial applications were for long-distance telecommunication applications by companies like MCI, AT&T, and Sprint. New types of fiber and coatings, and declining systems costs after 1983, led to many new applications by regional telephone companies (e.g., Bell South), cable television companies, and long-distance communication companies. Given the efforts by telephone companies to emphasize product standardization and compatibility of competing vendors' products, fewer single-mode than multimode fiber SKUs existed. Single-mode fiber represented approximately 90 percent of the market volume.

Corning sold almost all of its fiber to optical-fiber cablers. A few cablers accounted for approximately 80 percent of Corning's sales, with 200 customers making up the remaining 20 percent. Essentially, cablers packaged the optical fiber in a variety of materials to protect it during installation and to limit the effects of its installed environments. From a materials point of view, cablers added little to the value of the fiber, and the fiber itself was a large portion of the cost of fiber cabling. Excess capacity plagued the cabling industry, and barriers to entry were low. Telephone companies' purchases comprised 70 percent of the optical-cable market, and these companies were adept at creating a level playing field through specification standards and purchasing strategies. Product quality and service were important to the phone companies, but these parameters were viewed largely as requirements for entry. Bidding to attract the phone companies' business was fierce. Overall, profits for optical cablers tended to be low, which was consistent with the financial performance they achieved when these same cablers had been copper-wire cablers.

As the costs of fiber-optic systems declined, phone-company fiber-cable installation migrated from long-haul telecommunications trunks (e.g., MCI) through regional telecommunications (e.g., Bell South) interoffice trunks joining central-office switching systems to feeder cables connecting central-office switches directly to large businesses or to residential neighborhoods (see Figure 1). Phone companies were betting that optical systems' costs would decline to the degree that they would be no different than the costs of a copper wire system for final telephone line connections to residences (distribution and drop cables). When the fiber could be installed to the home, the phone companies would be able to take advantage of fiber's unlimited capacity to provide a raft of new information services such as video entertainment on demand, home shopping, and home education. This development would allow the phone companies to become the aggressive, high-growth information firms they had envisioned at the time of divestiture.

The cable television market also used single-mode fiber, to improve picture quality and channel capacity and as a defensive posture against the phone companies, who were interested in entering the home entertainment video market. Cable TV's mass deployment of fiber had lagged the phone companies' by five years, but growth since 1988 had been strong.

Beyond the phone companies and cable TV markets, another large and growing segment was premises wiring— banks, corporate offices, universities, hospitals, industrial complexes, and brokerage houses. These customers made up the market for multimode fiber. Standards had not progressed as far in this segment, and several different multimode glass and fiber designs serviced the market. Given the lack of concentrated purchasing observed in the phone company segment, the buying patterns were not as orderly. Many fiber cablers and systems integrators would often bid on the same premises job, and quote turnaround times and cable lead times were key determinants in establishing the winning bidder.

TELEPHONE OUTSIDE PLANT NETWORK

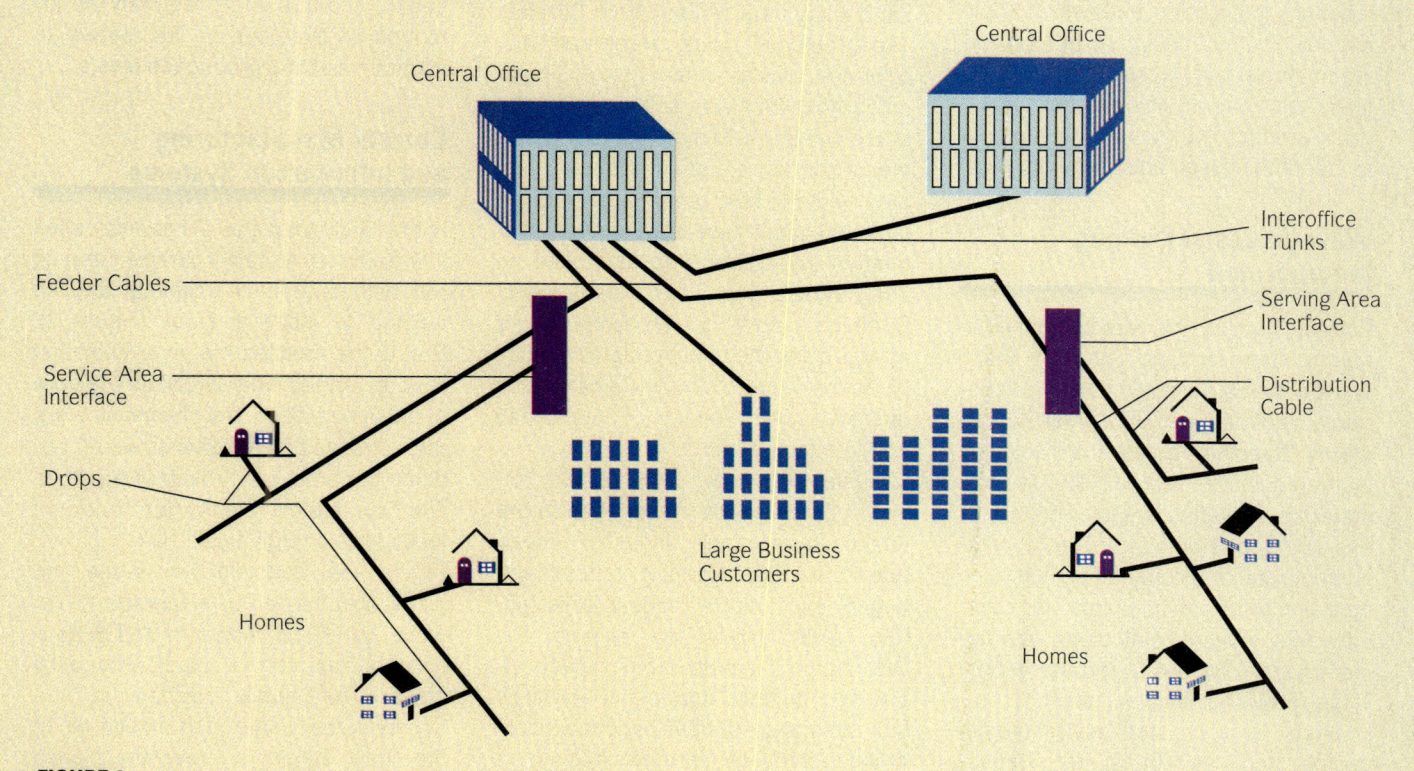

FIGURE 1
Telephone Outside Plant Network.

Cablers passed these segment pressures directly to Corning and other suppliers—AT&T and Spectran. While Corning and AT&T devoted a large percentage of their fiber capabilities to single mode, Spectran owed its existence to the multimode market. Spectran used attractive pricing, rapid quote turnaround, and competitive lead times to attract business.

Another interesting segment was the undersea telecommunications market. Transoceanic cables had been developed and installed linking the U.S. with Europe and Japan. Undersea cables were installed around the perimeter of Italy in time to be used for transmitting the World Cup Soccer matches. In these applications long-length, low-loss, high-strength fibers were used to reduce the installed system cost. Increased interest was developing in an altered single-mode fiber design, which optimized optical performance at longer wavelengths, thus resulting in lower-loss fibers and further reductions in installed system cost.

Beyond these current markets, new segments were on the horizon for fiber, including fiber for tethered weapons, navigation, and sensor applications. Product designs were still being finalized, but it was clear that new glass and coating designs beyond today's product lines would be required to meet these segments' requirements.

Waveguides at Corning Incorporated

Corning, Inc., in 1990 was composed of four primary sectors: Specialty Glass and Ceramics, Communications, Laboratory Services, and Consumer Housewares. Specialty Glass and Ceramics marketed more than 40,000 specialty materials, including eyeglass materials, and auto-emission filters. The Communications sector produced optical fiber, opto-electrical components for fiber networks, video display glass, and liquid crystal displays. Laboratory Services provided clinical testing, life-science research, and environmental testing services. Consumer Housewares produced such well-known products as Corning Ware®, Revere Ware®, and Corelle® dinnerware.

In 1989–90 the Communications sector contributed approximately 21 percent to Corning's revenues and 37 percent to its profits—increases of more than 35 percent in both categories. A significant contribution to corporate profits came from optical waveguides. Corning's quality and delivery had consistently provided a significant profit margin on this product.

Corning developed the first technically feasible optical fiber in 1970. The company then worked for eight years refining the technology and developing a proprietary low-cost manufacturing method. Despite years of only moderate interest from telephone companies and cablers, Corning funded the research and, in 1979, built a manufacturing plant in Wilmington. The plant operated for three years producing only samples and small orders for pilot projects before its first major order was received, which followed the deregulation of the telecommunications industry in 1982.

At that time MCI announced plans to build a nationwide fiber-optic network and ordered one hundred thousand kilometers of fiber from Corning. The order, ten times larger than any prior one, was for a new type of single-mode fiber that was still experimental at the company. To meet MCI's requirements, therefore, Corning moved a new generation of fiber technology from the lab to the plant floor, installed new production equipment, and embarked on one of the largest plant expansions in Corning's history. By 1986, sixteen years after proving the commercial feasibility of optical fiber, Corning's fiber-optics operations were running 24 hours a day and turning a profit.

The MCI order was quickly followed by others as competition in the telecommunications industry developed. In 1983 Corning funded the largest expenditure request in its history, $100 million, to expand the Wilmington plant to meet rapidly increasing demand and install Corning's fifth generation of fiber-optic manufacturing technology. Corning's dedication to its new technology and its willingness to invest allowed the company to compete with larger rivals such as AT&T and "Japan, Inc.," to become a world leader in waveguide manufacturing. In 1991 Corning Communications, having initiated a *total quality* effort to measure the performance of all business and manufacturing processes to determine competitive capabilities, was pursuing the Baldrige Award.

The initial growth phase, fueled by the needs of long-distance companies, had appeared endless, and to remain an industry's technological leader, Corning had averaged changes in production machinery every 12–24 months. In the second half of 1986, however, as Corning continued to increase its production capacity, the initial growth stopped. The market for long-distance lines was saturated, and increasingly customized fiber-optic, especially multimode, orders from the cable industry changed the demands on Corning's waveguide plant. By 1990 these new demands were not optimally satisfied by the manufacturing and information systems at the plant. By early 1991 construction to again increase the size and capacity of the plant substantially had begun, and this effort required the attention of everyone in the factory to maintain existing production levels.

Current Manufacturing and Information Systems

In the Laydown stage, a machine called a *lathe* systematically coated a ceramic rod with a precise chemical deposit buildup to make a *blank* (Figure 2). During the process the inner chemical buildup formed what would be the core of the optical fiber. The chemicals were then changed to build what would become the outer coat (clad) of the fiber. The completed blank, (or *preform*) looked like a large cigar.

In the Consolidation stage the blank was heated in a furnace to remove water and impurities and to consolidate the porous blank into pure glass. The blank purified in the Consolidation stage next moved on to the Draw stage. In Draw, the blanks (glass cigars) were placed in holders,

DESCRIPTION OF FIBER-OPTIC MANUFACTURING PROCESS

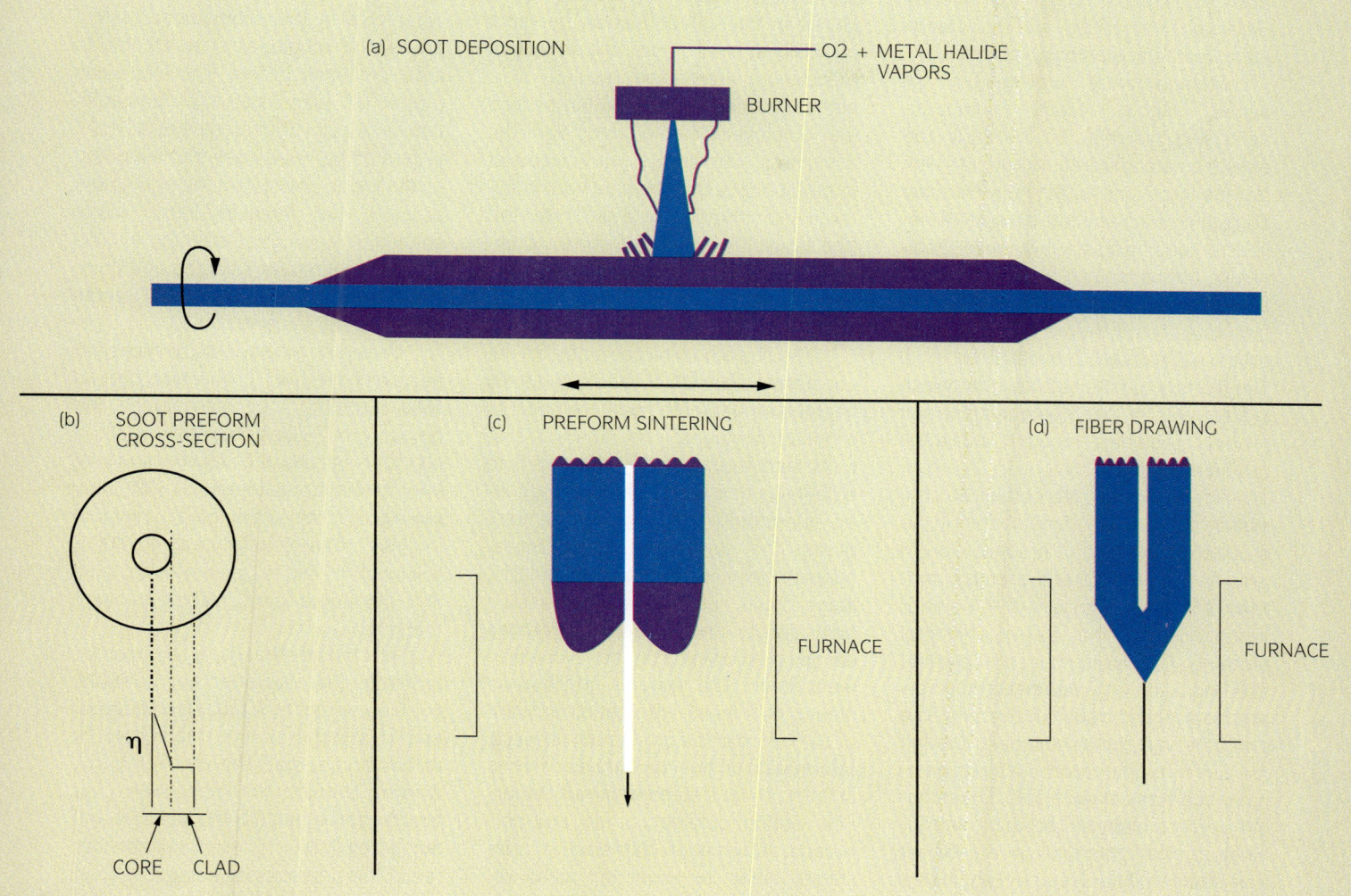

FIGURE 2
Description of Fiber-Optic Manufacturing Process.

and a small furnace heated the extreme tip of each blank, causing the melted tip to drop down a tower. The tip pulled along a small strand of optical fiber from the blank, which was threaded through a machine that applied different chemical coatings to the outside of the fiber and measured its width. At the bottom of the tower, a tractor pulled the fiber at a preset rate, and the fiber was collected on a take-up reel.

From Draw, the bulk reel of optical fiber moved to Off Line Screening (OLS), where tensile strength was measured. The reel then traveled to Measurement for a large battery of optical tests. The fiber was measured and cut to standard lengths and, in the Wind stage, taken off the special measurement spools and rewound on shipping spools.

Mike Jordan, planning and scheduling supervisor, had briefed Bob McAdoo on the complexity of production scheduling at the Wilmington plant: "*In making waveguides, the process is different from standard production like making automobiles. With cars, ten Chevy engines and ten Chevy bodies make ten Chevy cars, with some quality reworking. Here, in optical waveguides, we can mix ten batches of the same chemicals under the same conditions with the same computer-controlled processes. Sometimes we'll get seven batches that can be sold; sometimes we'll get ten. Each batch will differ slightly from the other batches. For example, the maximum length of optical fibers will vary as bad sections are cut out. Glass-geometry precision will differ slightly from batch to batch. So we don't know how many saleable end-products we'll get because of differences in selection yield. We also don't know how many end-products will be Oldsmobiles and how many will be Chevys, due to the distribution of characteristics. Luckily, we*

Corning Telecommunications Division

can substitute Oldsmobiles for Chevys here. Customers will take a higher quality cable for the same price. But this substitution costs us money. Selection, distribution, and substitution complicate the planning process."

Manufacturing waveguides required highly exact, computer-controlled systems, but the early emphasis on standard fiber products with few modifications for the long-distance companies had resulted in a system limited to keeping costs low while maintaining efficiency and high quality. The system was designed to control manufacturing at each step of the production process (Laydown, Consolidation, etc.). The primary function of the information system was to identify equipment and process problems in each individual production stage.

The tight controls coded into the system allowed few modifications in the product or production process. To get around the product and process controls, a small percentage of the plant's production was run as experimental products. Each production process had to be individually *tricked* into letting new products move through the system. The products were moved manually through the entire production process with computer overrides at each step. For example, new or customized products with diameters or lengths that were different from standard fibers required engineers to override set specifications in the Draw and Measurement systems. Since all fibers looked essentially identical to the naked eye, special fiber reels were identified with colored dots and batch numbers to flag them as requiring special processing. The manual intervention was not only time-consuming and labor-intensive, but also prone to human error.

Computer overrides often conflicted with standard costing information and with constants in production algorithms. Thus, costs could not be accumulated on special orders and new products. Inappropriate algorithm constants resulted in incorrect production information, and reported yields exceeded actual process inputs.

Information was captured by the system on each of the individual processes but was used to control only that process. No information was passed along by the system to the next production stage. Operators even keyed in reel identification numbers manually at each stage. This division of production information resulted in a vertically oriented information system that employees called, along with the associated computers, *stovepipes* of information. Each stovepipe was monitored and controlled by a separate staff (the stovepipe's *feudal lord*). Computers stored highly summarized information on products completed and in inventory.

The stovepipe infrastructure of the current system did not allow potentially useful information to be shared across production stages. The different systems had dramatically different field definitions and sizes, which offered little opportunity to integrate the data across the stovepipes. For example, measurement information from the OLS stage could not be used to eliminate later quality checks or to determine sampling strategies in the Measurement stage. The systems provided no means of feeding information forward or backward in the production process. Information on fiber defects discovered in later process steps required manual intervention, communication, and correction. Information gathered in prior stages, such as diameter measurements and usable fiber lengths determined in Draw, was unavailable to Measurement technicians, who might spend hours searching reels for a long usable fiber. Consolidating information from the different systems resulted in unacceptable delays in providing production information. In short, the stovepipe systems did not allow the plant to maximize the use of its capital-intensive equipment.

Designed to meet high demand for a few products, the system did not track work in process. All orders were matched to inventory. However, when a relatively stable supply of a few products had moved through the system, supervisors had been able to coordinate production based on inventory levels.

As the number of products multiplied and became more customized, and as customers demanded shorter lead times, a Sneaker Patrol, the plant's production and scheduling staff, had become responsible for determining what was in the plant and adjusting production schedules in an attempt to meet customer orders. The four-week production plan listed the number of blanks of each product type to start. As orders came in or were canceled and as the yields changed in the production process, the Sneaker Patrol made schedule revisions. Currently, numerous daily schedule changes and comprehensive changes were made weekly to the four-week plan.

Pressure to increase responsiveness can be seen in the fact that, in 1988, Corning fiber salespeople put pressure on Wilmington to respond in less than one day with delivery and cost information for customers; in 1991, they were pressuring Wilmington to respond in less than four hours. In 1991, Wilmington had a several-hour goal and monitored performance to meet that goal.

All changes that were based on information that was often two days old, were projected by hand. Most information was gathered and transmitted by the production staff, the Sneaker Patrol, walking through the plant with clipboards and changing the colored and numbered dots on different carts of fiber reels. This process was being stretched to the limit as the Wilmington plant continued to add new fiber products and prepared to add additional capacity.

Mike Jordan, who as planning and scheduling supervisor, was also head of the Sneaker Patrol, explained how the process was being stretched: *"A customer was buying multimode product of long length. This is not a standard product, so we have to begin a 'yellow-dot experiment,' where the particular yellow dot indicates 'produce long-length multimode.' The customer calls back in a few days and says he doesn't want the long length. Because we can't waste good in-process fiber, I have to go out and take off the yellow dot from this particular experiment and produce this in-process fiber for stock. The next day the same customer calls and says he* wants a different bandwidth multimode. I then have to run out again and find some in-process fiber of that bandwidth by looking around the plant and then put a yellow dot on that to indicate the length the customer wants. Can you imagine this happening many times each day? It does!"

The same information gathered for scheduling was used to quote order lead times to customers. Quoting a lead time one or two days longer than a competitor could lose an order. Missing a deadline or shipping incorrect product violated one of Corning's top cultural values. Currently, a significant percentage of customer orders were for shipment in less than five days, but the plant took more than six days to complete most of the orders, even though the production process required significantly less time. All other delays were caused by the logistics of moving between operations (a minimal amount of time) and scheduling conflicts and inefficiencies.

Mike O'Koren, the Wilmington plant manager, described the plant as computer intensive but reliant on "people intervention" and "customized people processes": "*The customers are wanting more one-of-a-kind orders with shorter lead times. Our record of error-free shipments and past turnaround time has made customer service a competitive advantage. Maintaining this advantage is crucial to our success. Right now we don't have a system in place that allows us to shrink lead times. The only way we do it now is with what people do in their heads. We promise orders based on what we think is on the shop floor. We've been stretched pretty thin. As our volume increases and the number of product choices multiplies the people system is going to break down.*"

Reliance on customized people processes and mutual production adjustments between feudal lords and the Sneaker Patrol had created a large informal communications network in the plant. Production processes had evolved to conform to this network.

Jordan estimated that the plant could accept orders for 10 percent more fiber a month if quote times could be reduced through the scheduling of a made-to-order manufacturing system. He explained that, in the information environment he envisioned, he could be much more effective: "*I want to be able to sit at home or in the office and, on the PC, identify what fiber is in stock or anywhere on the floor. Now I have to check what is in the inventory or on the floor to see what is there. Today we have almost zero visibility about ware in process.*"

Jordan hoped, however, that any new systems wouldn't be as difficult to implement as the last systems project with which he had been involved: "*Although this is my vision for fast response to our customer requests, the last information system project I was involved with, ATLAS, left me with a healthy dose of skepticism. ATLAS has worked out great, but not without some pain. Now we can see all orders, which customers place through the sales force at corporate, in 5 minutes. Before ATLAS, it took over 24 hours for us to get an order. I felt the project was badly undersourced. The system was being designed for multiple uses in multiple divisions. Coordination between all parties was difficult. Senior management in our sector didn't buy in initially, and without that pressure brought to bear, the project stagnated. It didn't work until we at Wilmington held our ground, insisted on getting the resources required, and fought for the project to be completed—the right way. After we at Wilmington started kicking, the guys at corporate got involved and insured that corporate IS [Information Systems] put the resources on the project for our sector. We learned a great deal during ATLAS, and it is a real lifesaver now. I just wonder if new systems will be as difficult to implement.*"

On a recent visit to the Wilmington plant, McAdoo had spoken with O'Koren about the effect of the proposed new information system on the people who composed the informal communications network. O'Koren thought the new system would provide tremendous benefits to customers, but he was less enthusiastic about the effect on plant personnel: "*Many people have done nothing but act as information transmitters in this network since the business was started. They feel very threatened. I think they're going to have to learn new jobs.*"

McAdoo noted that, as O'Koren was speaking, a large fish on his PC's aquarium display had turned and eaten several smaller fish.

The Appropriations Request

The decision to request $5 million to revamp waveguide manufacturing (see Figure 3) had not been straightforward. On the one hand, the waveguide project had always been a high-risk, high-return project. Historically, large appropriations requests had been granted, and they had paid off. On the other hand, the configuration and timing of the local-loop market appeared as uncertain as the long-distance market had in 1970.

Tom LaGarde, manager of IS at the Wilmington factory, had been heavily involved with the preparation of the request. He discussed with McAdoo how the implementation effort would be managed. "*At the highest level we have a review board consisting of senior managers at corporate that meet twice a year to make sure the project is not out of sync with the company. We have been asked to submit appropriation requests twice a year after the initial request is approved. As we present each request, we have to establish where we've been and where we are going and establish how much money has been spent and what will be needed. We brought in Global Analysis, a Big Five consulting firm, because we felt our corporate IS group, though talented, did not have the experience for this type of project. We're using a computer-based tool to plan, track, test, and manage the project—a tool that connects each project person. There is a great deal of technical risk beyond the sheer size and complexity of the project. We have no experience with the relational database technology, which has to provide rapid and flexible access to great quantities of*

FIGURE 3
Flexible Manufacturing Systems.

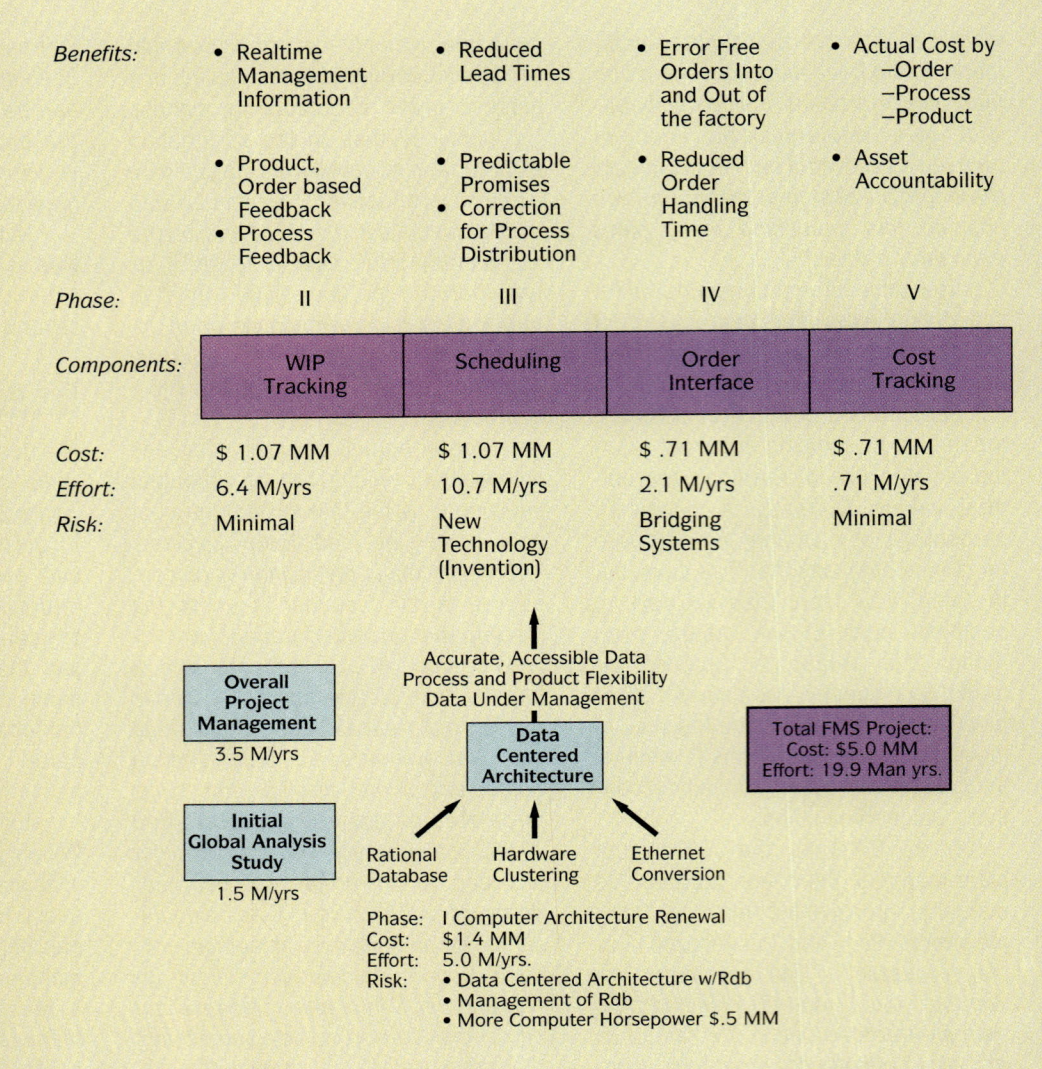

Benefits:	• Realtime Management Information	• Reduced Lead Times	• Error Free Orders Into and Out of the factory	• Actual Cost by —Order —Process —Product
	• Product, Order based Feedback • Process Feedback	• Predictable Promises • Correction for Process Distribution	• Reduced Order Handling Time	• Asset Accountability
Phase:	II	III	IV	V
Components:	WIP Tracking	Scheduling	Order Interface	Cost Tracking
Cost:	$ 1.07 MM	$ 1.07 MM	$ .71 MM	$ .71 MM
Effort:	6.4 M/yrs	10.7 M/yrs	2.1 M/yrs	.71 M/yrs
Risk:	Minimal	New Technology (Invention)	Bridging Systems	Minimal

Overall Project Management
3.5 M/yrs

Initial Global Analysis Study
1.5 M/yrs

Accurate, Accessible Data
Process and Product Flexibility
Data Under Management

Data Centered Architecture

Rational Database   Hardware Clustering   Ethernet Conversion

Total FMS Project:
Cost: $5.0 MM
Effort: 19.9 Man yrs.

Phase: I Computer Architecture Renewal
Cost: $1.4 MM
Effort: 5.0 M/yrs.
Risk: • Data Centered Architecture w/Rdb
• Management of Rdb
• More Computer Horsepower $.5 MM

information. The other dimension of technical risk is the finite-forward-scheduling component—which has never been developed before. We will break the project into seven teams of 5–7 people from about five organizations—contract programming houses, Global Analysis, corporate Engineering and IS, Digital, and the Wilmington factory. As for my organization, I'll have to provide support for the project. At the same time, the plant must have other information needs met. Combine this with a major plant expansion and the plant at capacity, and the difficulties inherent in the implementation become clear."

McAdoo picked up the appropriations request (see Figure 4) sitting on his desk to read through the body of the proposal. He knew he had to make a case to William Cunningham, manager of the entire Communications sector, to invest this much money on an information system. Furthermore, $5 million would require approval at the chairman level. Would changing the way information was managed at Wilmington convert a factory designed to produce standard products into a flexible manufacturing facility? Were there other, better, alternatives to FMS? McAdoo and his staff had considered the option that Corning not put any more money into waveguides. They had also looked for, but did not find, some other way to fix the current problem. The staff believed in FMS; after all, they had spent the last year in intensive analysis and design. But did they understand the industry forces, and did these forces require the type of strategy suggested by FMS? Finally, would the system work? How, given the ATLAS project delay and cost, could he recommend an information-systems project of this magnitude of this strategic importance?

McAdoo wanted to make sure his staff had thought through the issues carefully before he made a decision. Did his staff have answers to the myriad of important questions? Sighing, McAdoo got up and started the long walk to the meeting with his staff. He would then have the weekend to think things over, but on Monday he had to meet with Cunningham and make a recommendation on FMS.

FIGURE 4
Abstract from Appropriation Request.

Background

This is the first information systems project of this scope and scale undertaken by the Communications sector. Extensive outside assistance is planned to conduct the project because of its size and technical complexity. After several months of review and negotiations, we selected the consulting firm of Global Analysis for their expertise in building manufacturing support systems and methodology for conducting Business Area Analysis. We are extremely satisfied with that decision.

Corning began the analysis with Global Analysis on October 4, 1989. The objectives of the study were to develop a data architecture to serve as the foundation for FMS and to define a planning and factory scheduling system for the manufacture of optical waveguides. This study was completed on plan, March 23, 1990, and serves as the basis for defining the requirements of the systems that are planned for construction under this Appropriation Request.

Request

The vision for Flexible Manufacturing Systems is that every product made on the factory floor can be traced to a customer requirement, production forecast, or specific order (inventory or customer). This contrasts with our present system, which does not have this capability. In the current system, products are not tracked until they reach inventory. All current production is made for inventory, not for customer orders. Tracking production and linking specific product with customer orders is currently done manually. The FMS project constructed to automate and enhance that capability consists of two major components:

1. Information systems for planning, scheduling, tracking, and fulfilling customer order requirements in the factory.
2. A major renewal of the plant information infrastructure to include the plant computer network, the computer architecture, and plant databases.

The project will run from the 1989 planning stage through completion in 1993. Personnel from Corning, Global Analysis, DEC, and other outside contractors will be engaged in all phases of the project. Global Analysis will receive between 30–40% of the funds. The project will take approximately 19.9 man years to complete.

Project Structure

The FMS project can be partitioned into five major phases:
  I. Computer Architecture Renewal
 II. Ware-in-Process Tracking
III. Scheduling
 IV. Order Interface
  V. Cost Tracking

Each of the FMS phases consists of several projects that complete the implementation.

Phase I. Computer Architecture Renewal

To describe the computer architecture renewal, we have coined the term "Data Centered Architecture." This means an architecture for information management that is founded on the relationships between the fundamental elements of information that the business uses to operate (e.g., orders, products, processes, and equipment). These are key assets of the business and critical to operations. The Wilmington computer architecture is designed to serve the accessibility and accuracy of that asset. The new computer architecture will result in a data system that is highly accessible and places the key data assets under management to the benefit of all information-system users. The Data Centered Architecture will serve as a flexible information resource through an access structure that is known to all and accessible from any computer system in the Division.

In addition to a new design for the information system, there are three major technology components in the new architecture: (1) Digital Equipment Corporation's *RDB* database, which will manage the data, (2) Hardware Clustering, which allows direct access to the database by the plant manufacturing computers, and (3) Ethernet, which allows network access to the database by all business, process-control, and personal computers.

Phase II. Ware-in-Process Tracking

This phase consists of a system that links factory-floor machine events to the central database and provides user programs for data reporting and analysis. Individual orders, products, blanks, and fibers can be tracked in manufacturing, and process results can be analyzed quickly. The WIP Tracking phase will introduce the "Shop Order" into the factory as a tracking mechanism to link all products on the factory floor to a customer requirement. This information is not currently available. WIP Tracking also provides the shop-floor information required for the Scheduling and Cost Tracking phases of FMS.

Phase III. Scheduling

The scheduling system being developed for FMS takes into consideration three key attributes of the process of manufacturing optical waveguides. The manufacturing process produces a *distribution* of saleable optical fiber in terms of the performance capabilities of the product as opposed to discrete end products. In waveguide manufacture, there is the capability to *substitute* fiber of one characteristic for another. A characteristic of fiber-optical performance is that a fiber of higher performance can be sold against a lesser requirement. Finally, the manufacturing process itself provides *variable* output.

The scheduling system is a finite-capacity-planning system. In conjunction with process results from the WIP Tracking system, it will characterize the process distribution using actual historical data and allow the planner to predict with a set degree of certainty what the process output will be. The historical record will be used as the basis of the capacity plan, and this will yield a daily schedule for manufacturing. The Shop Orders specified in the schedule will be checked regularly to compensate for any unexpected process variability. This systematic approach to scheduling will result in reduced lead times for orders and a method for creating reliable and predictable promises for fiber to the customer, which in turn can result in shorter quoted lead times.

Phase IV. Order Interface

The plant has an interface to the corporate business data system (ATLAS) for both the initiation of orders and the fulfillment of orders for shipping. The FMS Order Interface will allow the plant to act on an order requested by the customer by delivering the order to the planning and scheduling systems established by the Scheduling Phase. In addition to glass and coating, information on optical, strength, and length requirements plus any other special labeling, invoicing, packing, or handling requirements will be communicated and checked for each order. The Order Interface is a systematic method to insure the plant's ability to fill orders in an error-free manner. There is a risk associated with bringing the two systems together, but this is recognized and will be a major focus of systems maintenance.

Phase V. Cost Tracking

The Cost Tracking phase is primarily a reporting function that takes advantage of the Shop Order tracking mechanism and its linkage to actual machine hours recorded in the database by the WIP Tracking phase. Cost Tracking will allow cost information to be automatically loaded into the FACTS corporate financial system. Also, it is essential in determining the cost of developmental products and the cost of all products generated for government contracts.

Flexible Manufacturing Systems Diagram

Figure 3 identifies the Benefits, Cost, Time, Effort, Risk, and Technology of each phase of the project and the time, cost, and effort for the total project. It also portrays the fundamental nature of the Data Centered Architecture to all components of FMS.

Alternatives

There are alternatives to FMS. One is to maintain the status quo. However, the manual nature of our current planning and scheduling systems in the face of increasing product-complexity does not meet the quality requirements that we have set for ourselves as an organization. Failure to select the correct fibers on a major order in 1989 made this clear. Another option is to build the new planning and scheduling systems without the information-systems renewal. This would result in a degree of benefit in plant scheduling but would not deliver the Lead-Time Reduction, Cost Tracking, or Accountability for Flexibility in adapting to new products and processes critical to the make-to-order business environment. Other options include increasing inventory or putting products on consignment at customer sites. Both of the options may significantly shorten lead times.

The business strategy that the Communications sector has put in place requires the Total Quality information systems that FMS delivers. A customer-order-based focus throughout the organization is fundamental to the ability to detect and exploit opportunities that are strategically targeted. FMS delivers the manufacturing practices and information systems that will enable that focus.

Energy, Impact, Environmental Control, and Raw-Material Statements

This project will result in no significant additional energy consumption, will not result in the need for any environmental control, and will not result in any additional raw-material requirements.

Corning Telecommunications Division (B): FMS Executive Summary

Background

As a world leader in the optical-fiber industry, the Corning Optical Waveguide Business has grown in recent years, both in volume and in the number of different products manufactured. Despite the technical complexity of fiber manufacturing, competitive pressure continues to require shorter lead times for product delivery.

The business computer systems in place at the Wilmington Plant have been developed over the past decade and, as in many high-growth industries, have generally been incrementally improved (as opposed to redesigned) in an attempt to keep pace with changes in the business. These systems are no longer capable of optimally providing the level and kind of support needed to facilitate Corning's continual plant expansions in the industry; therefore, a new systems capability is required. This capability has been named Flexible Manufacturing System (FMS).

The need for a new systems capability to support optical-fiber manufacturing at Wilmington is being driven by several factors, particularly the following:

- Market demand for shorter lead times
- Product proliferation
- Current system inflexibility
- Renewal of the computer architecture

The FMS project is a multi-year effort to provide enabling manufacturing systems for a high-volume, high-product-count, short-lead-time, make-to-order business environment. It involves the reconfiguration and integration of our plantwide computer network and data architecture and the implementation of new information systems. The FMS project goal is to allow the plant to manufacture directly to customer requirements. The intent is to provide the Optical Waveguide Business with the proper information support system for planning, scheduling, operations management, and control and to create a business system that is flexible enough to handle the rapidly changing aspects of the optical-fiber business.

Through FMS the demand for shorter lead times will be fulfilled by a real-time order-promising capability at the factory and increased efficiency in manufacturing scheduling. The impact of product proliferation will be reduced by building information systems that utilize a common database to eliminate the redundant and complex data structure of the existing systems. The current system inflexibility is the motivation to implement a new integrated information system for the manufacturing operation.

Benefits

The functional requirements of FMS have been developed by building a comprehensive description of the business needs identified by members of the Communications sector in Business Management, Sales and Customer Service, Production Supervision, Process and Product Engineering, Advanced Fiber Products, Computer Services, Quality Engineering, and others. The benefits that FMS will deliver are based on the requirements of the overall organization.

The goal of FMS is to allow the plant to manufacture directly to customer requirements. When a customer orders a product through ATLAS, it will be promised using a real-time capacity model, scheduled in the factory by Planning and Production, visible to the Operator on the floor, and checked before it leaves the plant to the exact specification it received at order entry into the ATLAS system.

The primary benefits of the FMS system are listed in Exhibit 1. These benefits highlight the system's potential contribution to the following:

- Flexibility to adapt to new products and production processes
- On-demand information on orders, production, and inventory
- Cost tracking for orders, experiments, and custom products

FMS will address several areas of responsiveness that are imperative to the survival of the business. Our Sales/Customer Service organizations have seen that reduced lead time can be a competitive edge. Customers know our price and quality. Many orders are now sold on the ship-date commitment. The requirement to compete in this environment is unavoidable. FMS will increase responsiveness in quoting, promising, and filling orders; decrease manufacturing processing time; and allow more rapid new product and process introductions. Through FMS and new technology in processes and products, we can continue to expand the business by addressing niche markets and finding new fiber applications.

Our business strategy is to provide unparalleled value to our customers through Customer Service, Total Quality, and Low Cost. FMS's ability to reduce lead time is a Customer Service advantage that will prevent the loss of market share and potentially result in increased market share. FMS will enable Total Quality efforts to provide the organization with the data required to measure all aspects of manufacturing. Making the right product at the right time will result in manufacturing efficiency and reduced cost.

It is envisioned that portions of FMS could be installed in other manufacturing facilities. FMS has been designed to facilitate that opportunity. It views the output of each process step as an end product, so that it could be applied to a smaller manufacturing organization as well.

Corning Telecommunications Division (C): FMS Progress Report

Jim Reid, in charge of managing Corning's Flexible Manufacturing Systems Project, assessed the status of the project: "We now have 4 project teams instead of the original 7. With production at capacity and construction for expansion starting, we haven't been able to test modules as we've developed them. We are now focusing on some critical technical issues and the relational database is proving to be a real bear. It is supposed to function for 24 hours a day, 7 days a week. It is taking us longer to get the system to run efficiently from the database than we had thought. The relational technology takes too much time to do all the joins. With the CPU cranking away, it takes up to 20 minutes for screens to appear for wareflow tracking. Our goal is a 10-second response time. Now we are looking at ways to recreate the database structure—to have less reliance on tables and logical joins and simply create permanent fields for information we know we will want. This isn't a show-stopper or even close, we just have to learn the technology and manage it better.

To our relief, we have a simulation completed for the finite-forward-scheduling module. We designed the module on a PC and then tested it with a month of real factory information. The calculations only took 40 minutes on the PC to schedule the entire factory, and it did it well. This was a new-invention area, and we're sailing through.

We also have developed a central repository on the Mac using database technology. This repository contains standards for screens, data definitions, code definitions, etc. As we develop a module, we put information about the module in the repository. All project teams have access to the repository, and we've been able to use about 80% of the modules we've designed for different parts of the overall system. Each project team gets all the information about naming files, fields, and designing screens from the repository. Our ability to coordinate and share knowledge is a real strong point.

Another problem had arisen when we discovered we couldn't buy a package for process manufacturing. It didn't work. We aren't tracking large batches in small numbers; we have thousands and thousands of batches of fiber running through. No package could handle it. Now we have to develop it from scratch. Most packages want to treat each fiber blank as a batch, but each fiber blank for us turns into many different fiber products for our customers. Our custom system will have to take into account this complexity, but we think we can handle it."

Tom LaGarde, manager of Information Systems at the Wilmington factory, commented on the progress thus far: "Jim [Reid] has been shorted some resources from my staff due to other expectations. Despite these difficulties, he has done a masterful job. Jim's development teams are moving at a pace faster than the organization can assimilate the new FMS technology. The plant is slowing Jim down. His resources are very expensive, so he has decided to spread the resources out over a longer period of time to better time his technical development efforts with our organizational learning capacity. There is also more and more attention being given to the plant expansion, and this slows Jim down. Jim is competing for resources with all these activities going on and had decided to develop FMS in a serial fashion rather than a parallel fashion—saving money for Corning and keeping pace with what parts of FMS can be adopted at the plant."

This case was prepared by Assistant Professor Andrew C. Boynton, Darden School, University of Virginia, and Ph.D. candidate Michael E. Shank, University of North Carolina, Chapel Hill, Copyright ©1991 by the Darden Graduate Business School Foundation, Charlottesville, Virginia.

Case Study Questions

1. Use the competitive forces and value chain models to analyze the Corning Telecommunications Division. What competitive forces did Corning have to deal with? What were the strategic advantages of switching to a flexible manufacturing system for optical waveguides?

2. What were the problems with Corning's existing manufacturing system for optical waveguides? How serious were they? What management, organization, and technology factors contributed to these problems?

3. What management, organization, and technology issues had to be addressed to implement a flexible manufacturing system successfully?

4. What were the dangers and risks of this project?

5. What criteria would you have used to determine whether Corning should invest in this project?

6. Should Corning have made the $5 million investment in the new flexible manufacturing system? Explain your answer. Analyze the status of the project.

Appendix A: Functional Information Systems

This appendix provides more detail on how organizations use information systems from a functional perspective. Information systems can be classified by the specific organizational function they serve as well as by organizational level. The major organizational functions consist of sales and marketing, manufacturing, finance, accounting, and human resources. We now describe typical information systems that support each of these functions, showing functional applications for each organizational level.

SALES AND MARKETING SYSTEMS

The sales and marketing function is responsible for selling the organization's product or service. Marketing is concerned with identifying the customers for the firm's products or services, determining what they need or want, planning and developing products and services to meet their needs, and advertising and promoting these products and services. Sales is concerned with contacting customers, selling the products and services, taking orders, and following up on sales.

Table A.1 shows that information systems are used in sales and marketing in a number of ways. At the strategic level, sales and marketing systems monitor trends affecting new products and sales opportunities, support planning for new products and services and monitor the performance of competitors. At the management level, sales and marketing systems support market research, advertising and promotional campaigns, and pricing decisions. They analyze sales performance and the performance of the sales staff. Knowledge-level sales and marketing systems support marketing analysis workstations. At the operational level, sales and marketing systems assist in locating and contacting prospective customers, tracking sales, processing orders, and providing customer service support.

A typical sales information system is one for recording sales using a point-of-sale device, which is illustrated in Figure A.1. A point-of-sale device captures data about each item sold at the time the sale takes place. For example, when a purchase is made

Table A.1 Examples of Sales and Marketing Information Systems

System	Description	Organization Level
Order Processing	Enter, process, and track orders	Operational
Point-of-Sale System	Record sales data	Operational
Sales Region Analysis	Analyze performance of sales territories	Management
Market Analysis	Identify customers and markets using data on demographics, markets, consumer behavior, and trends	Knowledge
Pricing Analysis	Determine prices for products and services	Management
Sales Trend Forecasting	Prepare 5-year sales forecasts	Strategic

at a Wal-Mart store, described in Chapter 2, point-of-sale terminals record the bar code of each item passing the checkout counter and send a purchase transaction directly to a central computer at Wal-Mart headquarters. The computer collects the sales data (which identify each item sold and the amount of the sale) and consolidates them for further management analysis. Wal-Mart managers examine these sales data to monitor sales activity and buying trends. The data are also used for placing orders to suppliers to replenish inventory of fast-selling goods. Figure A.1 illustrates how this point-of-sale system works.

MANUFACTURING AND PRODUCTION SYSTEMS

The manufacturing and production function is responsible for actually producing the firm's goods and services. Manufacturing and production systems deal with the planning, development, and maintenance of production facilities; the establishment of production goals; the acquisition, storage, and availability of production materials; and the scheduling of equipment, facilities, materials, and labor required to fashion finished products.

Table A.2 shows some typical manufacturing and production information systems arranged by organizational level. Strategic-level manufacturing systems deal with the firm's long-term manufacturing goals, such as where to locate new plants or whether to invest in new manufacturing technology. At the management level, manufacturing and production systems analyze and monitor manufacturing and production costs and resources. Knowledge manufacturing and production systems create and distribute design knowledge or expertise to drive the production process, and operational manufacturing and production systems deal with the status of production tasks.

Most manufacturing and production systems use some sort of inventory control system, illustrated in Figure A.2. Data about each item in inventory, such as the number of units depleted because of a shipment or purchase or the number of units replen-

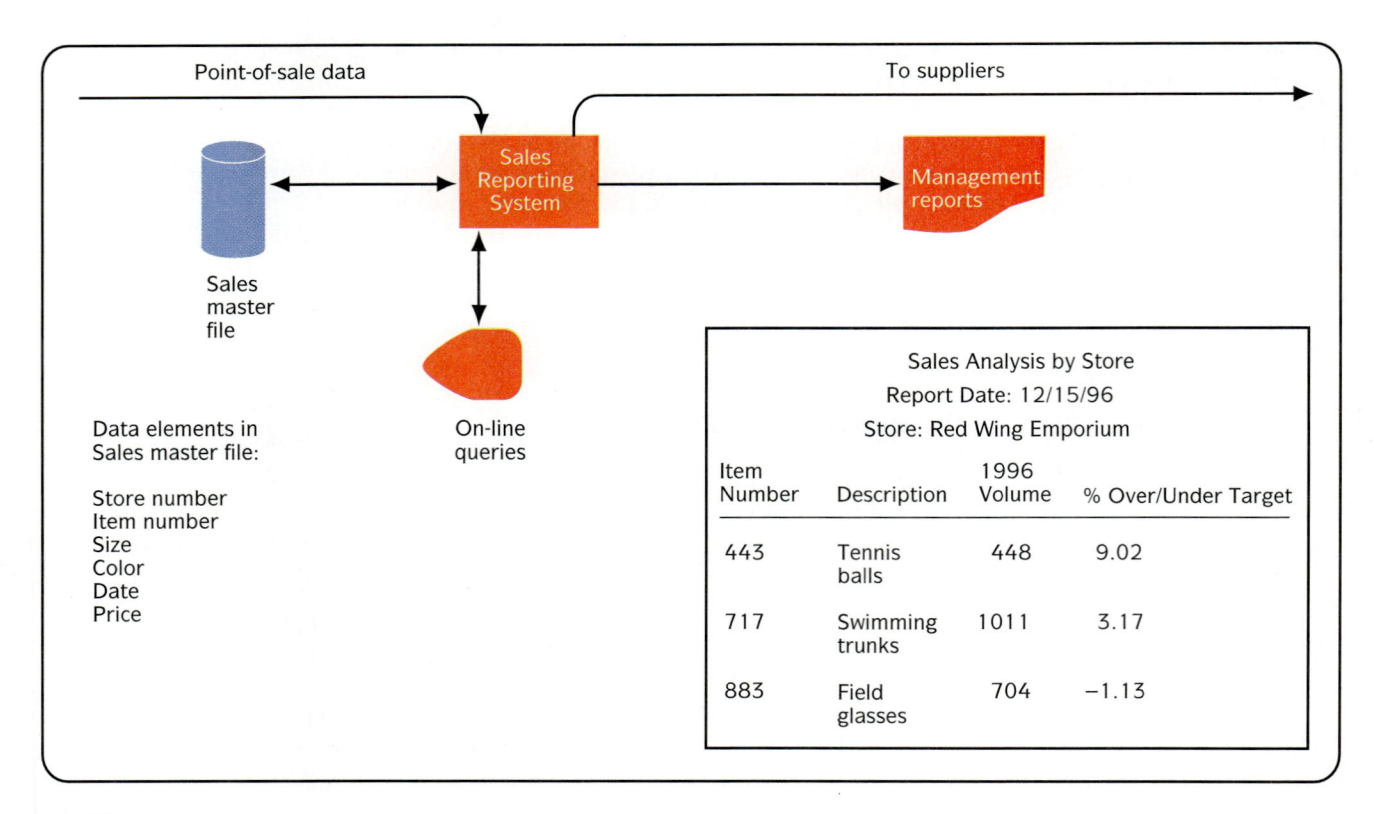

FIGURE A.1

Table A.2 — Examples of Manufacturing and Production Information Systems

System	Description	Organization Level
Plant Scheduling	Schedule the production of a product by coordinating jobs, labor, supplies, and finances	Operational
Material Movement Control	Track purchases, receipts, and shipments	Operational
Machine Control	Control the actions of machines and equipment	Operational
Computer-Aided Design (CAD)	Design new products	Knowledge
Production Planning	Decide when and how much products should be produced	Management
Inventory Control	Determine and maintain optimal level of stock for goods in process and finished goods	Management
Facilities Location	Decide where to locate new production facilities	Strategic

ished by reordering or returns are either scanned or keyed into the system. The inventory master file contains basic data about each item—the unique identification code for each item, the description of the item, the number of units on hand, the number of units on order, and the reorder point—the number of units in inventory that triggers a decision to reorder in order to prevent a stockout. (Companies can estimate the number of items to reorder or they can use a formula for calculating the least expensive quantity

Data elements in Inventory master file:

- Item code
- Description
- Units on hand
- Units on order
- Reorder point

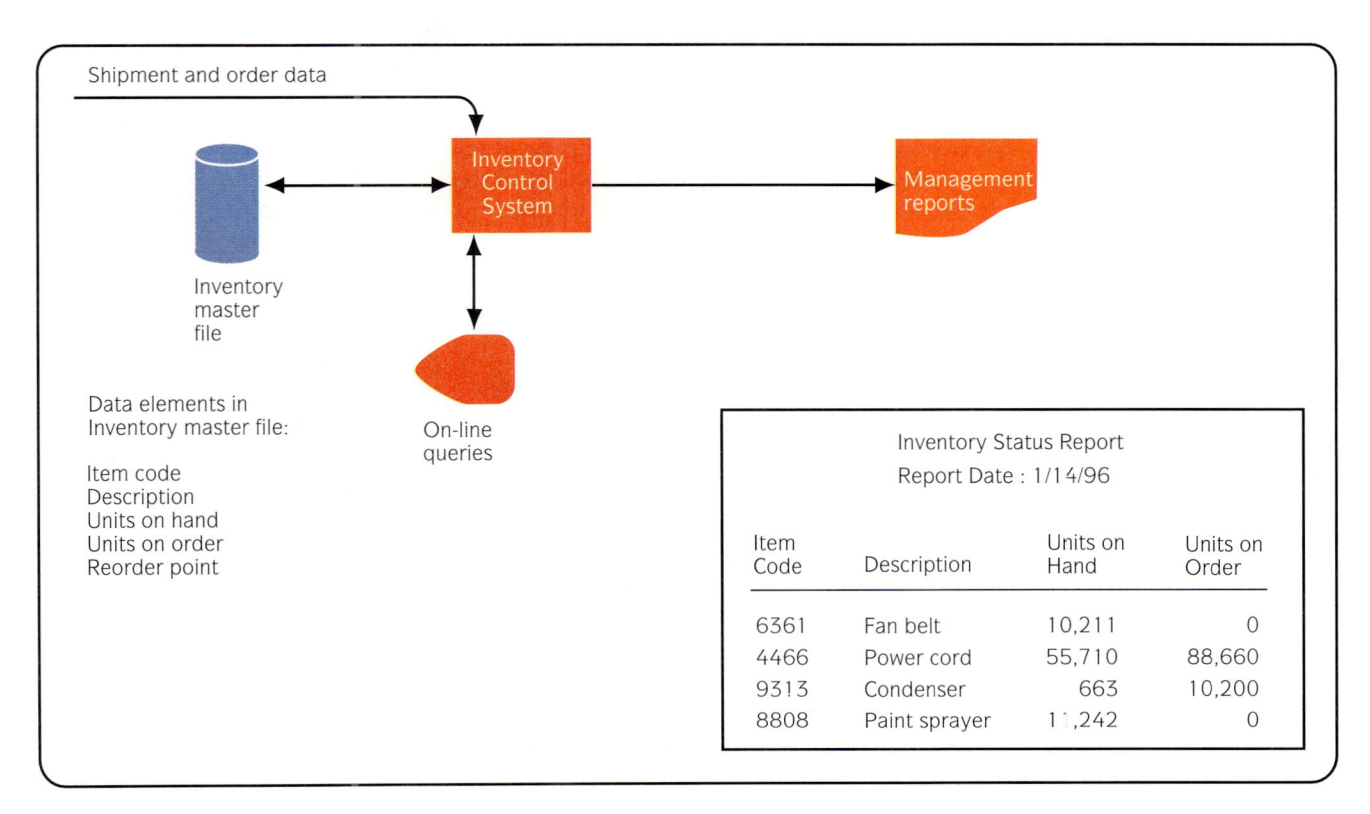

Inventory Status Report
Report Date : 1/14/96

Item Code	Description	Units on Hand	Units on Order
6361	Fan belt	10,211	0
4466	Power cord	55,710	88,660
9313	Condenser	663	10,200
8808	Paint sprayer	11,242	0

FIGURE A.2

to order called the *economic order quantity*.) The system produces reports such as the number of each item available in inventory, the number of units of each item to reorder, or items in inventory that must be replenished.

Many firms are trying to create a seamless manufacturing process by integrating the various types of automated manufacturing systems, using computers and communication technology. The data produced in one system are immediately available to be used by other systems. Leading-edge applications such as the computer-aided design/computer-aided manufacturing (CAD/CAM) system used by Odense Shipyards, which is described in the Window on Technology in Chapter 2, are even using the data from computer-generated designs to drive the actual fabrication and assembly of products. Before computer-integrated manufacturing, design engineers had to draft plans on paper and then hand them over to experts in manufacturing. The product development cycle was prolonged because the process required so many manual steps and handoffs.

FINANCE AND ACCOUNTING SYSTEMS

The finance function is responsible for managing the firm's financial assets, such as cash, stocks, bonds, and other investments in order to maximize the return on these financial assets. The finance function is also in charge of managing the capitalization of the firm (finding new financial assets in stocks, bonds, or other forms of debt). In order to determine whether the firm is getting the best return on its investments, the finance function must obtain a considerable amount of information from sources external to the firm.

The accounting function is responsible for maintaining and managing the firm's financial records—receipts, disbursements, depreciation, payroll—to account for the flow of funds in a firm. Finance and accounting share related problems— how to keep track of a firm's financial assets and fund flows. They provide answers to questions such as these: What is the current inventory of financial assets? What records exist for disbursements, receipts, payroll, and other fund flows?

Table A.3 shows some of the typical finance and accounting systems found in a typical large organization. Strategic-level systems for the finance and accounting function establish long-term investment goals for the firm and provide long-range forecasts of the firm's financial performance. At the management level, information systems help managers oversee and control the firm's financial resources. Knowledge systems support finance and accounting by providing analytical tools and workstations for designing the right mix of investments to maximize returns for the firm. Operational systems in finance

Table A.3 Examples of Finance and Accounting Information Systems

System	Description	Organization Level
Payroll	Produce paychecks and maintain payroll records	Operational
Accounts Receivable	Track money owed the firm	Operational
Cash Management	Track firm's receipts and disbursements to determine funds available for investment	Operational
Portfolio Analysis	Design the firm's portfolio of investments	Knowledge
Budgeting	Prepare short-term budgets	Management
Capital Investment Analysis	Evaluate the profitability of long-term capital expenditures	Management
Profit Planning	Plan long-term profits	Strategic

and accounting track the flow of funds in the firm through transactions such as paychecks, payments to vendors, securities reports, and receipts.

A typical finance and accounting system found in all businesses is an accounts receivable system (see Figure A.3). An accounts receivable system keeps track of the money owed to the firm by its customers. Every customer purchase generates an *account receivable*—that is, the customer owes the firm money. Some customers pay immediately in cash, and others are granted credit. The accounts receivable system records the data from every invoice in a master file that also contains information on each customer, including credit rating. As the business goes on day after day, the system also keeps track of all the bills outstanding and can produce a variety of reports, both on paper and on computer screens, to help the business collect bills. The system also answers queries regarding a customer's payment history and credit rating. This system supplies information to the general ledger system, which tracks all cash flows of the firm.

HUMAN RESOURCES SYSTEMS

The human resources function is responsible for attracting, developing, and maintaining the firm's work force. Human resources identifies potential employees, maintains complete records on existing employees, and creates programs to develop employees' talents and skills.

Strategic-level human resources systems identify the manpower requirements (skills, educational level, types of positions, number of positions, and cost) for meeting the firm's long-term business plans. At the management level, human resources systems help managers monitor and analyze the recruitment, allocation, and compensation of employees. Knowledge systems for human resources support analysis activities related to job design, training, and the modeling of employee career paths and reporting rela-

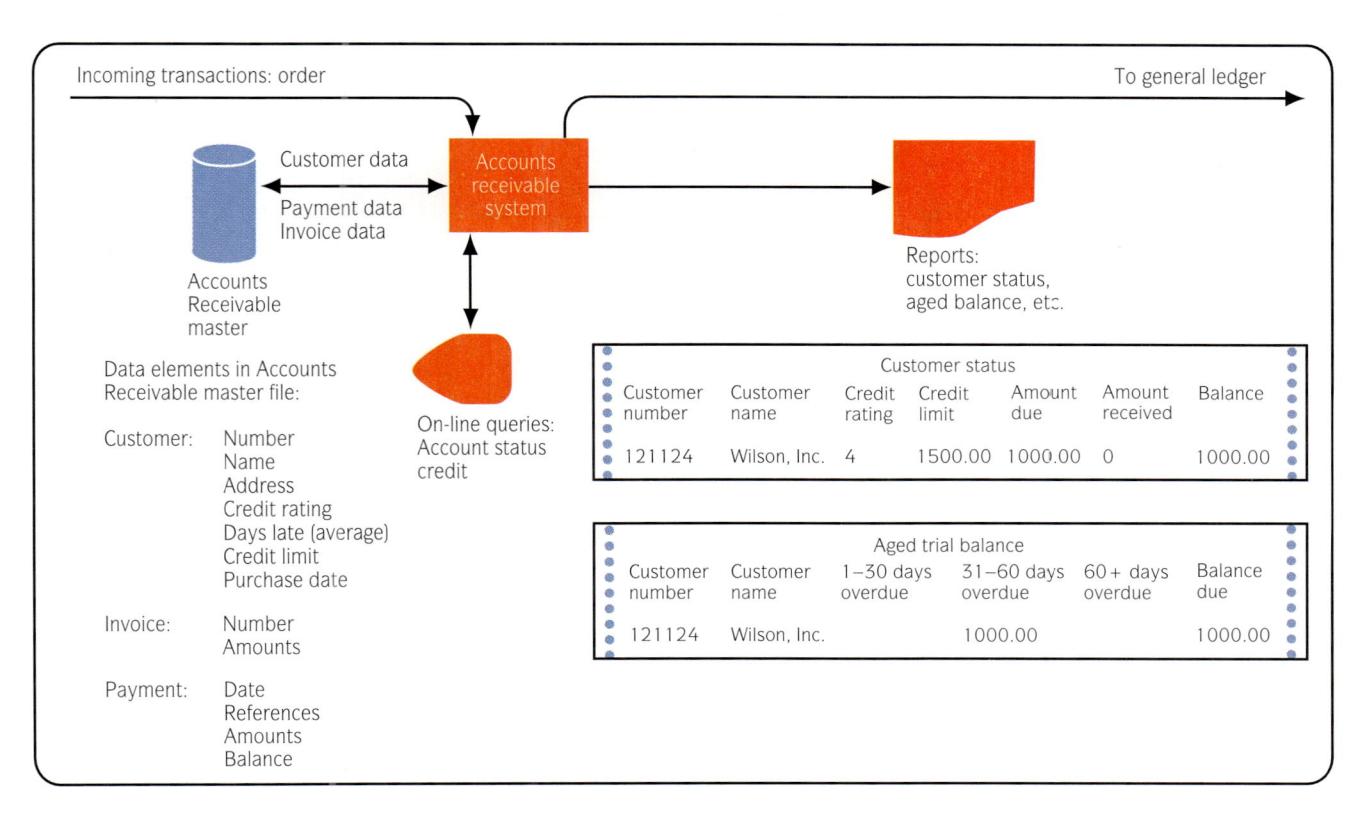

FIGURE A.3

Table A.4   Examples of Human Resources Information Systems

System	Description	Organization Level
Employee Record Keeping	Maintain records of employees	Operational
Training and Development	Track employee training, skills, and performance appraisals	Operational
Career Pathing	Design career paths for employees	Knowledge
Compensation Analysis	Analyze the range and distribution of employee wages, salaries, and benefits	Management
Contract Cost Analysis	Analyze the impact of projected changes in labor union contracts to the company's human resources costs	Management
Manpower Planning	Plan the long-term labor force needs of the organization	Strategic

tionships. Human resources operational systems track the recruitment and placement of the firm's employees (see Table A.4).

Figure A.4 illustrates a typical human resources system for employee record keeping. It maintains basic employee data, such as the employee's name, age, sex, marital status, address, educational background, salary, job title, date of hire, and date of termination. The system can produce a variety of reports, such as lists of newly hired employees, employees who are terminated or on leaves of absence, employees classified by job type or educational level, or employee job performance evaluations. Such systems are typically designed to provide data that can satisfy federal and state record keeping requirements for Equal Employment Opportunity (EEO) and other purposes.

```
Employee data (various departments) ──────►  [Human Resources System]  ──────► To payroll
                                                      │
         [Employee master file] ◄────────►           │  ──────► [Management reports]
                                                      │
                                              [On-line queries]
```

Data elements in employee master file:

Employee: Number
             Name
             Address
             Department
             Age
             Marital status
             Sex
             Salary
             Educational background
             Job title
             Date of hire
             Date of termination
             Termination reason

Termination Report

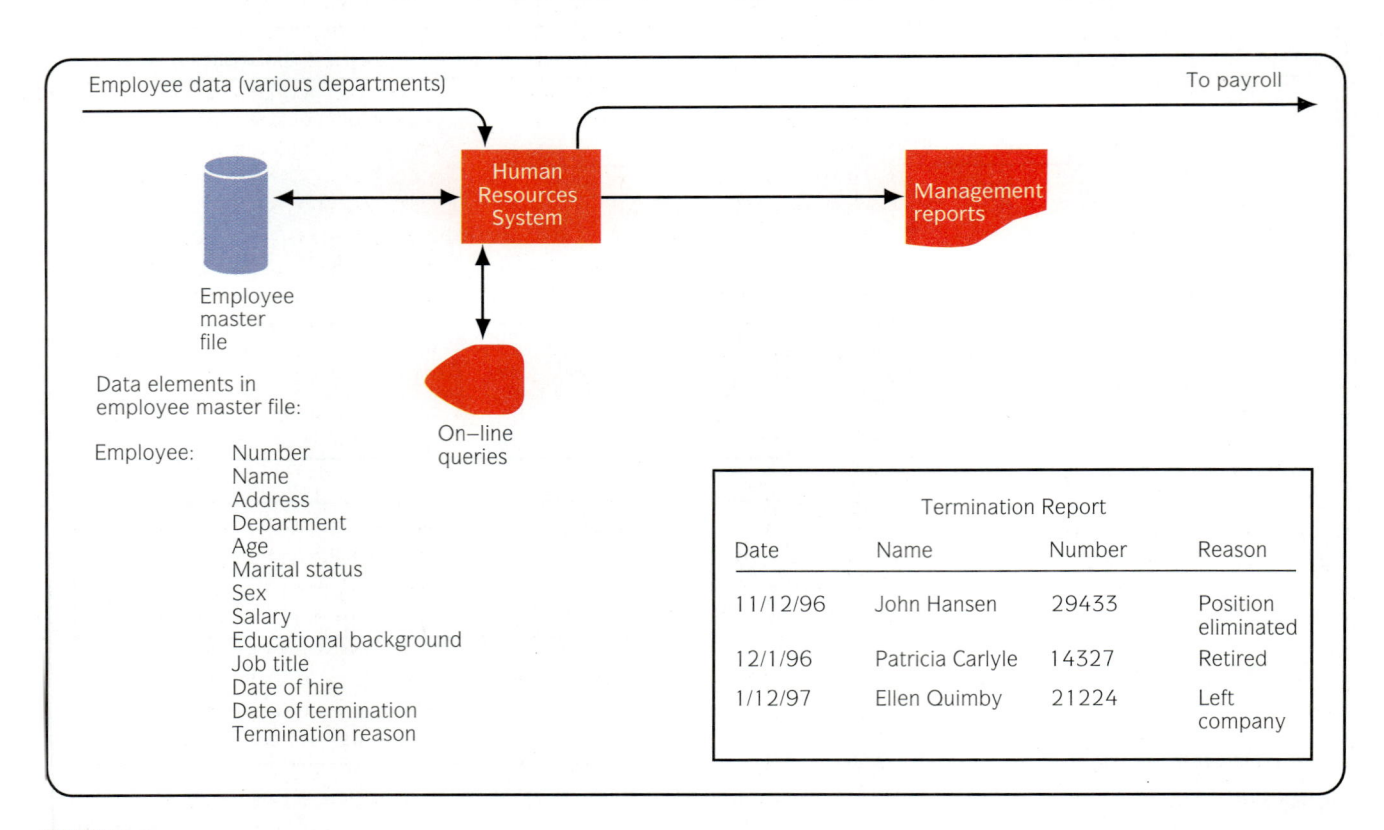

Date	Name	Number	Reason
11/12/96	John Hansen	29433	Position eliminated
12/1/96	Patricia Carlyle	14327	Retired
1/12/97	Ellen Quimby	21224	Left company

FIGURE A.4

Glossary

Acceptance testing: Provides the final certification that the system is ready to be used in a production setting.

Accountability: The mechanisms for assessing responsibility for decisions made and actions taken.

Ada: A programming language that is portable across different brands of soft hardware; is used for both military and nonmilitary applications.

Adhocracy: A task force organization, such as a research organization, designed to respond to a rapidly changing environment and characterized by large groups of specialists organized into short-lived multidisciplinary task forces.

Administrative controls: Formalized standards, rules, procedures, and disciplines to ensure that the organization's controls are properly executed and enforced.

Agency theory: An economic theory that views the firm as a nexus of contracts among self-interested individuals rather than a unified, profit-maximizing entity.

AI shell: The programming environment of an expert system.

Analog signal: A continuous wave form that passes through a communications medium. Used for voice communications.

Anti-virus software: Software designed to detect and often eliminate computer viruses from an information system.

Application controls: Specific controls unique to each computerized application.

Application generator: Software that can generate entire information system applications; the user needs only to specify what needs to be done and the application generator creates the appropriate program code.

Application software: Programs written for a specific business application in order to perform functions specified by end users.

Application software package: A set of prewritten, precoded, application software programs that are commercially available for sale or lease.

Applications portability: The ability to operate the same software on different hardware platforms.

Archie: A tool for locating data on the Internet that performs key word searches of an actual database of documents, software, and data files available for downloading from servers around the world.

Arithmetic-logic unit (ALU): Component of the CPU that performs the principal logical and arithmetic operations of the computer.

Artificial intelligence: The effort to develop computer-based systems that can behave like humans, with the ability to learn languages, accomplish physical tasks, use a perceptual apparatus, and emulate human expertise and decision making.

ASCII: American Standard Code for Information Interchange. A 7- or 8-bit binary code used in data transmission, microcomputers, and some large computers.

Assembly language: A programming language developed in the 1950s, that resembles machine language but substitutes mnemonics for numeric codes.

Asynchronous transfer mode (ATM): A networking technology that parcels information into 8-byte cells, allowing data to be transmitted between computers of different vendors at any speed.

Asynchronous transmission: The low-speed transmission of one character at a time.

Attribute: Piece of information describing a particular entity.

Automation: Using the computer to speed up the performance of existing tasks.

Backward chaining: A strategy for searching the rule base in an expert system that acts like a problem solver by beginning with a hypothesis and seeking out more information until the hypothesis is either proved or disproved.

Bandwidth: The capacity of a communications channel as measured by the difference between the highest and lowest frequencies that can be transmitted by that channel.

Bar code: A form of OCR technology widely used in supermarkets and retail stores in which identification data are coded into a series of bars.

Baseband: LAN channel technology that provides a single path for transmitting text, graphics, voice, or video data at one time.

BASIC (Beginners All-purpose Symbolic Instruction Code): General-purpose programming language used with microcomputers and for teaching programming.

Batch control totals: A type of input control that requires counting transactions or any quantity field in a batch of transactions prior to processing for comparison and reconciliation after processing.

Batch processing: A method of processing information in which transactions are accumulated and stored until a specified time when it is convenient and/or necessary to process them as a group.

Baud: A change in signal from positive to negative or vice-versa that is used as a measure of transmission speed.

Behavioral models: Descriptions of management based on behavioral scientists' observations of what managers actually do in their jobs.

Bit: A binary digit representing the smallest unit of data in a computer system. It can only have one of two states, representing 0 or 1.

Bit mapping: The technology that allows each pixel on the screen to be addressed and manipulated by the computer.

Bottom-up approach: In the history of artificial intelligence, the effort to build a physical analog to the human brain.

Bounded rationality: The idea that people will avoid new uncertain alternatives and stick with tried-and-true rules and procedures.

Briefing books: On-line data in the form of fixed-format reports for executives.

Broadband: LAN channel technology that provides several paths for transmitting text, graphics, voice, or video data so that different types of data can be transmitted simultaneously.

Browser: A software tool that supports graphics and hyperlinks and is needed to navigate the Web.

Bugs: Program code defects or errors.

Bureaucracy: Formal organization with a clear-cut division of labor, abstract rules and procedures, and impartial decision making that uses technical qualifications and professionalism as a basis for promoting employees.

Bureaucratic models: Models of decision making where decisions are shaped by the organization's standard operating procedures (SOPs).

Business driver: A force in the environment to which businesses must respond and that influences the direction of business.

Business process: A set of logically related tasks performed to achieve a defined business outcome.

Business reengineering: The radical redesign of business processes, combining steps to cut waste and eliminating repetitive, paper-intensive tasks in order to improve cost, quality, and service, and to maximize the benefits of information technology.

Bus network: A network topology linking a number of computers by a single circuit with all messages broadcast to the entire network.

Byte: A string of bits, usually eight, used to store one number or character stored in a computer system.

C: A powerful programming language with tight control and efficiency of execution; is portable across different microprocessors and is used primarily with microcomputers.

Cache: High-speed storage of frequently used instructions and data.

Capital budgeting: The process of analyzing and selecting various proposals for capital expenditures.

Carpal tunnel syndrome (CTS): A type of RSI in which pressure on the median nerve through the wrist's bony carpal tunnel produces pain.

Case-based reasoning (CBR): Artificial intelligence technology that represents knowledge as a database of cases.

CD-ROM: Compact disk read-only memory. Read-only optical-disk storage used for imaging, reference, and database applications with massive amounts of data and for multimedia.

Cellular telephone: A device that transmits voice or data, using radio waves to communicate with radio antennas placed within adjacent geographic areas called *cells*.

Centralized processing: Processing that is accomplished by one large central computer.

Central processing unit (CPU): The area of the computer system that manipulates symbols, numbers, and letters and controls the other parts of the computer system.

Change agent: In the context of implementation, the individual acting as the catalyst during the change process to ensure successful organizational adaptation to a new system or innovation.

Channels: The links by which data or voice are transmitted between sending and receiving devices in a network.

Chatting: Live, interactive conversations over a public network.

Choice: Simon's third stage of decision making, when the individual selects among the various solution alternatives.

Class: A feature of object-oriented programming so that all objects belonging to a certain class have all of the features of that class.

Classical model of management: Traditional descriptions of management that focused on its formal functions of planning, organizing, coordinating, deciding, and controlling.

Client: The user point-of-entry for the required function. Normally a desktop computer, workstation, or laptop computer, the user generally interacts directly only with the client, typically through a graphical user interface, using it to input and retrieve data, and to analyze and report on them.

Client/server model: A model for computing that splits the processing between clients and servers on a network, assigning functions to the machine most able to perform the function.

Coaxial cable: A transmission medium consisting of thickly insulated copper wire. Can transmit large volumes of data quickly.

COBOL (COmmon Business Oriented Language): The predominant programming language for business applications because it can process large data files with alphanumeric characters.

Cognitive style: An underlying personality disposition toward the treatment of information, selection of alternatives, and evaluation of consequences.

Combinatorial explosion: In computer processing, the overload that results when trying to test more rules to reach a solution than the computer is capable of handling.

Competitive forces model: A model used to describe the interaction of external threats and opportunities that affect an organization's strategy and ability to compete.

Compiler: Special system software that translates a higher-level language into machine language for execution by the computer.

Compound document: An electronic document that consists of differing types of information acquired from separate sources such as graphics, database, spreadsheet, and text-based programs.

Computer abuse: The commission of acts involving a computer that may not be illegal but are considered unethical.

Computer-aided design (CAD): An information system that automates the creation and revision of designs using sophisticated graphics software.

Computer-aided software engineering (CASE): The automation of step-by-step methodologies for software and systems development to reduce the amount of repetitive work the developer needs to do.

Computer-based information systems (CBIS): Information systems that rely on computer hardware and software for processing and disseminating information.

Computer crime: The commission of illegal acts through the use of a computer or against a computer system.

Computer generations: The major transitions in computer hardware; each generation is distinguished by a different technology for the components that do the processing.

Computer hardware: The physical equipment used for input, processing, and output work in an information system.

Computer matching: The processing control that matches input data to information held on master files.

Computer mouse: A handheld input device whose movement on the desktop controls the position of the cursor on the computer display screen.

Computer operations controls: The procedures to ensure that programmed procedures are consistently and correctly applied to data storage and processing.

Computer software: The detailed preprogrammed instructions that coordinate computer hardware components in an information system.

Computer virus: A rogue software program that is difficult to detect and spreads rapidly through computer systems, destroying data or disrupting processing and memory systems.

Computer vision syndrome (CVS): An eye-strain condition related to cathode ray tube (CRT) use, with symptoms including headaches, blurred vision, and dry, irritated eyes.

Concentrator: A telecommunications computer that collects and temporarily stores messages from terminals for batch transmission to the host computer.

Connectivity: A measure of how well computers and computer-based devices communicate and share information with one another without human intervention.

Connectivity audit: A method for examining the amount of connectivity an organization has by examining five areas of connectivity such as network standards, user interfaces, and applications.

Context diagram: An overview data flow diagram depicting an entire system as a single process with its major inputs and outputs.

Control aids: The capabilities that allow the user to control the activities and functions of the DSS.

Controller: A specialized computer that supervises communications traffic between the CPU and the peripheral devices in a telecommunications system.

Controls: All of the methods, policies, and procedures that ensure protection of the organization's assets, accuracy and reliability of its records, and operational adherence to management standards.

Control unit: The component of the CPU that controls and coordinates the other parts of the computer system.

Conversion: The process of changing from the old system to the new system.

Conversion plan: Provides a schedule of all activities required to install a new system.

Cooptation: Bringing the opposition into the process of designing and implementing the solution without giving up control over the direction and nature of the change.

Copyright: A statutory grant that protects creators of intellectual property against copying by others for any purpose for a period of 28 years.

Core systems: Systems that support functions that are absolutely critical to the organization.

Cost benefit ratio: A method for calculating the returns from a capital expenditure by dividing the total benefits by total costs.

Counterimplementation: A deliberate strategy to thwart the implementation of an information system or an innovation in an organization.

Critical success factors (CSFs): A small number of easily identifiable operational goals shaped by the industry, the firm, the manager, and the broader environment that are believed to assure the success of an organization. Used to determine the information requirements of an organization.

Custom manufacturing: Use of software and computer networks to finely control production so that products can be easily customized with no added cost for small production runs.

Customization: The modification of a software package to meet an organization's unique requirements without destroying the integrity of the package software.

Cylinder: Represents circular tracks on the same vertical line within a disk pack.

Data: Streams of raw facts representing events occurring in organizations or the physical environment before they have been organized and arranged into a form that people can understand and use.

Data administration: A special organizational function for managing the organization's data resources, concerned with data planning, information policy, maintenance of data dictionaries, and data quality standards.

Database: A collection of data organized to service many applications at the same time by organizing data so that they appear to be in one location.

Database administration: Refers to the more technical and operational aspects of managing data, including physical database design and operation.

Database management system (DBMS): Special software to create and maintain a database and enable individual business applications to extract the data they need without having to create separate files or data definitions in their computer programs.

Data bus width: The number of bits that can be moved at one time between the CPU, primary storage, and the other devices of a computer.

Dataconferencing: Teleconferencing in which two or more users are able to edit and directly modify data files simultaneously.

Data conversion: Process of properly transcribing data from one form into another form for computer transactions.

Data definition language: The component of a database management system that defines each data element as it appears in the database.

Data dictionary: An automated or manual tool for storing and organizing information about the data maintained in a database.

Data element: A field.

Data flow diagram (DFD): Primary tool in structured analysis that graphically illustrates the system's component processes and the flow of data between them.

Data flows: The movement of data between processes, external entities, and data stores in a data flow diagram.

Data management software: Software used for creating and manipulating lists, creating files and databases to store data, and combining information for reports.

Data manipulation language: A language associated with a database management system that is employed by end users and programmers to manipulate data in the database.

Data quality audit: Survey of files and samples of files for accuracy and completeness of data in an information system.

Data redundancy: The presence of duplicate data in multiple data files.

Data security controls: Controls to ensure that data files on either disk or tape are not subject to unauthorized access, change, or destruction.

Data stores: Manual or automated inventories of data.

Data warehouse: Database with reporting and query tools that stores current and historical data from operational systems that has been consolidated for management reporting and analysis.

Data workers: People such as secretaries or bookkeepers who process and disseminate the organization's paperwork.

Debugging: The process of discovering and eliminating the errors and defects—the bugs—in program code.

Decisional roles: Mintzberg's classification for managerial roles where managers initiate activities, handle disturbances, allocate resources, and negotiate conflicts.

Decision-support systems (DSS): Computer systems at the management level of an organization that combine data and sophisticated analytical models to support semi-structured and unstructured decision making.

Decision trees: Sequential tree-like diagrams that present the conditions affecting a decision and the actions that can be taken. The branches represent the paths that may be taken in the decision-making process.

Dedicated lines: Telephone lines that are continuously available for transmission by a lessee. Typically conditioned to transmit data at high speeds for high-volume applications.

Descartes's rule of change: A principle that states that if an action cannot be taken repeatedly, then it is not right to be taken at any time.

Design: Simon's second stage of decision making, when the individual conceives of possible alternative solutions to a problem.

Design: Stage in the systems lifecycle that produces the logical and physical design specifications for the systems solution.

Desktop publishing: Technology that produces professional-quality documents combining output from word processors with design, graphics, and special layout features.

Development methodology: A collection of methods, one or more for every activity within every phase of a development project.

Digital image processing: Technology that converts documents and graphic images into computerized form so that they can be stored, processed, and accessed by computer systems.

Digital scanners: Input devices that translate images such as pictures or documents into digital form for processing.

Digital signal: A discrete wave form that transmits data coded into two discrete states as 1-bits and 0-bits, which are represented as on–off electrical impulses. Used for data communications.

Direct access storage device (DASD): Refers to magnetic disk technology which permits the CPU to locate a record directly, in contrast to sequential tape storage that must search the entire file.

Direct cutover: A risky conversion approach where the new system completely replaces the old one on an appointed day.

Direct file access method: Method of accessing records by mathematically transforming the key fields into the specific address for the records.

Direct file organization: Method of storing records so that they can be accessed in any sequence without regard to their actual physical order on storage media.

Distributed database: A database that is stored in more than one physical location. Parts or copies of the database are physically stored in one location and other parts are stored and maintained in other locations.

Distributed processing: The distribution of computer processing work among multiple computers linked by a communication network.

Divisionalized bureaucracy: Combination of many machine bureaucracies, each producing a different product or service, under one central headquarters.

Documentation: Descriptions of how an information system works from either a technical or end-user standpoint.

Document imaging systems: Systems that employ digital image processing to store, retrieve, and manipulate a digitized image of a document, allowing the document itself to be discarded.

Domestic exporter: Global strategy characterized by heavy centralization of corporate activities in the home country of origin.

DOS: Operating system for 16-bit microcomputers based on the IBM Personal Computer standard.

Downsizing: The process of transferring applications from large computers to smaller ones.

Downtime: Periods of time in which an information system is not operational.

Drill down: The ability to move from summary data down to lower and lower levels of detail.

DSS database: A collection of current or historical data from a number of applications or groups.

DSS software system: DSS component that permits easy interaction between the users of the system and the DSS database and model base.

EBCDIC: Extended Binary Coded Decimal Interchange Code. Binary code representing every number, alphabetic character, or special character with 8 bits, used primarily in IBM and other mainframe computers.

Economic feasibility: Determines whether the benefits of the proposed solution outweigh the costs.

Edit checks: Routines performed to verify input data and correct errors prior to processing.

Electronic calendaring: Software that tracks appointments and schedules in an office.

Electronic commerce: The process of doing business electronically involving the automation of various business-to-business transactions.

Electronic data interchange (EDI): Direct computer-to-computer exchange between two organizations of standard business transaction documents.

Electronic mail: The computer-to-computer exchange of messages.

Electronic market: A marketplace that is created by computer and communication technologies which link many buyers and sellers via inter-organizational systems.

Electronic meeting software: Software designed to enhance the productivity of face-to-face meetings or of meetings among participants in scattered locations.

Electronic meeting system (EMS): Collaborative GDSS that uses information technology to make group meetings more productive by facilitating communication as well as decision making. Supports meetings at the same place and time or in different places and times.

End user: Representative of a department outside of the information systems group for whom information systems applications are developed.

End-user development: The development of information systems by end users with little or no formal assistance from technical specialists.

End-user interface: The part of the information system through which the end user interacts with the system, such as on-line screens and commands.

End-user software: Software tools that permit the development of applications by end users with little or no professional programmer intervention or that enhance the productivity of professional programmers.

Enterprise analysis: An analysis of organizationwide information requirements by looking at the entire organization in terms of organizational units, functions, processes, and data elements; helps identify the key entities and attributes in the organization's data.

Enterprise networking: An arrangement of the organization's hardware, software, telecommunications, and data resources to put more computing power on the desktop and create a companywide network linking many smaller networks.

Entity: A person, place, or thing about which information must be kept.

Entity-relationship diagram: Methodology for documenting databases illustrating the relationship between various entities in the database.

Entrepreneurial structure: Young, small firm in a fast-changing environment dominated by a single entrepreneur and managed by a single chief executive officer.

Environmental factors: Factors external to the organization that influence the adoption and design of information systems.

EPROM: Erasable programmable read-only memory. Subclass of ROM chip that can be erased and reprogrammed many times.

Ergonomics: The interaction of people and machines in the work environment, including the design of jobs, health issues, and the end-user interface of information systems.

Ethical no-free-lunch rule: Assumption that all tangible and intangible objects are owned by someone else unless there is a specific declaration otherwise and that the creator wants compensation for his work.

Ethics: Principles of right and wrong that can be used by individuals acting as free moral agents to make choices to guide their behavior.

Executive support systems (ESS): Information systems at the strategic level of an organization designed to address unstructured decision making through advanced graphics and communications.

Expert system: Knowledge-intensive computer program that captures the expertise of a human in limited domains of knowledge.

External entities: Originators or receivers of information outside the scope of the system portrayed in the data flow diagram. Sometimes called *outside interfaces*.

External integration tools: Project management technique that links the work of the implementation team to that of users at all organizational levels.

Facsimile (Fax): A machine that digitizes and transmits documents with both text and graphics over telephone lines.

Fair Information Practices (FIP): A set of principles originally set forth in 1973 that governs the collection and use of information about individuals and forms the basis of most U.S. and European privacy law.

Fault-tolerant computer systems: Systems that contain extra hardware, software, and power supply components that can back the system up and keep it running to prevent system failure.

Feasibility study: A way to determine whether a solution is achievable, given the organization's resources and constraints.

Feedback: Output that is returned to the appropriate members of the organization to help them evaluate or correct input.

Fiber-optic cable: Fast, light, and durable transmission medium consisting of thin strands of clear glass fiber bound into cables. Data are transmitted as light pulses.

Field: A grouping of characters into a word, group of words, or complete number.

File: A group of records of the same type.

File server: Computer in a network that stores various programs and data files for users of the network. Determines access and availability in the network.

File transfer protocol (FTP): Tool for retrieving and transferring files from a remote computer.

Firewall: Security system with specialized software to prevent outsiders from invading a private network.

Floppy disk: Removable magnetic disk primarily used with microcomputers. The two most common standard sizes are 3.5-inch and 5.25-inch disks that are made up of polyester film with magnetic coating.

Focused differentiation: Competitive strategy for developing new market niches where a business can compete in the target area better than its competitors.

Formal control tools: Project management technique that helps monitor the progress toward completion of a task and fulfillment of goals.

Formal planning tools: Project management technique that structures and sequences tasks, budgeting time, money, and technical resources required to complete the tasks.

FORTRAN (FORmula TRANslator): Programming language developed in 1956 for scientific and mathematical applications.

Forward chaining: Strategy for searching the rule base in an expert system that begins with the information entered by the user and searches the rule base to arrive at a conclusion.

Forward engineering: The final step in reengineering when the revised specifications are used to generate new, structured program code for a structured and maintainable system.

Fourth-generation language: A programming language that can be employed directly by end users or less skilled programmers to develop computer applications more rapidly than conventional programming languages.

Frame relay: Shared network service technology that packages data into bundles for transmission but does not use error correction routines. Cheaper and faster than packet switching.

Frames: Method of organizing expert system knowledge into chunks, but the relationships are based on shared characteristics determined by the user rather than a hierarchy.

Franchiser: A firm where the product is created, designed, financed, and initially produced in the home country, but must rely heavily on foreign personnel for further production, marketing, and human resources.

Front-end processor: Small computer managing communications for the host computer in a network.

Fuzzy logic: Rule-based AI that tolerates imprecision by using nonspecific terms called *membership functions* to solve problems.

Garbage can model: A model of decision making that states that organizations are not rational and that decisions are solutions that become attached to problems for accidental reasons.

Gateway: Communications processor that connects dissimilar networks by providing the translation from one protocol to another.

General controls: Overall controls that establish a framework for controlling the design, security, and use of computer systems throughout an organization.

Genetic algorithms: Problem-solving methods that promote the evolution of solutions to specified problems using the model of living organisms adapting to their environment.

Gigabyte: Approximately one billion bytes. Unit of computer storage capacity.

Global culture: The development of common expectations, shared artifacts, and social norms among different cultures and peoples.

Gopher: A character-oriented tool for locating data on the Internet that enables the user to locate essentially all textual information stored on Internet servers through a series of easy-to-use, hierarchical menus.

Graphical user interface: The part of an operating system that users interact with that uses graphic icons and the computer mouse to issue commands and make selections.

Graphics language: A computer language that displays data from files or databases in graphic format.

Group decision-support system (GDSS): An interactive computer-based system to facilitate the solutions to unstructured problems by a set of decision makers working together as a group.

Groupware: Software that recognizes the significance of groups in offices by providing functions and services that support the collaborative activities of work groups.

Hacker: A person who gains unauthorized access to a computer network for profit, criminal mischief, or personal pleasure.

Hard disk: Magnetic disk resembling a thin steel platter with an iron oxide coating; used in large computer systems and in many microcomputers.

Hardware controls: Controls to ensure the physical security and correct performance of computer hardware.

Hierarchical data model: One type of logical database model that organizes data in a treelike structure. A record is subdivided into segments that are connected to each other in one-to-many parent-child relationships.

High-level language: Programming languages where each source code statement generates multiple statements at the machine-language level.

Home page: A World Wide Web text and graphical screen display that welcomes the user and explains the organization that has established the page.

Hypermedia database: An approach to data management that organizes data as a network of nodes linked in any pattern established by the user.

Hypertext Markup Language (HTML): A programming tool that uses hypertext to establish links to other documents in the same or remote computers.

Immanuel Kant's Categorical Imperative: A principle that states that if an action is not right for everyone to take it is not right for anyone.

Implementation: Simon's final stage of decision making, when the individual puts the decision into effect and reports on the progress of the solution.

Implementation: All of the organizational activities working toward the adoption, management, and routinization of an innovation.

Implementation controls: Audit of the systems development process at various points to make sure that it is properly controlled and managed.

Incremental decision making: Choosing policies most like the previous policy.

Index: A table or list that relates record keys to physical locations on direct access files.

Indexed sequential access method (ISAM): File access method to directly access records organized sequentially using an index of key fields.

Index server: In imaging systems, a device that stores the indexes that allow a user to identify and retrieve a specific document.

Inference engine: The strategy used to search through the rule base in an expert system: can be forward or backward chaining.

Information: Data that have been shaped into a form that is meaningful and useful to human beings.

Informational roles: Mintzberg's classification for managerial roles, where managers act as the nerve centers of their organizations, receiving and disseminating critical information.

Information architecture: The particular form that information technology takes in a specific organization to achieve selected goals or functions.

Information center: A special facility within an organization that provides training and support for end-user computing.

Information partnership: A cooperative alliance formed between two corporations for the purpose of sharing information to gain strategic advantage.

Information policy: Formal rules governing the maintenance, distribution, and use of information in an organization.

Information portability: The sharing of computer files among different hardware platforms and software applications.

Information requirements: A detailed statement of the information needs that a new system must satisfy; identifies who needs what information, and when, where, and how the information is needed.

Information rights: The rights that individuals and organizations have with respect to information which pertains to themselves.

Information superhighway: High-speed digital telecommunications networks that are national or worldwide in scope and accessible by the general public rather than restricted to use by members of a specific organization or set of organizations such as a corporation.

Information system: Interrelated components that collect, process, store, and disseminate information to support decision making, control, analysis, and visualization in an organization.

Information systems department: The formal organizational unit that is responsible for the information systems function in the organization.

Information systems managers: Leaders of the various specialists in the information systems department.

Information systems plan: A road map indicating the direction of systems development, the rationale, the current situation, the management strategy, the implementation plan, and the budget.

Information work: Work that primarily consists of creating or processing information.

Information workers: People in the labor force who primarily create, work with, or disseminate information.

Inheritance: Features of object-oriented programming in which a specific class of objects receives the features of a more general class.

Input: The capture or collection of raw data from within the organization or from its external environment for processing in an information system.

Input authorization: Proper authorization, recording, and monitoring of source documents as they enter the computer system.

Input controls: Procedures to check data for accuracy and completeness when they enter the system, including input authorization, batch control totals, and edits.

Installation: Systems lifecycle stage consisting of testing, training, and conversion; the final steps required to put a system into operation.

Institutional factors: Factors internal to the organization that influence the adoption and design of information systems.

Intangible benefits: Benefits that are not easily quantified; they include more efficient customer service or enhanced decision making.

Integrated Services Digital Network (ISDN): International standard for transmitting voice, video, and data to support a wide range of service over the public telephone lines.

Integrated software package: A software package that provides two or more applications, such as spreadsheets and word processing, providing for easy transfer of data between them.

Intellectual property: Intangible property created by individuals or corporations which is subject to protections under trade secret, copyright, and patent law.

Intelligence: The first of Simon's four stages of decision making, when the individual collects information to identify problems occurring in the organization.

Interaction theory: User-resistance theory stating that resistance is caused by the interaction of people and systems factors.

Internal integration tools: Project management technique that ensures that the implementation team operates as a cohesive unit.

International information systems infrastructure: The basic information systems required by organizations to coordinate worldwide trade and other activities.

Internet: An international network of networks connecting more than 20 million people from 100 countries; it is the largest information superhighway in the world.

Internetworking: The linking of separate networks, each of which retains its own identity, into an interconnected network.

Interoperability: The ability of a software application to operate on two different machine platforms while maintaining the identical user interface and functionality.

Inter-organizational systems: Information systems that automate the flow of information across organizational boundaries and link a company to its customers, distributors, or suppliers.

Interpersonal roles: Mintzberg's classification for managerial roles where managers act as figureheads and leaders for the organization.

Interpreter: A special language translator that translates each source code statement into machine code and executes it one at a time.

Intranet: An internal network based on World Wide Web technology.

Intuitive decision makers: Cognitive style that describes people who approach a problem with multiple methods in an unstructured manner, using trial and error to find a solution.

Iteration construct: The logic pattern in programming where certain actions are repeated while a specified condition occurs or until a certain condition is met.

Iterative: Process of repeating the steps to build a system over and over again.

Java: Object-oriented programming language that can deliver only the software functionality needed for a particular task as a small applet downloaded from a network. Can run on any computer and operating system.

Joint application design (JAD): A design method which brings users and IS professionals into a room together for an interactive design of the system.

Jukebox: A device for storing and retrieving many optical disks.

Key field: A field in a record that uniquely identifies instances of that record so that it can be retrieved or updated.

Kilobyte: One thousand bytes (actually 1024 storage positions). Used as a measure of microcomputer storage capacity.

Knowledge and information-intense products: Products that require a great deal of learning and knowledge to produce.

Knowledge base: Model of human knowledge that is used by expert systems.

Knowledge engineer: Specialist who elicits information and expertise from other professionals and translates it into a set of rules, frames, or semantic nets for an expert system.

Knowledge-level decision making: Evaluating new ideas for products and services, ways to communicate new knowledge and distribute information.

Knowledge-level systems: Information systems that support knowledge and data workers in an organization.

Knowledge workers: People such as engineers, scientists, or architects who design products or services or create new knowledge for the organization.

Knowledge work systems (KWS): Information systems that aid knowledge workers in the creation and integration of new knowledge in the organization.

Legitimacy: The extent to which one's authority is accepted on grounds of competence, vision, or other qualities.

Liability: The existence of laws that permit individuals to recover the damages done to them by other actors, systems, or organizations.

Local-area network (LAN): Telecommunications network that requires its own dedicated channels and that encompasses a limited distance, usually one building or several buildings in close proximity.

Logical design: Lays out the components of the information system and their relationship to each other as they would appear to users.

Logical view: Representation of data as they would appear to an application programmer or end user.

Low-orbit satellites: Satellites that travel much closer to the earth than traditional satellites and so are able to pick up signals from weak transmitters while consuming less power.

Machine bureaucracy: Large bureaucracy organized into functional divisions that centralizes decision making, produces standard products, and exists in a slow-changing environment.

Machine cycle: Series of operations required to process a single machine instruction.

Machine language: Programming language consisting of the 1s and 0s of binary code.

Magnetic disk: A secondary storage medium in which data are stored by means of magnetized spots on a hard or floppy disk.

Magnetic ink character recognition (MICR): Input technology that translates characters written in magnetic ink into digital codes for processing.

Magnetic tape: Inexpensive and relatively stable secondary storage medium in which large volumes of information are stored sequentially by means of magnetized and nonmagnetized spots on tape.

Magneto-optical disk: Optical disk system that is erasable. Data are recorded by a high-powered laser beam that heats tiny spots in the magnetic media.

Mainframe: Largest category of computer, classified as having 50 megabytes to over 1 gigabyte of RAM.

Maintenance: Changes in hardware, software, documentation, or procedures to a production system to correct errors, meet new requirements, or improve processing efficiency.

Management control: Monitors how efficiently or effectively resources are utilized and how well operational units are performing.

Management information systems (MIS): Computer systems at the management level of an organization that serve the functions of planning, controlling, and decision making by providing routine summary and exception reports.

Management-level systems: Information systems that support the monitoring, controlling, decision making, and administrative activities of middle managers.

Managerial roles: Expectations of the activities that managers should perform in an organization.

Man-month: The traditional unit of measurement used by systems designers to estimate the length of time to complete a project. Refers to the amount of work a person can be expected to complete in a month.

Master file: Contains all permanent information and is updated during processing by transaction data.

Megabyte: Approximately one million bytes. Unit of computer storage capacity.

Megahertz: A measure of cycle speed, or the pacing of events in a computer; one megahertz equals one million cycles per second.

Memory aids: In DSS, capabilities to update and refresh memory, including databases, views of data, work spaces, and libraries.

Microcomputer: Desktop or portable computer with 640 kilobytes to 64 megabytes of RAM.

Microeconomic model: Model of the firm that views information technology as a factor of production that can be freely substituted for capital and labor.

Microprocessor: Very large-scale integrated circuit technology that integrates the computer's memory, logic, and control on a single chip.

Microsecond: One-millionth of a second.

Microwave: High-volume, long-distance, point-to-point transmission in which high-frequency radio signals are transmitted through the atmosphere from one terrestrial transmission station to another.

Middle managers: People in the middle of the organizational hierarchy who are responsible for carrying out the plans and goals of senior management.

Migration: The ability to move software from one generation of hardware to another more powerful generation.

Millisecond: One-thousandth of a second.

Minicomputer: Middle-range computer with about 10 megabytes to over 1 gigabyte of RAM.

MIS audit: Identifies all the controls that govern individual information systems and assesses their effectiveness.

Mobile data networks: Wireless networks that enable two-way transmission of data files cheaply and efficiently.

Model: An abstract representation that illustrates the components or relationships of a phenomenon.

Model base: A collection of mathematical and analytical models that can easily be made accessible to the DSS user.

Modem: Device for translating digital signals into analog signals and vice-versa.

Module: A logical unit of a program that performs one or a small number of functions.

Muddling through: Method of decision making involving successive limited comparisons where the test of a good decision is whether people agree on it.

Multidimensional database model: Database model that represents relationships between data as a multidimensional structure, which can be visualized as cubes of data. Can create complex views of data for sophisticated reporting and analysis.

Multimedia: Technologies that facilitate the integration of two or more types of media such as text, graphics, sound, voice, full-motion video, or animation into a computer-based application.

Multinational: Global strategy that concentrates financial management and control out of a central home base while decentralizing production, sales, and marketing operations to units in other countries.

Multiplexer: Device that enables a single communications channel to carry data transmissions from multiple sources simultaneously.

Multiprocessing: An operating system feature for executing two or more instructions simultaneously in a single computer system by using more than one central processing unit.

Multiprogramming: A method of executing two or more programs concurrently using the same computer. The CPU only executes one program but can service the input/output needs of others at the same time.

Multitasking: The multiprogramming capability of primarily single-user operating systems, such as those for microcomputers.

Nanosecond: One-billionth of a second.

Negligence: Finding of fault when a producer's product causes physical or economic harm to individuals that could and should have been prevented.

Net present value: The amount of money an investment is worth, taking into account its cost, earnings, and the time value of money.

Network data model: A logical database model that is useful for depicting many-to-many relationships.

Network operating system: Special software that manages the file server in a LAN and routes and manages communications on the network.

Network topology: The shape or arrangement of a network.

Neural network: Hardware or software that attempts to emulate the processing patterns of the biological brain.

Object code: Program instructions that have been translated into machine language so that they can be executed by the computer.

Object-oriented database: Approach to data management that stores both data and the procedures acting on the data as objects that can be automatically retrieved and shared.

Object-oriented programming: Approach to software development that combines data and procedures into a single object.

Object-oriented software development: Approach to software development that de-emphasizes procedures and shifts the focus from modeling business processes and data to combining data and procedures to create objects.

Office activities: The principal activities performed at offices; these include managing documents, scheduling and communicating with people, managing data, and managing projects.

Office automation systems (OAS): Computer systems, such as word processing, voice mail systems, and videoconferencing systems, that are designed to increase the productivity of information workers in the office.

On-line processing: A method of processing information in which transactions are entered directly into the computer system and processed immediately.

On-line transaction processing: Transaction processing mode in which transactions entered on-line are immediately processed by the computer.

Open systems: Software systems that can operate on different hardware platforms because they are built on public nonproprietary operating systems, user interfaces, application standards, and networking protocols.

Open Systems Interconnect (OSI): International reference model for linking different types of computers and networks.

Operating system: The system software that manages and controls the activities of the computer.

Operational control: Deciding how to carry out tasks specified by upper and middle management and establishing criteria for completion and resource utilization.

Operational feasibility: Determines whether the proposed solution is desirable within the existing managerial and organizational framework.

Operational-level systems: Information systems that monitor the elementary activities and transactions of the organization.

Operational managers: People who monitor the day-to-day activities of the organization.

Operations: In DSS, logical and mathematical manipulations of data.

Optical character recognition (OCR): Form of source data automation in which optical scanning devices read specially designed data and translate the data into digital form for the computer.

Optical disk: Secondary storage device on which data are recorded and read by laser beams rather than by magnetic means.

Organization (behavioral definition): A collection of rights, privileges, obligations, and responsibilities that are delicately balanced over a period of time through conflict and conflict resolution.

Organization (technical definition): A stable formal social structure that takes resources from the environment and processes them to produce outputs.

Organizational culture: The set of fundamental assumptions about what products the organization should produce, how and where it should produce them, and for whom they should be produced.

Organizational impact analysis: Study of the way a proposed system will affect organizational structure, attitudes, decision making, and operations.

Organizational models: Models of decision making that take into account the structural and political characteristics of an organization.

OS/2: Powerful operating system used with the 32-bit IBM/Personal System/2 microcomputer workstations that supports multitasking, networking, and more memory-intensive applications than DOS.

Output controls: Ensure that the results of computer processing are accurate, complete, and properly distributed.

Outsourcing: The practice of contracting computer center operations, telecommunications networks, or applications development to external vendors.

Packet switching: Technology that breaks blocks of text into small fixed bundles of data and routes them in the most economical way through any available communications channel.

Page: Small section of a program, which can be easily stored in primary storage and quickly accessed from secondary storage.

Paging system: A wireless transmission technology in which the pager beeps when the user receives a message; used to transmit short alphanumeric messages.

Paradigm shift: Radical reconceptualization of the nature of the business and the nature of the organization.

Parallel processing: Type of processing in which more than one instruction can be processed at a time by breaking down a problem into smaller parts and processing them simultaneously with multiple processors.

Parallel strategy: Conservative conversion approach where both the old system and its replacement are run together until everyone is assured that the new one functions correctly.

Parity: An extra bit built into the EBCDIC and ASCII codes used as a check bit to ensure accuracy.

Particularism: Making judgments and taking actions on the basis of narrow or personal characteristics.

Pascal: Programming language used on microcomputers and to teach sound programming practices in computer science courses.

Patent: A legal document that grants the owner an exclusive monopoly on the ideas behind an invention for 17 years; designed to ensure that the inventors of new machines or methods are rewarded for their labor while making widespread use of their inventions.

Pen-based input: Input devices such as tablets, notebooks, and notepads consisting of a flat-screen display tablet and a pen-like stylus that digitizes handwriting.

People-oriented theory: User-resistance theory focusing on factors internal to users.

Personal communication services (PCS): A new, wireless, cellular technology that uses lower-power, higher-frequency radio waves than does cellular technology and so can be used with smaller-sized telephones inside buildings and tunnels.

Personal digital assistants: Small, pen-based, handheld computers with built-in wireless telecommunications capable of entirely digital transmission.

Personal information manager: Packaged database tool designed to support specific office data management tasks for an information worker.

Phased approach: Introduces the new system in stages either by functions or by organizational units.

Physical design: The process of translating the abstract logical model into the specific technical design for the new system.

Physical view: The representation of data as they would be actually organized on physical storage media.

Pilot study: A strategy to introduce the new system to a limited area of the organization until it is proven to be fully functional.

Pixel: The smallest unit of data for defining an image in the computer. The computer reduces a picture to a grid of pixels. The term *pixel* comes from *picture element*.

PL/1 (Programming Language 1): Programming language developed by IBM in 1964 for business and scientific applications.

Pointer: A special type of data element attached to a record that shows the absolute or relative address of another record.

Political models: Models of decision making where decisions result from competition and bargaining among an organization's interest groups and key leaders.

Portfolio analysis: An analysis of the portfolio of potential applications within a firm to determine the risks and benefits and select among alternatives for information systems.

Post-implementation: Final stage of the systems lifecycle in which the system is used and evaluated while in production and is modified to make improvements or meet new requirements.

Present value: The value, in current dollars, of a payment or stream of payments to be received in the future.

Primary activities: Activities most directly related to the production and distribution of a firm's products or services.

Primary storage: Part of the computer that temporarily stores program instructions and data for use by the CPU.

Printer: A computer output device that provides paper hard-copy output in the form of text or graphics.

Privacy: The claim of individuals to be left alone, free from surveillance or interference from other individuals, organizations, or the state.

Private branch exchange (PBX): Central switching system that handles a firm's voice and digital communications.

Processing: The conversion of raw input into a form that is more meaningful to humans.

Processing controls: Routines for establishing that data are complete and accurate during processing.

Process specification: Describes the logic of the transformations occurring within the lowest-level processes of the data flow diagrams.

Product differentiation: Competitive strategy for creating brand loyalty by developing new and unique products and services that are not easily duplicated by competitors.

Production: The stage after the new system is installed and the conversion is complete; during this time the system is reviewed by users and technical specialists to determine how well it has met its original goals.

Production or service workers: People who actually produce the products or services of the organization.

Professional bureaucracy: Knowledge-based organization such as a law firm or hospital that is dominated by department heads with weak centralized authority; operates in a slowly changing environment.

Program: A series of statements or instructions to the computer.

Program-data dependence: The close relationship between data stored in files and the software programs that update and maintain those files. Any change in data organization or format requires a change in all the programs associated with those files.

Programmers: Highly trained technical specialists who write computer software instructions.

Programming: The process of translating the system specifications prepared during the design stage into program code.

Program security controls: Controls designed to prevent unauthorized changes to programs in systems that are already in production.

Project definition: Stage in the systems lifecycle that determines whether or not the organization has a problem and whether or not the problem can be solved by launching a system project.

Project management software: Software that facilitates the development, scheduling, and management of a project by breaking the complex project into simpler subtasks, each with its own completion time and resource requirements.

PROM: Programmable read-only memory. Subclass of ROM chip used in control devices because it can be programmed once.

Protocol: Set of rules and procedures that govern transmission between the components in a network.

Prototype: Preliminary working version of an information system for demonstration and evaluation purposes.

Prototyping: Process of building an experimental system quickly and inexpensively for demonstration and evaluation so that users can better determine information requirements.

Pseudocode: Method for expressing program logic that uses plain English statements rather than graphic symbols, trees, tables, or programming languages to describe a procedure.

Query language: A high-level computer language used to retrieve specific information from databases or files.

RAM: Random access memory: Primary storage of data or program instructions that can directly access any randomly chosen location in the same amount of time.

Rationalization of procedures: The streamlining of standard operating procedures, eliminating obvious bottlenecks, so that automation makes operating procedures more efficient.

Rational model: Model of human behavior believing that people, organizations, and nations make consistent, value-maximizing calculations within certain constraints.

Record: A group of related fields.

Reduced instruction set computing (RISC): Technology used to enhance the speed of microprocessors by embedding only the most frequently used instructions on a chip.

Reference model: A generic framework for thinking about a problem.

Register: Temporary storage location in the ALU or control unit where small amounts of data and instructions reside for thousandths of a second just before use.

Relational data model: A type of logical database model that treats data as if they were stored in two-dimensional tables. It can relate data stored in one table to data in another as long as the two tables share a common data element.

Repetitive stress injury (RSI): Occupational disease that occurs when muscle groups are forced through the same, repetitive actions often with high impact loads or thousands of repetitions of low impact loads.

Report generator: Software that creates customized reports in a wide range of formats that are not routinely produced by an information system.

Representations: In DSS, conceptualization of information in the form of graphs, charts, lists, reports, and symbols to control operations.

Request for Proposal (RFP): Detailed list of questions submitted to vendors of packaged software or other computer services to determine if the vendor's product can meet the organization's specific requirements.

Resource allocation: Determination of how costs, time, and personnel are assigned to different activities of a systems development project.

Responsibility: Accepting the potential costs, duties, and obligations of one's decisions.

Reverse engineering: The process of taking existing programs, files and database descriptions and converting them into corresponding design-level components that can then be used to create new applications.

Ring network: Network topology in which all computers are linked by a closed loop in a manner that passes data in one direction from one computer to another.

Risk assessment: Determining the potential frequency of occurrence of a problem and the potential damage if the problem were to occur. Used to determine the cost/benefit of a control.

Risk Aversion Principle: Principle that one should take the action which produces the least harm or incurs the least cost.

ROM: Read-only memory. Semiconductor memory chips that contain program instructions. These chips can only be read from; they cannot be written to.

Rule base: The collection of knowledge in an AI system that is represented in the form of IF–THEN rules.

Rule-based expert system: An AI program that has a large number of interconnected and nested IF–THEN statements, or rules, that are the basis for the knowledge in the system.

Run control totals: Procedures for controlling completeness of computer updating by generating control totals that reconcile totals before and after processing.

Satellite: Transmission of data using orbiting satellites to serve as relay stations for transmitting microwave signals over very long distances.

Schema: The logical description of an entire database, listing all the data elements in the database and the relationships among them.

Scoring model: A quick method for deciding among alternative systems based on a system of ratings for selected objectives.

Search engine: A tool for locating specific sites or information on the Internet. Primarily used to search the World Wide Web.

Secondary storage: Relatively long-term, nonvolatile storage of data outside the CPU and primary storage.

Sector: Method of storing data on a floppy disk in which the disk is divided into pie-shaped pieces or sectors. Disk storage location can be identified by sector and data record number.

Security: Policies, procedures, and technical measures used to prevent unauthorized access, alteration, theft, or physical damage to information systems.

Segregation of functions: Principle of internal control to divide responsibilities and assign tasks among people so that job functions do not overlap to minimize the risk of errors and fraudulent manipulation of the organization's assets.

Selection construct: The logic pattern in programming where a stated condition determines which of two or more actions can be taken depending on which satisfies the stated condition.

Semantic nets: Expert systems that use the property of inheritance to organize and classify knowledge when the knowledge base is composed of easily identifiable chunks or objects of interrelated characteristics.

Semiconductor: An integrated circuit made by printing thousands and even millions of tiny transistors on a small silicon chip.

Senior managers: People at the highest organizational level who are responsible for making long-range decisions.

Sensitivity analysis: Models that ask what-if questions repeatedly to determine the impact of changes in one or more factors on outcomes.

Sequence construct: The sequential single steps or actions in the logic of a program that do not depend on the existence of any condition.

Sequential file organization: A method of storing records in which records must be retrieved in the same physical sequence in which they are stored.

Server: Satisfies some or all of the user's requests for data and/or functionality, such as storing and processing shared data and performing back-end functions not visible to users, such as managing peripheral devices and controlling access to shared databases. It might be anything from a supercomputer or mainframe to another desktop computer.

Sociotechnical design: Design to produce information systems that blend technical efficiency with sensitivity to organizational and human needs.

Software: The detailed instructions that control the operation of a computer system.

Software controls: Controls to ensure the security and reliability of software.

Software metrics: Objective assessments of the software used in a system in the form of quantified measurements.

Software package: A prewritten, precoded, commercially available set of programs that eliminates the need to write software programs for certain functions.

Software reengineering: Methodology that addresses the problem of aging software by salvaging and upgrading it so that the users can avoid a long and expensive replacement project.

Source code: Program instructions written in a high-level language before translation into machine language.

Source data automation: Input technology that captures data in computer-readable form at the time and place the data are created.

Spaghetti code: Unstructured, confusing program code with tangled logic that metaphorically resembles a pot of cooked spaghetti.

Spreadsheet: Software displaying data in a grid of columns and rows, with the capability of easily recalculating numerical data.

Standards: Approved reference models and protocols as determined by standard-setting groups for building or developing products or services.

Standard operating procedures (SOPs): Precise, defined rules for accomplishing tasks that have been developed to cope with expected situations.

Standing data: Data that are permanent and affect transactions flowing into and out of a system.

Star network: Network topology in which all computers and other devices are connected to a central host computer. All communications between network devices must pass through the host computer.

Storage technology: Physical media and software governing the storage and organization of data for use in an information system.

Stored program concept: The idea that a program cannot be executed unless it is stored in a computer's primary storage along with required data.

Strategic decision making: Determining the long-term objectives, resources, and policies of an organization.

Strategic information systems: Computer systems at any level of the organization that change the goals, operations, products, services, or environmental relationships to help the organization gain a competitive advantage.

Strategic-level systems: Information systems that support the long-range planning activities of senior management.

Strategic transition: A movement from one level of sociotechnical system to another. Often required when adopting strategic systems that demand changes in the social and technical elements of an organization.

Structure chart: System documentation showing each level of design, the relationship among the levels, and the overall place in the design structure; can document one program, one system, or part of one program.

Structured: Refers to the fact that techniques are instructions that are carefully drawn up, often step-by-step, with each step building upon a previous one.

Structured analysis: Method for defining system inputs, processes, and outputs and for partitioning systems into subsystems or modules that show a logical graphic model of information flow.

Structured decisions: Decisions that are repetitive, routine, and have a definite procedure for handling them.

Structured design: Software design discipline, encompassing a set of design rules and techniques for designing a system from the top down in a hierarchical fashion.

Structured programming: Discipline for organizing and coding programs that simplifies the control paths so that the programs can be easily understood and modified. Uses the basic control structures and modules that have only one entry point and one exit point.

Structured Query Language (SQL): The emerging standard data manipulation language for relational database management systems.

Subschema: The logical description of the part of a database required by a particular function or application program.

Supercomputer: Very sophisticated and powerful computer that can perform very complex computations extremely rapidly.

Support activities: Activities that make the delivery of the primary activities of a firm possible.

Switched lines: Telephone lines that a person can access from his or her terminal to transmit data to another computer, the call being routed or switched through paths to the designated destination.

Switching costs: The expense a customer or company incurs in lost time and resources when changing from one supplier or system to a competing supplier or system.

Synchronous transmission: High-speed simultaneous transmission of large blocks of data.

System failure: An information system that either does not perform as expected, is not operational at a specified time, or cannot be used in the way it was intended.

System flowchart: Graphic design tool that depicts the physical media and sequence of processing steps used in an entire information system.

System-oriented theory: User-resistance theory focusing on factors inherent in the design of the system.

System residence device: The secondary storage device on which a complete operating system is stored.

System 7: Operating system for the Macintosh computer which supports multitasking and has powerful graphics and multimedia capabilities.

Systems analysis: The analysis of a problem which the organization will try to solve with an information system.

Systems analysts: Specialists who translate business problems and requirements into information requirements and systems.

Systems design: Details how a system will meet the information requirements as determined by the systems analysis.

Systems development: The activities that go into producing an information systems solution to an organizational problem or opportunity.

Systems lifecycle: Traditional methodology for developing an information system that partitions the systems development process into six formal stages that must be completed sequentially with a very formal division of labor between end users and information systems specialists.

System software: Generalized programs that manage the resources of the computer.

Systems study: Stage in the systems lifecycle that analyzes the problems of existing systems, defines the objectives to be attained by a solution, and evaluates various solution alternatives.

System testing: Tests the functioning of the information system as a whole in order to determine if discrete modules will function together as planned.

Tangible benefits: Benefits that can be quantified and assigned monetary value; they include lower operational costs and increased cash flows.

Technical feasibility: Determines whether a proposed solution can be implemented with the available hardware, software, and technical resources.

Technostress: Stress induced by computer use whose symptoms include aggravation, hostility toward humans, impatience, and enervation.

Telecommunications: Communication of information by electronic means, usually over some distance.

Telecommunications software: Special software for controlling and supporting the activities of a telecommunications network.

Telecommunications system: Collection of compatible hardware and software arranged to communicate information from one location to another.

Telecommunications technology: Physical devices and software that link various hardware components and transfer data from one physical location to another.

Teleconferencing: Ability to confer with a group of people simultaneously using the telephone or electronic mail group communication software.

Telnet: Network tool that allows someone to log onto one computer system while doing work on another.

Terabyte: Approximately 1 trillion bytes; unit of computer storage capacity.

Testing: The exhaustive and thorough process that determines whether the system produces the desired results under known conditions.

Test plan: Prepared by the development team in conjunction with the users; it includes all of the preparations for the series of tests to be performed on the system.

Time sharing: The sharing of computer resources by many users simultaneously by having the CPU spend a fixed amount of time on each user's program before proceeding to the next.

Top-down: An approach that progresses from the highest most abstract level to the lowest level of detail.

Top-down approach: In the history of artificial intelligence, the effort to develop a logical analog to how the brain works.

Total quality management (TQM): A concept that makes quality control a responsibility to be shared by all people in an organization.

Touch screen: Input technology that permits the entering or selecting of commands and data by touching the surface of a sensitized video display monitor with a finger or pointer.

Track: Concentric circle on the surface area of a disk on which data are stored as magnetized spots; each track can store thousands of bytes.

Trade secret: Any intellectual work or product used for a business purpose that can be classified as belonging to that business provided it is not based on information in the public domain.

Traditional file environment: A way of collecting and maintaining data in an organization that leads to each functional area or division creating and maintaining its own data files and programs.

Transaction cost theory: Economic theory that states that firms exist because they can conduct marketplace transactions internally more cheaply than they can with external firms in the marketplace.

Transaction file: In batch systems, the file in which all transactions are accumulated to await processing.

Transaction processing systems (TPS): Computerized systems that perform and record the daily routine transactions necessary to the conduct of the business; they serve the operational level of the organization.

Transborder data flow: The movement of information across international boundaries in any form.

Transform algorithm: Mathematical formula used to translate a record's key field directly into the record's physical storage location.

Transmission Control Protocol/Internet Protocol (TCP/IP): U.S. Department of Defense reference model for linking different types of computers and networks.

Transnational: Truly globally managed firms that have no national headquarters; value-added activities are managed from a global perspective without reference to national borders, optimizing sources of supply and demand and taking advantage of any local competitive advantage.

Tuple: A row or record in a relational database.

Twisted wire: Transmission medium consisting of pairs of twisted copper wires. Used to transmit analog phone conversations but can be used for data transmission.

Unit testing: The process of testing each program separately in the system. Sometimes called *program testing*.

UNIX: Operating system for microcomputers, minicomputers, and mainframes that is machine-independent and supports multi-user processing, multitasking, and networking.

Unstructured decisions: Nonroutine decisions in which the decision maker must provide judgment, evaluation, and

insights into the problem definition; there is no agreed-upon procedure for making such decisions.

Usenet: Forums in which people share information and ideas on a defined topic through large electronic bulletin boards where anyone can post messages on the topic for others to see and respond to.

User-designer communications gap: The differences in backgrounds, interests, and priorities that impede communication and problem-solving among end users and information systems specialists.

User interface: The part of the information system through which the end user interacts with the system; type of hardware and the series of on-screen commands and responses required for a user to work with the system.

Utilitarian Principle: Principle that one should take the action that achieves the higher or greater value.

Utility program: System software consisting of programs for routine, repetitive tasks, which can be shared by many users.

Value-added networks (VAN): Private, multipath, data-only, third-party-managed networks that are used by multiple organizations on a subscription basis.

Value chain model: Model that highlights the activities that add a margin of value to a firm's products or services where information systems can best be applied to achieve a competitive advantage.

Vendor-managed inventory: Approach to inventory management that assigns the supplier the responsibility to make inventory replenishment decisions based on order, point-of-sale data, or warehouse data supplied by the customer.

Very high-level programming language: Programming language using fewer instructions than conventional languages. Used primarily as a professional programmer productivity tool.

Videoconferencing: Teleconferencing with the capability of participants to see each other over video screens.

Video display terminal (VDT): A screen, also referred to as a *cathode ray tube* (CRT). Provides a visual image of both user input and computer output.

Videotext: Multimedia delivery of information to remote terminals typically used for consumer or commercial delivery systems such as electronic shopping, banking, news, and financial database services.

Virtual organization: Organization using networks linking people, assets, and ideas to create and distribute products and services without being limited by traditional organizational boundaries or physical location.

Virtual private networks (VPNs): The ability to custom configure a network and use whatever portion of the public switched network is needed to do the job while only charging for the services used; provided by the local phone company to each corporate user.

Virtual reality systems: Interactive graphics software and hardware that create computer-generated simulations that provide sensations that emulate real-world activities.

Virtual storage: A way of handling programs more efficiently by the computer by dividing the programs into small fixed or variable-length portions with only a small portion stored in primary memory at one time.

Voice input device: Technology that converts the spoken word into digital form for processing.

Voice mail: System for digitizing a spoken message and transmitting it over a network.

Voice output device: Converts digital output data into spoken words.

WAIS (Wide Area Information Server): A tool for locating data on the Internet that requires the name of the databases to be searched based upon key words.

Walkthrough: A review of a specification or design document by a small group of people carefully selected based on the skills needed for the particular objectives being tested.

Warranty: A representation expressed by the seller of goods representing that the goods are fit for purchase and use.

Web site: All of the World Wide Web pages maintained by an organization.

Wide-area network (WAN): Telecommunications network that spans a large geographical distance. May consist of a variety of cable, satellite, and microwave technologies.

Windows: A graphical user interface shell that runs in conjunction with the DOS microcomputer operating system. Supports multitasking and some forms of networking.

Windows 95: A 32-bit operating system with a streamlined graphical user interface that can support software written for DOS and Windows but can also run programs that take up more than 640 K of memory. Features multitasking, multithreading, and powerful networking capabilities.

Windows NT: Powerful operating system developed by Microsoft for use with 32-bit microcomputers and workstations based on Intel and other microprocessors. Supports networking, multitasking, and multiprocessing.

Word length: The number of bits that can be processed at one time by a computer. The larger the word length, the greater the speed of the computer.

Word processing: Office automation technology that facilitates the creation of documents through computerized text editing, formatting, storing, and printing.

Word processing software: Software that handles electronic storage, editing, formatting, and printing of documents.

Work-flow management: The process of streamlining business procedures so that documents can be moved easily and efficiently from one location to another.

Workstation: Desktop computer with powerful graphics, mathematical processing, and communications capabilities as well as the ability to perform several complicated tasks at one time. Often used in scientific or design work.

World Wide Web: A set of standards for storing, retrieving, formatting, and displaying information using a client/server architecture, graphical user interfaces, and a hypertext language that enables dynamic links to other documents.

WORM: Write Once, Read Many. Optical disk system that allows users to record data only once; data cannot be erased but can be read indefinitely.

Name Index

Abene, Mark, 113
Ada, Countess of Lovelace, 177
Adams, Robert B., 425
Ahituv, Niv, 340
Aiken, Peter H., 341, 361
Alavi, Maryam, 342, 349, 413
Allen, Brandt R., 23, 43
Allison, Graham T., 85
Alter, Steven, 77, 320
Anderson, Philip, 68
Anthes, Gary H., 424, 435
Anthony, R. N., 31
Aristide, Jean-Bertrand, 479
Arthur, Lowell Jay, 342

Badrinath, B. R., 240
Bailey, Wayne, 159–60
Baker, Michael A., 291
Banker, Rajiv D., 440
Banker, Virginia, 385
Barney, Jay B., 53
Barrett, Stephanie S., 19
Barth, Dan, 337
Bélanger, Marc, 94
Bell, Alexander, 230
Benjamin, Mike, 186
Benjamin, Robert I., 19
Berners-Lee, Tim, 276
Berson, Selwyn, 423
Betts, Mitch, 409
Bikson, Tora K., 291
Bjerklie, David, 101
Bogle, Bob, 427
Bostrom, Robert P., 300, 419
Boynton, Andrew C., 23, 43
Brandel, Mary, 255
Branig, Charles, 121
Brennan, Edward A., 89
Brooks, Garth, 124
Brynjolfsson, Erik, 371
Burns, Alan R., 51–53
Burtka, Michael, 394
Buss, Martin, 328

Caldwell, Bruce, 46
Calliau, Robert, 276
Carlson, E. D., 405, 407
Carmel, Erran, 217
Carr, Houston H., 448
Carroll, Glenn R., 68
Carton, Barbara, 29–30
Carvajal, Dorren, 105
Casey, Jim, 8
Caviston, Jerry, 281
Celko, Joe, 271
Cerveny, Robert P., 342
Champy, James, 306
Clemons, Eric K., 44

Clinton, Bill, 118
Cohen, Yeshayahu, 217
Cordell, Ron, 280
Cortese, Amy, 278
Courtney, James F., 413
Cox, Butler, 466

Dairies, Johanna, 193
Datar, Srikant M., 440
Davenport, Thomas H., 309
Davidson, W. H., 310
Davis, Gordon B., 12, 39
Dekleva, Sasa M., 358
Deming, W. Edwards, 50
Denning, Dorothy E., 103
Dennis, Alan R., 416, 417, 419
DePompa, Barbara, 45, 152
DeSanctis, Geraldine, 413
Dispaux, Jean-Claude, 484
Doyle, J. Michael, 56–58
Drucker, Peter, 74–75
Dunkle, Debora, 72
Dutton, William H., 12

Earl, Michael J., 350
Eastwood, Al, 264
El Sawy, Omar A. L., 410, 421
El Sherif, Hisham, 410
Elam, Joyce L., 423
Eveland, J. D., 291

Fayol, Henri, 78
Feeny, David, 351
FitzGerald, Niall, 295
Flannery, Lauren S., 349
Ford, Henry, 66
Franz, Charles, 321
Fraser, Martin D., 340
Freedman, David, 37
Freeman, John, 68
Frye, Colleen, 255
Fuerst, William L., 53
Fuller, Mary K., 349
Furger, Roberta, 115

Gabriel, Trip, 113
Gallupe, R. Brent, 413
Garrity, Edward J., 342
Gault, Stanley C., 261–62
Geffen, David, 284
Gehlen, Harry, 225–26
George, Joey F., 416, 417, 419
Ginzberg, Michael, 77, 320, 328
Godwin, Michael, 252
Goldberg, Michael, 220
Goodhue, Dale L., 223
Goodman, S. E., 284
Gore, Al, 118

Gorry, G. Anthony, 82
Graham, Robert L., 104
Green, Jesse, 347
Greenbaum, Joshua, 172
Grobowski, Ron, 413, 419
Grover, Varn, 50, 53
Guhan, Subashish, 50, 53
Gurbaxani, V., 72
Gutek, Barbara A., 291

Hamilton, Ken, 230
Hammer, Michael, 306, 310
Hannan, Michael T., 68
Harel, Elie C., 347
Harrison, Ed, 21
Heinen, J. S., 300
Helke, Jan, 323
Helms, Glenn L., 320
Henderson, John C., 405, 407
Hitt, Lorin, 371
Ho, Teck Hua, 419
Hogue, Jack T., 405
Holland, John H., 393
Holstein, William K., 425
Hopper, Grace M., 176
Hopper, Joe, 120–22
Hopper, Max, 53, 142

Imielinski, Tomasz, 240
Ives, Blake, 38, 468

Jarvenpaa, Sirkka L., 38, 468
Jessup, Len M., 416, 417
Joachimsthaler, Erich A., 413
Joes, Kathryn, 107
Johnson, Deborah G., 108
Johnson, Michael, 296
Johnston, Russell, 19, 49
Jones, David, 27
Jones, T.C., 347
Joshi, Kailash, 321
Junger, Mathias, 140
Juran, Joseph, 50

Kahneman, D., 84
Kambil, Ajit, 49
Kant, Immanuel, 99, 119
Kaplan, Jerry, 1–2
Katzenberg, Jeffrey, 284
Keen, Peter G. W., 32, 75, 84, 251, 321, 405, 413, 467
Kellogg, Collins, 368
Kemeny, John, 176
Kemerer, Chris F., 440
Kennedy, John F., 85
Kettinger, William J., 50, 53
King, John, 43, 72, 413
King, Julia, 107

King, William R., 310
Kirsch, Laurie J., 223
Klein, Lisa R., 281, 481
Kling, Rob, 12, 75
Koch, Christopher, 2
Koh, Chang E., 423
Kolb, D. A., 77
Konsynski, Benn R., 49
Kotter, John T., 78, 79
Kraemer, Kenneth L., 72, 413
Kruger, Manfred, 484
Kumar, Kuldeep, 340
Kurtz, Thomas, 176

Laberis, Bill, 290
Lacity, Mary C., 351
Lane, Joe, 72
LaPlante, Alice, 51
Lasher, Donald R., 38
Laudon, Kenneth C., 72, 75, 77, 215, 320, 441
Leavitt, Harold J., 77
Lehman, Sheila, 291
Leidner, Dorothy E., 423
Lentzcsh, Craig, 58
Leonard-Barton, Dorothy, 5
Lewis, Brad, 391
Lientz, Bennett P., 317
Liker, Jeffrey K., 12
Lindblom, C. E., 84
Littlewood, Bev, 440
Lobdell, Greg, 422
Lord Byron, 177
Lucas, Henry C. Jr., 318
Luotonen, Ari, 276

MacFatan, F. W., 72
Madsen, Kim Halskov, 341
Maes, Pattie, 253
Magay, Keith, 427
Malcolm, Andrew H., 85
Malone, Thomas W., 19
Mandelkern, David, 170
Markoff, John, 105, 148
Markus, M. Lynne, 323
Martin, Dennis, 438
Martinez, Arthur C., 89–90
Martz, Ben, 413, 419
Mata, Thomas J., 53
Matlin, Gerald, 328
Mazzucchelli, Louis, 440
McCann, Jim, 52
McCarthy, John, 178
McCune, Jenny C., 378
McDonough, Jim, 264
McFarlan, F. Warren, 49, 319
McGoff, Chris, 413, 419
McHenry, William K., 217
McKay, Brendan, 274
McKenney, James L., 84
McPartlin, John P., 432
Meador, Charles L., 413
Megadeth, 124
Michaels, Jenna, 377
Mintzberg, Henry, 67, 75, 79, 80, 87
Miranda, Shalia M., 419
Moad, Jeff, 44, 310
Mohan, Lakshmi, 425
Morris, Robert, 434
Morris, Robert T., 113
Morse, Alan, 170
Morton, M. S., 32, 405
Motiwalla, Luvai F, 395

Mulvey, John M., 108
Mumford, Enid, 325
Muntz, Alice, 361
Murphy, Hanna, 476

Naj, Amal Kumar, 376
Nash, Jim, 385
Nath, Ravinder, 464
Nelson, R. Ryan, 349
Neumann, Seev, 340
Nielsen, Henrik Frystyk, 276
Nilakanta, Sree, 255
Nobilski, Linda, 337
Nolan, Richard L., 328
Nunamaker, Jay, 419
Nunamaker, Jay F. Jr., 395, 413, 416, 417, 419

O'Brien, David, 61–62
O'Connor, Dennis E., 385
Olson, Margrethe H., 12, 39
Orwell, George, 110
Oz, Effy, 100

Pascal, Blaise, 177
Pelleschi, Mario, 226
Plaskett, Thomas G., 58
Porter, Michael, 43, 47
Premkumar, G., 255
Press, S. I., 284
Prouix, Claude, 180

Quelch, John A., 281, 481

Radziszowsky, Dr. Stanislaw, 274
Rainer, R. Kelly, 423
Rainer, Rex Kelley, Jr., 448
Ramamurthy, K., 255
Raman, K. S., 72, 419
Ramirez, Anthony, 101
Rebello, Joseph, 43
Reynolds, George, 170
Richards, Russ, 361
Rifkin, Glenn, 101, 113, 409
Rigdon, Joan E., 109
Roach, Stephen S., 371
Robey, Daniel, 321, 323
Roche, Edward M., 23, 468
Rockart, John F., 41, 303, 349
Roitman, David B., 12
Roskies, Ethel, 12
Ruth, S. R., 284
Rutkowski, A. M., 284
Ryan, Claude, 8

Sachs, Eric, 422
Sallarulo, Paul, 337
Samuelson, Pamela, 105
Sandenbergh, Margot, 155
Sanders, G. Lawrence, 342, 413
Schein, Edgar H., 67
Schilling, David A., 405, 407
Schmieder, Frank, 56, 58
Schneider, Don, 73
Schnorr, Teresa M., 117
Schwader, Heather A., 291
Scott-Morton, Michael S., 82
Secret, Arthur, 276
Segors, Albert H., 50, 53
Shearer, John W., 121
Sheng, Olivia R. Liu, 395
Shoars, Alana, 101, 252
Shore, Edwin B., 74

Short, James E., 49, 309
Simon, H. A., 83, 407
Simpson, Pat, 162
Sinatra, Frank, 124
Singleton, Eric, 465
Smith, Richard D., 52
Snyder, Charles A., 448
Spector, David, 307
Spielberg, Steven, 284
Sprague, R. H., 405, 407
Stahl, Stephanie, 477
Stanton, Steven A., 310
Staszko, Greg, 366
Steffy, Dr. Chris, 332
Steinbart, Paul John, 464
Stevens, William K., 117
Straub, Detmar W., 465
Strigini, Lorenzo, 440
Sviokla, John J., 385
Swanson, E. Burton, 317, 349

Tabaksblat, Morris, 295
Tabor, Mary W., 113
Thomborson, Clark D., 141
Thompson, Thomas, 56–58
Tierney, William, 368, 369
Treacy, Michael F., 41, 303
Trice, Mike, 451
Trippi, Robert, 390
Tuer, David, 62
Turban, Efraim, 390
Turner, Jon A., 325
Tushman, Michael L., 68
Tversky, A., 84

Vaishnavi, Vijay K., 340
Valacich, Joseph S., 417, 419
Vassiliou, Yannis, 178
Venkatraman, N., 49
Verasdonck, Robert, 317
Vetter, Ronald J., 250
Vijayan, Jaikumar, 220
Vincent, Marc, 404
Vitale, Michael J., 19, 49
Vogel, Douglas R., 395, 413, 416, 417, 419

Walls, Joseph G., 421
Watson, Hugh J., 423
Watson, Richard T., 419
Weber, Bruce W., 44
Weber, Max, 65–66
Wegman, David, 180
Weir, Mary, 325
Weiser, Mark, 152
Weiss, Ira R., 320, 349
Westin, Alan F., 291
Widmeyer, George R., 421
Wilder, Clinton, 280
Willcocks, Leslie P., 351
Williamson, Miday, 154
Wilson, Linda, 109, 441
Wirth, Niklaus, 177
Wybo, Michael D., 223

Yap, C. S., 72
Yarmuth, Robert, 193
Yates, JoAnne, 19

Zachman, J. A., 301
Zerrenner, Walter, 332
Zweig, Dani, 440

Organizations Index

Absolutely Fresh Flowers, 19
Accurate Inventory Management (AIM), 159–60
Advance Supply & Pump Co., 121
Advanced Research Projects Agency, 434
Aetna Insurance, 114
Allstate Insurance, 88
Alyeska Pipeline Service Company, 85
Amdahl, 180, 264
America Online, 251, 253, 272
American Airlines, 49, 53, 57, 108, 142
American Bar Association (ABA), 100
American Express, 45, 98, 117
American Medical Association (AMA), 100
American National Standards Institute (ANSI), 128, 478
American Society of Mechanical Engineers (ASME), 100
Amoco, 237
AMR Corporation, 108
Apple Computer, 1, 65, 104, 105, 137, 186, 188, 217, 240, 364
ASK Group, Inc., 217
Aspen, Colorado, Police Department, 65
Association of Computing Machinery (ACM), 100
Atlantic Portfolio Analytics and Management, 142
AT&T, 1, 17, 101, 113, 118, 121, 124, 177, 190, 229, 231, 232, 248, 251, 273, 288, 437
AT&T Global Information Services, 121
Avex Electronics, Inc., 47

Banc One Corporation, 306, 307, 308, 309
Banc One Mortgage, 306
BankAmerica Corporation, 282, 433
Bankers Association of Foreign Trade, 229
Baxter Healthcare International, Inc., 45–46, 49, 89, 250, 306
Bell Atlantic, 232, 239
Bell Laboratories, 172, 177
Bell South, 239
Bell Telephone, 76
BGS Systems, 140
Boeing Corporation, 89, 397–400
Budd Company, 18
Buitoni, 483
Burgman Industries, 121
Burlington Northern Railroad, 248
Burroughs Corp., 121

Calyx and Corolla, 17
Camstar Systems, Inc., 53
Cap Gemini America, 366
Carlson Travel Group, 476
Carnation, 483

Carnegie-Mellon University, 385, 434
Carrier Corporation, 50–51
Caterpillar Corporation, 16, 467
Cedar Sinai Medical Center, 438
Champlin Petroleum, 408
Chancellor Capital Management, Inc., 377
Charles Schwab, Inc., 21
Chase Manhattan Bank N.A., 116
Chevron Corporation, 364
Chiat/Day Inc., 76
Chrysler Corporation, 18, 19, 45, 74, 467
Circuit City Stores, Inc., 89
Citibank, 44, 49, 53, 190
Coldwell Banker, 88, 281
Colgate-Palmolive, 295
Comdisco Disaster Recovery Services, 437, 438
Communications Workers of America (CWA), 101
Compaq Computer, 116, 125, 284, 386, 387
CompuServe, 106, 108, 251, 253, 272
Computer Associates (CA), 225
Computer Sciences Corporation (CSC), 366
Comshare, 423
Consultative Committee on International Telegraphy and Telephony (CCITT), 287–88
Continental Can Co., 100–101
Continental Grain, 249
Coopers & Lybrand, 365, 366
Coors Brewing Company, 394
Cornell University, 113, 434
Countrywide Funding Corp., 385
C.R. England & Sons Inc., 310
Cray, 142
Cummins Engine Company, 255
Cushman & Wakefield (C&W), 80
Cygnus Support, 278, 284

Data Processing Management Association (DPMA), 100
Dataquest, Inc., 435
Dayton Hudson, 249
Dean Witter, 88
Deere Power, 262
Dell Computer, 280–81
Deloitte & Touche, 366
Demand Management Inc., 125
Dialog, 253
Digital Equipment Corporation (DEC), 154, 180, 188, 280, 288, 296, 346, 365, 385, 476, 478, 484
Discount Tire, 262
Discover Card, 88, 89
Dow Chemical Company, 364
Dow Jones News Retrieval, 253
DreamWorks SKG, 284

DuPont Company, 342

E. Kinast Distributors Inc., 121
Eastman Kodak, 252, 365
1-800-Flowers, 51, 52
Electronic Data Systems Inc. (EDS), 107, 365
Electronic Frontier Foundation, 252
Eli Lilly, 252
EMASS Storage Systems, 97–98
Entek Manufacturing, 280
Environmental Systems Research Institute, Inc. (ESRI), 193
Epson, 247
Epson America Inc., 101, 252
Equico Capital Corporation, 408
Equifax, Inc., 113
Ernst & Young, 76, 378, 379, 484
Estée Lauder, 255
Ethos Corporation, 237
Expersoft Corp., 186
Exxon Corporation, 85, 364, 437

Federal Aviation Administration (FAA), 400
Federal Bureau of Investigation (FBI), 77, 103, 441, 452
Federal Express, 17, 47, 53, 117, 252, 278
Fidelity Disciplined Equity, 391
Fidelity Investments, 455
Fingerhut Co., 45
First Bank of South Dakota, 49
First National Management Corporation of Atlanta, 441
Florida State University, 434
1-800-Flowers, 51, 52
Ford Motor Company, 17, 306, 391, 410, 411
Forrester Research, 290
Fox Run Capital Associates, 58
Frank Russell Company, 409
Frito-Lay Corporation, 21

Gartner Group, 290, 365
Geer DuBois, 441
General Dynamics, 408
General Electric, 229, 261, 376, 391, 394
General Magic, 254
General Motors, 17, 45, 67, 75, 150, 252, 467
Gillette Company, 29–31, 43, 48, 49
Go Corporation, 1
Goodyear Tire & Rubber Co., 261–64
Greyhound Lines Inc., 56–58
GTE, 251

Hallmark Cards, 252
Harvard University, 275
Heinz, 483
Hershey, 483

Hewlett-Packard Inc., 104, 180, 296, 365, 483, 484
Hills Brothers, 483
Hoechst Celanese Corporation, 323
Holiday Inn, 45
Home Depot, Inc., 89
Hopper Specialty Co., 120–22
Howrey & Simon, 255
Hyatt Hotels Corporation, 47, 280

IBM, 1, 17, 20, 76, 117, 125, 128, 137, 139, 142, 170, 172, 177, 180, 188, 210, 212, 225, 239, 247, 264, 288, 292, 296, 301, 332, 337, 365, 399, 417, 419, 427, 434, 438, 470, 475, 476, 478, 483, 484
Indiana University School of Medicine, 368
Inference Corp., 388
Information Technology Association of America (ITAA), 100
Institute for Certification of Computer Professionals (ICP), 100
Intel, 137, 155, 364, 366, 467
Intergraph Corp., 376
Internal Revenue Service, 130
International Brotherhood of Electrical Workers (IBEW), 101
International Standards Organization, 286
Iomega Corporation, 51

J.C. Penney, 89, 240, 241
J. D. Edwards & Company, 125
John Deere Harvester Works, 20
J. P. Morgan, 110, 307
Juniper Lumber, 408

Kellogg, 483
Kmart, 47, 89, 408
KPMG Peat Marwick, 366
Kraft General Foods, 45

Lands' End, 89
Lawrence Livermore National Laboratory, 282
Lawson Software, 125
Levi Strauss & Co., 44, 116
Lexis, 253
Library of Congress, 275
Lipper Analytical Services, 455
Livingston Products, Inc., 229
L. L. Bean Inc., 51, 89
Lombard Institutional Brokerage, 21
Lotus Development Corporation, 257

MapInfo Corp, 424
Marion Merrell Dow Pharmaceutical, 154
Marshall Field's, 249
McCaw Cellular, 239
McDonnell Douglas, 397
MCI, 49, 248, 251
Mellon Bank, 389
Merck and Co., 17
Mercury Interactive Corp., 451
Merrill Lynch and Co., 21
Methodist Hospital, 332

Michelin Corporation, 247
Microsoft Corporation, 1, 104, 105, 116, 170, 171, 174, 181, 182, 184, 186, 188, 210, 253, 257, 273, 292, 365, 412, 422, 434
MicroWorlds, Inc., 411
M.I.T., Sloan School of Management, 411
Mitre Corporation, 284
Motorola, 20, 137, 239
Muze Inc., 149

NASA, 173, 174
National Association of Securities Dealers (NASD), 455
National Center for Supercomputing Applications, 278
National Computer Security Association (NCSA), 435
National Gypsum, 408
NCR, 120–22
Netscape Communications Inc., 278
New York Telephone, 113
Nexis, 253
Nordstrom, 252
Northwest Airlines, 49
Novell, 292
Nynex, 239

Olivetti, 247
Onsale, 1–2, 6, 7, 18
Oracle, 210, 296, 346, 484
Otis Elevators, 239

Pacific Bell (PacBell), 113, 114
Pacific Gas & Electric, 257
Pacific Telesis Group, 114
Pan Am Corporation, 58
Perrier, 483
Philips Electronics, 148, 220
Phillips Petroleum Co., 56
Pitney Bowes, 408
Pratt & Whitney, 423
Proctor & Gamble, 73, 295, 483
Prodigy, 106, 108, 251, 253, 272
Public Access Network Corp., 434
Pyramid Technology, 142

Quotron, 253

Ram Broadcasting, 239
Rand Corporation, 67
Redstone Advisors, 403–4
Rite Aid Pharmacy, 237
Rochester Institute of Technology, 274
RoweCom, 307
RSA Data Security Inc., 434
Rubbermaid, 261

SABRE Group AA, Inc., 142
Saks Fifth Avenue, 45, 89
Sand Dollar Management Co., 162–63
Sandia Labs, 252
Sanyo Fisher USA, 393
SAP America, Inc., 365

Schneider National, 72, 73, 306
Sears, Roebuck & Co., 47, 88–90, 262
Security First Network Bank, 47
Sequent, 180
Shell Pipeline Corporation, 107
Silicon Graphics, 284
Sloan School of Management at M.I.T., 411
Snapple, 295
Software Publishers Association (SPA), 105–6
Sonny's Bar-B-Q, 192–93
Sony, 148
Southern Railway, 408
Southwestern Bell Corporation, 113
Sperry Univac, 346
Sprint, 232, 239, 296
State Street Bank and Trust Co. of Boston, 43
Stouffer's, 483
Stratton Oakmont, 108
Sun, 180, 186, 187, 188, 288
Sungard Recovery Services, 437, 438
Sybase, 296, 332

Tandem, 180
Taylor Management Systems Inc., 121
Telenet, 251
Tetrad Computer Applications, 193
Texaco, Inc., 206
Texas Instruments, 212, 360
Texas Oil and Gas Corporation, 408
Time-Warner, 148, 232
Tire & Auto Service, 264
Toshiba, 148
Toys 'R' Us, 89
Trane Co., 307
TRW, Inc., 440

Unify Corporation, 296
Unisys Corp., 121, 225, 268, 292
United Airlines, 65, 408
United Parcel Service (UPS), 8, 9, 10–11, 35, 53, 149, 221
United Services Automobile Association (USAA), 38, 309, 374
University of California, 275
U.S. Postal Service, 150
US West, 283

Verity Inc., 254
Versant Object Technology Corp., 217
Victoria's Secret Stores, 220
Visa USA Inc., 437
Vogue Tyre & Rubber Co., 121

Wal-Mart Stores, 46–47, 48, 89, 98, 142, 155, 262
Wang Laboratories, 68
Western Call & Decoy, 230
WMS Industries, 252
Wolf Communications, 422
Worthington Industries, 229

Zeneca Pharmaceuticals, 427

International Organizations Index

Accor Group, 476
African Internet Development Action Team, 479
Air Canada, 360
Airboss, 51-53
Airbus Industrie, 397
American Airlines, 49, 53, 57, 108, 142, 408
ANA, 398
Andersen Consulting, 298, 332, 365
Arrow International, 461
AT&T, 1, 17, 101, 113, 118, 121, 124, 177, 190, 229, 231, 232, 248, 251, 273, 288, 437
Australian National University, 274
Avalon Software Inc., 346

Bass PLC, 292
Baxter Healthcare International, Inc., 45–46, 49, 89, 250, 306
Bell Canada, 152, 180
BHP Mineral International Inc., 120
BHW Bausparkasse AG, 225–26
Borland International Inc., 210
British Airways, 45, 398

Calvin Klein Cosmetics, 295
Canadian Union of Public Employees, 94
Carlson Wagonlit Travel, 476
Carp Systems International, 408
Citibank, 44, 49, 53, 190, 474, 475
Citibank Asia-Pacific, 474, 475
Club Mediterranée, 479
ClubCorp International, 336-38
Coca Cola, 463
Computer Sciences Corp. (CSC), 351, 366
Credit Industriel et Commercial de Paris, 172

Dassault Aviation SA, 399
Deutsche Bank, 140
Deutsche Telekom, 232
DHL Worldwide Express, 254

E.I. du Pont de Nemours & Company, 364
Electronic Share Information Ltd. (ESI), 26–27
EuroMarketing Systems, 217
Europcar Interrent, 317

European Association of Securities Dealers, 26

Federal Express, 17, 47, 53
Ford Motor Company, 17, 306, 351, 391, 410, 411
France Télécom, 232
Frito-Lay, Inc., 21, 408, 463

Gillette Company, 29–31

Hoechst International, 323
Holiday Inn, 45
Holiday Inn Worldwide, 292
Hong Kong's Provisional Airport Authority, 376
Hyatt Hotels, 47

International Civil Aviation Authority, 376

Japan Airlines, 398
Jetset, 476

Kentucky Fried Chicken, 467
Komag, 53
Kommunedata, 211

Lever Brothers, 295
Lexmark International, 116
Loma Engineering Ltd., 388
London Stock Exchange (LSE), 26–27

Magic Software Enterprises Ltd., 180
Maritz, 476
Matsushita Electric Works, 375
McDonald's, 467, 468
Michelin Italia, 247
Mitsubishi Heavy Industries, 393
Molex Corporation, 458–59
Mott Consortium, 376
Mrs. Fields Cookies, 467

National Westminster Bank, 215
Nestlé SA, 251, 295, 483, 484
New Zealand Inland Revenue Department, 298, 305
Northwest Airlines, 49

Odense Steel Shipyards, 36, 37, 309
Office of Fair Trading, 27
Ontario Hydro, 186

PanCanadian Petroleum, 61–63, 65, 72
Pizza Pizza Ltd., 93–94, 99
Price Waterhouse, 365
Protravel, 476

Quest International, 296

Richmond Savings, 271

Saab, 346
Saab-Scania, 346
Sandenbergh Pavon Ltd., 155
SAP A.G., 364–66
Schlumberger Ltd., 280
ShareLink Ltd., 27
Society for Worldwide Interbank Financial Telecommunications, 477
SoliNet, 94
Sprint International, 232, 239, 296
Swissair, 430-31

Telecom Italia, 232
Texas Instruments, 212, 360
Thomson Financial Services, 403–4
Thorn EMI PLC., 124–26
T.J. Lipton, 295
Tradepoint Financial Networks, 26
Trimark Investment Management, 142

Unilever, 295–96
United Airlines, 65, 398, 400
United Food and Commercial Workers' (UFCW), 93-94
United Parcel Service (UPS), 8, 9, 10–11, 35, 53, 149, 221
University of Hohenheim, 414

Volkswagen, 217

Wagonlit Travel, 476

Yasuda Fire and Marine Insurance Co., 409

Subject Index

A

Abuse
  alcohol
    technostress and, 117
  computer
    defined, 112
    Computer Fraud and Abuse Act, 113
  drug
    technostress and, 117
  of information systems, 24
Acceptance testing, 315
Access
  telecommunications and, 258–59, 260
Accountability, 96, 97, 98–99
  code of ethics and, 117, 119
  defined, 98
Accountants
  as data workers, 36
Accounting
  information architecture and, 24
  information systems for, 9, 32–36
Ad hoc reports
  data warehouses and, 219
  files and, 203
Ada programming language, 177, 191
Adhocracies
  described, 67
  environments of, 68
Administrative controls, 443–44
Advanced Planning System (APS)
  for manufacturing, 408, 409, 412
Agency theory, 74
Agents
  for change, 318
    legitimacy of, 474
  intelligent, 253, 254
AI shell
  expert systems and, 383–84
Airlines
  data quality problems in, 110
  reservation systems for, 53, 57
    data models for, 210
Alcohol abuse
  technostress and, 117
Algorithms
  genetic, 393–94, 396
  transform, 200
Alliances
  strategic, 49
Alpha chips, 154
Alta Vista
  Internet and, 278
Alternative systems lifecycles, 340–52
ALU, 133, 157
Amateur Action
  liability for Internet pornography and, 108

American Standard Code for Information Interchange (ASCII)
  defined, 127, 157
  list of, 129
  main memory and, 132
American Venture Capital Exchange, 230
Amoco Retail Systems Technology Architecture (ARSTA), 237
Analog signals, 234
Analysis
  capital investment
    systems for, 34
  enterprise, 301–03, 330
  ethical
    consequences and, 99, 119
  of ethical conflicts, 99
  information systems and, 6, 25, 34
  portfolio
    for information systems investments, 327–28, 330
  relocation
    systems for, 32, 34
  strategic, 303, 330
  structured, 352–54, 363
  systems. See Systems analysis
  of trends
    systems for, 32
Analysts
  systems
    defined, 70
Anonymity
  group decision support systems and, 419
Anti-piracy laws
  intellectual property and, 106
Antivirus software, 112, 435
APL
  high-level programming language, 179
Applets
  in Java, 187–88
Application controls, 442, 444–45
Application generators, 178, 179
Application software, 173–83, 190, 191
  backlog, 190
  defined, 164
  packages, 180–83, 191, 342–46, 362
    customization of, 344, 345
    defined, 342
    examples of, 344
    selecting, 344, 346
  programming languages. See Programming languages
Archie
  Internet and, 276, 277, 278, 293
Architects
  as knowledge workers, 9
Architectures
  comparison of computer, 156

information. See Information architecture
Von Neumann, 155
Ardis, 230
Arithmetic-logic units (ALU), 133, 157
ARSTA, 237
Artificial intelligence, 380–85, 396
  defined, 380
  design re-use and, 388
  finding applications for, 395
  intelligent machines for, 380, 396
  natural language and, 380, 396
  perceptive systems and, 380, 396
  programming languages for, 178
  robotics and, 380, 396
ASCII. See American Standard Code for Information Interchange (ASCII)
Assemblers
  as production workers, 9
Assembly language, 174, 175–76, 191
  defined, 168, 191
Asynchronous transfer mode (ATM), 250
Asynchronous transmissions, 242, 259
ATM. See Asynchronous transfer mode (ATM)
ATMs. See Automatic teller machines (ATMs)
ATS, 196
Attributes
  data administration and, 222
  defined, 198, 212
Auction bidding systems
  Internet and, 1–2
Auditing, 448–49
Audits
  data and quality, 452
  MIS, 448–49
Australia
  design/development of 1994 Ford Mustang and, 17
Authorization
  of input, 445
Auto-by-Tel, 281
Automated Titles System (ATS), 196
Automatic teller machines (ATMs)
  liability and, 107
  product differentiation and, 44, 53
Automation, 304, 329
  custom manufacturing and, 20
  source data, 149–50
Automobiles
  CAD and, 37
  design/development of Ford Mustang (1994), 17
  just-in-time delivery systems and, 45
  manufacturing of
    standard operating procedures in, 66

B

Backup
　facilities
　　liability and, 107
　tape
　　for microcomputers, 143
Backward chaining
　in expert systems, 384, 396
Bandwidth, 241, 242, 259
Banking
　data quality problems in, 110
　debit cards
　　product differentiation and, 44
　downsizing in, 114
　hierarchical databases and, 212
　virtual
　　product differentiation and, 47
Bar codes
　data quality and, 110
　defined, 149
　in mailing list software, 163
　in package tracking systems, 8, 11
　in video rental stores, 159–61
　in warehousing, 240, 241
Baseband channel technology, 247–48
Basic Input Output System (BIOS), 132
BASIC programming language, 168, 176–77, 191
Batch processing
　defined, 150–51, 157
Baud, 240, 242
BayNet World, 281
Beginners All-purpose Symbolic Instruction Code (BASIC), 168, 176–77, 191
Behavioral theories
　on information systems and organizations, 11, 12, 25, 74–75, 77
　models of management and, 78–79, 87
Benchmarks
　quality and, 51
Benefits
　tangible/intangible, 326, 329
"Big Brother" society
　quality of life and, 110–11
Billing
　relationship
　　data mining and, 45
Binary codes, 126–28, 173
Binary digits. See Bits
BIOS, 132
Bits, 126–28, 157
　defined, 126, 197
　mapping of, 150–51
　parity, 128, 442
Blizzards
　information systems and, 112
　liability, 107
Blue-collar workers
　in labor force, 5
　reengineering and, 113
Bookkeepers
　as data workers, 9
Books
　briefing, 420
BPI
　tape storage density measurement, 143
Brainstorming tools
　electronic
　　group decision support systems and, 416
Briefing books, 420
Broadband channel technology, 248

Brokers
　discount
　　Internet and, 21
Brown Bag Software vs. Symantec, 104–05
Browsers, 276–78, 379
Budgeting
　systems for, 34
Bugs
　program, 439
Bulletin boards. *See also* Collaborative work
　liability and, 107, 108, 109
　PanCanadian Petroleum employee bulletin board and, 62
　privacy and, 103
Bureaucracies, 65–67, 75
　defined, 65
　models of
　　decision-making and, 84–85, 87
　Sears and, 90
Bus networks, 243–44, 259
Buses
　reservation systems for, 56–58
Business drivers, 462
Business enterprises
　Internet and. *See* Internet
　reorganizing, 469–70
　transformation of
　　technology and, 5–6, 25
Business plan
　information systems plan and, 300–301, 330
Business processes, 306, 471–72
Business reengineering, 306–08, 309–10, 329
　Internet and, 307
Business strategies
　information systems and, 13, 21, 25, 31–33
　challenge of, 22–23
　strategic role of, 29–60
Business systems planning, 301–3, 330
Business value
　determining
　　of information systems, 326–29, 330
Bytes, 127–28, 130–32, 157
　defined, 127, 197
Bytes per inch (BPI)
　tape storage density measurement, 143

C

C programming language, 168, 177, 191
Cable communications
　Cable Communications Policy Act of 1984, 103
　privacy laws on, 102, 103
Cache
　defined, 143
CAD. *See* Computer-aided design software (CAD)
Calendars
　systems for, 34, 36
Capacity
　computer
　　vs. costs, 152
Capital budgeting models, 326–27, 330
Capital investment analysis
　systems for, 34
Carpal tunnel syndrome (CTS), 115, 116
　defined, 115
Cartridges
　tape, 143
CASE
　for system building, 358–60, 361, 363

tools, 359
Case-based reasoning (CBR)
　organizational intelligence and, 386–87, 396
Cash flow
　information systems and Fortune 500 companies, 13
Catalog sales
　information systems and, 89
Catastrophes
　information systems and, 112
CATeam Room, 414–15
Cathode ray tubes (CRTs), 150. *See also* Computer terminals
CBIS. *See* Computer-based information systems (CBIS)
CBR, 438
　organizational intelligence and, 386–87
CCDs, 160
CDPD, 239
Cellular Digital Packet Data (CDPD), 239
Cellular phones
　privacy and, 103
　virtual offices and, 76
　wireless transmissions and, 238–39, 481
Census data
　on CD-ROM, 193
Central processing units (CPUs)
　defined, 131, 157
　primary storage and, 131–32
　speed of, 130
Centralization
　business and, 5–6
　vs. decentralization, 291, 293
Centralized processing
　defined, 138
Chance
　in organizations
　　technology and, 63, 64
Change
　agents, 318
　　legitimacy of, 474
　Descartes' rule of, 100, 119
　organizational. *See* Organizational change
　technological
　　management challenges of, 157
Channels
　defined, 235
　telecommunications, 235–40, 259
　　characteristics of, 240–42
Charge-coupled devices (CCDs), 160
Chatting, 274, 293
Check bit. *See* Parity bit
Chief information officer (CIO), 222
Child segments
　in IMS, 208
Chips
　superchips, 154
　word length and, 136
Choice
　stage of decision-making, 83
CIO, 222
Classes
　object-oriented programming and, 185
Classical model of management, 87
　defined, 78
Classified weapons research
　supercomputers and, 141
Clerks
　as data workers, 9, 36
Clients
　in client/server model, 270, 293
Client/server model

case study, 364–66
of enterprise networking, 270–71, 292, 293
hidden costs of, 289–90
Coaxial cables
telecommunications and, 233, 259
COBOL, 168, 174–75, 176, 191
Cognitive models
of human reasoning
information systems and, 12
Cognitive style
in decision-making, 84, 87
Collaborative work. *See also* Group collaboration systems; Group decision support systems
design/development of 1994 Ford Mustang, 17
groupware and. *See* Groupware
information systems and, 4–5, 17
Internet and, 15
Colleges
systems for, 36
Commander EIS, 422, 423
Commerce. *See* Electronic commerce; Electronic markets
Commercial digital information services, 253, 260
COmmon Business Oriented Language (COBOL), 168, 174–75, 176, 191
Common sense
artificial intelligence and, 380–81
Communications. *See also* Telecommunications
cable
privacy laws on, 102, 103
Cable Communications Policy Act of 1984, 103
concentrators and, 242
controllers and, 242, 259
devices for, 126, 127, 157
electronic
privacy laws on, 102, 103
Electronic Communications Privacy Act of 1986, 103, 252
front-end processors and, 242, 259
information systems and, 6, 25, 36
Internet and, 278, 280, 293
multiplexers and, 243, 259
satellites and, 481
Communications processors, 242–43, 259
Compact disk read-only memory (CD-ROM), 146–48
census data on, 193
defined, 146, 158
multimedia and, 153–54
rental of multimedia and, 160
zip code software on, 193
Companies. *See* Business enterprises
Compaq 486
music industry and, 125
Compatibility
for telecommunications, 259
Competition
time-based
economic transformation and, 4–5
quality of life and, 111
Competitive advantage
sustainability of, 53
Competitive forces model, 43–47, 54
defined, 43
Compiler
defined, 168, 169, 174, 191

Complexity
of information systems, 13
managing, 321
Comprehensive Business Recovery (CBR), 438
Compromise
in organizational decision-making, 85
CompuServe. *See also* Internet
liability and, 108
responsibility and, 106
Computability theories
technical approach to information systems and, 11
Computation methods
technical approach to information systems and, 11
Computer abuse
defined, 112
Computer Aided Team Room (CATeam Room), 414–15
Computer crime, 119
defined, 112
examples of, 113
Computer Fraud and Abuse Act, 113
Computer generations
defined, 134
history of, 134–35
Computer hardware
components, 126–57
defined, 10
evolution of, 134–37
failure of, 432
information architecture and, 24
information systems and, 13
platform standardization
challenge of, 474–75
systems integration and, 475–77
Computer literacy
managers and, 7, 25
Computer matching, 446
Computer Matching and Privacy Protection Act of 1988, 103
Computer mouse, 148, 158
Computer operations controls, 443
Computer science
MIS and, 12
technical approach to information systems and, 11
Computer Security Act of 1987, 103
Computer software. *See* Software
Computer Software Copyright Act, 104
Computer terminals
access penetration, 432
point-of-sale, 89
radiation from, 116–17
telecommunications systems and, 233
VGA standard grids, 127
video display
defined, 150, 158
Computer vision syndrome (CVS), 115, 116
defined, 115
Computer-aided design software (CAD)
1994 Ford Mustang design/development and, 17
automobile manufacturing and, 37
defined, 375, 396
Hong Kong airport and, 376
object-oriented databases and, 216
Odense Shipyards and, 36, 37
operating system for, 174
organizational flexibility and, 19
quality and, 51–53
razor design and, 30

resolution capabilities required for, 151
tire design and, 51–53
workstations and, 140, 141
Computer-aided software engineering (CASE)
for system building, 358–60, 361, 363
Computer-based information systems (CBIS)
defined, 6–7
purpose of, 25
related to all information systems, 40
Computers
abuse of
defined, 112
capacity of
vs. costs, 152
comparison of architectures, 156
Computer Fraud and Abuse Act, 113
costs *vs.* capacity, 152
credit reporting and, 113
crimes
defined, 112
hackers and Internet, 113, 293, 433
data mining
supercomputers and, 141
downsizing and
defined, 138
Deutsche bank and, 140
managing, 291
ethics
copying software and, 105, 106
fault-tolerant, 437
fifth generation, 155, 157
first generation, 135
fourth generation, 135
generations of, 134–35
hardware and inputs/outputs, 10
integrated circuits and
third generation, 135, 157
laptop
virtual offices and, 76
literacy
managers and, 7, 25
Macintosh, 172, 174
magnetic drums and
first generation, 135
mainframe. *See also* Mainframe computers
defined, 137, 157
massively parallel, 155–56
matching, 446
mice, 148, 158
microminiaturization and fourth generation, 135
minicomputers
defined, 137, 157
miscarriages and, 116–17
operations controls, 443
problem related to miscarriages, 116–17
related diseases and, 116
supercomputers and, 141
third generation of
silicon chips, 135
Concentrators
communications and, 242
Configuration
system, 126
Conflicts
ethical analysis and, 99
organizational politics and, 10
Connectivity, 285–87, 294
challenges of, 477–79
Decnet and, 478
defined, 285
models of, 285–87

planning for, 292–93
Society for Worldwide Interbank Financial Telecommunications and, 477–78
standards for, 285, 287–88
Systems Network Architecture and, 478
telecommunications and, 258–59, 260
Consensus databases
privacy and, 103
Consequences
ethical analysis and, 99, 119
Conspiracy
Internet and, 113
Constituencies
organizational, 68–69
Constitution
privacy guarantees in, 102
Control unit
defined, 133–34, 157
Controlling
communications and, 242, 259
managers and, 78, 87
MIS for, 38–40
Controls
administrative, 443–44
aids
in decision support systems, 407
application, 442, 444–45
data security, 443–44
general, 442
in a global economy, 3–4, 481–82
hardware, 442
on implementation, 442
information systems and, 6, 21, 24–25, 25
input, 445
management
defined, 82
operational
defined, 82
output, 447
procedures and methods, 441
for processing, 446
program security, 442
run totals, 446
software, 442
tools for, 321
Conversion plans, 316
Conversions, 315–16, 330, 445
Cooperative processing
defined, 138–39
example of, 140
Cooptation, 473
Coordination
information systems and, 6, 25
managers and, 78
Copyrights
defined, 104
Federal Copyright Act of 1790 and, 104
infringement of, 108
"look and feel," 104
intellectual property and, 104–05
professional ethics and, 101
Core business processes, 471–72
"Core" institutional activities
information systems and, 13–14
Core systems, 471–72
Cost-benefit ratio, 326
Costs
computer
vs. capacity, 152
hidden
of client/server model, 289–90
low-cost producer, 46–47

of switching, 44–46
telecommunications, 258–59, 260
Internet and, 278
transaction cost theory, 74
of transactions
lower from technology, 4–5
Counterimplementation, 321
CPUs. See Central processing units (CPUs)
Crashes
disk drives and, 146
Credit history
ethical issues on, 103
Credit reporting
computer crimes and, 113
privacy laws on, 102, 103
Crimes
computer
credit reporting and, 113
defined, 112
examples of, 113
Internet and, 113, 293, 433
National Crime Information Center and, 215
Critical success factors (CSFs), 303, 330, 421
Crop planters
custom manufacturing of, 20
CRTs, 150
CSFs, 303, 330, 421
CTS, 115, 116
Culture
in organizations
defined, 66
information systems and, 7, 9, 63, 66–67, 69, 77, 86
Sears and, 90
Custom manufacturing
in business, 5–6
defined, 18, 19
the new automation, 20
Customer service
imaging systems and, 38
Customization
of application software packages, 344, 345
CVS, 115, 116
Cycle speed, 136, 157
Cycle time
quality and, 51
Cylinders
defined, 144

D

DASD
defined, 146
Data
access methods for
files and, 199–200
technical approach to information systems and, 11
defined, 6
hierarchy, 198
historical
data warehouses and, 218–19, 224
information architecture and, 24
management of, 197–225
databases, 203–07, 223
files, 197–203, 223
operational
vs. warehouse data, 219
program-data dependence and, 202–03, 207, 223
quality of
audit of, 452

reported problems in, 110, 441
responsibility for, 109, 117, 120–22
redundancy, 202, 207, 223
standing, 447
storage methods
ethical issues on, 97–98
technical approach to information systems and, 11
Data administration, 222, 224
client/server model and, 291–92
Data bus width
defined, 136, 158
Data conversion, 445
Data definition language, 203, 223
Data dictionary, 203–5, 211, 223
data administration and, 222
data quality and, 452
Data elements, 205
Data file approach, 201
Data flow diagram (DFD), 353
Data manipulation languages, 203–04, 223
Data mining
ethical considerations on, 98
focused differentiation and, 44, 45
supercomputers and, 141
Data planning, 222, 224
Data quality audits, 452
Data redundancy
databases and, 207
files and, 202, 223
Data security controls, 443–44
Data warehouses, 218–20, 224
Data workers
defined, 9, 36, 372
Database management systems (DBMSs), 203–07, 223. See also Databases
advantages of, 207
management requirements for, 220–23, 224
Databases
administration of, 222
creating, 212
data management and, 203–7
data warehouses, 218–20, 224
design of, 207–12
distributed, 213–15, 223
documentation of, 222
DSS, 411–12
hypermedia, 215–17, 224
information systems and, 13
management requirements for, 220–26
management systems for, 182
application generators and, 179
query tools for, 178
multidimensional, 217–18, 224
National Trade Database, 228–30
object-oriented, 215–17, 224
partitioning of, 213–15, 224
replication and, 213–15, 224
trends in, 213–20, 223
Dataconferencing, 255
DB2
relational data model, 210, 211, 225–26
dBaseIV, 182
relational data model, 210
DBMSs, 203–07
DealerNet, 281
Debit cards
product differentiation and, 44
Debugging
systems quality and, 451
Decentralization
business and, 5–6

Subject Index 547

of enterprise
  from technology, 4–5
vs. centralization, 291, 293
Decision support systems (DSS), 33, 404–13, 425. *See also* Executive support systems (ESS)
  characteristics of, 34, 40–41, 86, 406–07, 408
  components of, 40, 405, 411–12
  defined, 40, 405
  group. *See* Group decision support systems (GDDS)
  integration with, 42, 53
  for manufacturing, 408–09
  types of, 34, 40–41, 54
  vs. MIS, 405–07
Decisional roles
  of managers
    defined, 79
    information systems for, 81, 87
Decision-making
  enhancing management, 405–27
  ethics and, 119
  information systems and, 6, 25, 32, 38
  knowledge-level, 82
  managers and, 79, 81–86, 87
  models of, 84–85
  practicing, 411
  process of, 82–83
  stages of, 83
  strategic
    defined, 82
  systems design and, 85–86
Decisions
  structured, 82, 87
  unstructured, 82, 86, 87
  defined, 83
Decnet, 478
Dedicated lines, 248
Delivery Information Acquisition Device (DIAD)
  UPS and, 8, 11, 149
Delivery systems
  global, 3–4
Department of Defense (DoD)
  COBOL and, 176
Departments
  in organizations
    information systems for, 68–69
Dependence
  on information systems, 111–12
Descartes' rule of change, 119
  defined, 100
Design
  business redesign with Internet, 307
  of databases, 207–12
  logical, 313
  physical, 313
  re-use with artificial intelligence, 388
  sociotechnical, 325
  stage of decision-making, 83
  structured, 354, 363
  of systems. *See also* Computer-aided design software (CAD)
    decision-making and, 85–86, 87
    managers and, 80–81
    organizational theories and, 77–78
    organizations and, 16–21, 22–23, 77–78
    in traditional systems lifecycle, 339, 362
    in virtual corporations, 18
Desktop publishing
  defined, 38
  office automation systems and, 36, 38

DFD, 353
DIAD, 8, 11, 149
Dictionaries
  group decision support systems and, 417
Differentiation
  focused, 44, 47
  product, 43–44, 47
Digital cash, 272
Digital information services, 253, 260
Digital scanners, 150, 158
Digital signals, 234
Dilemmas
  ethical analysis and, 99, 119
  real-world examples of, 100–102
Direct access storage devices (DASD)
  defined, 146
Direct cutover
  for conversions, 316
Direct file access method, 200
Direct file organization, 199, 223
Disaster recovery plans
  client/server and, 438
  liability and, 107
Disasters, 436–37
Diseases
  computer-related, 116
Disk drives, 145
Disk packs, 145
Diskettes
  high-density
    data storage in microcomputers and, 143
Disks
  compact disk read-only memory, 146–48
  crashes of, 146
  drives, 145
  floppy. *See* Floppy disks
  hard, 143, 144
  key-to-disk machines and, 148
  magnetic. *See* Magnetic disks
  magneto-optical, 148
  optical, 146–48, 158
  packs, 145
  Redundant Array of Inexpensive. *See* Redundant Array of Inexpensive Disks (RAID)
Dismissal
  Software Code of Ethics and, 106
  wrongful
    ethics and, 101
Distance
  telecommunications and, 258–59, 260
Distributed databases
  defined, 213–15, 223, 225–26
Distributed processing
  defined, 138, 213
Divisionalized bureaucracies
  described, 67
  environments of, 68
Divisions
  in organizations
    information systems for, 68–69
Doctors
  as knowledge workers, 36
Documentation
  for conversions, 316
Documents
  systems for imaging, 34, 38, 373–74
  word processing systems and, 36, 38
DoD
  COBOL and, 176
Domestic exporter, 467

DOS
  defined, 170, 191
  NASA and, 174
Dow Jones News/Retrieval
  executive support systems and, 41
Downsizing
  computer
    defined, 138
    Deutsche bank and, 140
  organizational
    examples of, 114
    hierarchies and, 16
    information systems and, 25
    middle managers and, 17
    virtual offices and, 76
Downtime, 290
Drag-and-drop
  visual programming technique, 185, 186
Drill down
  executive support systems and, 420
Drug abuse
  technostress and, 117
DSS. *See* Decision support systems (DSS)
Due process
  defined, 98
  ethics and, 98–99, 119

E

Early retirement
  technostress and, 117
Earthquakes
  information systems and, 112
EasyLink, 229
EBCDIC. *See* Extended Binary Coded Decimal Interchange Code (EBCDIC)
Economic feasibility, 312
Economic theories
  on organizations and information systems, 74
Economics
  behavioral approach to information systems and, 12
Economies
  in Germany
    transformation to service economies, 3–4
  global
    effects on business, 3, 25, 481–82
  industrial
    transformation of, 3–4
  in Japan
    transformation to service economies, 3–4
  service
    effects on business, 3–4
  transformation of
    time-based competition and, 4–5
  in United States
    transformation to service economies, 3, 25
EDI. *See* Electronic data interchange (EDI)
Edifact, 229, 477
Edit checks, 445–46
Education
  client/server and, 291
  Internet and, 15
  privacy laws on, 102, 103
Efficiency
  data models and, 210, 212
Egyptian Cabinet
  decision making and, 409–10
Electromagnetic spectrum, 236
Electronic commerce
  enterprise networking and, 271–72

Internet and, 19, 25, 26–27, 271–72, 280–81, 293
  telecommunications and, 18–19, 25, 271–72
Electronic communications
  privacy laws on, 102, 103
Electronic Communications Privacy Act of 1986, 103, 252
Electronic data interchange (EDI), 255–56, 260, 480
  Internet and, 281, 282
  standards for, 229, 288, 477–78
Electronic funds transfer, 272
Electronic mail (E-mail), 251–52, 260
  brokerage orders via, 21
  code of ethics and, 117
  Internet and, 251, 274, 293
  Japanese and, 463
  office automation systems and, 36, 373
  privacy and, 101, 103
  remote workers and, 17
  standards for, 288
Electronic markets. *See also* Electronic commerce
  defined, 18–19
  financial, 26–27
  global economy and, 3, 481
  Internet and, 19, 25
Electronic meeting system (EMS)
  benefits of, 418–19
  group decision support systems and, 417–18
Electronic shopping malls
  on the Internet, 19
E-mail. *See* Electronic mail (E-mail)
EMASS systems
  ethical issues and, 98
Embezzlement, 448
Employee record keeping
  transaction processing systems for, 33, 34
Employee Resource System (ERS), 80
Employment screening
  ethical issues on, 103
Empowerment
  information systems and, 4–5, 16, 19, 111
Encryption
  of telephone transmissions
    privacy and, 103
End-user development, 347–49, 362
  management of, 348–49, 362
  tools for, 347–48, 362
End-user interface, 342
Engineering
  forward, 361
  reverse, 361, 362
  supercomputers and, 141
Engineers
  as knowledge workers, 9, 36
England
  design/development of 1994 Ford Mustang and, 17
Enterprise analysis, 301–03, 330
Enterprise networking, 266–96, 293
  business drivers of, 271
  client/server model, 270–71, 289–90, 292, 293
  defined, 268
  electronic commerce and, 271–72
  Internetworking, 270
  networks. *See* Networks
  operating systems for, 288–89
  problems of, 289–91, 294
  security and, 290–91, 293–94

standards for, 285, 287–88, 294
Entertainment
  Internet and, 15
Entities
  databases and, 212
  defined, 198
  key, 222
Entity-relationship diagram, 212, 213
Entrepreneurial structures
  described, 67
  environments of, 68
Environmental factors
  affecting information systems, 72, 77
Environments
  organizational
    information systems and, 63, 64, 68, 69, 77, 86
EPROM, 132–33, 157
Erasable programmable read-only memory (EPROM)
  defined, 132–33, 157
Ergonomics
  defined, 325
  effects on decision making, 414
  risk factors, 115, 116
  systems design and, 325
Errors
  ethics and, 117
  information systems and, 24, 432
  liability for, 107, 109
  software
    management challenges and, 190
  telecommunications and, 243
  user, 448
  wireless transmissions and, 240
ERS, 80
ESS. *See* Executive Support Systems (ESS)
Ethical "no free lunch" rule, 119
  defined, 100
Ethics
  1984 and, 110–11
  analysis process, 99, 119
  candidate principles for, 99–100
  copying computer software and, 105, 106
  Corporate Code of Ethics and, 117
  corporate policy for IS on, 119
  defined, 95
  Fortune 500 and, 117
  intellectual property and. *See* Intellectual property
  liability and. *See* Liability
  moral risks from technology, 118–19
  privacy and. *See* Privacy
  professional codes of, 100, 101
  quality and, 109–10, 117
  social and political issues and, 95–96
  Software Code of Ethics and, 106
  technology trends raising issues, 97–98
EuroElan, 217
Evolutionary development
  of transnational systems, 472, 481
Execution cycle, 133–34
Executive information system (EIS), 225
Executive support systems (ESS), 33–34, 420–25
  benefits of, 423, 426
  characteristics of, 34, 425
  defined, 41, 420
  examples of, 423–25
  integration with, 42, 53
  role of, 41, 420, 425
  types of, 34, 41–42, 54

Expert systems
  AI shell, 383–84
  backward chaining in, 384, 396
  building, 384, 395
  capture of knowledge and, 381–85, 396
  defined, 381
  examples of, 385
  forward chaining in, 384, 396
  inference engine in, 384, 396
  knowledge base in, 381, 396
  knowledge frames and, 382–83, 396
  problems with, 385
  rule-based, 381–82, 396
  semantic nets and, 382, 383, 396
  vs. neural networks, 388–90, 396
Extended Binary Coded Decimal Interchange Code (EBCDIC)
  defined, 128, 157
  list of, 129
  main memory and, 132

F

Facsimile machines (fax), 252–53, 260
Facts
  in ethical analysis, 99, 119
Fair Credit Reporting Act, 1970, 103
Fair Information Practices (FIP)
  described, 102
Family
  boundaries between work and, 111
Family Educational Rights and Privacy Act of 1978, 103
Farm workers
  in labor force, 5
Fault-tolerant computer systems, 437
Fax machines, 252–53, 260
FDDI
  fiber-optic transmission standard, 288
Feasibility study, 312
Federal Copyright Act of 1790, 104
Federal Managers Financial Integrity Act of 1982, 103
Feedback
  defined, 6–7
Fiber-optic cable
  telecommunications and, 233, 259
  transmission standards for, 288
Fields
  defined, 197
Fifth generation computers, 155, 157
File servers, 247
File Transfer Protocol (FTP)
  Internet and, 276, 293
Files
  access methods
    direct, 200
    indexed sequential, 199–200
  data management and, 197–203, 223
  defined, 197
  flat, 201
  traditional organization of, 201, 202
Filing
  office automation systems and, 36
Finance
  information architecture and, 24
  information systems for, 9, 32–36
  in virtual corporations, 18
Financial records
  privacy laws on, 102, 103
FIP, 102
Firewalls, 282
Flat files, 201

Flattening
  enterprise
    in business, 5–6, 74–75
    client/server computing and, 271
    information systems and, 4–5, 16–17
Flexibility
  data models and, 210–11, 212, 223
  of enterprise
    from technology, 4–5, 6
    telecommunications technology
      and, 17–19
  executive support systems and, 423
Floods
  information systems and, 112
Floppy disks, 144. *See also* Magnetic disks
  defined, 145
Flowers
  quality programs and, 51
  selling via Internet
    Absolutely Fresh Flowers, 19
    Calyx and Corolla, 17
FOCUS, 178, 179
Focused differentiation, 44
  Internet and, 47
Ford Mustang (1994)
  design/development of, 17
Forecasting models
  for decision making purposes, 412
Formal plans
  in business, 5–6, 21
Formal rules
  in business, 5–6
  information systems and, 13
Formal systems
  defined, 6–7
FORmula TRANslator (FORTRAN), 168, 174–75, 176, 191
FORTRAN, 168, 174–75, 176, 191
Fortune 500 companies
  cash flow and information systems
    in, 13
  code of ethics and, 117
  organizational structures in, 67
Fortune 1000 companies
  reengineering in, 113
Forums
  Internet and, 274, 293
Forward chaining
  in expert systems, 384, 396
Forward engineering, 361
Fourth generation computers, 135
Fourth generation languages, 178–79, 191
Frame of reference
  in decision-making, 84, 87
Frame relay, 250
Frames
  knowledge
    expert systems and, 382–83, 396
Franchisers, 467
Fraud
  information systems and, 24
  Internet and, 113
  liability for
    Internet and, 108
Freedom of Information Act, 1968 as
  Amended, 103
Front-end processors
  communications and, 242, 259
FTP
  Internet and, 276, 293
Full-duplex transmissions, 242, 259
Functional information systems, 32, 33
Fuzzy logic, 391–93, 396

G

Gallup Poll
  executive support systems and, 41
GAMIS, 424
Gantt charts, 321–22
"Garbage can" model of decision-making, 85
Gateways, 247
GDDS, 413–20
GEIS, 229, 249
General controls, 442
General Electric Information Systems (GEIS), 229, 249
General Moral Imperative
  professional conduct standards, 101
General Services Administration (GSA)
  executive support systems and, 424
Generalists
  in businesses, 5–6
Generations
  computer, 134–35
Genetic algorithms, 393–94, 396
Geographic information system (GIS), 189, 192–93, 424
Geological Information System
  for oil production, 62–63
Germany
  effects of global economy on, 3
  transformation to service economies
    in, 3–4
Gigabytes
  defined, 130
GIS, 189, 192–93, 424
Glenn Asset Management Information
  System (GAMIS), 424
Global business strategy
  systems structure and, 467–68, 483–84
    centralized, 467
    decentralized, 468
    duplicated, 467
    networked, 468
Global culture, 462–63
Global economies of scale, 463, 481
Global economy
  effects on business, 3–4, 23, 25, 481
  Globalization Challenge, 23
  networks and, 228–30
Global markets, 463
Global operations, 463, 481
Global systems
  delivery, 3–4
  managing, 470–74
Global Trade Point Network, 228–30
Global work groups, 4
Globalization. *See* Global economy
Goals
  organizational, 68–69, 86
Golden Rule
  ethics and, 99, 119
Gophers
  Internet and, 275–76, 278, 293
Governments
  Fair Information Practices Principles
    and, 102
  Internet and, 15
  regulations for, 21
Graphical user interfaces (GUIs), 169–70
  standard for, 288
Graphics languages, 178, 179, 181, 191
Gross national product
  knowledge/information work and, 4
Group collaboration systems
  groupware and. *See* Groupware

Internet and, 378–80
  sharing of knowledge and, 377–80
Group decision support systems (GDDS), 413–20, 425
  tools for, 416–17
Groups
  in organizations
    information systems for, 68–69
Groupware, 256–57, 260, 378, 396, 480.
  See also Group decision support
  systems
GSA
  executive support systems and, 424
GUIs, 169–70

H

Hackers
  defined, 433
  Internet
    computer crime and, 113, 293, 433
Half-duplex transmissions, 242, 259
Hard disks. *See also* Magnetic disks
  data storage in microcomputers
    and, 143
  defined, 144
Hardware. *See* Computer hardware
Hardware controls, 442
Health risks
  information technology and, 114–17, 119
Healthcare
  information systems and, 24
  inventory management and, 45–46
Hierarchical data model, 198, 208, 210–12, 223
Hierarchies
  data, 198, 208, 210–12, 223
  in organizations, 5–6, 8, 65–66, 77, 86
  downsizing and, 16, 113, 114
High Performance Computing Act, 118
Higher-order values
  ethical analysis and, 99
High-level languages, 175, 191. *See also*
  Programming languages
Historical data
  data warehouses and, 218–19, 224
Home
  shopping at
    electronic malls and, 19
    Internet and, 1–2
  working at, 17
Home pages
  Internet and, 278, 283
Home Shopping Network, 19
Hong Kong airport
  CAD software and, 376
Horizontal organizations, 75
Hoteling systems
  virtual offices and, 76
Hotels
  Internet and, 47
  reservation systems for, 33, 200, 280
HTML, 276, 282
Human errors
  liability for, 107
Human factor
  in systems design, 324–25
Human resources
  information architecture and, 24
  information systems for, 9, 14, 32–36
  ethics and, 100–101
Hurricanes
  information systems and, 112

HyperCard, 217, 218
Hypermedia databases, 215-17, 224
Hypertext Markup Language (HTML), 276, 282

I

Icons, 169
Idea organizers
  electronic
    group decision support systems and, 416
IDMS
  network database management system, 225-26
Imaging systems
  for documents, 34, 38, 373-74
  USAA network, 38
Immanuel Kant's Categorical Imperative
  defined, 99, 119
Implementation
  stage of decision-making, 83
IMS, 208, 212
Incremental development
  of transnational systems, 472, 481
Index server
  document imaging and, 373-74
Indexed sequential access method (ISAM), 199-200, 223
Indexes
  to files, 199
Individual models
  of decision-making, 84, 87
Individuals
  in organizations
    information systems for, 68-69
Industrial economies
  transformation of, 3-4
IndustryNet, 229
Inference engine
  expert systems and, 384, 396
Infoglut, 422
Information
  defined, 6
  Internet and, 15
  knowledge work systems and, 372-79
  partnerships
    defined, 49
  retrieval of
    Internet and, 275, 293
Information architecture
  creation of, 25
  defined, 23-24, 268
  development of, 71
  management information systems and, 24, 480
Information center, 349, 363
Information Management System (IMS)
  database management system, 208, 212
Information policy, 222
Information requirements, 313, 329, 330
Information rights, 119
  corporate code of ethics and, 117
  defined, 96
Information services
  commercial digital, 253, 260
Information superhighway, 231-33
  defined, 231
Information systems
  computer-based. See also Computer-based information systems (CBIS)
  for accounting. See Accounting, information systems for

behavioral approach to, 11, 12, 25
business perspective on, 7-11
catastrophes and, 112
changing management process and, 21-22
contemporary approaches to, 11-12
controlling, 430-56, 453
defined, 6-7
departments
  defined, 70
design of. See Design
determining business value of, 326-29, 330
effects on organizations, 72-77, 300-310
errors in
  liability for, 109, 117
evolution of role of, 70-78
for finance. See Finance, information systems for
functional, 32, 33
international, 460-66
investment challenge of, 23-24
kinds of, 31-43, 53-54
knowledge management and, 370-71
knowledge-level, 31-33
literacy for managers and, 7, 25
management issues on, 22-25, 49-50
management-level, 31-33
managers
  defined, 70
for manufacturing. See Manufacturing, information systems for
for marketing. See Marketing, information systems for
office automation systems. See Office automation systems (OAS)
operational-level, 31, 32-33
organizational design and, 16-21, 22-23
organizations and, 7-10, 13-22, 63-78, 87, 300-310
  behavioral theories on, 74-75, 77
  economic theories on, 74
  implications for systems design, 77-78, 80-81
  resistance in, 77, 78
  power of, 14-16
  ethical issues on, 97
roles of
  organizational, 13-22, 70-78
  strategic, 29-60
for sales. See Sales, information systems for
sociotechnical approach to, 12, 25, 300, 329
strategic-level, 31-33, 43
technical approach to, 11, 25
types of, 31-43, 53-54
for human resources. See Human resources, information systems for
transaction processing systems. See Transaction processing systems (TPS)
Information systems plan
  business plan and, 300-301, 330
Information work, 372
Informational roles
  of managers
    defined, 79
  information systems for, 81
Information-based service economies. See Service economies
Infrared transmissions, 236, 259
Ingress
  relational databases and, 217

testing tools and, 451
Inheritance
  object-oriented programming and, 185-87
Input authorization, 445
Input controls, 445
Inputs
  computer hardware and, 10
  defined, 6
  devices for, 148-50, 157
  to information systems, 34
  pen-based, 149
Insider trading
  Greyhound bus company and, 58
Installation
  in traditional systems lifecycle, 340, 362
Institutional factors
  affecting information systems, 72
Instruction cycle, 133-34
Instructions. See Computer software
Insurance companies
  downsizing in, 114
  expert systems in, 385
  hierarchical databases and, 212
  imaging systems in, 38
  microfilm/microfiche in, 151
  underwriting work-flow systems in, 20, 22
Intangible benefits, 326, 329
Integrated circuits
  third generation computers and, 135, 157
Integrated Services Digital Network (ISDN), 287-88, 294, 478, 480, 482
  ethical issues and, 98
Integrated software packages, 182-83
Integration
  among various systems, 42-43, 53, 54
  hardware and systems, 475-77
  tools for
    external, 321
    internal, 321
Intellectual property
  defined, 104
  ethical issues and, 105-06
  patents and, 105
  professional ethics and, 101
  rights described, 96, 97, 119
  shareware and, 106
Intelligence
  stage of decision-making, 83
Intelligent agents, 253, 254
International information systems, 460-66
  infrastructure, 460
International Value-Added Network Services (IVANs), 478-79
Internet, 272-82, 284-85, 293
  accountability, 106
  address components, 275
  Alta Vista and, 278
  Archie and, 276, 277, 278
  auctions and, 1-2
  benefits of, 278-81
  browsers, 276-78, 379
  bundled services, 232
  business redesign with, 307
  chatting, 274, 293
  commerce on, 19, 25, 26-27, 271-72, 280-81
  computer crime and, 113, 293, 433
  control, 106
  data warehouses and, 220
  databases and, 221
  defined, 15-16
  electronic data interchange. See Electronic data interchange (EDI)

e-mail, 251
ethical issues and, 98
  intellectual property and, 105
financial trading and, 19, 21
FTP and, 276
global trade and, 229
gophers, 275–76, 278
group collaboration and, 378–80
groupware on, 257, 396
hackers and, 113, 293, 433
home pages on, 278, 283
home shopping on, 1–2
information retrieval on, 275
information sharing on, 14, 17
information superhighway and, 233
intelligent agents and, 254
international challenges of, 479, 480
intranet. *See* Intranets
Java and, 188
kiosks and, 154–55
legal issues, 285
liability and, 106
managers and, 79, 80
PanCanadian Petroleum employee bulletin board, 62
pornography and, 106, 108
remote workers and, 17, 25
search engines and, 278
security and, 21, 281, 284, 293–94
servers, 273
shopping malls on, 19
strategic uses of, 47
Telnet and, 274–75, 293
UPS and, 8
Usenet and, 274, 293
Veronica and, 277
viruses
  information systems and, 112, 113, 434
WAIS and, 276, 277, 278, 293
web, 276–78, 379–80
Yahoo and, 278
Internet Shopping Network, 19
Internetworking, 270
Interorganization level
  information systems for, 68–69
Interorganizational systems
  defined, 19
Interpersonal roles
  of managers
    defined, 79
    information systems for, 81, 87
Interpreter
  defined, 168, 191
Intranets, 282–83, 293, 396
Intuitive decision-makers
  described, 84
Inventory
  control
    systems for, 34
  custom manufacturing and, 20
  elimination of, 17
  replenishment systems, 45–46
  stockless supply method of management, 45–46, 49
  systems for managing healthcare, 45–46
  Warehouse Manager system, 119–21
Inventory Express
  UPS warehouse system, 8
Investment workstations, 377
Investments
  financial
    challenge for information systems, 23–24
    Russell/Yasuda model and, 409
Invoiceless processing, 306

ISAM, 199–200, 223
ISDN, 98, 287–88, 294, 478, 480, 482
Iteration construct
  in structured programming, 355
Iterative processes, 341
IVANs, 478–79

J

Japan
  design/development of 1994 Ford Mustang and, 17
  effects of global economy on, 3
  transformation to service economies in, 3–4
Java, 187–89, 191
Java virtual machine (JVM), 188
Jeans
  product differentiation in, 44
Job turnover
  technostress and, 117, 119
Join
  relational data model and, 209, 211
Jukebox, 373
Jurisdiction
  Internet and, 108
Just in time
  delivery systems
    automobiles and, 45–46
    products and, 17
JVM, 188

K

Kant's Categorical Imperative
  defined, 99, 119
Key fields
  defined, 198, 212
Keyboards
  causing repetitive stress injuries, 114–15, 116, 158
  ergonomic, 116
Keypunching, 148
Key-to-disk machines, 148
Key-to-tape machines, 148
Kilobytes
  defined, 130
Kiosks
  mobile data networks and, 239
  multimedia and, 154
Knowledge bases
  in expert systems, 381, 396
Knowledge engineers, 384
Knowledge management, 370–400
  artificial intelligence and, 380–85, 396
  capture of knowledge
    expert systems and, 381–85, 396
  creation of knowledge
    knowledge work systems and, 374–77
  distribution of knowledge
    Internet and, 280, 293
    office information systems and, 372–73
  information systems and, 370–71
  knowledge work and productivity, 371–72, 395
  knowledge work systems and, 372–79
  organizational intelligence, 386–87
  sharing of knowledge
    group collaboration systems and, 377–80
Knowledge work systems (KWS), 33, 34, 374–77
  characteristics of, 34, 36, 38, 374
  creation of knowledge and, 374–77
  defined, 36, 374
  information and, 372–79

integration with, 42, 53
productivity and, 371–72, 395
requirements of, 374
types of, 34, 36, 38, 375–76
Knowledge workers
  defined, 9, 372
  systems for, 31–33, 35
Knowledge-based service economies. *See* Service economies
Knowledge-level decision-making
  defined, 82
Knowledge-level systems, 31–33, 54
  defined, 31
  information architecture and, 24
KWS. *See* Knowledge work systems (KWS)

L

Labor
  division of
    in business, 5–6, 65–66
Labor force
  composition of, 5
  knowledge/information work and, 4
Languages. *See* Programming languages
LANs. *See* Local area networks (LANs)
Laptop computers
  virtual offices and, 76
Laws
  anti-piracy
    intellectual property and, 106
  copyright
    "Merger doctrine" and, 104
  on privacy, 102, 103
Lawsuits
  companies and employee e-mail, 252
  for repetitive stress injuries, 116
  for software failure, 120–22
Lawyers
  as knowledge workers, 36
Leadership
  business management and, 10, 21
  organizational, 68–69, 78, 86
Learning
  organizational change and, 12
Legitimacy
  as change agent, 474
Liability
  defined, 98
  ethics and, 98–99, 108
  Internet and, 108
  political issues on, 109
  recent problem situations with, 107–08
  social issues and, 108–09
  telecommunications and, 108
Libel
  liability for
    Internet and, 108, 109
Library of Congress, 118
License agreements
  ethics and, 106, 117
Life
  quality of
    information systems and, 97, 110–17, 118, 119
Linkage editter, 168, 169
LISP, 178
Literacy
  computer
    managers and, 7, 25
  information systems
    managers and, 7, 25
Load modules
  defined, 168, 169

Local area networks (LANs)
  image processing and, 38
  managing, 259
  telecommunications and, 246–48, 260
Location assignment
  operating system and, 165
Location independence
  of enterprise
    from technology, 4–5
Logic
  fuzzy, 391–93, 396
Logical application groups
  in enterprise analysis, 302
Logical design, 313
Logical views
  of data, 206, 223
Logistics
  in virtual corporations, 18
"Look and feel" copyright infringement, 104
Los Angeles Superior Court
  e-mail monitoring and, 101
Lotus
  1-2-3
    executive support systems and, 421
    high-level languages and, 175
    spreadsheets and, 182
  cc:Mail
    music industry and, 125
  Notes, 257, 284, 378, 379
Low-cost producer, 46–47
  Internet and, 47
Low-frequency radio transmissions, 236, 259
Low-orbit satellites
  wireless transmissions and, 237, 259
Loyalty
  in business, 5–6
Lupron, 427

M

Machine bureaucracies
  described, 67
  environments of, 68
Machine cycle
  defined, 133–34
Machine language
  defined, 173, 191
Machines
  intelligent
    for artificial intelligence, 380, 396
Machinists
  as production workers, 9
Macintosh computers, 172, 174
  Java and, 188
Magic
  high-level programming language, 179, 180
Magnetic disks
  data storage in microcomputers and, 143
  defined, 144, 158
  key-to-disk machines and, 148
  secondary storage and, 132, 144–46
  storage technology and, 10
Magnetic drums
  first generation computers and, 135
Magnetic ink character recognition (MICR), 149, 158
Magnetic tapes, 143–44
  data storage in microcomputers and, 143
  defined, 143
  key-to-tape machines and, 148
  secondary storage and, 132
  storage technology and, 10

Magneto-optical disks
  defined, 148
Mail
  electronic and voice
    office automation systems and, 36, 373
Mailing list software, 162–63
Mainframe computers
  defined, 137, 157
  desktop power and, 14
  Deutsche bank and, 140
  image processing and, 38
  speed of, 130
  storage/memory in, 130
Maintenance
  client/server implementation and, 440
  systems development cycle and, 317–18, 330
Management
  behavioral models of, 78–79, 87
  classical model of, 78, 87
  decision support systems for. See Decision support systems (DSS)
  of end-user development, 348–49, 362
  in flatter organizations, 16
  in a global economy, 3–4, 25
  of implementation complexity, 321
  information systems and, 9–10, 21–22, 31–33, 34, 54. See also Management Information Systems (MIS)
  decision support systems for, 34, 54
  defined, 32–33
  of networking, 289, 294
    local area, 259
  requirements for databases, 220–23, 224
  support of systems projects, 319
  transaction systems for, 38–40
Management control
  defined, 82
Management information systems (MIS), 33
  characteristics of, 34, 38–40
  defined, 38
  information architecture and, 24, 480
  integration with, 42, 53
  study of, 12
  types of, 34, 38–40, 54
  vs. decision support systems, 405–07
Management science
  MIS and, 12
  technical approach to information systems and, 11
Management-level systems, 31–33, 54
Managerial roles
  defined, 79
Managers
  as data workers, 36
  decision-making and, 81–86, 87
  Fair Information Practices Principles and, 102
  information systems
    defined, 70
  information systems and, 13, 49–50
  Internet and, 79, 80
  middle. See Middle managers
  operational. See Operational managers
  roles of, 78–86
  senior. See Senior managers
  systems design and, 80–81
  systems for, 35
Managing global systems, 470–74, 481
Manpower planning
  executive support systems for, 34
Manual systems
  described, 7
Manufacturing

custom. See Custom manufacturing
data quality problems in, 110
decision support system for, 408–09
design
  computer-aided. See Computer-aided design software (CAD)
  information architecture and, 24
  information systems for, 9, 32–36
  scheduling software for custom, 20
  in virtual corporations, 18
Manufacturing Execution System (MES), 53
MapInfo geographic information software, 193
Market
  electronic. See Electronic market
Market research
  ethical issues on, 103
  systems for, 36
Marketing
  information architecture and, 24
  information systems for, 9, 32–36
  in virtual corporations, 18
Mass marketing
  privacy and, 103
Mass-customized products. See Custom manufacturing
Massively parallel computers, 155–56
Mass-production
  vs. custom manufacturing, 20
Master files
  defined, 150
Masters of Deception (MOD)
  Internet hackers, 113, 433
Matching
  computer, 446
Matchpoint, 281
MCI:Mail account
  dismissal due to, 101
Media
  storage technology, 10
Meetings
  electronic, 418–20
Megabytes
  defined, 130
Megahertz (MHz)
  defined, 136
Memory. See Storage
Memory aids
  in decision support systems, 407
"Merger doctrine"
  copyright law and, 104
MESA
  system for production precision, 53
Metaphor
  for data access, 264
Methodologies
  computer-aided software engineering, 358–60, 361, 363
  Critical Success Factor methodology, 421
  development, 352
  object-oriented, 356–58, 359, 363
  quality and, 449–50
  software reengineering, 360–61, 363
  structured, 352–56, 362, 363
  for system building, 352–61, 362
Methods
  object-oriented programming and, 184
Metrics
  software, 450–51
MHz. See Megahertz
Mice
  computer, 148, 158
MICR. See Magnetic ink character recognition (MICR)

Subject Index 553

Microcomputers
  defined, 137–38, 157
  operating systems for, 170–73
  storage devices in, 143
  tools for, 181–83
  vs. workstations, 141
Microfiche, 151, 158
Microfilm, 151, 158
Microminiaturization
  fourth generation computers and, 135
Microprocessors, 135–37
  common, 137
  defined, 135
  power of, 14
  speed of, 130
  storage/memory in, 130
Microseconds
  defined, 130
Microsoft
  Access, 182
    relational data model, 210
  Excel, 182, 421
  Exchange, 257
  Word, 181, 182
Microwave transmissions, 236, 259
Middle managers
  defined, 10
  downsizing and, 17, 113, 114
  reengineering and, 113
  systems for, 32–33
Milliseconds
  secondary storage devices and, 128, 130
Minicomputers
  defined, 137, 157
Mining
  data
    ethical considerations on, 98
MIS. *See* Management information systems (MIS)
MIS audit, 448–49
Mobile data networks
  wireless transmissions and, 239
MOD, 113
Model base, 412
Modeling
  workstations and, 141
Models
  capital budgeting, 326–27, 330
  of connectivity, 285–87, 294
  of decision-making, 84–85, 87
    "Garbage can," 85
  forecasting
    for decision making purposes, 412
  hierarchical data, 208, 210–12
  network data, 208–09, 210–12
  Open Systems Interconnect, 286–87
  optimization
    for decision making purposes, 412
  reference, 285
  relational data, 209–12
  Roundabout Table, 414–15
  Russell/Yasuda
    for financial investing, 409
  scoring, 328–29
  sensitivity analysis
    for decision making purposes, 412
  Transmission Control Protocol/Internet Protocol, 286, 478
  value chain, 47–48, 54
  virtual stock-exchange, 27
Modems
  telecommunications and, 234, 235, 259
Modules
  in structured programming, 354–55

Monitoring
  operating system and, 166
Morale
  virtual offices and, 76
Mouse, 148
Multidimensional databases, 217–18, 224
Multimedia, 152–54, 158
  defined, 152
  rental of CD-ROM titles, 160
Multinational, 467
Multiplexers
  communications and, 243, 259
  telecommunications and, 234
Multiprocessing
  operating system and, 168, 190, 191
Multiprogramming
  operating system and, 166–67, 190, 191
Multitasking
  microcomputers and, 170–72
  operating system and, 167, 190, 191
Multithreading
  microcomputers and, 171
Music industry
  information systems and, 124–25
Mutuality of interest
  Fair Information Practices and, 102

N

Nanoseconds
  defined, 130
National Center for Health Statistics
  repetitive stress injuries and, 114–15
National Crime Information Center, 215
National Institute of Science and Technology (NIST), 110
National Research Education Network (NREN)
  ethical issues and, 98, 118
National Trade Database, 228–30
National Westminster Bank, 215
Natural Keyboard, 116
Natural language
  artificial intelligence and, 380, 396
Net present value, 326, 330
Network data model, 208–09, 210–12, 223, 226
  IDMS, 225–26
Network Neighborhood, 174
Networking. *See* Enterprise networking
Networks
  bus, 243–44, 259
  Decnet and, 478
  defined, 10, 11
  downtime in, 290
  enterprise. *See* Enterprise networking
  for financial trading, 21
  information superhighway, 231–33
  liability and, 107
  local area
    image processing and, 38
    telecommunications and, 246–48, 260
    microcomputers and, 171–72
  mobile data, 239
  neural, 387–91, 396
  operating systems for, 247
  outages of
    information systems and, 112
  ring, 244–45, 259
  security and, 290–91, 293–94
  Society for Worldwide Interbank Financial Telecommunications and, 477–78
  star, 243, 244, 259
  supernetworks and, 118

  teams and, 16–17
  topologies and telecommunications, 243–45, 259
  types of telecommunications, 243–50
  value-added, 249–50, 260
  virtual organizations and, 17, 18, 25
  Virtual Private Networks and, 480–81
  wide-area, 248–49, 260
Neural networks, 387–91, 396
New Jersey
  UPS processing in, 8
New products
  systems for, 36
New York State Office of General Services (OGS), 424–25
Newspaper records
  privacy laws on, 102, 103
Newton MessagePad, 240
1984
  ethics and, 110–11
NIST, 110
Nomad2
  high-level programming language, 179
Nomad computing
  quality of life and, 111
Nondisclosure agreements
  trade secrets and, 104
NREN, 98, 118
Number systems
  in computers, 127

O

OAS. *See* Office automation systems (OAS)
Object code
  defined, 168, 169
Object request brokers (ORBs)
  object-oriented programming and, 186
Object-oriented databases, 215–17, 224, 225–26
Object-oriented methodology
  for system building, 356–58, 359, 363
Object-oriented programming, 184–89, 191
  concepts of, 185–87
Object-oriented software development, 356–58, 359, 363
Objects
  object-oriented programming and, 184, 191
OCR. *See* Optical character recognition (OCR)
Office automation systems (OAS), 33, 395
  characteristics of, 34, 36, 38, 372–74
  defined, 36, 373
  integration with, 42, 53
  types of, 34, 36, 38, 372–74
Office information systems
  distribution of knowledge and, 372–73
Office space
  reduction of
    remote workers and, 17
Offices
  remote, 16
  virtual, 75, 76
Oil production
  information systems for, 61–63
OLE (Object Linking and Embedding), 186
On-line analytical processing (OLAP)
  executive support systems, 427
On-line processing
  defined, 150–51, 158
Open systems
  defined, 285

Open Systems Interconnect (OSI), 286–87, 288, 294, 478
Operating systems
  for CAD software, 174
  defined, 165
  functions of, 165–68, 190, 191
  for microcomputers, 170–73
  network, 247
  standards for, 288–89
Operational control
  defined, 82
Operational data, *vs.* warehouse data, 219
Operational feasibility, 312–13
Operational managers
  defined, 10
  information systems and, 13, 25, 31
  systems for, 31–33
Operational-level systems, 31–33, 53–54
  defined, 31
  information architecture and, 24
  for transaction processing, 33–36
Operations
  in decision support systems, 407
Operations research
  MIS and, 12
  technical approach to information systems and, 11
Optical character recognition (OCR), 149, 158
Optical disks, 146–48, 158
  CD-ROM. *See* Compact disk read-only memory
  data storage in microcomputers and, 143
  defined, 146
  image storage and, 38
  magneto-optical, 148
  replacing microfilm/microfiche, 151
  storage technology and, 10
  write once/read many, 148
Optimization
  of systems
    sociotechnical perspective on, 12
Optimization models
  for decision making purposes, 412
Options
  ethical analysis and, 99, 119
Oracle
  relational data model, 210
ORBs
  object-oriented programming and, 186
Organizational change, 12
  culture and, 67, 77
  environments and, 68–69, 77
  information systems and, 77–78, 87, 300–310, 329
  management of, 86, 318–25
  networks and, 289, 291, 294
  systems development and, 304–06, 330
Organizational impact analysis, 324
Organizational intelligence
  case-based reasoning and, 386–87, 396
Organizational models
  of decision-making, 84–85, 87
Organizational network level
  information systems for, 68–69
Organizations
  bureaucracies in, 65–67, 75
  change in, 12, 67, 77–78, 86, 87, 289, 291, 294, 300–310, 318–25, 329–30, 481
  common features of, 65–67, 69
  culture of
    information systems and, 7, 9, 63, 66–67, 69, 77, 86

defined
  behaviorly, 64, 65
  technically, 64, 65
effects of information systems on, 72–78
environments of
  information systems and, 63, 64, 68, 69, 77, 86
hierarchies in, 5–6, 8, 65–66, 77, 86
  downsizing and, 16, 113, 114
impacts of information systems on, 308
information architecture and, 23, 25, 71
information systems and, 7–10, 63–70, 87
  behavioral theories on, 74–75, 77
  design of, 16–21, 22, 77–78, 80–81. *See also* Systems design
  economic theories on, 74
  redesign of, 22–23
  resistance to, 77, 78
  role of, 13–22, 70–78
levels in, 68–70
manager role in, 78–86
politics in
  decision-making and, 85, 86
  technology and, 7, 10, 63, 64, 66, 69, 77
standard operating procedures in
  technology and, 7–8, 63, 64–65, 66, 69, 77, 86
structures in
  technology and, 5–6, 7–8, 63, 64–65, 69, 77
  types of, 67–68, 78
technology and, 12, 63, 77, 86
unique features of, 67–70
virtual. *See* Virtual organizations
OS/2, 170, 172, 191
OSI, 286–87, 288, 294, 478
Output controls, 447
Output devices, 150–52, 157
Outputs
  computer hardware and, 10
  defined, 6–7
  of information systems, 34
Outsourcing, 349–52, 363
Overcharging
  bar coding and, 110

P

Package tracking software, 8, 9, 10–11, 47, 53, 254
Packers
  as production workers, 9
Packet switching, 250
  standard for, 288
Pagers
  custom manufacturing of, 20
Pages
  home
    Internet and, 278, 283
  of programs, 167–68
Paging systems
  wireless transmissions and, 237–38
Pakistani virus
  information systems and, 112
Paper and pencil technology
  information systems and, 7
Paradigm shift, 306, 329
Paradox, 182
  relational data model, 210
Parallel processing
  defined, 141, 157
  massively parallel computers and, 155–56
  supercomputers and, 141–43

Parallel strategy
  for conversions, 315–16
Parent segments
  in IMS, 208
Parity bit
  defined, 127
Participation
  group decision support systems and, 418–19
Particularism, 464
Partitioning
  of databases, 213–15, 224
Partnerships
  information, 49
  strategic, 49
Part-time work
  virtual offices and, 76
Pascal, 177, 191
Patents
  defined, 105
  intellectual property and, 104–05
  professional ethics and, 101
Pattern-recognition
  neural networks and, 389
Payroll
  transaction processing systems for, 14, 33, 34, 35
PBX, 245–46, 260
PCensus software, 193
Pen-based input, 149, 158
Penthouse Magazine
  Internet liability and, 108
Pentium microprocessors, 136, 137, 154, 174
Perceptive systems
  artificial intelligence and, 380, 396
Performance
  computer
    prices and, 134
  measurement of
    quality and, 51
Personal communication services (PCS)
  wireless transmissions and, 239
Personal digital assistants (PDA)
  wireless transmissions and, 240
Personal Pair
  jeans product differentiation, 44
PERT, 321–22
Petroleum
  supercomputers and, 141
Phased approach
  for conversions, 316
Physical design, 313
Physical views
  of data, 206, 223
Picoseconds
  defined, 130
Pictures
  representing in computers, 127
Pilot study
  for conversions, 316
Pixel
  defined, 127
PL/1, 177, 191
Planning
  for connectivity, 292–93
  data, 222, 224
  executive support systems for, 34
  formal tools for, 321
  improved pre-planning
    group decision support systems and, 418
  managers and, 78, 87
  MIS for, 38–40
Plans
  business

information systems plan and, 300–301, 330
for conversions, 316
for disaster recovery liability and, 107
formal
 in business, 5–6, 21
test, 315
for testing, 315
PLEXSYS, 416
Plotters, 152, 158
Pointers
 in IMS, 208
 in network data model, 209
Point-of-sale terminals, 89
Policy formation tools
 group decision support systems and, 417
Political issues
 on intellectual property, 105–06
 on liability, 109
 on privacy, 103
 on quality, 110
Political models
 of decision-making, 85, 87
Political science
 behavioral approach to information systems and, 11, 12
Politics
 in organizations
  decision-making and, 85
  technology and, 7, 10, 63, 64, 66, 69, 77, 86
Pop-up boxes, 169
Pornography
 liability for
  Internet and, 106, 108
Portfolio analysis
 for information systems investments, 327–28, 330
Post, Telegraph, and Telephone authorities (PTT), 478, 480, 482
Postal systems
 privacy and, 103
Post-implementation
 in traditional systems lifecycle, 340, 362
Power
 computing
  ethical considerations and, 97
 organizational, 68–69, 85, 87
Power failure, 448
Power outages
 information systems and, 112
Power-PC processor, 137, 154
Pre-planning
 group decision support systems and, 418
Present value, 326
Prices
 computer
  performance and, 134
Pricing
 systems for, 36
Primary activities
 defined, 48
Primary memory. *See* Primary storage
Primary storage
 central processing units and, 131–32
 defined, 130, 157
 virtual storage and, 167
 vs. secondary storage, 143
Printers
 defined, 150, 151, 158
Privacy
 code of ethics and, 117, 119

defined, 102
ethical issues on, 103
Federal laws on, 102, 103
information systems and, 25
networks and, 252
political issues on, 103
professional ethics and, 101
social issues on, 103
wireless transmission and, 240
Privacy Act of 1974, 102
Privacy Act of 1974 as Amended, 103
Privacy Protection Act of 1980, 103
Private branch exchanges (PBX), 245–46, 260
Procedures. *See also* Standard operating procedures (SOPs)
 rationalization of, 304–05, 329
Process specifications, 354
Processes
 business, 471–72
Processing
 computer hardware and, 10
 defined, 6
 in information systems, 34
Processing controls, 446
Prodigy
 liability and, 108
 responsibility and, 106
Product differentiation, 43–44
 defined, 43
 Internet and, 47
Product life
 economic transformation and, 4–5
Production
 systems development cycle and, 316–17, 318, 330
Production workers
 defined, 9
Productivity
 downsizing and, 114
 economic transformation and, 4–5
 growth among white-collar workers, 22
 knowledge work and, 371–72, 395
 office automation systems and, 36, 372–74
 virtual offices and, 76
Professional bureaucracies
 described, 67
Professional codes of ethics, 100, 101
Professionalism
 in business, 5–6
Profit planning
 executive support systems for, 34
Program security controls, 442
Program-data dependence
 databases and, 207
 files and, 202–03, 223
Programmable read-only memory (PROM)
 defined, 132–33, 157
Programmers, 164
 defined, 70
Programming, 315, 330
 complexity
  data models and, 210–12
 languages. *See* Programming languages
 structured, 354–55, 363
 in traditional systems lifecycle, 339, 362
Programming language translation
 system software and, 168, 169, 190
Programming languages, 173–79
 Ada, 177, 191
 application generators, 178, 179
 assembly, 174, 175–76, 191
 C programming language, 168, 177, 191

COBOL. *See* COmmon Business Oriented Language (COBOL)
FOCUS, 178, 179
FORTRAN. *See* FORmula TRANslator (FORTRAN)
 fourth generation, 178–79, 191
 generations of, 173–75, 191
 graphics, 178, 179, 181, 191
 high-level, 175, 191
 Java, 187–89, 191
 LISP, 178
 machine, 173–74, 191
 Pascal, 177, 191
 PL/1, 177, 191
 Prolog, 178, 191
 query, 178, 179, 191
 Query-by-Example, 178, 179
 report generators, 179, 191
 very high-level programming languages, 179, 191
Programs
 defined, 164
 software. *See* Computer software
Project
 relational data model and, 209, 211
Project definition, 338, 362
Prolog, 178
PROM. *See* Programmable read-only memory (PROM)
Properties OnLine, 281
Property rights
 ethics and, 101, 117, 119
 intellectual. *See* Intellectual property
Property tracking systems
 real estate and, 80
Protocols
 for connectivity, 285, 294
 File Transfer Protocol
  Internet and, 276, 293
 for telecommunications, 234, 259
Prototype, 340
Prototyping, 340–42, 362, 363
 executive support systems and, 421
PSearch-USA software, 193
Psychology
 behavioral approach to information systems and, 11, 12
PTT, 478, 480, 482
Public domain
 trade secrets and, 104
Publishing
 desktop. *See* Desktop Publishing
Pull-down menus, 169
Punched cards
 first generation computers and, 135
Purchasing
 management challenges of technology, 157

Q

Quality
 benchmarks and, 51
 cycle time and, 51
 data. *See* Data, quality of
 debugging and, 451
 defined, 50
 ethics and, 109–10, 117
 information systems and, 50–53, 54, 109–10
 of life
  information systems and, 97, 110–17, 118, 119
 methodologies and, 449–50
 performance measurement and, 51

political issues on, 110
social issues on, 110
standards for, 97, 110, 119
testing and, 451
tools for, 452
walkthroughs and, 451
zero defects and, 50, 109, 440
Query languages, 178, 179, 191, 223
Query tools
 data warehouses and, 219
Query-by-Example, 178, 179
Questionnaires
 electronic
  group decision support systems for, 416

R

Racial inequity
 information systems and, 113–14
Radiation
 from terminals, 116–17
Radiation emission standards
 for VDTs, 116–17
RAID. *See* Redundant Array of Inexpensive Disks (RAID)
RAM. *See* Random Access Memory (RAM)
RAM Mobile Data, 230
Random Access Memory (RAM)
 defined, 132
 evolution of computers and, 135
 multimedia and, 153
 primary storage and, 143
Random file organizations, 199, 223
Rational model
 of decision-making, 84, 87
Rationalization of procedures, 304–05, 329
Read-only memory (ROM)
 defined, 132, 157
 primary memory and, 143
Real estate
 Internet and, 80, 281
Records
 defined, 197
Reduced instruction set computing (RISC)
 defined, 136–37
Redundancy
 of data
  databases and, 207
  files and, 202, 223
  network data model and, 209
Redundant Array of Inexpensive Disks (RAID)
 defined, 145
Reengineering
 blue-collar workers and, 113
 Boeing Company and, 397–400
 business. *See* Business reengineering
 in Fortune 1000 companies, 113
 middle managers and, 113
 software, 360–61
Reengineering work, 113
Reference model, 285
Register
 defined, 143
Regulations
 anti-piracy laws
  intellectual property and, 106
 Cable Communications Policy Act of 1984, 103
 Computer Fraud and Abuse Act, 113
 Computer Matching and Privacy Protection Act of 1988, 103
 Computer Security Act of 1987, 103
 Computer Software Copyright Act, 104

Electronic Communications Privacy Act of 1986, 103, 252
Fair Credit Reporting Act, 1970, 103
Fair Information Practices, 102
Family Educational Rights and Privacy Act of 1978, 103
Federal Copyright Act of 1790 and, 104
Federal Managers Financial Integrity Act of 1982, 103
Freedom of Information Act, 1968 as Amended, 103
High Performance Computing Act, 118
Privacy Act of 1974, 102
Privacy Act of 1974 as Amended, 103
Privacy Protection Act of 1980, 103
Right to Financial Privacy Act of 1978, 103
Telecommunications Act of 1996, 232
Video Privacy Protection Act of 1988, 103
Relational data model, 209–12, 223
Relationship billing
 data mining and, 45
Relationships
 data
  administration and, 222
Reliability
 networks and, 290–91
Relocation analysis
 systems for, 32, 34
Repetitive stress injuries (RSI), 114–15, 116
 defined, 114
Replication
 databases and, 213–15, 224
Reports
 ad hoc
  files and, 203
 data warehouses and, 219
 generators of, 179, 191
 in MIS, 38–40
Representations
 in decision support systems, 407
Request for Proposal (RFP), 346
Requirements
 management
  for database management systems, 220–23, 224
 for databases, 220–26
 for new employees, 22
 for systems analysis, 313, 329, 330
Research
 systems for
  market, 36
  operations, 11–12
Resource allocation
 operating system and, 165
 during systems development, 450
Responsibility
 challenge for information systems and, 24–25
 defined, 98
 ethics and, 98–99
Retail sales
 information systems and, 88–90
Retirement
 early
  technostress and, 117
Reverse engineering, 361, 362
RFP, 346
Right to Financial Privacy Act of 1978, 103
Rights
 information, 119
  corporate code of ethics and, 117
 defined, 96
Ring networks, 244–45, 259

Riots
 information systems and, 112
RISC. *See* Reduced instruction set computing (RISC)
Risk assessment, 447–48
Risk Aversion Principle, 119
 defined, 100
Risks
 in decision-making, 84
 ergonomic, 115, 116
 health
  information technology and, 114–17, 119
 moral
  from technology, 118–19
 Risk Aversion Principle and, 119
 in systems implementation, 319–20, 329
  controlling, 323
Robotics
 artificial intelligence and, 380, 396
Robots
 for custom manufacturing, 20
 EPROM chips for, 133
 for ship building, 37
ROM. *See* Read-only memory (ROM)
Root segments
 in IMS, 208
Roundabout Table Model, 414–15
RSI, 114–15, 116
Rule-based expert systems, 381–82, 396
Rules
 formal
  in business, 5–6
  information systems and, 13
 rule-based expert systems and, 381–82, 396
Run control totals, 446
Russell/Yasuda model
 for financial investing, 409

S

SABRE, 53, 57
Sales
 automation, 261–64
 information architecture and, 24
 information systems for, 9, 32–36
 in virtual corporations, 18
Satellites
 communication, 481
 information systems for, 9, 32–36
 television
  bundled services and, 232
  trucking industry and, 73
 wireless transmission, 236–37, 238, 259
Scanners
 bar code. *See* Bar codes
 digital, 150, 158
 imaging systems and, 38, 373
Scheduling
 office automation systems and, 36
 operating system and, 165–66
Science
 Internet and, 15
Scientists
 as knowledge workers, 9, 36
Scope
 of information systems, 13, 14
Scoring models, 328–29
Screens
 touch, 149
Search engines
 Internet and, 278, 293
 intranet and, 283

Second generation computers, 135
Secondary storage
  defined, 132, 143, 157
  speed of, 128, 130
Seconds
  retrieval time, 130
Secretaries
  as data workers, 9, 36
Sectors
  for data storage, 145–46
  defined, 145
Security
  database administration, 222
  e-mail, 252
  files and, 203, 223
  information systems, 24
  Internet, 21, 281, 284, 293–94, 453
  Java, 188
  networks, 290–91
  object-oriented databases and, 217
  operating system, 166
  telecommunications, 243, 258–59, 260
  wireless transmission, 240
Segments
  in IMS, 208
Segregation of functions, 444
Select-Ease Keyboard, 116
Selection construct
  in structured programming, 355
Semantic nets
  expert systems and, 382, 383, 396
Semiconductors
  defined, 132
  memory and, 132–33
  third generation computers and, 135
Senior managers
  defined, 10
  information systems and, 13
  systems for, 32–33, 43
Sensitivity analysis models
  for decision making purposes, 412
Sensors, 150, 158
Sequence construct
  in structured programming, 355
Sequential file organizations, 199, 223
Sequential processing
  vs. parallel processing, 141, 156, 157
Servers
  in client/server model, 270–71, 293
  index
    document imaging and, 373–74
Service economies
  effects on business, 3–4
Service workers
  defined, 9
Shareware software, 106
Shingo Prize for Excellence in American
    Manufacturing, 51
Ship building
  Odense Steel Shipyards CAD systems for,
    36, 37
Shipping
  transaction processing systems for, 33
Shopping
  at home
    Internet and, 1–2
  malls on the Internet, 19
Silicon chips
  third generation computers and, 135
Simplex transmissions, 242, 259
Simulations
  of decision-making process, 411
  workstations and, 141
Site Solutions, 80

SNA, 478
Social class inequity
  information systems and, 113–14
Social contact
  legal right to, 93–94
  virtual offices and, 76
Social issues
  on intellectual property, 105
  on liability, 108–09
  on privacy, 103
  on quality, 110
Social Security Master Beneficiary File
  ethical issues and, 97–98
Social well-being
  information systems and, 24
Society for Worldwide Interbank Financial
    Telecommunications (SWIFT),
    477–78
Sociology
  behavioral approach to information
    systems and, 11, 12
Sociotechnical approach
  to information systems, 12, 25, 300, 329
  strategic transitions and, 49, 54
Software
  application. See Application software
  controls, 442
  copying
    ethics and, 105, 106
  defined, 10, 164
  DSS software system and, 412
  errors in
    management challenges with, 190
  failure of, 432
  information architecture and, 24, 71
  information systems and, 7, 13
  infrastructure and, 479–80
  mailing list, 162–63
  metrics, 450–51
  object-oriented programming, 184–89,
    356–58, 363
  reengineering, 360–61
  system. See System software
  for telecommunications, 234, 243, 259
  trade secrets and, 104
  types of, 164–83
  utility
    system software and, 168, 190
Software Code of Ethics, 106
SOPs. See Standard operating procedures
    (SOPs)
Source code
  defined, 168, 169
Specialists
  in businesses, 5–6
Speed
  cycle, 136
  processing in computers, 128, 130
  RISC processors and, 136
  transmission. See Transmissions,
    speed of
Spreadsheet software, 181–82, 183
SQL, 204, 211, 225
Stakeholder identification tools
  group decision support systems
    and, 417
Stakeholders
  ethical analysis and, 99, 119
Standard operating procedures (SOPs)
  defined, 9, 66
  technology and, 7–8, 63–64, 65–66, 69,
    77, 86
Standards
  for computer terminals, 127

  for connectivity, 285, 287–88, 294
  for electronic data interchange, 229, 288,
    477–78
  for e-mail, 288
  fiber-optic transmissions, 288
  for graphical user interfaces, 288
  for networking, 285, 287–88
  for operating systems, 288–89
  for packet switching, 288
  for professional conduct, 101
  for quality, 97, 110, 119
  for radiation emission
    from VDTs, 117
  for telecommunications, 259
Standing data, 447
Star networks, 243, 244, 259
Stock exchange
  first on-line, 26–27
  virtual model of, 27
Stockless supply method
  of inventory management, 45–46, 49
Storage
  virtual, 167–68
Storage devices
  in microcomputers, 143
  speed of, 128, 130
Storage technology
  defined, 10, 11
  ethical issues on, 97–98
  primary storage. See Primary storage
  secondary storage. See Secondary storage
Store-Simplification Program, 89
Strategic alliances, 49
Strategic analysis, 303, 330
Strategic Business Challenge
  of information systems, 22–23
Strategic decision-making
  defined, 82
Strategic information systems
  defined, 43
  vs. strategic-level systems, 43
Strategic partnerships, 49
Strategic transitions, 54
  defined, 49
Strategic-level systems
  defined, 32–33
  executive support systems as, 34
  information architecture and, 24, 25
  vs. strategic information systems, 43
Strategies. See Business strategies,
    information systems and
Streaming tape backup
  for microcomputers, 143
Stress
  technology and, 115–17
Structured analysis, 352–54, 363
Structured decisions, 82, 87
  defined, 83
Structured design, 354, 363
Structured methodologies
  for system building, 352–56, 362, 363
Structured programming, 354–55, 363
Structured Query Language (SQL), 204,
    211, 225
Structures
  in organizations, 5–6, 7–8, 64, 69
  technology and, 63, 64–65, 77
  types of, 67–68, 78
Supercomputers, 118, 157
  defined, 138
  parallel processing and, 141–43
Superhighway
  national digital, 118
Supernetwork, 118

Support activities
  defined, 48
Supreme Court
  computer software patent decision, 105
SWIFT, 477–78
Switched lines, 248
Switching costs, 44–46
  defined, 44
Symbolic languages, 174, 175–76, 191
Synchronous transmissions, 242, 259
System 7, 170, 172–73, 191
System residence device
  defined, 166
System software, 165–73, 190
  defined, 164
  graphical user interfaces in, 169–70
  operating system in, 165–68, 170–73
Systematic decision-makers
  described, 84
Systems
  building of, 338–65
    alternative systems lifecycles, 340–52, 362
    application software packages, 342–46, 362
    end-user development, 347–49, 362
    outsourcing, 349–52, 363
    prototyping, 340–42, 362, 363
    software reengineering, 360–61, 363
    traditional systems lifecycle, 338–40, 352, 362, 363
  core, 471–72
  flowcharts of, 355, 358
  formal. *See* Formal systems
  hardware integration and, 475–77
  implementation of, 318–25, 330
  information. *See* Information systems
  interorganizational. *See* Interorganizational systems
  managing global, 470–74, 481
  study of
    in traditional systems lifecycle, 338–39, 362
  testing of, 315
Systems analysis, 311–13, 318, 330. *See also* Analysis
Systems analysts
  defined, 70
Systems design, 313–14, 330. *See also* Design
Systems development, 314–18, 330
  organizational change and, 304–6, 329
  overview of, 310–11, 330
  resource allocation during, 450
  systems analysis in, 311–13, 330
  systems design in, 313–14, 330
Systems implementation, 318–25, 330
  management of, 320–23
  management support and, 319
  risks in, 319–20, 329
Systems lifecycles
  alternative, 340–52
  defined, 338
  traditional, 338–40, 352, 362, 363
    problems with, 340
Systems Network Architecture (SNA), 478

T

Tables
  relational data model and, 209
Tangible benefits, 326, 329
Tapes. *See* Magnetic tapes

Task forces
  in business, 5–6
TCP/IP, 286, 288, 294, 478
Teams
  in business, 5–6
Teamwork
  information systems and, 4–5, 17
Technical approach
  to information systems, 11, 25
Technical feasibility, 312
Technologies
  challenges of, 474–80
  ethical issues and, 97–98
  information systems, 10–11
  moral risks of, 118
  organizations and, 12
  paper and pencil
    information systems and, 7
  power of, 14–16
    ethical issues on, 97
  storage. *See* Storage technology
  telecommunications. *See* Telecommunications
  transformation of business enterprises and, 4–5, 5–6, 25
  trickle-down, 113
Technostress, 115–17
  defined, 115
Telecommunications, 228–64
  analog signals and, 234
  challenges of, 475, 477–79
  channels, 235–40, 240–42, 259
  components of, 233–34
  computers and, 230–31
  defined, 10, 11, 230
  digital signals and, 234
  electronic commerce and, 18–19, 25, 271–72, 280–81
  electronic data interchange and, 255–56, 477–78
  ethical issues and, 98
  facilitating applications, 251–53, 260
  factors affecting, 258–59
  flexibility of organizations and, 17–19
  functions of, 234
  groupware and, 256–57, 260
  information architecture and, 24, 25
  information systems and, 13
  Internet and. *See* Internet
  kiosks and, 154–55
  LANs and, 246–48, 260
  liability and, 108
  networks and
    topologies and, 243–45, 259
    types of, 243–50
    value-added, 249–50, 260
  planning and, 257–58, 260
  private branch exchanges and, 245–46, 260
  processors, 242–43, 259
  protocols for, 234, 259
  remote workers and, 17, 25
  software
    defined, 243, 259
  standards for, 259
  systems, 233–43, 259
    defined, 233
  vulnerability of, 432–33
  WANs and, 248–49, 260
Telecommunications Act of 1996, 232
Telecommuting
  quality of life and, 111
Teleconferencing, 253, 255, 260
Telephone lines
  dedicated, 248

Internet and, 15
  switched, 248
Telephone systems
  as "common carriers," 107
  computer fraud and, 113
  deregulation of, 232
  monitoring, 180
Telephone transmissions
  encrypted
    privacy and, 103
Telephones
  cellular, 238–39, 481
Telnet, 274–75, 293
Terabytes
  defined, 130
Teraflop
  defined, 157
Terminals
  computer. *See* Computer terminals
Termination. *See* Dismissal
Test plans, 315
Testing, 315, 330
  ethics and, 109–10
  quality and, 451
  system failure lawsuits and, 120–22
Thefts, 432
  computer crime and, 112–13
  intellectual property and, 105
Thinkpads
  wireless transmissions and, 239
Third generation computers, 135
Time sharing
  operating system and, 168, 190, 191
Time-based competition
  economic transformation and, 4–5
  quality of life and, 111
Tire design
  CAD and, 51–53
Tools
  for CASE development, 359, 361
  for end-user development, 347–48, 362
Topologies
  network telecommunications and, 243–45, 259
Total quality management (TQM)
  defined, 50
Totals
  batch control, 445
Touch screens, 149, 155, 158
TPS. *See* Transaction processing systems (TPS)
Tracks
  defined, 144
Trade secrets
  defined, 104
  intellectual property and, 104, 105
Traditional systems lifecycle. *See* Systems lifecycle, traditional
Training
  client/server, 291
  management challenges for IT, 157
  multimedia and, 154
  organizational change and, 12
  transaction processing systems for, 34
Transaction files
  defined, 150
Transaction processing systems (TPS)
  characteristics of, 33–36
  defined, 33
  hierarchical databases and, 212
  integration with, 42, 53
  types of, 33–36, 53–54
Transactions
  costs of, 74

Subject Index *559*

lower
  from technology, 4–5
  Internet and, 15
  processing systems for. *See* Transaction processing systems (TPS)
Transborder data flow, 464
Transform algorithm
  direct file access and, 200
Transistors
  second generation computers and, 134–35, 157
Translations
  of programming language
    system software and, 168, 169, 190
Transmission Control Protocol/Internet Protocol (TCP/IP), 286, 288, 294, 478
Transmissions
  directions of, 242
  modes of, 242
  speed of, 240–42
Transnational systems, 468
  benefits of, 473–74
  development of
    evolutionary, 472, 481
    "grand design," 472
    incremental, 472, 481
  strategy for, 468–73
Transportation
  networks and, 266–68
Travel
  infrastructure mergers in, 476
  reservation systems for
    airline, 53, 57
    bus, 56–58
    hotel, 33, 200, 280
Travelocity
  Internet and, 281
Travelocity
  Internet and, 281
TravelWeb
  Internet and, 45, 280
Trends
  in databases, 213–20, 223
  in information technology, 152–57, 158
  systems for analysis of, 32
  technology
    raising ethics issues, 97–98
Trial and error
  in decision-making, 84
Trickle-down technology, 113
TRIPS
  bus management system, 56–58
Trucking industry
  information systems and, 73
Tuples
  relational data model and, 209
Turnover
  technostress and, 117
Twisted wire
  telecommunications and, 233, 259

U

Unemployment
  downsizing and, 114
Unit testing, 315
United Nations
  global trade and, 228–30
United States
  effects of global economy on, 3, 25
  transformation to service economies in, 3–4, 25

Universities
  organizational culture in, 67
  proposed network connecting, 118
  systems for, 36
Unix, 170, 172, 174, 191, 294
  Java and, 188
  operating systems standards and, 288–89, 294
Unstructured decisions, 82, 86, 87
  defined, 83
U.S. census data
  on CD-ROM, 193
U.S. Department of Defense (DoD)
  COBOL and, 176
U.S. General Services Administration
  executive support systems and, 424
Usenet, 274, 293
User exits
  in application generators, 179
User-designer communication gap, 319
Users
  of databases, 222
  of information systems, 33, 34
    defined, 70
  involvement of
    decision support systems and, 412–13
  role in systems design, 314, 319
Utilitarian Principle, 119
  defined, 100
Utility software
  system software and, 168, 190
Utilization
  telecommunications and, 258–59, 260

V

Vacuum tube technology
  first generation computers and, 134–35, 157
Valdez oil spill, 437
  decision-making and, 85
Value chain model, 47–48, 54
  defined, 47
Value-added networks (VAN), 249–51, 260, 282
  international. *See* International Value-Added Network Services (IVANs)
Values
  ethical analysis and, 99, 119
VAN, 249–51, 260, 282
Vaporware, 225
VDTs. *See* Video display terminals (VDTs)
Veronica
  Internet and, 277
Versant
  object-oriented databases and, 217
Vertical organizations, 75
Very high-level programming languages, 179, 191
Very Large-Scale Integrated Circuits (VLSIC)
  fourth generation computers and, 135, 157
VGA
  computer terminals and, 127
Video display terminals (VDTs)
  defined, 150, 158
  radiation from, 116–17
Video Privacy Protection Act of 1988, 103
Video rental stores
  use of bar codes in, 159–61
Video rentals
  privacy laws on, 102, 103

Videoconferencing
  defined, 255
  office automation systems and, 36
  remote workers and, 17
Virtual offices, 75
  management of, 76
Virtual organizations
  defined, 17, 18
Virtual Private Networks (VPNs), 480–81
Virtual reality, 375–76, 377
Virtual stock-exchange model, 27
Virtual storage
  operating system and, 167–68, 190, 191
Viruses
  computer, 434–36
  Internet
    information systems and, 112, 113
  Pakistani
    information systems and, 112
Visual programming, 185
  drag-and-drop, 185, 186
Visualization
  information systems and, 6, 25
Voice input devices, 150, 158
Voice mail, 252, 260
  office automation systems and, 36, 373
Voice output devices, 152, 158
Von Neumann Architecture, 155
Voter Education Kiosks
  in South Africa, 155
Voting tools
  group decision support systems and, 416
Voyage-estimating system
  for metals company, 40–41
VPNs, 480–81
Vulnerability
  information systems and, 111–12, 119, 431–33

W

WAIS, 276, 277, 278, 293
Walkthroughs
  systems quality and, 451
WANs, 248–49, 260
Warehouse data
  vs. operational data, 219
Warehouse Manager
  inventory system, 119–21
Warehouses
  bar codes and, 240, 241
  elimination of, 17
Weapons research
  supercomputers and, 141
Weather forecasting
  supercomputers and, 141
Web. *See also* Internet, web sites, 278, 279
Web sites, 278, 279
White collar workers
  in labor force, 5
  productivity growth among, 22
Wide Area Information Servers (WAIS), 276, 277, 278, 293
Wide-area networks (WANs), 248–49, 260
Windows
  defined, 170–71, 174
  Java and, 188
Windows 95, 170–71, 174, 191
Windows NT, 170–71, 174, 191
Windshield time, 264

Wireless transmissions, 236–40, 259
   cellular telephones and, 238–39, 481
   IBM Thinkpads and, 239
   microwave, 236, 259
   mobile data networks and, 239
   paging, 237–38
   personal communication services, 239
   personal digital assistants, 240
   satellites and, 236–37, 238, 259, 481
Wiretapping
   Internet and, 113
Word length
   chip speed and, 136
   defined, 136, 157
Word processing
   defined, 36
   software, 181
   systems for, 34, 36, 38, 373
Word spotting
   telephone operator jobs and, 101
WordPerfect, 181
Work groups. *See also* Teams
   global, 4
Workers
   blue-collar, 5
      reengineering and, 113
   data. *See* Data workers
   farm
      in labor force, 5
   knowledge. *See* Knowledge workers
   production. *See* Production workers
   productivity
      growth among white-collar, 22
   remote
      e-mail and, 17
      Internet and, 17, 25
   service. *See* Service workers
   white collar
      in labor force, 5
      productivity growth among, 22
Work-flow
   information technology and, 19–21, 25
   management of, 309, 329
Workplace
   privacy and, 103
Workstations
   CAD/CAM processing and, 140, 141
   defined, 137–38, 157
   for investment specialists, 377
   RISC and, 136
   vs. microcomputers, 141
World Wide Web. *See also* Internet, web
   defined, 276, 293
WORM. *See* Write once/read many (WORM)
Write once/read many (WORM)
   defined, 148

X

X.12
   electronic data interchange, 288, 478
X.25
   packet switching standard, 288
X.400
   e-mail standard, 288
Xenix, 170

Y

Yahoo
   Internet and, 278

Z

Zeneca Integrated Contracting System (ZICS), 427
Zero defects
   in larger programs, 440
   quality and, 50, 109
ZICS, 427
Zip code software
   on CD-ROM, 193
Zolodex, 427

Photo Credits

Page   Photographer/Source

CHAPTER 1

- 1   Courtesy of ONSALE
- 8   John Abbott
- 14   Donna Cox/Robert Patterson/NCSA/Illinois State University
- 20   Hewlett Packard

CHAPTER 2

- 29   Brian Smith/Gamma-Liaison, Inc.
- 37   Bob Sacha Photography
- 47   Louis Psihoyos/Matrix International
- 52   1-800-FLOWERS

CHAPTER 3

- 61   Daniel Wiener/Canadian Pacific
- 73   Schneider National, Inc.
- 76   Lizzie Himmel
- 81   Computer Associates International, Inc.

CHAPTER 4

- 93   Fred Lum/The Globe and Mail
- 97   Courtesy of Telnet
- 111   James Schnepf/Gamma-Liaison, Inc.
- 115   Stephen Ferry/Gamma-Liaison, Inc.

CHAPTER 5

- 124   Kindra Clineff/Picture Cube, Inc.
- 136   Courtesy of Intel Corporation
- 139   Courtesy of Boeing Corporation
- 139   Courtesy of IBM
- 147   Courtesy of IBM
- 153   Courtesy of IBM

CHAPTER 6

- 162   Tom McCarthy/Picture Cube, Inc.
- 171   Waggener Edstrom/Microsoft Corporation
- 181   Courtesy of SPSS, Inc.
- 184   Courtesy of Microsoft Corporation
- 185   Courtesy of The Gupta Corporation
- 189   Courtesy of Strategic Mapping, Inc.
- 190   Courtesy of Citibank

CHAPTER 7

- 195   Fritz Prenzel/Tony Stone Images
- 206   Courtesy of Texaco, Inc.
- 216   Courtesy of Versant Object Technology

CHAPTER 8

- 228   Bob Daemmrich/The Image Works
- 237   Will Crocket/Amoco Chemical Company
- 238   Courtesy of Motorola, Inc.
- 239   Courtesy of CompuServe, Inc.
- 249   James Schnepf/Ameritech
- 251   Courtesy of CompuServe, Inc.

CHAPTER 9

- 266   Thomas Grennara Photography
- 277   Ziff-Davis Publishing Company

CHAPTER 10

- 298   Courtesy of New Zealand Inland Revenue Service
- 309   Jim Langley/Banc One Mortgage
- 312   Matthew Borkoski/Stock Boston
- 325   Courtesy of Computerworld, Inc.

CHAPTER 11

- 336   John Coletti/Picture Cube, Inc.
- 345   S A P of America
- 348   Software AG Corporation
- 349   George Haling/Photo Researchers, Inc.

CHAPTER 12

- 368   Yvonne Hemsey/Gamma-Liaison, Inc.
- 377   Miller Freeman, Inc.
- 390   Courtesy of Neuromedical Systems, Inc.
- 390   Red Morgan Photography
- 392   Courtesy of Sanyo Fisher Corporation

CHAPTER 13

- 403   Siteman/Monkmeyer Press
- 411   Courtesy of Computerworld, Inc.
- 414   Courtesy of Lehrstuhl fur Wirtschaftsinformatik
- 417   Ventana Corporation
- 422   Courtesy of Comshare

CHAPTER 14

- 430   Courtesy of Swiss Air Transport Company
- 436   McAfee Associates, Inc.
- 438   Courtesy of Sungard Recovery Services, Inc.
- 452   Allen Green/Photo Researchers, Inc.

CHAPTER 15

- 458   Jon Feingersh/The Stock Market
- 461   Courtesy of Arrow International, Inc.
- 468   Kees/Sygma
- 478   Doug Wilson
- 480   Lotus Development Corp.

Contributors

🇦🇺 **AUSTRALIA**
Joel B. Barolsky, University of Melbourne

🇨🇦 **CANADA**
Len Fertuck, University of Toronto

FINLAND
Tapio Reponen, Turku School of Economics and Business Administration

GERMANY
Helmut Krcmar, Hohenheim University
Bettina Schwarzer, Hohenheim University

SWITZERLAND
Andrew C. Boynton, International Institute for Management Development

🇺🇸 **UNITED STATES OF AMERICA**
Michael E. Shank, University of North Carolina, Chapel Hill

Consultants

🇦🇺 **AUSTRALIA**
Robert MacGregor, University of Wollongong
Alan Underwood, Queensland University of Technology
Peter Weill, University of Melbourne

🇨🇦 **CANADA**
Wynne W. Chin, University of Calgary
Len Fertuck, University of Toronto
Robert C. Goldstein, University of British Columbia
Rebecca Grant, University of Victoria
Kevin Leonard, Wilfrid Laurier University
Anne B. Pidduck, University of Waterloo

GREECE
Anastasios V. Katos, University of Macedonia

HONG KONG
Enoch Tse, Hong Kong Baptist University

INDIA
Sanjiv D. Vaidya, Indian Institute of Management, Calcutta

ISRAEL
Phillip Ein-Dor, Tel-Aviv University
Peretz Shoval, Ben Gurion University

MEXICO
Noe Urzua Bustamante, Universidad Tecnológica de México

NETHERLANDS
E.O. de Brock, University of Groningen
Theo Thiadens, University of Twente

PUERTO RICO, Commonwealth of the United States
Brunilda Marrero, University of Puerto Rico

SWITZERLAND
Andrew C. Boynton, International Institute for Management Development

🇬🇧 UNITED KINGDOM

🏴󠁧󠁢󠁥󠁮󠁧󠁿 ENGLAND
  G.R. Hidderley, University of Central England, Birmingham
  Jonathan Liebenau, London School of Economics and Political Science
  Kecheng Liu, Staffordshire University

🏴󠁧󠁢󠁳󠁣󠁴󠁿 SCOTLAND
  William N. Dyer, Falkirk College of Technology

🇺🇸 UNITED STATES OF AMERICA
Chandra S. Amaravadi, Western Illinois University
Jon W. Beard, University of Richmond
Doug Brinkley, Naval Postgraduate School
Tung Bui, Naval Postgraduate School
Kimberly Cass, Marquette University
Jason Chen, Gonzaga University
P.C. Chu, Ohio State University, Columbus
Frank S. Davis, Jr., Bloomsburg University
William DeLone, American University
Vasant Dhar, New York University
Robert A. Fleck, Jr., Columbus College
Mark A. Fuller, Baylor University
Amita Goyal, Virginia Commonwealth University
Jeet Gupta, Ball State University
Vijay Gurbaxani, University of California, Irvine
William L. Harrison, Oregon State University
Bart Hodge, Virginia Commonwealth University
George Jacobson, California State University, Los Angeles
Rob Kauffman, University of Rochester
Susan Kinney, Wake Forest University
Rob Kling, University of California, Irvine
Gerald Kohers, Sam Houston State University
Roger Letts, Fairleigh Dickinson University
Barbara Libby, Niagra University
Jane Mackay, Texas Christian University
Efrem G. Mallach, University of Massachusetts, Lowell
Kipp Martin, University of Chicago
Richard O. Mason, Southern Methodist University
Khris McAlister, University of Alabama, Birmingham
Sheizaf Rafaeli, University of Michigan
Brian Reithel, University of Mississippi
James Riha, Northern Illinois University
Edward M. Roche, Seton Hall University
Naveed Saleem, University of Houston, Clear Lake
Werner Schenk, University of Rochester
Cort Schlichting, Spring Hill College
Ivan J. Singer, University of Hartford
Jill Y. Smith, University of Denver
Don Springer, University of Portland
William H. Starbuck, New York University
Kathy Stevens, Merrimack College
Dennis Strouble, Bowling Green State University
E. Burton Swanson, University of California, Los Angeles
John L. Swearingen, Bryant College
Bernadette Szajna, Texas Christian University
Kranti Toraskar, Penn State University
Duane Truex, State University of New York, Binghamton
B.S. Vijayaraman, University of Akron
Patrick J. Walsh, State University of New York, Binghamton
Diane Walz, University of Texas, San Antonio
Erma Wood, University of Arkansas, Little Rock